Office 2003
Brief

GO!
with Microsoft®

Office 2003
Brief

John Preston, Sally Preston, Robert L. Ferrett, Linda Foster-Turpen, and Alicia Vargas

Shelley Gaskin, Series Editor

PEARSON
Prentice Hall

Upper Saddle River, New Jersey

Library of Congress Cataloging-in-Publication Data

Go! with Microsoft Office 2003 : brief / Shelley Gaskin... [et al.]
   p. cm.
Includes index.
   ISBN 0-13-144420-4 (spiral: alk. paper)—ISBN 0-13-145118-9 (perfect bound: alk. paper)
   1. Microsoft Office. 2. Business—Computer programs. I. Preston, John M.
HF5548.4.M525G6 2003
005.5—dc22

2003021912

Vice President and Publisher: Natalie E. Anderson	**Manufacturing Buyer:** Tim Tate
Executive Acquisitions Editor: Jodi McPherson	**Design Manager:** Maria Lange
Marketing Manager: Emily Williams Knight	**Art Director:** Pat Smythe
Marketing Assistant: Nicole Beaudry	**Cover Designer:** Brian Salisbury
Associate Director IT Product Development: Melonie Salvati	**Cover Photo:** Steve Bloom/Getty Images, Inc.
Senior Project Manager, Editorial: Mike Ruel	**Interior Designer:** Quorum Creative Services
Project Manager, Supplements: Melissa Edwards	**Interior Illustrator:** Black Dot Group
Senior Media Project Manager: Cathi Profitko	**Full Service Composition:** Black Dot Group
Editorial Assistants: Jasmine Slowik, Jodi Bolognese, Alana Meyers	**Printer/Binder:** Von Hoffmann Corporation
Manager, Production: Gail Steier de Acevedo	**Cover Printer:** Phoenix Color Corporation
Senior Project Manager, Production: Tim Tate	

Credits and acknowledgments borrowed from other sources and reproduced, with permission, in this textbook are as follows or on the appropriate page within the text.

Page 95 Courtesy of Pro Golf of America, Inc.
Page 95 www.dol.gov
Page 100 Courtesy of Baker's Ribs, Fort Worth, Texas
Page 102 www.dol.gov
Page 102 www.dol.gov
Page 103 Courtesy of Pro Golf of America, Inc.
Page 104 Courtesy The Denver Post Online
Page 104 Courtesy Penn State University
Page 105 Courtesy CNN Interactive
Page 106 Courtesy CNN Interactive
Page 107 Courtesy CNN Interactive
Page 107 Courtesy CNN Interactive
Page 108 Courtesy CNN Interactive
Page 108 www.usgoverment.com
Page 109 www.navy.mil
Page 119 Courtesy The Denver Post Online
Page 121 Courtesy The Denver Post Online
Page 122 Courtesy The Denver Post Online
Page 123 Courtesy The Denver Post Online
Page 139 ©Corbis
Page 140 ©Corbis
Page 141 ©Corbis; ©Getty Images, Inc.; Courtesy, Hewlett-Packard Development Company, L.P.
Page 144 ©Corbis
Page 145 Figure 1.12 Courtesy, Hewlett-Packard Development Company, L.P.; ©Getty Images, Inc.
Figure 1.13 Courtesy, Hewlett-Packard Development Company, L.P.
Page 146 ©Corbis
Page 147 ©Corbis
Page 148 ©Corbis
Page 150 ©Corbis
Page 155 ©Corbis
Page 156 ©Corbis

Microsoft, Windows, PowerPoint, Outlook, FrontPage, Visual Basic, MSN, The Microsoft Network, and/or other Microsoft products referenced herein are either trademarks or registered trademarks of Microsoft Corporation in the U.S.A. and other countries. Screen shots and icons reprinted with permission from the Microsoft Corporation. This book is not sponsored or endorsed by or affiliated with Microsoft Corporation.

Microsoft and the Microsoft Office User Specialist logo are trademarks or registered trademarks of Microsoft Corporation in the United States and/or other countries. Pearson Education is independent from Microsoft Corporation and not affiliated with Microsoft in any manner. This text may be used in assisting students to prepare for a Microsoft Office Specialist Exam. Neither Microsoft, its designated review company, nor Pearson Education warrants that use of this text will ensure passing the relevant exam.

Copyright © 2004 by Pearson Education, Inc., Upper Saddle River, New Jersey, 07458. All rights reserved. Printed in the United States of America. This publication is protected by Copyright and permission should be obtained from the publisher prior to any prohibited reproduction, storage in a retrieval system, or transmission in any form or by any means, electronic, mechanical, photocopying, recording, or likewise. For information regarding permission(s), write to the Rights and Permissions Department.

10 9 8 7 6 5 4 3 2
ISBN 0-13-145118-9

We dedicate this book to our granddaughters, who bring us great joy and happiness: Clara and Siena & Alexis and Grace.

—John Preston, Sally Preston, and Robert L. Ferrett

I would like to dedicate this book to my awesome family. I want to thank my husband, Dave Alumbaugh, who always lets me be exactly who I am; my kids, Michael, Jordan, and Ceara, who give me hope and my drive for everything that I do; my mom, who never gives up; and my dad, who has been my light, my rock, and one of my best friends every day that I can remember. I love you all and . . . thanks for putting up with me.

—Linda Foster-Turpen

This book is lovingly dedicated to Guadalupe Perez, whose stories enriched the lives of every audience, big or small, young or old, friend or stranger.

—Alicia Vargas

This book is dedicated to my students, who inspire me every day, and to my husband, Fred Gaskin.

—Shelley Gaskin

What does this logo mean?

It means this courseware has been approved by the Microsoft® Office Specialist Program to be among the finest available for learning **Microsoft® Office Word 2003, Microsoft® Office Excel 2003, Microsoft® Office PowerPoint® 2003,** and **Microsoft® Office Access 2003**. It also means that upon completion of this courseware, you may be prepared to take an exam for Microsoft Office Specialist qualification.

What is a Microsoft Office Specialist?

A Microsoft Office Specialist is an individual who has passed exams for certifying his or her skills in one or more of the Microsoft Office desktop applications such as Microsoft Word, Microsoft Excel, Microsoft PowerPoint, Microsoft Outlook, Microsoft Access, or Microsoft Project. The Microsoft Office Specialist Program typically offers certification exams at the "Specialist" and "Expert" skill levels.* The Microsoft Office Specialist Program is the only program approved by Microsoft for testing proficiency in Microsoft Office desktop applications and Microsoft Project. This testing program can be a valuable asset in any job search or career advancement.

More Information:

To learn more about becoming a Microsoft Office Specialist, visit **www.microsoft.com/officespecialist**

To learn about other Microsoft Office Specialist approved courseware from Pearson Education, visit **www.prenhall.com/phit**

*The availability of Microsoft Office Specialist certification exams varies by application, application version, and language. Visit www.microsoft.com/officespecialist for exam availability.

Microsoft, the Microsoft Office Logo, PowerPoint, and Outlook are trademarks or registered trademarks of Microsoft Corporation in the United States and/or other countries, and the Microsoft Office Specialist Logo is used under license from owner.

GO!
Series for Microsoft® Office System 2003

Series Editor: Shelley Gaskin

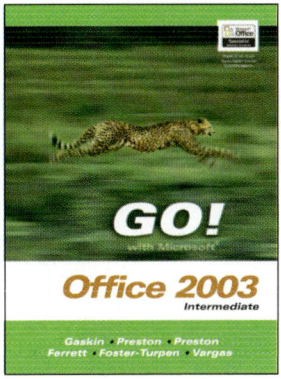

Office
Getting Started
Brief
Intermediate
Advanced

Word
Brief
Volume 1
Volume 2
Comprehensive

Excel
Brief
Volume 1
Volume 2
Comprehensive

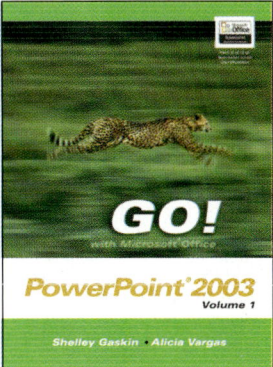

PowerPoint
Brief
Volume 1
Volume 2
Comprehensive

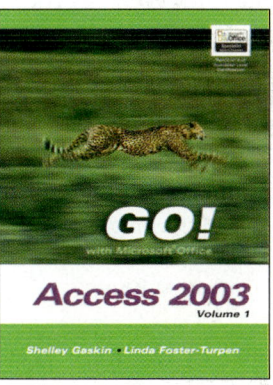

Access
Brief
Volume 1
Volume 2
Comprehensive

GO! Series Reviewers

We would like to thank the following "Super Reviewers" for both their subject matter expertise and attention to detail from the instructors' perspective. Your time, effort, hard work, and diligence has helped us create the best books in the world. Prentice Hall and your author partners thank you:

Rocky Belcher	Sinclair CC
Judy Cameron	Spokane CC
Gail Cope	Sinclair CC
Larry Farrer	Guilford Tech CC
Janet Enck	Columbus State CC
Susan Fry	Boise State
Lewis Hall	Riverside CC
Jeff Howard	Finger Lakes CC
Jason Hu	Pasadena City College
Michele Hulett	Southwestern Missouri State U.
Donna Madsen	Kirkwood CC
Cheryl Reindl-Johnson	Sinclair CC
Jan Spaar	Spokane CC
Mary Ann Zlotow	College of DuPage

We would also like to thank our valuable student reviewers who bring us vital input from those who will someday study from our books:

Nicholas J. Bene	Southwestern Missouri State U.
Anup Jonathan	Southwestern Missouri State U.
Kimber Miller	Pasadena City College
Kelly Moline	Southwestern Missouri State U.
Adam Morris	Southwestern Missouri State U.
Robert Murphy	Southwestern Missouri State U.
Drucilla Owenby	Southwestern Missouri State U.
Vince Withee	Southwestern Missouri State U.

Finally, we have been lucky to have so many of you respond to review our chapter manuscripts. You have given us tremendous feedback and helped make a fantastic series. We could not have done it without you.

Abraham, Reni	Houston CC	Challa, Chandrashekar	Virginia State University
Agatston, Ann	Agatston Consulting	Chamlou, Afsaneh	NOVA Alexandria
Alejandro, Manuel	Southwest Texas Junior College	Chapman, Pam	Wabaunsee CC
Ali, Farha	Lander University	Christensen, Dan	Iowa Western CC
Anik, Mazhar	Tiffin University	Conroy-Link, Janet	Holy Family College
Armstrong, Gary	Shippensburg University	Cosgrove, Janet	Northwestern CT Community
Bagui, Sikha	Univ. West Florida		Technical College
Belton, Linda	Springfield Tech. Com College	Cox, Rollie	Madison Area Technical College
Bennett, Judith	Sam Houston State University	Crawford, Hiram	Olive Harvey College
Bishop, Frances	DeVry Institute- Alpharetta (ATL)	Danno, John	DeVry University/
Branigan, Dave	DeVry University		Keller Graduate School
Bray, Patricia	Allegany College of Maryland	Davis, Phillip Md.	Del Mar College
Buehler, Lesley	Ohlone College	Doroshow, Mike	Eastfield College
Buell, C	Central Oregon CC	Douglas, Gretchen	SUNY Cortland
Byars, Pat	Brookhaven College	Driskel, Loretta	Niagara CC
Cacace, Rich	Pensacola Jr. College	Duckwiler, Carol	Wabaunsee CC
Cadenhead, Charles	Brookhaven College	Duncan, Mimi	University of Missouri-St. Louis
Calhoun, Ric	Gordon College	Duvall, Annette	Albuquerque Technical
Carriker, Sandra	North Shore CC		Vocational Institute

Reviewers continues

Reviewers continued

Ecklund, Paula	Duke University	Menking, Rick	Hardin-Simmons University
Edmondson, Jeremy	Mount Pisgah School	Meredith, Mary	U. of Louisiana at Lafayette
Erickson, John	University of South Dakota	Mermelstein, Lisa	Baruch College
Falkenstein, Todd	Indiana University East	Metos, Linda	Salt Lake CC
Fite, Beverly	Amarillo College	Meurer, Daniel	University of Cincinnati
Foltz, Brian	East Carolina University	Monk, Ellen	University of Delaware
Friedrichsen, Lisa	Johnson County CC	Morris, Nancy	Hudson Valley CC
Fustos, Janos	Metro State	Nadas, Erika	Wright College
Gallup, Jeanette	Blinn College	Nadelman, Cindi	New England College
Gentry, Barb	Parkland College	Ncube, Cathy	University of West Florida
Gerace, Karin	St. Angela Merici School	Nicholls, Doreen	Mohawk Valley CC
Gerace, Tom	Tulane University	Orr, Claudia	New Mexico State University
Ghajar, Homa	Oklahoma State University	Otieno, Derek	DeVry University
Gifford, Steve	Northwest Iowa CC	Otton, Diana Hill	Chesapeake College
Gregoryk, Kerry	Virginia Commonwealth State University	Oxendale, Lucia	West Virginia Institute of Technology
Griggs, Debra	Bellevue CC	Paiano, Frank	Southwestern College
Grimm, Carol	Palm Beach CC	Proietti, Kathleen	Northern Essex CC
Helms, Liz	Columbus State CC	Pusins, Delores	HCCC
Hernandez, Leticia	TCI College of Technology	Reeves, Karen	High Point University
Hogan, Pat	Cape Fear CC	Rhue, Shelly	DeVry University
Horvath, Carrie	Albertus Magnus College	Richards, Karen	Maplewoods CC
Howard, Chris	DeVry University	Ross, Dianne	Univ. of Louisiana in Lafayette
Huckabay, Jamie	Austin CC	Rousseau, Mary	Broward CC
Hunt, Laura	Tulsa CC	Sams, Todd	University of Cincinnati
Jacob, Sherry	Jefferson CC	Sandoval, Everett	Reedley College
Jacobs, Duane	Salt Lake CC	Sardone, Nancy	Seton Hall University
Johnson, Kathy	Wright College	Scafide, Jean	Mississippi Gulf Coast CC
Jones, Stacey	Benedict College	Scheeren, Judy	Westmoreland County CC
Kasai, Susumu	Salt Lake CC	Schneider, Sol	Sam Houston State University
Keen, Debby	Univ. of Kentucky	Scroggins, Michael	Southwest Missouri State University
Kirk, Colleen	Mercy College		
Kliston, Linda	Broward CC	Sever, Suzanne	Northwest Arkansas CC
Kramer, Ed	Northern Virginia CC	Sheridan, Rick	California State University-Chico
Laird, Jeff	Northeast State CC	Sinha, Atin	Albany State University
Lange, David	Grand Valley State	Smith, T. Michael	Austin CC
LaPointe, Deb	Albuquerque TVI	Smith, Tammy	Tompkins Cortland CC
Lenhart, Sheryl	Terra CC	Stefanelli, Greg	Carroll CC
Letavec, Chris	University of Cincinnati	Steiner, Ester	New Mexico State University
Lightner, Renee	Broward CC	Sterling, Janet	Houston CC
Lindberg, Martha	Minnesota State University	Stroup, Tracey	Pasadena City College
Linge, Richard	Arizona Western College	Sullivan, Angela	Joliet Junior College
Loizeaux, Barbara	Westchester CC	Szurek, Joseph	University of Pittsburgh at Greensburg
Lopez, Don	Clovis- State Center CC District		
Low, Willy Hui	Joliet Junior College	Taylor, Michael	Seattle Central CC
Lowe, Rita	Harold Washington College	Thangiah, Sam	Slippery Rock University
Lucas, Vickie	Broward CC	Thompson-Sellers, Ingrid	Georgia Perimeter College
Lynam, Linda	Central Missouri State University	Tomasi, Erik	Baruch College
		Toreson, Karen	Shoreline CC
Machuca, Wayne	College of the Sequoias	Turgeon, Cheryl	Asnuntuck CC
Madison, Dana	Clarion University	Turpen, Linda	Albuquerque TVI
Maguire, Trish	Eastern New Mexico University	Upshaw, Susan	Del Mar College
Malkan, Rajiv	Montgomery College	Vargas, Tony	El Paso CC
Manning, David	Northern Kentucky University	Vicars, Mitzi	Hampton University
Marghitu, Daniela	Auburn University	Vitrano, Mary Ellen	Palm Beach CC
Marks, Suzanne	Bellevue CC	Wahila, Lori	Tompkins Cortland CC
Marquez, Juanita	El Centro College	Wavle, Sharon	Tompkins Cortland CC
Marucco, Toni	Lincoln Land CC	White, Bruce	Quinnipiac University
Mason, Lynn	Lubbock Christian University	Willer, Ann	Solano CC
Matutis, Audrone	Houston CC	Williams, Mark	Lane CC
McCannon, Melinda (Mindy)	Gordon College	Wimberly, Leanne	International Academy of Design and Technology
McClure, Darlean	College of Sequoias		
McCue, Stacy	Harrisburg Area CC	Worthington, Paula	NOVA Woodbridge
McEntire-Orbach, Teresa	Middlesex County College	Yauney, Annette	Herkimer CCC
McManus, Illyana	Grossmont College	Zavala, Ben	Webster Tech

Reviewers

About the Authors/Acknowledgments

About John Preston, Sally Preston, and Robert L. Ferrett

John Preston is an Associate Professor at Eastern Michigan University in the College of Technology, where he teaches microcomputer application courses at the undergraduate and graduate levels. He has been teaching, writing, and designing computer training courses since the advent of PCs and has authored and co-authored over 60 books on Microsoft Word, Excel, Access, and PowerPoint. He is a series editor for the *Learn 97*, *Learn 2000*, and *Learn XP* books. Two books on Microsoft Access that he co-authored with Robert Ferrett have been translated into Greek and Chinese. He has received grants from the Detroit Edison Institute and the Department of Energy to develop Web sites for energy education and alternative fuels. He has also developed one of the first Internet-based microcomputer applications courses at an accredited university. He has a BS from the University of Michigan in Physics, Mathematics, and Education and an MS from Eastern Michigan University in Physics Education. His doctoral studies were in Instructional Technology at Wayne State University.

Sally Preston is president of Preston & Associates, which provides software consulting and training. She teaches computing in a variety of settings, which provides her with ample opportunity to observe how people learn, what works best, and what challenges are present when learning a new software program. This diverse experience provides a complementary set of skills and knowledge that blends into her writing. Prior to writing for the *GO! series*, Sally was a co-author on the *Learn* series since its inception and has authored books for the *Essentials* and *Microsoft Office User Specialist (MOUS) Essentials* series. Sally has an MBA from Eastern Michigan University. When away from her computer, she is often found planting flowers in her garden.

Robert L. Ferrett recently retired as the director of the Center for Instructional Computing at Eastern Michigan University, where he provided computer training and support to faculty. He has authored or co-authored more than 60 books on Access, PowerPoint, Excel, Publisher, WordPerfect, and Word and was the editor of the *1994 ACM SIGUCCS Conference Proceedings*. He has been designing, developing, and delivering computer workshops for nearly two decades. Before writing for the *GO! series*, Bob was a series editor for the *Learn 97*, *Learn 2000*, and *Learn XP* books. He has a BA in Psychology, an MS in Geography, and an MS in Interdisciplinary Technology from Eastern Michigan University. His doctoral studies were in Instructional Technology at Wayne State University. For fun, Bob teaches a four-week Computers and Genealogy class and has written genealogy and local history books.

Acknowledgments from John Preston, Sally Preston, and Robert L. Ferrett

We would like to acknowledge the efforts of a fine team of editing professionals, with whom we have had the pleasure of working. Jodi McPherson, Jodi Bolognese, Mike Ruel, and Shelley Gaskin did a great job managing and coordinating this effort. We would also like to acknowledge the contributions of Tim Tate, Production Project Manager, and Emily Knight, Marketing Manager, as well as the many reviewers who gave invaluable criticism and suggestions.

About Linda Foster-Turpen

Linda Foster-Turpen is an instructor in Computer Information Systems at Albuquerque TVI in Albuquerque, New Mexico, where she teaches and has developed computer applications courses. Linda received her B.B.A. in Accounting as well as her M.B.A. in MIS and M.B.A. in Accounting from the University of New Mexico. She has developed new courses for her college including courses in Intranets/Extranets, Management Information Systems, and Distance Learning courses in introductory computer applications and Microsoft Access.

In addition to teaching and authoring, Linda likes to hike and backpack with her family. She lives in Corrales, New Mexico, with her husband Dave, her three children, Michael, Jordan, and Ceara, and their animals.

Acknowledgments from Linda Foster-Turpen

I would like to thank everyone at Prentice Hall (and beyond) who was involved with the production of this book. To my reviewers, your input and feedback were appreciated more than you could know. I would not want to write a book without you! To my technical editors, Jan Snyder and Mary Pascarella, thank you for your attention to detail and for your comments and suggestions during the writing of this book. A big thank you to Emily Knight in Marketing, Gail Steier de Acevedo and Tim Tate in Production, and Pat Smythe and Maria Lange in Design for your contributions. To the series editor, Shelley Gaskin, thank you for your wonderful vision for this book and the entire *GO! Series*. Your ideas and inspiration were the basis for this whole project from its inception. To the Editorial Project Manager, Mike Ruel, thanks for making sure all of my ducks were always in a row, and to the Executive Editor, Jodi McPherson, thank you for your faith and confidence in me from the beginning. A huge thanks to my students, you are the reason these books are written! I would also like to thank my colleagues at TVI for giving me a sounding board from which I could bounce ideas or just vent my frustrations. Any book takes a team of people, and I was most fortunate to have all of you on mine. I also want to thank God for . . . everything.

About Alicia Vargas

Alicia Vargas is a faculty member in Business Information Technology at Pasadena City College. She holds a master's and a bachelor's degree in Business Education from California State University, Los Angeles and has authored several textbooks and training manuals on Microsoft Word, Microsoft Excel, and Microsoft PowerPoint.

Acknowledgments from Alicia Vargas

There are many people at Prentice Hall whose dedication and commitment to educational excellence made this book possible. Among those people are Jan Snyder and Mary Pascarella, technical editors extraordinaire, whose work ensured the consistency and credibility of the manuscript; Tim Tate, Production Project Manager, and Emily Knight, Marketing Manager, whose work guaranteed the success of the final product; and Tracey Stroup, whose creative mind made many of the presentations possible. My thanks to all of you and your teams! I would also like to *especially* thank Mike Ruel, Editorial Project Manager, whose humor kept me on task and made the deadlines bearable; Shelley Gaskin, Series Editor, mentor, and friend, whose understanding of college students and their learning is the basis for this series; and Jodie McPherson, Executive Editor, whose energy and intelligence made the *GO! Series* a reality.

On a personal note, I would like to thank my parents, whose commitment to family and education became the foundation for who I am and what I do; and my family and friends whose support makes it all possible. Finally, and most importantly, I would like to thank my husband, Vic, and my three children, Victor, Phil, and Emmy. They keep me busy, they keep me laughing, but most of all, they just keep me! This one's for us!

About Shelley Gaskin

Shelley Gaskin, Series Editor, is a professor of business and computer technology at Pasadena City College in Pasadena, California. She holds a master's degree in business education from Northern Illinois University and a doctorate in adult and community education from Ball State University. Dr. Gaskin has 15 years of experience in the computer industry with several Fortune 500 companies and has developed and written training materials for custom systems applications in both the public and private sector. She is also the author of books on Microsoft Outlook and word processing.

Acknowledgments from Shelley Gaskin

Many talented individuals worked to produce this book, and I thank them for their continuous support. My Executive Acquisitions Editor, Jodi McPherson, gave me much latitude to experiment with new things. Editorial Project Manager Mike Ruel worked with me through each stage of writing and production. Emily Knight and the Prentice Hall Marketing team worked with me throughout this process to make sure both instructors and students are informed about the benefits of using this series. Also, very big thanks and appreciation goes to Prentice Halls' top-notch Production and Design team: Associate Director Product Development Melonie Salvati, Manager of Production Gail Steier de Acevedo, Senior Production Project Manager and Manufacturing Buyer Tim Tate, Design Manager Maria Lange, Art Director Pat Smythe, Interior Designer Quorum Creative Services, and Cover Designer Brian Salisbury.

Thanks to all!
Shelley Gaskin, Series Editor

Why I Wrote This Series

Dear Professor,

If you are like me, you are frantically busy trying to implement new course delivery methods (e.g., online) while also maintaining your regular campus schedule of classes and academic responsibilities. I developed this series for colleagues like you, who are long on commitment and expertise but short on time and assistance.

The primary goal of the **GO! Series**, aside from the obvious one of teaching **Microsoft® Office 2003** concepts and skills, is ease of implementation using any delivery method—traditional, self-paced, or online.

There are no lengthy passages of text; instead, bits of expository text are woven into the steps at the teachable moment. This is the point at which the student has a context within which he or she can understand the concept. A scenario-like approach is used in a manner that makes sense, but it does not attempt to have the student "pretend" to be someone else.

A key feature of this series is the use of Microsoft procedural syntax. That is, steps begin with where the action is to take place, followed by the action itself. This prevents the student from doing the right thing in the wrong place!

The *GO! Series* is written with all of your everyday classroom realities in mind. For example, in each project, the student is instructed to insert his or her name in a footer and to save the document with his or her name. Thus, unidentified printouts do not show up at the printer nor do unidentified documents get stored on the hard drives.

Finally, an overriding consideration is that the student is not always working in a classroom with a teacher. Students frequently work at home or in a lab staffed only with instructional aides. Thus, the instruction must be error-free, clearly written, and logically arranged.

My students enjoy learning the Microsoft Office software. The goal of the instruction in the *GO! Series* is to provide students with the skills to solve business problems using the computer as a tool, for both themselves and the organizations for which they might be employed.

Thank you for using the **GO! Series for Microsoft® Office System 2003** for your students.

Regards,

Shelley Gaskin

Shelley Gaskin, Series Editor

Preface

Philosophy

Our overall philosophy is ease of implementation for the instructor, whether instruction is via lecture, lab, online, or partially self-paced. Right from the start, the *GO! Series* was created with constant input from professors just like you. You've told us what works, how you teach, and what we can do to make your classroom time problem free, creative, and smooth running—to allow you to concentrate on not what you are teaching from but who you are teaching to—your students. We feel that we have succeeded with the *GO! Series*. Our aim is to make this instruction high quality in both content and presentation, and the classroom management aids complete—an instructor could begin teaching the course with only 15 minutes advance notice. An instructor could leave the classroom or computer lab; students would know exactly how to proceed in the text, know exactly what to produce to demonstrate mastery of the objectives, and feel that they had achieved success in their learning. Indeed, this philosophy is essential for real-world use in today's diverse educational environment.

How did we do it?

- All steps utilize **Microsoft Procedural Syntax**. The *GO! Series* puts students where they need to be, before instructing them what to do. For example, instead of instructing students to "Save the file," we go a few steps further and phrase the instruction as "On the **Menu** bar, click **File**, then select **Save As**."

- A unique teaching system (packaged together in one easy to use **Instructor's Edition** binder set) that enables you to teach anywhere you have to—online, lab, lecture, self-paced, and so forth. The supplements are designed to save you time:

    - *Expert Demonstration Document*—A new project that mirrors the learning objectives of the in-chapter project, with a full demonstration script for you to give a lecture overview quickly and clearly.

    - *Chapter Assignment Sheets*—A sheet listing all the assignments for the chapter. An instructor can quickly insert his or her name, course information, due dates, and points.

    - *Custom Assignment Tags*—These cutout tags include a brief list of common errors that students could make on each project, with check boxes so instructors don't have to keep writing the same error description over and over! These tags serve a dual purpose: The student can do a final check to make sure all the listed items are correct, and the instructor can check off the items that need to be corrected.

- ***Highlighted Overlays***—These are printed and transparent overlays that the instructor lays over the student's assignment paper to see at a glance if the student changed what he or she needed to. Coupled with the Custom Assignment Tags, this creates a "grading and scoring system" that is easy for the instructor to implement.
- ***Point Counted Chapter Production Test***—Working hand-in-hand with the Expert Demonstration Document, this is a final test for the student to demonstrate mastery of the objectives.

Goals of the GO! Series

The goals of the *GO! Series* are as follows:

- Make it *easy for the instructor to implement* in any instructional setting through high-quality content and instructional aids and provide the student with a valuable, interesting, important, satisfying, and clearly defined learning experience.
- Enable true diverse delivery for today's diverse audience. The *GO! Series* employs various instructional techniques that address the needs of all types of students in all types of delivery modes.
- Provide *turn-key implementation* in the following instructional settings:
    - Traditional computer classroom—Students experience a mix of lecture and lab.
    - Online instruction—Students complete instruction at a remote location and submit assignments to the instructor electronically—questions answered by instructor through electronic queries.
    - Partially self-paced, individualized instruction—Students meet with an instructor for part of the class, and complete part of the class in a lab setting.
    - Completely self-paced, individualized instruction—Students complete all instruction in an instructor-staffed lab setting.
    - Independent self-paced, individualized instruction—Students complete all instruction in a campus lab staffed with instructional aides.
- Teach—*to maximize the moment*. The *GO! Series* is based on the Teachable Moment Theory. There are no long passages of text; instead, concepts are woven into the steps at the teachable moment. Students always know what they need to do and where to do it.

Pedagogical Approach

The *GO! Series* uses an instructional system approach that incorporates three elements:

- *Steps are written in* **Microsoft Procedural Syntax**, which prevents the student from doing the right thing but in the wrong place. This makes it easy for the instructor to teach instead of untangle. It tells the student where to go first, then what to do. For example—"On the File Menu, click Properties."

- *Instructional strategies* including five new, unique ancillary pieces to support the instructor experience. The foundation of the instructional strategies is performance based instruction that is constructed in a manner that makes it *easy for the instructor* to demonstrate the content with the GO Series Expert Demonstration Document, guide the practice by using our many end-of-chapter projects with varying guidance levels, and assess the level of mastery with tools such as our Point Counted Production Test and Custom Assignment Tags.

- *A physical design* that makes it *easy for the instructor* to answer the question, "What do they have to do?" and makes it easy for the student to answer the question, "What do I have to do?" Most importantly, you told us what was needed in the design. We held several focus groups throughout the country where we showed **you** our design drafts and let you tell us what you thought of them. We revised our design based on your input to be functional and support the classroom experience. For example, you told us that a common problem is students not realizing where a project ends. So, we added an "END. You have completed the Project" at the close of every project.

Microsoft Procedural Syntax

Do you ever do something right but in the wrong place?

That's why we've written the *GO! Series* step text using Microsoft procedural syntax. That is, the student is informed where the action should take place before describing the action to take. For example, "On the menu bar, click File," versus "Click File on the menu bar." This prevents the student from doing the right thing in the wrong place. This means that step text usually begins with a preposition—a locator—rather than a verb. Other texts often misunderstand the theory of performance-based instruction and frequently attempt to begin steps with a verb. In fact, the objectives should begin with a verb, not the steps.

The use of Microsoft procedural syntax is one of the key reasons that the *GO! Series* eases the burden for the instructor. The instructor spends less time untangling students' unnecessary actions and more time assisting students with real questions. No longer will students become frustrated and say "But I did what it said!" only to discover that, indeed, they *did* do "what it said" but in the wrong place!

Chapter Organization—Color-Coded Projects

All of the chapters in every *GO! Series* book are organized around interesting projects. Within each chapter, all of the instructional activities will cluster around these projects without any long passages of text for the student to read. Thus, every instructional activity contributes to the completion of the project to which it is associated. Students learn skills to solve real business problems; they don't waste time learning every feature the software has. The end-of-chapter material consists of additional projects with varying levels of difficulty.

The chapters are based on the following basic hierarchy:

Project Name
    Objective Name (begins with a verb)
        Activity Name (begins with a gerund)
            Numbered Steps (begins with a preposition or a verb using Microsoft Procedural Syntax.)

Project Name → **Project 1A Exploring Outlook 2003**

Objective Name → **Objective 1**
Start Outlook and Identify Outlook Window Elements

Activity Name → **Activity 1.1** Starting Outlook

Numbered Steps → **1** On the Windows taskbar, click the Start button, determine from your instructor or lab coordinator where the Microsoft Office Outlook 2003 program is located on your system, and then click Microsoft Office Outlook 2003.

A project will have a number of objectives associated with it, and the objectives, in turn, will have one or more activities associated with them. Each activity will have a series of numbered steps. To further enhance understanding, each project, and its objectives and numbered steps, is color coded for fast, easy recognition.

Preface xvii

In-Chapter Boxes and Elements

Within every chapter there are helpful boxes and in-line notes that aid the students in their mastery of the performance objectives. Plus, each box has a specific title—"Does Your Notes Button Look Different?" or "To Open the New Appointment Window." Our GO! Series Focus Groups told us to add box titles that indicate the information being covered in the box, and we listened!

Alert!

Does Your Notes Button Look Different?

The size of the monitor and screen resolution set on your computer controls the number of larger module buttons that appear at the bottom of the Navigation pane.

Alert! boxes do just that—they alert students to a common pitfall or spot where trouble may be encountered.

Another Way

To Open the New Appointment Window

You can create a new appointment window using one of the following techniques:

- On the menu bar, click File, point to New, and click Appointment.
- On the Calendar Standard toolbar, click the New Appointment button.

Another Way boxes explain simply "another way" of going about a task or shortcuts for saving time.

Note — Server Connection Dialog Box

If a message displays indicating that a connection to the server could not be established, click OK. Even without a mail server connection, you can still use the personal information management features of Outlook.

Notes highlight additional information pertaining to a task.

More Knowledge — Creating New Folders

A module does not have to be active in order to create new folders within it. From the Create New Folder text box, you can change the type of items that the new folder will contain and then select any location in which to place the new folder. Additionally, it is easy to move a folder created in one location to a different location.

More Knowledge is a more detailed look at a topic or task.

Organization of the GO! Series

The *GO! Series for Microsoft® Office System 2003* includes several different combinations of texts to best suit your needs.

- **Word, Excel, Access, and PowerPoint 2003** are available in the following editions:

    - **Brief:** Chapters 1–3 (1–4 for Word 2003)

    - **Volume 1:** Chapters 1–6
      ~ Microsoft Office Specialist Certification

    - **Volume 2:** Chapters 7–12 (7–8 for PowerPoint 2003)

    - **Comprehensive:** Chapters 1–12 (1–8 for PowerPoint 2003)
      ~ Microsoft Office Expert Certification for Word and Excel 2003.

- Additionally, the *GO! Series* is available in four combined **Office 2003** texts:

    - **Microsoft® Office 2003 Getting Started** contains the Windows XP Introduction and first chapter from each application (Word, Excel, Access, and PowerPoint).

    - **Microsoft® Office 2003 Brief** contains Chapters 1–3 of Excel, Access, and PowerPoint, and Chapters 1–4 of Word. Four additional supplementary "Getting Started" books are included (Internet Explorer, Computer Concepts, Windows XP, and Outlook 2003).

    - **Microsoft® Office 2003 Intermediate** contains Chapters 4–8 of Excel, Access, and PowerPoint, and Chapters 5–8 of Word.

    - **Microsoft® Office 2003 Advanced** version picks up where the Intermediate leaves off, covering advanced topics for the individual applications. This version contains Chapters 9–12 of Word, Excel, and Access.

Microsoft Office Specialist Certification

The *GO! Series* has been approved by Microsoft for use in preparing for the Microsoft Office Specialist exams. The Microsoft Office Specialist program is globally recognized as the standard for demonstrating desktop skills with the Microsoft Office System of business productivity applications (Microsoft Word, Microsoft Excel, Microsoft Access, Microsoft PowerPoint, and Microsoft Outlook). With Microsoft Office Specialist certification, thousands of people have demonstrated increased productivity and have proved their ability to utilize the advanced functionality of these Microsoft applications.

Instructor and Student Resources

Instructor's Resource Center and Instructor's Edition

The *GO! Series* was designed for you—instructors who are long on commitment and short on time. *We asked you how you use our books and supplements and how we can make it easier for you and save you valuable time.* We listened to what you told us and created this Instructor's Resource Center for you—different from anything you have ever had access to from other texts and publishers.

What is the Instructor's Edition?

1) Instructor's Edition

New from Prentice Hall, exclusively for the *GO! Series*, the Instructor's Edition contains the entire book, wrapped with vital margin notes—things like objectives, a list of the files needed for the chapter, teaching tips, Microsoft Office Specialist objectives covered, and MORE! Below is a sample of the many helpful elements in the Instructor's Edition.

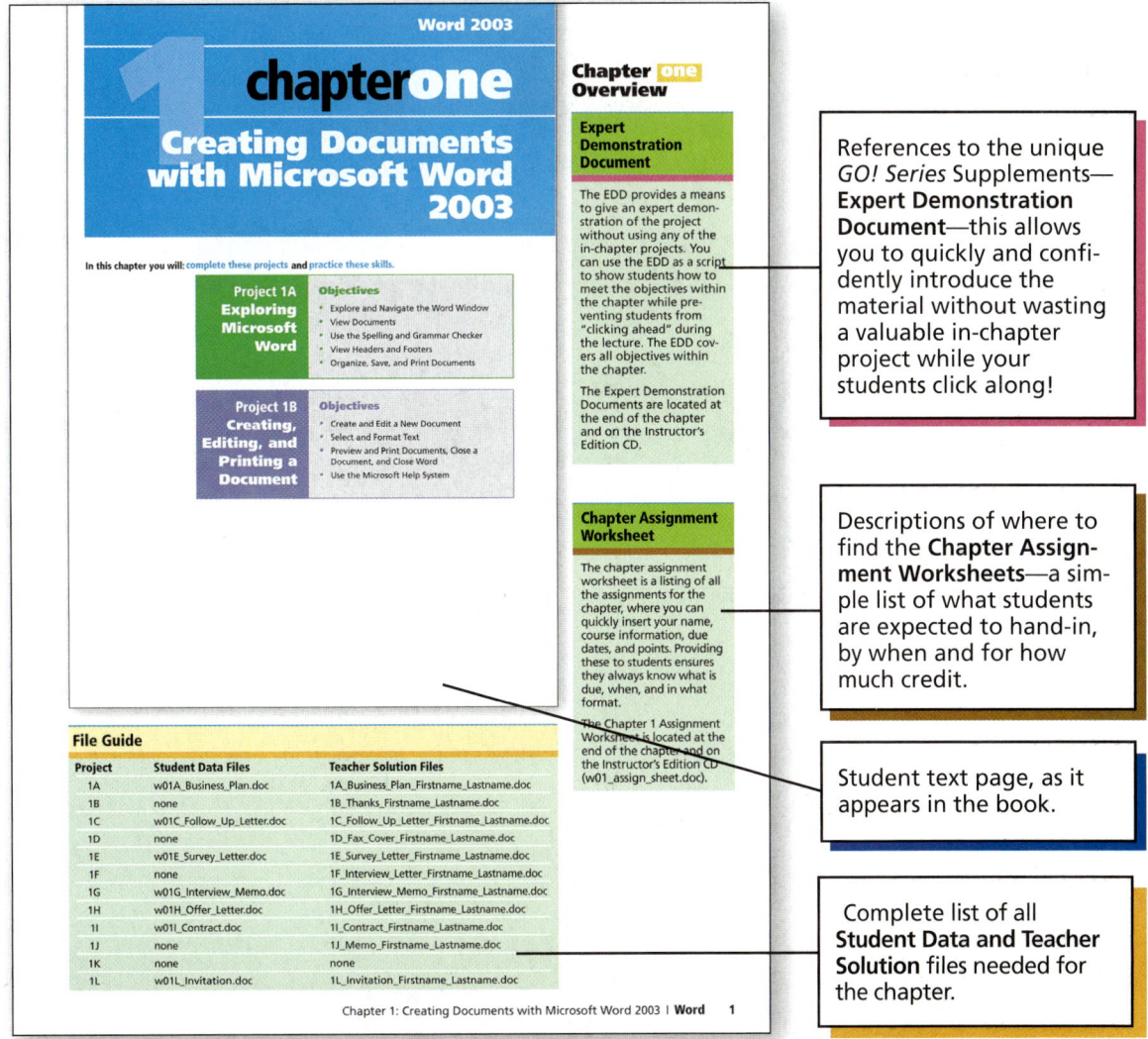

Preface   xxi

Reference to Prentice Hall's Companion Website for the *GO! Series*: **www.prenhall.com/go**

www.prenhall.com/go

The Companion Website is an online training tool that includes personalization features for registered instructors. Data files are available here for download as well as access to additional quizzing exercises.

Each chapter also tells you where to find another unique *GO! Series* Supplement—the **Custom Assignment Tags**—use these in combination with the highlighted overlays to save you time! Simply check off what the students missed or if they completed all the tasks correctly.

Custom Assignment Tags

Custom Assignment Tags, which are meant to be cut out and attached to assignments, serve a dual purpose: the student can do a final check to make sure all the listed items are correct, and the instructor can quickly check off the items that need to be corrected and simply return the assignment.

The Chapter 1 Custom Assignment Tags are located at the end of the chapter and on the Instructor's Edition CD (w01_assign_tags.doc).

The Perfect Party

The Perfect Party store, owned by two partners, provides a wide variety of party accessories including invitations, favors, banners and flags, balloons, piñatas, etc. Party-planning services include both custom parties with pre-filled custom "goodie bags" and "parties in a box" that include everything needed to throw a theme party. Big sellers in this category are the Football and Luau themes. The owners are planning to open a second store and expand their party-planning services to include catering.

© Getty Images, Inc.

Getting Started with Microsoft Office Word 2003

Word processing is the most common program found on personal computers and one that almost everyone has a reason to use. When you learn word processing you are also learning skills and techniques that you need to work efficiently on a personal computer. Use Microsoft Word to do basic word processing tasks such as writing a memo, a report, or a letter. You can also use Word to do complex word processing tasks, including sophisticated tables, embedded graphics, and links to other documents and the Internet. Word is a program that you can learn gradually, adding more advanced skills one at a time.

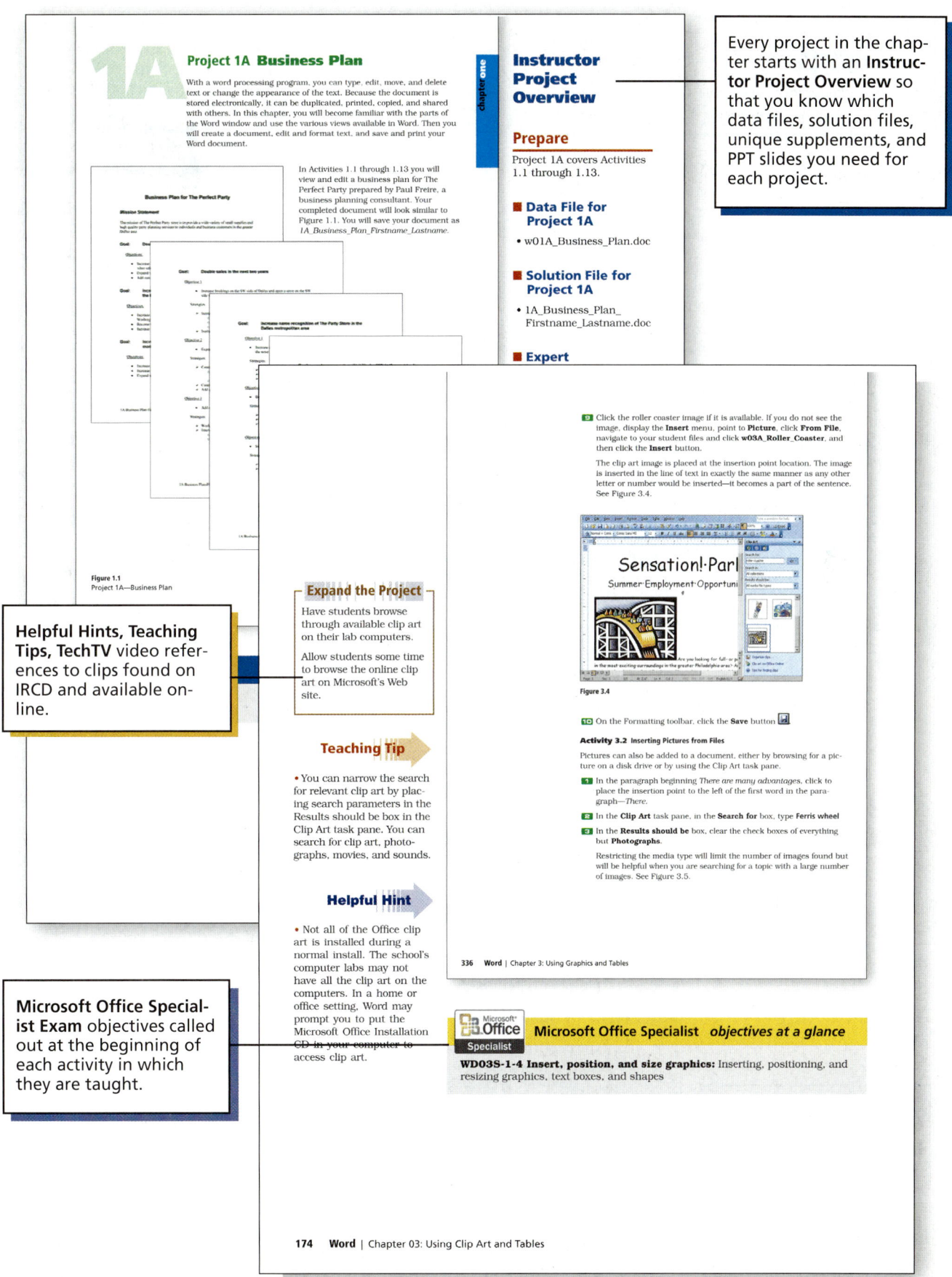

Every project in the chapter starts with an **Instructor Project Overview** so that you know which data files, solution files, unique supplements, and PPT slides you need for each project.

Helpful Hints, Teaching Tips, TechTV video references to clips found on IRCD and available online.

Microsoft Office Specialist Exam objectives called out at the beginning of each activity in which they are taught.

Preface xxiii

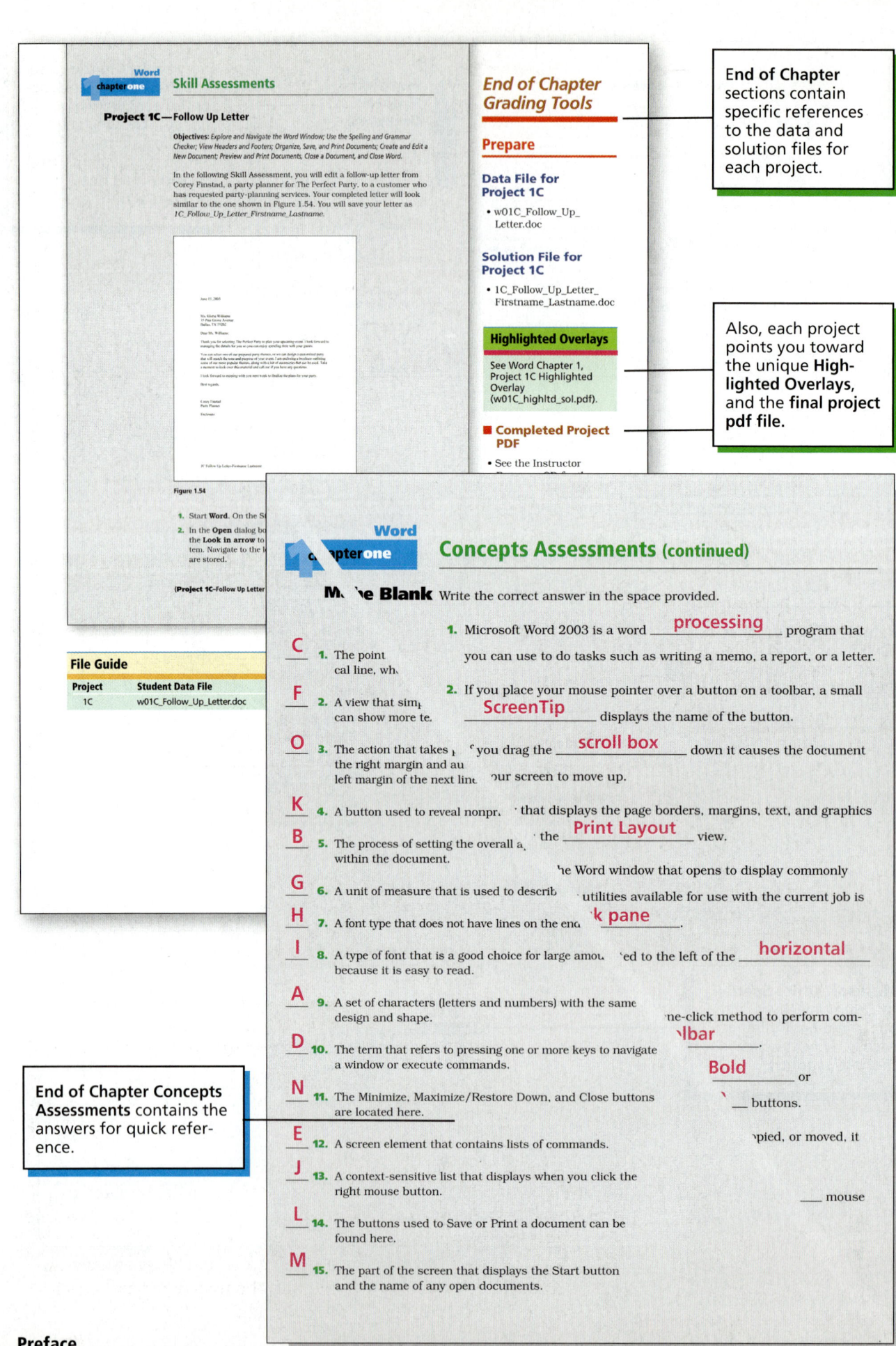

xxiv   Preface

Chapter summary pages contain links to Glossary and Key Terms, as well as information about Online Courses and Prentice Hall's Train and Assess Generation IT—online training and assessment.

Another supplement exclusive to the *GO! Series* is the **Point Counted Production Test.** Reminders are put on each chapter summary page, the printed documents are provided in the back of each chapter, and we also provide electronic versions in Word format on the IE CD-ROM for easy customization.

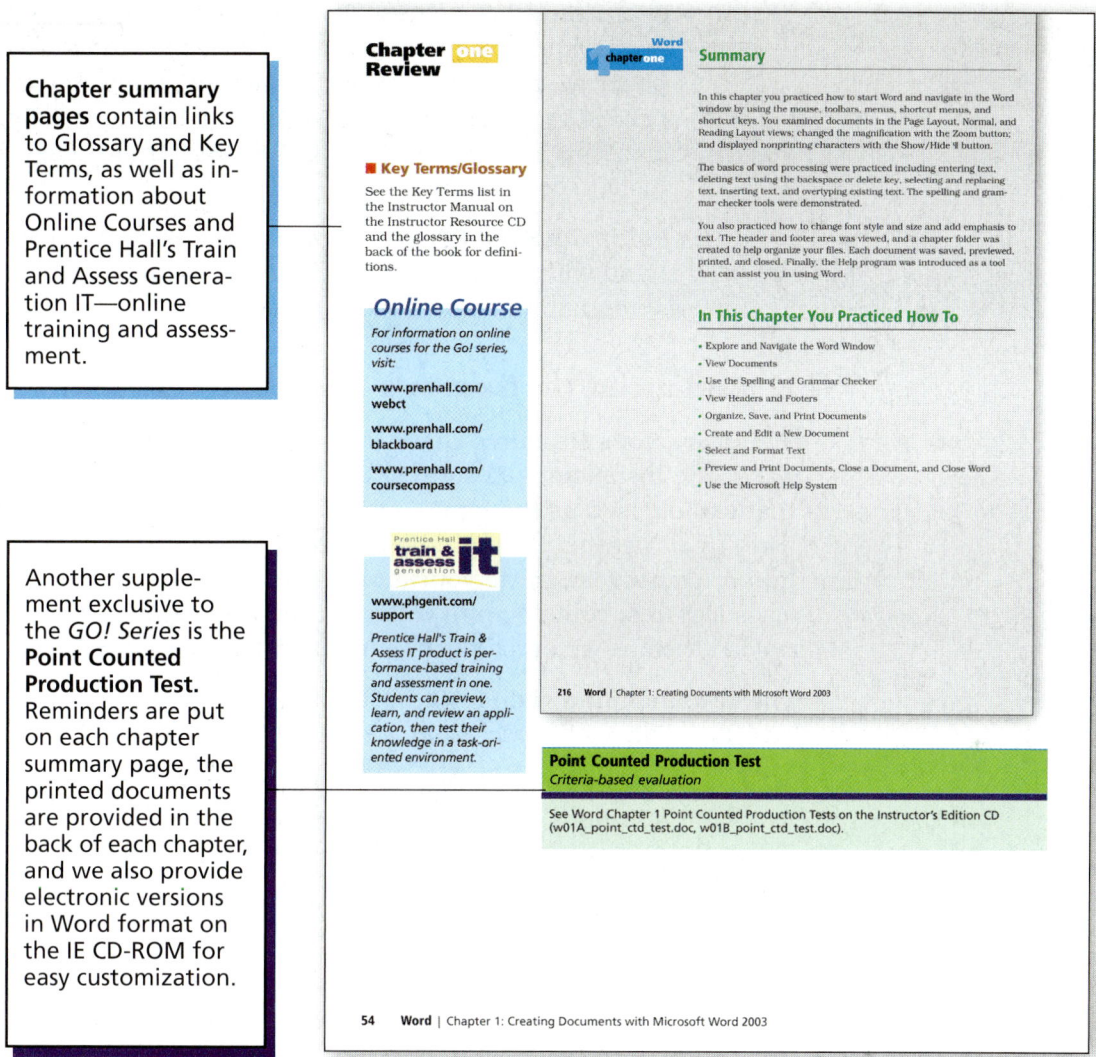

The Instructor's Edition also contains printed copies of these supplement materials *unique* to the *GO! Series*:

- **Expert Demonstration Document (EDD)**—A mirror image of each in-chapter project, accompanied by a brief script. The instructor can use it to give an expert demonstration of each objective that will be covered in the chapter, without having to use one of the chapter's projects. This EDD also prevents students from "working ahead during the presentation," as they do not have access to this document/project.

- **Chapter Assignment Sheets**—With a sheet listing all the assignments for the chapter, the instructor can quickly insert his or her name, course information, due dates, and points.

- **Custom Assignment Tags**—These cutout tags include a brief list of common errors that students could make on each project, with check boxes so instructors don't have to keep writing the same error description over and over! These tags serve a dual purpose: The student can do a final check to make sure all the listed items are correct, and the instructor can check off the items that need to be corrected.

- **Highlighted Overlays**—These are printed and transparent overlays that the instructor lays over the student's assignment paper to see at a glance if the student changed what he or she needed to. Coupled with the Custom Assignment Tags, this creates a "grading and scoring system" that is easy for the instructor to implement.

- **Point Counted Chapter Production Test**—Working hand-in-hand with the EDD, this is a final test for the student to demonstrate mastery of the objectives.

2) Enhanced Instructor's Resource CD-ROM

The Instructor's Resource CD-ROM is an interactive library of assets and links. The Instructor's Resource CD-ROM writes custom "index" pages that can be used as the foundation of a class presentation or online lecture. By navigating through the CD-ROM, you can collect the materials that are most relevant to your interests, edit them to create powerful class lectures, copy them to your own computer's hard drive, and/or upload them to an online course management system.

The new and improved Prentice Hall Instructor's Resource CD-ROM includes tools you expect from a Prentice Hall text:

- The Instructor's Manual in Word and PDF formats—includes solutions to all questions and exercises from the book and Companion Website
- Multiple, customizable PowerPoint slide presentations for each chapter
- Data and Solution Files
- Complete Test Bank
- Image library of all figures from the text
- TestGen Software with QuizMaster
    - TestGen is a test generator that lets you view and easily edit test bank questions, transfer them to tests, and print in a variety of formats suitable to your teaching situation. The program also offers many options for organizing and displaying test banks and tests. A built-in random number and text generator makes it ideal for creating multiple versions of tests that involve calculations and provides more possible test items than test bank questions. Powerful search and sort functions let you easily locate questions and arrange them in the order you prefer.
    - QuizMaster allows students to take tests created with TestGen on a local area network. The QuizMaster utility built into TestGen lets instructors view student records and print a variety of reports. Building tests is easy with TestGen, and exams can be easily uploaded into WebCT, Blackboard, and CourseCompass.

3) Instructor's Edition CD-ROM

The Instructor's Edition CD-ROM contains PDF versions of the Instructor's Edition as well as Word versions of the *GO! Series* unique supplements for easy instructor customization.

Training and Assessment—www2.phgenit.com/support

Prentice Hall offers performance-based training and assessment in one product—Train&Assess IT. The training component offers computer-based training that a student can use to preview, learn, and review Microsoft Office application skills. Web or CD-ROM delivered, Train IT offers interactive, multimedia, computer-based training to augment classroom learning. Built-in prescriptive testing suggests a study path based not only on student test results but also on the specific textbook chosen for the course.

The assessment component offers computer-based testing that shares the same user interface as Train IT and is used to evaluate a student's knowledge about specific topics in Word, Excel, Access, PowerPoint, Outlook, the Internet, and Computing Concepts. It does this in a task-oriented environment to demonstrate proficiency as well as comprehension of the topics by the students. More extensive than the testing in Train IT, Assess IT offers more administrative features for the instructor and additional questions for the student.

Assess IT also allows professors to test students out of a course, place students in appropriate courses, and evaluate skill sets.

Companion Website @ www.prenhall.com/go

This text is accompanied by a Companion Website at www.prenhall.com/go. Features of this new site include an interactive study guide, downloadable supplements, online end-of-chapter materials, additional practice projects, Web resource links, and technology updates and bonus chapters on the latest trends and hottest topics in information technology. All links to Web exercises will be constantly updated to ensure accuracy for students.

CourseCompass—www.coursecompass.com

CourseCompass is a dynamic, interactive online course-management tool powered exclusively for Pearson Education by Blackboard. This exciting product allows you to teach market-leading Pearson Education content in an easy-to-use, customizable format.

Blackboard—www.prenhall.com/blackboard

Prentice Hall's abundant online content, combined with Blackboard's popular tools and interface, result in robust Web-based courses that are easy to implement, manage, and use—taking your courses to new heights in student interaction and learning.

WebCT—www.prenhall.com/webct

Course-management tools within WebCT include page tracking, progress tracking, class and student management, gradebook, communication, calendar, reporting tools, and more. Gold Level Customer Support, available exclusively to adopters of Prentice Hall courses, is provided free-of-charge on adoption and provides you with priority assistance, training discounts, and dedicated technical support.

TechTV—www.techtv.com

TechTV is the San Francisco-based cable network that showcases the smart, edgy, and unexpected side of technology. By telling stories through the prism of technology, TechTV provides programming that celebrates its viewers' passion, creativity, and lifestyle.

TechTV's programming falls into three categories:

1. **Help and Information**, with shows like *The Screen Savers*, TechTV's daily live variety show featuring everything from guest interviews and celebrities to product advice and demos; *Tech Live*, featuring the latest news on the industry's most important people, companies, products, and issues; and Call for Help, a live help and how-to show providing computing tips and live viewer questions.

2. **Cool Docs**, with shows like *The Tech Of...*, a series that goes behind the scenes of modern life and shows you the technology that makes things tick; *Performance*, an investigation into how technology and science are molding the perfect athlete; and *Future Fighting Machines*, a fascinating look at the technology and tactics of warfare.

3. **Outrageous Fun**, with shows like *X-Play*, exploring the latest and greatest in videogaming; and *Unscrewed* with Martin Sargent, a new late-night series showcasing the darker, funnier world of technology.

For more information, log onto www.techtv.com or contact your local cable or satellite provider to get TechTV in your area.

Visual Walk-Through

Project-based Instruction
Students do not practice features of the application; they create real projects that they will need in the real world. Projects are color coded for easy reference.

Projects are named to reflect skills the student will be practicing, not vague project names.

Word 2003

chapter one
Creating Documents with Microsoft Word 2003

In this chapter you will: **complete these projects** and **practice these skills**.

Project 1A
Exploring Microsoft Word

Objectives
- Explore and Navigate the Word Window
- View Documents
- Use the Spelling and Grammar Checker
- View Headers and Footers
- Organize, Save, and Print Documents

Project 1B
Creating, Editing, and Printing a Document

Objectives
- Create and Edit a New Document
- Select and Format Text
- Preview and Print Documents, Close a Document, and Close Word
- Use the Microsoft Help System

Learning Objectives
Objectives are clustered around projects. They help students to learn how to solve problems, not just learn software features.

The Greater Atlanta Job Fair

The Greater Atlanta Job Fair is a nonprofit organization that holds targeted job fairs in and around the greater Atlanta area several times each year. The fairs are widely marketed to companies nationwide and locally. The organization also presents an annual Atlanta Job Fair that draws over 2,000 employers in more than 70 industries and generally registers more than 5,000 candidates.

©Getty Images, Inc.

Getting Started with Outlook 2003

Do you sometimes find it a challenge to manage and complete all the tasks related to your job, family, and class work? Microsoft Office Outlook 2003 can help. Outlook 2003 is a personal information management program (also known as a PIM) that does two things: (1) it helps you get organized, and (2) it helps you communicate with others efficiently. Successful people know that good organizational and communication skills are important. Outlook 2003 electronically stores and organizes appointments and due dates; names, addresses, and phone numbers; to do lists; and notes. Another major use of Outlook 2003 is its e-mail and fax capabilities, along with features with which you can manage group work such as the tasks assigned to a group of coworkers. In this introduction to Microsoft Office Outlook 2003, you will explore the modules available in Outlook and enter data into each module.

Each chapter opens with a story that sets the stage for the projects the student will create, not force them to pretend to be someone or make up a scenario themselves.

Each chapter has an introductory paragraph that briefs students on what is important.

Visual Summary
Shows students up front what their projects will look like when they are done.

Project Summary
Stated clearly and quickly in one paragraph with the Visual Summary formatted as a caption so your students won't skip it.

Objective
The skills they will learn are clearly stated at the beginning of each project and color coded to match projects listed on the chapter opener page.

Teachable Moment
Expository text is woven into the steps—at the moment students need to know it—not chunked together in a block of text that will go unread.

xxx   **Visual Walk-Through**

Steps
Color coded to the current project, easy to read, and not too many to confuse the student or too few to be meaningless.

Sequential Page Numbering
No more confusing letters and abbreviations.

End of Project Icon
All projects in the *GO! Series* have clearly identifiable end points, useful in self-paced or on-line environments.

Microsoft Procedural Syntax
All steps are written in Microsoft Procedural Syntax in order to put the student in the right place at the right time.

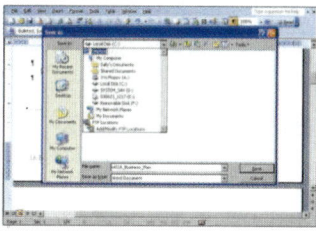

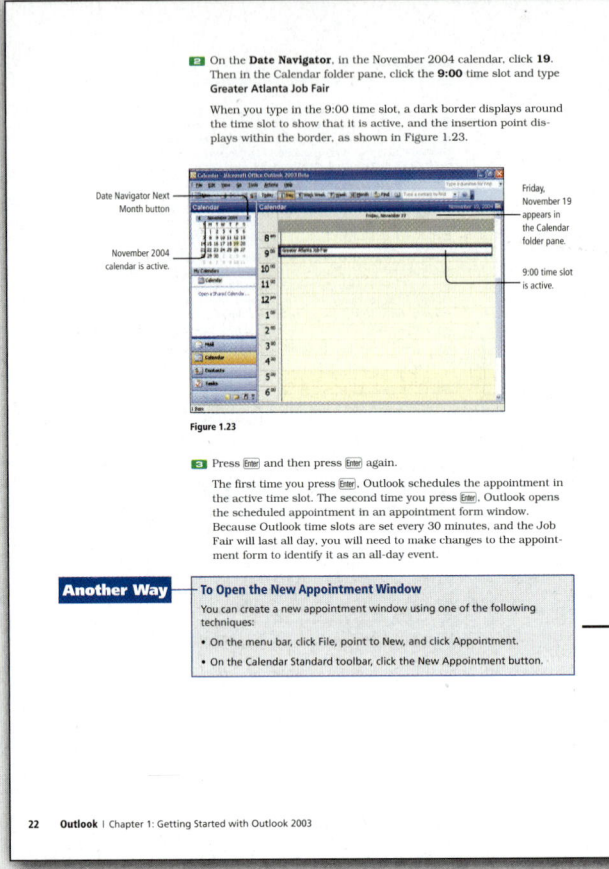

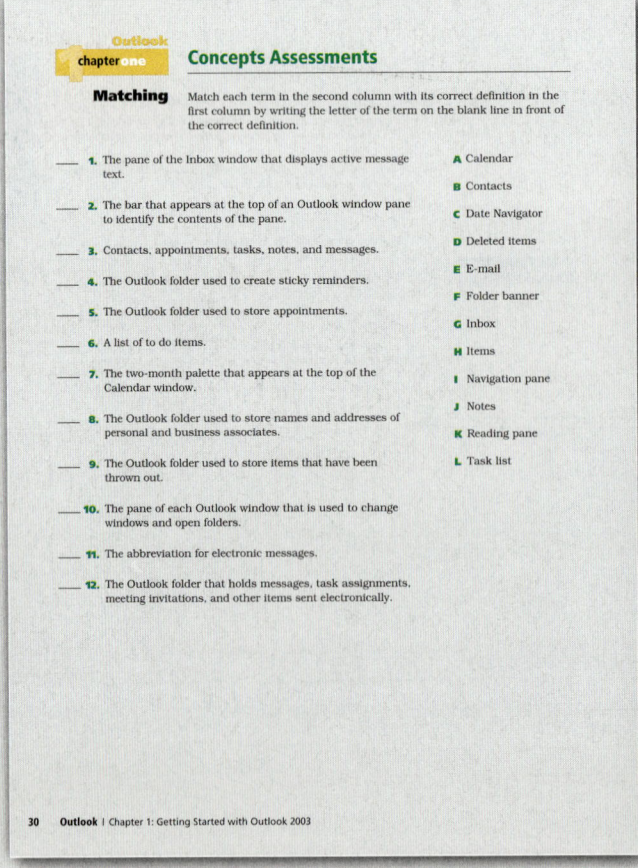

Alert box
Draws students' attention to make sure they aren't getting too far off course.

Another Way box
Shows students other ways of doing tasks.

More Knowledge box
Expands on a topic by going deeper into the material.

Note box
Points out important items to remember.

End-of-Chapter Material
Take your pick... Skills Assessment, Performance Assessment, or Mastery Assessment. Real-world projects with high, medium, or low guidance levels.

xxxii   Visual Walk-Through

Objectives List

Each project in the GO! Series end-of-chapter section starts with a list of the objectives covered, in order to easily find the exercises you need to hone your skills.

Performance Assessments

Project 1D — Creating Folders for College Fairs

Objectives: *Start Outlook and Create Outlook Folders.*

The fairs for Mercer College and Georgia Tech have been set for April 2005. As a result, you need to create folders to hold vendor information for the fairs. When you have created the contact folders for these two fairs, your Contacts list will appear as in Figure 1.35.

Figure 1.35

1. Start Outlook, open the **Contacts** module, open the main **Contacts** folder, and on the menu bar, click **File**, point to **Folder**, and click **New Folder** to open the **Create New Folder** dialog box.

2. In the **Name** text box, type **Mercer College Fair 2005** ensure that **Contact Items** appears in the **Folder contains** text box, and click **OK**.

3. Repeat the procedures in Steps 1 and 2 to create another contacts folder named **Georgia Tech Fair 2005**

 You have completed Project 1D

End of Each Project Clearly Marked

Groups of steps that the student performs; the guided practice in order to master the learning objective.

On the Internet

In this section, students are directed to go out to the Internet for independent study.

On the Internet

Locating Friends on the Web

The World Wide Web not only stores information about companies, Web sites for bidding on items, and so forth, but it also contains telephone book information as well as e-mail addresses for many people—especially those who are students at universities! Search the Web for the colleges that three of your friends attend. After you locate the sites, search each university's e-mail directory for one of your friends. Then record these friends and their university e-mail addresses in your contacts list. Print a copy of each contact form as you create it.

GO! with Help

Training on Outlook

Microsoft Online has set up a series of training lessons at its online Web site. You can access Microsoft.com and review these training sessions directly from the Help menu in Outlook. In this project, you will work your way through the links on the Microsoft Web site to see what training topics they currently offer for Outlook. Log onto the required networks, connect to the Internet, and then follow these steps to complete the exercise.

1. If necessary, start Outlook. On the menu bar, click **Help** and then click **Office on Microsoft.com**.

   The Microsoft Office Online Web page opens in the default browser window.

2. On the left side of the Microsoft Office Online Web page, click the **Training** link.

   The Training Home Web page opens.

3. On the Training Home page, under Browse Training Courses, click **Outlook**.

   The Outlook Courses Web page opens.

4. On the Outlook Courses Web page list, click **Address your e-mail: Get it on the To line fast**.

   The Overview Web page displays information about the training session, identifies the goals of the session, and displays links for continuing the session. Navigation buttons appear in a grey bar toward the top of the Overview page for playing, pausing, and stopping the session. Yellow arrows appear above the navigation bar to advance to the next session page.

5. In the upper right side of the Overview page, on the gray navigation bar, click **Play**.

GO! with Help

A special section where students practice using the HELP feature of the Office application.

Visual Walk-Through xxxiii

Contents in Brief

Preface xiv

Getting Started

Getting Started with Windows XP 1

Getting Started with Outlook 2003 51

Getting Started with Internet Explorer 93

Basic Computer Concepts 135

Word

Chapter 1 **Creating Documents with Microsoft Word 2003** 163

Chapter 2 **Formatting and Organizing Text** 243

Chapter 3 **Using Graphics and Tables** 331

Chapter 4 **Creating Documents with Multiple Columns and Special Formats** 419

Excel

Chapter 1 **Getting Started with Excel 2003** 499

Chapter 2 **Editing Workbooks, Formulas, and Cells** 587

Chapter 3 **Formatting a Worksheet** 667

Access

Chapter 1 **Getting Started with Access Databases and Tables** 739

Chapter 2 **Forms and Reports** 819

Chapter 3 **Queries** 891

xxxv

PowerPoint

Chapter **1** **Getting Started with PowerPoint 2003** **963**

Chapter **2** **Creating a Presentation** **1035**

Chapter **3** **Formatting a Presentation** **1091**

Task Guides **1155**
Glossary **1207**
Index **1217**

Table of Contents

.... xiv

...ing with ...ows XP 1

Objective 1	Get Started with Windows	4
Objective 2	Resize, Move, and Scroll Windows	14
Objective 3	Maximize, Restore, Minimize, and Close a Window	18
Objective 4	Create a New Folder	22
Objective 5	Copy, Move, Rename, and Delete Files	27
Objective 6	Find Files and Folders	35
Objective 7	Compress Files	41
Summary		48
In This Chapter You Practiced How To		48
Concepts Assessments		49

Outlook 2003

Chapter 1 Getting Started with Outlook 2003 51

Objective 1	Start Outlook and Identify Outlook Window Elements	54
Activity 1.1	Starting Outlook	54
Objective 2	Create Outlook Folders	57
Activity 1.2	Creating Outlook Folders	57
Objective 3	Close Outlook	59
Activity 1.3	Closing Outlook	59
Objective 4	Store Addresses in the Contacts Folder	60
Activity 1.4	Creating Contacts	60
Objective 5	Edit and Print Contacts	66
Activity 1.5	Editing and Printing Outlook Contacts	66
Objective 6	Schedule Appointments in the Calendar	69

Activity 1.6	Changing the Calendar Window View	69
Activity 1.7	Scheduling Appointments in the Calendar	71
Activity 1.8	Printing Calendars	74
Objective 7	Record Tasks and Notes	75
Activity 1.9	Recording Tasks in the TaskPad	75
Summary		79
In This Chapter You Practiced How To		79
Concepts Assessments		80
Skill Assessments		82
Performance Assessments		85
Mastery Assessments		89
Problem Solving		90
On the Internet		90
GO! with Help		91

Internet Explorer

Chapter 1 Getting Started with Internet Explorer ...93

Objective 1	Start Internet Explorer 6.0 and Identify Screen Elements	96
Activity 1.1	Starting Internet Explorer	96
Objective 2	Navigate the Internet	99
Activity 1.2	Using the Standard Buttons Toolbar	99
Activity 1.3	Using the Address Bar	100
Activity 1.4	Using Hyperlinks	105
Activity 1.5	Using Internet Explorer History	109
Objective 3	Work with Favorites	111
Activity 1.6	Adding an Address to the Favorites List	111
Activity 1.7	Displaying a Favorite Web Site	112
Activity 1.8	Deleting a Web Address from Favorites	114
Objective 4	Search the Internet	116
Activity 1.9	Searching the Internet	116
Objective 5	Download Files	119
Activity 1.10	Downloading and Saving a Web Page	119
Objective 6	Print Web Pages	122
Activity 1.11	Printing Web Pages	122
Objective 7	Close Internet Explorer	124
Activity 1.12	Closing Internet Explorer	124

xxxvii

Summary	125
In This Chapter You Practiced How To	125
Concepts Assessments	126
Skill Assessments	128
Performance Assessments	130
Mastery Assessments	133
Problem Solving	133
On the Internet	134
GO! with Help	134

Computer Concepts

Chapter 1 Basic Computer Concepts 135

Objective 1	Define Computer and Identify Required Components	137
Objective 2	Identify the Types of Computers	138
Objective 3	Describe Hardware Devices	140
	System Unit	140
	Input Devices	143
	Output Devices	147
	Storage Devices	149
Objective 4	Identify Types of Software and Their Uses	150
	Operating Systems Software	150
	Applications Software	151
Objective 5	Describe Networks and Define Network Terms	154
	Local Area Networks (LANs)	155
	Wide Area Networks (WANs)	156
Summary		157
In This Chapter You Practiced How To		157
Concepts Assessments		158

Word 2003

Chapter 1 Creating Documents with Microsoft Word 2003 163

Objective 1	Explore and Navigate the Word Window	166
Activity 1.1	Starting Word and Identifying Parts of the Word Window	166
Activity 1.2	Opening an Existing Document	170
Activity 1.3	Accessing Menu Commands and Displaying the Task Pane	171
Activity 1.4	Navigating a Document Using the Vertical Scroll Bar	175
Activity 1.5	Navigating a Document Using the Keyboard	178
Objective 2	View Documents	**179**
Activity 1.6	Displaying Formatting Marks	179
Activity 1.7	Changing Views	180
Activity 1.8	Using the Zoom Button	181
Objective 3	Use the Spelling and Grammar Checker	**183**
Activity 1.9	Checking Individual Spelling and Grammar Errors	183
Activity 1.10	Checking Spelling and Grammar in an Entire Document	185
Objective 4	View Headers and Footers	**188**
Activity 1.11	Accessing Headers and Footers	188
Objective 5	Organize, Save, and Print Documents	**190**
Activity 1.12	Creating Folders for Document Storage and Saving a Document	190
Activity 1.13	Printing a Document From the Toolbar	193
Objective 6	Create and Edit a New Document	**195**
Activity 1.14	Creating a New Document	195
Activity 1.15	Entering Text and Inserting Blank Lines	196
Activity 1.16	Editing Text with the Delete and Backspace Keys	201
Activity 1.17	Inserting New Text and Overtyping Existing Text	202
Objective 7	Select and Format Text	**204**
Activity 1.18	Selecting Text	204
Activity 1.19	Changing Font and Font Size	206
Activity 1.20	Adding Emphasis to Text	209
Objective 8	Preview and Print Documents, Close a Document, and Close Word	**210**
Activity 1.21	Previewing and Printing a Document and Closing Word	210
Objective 9	Use the Microsoft Help System	**213**
Activity 1.22	Typing a Question for Help	213

Summary	216
In This Chapter You Practiced How To	216
Concepts Assessments	217
Skill Assessments	219
Performance Assessments	228
Mastery Assessments	236
Problem Solving	240
On the Internet	242
GO! with Help	242

Chapter 2 Formatting and Organizing Text ... 243

Objective 1 Change Document and Paragraph Layout   246
- Activity 2.1   Setting Margins   246
- Activity 2.2   Aligning Text   248
- Activity 2.3   Changing Line Spacing   250
- Activity 2.4   Adding Space After Paragraphs   252
- Activity 2.5   Indenting Paragraphs   255
- Activity 2.6   Using the Format Painter   256

Objective 2 Change and Reorganize Text   257
- Activity 2.7   Finding and Replacing Text   257
- Activity 2.8   Selecting and Deleting Text   259
- Activity 2.9   Cutting and Pasting Text   261
- Activity 2.10 Copying and Pasting Text   264
- Activity 2.11 Dragging Text to a New Location   266
- Activity 2.12 Undoing and Redoing Changes   268

Objective 3 Create and Modify Lists   271
- Activity 2.13 Creating a Bulleted List   271
- Activity 2.14 Creating a Numbered List   272
- Activity 2.15 Formatting Lists   274
- Activity 2.16 Customizing Bullets   276

Objective 4 Work with Headers and Footers   279
- Activity 2.17 Inserting and Formatting Page Numbers   279
- Activity 2.18 Inserting AutoText   281
- Activity 2.19 Inserting the Current Date and Time   282

Objective 5 Insert Frequently Used Text   283
- Activity 2.20 Recording AutoCorrect Entries   283
- Activity 2.21 Using AutoCorrect Shortcuts   286
- Activity 2.22 Recording and Inserting AutoText   288
- Activity 2.23 Inserting Symbols   290

Objective 6 Insert References   292
- Activity 2.24 Inserting Footnotes   292

Activity 2.25 Formatting Footnotes	296
Activity 2.26 Creating a Reference Page	297
Activity 2.27 Formatting a Reference Page	298
Summary	301
In This Chapter You Practiced How To	301
Concepts Assessments	302
Skill Assessments	304
Performance Assessments	315
Mastery Assessments	324
Problem Solving	328
On the Internet	330
GO! with Help	330

Chapter 3 Using Graphics and Tables 331

Objective 1 Insert Clip Art and Pictures   334
- Activity 3.1   Inserting Clip Art   334
- Activity 3.2   Inserting Pictures from Files   336

Objective 2 Modify Clip Art and Pictures   338
- Activity 3.3   Wrapping Text around Graphic Objects   338
- Activity 3.4   Resizing a Graphic Object   341
- Activity 3.5   Moving a Graphic Object   343

Objective 3 Work with the Drawing Toolbar   344
- Activity 3.6   Inserting a Text Box   344
- Activity 3.7   Moving and Resizing a Text Box   346
- Activity 3.8   Inserting an Arrow   347
- Activity 3.9   Inserting an AutoShape   349

Objective 4 Work with Tab Stops   353
- Activity 3.10 Setting Tab Stops   354
- Activity 3.11 Formatting and Removing Tab Stops   357
- Activity 3.12 Using Tab Stops to Enter Text   359
- Activity 3.13 Moving Tab Stops   362

Objective 5 Create a Table   365
- Activity 3.14 Creating a Table   365
- Activity 3.15 Adding a Row to a Table   368
- Activity 3.16 Changing the Width of a Table Column   370
- Activity 3.17 Adding a Column to a Table   371

Objective 6 Format Tables   373
- Activity 3.18 Formatting Text in Cells   373
- Activity 3.19 Shading Cells   375
- Activity 3.20 Changing the Table Border   377
- Activity 3.21 Centering a Table   380

Table of Contents xxxix

Objective 7	Create a Table from Existing Text	381
Activity 3.22	Converting Text to Tables	381
Activity 3.23	Applying a Predefined Format to a Table	384
Activity 3.24	Merging Cells and Aligning Text Vertically	385

Summary	389
In This Chapter You Practiced How To	389
Concepts Assessments	390
Skill Assessments	392
Performance Assessments	401
Mastery Assessments	409
Problem Solving	414
On the Internet	417
GO! with Help	418

Chapter 4 Creating Documents with Multiple Columns and Special Formats 419

Objective 1	Create a Decorative Title	422
Activity 4.1	Inserting WordArt	422
Activity 4.2	Formatting WordArt	424
Activity 4.3	Adding a Border Line	426
Objective 2	Create Multicolumn Documents	428
Activity 4.4	Changing One Column to Two Columns	428
Activity 4.5	Formatting Multiple Columns	429
Activity 4.6	Inserting a Column Break	431
Objective 3	Add Special Paragraph Formatting	433
Activity 4.7	Adding a Border to a Paragraph	433
Activity 4.8	Shading a Paragraph	435
Objective 4	Use Special Character Formats	436
Activity 4.9	Changing Font Color	436
Activity 4.10	Using Small Caps	437
Objective 5	Insert Hyperlinks	441
Activity 4.11	Inserting Text Hyperlinks	441
Activity 4.12	Adding a Hyperlink to a Graphic	444
Activity 4.13	Modifying Hyperlinks	445
Objective 6	Preview and Save a Document as a Web Page	447
Activity 4.14	Previewing a Document as a Web Page	447
Activity 4.15	Saving a Document as a Web Page	448

Objective 7	Locate Supporting Information	451
Activity 4.16	Using Collect and Paste to Gather Images	451
Activity 4.17	Collecting Information from Other Documents	454
Activity 4.18	Finding Supporting Information Using the Research Tool	455
Activity 4.19	Pasting Information from the Clipboard Task Pane	458
Activity 4.20	Using the Thesaurus	461
Objective 8	Find Objects with the Select Browse Object Button	463
Activity 4.21	Using the Select Browse Object Menu to Find Document Elements	463

Summary	467
In This Chapter You Practiced How To	467
Concepts Assessments	468
Skill Assessments	470
Performance Assessments	480
Mastery Assessments	489
Problem Solving	496
On the Internet	498
GO! with Help	498

Excel 2003

Chapter 1 Getting Started with Excel 2003 ... 499

Objective 1	Start Excel and Navigate a Workbook	502
Activity 1.1	Starting Excel and Identifying the Parts of the Window	502
Activity 1.2	Using the Menu Bar, ScreenTips, and the Toolbars	506
Activity 1.3	Opening an Existing Workbook	509
Activity 1.4	Selecting Columns, Rows, Cells, Ranges, and Worksheets	512
Activity 1.5	Navigating Using the Scroll Bars	518
Activity 1.6	Navigating Using the Name Box	520
Activity 1.7	Navigating Among the Worksheets in a Workbook	522
Activity 1.8	Viewing a Chart	523
Activity 1.9	Renaming a Sheet Tab	524
Objective 2	Create Headers and Footers	525
Activity 1.10	Creating Headers and Footers	525
Objective 3	Preview and Print a Workbook	529
Activity 1.11	Previewing and Printing a Workbook	529

Objective 4	Save and Close a Workbook and Exit Excel	530
Activity 1.12	Creating a New Folder and Saving a Workbook with a New Name	530

Objective 5	Create a New Workbook	534
Activity 1.13	Creating a New Workbook	534
Activity 1.14	Saving and Naming a New Workbook	536

Objective 6	Enter and Edit Data in a Worksheet	537
Activity 1.15	Entering Text	537
Activity 1.16	Using AutoComplete to Enter Data	540
Activity 1.17	Entering Numbers	542
Activity 1.18	Typing Dates into a Worksheet	543
Activity 1.19	Editing Data in Cells	545
Activity 1.20	Using Undo and Redo	548
Activity 1.21	Clearing a Cell	548

Objective 7	Create Formulas	549
Activity 1.22	Typing a Formula in a Cell	549
Activity 1.23	Using Point and Click to Enter Cell References in a Formula	551
Activity 1.24	Summing a Column of Numbers with AutoSum	553

Objective 8	Use Zoom and the Spelling Checker Tool	555
Activity 1.25	Zooming a Worksheet	555
Activity 1.26	Checking for Spelling Errors in a Worksheet	557

Objective 9	Print a Worksheet Using the Print Dialog Box	558
Activity 1.27	Previewing the Worksheet	558
Activity 1.28	Closing a Workbook from the File Menu	559

Objective 10	Use Excel Help	559
Activity 1.29	Using the Type a question for help Box	559

Summary	562
In This Chapter You Practiced How To	562
Concepts Assessments	563
Skill Assessments	565
Performance Assessments	574
Mastery Assessments	581
Problem Solving	585
On the Internet	586
GO! with Help	586

Chapter 2 Editing Workbooks, Formulas, and Cells 587

Objective 1	Enter Constant Values with AutoFill and the Fill Handle	590
Activity 2.1	Inserting Titles and Headings	590
Activity 2.2	Creating a Series Using AutoFill	592
Activity 2.3	Duplicating Data Using AutoFill	594

Objective 2	Insert, Delete, and Adjust Rows and Columns	596
Activity 2.4	Adjusting Column Width and Row Height	596
Activity 2.5	Inserting and Deleting Rows and Columns	599

Objective 3	Align Cell Contents Horizontally	602
Activity 2.6	Aligning Cell Contents	602
Activity 2.7	Using Merge and Center	603

Objective 4	Copy and Move Cell Contents	604
Activity 2.8	Copying Cell Contents	604
Activity 2.9	Copying Multiple Selections Using Collect and Paste	608
Activity 2.10	Copying an Entire Worksheet to a New Worksheet	609
Activity 2.11	Pasting Data from Another Workbook	610
Activity 2.12	Moving Cell Contents Using the Cut Command	614
Activity 2.13	Moving Cell Contents Using Drag-and-Drop	616

Objective 5	Format Numbers Using the Toolbar	618
Activity 2.14	Formatting Cells with the Currency Style Button	618
Activity 2.15	Formatting Cells with the Percent Style Button	620
Activity 2.16	Increasing and Decreasing Decimal Places	621
Activity 2.17	Formatting Cells with the Comma Style Button	622

Objective 6	Edit Formulas	623
Activity 2.18	Selecting Ranges Using the AutoSum Function	623
Activity 2.19	Editing Within the Formula Bar	629
Activity 2.20	Editing Within a Cell Using Edit Mode	632

Objective 7	**Copy Formulas**	**633**
Activity 2.21	Copying a Formula with Relative Cell References Using the Fill Handle	633
Activity 2.22	Copying Formulas Containing Absolute Cell References	635
Objective 8	**Conduct a What-if Analysis**	**639**
Activity 2.23	Conducting a What-if Analysis	639
Objective 9	**Display and Print Underlying Formulas**	**640**
Activity 2.24	Displaying and Printing Underlying Formulas	640
Objective 10	**Change Page Orientation**	**641**
Activity 2.25	Changing Page Orientation	641
Summary		643
In This Chapter You Practiced How To		643
Concepts Assessments		644
Skill Assessments		645
Performance Assessments		654
Mastery Assessments		660
Problem Solving		665
On the Internet		665
GO! with Help		666

Chapter 3 Formatting a Worksheet 667

Objective 1	**Change Number Format**	**670**
Activity 3.1	Using the Format Cells Dialog Box to Format Numbers	670
Activity 3.2	Selecting and Applying the Currency Format	674
Objective 2	**Change Alignment of Cell Contents**	**675**
Activity 3.3	Changing Horizontal Alignment Using the Format Cells Dialog Box	675
Activity 3.4	Indenting Cell Contents	677
Activity 3.5	Filling a Cell	678
Activity 3.6	Aligning Cell Contents Vertically	679
Activity 3.7	Rotating Text	681
Activity 3.8	Wrapping Text in a Cell	682
Objective 3	**Apply Cell Formatting**	**684**
Activity 3.9	Changing the Font and Font Size	684
Activity 3.10	Merging Cells	689
Activity 3.11	Applying Cell Borders	690
Activity 3.12	Applying Cell Shading	693
Activity 3.13	Using Format Painter	695
Activity 3.14	Clearing Cell Formats	697

Objective 4	**Apply Workbook Formatting**	**699**
Activity 3.15	Selecting Page Orientation, Scaling, and Paper Size	699
Activity 3.16	Setting Margins and Centering the Worksheet	701
Activity 3.17	Creating Headers and Footers with Inserted Pictures	703
Activity 3.18	Setting Header and Footer Margins	708
Objective 5	**Print Gridlines, Print Row and Column Headings, and Set Print Quality**	**710**
Activity 3.19	Printing Gridlines, Printing Row and Column Headings, and Setting Print Quality	710
Objective 6	**View and Insert Comments in a Cell**	**712**
Activity 3.20	Viewing and Inserting Comments in a Cell	712
Summary		714
In This Chapter You Practiced How To		714
Concepts Assessments		715
Skill Assessments		717
Performance Assessments		726
Mastery Assessments		733
Problem Solving		737
On the Internet		738
GO! with Help		738

Access 2003

Chapter 1 Getting Started with Access Databases and Tables 739

Objective 1	**Rename a Database**	**742**
Activity 1.1	Renaming a Database	742
Objective 2	**Start Access, Open an Existing Database, and View Database Objects**	**744**
Activity 1.2	Starting Access and Opening an Existing Database	744
Activity 1.3	Viewing the Database Window	750
Activity 1.4	Opening a Table	752
Activity 1.5	Viewing a Table	756

Activity 1.6	Viewing a Query	758
Activity 1.7	Viewing a Form	759
Activity 1.8	Viewing and Printing a Report	761
Objective 3	**Create a New Database**	**766**
Activity 1.9	Creating a New Database	766
Objective 4	**Create a New Table**	**767**
Activity 1.10	Adding Fields to a Table	767
Activity 1.11	Switching Between Views	771
Objective 5	**Create a Primary Key and Add Records to a Table**	**772**
Activity 1.12	Creating a Primary Key in a Table	772
Activity 1.13	Adding Records to a Table	774
Objective 6	**Close and Save a Table**	**775**
Activity 1.14	Closing and Saving a Table	775
Objective 7	**Open a Table**	**776**
Activity 1.15	Opening a Table	776
Objective 8	**Modify the Table Design**	**777**
Activity 1.16	Deleting Fields	777
Activity 1.17	Adding Fields	779
Objective 9	**Print a Table**	**780**
Activity 1.18	Printing a Table	780
Objective 10	**Edit Records in a Table**	**782**
Activity 1.19	Editing a Record	782
Activity 1.20	Deleting a Record	783
Activity 1.21	Resizing Columns and Rows	784
Activity 1.22	Hiding Columns	787
Objective 11	**Sort Records**	**789**
Activity 1.23	Sorting Records in a Table	789
Objective 12	**Navigate to Records in a Table**	**790**
Activity 1.24	Navigating Among Records Using the Navigation Area	790
Activity 1.25	Navigating Among Records Using the Keyboard	791
Objective 13	**Close and Save a Database**	**792**
Activity 1.26	Closing and Saving a Database	792
Objective 14	**Use the Access Help System**	**793**
Activity 1.27	Using the Access Help System	793
Summary		796
In This Chapter You Practiced How To		796
Concepts Assessments		797
Skill Assessments		799
Performance Assessments		807
Mastery Assessments		813
Problem Solving		817
On the Internet		818
GO! with Help		818

Chapter 2 Forms and Reports.................... 819

Objective 1	**View and Navigate to Records with a Form**	**822**
Activity 2.1	Viewing and Navigating to Records Using a Form	822
Objective 2	**Create an AutoForm**	**825**
Activity 2.2	Creating an AutoForm	825
Objective 3	**Save and Close an AutoForm**	**827**
Activity 2.3	Saving and Closing an AutoForm	827
Objective 4	**Use a Form to Add Records to and Delete Records from a Table**	**828**
Activity 2.4	Adding Records to a Table Using a Form	828
Activity 2.5	Deleting Records from a Table Using a Form	829
Objective 5	**Create a From with the Form Wizard**	**833**
Activity 2.6	Creating a Form Using the Form Wizard	833
Objective 6	**Modify a Form**	**836**
Activity 2.7	Switching Between Views in a Form and Adding a Form Header	836
Activity 2.8	Moving and Resizing Fields in a Form	841
Activity 2.9	Adding a Page Footer to a Form	848
Objective 7	**Create a Report with the Report Wizard**	
		850
Activity 2.10	Creating a Report Using the Report Wizard	850
Objective 8	**Save a Report**	**853**
Activity 2.11	Saving a Report	853
Objective 9	**Modify the Design of a Report**	**853**
Activity 2.12	Switching Between Report View and Design View	853
Activity 2.13	Moving and Resizing Fields in a Report	855
Activity 2.14	Adding a Page Footer and a Report Footer to a Report	862
Objective 10	**Print a Report**	**864**
Activity 2.15	Printing a Report	864
Summary		865
In This Chapter You Practiced How To		865
Concepts Assessments		866
Skill Assessments		868
Performance Assessments		878
Mastery Assessments		884
Problem Solving		888

Table of Contents **xliii**

On the Internet		889
GO! with Help		890

Chapter 3 Queries 891

Objective 1 Create a New Select Query **894**
- Activity 3.1 Creating a New Query, Using the Select Query Window, and Adding Fields to the Design Grid — 894

Objective 2 Run, Save, and Close a Query **899**
- Activity 3.2 Running, Saving, and Closing A Query — 899

Objective 3 Open and Edit an Existing Query **900**
- Activity 3.3 Opening an Existing Query and Switching Between Views — 900
- Activity 3.4 Editing a Query — 901

Objective 4 Specify Text Criteria in a Query **904**
- Activity 3.5 Specifying Text Criteria in a Query — 904
- Activity 3.6 Printing a Query — 910

Objective 5 Use Wildcards in a Query **912**
- Activity 3.7 Using the * Wildcard in a Query — 912
- Activity 3.8 Using the ? Wildcard in a Query — 916
- Activity 3.9 Specifying Criteria Using a Field Not Displayed in the Query Result — 918

Objective 6 Specify Numeric Criteria in a Query **921**
- Activity 3.10 Specifying Numeric Criteria in a Query — 921
- Activity 3.11 Using Comparison Operators — 922

Objective 7 Use Compound Criteria **925**
- Activity 3.12 Using AND in a Query — 925
- Activity 3.13 Using OR IN A Query — 926

Objective 8 Sort Data in a Query **927**
- Activity 3.14 Sorting Data in a Query — 927
- Activity 3.15 Modifying the Query Design and Sorting Data Using Multiple Fields in a Query — 928

Objective 9 Use Calculated Fields in a Query **934**
- Activity 3.16 Using Calculated Fields in a Query — 934

Objective 10 Group Data and Calculate Statistics in a Query **939**
- Activity 3.17 Grouping Data in a Query — 939
- Activity 3.18 Using the AVG, SUM, MAX, and MIN Functions in a Query — 941

Summary	944
In This Chapter You Practiced How To	944
Concepts Assessments	945
Skill Assessments	947
Performance Assessments	954
Mastery Assessments	958
Problem Solving	961
On the Internet	962
GO! with Help	962

PowerPoint 2003

Chapter 1 Getting Started with PowerPoint 2003 963

Objective 1 Start and Exit PowerPoint **966**
- Activity 1.1 Starting PowerPoint and Opening a Presentation — 966
- Activity 1.2 Identifying Parts of the PowerPoint Window — 969
- Activity 1.3 Accessing the Menu Commands — 972
- Activity 1.4 Identifying and Displaying Toolbars and ScreenTips — 975
- Activity 1.5 Closing and Displaying the Task Pane — 976
- Activity 1.6 Creating a New Folder and Saving a File — 977
- Activity 1.7 Closing a File — 979
- Activity 1.8 Exiting PowerPoint — 980

Objective 2 Edit a Presentation Using the Outline/Slides Pane **980**
- Activity 1.9 Editing a Presentation Using the Outline — 980
- Activity 1.10 Promoting and Demoting Outline Text — 983
- Activity 1.11 Deleting a Slide — 985
- Activity 1.12 Moving a Slide — 986

Objective 3 Format and Edit a Presentation Using the Slide Pane **987**
- Activity 1.13 Editing Text Using the Slide Pane — 987
- Activity 1.14 Changing Slide Layout — 988
- Activity 1.15 Checking the Spelling of a Presentation — 991
- Activity 1.16 Adding Speaker Notes to a Presentation — 992

Objective 4 View and Edit a Presentation in Slide Sorter View **994**
- Activity 1.17 Selecting Multiple Slides — 994
- Activity 1.18 Moving and Deleting Slides in Slide Sorter View — 996

Objective 5 View a Slide Show **997**
- Activity 1.19 Viewing a Slide Show — 997

Objective 6	Create Headers and Footers	999
Activity 1.20	Creating Headers and Footers on Slides	999
Activity 1.21	Creating Headers and Footers on Handouts and Notes Pages	1000
Objective 7	**Print a Presentation**	**1002**
Activity 1.22	Previewing and Printing Handouts and Slides	1002
Activity 1.23	Printing Notes Pages	1005
Objective 8	**Use PowerPoint Help**	**1007**
Activity 1.24	Using PowerPoint Help	1007
Summary		1009
In This Chapter You Practiced How To		1009
Concepts Assessments		1010
Skill Assessments		1012
Performance Assessments		1020
Mastery Assessments		1028
Problem Solving		1032
On the Internet		1034
GO! with Help		1034

Chapter 2 Creating a Presentation 1035

Objective 1	Create a Presentation	1038
Activity 2.1	Creating a Presentation Using the AutoContent Wizard	1038
Activity 2.2	Modifying AutoContent Presentation Text	1040
Activity 2.3	Inserting Slides from an Existing Presentation	1044
Activity 2.4	Inserting a New Slide	1045
Objective 2	**Modify Slides**	**1046**
Activity 2.5	Finding and Replacing Text	1046
Activity 2.6	Using the Undo and Redo Commands	1048
Objective 3	**Create a Presentation Using a Design Template**	**1050**
Activity 2.7	Creating a Presentation from a Design Template	1050
Activity 2.8	Changing the Design Template for a Single Slide	1052
Activity 2.9	Changing the Design Template for the Entire Presentation	1053
Activity 2.10	Changing the Design Template for Selected Slides	1054

Objective 4	Import Text from Word	1054
Activity 2.11	Importing a Word Outline	1054
Objective 5	**Move and Copy Text**	**1056**
Activity 2.12	Moving and Copying Text Using Drag-and-Drop	1056
Activity 2.13	Moving Text Using the Clipboard	1059
Activity 2.14	Copying Text Using the Clipboard	1061
Activity 2.15	Moving Multiple Selections Using Collect and Paste	1062
Summary		1064
In This Chapter You Practiced How To		1064
Concepts Assessments		1065
Skill Assessments		1067
Performance Assessments		1076
Mastery Assessments		1084
Problem Solving		1089
On the Internet		1090
GO! with Help		1090

Chapter 3 Formatting a Presentation 1091

Objective 1	Format Slide Text	1094
Activity 3.1	Changing Fonts and Font Sizes	1094
Activity 3.2	Replacing Fonts	1095
Activity 3.3	Changing Font Styles and Font Effects	1096
Activity 3.4	Using the Repeat Key	1098
Activity 3.5	Changing Font Colors	1098
Activity 3.6	Copying Formatting Using Format Painter	1101
Activity 3.7	Changing Text Case	1103
Activity 3.8	Changing Text Alignment	1104
Objective 2	**Modify Placeholders**	**1105**
Activity 3.9	Selecting Placeholder Text	1105
Activity 3.10	Sizing a Placeholder	1106
Activity 3.11	Moving a Placeholder	1108
Objective 3	**Modify Slide Master Elements**	**1110**
Activity 3.12	Displaying and Modifying the Title Master	1110
Activity 3.13	Displaying and Modifying the Slide Master	1112
Objective 4	**Apply Bullets and Numbering**	**1114**
Activity 3.14	Modifying Bullet Characters	1114
Activity 3.15	Inserting Picture Bullets	1116
Activity 3.16	Removing Bullets from Slide Text	1117
Activity 3.17	Applying Numbering to a List	1118

Objective 5 Customize a Color Scheme   **1120**
    Activity 3.18 Applying a Slide Color Scheme   1120
    Activity 3.19 Modifying a Slide Color Scheme   1121

Objective 6 Modify the Slide Background   **1122**
    Activity 3.20 Copying Applying a Gradient Fill Background   1122
    Activity 3.21 Applying a Textured Background   1124
    Activity 3.22 Omitting Background Graphics from a Slide   1125

Objective 7 Apply an Animation Scheme   **1126**
    Activity 3.23 Applying Animation Schemes to Slides   1126

Summary   1128
In This Chapter You Practiced How To   1128
Concepts Assessments   1129
Skill Assessments   1131
Performance Assessments   1140
Mastery Assessments   1148
Problem Solving   1152
On the Internet   1153
GO! with Help   1154

Task Guides 1155
Word 2003   1155
Excel 2003   1171
Access 2003   1183
PowerPoint 2003   1197

Glossary 1207
Index 1217

Windows XP

chapter one

Getting Started with Windows XP

In this chapter, you will: practice these skills.

Project 1A **Working with Windows XP and Managing Files**	**Objectives** • Get Started with Windows • Resize, Move, and Scroll Windows • Maximize, Restore, Minimize, and Close a Window • Create a New Folder • Copy, Move, Rename, and Delete Files • Find Files and Folders • Compress Files

Getting Started with Windows XP

Windows is an *operating system* that coordinates the activities of your computer. It controls how your screen is displayed, how you open and close programs, the startup and shutdown procedures for your computer, and general navigation.

Before you can use Microsoft Office effectively, you need to have at least a basic familiarity with the Microsoft Windows operating system. You need to know how to work with the Start button and taskbar and how to open, close, move, and resize windows.

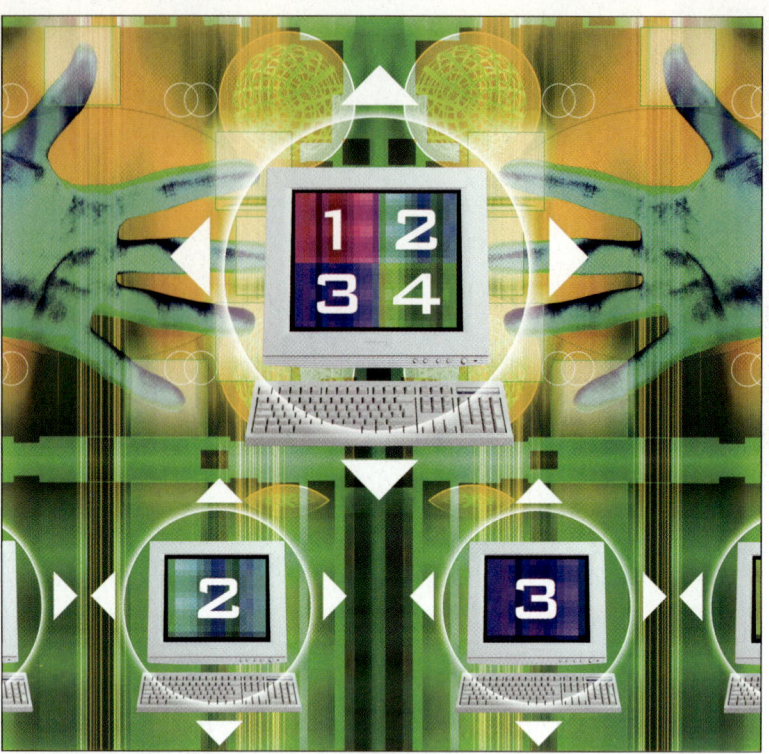

Introduction

It is important that you understand the difference between Windows (with a capital "W") and windows (with a lowercase "w"). When you see the word *Windows*, it will often be accompanied by the version, such as Windows 98, Windows NT, Windows 2000, or Windows XP (the version introduced in this chapter). These operating systems are similar and use what is known as a *graphical user interface (GUI)*. A graphic user interface uses graphics or pictures to represent commands and actions. It also enables you to see document formatting as it looks when printed. When you see the word *Windows* with a capital *W*, it always refers to the operating system that runs the computer.

A *window* (lowercase "w"), on the other hand, refers to a rectangular area on the screen, sometimes the whole screen, that is used to display files or documents. A window can be opened and closed. It can also be resized and moved around the screen. You can have more than one window open at a time on the screen. These windows can overlap one another, or one window can take up the whole screen, with other windows hidden behind it. You can also reduce a window to the size of a button, to be opened and closed using only a click of the mouse.

Project 1A **Working with Windows XP and Managing Files**

Using Office 2003 effectively requires a good working knowledge of the Windows XP operating system. You will need to know how to open, close, and resize a window; how to keep more than one window open at a time, and how to manage files.

In completing the exercises for Objectives 1.1 through 1.7, you will practice navigating Windows XP. You will also work with files and folders and compress and decompress files for easy file transfer. See Figure 1.1.

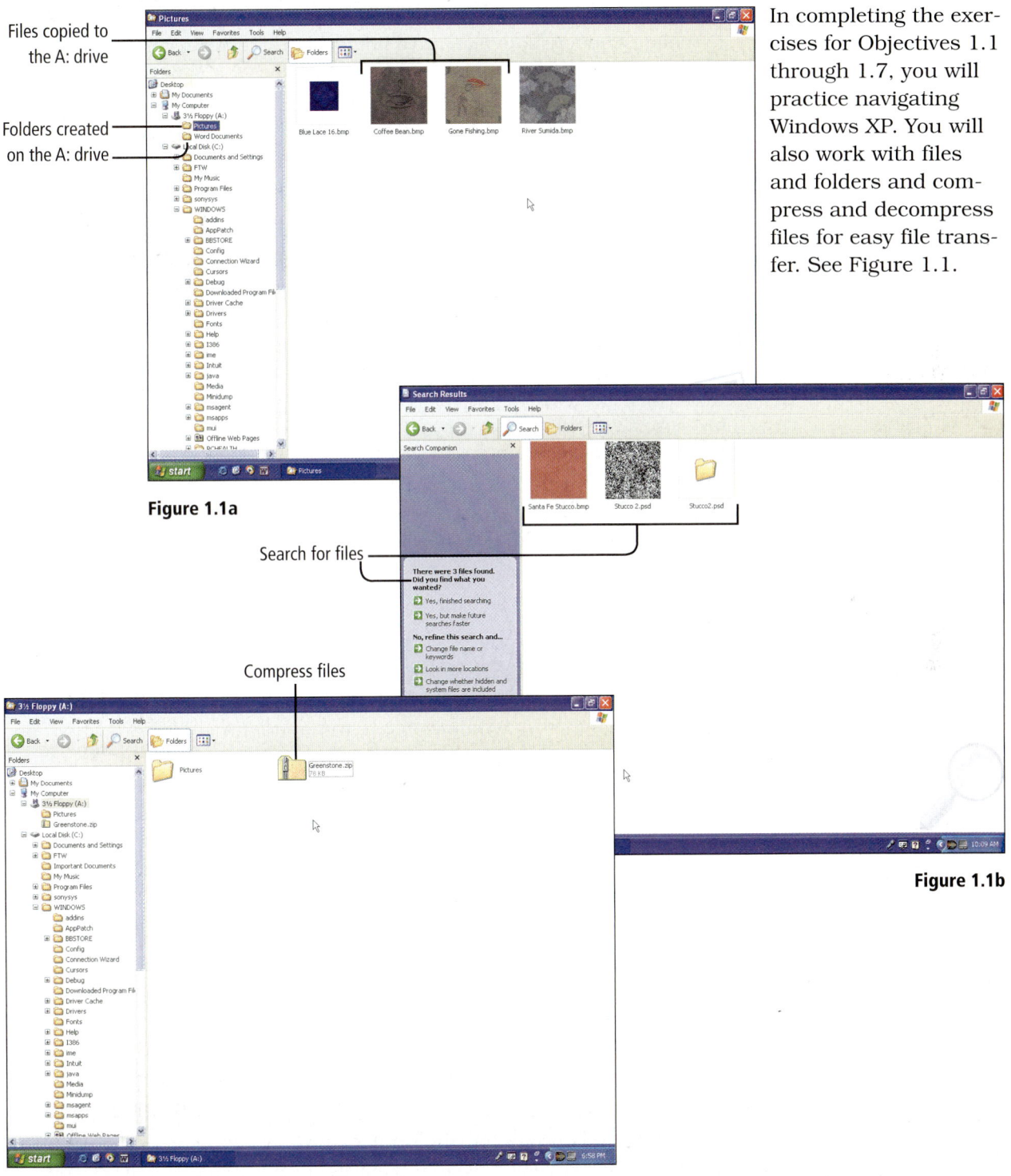

Figure 1.1a

Figure 1.1b

Figure 1.1c
a) Windows XP My Computer view, b) Searching for files, c) compressing ("zipping" files)

> **Note** — What You Need to Know First
>
> Much of the work you will do on a computer involves creating files. After you create a document, you need to save it before you turn off the computer. After the power is turned off, any work is lost unless it has been saved to a storage device. When you save your work, it is saved as a *file* and is usually stored on a disk drive or a network drive. Most of the time you store files on the **hard disk drive**, a *floppy disk drive*, or similar type of storage device. If you are going to become a regular computer user, you need to know how to effectively use disks to store files. You also need to know how to compress one or more files into a single file. This enables you to copy files more quickly and saves a great deal of time when you are sending files as attachments to e-mails.
>
> Your computer's hard disk drive is the main storage device on your computer. It stores the programs that run on your computer in addition to the files that you create. A hard drive is usually identified on your computer by the notation C:\ (and sometimes D:\, E:\, and so on for additional drives). A floppy disk drive provides storage on a floppy disk and is generally identified on your computer by the notation 3½ Floppy (A:). The advantage of using a floppy disk is the ability to take the disk with you and use it in other computers.
>
> You may also have access to files on another type of storage device, a **CD-ROM**. CD-ROM stands for Compact Disc-Read Only Memory. This is a storage device from which you can read and open files. If you are using files stored on a CD-ROM, you will need to open a file from the disc and then save it to a writable disk or copy a file from the CD-ROM to another disk and then open it. Many computers now have writable CD drives built in. They can store information on one of two types of CDs—a CD that can be written to but not erased (**CD-R**) or a CD that can be written to and erased many times (**CD-RW**).

Objective 1
Get Started with Windows

In most cases, starting Windows is an automatic procedure. You turn on your computer, and Windows (whichever version you are using) eventually appears. Some versions require that you log in, and some do not. If you are using a different version of Windows, some of the procedures used in this lesson will work differently. Also, note that Windows XP is available in two versions—a Professional Edition and a Home Edition. They are very similar, especially for basic tasks.

One of the strengths of Windows XP is its flexibility. It can be customized in endless ways. If you are working in a lab, security measures will be added to the operating system, and some of the most common Windows features may be disabled. The look of your screen will also vary, depending on the software that has been installed. Because of this, your screen will look different from the screens displayed throughout this lesson.

The **Start button** is a very important part of the Windows desktop. You can use it to start programs, set up your printer, get help, and shut down your computer. You will probably use this button more than any other.

In the following steps, you learn how to start Windows, use the mouse, and use the Start button to open a built-in calculator application.

1 Turn on your computer.

After a few seconds, a Welcome screen, also known as a Logon screen, is displayed, as shown in Figure 1.2. The exact look of the screen depends on the version of Windows being used and the number of users that have been identified. If you are working in a lab, you will probably have special instructions on how to log on to the computer.

Different users can log onto the same computer

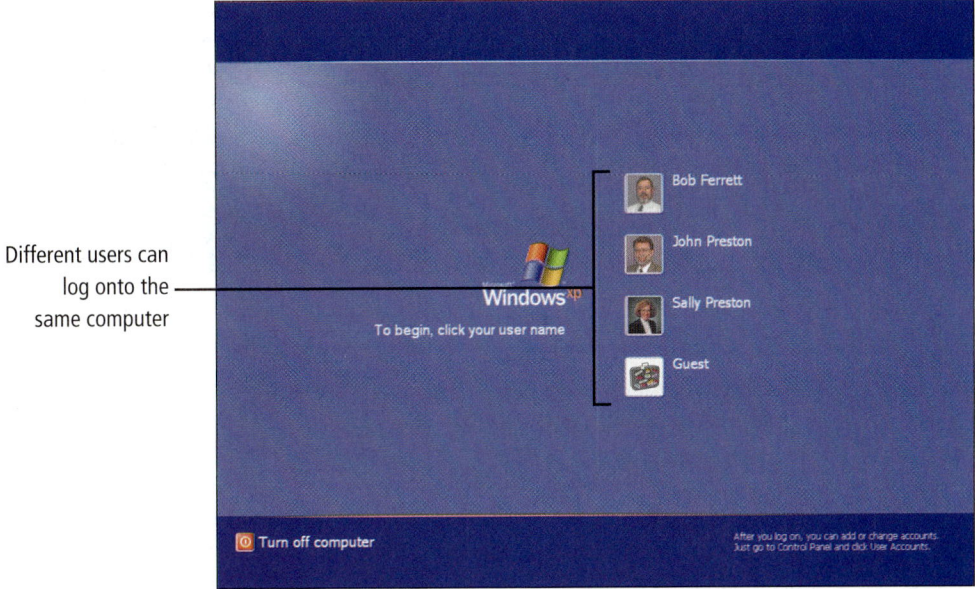

Figure 1.2

Note — If You Do Not See This Screen

If your computer is set up with only one user, you will not see this screen. Rather, the first screen will be the desktop.

2 On the **Welcome** screen, click the appropriate picture or name. If you are working in a computer lab, log on according to your instructor's directions.

The Windows desktop displays, as shown in Figure 1.3. The look of the screen will vary, depending on which version of Windows you are using. The figures in this chapter show Windows XP Home Edition. Common Windows elements are identified in the table in Figure 1.4.

Project 1A: Working with Windows XP and Managing Files | **Windows XP**   5

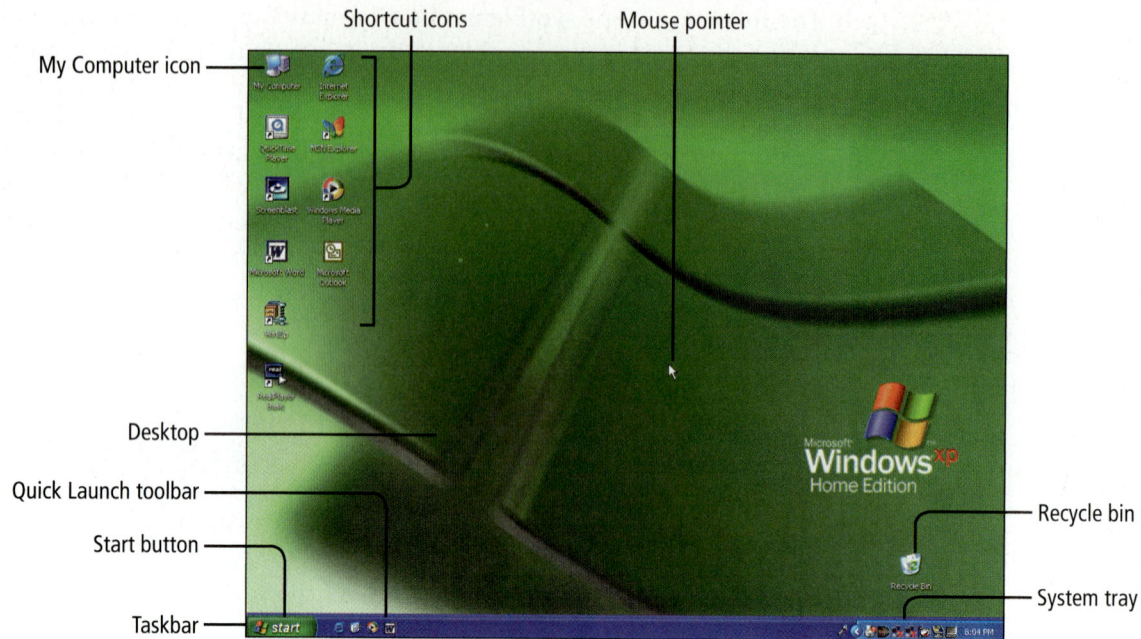

Figure 1.3

Windows Screen Elements

Element	Function
Desktop	The basic screen from which Windows and applications are run. The desktop consists of program icons, a taskbar, a Start button, and a mouse pointer.
Icon	Graphic representation; often a small image on a button that enables you to run a program or program function.
Mouse pointer	The arrow, I-beam, or other symbol that indicates a location or position on your screen. It is also called the pointer.
My Computer icon	An icon that gives you access to the files and folders on your computer.
Quick Launch toolbar	An area to the right of the Start button that contains shortcut icons for commonly used programs.
Recycle bin	A storage area for files that have been deleted. Files can be either recovered from the Recycle bin or permanently removed.
System tray	A notification area on the right side of the taskbar that keeps you informed about processes that are occurring in the background, such as antivirus software, network connections, and other utility programs. The system tray often displays the time.
Taskbar	A bar, usually at the bottom of the screen, that contains the Start button, buttons representing open programs, and other buttons that will activate programs.

Figure 1.4

Alert! — What If Your Computer Asks for a Password?

If you are using a computer in a lab or on a network, a box, called a *dialog box*, may open and ask for a username and password. In some cases, you can press Esc, press Enter, or click the Cancel button, which will bypass the security. If this doesn't work, ask your instructor or network administrator how to proceed.

More Knowledge — Taskbar Location

The taskbar may not appear at the bottom of the desktop. If you cannot see the taskbar, it may have been hidden. To see it, move the mouse pointer to the bottom of the screen. The taskbar should pop up. The taskbar also may not appear at the location shown in the figure. It may have been moved to the top or to the left or right side of the desktop.

3 Move the mouse across a flat surface such as a mouse pad to control the pointer on your screen. On the desktop, position the tip of the pointer in the center of the **My Computer** icon and click once, using the left mouse button. (If the **My Computer** icon is not visible, click the **My Documents** icon or other appropriate icon.)

The My Computer window is displayed, as shown in Figure 1.5. A window is a box that displays information or a program. Common window elements are identified in the table in Figure 1.6. When a window is open, the name of the window is displayed in the title bar and in a button on the taskbar, at the bottom of the desktop.

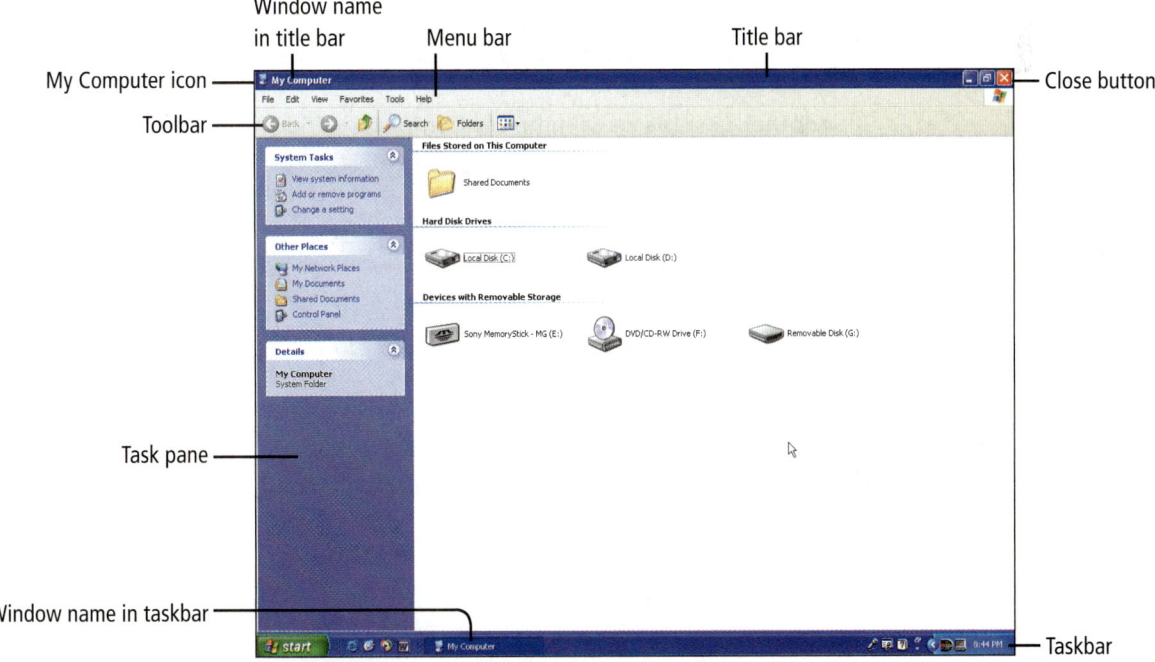

Figure 1.5

Project 1A: Working with Windows XP and Managing Files | **Windows XP**

Parts of a Window

Part	Function
Menu	A list of associated commands available from a command in a menu bar or from a list opened by right-clicking an object.
Menu bar	The bar, directly beneath the title bar, that contains commands. These commands are words, not icons.
ScreenTip	A small box containing the name of a button that pops up when you pause the mouse pointer over it.
Status bar	The bar at the bottom of a window that gives additional information about the window.
Task pane	A pane that opens on the side of a window and that is used to display commonly used tools.
Title bar	The line at the top of a window that contains the name of the application and document, along with the Minimize, Maximize/Restore Down, and Close buttons.
Toolbar	The bar, usually directly beneath the menu bar, that contains commands. These commands are buttons with icons, not words.

Figure 1.6

Alert!

Did the Window Open?

If the My Computer window did not open, the single-click selected the icon. This means that Windows has been set to require a double-click to open the window. If necessary, quickly double-click the left mouse button while holding the mouse pointer steady over the icon. If this does not work, it may be that you moved the mouse while you were double-clicking the button. It may also mean that you did not click the mouse button fast enough. In either case, try again. If you are unfamiliar with a mouse, it may take a while to become proficient.

Another possible reason the My Computer window may not open is that your computer is in a lab with security installed. Some levels of security will not allow you to open the My Computer window. If this is the case, ask your instructor how to proceed.

4 In the upper right corner of the **My Computer** window title bar, click the **Close** button ☒.

The My Computer window closes. If you have difficulty identifying buttons on a window, move the mouse pointer slowly over the buttons until you can see the ScreenTip that identifies each button.

5 On the **My Computer** icon, click the right mouse button.

A *shortcut menu* displays. Shortcut menus are context-sensitive menus used to perform operations quickly without having to use a menu bar or a toolbar. A context-sensitive menu provides quick access to commands that are appropriate to the window area clicked on. On this shortcut menu, the Open command is displayed in bold because it is the default action that occurs when you double-click this icon. See Figure 1.7.

The command in bold is the default action

Shortcut menu

Figure 1.7

More Knowledge — Using Shortcut Menus

The shortcut menu you activated by clicking the right mouse button on the My Computer icon displays commands that are appropriate for the selected object. Right-clicking displays a context-sensitive menu for most objects in Windows and in Microsoft Office applications. Try right-clicking an object first instead of using a toolbar or menu. You will find shortcut menus can be great timesavers.

6 In the shortcut menu, move the mouse pointer over the word **Open**.

The Open command is highlighted, which means it is selected.

7 Click the left mouse button once. Click the disk drive that is labeled **Local Disk (C:)**.

The My Computer window displays. This action performs exactly the same task as single-clicking (or double-clicking) the icon. In both Microsoft Windows and Microsoft Office, nearly every procedure and task can be performed several ways! The specifications of the hard drive are displayed in the Details area of the task pane. If the Details area does not display any information, click the expand/collapse arrow next to Details to expand this section of the task pane. See Figure 1.8.

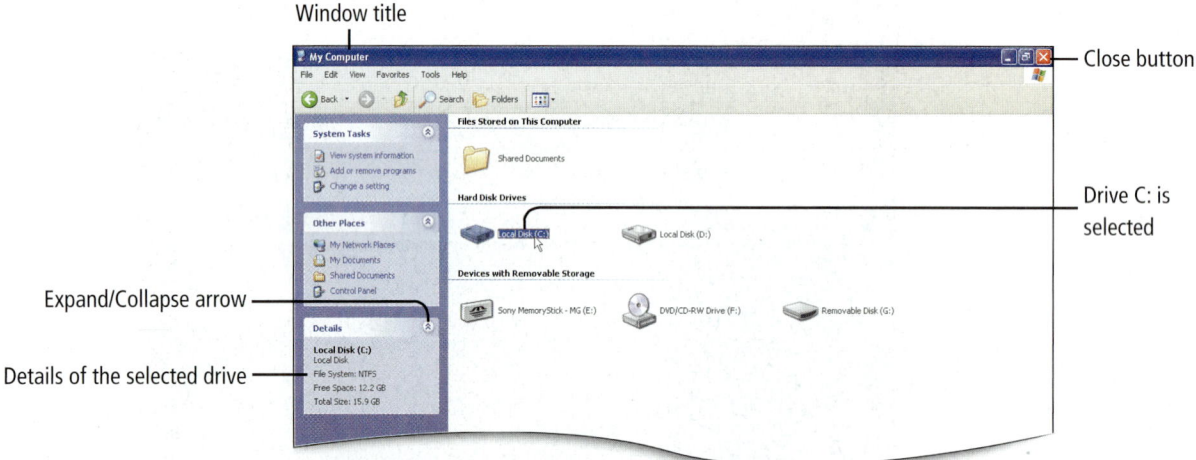

Figure 1.8

Note — Clicking the Mouse Buttons

The first five steps of this lesson demonstrate three basic techniques for using the mouse. The most common is to click once using the left mouse button. Throughout the rest of this book, when you are instructed to click the mouse, it means click the left mouse button once. To double-click the mouse means to click the left mouse button twice in rapid succession. This action is used to open programs, open files, or initiate other default actions. The third technique—right-click—uses a single click of the right mouse button. This action is used to open shortcut menus. Later you will learn how to use the mouse to click and drag.

8 In the **My Computer** window title bar, click the **Close** button .

Move the pointer to the **Start** button and click it once using the left mouse button.

The Start menu displays. Notice that some of the commands have arrows on the right, as shown in Figure 1.9. These arrows indicate that a **submenu** is available for a command. A submenu is a second-level menu. The items on the left side of the Start menu in the figure will be different from those on your screen, and the right side will be somewhat different. You can customize the Start menu to include shortcuts to programs and files you use often.

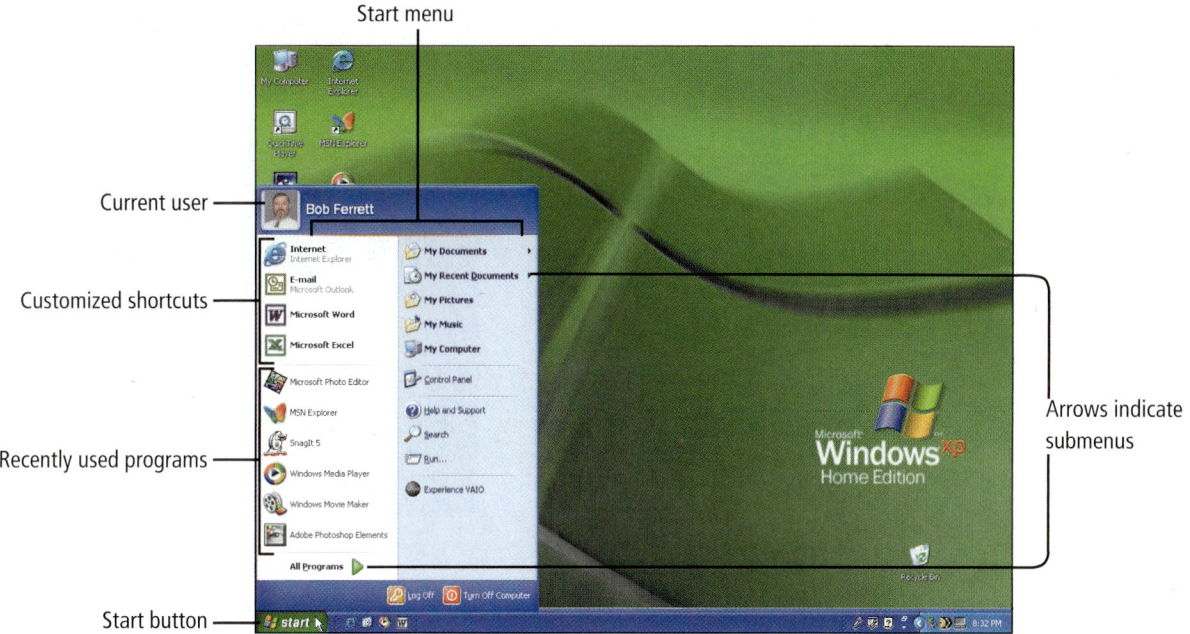

Figure 1.9

More Knowledge — Keeping Recently Used Documents Handy

The My Recent Documents menu displays files you have used recently. It is shown by default in Windows XP Professional Edition but is not displayed in the Home Edition. If you are using the Home Edition on your own computer, you can turn on this useful feature using the following procedure. Right-click the Start button and click Properties from the shortcut menu. Click the Start Menu tab at the top of the dialog box (you will learn more about dialog boxes later in this chapter). Click the Customize button, click the Advanced tab at the top of the dialog box, and then click the *List my most recently opened documents* box. Click OK twice to close both dialog boxes. If you do not feel comfortable doing this yet, wait until you finish this chapter, and then come back and try it!

[9] In the **Start** menu, move the pointer to the **All Programs** command, but do not click the mouse button.

The All Programs menu displays. Your menu will look somewhat different from Figure 1.10 because your computer will have different programs installed. Folders in the menu contain more programs, or more folders, or some of each. Programs that were recently installed are shown with a light shaded background.

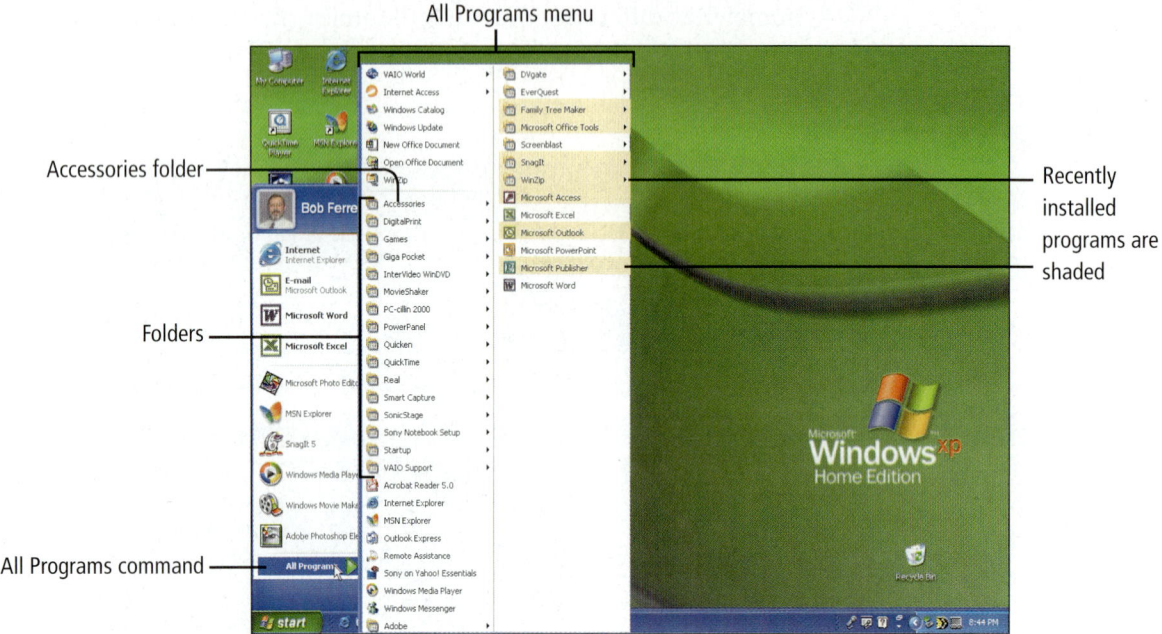

Figure 1.10

[10] In the **All Programs** menu, move the pointer up to the **Accessories** command, but do not click the mouse button.

The Accessories submenu displays.

[11] In the **Accessories** submenu, move the pointer down to the **Calculator** command.

The Calculator command is highlighted, as shown in Figure 1.11.

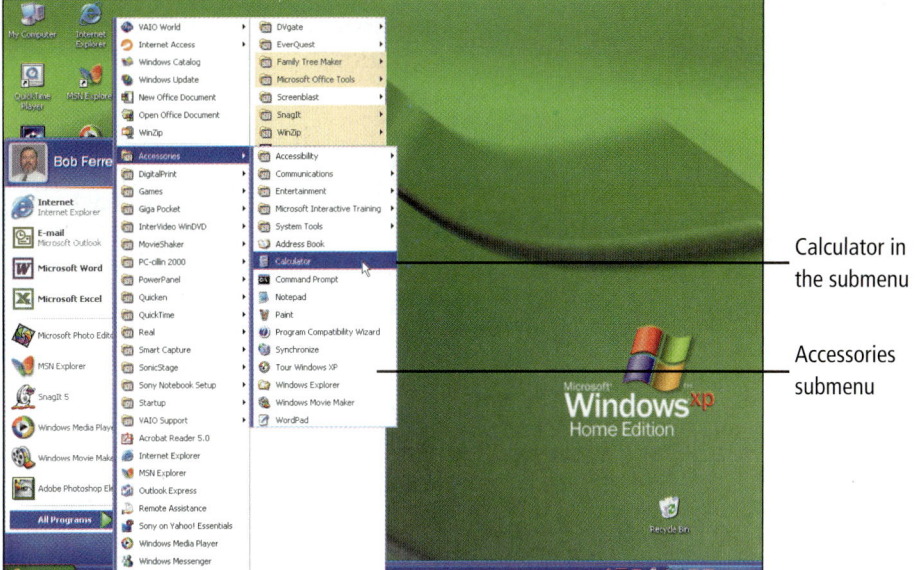

Figure 1.11

> ### More Knowledge — Using Accessories While Other Programs Are Open
>
> You can use the Accessories programs from the Start menu while you are using other Office programs. For example, you might want to make a quick calculation while you are typing a document in Microsoft Word. You can go to the Start button and open the calculator, make the calculation, and then place the answer in your Word document without ever closing Word.

12 Using the left mouse button, click the **Calculator** command.

The Start menu closes, and the Calculator window displays.

13 Try using the calculator. Point and click numbers and keys exactly as you would press keys on a calculator. See Figure 1.12.

Figure 1.12

Project 1A: Working with Windows XP and Managing Files | **Windows XP** 13

14 In the **Calculator** title bar, click the **Close** button ☒ to close the calculator window.

Objective 2
Resize, Move, and Scroll Windows

Another Windows skill you need is the ability to resize and move windows. When a window opens on your screen, it generally opens in the same size and shape as it was when last used. If you are using more than one window at a time, you may want to increase or decrease the size of a window so that you can see the information you need. Moving a window on your desktop is another way to help you see what you need.

In many cases, your computer will not be able to display all the information contained in a document. Scroll bars are included if the information in a window extends beyond the right or lower edges of the window. The *horizontal scroll bar* enables you to move left and right to view information that extends beyond the left or right edge of the screen. The *vertical scroll bar* enables you to move up and down to view information that extends beyond the top or bottom of the screen.

In the following steps, you open, resize, and move the My Computer window. You also use the scroll bars in the My Computer window to look at information that does not fit on the screen.

1 On the desktop, click (or double-click) the **My Computer** icon.

The My Computer window opens.

> **Note — If the My Computer Window Fills the Screen**
>
> The My Computer window may open in a view that fills the screen. If this is the case, click the Restore Down button, which is the middle of three buttons on the right end of the title bar, to return the window to a smaller size.

2 Move the pointer to the lower right corner of the window. (You can use any of the corners for this example.)

The pointer changes to a diagonal two-headed arrow, as shown in Figure 1.13. When the mouse pointer is in this shape, you can use it to change the size and shape of the window.

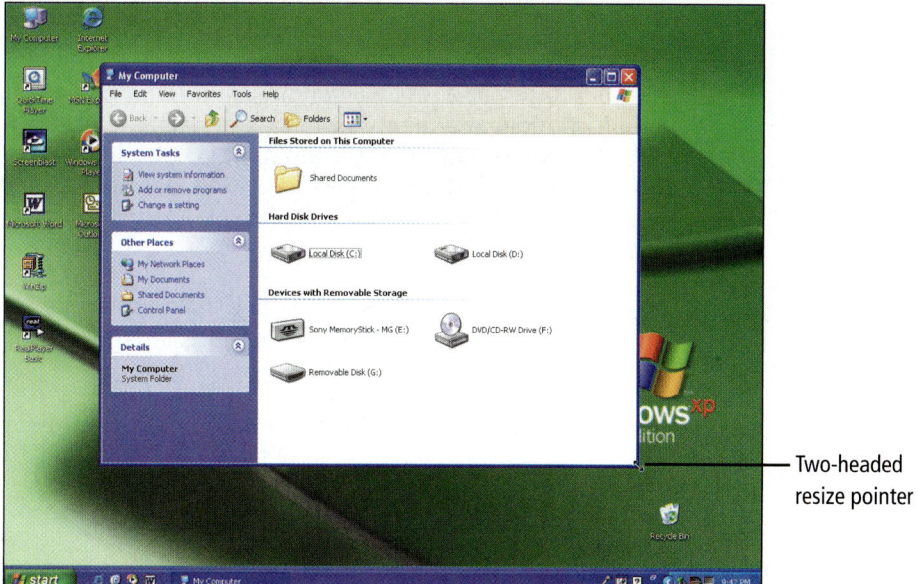

Figure 1.13

3. Hold down the left mouse button, drag diagonally up and to the left, and then release the mouse button. If you are using a different corner, drag toward the opposite corner of the window.

Compare your screen with Figure 1.14. Notice that a scroll bar displays on the right side of the window. A scroll bar appears whenever the window contains more than it can display.

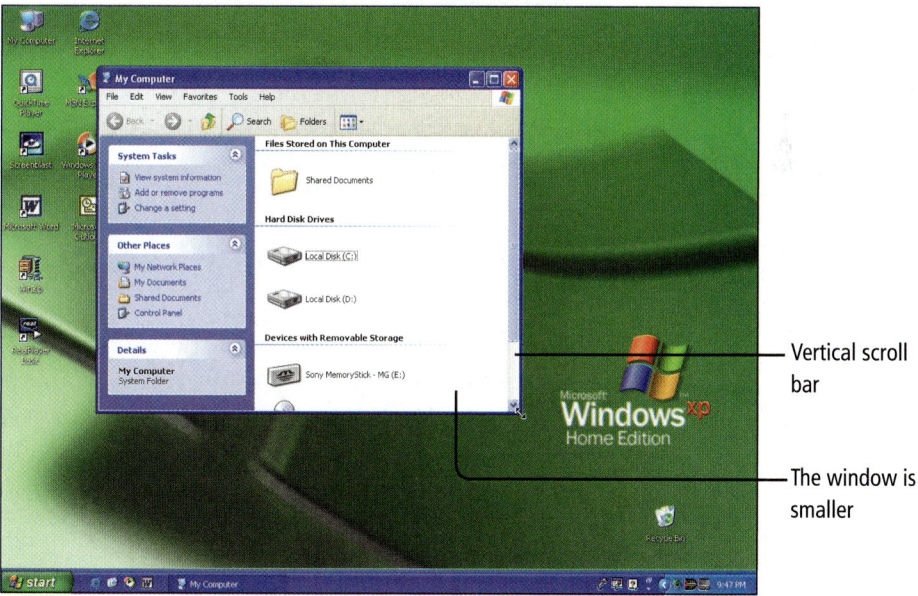

Figure 1.14

Project 1A: Working with Windows XP and Managing Files | **Windows XP** 15

> **Note — Another Way to Resize a Window**
>
> You can also resize a window by clicking and dragging on one side of the window at a time. To increase or decrease the width of the window, click and drag on the left or right edge. To change the height of a window, click and drag on the upper or lower edge of the window.

4 On the **My Computer** title bar, move the pointer to a blank area. Click and hold down the left mouse button, drag down and to the right, and release the mouse button.

When you release the mouse button, the window drops into the new location. See Figure 1.15.

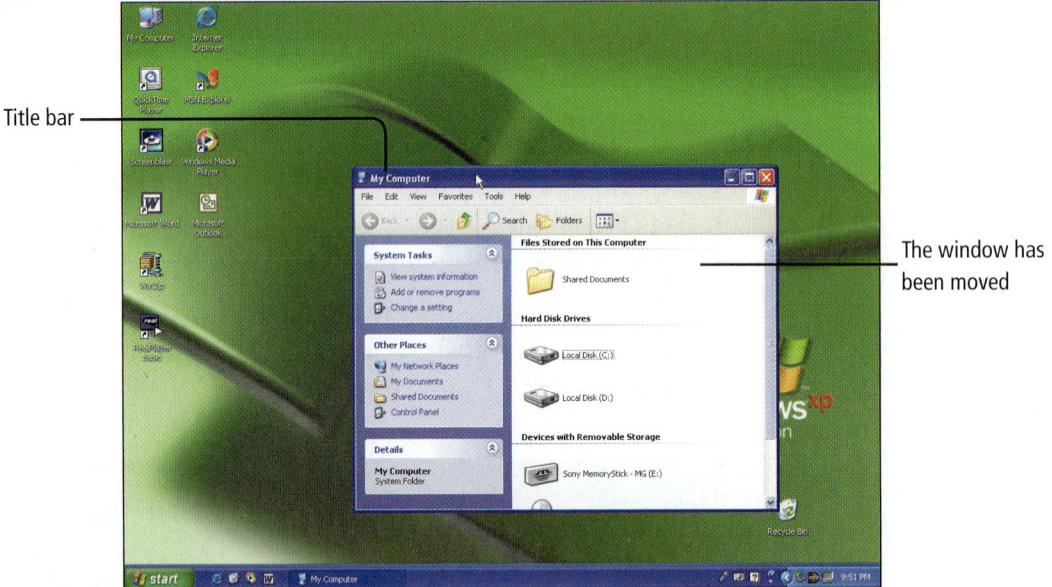

Figure 1.15

5 At the bottom of the vertical scroll bar, point to the **down arrow** and click.

The items at the bottom of the window scroll up so that you can see the folders and icons that were not visible before, as shown in Figure 1.16. You can click and hold down the left mouse button on the down arrow to scroll rapidly through many items.

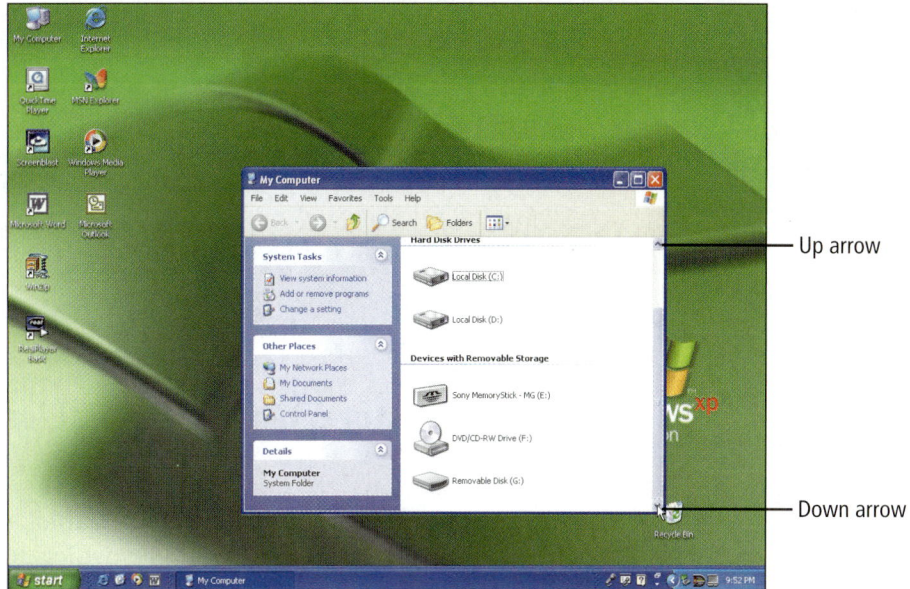

Figure 1.16

6 On the **up arrow** on the same scroll bar, click and hold down the left mouse button.

The list scrolls up until the first item is displayed.

7 In the vertical scroll bar, using the left mouse button, click the scroll box and drag down.

The ***scroll box*** enables you to move quickly up or down a window. The location of the scroll box indicates your relative location in the window. It also gives you more control as you scroll because you can see the information as it moves up or down the window. See Figure 1.17.

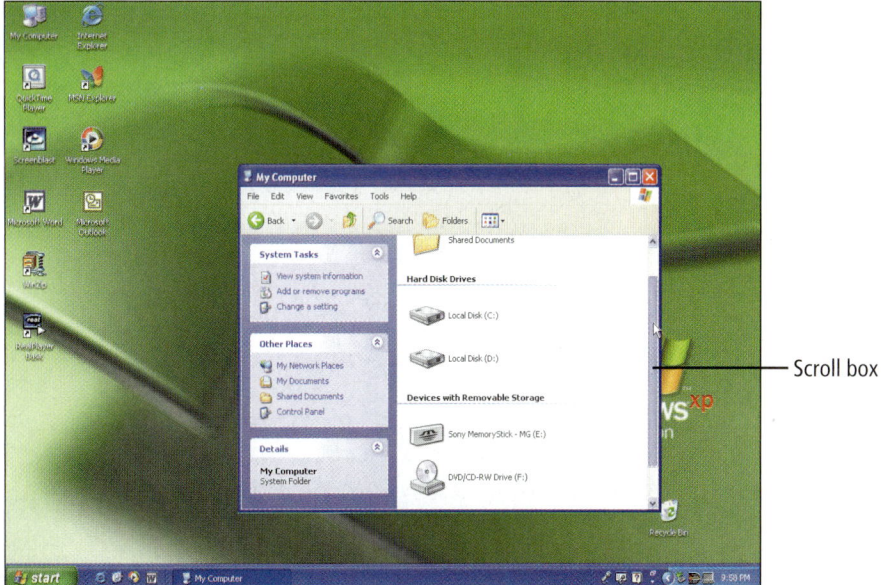

Figure 1.17

Project 1A: Working with Windows XP and Managing Files | **Windows XP** 17

More Knowledge — More on Using the Scroll Bars

You can move up or down a screen at a time by clicking in the gray area above or below the vertical scroll box. You can also move left or right a screen at a time by clicking in the gray area to the left or right of the horizontal scroll box. The size of the scroll box indicates the relative size of the display to the whole document. If the scroll box is small, it means that the display is a small portion of the whole document.

Objective 3
Maximize, Restore, Minimize, and Close a Window

To meet the previous objective, you resized the My Computer window. You can **maximize** the window, which enables the window to take up the whole screen, and **restore** the window, which takes it back to the size it was before being maximized. You can also **minimize** a window, removing it from the screen and representing it as a button on the taskbar until it is needed again.

In the following steps, you maximize, restore, minimize, and close the My Computer window.

1 In the upper right corner of the **My Computer** window, on the **My Computer** title bar, place the pointer on the **Maximize** button.

The Maximize button is the middle button in the group of three. When you point to it, a ScreenTip displays, as shown in Figure 1.18. ScreenTips tell you the name and function of a button.

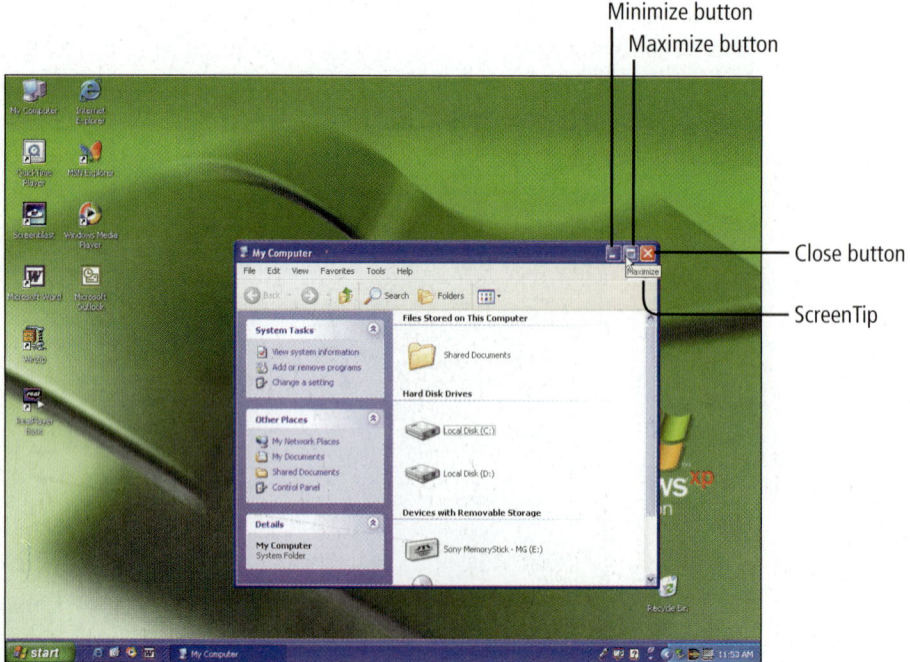

Figure 1.18

2 Using the left mouse button, click the **Maximize** button 🗖. Alternatively, you can maximize or restore a window by double-clicking anywhere in the window's title bar.

The My Computer window now occupies the entire screen, as shown in Figure 1.19. The Maximize button is replaced by the Restore Down button, which has a different icon.

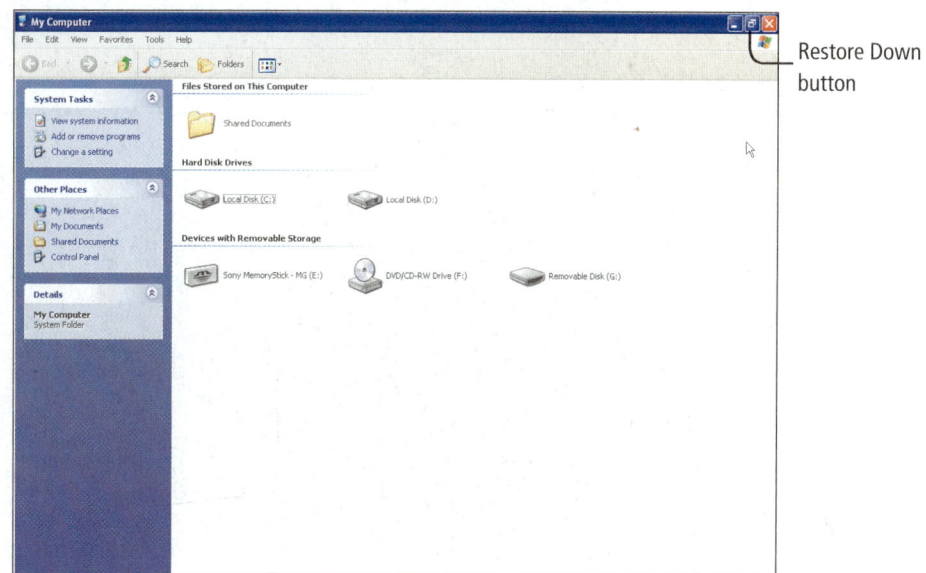

Figure 1.19

3 On the **My Computer** title bar, click the **Restore Down** button 🗗.

The window returns to the size it was before you clicked the Maximize button. See Figure 1.20.

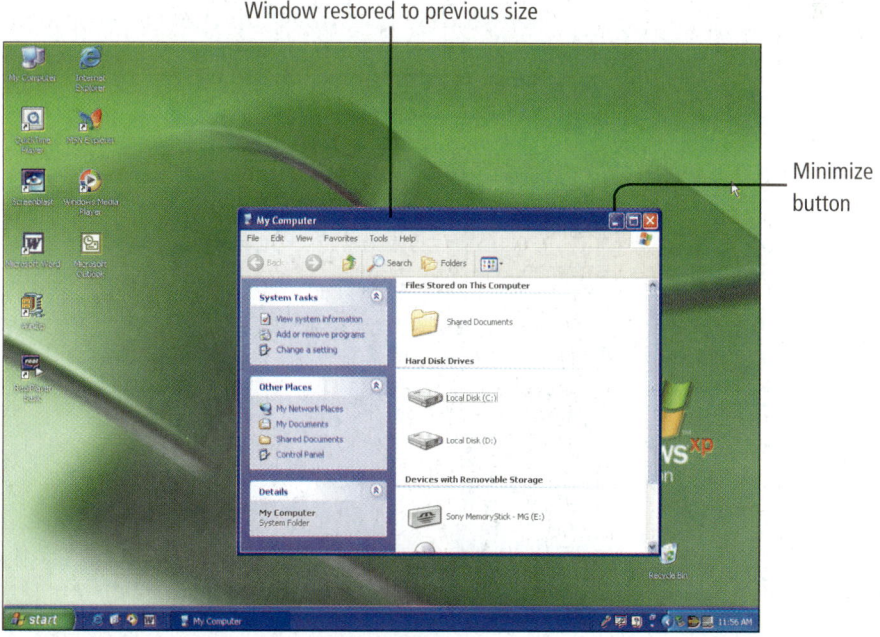

Figure 1.20

Project 1A: Working with Windows XP and Managing Files | **Windows XP** 19

4 On the **My Computer** title bar, click the **Minimize** button.

The My Computer program is still running but the window is minimized. It is represented by a button on the taskbar at the bottom of the screen, as shown in Figure 1.21. The window has not been closed, only temporarily hidden.

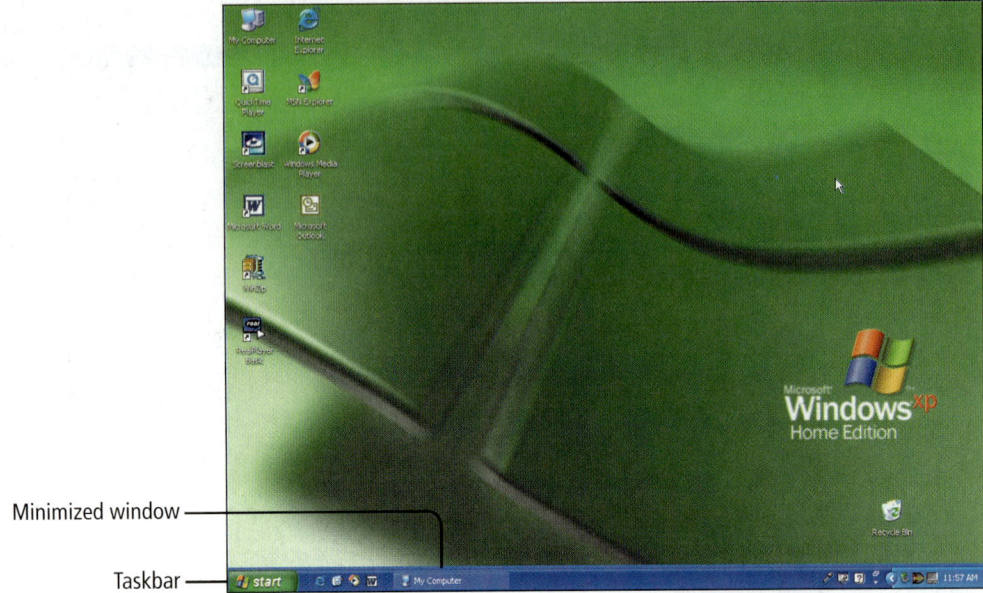

Minimized window

Taskbar

Figure 1.21

5 On the taskbar, click the **My Computer** button.

The window reappears in the same location as it occupied when you clicked the Minimize button.

6 On the **My Computer** title bar, click the **Maximize** button to maximize the **My Computer** window.

The window now takes up the whole screen, as shown in Figure 1.22.

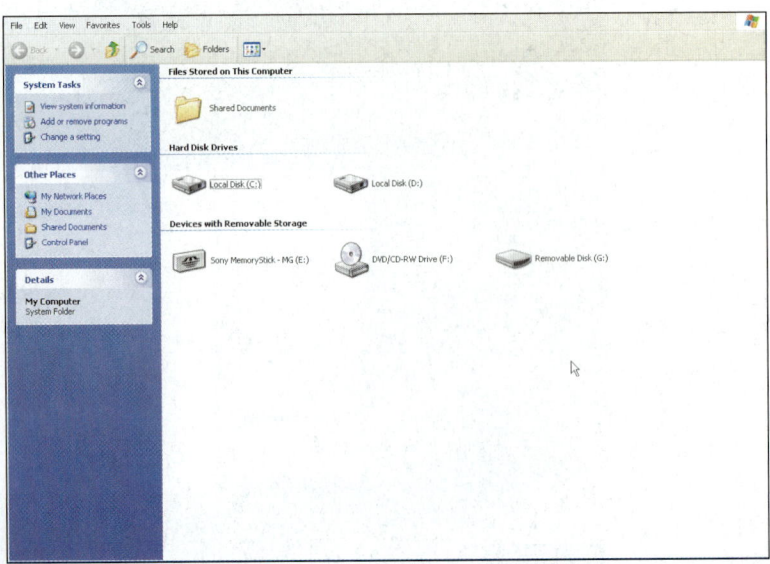

Figure 1.22

20   **Windows XP** | Chapter 1: Getting Started with Windows XP

7 On the taskbar, click the **Start** button ![start], click **All Programs**, click **Accessories**, and then click **Calculator**.

The calculator program opens.

8 Click anywhere on the **My Computer** window.

Notice that the My Computer window is brought to the front. The calculator is still open, but you cannot see the calculator window. This means that you cannot click it to bring the window to the front, but you can use the taskbar. See Figure 1.23.

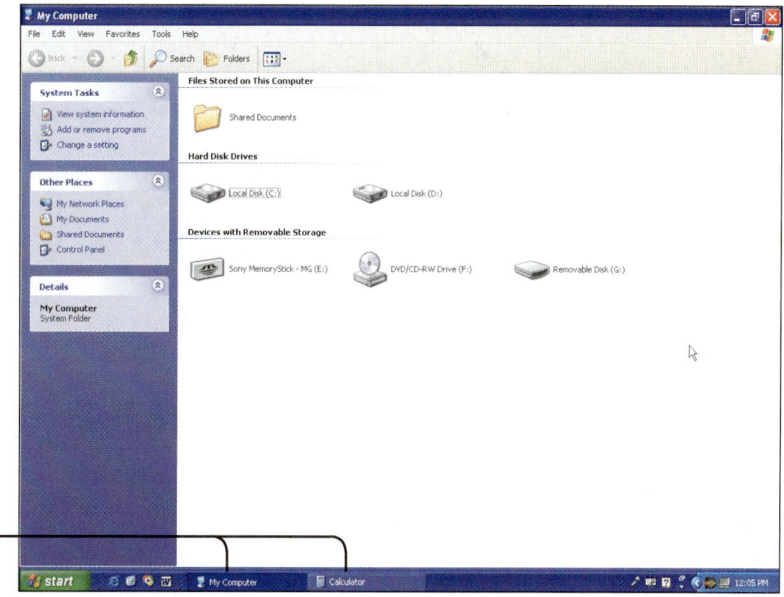

Two programs are running at the same time

Figure 1.23

9 On the taskbar, click the **Calculator** button.

The calculator window moves to the front and is now ready to use, as shown in Figure 1.24.

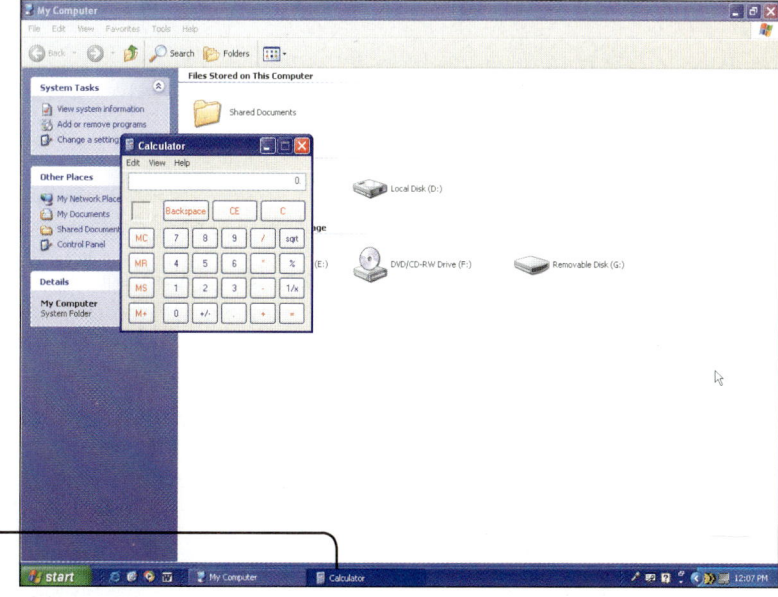

Calculator button in the taskbar

Figure 1.24

Project 1A: Working with Windows XP and Managing Files | **Windows XP**   21

10 On the **Calculator** title bar, click the **Close** button ❌. In the **My Computer** window title bar, click the **Close** button ❌.

> **More Knowledge** — **Keeping More Than One Application Window Open at a Time**
>
> The ability to keep more than one window open at a time will become more and more important as you become more familiar with Microsoft Office. If you want to take information from two word processing documents to create a third document, you can open all three documents and use the taskbar to move back and forth among them, copying and pasting text from one document to another. You can also copy a chart from Excel and paste it into Word or take a table of data and paste it into PowerPoint. You can even have the same document open in two windows. Having multiple documents open greatly reduces the amount of time it takes to do many everyday computer tasks.

Objective 4
Create a New Folder

Folders are used to organize files or other folders. As you use the computer more and more, you will accumulate files that you want to save. If you put all the files in one place, searching for the right one might be difficult. Folders enable you to store your important files by type or by subject and make handling them more manageable. In most cases, you will use folders on hard drives or other drives that have large capacities. You can also create folders on floppy disks.

In the following steps, you will create your folders on a floppy disk. You will need to have a floppy disk available. If you are using your own computer, you might want to create the folders in the My Documents folder. If you are using a computer in a lab, you may have space assigned to you on a shared drive. You can create these folders on another drive if you wish.

1 In the taskbar, click the **Start** button [start] and click **My Computer**.

The My Computer window opens.

2 On the toolbar, click the **Folders** button [Folders].

The task pane changes to a Folders pane, displaying the drives and folders on your computer, as shown in Figure 1.25. This view makes it much easier to navigate your computer. The floppy drive, labeled 3½ Floppy (A:), is visible in both the Folders pane on the left and the Contents pane on the right. You can open it using either icon.

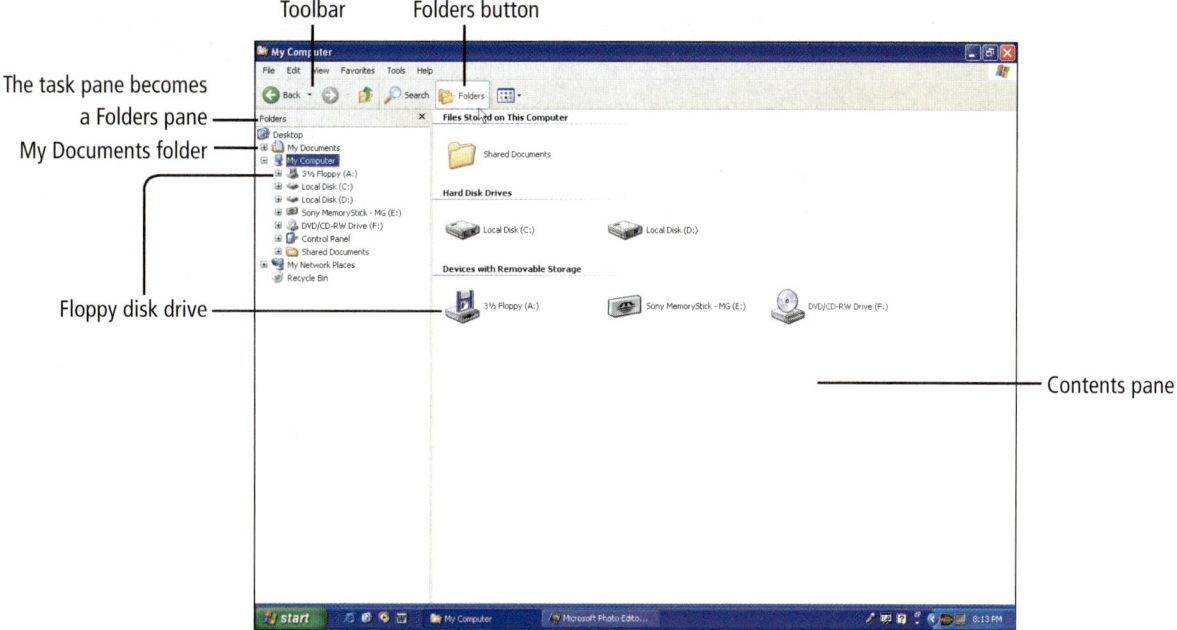

Figure 1.25

More Knowledge — Formatting a Floppy Disk

Floppy disks sometimes need to be formatted which prepares them to be used for the first time. If you want to use a disk that has previously been used in a Macintosh or you are using a disk that has been heavily used and you want to clean it up, you can reformat it by going to My Computer, right-clicking on the 3½ Floppy (A:) drive, and choosing Format from the shortcut menu.

3 Insert a floppy disk into drive A on your computer. In the **Folders** pane, click the **3½ Floppy (A:)** choice.

The contents of the disk in the A: drive are displayed in the Contents pane—in this case, the disk is empty.

4 In the **Contents** pane, right-click in a blank area. In the shortcut menu, move the pointer over the **New** command.

A submenu displays, showing the various items that can be created using the New command. See Figure 1.26.

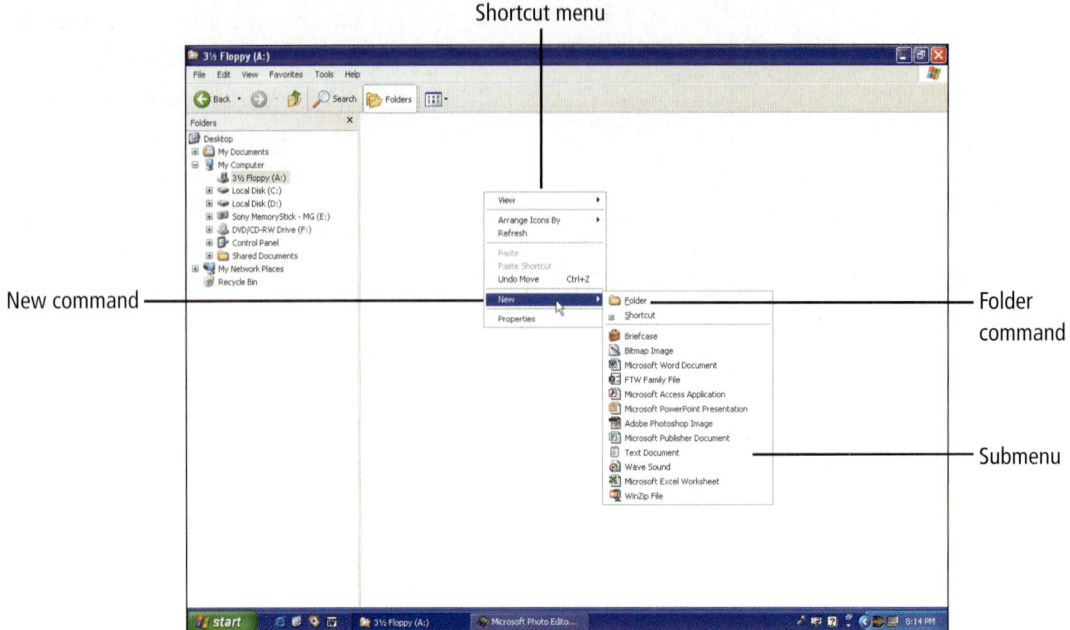

Figure 1.26

🔢 Move the pointer to the **Folder** command and click it using the left mouse button.

A new folder is created with the name of the folder displayed in the edit mode, as shown in Figure 1.27.

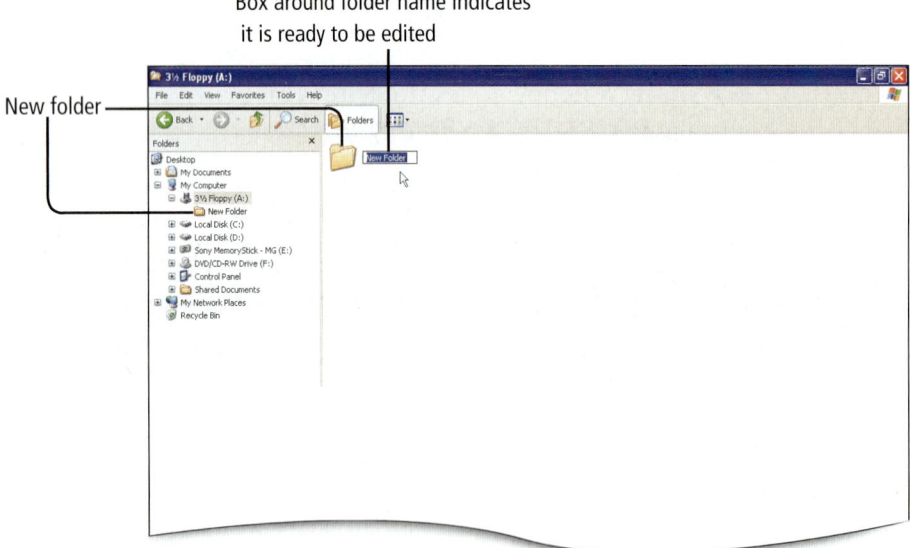

Figure 1.27

6 Over the default **New Folder** name, type **Word Documents** and press Enter.

The folder now has a meaningful name. See Figure 1.28.

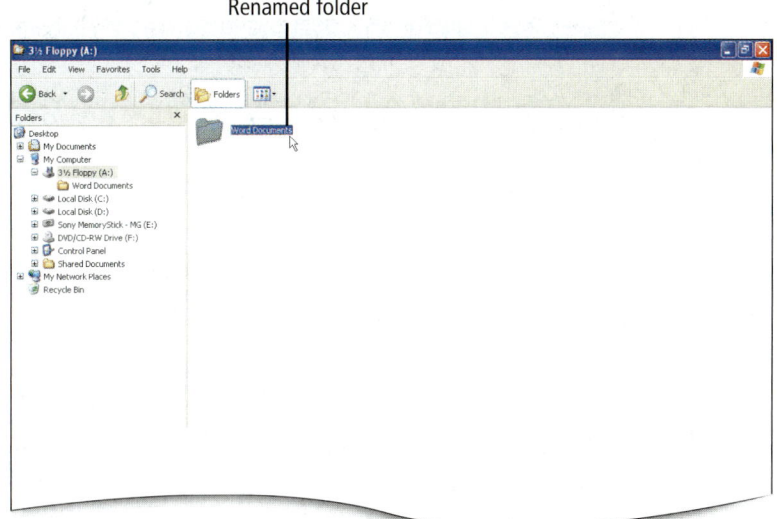

Figure 1.28

Another Way

Rename a Folder

If you accidentally press Enter before you have a chance to name the folder, you can still rename it. Right-click the folder, click Rename from the shortcut menu, type a new name, and then press Enter. Alternatively, you can click the folder once, pause, and then click the folder again.

7 From the **File** menu, click **New**.

A different submenu is displayed, but it also contains the Folder command, as shown in Figure 1.29.

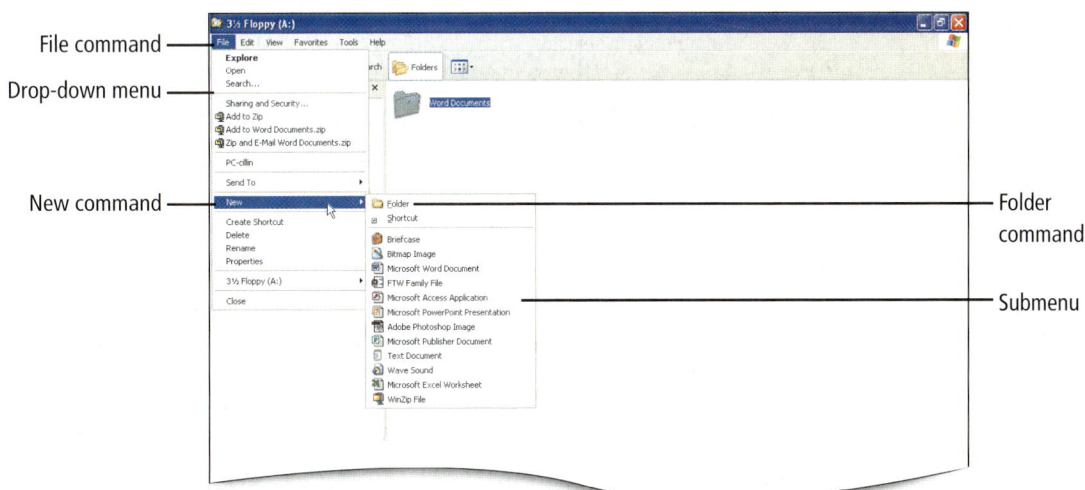

Figure 1.29

Project 1A: Working with Windows XP and Managing Files | **Windows XP** 25

8 In the submenu, click **Folder**. Type **Pictures** and press Enter.

You have now added two folders on your floppy disk. The folders are currently in the Icons view, but several other views are available. See Figure 1.30.

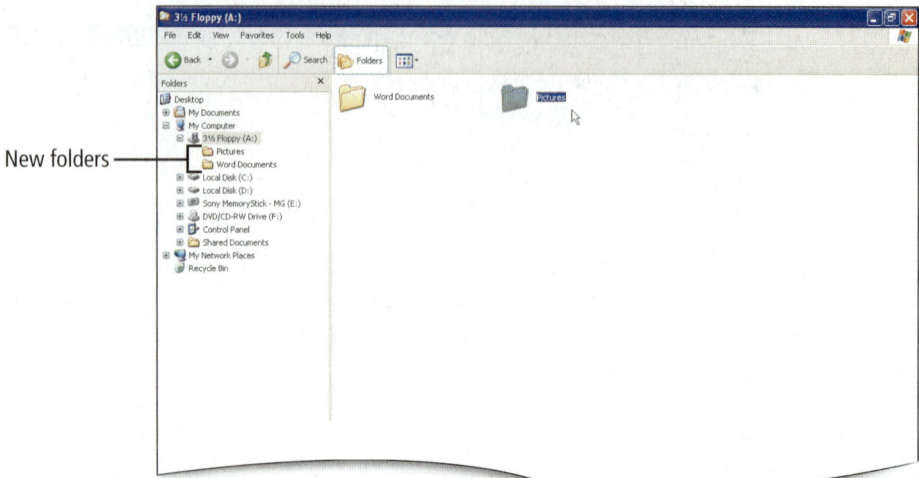

New folders

Figure 1.30

9 From the My Computer toolbar, click the **Views** button and then click **Details**.

The folders display in a list format, with more information, including the date they were last modified. Notice the order in which the folders appear.

10 At the top of the Name column, click the **Name** heading, which is called a *column selector* when clicked. Click the **Name** column selector again.

The folders are sorted in alphabetical order, from *a* to *z*, as shown in Figure 1.31. Clicking the column selector again would switch the order, from *z* to *a*.

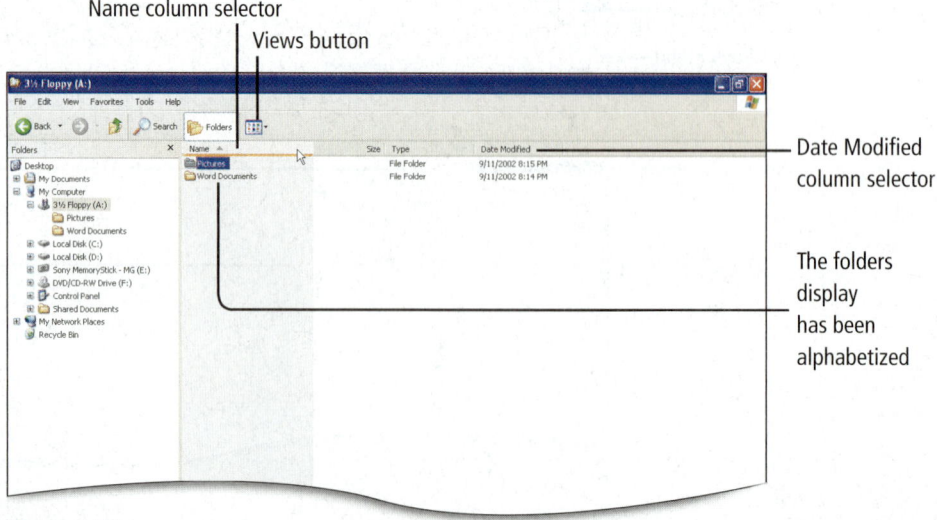

Name column selector
Views button
Date Modified column selector
The folders display has been alphabetized

Figure 1.31

26 **Windows XP** | Chapter 1: Getting Started with Windows XP

> **More Knowledge** — Sorting Files by Size, Date Modified, or File Type
>
> When you sort from smallest to largest file size, the folders within the folder being sorted are listed first in alphabetical order. If you sort by size from largest to smallest, the folder names are listed last in reverse alphabetical order. To see the cumulative size of the files within a folder, right-click on the folder and click Properties.

Objective 5
Copy, Move, Rename, and Delete Files

You will often need to copy files from one location to another. As you work through this book, you will want to make copies of your files to have them as backups. You can copy a file from a hard disk to a floppy disk, a network drive, or even a recordable CD. You may also want to copy files that you have worked on in a lab so that you can put them on the hard drive on your own computer. Knowing how to copy files is an important skill when using a computer.

As you use the Office applications more frequently, you will begin to accumulate a large number of documents. At some point, you will want to remove unnecessary files to reduce clutter on your hard drive, and you might also want to move documents into other folders to archive them. Finally, there are times when you would like to make the file names more descriptive. Windows makes it easy to change the name of a file.

In the following steps, you copy files into the folders you created in Objective 4. You also move and rename files and delete files and folders.

1 With the **My Computer** window still open, click the **plus (+)** to the left of the C: drive in the **Folders** pane to expand the folder.

The folders in the C: hard drive display, and the plus changes to a minus.

2 In the **Folders** pane, click the **WINDOWS** folder.

The folders in the WINDOWS folder display in the Folders pane on the left, and the folders and files in the WINDOWS folder display in the Contents pane on the right, as shown in Figure 1.32.

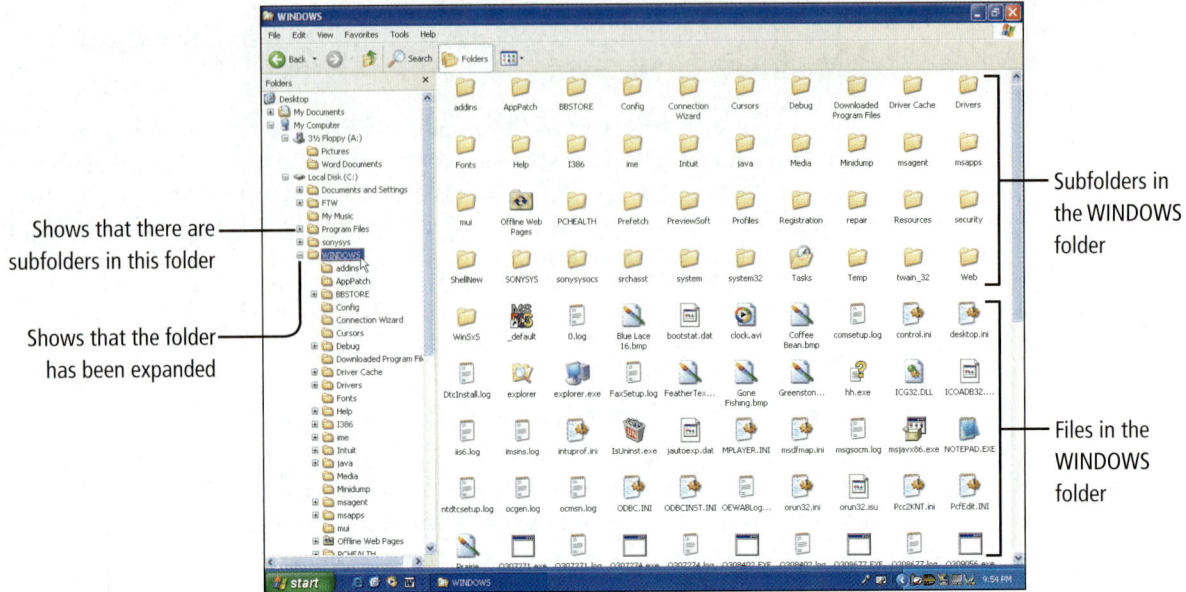

Figure 1.32

> **Note** — **If You Do Not See the Windows Folder**
>
> If you do not see the WINDOWS folder, open the WINNT folder instead. Substitute the WINNT folder for the WINDOWS folder for the rest of this lesson.

Alert! — **Can't Get into the Windows Folder?**

In some instances, because of lab security you will not be able to open the WINDOWS folder. If this is the case, find some other files in the My Documents folder or your shared network drive and substitute them for the ones used in the rest of this task. If you can get to the bitmap images but your images differ from the ones used, choose a different set of files.

3 In the My Computer toolbar, click the **Views** button and then click **Details**.

The subfolders in the WINDOWS folder display. The files in the folder extend below the bottom of the screen.

4 At the top of the **Type** column in the **Contents** pane, click the **Type** column selector twice, and then scroll down until you can see some of the bitmap images.

When you click the Type column selector, the folders are moved to the bottom, and the individual files appear at the top in reverse alphabetical order. Clicking it a second time changes the list to *a*-to-*z* order. Bitmap images are small graphics included with Windows XP. See Figure 1.33.

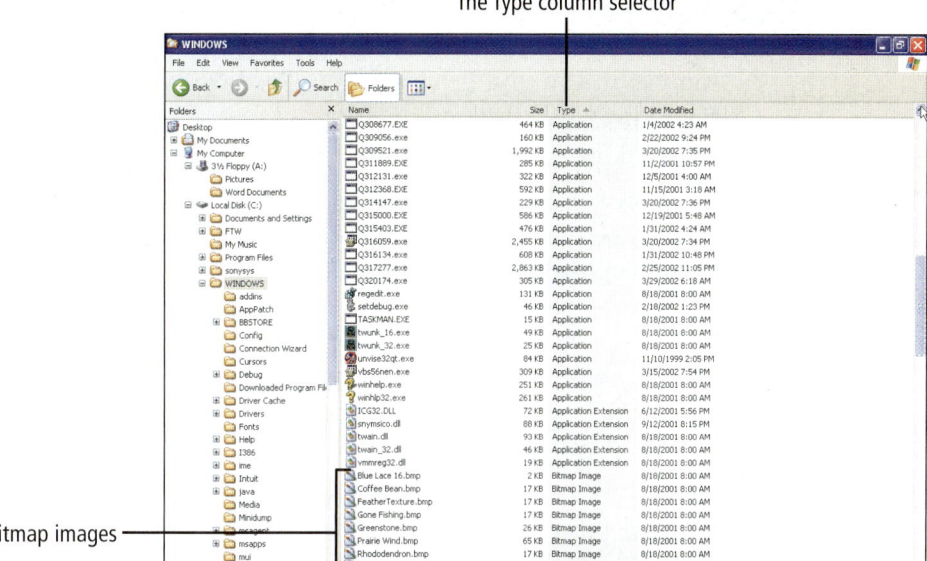

Figure 1.33

More Knowledge — Understanding and Displaying File Extensions

The files you see may display three letters following the file name, such as *.doc*. These are known as *file extensions*, and nearly all files have these extensions. Files created by Microsoft Office programs have a standard set of extensions that identify the type of program used to create the file. For example, Microsoft Word documents end in *.doc*, Excel spreadsheets end in *.xls*, PowerPoint presentations end with *.ppt*, and so on.

In this chapter, it is assumed that the file extensions are turned on. To turn the file extensions on or off, from the Tools menu click Folder Options, and then click the View tab if necessary. Click the check box to the left of the phrase *Hide extensions for known file types* and then click OK.

5 In the **Name** column in the **Contents** pane, click the **Blue Lace 16.bmp** file.

The file is selected.

Project 1A: Working with Windows XP and Managing Files | **Windows XP**   29

6 In the **Folders** pane, scroll up until you can see the **3½ Floppy (A:)** drive. On the **Blue Lace 16.bmp** file, click and hold down the left mouse button and drag it to the **Word Documents** folder on the **3½ Floppy (A:)** drive.

The A: drive is selected, and the file name is attached to the pointer, as shown in Figure 1.34. When you release the mouse button, the file will be copied. Files are copied when dragged to a different drive, and moved when dragged to a different location in the same drive.

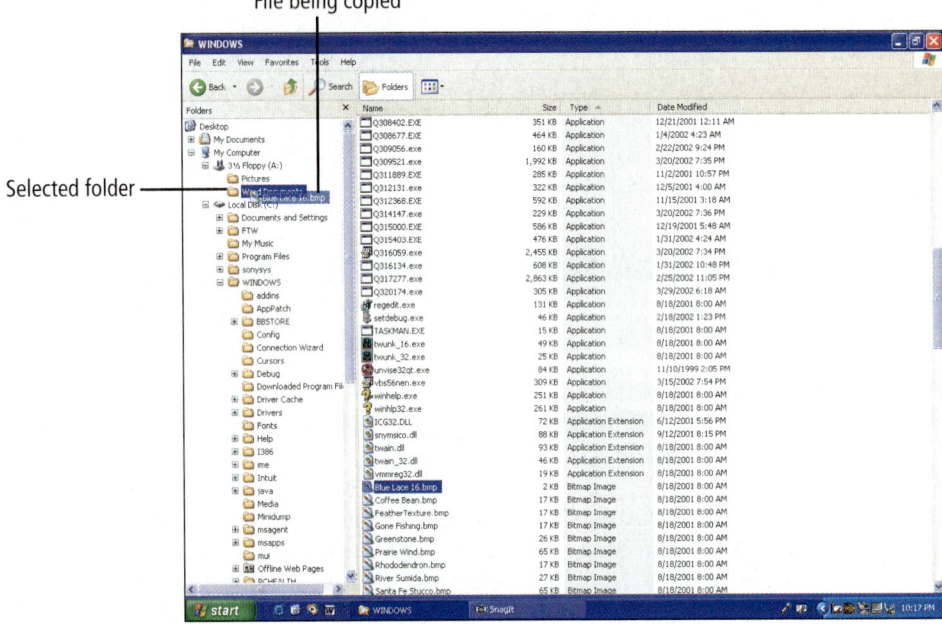

Figure 1.34

7 Release the mouse button.

A dialog box shows that the file is being copied. See Figure 1.35.

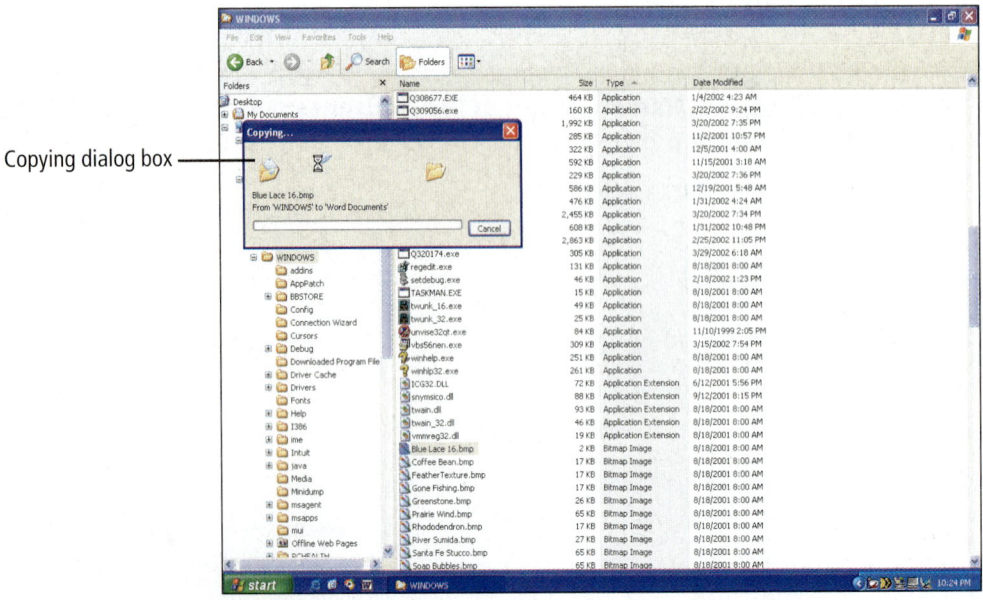

Figure 1.35

30   Windows XP | Chapter 1: Getting Started with Windows XP

Note — **Using the Shortcut Menu to Send Files to the Floppy Drive**

You can also copy files to a floppy drive by right-clicking on the file, clicking Send To, and then clicking 3½ Floppy (A:).

8 In the **Name** column in the **Contents** pane, click the **Coffee Bean.bmp** file. Hold down [Ctrl] and click the **Gone Fishing.bmp** file and the **River Sumida.bmp** file.

The [Ctrl] key enables you to select multiple files that are not next to each other. Compare your screen with Figure 1.36.

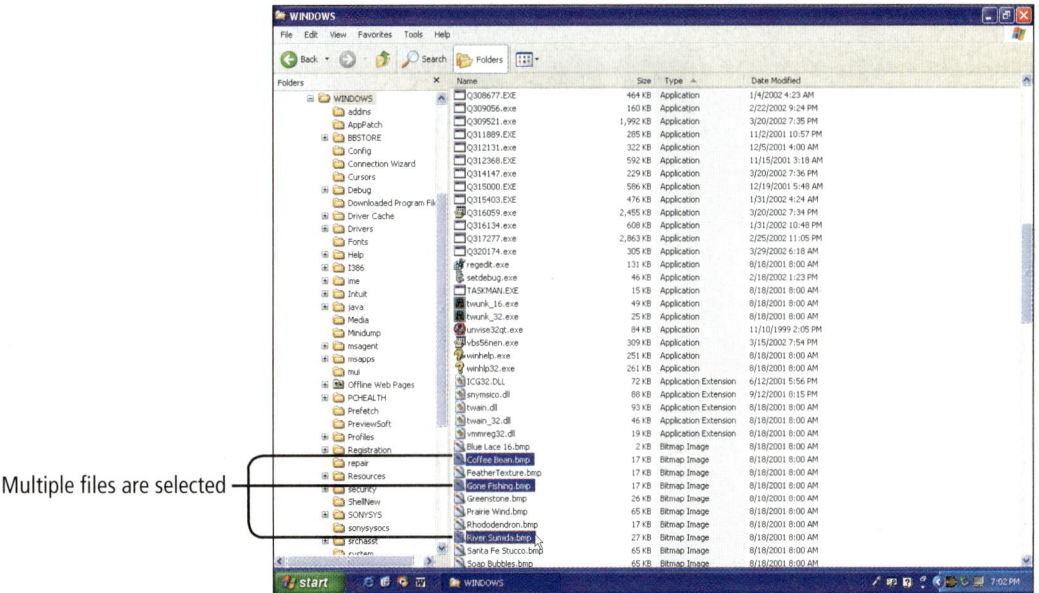

Multiple files are selected

Figure 1.36

More Knowledge — **Selecting Multiple Files**

If the files are all next to one another, you can click the first one, hold down [Shift], and then click the last file. The first and last file and all the files in between are selected. You can then right-click any one of the selected files and send them all to the floppy disk, or you can left-click any one of the files and drag them all to another location.

Project 1A: Working with Windows XP and Managing Files | **Windows XP** 31

9 In the **Contents** pane, click any one of the selected files, hold down the mouse button, and then drag the files to the **Pictures** folder on the **3½ Floppy (A:)** drive.

The files display lightly as you drag them to the Pictures folder.

10 In the **Folders** pane, when the **Pictures** folder is highlighted, release the mouse button. Click the **Pictures** folder. Click the **Views button arrow** and then click **Thumbnails**.

Small thumbnail images display in the Contents pane, as shown in Figure 1.37.

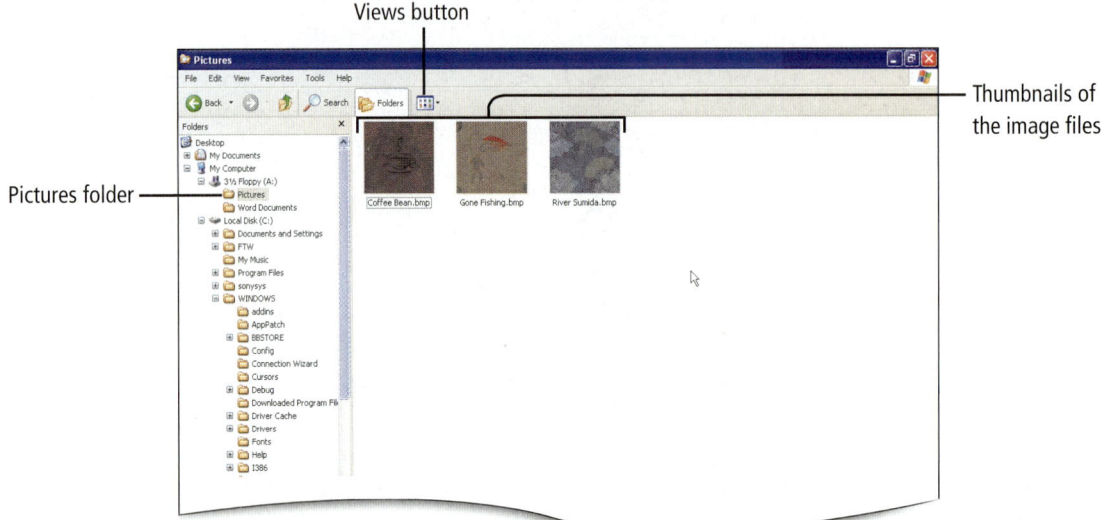

Figure 1.37

11 In the **Folders** pane, on the floppy drive, click the **Word Documents** folder. Drag the **Blue Lace 16.bmp** file from the **Word Documents** folder to the **Pictures** folder in drive A.

When you drag a file between two folders on the same disk, the file is moved instead of copied.

12 In the **Folders** pane, click the **Pictures** folder in drive A to be sure the fourth file was copied. If necessary, from the toolbar click the **Views** button and then click **Thumbnails**. See Figure 1.38.

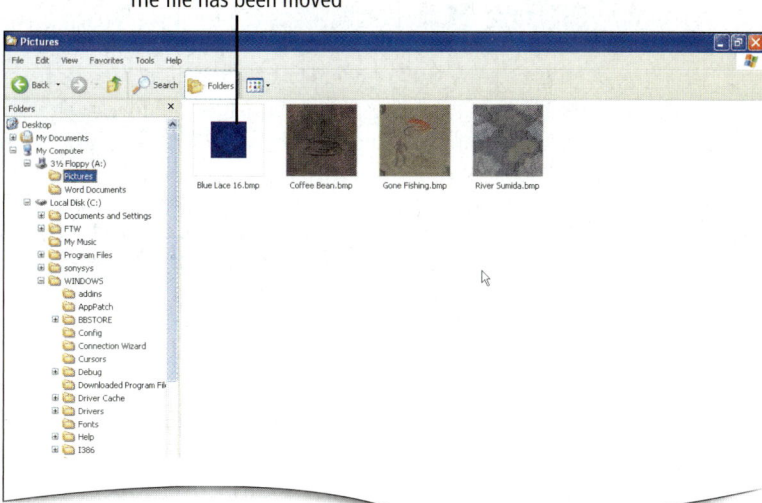

Figure 1.38

More Knowledge — Using Cut and Paste to Move Files

You can also move a file using the cut-and-paste method. To do this, right-click the file and click Cut from the shortcut menu. Click the new drive or folder to which you want to move the file, right-click in an open area, and then click Paste from the shortcut menu.

13 In the **Name** column in the **Contents** pane, right-click the **Blue Lace 16.bmp** file.

A shortcut menu displays, including a Rename command.

14 From the shortcut menu, click the **Rename** command. Type **Blue.bmp** and press [Enter].

When the file extensions are displayed, you need to include the extension when you rename the file. See Figure 1.39.

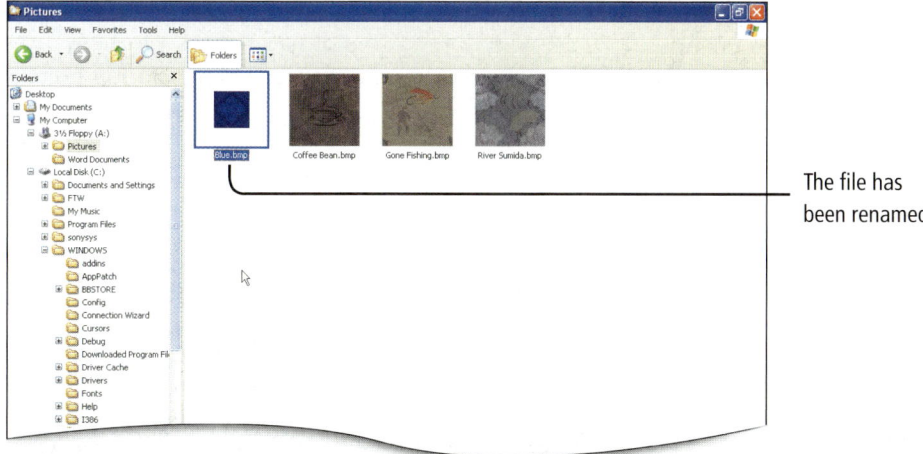

Figure 1.39

Project 1A: Working with Windows XP and Managing Files | **Windows XP** 33

More Knowledge — File Name Restrictions

There are several restrictions for naming files or folders. A file name can contain up to 255 characters, including spaces, although the file name cannot begin with a space. It also cannot contain the following characters: \ / : * ? " < > |

15 In the **Contents** pane **Name** column, right-click the **Word Documents** folder on drive A. From the shortcut menu, click **Delete**.

A dialog box asks whether you want to delete the folder and all its contents, as shown in Figure 1.40. Any files in the folder will be deleted along with the folder. You can delete files using this same method.

Note — If You Can't Delete a File

Sometimes you will try to delete a file and Windows Explorer will display a dialog box saying that the file cannot be deleted. This usually means that the file is open. You must close a document before you can delete it.

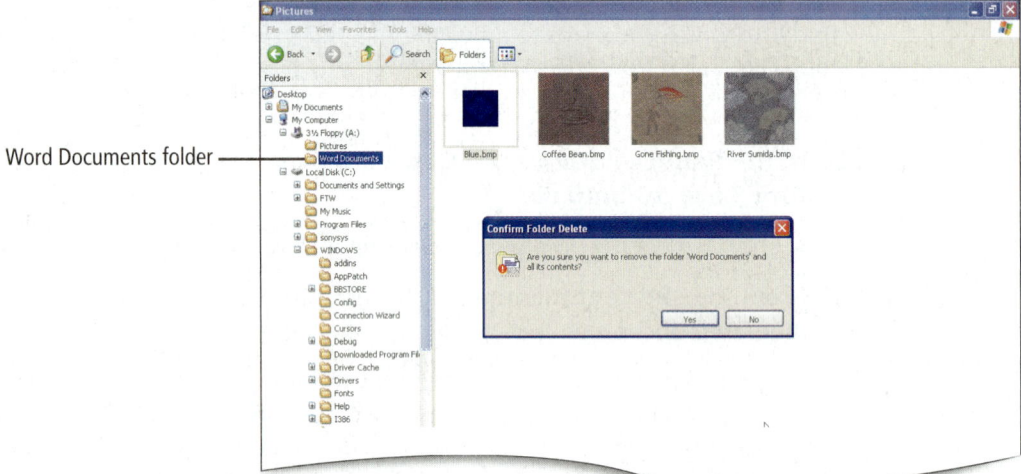

Word Documents folder

Figure 1.40

16 In the **Confirm Folder Delete** dialog box, click **Yes**.

The folder is deleted.

17 In the title bar, click the **Close** button ⊠ to close the **My Computer** window.

More Knowledge — Recovering Deleted Files

If you accidentally delete a file from a hard disk drive that you want to keep, there is a good chance you can recover it. Windows temporarily stores files deleted from your hard drive in a Recycle bin, which you can find on the desktop or in the My Computer Folders pane. You can open the Recycle bin in the same way as you open a file folder. If the discarded files have not been permanently removed, you can right-click the file name in the Contents pane and click Restore in the shortcut menu.

Alert!

Removing Read-Only Status from a File

Each file has certain properties that are established when the file is created. These include the date and time the file was created, the last time it was modified, the last time it was accessed, the type of file, and the file location. If you are using an earlier version of Windows, three file attributes—read-only, archive, and hidden—are also set and may need to be changed. For most files, the attribute is set as archive. However, files copied from a CD-ROM and some network drives using older versions of Windows may be read-only. You need to change this attribute in order to edit the file.

To change the attribute of a file that has been copied from a CD, right-click the file name and click Properties from the shortcut menu. Click the Read-only check box to deselect it and then click OK. If you have copied a number of files, you can select them all and use this method once to remove the read-only status from all the files.

Objective 6
Find Files and Folders

If you use a computer long enough, you will accumulate a large number of files and folders. You will also occasionally forget where you put a file, or what you called it. Windows XP provides a way to search the computer for files and folders, and even for text within a document. You can also specify the type of file or the date it was last modified.

In the following steps, you use several different methods to search for files and folders.

1 In the taskbar, click the **Start** button and then click **My Computer**.

The My Computer window opens.

2 On the toolbar, click the **Search** button.

The options in the task pane change, showing the search options for your computer. Notice that you can search for specific file types or you can search through all the files and folders. See Figure 1.41.

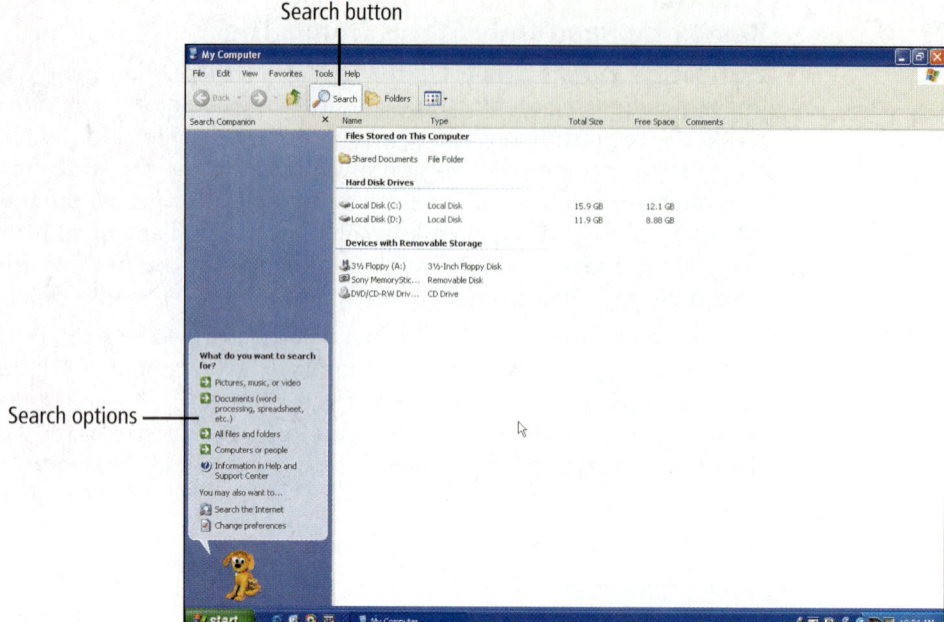

Figure 1.41

3 In the task pane, click the **All files and folders** option.

A search dialog box displays. This enables you to specify the file name (or part of a file name) or text contained in the file. It also enables you to narrow the search by specifying the search location. By default, the program is set to check all available drives.

4 In the **All or part of the file name** box, type **zapotec**

The actual file name is capitalized, but this search option is not case sensitive. See Figure 1.42.

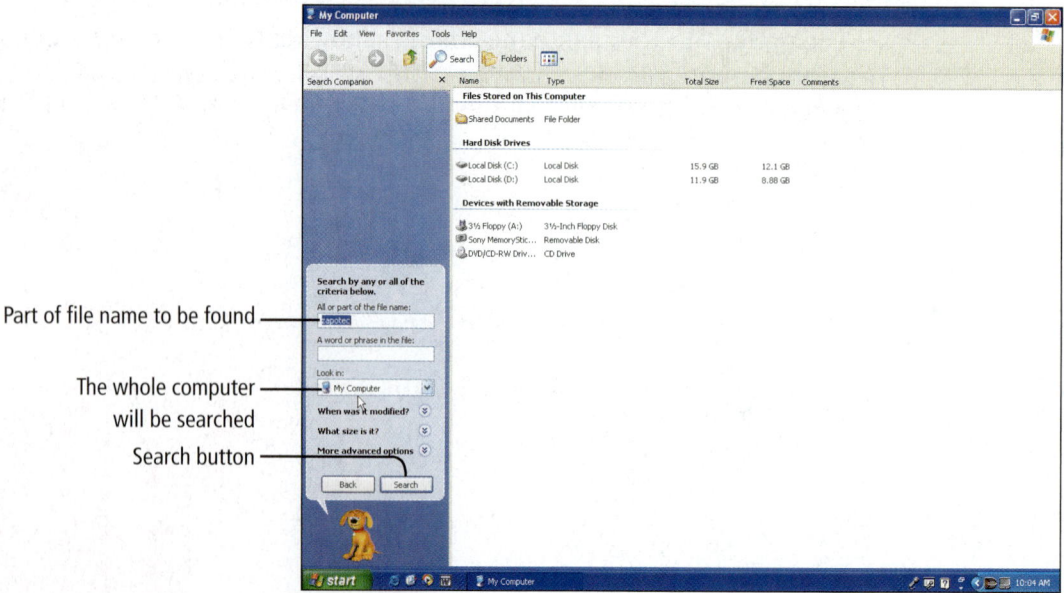

Figure 1.42

36 Windows XP | Chapter 1: Getting Started with Windows XP

Note — Narrowing Your Search

To narrow your search, open the drive you wish to search. When you click the Search button, the default location will be the open drive.

5 At the bottom of the task pane, click the **Search** button.

The search begins. Notice that a couple of files appear rather quickly, but the search program goes on and on. See Figure 1.43. (You may see only one file, depending on the way your computer has been set up.) This is because you did not specify a location, so the program is checking all storage locations on the computer. You can click the Stop button at any time if the procedure seems to be taking too long.

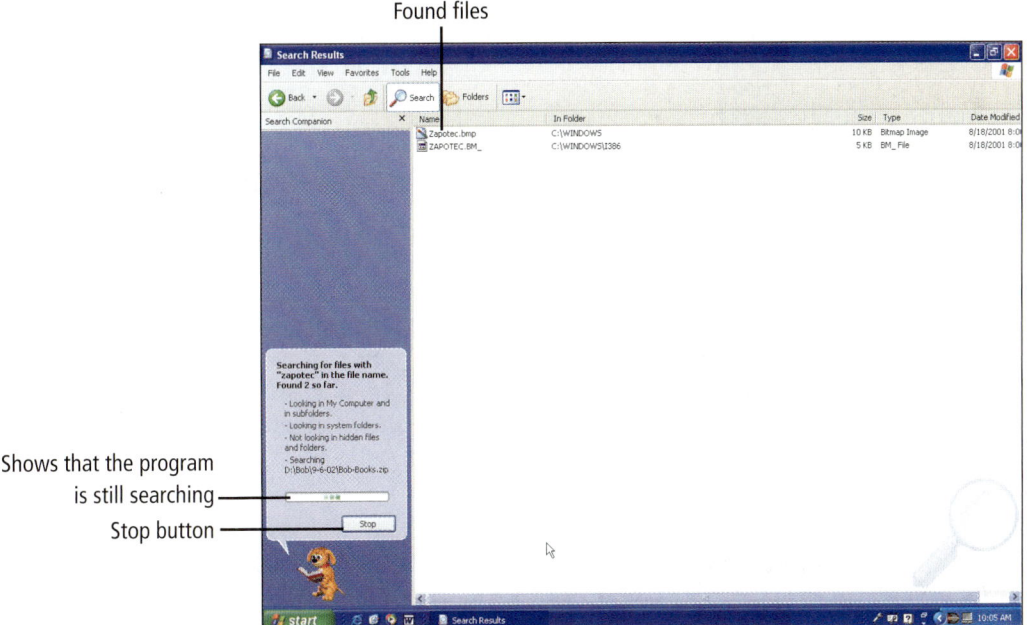

Figure 1.43

6 If necessary, at the bottom of the task pane, click **Stop** to stop the current search. Click the **Start a new search** option. Click the **Pictures**, **music**, or **video** option.

A new dialog box displays, showing the options for finding this type of file.

7 At the bottom of the task pane, click the **Pictures and Photos** check box. In the **All or part of the file name** box, type **stucco**

This is part of the Santa Fe Stucco.bmp file name. See Figure 1.44.

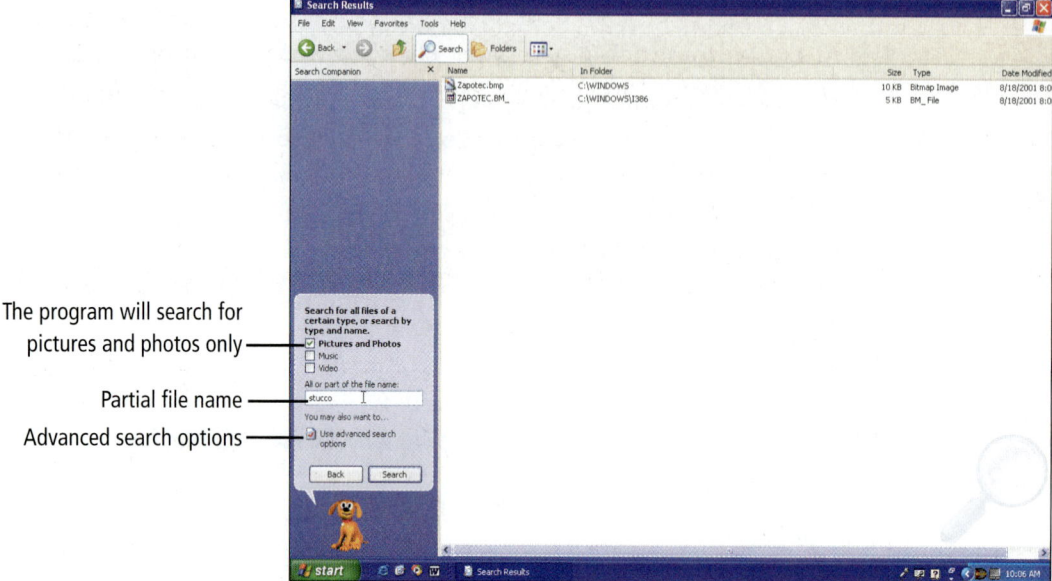

The program will search for pictures and photos only

Partial file name

Advanced search options

Figure 1.44

8 In the task pane, click the **Use advanced search options** check box.

An expanded dialog box displays.

9 At the right of the **Look in** box, click the arrow.

A menu of possible file locations is displayed, as shown in Figure 1.45.

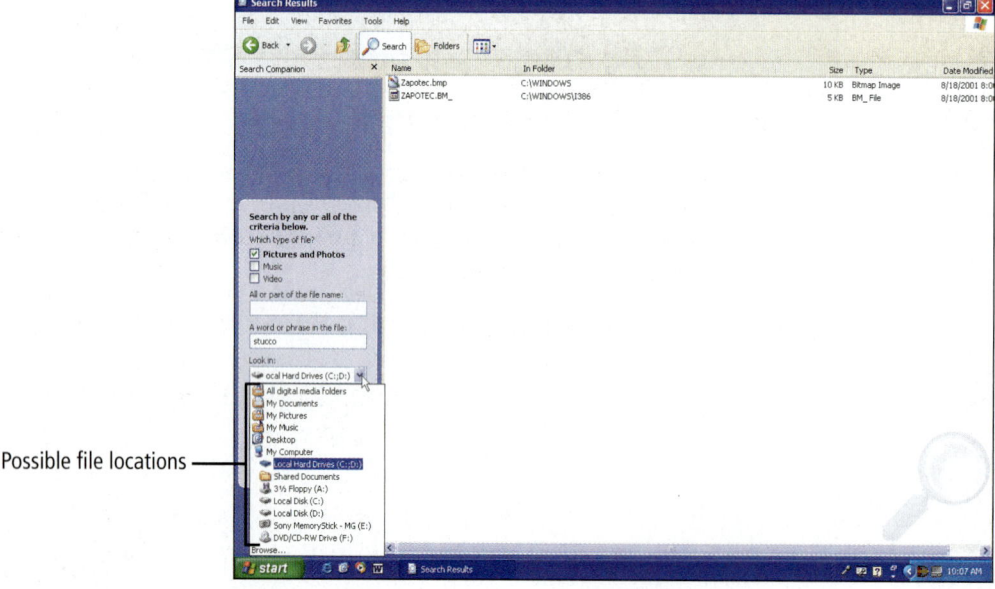

Possible file locations

Figure 1.45

38 Windows XP | Chapter 1: Getting Started with Windows XP

10 From the location list, click **Local Disk (C:)**.

This will greatly speed up your search.

11 At the bottom of the task pane, click the **Search** button.

The Santa Fe Stucco.bmp file is found, along with another file and a file folder, as shown in Figure 1.46. Again, your search results may show only one file. The search may still take several minutes, but it is much faster than a search of all files in all storage locations.

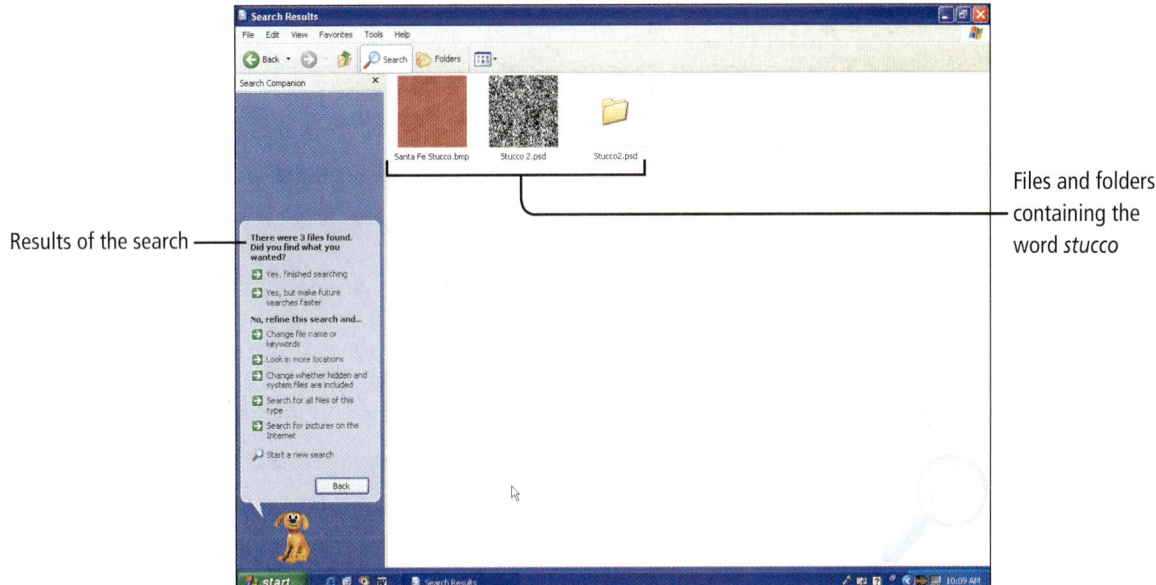

Results of the search

Files and folders containing the word *stucco*

Figure 1.46

12 Scroll down, if necessary, and click the **Start a new search** option. Click the **Documents (word processing, spreadsheet, etc.)** option.

This dialog box gives you greater control over the search. You can search for documents that have specified file extensions, or you can search for documents last modified during a certain time period. You can even combine the two.

13 In the task pane, click **Within the last week**, and type ***.doc** in the **All or part of the document name box**. If your computer is not used often, click **Past month** instead.

This restricts the search to Word documents (that have the .doc extension) modified in the past week. The asterisk is called a ***wildcard*** and means that you will be searching for anything that has the .doc extension. This is very helpful if you can't remember the file name or where you put it. See Figure 1.47.

Project 1A: Working with Windows XP and Managing Files | **Windows XP** 39

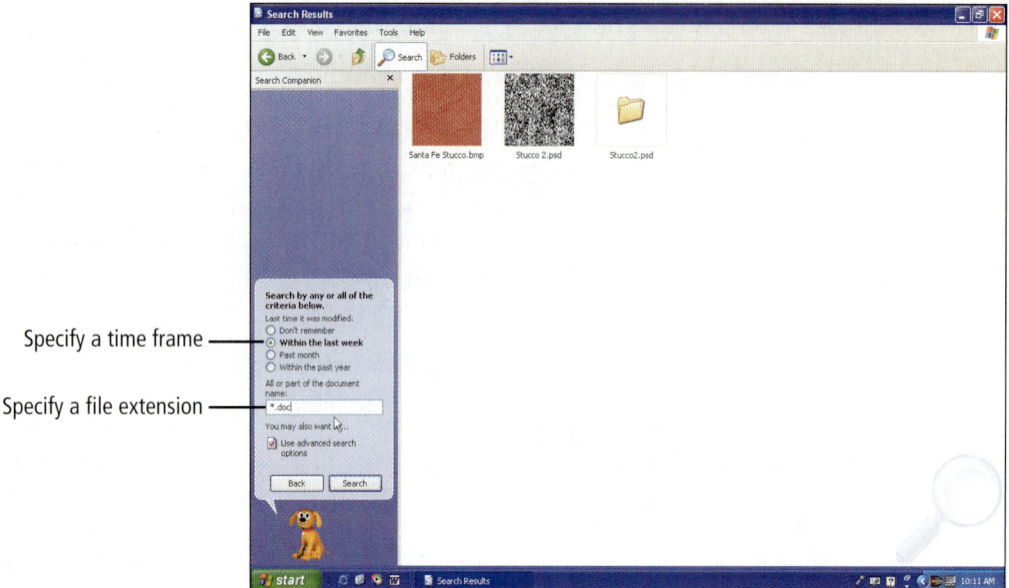

Specify a time frame
Specify a file extension

Figure 1.47

14 In the task pane, click the **Use advanced search options** check box, click the arrow to the right of the **Look in** box, and then click **Local Disk (C:)**. Click the **Search** button.

The Contents pane displays the files modified in the past week that have the .doc extension. The files found on your computer will be different from the ones shown in Figure 1.48.

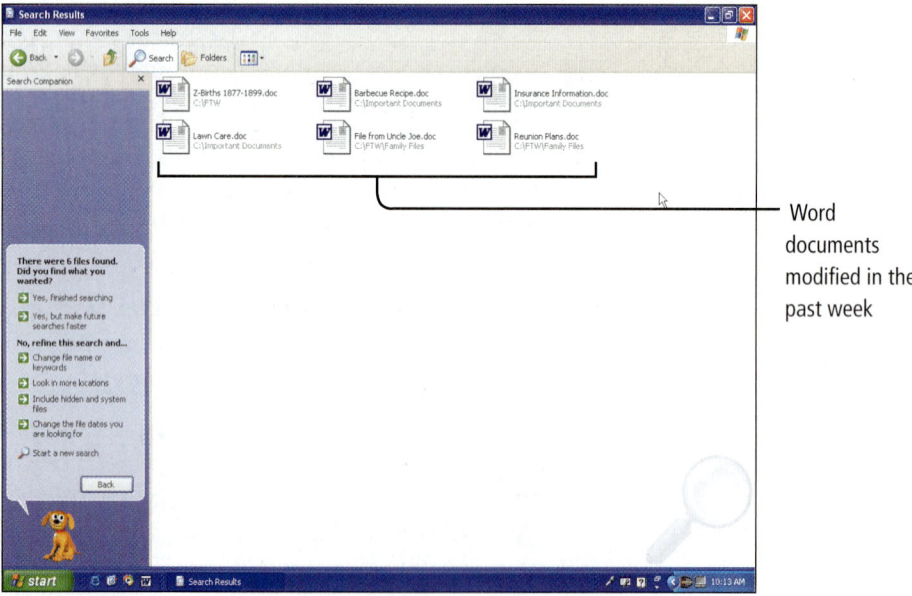

Word documents modified in the past week

Figure 1.48

40 Windows XP | Chapter 1: Getting Started with Windows XP

Objective 7
Compress Files

Circumstances may arise when you would like your file sizes to be smaller. For example, some files containing graphics can be larger than the capacity of a floppy disk. Also, when you send files as e-mail attachments, the smaller they are, the faster you can send them. In fact, if you are using a computer that has a modem, reducing the file size may mean the difference between successfully transmitting the file or having the system time out—end the online session—before the transfer is complete.

Windows XP includes a built-in compression feature. This enables you to quickly compress (zip) one or more files into a single file that uses a *.zip* file extension. These files can then be unzipped for editing on any other computer running Windows XP or any earlier version of Windows that has a third-party zip program installed. If you are using a third-party zip program, such as WinZip® or PKZIP®, you will need to use that program to complete this task—the procedure listed below will not work.

In the following steps, you compress a single file and then compress several files at the same time.

1 With the **My Computer** window open, click the **Folders** button to activate the **Folders** pane. In the toolbar, click the **Views** button and then click **Details**.

The search results are kept in a special temporary storage area, as shown in Figure 1.49.

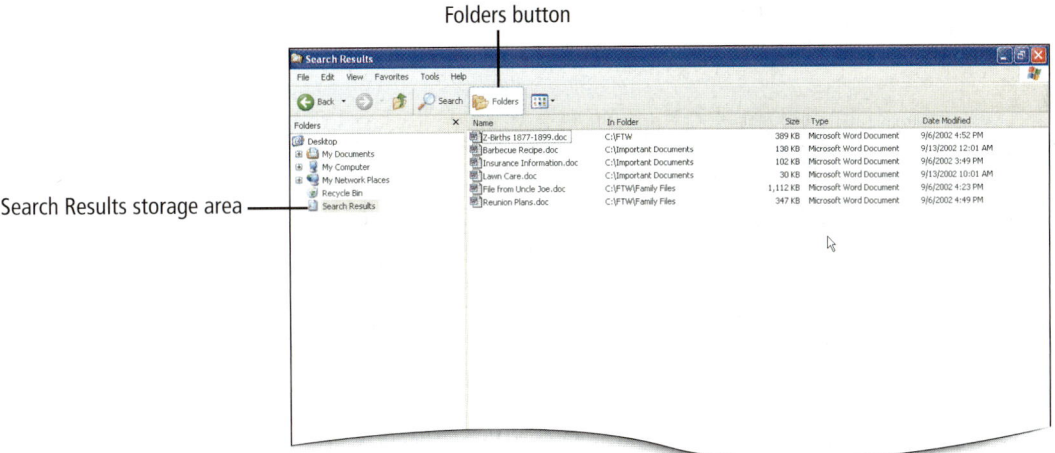

Figure 1.49

2 Click **My Computer**, open the **C:** drive, and open the **WINDOWS** (or **WINNT**) folder.

The Windows system files display in the Contents pane.

Project 1A: Working with Windows XP and Managing Files | **Windows XP** 41

3 Click the **Type** column selector and scroll down, if necessary, so that you can see the text document files (files that have a *.txt* extension if you have extensions turned on). Move the pointer over the **setuplog.txt** file. If you do not have this file, choose any other file that is listed as a text document.

A ScreenTip displays, providing information about the file, as shown in Figure 1.50. The setuplog.txt file is automatically created during setup. The size of this file will be different on each computer.

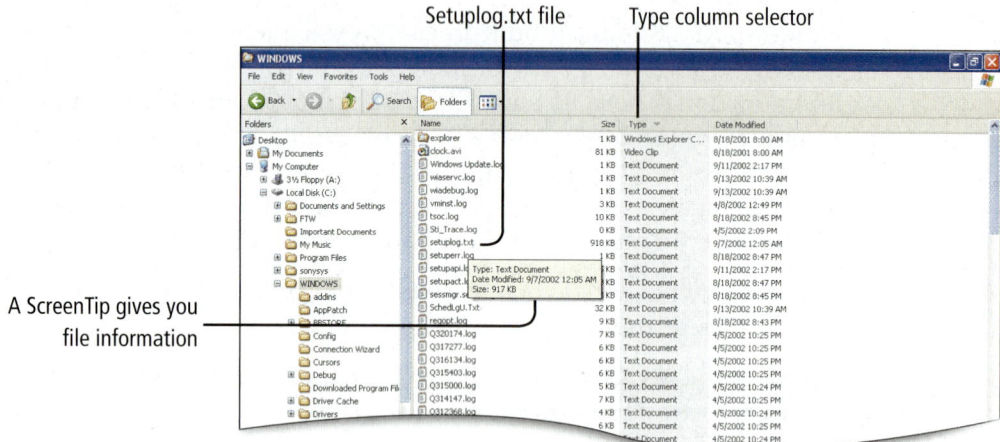

Figure 1.50

4 Right-click **setuplog.txt**, and move the pointer to **Send To**.

The Send To submenu is displayed, as shown in Figure 1.51. Your submenu will probably look somewhat different.

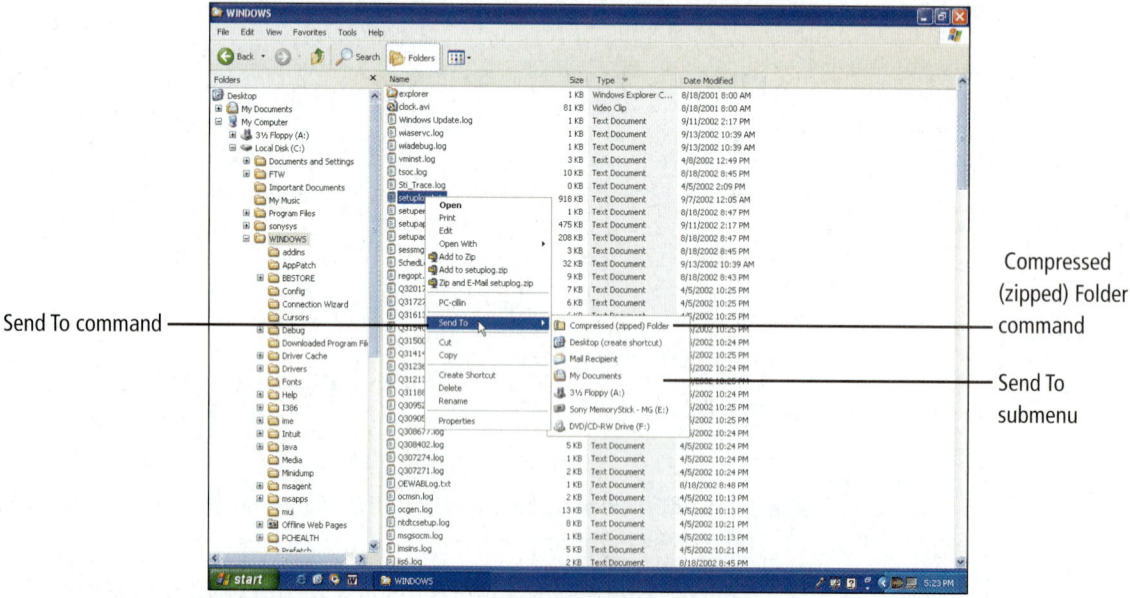

Figure 1.51

42 Windows XP | Chapter 1: Getting Started with Windows XP

5 From the shortcut menu, click the **Compressed (zipped) Folder** command.

A new file, called setuplog.zip (or the name of whichever text file you selected), is created. The file displays at the bottom of the Contents pane.

6 In the **Contents** pane, click the **Date Modified** column selector twice to show the recent documents first. If necessary, scroll to the top of the **Contents** pane.

In Figure 1.52, you can see that the file size has been reduced from 918 KB to 64 KB (your numbers will be different). Files created by different applications will compress at different rates. Some, like this text file, will compress by about 90 percent. Excel files often compress by about 75 percent, but PowerPoint files compress only by 10 percent or so.

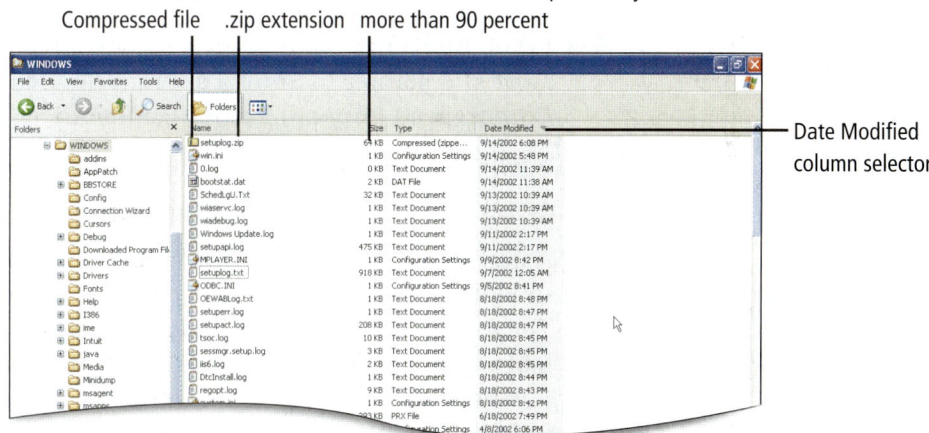

Figure 1.52

More Knowledge — File Associations and Compression Programs

You may see a dialog box when you click the Compressed (zipped) Folder command. Because every file type needs to be associated with a program, your computer may already associate files that have the *.zip* extension with a third-party program such as WinZip. The dialog box will ask whether you want to designate Compressed (zipped) Folders as the application for handling ZIP files (compressed files that have a *.zip* extension). If you are working in a lab, ask the lab manager how to answer this question. If you are working at home, click Yes unless you want to use another program to compress your files.

---

7 In the **Contents** pane, click the **Type** column selector twice, and scroll down so that you can see the bitmap files. Click the **Soap Bubbles.bmp** file, hold down Ctrl, and click the **Prairie Wind.bmp** and **Greenstone.bmp** files.

Project 1A: Working with Windows XP and Managing Files | **Windows XP** 43

You should have three files selected, as shown in Figure 1.53.

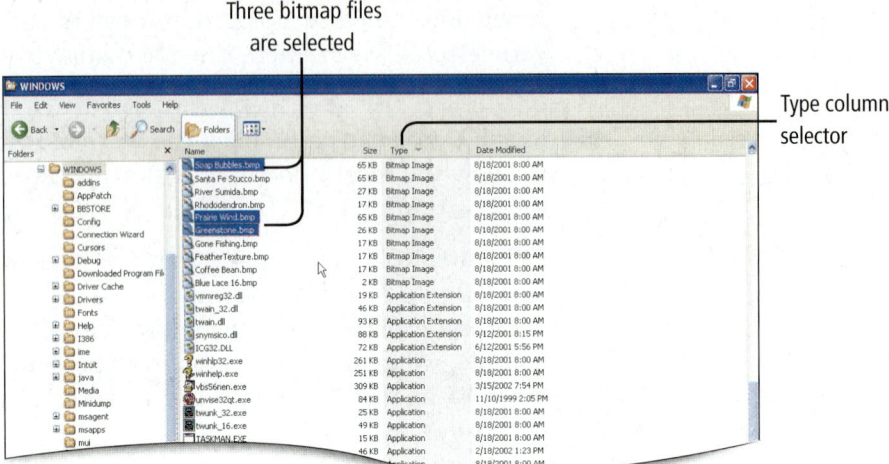

Figure 1.53

8. In the **Contents** pane, right-click any one of the selected files, and move the pointer to **Send To**. From the **Send To** submenu, click the **Compressed (zipped) Folder** command.

   The files are all placed in a single zipped folder.

9. Scroll to the bottom of the **Contents** pane.

   A new folder displays, as shown in Figure 1.54. The icon is a folder, unlike the icon that is displayed when you compress a single file. The folder means that multiple files have been compressed. The folder name is the name of whichever file you right-clicked, although it contains all three files. Notice that the files have been compressed to 78 KB from an original 156 KB, a size reduction of 50 percent.

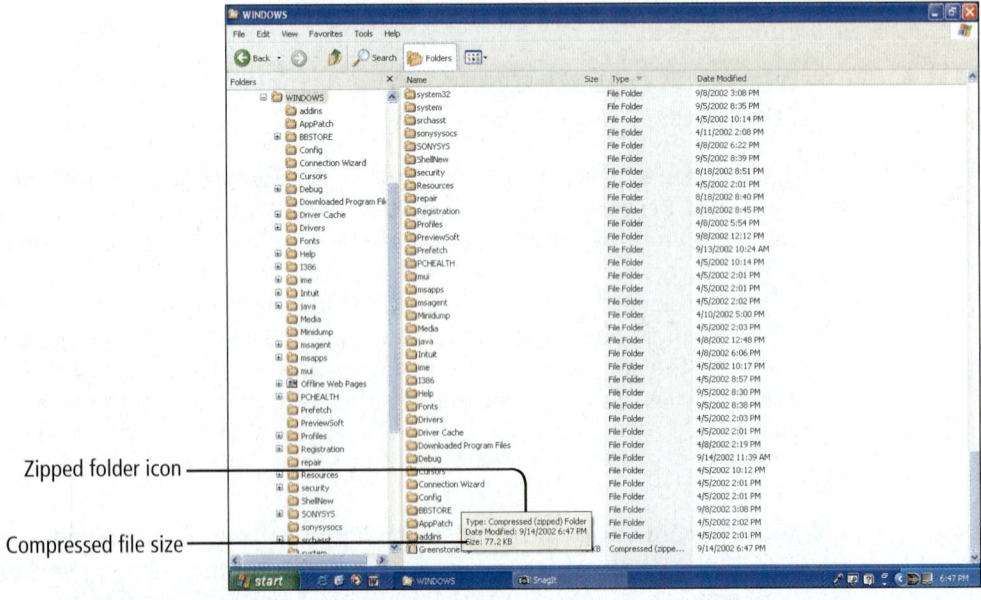

Figure 1.54

44 Windows XP | Chapter 1: Getting Started with Windows XP

10 In the **Folders** pane, scroll up until you can see the **3½ Floppy (A:)** icon. Drag the zipped folder, in this example the **Greenstone.zip** folder, to the floppy drive.

The zipped folder is copied to the floppy disk.

11 In the **Folders** pane, click the **3½ Floppy (A:)** drive.

The zipped folder appears next to the Pictures folder you created in Objective 5, as shown in Figure 1.55.

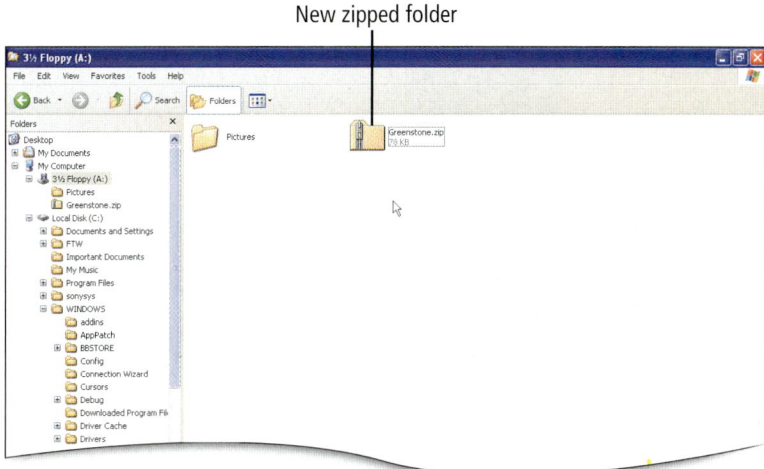

Figure 1.55

12 In the **Contents** pane, double-click the **Greenstone.zip** folder.

All the compressed files are displayed in a new window, as shown in Figure 1.56.

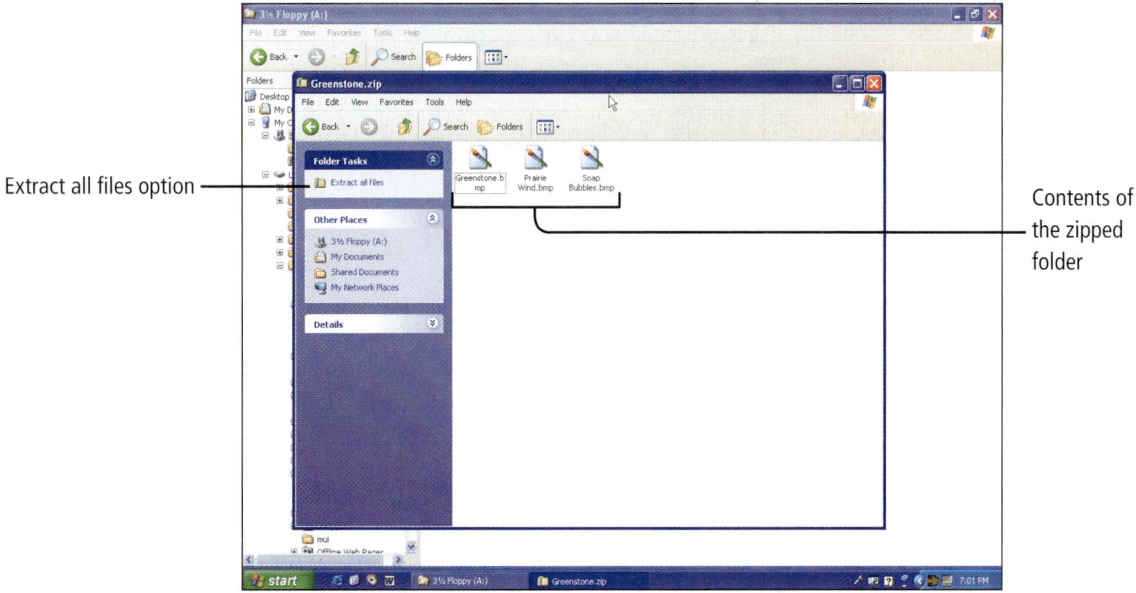

Figure 1.56

13 In the **Greenstone.zip** window, click the **Extract all files** option.

The first Extraction Wizard dialog box displays. See Figure 1.57.

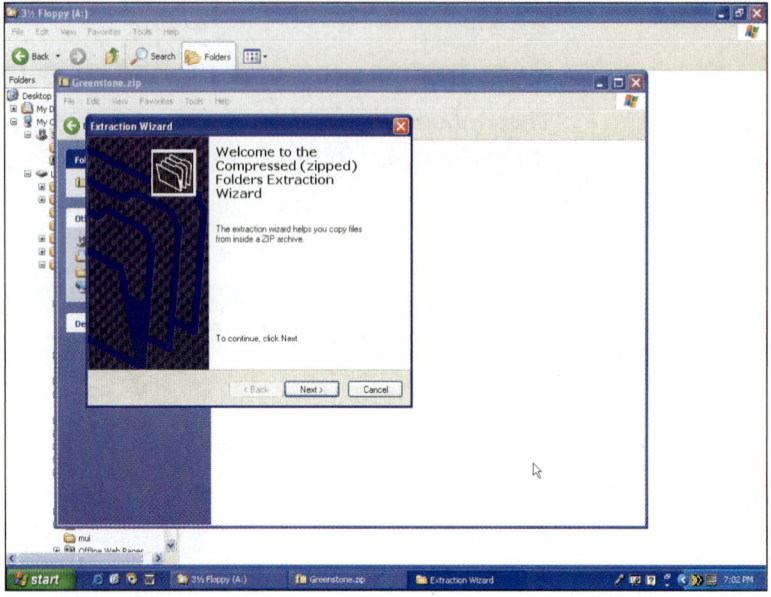

Figure 1.57

14 In the **Extraction Wizard** dialog box, click the **Next** button.

A second Extraction Wizard dialog box displays, as shown in Figure 1.58. You can designate the destination location of the extracted files. For this task, you will accept the default location, which is the floppy drive.

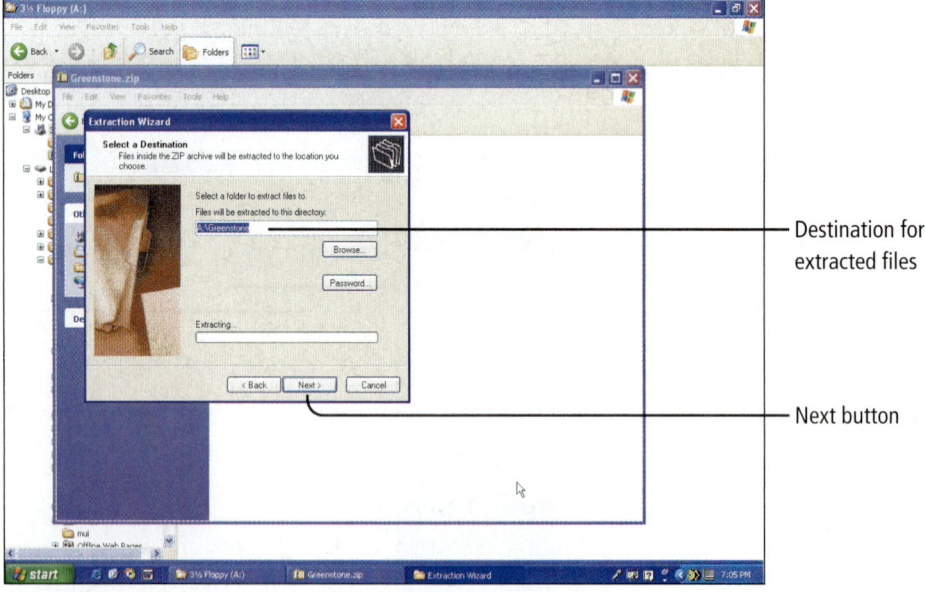

Figure 1.58

15 In the **Extraction Wizard** dialog box, click the **Next** button.

The files are extracted, and a third Extraction Wizard dialog box displays.

46   Windows XP | Chapter 1: Getting Started with Windows XP

16 In the **Extraction Wizard** dialog box, click the **Finish** button. Close all windows except the My Computer window.

The extracted files are stored in a new folder. The name of the folder is the same as the name of the zipped folder file name without the *.zip* extension, as shown in Figure 1.59.

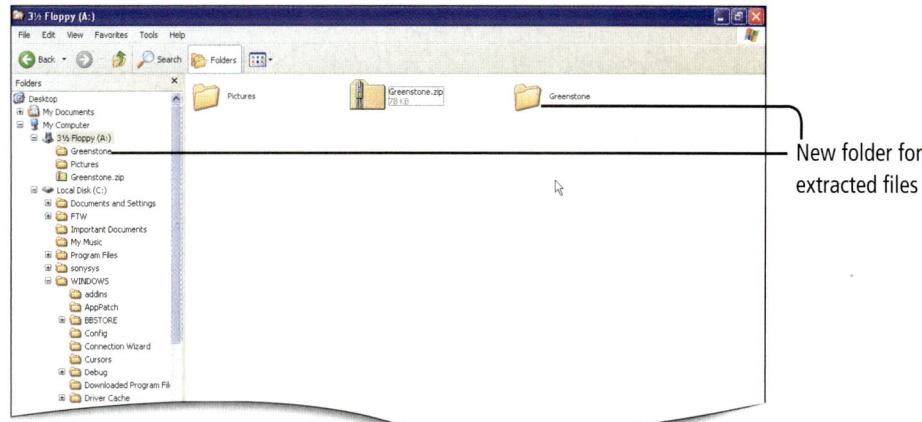

Figure 1.59

17 Under **Folders**, under drive A, double-click the **Greenstone** folder (not the zipped folder). From the toolbar, click the **Views** button, and then click **Details**.

The files have been restored to their original size, as shown in Figure 1.60.

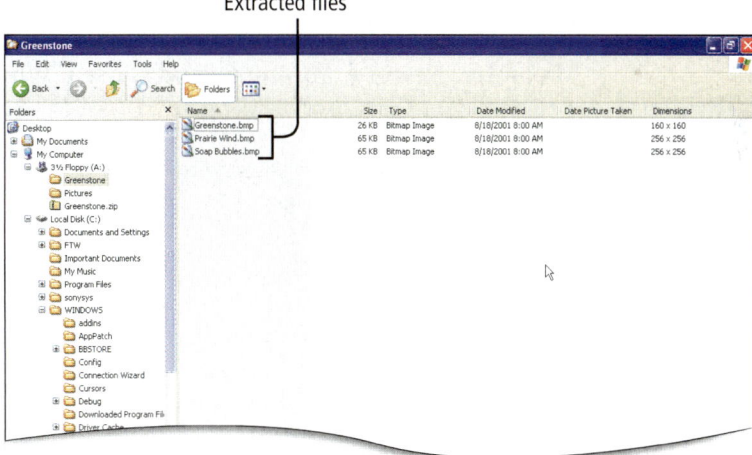

Figure 1.60

18 Submit the files as directed by your instructor. Delete the two *.zip* files you created in this task, and then close the **My Computer** window.

Another Way — Zipping a Folder

If you want to zip all of the files in a folder, it is easier to zip the folder than to select and zip the individual files. This method also has the advantage of giving the zip file the same name as the folder.

Summary

A working knowledge of Windows is necessary in order to use Microsoft Office effectively. In this chapter, you practiced setting up, organizing, and navigating the Windows desktop. You learned how to maximize, minimize, and restore windows and how to move windows on the desktop. You learned how to use the Windows taskbar, how to find files, and how to use the Start button.

Another Windows feature you worked with was managing your files. You created folders to store your documents and then moved files between folders. You copied, renamed, and deleted files and then learned how to compress one or more documents to save space and facilitate sending files over the Internet.

In This Chapter You Practiced How To

- Get Started with Windows
- Resize, Move, and Scroll Windows
- Maximize, Restore, Minimize, and Close a Window
- Create a New Folder
- Copy, Move, Rename, and Delete Files
- Find Files and Folders
- Compress Files

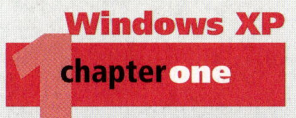

Concepts Assessments

Matching   Match each term in the second column with its correct definition in the first column by writing the letter of the term on the blank line in front of the correct definition.

____ **1.** A bar that contains the Start button, buttons representing open programs, and other buttons that will activate programs.

____ **2.** The moving arrow (or other object) on the screen that is used to select or activate objects and programs.

____ **3.** Enables you to view text that extends beyond the edges of the screen.

____ **4.** A box that displays information and usually consists of a title bar, menu bar, status bar, and toolbars, and always has a Minimize button.

____ **5.** Used to keep related files stored together in one location.

____ **6.** Character used to substitute for several characters in a file search.

____ **7.** Three-letter ending to a file name that identifies the file type but that may or may not be displayed.

____ **8.** Used to find files or folders.

____ **9.** Area at the top of the window that displays the file name and also contains the Minimize, Maximize/Restore Down, and Close buttons.

____ **10.** Lets you see your document in its final format.

A. A window
B. Title bar
C. Mouse pointer
D. Graphical User Interface (GUI)
E. Taskbar
F. Wildcard
G. Folder
H. Search button
I. Scroll bar
J. Extension

Concepts Assessments (continued)

Fill in the Blank Write the correct answer in the space provided.

1. A(n) _____, which consists of the last three characters of a file name, indicates which program was used to create the file.

2. A(n) _____ is a graphic representation that enables you to run a program or use a program function.

3. Windows XP is an example of a(n) _____, which coordinates the activities of a computer.

4. The _____ button on the left end of the taskbar is used to run programs, change system settings, or find help.

5. To make a window fill the screen, use the _____ button from the title bar.

6. When more than one document or program is open at the same time, you can switch back and forth between them by clicking the appropriate button in the _____.

7. A(n) _____ is a second-level menu that is accessed using a menu command.

8. When you delete a file, it is stored in a temporary area called the _____, from which it can often be recovered.

9. You can hide a program or document without closing it by clicking the _____ button.

10. In My Computer, you can sort file names alphabetically by clicking the _____ column selector.

Outlook 2003

chapter one

Getting Started with Outlook 2003

In this chapter, you will: complete this project and practice these skills.

Project 1A
Exploring Outlook 2003

Objectives
- Start Outlook and Identify Outlook Window Elements
- Create Outlook Folders
- Close Outlook
- Store Addresses in the Contacts Folder
- Edit and Print Contacts
- Schedule Appointments in the Calendar
- Record Tasks and Notes

The Greater Atlanta Job Fair

The Greater Atlanta Job Fair is a nonprofit organization that holds targeted job fairs in and around the greater Atlanta area several times each year. The fairs are widely marketed to companies nationwide and locally. The organization also presents an annual Atlanta Job Fair that draws over 2,000 employers in more than 70 industries and generally registers more than 5,000 candidates.

©Getty Images, Inc.

Getting Started with Outlook 2003

Do you sometimes find it a challenge to manage and complete all the tasks related to your job, family, and class work? Microsoft Office Outlook 2003 can help. Outlook 2003 is a personal information management program (also known as a PIM) that does two things: (1) it helps you get organized, and (2) it helps you communicate with others efficiently. Successful people know that good organizational and communication skills are important. Outlook 2003 electronically stores and organizes appointments and due dates; names, addresses, and phone numbers; to do lists; and notes. Another major use of Outlook 2003 is its e-mail and fax capabilities, along with features with which you can manage group work such as the tasks assigned to a group of coworkers. In this introduction to Microsoft Office Outlook 2003, you will explore the modules available in Outlook and enter data into each module.

Project 1A Exploring Outlook 2003

As a personal information manager, Outlook organizes your information within various *modules*. Modules are separate storage areas named to identify the type of information they hold, for example, e-mail messages, contacts, events, tasks, or notes.

In Activities 1.1 through 1.9, you will use Outlook to organize the activities and information related to the Greater Atlanta Job Fair for Mr. Ben Ham, the administrative manager. You will examine the e-mail capability of Outlook. In addition, you will store the names and addresses of people and companies associated with the Job Fair, schedule dates for Job Fair–related events, record a list of tasks to accomplish, and create electronic notes. The items you create will resemble those shown in Figure 1.1.

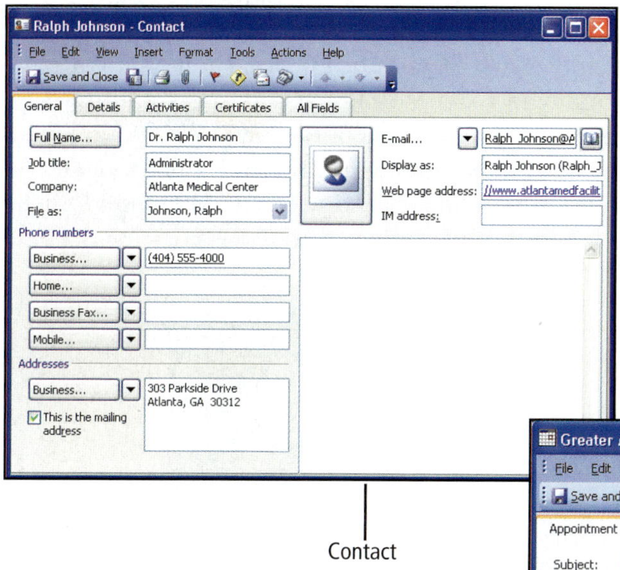

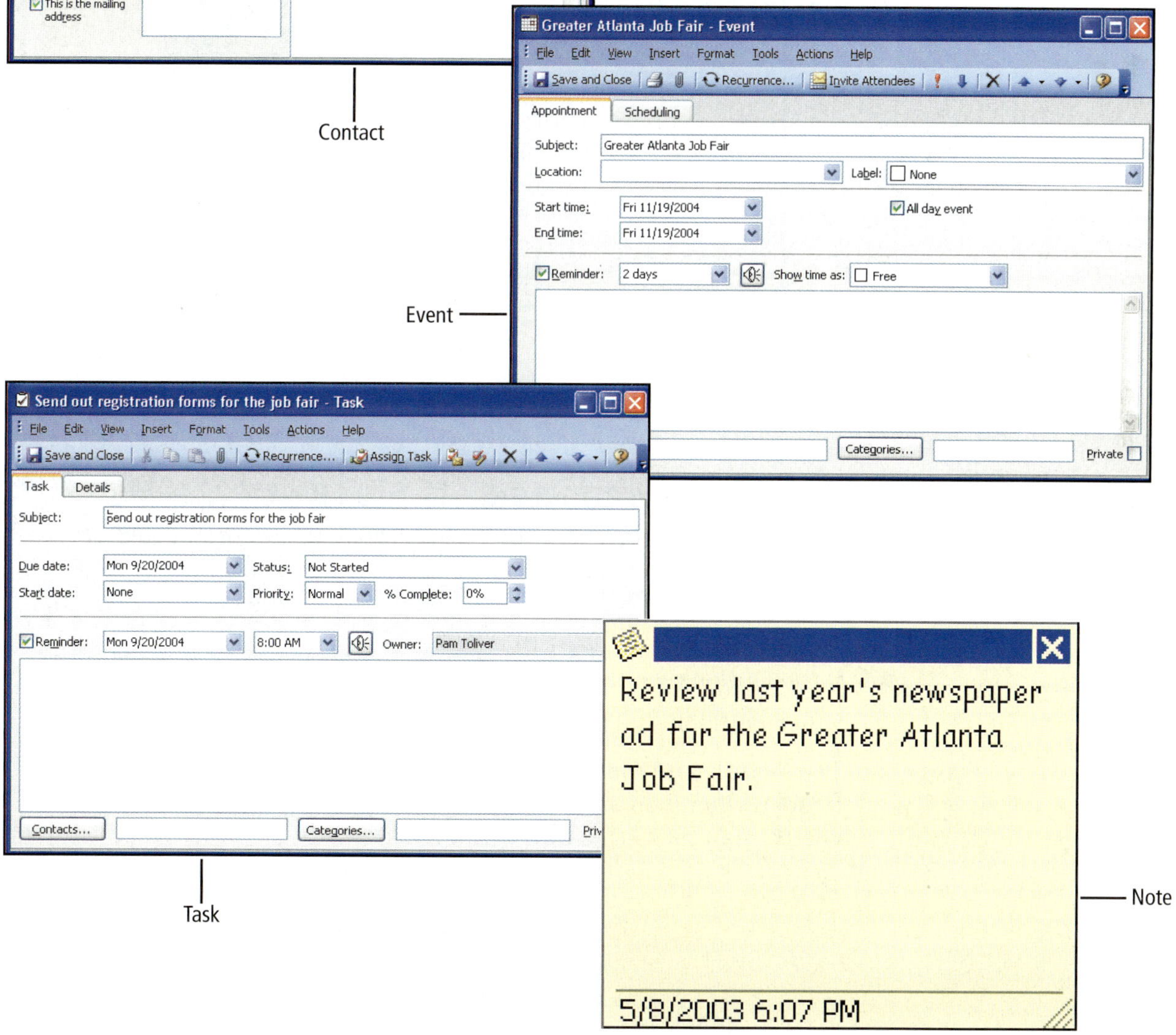

Figure 1.1
Project 1A—Outlook Items

Objective 1
Start Outlook and Identify Outlook Window Elements

Activity 1.1 Starting Outlook

1 Find out from your instructor or lab coordinator where the microsoft office 2003 program is located on your system. On the Windows taskbar, click the **Start** button, then click **Microsoft Office Outlook 2003**.

Organizations and individuals store computer programs in a variety of ways. In organizations where Outlook is used as the standard e-mail program, it may display at the top of the Start menu along with Internet Explorer. Or it may display on the All Programs list, either by itself or on a submenu associated with the Microsoft Office suite. Refer to Figure 1.2 for an example.

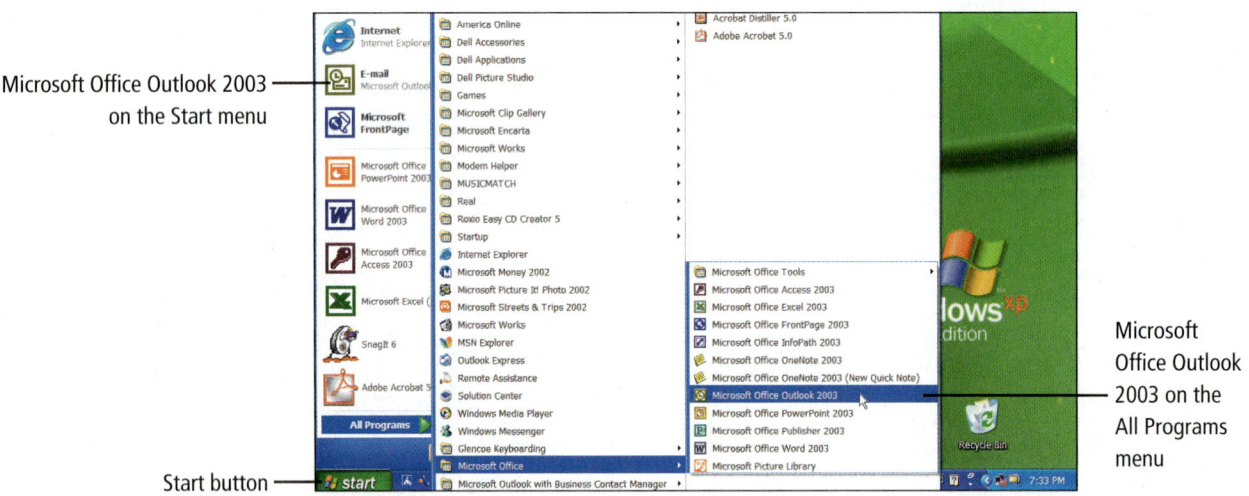

Microsoft Office Outlook 2003 on the Start menu

Microsoft Office Outlook 2003 on the All Programs menu

Start button

Figure 1.2

> **Alert!** **Server Connection Dialog Box**
> If a message displays indicating that a connection to the server could not be established, click OK. Even without a mail server connection, you can still use the personal information management features of Outlook.

2 If the Outlook window is not already maximized, on the Microsoft Office Outlook 2003 title bar, click the **Maximize** button.

The default and most common Outlook setup is for the Mail module to open when you start Outlook 2003. The Mail module organizes your e-mail messages into various folders.

More Knowledge — Folders

Outlook uses the *Inbox* folder to store incoming e-mail message items from your connected mail server. Other folders are included in the default setup of the Mail module. You can add additional folders and delete folders, according to your needs.

3 Take a moment to study the Outlook screen elements identified in Figure 1.3 and described in the table in Figure 1.4.

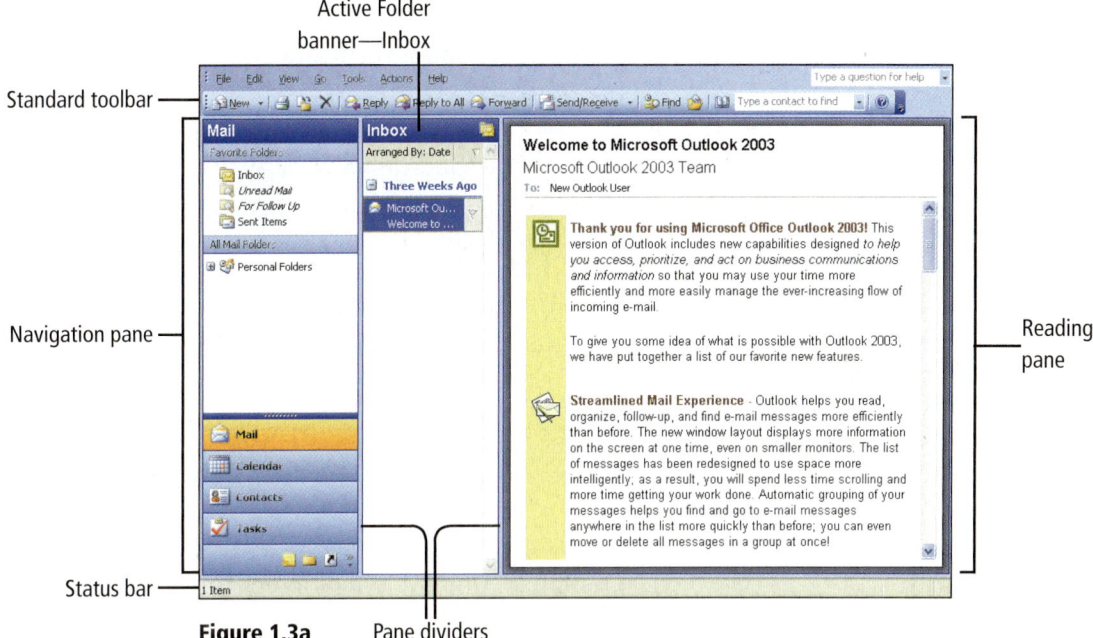

Figure 1.3a

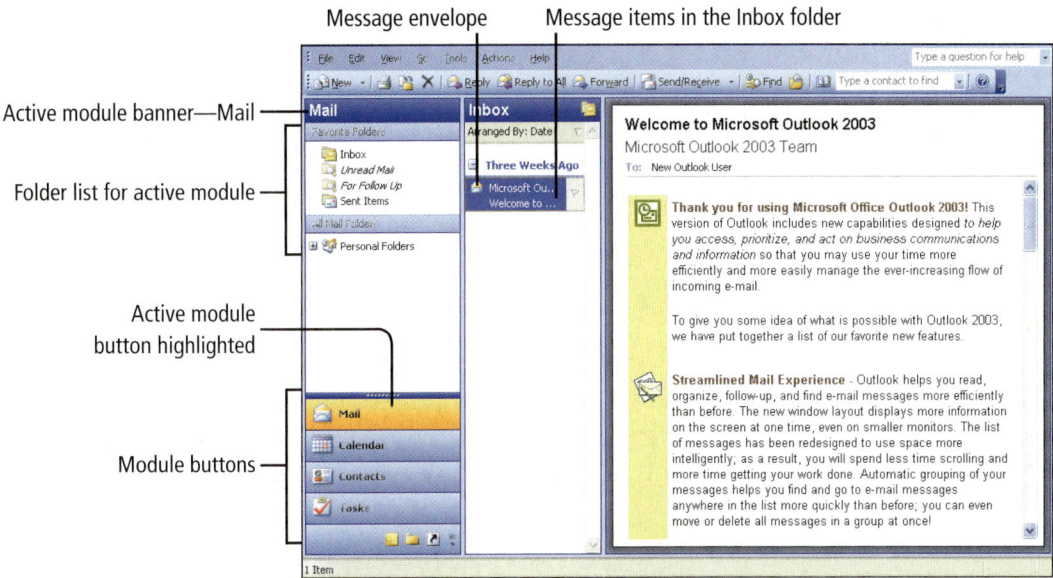

Figure 1.3b

Microsoft Outlook 2003 Screen Elements

Screen Element	Description
Standard toolbar	Contains buttons that provide a one-click method to activate the most common menu commands. Buttons differ depending on the module that is open.
Reading pane	Displays the active message when a mail folder is open or the active item in other modules.
Active Folder banner—Inbox	Identifies the active folder—the folder highlighted in the Navigation pane.
Active Module banner—Mail	Displays the name of the active module.
Pane dividers	Separate panes of the active window. Pane dividers change as you display different modules.
List of folders for the active module	Displays a list of the folders that hold the items within the active module.
Navigation pane	Displays buttons for each Outlook module.
Navigation pane banner	Identifies the active module.
Module buttons	Identifies the modules available.
Status bar	Displays information about the amount of information stored in the active module and displays program activity as it occurs.
Active module button	Displays as a different color to identify the active module.
Message items in the Inbox folder	Displays as a closed envelope until the message is opened, after which it displays as open.

Figure 1.4

Objective 2
Create Outlook Folders

Each Outlook 2003 module has some predefined folders in which you can store items. You will likely want to create additional folders with names that meet your individual needs. For example, if you routinely receive e-mail messages regarding your daughter's softball team, you could create a folder to store and organize only those messages. Creating folders to meet your individual needs is how Outlook helps to keep you organized. In Activity 1.2, you will create an additional Mail folder for Mr. Ham to store messages related to the Greater Atlanta Job Fair.

Activity 1.2 Creating Outlook Folders

1 On the Mail module Navigation pane, under **All Mail Folders**, click the **expand** (+) button to the left of **Personal Folders**.

The list of default Mail module folders, as well as any others that have been created for your logon, displays and the expand button changes to the collapse (-) button. Each folder name identifies the type of mail item stored in it. Folders containing unread items display in bold letters, and the number of unread messages displays in parentheses beside the folder.

2 On the menu bar, click **File**, point to **Folder**, and then click **New Folder**.

The Create New Folder dialog box shown in Figure 1.5 displays.

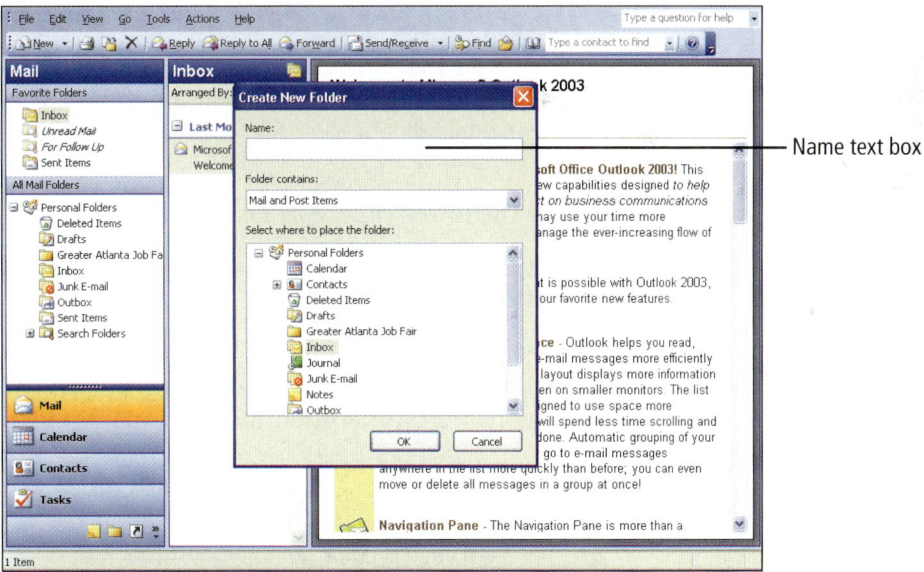

Figure 1.5

Project 1A: Exploring Outlook 2003 | **Outlook**   57

3 In the **Create New Folder** dialog box, click to position the insertion point in the **Name** box, and then type **Greater Atlanta Job Fair**

4 Under **Folder contains**, be sure that *Mail and Post Items* displays.

5 Under **Select where to place the folder**, click to highlight **Personal Folders** so that the folder is created as an additional folder within the folder list entitled Personal Folders, as in Figure 1.6.

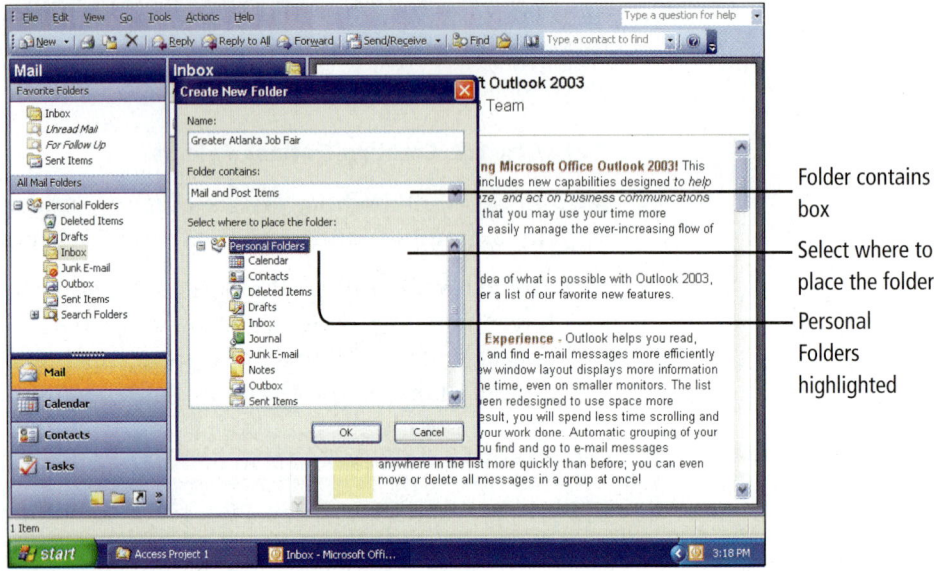

Figure 1.6

Note Creating Personal Folders

Because the Mail module was active when you started creating the new folder, Outlook selects Mail and Post Items for the Folder contains setting. By selecting Personal Folders, the new folder is created within the Personal Folders list.

6 At the lower right corner of the dialog box, click **OK**.

7 In the Navigation pane, under **All Mail Folders**, click the **Greater Atlanta Job Fair** folder.

The Greater Atlanta Job Fair mail folder opens in the pane that previously displayed the contents of the Inbox. Notice in Figure 1.7 that the folder banner identifies the open mail folder.

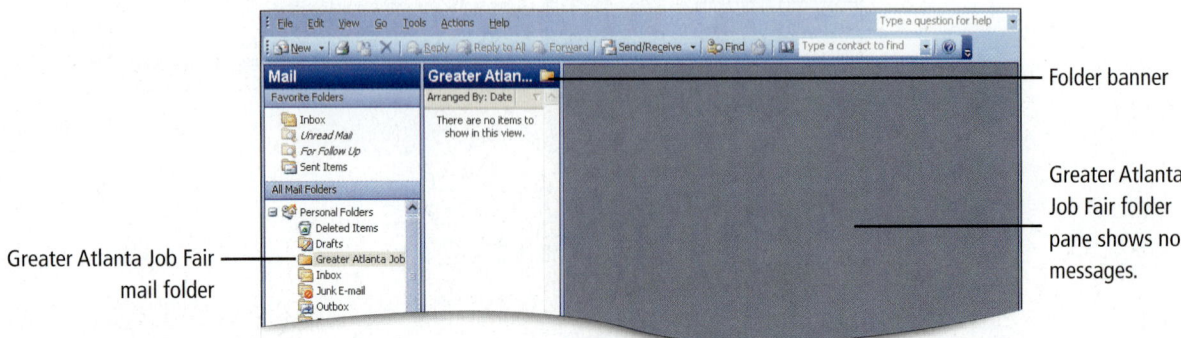

Figure 1.7

More Knowledge — Creating New Folders

A module does not have to be active in order to create new folders within it. From the Create New Folder text box, you can change the type of items that the new folder will contain and then select any location in which to place the new folder. Additionally, it is easy to move a folder created in one location to a different location.

Objective 3
Close Outlook

Many Outlook users keep Outlook open and running on their computers while they work in other Office applications. In that manner, they can quickly check for e-mail, check the Calendar module for appointments, look up the phone numbers of contacts, and so forth.

Activity 1.3 Closing Outlook

1 On the Outlook title bar, click the program **Close** button ☒.

Outlook closes or displays a message delivery warning box in which you can take appropriate action.

2 If the message delivery warning box displays, click **Yes** to close Outlook without delivering messages.

Another Way

To Close Outlook

Use any of the following techniques to close Outlook:

- On the Outlook application title bar, click the Close button ☒.
- On the Outlook menu, click File and then click Exit.
- Press [Alt] + [F4].
- On the Windows taskbar, right-click the Outlook program button and click Close.

Note — Sending and Receiving E-mail

To use the Mail module in Outlook to send and receive e-mail messages, you must have an e-mail address that is registered on a mail server, and the mail server must be connected to your computer. In a company, school, or other organization, the mail server is determined by the system administrator. In your home, you can subscribe and connect to an Internet mail server such as Microsoft Network (MSN).

Objective 4
Store Addresses in the Contacts Folder

Within the *Contacts module*, the module where Outlook stores address book information, there are folders to store contact items. Recall that a contact is information about a person or organization, such as those you would write in an address book—the names, addresses, phone numbers, and company names about friends, family members, and business associates. By storing the information electronically, you can update contact information, print changes, send letters to contacts, and send e-mail messages to contacts. Many organizations set up electronic address books, such as Outlook Contacts, on the computer workstation of every employee.

In Activity 1.4, you will create two contacts in Mr. Ham's Outlook address book and display contacts using different views.

Activity 1.4 Creating Contacts

1 Start Outlook and, if necessary, click **OK** in response to the alert message. On the Navigation pane, click the **Contacts** button .

2 Take a moment to study the features of the Contacts module panes shown in Figure 1.8 and described in the table in Figure 1.9.

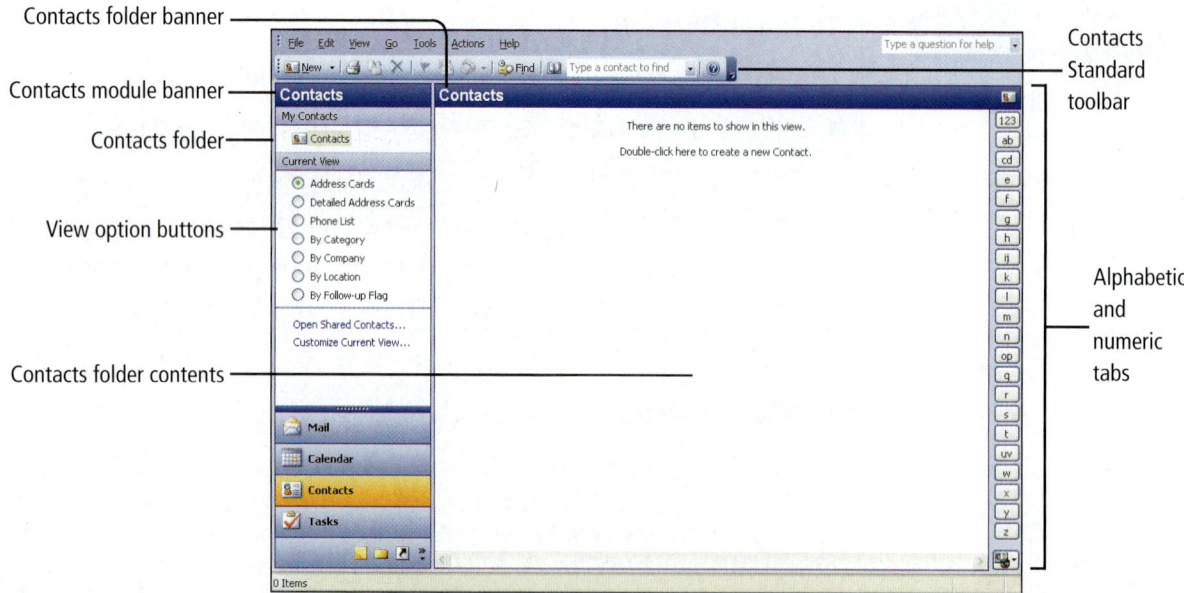

Figure 1.8

Contacts Module Screen Elements

Screen Element	Description
Contacts module banner	Identifies the active module.
Contacts Standard toolbar	Displays buttons for performing tasks commonly associated with creating and displaying contacts.
Contacts folder	Stores the contact items that you create. You can create and name additional folders as needed.
Contacts folder banner	Identifies the active folder name.
Contacts view option buttons	Displays your contact information in various arrangements.
Alphabetic and numeric tabs	Resemble alphabetic tabs in paper address books to quickly find contacts alphabetically or numerically.
Folder contents pane	Displays the list of contacts stored in the active folder—in this case the Contacts folder.

Figure 1.9

3 On the Contacts Standard toolbar, click the **New Contact** button 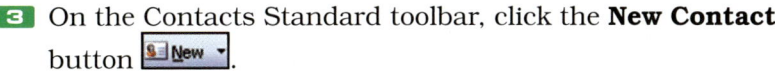.

The Untitled - Contact form displays, as shown in Figure 1.10. Recall that each module uses a predefined form to assist you in entering item information into the module.

Another Way

To Create New Contacts

There are several ways to create a new contact in Outlook such as:

- From the File menu, point to New and then click Contact.
- From the Contacts folder, press [Ctrl] + [N] or click the New Contact button on the Contacts Standard toolbar.
- From the Contacts folder, double-click a blank area of the folder contents.

4. Take a moment to study the form shown in Figure 1.10 and described in the table in Figure 1.11.

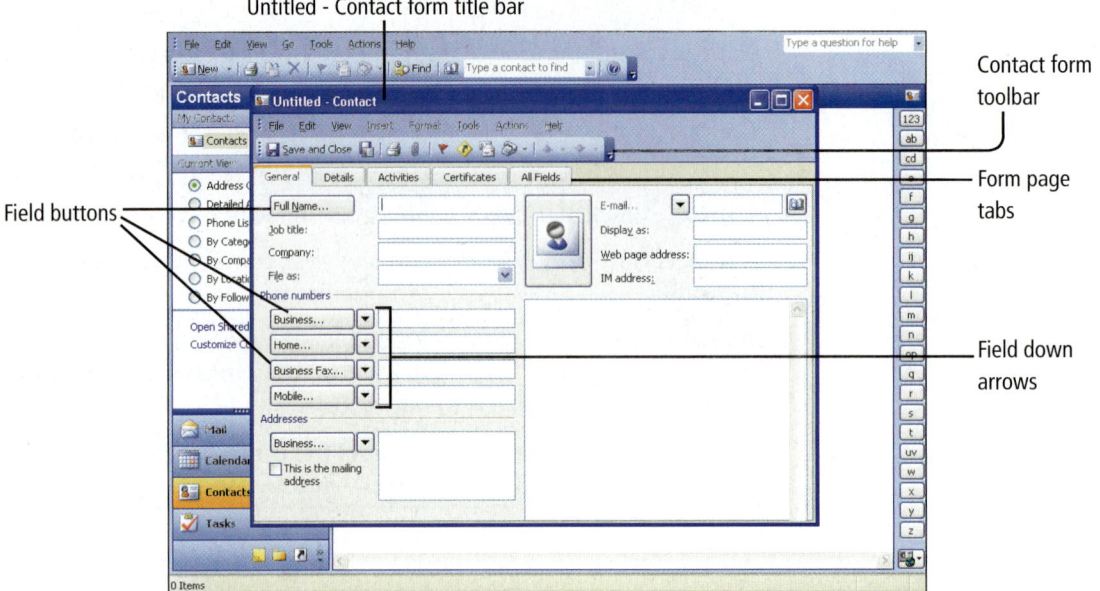

Figure 1.10

Contact Form Elements

Form Element	Description
Untitled - Contact form title bar	Displays the contact name after it is entered.
Form page tabs	Provide access to more form pages for entering additional information about the contact.
Field buttons	Open additional dialog boxes so that you can enter data into separate fields. For example, you can click the Full Name button to open a dialog box and enter the contact's last name in one box, first name in another box, and so on.
Field arrows	Display lists from which you can select the type of data you are entering. For example, under Phone numbers, you can click the Business down arrow and select Home to identify the phone number as the home phone number.
Contact form toolbar	Displays buttons for performing the most frequent tasks associated with saving and using the Contact form.

Figure 1.11

5 On the **General** tab of the **Untitled - Contact** form, click to position the insertion point in the **Full Name** box and type **Dr. Ralph Johnson**

6 Press Tab and in the **Job title** box type **Administrator**

Notice that in the File as box, *Johnson, Ralph* is inserted. When you search for your contacts, Outlook will use this common filing arrangement, similar to the way telephone directories arrange names.

7 Press Tab and in the **Company** box type **Atlanta Medical Center**

Compare your screen to Figure 1.12.

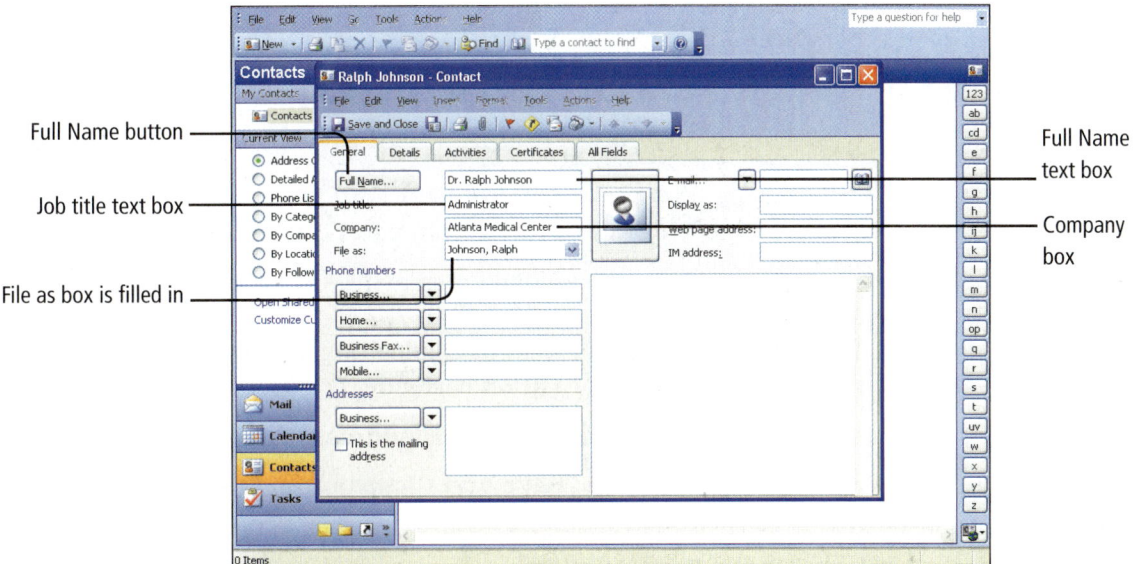

Figure 1.12

8 Click the **Full Name** button.

The Check Full Name dialog box displays with the Name details filled in. Outlook divides the Full Name information into Title, First, Middle, Last, and Suffix fields when the name is entered properly. If Outlook is unable to recognize the distinct name fields, this dialog box will display so that you can be sure that Outlook interprets your information correctly.

9 Click **OK** to close the **Check Full Name** dialog box. Then position the insertion point in each of the following fields and complete the information for the first contact, as shown in Figure 1.13:

Business phone number:	**(404) 555-4000**
Address:	**303 Parkside Drive**
	Atlanta, GA 30312
E-mail:	**Ralph_Johnson@AMF.com**
Web page address:	**www.atlantamedfacility.com**

Project 1A: Exploring Outlook 2003 | **Outlook**   63

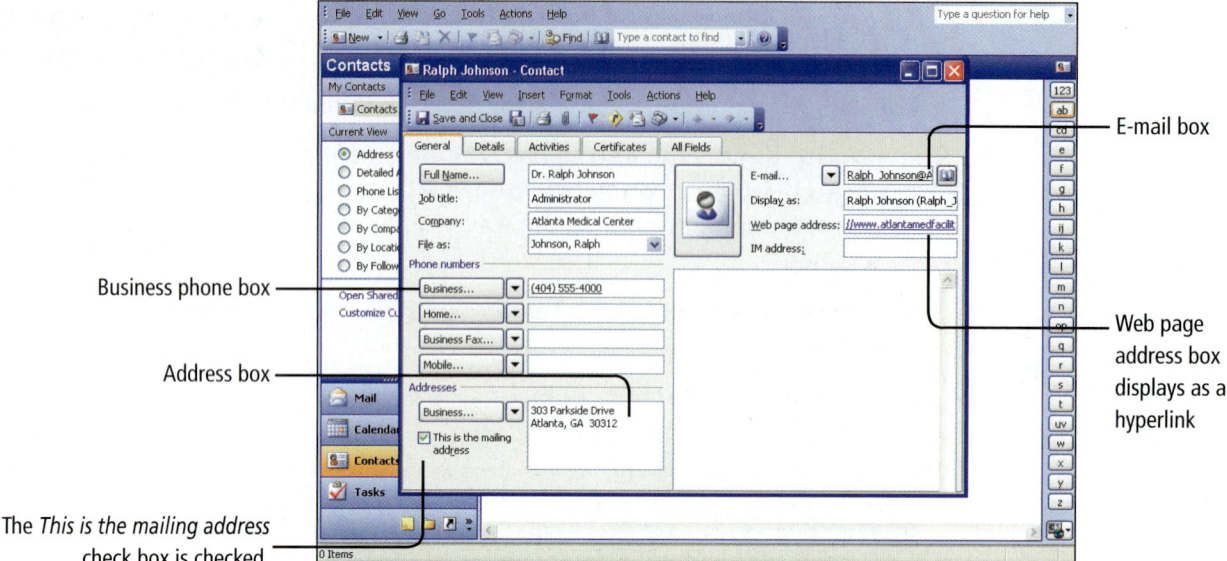

Business phone box

Address box

The *This is the mailing address* check box is checked.

E-mail box

Web page address box displays as a hyperlink

Figure 1.13

10 To the left of the address that you typed, click the **Business** button.

The Check Address field displays. Outlook divides the Address details into Street, City, State/Province, ZIP/Postal code, and Country/Region. Use this dialog box to check that Outlook interpreted your information correctly.

11 Click **OK** to close the **Check Address** dialog box. On the Standard toolbar, click the **Save and Close** button to save the contact.

In the Contacts folder pane, notice that Dr. Johnson's name is added, as shown in Figure 1.14.

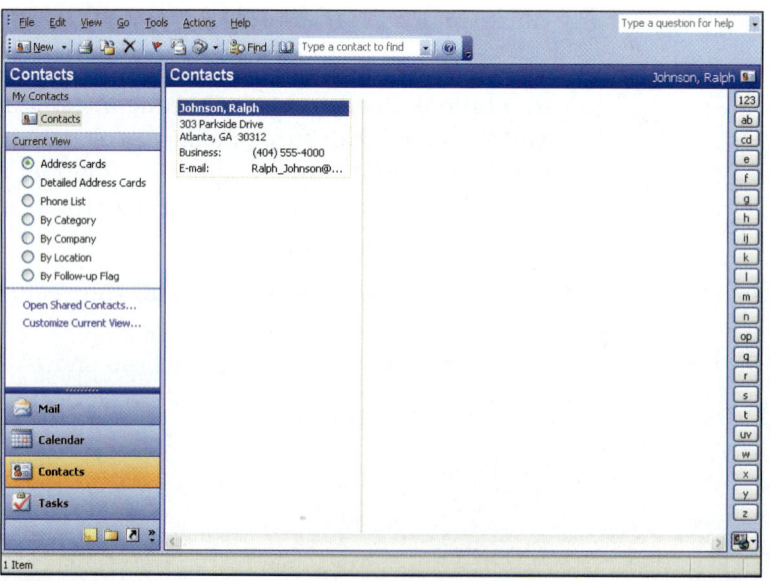

Figure 1.14

64 **Outlook** | Chapter 1: Getting Started with Outlook 2003

12 Repeat the procedures outlined in Steps 3–11 to create a contact form that contains your own personal information. When you are finished, click the **Save and Close** button .

The Contacts folder pane displays your contact form alphabetically with any other contacts in the folder.

13 In the Navigation pane, under **Current View**, click the **Detailed Address Cards** option button and compare your screen to Figure 1.15.

Your information will, of course, differ from the figure, but you can see that in this view, more of the information for the contact is shown. If you find errors, double-click the contact's small title bar to open it and make the necessary corrections. Notice that Outlook arranges the contacts alphabetically by last name.

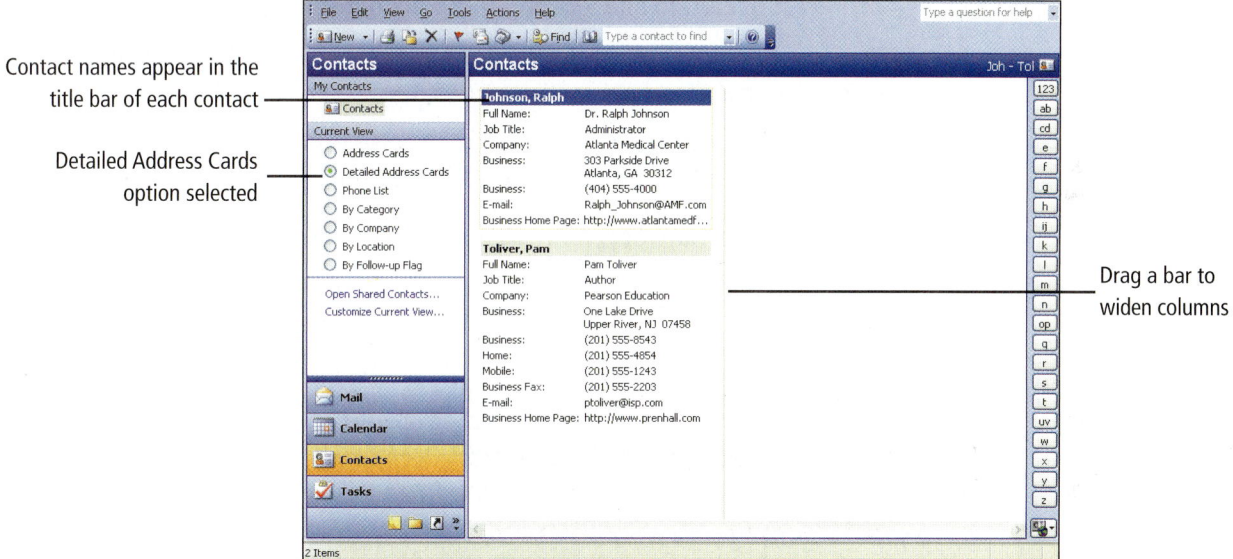

Figure 1.15

Objective 5
Edit and Print Contacts

When contact information changes, you can update contact information individually by opening the contact and making the necessary edits and then clicking the Save and Close button. This will store the updated information.

Although you probably work at your computer frequently, there will be times when you would like a printed copy of all or some of your contacts, arranged in an easy-to-read format. For example, perhaps you are taking a business trip and need a list of the contacts in the city you are visiting. Or you might be taking your daughter's softball teammates on a road trip and want a printed list of each player's parents and home phone numbers.

Activity 1.5 Editing and Printing Outlook Contacts

1 In the Contacts module Navigation pane, under **Current View**, click the **Phone List** option button.

The display in the Contacts folder pane changes to display a list of contacts formatted as a table of rows and columns.

2 On the Standard toolbar, click the **Print** button.

The Print dialog box displays, as shown in Figure 1.16.

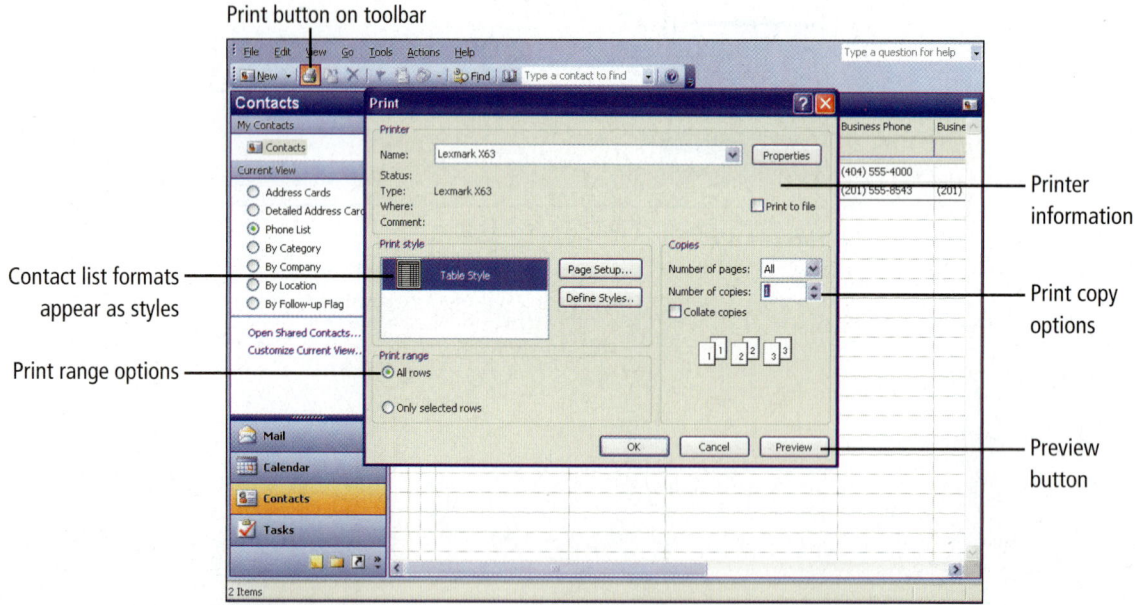

Figure 1.16

Another Way

To Print Contacts

Alternatively, you can display the File menu and click Print.

3 In the lower right corner, click the **Preview** button.

The Phone List view displays as a full page in the Print Preview window as it will print on paper.

4 In the **Print Preview** window, move the mouse pointer, which is in the form of a magnifying glass, to the top of the document and click the left mouse button once.

The document enlarges to give you a better view. You can see that if you were traveling, this would be a convenient list to carry along with you.

5 On the Print Preview toolbar, click the **Close** button.

The Print Preview window closes, and the Outlook window displays.

6 In the Navigation pane, under **Current View**, click the **Address Cards** option.

The Address Cards view redisplays.

7 In the **Contacts** folder pane, double-click the title bar for the **Johnson, Ralph** contact, double-click the text in the **Job title** box to select the title *Administrator*, and then type **Human Resources Director** as shown in Figure 1.17.

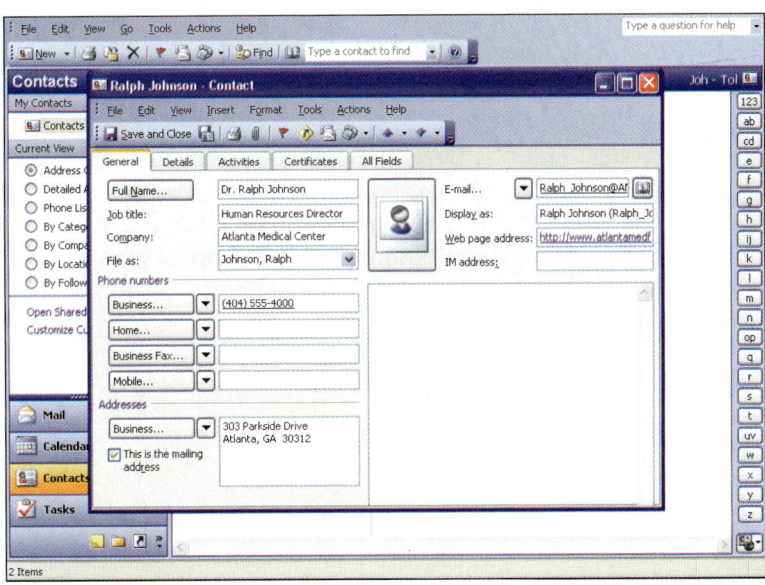

Figure 1.17

Double-clicking the title bar of a contact opens the contact in its original window. Double-clicking the Job title box positions the insertion point in the box and selects the text within it so that typing new text replaces the original text.

8 On the Contact form toolbar, click the **Save and Close** button.

Outlook updates the contact information and closes the contact.

9 In the Navigation pane, under **Current View**, click the **Detailed Address Cards** option button and notice that the Job Title was updated to *Human Resources Director*. If necessary, drag the right boundary to view the entire address card as shown in Figure 1.18.

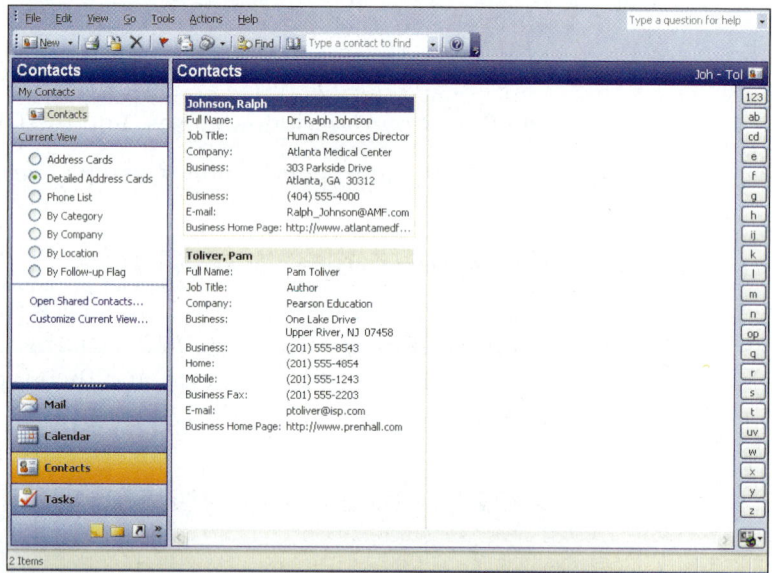

Figure 1.18

10 On the Standard toolbar, click the **Print** button. In the displayed Print dialog box, under **Print style**, click **Card Style**, and then click **OK**.

Outlook prints the contacts in the Address Card view with multiple contacts on each page.

Objective 6
Schedule Appointments in the Calendar

Use the Outlook Calendar module to record appointments on the day, date, and time the appointment is scheduled to occur, just as you would record meetings and appointments on a paper calendar. You can enter appointments either by typing directly into the Calendar pane or by typing into a form formatted to help you organize appointments. In Activities 1.6 through 1.8, you will use the Calendar module to change the Calendar view and record and print appointments in the Calendar.

Activity 1.6 Changing the Calendar Window View

1 On the Navigation pane, click the **Calendar** button. When the Calendar module displays, move to the menu bar, click **View**, and then click **Day**.

The Calendar module displays in the Day view similar to the one shown in Figure 1.19.

> **Note** — Calendar Views
>
> Views in the Calendar module provide different ways for you to look at your calendar. For example, you can view your calendar for the day, week, or month. You can also navigate to a specific date using the *Date Navigator*—the monthly calendar palette that displays at the top of the Calendar Navigation pane.

2 Take a moment to study the elements of the Calendar module shown in Figure 1.19 and described in the table in Figure 1.20.

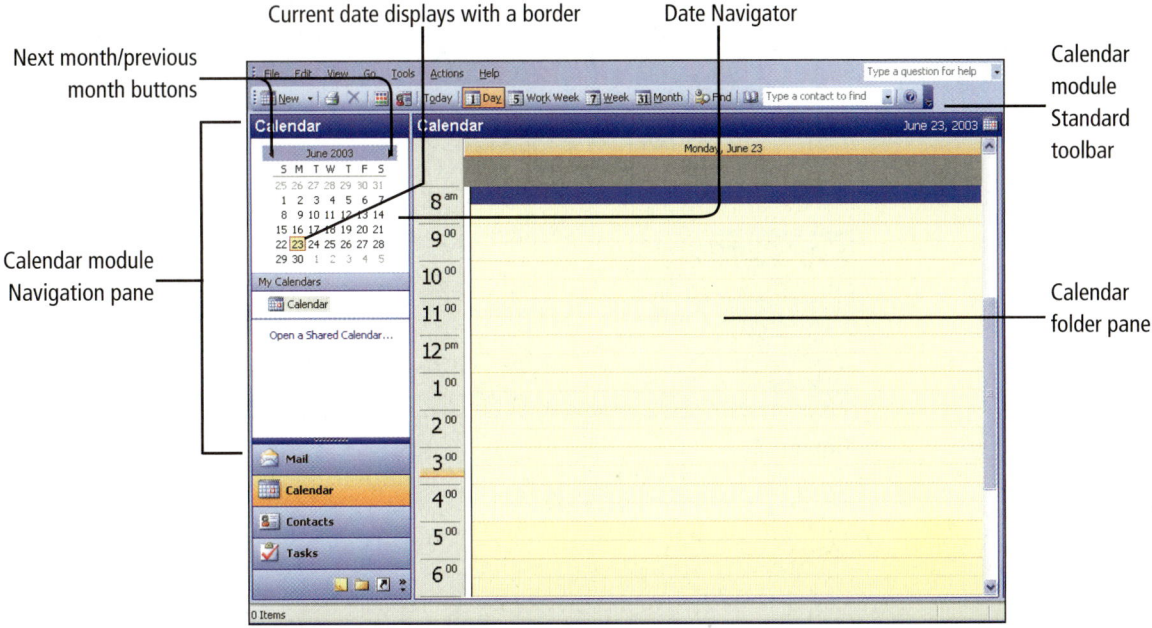

Figure 1.19

Project 1A: Exploring Outlook 2003 | **Outlook**   69

Calendar Module Screen Elements

Calendar Element	Description
Calendar module Navigation pane	Displays the default Calendar folder and the date navigator.
Calendar module Standard toolbar	Displays buttons for creating new appointments and changing the Calendar folder pane view.
Calendar folder pane	Displays the current day/date and time palette for recording and reviewing appointments.
Date Navigator	Displays one or two monthly calendars from which you can navigate to different dates.
Next month/previous month buttons	Display the previous or next month calendar palette in the Date Navigator.
Current date	Identifies the current date when the corresponding month palette displays in the Date Navigator.

Figure 1.20

3 On the Standard toolbar, click the **Work Week** button .

Five calendar days—beginning with Monday of the current week—display side by side similar to Figure 1.21. Various views can be accessed from the toolbar buttons or from the View menu.

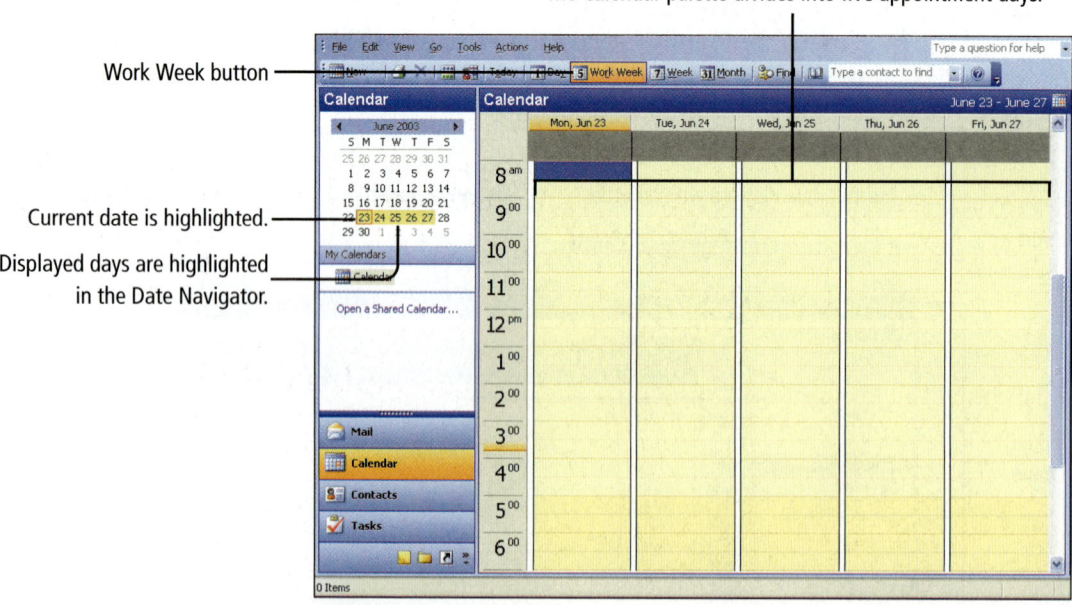

Figure 1.21

70   Outlook | Chapter 1: Getting Started with Outlook 2003

4 On the Standard toolbar, click the **Month** button.

The active month displays as a full-month calendar similar to Figure 1.22.

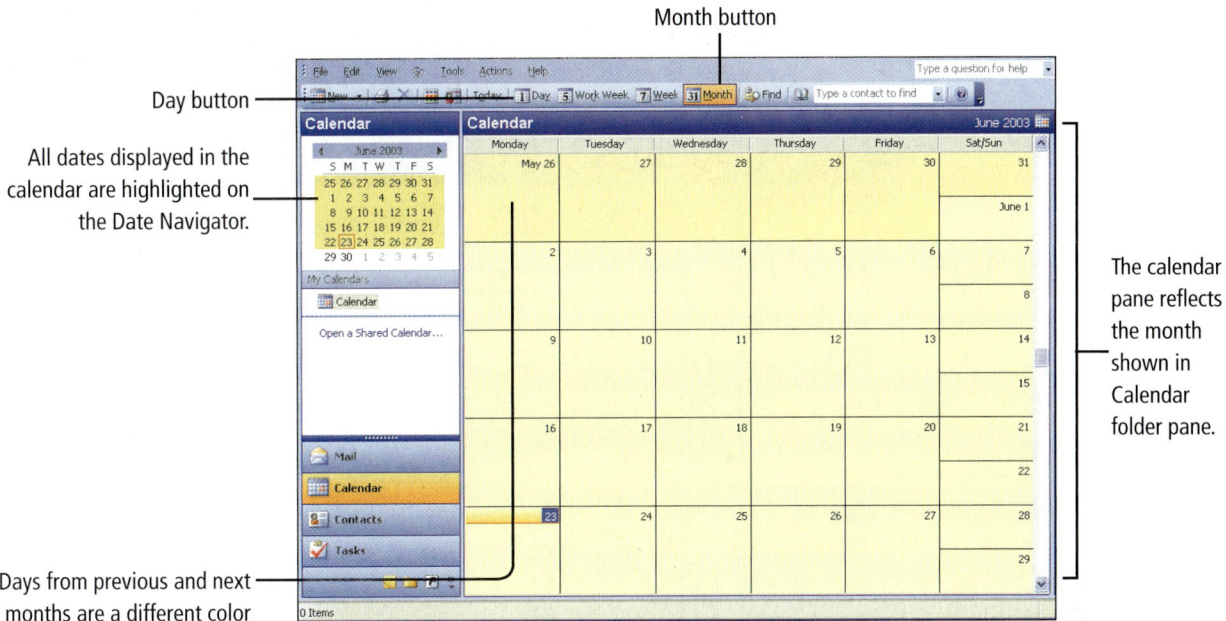

Figure 1.22

5 On the Standard toolbar, click the **Day** button.

The Calendar folder pane displays in the Day view, which is Outlook's default view.

Activity 1.7 Scheduling Appointments in the Calendar

For simple appointments, you can type directly on the daily calendar. When you need to include detailed information about an appointment, such as setting a meeting reminder or noting the location of a meeting, Outlook provides a **New Appointment** dialog box for you to set various options.

1 In the Navigation pane, on the **Date Navigator**, click the **Next Month arrow** button until November 2004 (or November of next year) displays.

2 On the **Date Navigator**, in the November 2004 calendar, click **19**. Then in the Calendar folder pane, click the **9:00** time slot and type **Greater Atlanta Job Fair**

When you type in the 9:00 time slot, a dark border displays around the time slot to show that it is active, and the insertion point displays within the border, as shown in Figure 1.23.

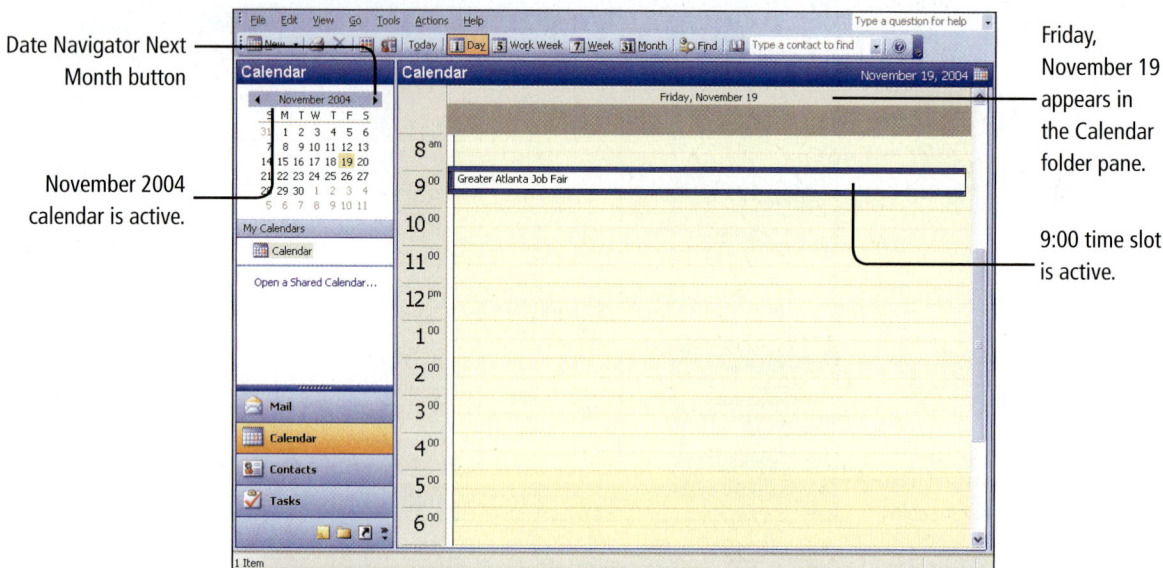

Figure 1.23

3 Press Enter and then press Enter again.

The first time you press Enter, Outlook schedules the appointment in the active time slot. The second time you press Enter, Outlook opens the scheduled appointment in an appointment form window. Because Outlook time slots are set every 30 minutes, and the Job Fair will last all day, you will need to make changes to the appointment form to identify it as an all-day event.

Another Way

To Open the New Appointment Window

You can create a new appointment window using one of the following techniques:

- On the menu bar, click File, point to New, and click Appointment.
- On the Calendar Standard toolbar, click the New Appointment button New.

4 In the appointment form window, select (click to place a check mark in) the **All day event** check box. If necessary, select the **Reminder** check box. Click the **Reminder arrow** and click **2 days**.

When you select the Reminder check box, the Reminder box becomes available so that you can set the reminder to occur 2 days before the event. Figure 1.24 shows the appointment with active settings.

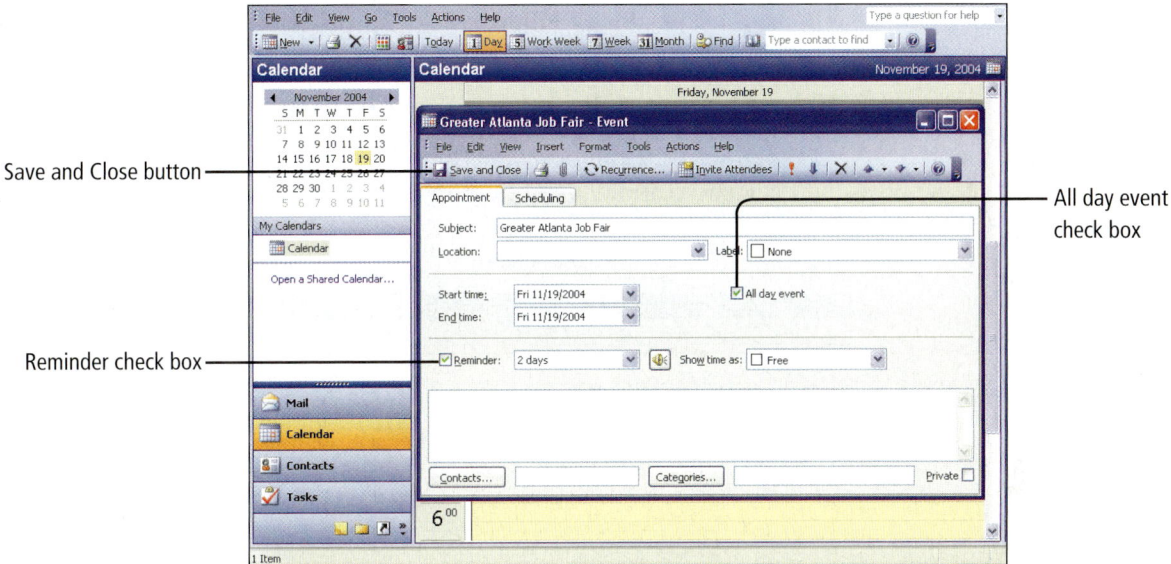

Figure 1.24

5 In the appointment form window, click the **Save and Close** button .

Outlook saves changes to the appointment and closes the appointment form window. When you schedule an appointment as an all-day event, Outlook moves the appointment from its original time slot and places it as a banner at the top of the daily calendar palette, as shown in Figure 1.25.

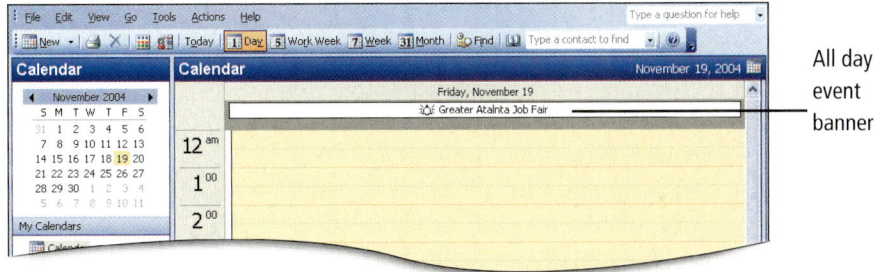

Figure 1.25

Project 1A: Exploring Outlook 2003 | **Outlook**   73

Activity 1.8 Printing Calendars

When you print from the Calendar module, you have many choices for printing your calendar in a format useful to you. The amount of appointment detail printed depends on the style you choose to print and the range of dates that you specify.

1 On the **Date Navigator**, navigate to November 19, 2004 (or November 19 of next year).

2 On the Standard toolbar, click the **Print** button . In the displayed Print dialog box, under **Print style**, click **Monthly Style**.

3 In the **Print** dialog box, click the **Preview** button.

The monthly calendar for the active month displays in the Print Preview window, as shown in Figure 1.26.

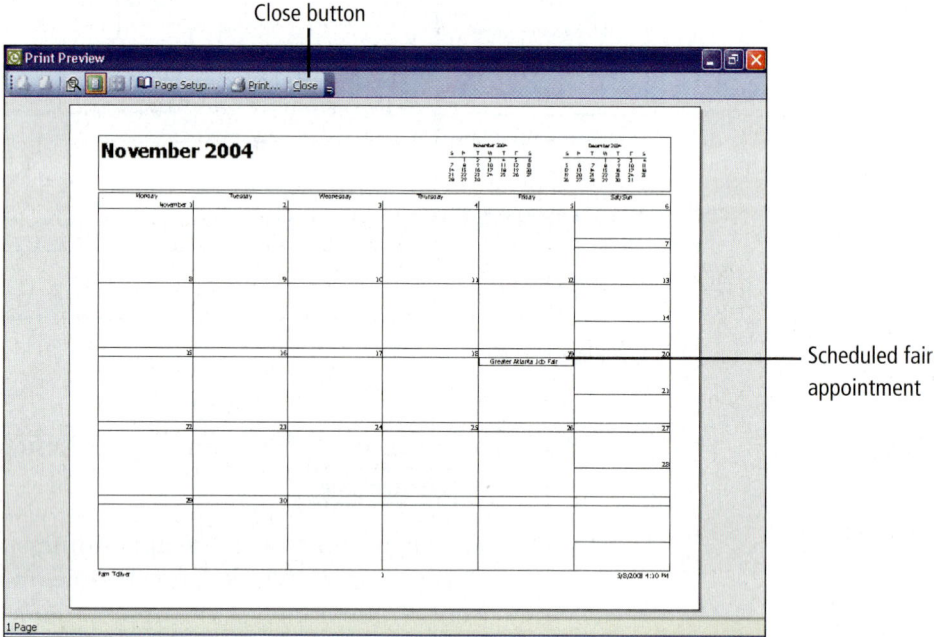

Figure 1.26

4 On the Print Preview window toolbar, click the **Close** button to close the Print Preview window.

Objective 7
Record Tasks and Notes

You can use Outlook to arrange your lists of things to do and those notes you write to yourself on either small pieces of paper or sticky notes. The ***Tasks module*** contains the Tasks folder in which you can store your to do items. The ***Notes module*** contains the Notes folder that stores the notes you write to yourself.

One advantage to using Outlook to record and store to do lists is that you can record the items in the Calendar folder pane where you store appointments. Although the task items are actually stored in the Tasks module Tasks folder, you can read the tasks each time you check your calendar appointments. In Activity 1.9, you will use the TaskPad in the Calendar module to record to do items and the Notes module to record notes.

Activity 1.9 Recording Tasks in the TaskPad

1 On the Navigation pane, click the **Calendar** button and use the **Date Navigator** to display November 19, 2004 (or November 19 of next year).

The Calendar folder pane displays November 19, 2004 (or the year you select).

2 On the Standard toolbar, click **Day** to display the calendar in the Day view. On the menu bar, click **View** and then click **TaskPad**.

The TaskPad pane opens, and the Date Navigator moves to the right side of the Calendar folder pane above the TaskPad. The task entry bar displays at the top of the TaskPad and is used to type task text.

On the Calendar module pane, the *My Calendars* area moves to the position previously occupied by the Date Navigator, as shown in Figure 1.27.

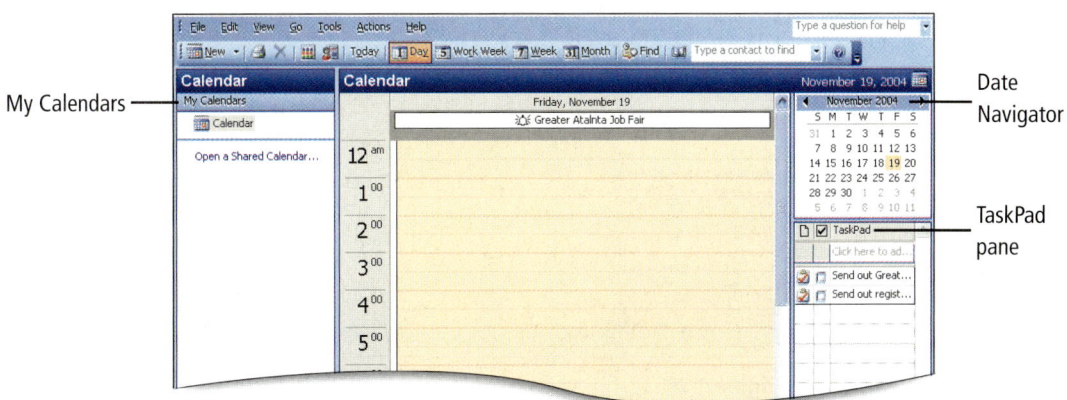

Figure 1.27

Project 1A: Exploring Outlook 2003 | **Outlook**   75

3 In the TaskPad pane task entry bar, click the text **Click here to add a new task**.

Figure 1.28 shows the instruction text in the task pad. When you click the instruction text, the text box is cleared, and an insertion point displays.

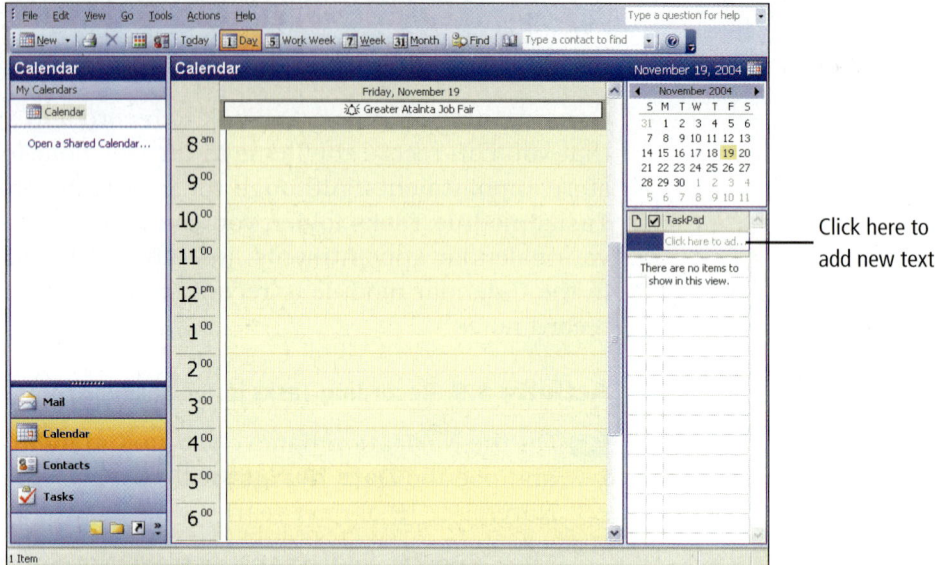

Click here to add new text

Figure 1.28

4 Type **Send out registration forms for job fair** and then press Enter.

The task displays on the task list, as shown in Figure 1.29.

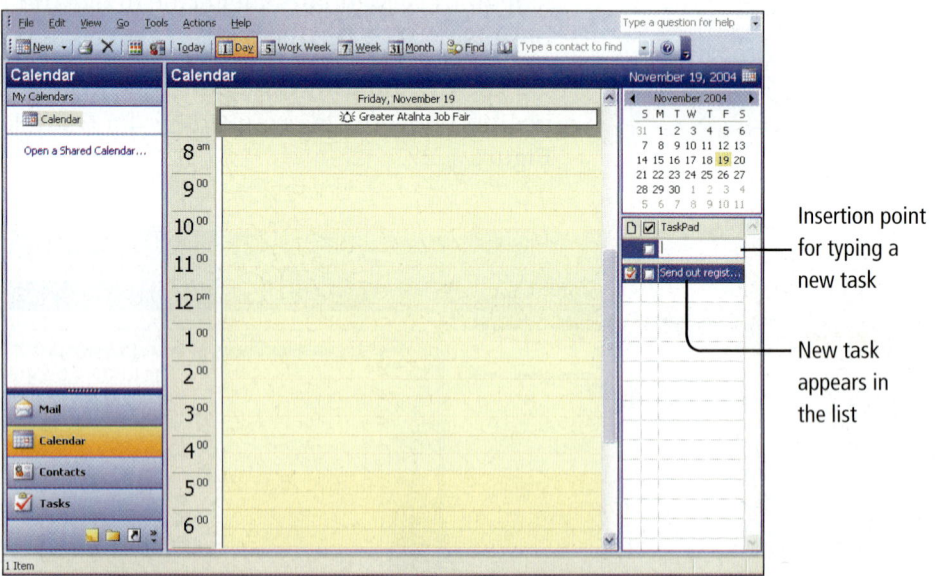

Insertion point for typing a new task

New task appears in the list

Figure 1.29

5 On the TaskPad pane, to the left of the task, double-click the task clipboard for the task you just entered.

The Task form opens in a separate window, as shown in Figure 1.30. You can use the features in the Task form window to set a due date to complete the task.

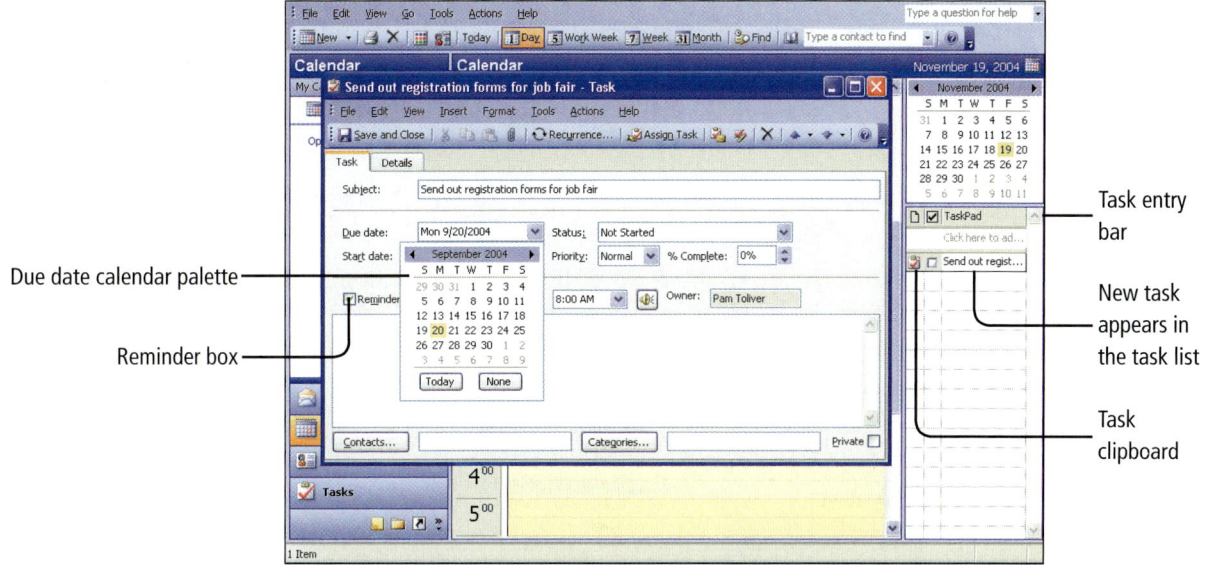

Figure 1.30

6. In the Task form window, click the **Due date arrow**.

7. On the monthly drop-down palette, click the **Next month** or **Previous month** button to navigate to **September 2004** (or September of next year) and click **20** in the September calendar.

    The date displays in the Due date box. Notice the reminder is set to notify you at 8:00 AM on that date so that you will be sure to remember to send out the forms.

8. On the Standard toolbar, click the **Save and Close** button.

    Outlook monitors task due dates and identifies overdue tasks by changing the task text color to red.

9. On the Navigation pane, click the **Notes** button.

    The Notes module opens. In the Notes module Navigation pane, notice the view options for arranging notes.

Alert!

Does Your Notes Button Look Different?

The size of the monitor and screen resolution set on your computer controls the number of larger module buttons that appear at the bottom of the Navigation pane. As a result, your Notes button may appear in a format similar to the Mail, Calendar, Contacts, and Tasks buttons. If you don't see the Notes button shown in Step 9, look for the Notes button and click it.

Project 1A: Exploring Outlook 2003 | **Outlook** 77

10 On the **Notes** folder pane, double-click a blank area.

A new note opens in the Notes folder pane, with an insertion point positioned within the note. If necessary, you can drag the note by its blue bar into a different area of the screen.

11 Click in the new note box and type **Review last year's newspaper ad for the Greater Atlanta Job Fair**

The completed note displays, as shown in Figure 1.31.

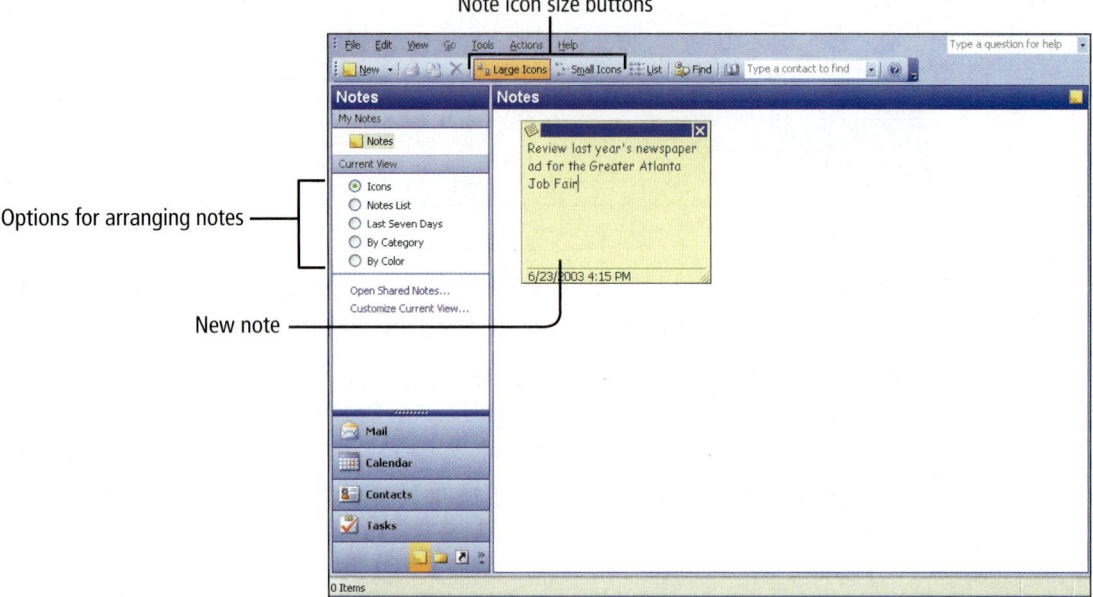

Figure 1.31

12 In the **Notes** folder pane, click a blank area.

The note closes, but the note text displays below the note.

13 Close Outlook.

End You have completed Project 1A

78   **Outlook** | Chapter 1: Getting Started with Outlook 2003

Summary

In this chapter, you explored the basic modules contained in Microsoft Office Outlook 2003. You saw how Outlook can function as a method to manage your e-mail messages. You also practiced using Outlook as a personal information manager to organize appointments, maintain a list of tasks to accomplish, write electronic notes, and update business and personal contacts.

In This Chapter You Practiced How To

- Start Outlook
- Identify Outlook screen elements
- Identify Outlook features and their uses
- Create Outlook folders
- Close Outlook
- Store contacts in the contacts list
- Edit and print contacts
- Change module views
- Schedule appointments in the calendar
- Print from Outlook
- Record tasks and Notes

Concepts Assessments

Matching Match each term in the second column with its correct definition in the first column by writing the letter of the term on the blank line in front of the correct definition.

____ 1. The pane of the Inbox window that displays active message text.

____ 2. The bar that appears at the top of an Outlook window pane to identify the contents of the pane.

____ 3. Contacts, appointments, tasks, notes, and messages.

____ 4. The Outlook folder used to create sticky reminders.

____ 5. The Outlook folder used to store appointments.

____ 6. A list of to do items.

____ 7. The two-month palette that appears at the top of the Calendar window.

____ 8. The Outlook folder used to store names and addresses of personal and business associates.

____ 9. The Outlook folder used to store items that have been thrown out.

____ 10. The pane of each Outlook window that is used to change windows and open folders.

____ 11. The abbreviation for electronic messages.

____ 12. The Outlook folder that holds messages, task assignments, meeting invitations, and other items sent electronically.

A Calendar
B Contacts
C Date Navigator
D Deleted items
E E-mail
F Folder banner
G Inbox
H Items
I Navigation pane
J Notes
K Reading pane
L Task list

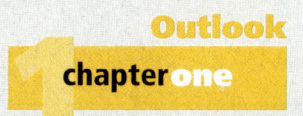

Concepts Assessments (continued)

Fill in the Blank Write the correct answer in the space provided for each statement.

1. When viewing messages in the Inbox, messages that have been read are identified by a(n) _____.

2. To access a different month in the Calendar folder, use the _____.

3. To open a blank form for adding a new item, click the _____ button.

4. To enter a name for a new contact into separate name fields on the Contact form, click the _____ button.

5. To attach a file to an e-mail message, click the _____ button on the message Standard toolbar.

6. To display a full month calendar in the Calendar window, click the _____ button.

7. Buttons that are shown on the Navigation pane are used to access Outlook _____.

8. To read e-mail without opening the message in a separate window, display the _____.

9. You can customize the Calendar window so that it displays a calendar palette, a Date Navigator, and the _____.

10. Two tools are available for responding to e-mail messages: _____ and _____.

Skill Assessments

Project 1B — Creating Additional Contacts

Objectives: *Start Outlook, Store Addresses in the Contacts Folder, and Edit and Print Contacts.*

Four additional vendors have registered for the Greater Atlanta Job Fair. In this project, you will create contacts for the additional fair vendors. When you have completed the contacts, the Address Card view of the Contacts folder will display the five vendors shown in Figure 1.32.

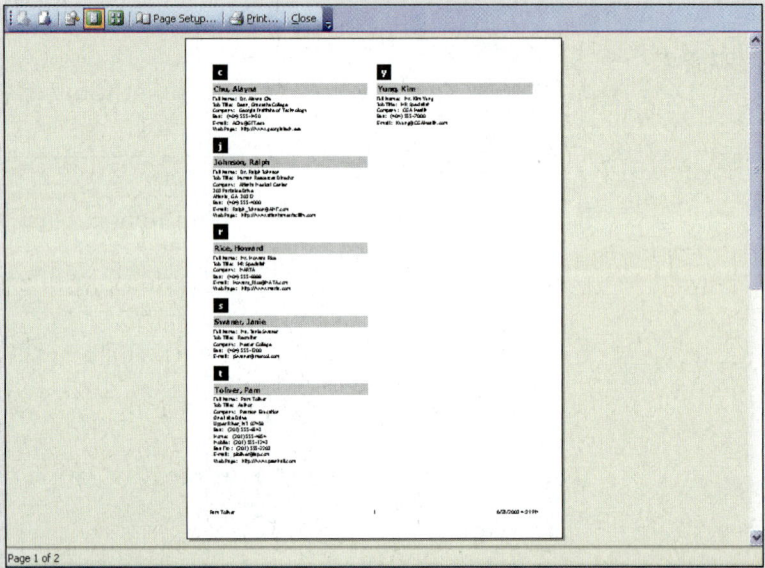

Figure 1.32

1. On the Navigation pane, click the **Contacts** button.

   The Contacts module opens in the Outlook window.

2. On the Contacts Standard toolbar, click the **New Contact** button.

   A new Contact form opens.

3. In the new contact form, type the information displayed for the first vendor shown in the table in Figure 1.33. Then save and close the contact.

(**Project 1B**–Creating Additional Contacts continues on the next page)

Outlook chapter one
Skill Assessments (continued)

(Project 1B–Creating Additional Contacts continued)

Fair Vendor Contacts

Full Name	Job Title	Company	Business Phone	E-mail	Web Page
Ms. Janie Swaner	Recruiter	Mercer College	(404) 555-1200	JSwaner@mercol.com	www.mercer.edu
Mr. Kim Yung	HR Specialist	CGA Health	(404) 555-7000	Kyung@CGAHealth.com	www.cgahealth.com
Dr. Alayna Chu	Dean	Graduate College Georgia Institute of Technology	(404) 555-1450	AChu@GIT.edu	www.georgiatech.edu
Mr. Howard Rice	HR Specialist	MARTA	(404) 555-8888	Howard_Rice@MATA.com	www.marta.com

Figure 1.33

4. Repeat Steps 2 and 3 to complete additional new contact forms for the remaining three vendors listed in the table in Figure 1.33, saving and closing each new record as you complete it.

5. In the Contacts Navigation pane, click the **Detailed Address Cards** view and print a copy of the Contacts list using the **Card Style**.

End You have completed Project 1B

Project 1C—Scheduling Fair Dates

Objectives: *Start Outlook, Schedule Appointments in the Calendar, Print the Calendar, and Close Outlook.*

In addition to the Greater Atlanta Job Fair, the organization sponsors job fairs at most of the colleges in Atlanta and the surrounding area. Because it is important to schedule these fairs 12 to 18 months in advance, fair dates for Mercer College and Georgia Tech have been set for April 2005. The appointment entries for these two fairs will appear on the weekly calendar printout shown in Figure 1.34.

(Project 1C–Scheduling Fair Dates continues on the next page)

Skill Assessments (continued)

(Project 1C–Scheduling Fair Dates continued)

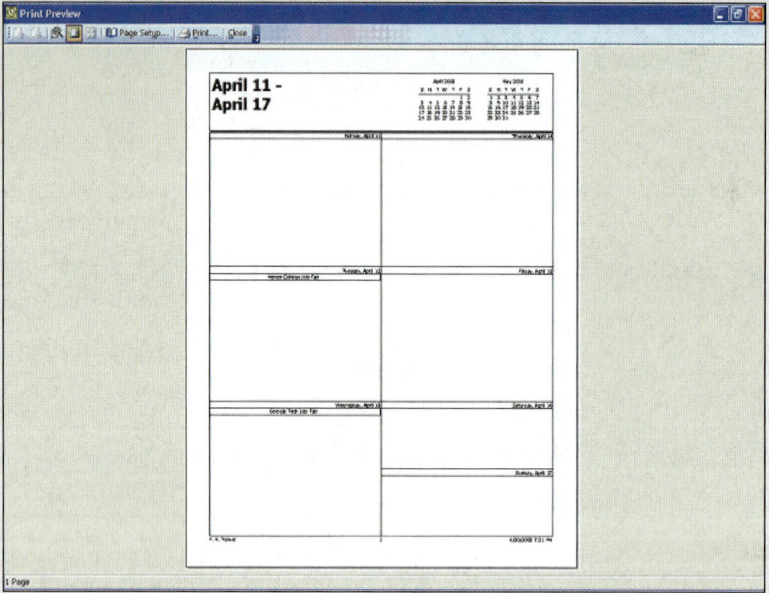

Figure 1.34

1. Start Outlook if it is not running. On the Navigation pane, click the **Calendar** button.

2. Use the **Date Navigator** to navigate to **April 2005**. In April on the Date Navigator, click **12** and drag across **13** to display both days in the calendar.

3. Double-click the **9:00** time slot for April 12 to open a new appointment form, click the **Subject** text box, type **Mercer College Job Fair** click the **All day event** check box, and save and close the appointment.

4. Repeat the procedures identified in Step 3 to create an all day event for April 13 for the Georgia Tech Job Fair, print a copy of the Calendar folder using the **Weekly Style** for the week of the new fairs, and then close Outlook.

End You have completed Project 1C

chapter one

Performance Assessments

Project 1D — Creating Folders for College Fairs

Objectives: *Start Outlook and Create Outlook Folders.*

The fairs for Mercer College and Georgia Tech have been set for April 2005. As a result, you need to create folders to hold vendor information for the fairs. When you have created the contact folders for these two fairs, your Contacts list will appear as in Figure 1.35.

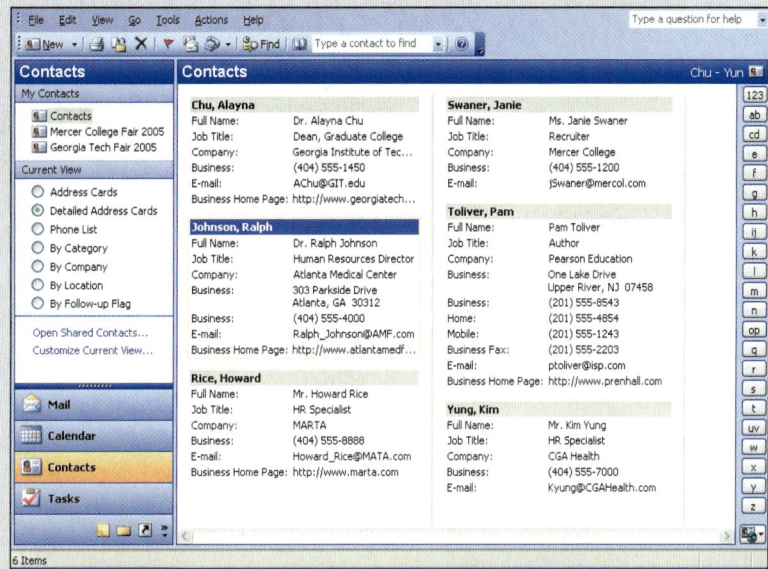

Figure 1.35

1. Start Outlook, open the **Contacts** module, open the main **Contacts** folder, and on the menu bar, click **File**, point to **Folder**, and click **New Folder** to open the **Create New Folder** dialog box.

2. In the **Name** text box, type **Mercer College Fair 2005** ensure that **Contact Items** appears in the **Folder contains** text box, and click **OK**.

3. Repeat the procedures in Steps 1 and 2 to create another contacts folder named **Georgia Tech Fair 2005**

End You have completed Project 1D

Project 1D: Creating Folders for College Fairs | **Outlook**

Performance Assessments (continued)

Project 1E — Copying Contacts to New Folders

Objectives: *Start Outlook, Store Addresses in the Contacts Folder, and Close Outlook.*

Two of the vendors registered for the Greater Atlanta Job Fair in November 2004 will also participate in the Georgia Tech Job Fair on April 13, 2005. Instead of retyping the information for the contacts, you can copy the contact from the Contacts folder into the Georgia Tech Job Fair 2005 folder to create the Contact list shown in Figure 1.36.

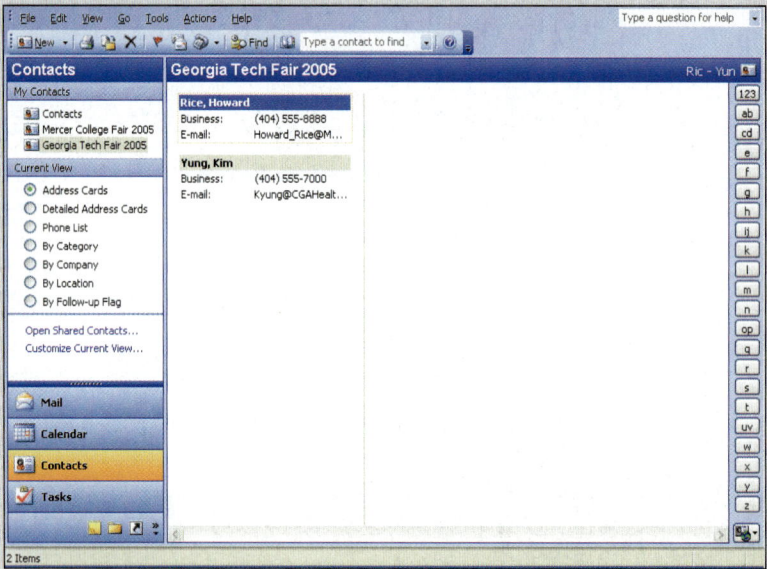

Figure 1.36

1. Start Outlook and open the **Contacts** module.

2. Click the title bar for the **Kim Yung** contact, press and hold the Ctrl key, and click the **Howard Rice** contact to select both contacts.

3. Press and hold the Ctrl key, drag the title bar for one of the selected records to the My Contacts area of the Navigation pane, and then point to the **Georgia Tech Fair 2005** folder.

4. Release the mouse button and then release the Ctrl key.

   If you accidentally place the contacts in the wrong folder or if the contacts disappear from their original folder, press Ctrl + Z to reverse the action and try again.

5. Open the **Georgia Tech Fair 2005** contacts folder to view the copied contacts and close Outlook if you have completed your work.

End You have completed Project 1E

Outlook
chapter one
Performance Assessments (continued)

Project 1F — Mass Mailing to Contacts

Objectives: *Start Outlook, Create and Send E-mail Messages, Print E-mail Messages, Schedule Appointments in the Calendar, Print Appointments, Record Tasks, and Close Outlook.*

Now that several vendors have registered for the Greater Atlanta Job Fair in November 2004, you can send them an e-mail message to let them know that their registration forms have been received. In this project, you will create the message shown in Figure 1.37.

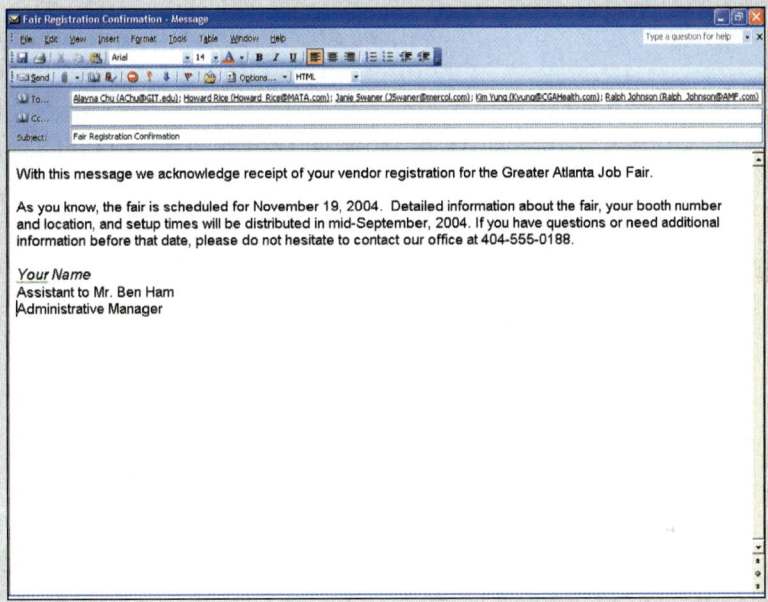

Figure 1.37

1. Start Outlook, open the **Mail** folder list, open the **Inbox** folder, and click the **New Mail Message** button to create a new mail message.

2. In the Untitled Mail message window, click the **To** button at the left end of the To text box to open the **Select Names** dialog box.

   When you point to the word *To*, a highlighted button appears.

3. In the **Select Names** dialog box, click the **Show Names from the** down arrow and click **Contacts** to show the names and e-mail addresses of contacts in the folder.

4. In the dialog box list box, click **Alayna Chu** (the first name in the list), press and hold the [Shift] key and click **Ralph Johnson** (the last name in the list) to select all names in the list.

5. In the dialog box, under **Message Recipients**, click the **To** button to add selected names to the box, and then click **OK**.

(**Project 1F**–Mass Mailings to Contacts continues on the next page)

Performance Assessments (continued)

(Project 1F–Mass Mailings to Contacts continued)

6. Press Tab twice to move to the **Subject** text box, type **Fair Registration Confirmation**, and then press Tab to move to the message area.

7. Type the message shown in Figure 1.37, click the **Save** button to save the message in the **Drafts** folder, and then click the **Print** button to print the message.

8. Open the Calendar module, open the Calendar folder, navigate to September 15, 2004, and in the TaskPad type **Send out Greater Atlanta Job Fair vendor details**

9. Drag the task clipboard to the dark area between the daily time scale and the day/date banner at the top of the daily palette to open a task appointment window for the task, as shown in Figure 1.38.

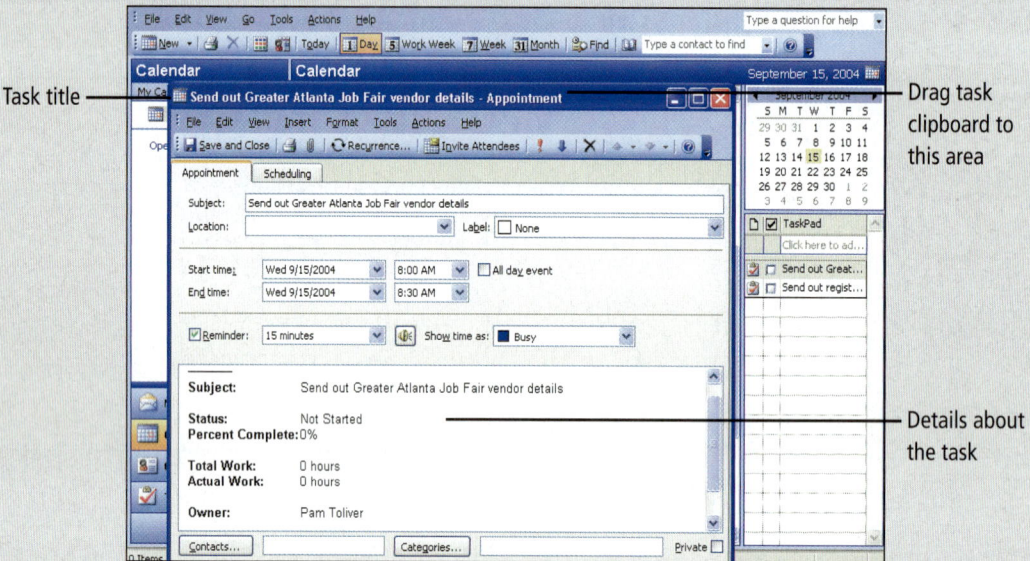

Figure 1.38

10. On the task appointment window, click the **Print** button to print the appointment and then click the **Save and Close** button to save the task appointment. Close Outlook if you have completed your work.

End You have completed Project 1F

Mastery Assessments

Project 1G — Responding to Messages and Sending Attachments

Objectives: *Start Outlook, Respond to E-mail Messages, Attach Files to E-mail Messages, View and Save E-mail Attachments, and Close Outlook.*

Each year, the Greater Atlanta Job Fair provides area colleges with flyers announcing the job fair. The flyer is ready for distribution, but the list of colleges to receive the message is not yet complete. You have, however, received a notice from your instructor asking you to submit a copy of the flyer for review. You will respond to the message with the message shown in Figure 1.39.

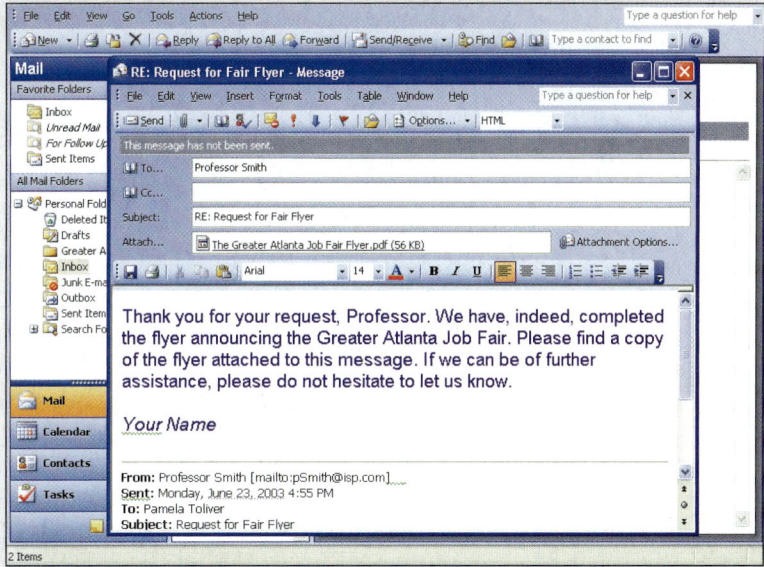

Figure 1.39

1. Open the Inbox folder and open the message from your instructor with the subject line *Request for Fair Flyer*.

2. Reply to the message by typing the response shown in Figure 1.39, attach the file *The Greater Atlanta Job Fair Flyer.pdf*, add your e-mail address to the **Cc** text box, and send the response.

3. Retrieve messages, open the copy of the response you sent to yourself, and open the flyer attachment and review it. Then close the flyer, close Acrobat, and close all open messages in Outlook.

End You have completed Project 1G

Problem Solving

Project 1H—Tracking Personal Appointments

Objectives: *Start Outlook, Schedule Appointments in the Calendar, Use Help, Print Calendar Information, and Close Outlook.*

The main Outlook Calendar folder is currently available for storing personal appointments, assignments, and class times. Use the Calendar folder to record important class assignments, lab appointments, class tests, holidays, and special days in the current semester. Then review information about Recurring Appointments in the Help file and see if you can use the feature to record classes that occur at regular intervals—the same days and times each week. When you are finished, print the monthly calendars for each month of the semester.

 You have completed Project 1H

On the Internet

Locating Friends on the Web

The World Wide Web not only stores information about companies, Web sites for bidding on items, and so forth, but it also contains telephone book information as well as e-mail addresses for many people—especially those who are students at universities! Search the Web for the colleges that three of your friends attend. After you locate the sites, search each university's e-mail directory for one of your friends. Then record these friends and their university e-mail addresses in your contacts list. Print a copy of each contact form as you create it.

GO! with Help

Training on Outlook

Microsoft Online has set up a series of training lessons at its online Web site. You can access Microsoft.com and review these training sessions directly from the Help menu in Outlook. In this project, you will work your way through the links on the Microsoft Web site to see what training topics they currently offer for Outlook. Log onto the required networks, connect to the Internet, and then follow these steps to complete the exercise.

1. If necessary, start Outlook. On the menu bar, click **Help** and then click **Office on Microsoft.com**.

   The Microsoft Office Online Web page opens in the default browser window.

2. On the left side of the Microsoft Office Online Web page, click the **Training** link.

   The Training Home Web page opens.

3. On the Training Home page, under Browse Training Courses, click **Outlook**.

   The Outlook Courses Web page opens.

4. On the Outlook Courses Web page list, click **Address your e-mail: Get it on the To line fast**.

   The Overview Web page displays information about the training session, identifies the goals of the session, and displays links for continuing the session. Navigation buttons appear in a grey bar toward the top of the Overview page for playing, pausing, and stopping the session. Yellow arrows appear above the navigation bar to advance to the next session page.

5. In the upper right side of the Overview page, on the gray navigation bar, click **Play**.

   When the first page is complete, the audio stops.

6. At the top of the Overview page, above the gray navigation bar, click **Next** and repeat the procedures outlined in Step 5 to review the training session to determine if you believe it rates five stars.

7. Click the **Close** button in the upper right corner of the browser title bar to close the browser window.

Internet Explorer

chapter one

Getting Started with Internet Explorer

In this chapter, you will: complete this project and practice these skills.

**Project 1A
Exploring Internet Explorer 6.0**

Objectives
- Start Internet Explorer and Identify Screen Elements
- Navigate the Internet
- Work with Favorites
- Search the Internet
- Download Files
- Print Web Pages

The Management Association of Pine Valley

The Management Association of Pine Valley is an employers' association that provides human resources consulting, organizational development, and training to member companies. Members are small and mid-size companies with up to 1,000 employees.

Based on the results of member surveys, the association has recently added new training classes to address the growing number of businesses that access the Internet.

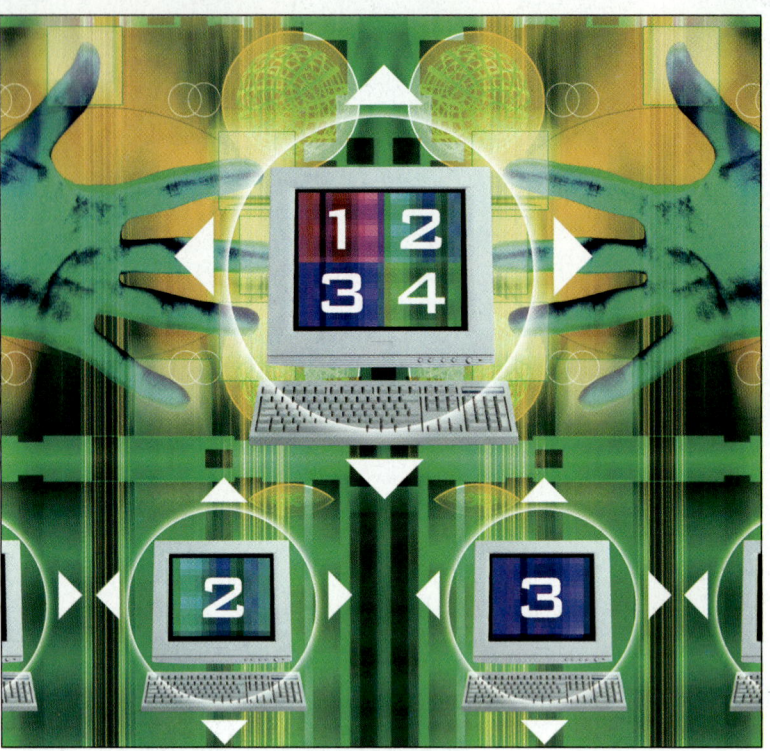

Getting Started with Internet Explorer 6.0

Microsoft Internet Explorer is a Web-browsing program used to explore the *Internet* and to unravel the mysteries of the *World Wide Web*. Internet Explorer enables the user to connect to the Internet to search for information, display Web pages, and send and receive e-mail.

The Internet got its start in the 1960s as an experiment by the Department of Defense as a way for mainframes to communicate with other mainframes. It has evolved into the largest online computer network in the world—one accessed by millions of people every day.

This introduction to Internet Explorer 6.0 provides a basic overview of Internet Explorer features and how to use them to explore the Internet. You will learn how to access Web sites, navigate the Internet, save your favorite Web sites, search for information, download files, and print Web pages.

Project 1A Exploring Internet Explorer 6.0

The interwoven affect created by interconnecting networks all over the world establishes a web-like structure from which the World Wide Web gets its name. As a Web browser, Internet Explorer 6.0 provides the tools you need to access data on the Internet. However, connecting to the Internet requires much more than simply installing and starting Internet Explorer 6.0. See the Alert box on page 4 to identify some steps you must take before you can connect to the Internet and some terms with which you should become familiar.

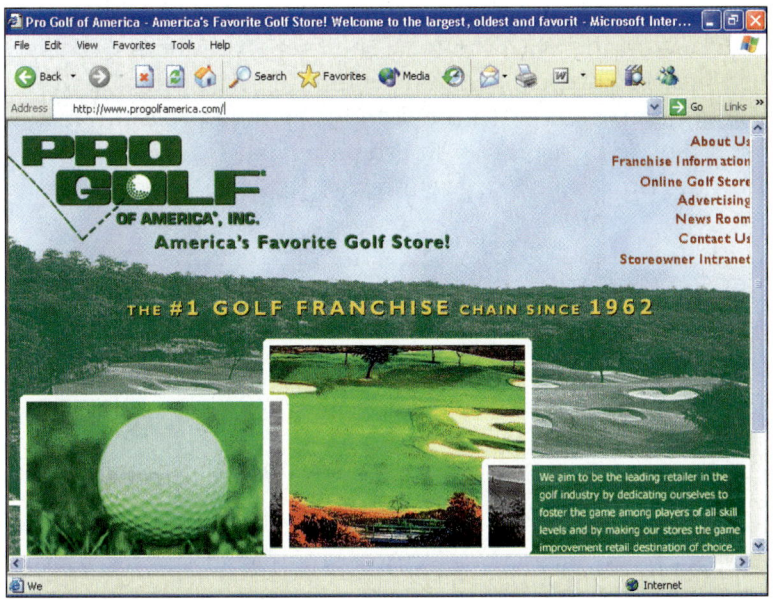

As you explore the features of the Internet, you will see Web pages similar to those shown in Figure 1.1. In Activities 1.1 through 1.12 you will become familiar with Internet Explorer 6.0. You will examine its standard toolbars and features, learn how to use a Web address to visit a Web site, and store Web addresses in your Favorites folder for future reference. In addition, you will learn the basics of searching the Internet to find information and how to download, save, and print a Web page.

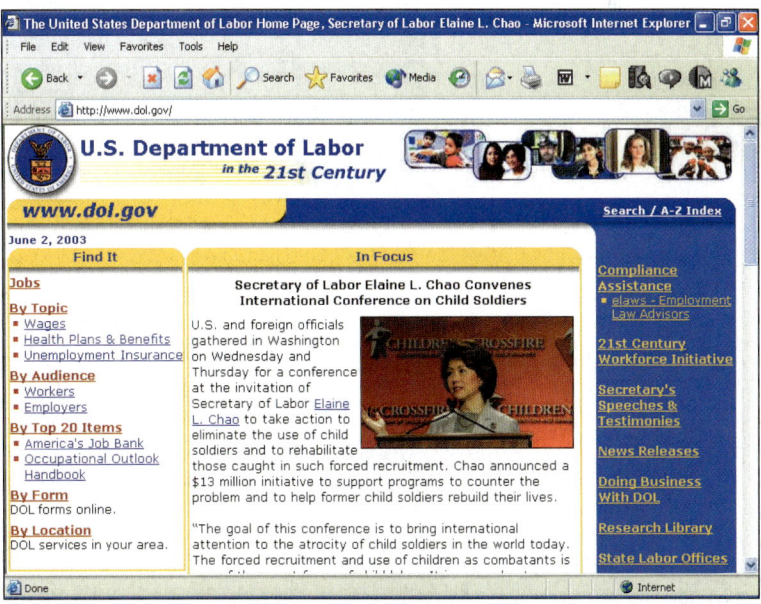

Figure 1.1
Project 1A—Internet Explorer window

Project 1A: Exploring Internet Explorer 6.0 | **Internet Explorer** 95

Objective 1
Start Internet Explorer 6.0 and Identify Screen Elements

In the following activity, you start Internet Explorer 6.0 and identify features of the Internet Explorer program window. The way you start Internet Explorer will vary depending on the version of Windows you are using and the way the system has been set up by your college or organization. The standard installation of Windows places Internet Explorer at the top of the Start menu.

Activity 1.1 Starting Internet Explorer

1 On the taskbar, click the **Start** button .

Organizations, labs, and individuals often customize the arrangement of programs on the Start menu. If Internet Explorer is used as the standard browser program on your computer, it appears at the top of the Start menu along with the standard e-mail program. In other cases, it may appear on the All Programs list. Figure 1.2 shows two places on the Start menu where Internet Explorer appears.

Figure 1.2

Alert!

Before Connecting to the Internet

You must install a modem or other hardware that can connect you to a *network*—a group of computers connected in some way to each other—that can access the Internet. Although businesses, schools, and other large organizations often have their own networks established and provide Internet service to their students and employees, individuals need to go through a service provider for Internet service.

You must establish an account with an *Internet Service Provider (ISP)*. ISPs such as AT&T, AOL, and Earthlink set up large computers that acts as *servers* or *hosts* to other computers and allows their *clients*—computers that connect to servers or hosts—to connect via telephone, cable, and DSL lines.

2 On the Start menu, click **Internet** and maximize the window if it is not already maximized.

Each time you start Internet Explorer when you are connected to the Internet, the *home page* that has been set up on your computer opens. The default home page for Internet Explorer 6.0 is the MSN (Microsoft Network) Web page. Many organizations, schools, labs, and individuals customize the home page that opens on computers they own, so the home page set up on your computer may be different from the MSN Web page.

A *Web page* is an individual page of information, similar to a page of a document, that displays as a screen containing links, frames, pictures, and other features of interest to many users. A *Web site* is a group of related Web pages published to a specific location on the World Wide Web. Each Web site has its own unique address.

3 On the Microsoft Internet Explorer menu bar, click **Favorites**; then click **MSN.com** and study the screen elements unique to Internet Explorer.

An MSN Web page that resembles the one shown in Figure 1.3 opens. Because companies are constantly updating their Web pages, the figure you see may vary somewhat from the one shown in Figure 1.3. Notice that the address of the MSN Web site appears in the Address Bar shown in Figure 1.3. Each unique feature is described in more detail in the table in Figure 1.4.

Figure 1.3

Project 1A: Exploring Internet Explorer 6.0 | **Internet Explorer**

Microsoft Internet Explorer Screen Elements

Screen Element	Description
Title bar	Identifies the application as Microsoft Internet Explorer and also displays the name of the active Web page.
Favorites menu	Contains shortcuts to access Web sites you visit frequently.
Standard Buttons toolbar	Contains shortcuts for performing frequent tasks.
Address bar	Displays the address of the active Web page.
Tabs	Access pages of the active Web site.
Mouse pointer	Appears as a pointing hand when you point to a link.
Links	Text that connects to other Web sites or Web pages. When you click the text, Internet Explorer "jumps" to the related site or page.

Figure 1.4

More Knowledge — Home Pages and Portals

The default home page installed when Windows is set up on your computer is a Microsoft site because Internet Explorer is a Microsoft program. Schools, businesses, and individuals that have Web sites often change the default settings to display their sites as the home page. As part of the installation process, ISPs such as AOL and Earthlink and sites such as eBay and Yahoo! offer to change the home page to their Web sites to make accessing e-mail and other frequently used features easier. These home pages, including MSN, act as *portals* or launching sites to other Web pages. They contain links to access frequently visited sites, up-to-the-minute news, weather reports, and maps and directories. The portal pages are also customizable so that you can replace the standard links and information presented on the page with features you use.

On school, lab, and business computers, changing the home page is usually not recommended. However, on your personal computer, you can change the home page. Simply display the page you want to set as the home page. Then, on the menu bar, choose Tools and select Internet Options to open the Internet Options dialog box. Click the General tab and then click the Use Current button under Home page at the top of the dialog box. Click OK to set your new home page.

Objective 2
Navigate the Internet

Most Web pages contain links that you can use to navigate to other sites on the Internet. In addition, Internet Explorer contains tools such as the Standard Buttons tool bar, a history list, and the Address bar that you can use to navigate the Web. In Activities 1.2 through 1.5, you use each of these tools to access different Web sites.

Activity 1.2 Using the Standard Buttons Toolbar

1 On the Standard Buttons toolbar, click the **Back** button.

Internet Explorer displays your home page—the page that opened when you started the program. The Forward button becomes available.

2 On the Standard Buttons toolbar, point to the Forward button.

Although the Web page displayed in Figure 1.5 may be different on your computer, when you point to the Forward button, a screen tip identifies the Web page that will appear when you click the button.

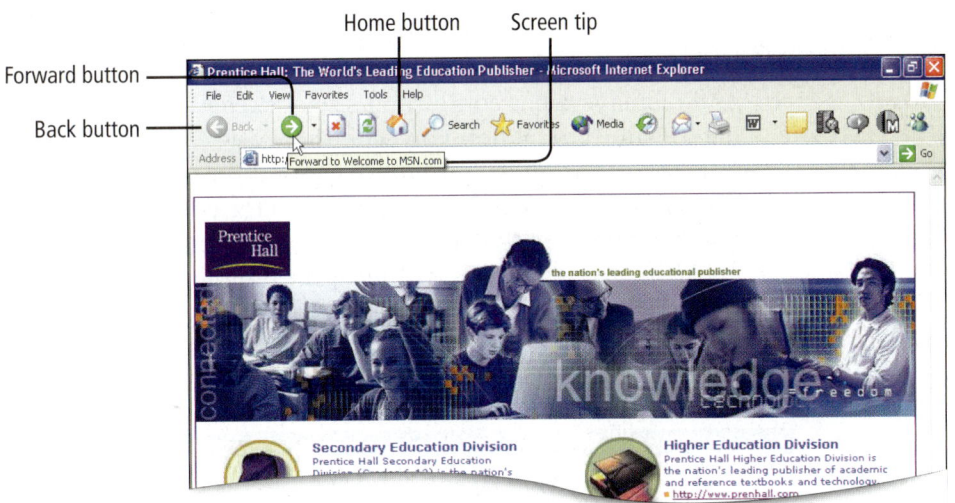

Figure 1.5

3 On the Standard Buttons toolbar, click the **Forward** button.

The MSN page displays again.

4 On the Standard Buttons toolbar, click the **Home** button as seen in Figure 1.5.

Regardless of how many Web pages you view or Web sites you visit, clicking the Home button returns you to the site that you have set as the home page.

> **More Knowledge** — Home, Back, and Forward Buttons
>
> The Home, Back, and Forward buttons on the Standard Buttons toolbar provide shortcuts to navigating sites you have visited during the current session using Internet Explorer. The Home button displays the Home page that is set on your computer and the Back button displays the previous Web page you viewed. The Forward button remains unavailable until you click the Back button. When it becomes available, you can use it to return to the page that was displayed before you clicked the Back button.

Activity 1.3 Using the Address Bar

1. Start Internet Explorer, if necessary, and at the top of the Internet Explorer window, click the **Address Bar** box.

   The existing Web address appears highlighted to show that it is selected.

2. With the current Web address selected, type **www.bakersribs.com** and press Enter.

   Although the existing Web address is selected, typing a new address replaces the selected text. As you type, a drop-down list may appear. Internet Explorer remembers the last 25 Web addresses you entered and displays a list containing site addresses that start with the characters you type. When you type the www, Internet Explorer displays a list of all the sites you have accessed recently that begin with www. The list gets shorter with each character you type. If you see the site you are typing in the Address Bar box on the drop-down list, you can click the item in the list rather than typing the complete address.

   When you press Enter, Internet Explorer retrieves the Baker's Ribs Web page www.bakersribs.com shown in Figure 1.6.

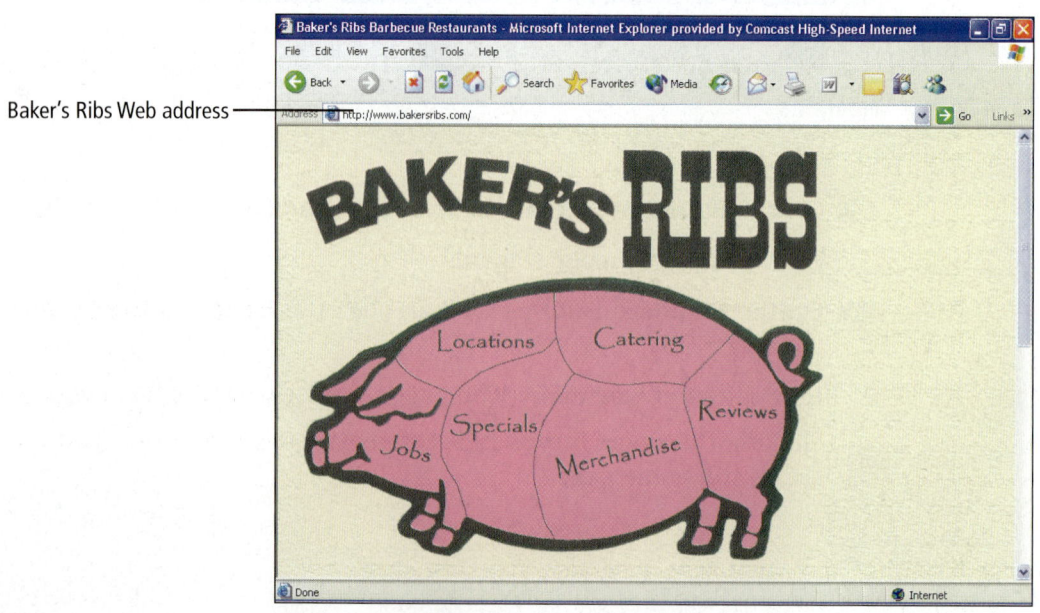

Baker's Ribs Web address

Figure 1.6

100 Internet Explorer | Chapter 1: Getting Started with Internet Explorer

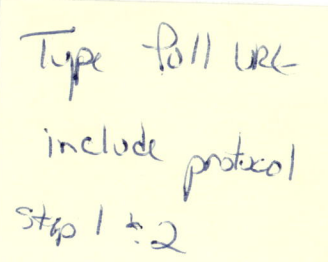

— What Makes Up a URL

...may have noticed in Figure 1.5, the Address bar displays the address ... World Wide Web that accesses a Web site. Each Web address is often ...ed to as a *URL*, which stands for Uniform Resource Locator. Each URL ... ecific components the make up the Web address so that browsers can find it. The table in Figure 1.7 identifies each piece of the Web address, using, for example, *http://www.prenticehall.com/catalog/index.html*.

Anatomy of a Web Address

Part of Web address	Description
http	The abbreviation for Hypertext Transfer Protocol—the standard **protocol** or method for retrieving Web sites. Another protocol is *ftp*, or File Transfer Protocol, which is often used for posting files to a Web site.
://	Three characters identified by Internet creators for separating the protocol from the rest of the Web address. These particular three characters were identified because they had never appeared together in computer programs and other computer-related contexts.
www.prenticehall.com	The domain name. In this case, the domain name includes the abbreviation for World Wide Web (www), the name of the business, and the domain type—.com stands for commercial. Not all domain names start with www, but many do. Other domain types include .edu (education), .gov (government), .org (organization), .net (network), .mil (military), and .mus (music). Most countries have their own domain type such as .ca for Canada and .fr for France.
catalog/index.html	The path within the Web site that contains the folder name (catalog) and page name (index.html).

Figure 1.7

3 Click the **Address Bar** box again, type **www.dol.gov** and press Enter.

The U.S. Department of Labor Web site opens, as shown in Figure 1.8. The *.gov* in the Web address identifies the site as a government site.

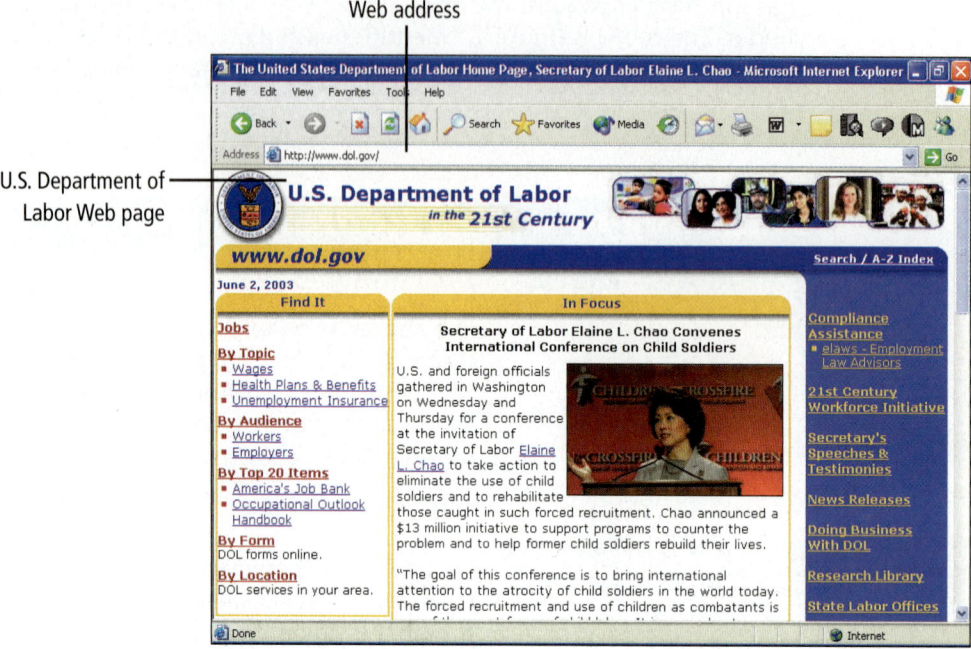

Figure 1.8

4 At the right end of the **Address Bar** box, click the Address Bar box **down arrow** and point to the *http://www.bakersribs.com* Web address.

The list of recently accessed Web sites on your computer will be different from those shown in Figure 1.9. The sites listed represent those most frequently visited on your computer.

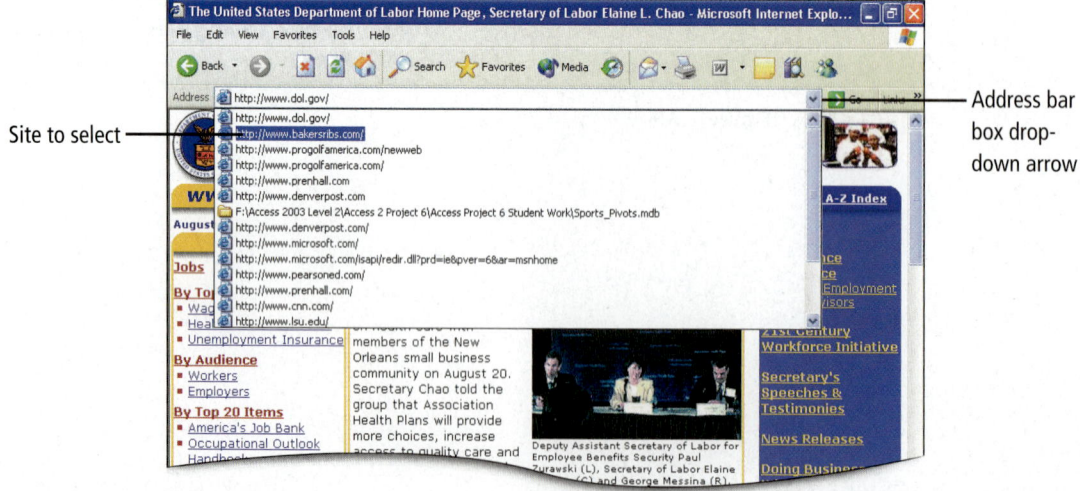

Figure 1.9

---

102 **Internet Explorer** | Chapter 1: Getting Started with Internet Explorer

5 In the drop-down list, click the Baker's Ribs Web address.

Internet Explorer retrieves the Baker's Ribs Web site again.

6 In the **Address Bar** box, type **www.progolfamerica.com** and press Enter.

Internet Explorer retrieves the Pro Golf of America Web page shown in Figure 1.10.

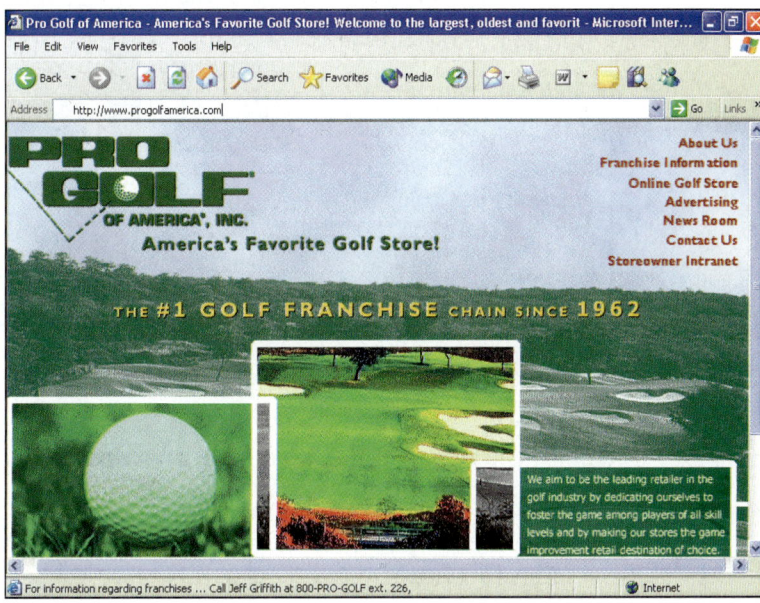

Figure 1.10

7 On the Standard Buttons toolbar, click **Back** to display the Baker's Ribs Web site again, and then click **Forward** to return to the Pro Golf of America site.

8 In the **Address Bar** box, type **www.denverpost.com** and press Enter.

The Denver Post Web site opens. As you view the Web site, notice that text and images on the right side of the site change.

Site address

Figure 1.11

9 In the Address Bar box, type **www.psu.edu** and press Enter.

The *.edu* extension is reserved for schools, colleges, and universities. Internet Explorer retrieves the Penn State Web site shown in Figure 1.12.

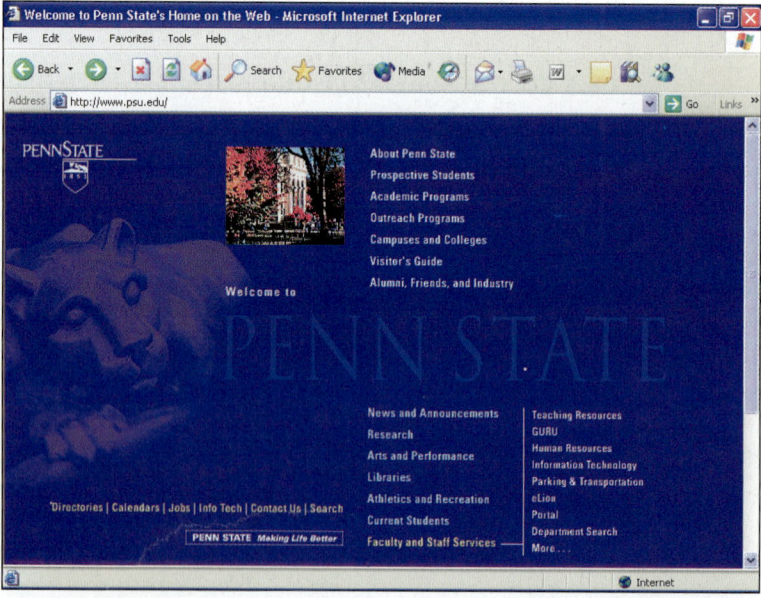

Figure 1.12

10 On the Standard Buttons toolbar, click the **Home** button.

Internet Explorer retrieves the home page set up on your computer.

104   Internet Explorer | Chapter 1: Getting Started with Internet Explorer

More Knowledge — Pop-Up Windows

Pop-up windows open as you navigate pages and sites on the Web. Pop-up windows display information related to the site and normally appear in separate windows. Pop-up windows serve a variety of purposes. Some pop-up windows solicit feedback on topics of interest; others offer goods and services for sale. When a pop-up window opens, you have the choice of closing the window or reading the information contained in the window and taking appropriate action.

Activity 1.4 Using Hyperlinks

Most Web sites contain **hyperlinks** that provide another navigation tool for browsing Web pages. Hyperlinks can be text, buttons, pictures, and other objects displayed on Web pages that access other Web pages or display other sections of the active page. Linked Web pages can be pages within the same Web site or Web pages on sites of other companies, schools, or businesses. In this activity, you will use hyperlinks to display Web pages.

1 Start Internet Explorer, if necessary, and in the **Address Bar** box, type **www.cnn.com** and press Enter.

Internet Explorer retrieves the CNN.com home page that appears similar to the one shown in Figure 1.13. As you review Figure 1.13, notice that the mouse pointer appears as a pointing hand when you point to an item that links to another Web page. Many Web pages contain navigation panes that connect to other pages on the site and have a home page within their site that displays each time you access the site.

Figure 1.13

2 On the CNN.com navigation pane, click **World**.

The World page of the CNN.com Web site opens, as shown in Figure 1.14. Notice that the address in the Address bar still shows the CNN Web site, but the path has expanded to identify the path on the CNN Web site for the page displayed.

Figure 1.14

Alert!

Web Site Doesn't Appear?

Because Web sites such as CNN are updated frequently, the links on the Web site and news displayed also change. If the World link does not appear, follow the direction of your instructor to navigate to a different link.

3 On the Standard Buttons toolbar, click the **Back** button.

The CNN.com home page appears.

4 Just below the CNN.com title, point to the picture.

Although the picture you see will be different from the one shown in Figure 1.14, CNN.com traditionally places a picture related to the top story of the day on its home page. When you point to the picture, the mouse pointer appears as a pointing hand and the Image toolbar shown in Figure 1.15 opens.

Figure 1.15

5 Click the picture.

The item on the site navigation bar related to the picture is activated, and the story related to the picture appears onscreen. Although in Figure 1.16 the story is related to the law area, the story related to the picture you click may be associated with a different area on the site navigation pane.

Figure 1.16

Project 1A: Exploring Internet Explorer 6.0 | **Internet Explorer** 107

6 On the CNN.com navigation pane, click **Weather**.

The Weather page of the CNN.com Web site opens, as shown in Figure 1.17.

Figure 1.17

So far, all the links you have used connect to other pages within the CNN.com Web site. Other sites contain links that connect you to other Web sites.

7 In the **Address Bar** box, type **www.usgovernment.com** and press [Enter].

Internet Explorer retrieves the USGovernment.com Web site as shown in Figure 1.18.

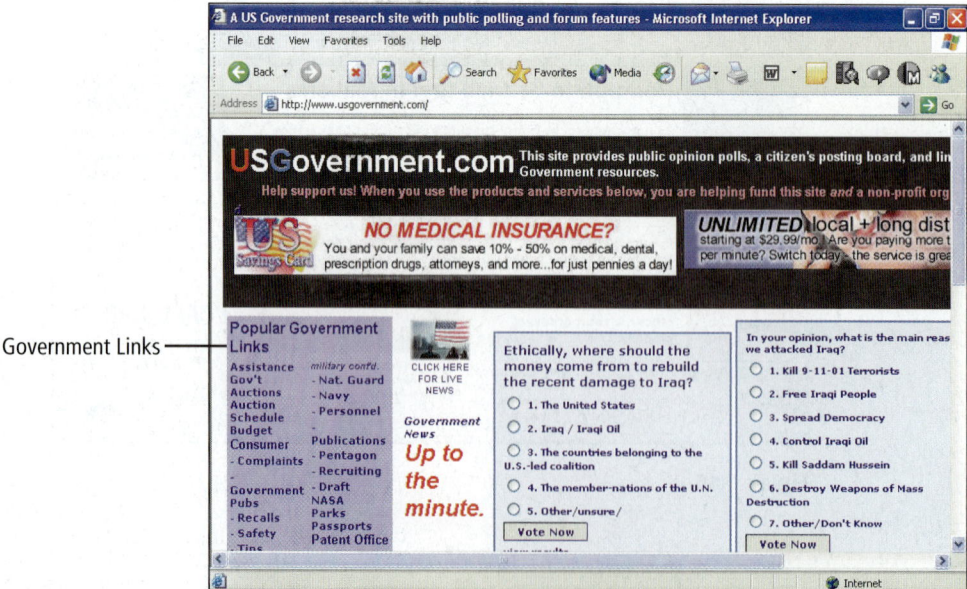

Figure 1.18

8 In the Popular Government Links panel, click **Navy** or the link identified by your instructor.

- Internet Explorer opens the new Web site in a new window, as shown in Figure 1.19. Each Web page contains settings that control whether linked pages open in a separate window or in the same window. In addition, settings that are active on your computer control linked page display.

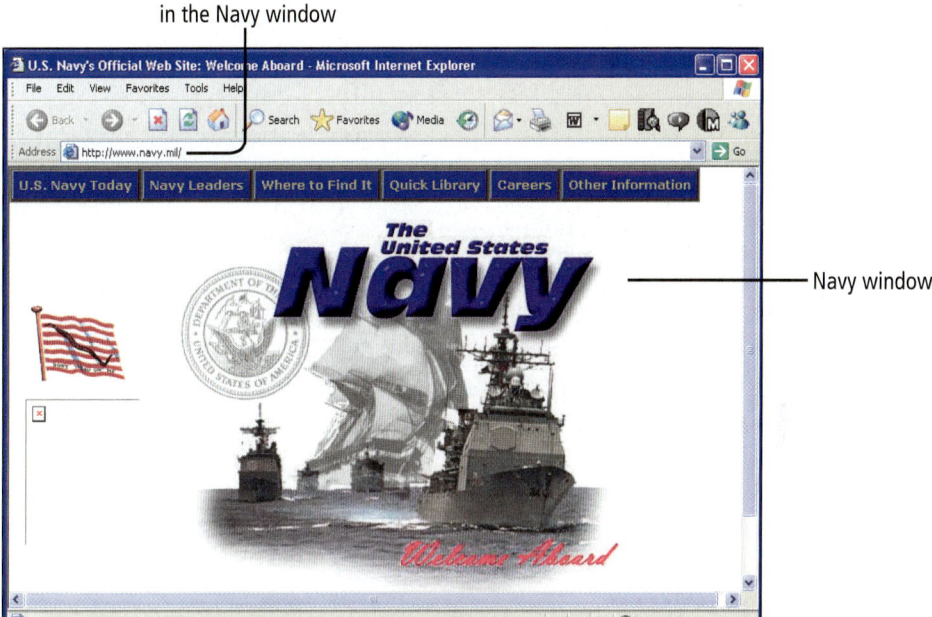

Figure 1.19

9 On the U.S. Navy's Official Web Site title bar, click the **Close** button.

The separate window closes.

10 On the Standard Buttons toolbar, click the **Home** button to return to your home page.

Activity 1.5 Using Internet Explorer History

The Internet Explorer History list tracks recently visited Web pages and sites. You can display the History list and select an item to access a recently visited site. By default, Internet Explorer tracks sites visited in the last 20 days. To reduce the amount of disk storage space required to maintain the History list, you can customize the settings to change the number of days tracked and to clear the list. In this activity, you will use the History list to display recently visited sites.

1 Start Internet Explorer, if necessary, and on the Standard Buttons toolbar, click the **History** button.

The History pane appears on the left side of the Internet Explorer window, as shown in Figure 1.20. The listings of items on your computer will be different from those shown in the figure. However, many of the listings shown for *Today* should be the same. Notice that the links to sites accessed today appear in alphabetical order.

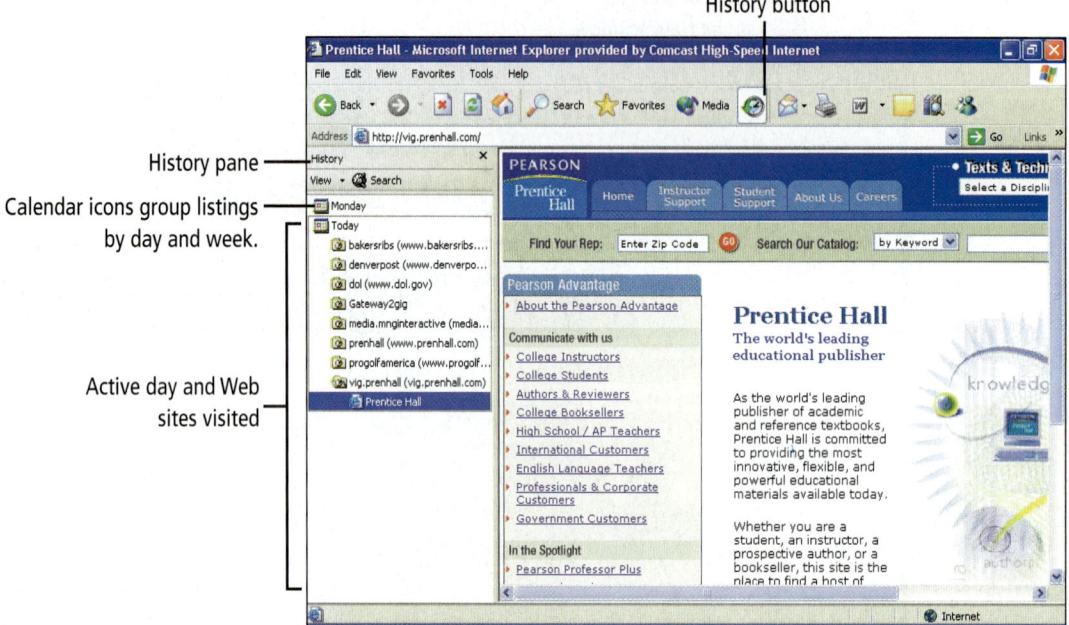

Figure 1.20

2 On the History pane, click the *dol (www.dol.gov)* link.

The Web site name associated with the address appears below the link, as shown in Figure 1.21.

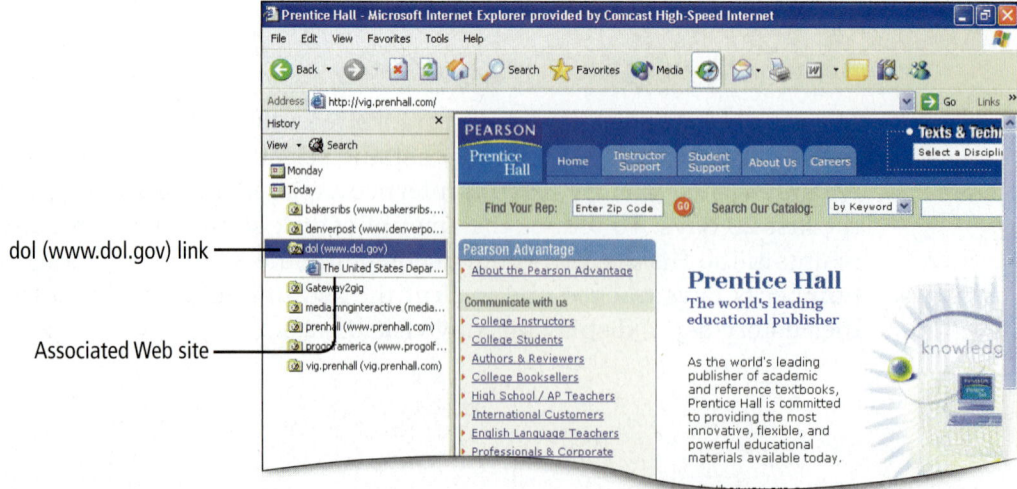

Figure 1.21

3 On the History pane, click *The United States Department of Labor* link.

Internet Explorer displays the U.S. Department of Labor Web site.

4 On the Standard Buttons toolbar, click the **History** button again to hide the History pane.

The History button acts as a toggle to display and hide the History pane.

> ### More Knowledge — Setting History Options
>
> The default setting for the History pane displays Web pages visited the last 20 days. You can change the options that control the History pane and also clear the History list by setting Internet Options. On the Internet Explorer menu bar, click Tools and then click Internet Options to open the Internet Options dialog box. In the dialog box, click the Clear History button to remove all site listings; then click Yes to confirm the deletion. You can also click the spin buttons beside *Days to keep pages in history* to increase or decrease the number of days tracked on the History pane.

Objective 3
Work with Favorites

The History list tracks sites you visit each time you start Internet Explorer—many of which you may never visit again. The **Favorites** list contains Web addresses for sites you plan to visit frequently; you intentionally add addresses to the Favorites list. When you install Internet Explorer, a short list of Microsoft sites is added to the Favorites list. You can delete these addresses, add new listings, and organize favorite site addresses in folders. In Activities 1.6 through 1.8, you will add a new favorite, navigate to a site listed in favorites, and delete a favorite.

Activity 1.6 Adding an Address to the Favorites List

In this activity, you will display a Web page and add it to the Favorites list using the **Add Favorite** dialog box.

1 Start Internet Explorer, if necessary, and in the **Address Bar** box, type **www.prenhall.com** and press [Enter].

The Prentice Hall Web site opens.

2 On the menu bar, click **Favorites**, and then click **Add to Favorites**.

The Add Favorite dialog box shown in Figure 1.22 opens. The name of the Web site appears in the Name box. A list of folders on the Favorites menu is shown in the *Create in* box at the bottom of the Add Favorite dialog box. When you have a number of sites that are related to a specific topic, you can create a new folder and use it to store related site addresses. You can also check the *Make available offline* check box (the little square beside *Make available offline*) to download the Web page and store it on your computer for use when you are offline—no longer connected to the Internet.

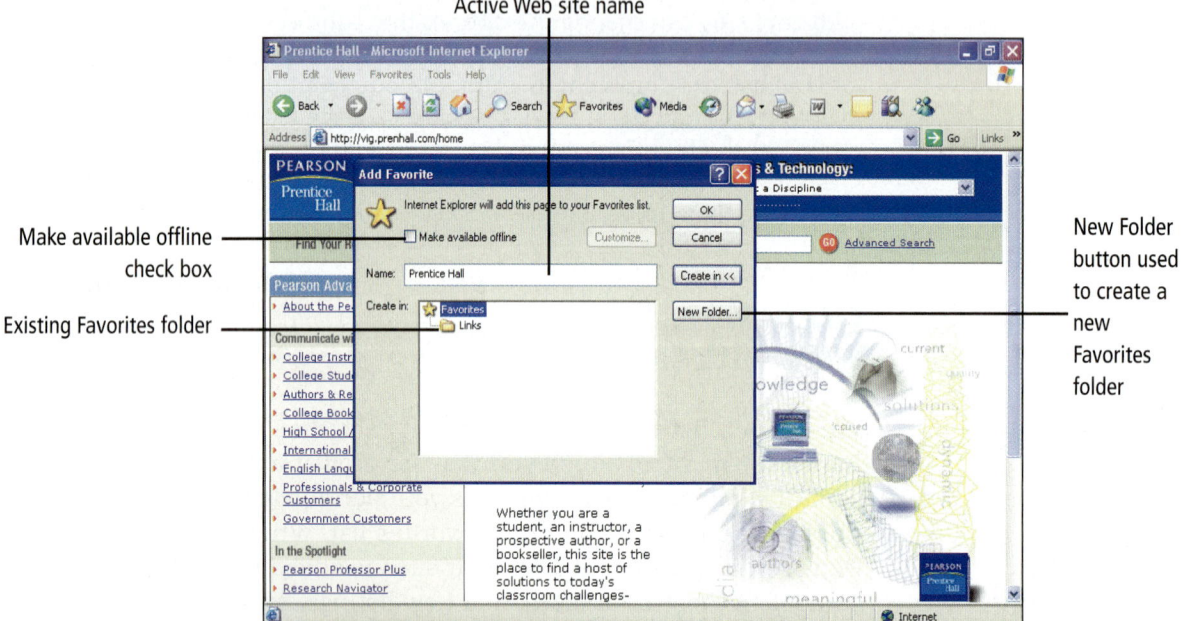

Figure 1.22

3 In the **Favorites** dialog box, click **OK**.

Internet Explorer adds the Prentice Hall Web page address to the Favorites list.

4 On the Standard Buttons toolbar, click the **Home** button to display your home page.

Returning to the home page on your computer enables you to see results when you use the Favorites list to display a Web page.

Activity 1.7 Displaying a Favorite Web Site

In this activity, you use the Favorites list to display a Web site. You also use the Favorites button on the Standard Buttons toolbar to display the Favorites pane.

1 On the menu bar, click **Favorites**.

Your Favorites list, similar to the one in Figure 1.23, appears. Notice the link to the Prentice Hall Web site.

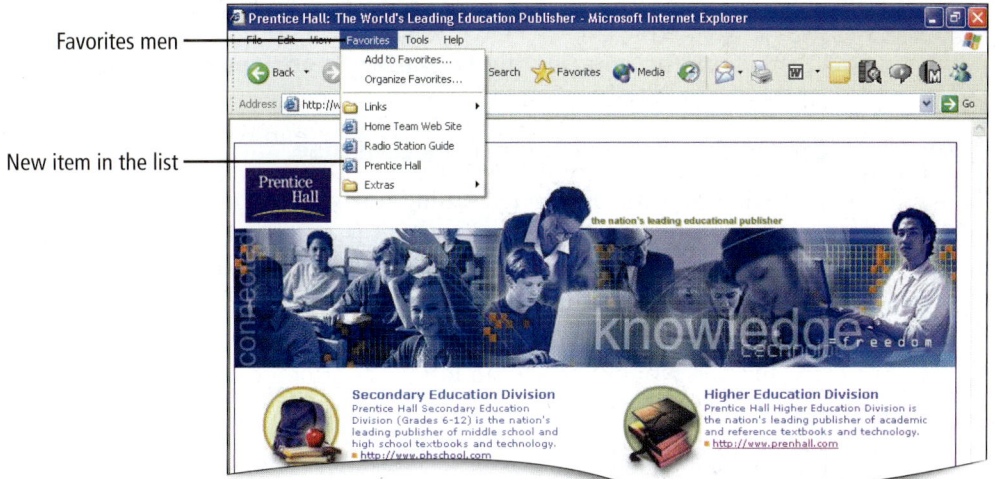

Figure 1.23

2. Click **Prentice Hall**.

   Internet Explorer retrieves the Prentice Hall Web page.

3. On the Standard Buttons toolbar, click the **Favorites** button.

   A Favorites pane that is similar to the History pane opens on the left side of the Internet Explorer window. As you review features on the Favorites pane shown in Figure 1.24, notice the Add button that appears at the top of the pane. You can use the Add button to open the Add Favorite dialog box.

Figure 1.24

Project 1A: Exploring Internet Explorer 6.0 | **Internet Explorer**   113

Activity 1.8 Deleting a Web Address from Favorites

In this activity, you use the **Organize Favorites** dialog box to remove an address from the Favorites list.

1 On the Favorites pane, click **Organize**.

The Organize Favorites dialog box shown in Figure 1.25 opens to display a list of items contained on the Favorites list and action buttons for creating folders, renaming items, moving items to folders, and removing items from favorites. You can also use the *Make available offline* check box in this dialog box to download a favorite Web site for use when you are no longer connected to the Internet.

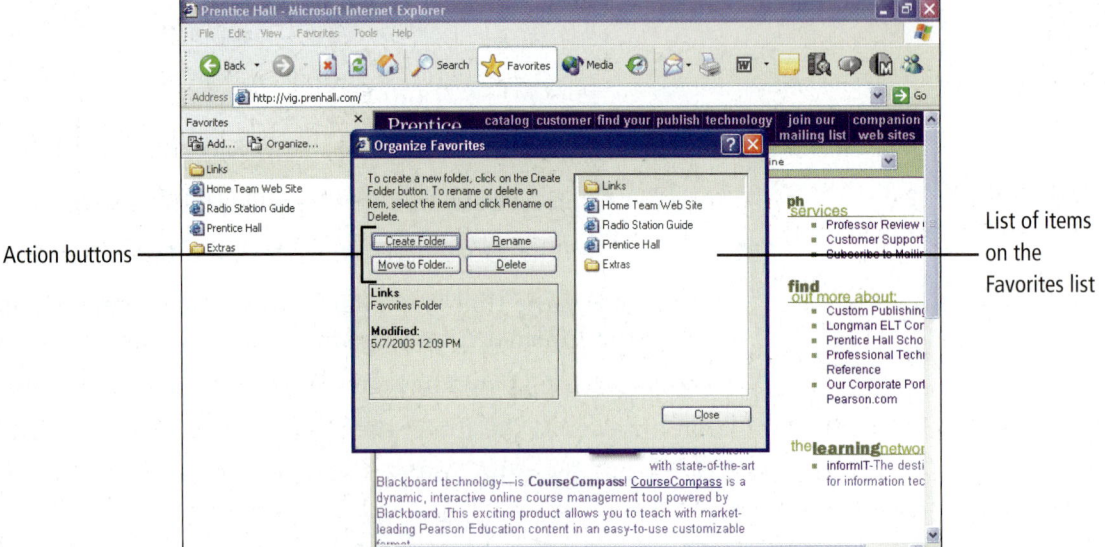

Figure 1.25

2 In the Organize Favorites dialog box list of items on the Favorites list, click **Prentice Hall** to select it.

The Prentice Hall item appears highlighted.

3 In the Organize Favorites dialog box, click the **Delete** button.

Internet Explorer displays the Confirm File Delete message box, which prompts you to ensure that you want to delete the item from the Favorites list, as shown in Figure 1.26.

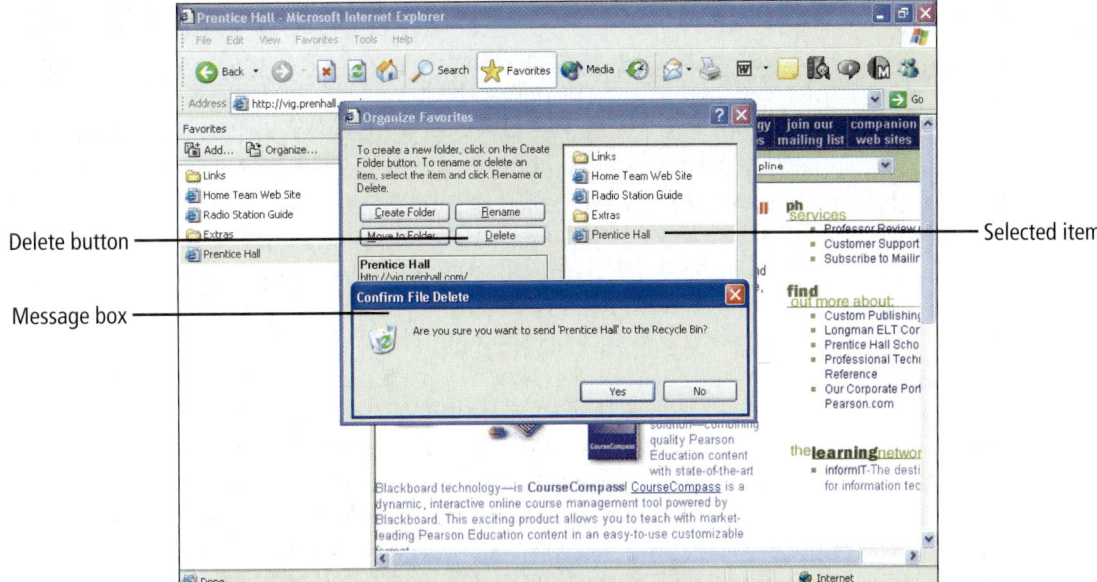

Figure 1.26

4 In the Message box, click **Yes**; then, in the **Organize Favorites** dialog box, click **Close**.

Internet Explorer removes the Prentice Hall Web site from the Favorites list and closes the Organize Favorites dialog box.

5 On the Standard Buttons toolbar, click the **Favorites** button to close the Favorites pane.

Objective 4
Search the Internet

When you know the name of a business or the Web address you want to locate, accessing the site presents little challenge. When you want to locate information about topics from a variety of sources, finding sites for businesses, journals, and other sources presents a greater challenge because of the vast expanse of the Internet. As a result, many businesses have created **search engines**, programs designed to search the Internet for sites containing specific text.

One of the most powerful features available in Internet Explorer is a search capability that connects to many popular search engines to locate sites that may contain the information you are seeking. The Search pane is similar to the History and Favorites panes; it displays the Search Companion to assist you in your search for topics. In this activity, you will search the Internet for topics related to computer training.

Activity 1.9 Searching the Internet

1 Start Internet Explorer, if necessary, and on the Standard Buttons toolbar, click the **Search** button.

The Search Companions pane opens, as shown in Figure 1.27.

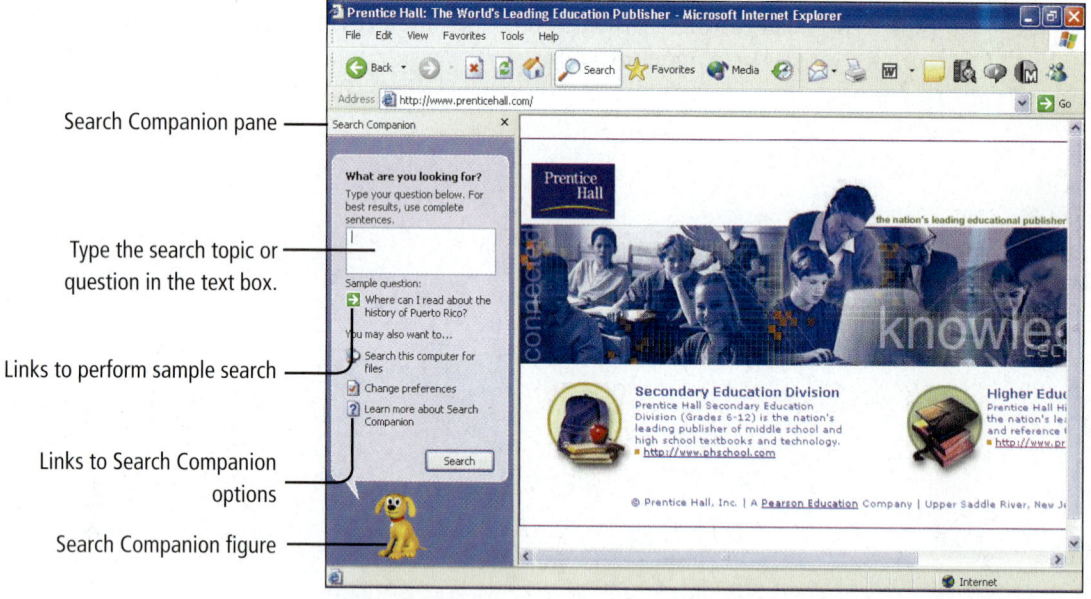

Figure 1.27

116   Internet Explorer | Chapter 1: Getting Started with Internet Explorer

2 In the **Search Companion** text box, type **"computer training"** including the quotation marks and press Enter.

Typing *computer training* without the quotes tells the Search Companion to look for two different terms. Placing the text in quotation marks ensures that the Search Companion looks for sites that contain the entire phrase. Figure 1.28 displays the search results from the Search Companion. Notice that the number of sites found during this particular search that contain the phrase *"computer training"* is 385. Internet Explorer displays links to the Web sites in order based on the number of references to the search text contained in the site.

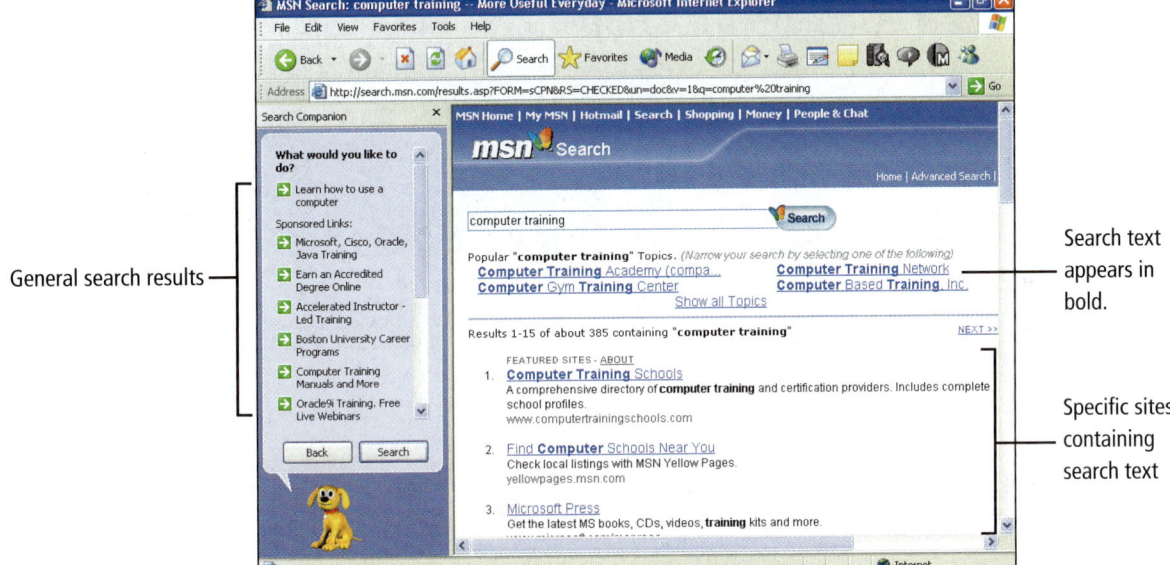

Figure 1.28

3 On the Search Companion pane, click the **Accelerated Instructor-Led Training** link.

The Training Camp Web page opens, as shown in Figure 1.29.

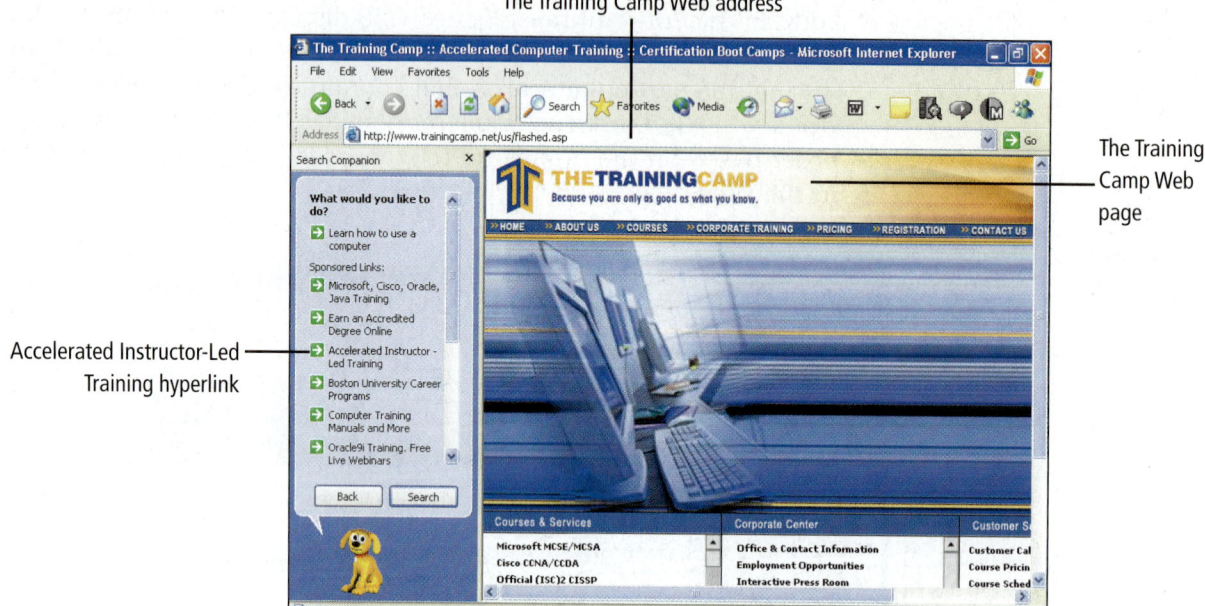

Figure 1.29

Alert!

Link Unavailable?
If the Accelerated Instructor-Led Training link is unavailable, click the link identified by your instructor.

4 On the Standard Buttons toolbar, click the **Back** button.

The MSN Search results page opens.

5 In the MSN Search results pane, click the link for **Computer Training Schools** or the link identified by your instructor.

Internet Explorer retrieves the site for Computer Training Schools or the site connected to the link you clicked.

6 On the Standard Buttons toolbar, click the **Search** button and then click the **Home** button.

The Search Companion pane closes. The Web page expands to cover the Internet Explorer window, and Internet Explorer retrieves your home page.

118 Internet Explorer | Chapter 1: Getting Started with Internet Explorer

Objective 5
Download Files

When you add a Web page to the Favorites list, you have the option of making the page available offline. Selecting the option ***downloads*** or saves a copy of the page on your computer hard drive or floppy disk so that you can review page contents after ending your Internet connection. You can also save Web pages and store them on your computer or disk so that you can review them later. When you save a Web page displayed in Internet Explorer, Internet Explorer creates a new folder in the location you indicate and stores graphics, pictures, and other features of the Web page in the folder so that when you view the file, it resembles the page displayed on the Web. Because of the widespread threat of computer viruses, as a general precaution, avoid downloading or saving files from unknown Web sites, and be sure your virus protection program is up to date before storing Web files on your computer.

In this activity, you will download a Web page, save it in the folder normally used to hold student files, and open the file from the folder.

Activity 1.10 Downloading and Saving a Web Page

1 In the **Address Bar** box, type **www.denverpost.com** and press Enter.

Internet Explorer retrieves the Denver Post Web site home page.

2 On the Internet Explorer menu bar, click **File**, and then click **Save As**.

The Save Web Page dialog box shown in Figure 1.30 opens.

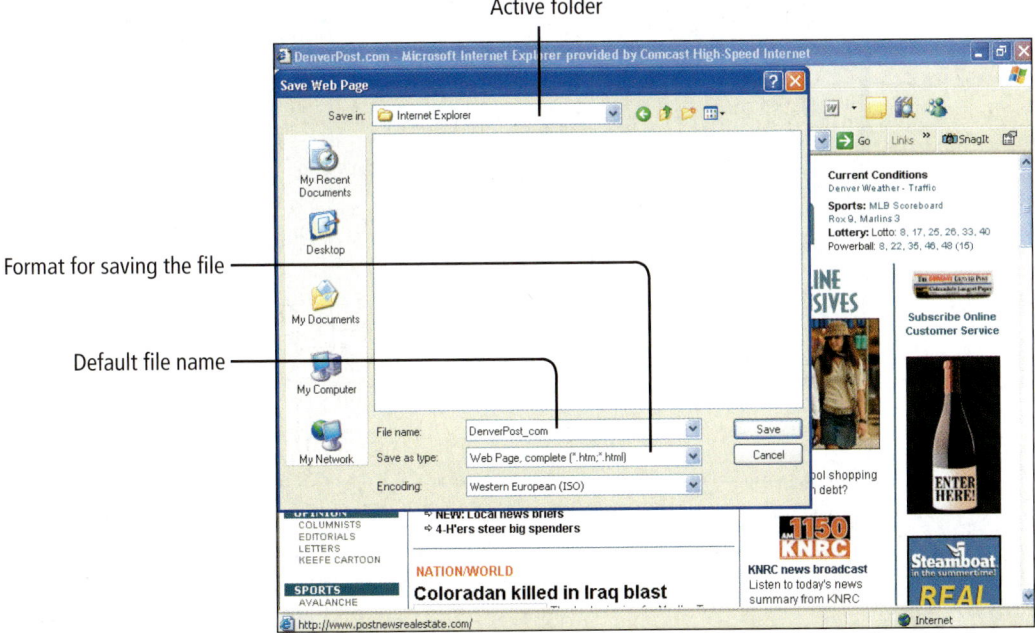

Figure 1.30

Project 1A: Exploring Internet Explorer 6.0 | **Internet Explorer** 119

3 In the **Save in** text box, open the folder in which you want to save the Web page and click **Save**.

Internet Explorer saves the Web page in the designated folder.

Alert! Can't Save the Page?
If the Web page contains settings that prevent you from downloading and saving the page, Internet Explorer displays a message box to tell you that it cannot be saved. Click OK in the message box to continue.

4 On the Standard Buttons toolbar, click the **Home** button. On the Internet Explorer menu bar, click **File** and then click **Open**.

The Open dialog box opens.

5 In the Open dialog box, click the **Browse** button.

The Microsoft Internet Explorer dialog box shown in Figure 1.31 opens. The *Look in* text box shows the folder in which you saved the Web page. Because you are opening a file in Internet Explorer, *HTML* files are listed. HTML stands for **Hypertext Markup Language**—the language used to format Web pages. Notice that Internet Explorer also created a folder to hold the files associated with the DenverPost_com Web page.

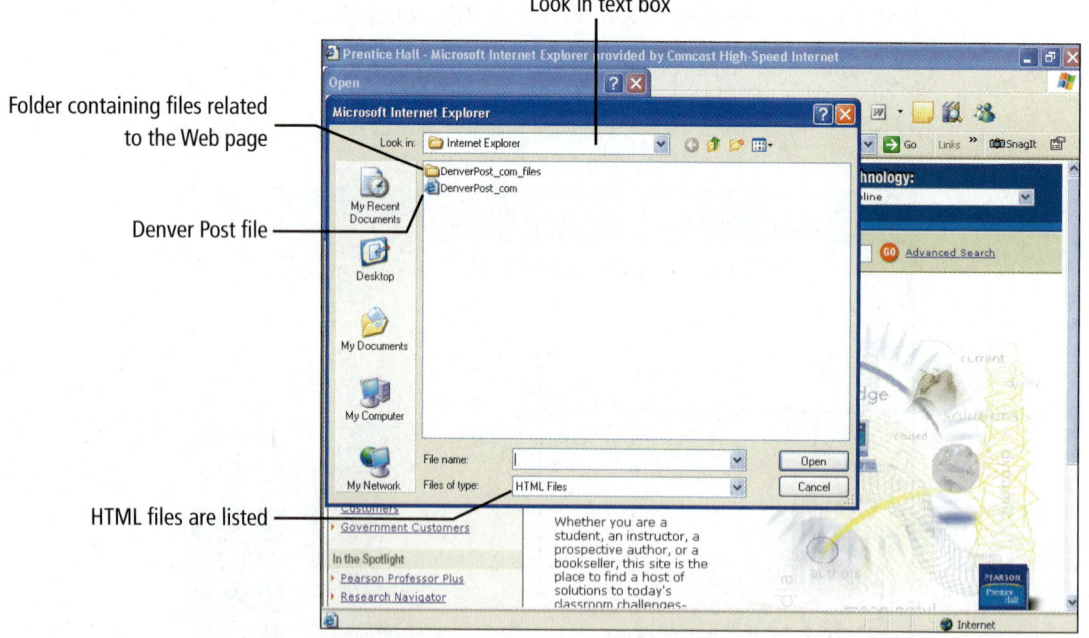

Figure 1.31

6 In the Microsoft Internet Explorer dialog box, double-click the **DenverPost_com** file.

The Web file name, drive, and folder name on your computer appears in the Open box of the Open dialog box.

7 In the **Open** dialog box, click **OK**.

The Web file opens in Internet Explorer, as shown in Figure 1.32.

Path and file name of file displayed in Internet Explorer

Figure 1.32

8 On the Standard Buttons toolbar, click **Home**.

More Knowledge — Creating New Folders

Downloading, as you used it in Activity 1.10, simply saves a Web page and associated files in the folder you specify. Downloading can also relate to downloading programs and other items from the Internet. For example, if you display the Microsoft.com Web site, you can download free trial packages, install them on your computer, and try them before you purchase them. When sites offer free downloads, a Download link usually appears on the page. When you click the link, Internet Explorer prompts you to save the file on your computer. The prompt message also provides an option to open or run the program from the server.

Many times, the programs you download from sites such as Microsoft save files on your computer so that you can install programs on your computer. As a result, it is generally recommended that you download and save the file on your computer before trying to install it. Again, be careful what you download and avoid downloading programs from unknown sites.

Project 1A: Exploring Internet Explorer 6.0 | **Internet Explorer** 121

Objective 6
Print Web Pages

As you have seen, Web pages are constructed to contain a variety of different elements—pictures, navigation panes, links, frames, text, and so forth. When you print Web pages, all elements displayed on the Web page print unless you select the specific text, picture, or frame you want to print. Most of the options contained in the **Print** dialog box in Internet Explorer are the same as those seen in the Print dialog box for other programs. However, the Print dialog box in Internet Explorer contains options that enable you to print pages that are linked to the active Web page and a table of pages linked to the Web page.

Because frames and objects are placed so closely together on the Web page, selecting just the information you want to print can be a challenge without activating a hyperlink or selecting additional information as well. In this activity, you will review options in the Print dialog box and print a Web page.

Activity 1.11 Printing Web Pages

1 In the **Address Bar** box, type **www.denverpost.com** and press Enter.

The Web site displays current information and news items.

2 On the menu bar, click **File** and then click **Print**.

The Print dialog box shown in Figure 1.33 opens.

Figure 1.33

Another Way

To Open the Print Dialog Box

You can display the Print dialog box by pressing Ctrl + P. Clicking the Print button bypasses the Print dialog box and prints the complete Web page.

3 On the **Print** dialog box, click the **Options** tab.

The Options page of the Print dialog box shown in Figure 1.34 opens. The options contained on this page are unique to Internet Explorer and are used to print a table of linked items and all pages liked to the Web page.

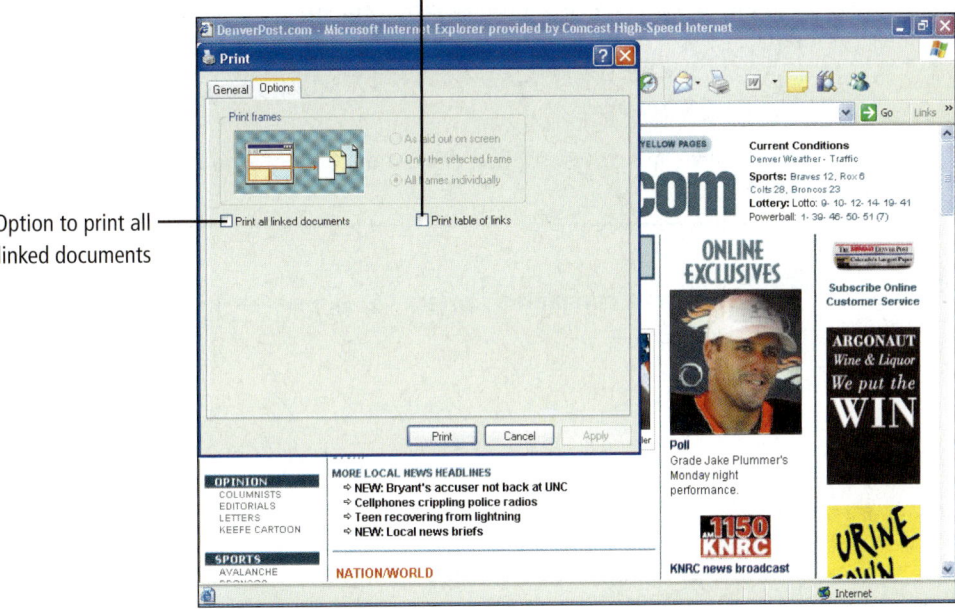

Figure 1.34

4 On the Print dialog box Options page, select the **Print table of links** check box and click **Print**.

Internet Explorer prints a copy of the Web page and a table identifying all items linked to the Web page.

Project 1A: Exploring Internet Explorer 6.0 | **Internet Explorer** 123

Objective 7
Close Internet Explorer

When you have completed your work in Internet Explorer, you can close Internet Explorer and end the Internet connection.

Activity 1.12 Closing Internet Explorer

1 On the Internet Explorer title bar, click the program **Close** button ☒.

2 Respond appropriately to messages, if prompted.

> **Another Way**
>
> **To Close Internet Explorer**
>
> *Use any of the following techniques to close Internet Explorer:*
>
> - On the Internet Explorer application title bar, click the Close button ☒.
> - On the Internet Explorer menu, click File, and then click Close.
> - Press Alt + F4.
> - On the Windows taskbar, right-click the Internet Explorer program button and click Close.

End **You have completed Project 1A**

Summary

In this project, you explored basic features for starting Internet Explorer, navigating among Web pages, and working with Favorites. You learned how to search for Web sites containing information about topics you specify, how to download and save Web pages, and how to print a Web page with a list of linked pages.

In This Chapter You Practiced How To

- Start Internet Explorer
- Use the Standard Buttons toolbar to navigate Web pages
- Use the Address bar to navigate Web pages
- Use hyperlinks to navigate Web pages
- Use Internet Explorer History to navigate Web pages
- Add an address to the Favorites list
- Display a Favorite Web site
- Delete a Web address from Favorites
- Search the Internet
- Download and save a Web page
- Print Web pages
- Close Internet Explorer

Concepts Assessments

Matching Match each term in the second column with its correct definition in the first column. Write the letter of the term on the blank line that appears beside each definition.

____ 1. Computers connected to a computer network.

____ 2. Copies of files moved from the Internet to your computer.

____ 3. Text, pictures, and other objects displayed on Web pages that are used to connect to other pages.

____ 4. The language used to format Web pages.

____ 5. A company that provides access to the Internet.

____ 6. A place on the Internet that connects you to other sites.

____ 7. The Web page that opens each time you start Internet Explorer.

____ 8. Programs designed to locate Web sites related to topics and questions you ask Internet Explorer.

____ 9. A set of connected computers.

____ 10. The complete address of a Web site.

____ 11. An individual screen that appears when you connect to the Internet.

____ 12. The retrieval method used to access pages on the Internet.

____ 13. A group of related pages on the Internet.

____ 14. A list of Web pages.

____ 15. Computers to which other computers connect.

A network

B Internet Service Provider (ISP)

C servers

D clients

E home page

F Web page

G Web site

H portals

I Uniform Resource Locator (URL)

J protocol

K hyperlinks

L Favorites

M search engines

N downloads

O hypertext markup language (HTML)

Concepts Assessments (continued)

Fill in the Blank Write the correct answer in the space provided for each statement.

1. Three characters that separate the protocol from the rest of the Web address are _____.

2. WWW stands for _____ _____ _____.

3. Government Web sites normally end with _____.

4. The Internet Explorer feature that tracks sites you visit over a period of time is the _____ feature.

5. The mouse pointer appears as a _____ when you point to a hyperlink on a Web page.

6. To display the previous Web page, on the Standard Buttons toolbar, click _____.

7. The _____ _____ is used to look up information on the Internet about topics or questions you type in the Search box.

8. The portion of a Web address that follows the www is called the _____.

9. Internet Explorer is a _____ program.

10. What part of a Web site is not usually typed when you type the site address? _____

Skill Assessments

Project 1B — Exploring Favorite Links

Objectives: *Display a Favorite Web Site, Use Links, Display Home Page*

The Links folder on the Favorites list contains sites that are installed when you install Internet Explorer on your computer. Most of these links connect you to Microsoft-sponsored sites on the Internet. To determine which of the links you want to keep, you can review each Web page contained in the Links folder.

1. On the Internet Explorer menu bar, click **Favorites**, point to **Links**, and click the **Free Hotmail** link.

    Hotmail is a free Internet mail service that you can use to send and receive e-mail. You would still need an ISP to connect to the internet to access your Hotmail account.

2. On the Internet Explorer menu bar, click **Favorites**, point to **Links**, and click the **Windows** link.

    The Windows page of the Microsoft.com Web site opens. Links enable you to download products from the Microsoft site, locate information about different versions of the Windows operating system, and find answers to frequently asked questions about Windows.

3. On the Internet Explorer menu bar, click **Favorites**, point to **Links**, and click the **Windows Media** link.

    WindowsMedia.com is the Microsoft site for updating your knowledge of songs and media-related topics.

4. On the Standard Buttons toolbar, click the **Home** button to display your home page.

End You have completed Project 1B

Skill Assessments (continued)

Project 1C — Deleting a Link Favorite

Objectives: *Start Internet Explorer, Delete a Web Address from Favorites*

As you have discovered, Internet Explorer installs several items on the Favorites list when you set up Internet Explorer on a computer. After exploring the Links installed during setup, you most likely have identified a link that you have no plans to use. You can delete the link from the Favorites list.

1. Start Internet Explorer, and on the menu bar, click **Favorites**.
2. On the Favorites menu list, click **Organize Favorites** to open the Organize Favorites dialog box.
3. In the Organize Favorites dialog box, in the list of favorites box, click the **Links** folder to display a list of links to Web sites.
4. In the list of Web sites in the Links folder, click a link that you want to delete, click the **Delete** button, and click **Yes** to delete the link.
5. In the Organize Favorites dialog box, click **Close**.

 You have completed Project 1C

Performance Assessments

Project 1D — Playing Music from a Favorite Link

Objectives: *Start Internet Explorer, Displaying a Favorite Web Site, Using Links*

In addition to Web sites stored in the Links folder of the Favorites menu, a Radio Station Guide is added to the Favorites list when you install Internet Explorer. You can use the Radio Station Guide to locate radio stations in your area and, if you have a sound card, you can listen to the radio as you work.

1. Start Internet Explorer, and on the menu bar, click **Favorites**.
2. On the Favorites menu list, click **Radio Station Guide** to open the Windowsmedia.com radio tuner site shown in Figure 1.35.

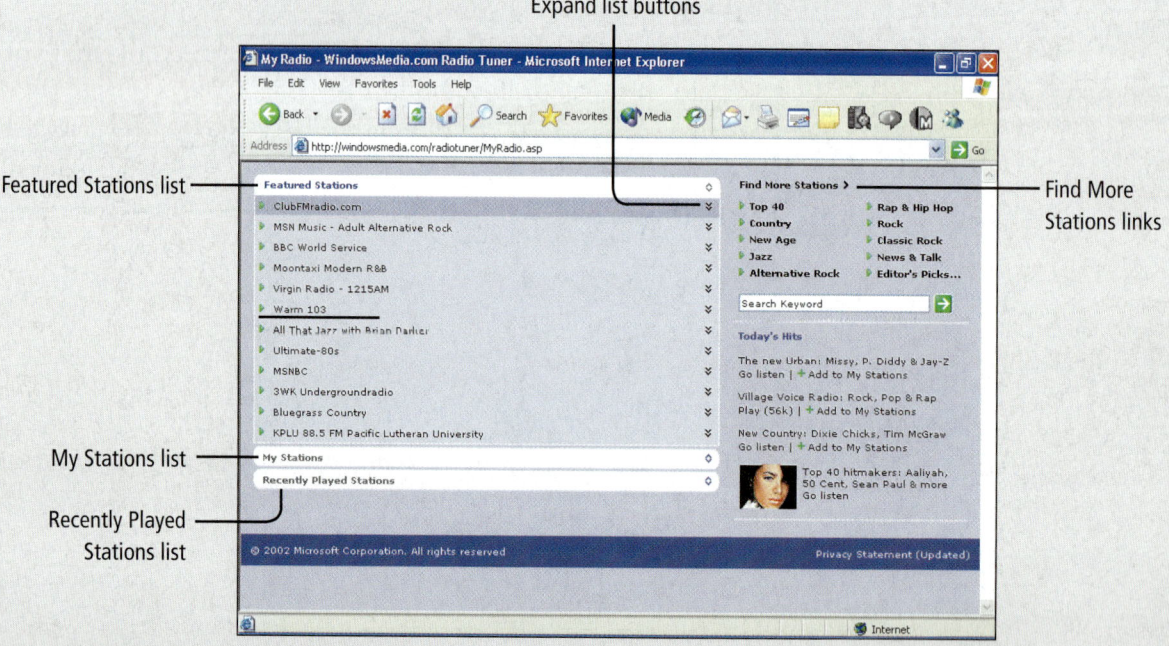

Figure 1.35

Each radio station in the Featured Stations list can be expanded to display additional links. You can use the additional links to add a radio station listed to the My Stations list for easier access.

3. In the Featured Stations list, click **MSNBC** to expand the listing.
4. Under the MSNBC listing, click **Play** to play the station.

Depending on the active settings on your computer, Internet Explorer may present a message box asking if you want to play the station in Internet Explorer.

(**Project 1D**–Playing Music from a Favorite Link continues on the next page)

Performance Assessments (continued)

(Project 1D–Playing Music from a Favorite Link continued)

5. Click **Yes** to play the station from Internet Explorer, if prompted.

   If you have a sound card, live radio from MSNBC plays, as shown in Figure 1.36.

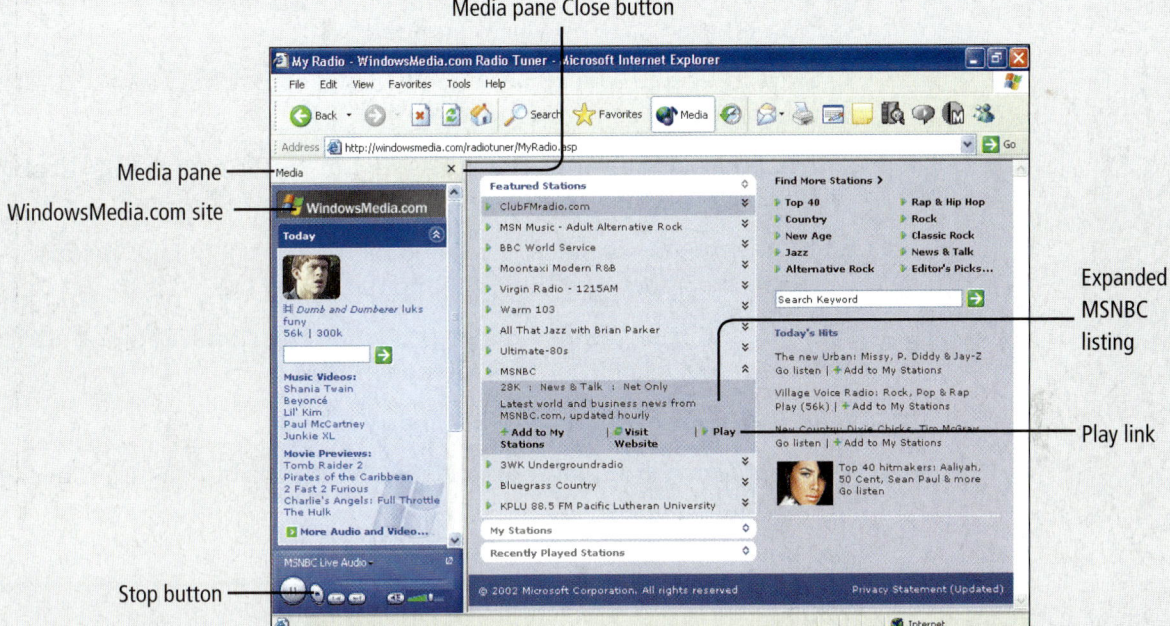

Figure 1.36

6. In the Media pane, click the **Stop** button to stop the live broadcast; then click the Media pane **Close** button to close the pane.

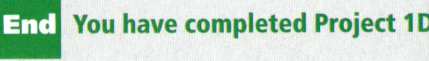 You have completed Project 1D

Project 1D: Playing Music from a Favorite Link | **Internet Explorer** 131

Performance Assessments (continued)

Project 1E — Setting a Home Page

Objectives: *Start Internet Explorer, Use the Address Bar, Set Internet Explorer Options*

The home pages set on computers in your lab or place of business are often set so that you cannot change them. However, you should be able to set the home page on your home computer. Follow these instructions to set up a home page on your computer:

1. Start Internet Explorer and in the Address Bar box, type **www.prenhall.com** and press [Enter].

   The Prentice Hall Web site opens. If you prefer setting a different Web site as your home page, open the site before continuing.

2. On the menu bar, click the **Tools** menu and then click **Internet Options** to open the Internet Options dialog box.

3. In the Internet Options dialog box, click the **General** tab. Under Home Page, click the **Use Current** button.

4. In the Internet Options dialog box, click **OK**.

5. Close Internet Explorer and then start it again to ensure that the new home page is set.

End You have completed Project 1E

Mastery Assessments

Project 1F — Searching for Picture Space

Objectives: *Start Internet Explorer, Search the Internet, Use Hyperlinks, Display a Home Page*

Many sites on the Internet offer free space for storing and sharing pictures. From these sites, friends and family can view pictures and order copies of those pictures they want to keep. You can locate these services by searching the Internet. Follow these steps to locate and explore sites to determine which one best meets your needs.

1. Start Internet Explorer, if necessary. On the Standard Buttons toolbar, open the Search Companion pane and search for **Free Photography Services**.

2. Display the Web pages for at least three sites listed in the search results and review and print information about the sites. Use buttons on the Standard Buttons toolbar to return to the list of search results after reviewing each site.

3. Close the Search Companion pane and display your home page.

 End You have completed Project 1F

Problem Solving

Project 1G — Locating Freebies

Objectives: *Search the Internet, Use Hyperlinks, Download Files*

As you become more familiar with the Internet, you will run across a large amount of free "stuff"—programs, computer equipment, computer services, and so forth—available from Web sites. Unfortunately, not all of these offers are legitimate. Search the Internet for "*free stuff*" and review some of the offers. As you explore the sites, remember that you should download programs and information only from sites you know and trust. See if you can determine which sites make legitimate offers and which do not.

 End You have completed Project 1G

On the Internet

Setting a Favorite

The World Wide Web stores information about individuals as well as companies. Many businesses store data about their clients and customers in databases on the Web so that they can place orders online. Families often store family trees on Web sites so that others can track their family history. Search the Internet for information about yourself to see what information is stored about you and others with your name. Then search again for information about your family name to see if family tree data is available and download data you believe connects to your family.
One of the most frequently visited federal government sites is that of the United States Postal Service. On the site, you can search for ZIP codes, calculate domestic or international mail rates, change your address, obtain a map to a post office, purchase stamps, track a package, and so forth. Locate the Web site for the U.S. Postal Service and add it to your Favorites list for easy reference.

GO! with Help

Searching Microsoft's Knowledge Base

Microsoft Corporation has developed a vast network of support services on the Internet. Using the services, users of Microsoft programs such as Internet Explorer can obtain answers to frequently asked questions (FAQs), post messages on bulletin boards, and search the knowledge base for information about specific products. Microsoft also posts patches and service packs for Microsoft products on the Internet. Connect to the Microsoft.com site on the Internet. Then use the panel on the left side of the site window to locate Support under Resources. Select the Knowledge Base link to connect to the Product Support Services. In the Advanced Search and Help pane, under Select a Microsoft Product, click the down arrow and select Internet Explorer 6. Press [Enter] to initiate the search. Then click the hyperlinks to open articles containing information about Internet Explorer 6. Download at least two articles and print copies of the articles that contain data and information you believe you can use as you explore the Internet.

Computer Concepts

chapter one

Basic Computer Concepts

In this chapter, you will: complete these skills.

Objectives

- Define Computer and Identify Required Components
- Identify the Types of Computers
- Describe Hardware Devices
- Identify Types of Software and Their Uses
- Describe Networks and Define Network Terms

Introduction

Computers have been intrinsically entwined in our lives for so many years now that most people consider them a necessary part of doing business. You see them at the grocery store, in banks, and in most any office. They are used to compile newspapers and magazines, books and publications. Doctors use them, accountants use them, government offices use them, and courts use them. Hotels, motels, banks, gasoline stations—all use some type of computer. They are installed in cars and homes to monitor systems and in utility meters, security systems, telephone systems, and a myriad of other systems to track usage. Computers have, in effect, proven to be an innovation that has changed our lives and the way we do business. As a result, learning to use a computer is basic to the core skills and knowledge required of most high-school and college graduates.

This introduction provides an overview of computers, what they do, and how they operate. You learn the basics of computer hardware and software and identify features of networks. As you explore computer technology, you identify the four stages of the information processing cycle shown in Figure 1.1 and how the four components required for a complete computer system address these stages.

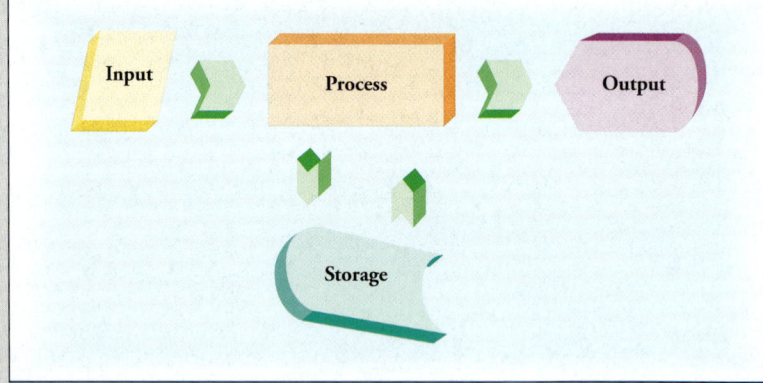

Figure 1.1

Objective 1
Define Computer and Identify Required Components

In its most basic form, a ***computer*** is a machine that computes. By today's standards, a computer is an electronic system that accepts, stores, processes, and reports data in a format that provides useful information. The definition describes the operations required to complete the information processing cycle: input, process, output, and storage. Figure 1.2 identifies the components required for a complete computer system. Each component is described in the table in Figure 1.3.

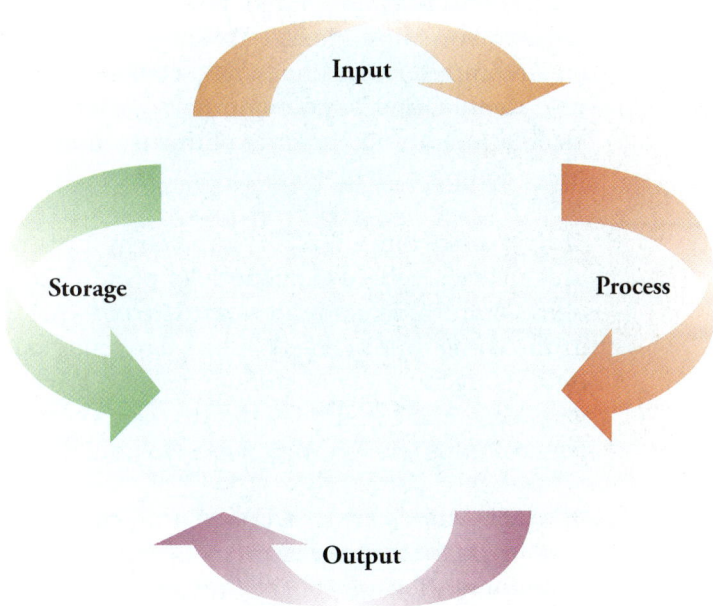

Figure 1.2

Components of a Computer System

Component	Description
Input	The means of getting data—facts and figures—into a computer
Process	Performing an arithmetic calculation or logical operation such as alphabetizing or sorting the data to change it into useful information
Output	The means of getting data and information out of a computer
Storage	Storing data for future use

Figure 1.3

If you compared a computer system with a stereo system, you would consider the CD as the storage device because the songs are stored on the CD, the cassette (or tray) in which you place the CD as the input device, the receiver as the processor, and the speakers as the output devices.

Objective 2
Identify the Types of Computers

Although computers come in a variety of sizes and shapes, the basic components required for completing the information processing cycle must be present in them all. There are four basic types of computers: supercomputers, mainframes, minicomputers, and microcomputers.

Supercomputers are large, powerful computers normally devoted to performing specialized tasks. You may have heard of Big Blue, the IBM® supercomputer that challenged chess players to chess matches—and beat them! Other supercomputers perform sophisticated mathematical calculations, track weather patterns, monitor satellites, and perform other complex, dedicated tasks.

Mainframe computers are large computers often found in businesses and colleges, where thousands of people use the computer to process data. Mainframe computers **multitask**—perform different types of tasks at the same time. They have the capability of storing vast amounts of data using a variety of storage devices. Early mainframe computers were very large and required separate rooms to house them. Today's mainframe computers are significantly smaller.

Minicomputers are often used in medium-sized businesses that have smaller data storage requirements than businesses using mainframe computers. Because of the increased capabilities of microcomputers, minicomputers are less common than they once were.

Microcomputers are the smallest of the four categories of computers. Within the microcomputer category, computers range in size from servers that have the storage capability of minicomputers (and small mainframes) to handheld devices that fit in your pocket. Some of the most common types of microcomputers include the following:

- **Desktop** computers sit on your desktop, floor, table, or other flat surface and have a detachable keyboard, mouse, monitor, and other pieces of equipment (see the section on hardware for detailed information). Two popular types of desktop computers include the Macintosh® computer made by Apple® Computer, Inc. and personal computers that are made by companies such as Hewlett-Packard, Dell®, IBM, Gateway®, and so forth.

- **Laptop** or **notebook** computers are smaller than desktop computers so that you can take them with you when you travel. They are designed to fit comfortably on your lap (thus the name *laptop*) or in your briefcase (thus the name *notebook*) to enable you to use them in a variety of places such as a car, on a train, in an airport, in the office, or at home. Although laptop and notebook computers normally have the keyboard, pointing device, and monitor screen built in, they also can be connected to detachable devices for office use.

- **Personal digital assistants (PDA)** or **handheld** computers vary in size and provide a convenient resource for maintaining an organized calendar and list of business and personal associates. PDAs and other handhelds are designed so that you can hold them in one hand and use a sticklike device to access features. Some of the more modern handheld computers come with a detachable keyboard for entering text and other data.

Figure 1.4 identifies three types of microcomputers.

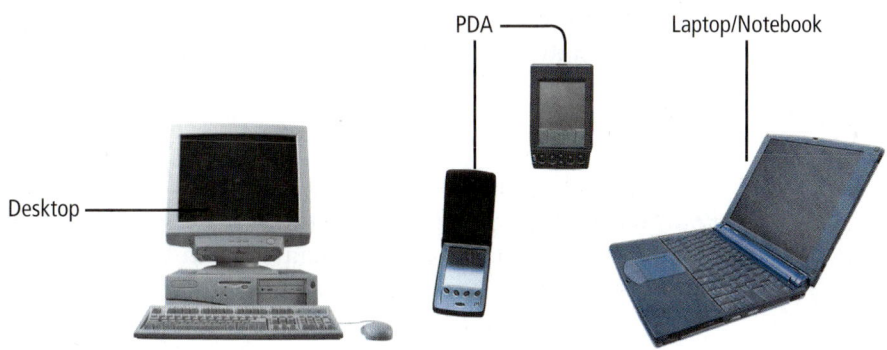

Figure 1.4

Objective 2: Identify the Types of Computers | **Computer Concepts**

Objective 3
Describe Hardware Devices

In the days when an adding machine was operated manually to perform calculations, only one piece of equipment was required. Modern computers are made up of numerous devices, each designed to perform one step in the information processing cycle. These devices are called **hardware**—the physical pieces that make up the computer system. Hardware appears both inside and outside the computer. Devices that attach to the outside of the main computer unit are called **peripherals**. The main computer unit, sometimes referred to as the **console** or **system unit**, houses the processor as well as other hardware units. Figure 1.5 shows a standard computer system and identifies the function each piece of hardware performs.

Figure 1.5

In the sections that follow, each type of hardware unit is presented separately so that you get an overview of each type of hardware. Samples of the most popular devices associated with hardware units are also presented. Keep in mind that companies that make hardware units constantly update their hardware designs. The devices shown here represent samples—what you find when you look at computers and computer hardware in stores may vary significantly.

System Unit

The system unit is the main computer unit that holds the processing hardware, electrical power supply, disk drives, circuit cards, ports for connecting other pieces of hardware peripherally, and a **motherboard**—also called the **system board**—that ties everything inside the system unit together. Figure 1.6 shows a motherboard similar to those found inside a system unit and identifies the main features normally found on the motherboard. The table in Figure 1.7 identifies and describes each item.

Figure 1.6

Motherboard Features	
Component	**Description**
Motherboard/System board	The main computer circuit board that connects all computer components.
Memory (RAM) chips	The temporary holding area inside the computer where data is stored electronically to make it accessible for processing. Data must be stored in memory so that the processor can access and process it. RAM stands for Random Access Memory.
CPU	The central processing unit that gets data from memory and processes the data by performing mathematical or logical operations.
Expansion slots	Hold expansion cards.
Expansion cards	Removable circuit cards for adding new peripherals or increasing computer capabilities.
Memory (RAM) slots	The slots on the motherboard into which you add memory (RAM) chips to increase the computer memory (RAM).

Figure 1.7

Many people imagine that the CPU or central processing unit is the largest piece of hardware located inside the system unit. As you can see, it is relatively small, but it is quite powerful. Most CPUs are **microprocessors**—*micro* meaning that they are very small. Some of the most commonly used processors are manufactured by Intel®, Motorola®, and Advanced Micro Devices®. Intel makes Celeron® and Pentium® processors and Advanced Micro Devices make Athlon® and Duron® chips—the processors most frequently found in PCs made by IBM, Gateway, Dell, Hewlett-Packard, and others. Motorola chips are most frequently found in Macintosh computers. The CPU consists of two parts—the **control unit** and the **arithmetic/logic** unit. The control unit retrieves data from memory so that it can be processed and sends it back to memory when the CPU is finished with it. The arithmetic/logic unit does the processing. Arithmetic processing includes performing mathematical calculations. Logical processing includes sorting data alphabetically or numerically, filtering data that meets specific criteria, and so forth.

CPUs are measured by the speed at which they are capable of processing data—also known as **clock speed**. Processing speed is measured in **megahertz** (MHz) and has grown from early computers that processed at less than 5 MHz to modern processors that operate at over 2,000 MHz or 2 **gigahertz**. In "computereze," **mega** refers to millions and **giga** refers to billions.

Another important feature of system units is memory. Computers contain two basic types of memory—ROM and RAM. Read only memory (ROM) comes built into the computer and, for the most part, remains inaccessible to users. It contains the instructions that enable the computer to turn on and run when you turn on the power. Random access memory (RAM) is the internal storage area for data with which you are working. It stores data temporarily while the data is being processed and empties out when you turn off the computer. Many people compare computer memory with human memory—it's full when you go into class to take a test and empties out as soon as you finish the test. Others compare RAM with a desk—you get out your work, put it on your desk, complete your work, and clean off your desk when you leave work or school. Memory (RAM) is measured by size. The more memory the computer has, the more efficiently it processes data. Referring to the desk model mentioned earlier, the bigger the desk, the more work you can have out. To understand memory size, it is important to compare terminology associated with memory. The table in Figure 1.8 identifies terms associated with unit measurements for both RAM and disk storage capacity.

Unit Measurement Terms

Term	Description
Byte	One character, such as a letter, number digit, space, tab, and so forth
Kilobyte (KB)	Roughly 1,000 bytes or characters
Megabyte (MB)	Roughly one million bytes or characters
Gigabyte (GB)	Roughly one billion bytes or characters

Figure 1.8

> **Note — Measuring Storage in Bytes**
>
> Computer storage media are also measured in bytes, kilobytes, megabytes, and gigabytes. As a result, it's easy to get RAM confused with hard disk storage capacity. Remember that one is memory and the other stores data and programs.

Memory capacity in most desktop and laptop PCs has grown from less than four kilobytes to more than 256 megabytes of RAM. Figure 1.9 shows how the memory and the CPU work together to process data.

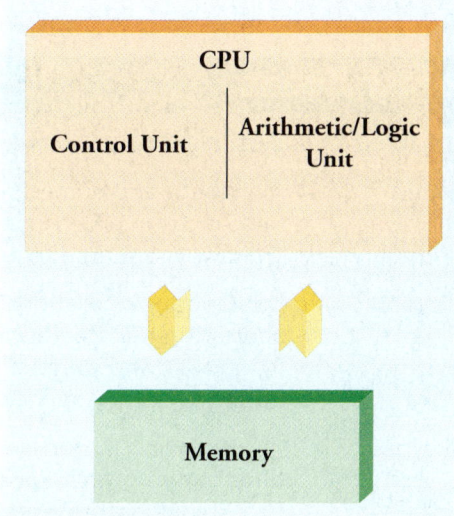

Figure 1.9

Input Devices

Input devices are pieces of hardware used to get data into the computer in a format that the computer can understand. The most common input devices include the mouse and keyboard. Input devices that are gaining popularity are scanners, digital cameras, PC tablets, microphones, and other audio and video devices.

Keyboards

Keyboards are essential input devices used to type data and text and to interact with the computer. Figure 1.10 shows a keyboard and identifies each group of keys and buttons. In addition, many of today's keyboards contain buttons and knobs for interacting with the Internet, controlling sound settings, and adjusting screen settings. These special keyboards are called ***multimedia keyboards*** and contain all the keys found on the enhanced keyboard as well as the media buttons and knobs. The table in Figure 1.11 identifies each group of keys on the keyboard and how they are used.

Figure 1.10

Keyboard Areas

Keyboard Area	Description
Typing keypad	Alphabetic and numeric keys that are arranged in the same order in which keys on a typewriter are arranged. These keys are used to enter text and other data.
Numeric keypad	Numeric and operational keys used to enter numbers and calculation operations such as multiply (*), divide (/), add (+), and subtract (-). The number keys are arranged as they appear on adding machines.
Function keypad	[F1] through [F12] perform special functions for different programs. For example, [F1] may display Help in one program and perform a different action in another program.
Extender keys	[Ctrl] and [Alt] are used in combination with other keys to access menus, control onscreen mouse actions, and perform other special actions.
Arrow keys	Move the insertion point to a different position in text and numbers.
Special keys	Move to specific locations, such as home and next page, and delete and insert text.
Multimedia buttons and knobs	Play, pause, stop, fast forward, and so forth multimedia audio and video items playing and sometimes connect directly to the Internet.
Indicator lights	Identify active number lock, caps lock, and scroll lock keys.

Figure 1.11

Not all keyboards contain all the elements shown in Figure 1.10. Most keyboards attach to the computer console using a special cord connected to the keyboard outlet. Some keyboards are cordless and use laser technology to enter data into the computer. Others connect to USB ports—new technology that has developed in the last few years to allow quick connection of peripherals to the front or back of a computer.

Mouse

A *mouse* is a small hand-sized unit that acts as a pointing device. With the advent of the first Microsoft Windows product, the mouse became an essential input device. A mouse may contain a ball that you roll around on a desktop mouse pad to point to items on the computer screen. A mouse may also contain a laser beam that guides the onscreen pointer. Each mouse contains from one to three buttons that you click to select items and open and close them. Figure 1.12 shows different types of mouse pointing devices available.

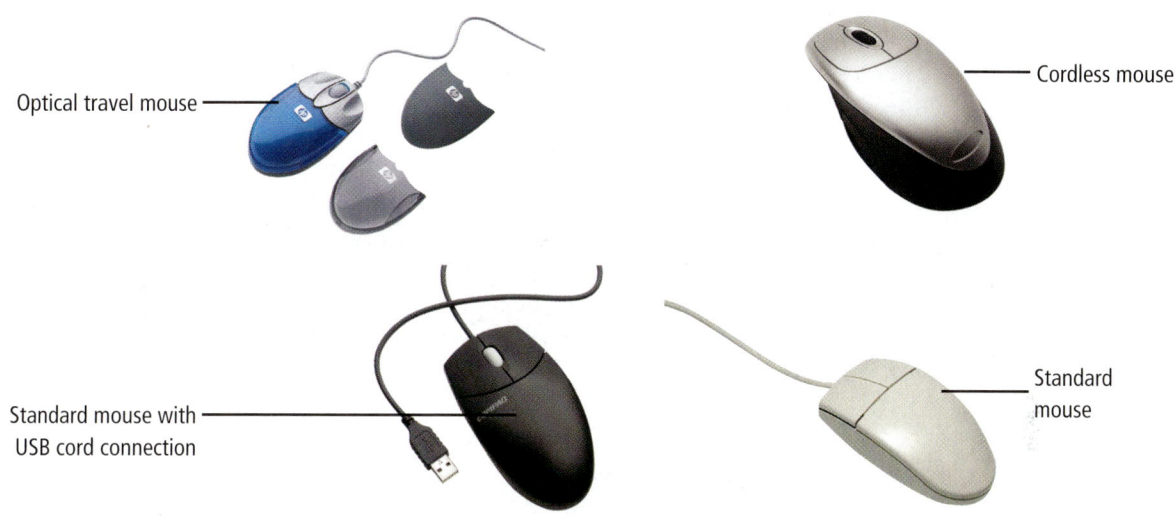

Figure 1.12

More Knowledge — Additional Input Devices

Although the keyboard and mouse are the two most common types of input devices, a number of other devices are gaining in popularity. Figure 1.13 shows a variety of devices on the market and identifies each.

Figure 1.13

Multimedia Input Devices

Multimedia is a term often associated with visual and audio media. As the capabilities of computers have grown to encompass more and more multimedia, the number of devices available to input multimedia files has also grown. Digital cameras have increased in popularity, and the quality of pictures they take has improved. Digital cameras take and record visual images digitally so that they can be downloaded directly into the computer right from the camera. In addition, video cameras often come equipped with PC cables that connect to the computer so that the videos can be converted into digital files. Voice-input devices, such as microphones, are also becoming more popular and can be used to record sound files in a digital format that can be interpreted by computers. With the right software, computers can convert sound recorded using microphones to text. Printers, commonly used as output devices for printing documents and other files, now serve as multipurpose devices that are also used to scan pictures, documents, and other items into the computer. As a result, multipurpose printers are now considered input devices.

Figure 1.14 shows examples of digital cameras, scanners, headphone/microphone sets, and video cameras popular for creating computer multimedia.

Figure 1.14

Output Devices

Output devices are pieces of hardware used to get data and information from the computer in a format that the user can understand. The most common output devices include monitors and printers. Multimedia output devices are also quite popular and are becoming more sophisticated.

Monitors

Many people consider the computer monitor as an essential piece of computer hardware but forget that monitors are essential output devices used to display data, text, and graphics. Some monitors, such as touch-screen monitors, even enable users to interact with the computer. Monitors output soft-copy—printed data and images that disappear when you turn off the computer. Monitors range in size from about 14 inches to more than 20 inches. They are measured diagonally from upper left to lower right to determine the size, just as television sets are measured. Monitor ***resolution*** identifies the number of ***pixels***—points of light—per square inch that appear on a monitor screen. As the number of pixels per square inch increases, the clarity of images and document text displayed on the monitor also increases because the light points are closer together.

Most monitors today are color monitors that can display at least 256 colors. Standard monitors are known as cathode ray tubes (CRTs) that range from about 10 to about 14 inches deep. CRT monitors can have a curved screen or a flat screen and are relatively inexpensive. Flat-*panel* monitors (not to be confused with flat-*screen* monitors) are much slimmer and range in depth from one or two inches to three or four inches. Flat-panel monitors use LCD (liquid crystal display) technology, which many people consider offers better resolution than CRT monitors, and the refresh rate—the rate at which objects appear onscreen—is faster. They are also much more expensive than CRT monitors. Figure 1.15 shows an example of a CRT monitor and a flat-panel monitor. If you compare the depth of the two monitors, you'll see why flat-panel monitors are becoming more popular.

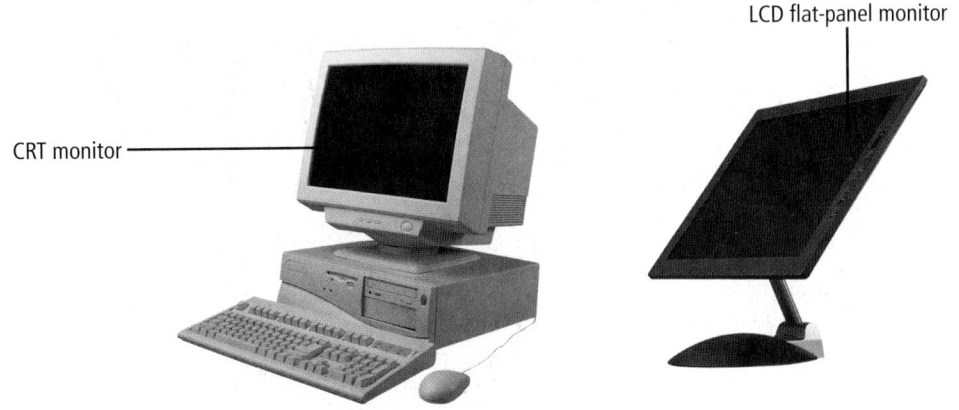

Figure 1.15

Printers

Printers are the devices normally associated with output. Printers produce hard-copy—a permanent paper printout—of data and information generated by a computer. Like monitors, printers vary in size, capabilities, and resolution (quality of print). Printing speed is, in most cases, dependent on print resolution—the higher the resolution and quality of the printout, the slower the print speed. Resolution in printed output is measured in **dpi**, or dots per inch. The higher the number of dots printed per inch of paper, the higher and clearer the print quality.

The two most common types of printers used by individuals who own personal computer systems are the ink-jet printer and the personal laser printer. Ink-jet printers normally print both black-and-white copy and color copy. As a result, they have become popular for printing pictures and other graphics. They work by shooting colored or black ink through a jet stream onto the paper. You can adjust the print resolution to print draft- (low-) quality copy or best- (high-) quality copy. Low-quality copy prints at up to 16 pages per minute, and high-quality copy prints at about 5 pages per minute. Ink-jet printers are relatively inexpensive to purchase.

Laser printers produce a high-quality printout. Although most laser printers produce black-and-white copy, color laser printers are also available. Laser printers are more expensive than ink-jet printers. They create copies using a laser beam to transfer toner from a drum inside the printer onto the paper.

Printers have also become multipurpose devices that serve as both input and output units. Many printers include scanning, faxing, and copying capabilities at a reasonable cost to consumers. Figure 1.16 shows two types of printers—an ink-jet printer and a laser printer.

Figure 1.16

Multimedia Output Devices

Multimedia output devices have been around much longer than multimedia input devices. Speakers have been used to output sound from video games, sound cards, and other audio sources. DVD sources output movies to computer monitors and sound through speakers or headphones. Communications software has improved to enable users to "talk face to face" by placing or receiving phone calls through the computer, transmitting audio through microphones and speakers and live video using computer cameras.

Data and multimedia projectors also output data and information from a computer. Frequently, they are used to enhance a business presentation by projecting the data from the computer onto a screen or wall.

Storage Devices

Storage devices are pieces of hardware used to store data and information. There are both internal and external storage devices, and they come in a variety of sizes and shapes. Most PC owners use both types of storage devices. Hard disk drives, floppy disk drives, DVD drives, CD-writers, and Zip® drives are examples of storage devices. Each storage device also requires a **storage medium** that actually holds the data. Hard disks, floppy disks, CDs, DVDs, Zip® disks, and tapes are examples of storage media. The hard disk and drive are fixed inside the computer system unit so that the hard disk is not removed. Other storage devices provide slots or trays for inserting and removing disks. Normally, these slots and trays appear in the front of the system unit for easy access.

Each storage device serves as both an input unit and an output unit. It reads the data contained on the storage medium and puts it into the computer memory—input. It also writes data from computer memory onto the medium so that it can be stored for future use—output.

As computer technology has evolved, the types of computer storage devices and size of the media have also evolved from 8-inch disks that stored about 50 pages of print to a CD that stores thousands of pages. In general, you are now able to store more data in a smaller space than ever before. Storage capacity of media is measured using the same terms used to measure the storage capacity of memory—bytes, kilobytes, megabytes, and gigabytes. As the capabilities of software programs have increased, the computer hard disk space required to store the programs has also increased. As a result, hard disks can now store many gigabytes of data. CDs normally store between 650 and 780 megabytes, and 3½-inch disks can store about 1.44 megabytes. ZIP® disks compress files so that they can store more data on a disk. Depending on the drive being used, they can store anywhere from about 100 megabytes of data to more than 250 megabytes. DVDs used to store and show movies often contain four layers that can hold 4.7 gigabytes on each layer! DVD cartridges can be read-only (DVD-ROM) so that you can view the videos on them or rewritable (DVD-RAM or DVD+RW) so that you can use them to record your own videos.

Figure 1.17 shows examples of a variety of storage media.

Figure 1.17

Objective 4
Identify Types of Software and Their Uses

Software is the term that describes the programs installed on computers. Computer programs contain the instructions that tell the computer what to do. Computers require two different types of software—operating systems software and applications software. It is easy to confuse the two types of software, especially when the software names are similar. Each is described here to help you differentiate between the two types.

Operating Systems Software

Operating systems software is the operating software that contains the instructions that the computer needs to start up and run—in essence, it enables the computer to operate. Systems software starts each time you turn on the computer, checks the computer each time you turn it on, ensures that everything is operating properly, locates new pieces of hardware, and performs other startup and housekeeping tasks. Systems software serves as an interface between you and the computer that enables you to access other programs, manage files, and perform other tasks.

Currently, three different types of operating systems are being used on microcomputer systems. Each of the systems is similar to the other two, and each has networking capabilities that make it popular.

- Windows: The Microsoft operating systems software that is installed on most PCs. Windows originated in the late 1980s and has survived many generations of products. Windows 3.0 introduced PC users to the *GUI* (graphical user interface) environment, where icons with pictures on them are used to issue computer commands rather than written word commands. Windows 3.1 and Windows 3.11 quickly followed so that they became known as the Windows 3.x generation. Windows 95 introduced the Start menu and taskbar. This generation of the Windows operating system includes Windows 98, Windows Millennium for personal use, Windows NT (new technology), and Windows 2000 for business use. Many consider Windows XP the start of the next generation of Windows products. It contains features that enhance networking and comes in two versions—the Home Edition for home users and the Professional Edition for businesses. A sample Windows XP desktop with the Start menu displayed is shown in Figure 1.18.

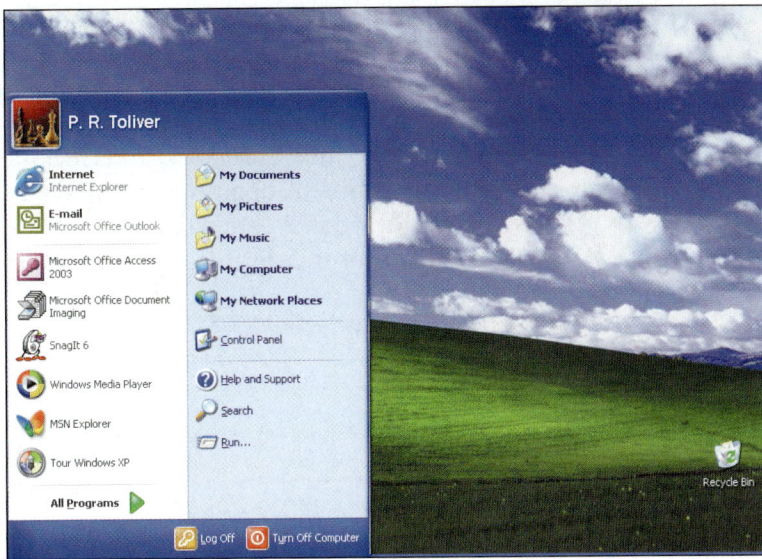

Figure 1.18

- Linux: Bell Labs developed the Linux operating system for PCs from the Unix operating system for minicomputers in the early 1980s. Today it is used by programmers to build custom operating systems. It is not recommended for computer beginners but is widely used among developers. It can be used to integrate PCs, minicomputers, and mainframes from different types of computer systems together on the same network.

- Macintosh: A special operating system is required to run on Macintosh computers. It was developed by Apple Computer, Inc., and is dedicated to run only on Macintosh computers. Apple has traditionally named its operating systems using the name *System* and named them consecutively so that users could easily identify their operating system as System 7, System 10, and so forth.

Microsoft names its products using years, such as Windows 2000, or common identifiers, such as Windows XP. It is easy to confuse the operating systems software with the applications software Microsoft Office. It, too, comes in versions such as Office 2000 and Office XP. However, just because your computer is running Windows XP does not mean that you also have Office XP, and vice versa.

Applications Software

The term ***applications software*** relates to the programs that enable you to accomplish the tasks that you need to complete using the computer. It includes different software programs designed to accomplish specific kinds of tasks.

Individuals and businesses commonly use five primary types of applications. Each of these types and how it is used include the following:

- Word processing: Creating, editing, formatting, and saving documents, and other text-based files—documents and data that are saved (stored) electronically so that you can retrieve and edit them. These files may include graphics, charts, and other graphic elements. Microsoft Word, Lotus® Word Pro®, and Corel® WordPerfect® are all examples of word-processing programs. A document displayed in the Microsoft Word 2003 program window is shown in Figure 1.19. Notice, as you review the document, that it contains a number of graphic elements.

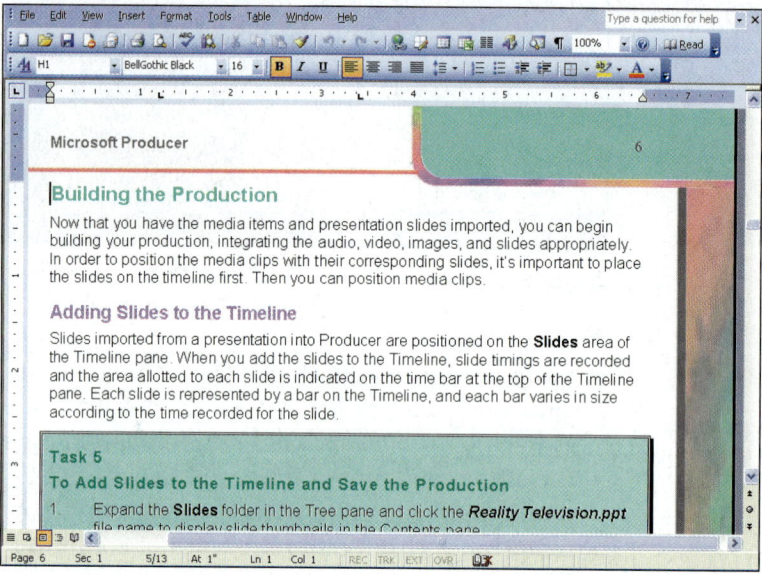

Figure 1.19

- Spreadsheets: Creating worksheets—documents similar to those used by accountants—containing data entered in columns and rows, performing calculations, creating scenarios, performing "what-if" analyses, charting and graphing data, and formatting worksheet layout. Microsoft Excel, Lotus 1-2-3®, and Corel Quattro Pro® are examples of spreadsheet programs. Figure 1.20 shows a worksheet in Microsoft Excel 2003.

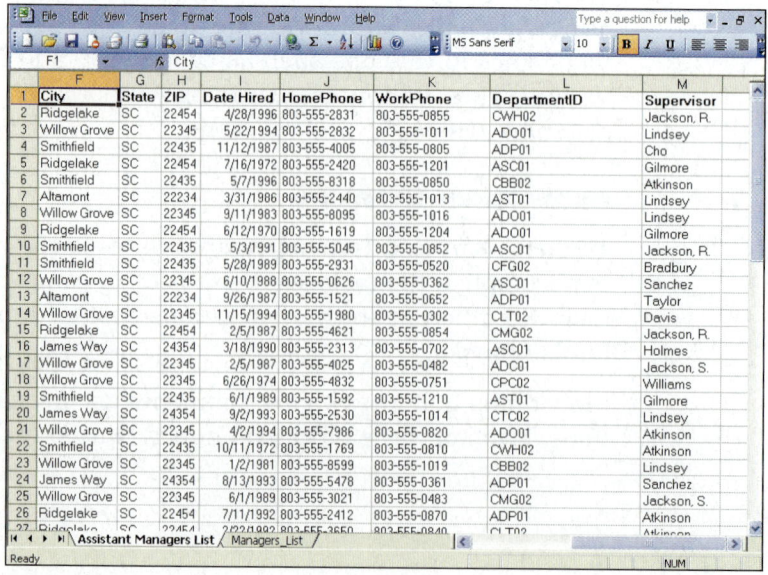

Figure 1.20

- Databases: Entering, storing, sorting, filtering, retrieving, summarizing, and reporting related data and records. Common database programs include Microsoft Access, Lotus Approach®, and Corel Paradox®. Figure 1.21 shows a group of database objects in Microsoft Access 2003.

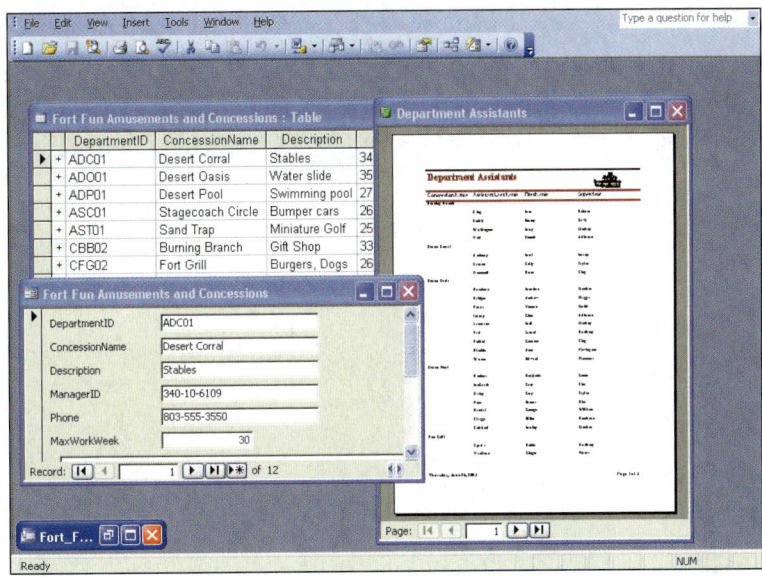

Figure 1.21

- Presentations: Creating graphic presentations that include audience handouts and other materials to be shown onscreen during an oral presentation or projected for audience viewing. Microsoft PowerPoint, Lotus Freelance Graphics®, and Corel Presentations™ are examples of presentations programs. Figure 1.22 shows a presentation displayed in Microsoft PowerPoint 2003.

Figure 1.22

Objective 4: Identify Types of Software and Their Uses | **Computer Concepts**

- Communications and organization: Sends and receives e-mail, stores names and addresses, maintains appointment schedules, records to-do tasks, and so forth. Microsoft Outlook, Lotus Notes®, and Corel Groupwise are examples of communications and organization software. Figure 1.23 displays an example of a calendar in Outlook 2003.

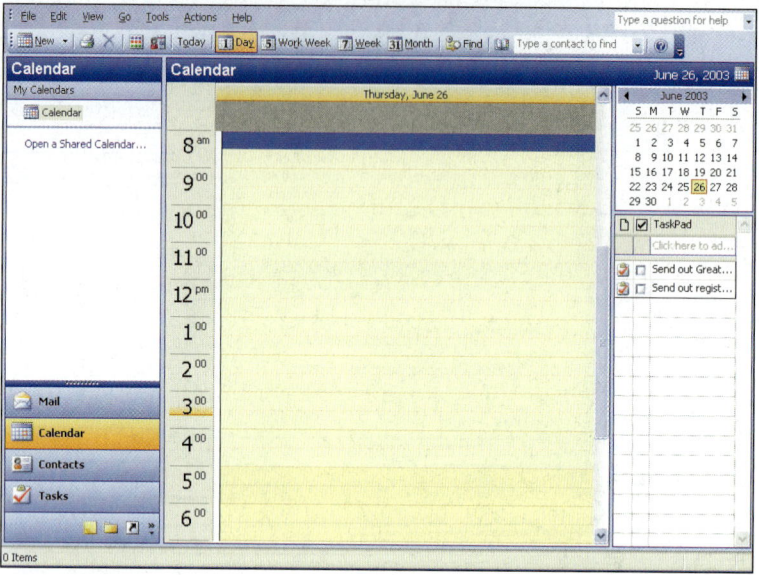

Figure 1.23

In addition to these main types of software, many companies have developed specialized applications to help users accomplish unique tasks. Publishing programs such as QuarkXPress™, Microsoft Publisher, and Adobe® PageMaker® help you lay out publications, Peachtree® Accounting, QuickBooks®, and other similar programs enable you to perform accounting tasks electronically, and programs such as Adobe® Photoshop® and Microsoft PhotoEditor enable you to perfect pictures.

In addition, many companies such as Microsoft, Corel, and Lotus package their programs as suites and offer the suites at a price less than you would spend if you purchased each program separately. Because products from the same company have many common elements such as basic window design and layout, toolbars containing similar tools that enable you to click a button to issue a command, dictionaries, and media galleries, many users find moving from one program in a suite to another much easier.

To identify other software programs and their uses, visit a computer shop or browse the shelves of home electronics or discount stores to see which programs they stock.

Objective 5
Describe Networks and Define Network Terms

Many people consider networks to be television or radio stations that work together to share the costs associated with broadcasting shows. A *computer network*, in its basic form, is two or more computers connected in some way so that they can share hardware (printers, storage devices), software programs, data, and other resources. Most networks consist of a **server** or **host** computer, **client** computers or **workstations**, printers, and other hardware devices. How computers and other devices are arranged and connected make up their **topography**. The three most common topographic layouts include the following:

- Star network: Includes a host computer to which all other computers (clients or workstations), printers, and other devices are connected.

- Bus network: Each computer, printer, and other device in the network connects to a central high-speed line. No host or server is used, and only one computer or device can transmit over the network at a time.

- Ring network: All devices connect to a circular line around which data travels in only one direction.

- Wireless network: Devices connect to other computers and network resources using radio signals, microwaves, satellite signals, and other wireless media.

Most computer networks use a combination of these topographies. Figure 1.24 displays samples of each of the topographies that connect physically.

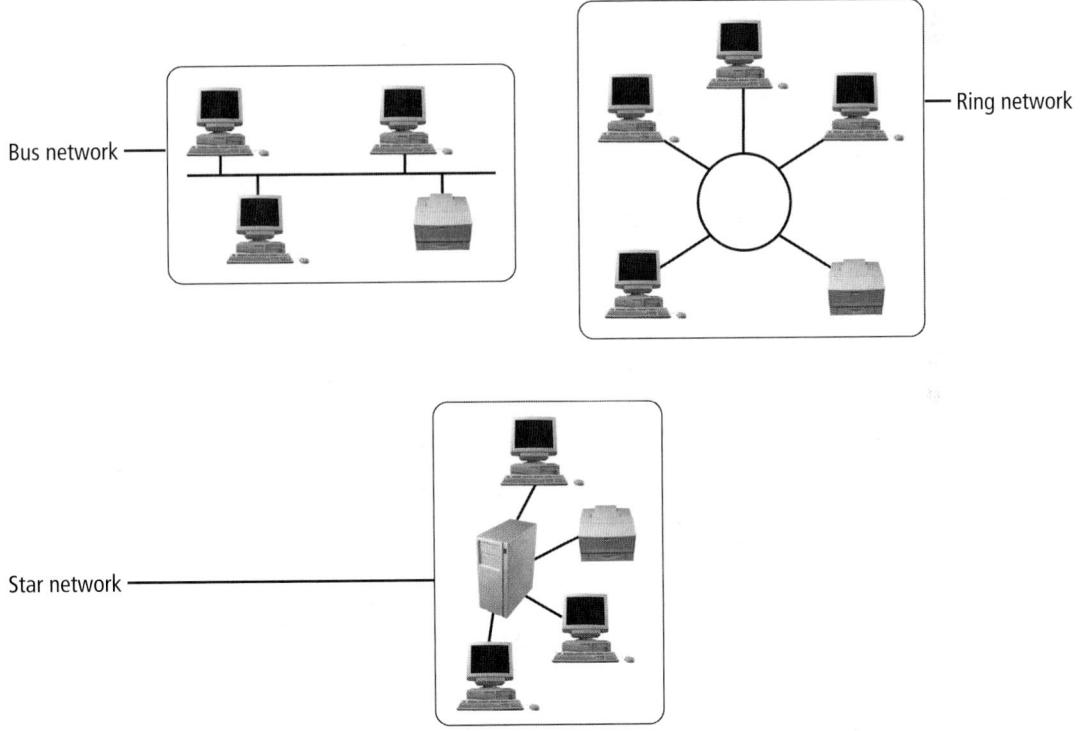

Figure 1.24

In general, networks can be categorized into two basic types geographically—local area networks (LANs) and wide area networks (WANs).

Local Area Networks (LANs)

Local area networks are networks established to connect computers and other hardware resources that are physically located in a relatively close space. They may all be in the same room, on the same floor of a building, or within the same building. Normally, LANs incorporate several smaller networks that may mix and match network topographies. For example, a star network from one office may connect to another star network in the building using a bus line. Most computers in a lab or building are connected using a LAN.

Wide Area Networks (WANs)

Wide area networks are networks established to connect computers and other hardware resources across a broader geographic area, such as across campus, across town, or across the country. Many WANs connect multiple LANs to form a much larger network. Telephone lines, digital cable lines, DLS lines, and fiberoptic lines are often used to connect resources to other resources or to resources of LANs and WANs. In many cases, hubs—computers or other connection devices that allow multiple network resources to connect to another device—provide a connection point to join the networks. In addition, a **bridge** or **gateway** may be used to connect the networks. A bridge connects two networks that contain similar hardware and other devices such as a LAN from a company office in one city with a LAN for the same company office in another city. A gateway enables hardware on one network to communicate with hardware and other resources on a different type of network.

The Internet is a great example of a WAN that spans the world. It is by far the largest known network that connects millions of LANs and WANs. To connect to the Internet, most LANs and WANs require a gateway to ensure that their hardware can communicate with the technology available on the Internet. Figure 1.25 shows how a LAN might connect to another LAN, to a WAN, and to the Internet.

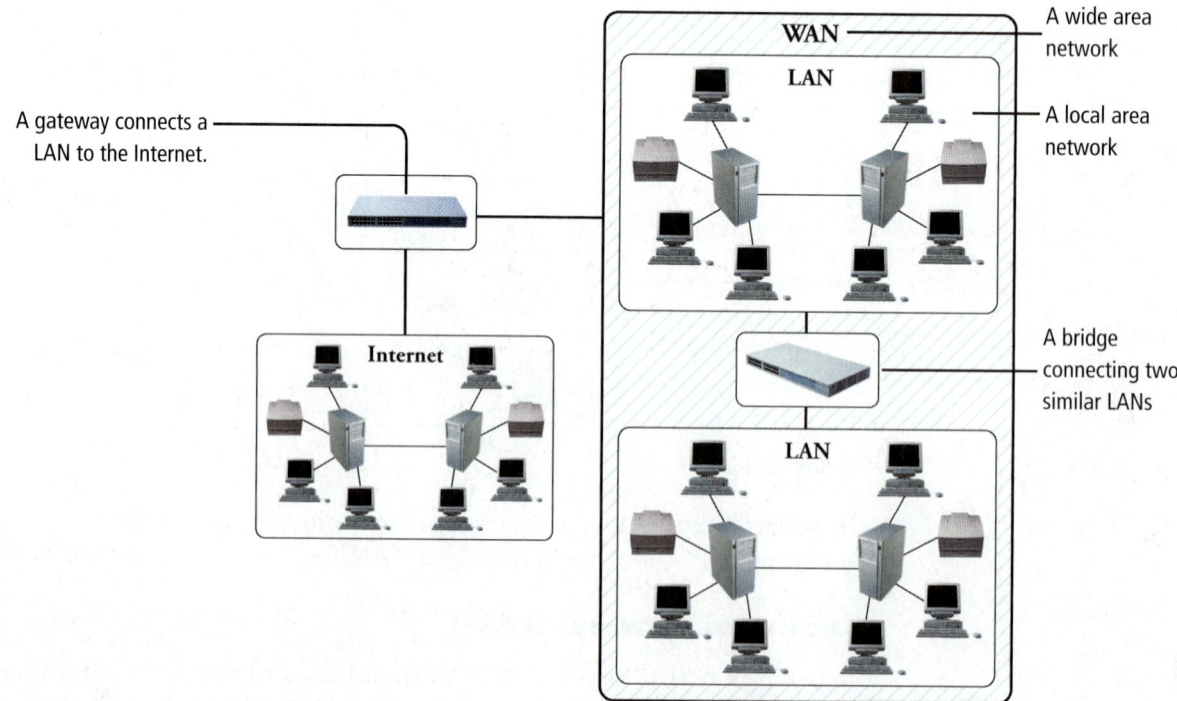

Figure 1.25

Computer Concepts
chapter one

Summary

In this chapter, you explored the basic components required to form a computer system, identified different types of computers, and learned about computer networks. You reviewed terms commonly associated with measuring computer storage and memory capacity as well as terms associated with determining computer speed. You identified common pieces of hardware used for input, output, and storage and learned what pieces of the computer system are housed in the system or console unit. You also explored the basic types of computer software—operating systems software and applications software—and learned how each type of software is used.

In This Chapter You Learned How To

- Correlate terms associated with measuring memory and disk storage capacity
- Define what a computer is and the four basic components required to form the system
- Describe hardware units used for input, output, and storage
- Describe types of networks and how they connect
- Determine the speed of a computer
- Identify hardware units that fit inside the system or console unit
- Identify types and sizes of computers
- Identify types of software and how they are used

Computer Concepts
chapter one

Concepts Assessments

Matching Matching each term in the second column with its correct definition in the first column by writing the letter of the term on the blank line in front of the correct definition.

____ 1. Computer programs.

____ 2. Programs that enable you to accomplish the tasks that you need to complete using the computer.

____ 3. Two or more computers connected in some way so that they can share hardware (printers, storage devices), software programs, data, and other resources.

____ 4. A computer to which other computers on a network are connected.

____ 5. Computers connected to a server/host on a network.

____ 6. The layout or design/arrangement of computers connected to a network.

____ 7. A connection between two networks that contain similar hardware and other devices.

____ 8. An electronic system that contains input, processing, output, and storage units.

____ 9. The physical components of a computer system.

____ 10. Hardware connected outside the main computer system unit.

____ 11. The hardware unit that contains the CPU, memory, hard disk, and power supply.

____ 12. The unit that contains the circuitry that enables a computer system to operate.

____ 13. The temporary storage available inside the computer.

____ 14. The processing unit.

____ 15. Spaces inside the computer console unit that enable you to add circuit boards to connect additional hardware.

A Applications software

B Bridge

C Computer

D Computer network

E Console/system unit

F CPU

G Expansion slots

H Hardware

I Memory (RAM)

J Motherboard/system board

K Peripherals

L Server/host

M Software

N Topography

O Workstations

158 Computer Concepts | Chapter 1: Basic Computer Concepts

Computer Concepts
chapter one

Concepts Assessments (continued)

Fill in the Blank Write the correct answer in the space provided for each statement.

1. The largest size of computer is the _____.

2. Four components required to form a computer system are _____, _____, _____, and _____.

3. The disk drive that is fixed inside the computer console is the _____ drive.

4. Another name for a laptop computer is _____.

5. A byte represents a _____.

6. A _____ connects computer networks that consist of different computer technologies.

7. A _____ enables numerous network recourses to "plug into" a single resource.

8. A _____ computer is a computer that is connected to a network.

9. _____ enables the computer to start and checks the system each time you turn it on.

10. Computer devices and tools that enable you to work with and hear audio from the computer and add video to files are called _____ devices.

(**Fill in the Blank** continues on the next page)

Concepts Assessments (continued)

(Fill in the Blank continued)

11. The two parts to the central processing unit are the _____ and the _____.

12. Clarity on a computer monitor is call the _____ and it is measured in _____.

13. The processing speed of a computer is also referred to as the _____.

14. The quality of a printed page is measured in dpi, which is an acronym for _____.

15. Disks are a type of _____.

Computer Concepts
chapter one
Concepts Assessments (continued)

Multiple Choice Circle the letter of the item that correctly answers the question.

1. Which of the following requires one byte of storage?

    a. Page

    b. Paragraph

    c. Sentence

    d. Character

2. Which of the following terms represents the fastest computer speed?

    a. 733 MHz

    b. 286 MHz

    c. 2 GHz

    d. 2 GB

3. Which of the following is *not* an input device?

    a. Keyboard

    b. Monitor

    c. Mouse

    d. Light pen

4. Which of the following is a storage device?

    a. Disk drive

    b. Monitor

    c. Memory

    d. Disk

5. Which of the following is *not* a size of computer?

    a. Mainframe

    b. Multitask

    c. Minicomputer

    d. Supercomputer

6. Before data can be processed by the computer, where must it be stored?

    a. On a disk

    b. In computer memory

    c. In the control unit

    d. On the monitor

(**Multiple Choice** continues on the next page)

Concepts Assessments (continued)

(Multiple Choice continued)

7. What term, related to computers, means billions?

    a. Byte

    b. Mega

    c. Giga

    d. Hertz

8. Which of the following is *not* a type of microcomputer?

    a. Desktop

    b. Laptop/notebook

    c. Personal digital assistant

    d. Microprocessors

9. Which of the following represents the largest amount of computer memory?

    a. Kilobyte (KB)

    b. Megabyte (MB)

    c. Gigabyte (GB)

    d. They are all equal.

10. What type of disk normally stores the greater amount of data?

    a. Floppy disk

    b. CD

    c. Zip® disk

    d. Hard disk

Word 2003

chapterone

ng Documents
crosoft Word
2003

In this chapter you will: complete these projects and practice these skills.

Project 1A **Exploring Microsoft Word**	**Objectives** • Explore and Navigate the Word Window • View Documents • Use the Spelling and Grammar Checker • View Headers and Footers • Organize, Save, and Print Documents
Project 1B **Creating, Editing, and Printing a Document**	**Objectives** • Create and Edit a New Document • Select and Format Text • Preview and Print Documents, Close a Document, and Close Word • Use the Microsoft Help System

The Perfect Party

The Perfect Party store, owned by two partners, provides a wide variety of party accessories including invitations, favors, banners and flags, balloons, piñatas, etc. Party-planning services include both custom parties with pre-filled custom "goodie bags" and "parties in a box" that include everything needed to throw a theme party. Big sellers in this category are the Football and Luau themes. The owners are planning to open a second store and expand their party-planning services to include catering.

© Getty Images, Inc.

Getting Started with Microsoft Office Word 2003

Word processing is the most common program found on personal computers and one that almost everyone has a reason to use. When you learn word processing you are also learning skills and techniques that you need to work efficiently on a personal computer. Use Microsoft Word to do basic word processing tasks such as writing a memo, a report, or a letter. You can also use Word to do complex word processing tasks, including sophisticated tables, embedded graphics, and links to other documents and the Internet. Word is a program that you can learn gradually, adding more advanced skills one at a time.

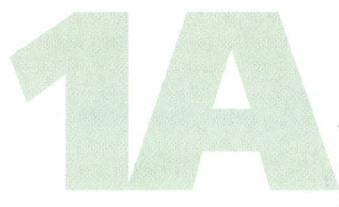

Project 1A Business Plan

With a word processing program, you can type, edit, move, and delete text or change the appearance of the text. Because the document is stored electronically, it can be duplicated, printed, copied, and shared with others. In this chapter, you will become familiar with the parts of the Word window and use the various views available in Word. Then you will create a document, edit and format text, and save and print your Word document.

In Activities 1.1 through 1.13 you will view and edit a business plan for The Perfect Party prepared by Paul Freire, a business planning consultant. Your completed document will look similar to Figure 1.1. You will save your document as *1A_Business_Plan_Firstname_Lastname.*

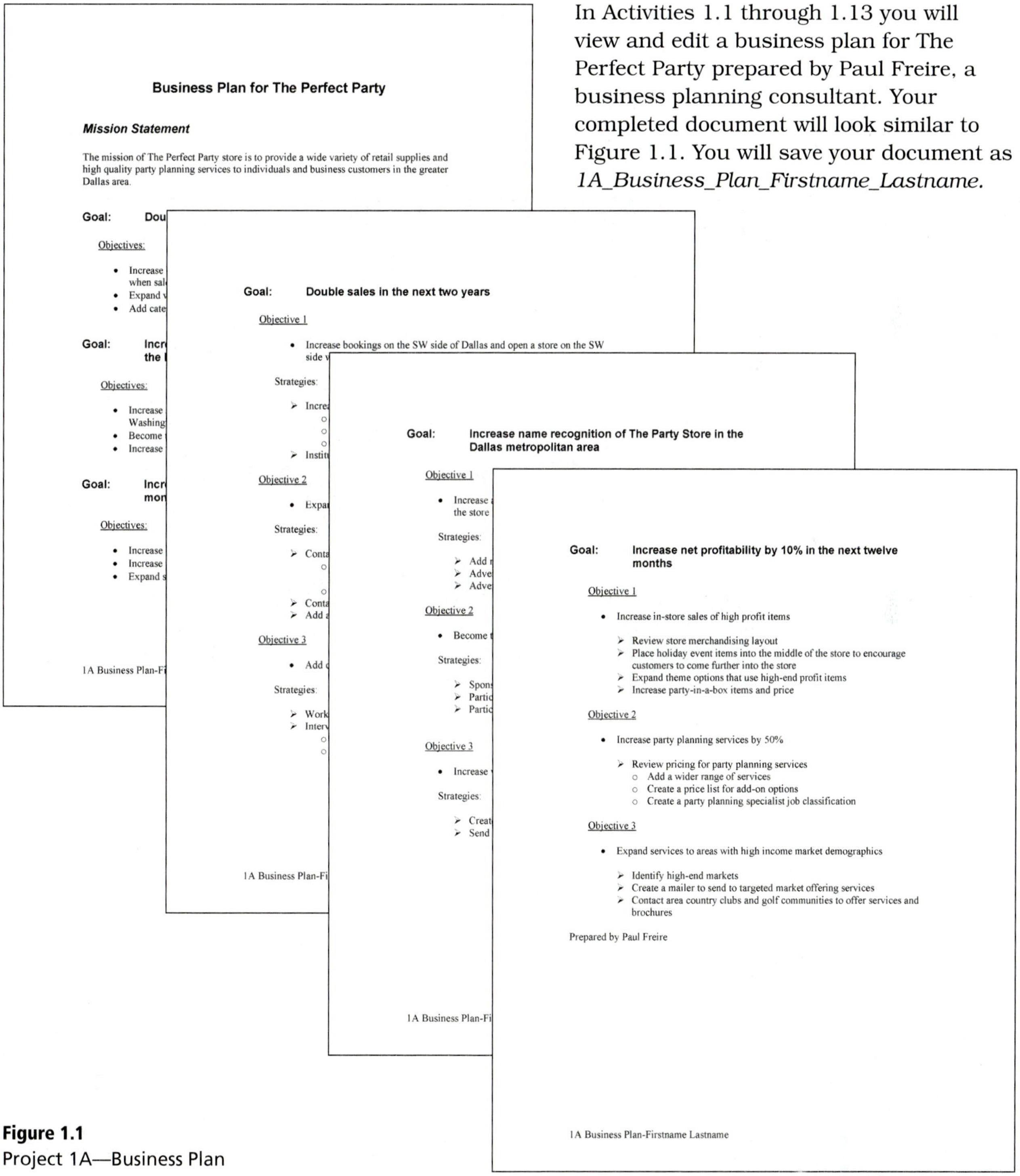

Figure 1.1
Project 1A—Business Plan

Project 1A: Business Plan | **Word**   165

Objective 1
Explore and Navigate the Word Window

Activity 1.1 Starting Word and Identifying Parts of the Word Window

1 On the left side of the Windows taskbar, point to and then click the **Start** button.

The Start menu displays.

2 On the computer you are using, locate the Word program and then click **Microsoft Office Word 2003**.

Organizations and individuals store computer programs in a variety of ways. The Word program might be located under All Programs or Microsoft Office or at the top of the main Start menu. Refer to Figure 1.2 as an example.

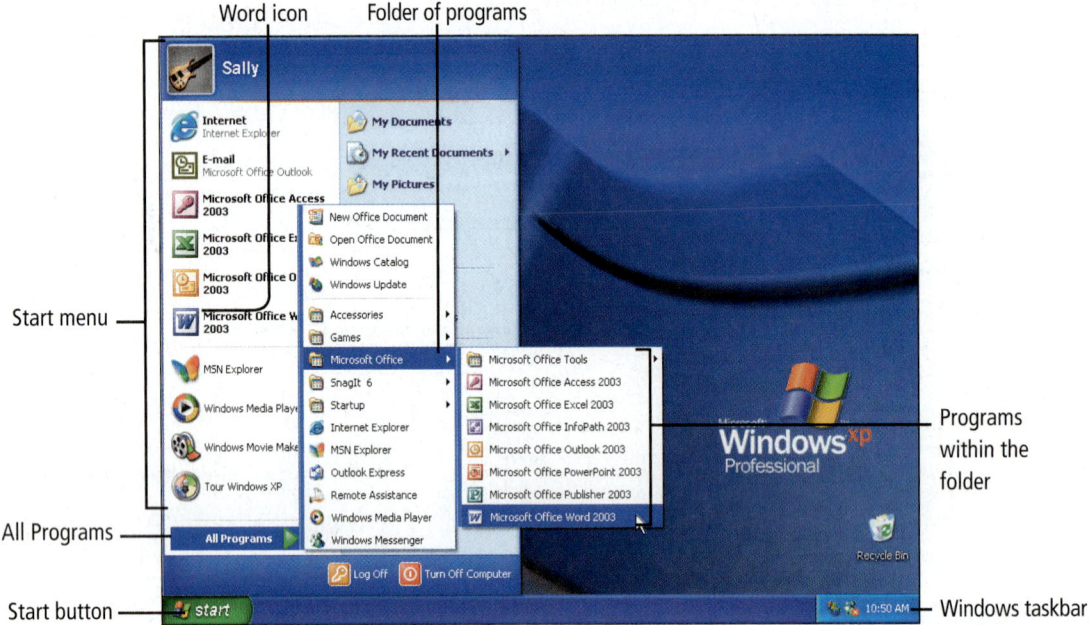

Figure 1.2

166   Word | Chapter 1: Creating Documents with Microsoft Word 2003

3 Look at the opening Word screen, and then take a moment to study the main parts of the screen as shown in Figure 1.3 and described in the table in Figure 1.4.

Alert!

Does your screen differ?
There are several ways to look at a document in the Word window. The appearance of the screen depends on various settings that your system administrator established when the program was installed and how the program has been modified since installation. In many cases, whether a screen element displays depends on how the program was last used.

4 On the Formatting toolbar, click the **Toolbar Options** button. If the Standard and Formatting toolbars are on two separate rows as shown in Figure 1.3, move the pointer into the Word document window and click to close the list without making any changes. If the toolbars are sharing a single row, click **Show Buttons on Two Rows**.

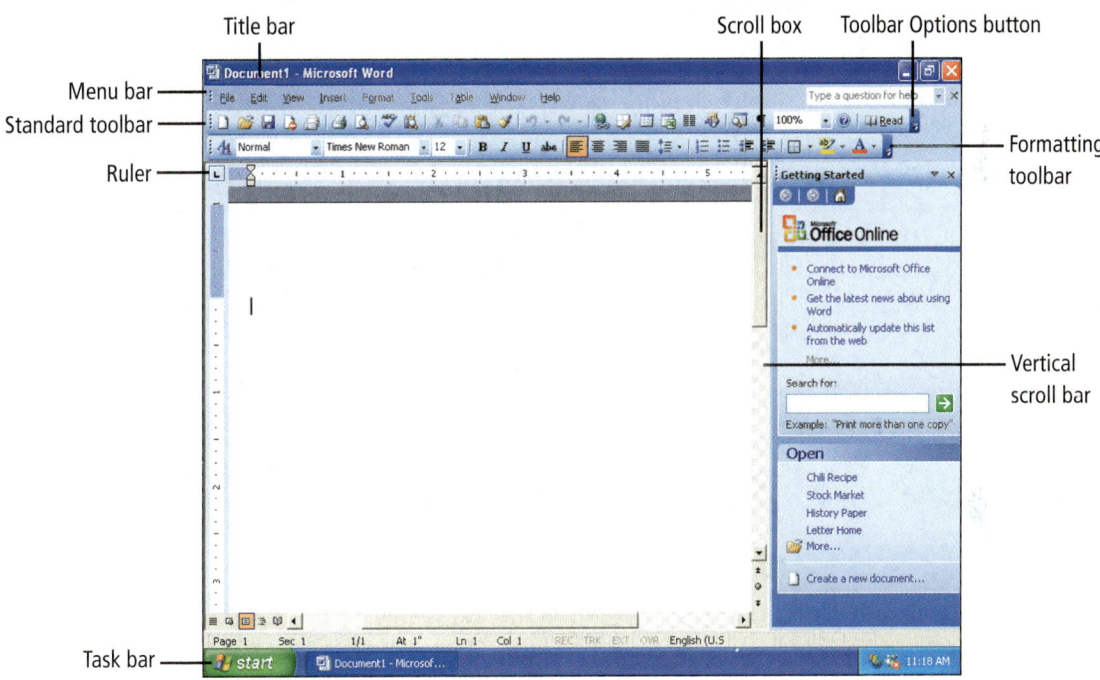

Figure 1.3a

Project 1A: Business Plan | **Word** 167

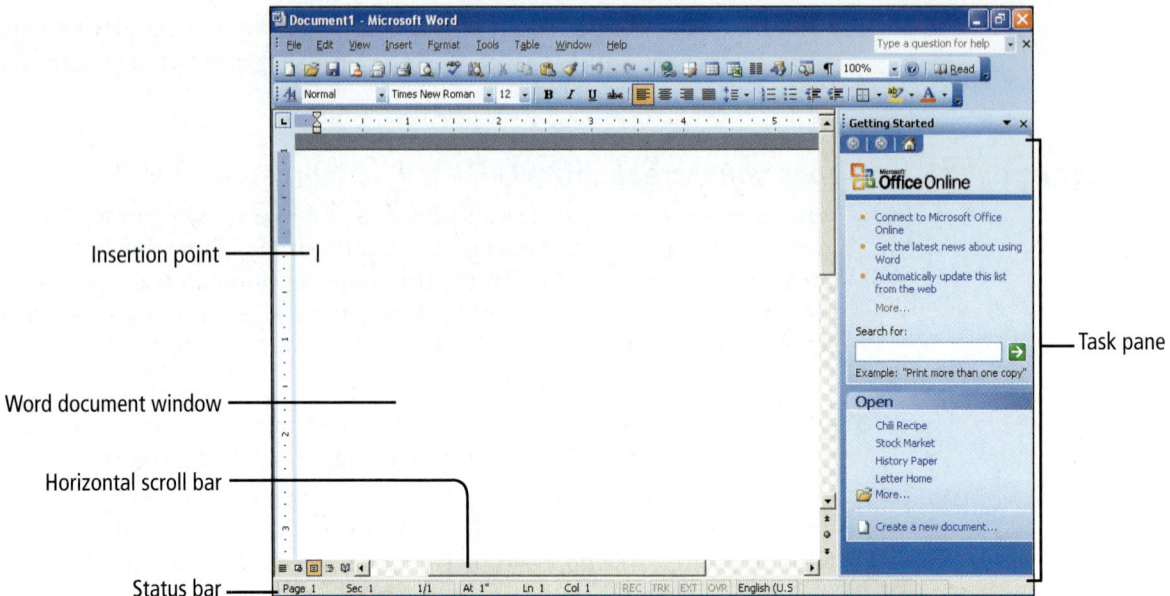

Figure 1.3b

It is easier to use the toolbars if all of the most commonly used buttons are displayed. Most Word users keep the Standard and Formatting toolbars displayed on separate rows.

> **More Knowledge** — Turning on Toolbars
>
> If a toolbar is missing entirely, point to an existing toolbar or to the menu bar and click the right mouse button (also known as right-clicking). On the shortcut menu that displays, point to the name of the toolbar you want to display and click the left mouse button. A shortcut menu is a context-sensitive menu of commands relevant to the particular item. Alternatively, display the View menu, click Toolbars, and then click the name of the toolbar you want to display. If a toolbar is open, a check mark displays to the left of the toolbar name.

Microsoft Word Screen Elements

Screen Element	Description
Title bar	Displays the program icon, the name of the document, and the name of the program. The Minimize, Maximize/Restore Down, and Close buttons are grouped on the right side of the title bar.
Menu bar	Contains a list of commands. To display a menu, click on the menu name.
Standard toolbar	Contains buttons for some of the most common commands in Word. It may occupy an entire row or share a row with the Formatting toolbar.
Formatting toolbar	Contains buttons for some of the most common formatting options in Word. It may occupy an entire row or share a row with the Standard toolbar.
Ruler	Displays the location of margins, indents, columns, and tab stops.
Vertical scroll bar	Enables you to move up and down in a document to display text that is not visible.
Horizontal scroll bar	Enables you to move left and right in a document to display text that is not visible.
Scroll box	Provides a visual indication of your location in a document. It can also be used with the mouse to drag a document up and down.
Toolbar Options button	Displays a list of all of the buttons associated with a toolbar. It also enables you to place the Standard and Formatting toolbars on separate rows or on the same row.
Word document window	Displays the active document.
Insertion point	Indicates, with a blinking vertical line, where text or graphics will be inserted.
Task pane	Displays commonly used commands related to the current task.
Taskbar	Displays the Start button and the name of any open documents. The taskbar may also display shortcut buttons for other programs.
Status bar	Displays the page and section number and other Word settings.

Figure 1.4

Activity 1.2 Opening an Existing Document

1 On the Standard toolbar, click the **Open** button.

The Open dialog box displays.

2 In the **Open** dialog box, click the **Look in arrow** at the right edge of the **Look in** box to view a list of the drives available on your system. See Figure 1.5 as an example—the drives and folders displayed on your screen will differ.

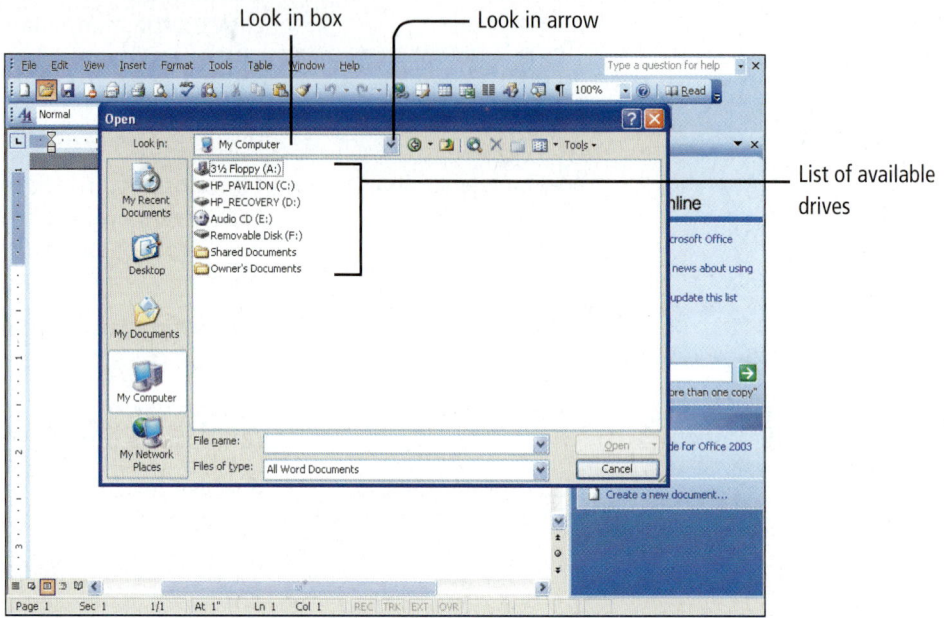

Figure 1.5

3 Navigate to the location where the student files for this textbook are stored.

4 Locate **w01A_Business_Plan** and click once to select it. Then, in the lower right corner of the **Open** dialog box, click the **Open** button. Alternatively, *double-click* the file name to open it—click the left mouse button twice in rapid succession.

The document displays in the Word window. See Figure 1.6.

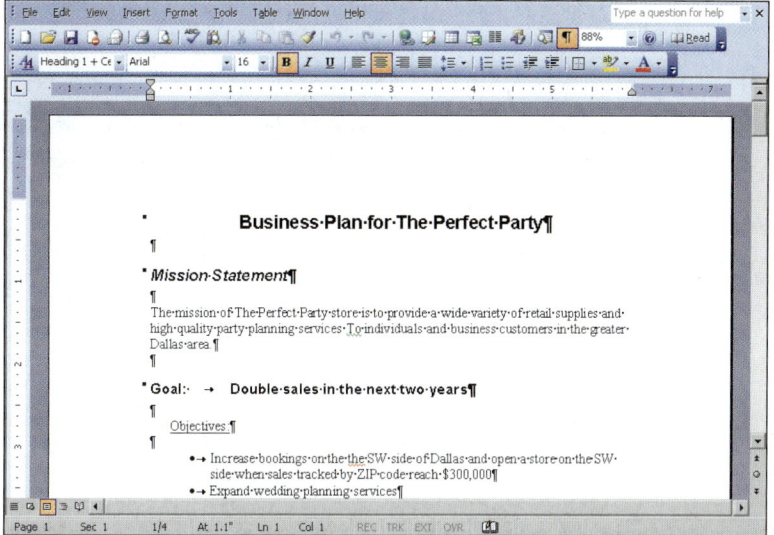

Figure 1.6

> **Note** — **Turning Off the Office Assistant**
>
> One of Word's Help features is an animated object called the Office Assistant. Many people like to turn this feature off. To hide the Office Assistant, click the right mouse button on the Office Assistant. In the menu that displays, click Hide with the left mouse button. The instruction in this textbook assumes that the Office Assistant is turned off.

Activity 1.3 Accessing Menu Commands and Displaying the Task Pane

Word commands are organized in *menus*—lists of commands within a category. The *menu bar* at the top of the screen provides access to the Word commands. The buttons on the toolbars provide one-click shortcuts to menu commands.

1 On the menu bar, click **View**.

The View menu displays in either the short format as shown in Figure 1.7, or in the full format, which displays all of the menu commands. If the full menu does not display, you can do one of three things:

- Wait a moment and the full menu will display if your system is set to do so.

- At the bottom of the menu, click the double arrows to expand the menu to display all commands.

- Before opening a menu, point to the menu name in the menu bar, and then double-click. This ensures that the full menu displays.

Project 1A: Business Plan | **Word** 171

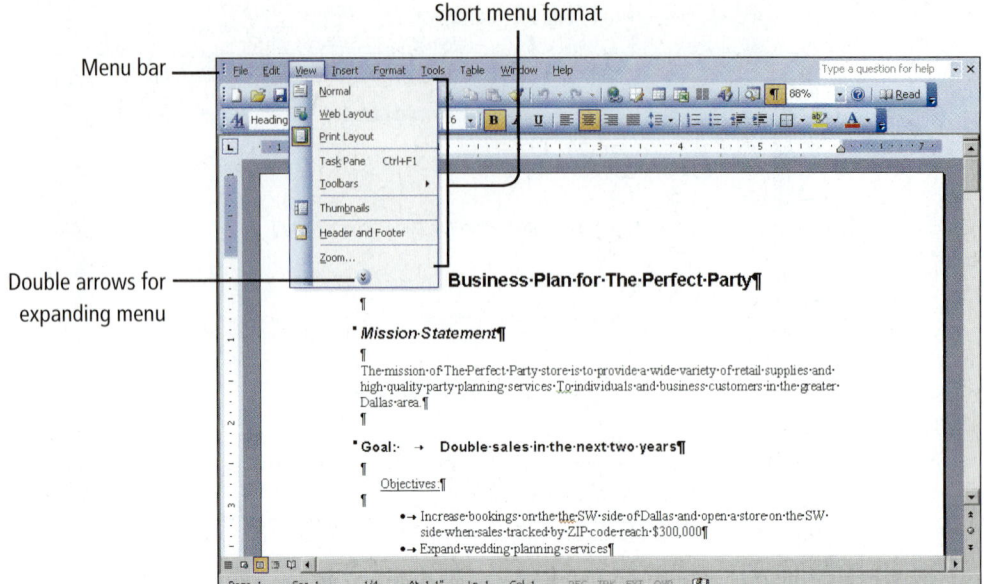

Figure 1.7

> **Note** — **Turning On Full Menus**
>
> The instruction in this textbook assumes that the full menus display when you click a menu command. To turn on full menus, go to the menu bar, click Tools, and then click Customize. In the Customize dialog box, click the Options tab, and then click the *Always show full menus* check box. Click the Close button to close the dialog box.

2 Be sure that the full menu is displayed as shown in Figure 1.8, and notice to the right of some commands there is a **keyboard shortcut**; for example, *Ctrl+F1* for the task pane.

A keyboard shortcut enables you to perform commands using a combination of keys from your keyboard. For example, if you press and hold down [Ctrl] and then press [F1], the result is the same as clicking View on the menu bar and then clicking Task Pane. Many commands in Word can be accomplished in more than one way.

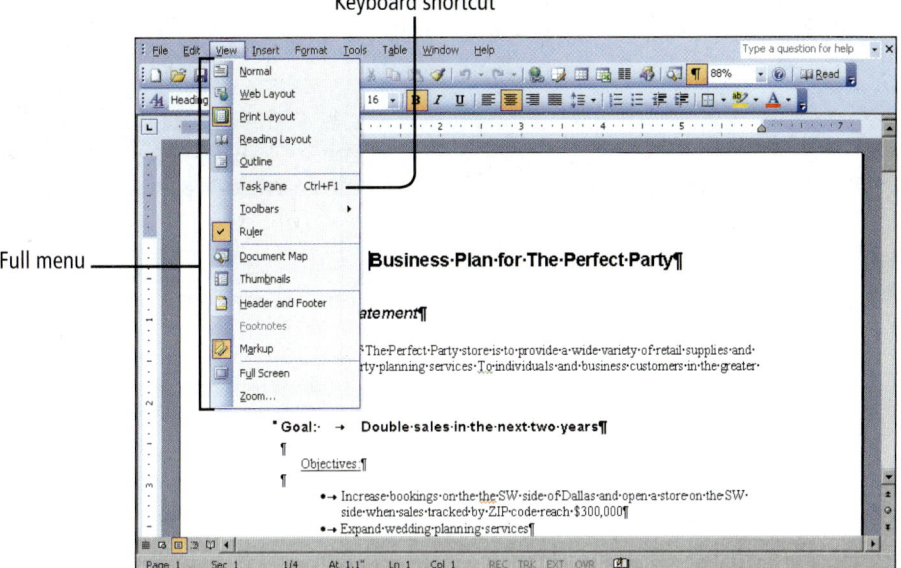

Figure 1.8

3. On the displayed **View** menu, to the left of some command names, notice the image of the button that represents this command on a toolbar.

   This is a reminder that you can initiate the command with one click from a toolbar, rather than initiating the command with multiple clicks from the menu.

4. On the displayed **View** menu, pause the mouse pointer over **Toolbars** but do not click.

   An arrow to the right of a command name indicates that a submenu is available. When you point to this type of menu command, a submenu displays. See Figure 1.9.

Project 1A: Business Plan | **Word** 173

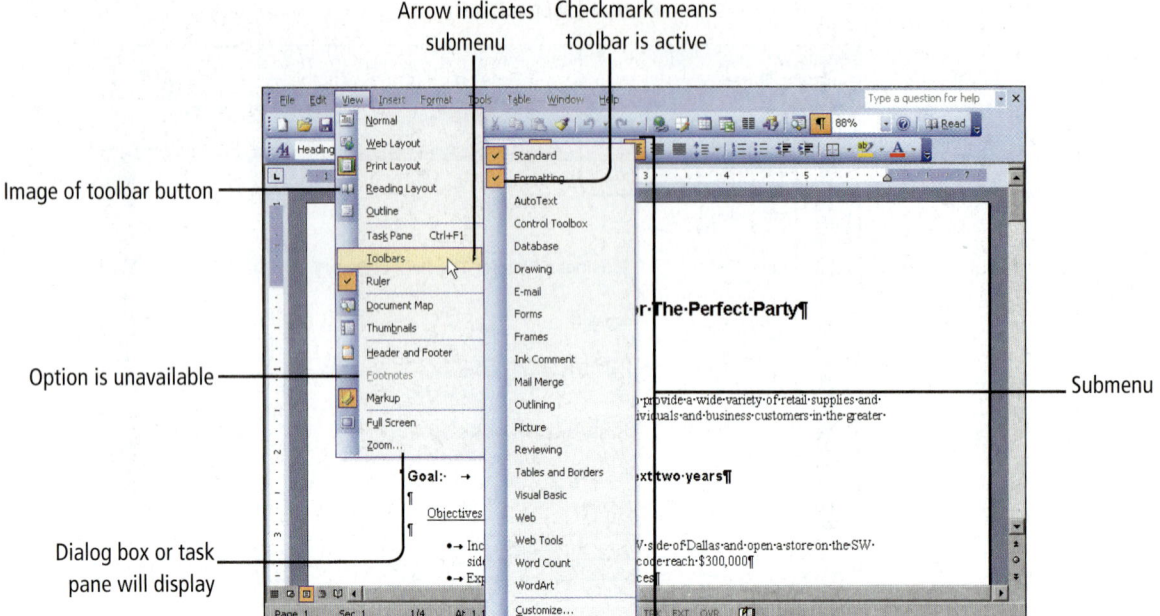

Figure 1.9

5 Look at the full **View** menu on your screen, and notice the various symbols and characters. These are standard across all Microsoft products. Take a moment to study the table in Figure 1.10 for a description of these elements.

Word Menu Characteristics

Characteristic	Description	Example
… (ellipsis)	Indicates that either a dialog box requesting more information or a task pane will display.	Zoom…
▶ (right arrow)	Indicates that a submenu—another menu of choices—will display.	Toolbars ▶
No symbol	Indicates that the command will perform immediately.	Web Layout
✔ (check mark)	Indicates that a command is turned on or active.	✔ Ruler
Gray option name	Indicates that the command is currently unavailable.	Footnotes

Figure 1.10

174   **Word** | Chapter 1: Creating Documents with Microsoft Word 2003

6 With the **View** menu still displayed, click **Task Pane**.

The Getting Started task pane displays as shown in Figure 1.11. If the task pane was already displayed, it will close. If the task pane was not visible, it will display on the right side of the screen. As you progress in your study of Word, you will see various task panes to assist you in accomplishing Word tasks.

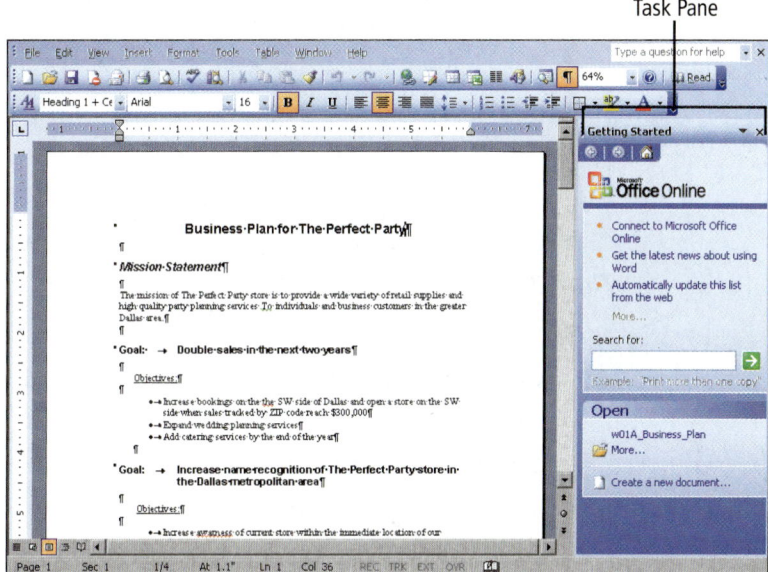

Figure 1.11

7 On the menu bar, click **View**, and then click **Task Pane** again to close the task pane.

For the remainder of this book the task pane should be closed, except when otherwise instructed.

Activity 1.4 Navigating a Document Using the Vertical Scroll Bar

Most Word documents are larger than the Word window. Therefore, there are several ways to ***navigate*** (move) in a document.

1 At the right of your screen, in the vertical scroll bar, locate the down arrow at the bottom of the bar as shown in Figure 1.12. Then, click the **down scroll arrow** five times.

Notice that the document scrolls up a line at a time. In this document, Word has flagged some spelling and grammar errors (red and green wavy lines), which you will correct in Activity 1.9.

Project 1A: Business Plan | **Word** 175

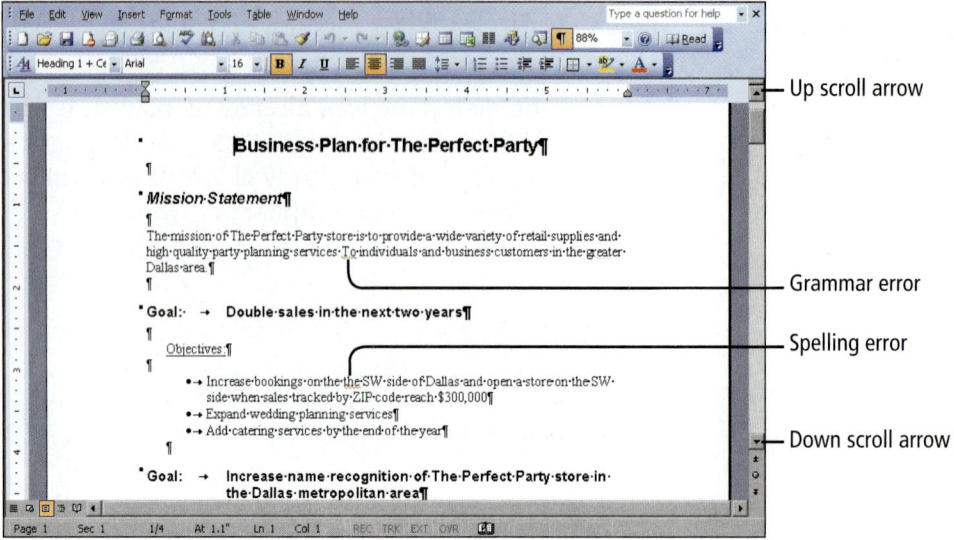

Figure 1.12

[2] Point to the **down scroll arrow** again, and then click and hold down the mouse button for several seconds.

The document text scrolls up continuously, a line at a time.

[3] At the top of the vertical scroll bar, point to the **up scroll arrow**, and then click and hold down the mouse button until you have scrolled back to the top of the document. As you do so, notice that the scroll box moves up in the scroll bar.

[4] At the top of the vertical scroll bar point to the scroll box, and then press and hold down the left mouse button.

A **ScreenTip**—a small box that displays information about, or the name of, a screen element—displays. In this instance, the ScreenTip indicates the page number and the first line of text at the top of the page. See Figure 1.13.

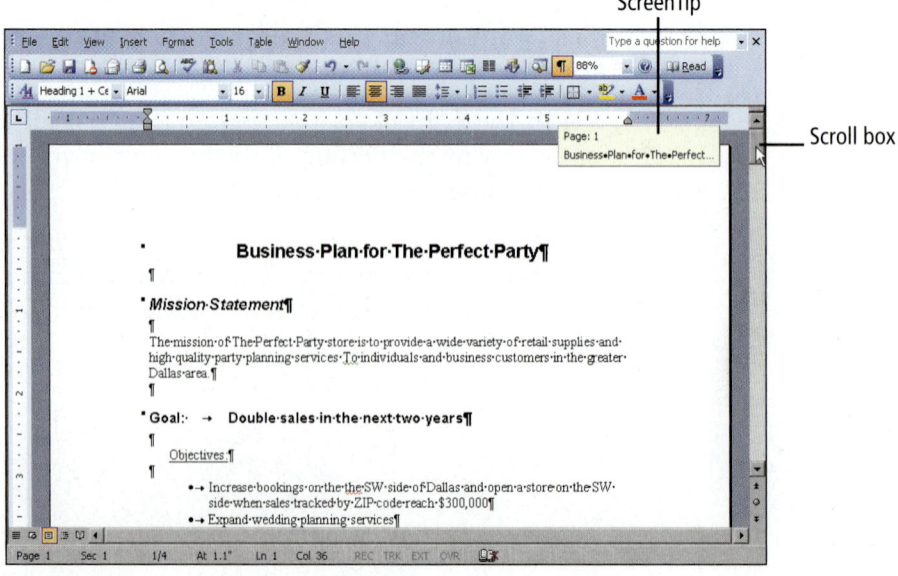

Figure 1.13

176   **Word** | Chapter 1: Creating Documents with Microsoft Word 2003

5 ***Drag*** (hold down the left mouse button while moving your mouse) the scroll box down to the bottom of the scroll bar. As you do so, watch the ScreenTip.

The ScreenTip changes as each new page reaches the top of the screen. See Figure 1.14.

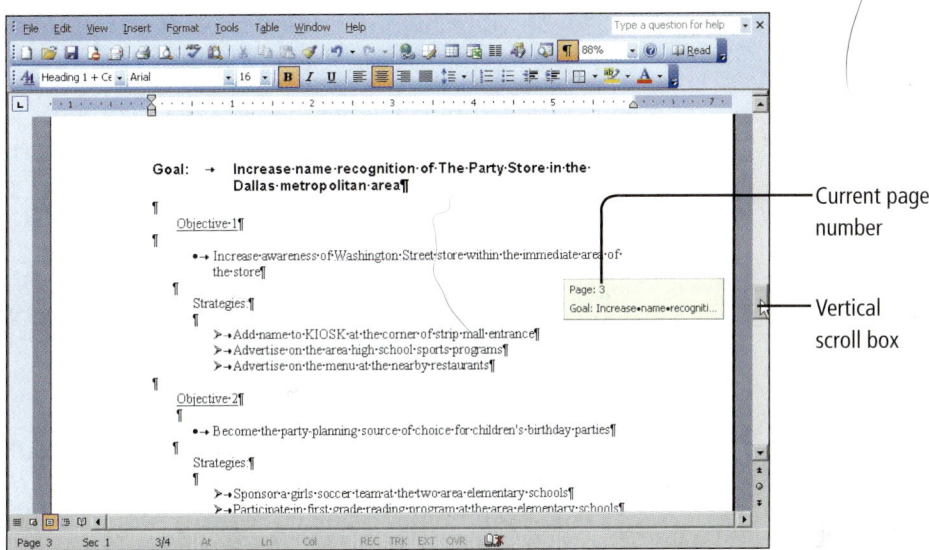

Figure 1.14

6 Release the mouse button, and then click in the gray area above the scroll box.

The document scrolls up one screen.

7 Practice clicking in the area above and below the scroll box.

This is a quick way to scan a document.

Another Way

Using the Wheel Button on the Mouse

If your mouse has a small wheel button between the left and right mouse buttons, you can scroll up and down in the document by rotating the wheel.

Activity 1.5 Navigating a Document Using the Keyboard

Keyboard shortcuts are another way to navigate your document quickly. Keyboard shortcuts provide additional navigation techniques that you cannot accomplish with the vertical scroll bar. For example, using keyboard shortcuts, you can move the insertion point to the beginning or end of a word or line.

1 On your keyboard, hold down [Ctrl] and press [Home].

The top of the document displays, and the insertion point moves to the left of the first word in the document.

2 Hold down [Ctrl] and press [End].

The text at the bottom of the last page in the document displays, and the insertion point moves to the right of the last word in the document.

3 Press [Page Up].

The document scrolls up one screen.

4 Press [End].

The insertion point moves to the end of the current line of text. Take a moment to study the table shown in Figure 1.15, which lists the most commonly used keyboard shortcuts.

Navigating a Document Using Keyboard Shortcuts

To Move	Press
To the beginning of a document	[Ctrl] + [Home]
To the end of a document	[Ctrl] + [End]
To the beginning of a line	[Home]
To the end of a line	[End]
To the beginning of the previous word	[Ctrl] + [←]
To the beginning of the next word	[Ctrl] + [→]
To the beginning of the current word (if insertion point is in the middle of a word)	[Ctrl] + [←]
To the beginning of the previous paragraph	[Ctrl] + [↑]
To the end of the next paragraph	[Ctrl] + [↓]
To the beginning of the current paragraph (if insertion point is in the middle of a paragraph)	[Ctrl] + [↑]
Up one screen	[Page Up]
Down one screen	[PageDown]

Figure 1.15

5 Hold down [Ctrl] and press [Home] to position the insertion point at the beginning of the document.

Objective 2
View Documents

In addition to different document views, there is a method to view characters on your screen that do not print on paper. Examples of these characters include paragraph marks, tabs, and spaces.

Activity 1.6 Displaying Formatting Marks

When you press [Enter], [Spacebar], or [Tab] on your keyboard, characters are placed in your document to represent these keystrokes. These characters do not print, and are referred to as *formatting marks* or *nonprinting characters*. Because formatting marks guide your eye in a document like a map and road signs guide you along a highway, these marks will be displayed throughout this instruction.

1 In the displayed document, look at the document title *Business Plan for The Perfect Party* and determine if a paragraph symbol (¶) displays at the end of the title as shown in Figure 1.16. If you do *not* see the paragraph symbol, on the Standard toolbar, click the **Show/Hide ¶** button ¶ to display the formatting marks.

Paragraph marks display at the end of every paragraph. Every time you press [Enter], a new paragraph is created, and a paragraph mark is inserted. Paragraph marks are especially helpful in showing the number of blank lines inserted in a document. Spaces are indicated by dots, and tabs are indicated by arrows as shown in Figure 1.16.

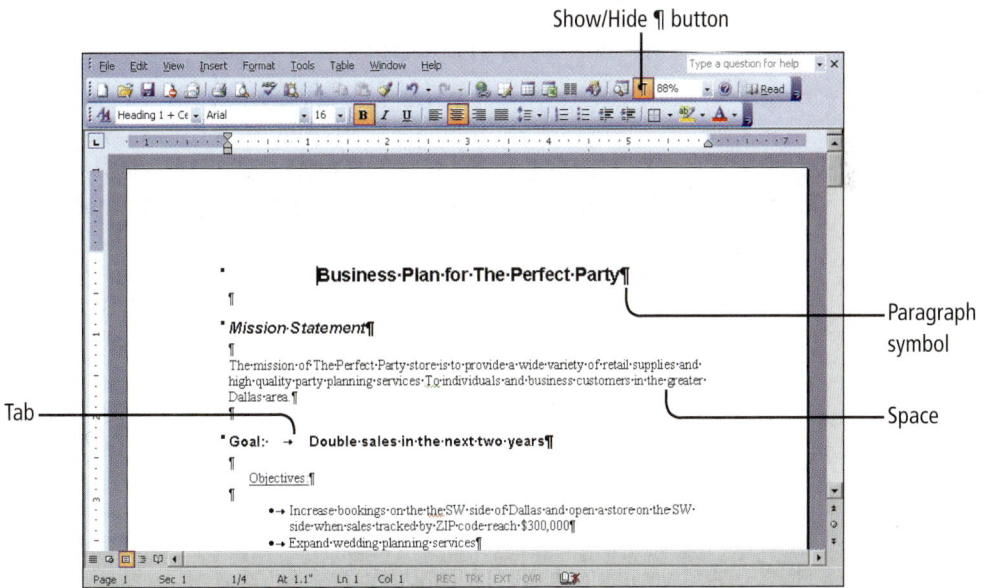

Figure 1.16

2 Click the **Show/Hide ¶** button ¶. This turns off the display of nonprinting characters. Then, click the **Show/Hide ¶** button ¶ once more to turn it on again.

Project 1A: Business Plan | **Word** 179

Another Way

Viewing Documents

There are five ways to view your document on the screen. Each view is useful in different situations.

- The Print Layout view displays the page borders, margins, text, and graphics as they will look when you print the document. Most Word users prefer this view for most tasks, and it is the default view.

- The Normal view simplifies the page layout for quick typing, and shows a little more text on the screen than the Print Layout view. Graphics, headers, and footers do not display.

- The Web Layout view shows how the document will look when saved as a Web page and viewed in a Web browser.

- The Reading Layout view creates easy-to-read pages that fit on the screen to increase legibility. This view does not represent the pages as they would print. Each screen page is labeled with a screen number, rather than a page number.

- The Outline view shows the organizational structure of your document by headings and subheadings and can be collapsed and expanded to look at individual sections of a document.

Activity 1.7 Changing Views

1 To the left of the horizontal scroll bar, locate the **View buttons**.

These buttons are used to switch to different document views. Alternatively, you can switch views using the commands on the View menu.

2 Click the **Normal View** button.

The work area covers the entire width of the screen. See Figure 1.17. Page margins are not displayed, and any inserted graphics, **headers**, or **footers** do not display. A header is information at the top of every page, and a footer is information at the bottom of every printed page.

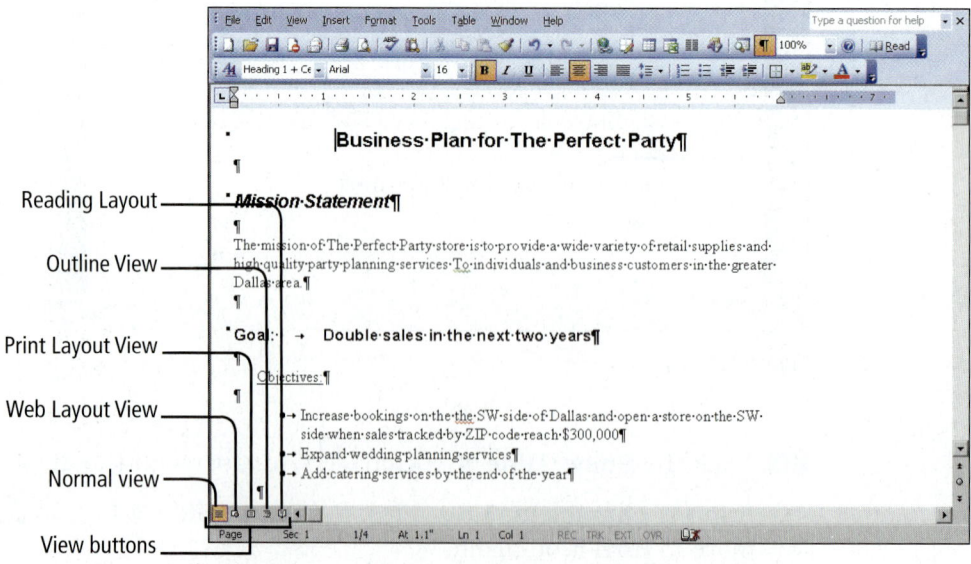

Figure 1.17

180   **Word** | Chapter 1: Creating Documents with Microsoft Word 2003

3 Click the **Reading Layout** button.

An entire page is displayed, and the text reaches nearly to the bottom. However, this is only about half of the text that is actually on the page as it is formatted and if it were printed. This view has its own toolbars and is optimized for easy reading. You can display side-by-side pages in longer documents, and you can *edit*—make changes to—the document in this view.

> **Note** — Opening the Reading Layout view
>
> The Reading Layout view is also accessible by clicking the Read button on the Standard toolbar.

4 At the top of the screen, in the Reading Layout toolbar, click **Close** button.

Closing the Reading Layout view returns you to the previous view, which was Normal view.

5 At the left of the horizontal scroll bar, click the **Print Layout View** button.

In this view you can see all of the elements that will display on paper when you print the document. The instruction in this textbook will use the Print Layout View for most documents.

Activity 1.8 Using the Zoom Button

To *zoom* means to increase or to decrease the viewing area of the screen. You can zoom in to look closely at a particular section of a document, and then zoom out to see a whole page on the screen. It is also possible to view multiple pages on the screen.

1 On the Standard toolbar, click the **Zoom button arrow**.

The Zoom list displays as shown in Figure 1.18.

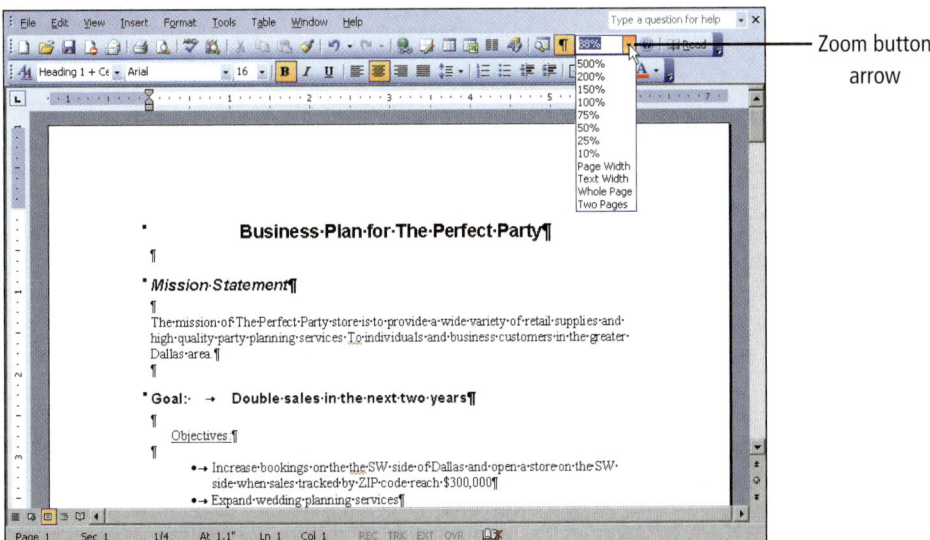

Figure 1.18

Project 1A: Business Plan | **Word** 181

2 On the displayed list, click **150%**.

The view of the text is magnified. See Figure 1.19.

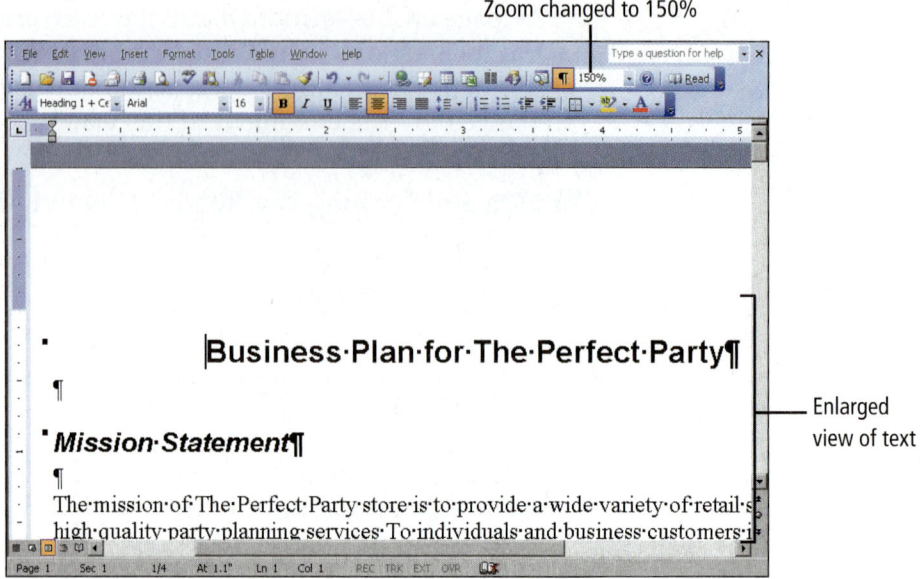

Figure 1.19

3 On the Standard toolbar, click the **Zoom button arrow** again and then click **Two Pages**.

Two full pages display on the screen. This magnification enables you to see how the text is laid out on the page and to check the location of other document elements, such as graphics.

4 On the vertical scroll bar, click the down scroll arrow five times.

Notice that you can now see parts of four pages, and you can see how the text flows from one page to another. See Figure 1.20.

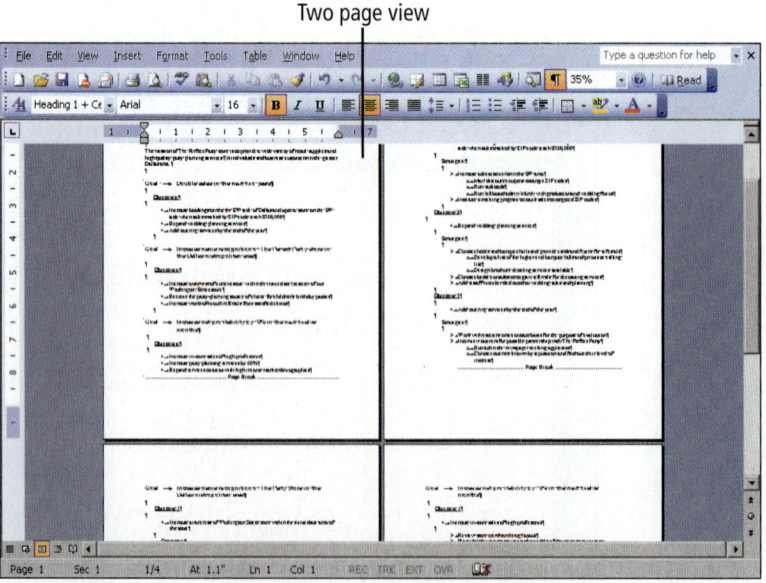

Figure 1.20

182 **Word** | Chapter 1: Creating Documents with Microsoft Word 2003

5 On the Standard toolbar, click the **Zoom button arrow** 100% and from the displayed list click **Page Width**.

This is a flexible magnification, displaying the maximum page width, regardless of the size of your screen. The size shown in the Zoom box will vary depending on screen size and resolution.

6 On the Standard toolbar, click on the number in the Zoom box to highlight the number currently displayed. Type **100** and then press Enter.

Typing a number directly into the Zoom box is another method of changing the zoom level.

Objective 3
Use the Spelling and Grammar Checker

As you type, Word compares your words to those in the Word dictionary and compares your phrases and punctuation to a list of grammar rules. Words that are not in the Word dictionary are marked with a wavy red underline. Phrases and punctuation that differ from the grammar rules are marked with a wavy green underline. Because a list of grammar rules applied by a computer program can never be exact, and because a computer dictionary cannot contain all known words and proper names, you will need to check any words flagged by Word as misspellings or grammar errors.

Finally, Word does not check for usage. For example, Word will not flag the word *sign* as misspelled, even though you intended to type *sing a song* rather than *sign a song*, because both are legitimate words contained within Word's dictionary.

Activity 1.9 Checking Individual Spelling and Grammar Errors

One way to check spelling and grammar errors flagged by Word is to right-click the flagged word or phrase and, from the displayed shortcut menu, select a suitable correction or instruction.

1 Hold down Ctrl and press Home to move the insertion point to the top of the document. Scan the text on the screen to locate green and red wavy underlines.

> **Note** — Activating Spelling and Grammar Checking
>
> If you do not see any wavy red or green lines under words, the automatic spelling and/or grammar checking has been turned off on your system. To activate the spelling and grammar checking, display the Tools menu, click Options, and then click the Spelling & Grammar tab. Under Spelling, click the *Check spelling as you type* check box. Under Grammar, click the *Check grammar as you type* check box. There are also check boxes for hiding spelling and grammar errors. These should not be checked. Close the dialog box.

2 In the second line of the *Mission Statement*, locate the word *To* with the wavy green underline. Position your mouse pointer over the word and right-click.

A shortcut menu displays as shown in Figure 1.21. A suggested replacement is shown in the top section of the shortcut menu. In this instance, Word has identified an incorrectly capitalized word in the middle of a sentence.

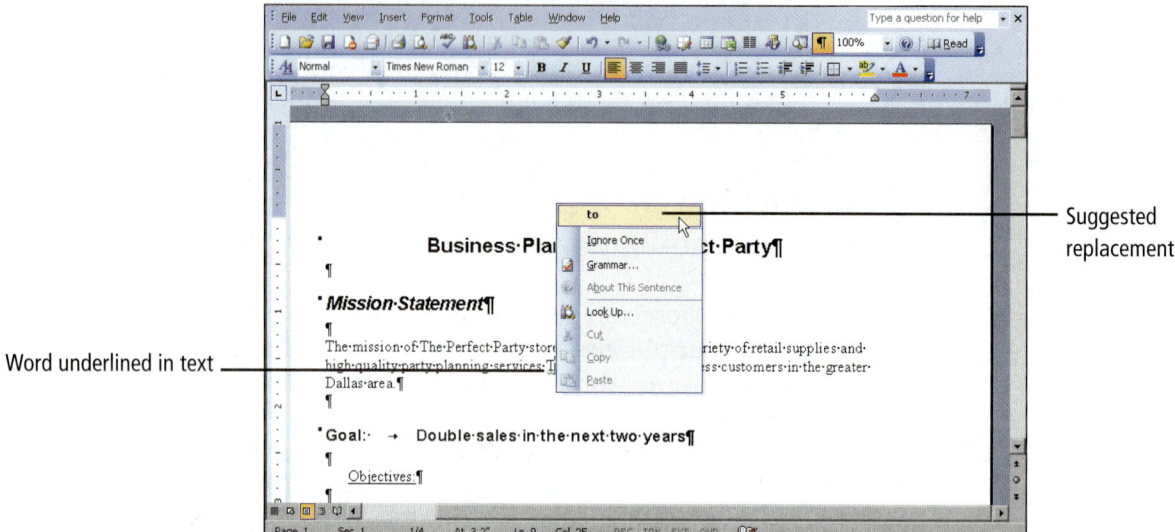

Figure 1.21

3 On the shortcut menu, click **to**.

The incorrect word is replaced.

4 In the first bullet point, find the word *the* with a wavy red underline. Position the mouse pointer over the word and right-click.

Word identified a duplicate word, and provides two suggestions—*Delete Repeated Word* or *Ignore*. See Figure 1.22. The second option is included because sometimes the same word will be used twice in succession.

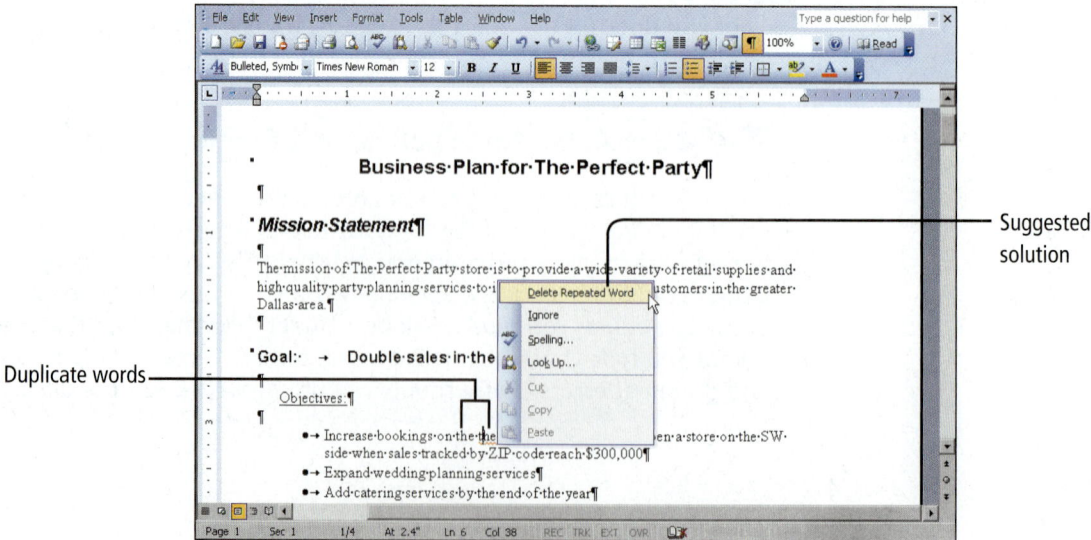

Figure 1.22

184   **Word** | Chapter 1: Creating Documents with Microsoft Word 2003

5 On the displayed shortcut menu, click **Delete Repeated Word**.

The repeated word is deleted.

Activity 1.10 Checking Spelling and Grammar in an Entire Document

Initiating the spelling and grammar checking feature from the menu or toolbar displays the Spelling and Grammar dialog box, which provides more options than the shortcut menus.

1 On the Standard toolbar, click the **Spelling and Grammar** button to begin a check of the document. If necessary, move your mouse pointer to the title bar of the dialog box, and drag the dialog box out of the way so you can see the misspelled word *awarness*.

The Spelling and Grammar dialog box displays. Under Not in Dictionary, a misspelled word is highlighted, and under Suggestions, two suggestions are presented. See Figure 1.23.

2 Take moment to study the spelling and grammar options available in the **Spelling and Grammar** dialog box as shown in the table in Figure 1.24.

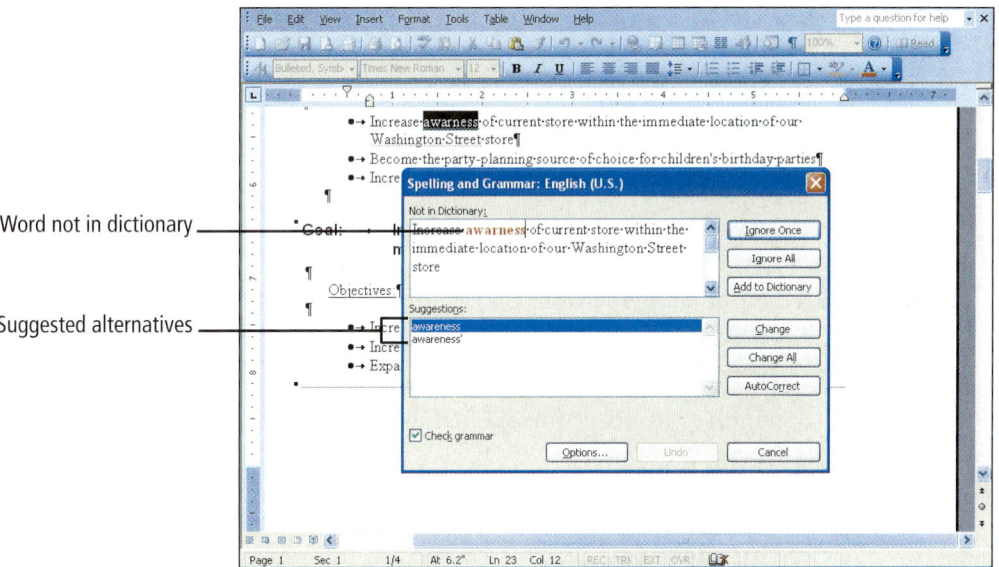

Figure 1.23

Spelling and Grammar Dialog Box Buttons

Button	Action
Ignore Once	Ignores the identified word one time, but flags it in other locations in the document.
Ignore All	Discontinues flagging any instance of the word anywhere in the document.
Add to Dictionary	Adds the word to a custom dictionary, which can be edited. This option does not change the built-in Microsoft Office dictionary.
Change	Changes the identified word to the word highlighted under Suggestions.
Change All	Changes every instance of the word in the document to the word highlighted under Suggestions.
AutoCorrect	Adds the flagged word to the AutoCorrect list, which will subsequently correct the word automatically if misspelled in any documents typed in the future.
Ignore Rule (Grammar)	Ignores the specific rule used to determine a grammar error and removes the green wavy line.
Next Sentence (Grammar)	Moves to the next identified error.
Explain (Grammar)	Displays the rule used to identify a grammar error.
Options	Displays the Spelling and Grammar tab of the Options dialog box.

Figure 1.24

3 Under **Suggestions**, make sure *awareness* is selected, and then click the **Change** button.

The correction is made and the next identified error is highlighted, which is another misspelled word, *merchandixing*.

4 Under **Suggestions**, make sure *merchandising* is selected, and then click the **Change** button.

The misspelled word is corrected, the next identified error is highlighted, and a number of suggestions are provided. This time the word is a proper noun, and it is spelled correctly. You could add this word to your dictionary, or choose to ignore it. See Figure 1.25.

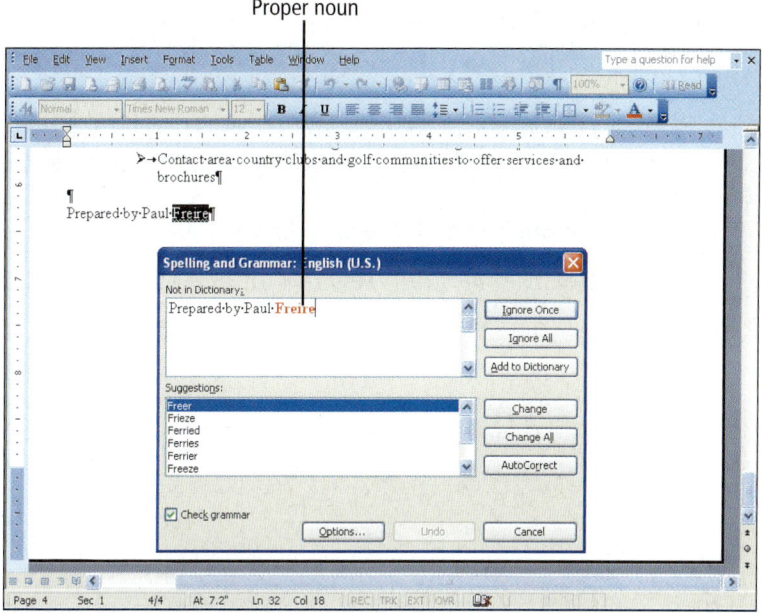

Figure 1.25

5 Click the **Ignore Once** button.

A dialog box displays indicating that the spelling and grammar check is complete. See Figure 1.26.

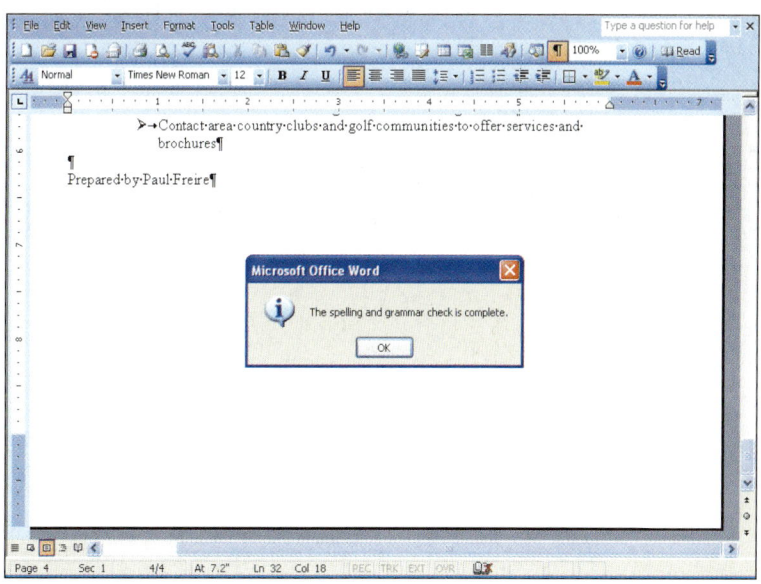

Figure 1.26

6 Click **OK** to close the dialog box.

Objective 4
View Headers and Footers

Headers and footers are areas reserved for text and graphics that repeat at the top (header) or bottom (footer) of each page in a document.

Activity 1.11 Accessing Headers and Footers

1 Display the **View** menu, and then click **Header and Footer**.

The first page of the document displays with the Header area outlined with a dotted line. By default, headers and footers are placed 0.5 inch from the top and bottom of the page, respectively. The Header and Footer toolbar displays, floating on your screen as shown in Figure 1.27.

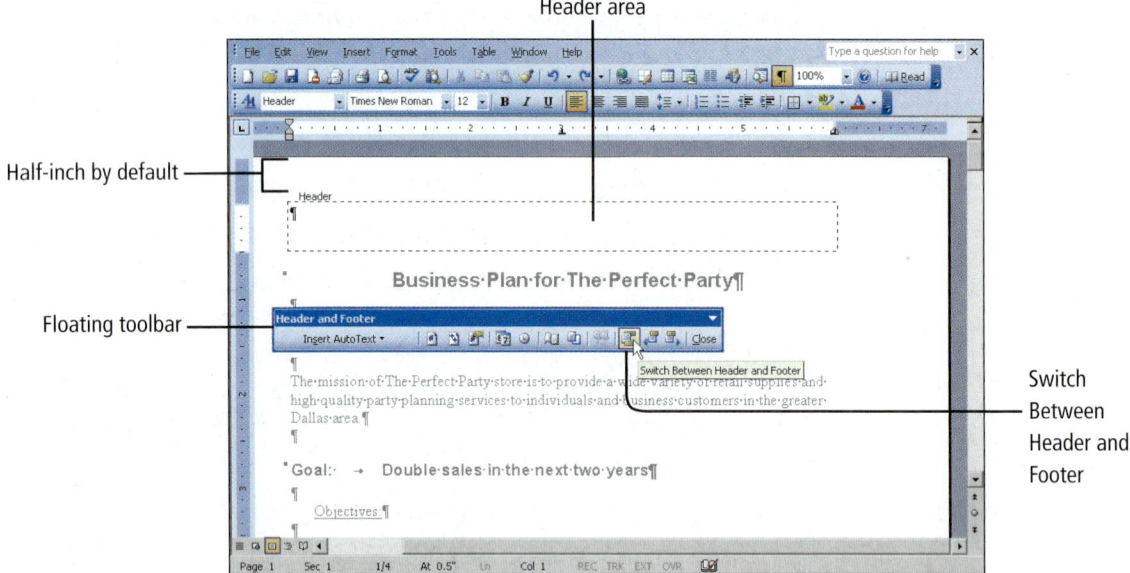

Figure 1.27

2 On the Header and Footer toolbar, click the **Switch Between Header and Footer** button.

The footer area displays with the insertion point blinking at the left edge of the footer area.

3 In the footer area, using your own name, type **1A Business Plan-Firstname Lastname** as shown in Figure 1.28.

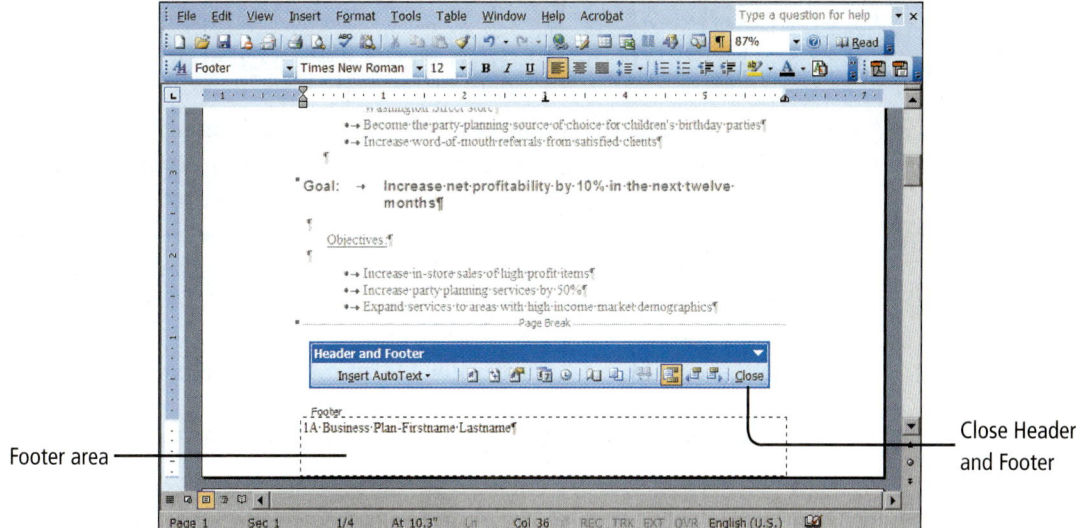

Figure 1.28

4 On the Header and Footer toolbar, click the **Close** button [Close]. Alternatively, double-click anywhere in the text area of the document to close the Header and Footer toolbar.

5 Scroll down until you can see the footer on the first page.

The footer displays in light gray as shown in Figure 1.29. Because it is a proper name, your name in the footer may display with wavy red lines.

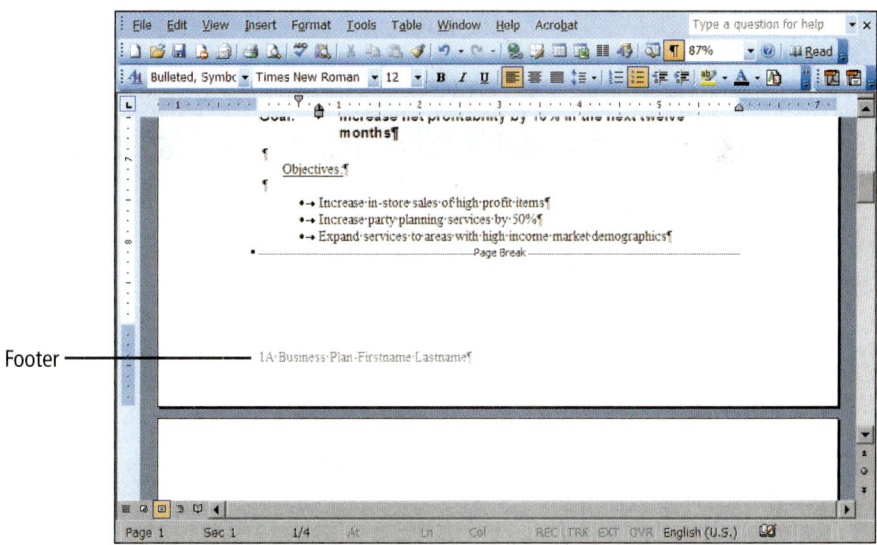

Figure 1.29

More Knowledge — Moving to the Header or Footer

A quick way to edit an existing header or footer is to double-click in the header or footer area. This will display the Header and Footer toolbar, and also place the insertion point at the beginning of the header or footer.

Project 1A: Business Plan | **Word** 189

Objective 5
Organize, Save, and Print Documents

In the same way that you use file folders to organize your paper documents, Windows uses a hierarchy of electronic folders to keep your electronic files organized. Check with your instructor or lab coordinator to see where you will be storing your documents (for example, on your own disk or on a network drive) and whether there is any suggested file folder arrangement. Throughout this textbook, you will be instructed to save your files using the file name followed by your first and last name. Check with your instructor to see if there is some other file naming arrangement for your course.

Activity 1.12 Creating Folders for Document Storage and Saving a Document

When you save a document file, the Windows operating system stores your document permanently on a storage medium—either a disk that you have inserted into the computer, the hard drive of your computer, or a network drive connected to your computer system. Changes that you make to existing documents, such as changing text or typing in new text, are not permanently saved until you perform a Save operation.

1 On the menu bar, click **File**, and then click **Save As**.

The Save As dialog box displays.

2 In the **Save As** dialog box, at the right edge of the **Save in** box, click the **Save in arrow** to view a list of the drives available to you as shown in Figure 1.30. Your list of drives and folders will differ from the one shown.

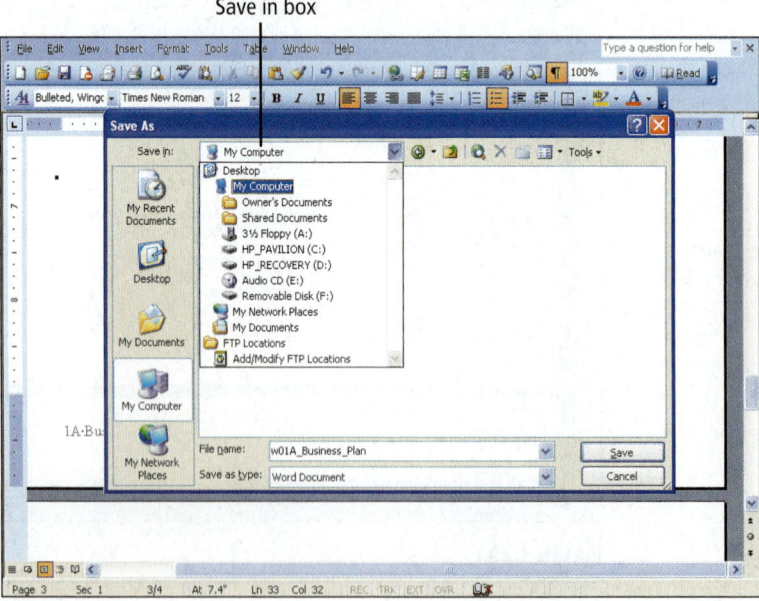

Figure 1.30

3 Navigate to the drive on which you will be storing your folders and projects for this chapter—for example, 3½ Floppy (A:) or the drive designated by your instructor or lab coordinator.

4 In the **Save As** dialog box toolbar, click the **Create New Folder** button.

The New Folder dialog box displays.

5 In the **Name** box, type **Chapter 1** as shown in Figure 1.31, and then click **OK**.

The new folder name displays in the Save in box, indicating that the folder is open and ready to store your document.

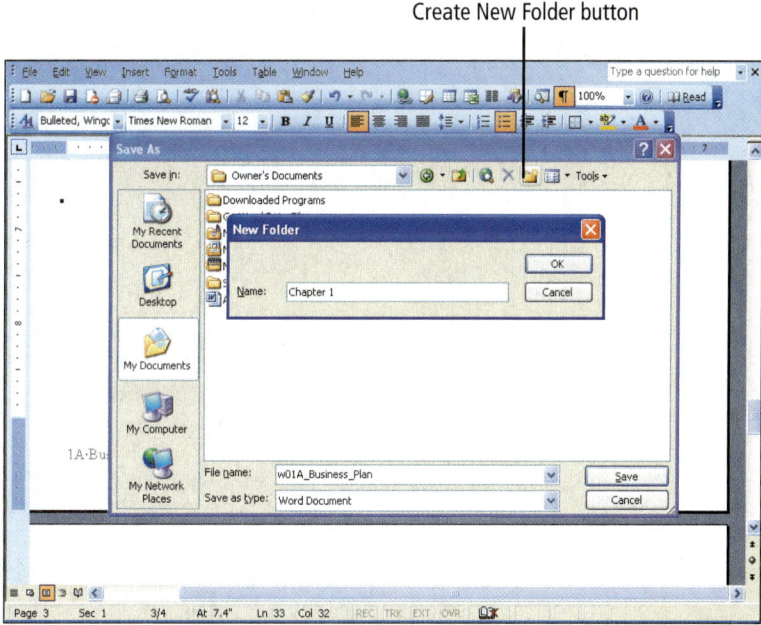

Figure 1.31

6 In the lower portion of the **Save As** dialog box, locate the **File name** box.

The file name *w01A_Business_Plan* may be highlighted in blue, in which case your new typing will delete the existing text.

More Knowledge — Renaming a Folder

You can rename folders as well as files. To rename a folder, right-click the folder in the Save As dialog box, click Rename from the shortcut menu, and then type a new folder name. This procedure also works in My Computer or Windows Explorer.

7 If necessary, select or delete the existing text, and then in the **File name** box, using your own first and last name, type **1A_Business_Plan_Firstname_Lastname** as shown in Figure 1.32.

The Microsoft Windows operating system recognizes file names with spaces. However, some Internet file transfer programs do not. To facilitate sending your files over the Internet using a course management system such as Blackboard, eCollege, or WebCT, in this textbook you will be instructed to save files using an underscore instead of a space. The underscore key is the shift of the ⌐ key, located two keys to the left of ←Bksp.

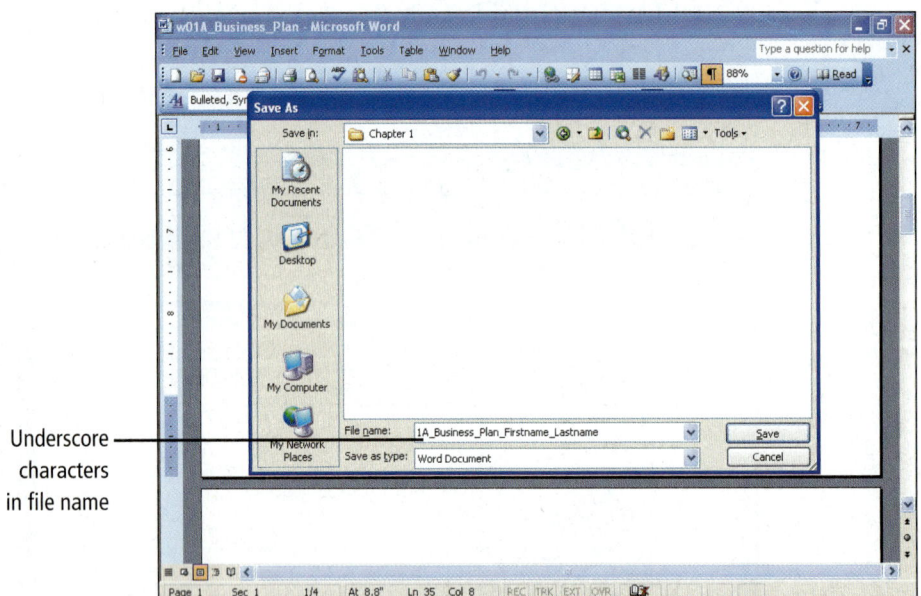

Underscore characters in file name

Figure 1.32

8 In the lower portion of the **Save As** dialog box, click the **Save** button, or press Enter.

Your file is saved in the new folder with the new file name.

More Knowledge — Saving Your Document Often

Save your documents frequently to avoid losing the information you have created in a new document or the changes you have made to an existing document. In rare instances, problems arise with your computer system or your electrical power source. After a document is saved, hardware or electrical problems will not harm your document. However, you could lose any new editing that you performed on the document after the last save operation.

Activity 1.13 Printing a Document from the Toolbar

In Activity 1.13, you will print your document from the toolbar.

1 On the Standard toolbar, click the **Print** button .

One copy of your document prints on the default printer. A total of four pages will print, and your name will print in the footer area of each page.

2 On your printed copy, notice that the formatting marks designating spaces, paragraphs, and tabs do not print.

3 From the **File** menu, click **Exit**, saving any changes if prompted to do so.

Both the document and the Word program close.

Another Way

Printing a Document

There are two ways to print a document:

- On the Standard or Print Preview toolbar, click the Print button, which will print a single copy of the entire document on the default printer.

- From the File menu, click Print to display the Print dialog box, from which you can select a variety of different options, such as printing multiple copies, printing on a different printer, and printing some but not all pages.

End You have completed Project 1A

Project 1B **Thank You Letter**

In Project 1A you opened and edited an existing document. In Project 1B you will create and edit a new document.

In Activities 1.14 through 1.22 you will create a letter from Gabriela Quinones, a co-owner of The Perfect Party, to Paul Freire, a business consultant who was involved in preparing the business plan. Your completed document will look similar to Figure 1.33. You will save your document as *1B_ Thanks_Firstname_Lastname*.

Figure 1.33
Project 1B—Thank you letter

194   Word | Chapter 1: Creating Documents with Microsoft Word 2003

Objective 6
Create and Edit a New Document

In Activities 1.14 through 1.17, you will practice the basic skills needed to create a new document, insert and delete text, and edit text.

Activity 1.14 Creating a New Document

1 Start Word. If necessary, close the Getting Started task pane by clicking the small Close button ⊠ in the upper right corner of the task pane.

When Word is started, a new blank document displays.

2 In the blue title bar, notice that *Document1* displays.

Word displays the file name of a document in both the blue title bar at the top of the screen and on a button in the taskbar at the lower edge of the screen—including new unsaved documents. The new unsaved document displays *Document1* or *Document2* depending on how many times you have started a new document during your current Word session. See Figure 1.34.

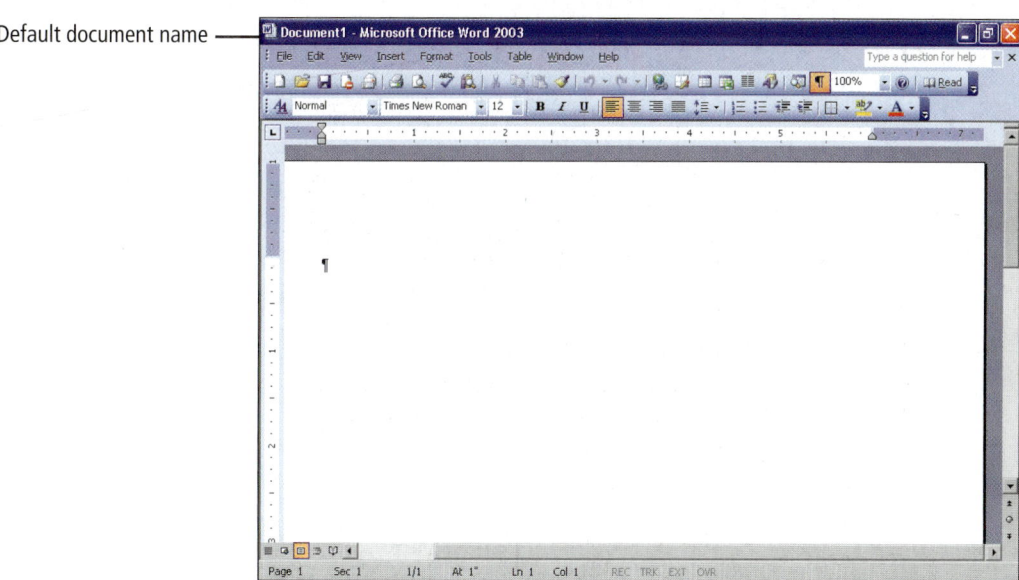

Default document name

Figure 1.34

Project 1B: Thank You Letter | **Word** 195

Another Way

Opening a New Document

There are five ways to begin a new document in Word:

- Start the Word program; a new blank document displays.
- On the Standard toolbar, click the New Blank Document button.
- From the menu bar, click File, and then click New.
- From the Getting Started task pane, under Open, click *Create a new document*.
- From the New Document task pane, under New, click *Blank document*.

Activity 1.15 Entering Text and Inserting Blank Lines

1 Verify that formatting marks are displayed. If necessary, click the Show/Hide ¶ button to display them. With the insertion point blinking in the upper left corner of the document to the left of the default first paragraph mark, type **Sept**

A ScreenTip displays *September (Press ENTER to Insert)* as shown in Figure 1.35. This feature, called **AutoComplete**, assists in your typing by suggesting commonly used words and phrases after you type the first few characters.

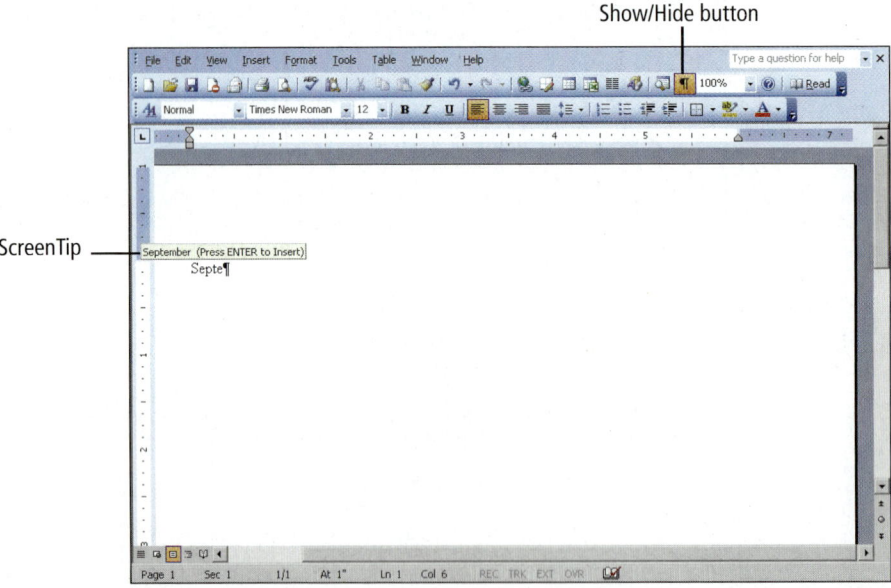

Figure 1.35

196 **Word** | Chapter 1: Creating Documents with Microsoft Word 2003

2 To finish the word *September*, press [Enter]. Press [Spacebar] once and then type **12, 2005** and press [Enter]. (If you are completing this activity during the month of September, AutoComplete may offer to fill in the current date. To ignore the suggestion, type as indicated.)

The first paragraph is complete and the insertion point is positioned at the beginning of the next line. A paragraph is created when you press [Enter]. Thus, a paragraph can be a single line like the date line, or a blank line.

A purple dotted underscore beneath the date indicates that Word has flagged this as a ***recognizer***. A recognizer indicates that Word recognizes this as a date. As you progress in your study of Microsoft Office, you will discover how dates such as this one can be added to other Office programs like Microsoft Outlook.

3 Press [Enter] three more times.

Three empty paragraphs, which function as blank lines, display below the typed date.

4 Type **Mr. Paul Freire** and then press [Enter].

5 On three lines, type the following address:

Business Consulting Services

123 Jackson Street, Suite 100

Dallas, TX 75202

6 Press [Enter] twice. Type **Dear Paul:** and then press [Enter] twice.

7 Type **Subject: Your participation in the planning retreat** and press [Enter] twice.

Compare your screen to Figure 1.36. The purple dotted line under the street address is another recognizer, indicating that you could add the address to your Microsoft Outlook address book or perform other useful tasks with the address. Additionally, the proper name *Freire* is flagged as misspelled because it is a proper name not contained in the Word dictionary.

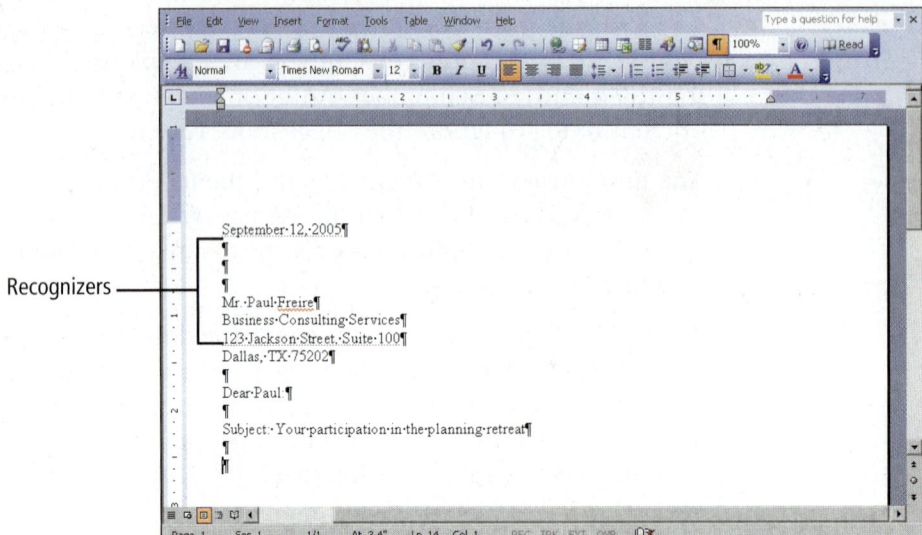

Figure 1.36

8 As you type the following text, press the [Spacebar] only once at the end of a sentence: **Thank you for participating in the retreat for The Perfect Party. We are really very excited about the next two years. One of the reasons our future looks so bright is because of the contributions you have made!** Press [Enter] twice.

As you type, the insertion point moves to the right, and when it reaches the right margin, Word determines whether or not the next word in the line will fit within the established right margin. If the word does not fit, Word will move the whole word down to the next line. This feature is ***wordwrap***.

Note — Spacing at the End of Sentences

Although you may have learned to press [Spacebar] twice at the end of a sentence, it is common practice now to space only once at the end of a sentence.

9 Type **I would also like to thank you personally for taking notes and also for summarizing the ideas expressed at the retreat.**

10 Press [Enter] two times. Type **Your** and when the ScreenTip *Yours truly, (Press ENTER to Insert)* displays, press [Enter] to have AutoComplete complete the closing of the letter.

11 Press [Enter] four times, and then type **Angie Nguyen**

Compare your screen to Figure 1.37.

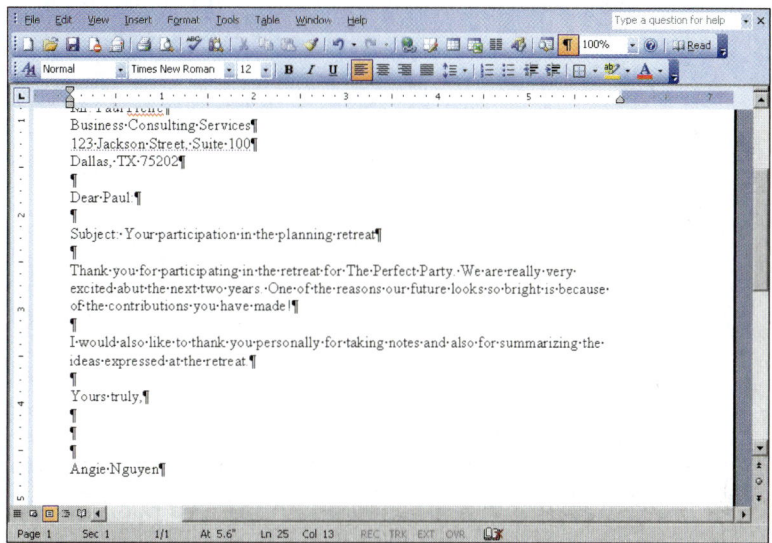

Figure 1.37

12 On the Standard toolbar, click the **Print Preview** button. If necessary, change the Zoom setting on the Print Preview toolbar to Whole Page to see the entire page as it will print.

Your document displays as it will print on paper. Notice that there is a large amount of blank space at the bottom of this short letter.

13 On the Print Preview toolbar, click **Close**. Display the **File** menu, and then click **Page Setup**.

14 On the displayed **Page Setup** dialog box, click the **Layout tab**. Under **Page**, click the **Vertical alignment arrow**. From the displayed list, click **Center** as shown in Figure 1.38.

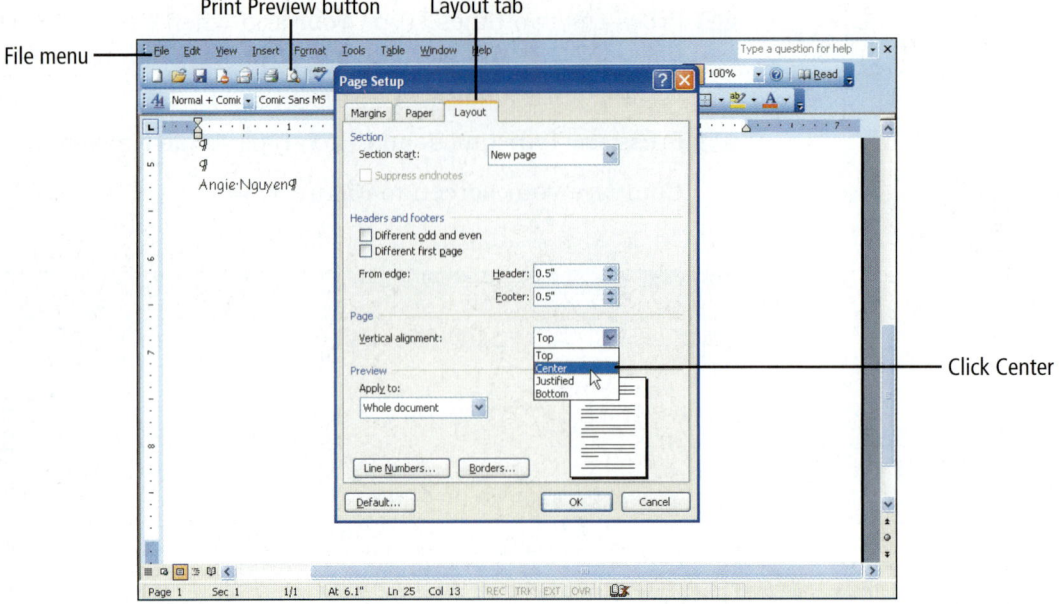

Figure 1.38

15. In the lower right corner of the **Page Setup** dialog box, click **OK**. On the Standard toolbar, click the **Print Preview** button.

    Your document displays as it will print on paper. The text is centered on the page between the top and bottom margin. You can see that vertically centering one-page letters results in a more attractive and professional looking document.

16. On the Print Preview toolbar, click the **Close** button. On the Standard toolbar, click the **Save** button.

    Because this document has never been saved, the Save As dialog box displays.

17. Use the **Save in arrow** to navigate to the **Chapter 1 folder** that you created in your storage location. In the lower portion of the **Save As** dialog box, in the **File name** box, delete any existing text and then type **1B_Thanks_Firstname_Lastname**

    Make sure you type your own first name and last name as the last two parts of the new file name.

18. In the lower right portion of the **Save As** dialog box, click the **Save** button or press Enter.

    Your file is saved in your Chapter 1 folder with the new file name.

Activity 1.16 Editing Text with the Delete and Backspace Keys

1 Scroll as necessary to view the upper portion of your document. In the paragraph beginning *Thank you*, at the end of the first line, click to position your insertion point to the left of the word *very*.

The insertion point is blinking to the left of the word *very*.

2 Press ←Bksp once.

The space between the words *really* and *very* is removed. See Figure 1.39.

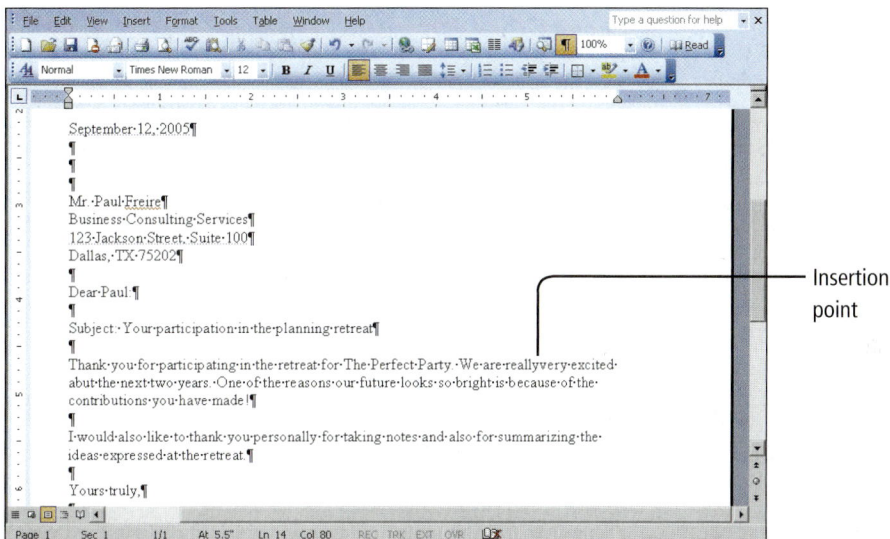

Figure 1.39

3 With the insertion point between the two words, press ←Bksp six times.

The word *really* is removed. Make sure there is only one dot (dots are the formatting marks that indicate spaces) between *are* and *very*. You can see that when editing text, it is useful to display formatting marks.

4 In the paragraph beginning *I would*, in the first line, locate the phrase *for summarizing* and then click to position the insertion point to the left of the word *for*.

5 Press ←Bksp five times.

The word *also* and the space between the words is removed.

6 Press Delete four times.

The word *for* to the right of the insertion point is removed, along with the space following the word. Make sure there is only one dot (space) between *and* and *summarizing*. See Figure 1.40.

Project 1B: Thank You Letter | **Word** 201

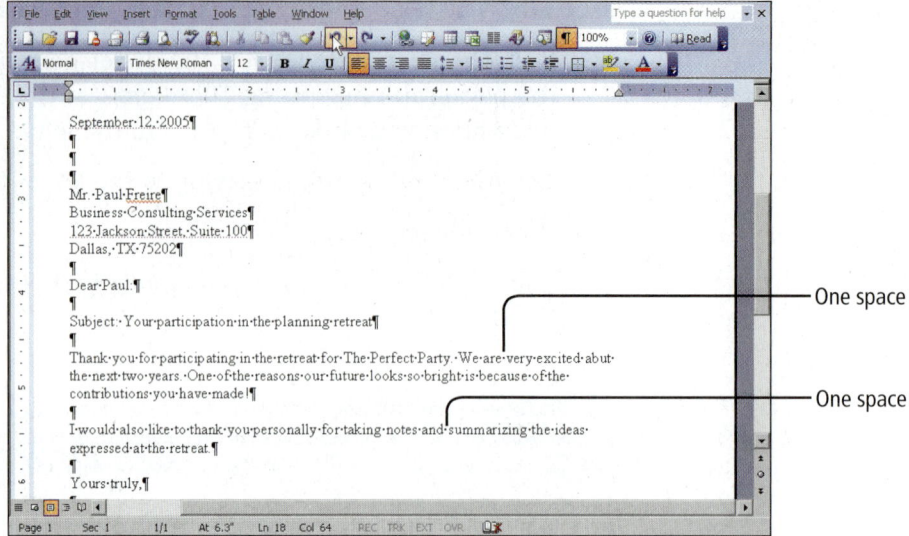

Figure 1.40

7 On the Standard toolbar, click the **Save** button to save the changes you have made to your document since your last save operation.

Another Way

Removing Characters

There are two ways to remove individual characters in a document:

- Press Delete to remove characters to the right of the insertion point.
- Press ←Bksp to remove characters to the left of the insertion point.

Activity 1.17 Inserting New Text and Overtyping Existing Text

When you place the insertion point in the middle of a word or sentence and start typing, the existing text moves to the right to make space for your new keystrokes. This is called **insert mode** and is the default setting in Word. If you press the Insert key once, **overtype mode** is turned on. In overtype mode, existing text is replaced as you type. When overtype mode is active, the letters *OVR* display in black in the status bar. When insert mode is active, the letters *OVR* are light gray.

1 In the paragraph beginning *Thank you*, in the first line, click to place the insertion point to the left of the word *retreat*.

The space should be to the left of the insertion point.

2 Type **planning** and then press Spacebar.

As you type, the existing text moves to the right to make space for your new keystrokes, and the overtype indicator (OVR) in the status bar is gray. See Figure 1.41.

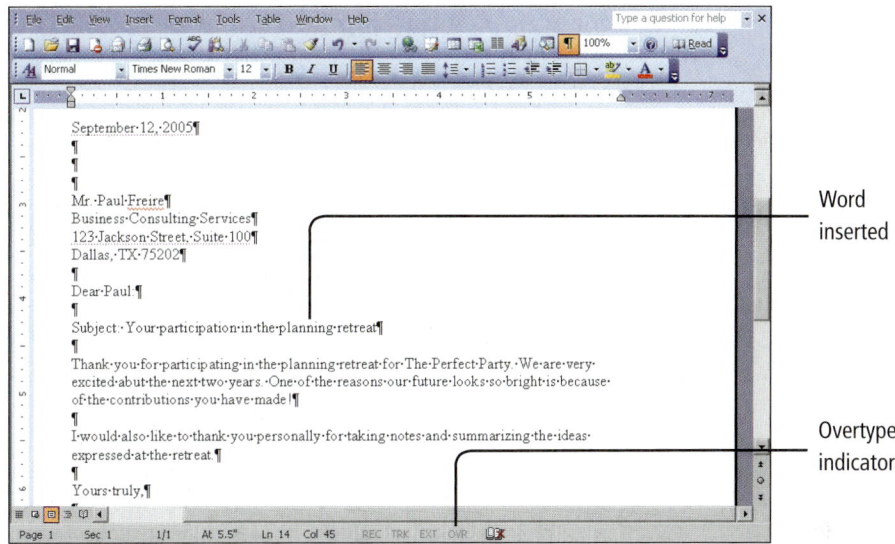

Figure 1.41

3 In the last line of the document, click to place the insertion point to the left of *Angie Nguyen*.

4 Press Insert, and notice that in the status bar, the OVR indicator is black, indicating that overtype mode is active.

When you begin to type, the new text will replace the old text, rather than move it to the right.

5 Type **Gabriela Quinones**

Notice that as you type, the characters replace the existing text.

6 Press Insert to turn off overtype mode. Alternatively, double-click the overtype indicator in the status bar.

7 On the Standard toolbar, click the **Save** button to save the changes you have made to your document.

Project 1B: Thank You Letter | **Word**   203

Objective 7
Select and Format Text

Selecting text refers to highlighting, by dragging with your mouse, areas of text so that the text can be edited, formatted, copied, or moved. Word recognizes a selected area of text as one unit, to which you can make changes. ***Formatting text*** is the process of setting the overall appearance of the text within the document by changing the color, shading, or emphasis of text.

Activity 1.18 Selecting Text

To perform an action on text—for example, to move, delete, or emphasize text—you must first select it. You can select text using either the mouse or the keyboard.

1 In the paragraph beginning *Thank you,* position the I-beam pointer to the left of *Thank,* hold down the left mouse button, and then drag to the right to select the first sentence including the ending period and its following space as shown in Figure 1.42. Release the mouse button.

The first sentence of the paragraph is selected. Dragging is the technique of holding down the left mouse button and moving over an area of text. Selected text is indicated when the background and color of the characters are reversed—the characters are white and the background is black as shown in Figure 1.42. Selecting takes a steady hand. If you are not satisfied with your result, click anywhere in a blank area of the document and begin again.

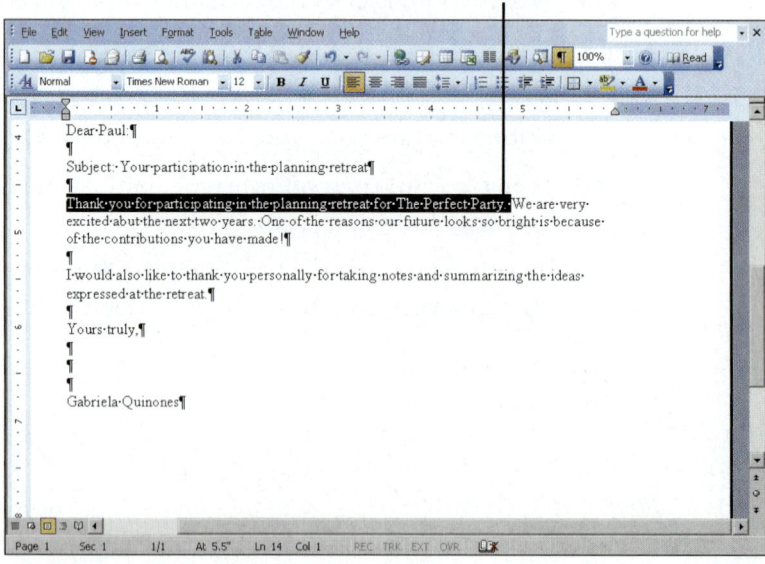

Figure 1.42

204 Word | Chapter 1: Creating Documents with Microsoft Word 2003

2 Click anywhere in the document to deselect the sentence. Then, in the same sentence, move the pointer over the word *Perfect* and double-click the mouse button.

The entire word is selected. Double-clicking takes a steady hand. The speed of the two clicks is not difficult (although you only have about a second between clicks), but you must hold the mouse perfectly still between the two clicks. If you are not satisfied with your result, try again.

3 Click anywhere to deselect the word *Perfect*. Then, move the pointer over the word *Perfect* and triple-click the mouse button.

The entire paragraph is selected. Recall that keeping the mouse perfectly still between the clicks is critical.

4 Hold down [Ctrl] and press [A].

The entire document is selected. See Figure 1.43. There are many shortcuts for selecting text. Take a moment to study the shortcuts shown in the table in Figure 1.44.

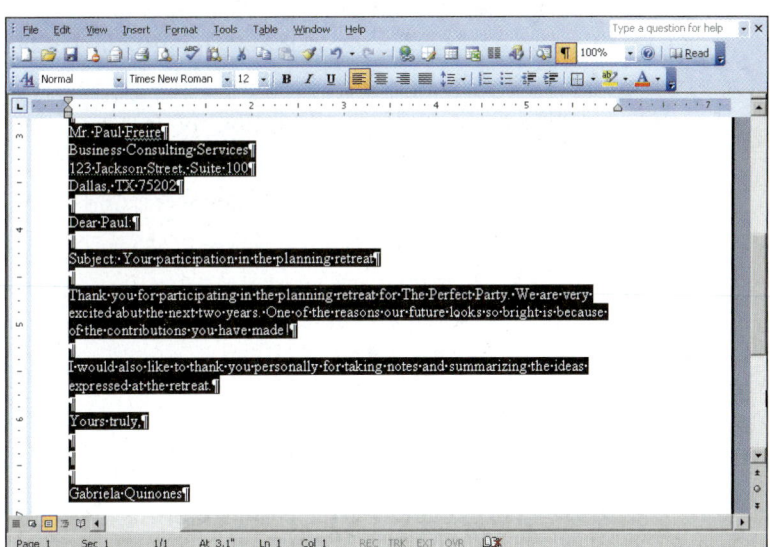

Figure 1.43

Project 1B: Thank You Letter | **Word** 205

Selecting Text in a Document

To Select	Do This
A portion of text	Click to position the insertion point at the beginning of the text you want to select, hold down Shift, and then click at the end of the text you want to select. Alternatively, hold down the left mouse button and drag from the beginning to the end of the text you want to select.
A word	Double-click the word.
A sentence	Hold down Ctrl and click anywhere in the sentence.
A paragraph	Triple-click anywhere in the paragraph; or, move the pointer to the left of the line, into the margin area. When the pointer changes to a right-pointing white arrow, double-click.
A line	Move the pointer to the left of the line. When the pointer turns to a right-pointing white arrow, click once.
One character at a time	Position the insertion point at the left of the first character, hold down Shift and press → or ← as many times as desired.
A string of words	Position the insertion point to the left of the first word, hold down Shift and Ctrl, and then press → or ←.
Consecutive lines	Hold down Shift and press ↑ or ↓.
Consecutive paragraphs	Hold down Shift and Ctrl and press ↑ or ↓.
The entire document	Hold down Ctrl and press A or move the pointer to the left of the line. When it turns to a right-pointing white arrow, triple-click.

Figure 1.44

5 Click anywhere in the document to cancel the text selection.

Activity 1.19 Changing Font and Font Size

A *font* is a set of characters with the same design and shape. There are two basic types of fonts—serif and sans serif. **Serif fonts** contain extensions or lines on the ends of the characters and are good choices for large amounts of text because they are easy to read. Examples of serif fonts include Times New Roman, Garamond, and Century Schoolbook. **Sans serif fonts** do not have lines on the ends of characters. Sans serif fonts are good choices for headings and titles. Examples of sans serif fonts include Arial, Verdana, and Comic Sans MS. The table in Figure 1.45 shows examples of Serif and Sans Serif fonts.

Examples of Serif and Sans Serif Fonts

Serif Fonts	Sans Serif Fonts
Times New Roman	Arial
Garamond	Verdana
Century Schoolbook	Comic Sans MS

Figure 1.45

1 Move the mouse pointer anywhere over the subject line in the letter and triple-click.

The entire paragraph is selected. Recall that a paragraph is defined as one paragraph mark and anything in front of it, which could be one or more lines of text or no text at all in the case of a blank line.

2 On the Formatting toolbar, locate the **Font Size button arrow** and click the arrow. On the displayed list, click **14** as shown in Figure 1.46.

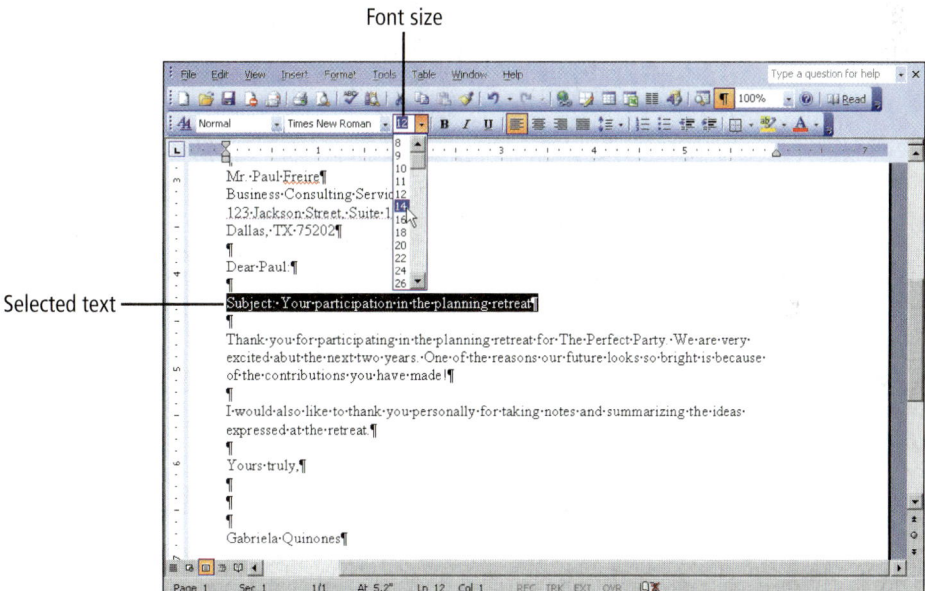

Figure 1.46

Fonts are measured in ***points***, with one point equal to 1/72 of an inch. A higher point size indicates a larger font size. For large amounts of text, font sizes between 10 point and 12 point are good choices. Headings and titles are often formatted using a larger font size. The word *point* is abbreviated as ***pt***.

Project 1B: Thank You Letter | **Word** 207

3 On the Formatting toolbar, locate the **Font button arrow** `Times New Roman` and click the arrow.

On the displayed list, the fonts are displayed in alphabetical order. Word assists in your font selection by placing fonts recently used on this computer at the top of the list.

4 Scroll the displayed list as necessary and then click **Arial**. Click anywhere in the document to cancel the selection.

5 Hold down Ctrl and press A to select the document.

6 With the document selected, click the **Font button arrow** `Times New Roman`. On the displayed list, scroll as necessary and then click **Comic Sans MS**.

The selected text changes to the Comic Sans MS font. In a letter, it is good practice to use only one font for the entire letter. This font is less formal than the default font of Times New Roman.

7 With the entire document selected, click the **Font Size button arrow** `12` and change the font size to **11**. Alternatively, you can type **11** in the Font Size box. Click anywhere in the document to cancel the text selection.

8 Compare your screen to Figure 1.47.

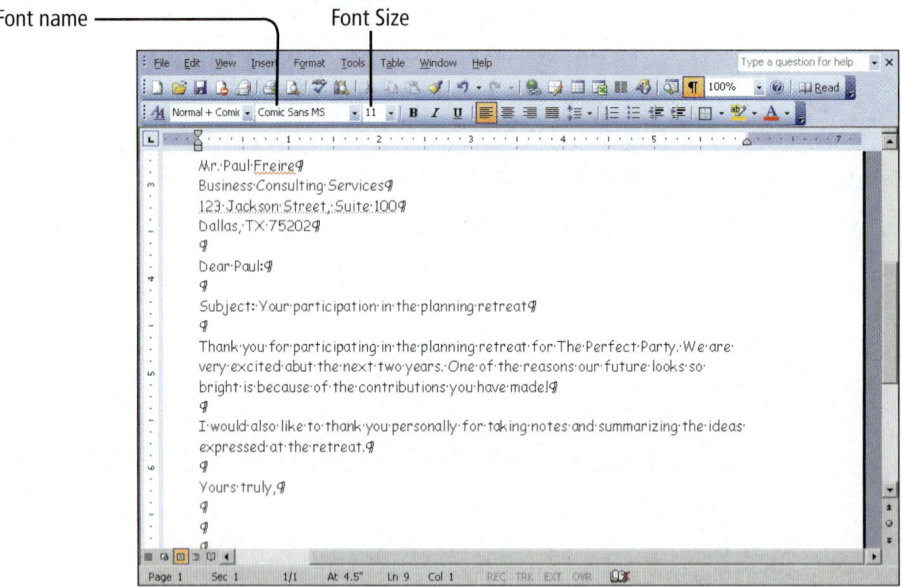

Figure 1.47

9 On the Standard toolbar, click the **Save** button 💾 to save the changes you have made to your document. Leave the document open for Activity 1.20.

Activity 1.20 Adding Emphasis to Text

Font styles emphasize text and are a visual cue to draw the reader's eye to important text. Font styles include bold, italic, and underline, although underline is not commonly used for emphasis. You can add emphasis to existing text, or you can turn the emphasis on before you start typing the word or phrase and then turn it off.

1 Move the pointer over the subject line and triple-click to select the paragraph.

2 On the Formatting toolbar, click the **Italic** button 𝐼.

Italic is applied to the paragraph that forms the Subject line.

3 In the paragraph beginning *Thank you*, use any method to select the text *The Perfect Party*.

Another Way

Applying Font Styles

There are three methods to apply font styles:

- On the Standard toolbar, click the Bold, Italic, or Underline button.
- From the menu bar, click Format, click Font, and apply styles from the Font dialog box.
- From the keyboard, use the keyboard shortcuts of [Ctrl] + [B] for bold, [Ctrl] + [I] for italic, or [Ctrl] + [U] for underline.

---

4 On the Formatting toolbar, click the **Bold** button **B**. Click anywhere in the document to cancel the selection.

5 On the Standard toolbar, click the **Print Preview** button 🔍 and compare your screen to Figure 1.48.

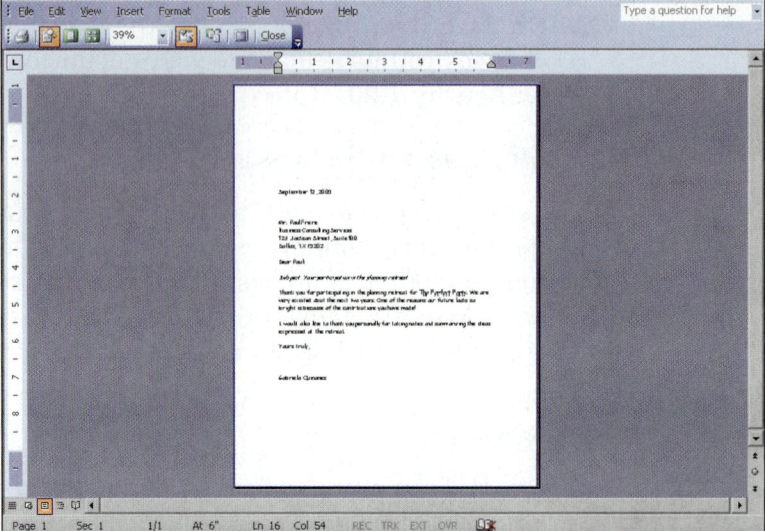

Figure 1.48

6 On the Print Preview toolbar, click **Close**.

7 In the inside address, right-click *Freire* and then click **Ignore All**. Correct any other spelling or grammar errors in your document.

8 On the Standard toolbar, click the **Save** button to save your changes.

> **More Knowledge** — Using Toggle Buttons
>
> The bold, italic, and underline buttons are toggle buttons; that is, you can click the button once to turn it on and again to turn it off.

Objective 8
Preview and Print Documents, Close a Document, and Close Word

While creating your document, it is helpful to check the print preview to make sure you are getting the result you want. Before printing, make a final check with print preview to make sure the document layout is exactly what you want.

Activity 1.21 Previewing and Printing a Document and Closing Word

1 From the **View** menu, click **Header and Footer**. (The large header area at the top is a result of vertically centering the document on the page.) On the displayed Header and Footer toolbar, click the **Switch Between Header and Footer** button.

The footer area displays. The insertion point is at the left edge of the footer area.

2 In the footer area, using your own name, type **1B Thanks-Firstname Lastname** as shown in Figure 1.49.

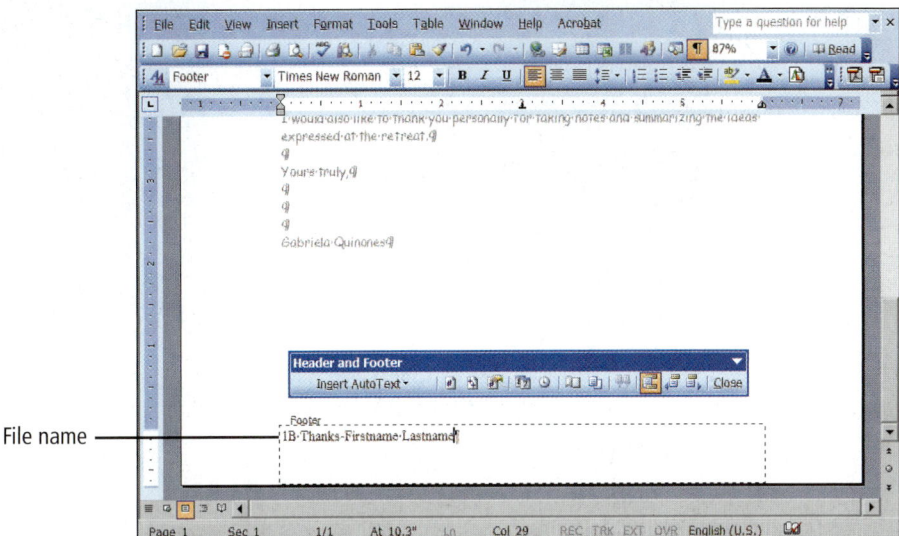

File name

Figure 1.49

3 Double-click anywhere in the text area of the document to close the Header and Footer toolbar. Alternatively, on the Header and Footer toolbar, click the Close button .

4 On the Standard toolbar, click the **Print Preview** button .

Your document displays exactly as it will print. The formatting marks, which do not print, are not displayed.

5 In the **Print Preview** window, move the mouse pointer anywhere over the document.

The pointer becomes a magnifying glass with a plus in it, indicating that you can magnify the view. See Figure 1.50.

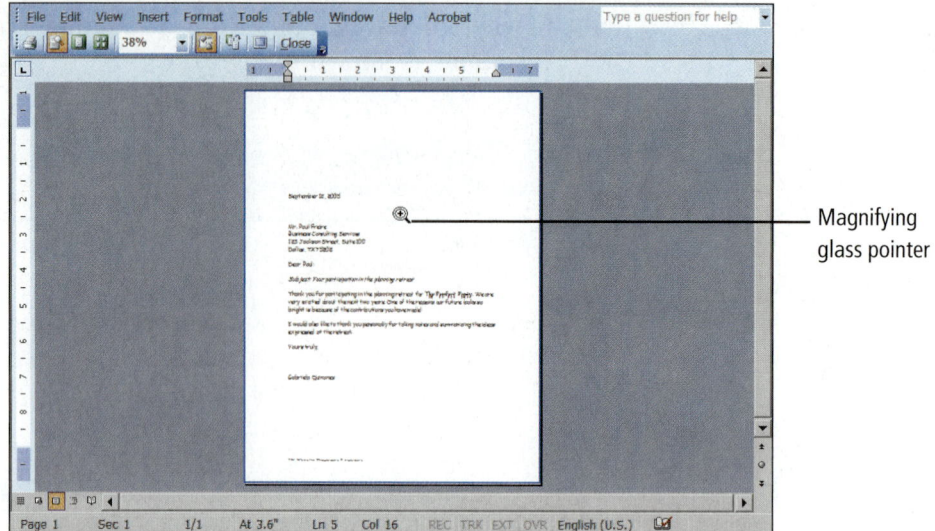

— Magnifying glass pointer

Figure 1.50

[6] Move the pointer over the upper portion of the document and click once.

The top portion of the document is magnified, and is easier to read. The pointer changes to a magnifying glass with a minus sign.

[7] Click anywhere on the document.

The full page displays again.

[8] On the Print Preview toolbar, click **Close**. On the Standard toolbar, click the **Save** button to save your changes.

[9] Display the **File** menu, and then click **Print**.

The Print dialog box displays. See Figure 1.51. Here you can specify which pages to print and how many copies you want. Additional command buttons for Options and Properties provide additional printing choices. The printer that displays will be the printer that is selected for your computer.

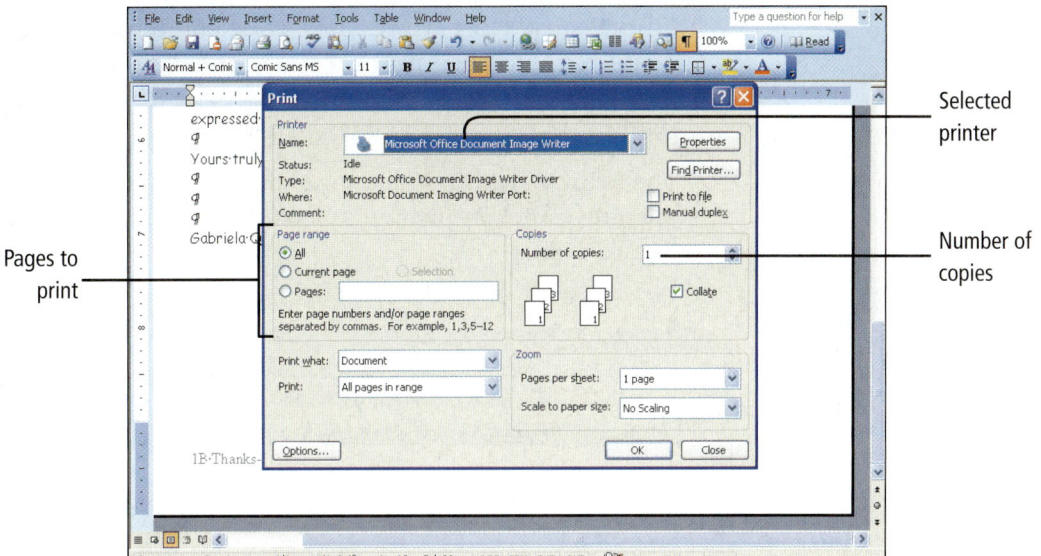

Figure 1.51

10 In the displayed **Print** dialog box, under **Copies**, change the number of copies to 2 by either typing **2** in the text box or clicking the **up arrow** in the spin box. See Figure 1.51. At the bottom of the **Print** dialog box, click **OK**.

Two copies will print.

11 From the **File** menu, click **Close**, saving any changes if prompted to do so. At the far right edge of the blue title bar, click the **Close** button ☒.

The Word program is closed.

Objective 9
Use the Microsoft Help System

As you work with Word, you can get assistance by using the Help feature. You can ask questions and Help will provide you with information and step-by-step instructions for performing tasks.

Activity 1.22 Typing a Question for Help

The easiest way to use Help is to type a question in the *Type a question for help* box, located at the right side of the menu bar.

Project 1B: Thank You Letter | **Word** 213

1 If necessary, start Word. Move your pointer to the right side of the menu bar and click in the **Type a question for help** box. With the insertion point blinking in the box, type **How do I open a file?** and then press Enter.

The Search Results task pane displays a list of topics related to opening a file. Your list may be quite different than the one shown in Figure 1.52.

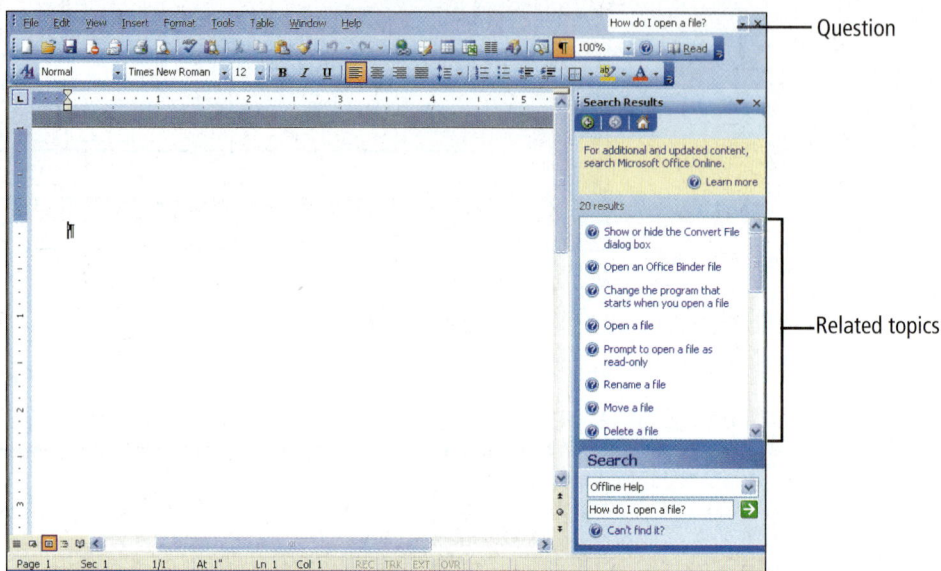

Figure 1.52

2 On the displayed list in the task pane, point to and then click **Open a file**.

The Microsoft Word Help window opens at listing instructions for opening a file. Text in blue at the bottom of the Help window indicates links to related instructions or related information.

3 At the bottom of the **Microsoft Office Word Help** window, click **Tips** to display additional information about opening files.

4 In the second bulleted item, point to and then click the blue highlighted words **task pane** to display a green definition of a task pane as shown in Figure 1.53.

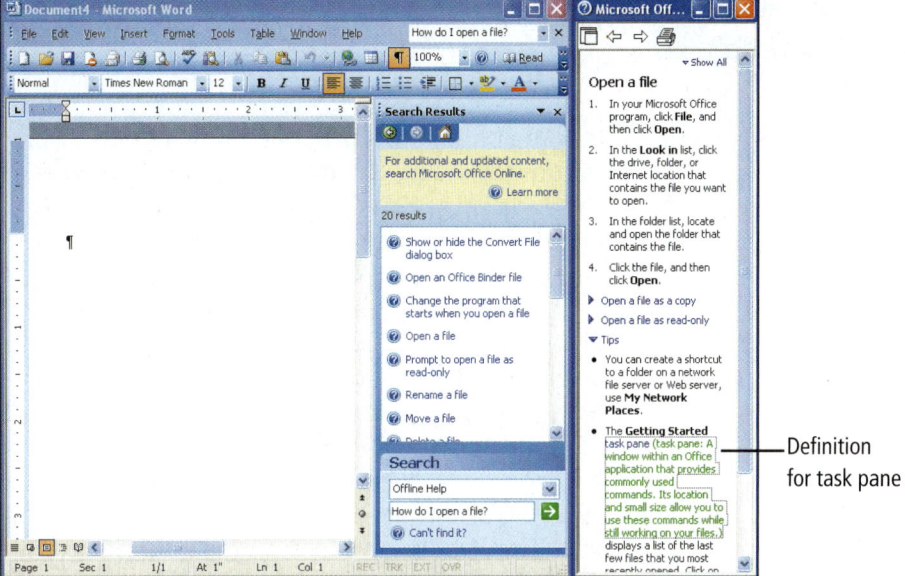

Figure 1.53

5 Click **task pane** again to close the definition.

6 In the **Microsoft Office Word Help** window, click the **Close** button ⊠.

On the **Search Results** task pane, click the **Close** button ⊠.

7 From the **File** menu, click **Exit** to close the Word program.

Another Way — Getting Help Using the Task Pane and the Office Assistant

You can access Help by clicking the Microsoft Word Help button on the Standard toolbar. This action opens the Help task pane. In the Search box, type a topic that you want to learn more about and then press [Enter]. Results are displayed in the Search Results task pane. The Office Assistant, an animated character that provides tips as you work, can be displayed from the Help menu by clicking Show the Office Assistant.

End You have completed Project 1B

Summary

In this chapter you practiced how to start Word and navigate in the Word window by using the mouse, toolbars, menus, shortcut menus, and shortcut keys. You examined documents in the Page Layout, Normal, and Reading Layout views; changed the magnification with the Zoom button; and displayed nonprinting characters with the Show/Hide ¶ button.

The basics of word processing were practiced including entering text, deleting text using the backspace or delete key, selecting and replacing text, inserting text, and overtyping existing text. The spelling and grammar checker tools were demonstrated.

You also practiced how to change font style and size and add emphasis to text. The header and footer area was viewed, and a chapter folder was created to help organize your files. Each document was saved, previewed, printed, and closed. Finally, the Help program was introduced as a tool that can assist you in using Word.

In This Chapter You Practiced How To

- Explore and Navigate the Word Window
- View Documents
- Use the Spelling and Grammar Checker
- View Headers and Footers
- Organize, Save, and Print Documents
- Create and Edit a New Document
- Select and Format Text
- Preview and Print Documents, Close a Document, and Close Word
- Use the Microsoft Help System

Chapter One Word: Concepts Assessments

Matching — Match each term in the second column with its correct definition in the first column by writing the letter of the term on the blank line in front of the correct definition.

____ 1. The point in the Word window, indicated by a blinking vertical line, where text will be inserted when you start to type.

____ 2. A view that simplifies the page layout for quick typing and can show more text on a smaller screen.

____ 3. The action that takes place when the insertion point reaches the right margin and automatically moves down and to the left margin of the next line.

____ 4. A button used to reveal nonprinting characters.

____ 5. The process of setting the overall appearance of the text within the document.

____ 6. A unit of measure that is used to describe the size of a font.

____ 7. A font type that does not have lines on the ends of characters.

____ 8. A type of font that is a good choice for large amounts of text because it is easy to read.

____ 9. A set of characters (letters and numbers) with the same design and shape.

____ 10. The term that refers to pressing one or more keys to navigate a window or execute commands.

____ 11. The Minimize, Maximize/Restore Down, and Close buttons are located here.

____ 12. A screen element that contains lists of commands.

____ 13. A context-sensitive list that displays when you click the right mouse button.

____ 14. The buttons used to Save or Print a document can be found here.

____ 15. The part of the screen that displays the Start button and the name of any open documents.

A Font
B Formatting
C Insertion point
D Keyboard shortcuts
E Menu bar
F Normal
G Point
H Sans serif
I Serif
J Shortcut menu
K Show/Hide ¶
L Standard toolbar
M Taskbar
N Title bar
O Wordwrap

Concepts Assessments (continued)

Fill in the Blank Write the correct answer in the space provided.

1. Microsoft Word 2003 is a word _____ program that you can use to do tasks such as writing a memo, a report, or a letter.

2. If you place your mouse pointer over a button on a toolbar, a small _____ displays the name of the button.

3. If you drag the _____ down it causes the document on your screen to move up.

4. The view that displays the page borders, margins, text, and graphics is known as the _____ view.

5. The portion of the Word window that opens to display commonly used commands or utilities available for use with the current job is known as the _____.

6. The View buttons are located to the left of the _____ scroll bar.

7. A row of buttons that provides a one-click method to perform common commands is called a _____.

8. To add emphasis to text, use the _____ or _____ or _____ buttons.

9. Before text can be edited, changed, formatted, copied, or moved, it must first be _____.

10. To display a shortcut menu, click the _____ mouse button.

Word chapter one

Skill Assessments

Project 1C—Follow Up Letter

Objectives: *Explore and Navigate the Word Window; Use the Spelling and Grammar Checker; View Headers and Footers; Organize, Save, and Print Documents; Create and Edit a New Document; Preview and Print Documents, Close a Document, and Close Word.*

In the following Skill Assessment, you will edit a follow-up letter from Corey Finstad, a party planner for The Perfect Party, to a customer who has requested party-planning services. Your completed letter will look similar to the one shown in Figure 1.54. You will save your letter as *1C_Follow_Up_Letter_Firstname_Lastname*.

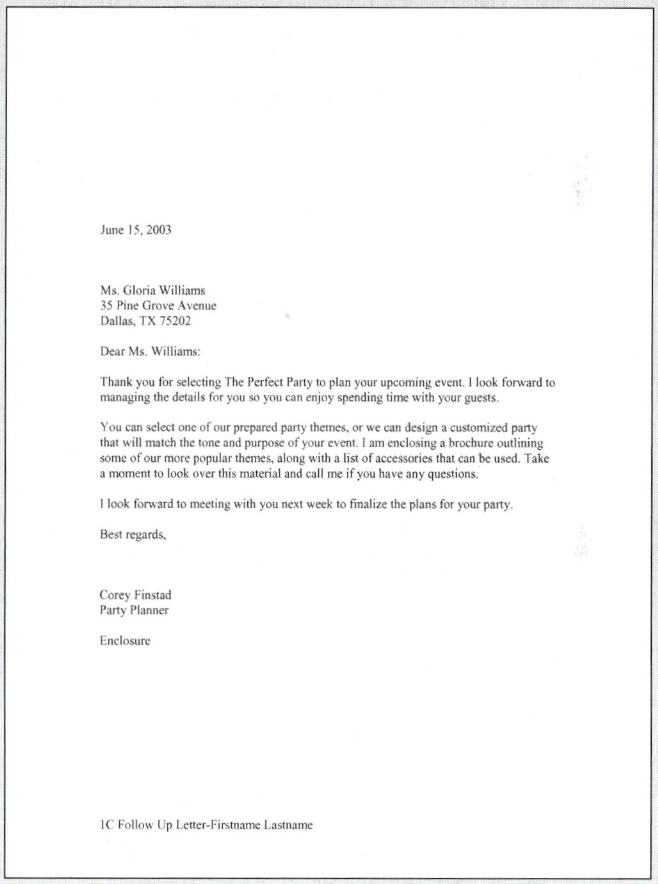

Figure 1.54

1. Start **Word**. On the Standard toolbar, click the **Open** button.

2. In the **Open** dialog box, at the right edge of the **Look in** box, click the **Look in arrow** to view a list of the drives available on your system. Navigate to the location where the student files for this textbook are stored.

(**Project 1C**–Follow Up Letter continues on the next page)

Skill Assessments (continued)

(Project 1C–Follow Up Letter continued)

3. Locate and click the file **w01C_Follow_Up_Letter**. In the lower portion of the **Open** dialog box, click the **Open** button.

4. If necessary, on the Standard toolbar click the **Show/Hide ¶** button to display formatting marks.

5. On the menu bar, click **File**, and then click **Save As**. In the **Save As** dialog box, click the **Save in arrow**, and then navigate to the location where you are saving your projects for this chapter. Recall that you created a Chapter 1 folder for this purpose.

6. In the **File name** box, using your own first and last name, type **1C_Follow_Up_Letter_Firstname_Lastname**

7. In the lower portion of the **Save As** dialog box click the **Save** button.

8. Be sure the insertion point is positioned to the left of the blank line at the top of the document. If necessary, hold down [Ctrl] and press [Home] to move the insertion point to the top of the document.

9. Begin typing today's date and let AutoComplete assist in your typing by pressing [Enter] when the ScreenTip displays. Press [Enter] four times. Notice the purple dotted line under the date, which is the recognizer that could add this date to your Outlook calendar. Type the following on three lines:

   Ms. Gloria Williams

   35 Pine Grove Avenue

   Dallas, TX 75202

10. Press [Enter] twice, type **Dear Ms. Williams:** and then press [Enter] once.

11. Hold down [Ctrl] and press [End] to move the insertion point to the end of the document. Press [Enter] twice, type **Best regards,** and then press [Enter] four times.

12. Finish the letter by typing the following on two lines:

    Corey Finstad

    Party Planner

13. Press [Enter] twice and type **Enclosure**

14. On the Standard toolbar, click the **Spelling and Grammar** button. The first error—a duplicated word—is highlighted, unless you made a typing error earlier in the document.

15. In the **Spelling and Grammar** dialog box, click the **Delete** button to delete the second occurrence of *the*. The next error is highlighted.

(Project 1C–Follow Up Letter continues on the next page)

Skill Assessments (continued)

(Project 1C–Follow Up Letter continued)

16. Under **Suggestions**, the first suggestion is correct. Click the **Change** button to change the misspelled word to the highlighted suggestion of *brochure*. The next error is highlighted.

17. Be sure *themes* is highlighted under **Suggestions**, and then click the **Change** button. Correct the next two errors, and then click **Ignore Once** to ignore the name *Finstad*. Click **OK** to close the box indicating the check is complete.

18. Drag the vertical scroll box to the top of the scroll bar to display the top of the document. In the paragraph beginning *Thank you*, double-click the word *handle* to select it and type **plan**

    Notice that your typing replaces the selected word.

19. In the paragraph beginning *You can select*, locate the first occurrence of the word *party*, click to the left of the word, type **prepared** and then press Spacebar once.

20. On the menu bar, click **View**, and then click **Header and Footer**. Click the **Switch Between Header and Footer** button. In the footer area, using your own name, type **1C Follow Up Letter-Firstname Lastname**

21. On the Header and Footer toolbar, click the **Close** button.

22. Display the **File** menu, click **Page Setup**, and then in the displayed **Page Setup** dialog box, click the **Layout tab**. Under **Page**, click the **Vertical alignment arrow**, and from the displayed list, click **Center**. Recall that vertically centering one-page letters results in a more attractive letter. In the lower right corner of the dialog box, click **OK**.

23. On the Standard toolbar, click the **Save** button to save the changes you have made to your document.

24. On the Standard toolbar, click the **Print Preview** button to make a final check of your letter before printing. On the Print Preview toolbar, click the **Print** button, and then on the same toolbar, click the **Close** button.

25. From the **File** menu, click **Close** to close the document, saving any changes if prompted to do so. Display the **File** menu again and click **Exit** to close Word. Alternatively, you can close Word by clicking the **Close** button at the extreme right end of the blue title bar.

End You have completed Project 1C

Skill Assessments (continued)

Project 1D — Fax Cover

Objectives: *Explore and Navigate the Word Window; Create and Edit a New Document; View Documents; View Headers and Footers; Select and Format Text; Preview and Print Documents, Close a Document, and Close Word.*

In the following Skill Assessment, you will create a cover sheet for a facsimile (fax) transmission. When sending a fax, it is common practice to include a cover sheet with a note describing the pages that will follow. Your completed document will look similar to Figure 1.55. You will save your document as *1D_Fax_Cover_Firstname_Lastname*.

FACSIMILE TRANSMITTAL SHEET

To: Michael Garcia, Rideout Elementary

From: Christina Stevens, The Perfect Party

Fax: 555-0101

RE: Party Supplies for First Grade Reading Program

The page to follow lists the party items we are happy to donate to Rideout Elementary to help launch the first grade reading program this fall. We are excited to be a part of this important project and look forward to working with you. If you have any questions, please contact me at 555-0188.

1D Fax Cover-Firstname Lastname

Figure 1.55

1. Start **Word** and make sure the **Show/Hide ¶** button is active so you can view formatting marks. If necessary, close the task pane.

2. On your keyboard, press [CapsLock]. With the insertion point at the top of the document, type **FACSIMILE TRANSMITTAL SHEET** and then press [Enter] twice. Press [CapsLock] again to turn the feature off.

(**Project 1D**–Fax Cover continues on the next page)

Skill Assessments (continued)

(Project 1D–Fax Cover continued)

3. On the Standard toolbar click the **Save** button. Because this new document has never been saved, the **Save As** dialog box displays. Click the **Save in arrow**, and then navigate to the location where you are saving your projects for this chapter. In the **File name** box type **1D_Fax_Cover_Firstname_Lastname** and in the lower portion of the **Save As** dialog box, click the **Save** button.

4. Type **To:** press Tab, type **Michael Garcia, Rideout Elementary** and then press Enter twice. Type the remainder of the fax headings as follows, pressing Tab after each colon (:) and pressing Enter twice at the end of each line. Refer to Figure 1.55.

   From: Christina Stevens, The Perfect Party

   Fax: 555-0101

   RE: Party Supplies for First Grade Reading Program

5. Type the following, and as you do so, remember to let wordwrap end the lines for you and to press the Spacebar only once at the end of a sentence:

   The page to follow lists the party items we are happy to donate to Rideout Elementary to help launch the first grade reading program this fall. We are excited to be a part of this important project and look forward to working with you. If you have any questions, please contact me at 555-0188.

6. On the Standard toolbar click the **Save** button to save your work.

7. Press Ctrl + A to select the entire document. On the Formatting toolbar, click the **Font arrow**, scroll as necessary, and then click **Tahoma**. Click anywhere in the document to cancel the selection.

8. Move the mouse pointer into the margin area to the left of *FACSIMILE TRANSMITTAL SHEET* until the pointer displays as a white arrow. Click to select the title line only. On the Formatting toolbar, click the **Font arrow**, scroll as necessary, and then click **Arial Black**. You can also type the first letter of the font to move quickly in the Font box. With the text still selected, click the **Font Size arrow**, and then click **16**. Click anywhere to cancel the text selection.

(Project 1D–Fax Cover continues on the next page)

Skill Assessments (continued)

(Project 1D–Fax Cover continued)

9. On the menu bar, click **View**, and then click **Header and Footer**. On the Header and Footer toolbar, click the **Switch Between Header and Footer** button. In the footer area, type **1D Fax Cover-Firstname Lastname** using your own name. On the Header and Footer toolbar, click the **Close** button.

10. On your screen, notice that the word *Rideout*, which appears twice, is flagged as misspelled, and *The* is flagged as a grammar error. On the Standard toolbar, click the **Spelling and Grammar** button.

11. At the first occurrence of *Rideout*, click **Ignore All**. This action will remove the red flag from the second occurrence of the word. For the grammar error *The*, click **Ignore Once**. Because the word *The* is part of the proper name of the company, it is correct as written. If the Spelling and Grammar checker stops on your name, click **Ignore Once**. Click **OK** when the check is complete or, if necessary, click the **Close** button on the title bar of the **Spelling and Grammar** dialog box.

12. On the Standard toolbar, click the **Save** button to save your changes.

13. On the Standard toolbar, click the **Print Preview** button. On the Print Preview toolbar, click the **Print** button, and then click the **Close** button. From the **File** menu, click **Close**.

14. At right end of the title bar, click the **Close** button to close Word.

 You have completed Project 1D

Skill Assessments (continued)

Project 1E — Survey Letter

Objectives: *Explore and Navigate the Word Window; View Documents; Create and Edit a New Document; Use the Spelling and Grammar Checker; Select and Format Text; View Headers and Footers; Organize, Save, and Print Documents; Preview and Print Documents, Close a Document, and Close Word.*

In the following Skill Assessment, you will edit a cover letter that will be sent with a survey to clients. Your completed document will look similar to Figure 1.56. You will save your document as *1E_Survey_Letter_Firstname_Lastname*.

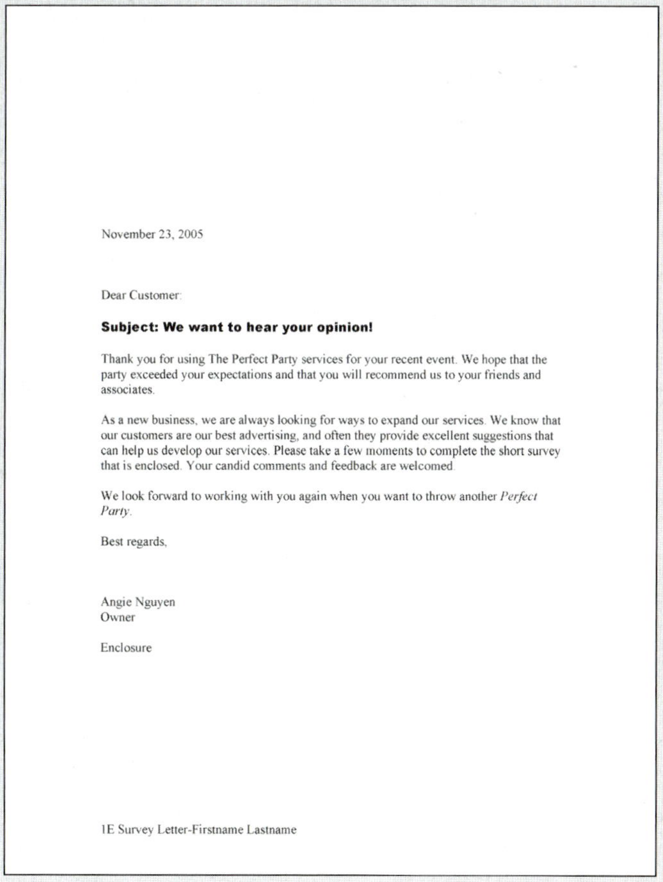

November 23, 2005

Dear Customer:

Subject: We want to hear your opinion!

Thank you for using The Perfect Party services for your recent event. We hope that the party exceeded your expectations and that you will recommend us to your friends and associates.

As a new business, we are always looking for ways to expand our services. We know that our customers are our best advertising, and often they provide excellent suggestions that can help us develop our services. Please take a few moments to complete the short survey that is enclosed. Your candid comments and feedback are welcomed.

We look forward to working with you again when you want to throw another *Perfect Party*.

Best regards,

Angie Nguyen
Owner

Enclosure

1E Survey Letter-Firstname Lastname

Figure 1.56

1. Start **Word**. On the Standard toolbar, click the **Open** button.
2. In the **Open** dialog box, at the right edge of the **Look in** box, click the **Look in arrow** to view a list of the drives available on your system. Navigate to the location where the student files for this textbook are stored.

(Project 1E–Survey Letter continues on the next page)

Skill Assessments (continued)

(Project 1E–Survey Letter continued)

3. Locate and click the file **w01E_Survey_Letter**. In the lower portion of the **Open** dialog box, click the **Open** button.

4. If necessary, on the Standard toolbar, click the **Show/Hide ¶** button to display formatting marks.

5. On the menu bar, click **File**, and then click **Save As**. In the **Save As** dialog box, click the **Save in arrow**, and then navigate to the location where you are saving your projects for this chapter.

6. In the **File name** box, using your own first and last name, type **1E_Survey_Letter_Firstname_Lastname** and then click the **Save** button.

7. Move the pointer into the left margin to the left of the subject line until the pointer takes the shape of a white arrow. Click once to select the subject line. On the Formatting toolbar, click the **Font arrow**, and then click **Arial Black**.

8. In the sentence beginning *We once again*, drag to select the phrase *We once again want to* and then press [Delete] to remove this phrase. Press [Delete] to delete the *t* in *thank*, and then type **T**

9. In the same paragraph, select the phrase *hopes and dreams* and then type **expectations** and adjust spacing if necessary.

10. In the same paragraph, click to place your insertion point to the left of the word *recommend* and type **will** and then press [Spacebar].

11. In the paragraph beginning *As a new*, right-click *advertising*, which is flagged as a spelling error. On the displayed shortcut menu, click *advertising*. In the same sentence double-click *ideas* to select it, and then type **suggestions** to replace it. In the same sentence replace the word *expand* with **develop**

12. In the same paragraph, right-click *moment*, which is flagged as a grammar error. From the displayed shortcut menu, click *moments*.

13. In the paragraph beginning *We look*, click to position the insertion point to the left of *Perfect Party*. Hold down [Shift] and [Ctrl] and then press [→] twice to select *Perfect* and then *Party*. Recall that this is a keyboard shortcut for selecting a string of words. On the Formatting toolbar, click the **Italic** button to apply the Italic font style to this phrase.

(Project 1E–Survey Letter continues on the next page)

Skill Assessments (continued)

(Project 1E–Survey Letter continued)

14. In the closing of the letter, click to position the insertion point to the left of *Sincerely* and then press [Insert] on your keyboard to activate Overtype mode. The OVR indicator on the status bar displays in black. Type **Best regards,** and then press [Delete] three times to delete the remaining unnecessary characters. Press [Insert] again to turn off Overtype mode and dim the OVR indicator.

15. Hold down [Ctrl] and press [End] to position the insertion point at the end of the document. Press [Enter] twice and then type **Enclosure**

16. On the menu bar, click **View**, and then click **Header and Footer**. On the Header and Footer toolbar, click the **Switch Between Header and Footer** button. In the footer area, type **1E Survey Letter-Firstname Lastname** and then on the Header and Footer toolbar, click the **Close** button.

17. From the **File** menu, click **Page Setup**, and then on the displayed **Page Setup** dialog box, click the **Layout tab**. Under **Page**, click the **Vertical alignment arrow**, and then click **Center**. In the lower right corner of the dialog box, click **OK**. Recall that one-page letters are commonly centered vertically on the page to give a more professional appearance.

18. On the Standard toolbar, click the **Save** button to save the changes you have made to your document. On the Standard toolbar, click the **Print Preview** button to view your document as it will print. On the Print Preview toolbar, click the **Print** button to print the letter, and then on the same toolbar, click the **Close** button.

19. From the **File** menu, click **Close** to close the document. At the right edge of the blue title bar, click the **Close** button to close Word.

 You have completed Project 1E

Word chapter one

Performance Assessments

Project 1F—Interview Letter

Objectives: *View Headers and Footers; Create and Edit a New Document; Organize, Save, and Print Documents; and Preview and Print Documents, Close a Document, and Close Word.*

In the following Performance Assessment, you will create a letter to schedule an interview for Gabriela Quinones with a catering service. Your completed document will look similar to Figure 1.57. You will save your document as *1F_Interview_Letter_Firstname_Lastname*.

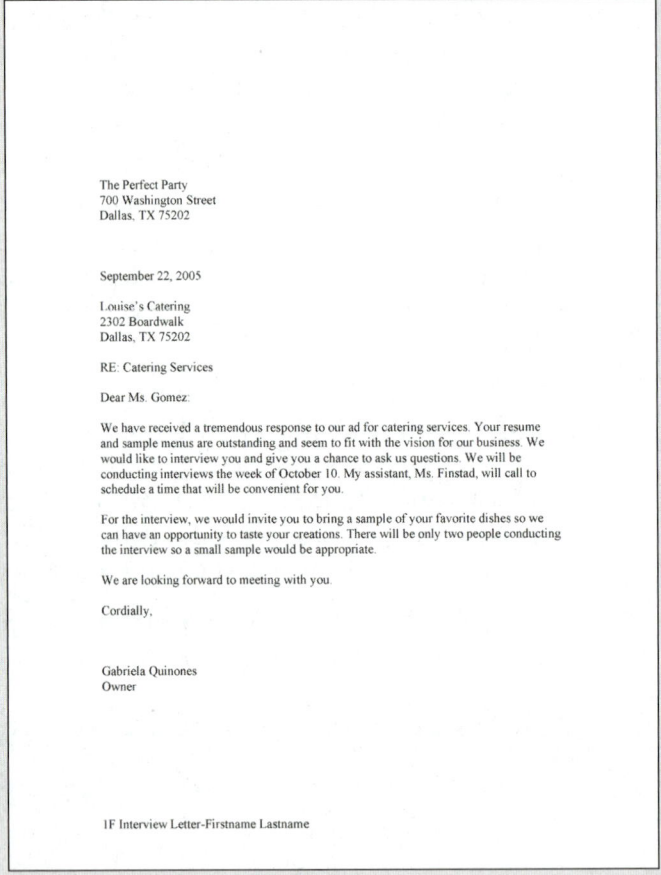

Figure 1.57

(Project 1F–Interview Letter continues on the next page)

228   Word | Chapter 1: Creating Documents with Microsoft Word 2003

Word
chapter one
Performance Assessments (continued)

(Project 1F–Interview Letter continued)

1. Start **Word** and, if necessary, close the task pane. Beginning at the top of the page type the address on three lines as shown:

   The Perfect Party
   700 Washington Street
   Dallas, TX 75202

2. Press Enter four times. Type **September 22, 2005** and press Enter twice. Type the following on three lines:

   Louise's Catering
   2302 Boardwalk
   Dallas, TX 75202

3. Press Enter two times and then type **RE: Catering Services**
   Press Enter two times and type the salutation **Dear Ms. Gomez:**

4. Press Enter twice and type the body of the letter as follows, pressing Enter two times at the end of each paragraph:

   We have received a tremendous response to our ad for catering services. Your resume and sample menus are outstanding and seem to fit with the vision for our business. We would like to interview you and give you a chance to ask us questions. We will be conducting interviews the week of October 10. My assistant, Ms. Finstad, will call to schedule a time that will be convenient for you.

   For the interview, we would invite you to bring a sample of your favorite dishes so we can have an opportunity to taste your creations. There will be only two people conducting the interview so a small sample would be appropriate.

   We are looking forward to meeting with you.

5. Press Enter twice and type **Cordially,** create three blank lines (press Enter four times), and then type the following on two lines:

   Gabriela Quinones
   Owner

(Project 1F–Interview Letter continues on the next page)

Performance Assessments (continued)

(**Project 1F**–Interview Letter continued)

6. On the Standard toolbar, click the **Save** button. In the **Save As** dialog box, navigate to the location where you are saving your projects for this chapter. In the **File name** box, using your own name, type **1F_Interview_Letter_Firstname_Lastname** and then click the **Save** button.

7. Display the **View** menu, and then click **Header and Footer**. Click the **Switch Between Header and Footer** button. In the footer area, using your own information, type **1F Interview Letter-Firstname Lastname**

8. Double-click in the body of the document to close the Header and Footer toolbar and return to the document.

9. Display the **File** menu, click **Page Setup**, and then click the **Layout tab**. Under **Page**, click the **Vertical alignment arrow**, and then click **Center**. Click **OK** to center the letter on the page.

10. Proofread the letter to make sure it does not contain any typographical or spelling errors. Use the Spelling and Grammar checker to correct any errors.

11. On the Standard toolbar, click the **Print Preview** button to see how the letter will print on paper. On the Print Preview toolbar, click the **Print** button to print the letter. Close Print Preview and then click the **Save** button to save your changes. Close the document and close Word.

End You have completed Project 1F

Performance Assessments (continued)

Project 1G—Interview Memo

Objectives: *Create and Edit a New Document; Select and Format Text; View Headers and Footers; and Organize, Save, and Print Documents.*

In the following Performance Assessment, you will edit a memo for Corey Finstad to Gabriela Quinones listing interviews that The Perfect Party has scheduled with catering firms. Your completed document will look similar to Figure 1.58. You will save your document as *1G_Interview_Memo_Firstname_Lastname*.

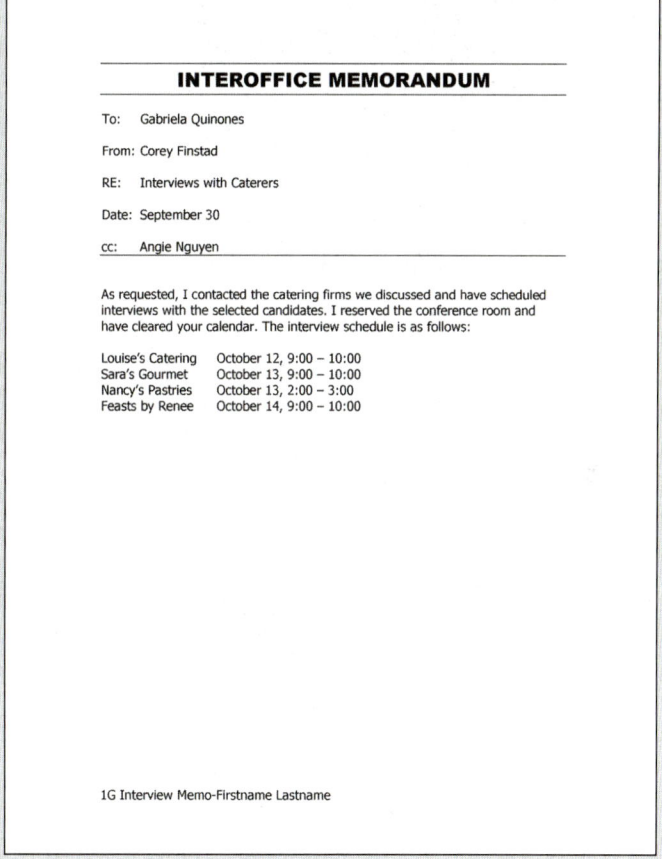

Figure 1.58

(**Project 1G**–Interview Memo continues on the next page)

Word chapter one

Performance Assessments (continued)

(Project 1G–Interview Memo continued)

1. Start **Word**. On the Standard toolbar, click the **Open** button. Navigate to the location where the student files for this textbook are stored. Locate and open the file *w01G_Interview_Memo*.

2. From the **File** menu, click **Save As**. In the **Save As** dialog box, navigate to the location where you are saving your projects for this chapter. In the **File name** box, type **1G_Interview_Memo_Firstname_Lastname** and then click the **Save** button.

3. Click after the colon in the word *To:* then press [Tab] and type **Gabriela Quinones**

   Press [↓] twice to move to right of *From:* then press [Tab] and type **Corey Finstad**

4. Use the same keystroke technique to complete the heading portion of the memo as shown:

   RE: Interviews with Caterers

   Date: September 30

   CC: Angie Nguyen

5. Click to position the insertion point at the beginning of the third empty line in the body of the memo, and then type the following:

   As requested, I contacted the catering firms we discussed and have scheduled interviews with the selected candidates. I reserved the conference room and have cleared your calendar. The interview schedule is as follows:

6. Press [Enter] twice. Type **Louise's Catering** Press [Tab] and type **October 12, 9:00 –10:00** and then press [Enter]. Repeat this pattern to enter the remainder of the interview dates.

Sara's Gourmet	October 12, 9:00–10:00
Chef Michelangelo	October 13, 9:00–10:00
Nancy's Pastries	October 13, 2:00–3:00
Feasts by Renee	October 14, 9:00–10:00

(Project 1G–Interview Memo continues on the next page)

Performance Assessments (continued)

(Project 1G–Interview Memo continued)

7. On the Standard toolbar, click the **Spelling and Grammar** button. Click **Ignore Once** to ignore the any proper names that are flagged and correct any other errors that may be identified.

8. Beginning with the paragraph *As requested*, select all of the text of the memo and change the font to **Tahoma**, which is the same font used in the top portion of the memo.

9. Navigate to the top of the document and select the text INTEROFFICE MEMORANDUM. Change the font to **Arial Black** and the font size to **18** point.

10. Display the **View** menu and click **Header and Footer**. Click the **Switch Between Header and Footer** button. In the footer area, using your own information, type **1G Interview Memo-Firstname Lastname**

    Select the text you just typed in the footer and change the font to **Tahoma**, **12** point. Double-click the body of the document to close the Header and Footer toolbar and return to the document.

11. On the Standard toolbar, click the **Save** button to save your changes. On the Standard toolbar, click the **Print Preview** button to preview the document before it is printed. Print the document. Close the file and close Word.

End You have completed Project 1G

Word Chapter One

Performance Assessments (continued)

Project 1H — Offer Letter

Objectives: *Explore and Navigate the Word Window; View Documents; Use the Spelling and Grammar Checker; View Headers and Footers; Create and Edit a New Document; Select and Format Text; and Preview and Print Documents, Close a Document, and Close Word.*

In the following Performance Assessment, you will edit a letter for Gabriela Quinones to Sara's Gourmet requesting a follow-up meeting to discuss a possible business partnership. Your completed document will look similar to Figure 1.59. You will save your letter as *1H_Offer_Letter_Firstname_Lastname*.

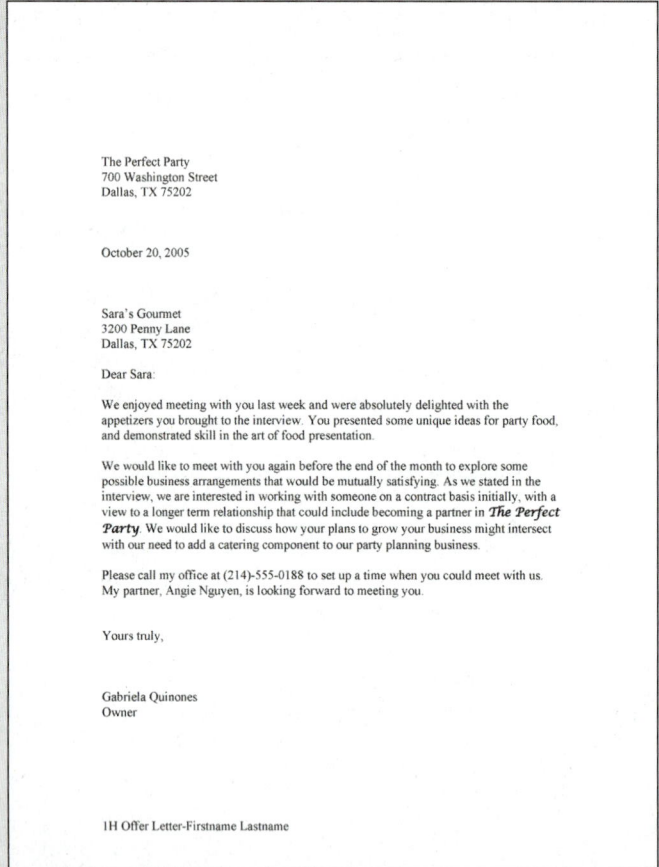

Figure 1.59

1. Start **Word**. On the Standard toolbar, click the **Open** button. Navigate to the location where the student files for this textbook are stored. Locate and open the file *w01H_Offer_Letter*.

2. Display the **File** menu, click **Save As**, and then use the **Save in arrow** to navigate to the location where you are storing your projects for this chapter. In the **File name** box, using your own information, type **1H_Offer_Letter_Firstname_Lastname**

(Project 1H–Offer Letter continues on the next page)

234   Word | Chapter 1: Creating Documents with Microsoft Word 2003

Performance Assessments (continued)

(Project 1H–Offer Letter continued)

3. In the paragraph that begins *We enjoyed meeting*, select *liked* and type **were absolutely delighted with** and then adjust the spacing if necessary.

4. In the same paragraph, select *interesting* and replace it with **unique** In the same sentence delete the word *alternatives*. In the same sentence, select the phrase *are very skillful* and replace it with **demonstrated skill**

5. In the paragraph that begins *We would like*, delete the word *once*. In the same sentence, replace the word *consider* with **explore** In the same sentence, place the insertion point at the end of the word *mutual* and type **ly**

6. There are some grammar and spelling errors that need to be corrected. Right-click on the duplicate or misspelled words and correct as necessary.

7. In the paragraph that begins with *We would like*, use the technique of Ctrl + Shift + → to select the three words *The Perfect Party* and then change the font to **Lucida Calligraphy**. If you do not have that font, choose a similar font from the list. Change the font size to **11** point. With the name still selected, click the **Bold** button.

8. Click in the blank line following *Yours truly* and add two more blank lines by pressing Enter two times. Three blank lines is the standard space allotted for a signature in a letter. Display the Page Setup dialog box and center the letter vertically on the page.

9. Display the **View** menu and then click **Header and Footer**. Click the **Switch Between Header and Footer** button. In the footer area, using your own information, type **1H Offer Letter-Firstname Lastname** Double-click in the body of the document to close the Header and Footer toolbar and return to the document.

10. Use Ctrl + Home to navigate to the top of the letter. On the Standard toolbar, click the **Read** button to display the document in Reading Layout view. Proofread the letter to make sure it is correct. In this format, two pages display to make the reading easier, but recall that this is not the page preview. When printed, the document will print on one page.

11. On the Reading Layout toolbar, click the **Close** button to return to the Page Layout view. Click the **Save** button to save your changes. Preview the letter in Print Preview and then print the document. Close the file and then close Word.

End You have completed Project 1H

Mastery Assessments

Project 1I—Contract

Objectives: *Explore and Navigate the Word Window; View Documents; View Headers and Footers; Create and Edit a New Document; Use the Spelling and Grammar Checker; Select and Format Text; Organize, Save, and Print Documents; and Preview and Print Documents, Close a Document, and Close Word.*

In the following Mastery Assessment, you will complete a contract that is given to clients of The Perfect Party. Your completed document will look similar to Figure 1.60. You will save your document as *1I_Contract_Firstname_Lastname.*

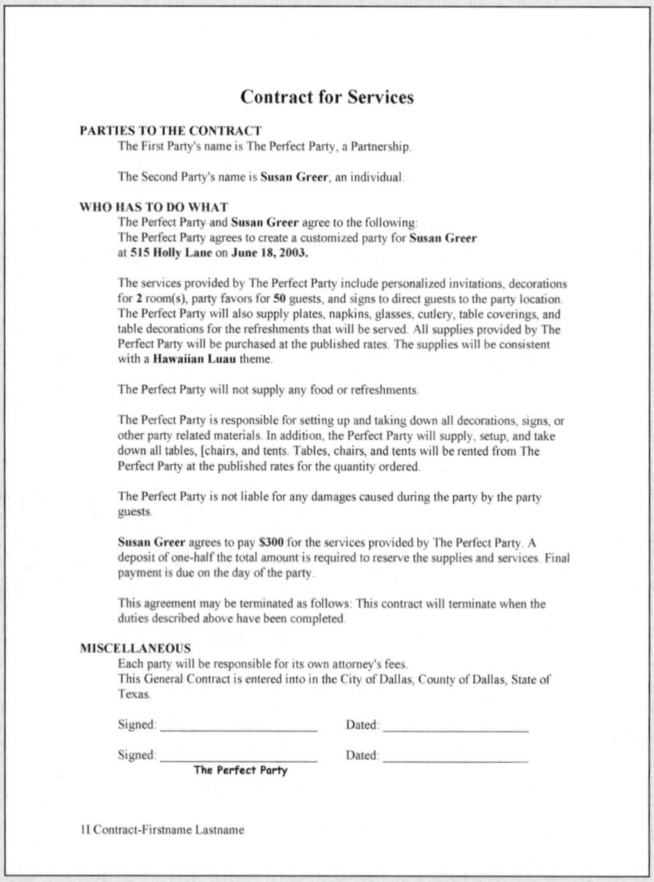

Contract for Services

PARTIES TO THE CONTRACT
The First Party's name is The Perfect Party, a Partnership.

The Second Party's name is **Susan Greer**, an individual.

WHO HAS TO DO WHAT
The Perfect Party and **Susan Greer** agree to the following:
The Perfect Party agrees to create a customized party for **Susan Greer** at **515 Holly Lane** on **June 18, 2003.**

The services provided by The Perfect Party include personalized invitations, decorations for **2** room(s), party favors for **50** guests, and signs to direct guests to the party location. The Perfect Party will also supply plates, napkins, glasses, cutlery, table coverings, and table decorations for the refreshments that will be served. All supplies provided by The Perfect Party will be purchased at the published rates. The supplies will be consistent with a **Hawaiian Luau** theme.

The Perfect Party will not supply any food or refreshments.

The Perfect Party is responsible for setting up and taking down all decorations, signs, or other party related materials. In addition, the Perfect Party will supply, setup, and take down all tables, [chairs, and tents. Tables, chairs, and tents will be rented from The Perfect Party at the published rates for the quantity ordered.

The Perfect Party is not liable for any damages caused during the party by the party guests.

Susan Greer agrees to pay **$300** for the services provided by The Perfect Party. A deposit of one-half the total amount is required to reserve the supplies and services. Final payment is due on the day of the party.

This agreement may be terminated as follows: This contract will terminate when the duties described above have been completed.

MISCELLANEOUS
Each party will be responsible for its own attorney's fees.
This General Contract is entered into in the City of Dallas, County of Dallas, State of Texas.

Signed: ____________________ Dated: ____________________

Signed: ____________________ Dated: ____________________
The Perfect Party

1I Contract-Firstname Lastname

Figure 1.60

1. Display the **Open** dialog box. Navigate to the student files, and then locate and open the file *w01I_Contract.* Display the **File** menu, click **Save As**, and then use the **Save in arrow** to navigate to the location where you are storing your projects for this chapter. In the **File name** box, type **1I_Contract_Firstname_Lastname**

2. Click the **Read** button to view this document and read through the contents of the contract. In the reading view, text size is increased to ease your reading of the document on the screen. Notice that there are three headings that are shown in all uppercase letters.

(Project 1I–Contract continues on the next page)

Mastery Assessments (continued)

(Project 1I–Contract continued)

3. On the Reading View toolbar, click the **Close** button to return to the Print Layout view. Use the **Spelling and Grammar** checker to correct the errors in the document. The last error flagged shows *State*, and suggests that this needs to be changed to *and State*. Click **Ignore Once** to ignore this occurrence.

4. Locate the three headings in uppercase letters. Select each one and add bold emphasis.

5. Locate the black lines in the document that represent blanks to be filled in. Press [Insert] on your keyboard to turn on the overtype feature. Alternatively, double-click the **OVR** button displayed in the Status bar at the bottom of the Word Window.

6. In the line beginning *The Second Party's name*, click to position your insertion point after the space following *is*. Type **Susan Greer** and notice that as you type, your typing will be displayed in bold. Make sure you do not type over any of the words in the contract. Then, use [Delete] or [←Bksp] to remove the unused portion of the black line. On the next two black lines, type **Susan Greer** again and delete the rest of both black lines. On the fourth black line, following the word *at*, type **515 Holly Lane** and delete the rest of the black line. At the beginning of the next black line, type the current date followed by a period and delete the rest of the black line. Delete unused portions of the black lines using [Delete] or [←Bksp] as needed in the remaining steps.

7. In the paragraph that begins with *The services provided*, type **2** for the number of rooms to be decorated, and type **50** for the number of guests. On the last black line in this paragraph, type **Hawaiian Luau** as the theme for the party.

8. Locate the next black line, and type **Susan Greer** and in the next black line type **300** following the dollar sign.

9. At the end of the contract, under *Signed*, select *The Perfect Party* and change the font size to **10**, change the font to **Comic Sans MS**, and add bold emphasis.

10. Display the footer area, and then, using your own information, type **1I Contract-Firstname Lastname**

11. Save the changes. Preview the document and then print it. Close the file. On the Status bar, double-click the **OVR** button to turn off the overtype feature. Close Word.

End You have completed Project 1I

Mastery Assessments (continued)

Project 1J—Memo

Objectives: *Create and Edit a New Document; View Documents; View Headers and Footers; Organize, Save, and Print Documents; Select and Format Text; Preview and Print Documents, Close a Document, and Close Word.*

In the following Mastery Assessment, you will create a memo for Christina Stevens requesting a copy of a contract from another Perfect Party employee and asking him to work at an upcoming event. Your completed memo will look similar to Figure 1.61. You will save your document as *1J_Memo_Firstname_Lastname*.

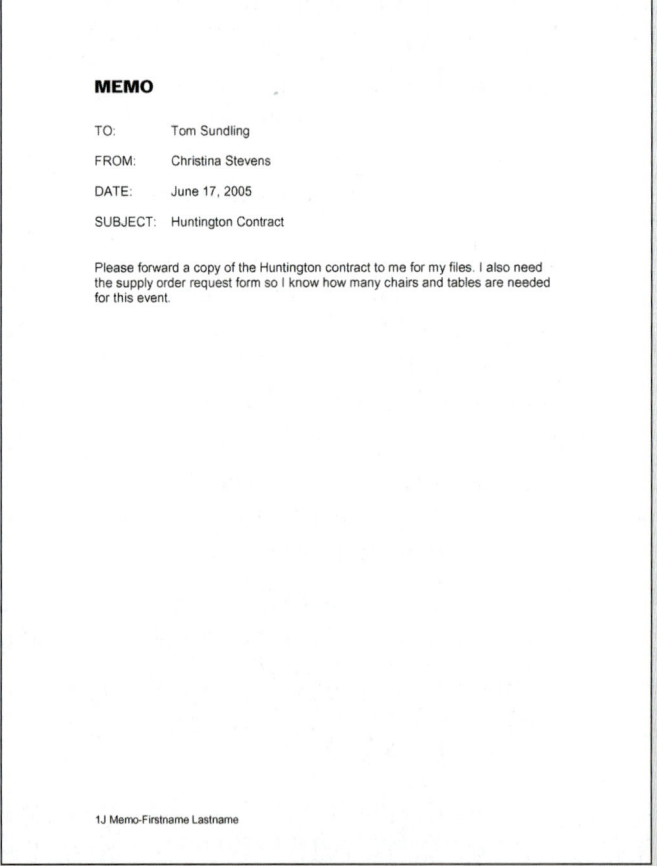

Figure 1.61

1. Open **Word** and begin with a new document. Change the font to **Arial Black**, and the font size to **16**. Press CapsLock, type **MEMO** and press Enter twice. Change the font to **12-point Arial**.

2. Save the project in your storage location as **1J_Memo_Firstname_Lastname**

(Project 1J–Memo continues on the next page)

Word chapter one

Mastery Assessments (continued)

(Project 1J–Memo continued)

3. Change the font to **12-point Arial**. Type **TO:** and press [Tab] twice. Type **Tom Sundling** and press [Enter] twice. Follow the same pattern to enter the remainder of the heading, pressing [Enter] twice to create a blank line between each heading line. You will need to press [Tab] twice after *DATE* and then type the current date for the date line. Use the appropriate number of tabs to line up the text. Press [CapsLock] to turn it off.

    FROM: Christina Stevens

    DATE:

    SUBJECT: Huntington Contract Party

4. Make sure the information entered in the memo heading aligns as shown in Figure 1.61. Save your document.

5. At the end of the Subject line, press [Enter] three times and type the body of the memo as follows:

    Please forward a copy of the Huntington contract to me for my files. I also need the supply order request form so I know how many chairs and tables are needed for this event.

6. Save your document. Create a footer and type **1J Memo-Firstname Lastname** and then format the text in the footer to **10-point Arial** font.

7. Proofread the document and use the Spelling and Grammar checker to correct any errors if necessary.

8. Print the memo, save your changes, and close the file.

End You have completed Project 1J

Word chapter one — Problem Solving

Project 1K — Party

Objectives: *Create and Edit a New Document; View Headers and Footers; Organize, Save, and Print Documents; Select and Format Text; Preview and Print Documents, Close a Document, and Close Word.*

Using the information provided, draft a letter for the owners of The Perfect Party describing the services available to potential customers. Save your document as *1K_Party_Firstname_Lastname*.

1. Open **Word**. Type the current date and press [Enter] four times to create two blank lines. Type **Dear** and then create a blank line.

2. Compose a letter that explains the services offered by The Perfect Party. The tone of the letter should be positive and sales oriented. The letter should answer the question "why do I need this service?" As you write the letter, use your own imagination along with the information in the beginning of the chapter that describes the company. The letter should contain three paragraphs—an introductory paragraph, a second paragraph describing the services offered, and a closing paragraph.

3. Add an appropriate closing, such as **Sincerely**
   Create three blank lines and then type:

   Angie Nguyen

   Owner

4. Proofread the letter and correct any spelling or grammar errors.

5. Change the font of the letter to a font and font size of your choosing.

6. Create a footer and, using your own information, type **1K Party-Firstname Lastname**

7. Preview the letter. Use the **Page Setup** dialog box to center the letter vertically on the page.

8. Save the letter in your storage location as **1K_Party_Firstname_Lastname** Print the letter. Close the file and close Word.

End You have completed Project 1K

Word chapter one

Problem Solving (continued)

Project 1L — Invitation

Objectives: *Create and Edit a New Document; View Headers and Footers; Organize, Save, and Print Documents; Select and Format Text; Preview and Print Documents, Close a Document, and Close Word.*

Create a sample invitation for The Perfect Party that could be used for birthday parties. Save your invitation as *1L_Invitation_Firstname_Lastname*.

1. From your student files, open the file *w01L_Invitation* and save it in your storage location as **1L_Invitation_Firstname_Lastname**. This document contains only a title. On separate lines add labels for information that is typically found on an invitation, such as who the party is for; when, where, and why it is being held; any party theme; refreshments provided; and an R.S.V.P line. Place a blank line between each line of information.

2. Change the font of the title to **Batang** and increase the font size so the title is large and easy to read. Add bold emphasis to the title. If Batang is not available on your computer, choose another font.

3. Format the labels to **12-point Batang**. Add bold emphasis to the labels.

4. Next to each label, add a statement in brackets that describes the information to enter in each empty space; for example, **[Enter address of party]**

5. Change the font of the instructions on each line to a font of your choice in an appropriate font size.

6. View the footer area and, using your own information, type **1L Invitation-Firstname Lastname**

7. Save your changes and print the invitation. Close the file and close Word.

End You have completed Project 1L

Word chapter one

On the Internet

Microsoft Word Specialist Certification

As you progress through this textbook, you will practice skills necessary to complete the Microsoft certification test for Word 2003. Access your Internet connection and go to the Microsoft certification Web site at **www.microsoft.com/traincert/mcp/officespecialist/requirements.asp**. Navigate to the Microsoft Word objectives for the certification exam. Print the Core (Specialist) objectives for the Microsoft Word user certification and any other information about taking the test.

GO! with Help

Getting Help While You Work

The Word Help system is extensive and can help you as you work. In this exercise, you will view information about getting help as you work in Word.

1. Start **Word**. On the Standard toolbar, click the **Microsoft Office Word Help** button. In the **Search for** box, on the **Microsoft Word Help** task pane type **help**. Click the green **Start searching** button to the right of the *Search for* box.

2. In the displayed **Search Results** task pane, click *About getting help while you work*. Maximize the displayed window, and at the top of the window, click the **Show All** link. Scroll through and read all the various ways you can get help while working in Word.

3. If you want, print a copy of the information by clicking the printer button at the top of Microsoft Office Word Help task pane.

4. Close the Help window, and then close Word.

Word 2003

chapter two

Formatting and Organizing Text

In this chapter, you will: complete these projects and practice these skills.

Project 2A
Changing the Appearance of a Document

Objectives
- Change Document and Paragraph Layout
- Change and Reorganize Text

Project 2B
Working with Lists and References

Objectives
- Create and Modify Lists
- Work with Headers and Footers
- Insert Frequently Used Text
- Insert References

Lake Michigan City College

Lake Michigan City College is located along the lakefront of Chicago—one of the nation's most exciting cities. The college serves its large and diverse student body and makes positive contributions to the community through relevant curricula, partnerships with businesses and nonprofit organizations, and learning experiences that allow students to be full participants in the global community. The college offers three associate degrees in 20 academic areas, adult education programs, and continuing education offerings on campus, at satellite locations, and online.

© Getty Images, Inc.

Formatting and Organizing Text

Typing text is just the beginning of the process of creating an effective, professional-looking document. Microsoft Word also provides many tools for formatting paragraphs and documents; tools to create shortcuts for entering commonly used text; and quick ways to copy, cut, and move text.

Word also provides tools to create specialized formats, such as endnotes, bulleted and numbered lists, and indented paragraphs.

In this chapter you will edit a report about a groupware database and how it is being used.

Project 2A Campus Software

You have practiced opening existing documents and creating and editing new documents. In this chapter you will go further and learn how to change paragraph layouts, work with lists, headers and footers, and references.

In Activities 2.1 through 2.12 you will edit a document that describes the groupware software used by Lake Michigan City College. Your completed document will look similar to Figure 2.1. You will save your document as *2A_Campus_Software_Firstname_Lastname.*

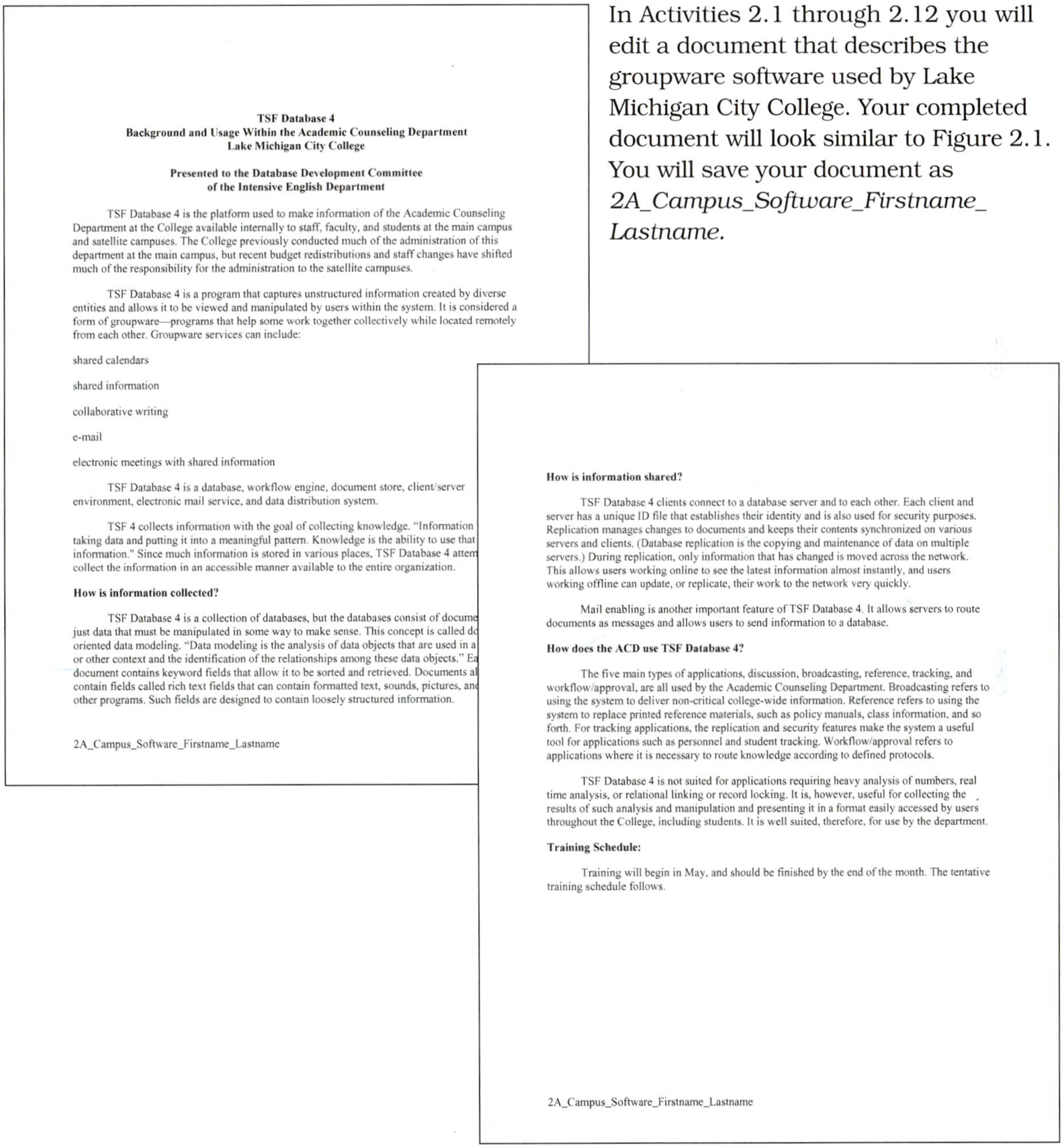

TSF Database 4
Background and Usage Within the Academic Counseling Department
Lake Michigan City College

Presented to the Database Development Committee
of the Intensive English Department

TSF Database 4 is the platform used to make information of the Academic Counseling Department at the College available internally to staff, faculty, and students at the main campus and satellite campuses. The College previously conducted much of the administration of this department at the main campus, but recent budget redistributions and staff changes have shifted much of the responsibility for the administration to the satellite campuses.

TSF Database 4 is a program that captures unstructured information created by diverse entities and allows it to be viewed and manipulated by users within the system. It is considered a form of groupware—programs that help some work together collectively while located remotely from each other. Groupware services can include:

shared calendars

shared information

collaborative writing

e-mail

electronic meetings with shared information

TSF Database 4 is a database, workflow engine, document store, client/server environment, electronic mail service, and data distribution system.

TSF 4 collects information with the goal of collecting knowledge. "Information taking data and putting it into a meaningful pattern. Knowledge is the ability to use that information." Since much information is stored in various places, TSF Database 4 attem collect the information in an accessible manner available to the entire organization.

How is information collected?

TSF Database 4 is a collection of databases, but the databases consist of docume just data that must be manipulated in some way to make sense. This concept is called dc oriented data modeling. "Data modeling is the analysis of data objects that are used in a or other context and the identification of the relationships among these data objects." Ea document contains keyword fields that allow it to be sorted and retrieved. Documents al contain fields called rich text fields that can contain formatted text, sounds, pictures, anc other programs. Such fields are designed to contain loosely structured information.

2A_Campus_Software_Firstname_Lastname

How is information shared?

TSF Database 4 clients connect to a database server and to each other. Each client and server has a unique ID file that establishes their identity and is also used for security purposes. Replication manages changes to documents and keeps their contents synchronized on various servers and clients. (Database replication is the copying and maintenance of data on multiple servers.) During replication, only information that has changed is moved across the network. This allows users working online to see the latest information almost instantly, and users working offline can update, or replicate, their work to the network very quickly.

Mail enabling is another important feature of TSF Database 4. It allows servers to route documents as messages and allows users to send information to a database.

How does the ACD use TSF Database 4?

The five main types of applications, discussion, broadcasting, reference, tracking, and workflow/approval, are all used by the Academic Counseling Department. Broadcasting refers to using the system to deliver non-critical college-wide information. Reference refers to using the system to replace printed reference materials, such as policy manuals, class information, and so forth. For tracking applications, the replication and security features make the system a useful tool for applications such as personnel and student tracking. Workflow/approval refers to applications where it is necessary to route knowledge according to defined protocols.

TSF Database 4 is not suited for applications requiring heavy analysis of numbers, real time analysis, or relational linking or record locking. It is, however, useful for collecting the results of such analysis and manipulation and presenting it in a format easily accessed by users throughout the College, including students. It is well suited, therefore, for use by the department.

Training Schedule:

Training will begin in May, and should be finished by the end of the month. The tentative training schedule follows.

2A_Campus_Software_Firstname_Lastname

Figure 2.1
Project 2A—Campus Software Document

Objective 1
Change Document and Paragraph Layout

Document layout includes **margins**—the space between the text and the top, bottom, left, and right edges of the page. Paragraph layout includes line spacing, indents, tabs, and so forth. Information about paragraph formats is stored in the paragraph mark at the end of a paragraph. When you press the Enter key, the new paragraph mark contains the formatting of the previous paragraph.

Activity 2.1 Setting Margins

You can change each of the four page margins independently. You can also change the margins for the whole document at once or change the margins for only a portion of the document.

1. Start Word. On the Standard toolbar, click the **Open** button. Navigate to the location where the student files for this textbook are stored. Locate **w02A_Campus_Software** and click once to select it. Then, in the lower right corner of the **Open** dialog box, click **Open**.

   The *w02A_Campus_Software* file opens. See Figure 2.2.

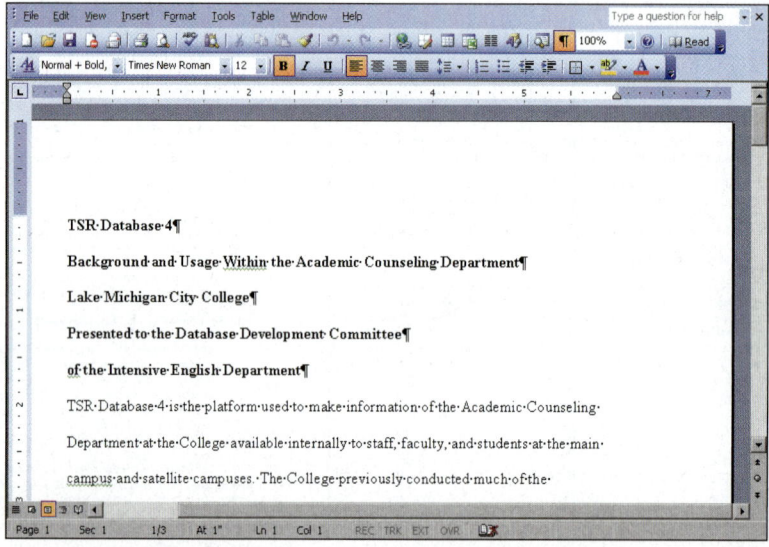

Figure 2.2

2. If your formatting marks are not displayed as shown in Figure 2.2, on the Standard toolbar, click the **Show/Hide ¶** button to display the formatting marks on your screen.

3. On the **File** menu, click **Save As**.

   The Save As dialog box displays.

4. Use the **Save in arrow** to navigate to the location where you are saving your files. In the **File name** box, delete the existing text, and using your own name, type **2A_Campus_Software_Firstname_Lastname**

5 Click **Save**.

The document is saved with a new name.

6 On the Standard toolbar, click the **Zoom button arrow** and click **Page Width**.

7 On the **File** menu, click **Page Setup**.

The Page Setup dialog box displays.

8 In the **Page Setup** dialog box, if necessary, click the **Margins tab**. Under **Margins**, with *1"* highlighted in the **Top** box, type **1.5**

This will change the top margin to 1.5 inches on all pages of the document. (Note: You do not need to type the inch (") mark.)

9 Press Tab two times to highlight the measurement in the **Left** box, type **1** and then press Tab again. With the measurement in the **Right** box highlighted, type **1**

The new margins will be applied to the entire document. Compare your Page Setup dialog box to Figure 2.3.

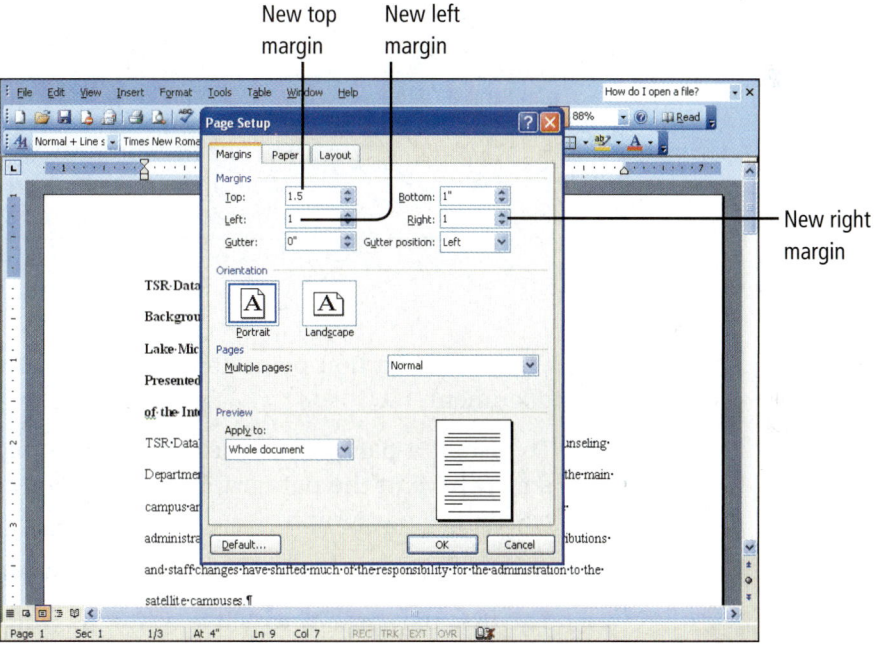

Figure 2.3

10 In the lower right corner of the dialog box, click **OK**.

The dialog box closes, and the new margins are applied to your document. The width of the document is displayed on the ruler. If the ruler is not displayed, from the View menu, click Ruler. With 1" left and right margins, the document width will be 6.5".

Activity 2.2 Aligning Text

Alignment is the placement of paragraph text relative to the left and right margins. Most paragraph text is ***aligned left***—aligned at the left margin, leaving the right margin uneven. Three other types of paragraph alignment are available: ***center alignment***, which is centered between the left and right margin, ***right alignment***, which is aligned on the right margin, and ***justified alignment***, which is text aligned on both the left and right margins. Examples are shown in the table in Figure 2.4.

Paragraph Alignment Options

Alignment	Button	Description and Example
Align Left		Align Left is the default paragraph alignment in Word. Text in the paragraph aligns at the left margin and the right margin is ragged.
Center		The Center alignment option aligns text in the paragraph so that it is centered between the left and right margins.
Align Right		Align Right is used to align text at the right margin. Using Align Right, the left margin, which is normally even, is ragged.
Justify		The Justify alignment option adds additional space between words so that both the left and right margins are even. Justify is often used when formatting newspaper-style columns.

Figure 2.4

1 Place the insertion point anywhere in the first line of text in the document.

To format a paragraph, you only need to have the insertion point somewhere in the paragraph—you do not need to select all of the text in the paragraph.

2 On the Formatting toolbar, click the **Center** button .

The first paragraph, which is a title, is centered.

3 Move the pointer into the left margin area, just to the left of the second line of text. When the pointer changes to a white arrow, drag down to select the second, third, fourth, and fifth lines of text as shown in Figure 2.5.

Recall that a paragraph consists of a paragraph mark and all the text in front of it. To format multiple paragraphs, they need to be selected.

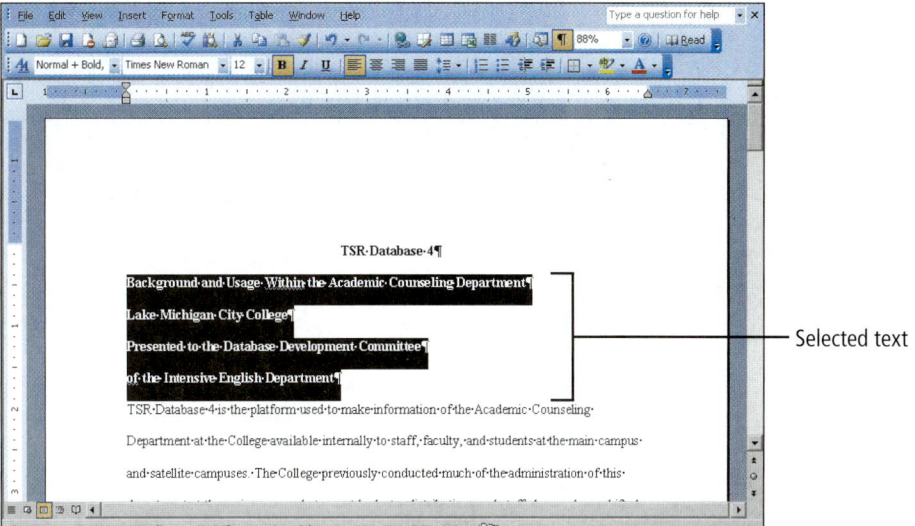

Figure 2.5

[4] On the Formatting toolbar, click the **Center** button.

All five of the title lines of bold text are centered. The last four lines are still selected. See Figure 2.6.

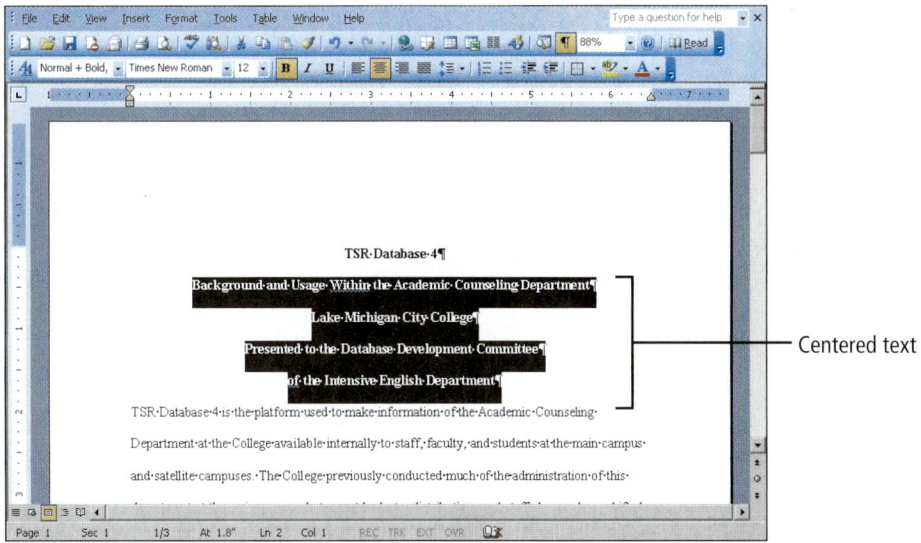

Figure 2.6

[5] Click the down arrow at the bottom of the vertical scrollbar until you can see all of the paragraph that begins *TSR Database 4 is the platform* and click anywhere in this paragraph. Make sure that you can see the first two or three lines of the following paragraph also.

[6] On the Formatting toolbar, click the **Justify** button.

Both the left and right edges of the paragraph are even. The other paragraphs are not affected. See Figure 2.7.

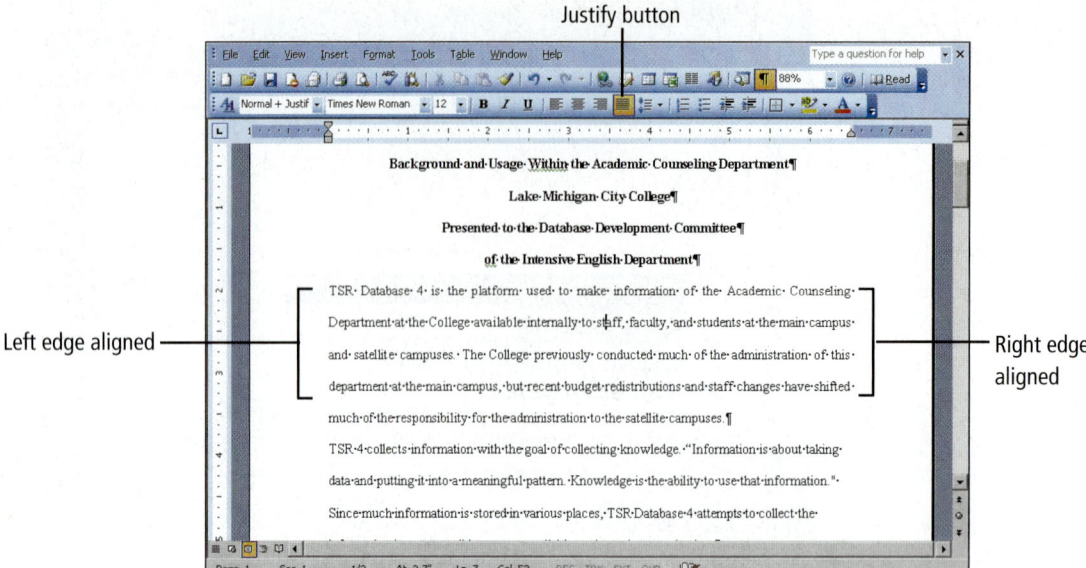

Figure 2.7

7 On the Formatting toolbar, click the **Align Left** button.

The paragraph is returned to the left aligned format.

Activity 2.3 Changing Line Spacing

Line spacing is the distance between lines of text in a paragraph. A single-spaced paragraph of 12-point text has six lines per vertical inch. If you double-space the same text, each line will be 24 points high (12 points of text, 12 points of space), or three lines per inch. See Figure 2.8.

Line Spacing Options

Spacing	Example
Single (1.0)	Most business documents are single spaced. This means that the spacing between lines is just enough to separate the text.
Double (2.0)	Many college research papers and reports, and many draft documents that need room for notes are double spaced; there is room for a full line of text between each document line.

Figure 2.8

1 Move the pointer to the left margin just to the left of the first title line. When the pointer changes to a white arrow, drag downward to highlight the first and second lines of the title.

2 On the Formatting toolbar, click the arrow on the right of the **Line Spacing** button.

A list displays. A check mark next to 2.0 indicates that the selected paragraphs are double spaced. See Figure 2.9.

250   Word | Chapter 2: Formatting and Organizing Text

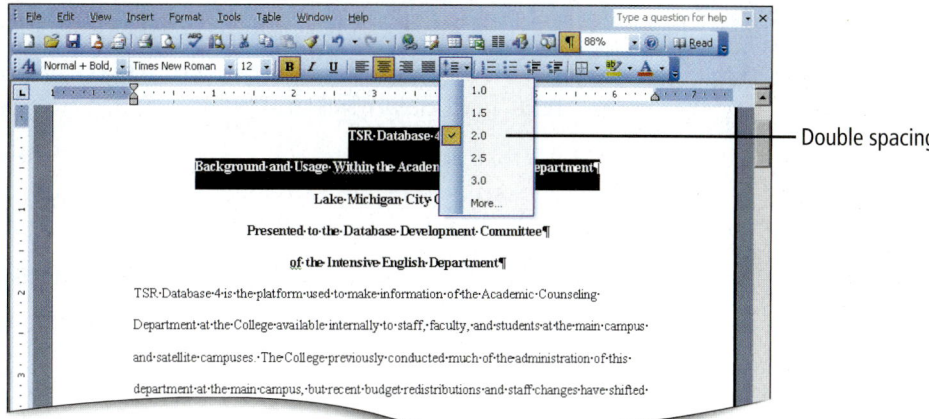

Figure 2.9

3 On the displayed **Line Spacing** list, click **1.0**.

The selected paragraphs are single spaced. The third title line is part of the first group of titles, so its spacing was left as double spaced to separate it from the following title lines. See Figure 2.10.

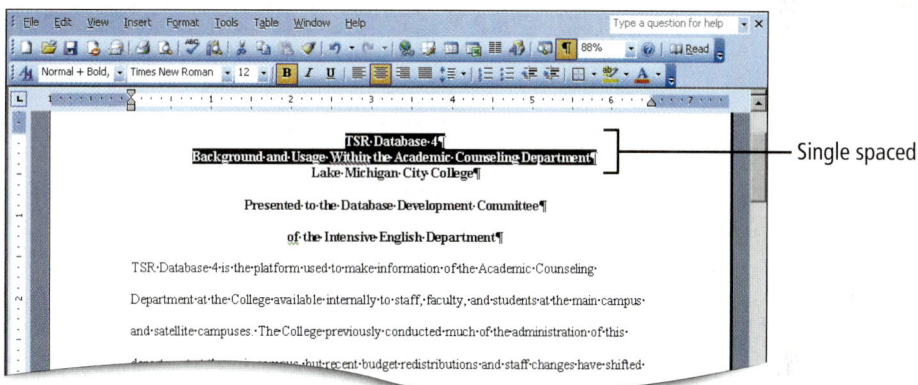

Figure 2.10

4 Click to place the insertion point anywhere in the fourth line of the title. On the **Formatting** toolbar, move the pointer over the **Line Spacing** button.

A ScreenTip displays, indicating *Line Spacing (1)*. This means that the last operation performed using this button is now the default when you click the button.

5 On the Formatting toolbar, click the **Line Spacing** button. Make sure you click the button and not the arrow on the right side of the button.

The line is single spaced.

6 In the paragraph that begins *TSR Database 4 is the platform*, click to place the insertion point to the left of the first word in the paragraph.

Project 2A: Campus Software | **Word** 251

7 Use the vertical scrollbar to scroll to the bottom of the document, position the I-beam pointer to the right of the last word in the text, hold down Shift and click.

All text between the insertion point and the point at which you clicked is selected. This Shift + click technique is convenient to select a block of text between two points that span several pages.

8 On the Formatting toolbar, click the **Line Spacing** button.

The selected text is formatted with single spacing.

9 Scroll to the top of the document and click anywhere to cancel the text selection.

Compare your screen to Figure 2.11.

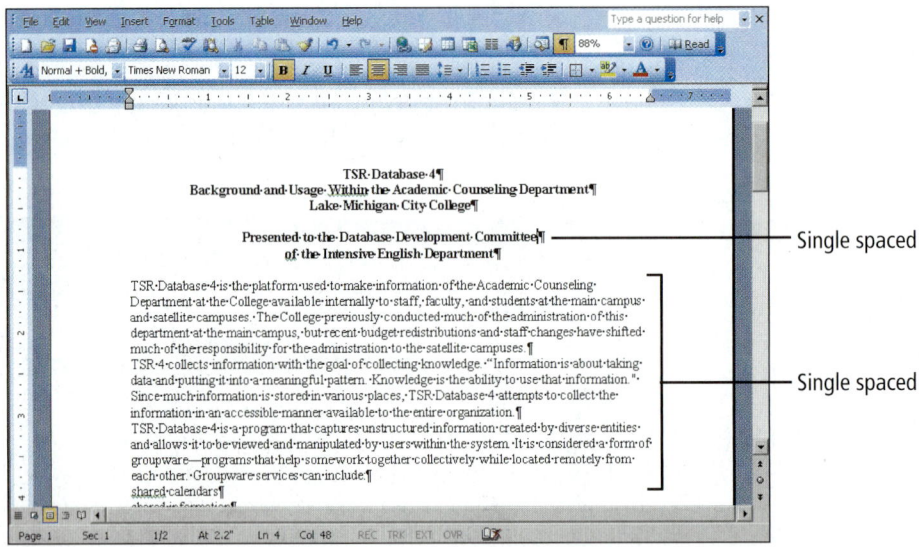

Figure 2.11

10 On the Standard toolbar, click the **Save** button.

Activity 2.4 Adding Space After Paragraphs

Adjusting paragraph spacing from the Paragraph dialog box gives you the most control, because you can control the space before or after paragraphs using points as the unit of measure. Remember, there are 72 points per inch.

1 Click anywhere in the paragraph that begins *TSR Database 4 is the platform*.

2 On the **Format** menu, click **Paragraph**.

The Paragraph dialog box displays. You can also open this dialog box by clicking the arrow on the Line Spacing button and clicking More from the displayed list.

3 If necessary, click the Indents and Spacing tab. Under **Spacing**, in the **After** box, click the up arrow twice.

The value in the box changes from 0 pt. to 12 pt. The up and down arrows, called *spin box arrows*, increment the point size by six points at a time. Alternatively, type a number of your choice directly into the text box. See Figure 2.12.

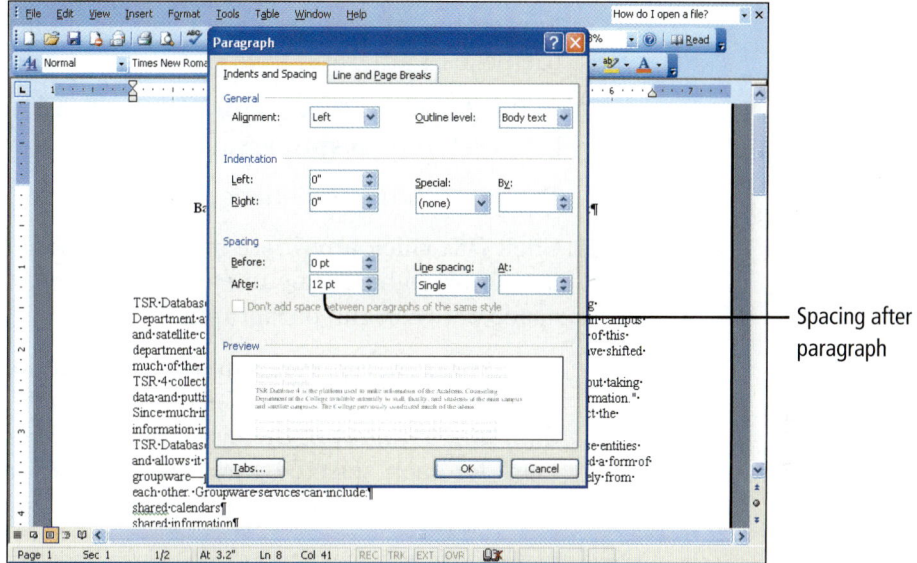

Figure 2.12

4 Click **OK**.

A 12-point space is added to the end of the paragraph. See Figure 2.13.

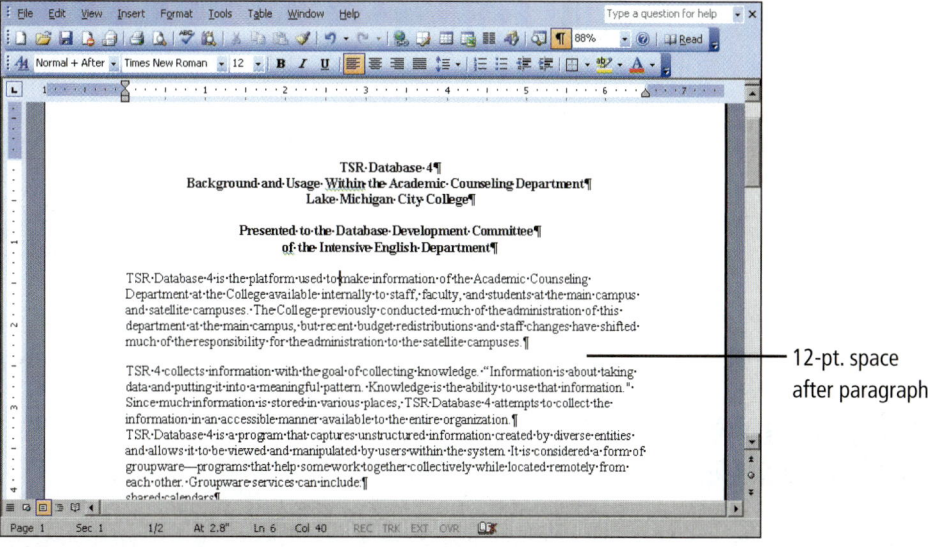

Figure 2.13

Project 2A: Campus Software | **Word**   253

5 In the paragraph that begins *TSR 4 collects information*, click to the left of first word in the paragraph. Use the vertical scrollbar to scroll to the end of the document, position the I-beam pointer [I] to the right of the last word in the document, hold down [Shift] and click.

The text between the insertion point and the end of the document is selected.

6 With the text selected, display the **Format** menu, and then click **Paragraph**. Alternatively, you can right-click in the selected text and then click Paragraph from the shortcut menu.

7 In the displayed **Paragraph** dialog box, under **Spacing**, in the **After** box, click the **up spin arrow** twice.

The value in the box changes from 0 pt. to 12 pt.

8 Click **OK**. Click anywhere in the document to cancel the selection. Scroll through the document to examine the result of adding extra space between the paragraphs.

Recall that paragraph formatting instructions are stored in the paragraph marks at the end of each paragraph. When you select more than one paragraph, these instructions are placed in the paragraph mark for each selected paragraph but not for any other paragraphs in the document. Compare your screen to Figure 2.14.

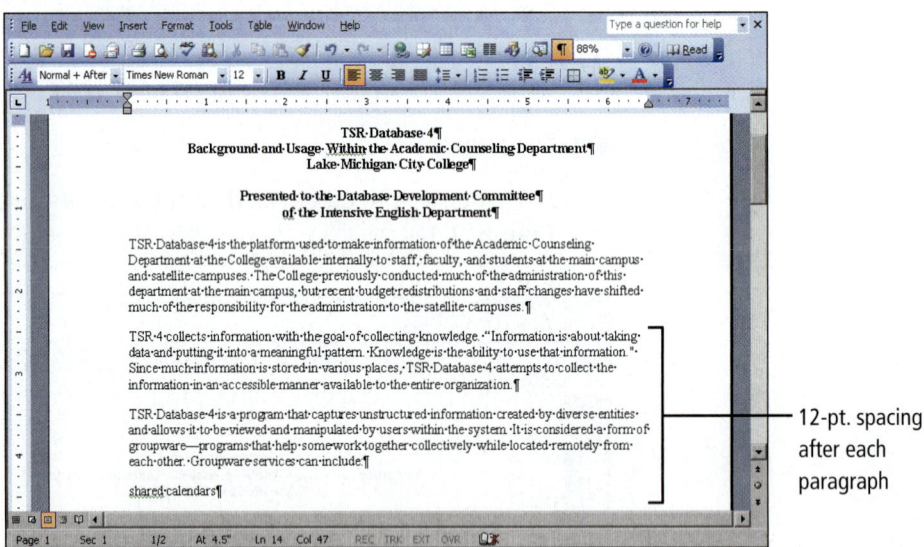

12-pt. spacing after each paragraph

Figure 2.14

9 On the Standard toolbar, click the **Save** button.

Another Way — Adding Space

You can add space to the end of a paragraph in the following ways:

- Press [Enter] to add a blank line.
- Change the line spacing to double.
- From the Paragraph dialog box, adjust the spacing after the paragraph.

Activity 2.5 Indenting Paragraphs

In addition to adding space at the end of paragraphs, indenting the first lines of paragraphs provides visual cues to the reader to help break the document up and make it easier to read.

1 Hold down [Ctrl] and press [Home] to move to the top of page 1. Then, click anywhere in the paragraph that begins *TSR Database 4 is the platform*.

2 On the **Format** menu, click **Paragraph**.

The Paragraph dialog box displays.

3 Be sure that the **Indents and Spacing tab** is displayed. Under **Indentation**, click the **Special arrow**, and from the displayed list, click **First line**.

4 Under **Indentation**, in the **By** box, make sure *0.5"* is displayed. See Figure 2.15.

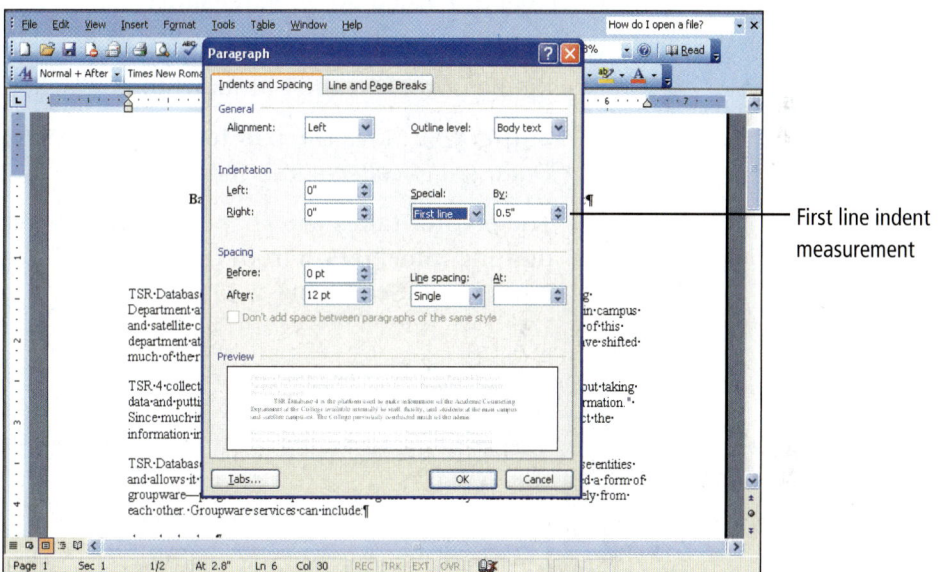

First line indent measurement

Figure 2.15

5 In the lower right corner of the dialog box, click **OK**.

The first line of the paragraph is indented by 0.5 inch, and the First Line Indent marker on the ruler moves to the 0.5 inch mark. See Figure 2.16.

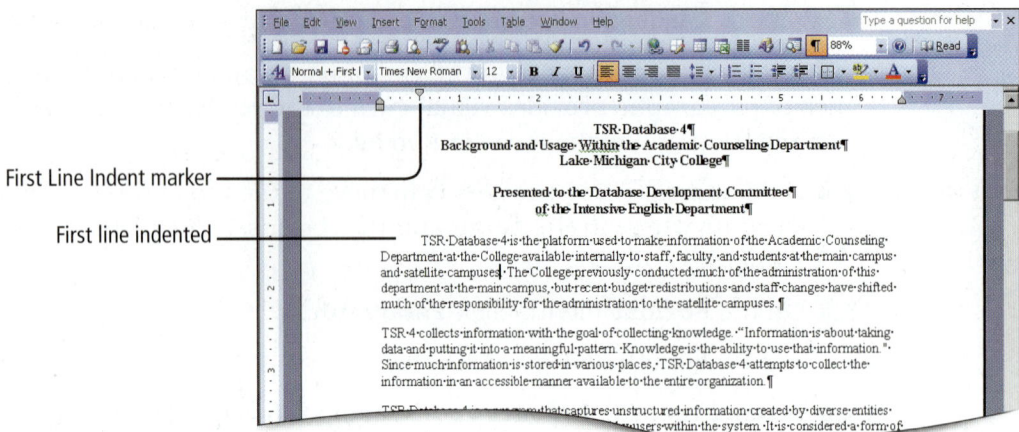

Figure 2.16

6 On the Standard toolbar, click the **Save** button.

Activity 2.6 Using the Format Painter

1 Click anywhere in the paragraph that begins *TSR Database 4 is the platform*. On the Standard toolbar, click the **Format Painter** button. Move the pointer over the next paragraph, beginning *TSR Database 4 collects information*.

The pointer takes the shape of a paintbrush, and contains the formatting information from the paragraph where the insertion point is positioned. See Figure 2.17.

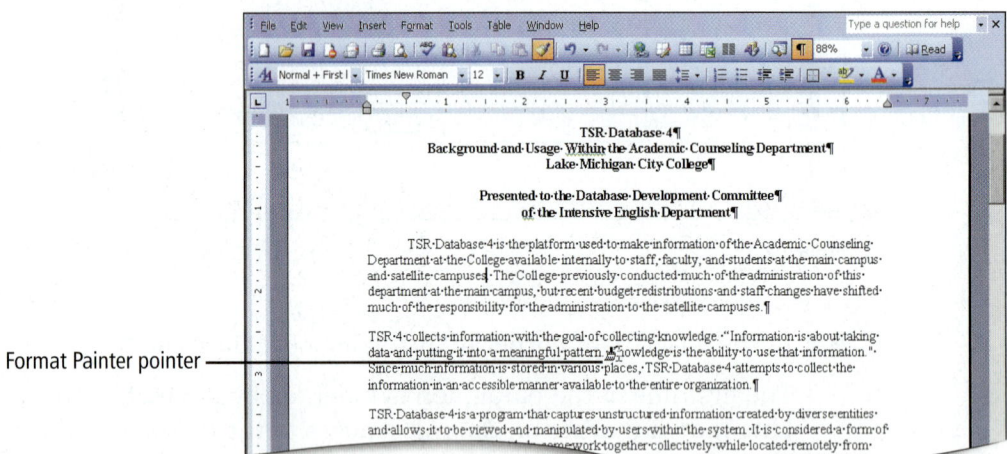

Figure 2.17

2 Click once.

The paragraph is formatted with the same formatting as the previous paragraph.

The pointer returns to its normal I-beam shape.

3 On the Standard toolbar, *double-click* the **Format Painter** button. Move the pointer over the paragraph that begins *TSR Database 4 is a program that captures*.

4 Click once.

The paragraph is indented, but this time the Format Painter paintbrush remains active.

5 Scroll down using the down scroll arrow and move the pointer over the paragraph that begins *TSR Database 4 is a database*. Click once.

6 Scroll down and click once in each of the remaining paragraphs that are not bold subheadings.

This is much faster than clicking on each paragraph and then opening the Paragraph dialog box to set the indentation parameters.

7 On the Standard toolbar, click the **Format Painter** button.

The Format Painter feature is turned off. You can also turn it off by pressing Esc.

8 On the Standard toolbar, click the **Save** button.

Objective 2
Change and Reorganize Text

Changing and reorganizing text is accomplished using Word tools such as the **Office Clipboard**, a temporary storage area that holds text. Text can be moved to the Office Clipboard by **copying** existing text, which leaves the original text in place, or by **cutting** text, which removes it from its original location. You can then **paste** the contents of the clipboard in a new location. There are keyboard shortcuts for many of these tools, as shown in Figure 2.18.

Activity 2.7 Finding and Replacing Text

Finding and then replacing text is a quick way to make a change in a document that occurs more than one time. For example, if you misspelled someone's last name, Word can search for all instances of the name and replace it with the correct spelling.

Keyboard Shortcuts for Editing Text

Keyboard Shortcut	Action
Ctrl + X	Cut text or graphic and place it on the Office Clipboard
Ctrl + C	Copy text or graphic and place it on the Office Clipboard
Ctrl + V	Paste the contents of the Office Clipboard
Ctrl + Z	Undo an action
Ctrl + Y	Redo an action
Ctrl + F	Find text
Ctrl + H	Find and replace text

Figure 2.18

1 Press Ctrl + Home to position the insertion point at the beginning of the document.

When you initiate a find-and-replace operation, it begins from the location of the insertion point and proceeds to the end of the document. If you begin a search in the middle of a document, Word will prompt you to return to the beginning of the document and continue the search.

2 On the **Edit** menu, click **Replace**.

3 In the displayed **Find and Replace** dialog box, in the **Find what** box, type **TSR**

4 In the **Find and Replace** dialog box, in the **Replace with** box, type **TSF**

5 Click **Find Next**.

The first instance of TSR is highlighted, and the Find and Replace dialog box remains open. See Figure 2.19.

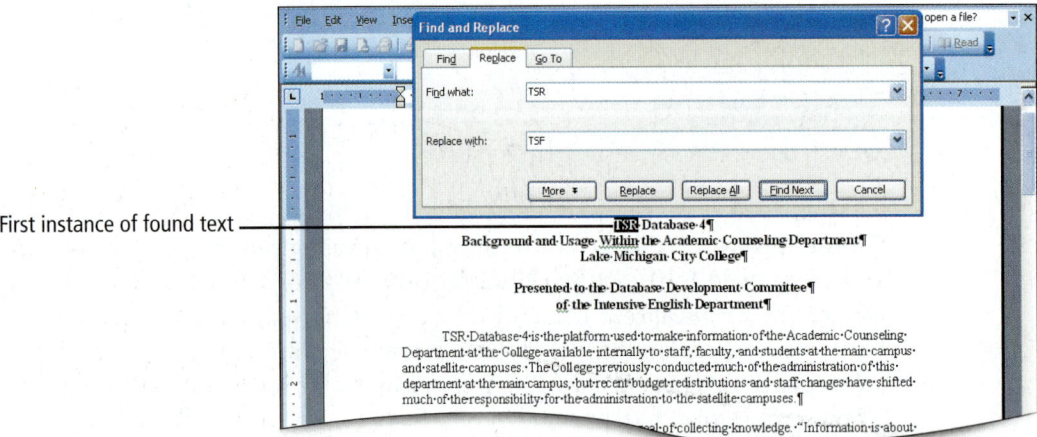

First instance of found text

Figure 2.19

6 Click the **Replace** button.

The first instance of TSR is replaced by TSF, and the next instance of TSR is highlighted. See Figure 2.20.

258   **Word** | Chapter 2: Formatting and Organizing Text

First TSR replaced

Second instance found

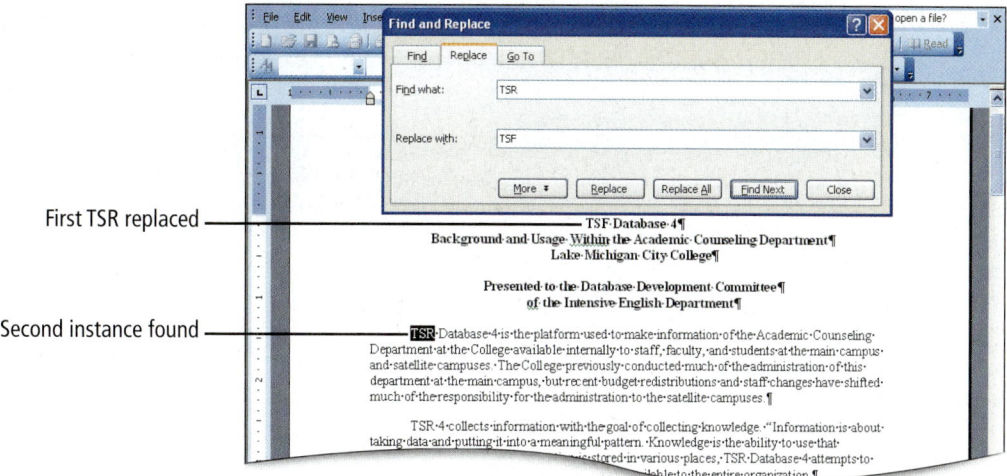

Figure 2.20

7 Click the **Replace All** button.

Every occurrence of TSR is replaced with TSF, and a dialog box indicates the number of replacements made. See Figure 2.21.

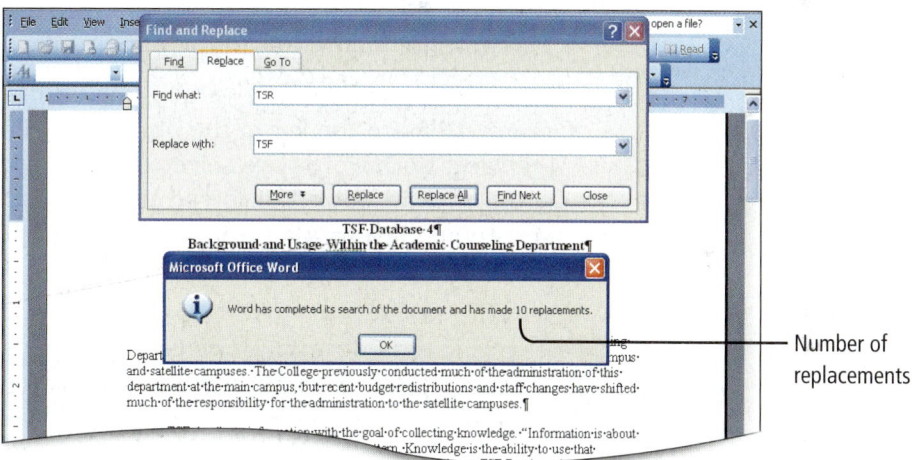

Number of replacements

Figure 2.21

8 Click **OK** to close the dialog box. In the **Find and Replace** dialog box click **Close**.

The Find and Replace dialog box closes.

Activity 2.8 Selecting and Deleting Text

You have practiced removing text one letter at a time using the Backspace key and the Delete key. For removing larger blocks of text, it is more efficient to select the block of text and then delete it.

1 Scroll down until you can see the lower portion of page 1 and locate the paragraph that begins *TSF Database 4 is a collection of databases*.

2 At the end of the fifth line in the paragraph, locate the word *can*, and then double-click to select the word. See Figure 2.22.

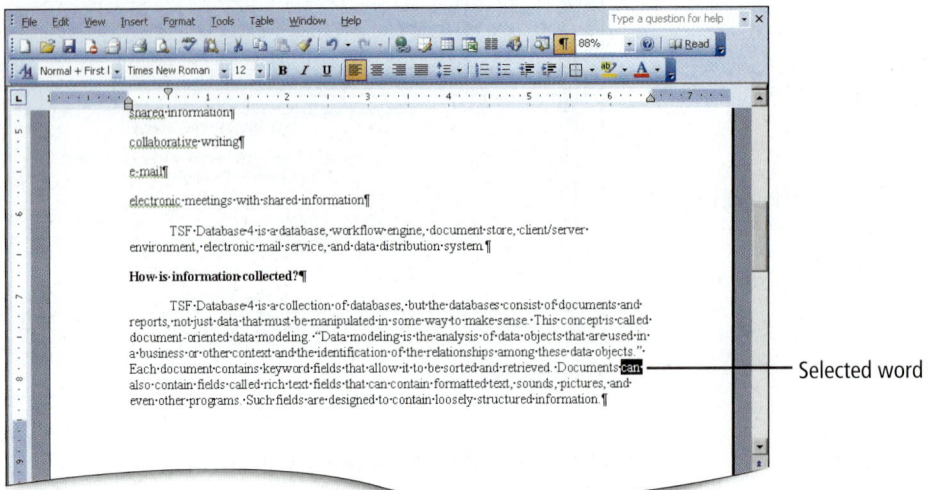

Figure 2.22

3 Press Delete.

The word is removed from the paragraph.

4 Locate the phrase *and reports* in the first sentence of the same paragraph. Click to the left of the phrase, hold down Ctrl + Shift, and press → twice. Both words are selected. See Figure 2.23. Alternatively, you could click to the left of the phrase and drag to select both words, or you could click at the beginning of the phrase and Shift + click at the end of the phrase.

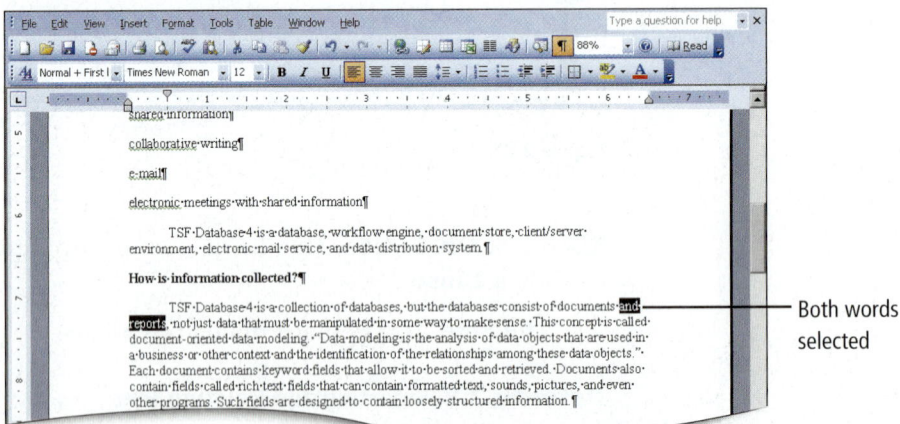

Figure 2.23

5 Press Delete.

Both words are deleted.

6 On the Standard toolbar, click the **Save** button.

Activity 2.9 Cutting and Pasting Text

You can move text from one location in a document to a different location in the same document with the commands cut and paste. The **cut** command moves text out of the document and onto the Office Clipboard—the temporary storage location for text or graphics. Then, use the **paste** command to paste the contents of the Office Clipboard into the new location.

1 Scroll down to view the upper portion of page 2, and locate the paragraph that begins *TSF Database 4 clients connect*.

2 Locate the second sentence, that begins with *Replication manages changes*. Hold down Ctrl and click anywhere in the sentence.

The entire sentence is selected. See Figure 2.24.

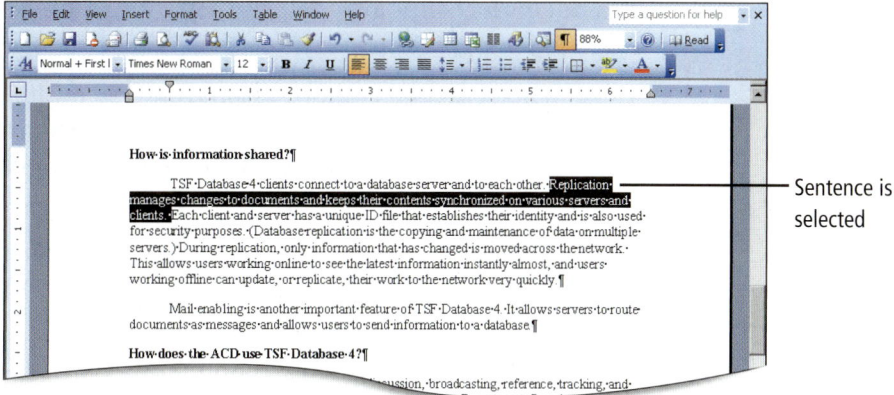

Figure 2.24

3 On the Standard toolbar, click the **Cut** button.

The sentence is removed from the document and moved to the Office Clipboard.

> **Note** — The Difference Between Using Delete, Backspace, and Cut
>
> When you use the Cut command to remove text, it is stored on the Office Clipboard and can be pasted into the same (or another) document. When you use Delete or Backspace to remove text, the text is not stored on the Office Clipboard. The only way you can retrieve text removed with Delete or Backspace is by using the Undo feature.

4 In the third line of the paragraph, click to position the insertion point to the left of the sentence that begins *(Database replication*. See Figure 2.25.

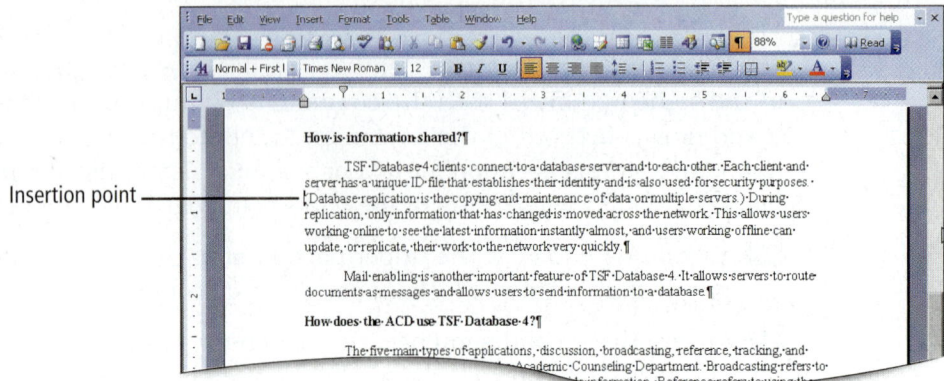

Figure 2.25

5 On the Standard toolbar, click the **Paste** button . Adjust the spacing before and after the sentence if needed.

The sentence is moved from the Office Clipboard and pasted into the document at the insertion point. A **smart tag** with a clipboard image also displays below the pasted sentence. A smart tag is a button that lets you control the result of certain actions, for example, a cut and paste operation.

6 Point to the smart tag until its ScreenTip *Paste Options* displays, and then click its small arrow.

A short menu provides commands related specifically to pasting, as shown in Figure 2.26. You can determine whether you want to format the pasted text the same as the surrounding text or retain its original formatting. Performing another screen action will cancel the display of the smart tag; alternatively press Esc to cancel its display.

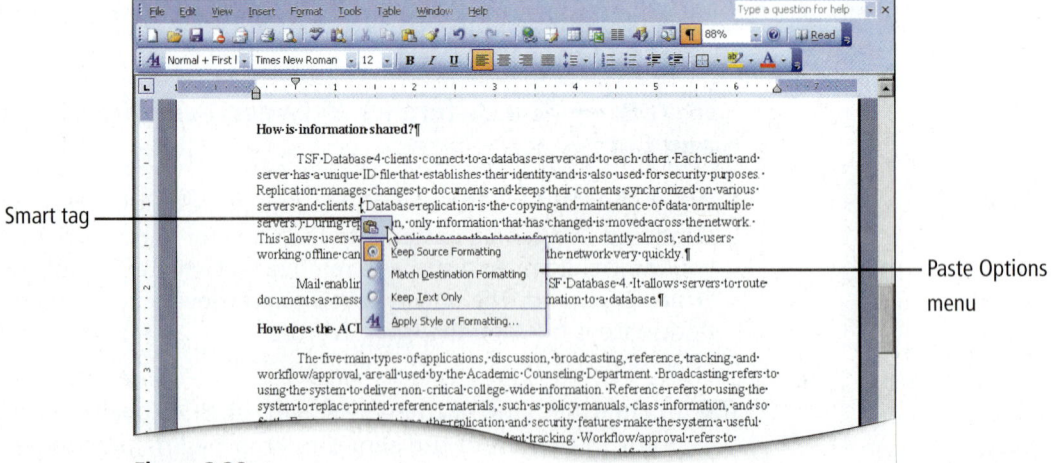

Figure 2.26

262 **Word** | Chapter 2: Formatting and Organizing Text

7 Click anywhere in the document to close the **Paste Options** menu.

8 Scroll up to position the insertion point at the top of page 1 on your screen, locate the paragraph that begins *TSF 4 collects information*, and then triple-click in the paragraph.

The entire paragraph is selected. Recall that double- and triple-clicking takes a steady hand. The speed of the clicks is important, but the mouse must also remain steady. If you did not select the entire paragraph, begin again. See Figure 2.27.

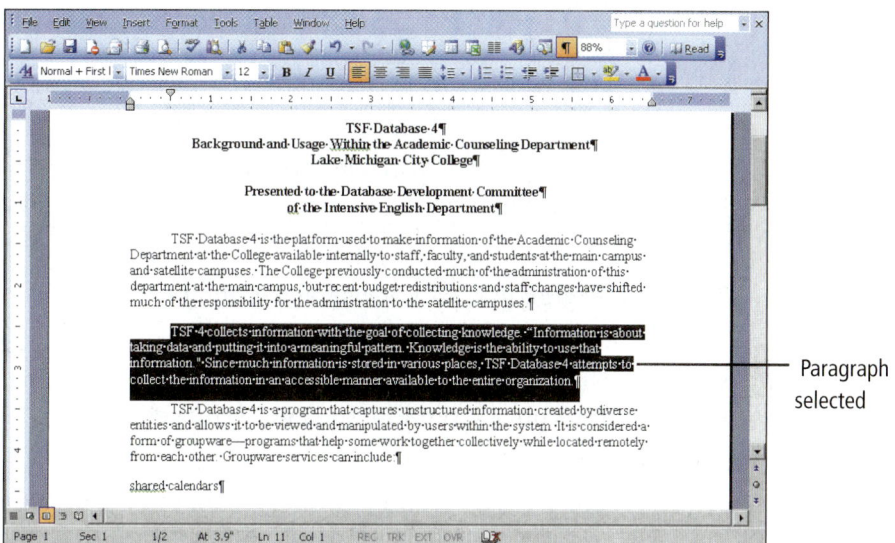

Paragraph selected

Figure 2.27

9 On the Standard toolbar, click the **Cut** button.

The paragraph is moved from the document onto the Office Clipboard.

Alert! — If the Clipboard Task Pane Opens

The Clipboard task pane may display on your screen depending on the options that have been set for the clipboard on your computer. If the Clipboard task pane opens, click the close button on the task pane title bar.

10 Scroll down as necessary and click to position the insertion point to the left of the word *How* in the subheading, *How is information collected?*

11 On the Standard toolbar, click the **Paste** button.

The paragraph is pasted from the Office Clipboard into the document at the insertion point, and the Paste Options smart tag displays. See Figure 2.28.

Project 2A: Campus Software | **Word** 263

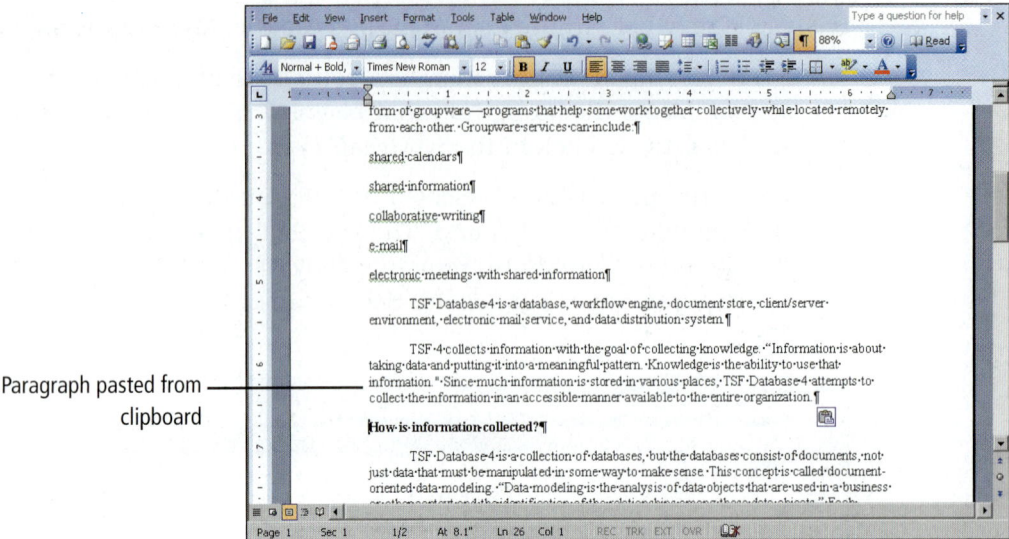

Paragraph pasted from clipboard

Figure 2.28

Activity 2.10 Copying and Pasting Text

The copy command places a copy of selected text on the Office Clipboard, which you can then paste to another location. Unlike the cut command, the copy command does not remove the selected text from its original location.

1 Be sure that the lower portion of page 1 is in view and then triple-click on the subheading *How is information collected?*

The subheading is selected. See Figure 2.29.

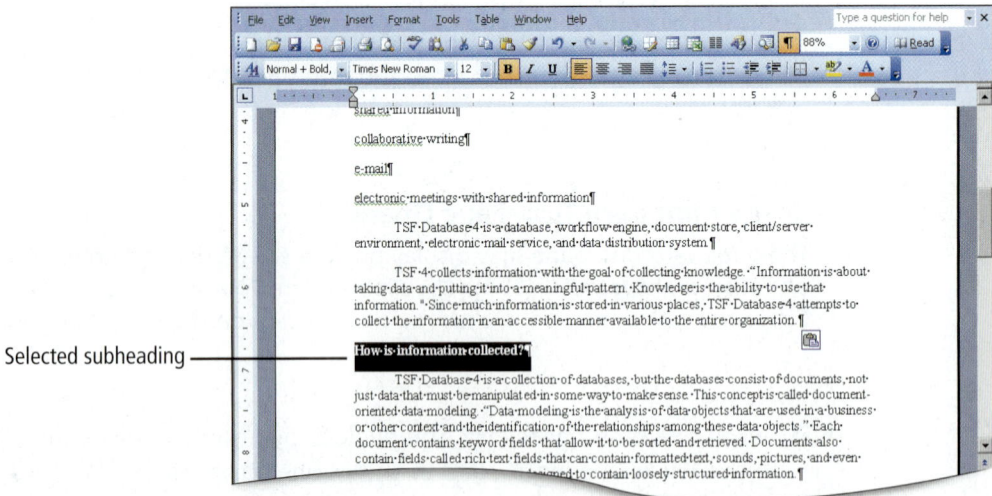

Selected subheading

Figure 2.29

2 On the Standard toolbar, click the **Copy** button. Alternatively, you can right-click on the selected text and click Copy from the shortcut menu, or press Ctrl + C.

The heading remains in its original location, but a copy has been moved onto the Office Clipboard.

3 Hold down [Ctrl] and press [End] to move to the end of the document.

4 In the last paragraph, click to position the insertion point to the left of the word *Training*. On the Standard toolbar, click the **Paste** button.

The text is copied from the Office Clipboard to the insertion point location. The spacing following the heading is also included because the information about the spacing following the paragraph is stored in its paragraph mark. See Figure 2.30.

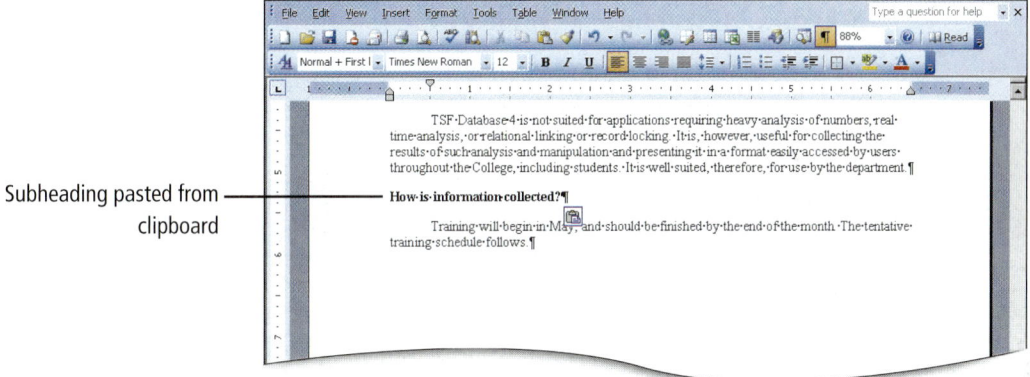

Figure 2.30

5 Triple-click on the new subheading to select it. Type **Training Schedule:** to replace the selected text.

The original text is replaced, but the formatting is retained. See Figure 2.31.

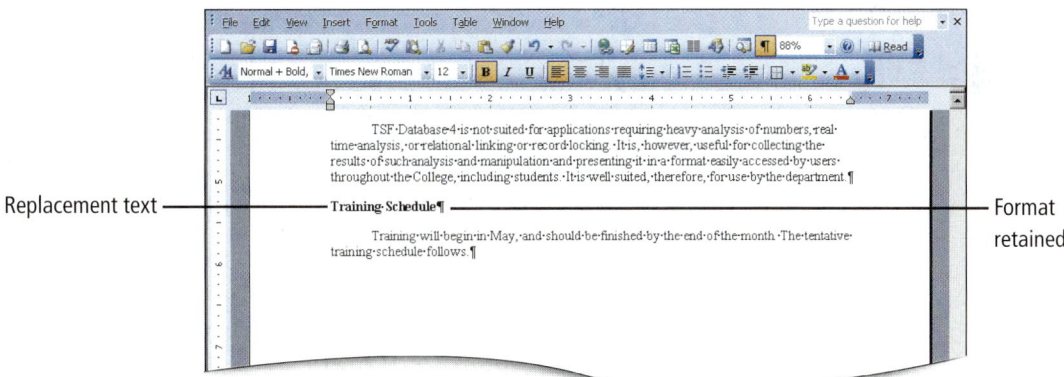

Figure 2.31

More Knowledge — Using the Office Clipboard Task Pane

If you use the copy command twice without pasting, a Clipboard task pane may open. This enables you to copy up to 24 pieces of text, graphics, and other objects into the Office Clipboard, and then paste them by selecting the desired item from the task pane. Clipboard task pane options are accessed by clicking the Options button at the bottom of the task pane. The Clipboard task pane can also be opened by clicking Edit on the menu bar, and then clicking Office Clipboard.

Project 2A: Campus Software | **Word** 265

Activity 2.11 Dragging Text to a New Location

Another method of moving text is **drag-and-drop**. This technique uses the mouse to drag selected text from one location to another. This method is useful if the text to be moved is on the same screen as the destination location.

1 Scroll as necessary to position the upper portion of page 2 at the top of your screen.

2 In the paragraph that begins *TSF Database 4 clients*, in the next to the last line, locate and select the word *almost*.

3 Move the pointer over the selected word.

The pointer becomes a white arrow that points up and to the left. This is the drag and drop pointer. See Figure 2.32.

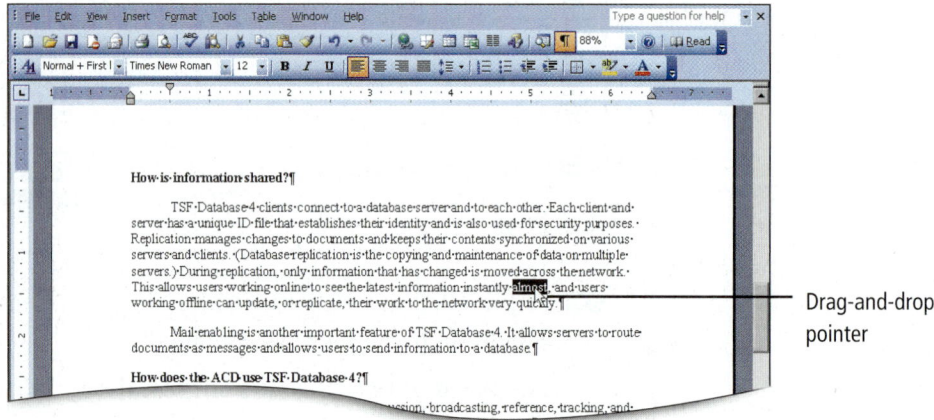

Drag-and-drop pointer

Figure 2.32

> **Note** — Turning on the Drag-and-Drop Option
>
> If you do not see the drag-and-drop pointer, you will need to turn this feature on. On the Tools menu, click Options, and then click the Edit tab. Under Editing options, select the *Drag-and-drop text editing* text box.

4 Hold down the left mouse button and drag to the left until the dotted vertical line that floats next to the pointer is positioned to the left of the word *instantly* and then release the left mouse button.

The word is moved to the insertion point location. The vertical line of the pointer assists you in dropping the moved text in the place where you want it. The small box attached to the pointer indicates that there is text attached to the pointer. See Figure 2.33.

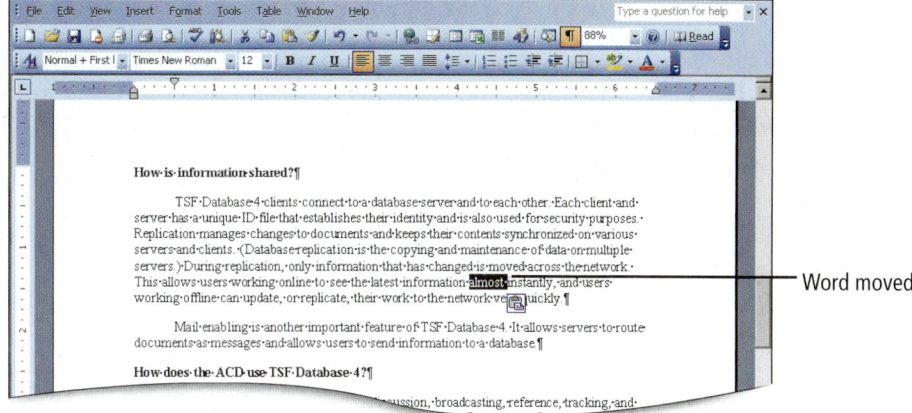

Figure 2.33

5 Press Ctrl + End to move to the end of the document. Then scroll as necessary so that you can view the last four paragraphs on your screen as shown in Figure 2.34.

6 Hold down Ctrl and click anywhere in the sentence *It is well suited, therefore, for use by the department* at the end of the second-to-last paragraph.

The sentence is selected.

7 Move the pointer over the selected sentence to display the drag-and-drop pointer, and then drag up to the paragraph above and position the vertical line to the right of the period at the end of *defined protocols.* as shown in Figure 2.34.

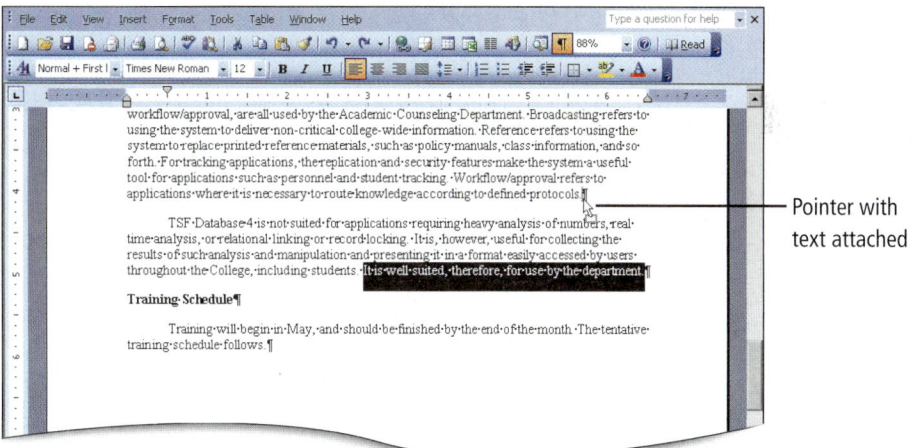

Figure 2.34

8 Release the mouse button. The sentence you moved becomes the last sentence in the paragraph. Notice that a space was automatically added before the sentence.

Project 2A: Campus Software | **Word** 267

Activity 2.12 Undoing and Redoing Changes

You can Undo one or more actions that you made to a document since the last time you saved it. An Undo action can be reversed with the Redo command.

1 On the Standard toolbar, click the **Undo** button.

The sentence you dragged and dropped returns to its original location as shown in Figure 2.35.

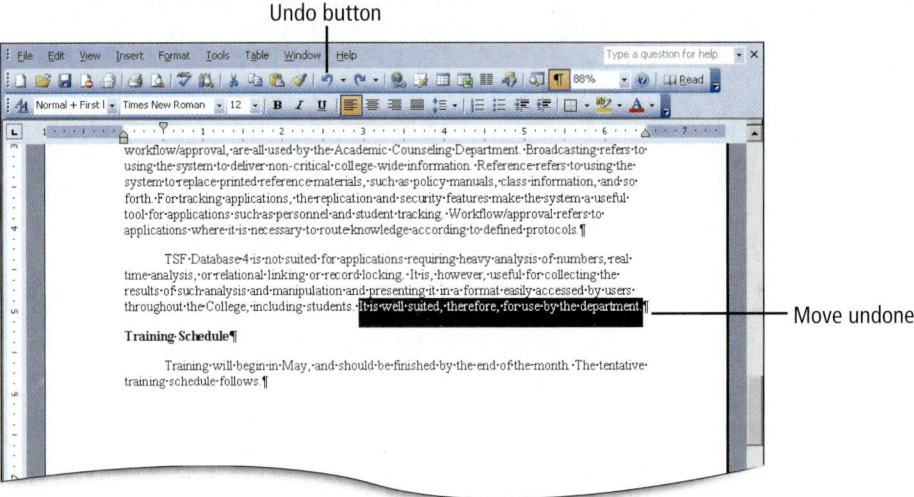

Figure 2.35

2 On the Standard toolbar, click the **Undo** button again.

The word you moved prior to moving the sentence returns to its original location.

3 On the Standard toolbar, click the **Redo** button.

The word is moved back. Clicking the Undo and Redo buttons changes one action at a time.

4 On the Standard toolbar, click the arrow on the right of the **Undo** button.

A list of changes displays showing all of the changes made since your last save operation. From the displayed list, you can click any of the actions and undo it, but all of the changes above the one you select will also be undone. See Figure 2.36.

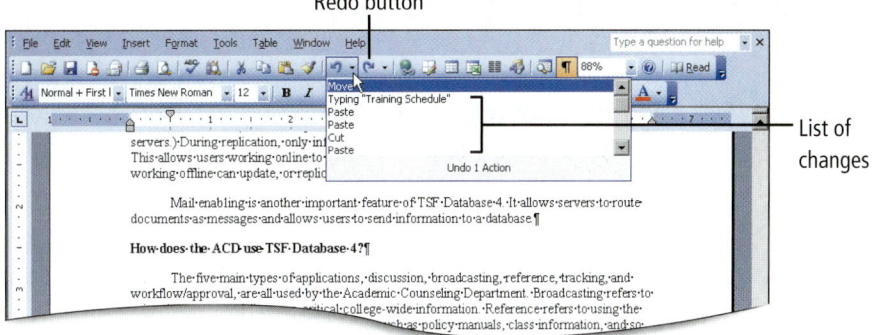

Figure 2.36

5. Click anywhere in the document to close the Undo menu without selecting any actions.

6. From the **View** menu, click **Header and Footer**.

7. From the Header and Footer toolbar, click the **Switch Between Header and Footer** button. Using your own name, type **2A Campus Software_Firstname_Lastname** in the footer.

8. On the Header and Footer toolbar, click the **Close** button.

9. On the Standard toolbar, click the **Save** button and then click the **Print Preview** button to preview the document. Close the Print Preview window. Use the PgUp and PgDn keys as necessary to view both pages in Print Preview. Make any necessary changes, and then click the **Print** button. Close the document saving any changes.

End You have completed Project 2A

Project 2B Software

Word has numerous features to help you create a report. In this project, you will use report features such as lists, headers and footers, and footnote references.

In Activities 2.13 through 2.27 you will make further changes to a document that describes the groupware software being used by Lake Michigan City College. This document is similar to the one you worked on in Project 2A. Your completed document will look similar to Figure 2.37. You will save your document as *2B_Software_Firstname_Lastname*.

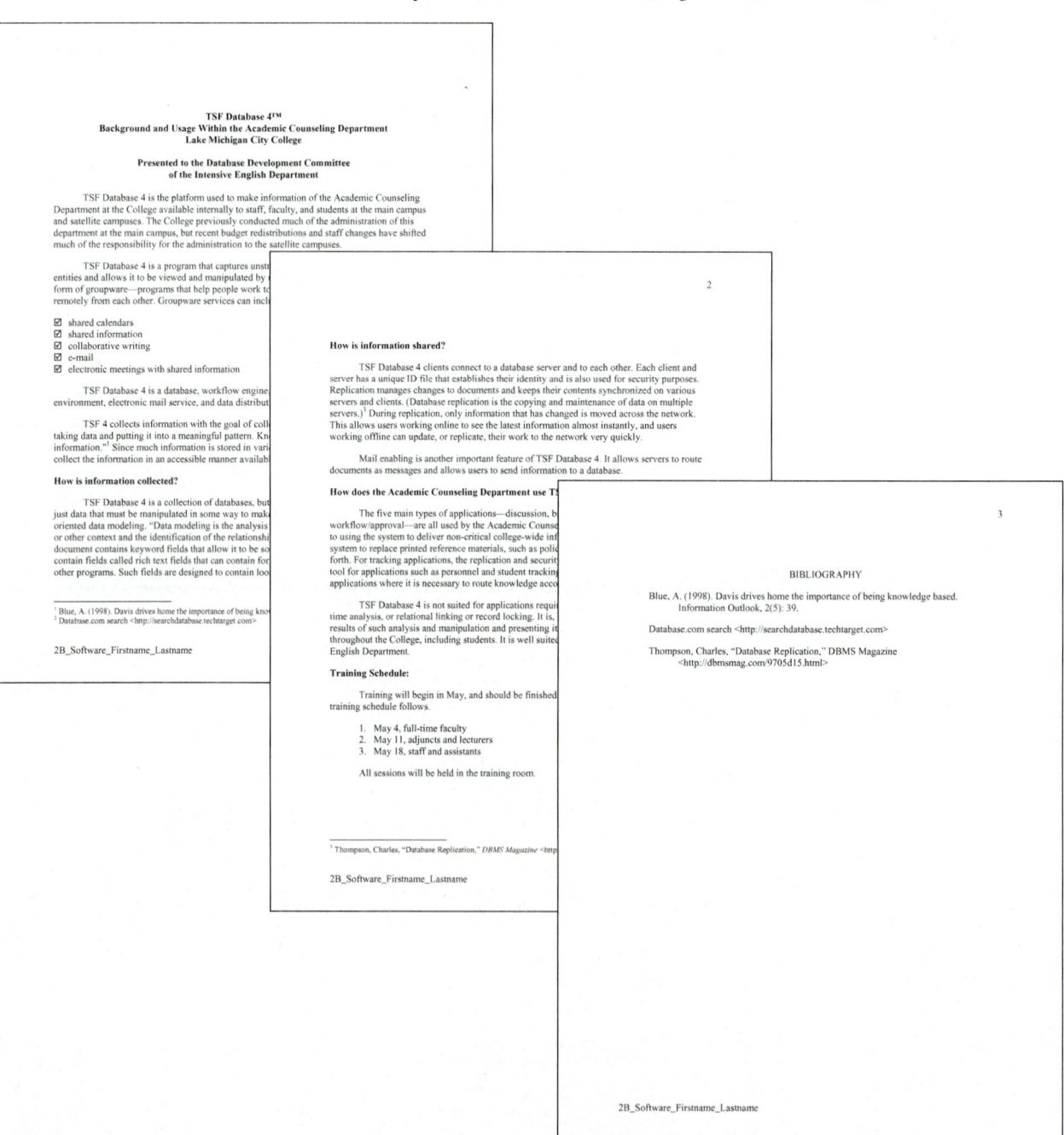

Figure 2.37
Project 2B—Software

Objective 3
Create and Modify Lists

Lists of information can be displayed two ways. A bulleted list uses bullets, which are text symbols such as small circles or check marks, to introduce each piece of information. Numbered lists use consecutive numbers to introduce each item in a list. Bulleted lists are used when the items in the list can be displayed in any order; numbered lists are used for items that have definite steps, a sequence of actions, or are in chronological order.

Activity 2.13 Creating a Bulleted List

1 Start Word. On the Standard toolbar, click the **Open** button. Navigate to the location where the student files for this textbook are stored. Locate **w02B_Software** and click once to select it. Then, in the lower right corner of the **Open** dialog box, click the **Open** button.

The *w02B_ Software* file opens.

2 If the formatting marks are not already displayed on your screen, on the Standard toolbar, click the Show/Hide ¶ button.

3 On the **File** menu, click **Save As**.

The Save As dialog box displays.

4 Use the **Save in arrow** to navigate to the location where you are saving your files. In the **File name** box, delete the existing text and, using your own name, type **2B_Software_Firstname_Lastname**

5 Near the bottom of the **Save As** dialog box, click **Save**.

The document is saved with a new name.

6 On the Standard toolbar, click the **Zoom button arrow** and click **Page Width**.

7 Scroll as necessary to display the middle of page 1 on your screen, and locate the five short paragraphs that begin with *shared calendars*.

8 Move the pointer into the left margin to the left of *shared calendars*, and when the pointer changes to a white arrow, drag down to select the five short paragraphs as shown in Figure 2.38.

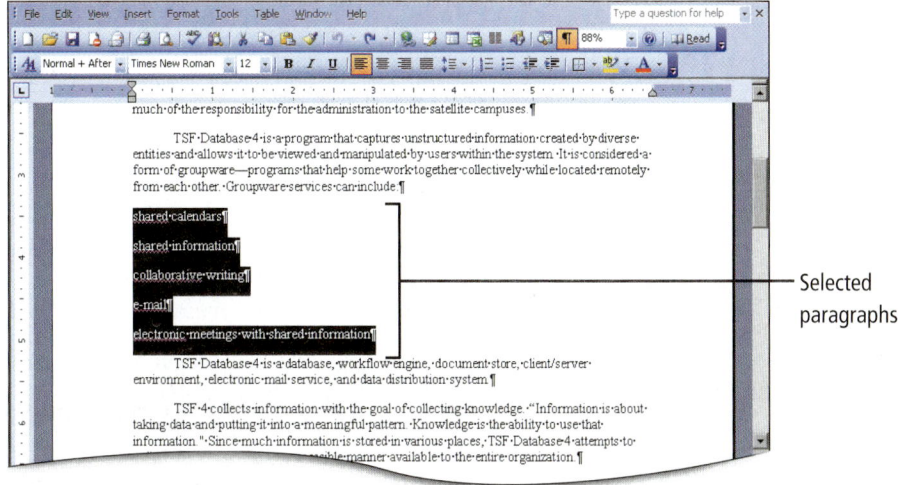

Selected paragraphs

Figure 2.38

Project 2B: Software | **Word** 271

To create a list from existing text, the paragraphs need to be selected.

9 On the Formatting toolbar, click the **Bullets** button.

A symbol is placed to the left of each of the five paragraphs, and the text is moved to the right. The bullet symbol displayed on your screen depends on previous bullet usage of the computer at which you are seated. The default bullet is a large, round, black dot centered vertically on the line of text.

10 Click anywhere in the document to deselect the text. Click the **Show/Hide ¶** button.

This enables you to see the bulleted list without the formatting marks. Notice that the line spacing remains the same as it was before you created the list. See Figure 2.39.

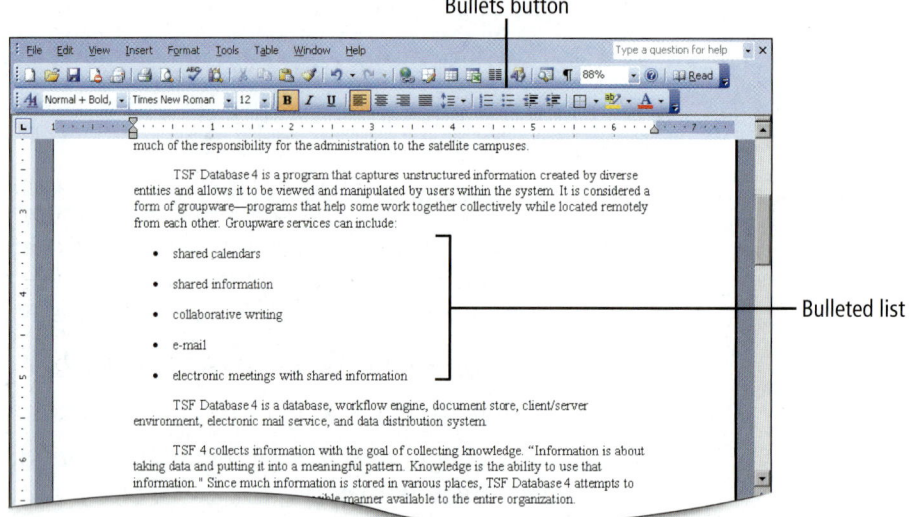

Figure 2.39

11 Click the **Show/Hide ¶** button again to turn on formatting marks.

12 On the Standard toolbar, click the **Save** button.

Activity 2.14 Creating a Numbered List

In the previous activity you created a list using existing text. You can also turn on the list feature and create a new list.

1 Press Ctrl + End to move to the end of the document and then press Enter once.

Notice that the insertion point is indented. This paragraph retains the formatting of the previous paragraph, which is stored in the paragraph mark you just created when you pressed Enter.

2 On the Formatting toolbar, click the **Numbering** button.

The number *1* is inserted to begin a numbered list as shown in Figure 2.40.

Numbering button

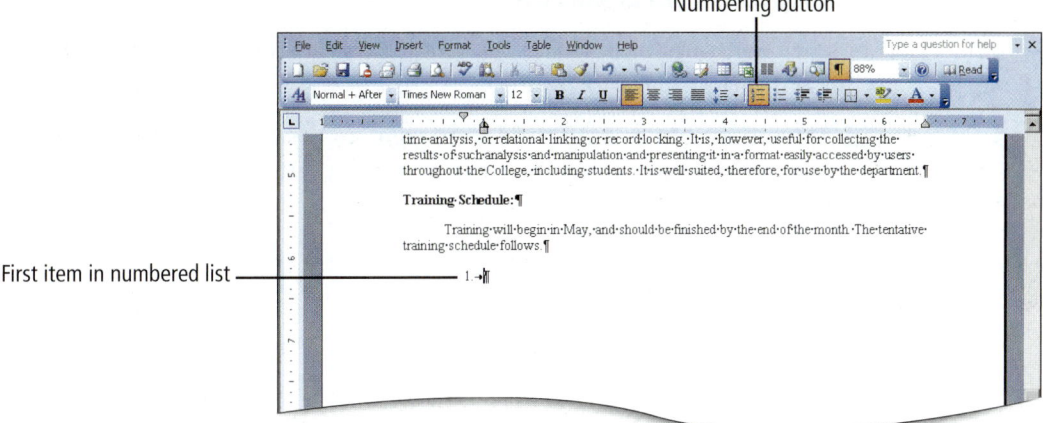

First item in numbered list

Figure 2.40

3 Type **May 4, full-time faculty** and press Enter.

The text is entered, and a second number is added.

4 Type **May 11, adjuncts and lecturers** and press Enter.

5 Type **May 18, staff and assistants** and press Enter.

Although this list will contain only the three lines you typed, the paragraph marker for the new paragraph retains the formatting of the previous paragraph, which is a numbered list. See Figure 2.41.

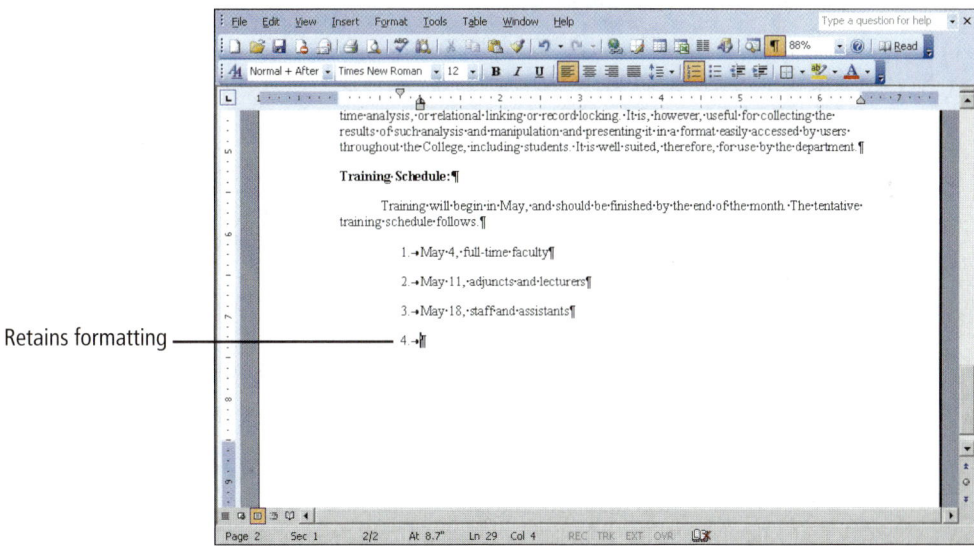

Retains formatting

Figure 2.41

6 On the Formatting toolbar, click the **Numbering** button again.

The numbering format is turned off. Both list buttons, Numbering and Bullets, act as a ***toggle switch***; that is, clicking the button once turns the feature on, and clicking the button again turns the feature off.

7 Type **All sessions will be held in the training room.**

8 On the Standard toolbar, click the **Save** button.

Project 2B: Software | **Word** 273

Activity 2.15 Formatting Lists

Lists are columns of paragraphs and can be formatted in the same way other paragraphs are formatted.

1 Move the pointer into the left margin to the left of *1.* and when the pointer changes to a white arrow, drag down to select the three numbered items.

The three items are selected, even though the list numbers are outside the highlighted area.

2 On the Formatting toolbar, click the **Decrease Indent** button.

All of the items in the list move to the left, and the decreased indent is reflected in the ruler. See Figure 2.42.

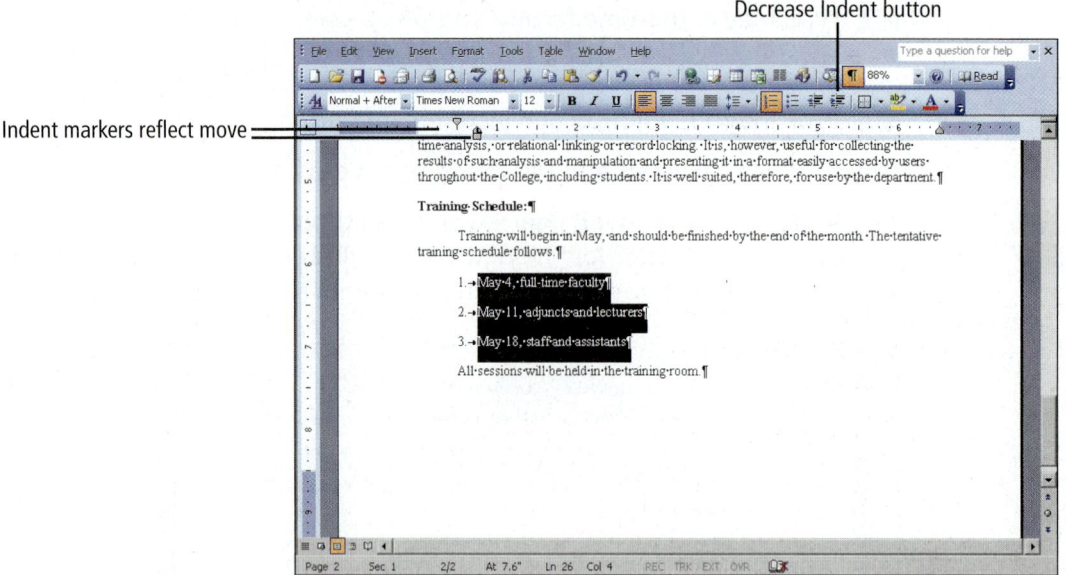

Figure 2.42

3 Select only the first two numbered items in the list.

4 On the **Format** menu, click **Paragraph**. If necessary, click the Indents and Spacing tab.

The Paragraph dialog box displays.

5 Under **Spacing**, in the **After** spin box, click the **down arrow** twice.

The value in the box changes from 12 pt. to 0 pt. as shown in Figure 2.43.

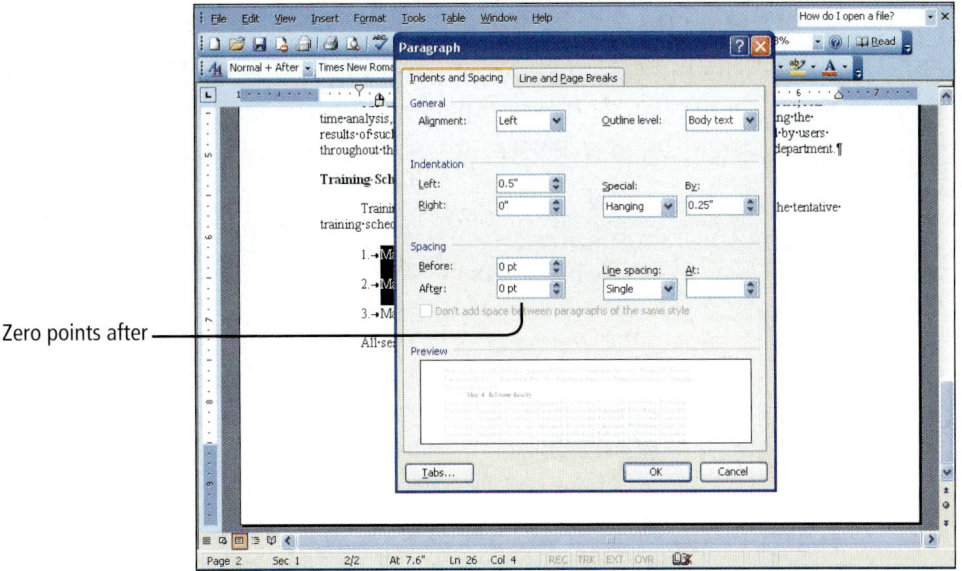

Zero points after

Figure 2.43

6 Click **OK**.

The extra spaces between the items in the list are removed resulting in single spacing. The space after the third item remains, because it was not selected. See Figure 2.44.

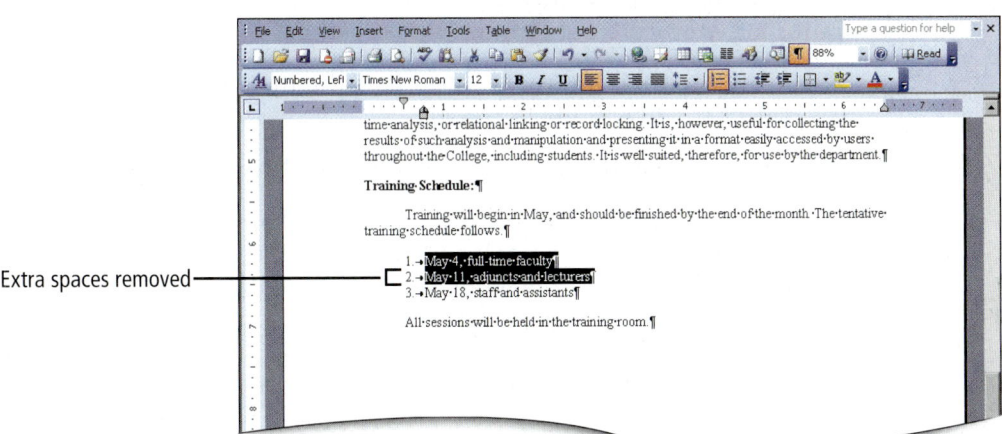

Extra spaces removed

Figure 2.44

7 Scroll up to view the bulleted list on page 1, position the pointer in the margin until it displays as a white arrow, and then drag downward to select the five bulleted items.

8 On the Formatting toolbar, click the **Decrease Indent** button.

All of the items in the list move to the left, and the ruler reflects the change.

9 Select the first four bulleted items in the list. On the **Format** menu, click **Paragraph**.

The Paragraph dialog box displays.

10 Under **Spacing**, in the **After** spin box, click the **down arrow** twice.

The value in the box changes from 12 pt. to 0 pt.

Project 2B: Software | **Word** 275

11 Click **OK**.

The bulleted list is now formatted in the same manner as the numbered list. The extra spacing after the last item remains to set it off from the next paragraph. See Figure 2.45.

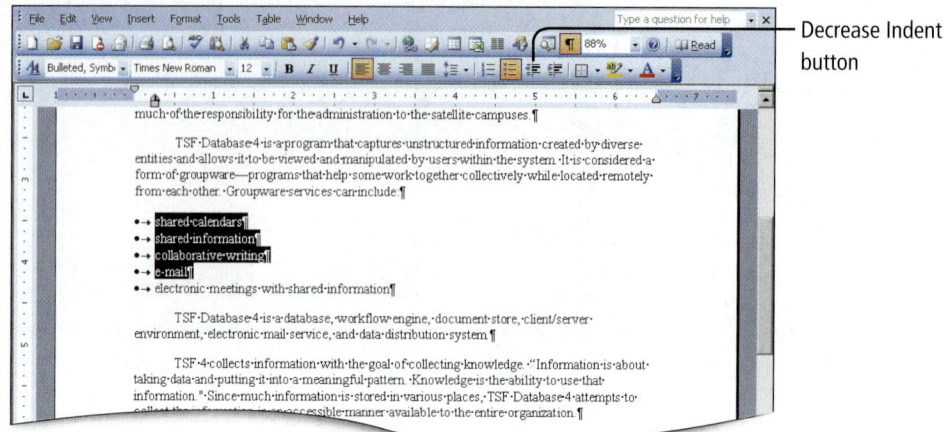

Figure 2.45

Activity 2.16 Customizing Bullets

You are not restricted to the bullet symbol that displays when you click the Bullets button. You can use any symbol from any font on your computer for your bullet character.

1 From the margin area to the left of the five bulleted items, drag to select the five items in the list.

2 On the **Format** menu, click **Bullets and Numbering**.

The Bullets and Numbering dialog box displays, showing you the most recently used bullets. Because the bullets displayed depend on previous usage at the computer at which you are seated, your screen may vary somewhat from Figure 2.46.

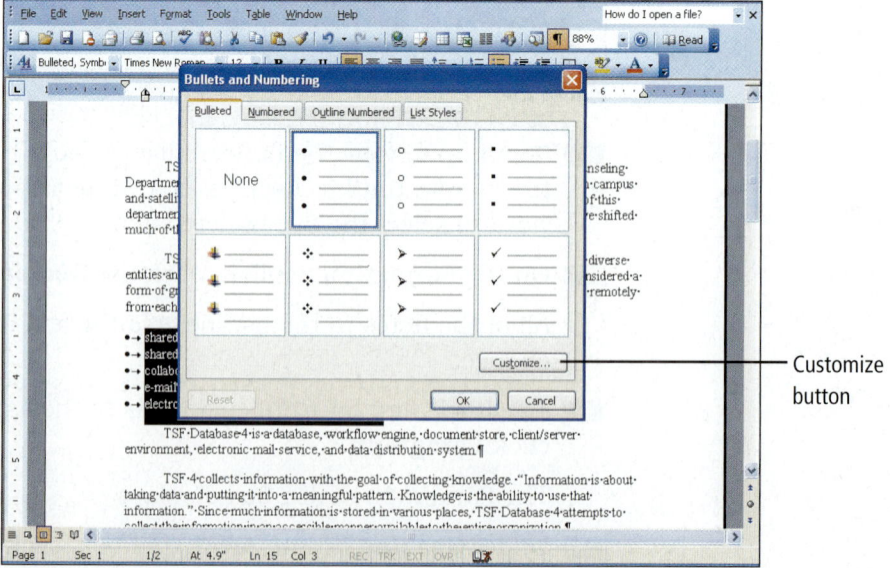

Figure 2.46

3 In the **Bullets and Numbering** dialog box, in the lower right corner click the **Customize** button.

The Customize Bulleted List dialog box displays, showing the options that are available for customizing a bullet character. See Figure 2.47.

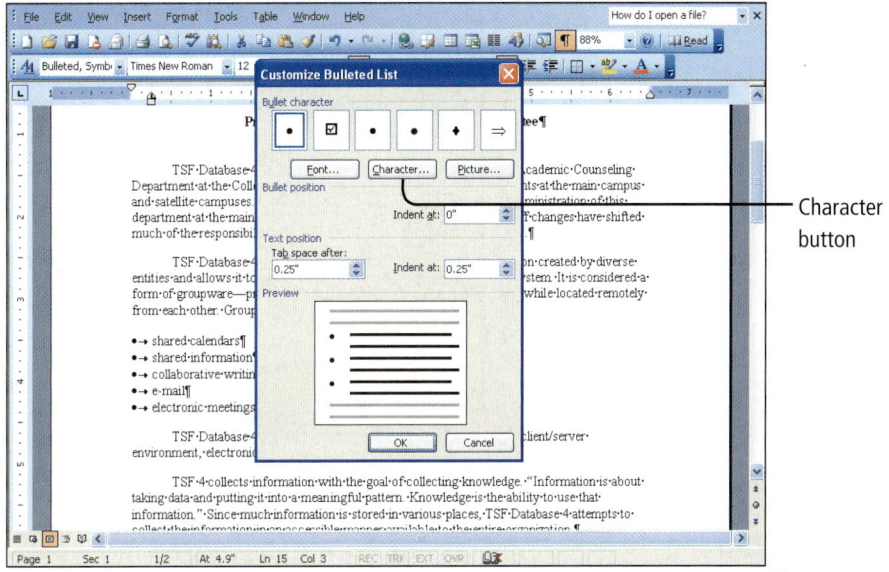

Character button

Figure 2.47

4 Under **Bullet character**, click the **Character** command button.

A table of characters displays in the Symbol dialog box. The character that is currently used for your list is highlighted. The font name of the current bullet symbol also displays. See Figure 2.48.

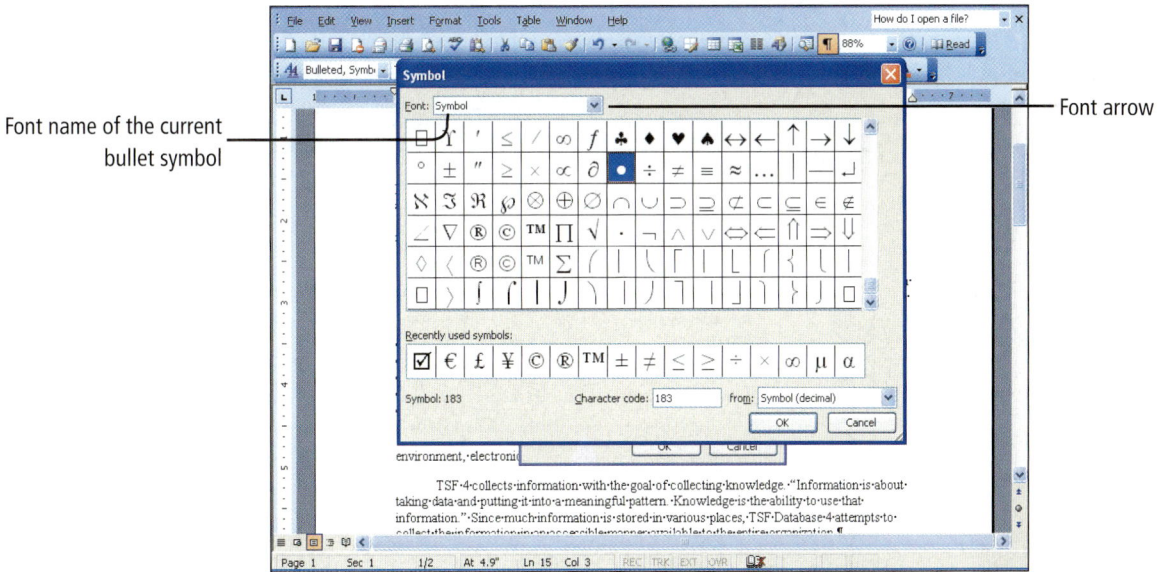

Font name of the current bullet symbol

Font arrow

Figure 2.48

5 At the top of the dialog box, click the **Font arrow** at the right of the font box, scroll as necessary, and then click **Wingdings**.

Project 2B: Software | **Word**   277

6 Use the scroll bar on the right of the dialog box to scroll down the list of Wingding characters until you reach the end. Click the check mark in the last row as shown in Figure 2.49.

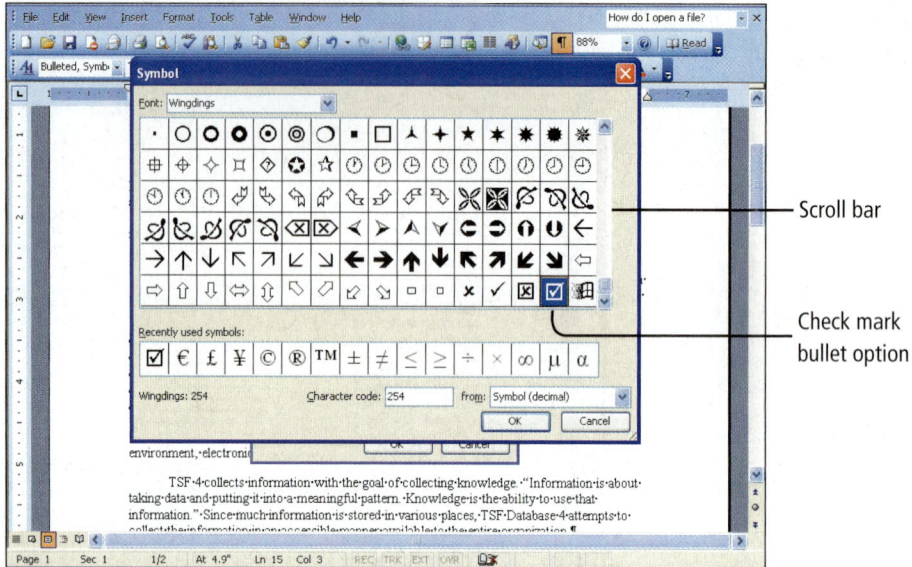

Figure 2.49

7 Click **OK** to close the **Symbol** dialog box. Click **OK** again to close the **Customize Bulleted List** dialog box.

8 Click anywhere in the document to deselect the list.

The bullet character is changed to check marks in boxes, as shown in Figure 2.50.

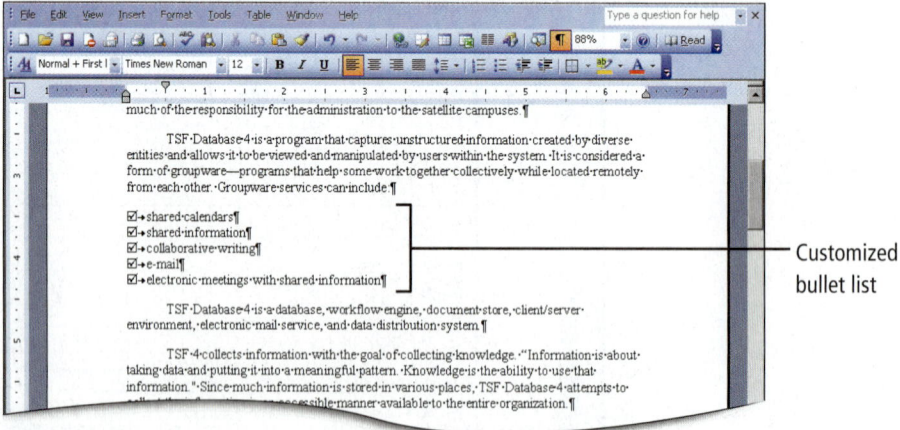

Figure 2.50

9 On the Standard toolbar, click the **Save** button.

Objective 4
Work with Headers and Footers

Text or graphics that you insert into a header or a footer display on every page of a document. On the first page of a document, it is common practice to suppress (hide) the header or footer, and Word provides an easy way to accomplish this. Within a header or footer, you can add automatic page numbers, dates, times, the file name, and pictures.

Activity 2.17 Inserting and Formatting Page Numbers

1 Position the insertion point at the top of the document. On the **View** menu, click **Header and Footer**.

The Header area displays.

2 On the Formatting toolbar, click the **Align Right** button.

The insertion point moves to the right edge of the header box.

3 On the Header and Footer toolbar, click the **Insert Page Number** button.

The page number, *1*, is inserted as shown in Figure 2.51.

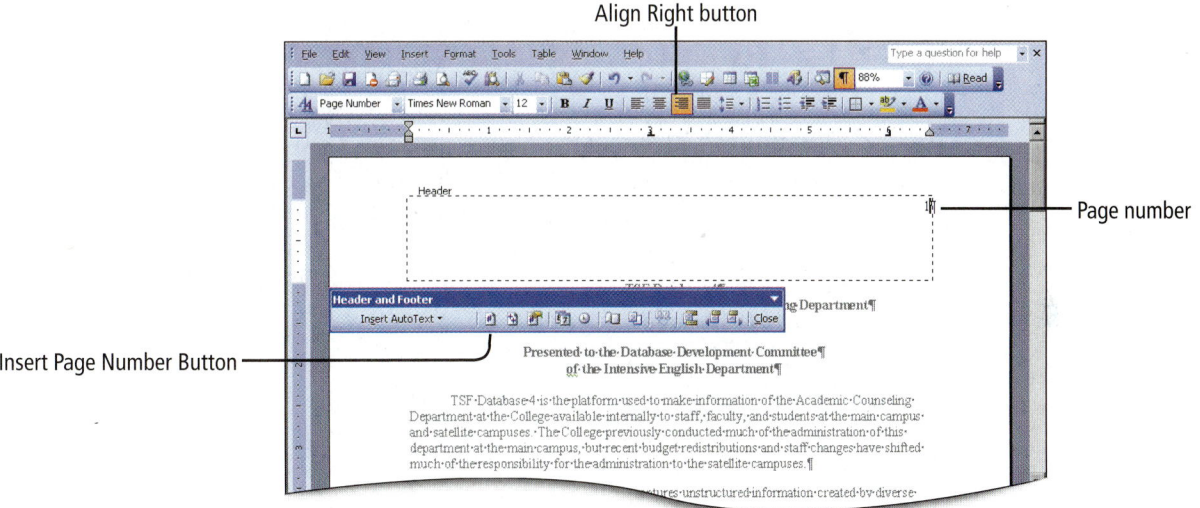

Figure 2.51

4 On the Header and Footer toolbar, click the **Page Setup** button.

The Page Setup dialog box displays.

5 On the **Page Setup** dialog box, click the **Layout tab**. Under **Headers and footers**, select (click to place a check mark in) the **Different first page** check box as shown in Figure 2.52.

The Different first page option enables you to remove the header or footer information from the first page.

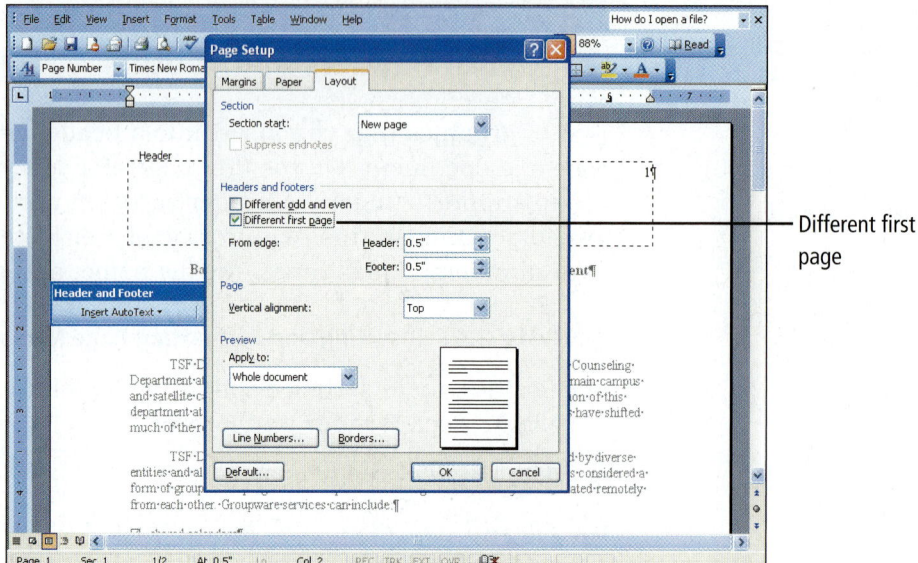

Figure 2.52

6 In the lower right corner of the dialog box, click **OK**.

The page number is removed from the header box and the name of the box changes to First Page Header.

7 Use the vertical scroll bar to scroll down and bring the top of page 2 into view.

The page number is displayed on the second page, and will be displayed on every page thereafter. This is an easy way to suppress the header on page 1. Notice that the name of the footer box at the end of page 1 has been changed to First Page Footer. This reflects the change you made to create a header and footer on the first page of your document that is different from those on the remaining pages. See Figure 2.53.

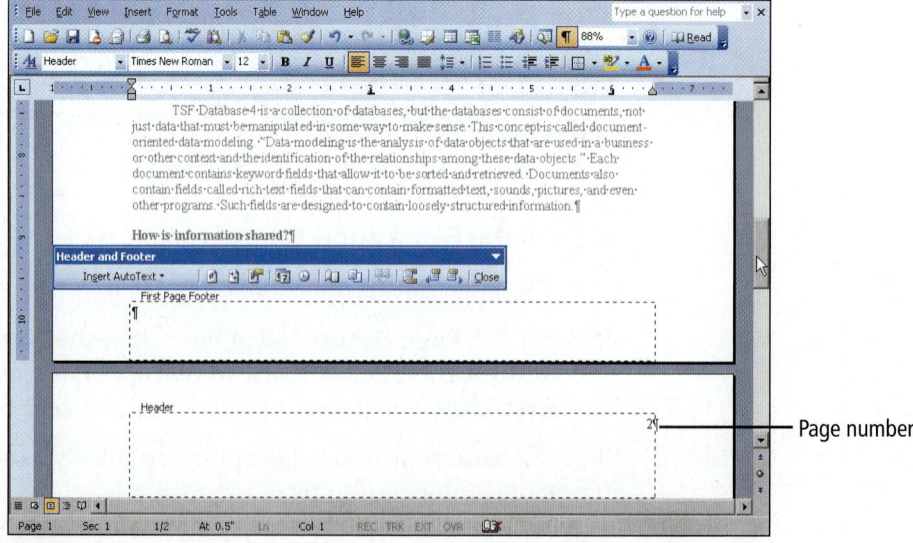

Figure 2.53

280 Word | Chapter 2: Formatting and Organizing Text

Activity 2.18 Inserting AutoText

1 On the Header and Footer toolbar, click the **Switch Between Header and Footer** button.

The insertion point is placed at the left edge of the First Page Footer box.

2 On the Header and Footer toolbar, click the **Insert AutoText** button. Take a moment to look at the items that can be inserted in the header or footer. See Figure 2.54.

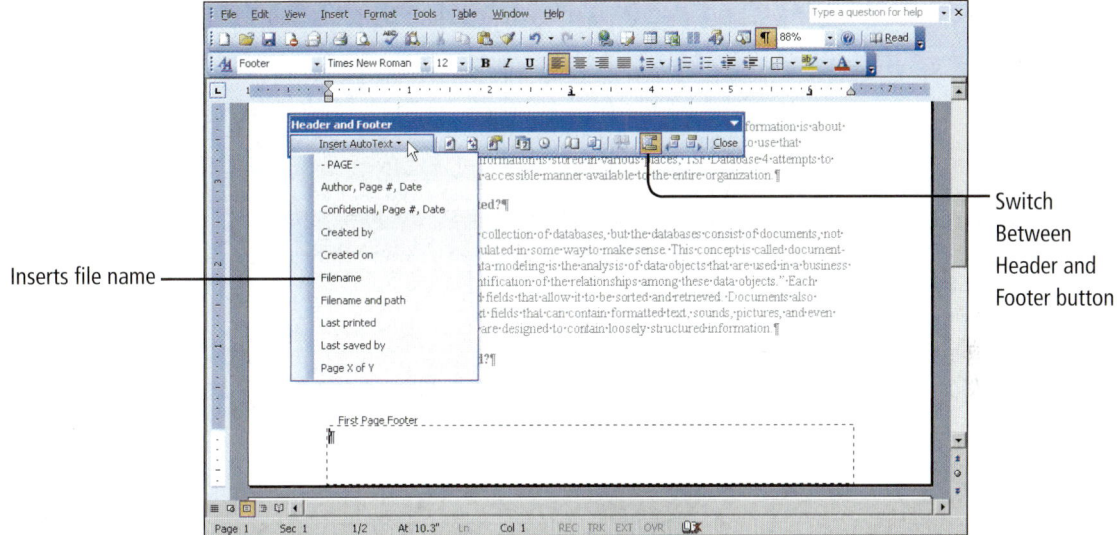

Figure 2.54

3 Click **Filename**.

The file name displays in the First Page Footer. The file extension *.doc* may or may not display, depending on your Word settings. See Figure 2.55.

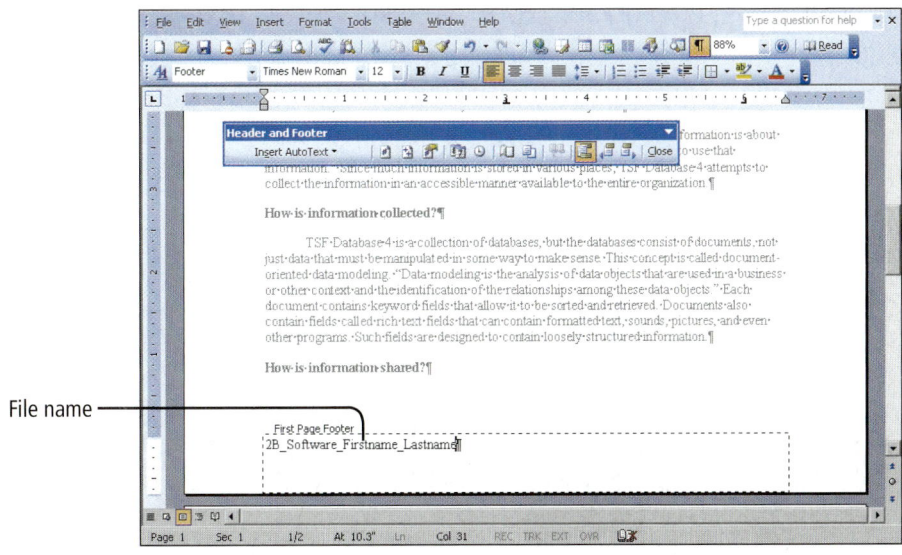

Figure 2.55

Activity 2.19 Inserting the Current Date and Time

1 Press Tab twice.

The insertion point moves to the right side of the footer box. Notice the location of the tab stop in the ruler bar.

2 On the Header and Footer toolbar, click the **Insert Date** button, and then type a comma and press the Spacebar once.

The current date displays.

3 On the Header and Footer toolbar, click the **Insert Time** button.

The current time displays. Your date and time will differ from the ones shown in Figure 2.56.

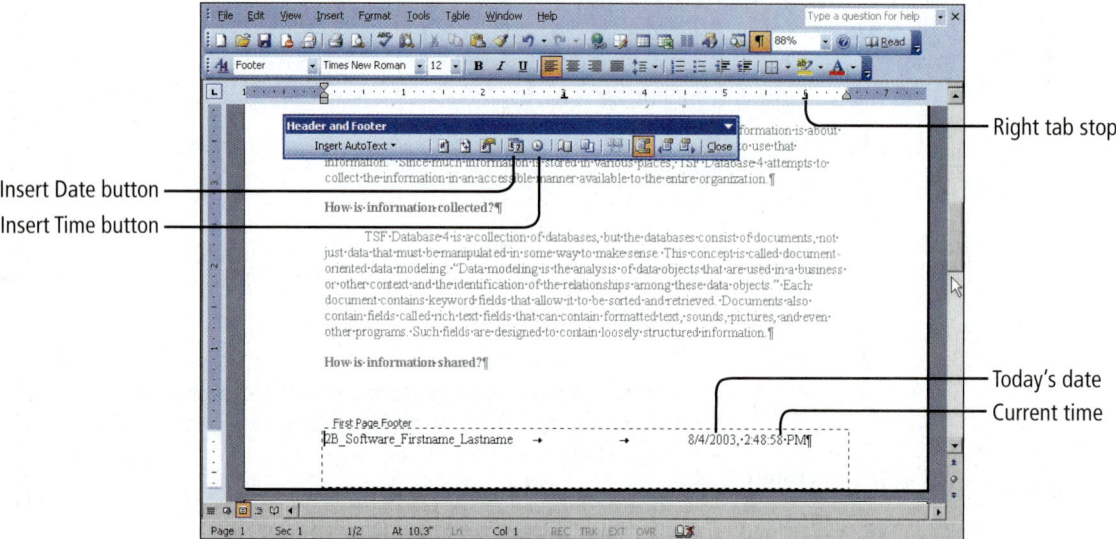

Figure 2.56

4 On the Header and Footer toolbar, click the **Close** button.

5 Scroll down as necessary to view the bottom of the first page and the top of the second page.

Notice that the text in the header and footer is gray, while the text in the document is black. When you are working in the header and footer, the header and footer text is black (active) and the document text is gray (inactive). See Figure 2.57.

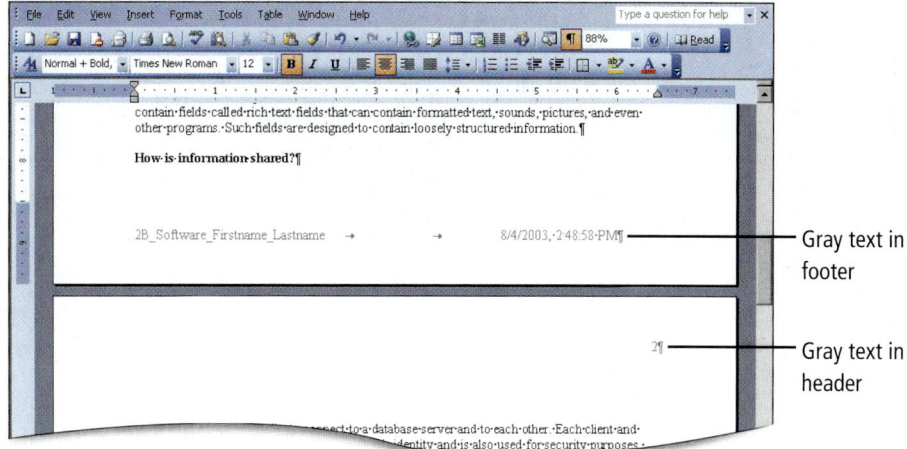

Figure 2.57

6 On the Standard toolbar, click the **Save** button.

Objective 5
Insert Frequently Used Text

AutoCorrect corrects common spelling errors as you type. When you type a word incorrectly, for example *teh*, Word automatically changes it to *the*.

If there are words that you frequently misspell, you can add them to the AutoCorrect list. Another feature, AutoText, lets you create shortcuts to quickly insert long phrases that are used regularly, such as a business name or your address, in a manner similar to AutoComplete.

Another type of frequently used text includes various symbols, such as the trademark symbol (™) or copyright symbol ©. These are accessed from the Insert Symbol dialog box.

Activity 2.20 Recording AutoCorrect Entries

You probably have words that you frequently misspell. You can add these to the AutoCorrect list for automatic correction.

1 On the **Tools** menu, click **AutoCorrect Options**.

The AutoCorrect dialog box displays as shown in Figure 2.58. All of the check boxes on the left of the dialog box are selected by default. Yours may be different.

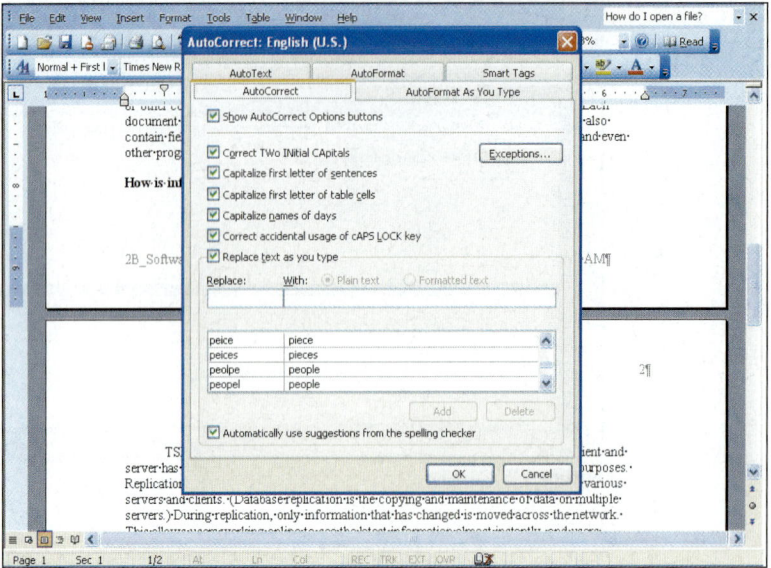

Figure 2.58

2 Under **Replace**, type **peepel**

3 Under **With**, type **people**

Your dialog box should be similar to Figure 2.59. If someone has already added this AutoCorrect entry, the Add button will change to a Replace button.

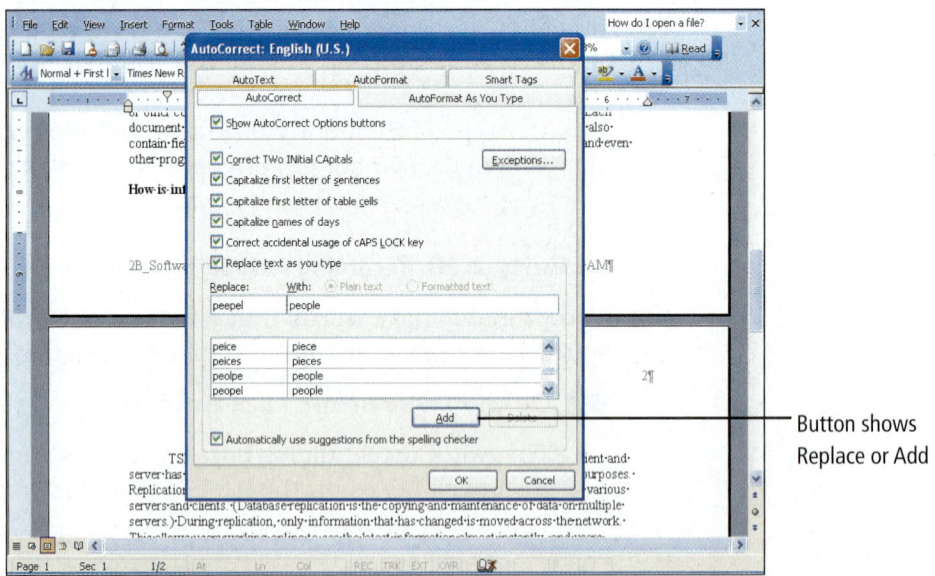

Button shows Replace or Add

Figure 2.59

4 Click **Add**. If the entry already exists, click **Replace** instead, and then click **Yes**.

The new entry is added to the AutoCorrect list. See Figure 2.60.

284   Word | Chapter 2: Formatting and Organizing Text

Added to the list

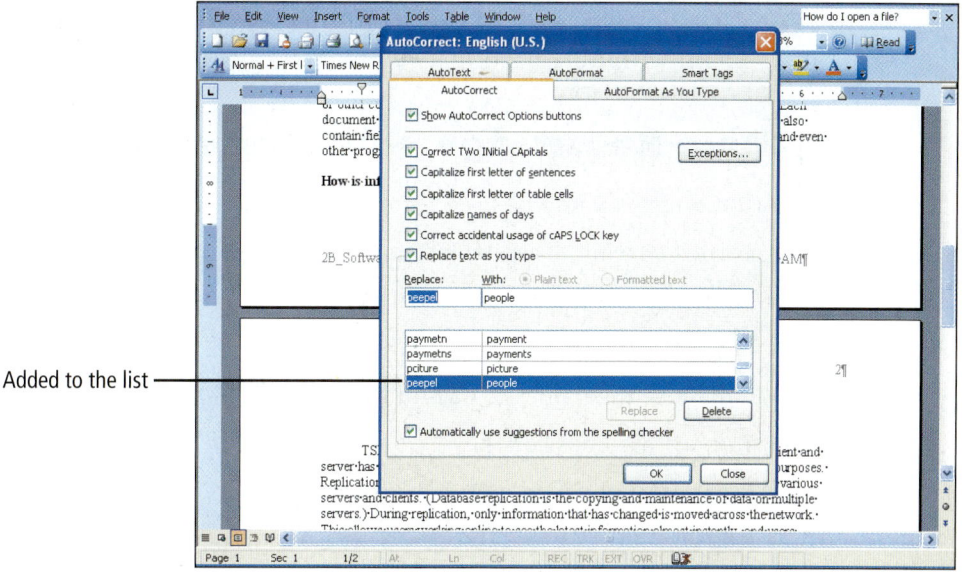

Figure 2.60

5 Click **OK**.

The dialog box closes.

6 Scroll to the top of page 1 and locate the paragraph that begins *TSF Database 4 is a program*, and then locate and double-click to select the word *some* in the third line.

7 Watch the screen, type **peepel** and then press Spacebar. If necessary, press ←Bksp to get rid of the extra space between words.

Notice that the misspelled word is automatically corrected.

8 Move the mouse pointer over the corrected word.

A blue line displays under the word. See Figure 2.61.

Corrected word

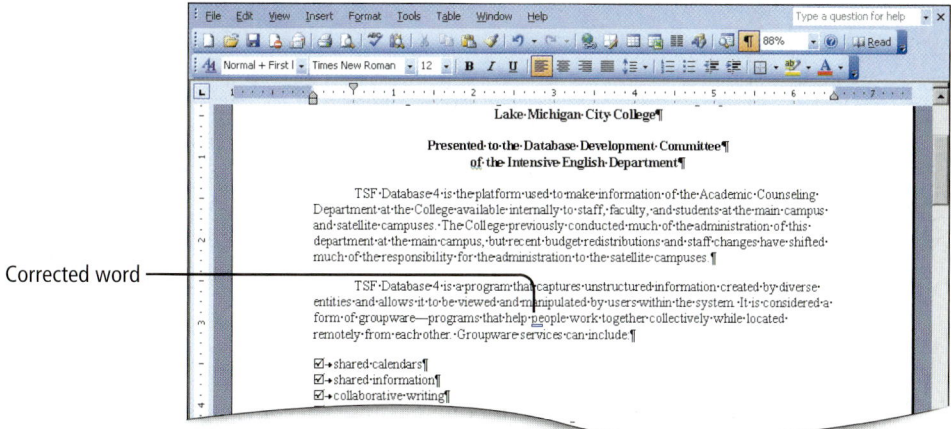

Figure 2.61

9 Move the pointer over the blue line until the **AutoCorrect Options** smart tag button displays, and then click the button.

The AutoCorrect options menu displays. Notice that you have several commands available. The Control AutoCorrect Options selection will display the AutoCorrect dialog box.

Project 2B: Software | **Word** 285

10 Click anywhere in the document to close the **AutoCorrect Options** menu without selecting a command.

> ### More Knowledge — Other Uses of AutoCorrect
>
> AutoCorrect can also be used to
>
> - Correct two initial capital letters
> - Capitalize the first letter of sentences
> - Capitalize the first letter of table cells
> - Capitalize the names of days of the week
> - Turn off the Caps Lock key
> - Create exceptions to automatic corrections
> - Add your own AutoCorrect entries to the AutoCorrect list

Activity 2.21 Using AutoCorrect Shortcuts

The AutoCorrect replacement is most commonly used to correct spelling errors, but it can also be used to insert symbols or to expand shortcut text into longer words or phrases.

1 Scroll to the top of the document. In the fifth line of the title, select the words *Intensive English Department*.

Make sure you do not select the paragraph mark at the end of the title. See Figure 2.62.

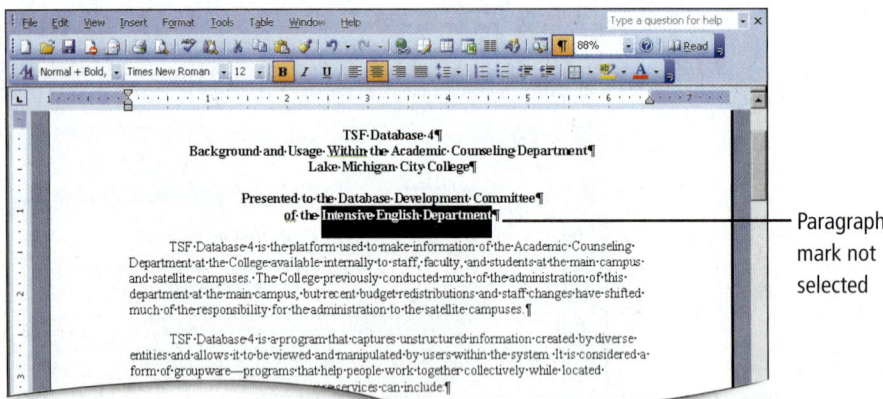

Figure 2.62

2 On the **Tools** menu, click **AutoCorrect Options**.

The AutoCorrect dialog box displays. Notice that the selected text displays in the With box. See Figure 2.63.

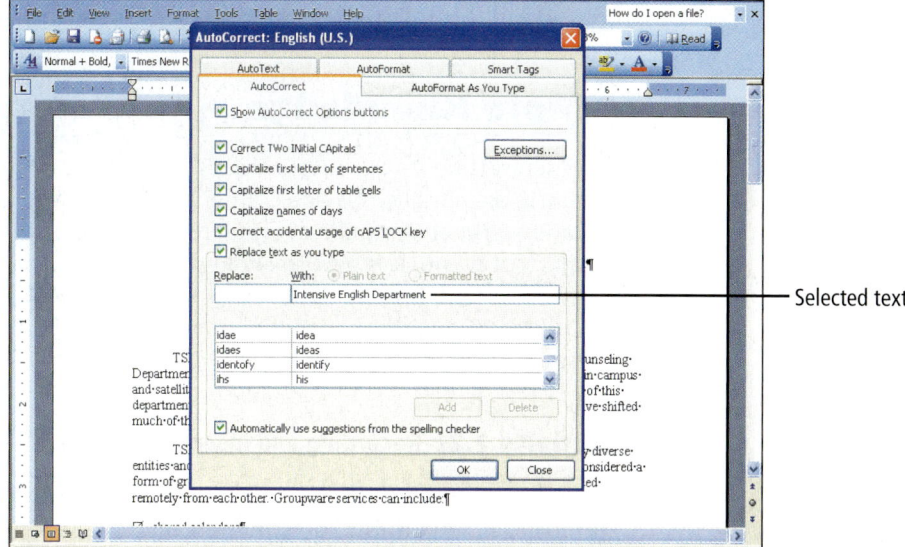

Figure 2.63

3 Under **Replace**, type **ied**, and then click **Add**. If this entry already exists, click the **Replace** button, and then click **Yes.**

The new shortcut is added to the list.

4 Click **OK** to close the **AutoCorrect** dialog box, and then press [Ctrl] + [End] to move to the end of the document.

5 Locate the *Training Schedule:* subheading and at the end of the sentence just above this subheading select the word *department* and the period at the end of the sentence.

6 Type **ied.**

When you type the period, the AutoCorrect feature replaces the shortcut text with the text you defined. In order to activate the replace feature, you need to follow the shortcut with a space, a paragraph mark, or a punctuation mark. See Figure 2.64.

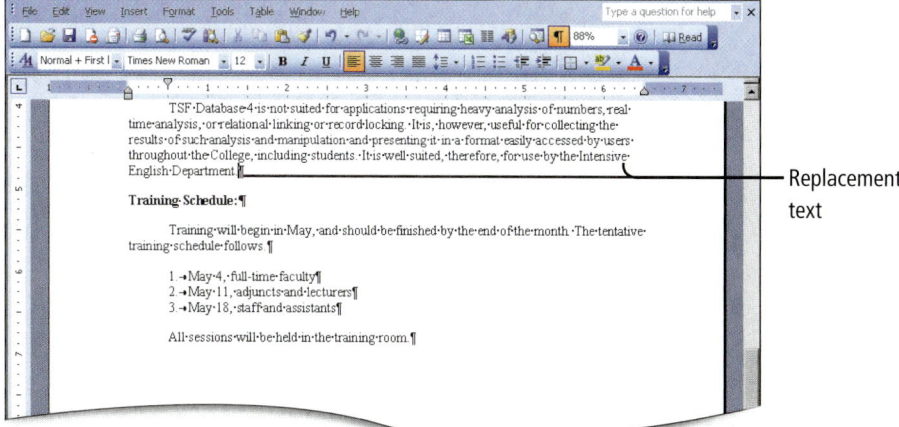

Figure 2.64

Project 2B: Software | **Word** 287

7 On the Standard toolbar, click the **Save** button.

> **More Knowledge** — Creating AutoCorrect Shortcuts
>
> When setting up an AutoCorrect shortcut, it is best not to use shortcut text that is an actual word or a commonly used abbreviation. Even though you can reverse an AutoCorrect replacement by using the AutoCorrect Options shortcut menu, it is best to avoid the problem by adding a letter to the shortcut text. For example, if you type both *LMCC* and *Lake Michigan City College* frequently, you might want to add *lmccx* (or just *lmx*) as an AutoCorrect shortcut for the text *Lake Michigan City College*.

Activity 2.22 Recording and Inserting AutoText

AutoText stores, with a unique name, text and graphics that you use frequently. For example, at Lake Michigan City College, individuals in the counseling department frequently type *Academic Counseling Department*.

1 Scroll to the top of the document. From the second title line, select *Academic Counseling Department*, but do not include the paragraph mark. See Figure 2.65.

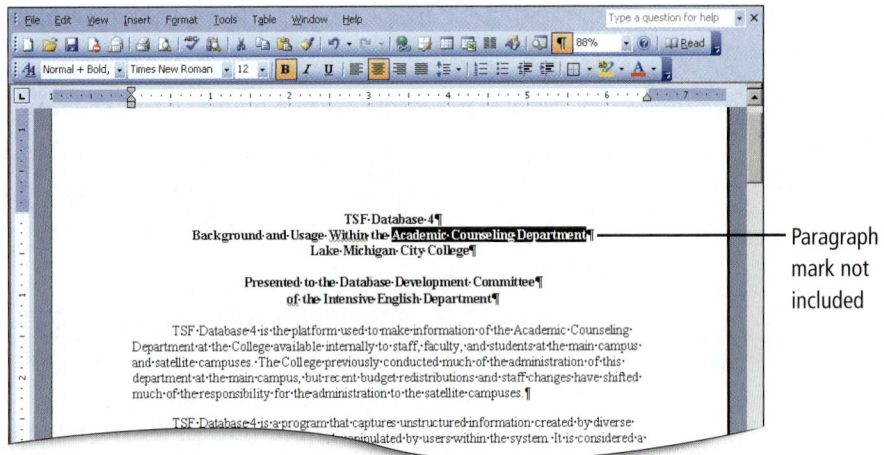

Paragraph mark not included

Figure 2.65

2 On the **Tools** menu, click **AutoCorrect Options**.

The AutoCorrect dialog box displays.

3 In the **AutoCorrect** dialog box, click the **AutoText tab**.

Notice that the selected text displays in the *Enter AutoText entries here* box. You can also type entries directly into this box. See Figure 2.66.

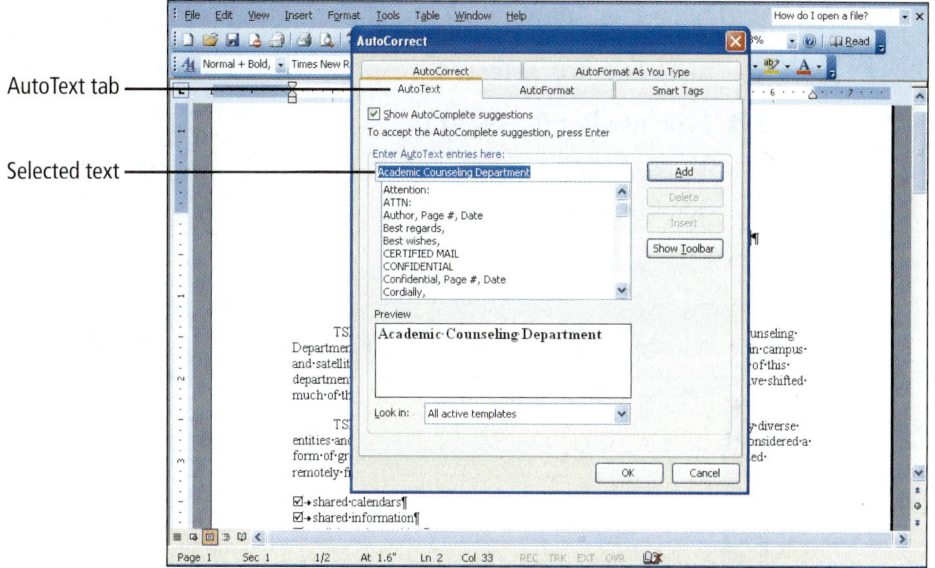

Figure 2.66

4. Click **Add**.

   The phrase is added to the AutoText entries, and the AutoCorrect dialog box closes. If the entry has already been created on this computer, click Yes to redefine the entry.

5. Click outside the selected text to deselect it. On the **Edit** menu, click **Find**.

   The Find and Replace dialog box displays. Using Find and Replace is not necessary to use AutoComplete—it just makes finding the text easier.

6. In the **Find what** box, type **acd** and then click **Find Next**.

   The next (and only) instance of ACD is found in the third subheading. See Figure 2.67.

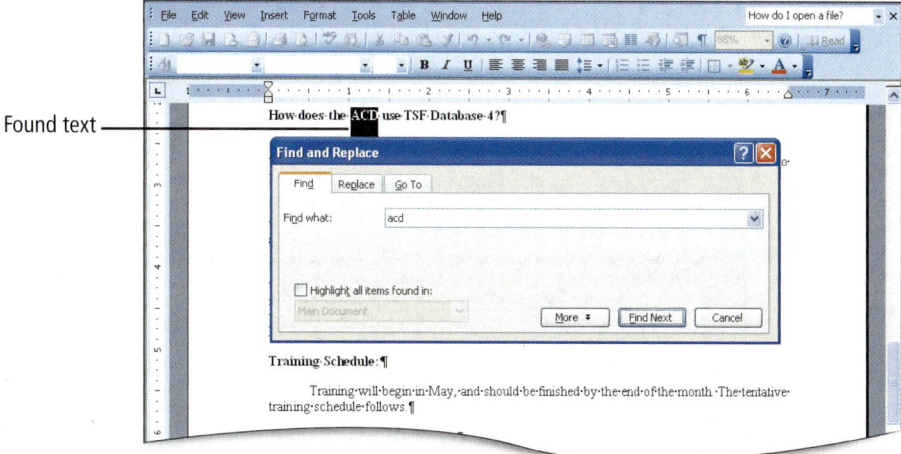

Figure 2.67

Project 2B: Software | **Word** 289

7 Click **Cancel** to close the Find and Replace dialog box.

ACD remains selected.

8 Type **acad** and look at the screen.

A ScreenTip displays the AutoCorrect entry that you just created. See Figure 2.68.

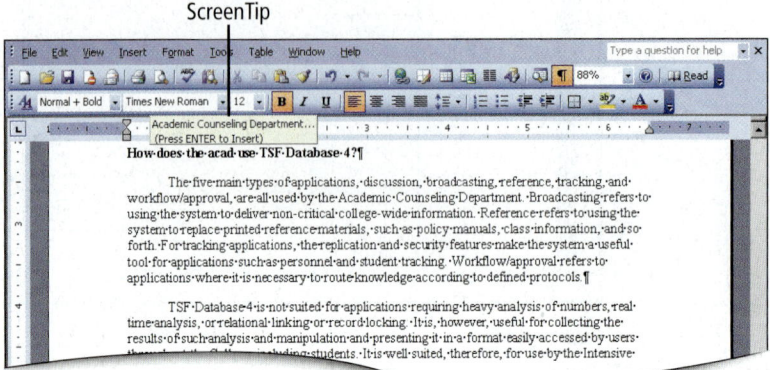

Figure 2.68

9 Press Enter.

ACD is replaced with the AutoText entry Academic Counseling Department. Notice that the text is bold, as it was in the document title. The character formatting of an AutoText entry is the same as its source text.

10 On the Standard toolbar, click the **Save** button.

Activity 2.23 Inserting Symbols

There are many symbols that are used occasionally, but not often enough to put on a standard keyboard. These symbols can be found and inserted from the Insert menu.

1 Scroll to view the middle of the second page, and locate the paragraph following the subheading *How does the Academic Counseling Department use TSF Database 4?*

2 After *The five main types of applications*, select the comma and space as shown in Figure 2.69.

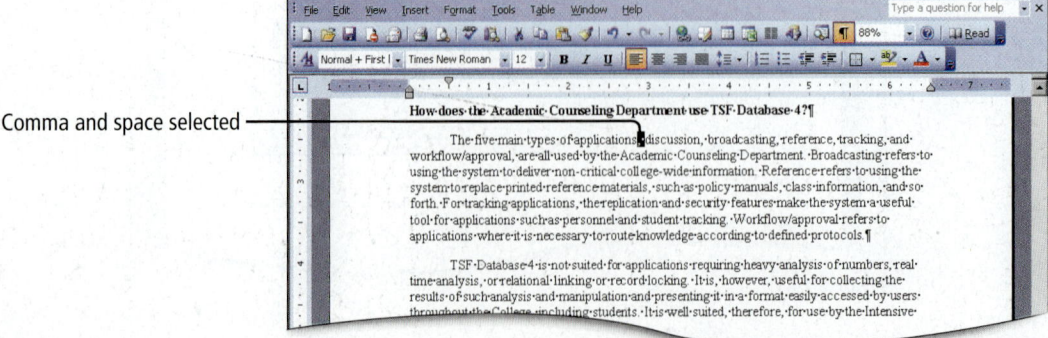

Figure 2.69

[3] On the **Insert** menu, click **Symbol**.

The Symbol dialog box displays. This is the same dialog box you used when you formatted bullets.

[4] Click the **Special Characters tab**.

A list of commonly used symbols displays. The keyboard shortcuts for inserting these commonly used symbols display to the right of the character name, as shown in Figure 2.70.

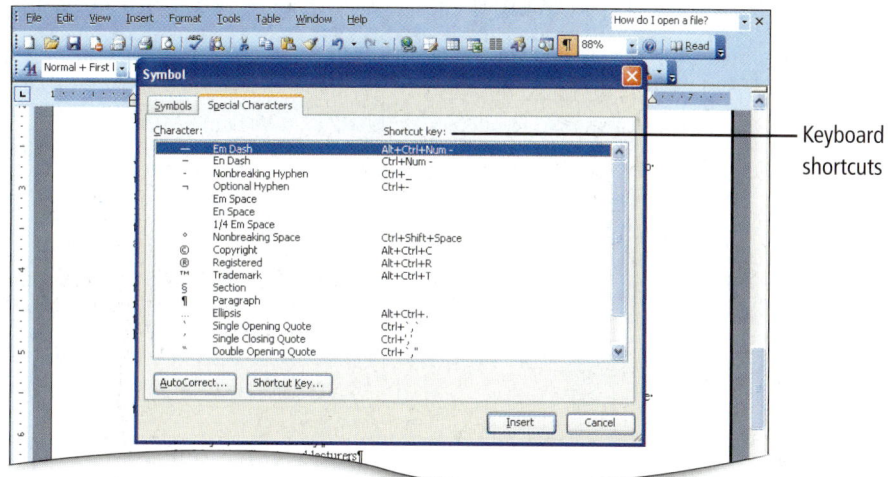

Keyboard shortcuts

Figure 2.70

[5] Be sure the *Em dash* is selected. In the lower right corner of the dialog box, click **Insert**, and then click **Close**.

An em dash replaces the selected text. An **em dash** is the word processing name for a long dash in a sentence. An em dash in a sentence marks a break in thought, similar to a comma but stronger.

[6] Select the em dash. On the Standard toolbar, click **Copy**.

[7] Near the end of the same sentence, in the second line, select the comma and space after *workflow/approval*. Click **Paste**.

A second em dash is inserted in the sentence. Because you used a paste operation to insert the em dash, the Paste Options smart tag also displays. See Figure 2.71.

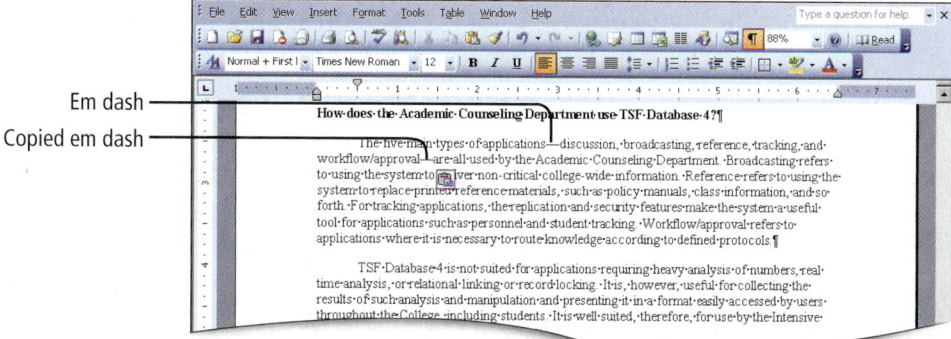

Em dash
Copied em dash

Figure 2.71

Project 2B: Software | **Word** 291

8 Navigate to the top of the document by pressing Ctrl + Home. Position the insertion point at the end of the first title line. Type **(tm)**

Although this symbol, which indicates a trademark, is available from the Symbol dialog box, it is also included in Word's AutoCorrect list. The parentheses are necessary for AutoComplete to insert a trademark symbol.

9 On the **Tools** menu, click **AutoCorrect Options** and then click the **AutoCorrect tab**.

Symbols that can be inserted automatically with AutoCorrect display at the top of the Replace With area. See Figure 2.72.

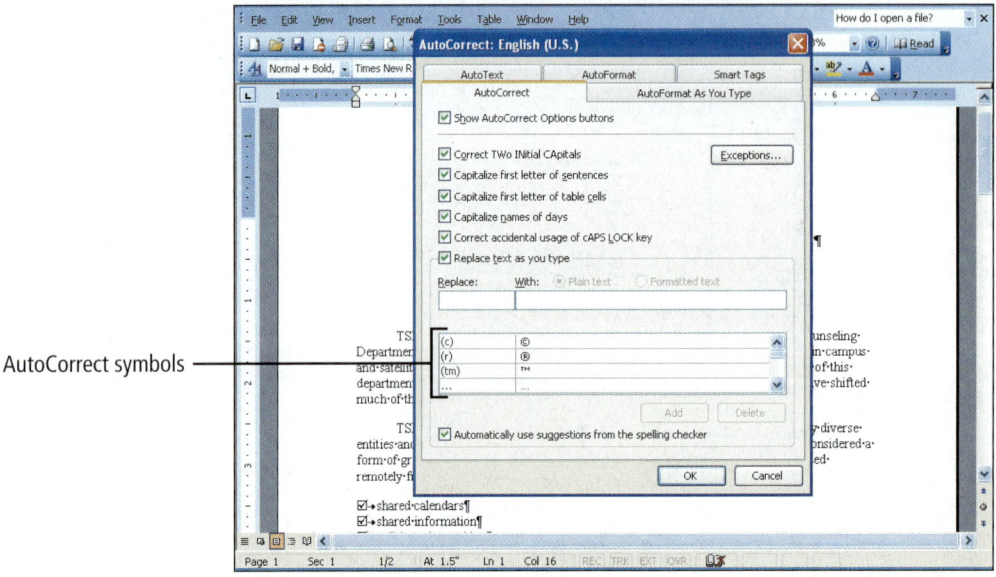

AutoCorrect symbols

Figure 2.72

10 Scroll the list to view additional symbol shortcuts. When you are finished, click **OK** to close the dialog box. On the Standard toolbar, click the **Save** button.

Objective 6
Insert References

Reports frequently include information taken from other sources, and these need to be credited. Within report text, numbers mark the location of information that has been taken from another source, called **references**. The numbers refer to **footnotes** (references placed at the bottom of the page containing the reference), or **endnotes** (references placed at the end of a document or chapter).

When footnotes or endnotes are included in a report, a page listing the references is also usually included. Such a list is usually titled *Bibliography, Works Cited, Sources* or *References.*

Activity 2.24 Inserting Footnotes

Footnotes can be added when you type the document or after the document is complete. They do not need to be entered in order, and if one is removed, the rest are renumbered.

1 In the lower half of page 1, in the paragraph that begins *TSF 4 collects information*, locate the quotation mark in the third line of text. Click to right of the quotation mark.

Direct quotes always need to be referenced.

2 On the **Insert** menu, point to **Reference** and then click **Footnote**.

The Footnote and Endnote dialog box displays.

3 Under **Location**, be sure the **Footnotes** option button is selected and that **Bottom of page** is selected. Under **Format**, be sure **Start at** is at **1**, and **Numbering** is **Continuous**.

4 If necessary, under **Format** click the **Number format** arrow and, from the displayed list, click **1**, **2**, **3**.

The number format is selected.

Under Apply changes, *Apply changes to* the *Whole document* is selected by default. Compare your Footnote and Endnote dialog box to Figure 2.73.

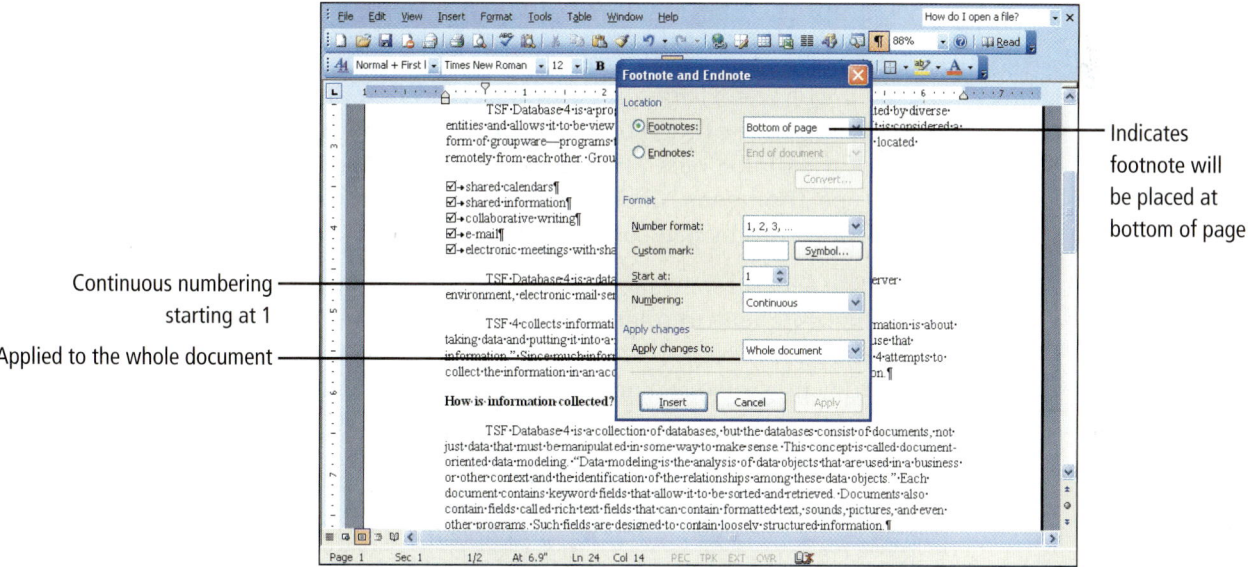

Figure 2.73

5 Click **Insert**.

A footnote area is created at the bottom of the page, and a footnote number is added to the text at the insertion point location. Footnote 1 is placed at the top of the footnote area, and the insertion point is moved to the right of the number. You do not need to type a footnote number.

6 Type **Blue, A. (1998). Davis drives home the importance of being knowledge based. Information Outlook, 2(5): 39.**

Footnote 1 is placed at the bottom of the page. See Figure 2.74.

Project 2B: Software | **Word** 293

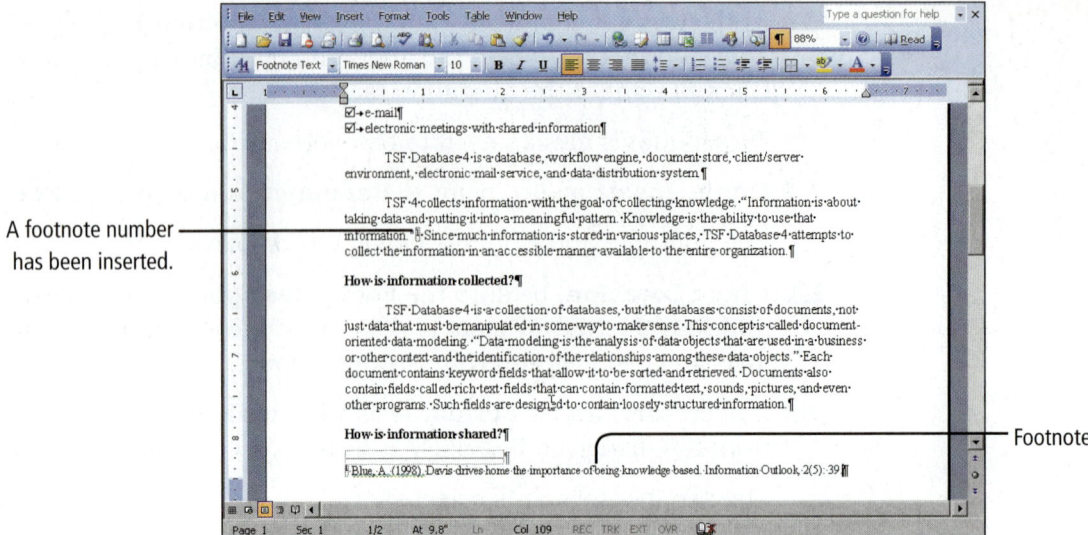

A footnote number has been inserted.

Footnote

Figure 2.74

7 Scroll as necessary to position the top of page 2 in view. In the paragraph that begins *TSF Database 4 clients connect*, in the fifth line, locate servers.) and click to the right of the parenthesis.

8 On the **Insert** menu, point to **Reference** and then click **Footnote**. Using the settings from your previous footnote, move to the bottom of the dialog box, click **Insert** and then in the inserted footnote box type **Thompson, Charles, "Database Replication," DBMS Magazine <http://dbmsmag.com/9705d15.html>**

The second footnote is placed at the bottom of the second page. The footnote feature places the footnote text on the same page as the referenced text and adjusts pages as necessary. The AutoCorrect feature may also replace straight quotes with curly quotes, depending on the settings on your computer. See Figure 2.75.

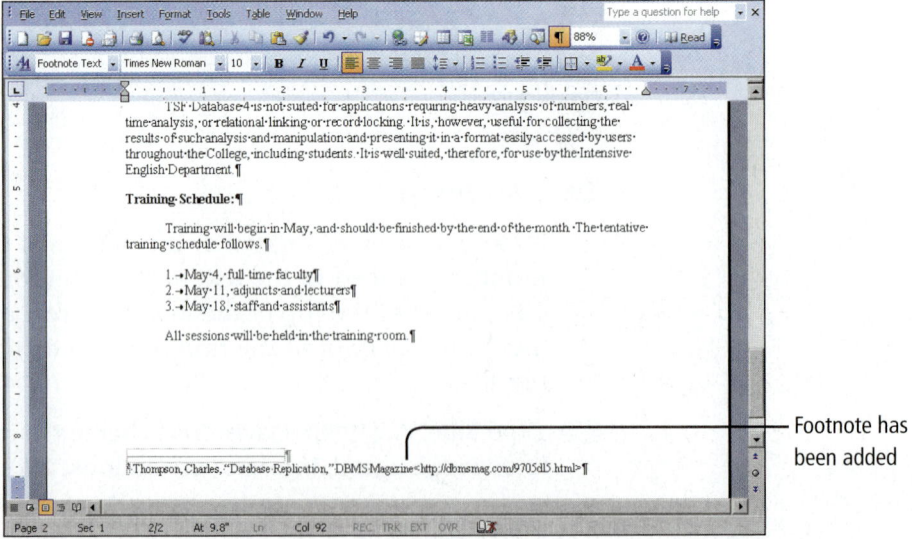

Footnote has been added

Figure 2.75

Alert! **If the Web Address Changes to a Hyperlink**

If you press the spacebar after you type the Web address in the footnote, the Web address text may be displayed in blue with an underline. This is the common format used to display a *hyperlink*—which is a link that can be used to open the Web page on the Internet that is related to this address. If this happens, click the Undo button once to reverse the formatting.

9 In the lower half of page 1, in the paragraph that begins *TSF Database 4 is a collection of*, locate the closing quotation mark near the end of the fourth line and position the insertion point to the right of the quotation mark.

10 On the **Insert** menu, point to **Reference**, and then click **Footnote**. Click **Insert**, and then type:
Database.com search <http://searchdatabase.techtarget.com>

This new footnote number is 2, and the footnote on page 2 becomes footnote 3. In this manner, Word makes it easy to insert footnotes in any order within your report, because it automatically renumbers and adjusts page endings. Compare your screen to Figure 2.76.

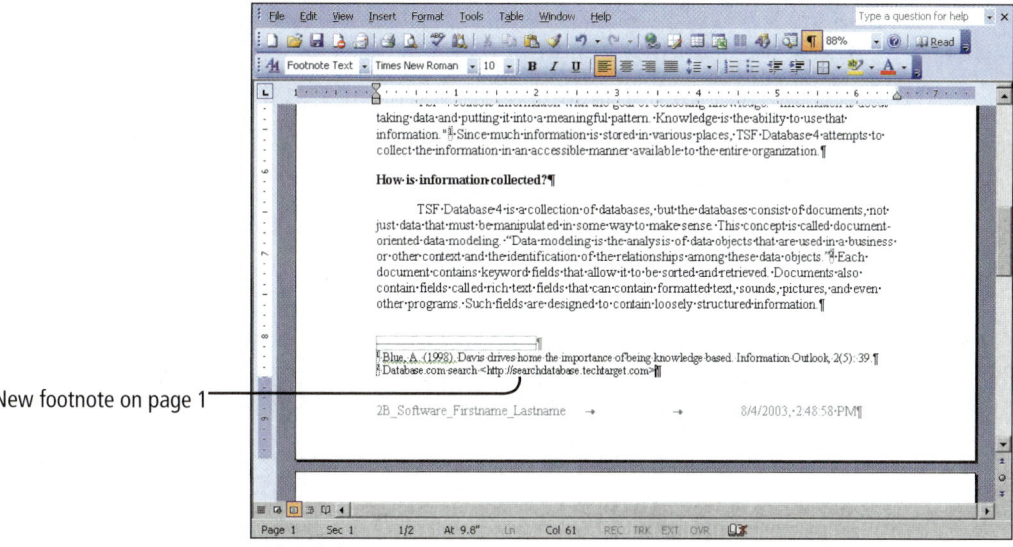

New footnote on page 1

Figure 2.76

11 Click to see if the *How is information shared?* subheading is at the bottom of the page. If so, position the insertion point to the left of the subheading, hold down [Ctrl] and press [Enter].

A manual page break is inserted, the subheading is moved to the second page, but the footnotes remain on the proper page. See Figure 2.77.

Project 2B: Software | **Word** 295

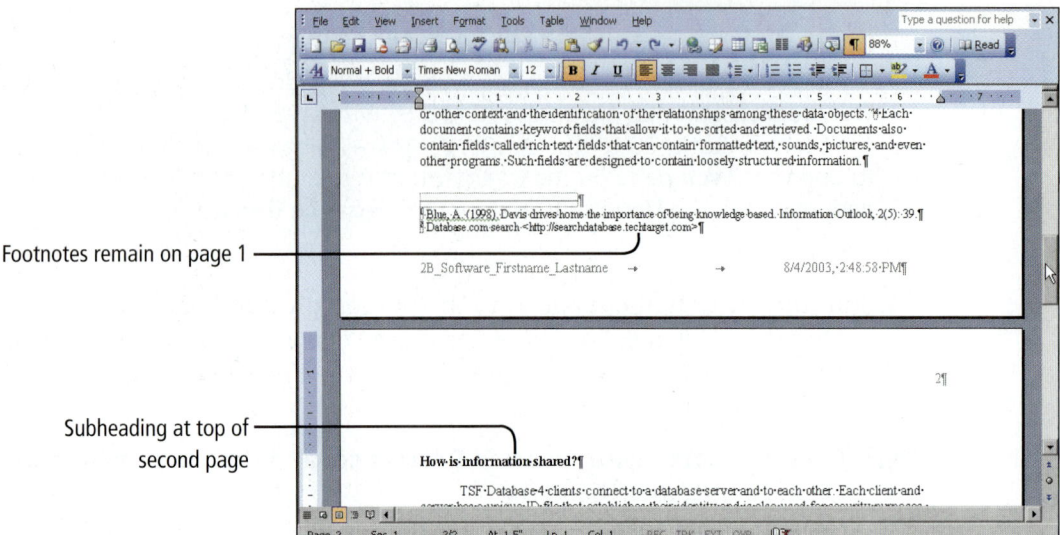

Footnotes remain on page 1

Subheading at top of second page

Figure 2.77

12 On the Standard toolbar, click the **Save** button.

Activity 2.25 Formatting Footnotes

Some parts of footnotes require special formatting. Magazine and book titles, for example, need to be italicized.

1 At the end of the first page, in the first footnote, locate and select the magazine title, *Information Outlook*.

2 Click the **Italic** button.

The magazine title is italicized as shown in Figure 2.78.

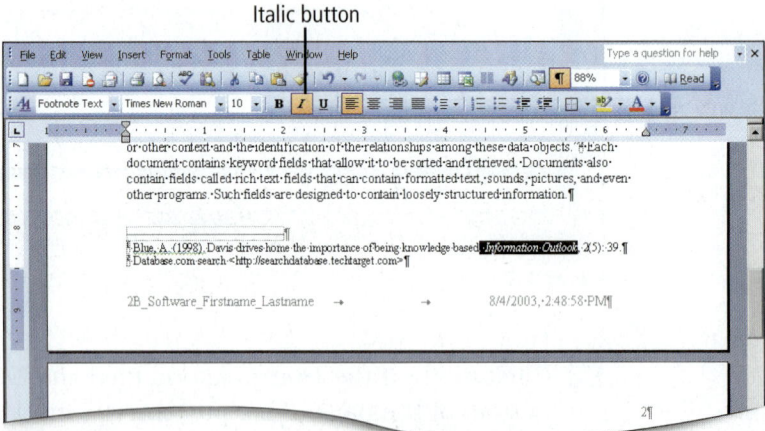

Italic button

Figure 2.78

3 Scroll to the bottom of the document, locate and select the magazine title, *DBMS Magazine*.

4 Click the **Italic** button.

The magazine title is italicized.

5 On the Standard toolbar, click the **Save** button.

Activity 2.26 Creating a Reference Page

In a long document, there will be many books, articles, and Web sites that have been referenced on the various pages. Some of them may be noted many times, others only once. It is common to include, at the end of a report, a single list of each source referenced. This list is commonly titled *References*, *Bibliography*, *Sources* or *Works Cited*.

1 Press Ctrl + End to navigate to the end of the document.

2 Hold down Ctrl and press Enter.

A manual page break is inserted, and a new page is created.

3 Press CapsLock, type **BIBLIOGRAPHY** and press Enter. Turn off CapsLock. See Figure 2.79.

The paragraphs are double spaced and indented because the paragraph mark for the last paragraph of the document contains those instructions. Notice the indents in the ruler.

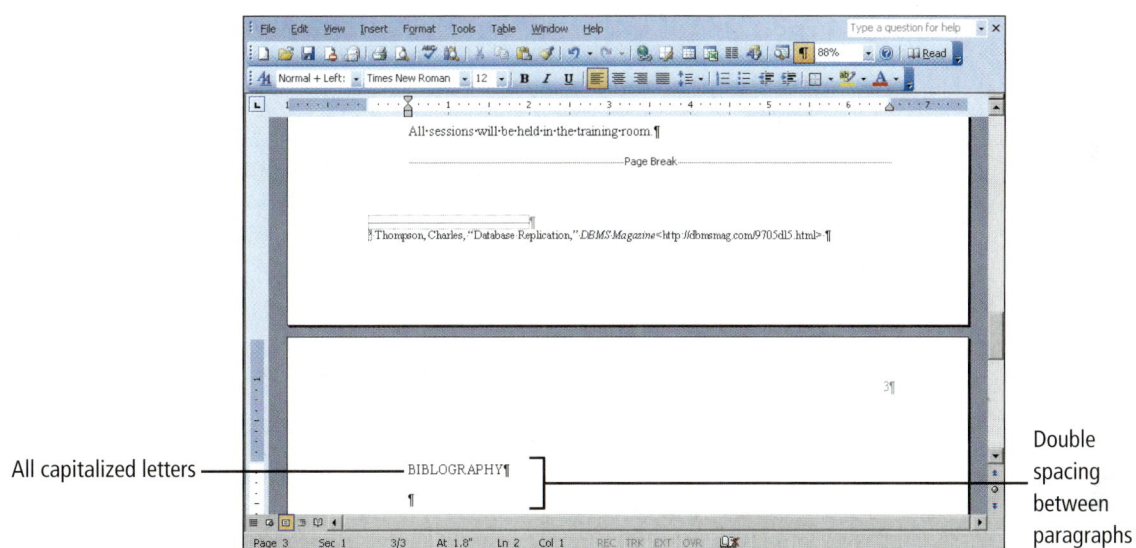

All capitalized letters

Double spacing between paragraphs

Figure 2.79

4 Type **Blue, A. (1998). Davis drives home the importance of being knowledge based. Information Outlook, 2(5): 39.** Press Enter.

5 Type **Thompson, Charles, "Database Replication," DBMS Magazine http://dbmsmag.com/9705d15.html** and then press Enter.

When you type the Internet address, it may change to blue. This means that you have created a live Internet link. If this happens, move the pointer over the link, point to the small blue box under the first letter in the Internet address to display a white arrow, click the displayed AutoCorrect Options smart tag, and from the displayed menu, click Undo Hyperlink.

6 Type **Database.com search <http://searchdatabase.techtarget.com>** and press Enter. If necessary, undo the hyperlink in the same manner as the previous step.

Compare your screen to Figure 2.80.

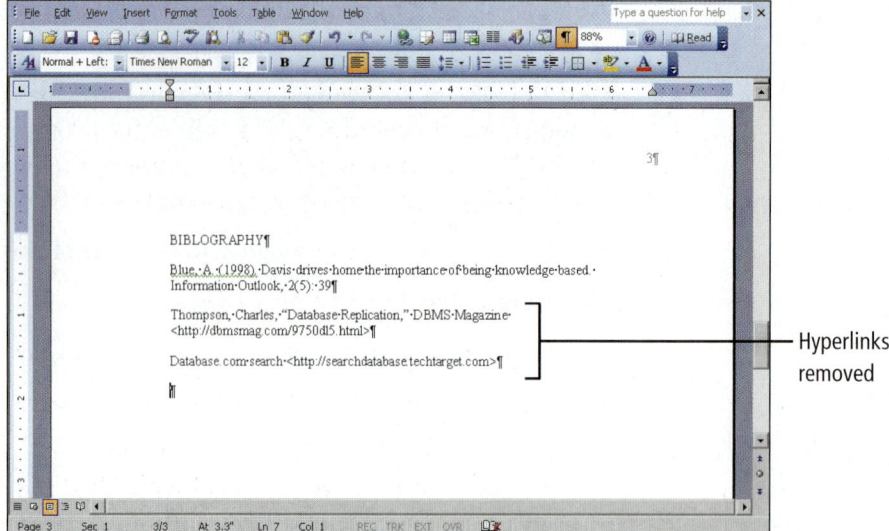

Figure 2.80

[7] On the Standard toolbar, click the **Save** button.

Activity 2.27 Formatting a Reference Page

Bibliographies have special formatting requirements. The title should be centered, the entries should be in alphabetical order, and the subsequent lines of an entry should be indented 0.5 inch to the right of the first line of the entry.

[1] Click anywhere in the title *BIBLIOGRAPHY*.

[2] On the Formatting toolbar, click the **Center** button.

The title is centered, but the centering is between the first line indent of 0.5" (instead of the left margin) and the right margin.

[3] On the **Format** menu, click **Paragraph**. On the **Indents and Spacing tab**, under **Indentation**, change the **Left** indent to 0. In the lower right corner of the dialog box, click **OK**.

[4] Select all three bibliographic entries. On the **Format** menu, click **Paragraph**.

[5] In the displayed **Paragraph** dialog box, under **Indentation**, change the **Left** indent to 0. Click the **Special arrow**, and from the displayed list, click **Hanging**. See Figure 2.81.

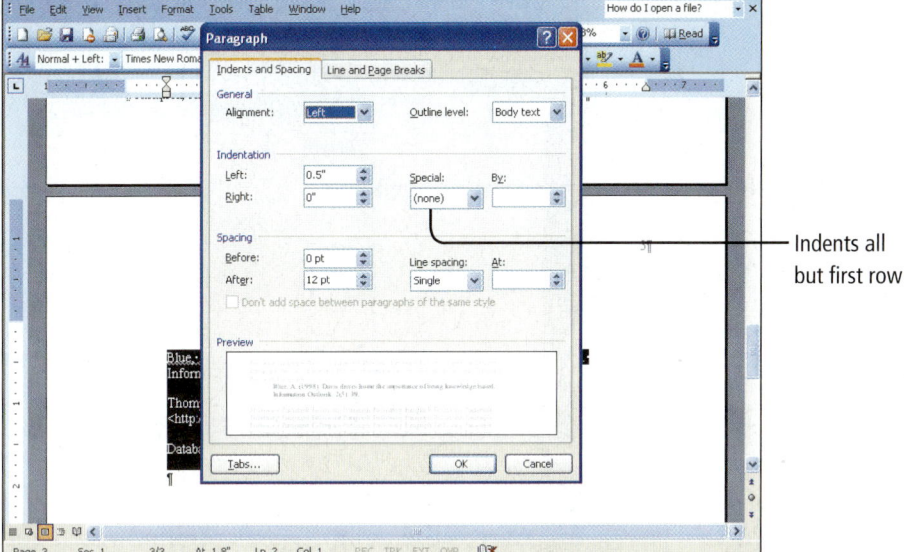

Indents all but first row

Figure 2.81

6 Click **OK** to close the dialog box.

This paragraph style is called a ***hanging indent***, where the first line extends to the left of the rest of the lines in the same paragraph. Notice the indent markers on the toolbar. See Figure 2.82.

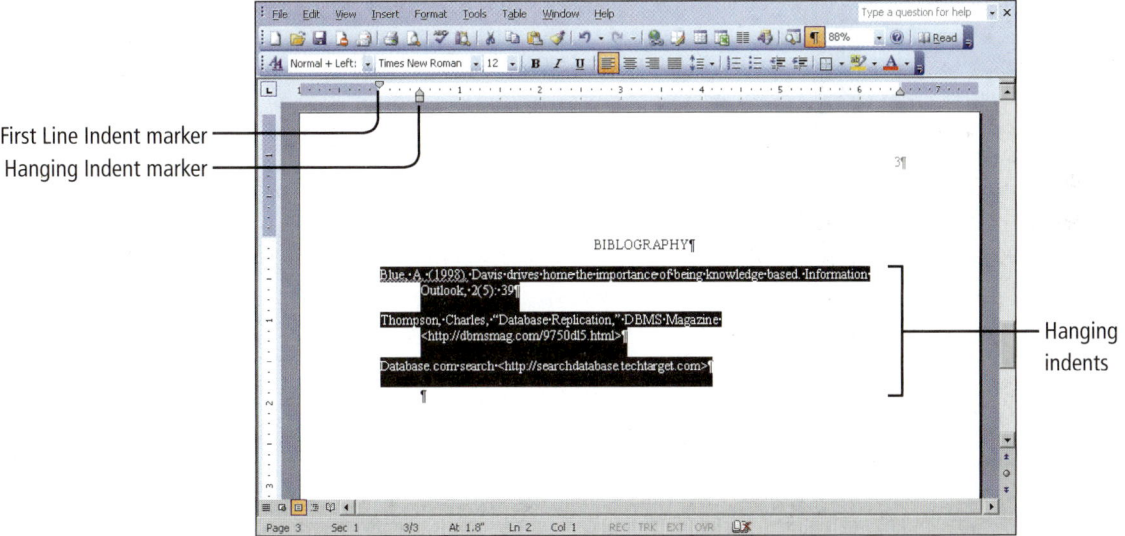

First Line Indent marker
Hanging Indent marker

Hanging indents

Figure 2.82

7 Be sure the three entries are still selected. From the **Table** menu, click **Sort**.

The Sort Text dialog box displays as shown in Figure 2.83.

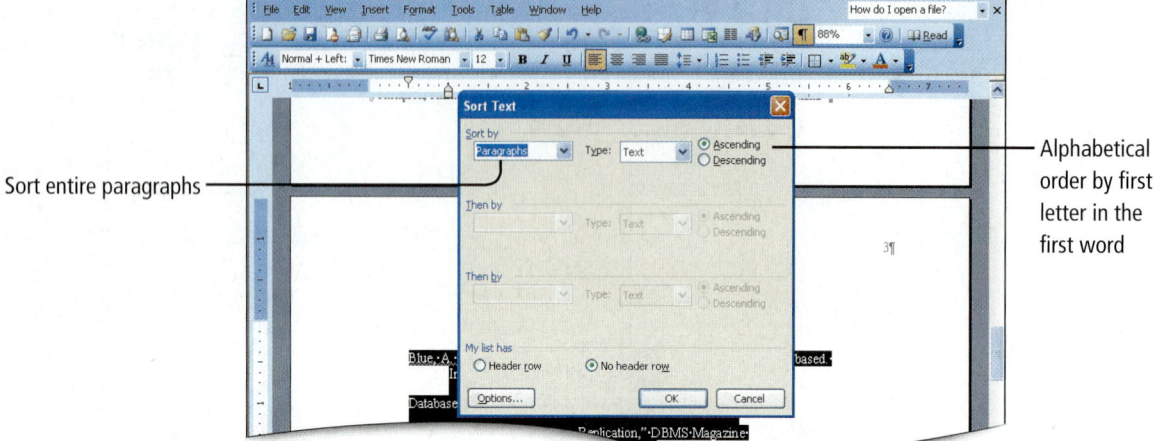

Figure 2.83

8. Accept the default sort options, which sort by paragraph in ascending (A-to-Z) order and click **OK**.

   The paragraphs are sorted alphabetically.

9. Click anywhere in the document to deselect the text.

   Compare your Bibliography page with Figure 2.84.

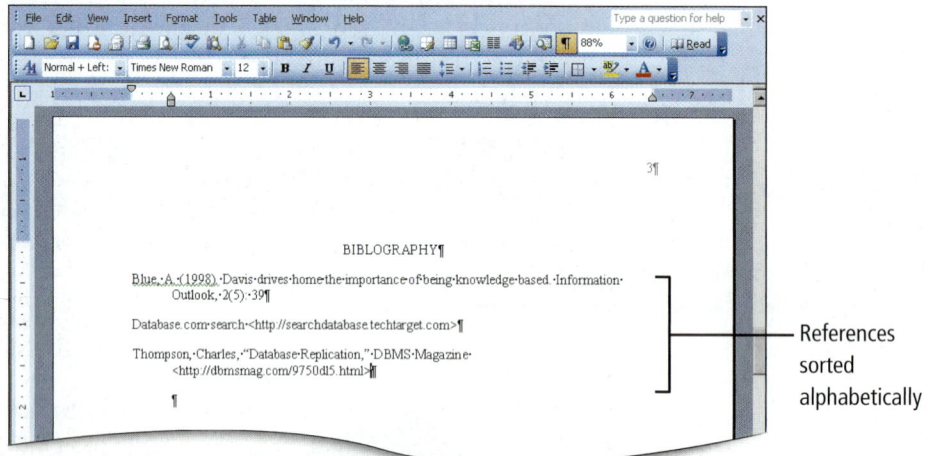

Figure 2.84

10. Move to page 2 and click anywhere in the text. From the **View menu**, display the **Header** and Footer toolbar, switch to the footer and on the Header and Footer toolbar, click **Insert AutoText**, and then click **Filename**. Close the **Header** and Footer toolbar.

    This is necessary because the Different First Page option was selected, and the footer you added earlier displays only on page 1. Adding the filename to the footer of page 2 displays the footer in the rest of the document.

11. On the Standard toolbar, click the **Save** button and then click the **Print Preview** button to preview the document. Close the Print Preview window. Make any necessary changes, and then click the **Print** button. Close the document and save any changes.

End You have completed Project 2B

300 Word | Chapter 2: Formatting and Organizing Text

Summary

In this chapter you practiced how to change the format of pages by setting the margins and how to change the format of paragraphs by changing indents, line spacing, and the spacing after paragraphs. You practiced applying the format from one paragraph to others using the Format Painter. Another paragraph formatting technique you used was creating bulleted and numbered lists and modifying the bullets from the Bullets and Numbering dialog box.

One of the most important features of word processing was presented in this chapter—moving and copying text. Both cut-and-paste and drag-and-drop techniques were demonstrated for moving text. You also practiced how to copy text and place it in a new location. You used the Find and Replace dialog box to locate text that you want to modify, and you practiced how to use the AutoCorrect, AutoText, AutoComplete, and Insert Symbols features.

In the header and footer areas, you accessed commands from the toolbar to add consecutive page numbers, the current date, the time, and the filename. Finally, you practiced how to add footnotes to a document, create a reference page with hanging indent paragraph format, and sort references in alphabetical order.

In This Chapter You Practiced How To

- Change Document and Paragraph Layout
- Change and Reorganize Text
- Create and Modify Lists
- Work with Headers and Footers
- Insert Frequently Used Text
- Insert References

Concepts Assessments

Matching Match each term in the second column with its correct definition in the first column by writing the letter of the term on the blank line in front of the correct definition.

____ 1. Text that is aligned on both the left and right margins.

____ 2. A temporary storage location that is used for text that is cut or copied.

____ 3. The button that is used to reverse a previous action.

____ 4. A small symbol that is used to begin each line of information in a list.

____ 5. A reference that is placed at the bottom of a page.

____ 6. The alignment of text in the middle of the document between the left and right margin.

____ 7. The Word feature that is primarily responsible for correcting commonly misspelled words.

____ 8. A paragraph style that positions the first line of text to the left of the rest of the paragraph.

____ 9. In most documents, paragraphs are aligned on this side of the page.

____ 10. The action that leaves text in its original location but also makes it available to place in a new location.

____ 11. The name of a dialog box that you can use to locate specific text.

____ 12. The command activated by the keyboard shortcut Ctrl + X.

____ 13. The command activated by the keyboard shortcut Ctrl + V.

____ 14. The area at the bottom of a page that shows the same information, or same type of information on every page of a document, with the possible exception of the first page.

____ 15. The type of menu that displays by right-clicking on selected areas of a document.

A AutoCorrect
B Bullet
C Centered
D Copy
E Cut
F Find and Replace
G Footer
H Footnote
I Hanging indent
J Justified
K Left
L Office Clipboard
M Paste
N Shortcut menu
O Undo

Concepts Assessments (continued)

Fill in the Blank Write the correct answer in the space provided.

1. The width between the text and the edge of the paper is known as the _____.

2. The placement of text relative to the left and right side of a paragraph is known as _____.

3. When you drag-and-drop text, it is _____ from one place to another.

4. When you paste text, the text is taken from the _____ and placed where the insertion point is positioned.

5. The keyboard shortcut used to copy text is Ctrl + _____.

6. If you need to create a list of items that is sequential, you should use a(n) _____ list.

7. When you click the Redo button, it reverses the action of the _____ _____.

8. If you want to create a shortcut that will automatically finish a frequently used phrase or name, use the _____ feature.

9. If you need to add a ™ ® or © to a document, display the _____ dialog box from the Insert menu.

10. A reference placed at the end of a document or a chapter is known as a(n) _____.

Skill Assessments

Project 2C—Computer Lab

Objectives: *Change Document and Paragraph Layout, Change and Reorganize Text, Create and Modify Lists, Work with Headers and Footers, Insert Frequently Used Text, and Insert References.*

In the following Skill Assessment, you will format and modify a document regarding the Computer Lab policies at Lake Michigan City College. Your completed document will look similar to the one shown in Figure 2.85. You will save your document as *2C_Computer_Lab_Firstname_Lastname*.

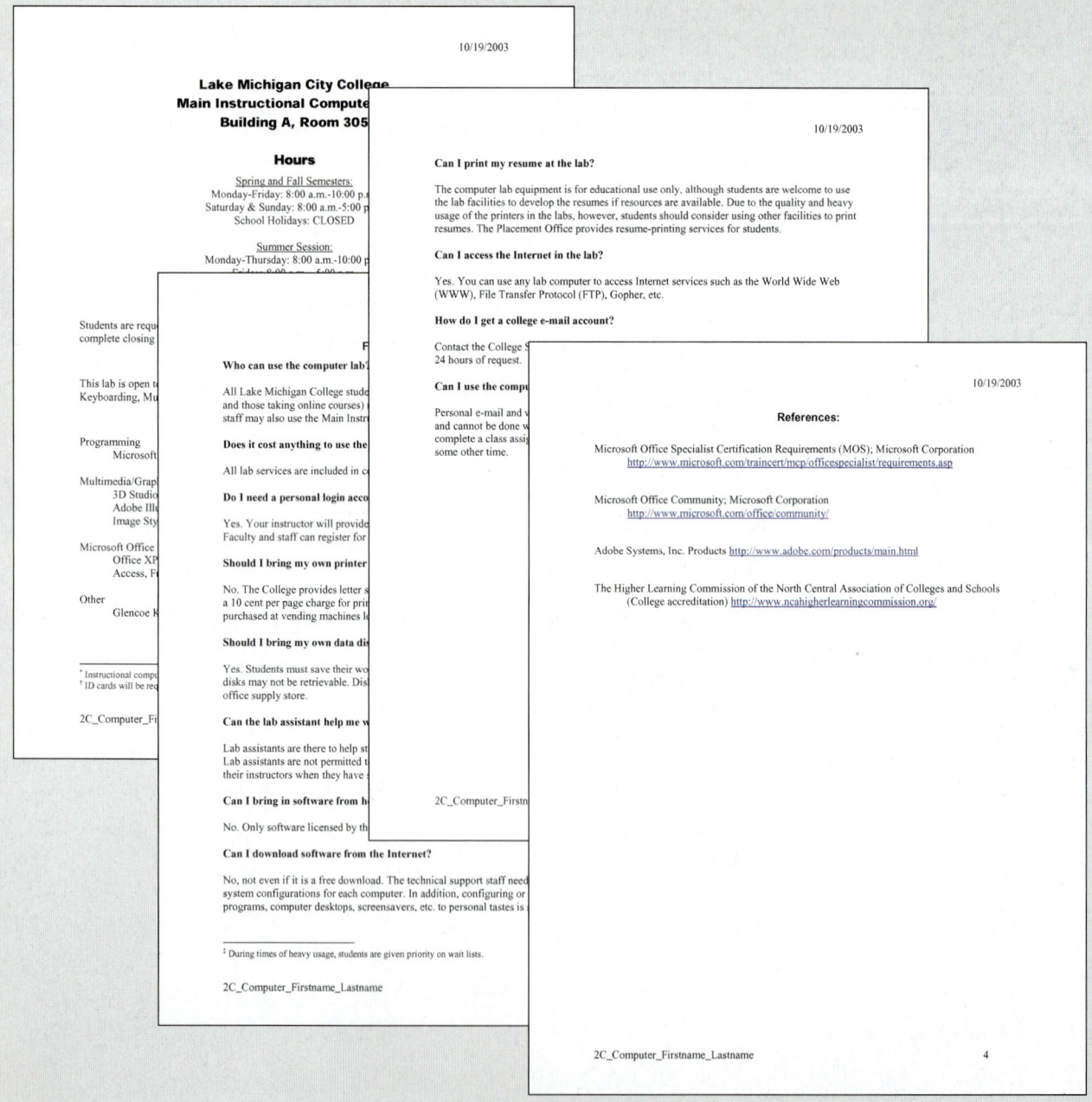

Figure 2.85

(Project 2C–Computer Lab continues on the next page)

304   Word | Chapter 2: Formatting and Organizing Text

Skill Assessments (continued)

(Project 2C–Computer Lab continued)

1. Start Word. On the Standard toolbar, click the **Open** button. Navigate to the location where the student files for this textbook are stored. Locate and open **w02C_Computer_Lab**. Be sure that non-printing characters are displayed. This is a three-page document; take a moment to scroll through the document to familiarize yourself with the overall content and layout.

2. Display the **File** menu and then click **Save As**. Navigate to the location where you are saving your projects for this chapter. In the **File name** box, type **2C_Computer_Lab_Firstname_Lastname** and then in the lower portion of the **Save As** dialog box, click the **Save** button.

3. Select the first four lines of text in the document, which comprise the document's title, two subtitles, and *Hours*. On the Formatting toolbar, click the **Center** button. With the four lines still selected, click the **Font button arrow**, click **Arial Black**, click the **Font Size button arrow**, and then click **14**. The title is centered and looks more distinctive.

4. Click anywhere to deselect. Select the title line and the first subtitle line—the first two lines of the document. Click the **Line Spacing button arrow** and, from the displayed list, click **1.0**. The line spacing for the first two lines of the document is changed, but the third line remains double-spaced so that it creates a space after effect.

5. Select the four lines of text that begin *Spring and Fall Semesters*. On the Formatting toolbar, click the **Center** button. Select the five lines of text that begin *Summer Session*, and click the **Center** button again. On the Standard toolbar, click **Save**.

6. Scroll to view the bottom of page 1, and click to position the insertion point at the beginning of the heading *Frequently Asked Questions*. Because it is not good document design to strand a subheading at the bottom of the page without any of its following information, press Ctrl + Enter to insert a hard page break if necessary and move this subheading to the next page.

7. Scroll to view the bottom of page 3, click to the left of the *References:* heading, and then press Ctrl + Enter to insert a page break and move the References portion to a separate page. This becomes page 4. Click the **Save** button.

(Project 2C–Computer Lab continues on the next page)

Skill Assessments (continued)

(Project 2C–Computer Lab continued)

8. Hold down **Ctrl** and press **Home** to move the insertion point to the top of the document. Click to place the insertion point at the end of *Main Instructional Computer Lab*. Display the **Insert** menu, point to **Reference**, and then click **Footnote**. In the **Footnote and Endnote** dialog box, under **Location**, be sure the **Footnotes** option button is selected and **Bottom of page** is displayed in the Footnotes box. Under **Format**, click the **Number format arrow**, and then click the sixth item in list, which is a group of symbols beginning with an *. These are appropriate to use when you are not making a specific reference to a document, but are noting additional information. In the lower left of the **Footnote and Endnote** dialog box, click **Insert**.

9. The insertion point is moved to the new footnote created at the bottom of page 1. Type the following note: **Instructional computer labs are also located at satellite campuses. See catalog or call campus for details.** Recall that you do not have to type the footnote symbol—Word places the symbol in the correct location for you.

10. Scroll to view the middle of page 1, and in the paragraph under the subheading *Courses Supported*, click to the right of the word *enrolled*. Display the **Insert** menu, point to **Reference**, and then click **Footnote**. In the displayed dialog box, in the lower left corner, click the **Insert** button to accept the settings. A new footnote is inserted, and the insertion point moves to the bottom of page 1. Type **ID cards will be required for entrance to lab.**

11. Navigate to the top of page 2. In the paragraph beginning *All Lake Michigan College students*, in the third line, click to place the insertion point to the right of the period following *Main Instructional Computer Lab*. Display the **Footnote and Endnote** dialog box, click the **Insert** button, and then type the following: **During times of heavy usage, students are given priority on wait lists.** This footnote, the third one you have added to the document, is placed at the bottom of page 2.

12. Navigate to page 4—the References page. Select the two lines beginning *Microsoft Office Specialist*. Hold down **Ctrl** and select the two lines beginning *Microsoft Office Community*. Continue to hold down **Ctrl** and select the text lines that form the remaining two references. All four references are selected, but the blank lines between them are not selected. From the **Format** menu, click **Paragraph**, and then click the **Indents and Spacing tab**. Under **Indentation**, click the **Special arrow** and then click **Hanging**. Under **Spacing**, in the **After** box, click the up arrow in the spin box to change the spacing after the paragraph to 12 pt. Click **OK**. The references are displayed with a hanging line indent and 12 points of space after each paragraph.

(Project 2C–Computer Lab continues on the next page)

Word chapter two

Skill Assessments (continued)

(Project 2C–Computer Lab continued)

13. Click anywhere to deselect. On the **View** menu, click **Header and Footer**. With the header area displayed, on the Formatting toolbar, click the **Align Right** button. On the Header and Footer toolbar, click the **Insert Date** button. The current date is placed on the right side of the header.

14. On the Header and Footer toolbar, click the **Switch Between Header and Footer** button. In the footer area, on the **Header and Footer** toolbar, click **Insert AutoText**, and then click **Filename**. Press Tab twice to move the insertion point to the right side of the footer. On the Header and Footer toolbar, click the **Insert Page Number** button, and then click the **Close** button.

15. On the Standard toolbar, click the **Save** button to save the changes you have made to your document.

16. Press Ctrl + Home. On the Standard toolbar, click the **Print Preview** button to make a final check of your document before printing. Use the scroll bar to view each page in the document, and notice how Word formatted and placed your footnotes on pages 1 and 2. On the Print Preview toolbar, click the **Print** button, and then, on the same toolbar, click the **Close** button.

17. From the **File** menu, click **Close** to close the document, saving any changes if prompted to do so. Display the **File** menu again and then click **Exit** to close Word. Alternatively, you can close Word by clicking the Close button at the extreme right end of the blue title bar.

End You have completed Project 2C

Project 2D — AFV Proposal

Objectives: *Change Document and Paragraph Layout, Create and Modify Lists, Work with Headers and Footers, and Insert Frequently Used Text.*

In the following Skill Assessment, you will format and edit a proposal for an Alternative Fuel Project that is being cosponsored by the college and several energy-related businesses. Your completed document will look similar to Figure 2.86. You will save your document as 2D_AFV_Proposal_Firstname_Lastname.

1. On the Standard toolbar, click the **Open** button. Navigate to the location where the student files for this textbook are stored. Locate and open **w02D_AFV_Proposal**. Be sure that nonprinting characters are displayed. This is a two-page document. Take a moment to scroll through the document to familiarize yourself with the content and layout.

(Project 2D–AFV Proposal continues on the next page)

Skill Assessments (continued)

(Project 2D–AFV Proposal continued)

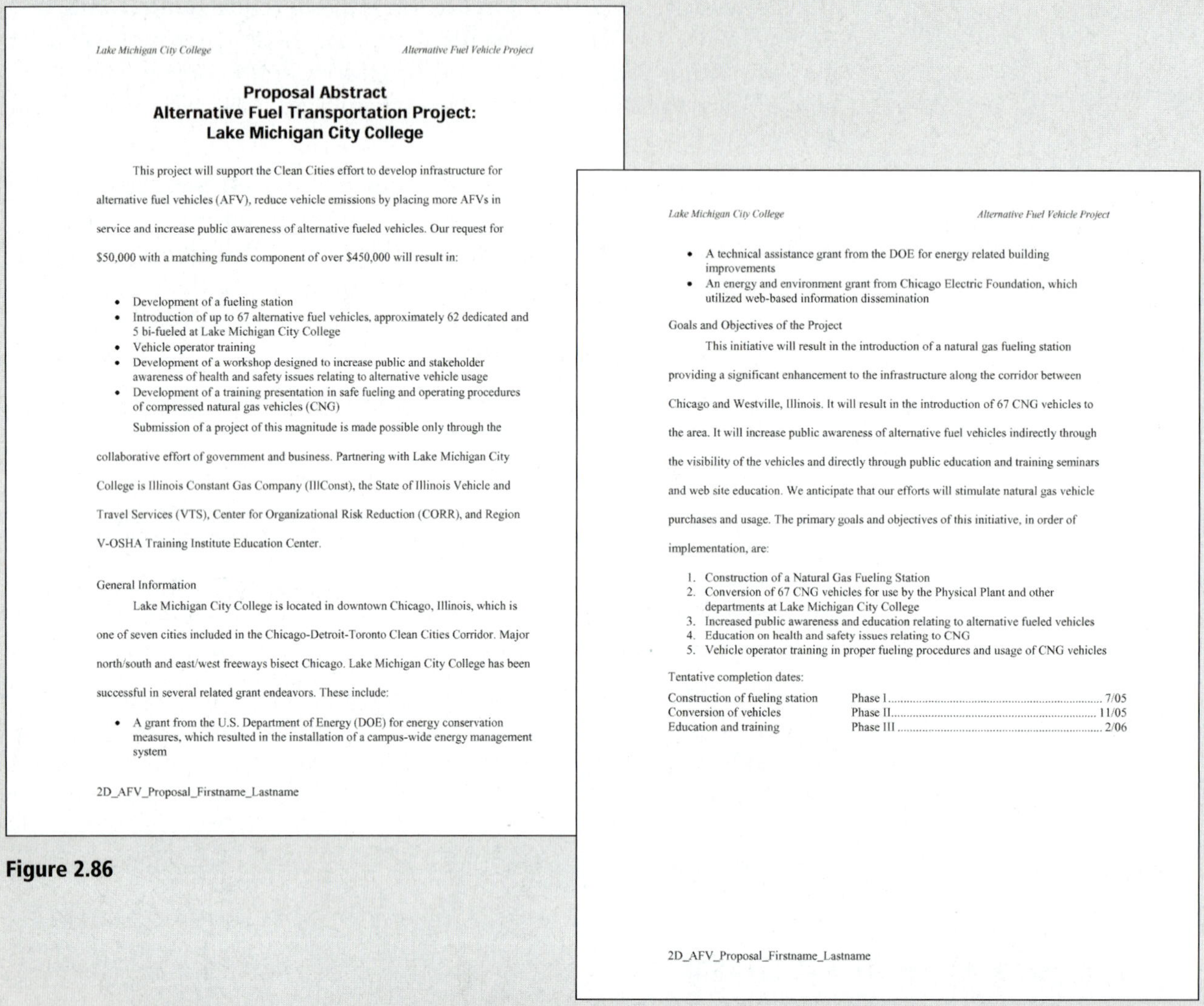

Lake Michigan City College *Alternative Fuel Vehicle Project*

Proposal Abstract
Alternative Fuel Transportation Project:
Lake Michigan City College

This project will support the Clean Cities effort to develop infrastructure for alternative fuel vehicles (AFV), reduce vehicle emissions by placing more AFVs in service and increase public awareness of alternative fueled vehicles. Our request for $50,000 with a matching funds component of over $450,000 will result in:

- Development of a fueling station
- Introduction of up to 67 alternative fuel vehicles, approximately 62 dedicated and 5 bi-fueled at Lake Michigan City College
- Vehicle operator training
- Development of a workshop designed to increase public and stakeholder awareness of health and safety issues relating to alternative vehicle usage
- Development of a training presentation in safe fueling and operating procedures of compressed natural gas vehicles (CNG)

Submission of a project of this magnitude is made possible only through the collaborative effort of government and business. Partnering with Lake Michigan City College is Illinois Constant Gas Company (IllConst), the State of Illinois Vehicle and Travel Services (VTS), Center for Organizational Risk Reduction (CORR), and Region V-OSHA Training Institute Education Center.

General Information

Lake Michigan City College is located in downtown Chicago, Illinois, which is one of seven cities included in the Chicago-Detroit-Toronto Clean Cities Corridor. Major north/south and east/west freeways bisect Chicago. Lake Michigan City College has been successful in several related grant endeavors. These include:

- A grant from the U.S. Department of Energy (DOE) for energy conservation measures, which resulted in the installation of a campus-wide energy management system

2D_AFV_Proposal_Firstname_Lastname

Lake Michigan City College *Alternative Fuel Vehicle Project*

- A technical assistance grant from the DOE for energy related building improvements
- An energy and environment grant from Chicago Electric Foundation, which utilized web-based information dissemination

Goals and Objectives of the Project

This initiative will result in the introduction of a natural gas fueling station providing a significant enhancement to the infrastructure along the corridor between Chicago and Westville, Illinois. It will result in the introduction of 67 CNG vehicles to the area. It will increase public awareness of alternative fuel vehicles indirectly through the visibility of the vehicles and directly through public education and training seminars and web site education. We anticipate that our efforts will stimulate natural gas vehicle purchases and usage. The primary goals and objectives of this initiative, in order of implementation, are:

1. Construction of a Natural Gas Fueling Station
2. Conversion of 67 CNG vehicles for use by the Physical Plant and other departments at Lake Michigan City College
3. Increased public awareness and education relating to alternative fueled vehicles
4. Education on health and safety issues relating to CNG
5. Vehicle operator training in proper fueling procedures and usage of CNG vehicles

Tentative completion dates:

Construction of fueling station	Phase I 7/05
Conversion of vehicles	Phase II 11/05
Education and training	Phase III 2/06

2D_AFV_Proposal_Firstname_Lastname

Figure 2.86

2. From the **File** menu, click **Save As**. Navigate to the location where you are saving your projects for this chapter. In the **File name** box, type **2D_AFV_Proposal_Firstname_Lastname** and then in the lower portion of the **Save As** dialog box, click the **Save** button.

3. The name of the college needs to be added to the title and in several locations throughout the document. This will be easier if you first create an AutoText entry for Lake Michigan City College. From the **Tools** menu, click **AutoCorrect Options**. In the **AutoCorrect** dialog box, click the **AutoText tab**. In the **Enter AutoText entries here** box type **Lake Michigan City College** and click the **Add** button. (If the Add button is dimmed and *Lake Michigan City College* displays in the list, another student has already added this text to AutoText. Click Cancel and go on to the next step. You will be able to use the existing AutoText entry.) This AutoText is added to the list. In the lower portion of the **AutoText** dialog box, click **OK**.

(Project 2D–AFV Proposal continues on the next page)

Skill Assessments (continued)

(Project 2D–AFV Proposal continued)

4. On the second line of the document, click to place the insertion point following the colon after *Alternative Fuel Transportation Project:* and then press [Enter]. On the new line, start typing **Lake Michigan City College** When the AutoText ScreenTip displays, press [Enter] to finish the text.

5. Select the first three lines in the document and, on the Formatting toolbar, click the **Center** button. Click the **Font button arrow**, click **Tahoma**, click the **Font Size button arrow**, click **16**, and then click the **Bold** button. Click anywhere to deselect the title lines.

6. There are several places in the document where the phrase *the college* needs to be replaced with the phrase *Lake Michigan City College*. From the **Edit** menu, click **Replace**. In the **Find what** box type **the college** In the **Replace with** box type **Lake Michigan City College** In the **Find and Replace** dialog box, click the **Find Next** button. When the first occurrence of *the college* is highlighted, click **Replace**. When the second occurrence of *the college* is highlighted, click **Replace**. When the next occurrence is highlighted, click **Replace All**. When the message box displays that Word has finished searching the document, click **OK**, and then close the **Find and Replace** dialog box. Click the **Save** button.

7. Hold down [Ctrl] and press [Home] to move to the top of the document. In the paragraph beginning *This project will*, at the end of the fourth line, click at the end of the paragraph, to the right of *result in:* and then press [Enter].

8. Beginning with *Development of a fueling*, select the next five short paragraphs—through *compressed natural gas vehicles (CNG)*. This is a list of results that are expected from the Alternative Fuel Project. With the list selected, on the Formatting toolbar, click the **Bullets** button.

9. The bullet symbol last used on your computer displays. With the list still selected, display the **Format** menu and then click **Bullets and Numbering**. In the first row, click the second box. If the second box is not solid black circles, in the lower left of the dialog box, click Reset and then click **Yes**. The selected box changes to its original setting—a solid black circle. Click **OK**.

10. Scroll as necessary to view the paragraphs below the bulleted list. Locate the subtitle *General Information*. Five lines below that, locate the paragraph that begins *A grant from*. Select the three paragraphs (five lines of text) beginning with *A grant from*. On the Formatting toolbar, click the **Bullets** button. The same bullet symbol that was used previously is applied to the list.

11. Scroll down to view the top portion of page 2. Select the six lines of text beginning with *Construction of a Natural*. On the Formatting toolbar, click the **Numbering** button. The result is five numbered items. Click the **Save** button.

(Project 2D–AFV Proposal continues on the next page)

Skill Assessments (continued)

(Project 2D–AFV Proposal continued)

12. Press **Ctrl** + **Home** to move to the top of the document, and then click to place the insertion point anywhere in the paragraph that begins *This project*. From the **Format** menu, click **Paragraph**. In the **Paragraph** dialog box, under **Indentation**, click the **Special arrow**, and then click **First line**. Under **Spacing**, click the **Line spacing arrow**, click **Double**, and then in the **Before** box, click the spin box up arrow once to display **6 pt**. Click **OK**.

13. The paragraph format that you just set will be applied to the other main paragraphs in the document. With the insertion point still in the formatted paragraph, on the Formatting toolbar, double-click the **Format Painter** button. Move the mouse pointer into a text portion of your document and verify that it takes on the shape of a paint brush. On this page, use the scroll bar to scroll down slightly below the first bulleted list, locate the paragraph that begins *Submission of a project* and then click in the paragraph. The paragraph format is applied, and the mouse pointer retains the paint brush. (If your mouse pointer no longer displays the paintbrush, double-click the Format Painter button again.)

14. Use the scroll arrow to move down slightly to view the paragraph beginning *Lake Michigan City College is located*—click in the paragraph to apply the formatting. Use the scroll bar to move to page 2, locate the paragraph that begins *This initiative will result*, and click in the paragraph. On the Formatting toolbar, click the **Format Painter** button once to turn it off.

15. Press **Ctrl** + **Home** to move to the top of the document. From the **View** menu, click **Header and Footer**. In the header area, type **Lake Michigan City College** (use AutoText to complete the entry if it displays), press **Tab** twice, and type **Alternative Fuel Vehicle Project** Select the text in the header and then, on the Formatting toolbar, click the **Italic** button.

16. On the Header and Footer toolbar, click the **Switch Between Header and Footer** button. On the Header and Footer toolbar, click the **Insert AutoText** button, point to **Header/Footer**, and then click **Filename** from the list that displays. Close the Header and Footer toolbar.

17. Click the **Save** button, then click the **Print Preview** button to see the document as it will print. Click the **Print** button, then close the file saving changes if prompted to do so.

End You have completed Project 2D

Skill Assessments (continued)

Project 2E — Delivery Suggestions

Objectives: *Change Document and Paragraph Layout, Change and Reorganize Text, Create and Modify Lists, Work with Headers and Footers, and Insert Frequently Used Text.*

In the following Skill Assessment, you will format and edit a paper that discusses technology needed for delivering online courses at Lake Michigan City College. Your completed document will look similar to Figure 2.87. You will save your document as 2E_Delivery_Suggestions_Firstname_Lastname.

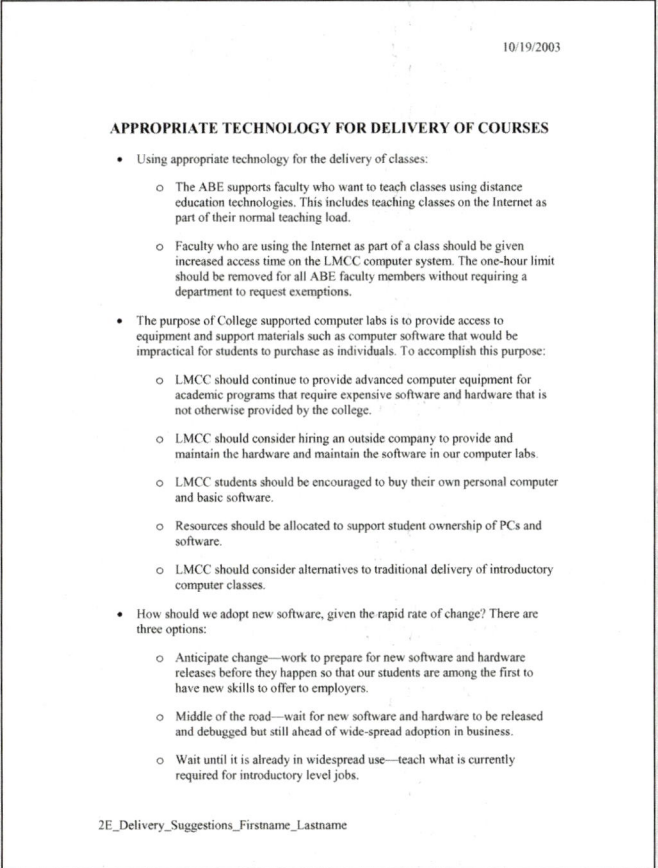

Figure 2.87

(Project 2E–Delivery Suggestions continues on the next page)

Skill Assessments (continued)

(Project 2E–Delivery Suggestions continued)

1. On the Standard toolbar, click the **Open** button. Navigate to the location where the student files for this textbook are stored. Locate and open **w02E_Delivery_Suggestions**. Be sure that nonprinting characters are displayed.

2. From the **File** menu, click **Save As**. Navigate to the location where you are saving your projects for this chapter. In the **File name** box, type **2E_Delivery_Suggestions_Firstname_Lastname** and then in the lower portion of the **Save As** dialog box, click the **Save** button.

3. Select the first line of the document and then, on the Formatting toolbar, click the **Center** button. From the **Format** menu, click **Change Case**. In the **Change Case** dialog box, click the **UPPERCASE** option button and then click **OK**. With the title still selected, on the Formatting toolbar, click the **Font Size button arrow**, click **14**, and then click the **Bold** button.

4. Click anywhere in the line beginning *1. Using*. Click the **Bullets** button. The last bullet symbol used on the computer at which you are seated is applied. Display the **Format** menu, and then click **Bullets and Numbering**. In the **Bullets and Numbering** dialog box, in the first row, click the second box. If the second box is not solid black circles, in the lower left of the dialog box, click Reset, and then click **Yes**. The selected box changes to its original setting—a solid black circle. Click **OK**.

5. On the Formatting toolbar, double-click the **Format Painter** button. When moved into the text area, the mouse pointer takes the shape of a paint brush. Use the scroll bar to scroll down until you see the next numbered paragraph beginning *1. The purpose of College supported* and then click in the numbered paragraph. A bullet replaces the number. Scroll down the document and click once in the next numbered paragraph, which begins *1. How should we*. On the Formatting toolbar, click the **Format Painter** button once to turn it off.

6. Scroll to position the second bulleted item and its following paragraphs into view on your screen. Select the paragraph that begins *Students should be*. On the Standard toolbar, click the **Cut** button. Click to place the insertion point at the beginning of the paragraph that begins *Resources should be allocated*. On the Standard toolbar, click the **Paste** button. The paragraph is moved.

7. Locate the paragraph under the second bulleted item that begins *We should consider hiring an outside company*. Select the word *software*, point to the selected word and drag it to the right of *hardware* and then release the mouse button. In the same sentence, select the second *and*, point to the selected word and drag it to the right of hardware, dropping it between *hardware* and *software*. Click to the left of *software*, and type **maintain the** The sentence should now read *…provide and maintain the hardware and maintain the software in our computer labs.*

(Project 2E–Delivery Suggestions continues on the next page)

Skill Assessments (continued)

(Project 2E–Delivery Suggestions continued)

8. Press Ctrl + Home to move to the top of the document. Under the first bulleted item, locate the paragraph that begins *Faculty who are using*. In the second line, select the text *LMCC* and click the **Copy** button.

9. In the second bulleted item, locate the paragraph that begins *The college should*. At the beginning of the paragraph, select the text *The college* and then click the **Paste** button. LMCC replaces the selected text.

10. In the first line of the next paragraph, select *We* and click the **Paste** button. In the next paragraph, select the *S* in *Students* click the **Paste** button, and then type **s** to provide the lower case letter at the beginning of the word *students*. Finally, select *We* at the beginning of the last paragraph under this bullet point and then click the **Paste** button.

11. Navigate to the top of the document and select the two paragraphs under the first bullet point. From the **Format** menu, click **Bullets and Numbering**. In the displayed dialog box, in the first row, click the third box, which should be a hollow circle. (If this bullet is not a hollow circle, in the lower left of the dialog box, click Reset. In the message box that displays, click Yes to reset the gallery position to the default setting. This resets the selected symbol to the default setting, which for the third box is a hollow circle.) Click **OK**. The selected text is formatted with a hollow circle bullet and is indented to the right under the first bullet.

12. Under the second bulleted item, select the five paragraphs that begin *LMCC should continue to provide*. On the Formatting toolbar, click the **Bullets** button and then click the **Increase Indent** button. When the bulleted text is indented, the bullets change to the hollow circle style.

13. Repeat this process to create the same style of bulleted list for the paragraphs that are listed under *How should we adopt*.

14. In the three bulleted items you just formatted, you will replace a colon (:) with an em dash. Position the bottom of the page into view on your screen. In the first bulleted item that begins *Anticipate*, select the colon and space following the text *Anticipate change*. From the **Insert** menu, click **Symbol**. In the **Symbol** dialog box, click the **Special Characters tab**. Make sure that **Em Dash** is highlighted, and then in the lower portion of the dialog box click **Insert**. The **Symbol** dialog box remains open on your screen.

(Project 2E–Delivery Suggestions continues on the next page)

Skill Assessments (continued)

(Project 2E–Delivery Suggestions continued)

15. Point to the title bar of the **Symbol** dialog box, and then drag it to the right of your screen so that you can view the last two bulleted items on the page. Select the colon and space that follows *Middle of the road*, and then in the **Symbol** dialog box, click **Insert**. Moving the dialog box as necessary, repeat this process to replace the colon and space in the final bulleted item, found after *widespread use*. Close the **Symbol** dialog box. Click **Save** to save your changes.

16. From the **View** menu, click **Header and Footer**. In the header area, press twice. On the Header and Footer toolbar, click the **Insert Date** button.

17. On the Header and Footer toolbar, click the **Switch Between Header and Footer** button. On the Header and Footer toolbar, click the **Insert AutoText** button, and then from the displayed list, click **Filename**. Close the Header and Footer toolbar.

18. From the **File** menu, click **Page Setup**. In the displayed **Page Setup** dialog box, click the **Margins tab**. Under **Margins**, click in the **Top** box and type **1.5** In the lower right corner of the dialog box, click **OK**.

19. On the Standard toolbar, click the **Save** button to save the changes to the document.

20. On the Standard toolbar, click the **Print Preview** button to view your document as it will print. On the Print Preview toolbar, click the **Print** button to print the document, and then on the same toolbar, click the **Close** button. Close the document and then close Word.

End You have completed Project 2E

Performance Assessments

Project 2F—Computer Virus Policy

Objectives: *Change Document and Paragraph Layout, Change and Reorganize Text, Create and Modify Lists, Work with Headers and Footers, Insert Frequently Used Text, and Insert References.*

In the following Performance Assessment, you will format and edit a report regarding the Lake Michigan City College computer virus policy. Your completed document will look similar to Figure 2.88. You will save your document as *2F_Computer_Virus_Firstname_Lastname*.

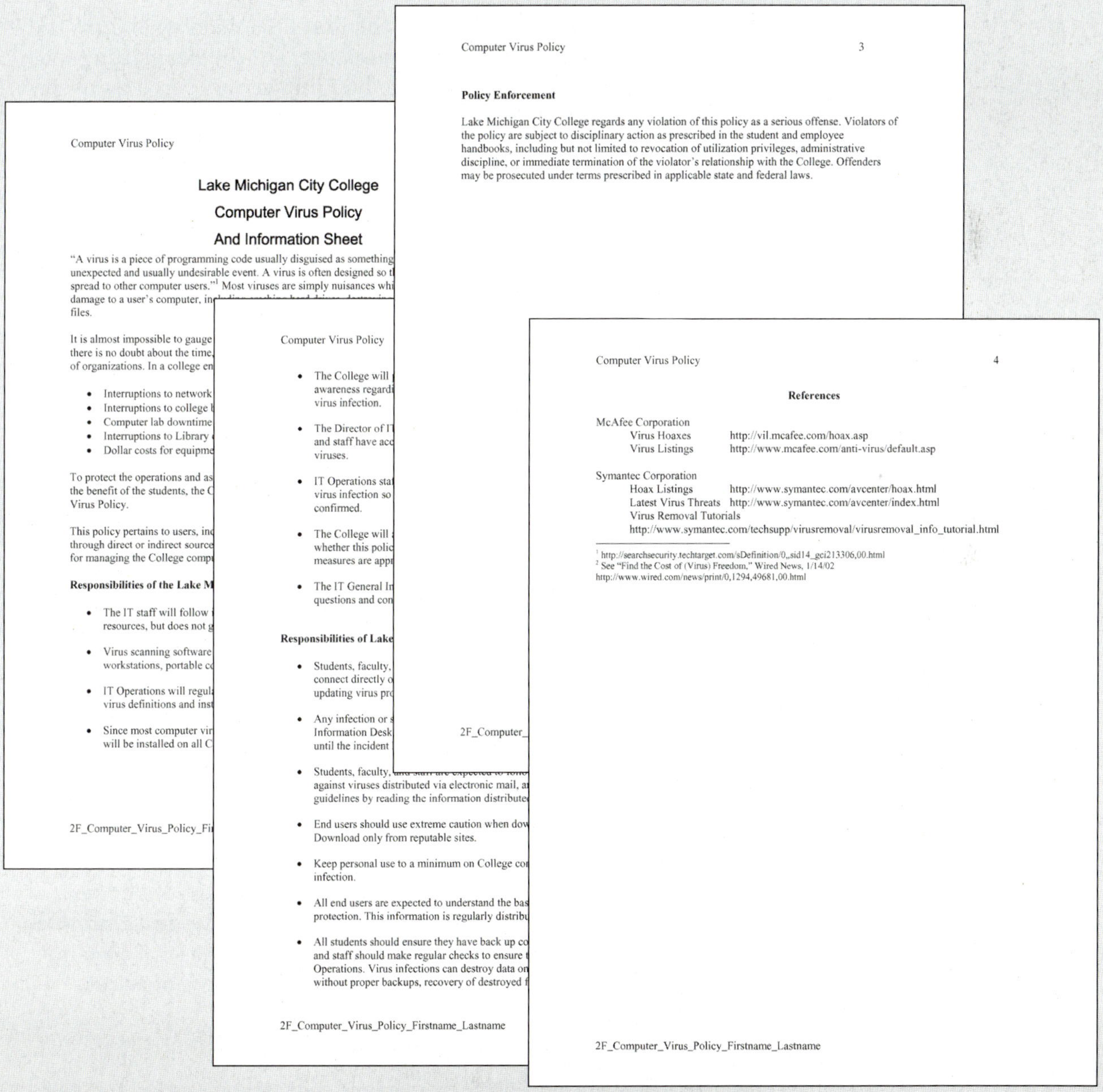

Figure 2.88

(Project 2F–Computer Virus continues on the next page)

Word chapter two

Performance Assessments (continued)

(Project 2F–Computer Virus Policy continued)

1. Click the **Open** button. Navigate to the location where the student files for this textbook are stored. Locate and open **w02F_Computer_Virus_Policy**. From the **File** menu click **Save As**. Navigate to the location where you are saving your projects for this chapter. In the **File name** box, and using your own name, type **2F_Computer_Virus_Policy_Firstname_Lastname** and then click the **Save** button.

2. From the **File** menu, click **Page Setup**. In the **Page Setup** dialog box, change the left margin to **1"** and the right margin to **1"** and then click **OK**.

3. At the top of the document, select the first line, which will form the title and begins *Lake Michigan City College*. On the Formatting toolbar, click the **Center** button. Click the **Font arrow**, scroll as needed and click **Arial Unicode MS**, click the **Font Size arrow**, and then click **16**. On the Formatting toolbar, click the **Bold** button. Place the insertion point at the end of the word *College* and press Enter. Place the insertion point at the end of the word *Policy* and press Enter again. The title is on three lines and is easier to read. If necessary, on the Standard toolbar, click the Show/Hide ¶ button to display nonprinting characters. Delete the spaces at the beginning of the second and third lines of the title.

4. The first two sentences in this document—beginning with *"A virus—*is a quote and needs to be referenced. In the third line of this paragraph, place the insertion point after the closing quote mark following *computer users."* From the **Insert** menu, point to **Reference**, and then click **Footnote**. In the **Footnote and Endnote** dialog box, under **Location**, click the **Endnotes** option button, and be sure **End of document** displays in the box to its right. Under **Format**, click the **Number format arrow**, and then click **1, 2, 3** from the list. Click **Insert**. In the endnote area type **http://searchsecurity.techtarget.com/sDefinition/0,,sid14_gci213306,00.html** but do not type a space or press Enter.

5. Because this is an Internet address, the Word program may automatically format it as a hyperlink—in blue and underlined—if you follow it with a space or Enter. If Word formats the address as a hyperlink, right-click on the address and click Remove Hyperlink.

6. Press Ctrl + Home. Locate the paragraph of text that begins *It is almost impossible* and place the insertion to the right of *viruses each year*—before the comma. Display the **Footnote and Endnote** dialog box again, click **Insert**, and then, without pressing Enter, but placing a space after the date, type **See "Find the Cost of (Virus) Freedom," Wired News, 1/14/02 http://www.wired.com/news/print/0,1294,49681,00.html**

    Your text may wrap at a different place than shown in Figure 2.88. Click the **Save** button.

(Project 2F–Computer Virus continues on the next page)

Performance Assessments (continued)

(Project 2F–Computer Virus Policy continued)

7. Near the top of the document, select the five one-line paragraphs starting with the paragraph that begins *Interruptions to network* and then click the **Bullets** button. (If the bullet that displays is not a solid round symbol, display the Format menu, click Bullets and Numbering, click the solid round bullet example, and then click OK.)

8. Position the lower portion of page 1 into view. In the paragraph beginning *The IT staff will follow,* click to left of the first word in the paragraph. Use the scroll arrow to view the top of the next page. Hold down [Shift] and, in the seventh line down, click after the period following the word *College.* This will select all the text paragraphs that follow this subheading. With these paragraphs selected, apply a solid round bullet. Display the **Format** menu, click **Paragraph**, and increase the spacing after to **12 pt**.

9. Using the technique in the previous step, select the paragraphs of text following the subheading *Responsibilities of Lake Michigan City College Students, Faculty, and Staff,* and use the same procedure to add solid round bullets and increase the space after to **12 pt**.

10. Navigate to the bottom of page 3, click to place the insertion point to the left of the word *References* and then press [Ctrl] + [Enter] to insert a page break and move this title to the next page. Select *References* and click the **Center** button.

11. On page 4, select *McAfee Corporation* and the two references listed under it. Click the **Cut** button. Place the insertion point to the left of *Symantec* and press the **Paste** button. The references are reordered. Insert an empty line between the Symantec and McAfee references.

12. Select the four lines listed under *Symantec Corporation*. Display the **Table** menu and then click **Sort**. In the **Sort Text** dialog box, under **Sort by**, be sure *Paragraphs* displays and then click **OK**. The references are resorted in alphabetical order. Right-click on any Web references that are formatted as hyperlinks (blue and underlined) and click **Remove Hyperlink**. Remove any empty paragraphs between the last reference and the beginning of the endnotes.

13. Display the **View** menu and then click **Header and Footer**. In the header area, type **Computer Virus Policy**, press [Tab] twice, and then click the **Insert Page Number** button. Switch to the footer area, click the **Insert AutoText** button, and insert the **Filename**. Close the Header and Footer toolbar.

14. Click the **Save** button, then click the **Print Preview** button. Compare the layout of your document to the figure. Click the **Print** button and then close the Print Preview window. Close the document, saving any changes and then close Word.

End You have completed Project 2F

Project 2F: Computer Virus Policy | **Word**

Project 2G—Interview Questions

Objectives: *Change Document and Paragraph Layout, Change and Reorganize Text, Create and Modify Lists, Work with Headers and Footers, Insert Frequently Used Text, and Insert References.*

In the following Performance Assessment, you will edit and format a list of questions from Lisa Huelsman, Associate Dean of Adult Basic Education, for use in an interview with candidates for a new Director of Distance Education at Lake Michigan City College. Your completed document will look similar to Figure 2.89. You will save your document as *2G_Interview_Questions_Firstname_Lastname*.

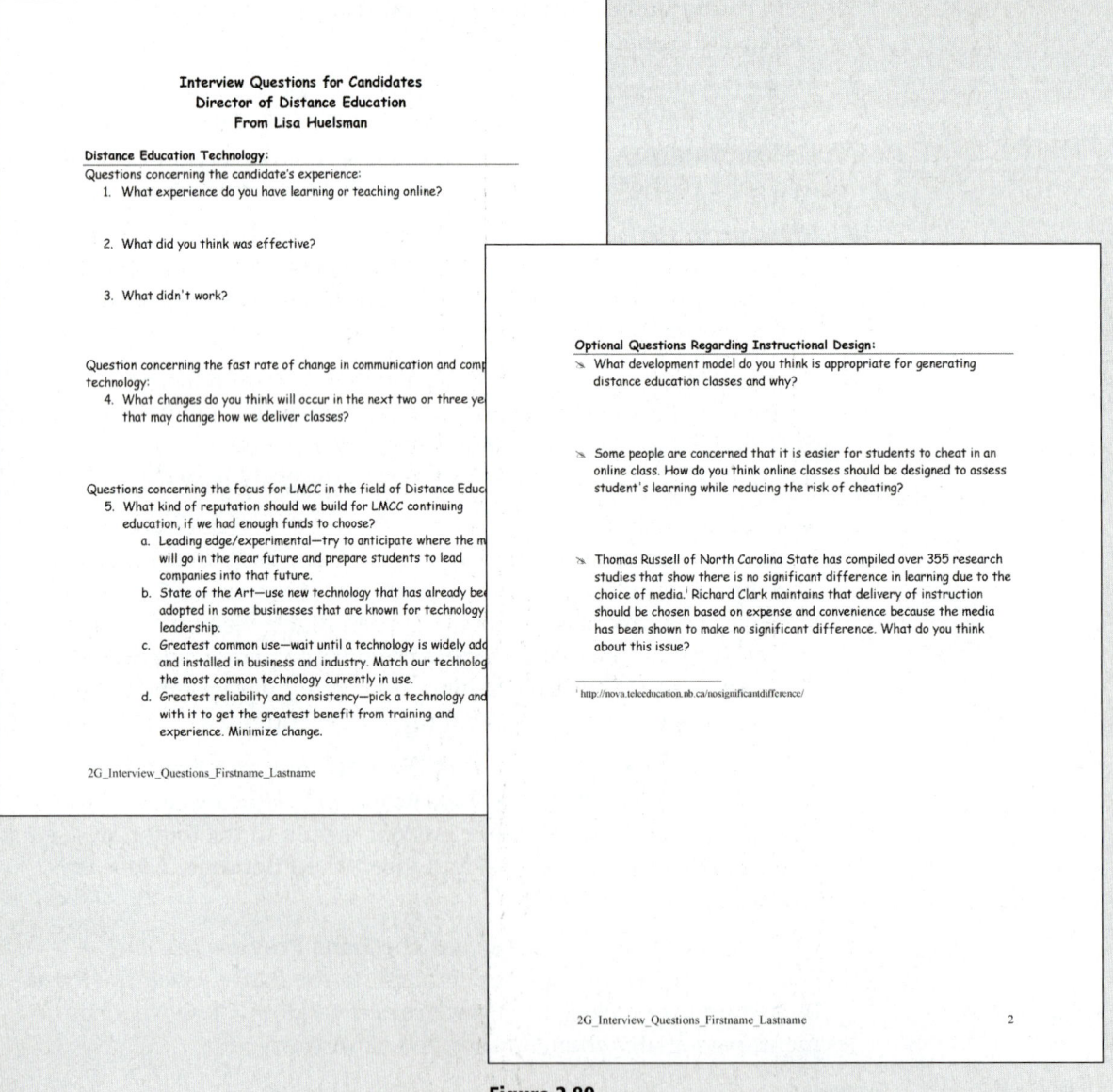

Figure 2.89

(Project 2G–Interview Questions continues on the next page)

Word chapter two

Performance Assessments (continued)

(Project 2G–Interview Questions continued)

1. Click the **Open** button. Navigate to the location where the student files for this textbook are stored. Locate and open **w02G_Interview_Questions**. From the **File** menu, click **Save As**. Navigate to the location where you are saving your projects for this chapter. In the **File name** box, using your own name, type **2G_Interview_Questions_Firstname_Lastname** and then click the **Save** button. Make sure that nonprinting characters are displayed and take a moment to scroll through this two-page document to familiarize yourself with the layout and content.

2. In the first line of the document that begins *Interview Questions*, place your insertion point after *Candidates* and press Enter. Type **Director of Distance Education** and then press Enter again. There are now three title lines. Delete the space to the left of the third line.

3. Select the three title lines. On the Formatting toolbar, click the **Center** button and then click the **Bold** button. Change the **Font Size** to **14**.

4. Locate the first question beginning with *What experience*. Three questions are listed concerning the experience of the candidate. Select the three questions and, on the Formatting toolbar, click the **Line Spacing** arrow and then click **3.0**. This increases the spacing between the questions, which will provide space for the interviewer to make notes during the interview.

5. With the three questions still selected, on the Formatting toolbar, click the **Numbering** button.

6. Position the middle of page 1 into view. Select the paragraph that begins *What changes*. From the **Format** menu, click **Paragraph** and then click the **Indents and Spacing tab**. Under **Spacing**, change the **After** box to **36**. You can either type 36 or use the spin box arrow to increase the number displayed. Click **OK** to close the **Paragraph** dialog box. Notice that in this instance, the Line Spacing button was not used, because doing so would increase the space between the two wrapped lines of the paragraph. Because the goal is to add some space after the question for handwritten notes, the Spacing After paragraph feature is useful here.

7. With the question still selected, on the Formatting toolbar, click the **Numbering** button. The question is numbered 1, starting the numbering sequence over again, and the AutoCorrect Options button displays. Point to the **AutoCorrect Options** button, click its arrow to display the list of options available, and then, from the displayed list, click **Continue Numbering**. The number for this question is changed to 4.

8. Scroll down a few lines, select the question beginning *What kind of reputation*, and then click the **Numbering** button. The question is numbered 5, continuing the numbering sequence.

(Project 2G–Interview Questions continues on the next page)

Project 2G: Interview Questions | **Word** 319

Word chapter two
Performance Assessments (continued)

(Project 2G–Interview Questions continued)

9. Select the four paragraphs following question 5, beginning with *Leading Edge*. Click the **Numbering** button. The numbering sequence continues—6 through 9. However, these paragraphs are a subset of question 5. With the four paragraphs still selected, on the Formatting toolbar, click the **Increase Indent** button. The paragraphs are indented and the numbers changed to letters a through d.

10. On the Standard toolbar, click the **Save** button. Each of the four paragraphs now labeled a. through d. has a colon followed by a space in the first line. In the paragraph beginning *a. Leading edge*, select the colon and its following space. From the **Insert** menu, click **Symbol**. In the **Symbol** dialog box, click the **Special Characters tab**; be sure that **Em Dash** is highlighted. Click **Insert**. The dialog box remains open on your screen. Select the colon and following space found in the first line of the paragraphs labeled, b., c., and d. and replace it by inserting an em dash from the **Symbol** dialog box. Move the dialog box on your screen as necessary and then close the dialog box.

11. Scroll as necessary to view page 2 on your screen. Select the paragraphs under *Instructional Design* including the two empty paragraphs between the questions. Display the **Paragraph** dialog box and increase the spacing after to **18**. Click **OK**. The space after formatting was applied to all of the paragraphs, including those without text.

12. With the paragraphs still selected, display the **Bullets and Numbering** dialog box and click the **Bulleted tab**. If necessary, click any bullet syles to activate the **Customize button**. In the lower right corner, click the **Customize button**. In the **Customize Bulleted List** dialog box, click the **Character button**. In the displayed **Symbol** dialog box, click the **Font** arrow, click **Wingdings**, scroll to the top of the list, and in the third row, click the first symbol-a hand with a pencil. Click **OK** twice. Then, click the **Decrease Indent** button as many times as necessary to align the bullets at the left margin.

    If the numbers continue sequentially with the number 6 from the previous list, instead of restarting at number 1, open the **Bullets and Numbering** dialog box and click again to select the **Restart Numbering** option button. Click **OK**.

13. From the **View** menu, click **Header and Footer**. Switch to the footer area and then, on the **Header and Footer** toolbar, click **Insert AutoText**. From the displayed list, click **Filename**. Press [Tab] and click the **Insert Page Number** button. Close the Header and Footer toolbar.

(Project 2G–Interview Questions continues on the next page)

Performance Assessments (continued)

(Project 2G–Interview Questions continued)

14. Press Ctrl + Home to move to the top of the document. In the first group of questions, the second and third questions need to be reversed. Select the question *What did you think was effective?* The number will not be highlighted. Point to the highlighted text. When the mouse pointer is in the shape of the white move arrow, drag the question and place the vertical line at the beginning of question 2— in front of the *W*—and then release the mouse button. The questions are reversed. On the Standard toolbar click the **Undo** button and then click the **Redo** button. Notice that the numbers stay in sequence.

15. Press Ctrl + End to move to the end of the document. In the paragraph beginning *Thomas Russell*, in the third line, click to place the insertion point following the period after the word *media*. From the **Insert** menu, point to **Reference** and then click **Footnote**. In the **Footnote and Endnote** dialog box, under **Location**, click the **Endnotes** option button and be sure **End of document** is displayed in its box. Under **Format**, click the **Number format arrow** and then click **i, ii, iii** from the list that displays. Click the **Insert** button. In the endnote area, type **http://nova.teleeducation.nb.ca/nosignificantdifference/**

16. Click the **Save** button and then click the **Print Preview** button to view the document. From the Print Preview toolbar, click the **Print** button and then, on the same toolbar, click the **Close** button. Close the document, saving changes if prompted to do so.

End You have completed Project 2G

Word chapter two

Performance Assessments (continued)

Project 2H—Virtual Tour

Objectives: *Change Document and Paragraph Layout, Change and Reorganize Text, Work with Headers and Footers, and Insert Frequently Used Text.*

In the following Performance Assessment, you will edit and format a report written by students of the Advanced Web Design class, regarding a Web site they plan to create for members of the local community. Your completed document will look similar to Figure 2.90. You will save your document as *2H_Virtual_Tour_Firstname_Lastname*.

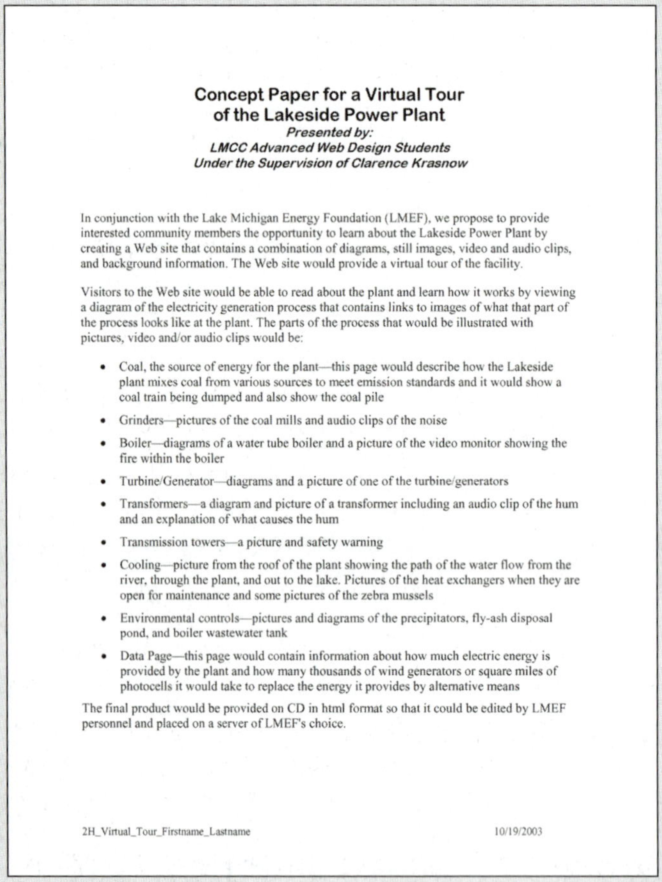

Figure 2.90

(**Project 2H**–Virtual Tour continues on the next page)

322 **Word** | Chapter 2: Formatting and Organizing Text

Performance Assessments (continued)

(Project 2H–Virtual Tour continued)

1. Click the **Open** button. Navigate to the location where the student files for this textbook are stored. Locate and open the file **w02H_Virtual_Tour**. From the **File** menu, click **Save As**. Navigate to the location where you are storing your projects for this chapter. In the **File name** box, using your own name, type **2H_Virtual_Tour_Firstname_Lastname**

2. From the **File** menu, click **Page Setup**. Change the left and right margin boxes to **1"**.

3. From the **Tools** menu, click **AutoCorrect Options** and then click the **AutoCorrect tab**. In the **Replace** box type: **xlmef** and in the **With** box type **Lake Michigan Energy Foundation**. Click the **Add** button and then click **OK**. If another student has already added this AutoCorrect entry, the Replace button will be indicated instead of the Add button. Click Replace, click Yes, and then click OK.

4. In the paragraph that begins with *In conjunction with*, in the first line, place the insertion point to the left of LMEF. Type **xlmef** and then press the spacebar. The name of the foundation replaces the shortcut you typed. Enclose *LMEF* in parentheses.

5. In the same paragraph, at the end of the third line, select *still images,*—be sure you include the comma and the space. Point to the selected text and drag it to the left of *video and audio clips* in the same sentence. Adjust the spacing if necessary.

6. Select the two paragraphs above the bulleted list, beginning with *In conjunction with*, point anywhere in the selected text and right-click, and then click **Paragraph** from the shortcut menu. Under **Spacing**, change the **After** box to **12**. Click **OK**.

7. In the bulleted list, rearrange the items into the following order: Coal, Grinders, Boiler, Turbine/Generator, Transformers, Transmission towers, Cooling, Environmental Controls, Data Page.

8. Press [Ctrl] + [Home] to move to the top of the document. Press [Ctrl] + [H] to open the **Find and Replace** dialog box. In the **Find what** box, type **web** In the **Replace with** box, type **Web** Click **Replace All**. Four replacements are made. Close the dialog box.

9. From the **View** menu, click **Header and Footer**. Switch to the footer area on the Header and Footer toolbar, click **Insert AutoText** and then click **Filename**. Press [Tab] two times to move to the right side of the footer area and then click the **Insert Date** button. Select the text in the footer and change the font size to **10 pt**. Close the Header and Footer toolbar.

10. Click the **Save** button and then click the **Print Preview** button. From the Print Preview toolbar, click the **Print** button and then, on the same toolbar, click the **Close** button. Close the document.

End You have completed Project 2H

Mastery Assessments

Project 2I — Organizations

Objectives: *Change Document and Paragraph Layout, Change and Reorganize Text, Create and Modify Lists, and Work with Headers and Footers.*

In the following Mastery Assessment, you will format and reorganize a list of the student organizations at LMCC. Your completed document will look similar to Figure 2.91. You will save your document as *2I_Organizations_Firstname_Lastname.*

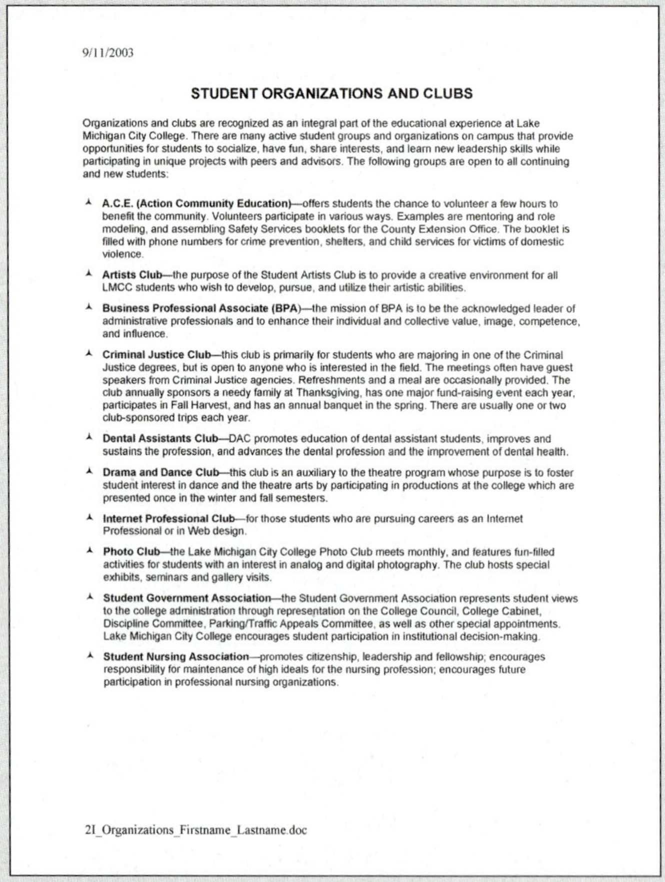
9/11/2003

STUDENT ORGANIZATIONS AND CLUBS

Organizations and clubs are recognized as an integral part of the educational experience at Lake Michigan City College. There are many active student groups and organizations on campus that provide opportunities for students to socialize, have fun, share interests, and learn new leadership skills while participating in unique projects with peers and advisors. The following groups are open to all continuing and new students:

- **A.C.E. (Action Community Education)**—offers students the chance to volunteer a few hours to benefit the community. Volunteers participate in various ways. Examples are mentoring and role modeling, and assembling Safety Services booklets for the County Extension Office. The booklet is filled with phone numbers for crime prevention, shelters, and child services for victims of domestic violence.
- **Artists Club**—the purpose of the Student Artists Club is to provide a creative environment for all LMCC students who wish to develop, pursue, and utilize their artistic abilities.
- **Business Professional Associate (BPA)**—the mission of BPA is to be the acknowledged leader of administrative professionals and to enhance their individual and collective value, image, competence, and influence.
- **Criminal Justice Club**—this club is primarily for students who are majoring in one of the Criminal Justice degrees, but is open to anyone who is interested in the field. The meetings often have guest speakers from Criminal Justice agencies. Refreshments and a meal are occasionally provided. The club annually sponsors a needy family at Thanksgiving, has one major fund-raising event each year, participates in Fall Harvest, and has an annual banquet in the spring. There are usually one or two club-sponsored trips each year.
- **Dental Assistants Club**—DAC promotes education of dental assistant students, improves and sustains the profession, and advances the dental profession and the improvement of dental health.
- **Drama and Dance Club**—this club is an auxiliary to the theatre program whose purpose is to foster student interest in dance and the theatre arts by participating in productions at the college which are presented once in the winter and fall semesters.
- **Internet Professional Club**—for those students who are pursuing careers as an Internet Professional or in Web design.
- **Photo Club**—the Lake Michigan City College Photo Club meets monthly, and features fun-filled activities for students with an interest in analog and digital photography. The club hosts special exhibits, seminars and gallery visits.
- **Student Government Association**—the Student Government Association represents student views to the college administration through representation on the College Council, College Cabinet, Discipline Committee, Parking/Traffic Appeals Committee, as well as other special appointments. Lake Michigan City College encourages student participation in institutional decision-making.
- **Student Nursing Association**—promotes citizenship, leadership and fellowship; encourages responsibility for maintenance of high ideals for the nursing profession; encourages future participation in professional nursing organizations.

2I_Organizations_Firstname_Lastname.doc

Figure 2.91

(Project 2I–Organizations continues on the next page)

Mastery Assessments (continued)

(Project 2I–Organizations continued)

1. Display the **Open** dialog box. Navigate to the student files and then locate and open the file **w02I_Organizations**. In the **File name** box, type **2I_Organizations_Firstname_Lastname** Display nonprinting characters. Display the **File** menu and click **Save As**. Navigate to the location where you are storing your projects for this chapter.

2. From the **File** menu, display the **Page Setup** dialog box. Change the left and right margins to **1 inch**, and close the dialog box. Center the title of the document.

3. Select the list of student organizations, beginning with *Student Government* and continuing down through the end of the document. Recall that you can click at the beginning point in the text, scroll to the end, press Shift, and then click at the end to select all of the text rather than dragging. Display the **Paragraph** dialog box, click the **Indents and Spacing tab**, and then, under **Spacing**, change the **After** box to **6**.

4. With the list of organizations still selected, display the **Bullets and Numbering** dialog box. Click the **Bulleted tab** and then click any of the bullet options. Click the **Customize** button and then click the **Character** button. In the **Symbol** dialog box, click the **Font arrow**, scroll, and then click **Wingdings**. Click a symbol of your choice that would serve as a bullet and then click **OK** twice to apply the bullet. Click the **Decrease Indent** button once to move the list to the left.

5. With the list of organizations still selected, from the **Table** menu, click **Sort**. Sort the list alphabetically by paragraph.

6. Display the footer area and then, using the **Insert AutoText** button, insert the **Filename**. Switch to the header area and insert the date at the left side of the header.

7. Save the changes. Preview and then print the document. Close the file.

End You have completed Project 2I

Mastery Assessments (continued)

Project 2J—Online Article

Objectives: *Change Document and Paragraph Layout, Change and Reorganize Text, Create and Modify Lists, Work with Headers and Footers, Insert Frequently Used Text, and Insert References.*

In the following Mastery Assessment, you will edit and format an article about one of the professors at LMCC who offers online classes. The completed article will look similar to Figure 2.92. You will save your document as *2J_Online_Article_Firstname_Lastname.*

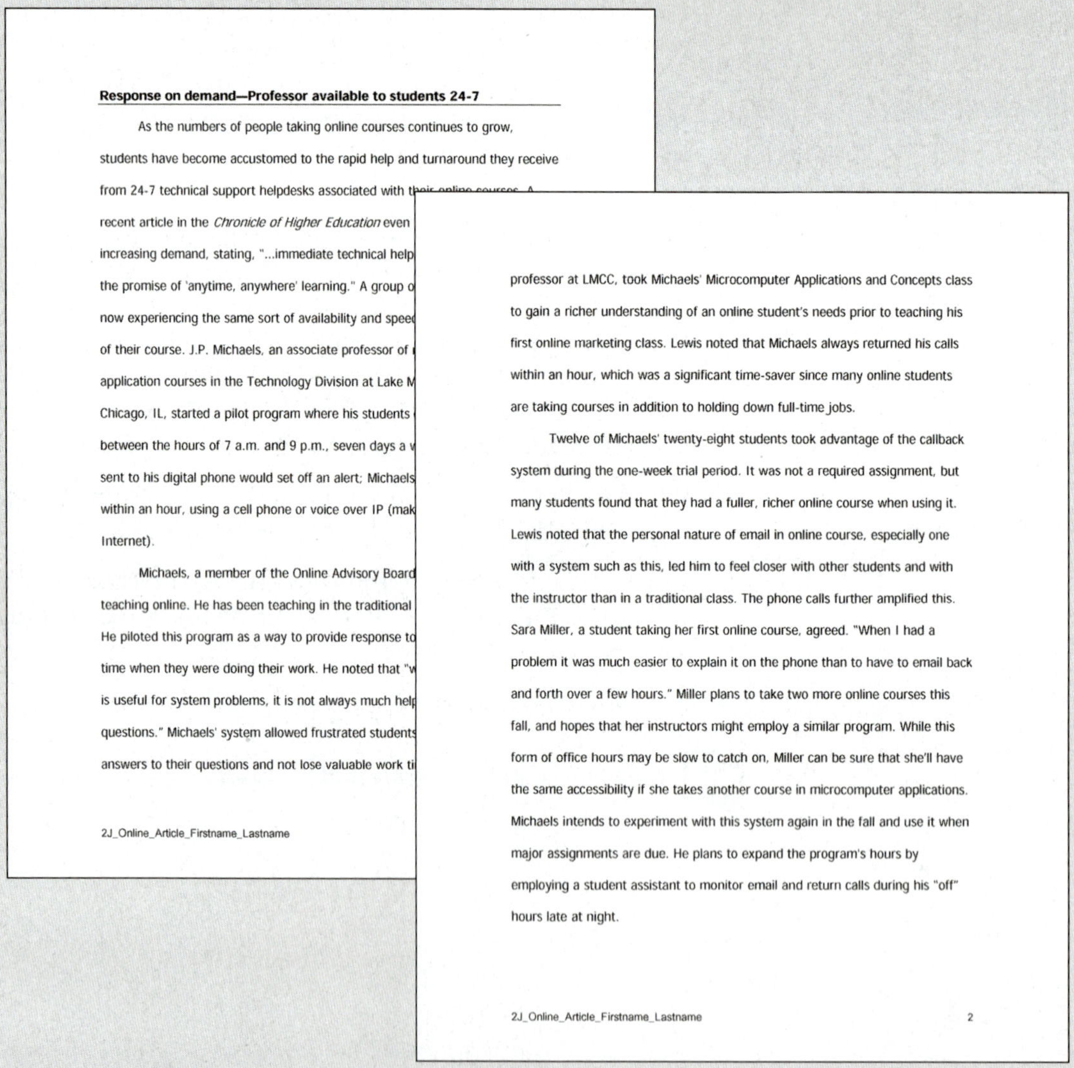

Response on demand—Professor available to students 24-7

As the numbers of people taking online courses continues to grow, students have become accustomed to the rapid help and turnaround they receive from 24-7 technical support helpdesks associated with their online courses. A recent article in the *Chronicle of Higher Education* even increasing demand, stating, "...immediate technical help the promise of 'anytime, anywhere' learning." A group o now experiencing the same sort of availability and speed of their course. J.P. Michaels, an associate professor of application courses in the Technology Division at Lake M Chicago, IL, started a pilot program where his students between the hours of 7 a.m. and 9 p.m., seven days a w sent to his digital phone would set off an alert; Michaels within an hour, using a cell phone or voice over IP (mak Internet).

Michaels, a member of the Online Advisory Board teaching online. He has been teaching in the traditional He piloted this program as a way to provide response to time when they were doing their work. He noted that "w is useful for system problems, it is not always much help questions." Michaels' system allowed frustrated students answers to their questions and not lose valuable work ti

2J_Online_Article_Firstname_Lastname

professor at LMCC, took Michaels' Microcomputer Applications and Concepts class to gain a richer understanding of an online student's needs prior to teaching his first online marketing class. Lewis noted that Michaels always returned his calls within an hour, which was a significant time-saver since many online students are taking courses in addition to holding down full-time jobs.

Twelve of Michaels' twenty-eight students took advantage of the callback system during the one-week trial period. It was not a required assignment, but many students found that they had a fuller, richer online course when using it. Lewis noted that the personal nature of email in online course, especially one with a system such as this, led him to feel closer with other students and with the instructor than in a traditional class. The phone calls further amplified this. Sara Miller, a student taking her first online course, agreed. "When I had a problem it was much easier to explain it on the phone than to have to email back and forth over a few hours." Miller plans to take two more online courses this fall, and hopes that her instructors might employ a similar program. While this form of office hours may be slow to catch on, Miller can be sure that she'll have the same accessibility if she takes another course in microcomputer applications. Michaels intends to experiment with this system again in the fall and use it when major assignments are due. He plans to expand the program's hours by employing a student assistant to monitor email and return calls during his "off" hours late at night.

2J_Online_Article_Firstname_Lastname 2

Figure 2.92

(Project 2J–Online Article continues on the next page)

Mastery Assessments (continued)

(Project 2J–Online Article continued)

1. Display the **Open** dialog box. Navigate to the student files and then locate and open the file **w02J_Online_Article**. Display the **File** menu, click **Save As**, and navigate to the location where you are storing your projects for this chapter. In the **File name** box, type **2J_Online_Article_Firstname_Lastname**

2. From the **File** menu, display the **Page Setup** dialog box. Change the left and right margins to **1.25"**.

3. Beginning with the paragraph *As the numbers*, select the entire body of the article, click the arrow on the **Line Spacing** button, and then click **2.0**.

4. With the text still selected, display the **Paragraph** dialog box, and then click the **Indents and Spacing tab**. Under **Indentation**, click the **Special arrow** and then click **First line**.

5. Position the insertion point at the top of the document and then display the **Find and Replace** dialog box. In the **Find what** box type **e-mail** and in the **Replace with** box type **email** Find and replace this word throughout the document.

6. Use the **Find and Replace** dialog box to locate **College of Technology** and replace it with **Technology Division** Make sure the insertion point is at the top of the document. Use the **Find and Replace** dialog box to locate the second occurrence of *Lake Michigan City College* and replace it with **LMCC** Finally, use the **Find and Replace** dialog box to find **Rosenthal** and replace each occurrence with **Miller**.

7. Move to the top of the document. In the paragraph beginning *As the numbers*, in the middle of the seventh line, locate the phrase *speed and availability*. Use drag-and-drop or cut-and-paste techniques to reword this to read *availability and speed*.

8. Press Ctrl + End to move to the end of the document. Select the last sentence in the document beginning with *Miller plans to take* (do not select the ending paragraph mark). In the same paragraph, locate the sentence that begins *While this form* and then use the drag-and-drop technique to move the selected sentence in front of the *While this form* sentence. Adjust the spacing if necessary. Be sure that you did not create a new paragraph.

9. View the footer area, click the **Insert AutoText** button, and then insert the **Filename**. Tab to the right side of the footer and insert the page number.

10. Save the changes. Preview and then print the document. Close the file.

End You have completed Project 2J

Project 2J: Online Article | **Word** 327

Problem Solving

Project 2K — Holidays

Objectives: *Change Document and Paragraph Layout, Change and Reorganize Text, Create and Modify Lists, Work with Headers and Footers.*

You will write a memo listing the holidays that will be taken during the calendar school year at Lake Michigan City College. You will save your document as *2K_Holidays_Firstname_Lastname*.

1. Open Word. Use the **Page Setup** dialog box to set the margins to **2 inches** at the top margin, and **1 inch** on the left and right sides.

2. Create a MEMO heading at the top of the document. Format the heading in a distinctive manner and align it on the right side of the page. Press Enter four times.

2. Type the heading of the memo as follows:

MEMO TO:	James Smith, Vice President of Student Affairs
FROM:	Henry Sabaj, Vice President of Academic Affairs
DATE:	August 1
SUBJECT:	College Holidays

3. Format the heading to be double-spaced and indent 1 inch from the left margin. Format the headings in uppercase bold.

4. Write one or two introductory sentences indicating that this is the list of holiday dates agreed to by the faculty and administration for the upcoming college year.

5. Use a calendar and create a bulleted list of official holiday names and dates for the September through May college year. Look at your own college calendar and include the dates for any winter or spring breaks that may be scheduled.

6. Format the list of holidays using a bullet symbol of your choice.

7. Save the memo in your storage location with the name **2K_Holidays_Firstname_Lastname**

8. View the footer area and insert the filename using AutoText.

9. Switch to the header area and type **Academic Affairs**

10. Preview and then print the memo. Close the file and close Word.

End You have completed Project 2K

Problem Solving (continued)

Project 2L — Computer Information Memo

Objectives: *Change Document and Paragraph Layout, Change and Reorganize Text, Create and Modify Lists, Work with Headers and Footers.*

In this Problem Solving assessment, you will write a memo to the Vice President of Academic Affairs listing the Computer Information Systems courses at LMCC. You will save your memo as *2L_Computer_Information_Memo_Firstname_Lastname*.

1. Open Word. Use the **Page Setup** dialog box to set the margins to **2"** at the top margin, and **1"** on the left and right sides.

2. Create a MEMO heading at the top of the document. Format the heading in a distinctive manner and center it on the page. Press Enter four times.

3. Type the heading of the memo as follows:

MEMO TO:	Henry Sabaj, Vice President of Academic Affairs
FROM:	Lisa Huelsman, Associate Dean of Adult Basic Education
DATE:	September 30
SUBJECT:	Computer Information Systems Courses

4. Format the heading area to be double-spaced and indent 1" from the left margin. Format the headings in uppercase bold.

5. Write one or two introductory sentences explaining that the list includes the current Computer Information Systems courses required for a certificate or degree at LMCC.

6. Using the course catalog and other information available via your college's Web site, create a bulleted list of the course numbers and names that are required as Computer Information Systems—or similar—classes at your college.

7. Add a closing to the memo requesting that Mr. Sabaj review the list for possible adjustments or modifications.

8. Save the memo in your storage location with the name **2L_Computer_Information_Memo_Firstname_Lastname**

9. View the footer area and insert the filename using AutoText.

10. Preview and then print the memo. Close the file and close Word.

End You have completed Project 2L

On the Internet

Finding More Bullet Styles To Use

The bullet symbols that display in the Symbols dialog box are used throughout Microsoft Office programs. You can also download and use symbols from other sites on the Internet.

1. Open your Web browser and go to a search engine such as www.google.com or www.yahoo.com. Type the key words **bullets** and **free** in the search box.

2. Look through the various sites for one you like that has a variety of interesting graphics that may be used for bullets. There are several that do not require that you sign up for advertising or provide your e-mail address.

3. Pick a bullet you like and right-click it. Click the **Save as Picture** option from the shortcut menu and save it to your disk.

4. Open a Word document and create a short bulleted list to demonstrate your new bullet.

5. Select the list and, on the Formatting toolbar, click the **Bullet** button.

6. From the **Format** menu, choose **Bullets and Numbering**. Click **Customize** and then **Picture**.

7. Click **Import**. In the **Add Clips to Organizer** dialog box, find the picture you saved to your disk, click it, and then click **Add**. Select your new picture, if necessary, click **OK**, and then click **OK** again to close the dialog boxes.

8. Close the file without saving the changes and then close Word.

GO! with Help

Restoring the Default Bullets and Numbering

If you have used a number of customized bullets in the Bullets and Numbering dialog box, you may want to restore the dialog box to its original configuration. The Word Help program gives you step-by-step instructions on how to restore a customized list format to its original setting.

1. Start Word. On the menu bar, in the *Type* a question for help box, type **How do I restore customized bullet list** and then press Enter.

2. Locate and then click the topic **Restore a customized list format to its original setting**.

3. Read the instructions that display and then follow the steps to restore the original settings to the Bullets and Numbering dialog box on your computer.

4. Close the Microsoft Word Help pane and then close the Search Results task pane.

Word 2003

chapter three

Using Graphics and Tables

In this chapter, you will: complete these projects and practice these skills.

Project 3A **Creating a Flyer**	**Objectives** • Insert Clip Art and Pictures • Modify Clip Art and Pictures • Work with the Drawing Toolbar

Project 3B **Formatting a Report**	**Objectives** • Work with Tab Stops • Create a Table • Format Tables • Create a Table from Existing Text

Sensation! Park

Sensation! Park is a "family fun center" theme park designed for today's busy families. The park offers traditional amusement park rides and arcade games along with new and popular water rides, surf pools, laser tag, video games, and a racetrack for all ages.

Situated on 100 acres, the park's mission is to provide a safe, clean, exciting environment where children and adults of all ages can find a game, ride, or event that suits their interests or discover something completely new!

© Getty Images, Inc.

Adding Graphics and Tables to a Document

Adding graphics can greatly enhance the effectiveness of documents. Digital images, such as those obtained from a digital camera or a scanner, can be inserted into documents. A ***clip*** is a media file, including art, sound, animation, or movies. ***Clip art*** images—which are predefined graphic images included with Microsoft Office or downloaded from the Web—can be effective if used appropriately. You can also create your own graphic objects by using the tools on the Drawing toolbar.

Tabs can be used to horizontally align text and numbers. The Tab key is used to move to ***tab stops***, which mark specific locations on a line of text. You can set your own tab stops and specify the alignment of each stop.

Tables are used to present data effectively and efficiently. The row and column format makes information easy to find and easy to read and helps the reader organize and categorize the data. The Word table feature has tools that enable you to format text, change column width and row height, change the background on portions or all of the table, and modify the table borders and lines.

Project 3A Job Opportunities

In this chapter, you will create a document and add a picture from a file and a clip art image provided by Microsoft. You will format, resize, and move the images. You will add tab stops, and you will create and format two tables.

In Activities 3.1 through 3.9, you will edit a job announcement flyer for Sensation! Park. You will add a picture and a clip art image. You will also add objects from the Drawing toolbar. Your completed document will look similar to Figure 3.1. You will save your document as *3A_Job_Opportunities_Firstname_Lastname*.

Figure 3.1
Project 3A—Job Opportunity Flyer

Objective 1
Insert Clip Art and Pictures

Graphic images can be inserted into a document from many sources. Clip art can be inserted from files provided with Microsoft Office or can be downloaded from the Microsoft Office Web site. Pictures can be scanned from photographs or slides, taken with a digital camera, or downloaded from the Web.

Activity 3.1 Inserting Clip Art

1 On the Standard toolbar, click the **Open** button. Navigate to the location where the student files for this textbook are stored. Locate **w03A_Job_Opportunities** and click once to select it. Then, in the lower right corner of the **Open** dialog box, click **Open**.

The w03A_Job_Opportunities file opens. See Figure 3.2.

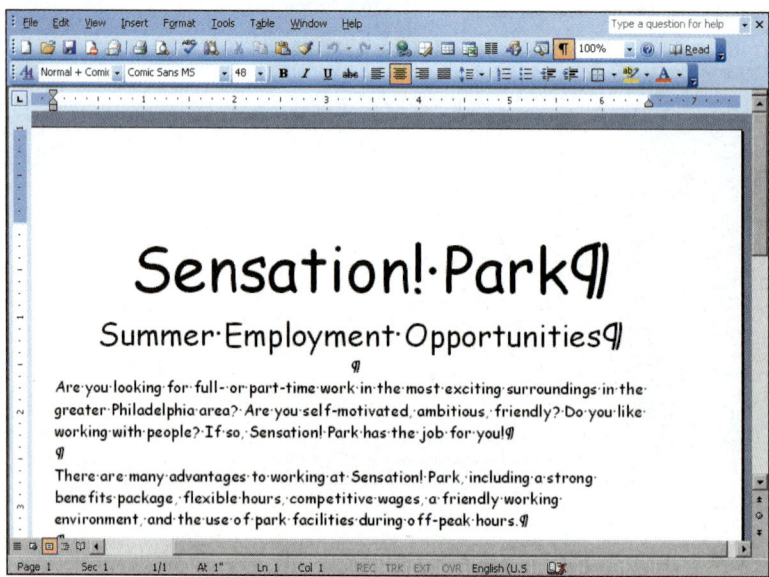

Figure 3.2

2 From the **File** menu, click **Save As**. In the **Save As** dialog box, click the **Save in** arrow and navigate to the location where you are storing your files for this chapter, creating a new Chapter 3 folder if you want to do so.

3 In the **File name** box, type **3A_Job_Opportunities_Firstname_Lastname** and then click **Save**.

The document is saved with a new name. Make sure you substitute your name where indicated.

4 If necessary, on the Standard toolbar, click the Show/Hide ¶ button to display the nonprinting characters.

5 In the paragraph near the top of the document beginning *Are you looking*, click to place the insertion point to the left of the first word in the paragraph—*Are*.

6 From the **Insert** menu, point to **Picture**, and then click **Clip Art**.

The Clip Art task pane opens.

7 In the **Search in** box, verify that *All collections* displays and, if necessary, click the arrow, and then select the **Everywhere** check box. In the **Results should be** box, verify that *All media file types* displays and, if necessary, click the arrow, and then select the **All media types** check box.

8 In the **Search for** box, delete any existing text, type **roller coaster** and then click the **Go** button. Locate the roller coaster image from the task pane as shown in Figure 3.3. Use the scroll bar if necessary.

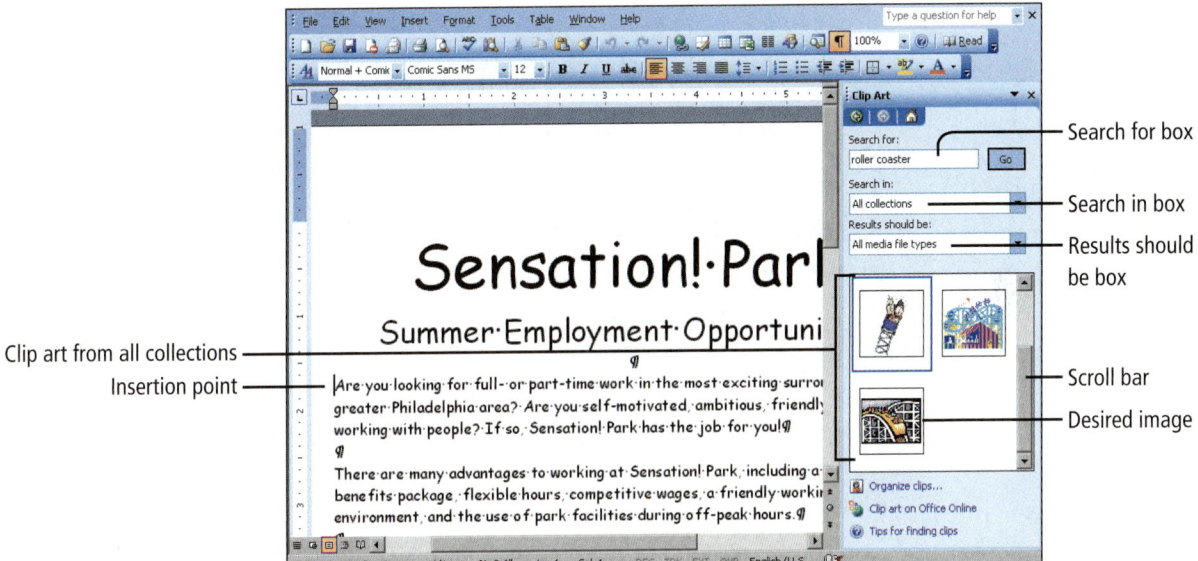

Figure 3.3

Alert! Is the Image Missing from your Task Pane?

Many colleges perform minimum installations of software, including Microsoft Office. This means that little or no clip art is included with the program. When the program searches for an image, it looks on the hard drive and also tries to access the clip libraries on the Microsoft Office Web site. If you are not connected to the Web, your screen will not display the images shown in Figure 3.3.

If you do not see the appropriate image, click Organize clips at the bottom of the Clip Art task pane. From the File menu, point to Add Clips to Organizer, and then click Automatically. After a few minutes, all images on your computer are identified and organized. If the appropriate image is still not available, display the Insert menu, point to Picture, click From File, navigate to the location in which your student files are stored, click w03A_Roller_Coaster and then click the Insert button. Alternatively, use a similar image from the task pane.

Project 3A: Job Opportunities | **Word** 335

9 Click the roller coaster image if it is available. If you do not see the image, display the **Insert** menu, point to **Picture**, click **From File**, navigate to your student files and click **w03A_Roller_Coaster**, and then click the **Insert** button.

The clip art image is placed at the insertion point location. The image is inserted in the line of text in exactly the same manner as any other letter or number would be inserted—it becomes a part of the sentence. See Figure 3.4.

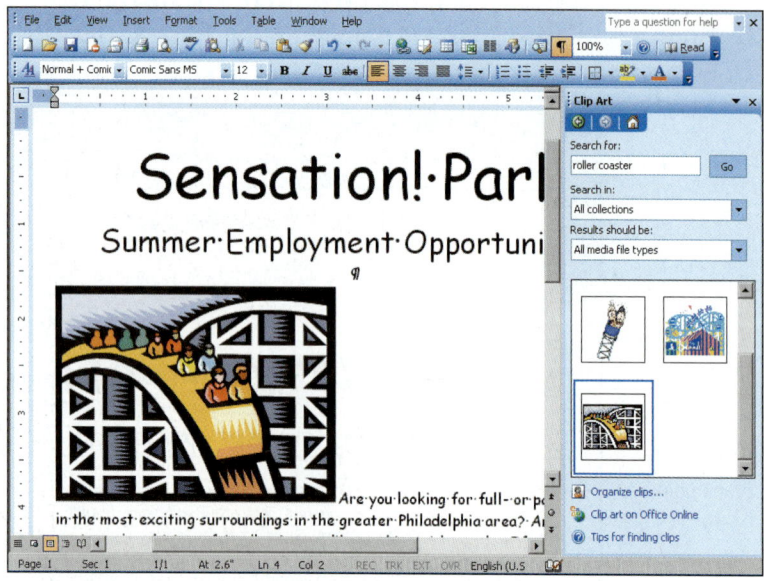

Figure 3.4

10 On the Formatting toolbar, click the **Save** button.

Activity 3.2 Inserting Pictures from Files

Pictures can also be added to a document, either by browsing for a picture on a disk drive or by using the Clip Art task pane.

1 In the paragraph beginning *There are many advantages*, click to place the insertion point to the left of the first word in the paragraph—*There*.

2 In the **Clip Art** task pane, in the **Search for** box, type **Ferris wheel**

3 In the **Results should be** box, clear the check boxes of everything but **Photographs**.

Restricting the media type will limit the number of images found but will be helpful when you are searching for a topic with a large number of images. See Figure 3.5.

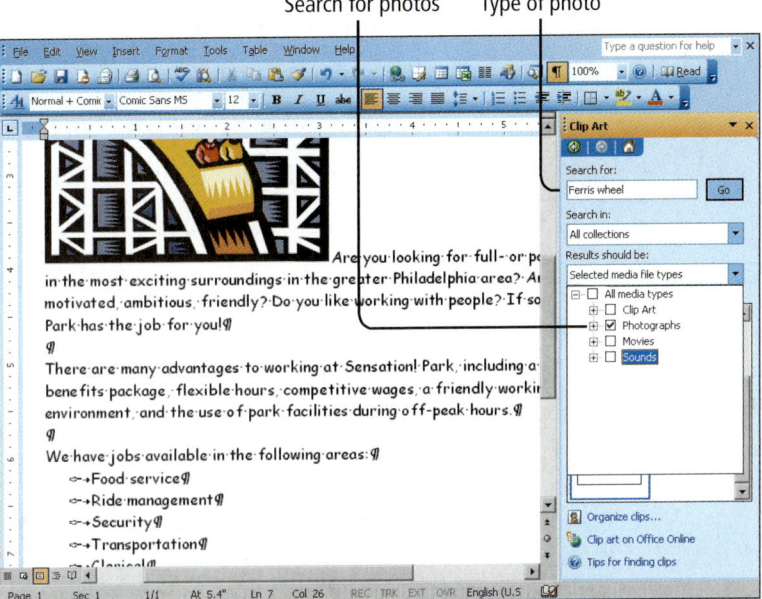

Figure 3.5

4 Click **Go**.

One or more Ferris wheel photographs display.

5 Click the Ferris wheel with the blue background. If the image is not available, select another similar image or display the **Insert** menu, point to **Picture**, click **From File**, navigate and click **w03A_Ferris_Wheel**, and click **Insert**. Scroll to the top of the second page.

The photograph is inserted at the insertion point location and the document expands to a second page. See Figure 3.6.

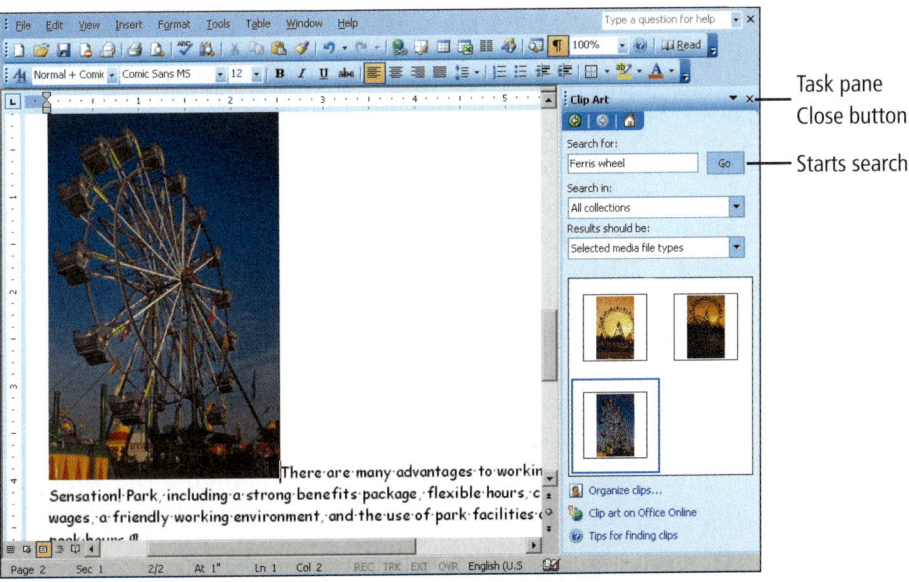

Figure 3.6

Project 3A: Job Opportunities | **Word**   337

6 On the **Clip Art** task pane title bar, click the **Close** button.

7 From the **View** menu, click **Header and Footer**.

The Header and Footer dialog box displays.

8 On the Header and Footer toolbar, click the **Switch Between Header and Footer** button.

The insertion point is positioned in the footer box.

9 On the Header and Footer toolbar, click the **Insert AutoText** button, and then click **Filename**.

The file name is inserted in the footer. The file extension .doc may or may not display, depending on your Word settings. See Figure 3.7.

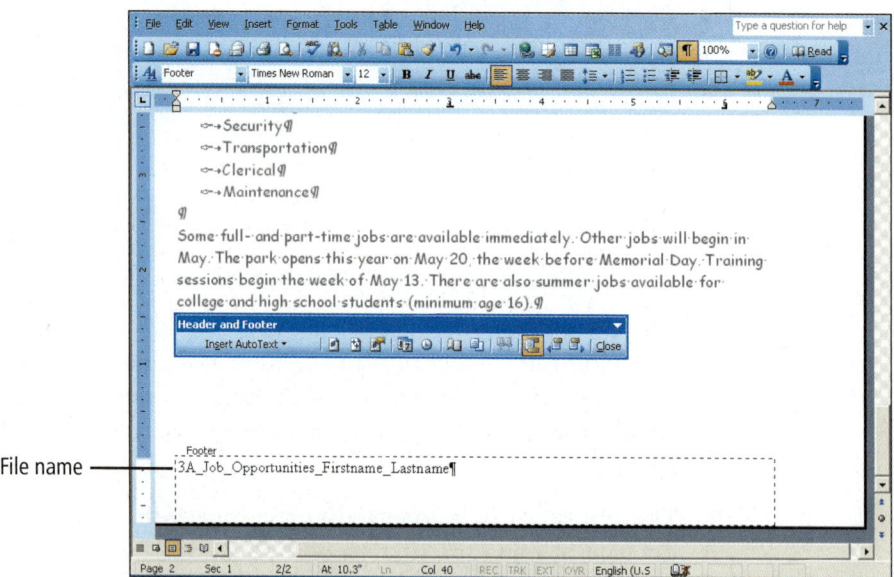

File name

Figure 3.7

10 On the Header and Footer toolbar, click the **Close** button.

11 On the Standard toolbar, click the **Save** button. Alternatively, press Ctrl + S to save your changes.

Objective 2
Modify Clip Art and Pictures

You can format clip art or pictures once you have placed them in a document. When images are placed in documents, they are placed inline. ***Inline images*** are just like characters in a sentence. You can change them to ***floating images***—images that can be moved independently of the surrounding text—by changing the wrapping options. You can also change the size of an image to make it fit better in your document.

Activity 3.3 Wrapping Text around Graphic Objects

Pictures and clip art images that are treated as characters in a sentence can cause awkward spacing in a document. To avoid this awkward spacing, you can format any graphic to move independently of the surrounding text.

1 Locate and click the first image (the roller coaster) that you inserted.

Sizing handles, small black boxes, display around the image border. These handles are used to increase or decrease the size of the image. The sizing handles also indicate that the image is selected. The Picture toolbar may also open, either floating over the document, or added to the other toolbars. See Figure 3.8.

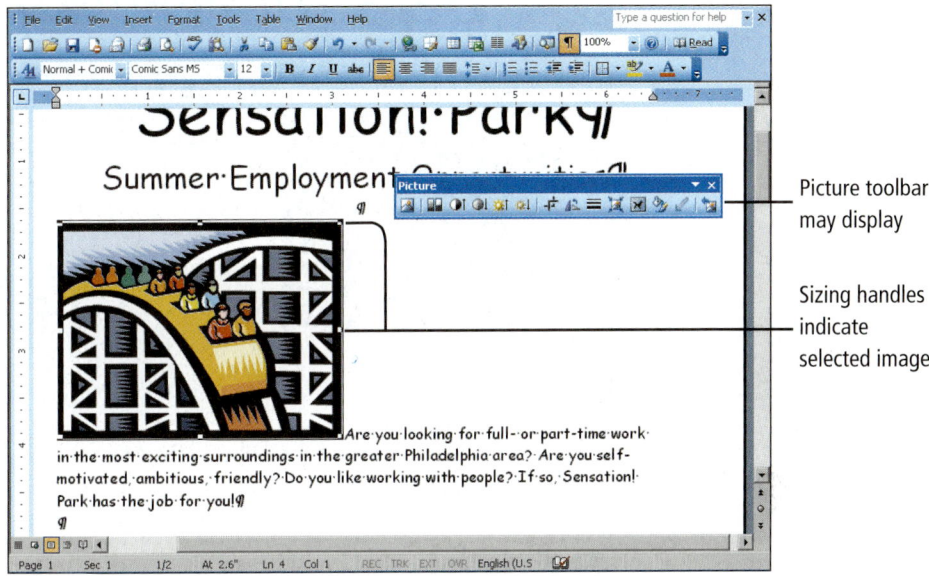

Figure 3.8

2 From the **Format** menu, click **Picture**. Alternatively, you can right-click the image and click Format Picture from the shortcut menu.

The Format Picture dialog box displays.

3 In the **Format Picture** dialog box, click the **Layout tab**

The wrapping and alignment options display on the Layout tab. See Figure 3.9.

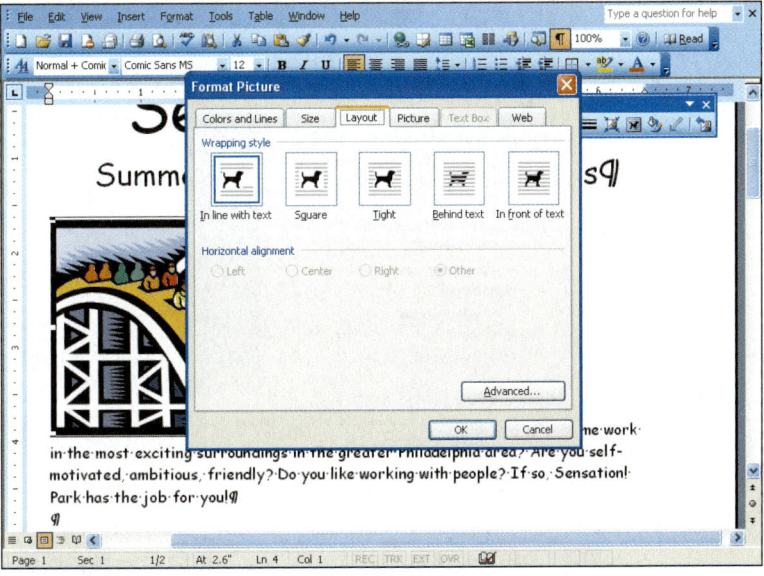

Figure 3.9

Project 3A: Job Opportunities | **Word** 339

4 Under **Wrapping style**, click **Tight**, and then click **OK**.

The text wraps tightly around the image, and the ferris wheel picture moves up from the second page. See Figure 3.10.

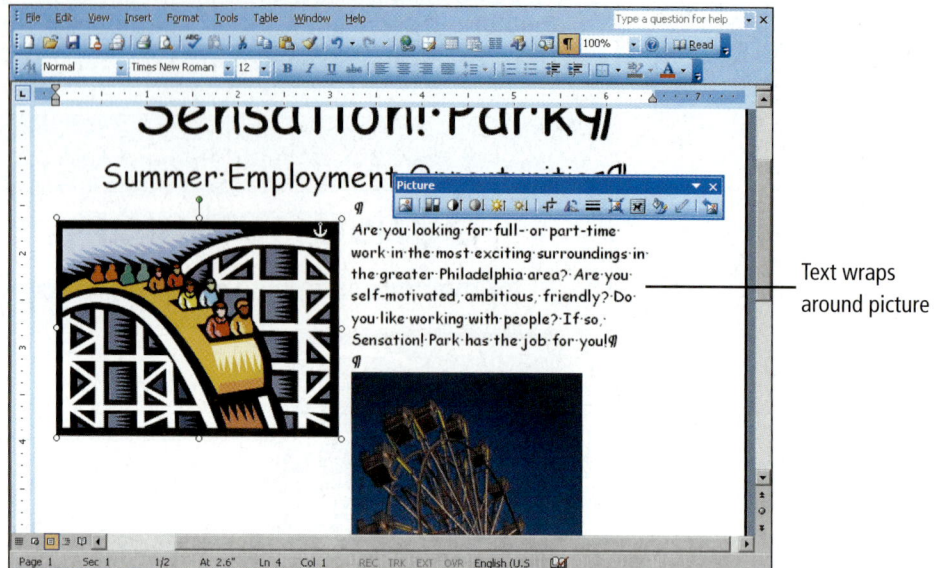

Text wraps around picture

Figure 3.10

5 Scroll down and click the Ferris wheel picture.

6 From the **Format** menu, click **Picture**, and then click the **Layout tab**.

7 Under **Wrapping style**, click **Tight**, and then click **OK**.

The text wraps around the second image. See Figure 3.11. Because the spaces to the right of the pictures are used to display text, the document now occupies one page instead of two.

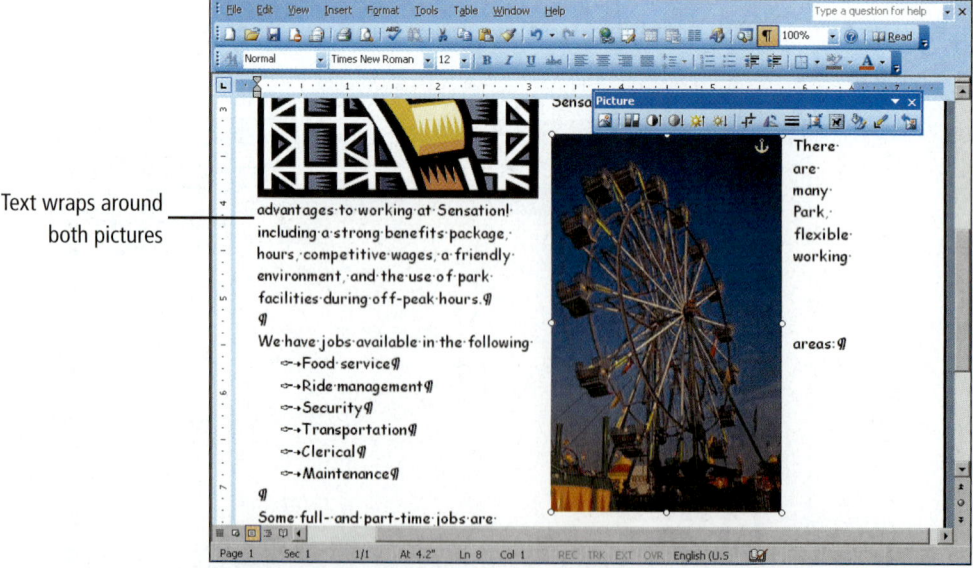

Text wraps around both pictures

Figure 3.11

8 On the Standard toolbar, click the **Save** button.

340 **Word** | Chapter 3: Using Graphics and Tables

Activity 3.4 Resizing a Graphic Object

Usually you will want to adjust the size of the clip art and pictures that you place in documents. Use the sizing handles to resize images.

1 Locate and click the first image you inserted (the roller coaster). Drag the image to the right side of the page so that its right edge aligns at approximately **6.5 inches on the horizontal ruler**.

Sizing handles, a *rotate handle*, and an *anchor* all display on or near the image. If your ruler is not displayed, from the View menu, click Ruler. You may need to use the horizontal scrollbar to move left to see the anchor. The table in Figure 3.12 describes the purpose of each of these formatting tools. Then refer to Figure 3.13 for placement of the image.

Graphic Formatting Marks, Handles, and Anchors

Mark	Purpose
Corner-sizing handles	Resizes images proportionally
Side-sizing handles	Stretches or shrinks the image in one direction
Rotate handle	Rotates the image clockwise or counterclockwise
Anchor	Indicates that the image is attached to the nearest paragraph

Figure 3.12

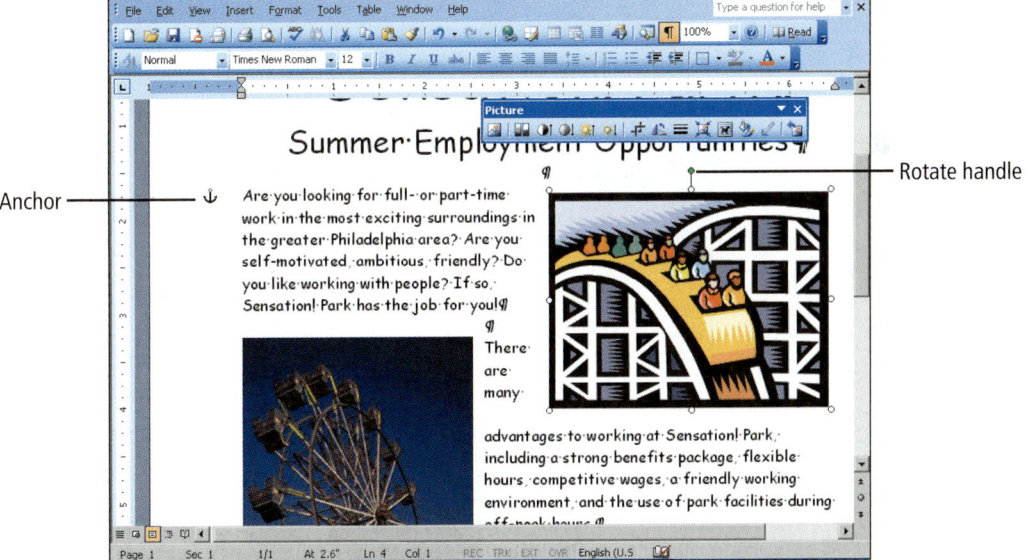

Figure 3.13

2 Locate the sizing handle in the middle of the lower edge of the roller coaster image and drag it up until the image is about an inch high. Check the ruler height on the vertical ruler, although it need not be exact.

Notice that the image shape is distorted. See Figure 3.14.

Project 3A: Job Opportunities | **Word** 341

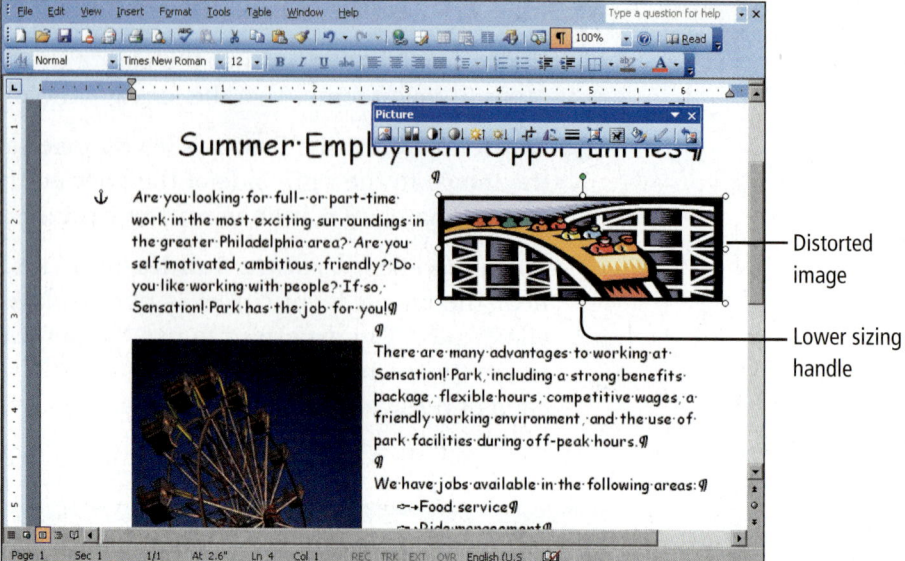

Figure 3.14

3 From the Standard toolbar, click the **Undo** button.

The image returns to its original size.

4 Locate the sizing handle on the lower right corner of the image and drag it up and to the left until the image is about an inch high.

Notice that the image is resized proportionally and not distorted. Do not be concerned if the words do not wrap exactly as shown in Figure 3.15.

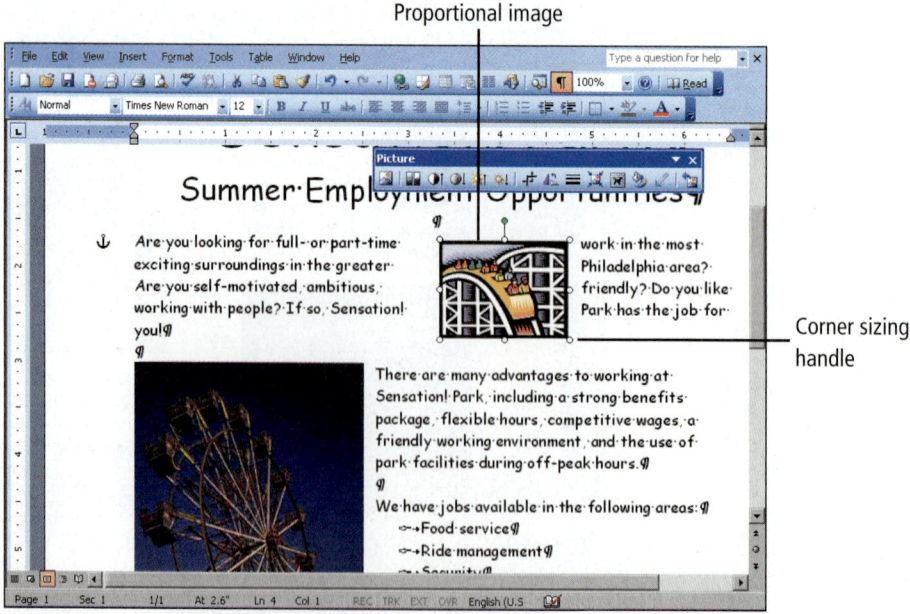

Figure 3.15

5 On the Standard toolbar, click the **Save** button.

Activity 3.5 Moving a Graphic Object

Once you have chosen one of the image wrapping options, you can move the image anywhere on the page.

1 Move the pointer to the middle of the roller coaster image but do not click.

The move pointer displays. See Figure 3.16.

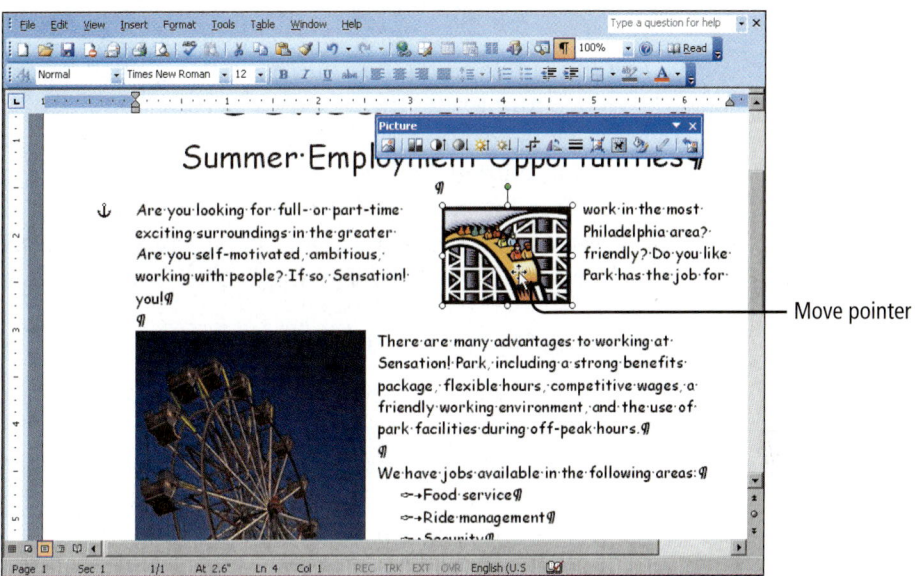

Figure 3.16

2 Click in the middle of the image and, as shown in Figure 3.17, drag it to the right of the paragraph beginning *Are you looking for*.

A dashed border around the pointer indicates the potential position of the image. See Figure 3.17.

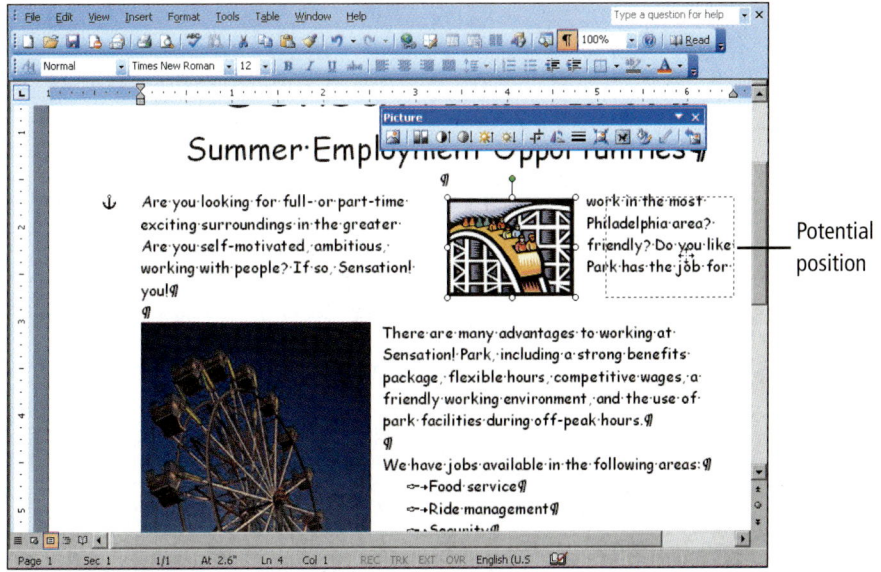

Figure 3.17

Project 3A: Job Opportunities | **Word**   343

3 Release the mouse button.

The image moves to the pointer location, and the text wraps at the left border of the image.

4 On the Standard toolbar, click the **Save** button 🖫.

Objective 3
Work with the Drawing Toolbar

The Drawing toolbar has tools to add text boxes, lines, arrows, boxes, circles, and predefined shapes to your document. Many of these drawing objects can be formatted; that is, you can increase line thickness and color, change font colors, and change the background colors and patterns. A drawing canvas is provided as a work area for complex drawings; however, when inserting and formatting simple drawing objects, it is more convenient to turn the drawing canvas off.

Activity 3.6 Inserting a Text Box

A ***text box*** is a movable, resizable container for text or graphics. A text box is useful to give text a different orientation from other text in the document because it is can be placed anywhere in the document. A text box can be moved around the document just like a floating image. A text box is a drawing object and, as such, can be placed outside the document margin, resized, and moved. This is easier if you first turn off the drawing canvas. As you progress in your study of Word, you will learn more about using the drawing canvas.

1 From the **Tools** menu, click **Options**, and then click the **General tab**.

2 Under **General options**, locate the last check box, **Automatically create drawing canvas when inserting AutoShapes** and, if necessary, clear (click to remove the check mark). Click **OK** to close the **Options** dialog box.

The drawing canvas is turned off.

3 Check to see the if your Drawing toolbar is displayed at the bottom of your screen. If it is not, right-click either toolbar to activate the Toolbars shortcut menu and then click Drawing.

The Drawing toolbar displays, usually at the bottom of the screen. You can also open the Drawing toolbar by clicking the Drawing button on the Standard toolbar.

4 Position your document so the bulleted list is near the top of your screen. On the Drawing toolbar, click the **Text Box** button 🄰 and then move the pointer into the document window.

The pointer changes to a crosshair. See Figure 3.18.

344 Word | Chapter 3: Using Graphics and Tables

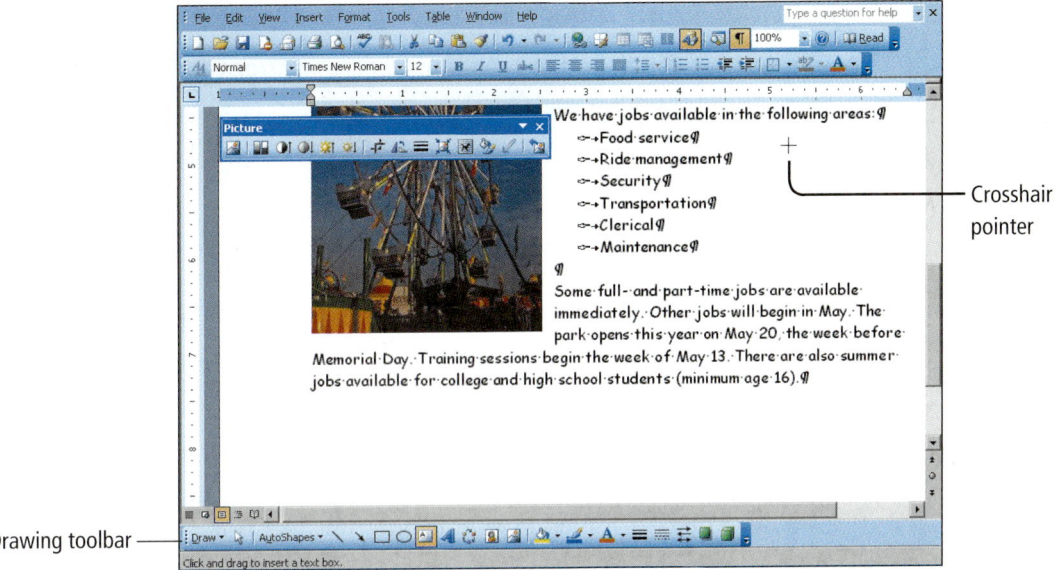

Figure 3.18

5 Position the crosshair pointer slightly to the right of *Food service* and then drag down and to the right to form an approximately 1½-inch square. Release the mouse button. Your measurement need not be exact.

A text box displays with the insertion point in the upper left corner, and the Text Box toolbar displays.

6 Type **The SuperSpeed Ferris Wheel, one of the new rides at Sensation! Park**

The text wraps within the text box. See Figure 3.19.

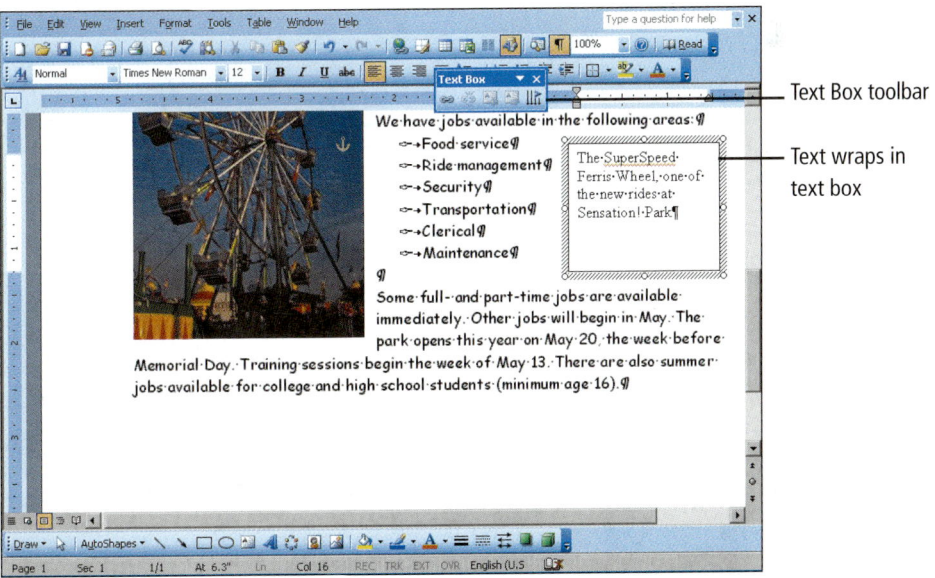

Figure 3.19

Project 3A: Job Opportunities | **Word** 345

Activity 3.7 Moving and Resizing a Text Box

1 On the Standard toolbar, click the **Zoom button arrow** , and then click **Page Width**.

2 Move the pointer over a border of the text box until a four-headed arrow pointer displays.

The pointer changes to a move pointer, which looks like a four-way arrow.

3 Drag the text box down to the empty area below the paragraph beginning *Some full- and part-time* as shown in Figure 3.20. A dashed border around the pointer indicates the potential position of the image.

4 Release the mouse button.

The text box is moved to the new location. See Figure 3.20.

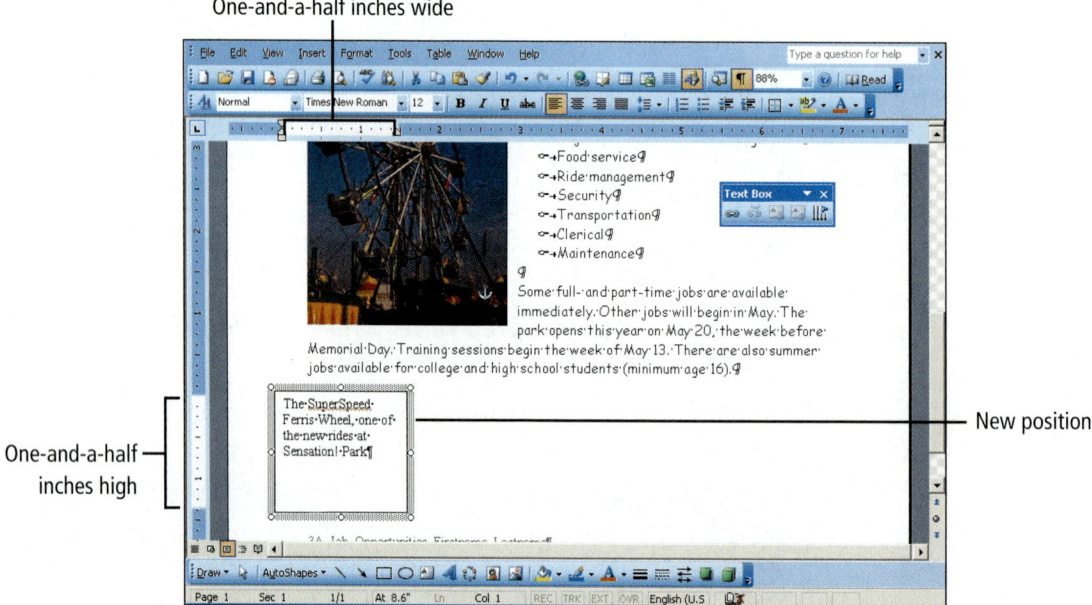

Figure 3.20

5 Scroll down until you can see the whole text box. If necessary, position the pointer over the center right sizing handle to display a two-headed pointer and then drag to the right to adjust the text box size until all the text in the box displays on three lines. Drag the lower center handle up slightly to remove excess white space in the text box.

6 On the Formatting toolbar, click the **Center** button .

The text is horizontally centered within the text box. Compare your screen to Figure 3.21.

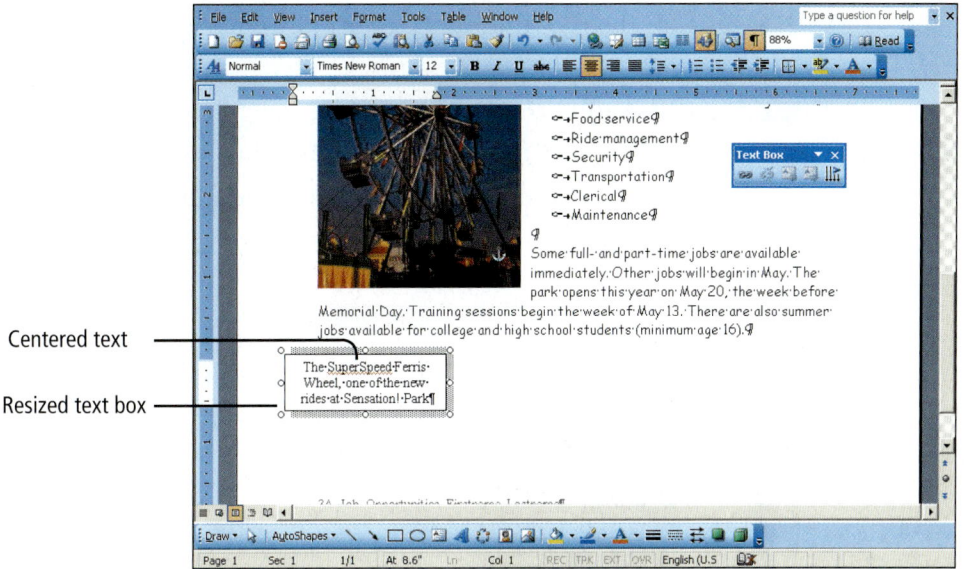

Centered text
Resized text box

Figure 3.21

[7] On the Standard toolbar, click the **Save** button.

Activity 3.8 Inserting an Arrow

Buttons on the Drawing toolbar enable you to create shapes—circles, boxes, lines, and arrows. Arrows are very useful to point out features in graphic objects such as photographs and maps.

[1] On the Drawing toolbar, click the **Arrow** button and move your pointer into the document window.

The pointer changes to a crosshair.

Alert! Does a Large Drawing Box Display?

If you did not deactivate the drawing canvas earlier, clicking buttons on the Drawing toolbar results in the insertion of a large *drawing canvas*, which is a work area for creating drawings. This work area is very handy for combining several graphic objects but gets in the way when you try to add simple shapes to a document. To turn off the drawing canvas, click the Close button on the Drawing Canvas toolbar and click in the drawing canvas area.

The drawing canvas can be deactivated by choosing Tools, Options from the menu. Click the General tab. Clear the *Automatically create drawing canvas when inserting AutoShapes* check box.

2 Position the crosshair pointer at the center of the left border of the text box.

3 Drag up and to the right to draw a line to the Ferris wheel picture and then release the mouse button.

The arrowhead points in the direction you dragged the arrow. See Figure 3.22.

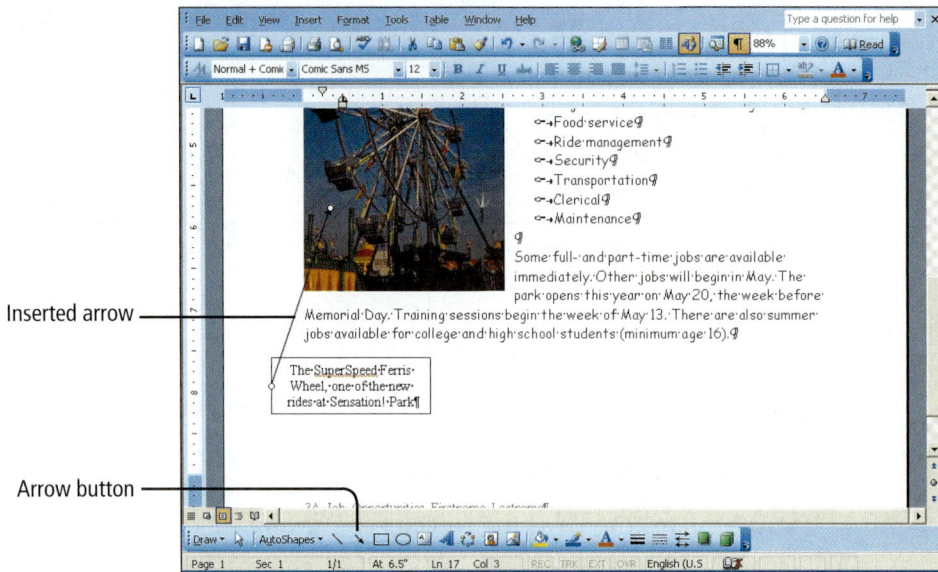

Figure 3.22

4 With the arrow still selected, move your pointer over the white sizing handle on the lower end of the arrow to display a two-headed pointer and then drag up to shorten the arrow until its lower end is near the left edge of the top border of the text box as shown in Figure 3.23.

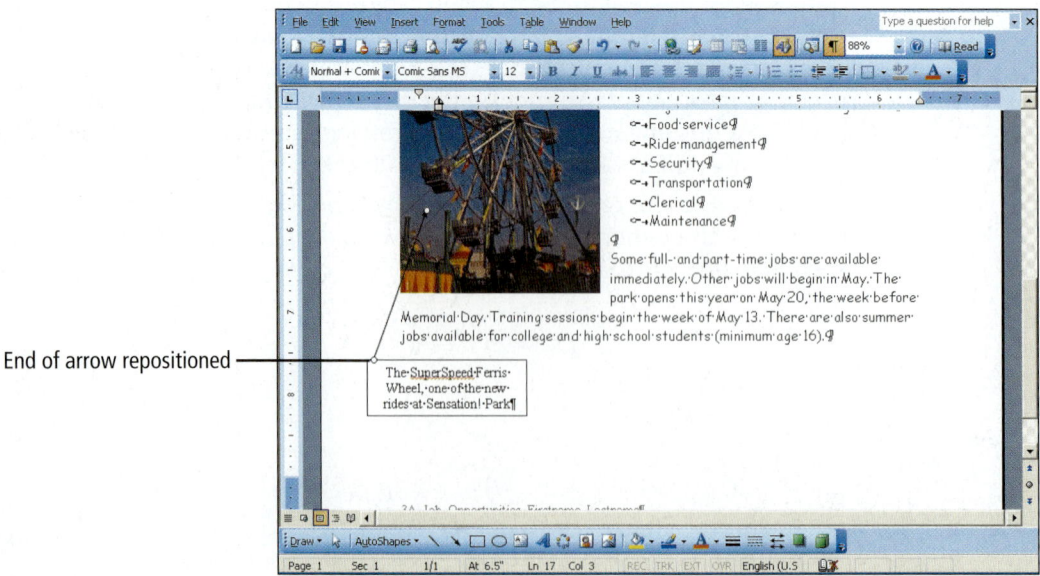

Figure 3.23

348 **Word** | Chapter 3: Using Graphics and Tables

5 Move the pointer over the selected arrow and right-click. From the shortcut menu, click **Format AutoShape** and, in the displayed **Format AutoShape** dialog box, click the **Colors and Lines tab**.

6 Under **Line**, click the **Weight spin** box up arrow three times to select **1.5 pt**.

7 Under **Arrows**, click the **End Size** arrow and, from the displayed menu, click the largest arrowhead—**Arrow R Size 9**.

Compare your dialog box to Figure 3.24.

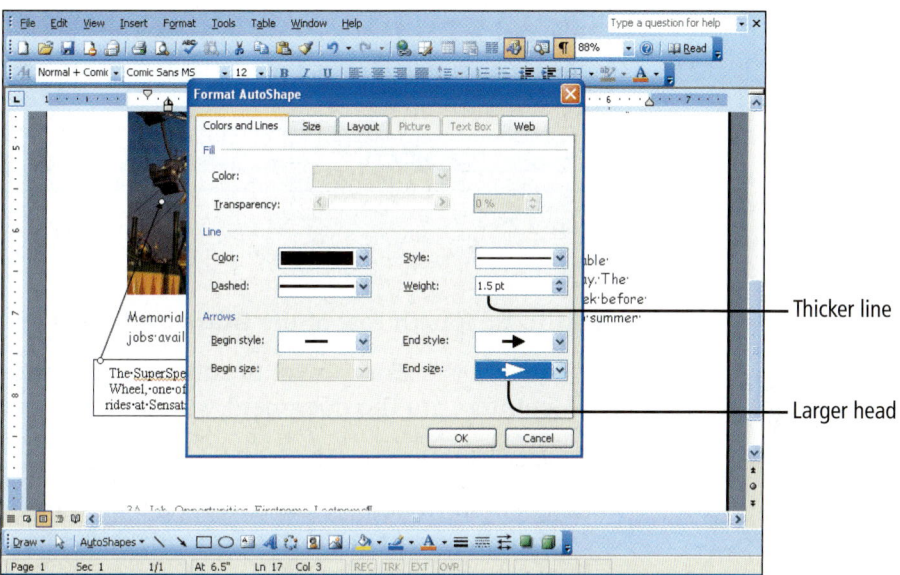

Figure 3.24

8 Click **OK**.

The arrow is thicker and has a larger arrowhead.

9 On the Standard toolbar, click the **Save** button.

Activity 3.9 Inserting an AutoShape

More than 150 predefined AutoShapes are available to use in documents. These include stars, banners, arrows, and callouts.

1 On the Drawing toolbar, click the **AutoShapes** button.

Point to the **Stars and Banners** button.

Sixteen star and banner shapes display. See Figure 3.25.

Project 3A: Job Opportunities | **Word** 349

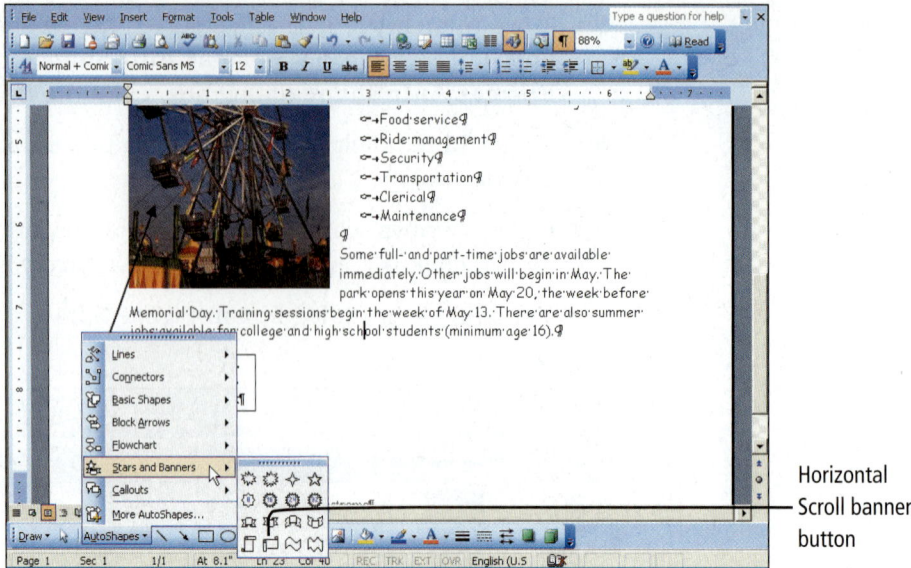

Figure 3.25

[2] In the fourth row of the **Stars and Banners** menu, click the second shape, the **Horizontal Scroll** banner button , and move your pointer into the document window.

A crosshair pointer displays.

[3] Position the crosshair to the right of the text box approximately **3 inches on the horizontal ruler**. As shown in Figure 3.25, drag down and to the right until the banner is about ¾ inch high and 3½ inches wide and release the mouse button. Use the horizontal and vertical rulers to help you determine the size of the banner. If you are not satisfied with your result, click Undo and begin again.

A banner is placed at the bottom of the flyer. See Figure 3.26.

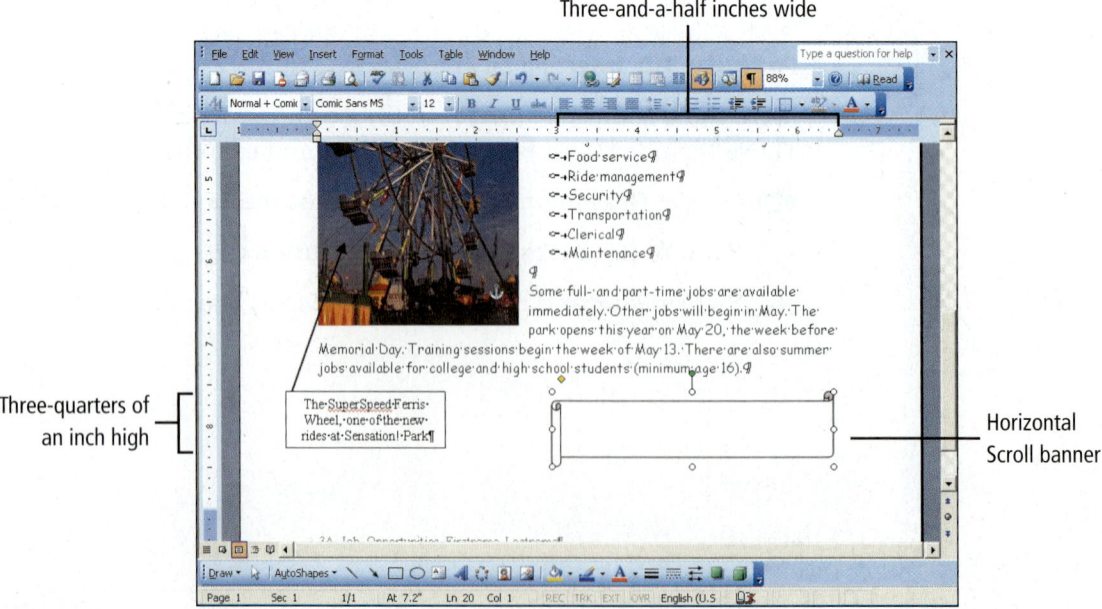

Figure 3.26

350 **Word** | Chapter 3: Using Graphics and Tables

4 Move the pointer over the banner and right-click. From the shortcut menu, click **Add Text**.

The insertion point is placed in the banner, and a slashed border surrounds the shape.

5 Type **Call 215.555.1776**

6 Select the text you just typed. From the Formatting toolbar, click the **Font Size arrow** and click **28**, as shown in Figure 3.27.

7 Be sure the text is still selected and then on the Formatting toolbar, click the **Bold** button. Adjust the height and width of the AutoShape as necessary.

8 On the Formatting toolbar, click the **Center** button. Use the sizing handles to adjust the banner until it looks similar to Figure 3.27. Click outside the banner to deselect it.

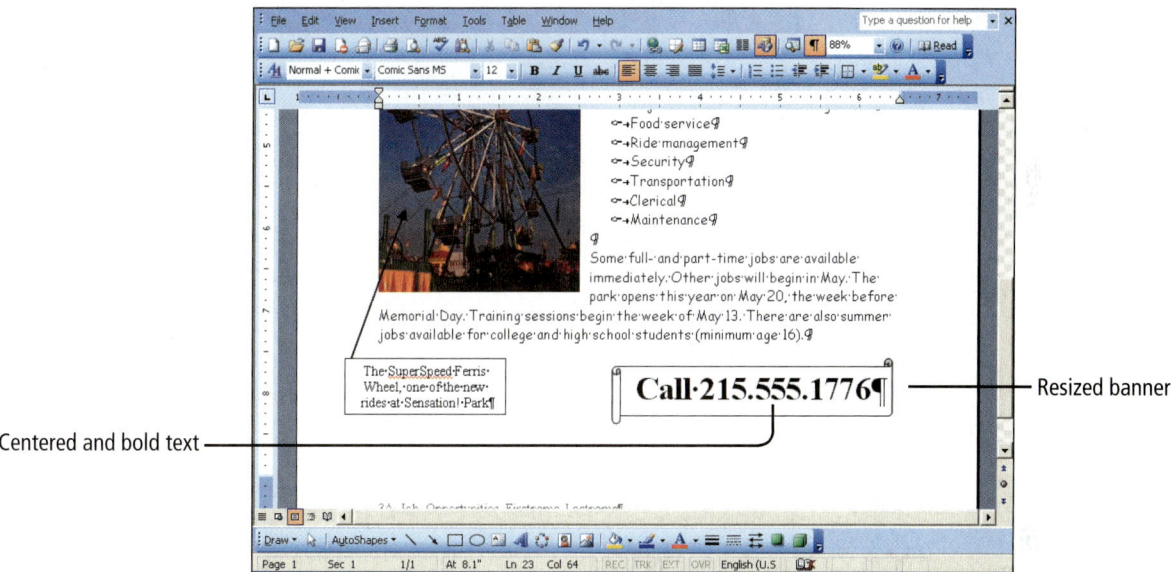

Centered and bold text

Resized banner

Figure 3.27

8 On the Standard toolbar, click the **Save** button. Then, on the Standard toolbar, click the **Print Preview** button to view your document.

9 On the Print Preview toolbar, click the **Print** button. Close the document.

End You have completed Project 3A

Project 3A: Job Opportunities | **Word** 351

Project 3B Park Changes

In Project 3A you worked with clip art and the drawing features of Word. Now you will use tabs and tables to align and organize lists of information.

In Activities 3.10 through 3.24 you will edit a list of changes in age and height restrictions for the rides and other attractions for the coming Sensation! Park season. You will add a tabbed list and two tables. Your completed document will look similar to Figure 3.28. You will save your document as 3B_Park_Changes_Firstname_Lastname.

Figure 3.28
Project 3B—Park Changes Memo

Objective 4
Work with Tab Stops

Tab stops are used to indent and align text. By default, tab stops are set every half inch, although the stops are not displayed on the horizontal ruler. Each time you press the tab key, the insertion point moves across the page a half inch. You can also customize tab stops by designating the location and characteristics of the tab stops. Custom tab stops override default tab stops that are to the left of the custom tab stop position. When you create a custom tab stop, its location and tab stop type is displayed on the ruler, as shown in Figure 3.29. The types of tab stops are shown in the table in Figure 3.29.

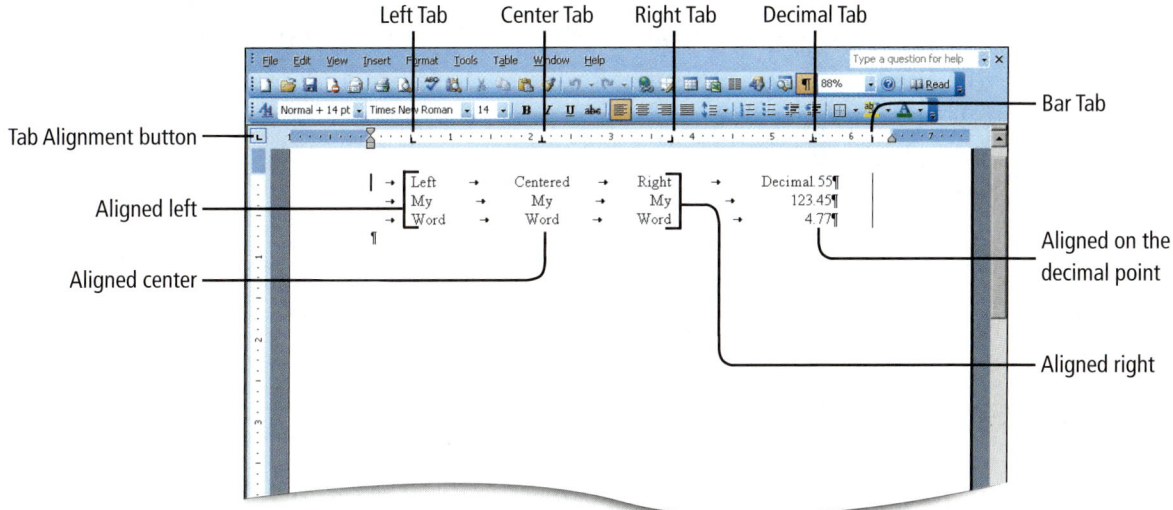

Figure 3.29

Tab Alignment Options

Type	Tab Alignment Button Displays This Marker	Description
Left		Text is left aligned at the tab stop and extends to the right.
Center		Text is centered around the tab stop.
Right		Text is right aligned at the tab stop and extends to the left.
Decimal		The decimal point aligns at the tab stop.
Bar		A vertical bar is inserted in the document at the tab stop.
First Line Indent		Indents the first line of a paragraph.
Hanging Indent		Indents all lines but the first in a paragraph.

Figure 3.30

Activity 3.10 Setting Tab Stops

Tab stops enable you to position text on a line. Tab stops can be set before or after typing text, but it is easiest to set them before you type the text.

1 On the Standard toolbar, click the **Open** button . Navigate to the location where the student files for this textbook are stored. Locate **w03B_Park_Changes** and click once to select it. Then, in the lower right corner of the **Open** dialog box, click **Open**.

The w03B_Park_Changes file opens. See Figure 3.31.

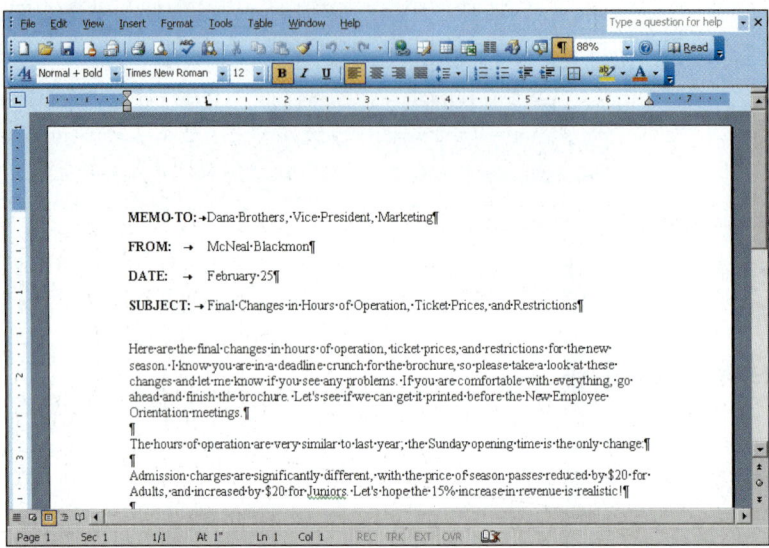

Figure 3.31

2 From the **File** menu, click **Save As**. In the **Save As** dialog box, click the **Save in** arrow and navigate to the location in which you are storing your files for this chapter.

3 In the **File name** box, type **3B_Park_Changes_Firstname_Lastname** and click **Save**.

The document is saved with a new name. Make sure you substitute your name where indicated.

4 In the paragraph beginning *The hours of operation*, position the insertion point after the colon at the end of the paragraph. Press Enter two times.

5 At the left end of the horizontal ruler, position the pointer over the **Tab Alignment** button .

A ScreenTip displays showing the type of tab currently selected, as shown in Figure 3.32.

354 **Word** | Chapter 3: Using Graphics and Tables

Options for tab alignment —

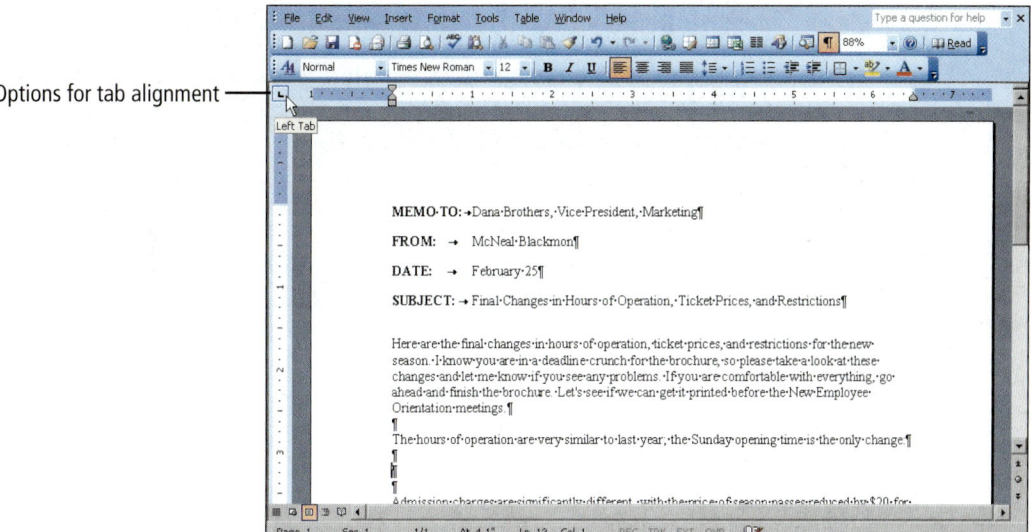

Figure 3.32

6 Click the **Tab Alignment** button once, move the mouse pointer away, and then point to the button again to display the next ScreenTip—*Center Tab*. Repeat this process to cycle through and view the ScreenTip for each of the types of tab stops, and then stop at the **Left Tab** button.

7 Move the pointer over the horizontal ruler and click at the **1 inch mark**.

A left tab stop is inserted in the ruler. See Figure 3.33. Left tab stops are used when you want the information to align on the left.

Left alignment tab at the 1-inch mark

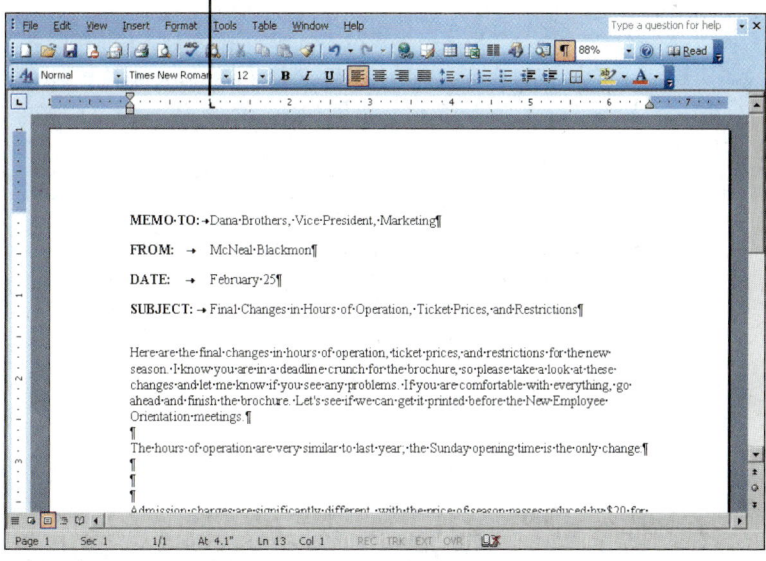

Figure 3.33

8 Click the **Tab Alignment** button two times to display the **Right Tab** button.

Project 3B: Park Changes | **Word** 355

9 At the **4 inch mark on the horizontal ruler**, click once.

A right tab stop is inserted in the ruler. See Figure 3.34. Right tab stops are used to align information on the right. As you type, the information will extend to the left of the tab stop.

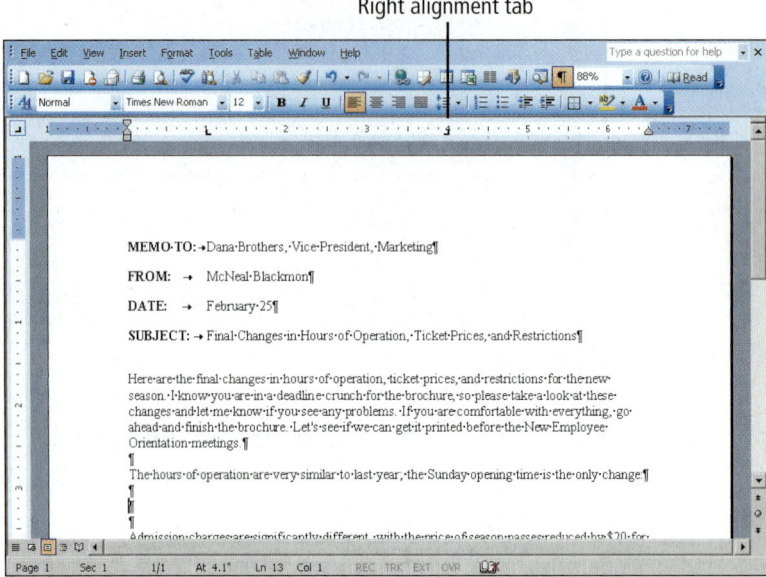

Figure 3.34

10 Click the **Tab Alignment** button six times to display the **Center Tab** button.

11 Click at the **5 inch mark on the horizontal ruler**, and then click again at the **6 inch mark**.

Two center tab stops are inserted in the ruler. See Figure 3.35. Center tab stops are used when you want the information to be centered over a particular point.

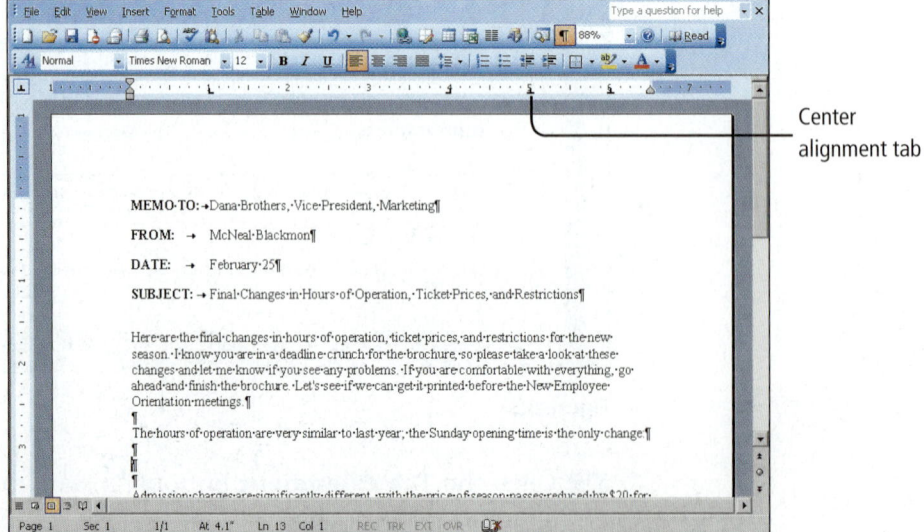

Figure 3.35

356   Word | Chapter 3: Using Graphics and Tables

Activity 3.11 Formatting and Removing Tab Stops

The Tabs dialog box enables you to add, remove, and format tab stops. You can also change the alignment of a tab stop.

1 From the **Format** menu, click **Tabs**.

The Tabs dialog box displays. The tabs you just added to the ruler for the paragraph at the insertion point location are displayed under the *Tab stop position*, as shown in Figure 3.36.

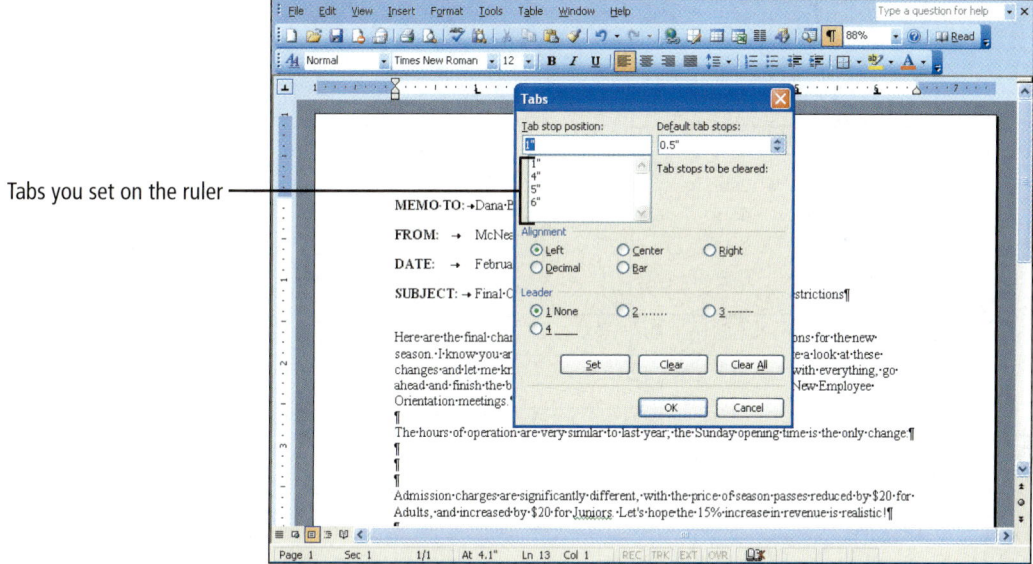

Figure 3.36

2 Under **Tab stop position**, click **4"**.

The tab stop at the 4-inch mark is selected.

3 At the bottom of the **Tabs** dialog box, click the **Clear** button.

The tab stop is ready to be removed, although it won't be removed until you close the dialog box. See Figure 3.37.

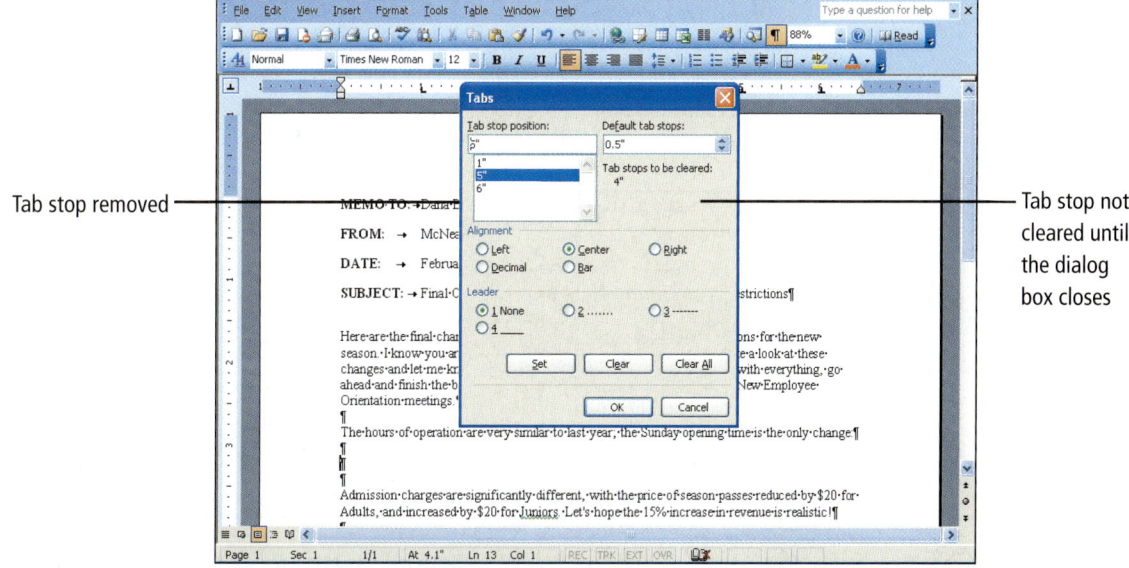

Figure 3.37

4 Under **Tab stop position**, click **5"**.

5 Under **Leader**, click the **2** option button. Near the bottom of the **Tabs** dialog box, click **Set**.

The Set button saves the change. The tab stop at the 5 inch mark now has a ***dot leader***. Dot leader tabs are used to help draw the reader's eye across the page from one item to the next. Later, when you tab to this spot, a row of dots will display. See Figure 3.38.

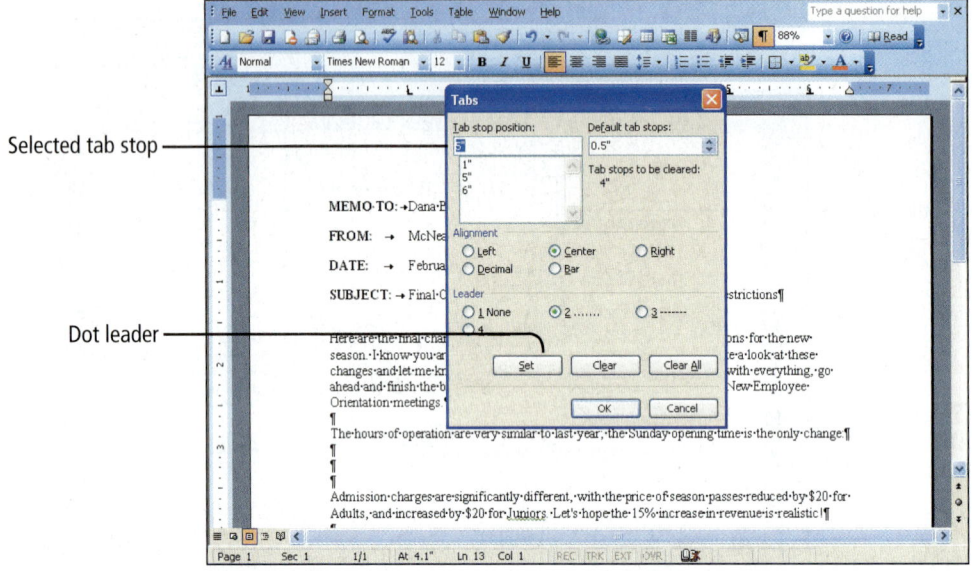

Figure 3.38

6 Under **Tab stop position**, click **5"**.

7 Under **Alignment**, click the **Right** option button. Near the bottom of the **Tabs** dialog box, click **Set**. Repeat this process to change the tab stop at the **6 inch mark** to a **Right** align tab stop as shown in Figure 3.39.

The tab stops at the 5- and 6-inch marks will be right aligned when the dialog box is closed.

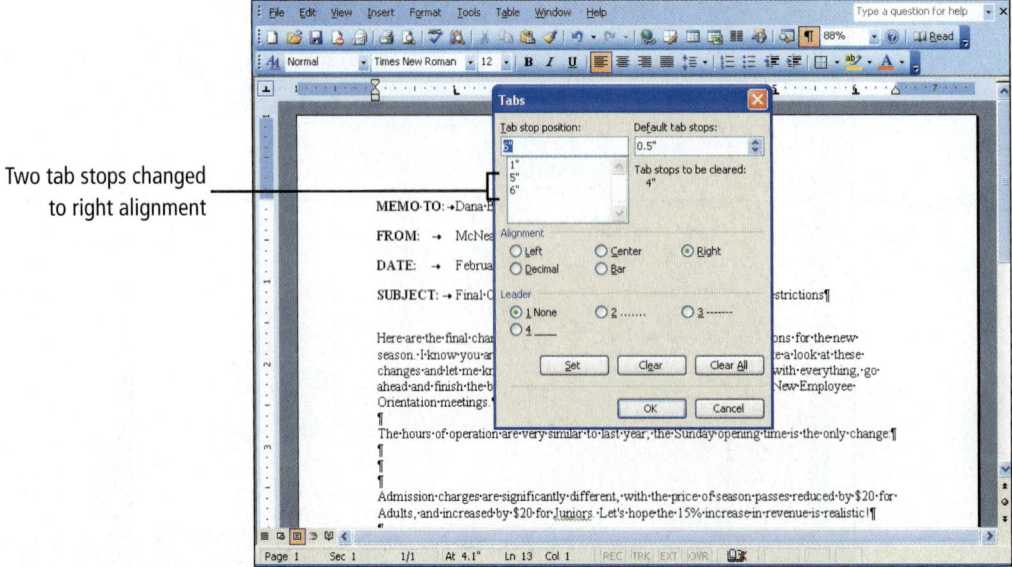

Figure 3.39

8 At the bottom of the **Tabs** dialog box, click **OK**.

Notice that the changes are reflected in the ruler. See Figure 3.40.

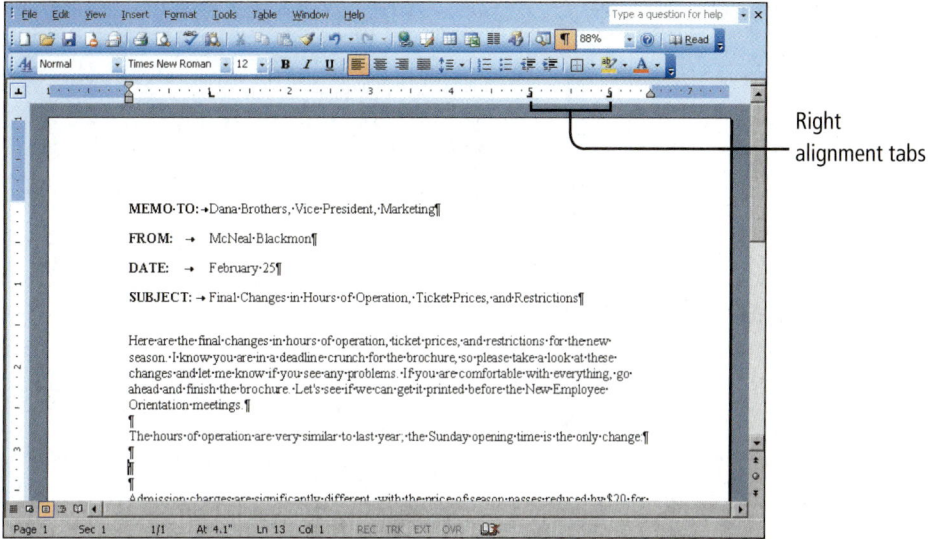

Figure 3.40

9 From the **View** menu, click **Header and Footer**. On the Header and Footer toolbar, click the **Switch Between Header and Footer** button.

10 On the Header and Footer toolbar, click the **Insert AutoText** button `Insert AutoText`, and then click **Filename**.

The filename is inserted in the footer. The file extension .doc may or may not display, depending on your Word settings.

11 On the Header and Footer toolbar, click the **Close** button `Close`.

12 On the Standard toolbar, click the **Save** button.

Activity 3.12 Using Tab Stops to Enter Text

1 With the insertion point positioned at the beginning of the line with the new tab stops, press `Tab`.

The insertion point moves to the first tab, which is at the 1 inch mark, and the nonprinting character for a tab (a small arrow) displays. See Figure 3.41.

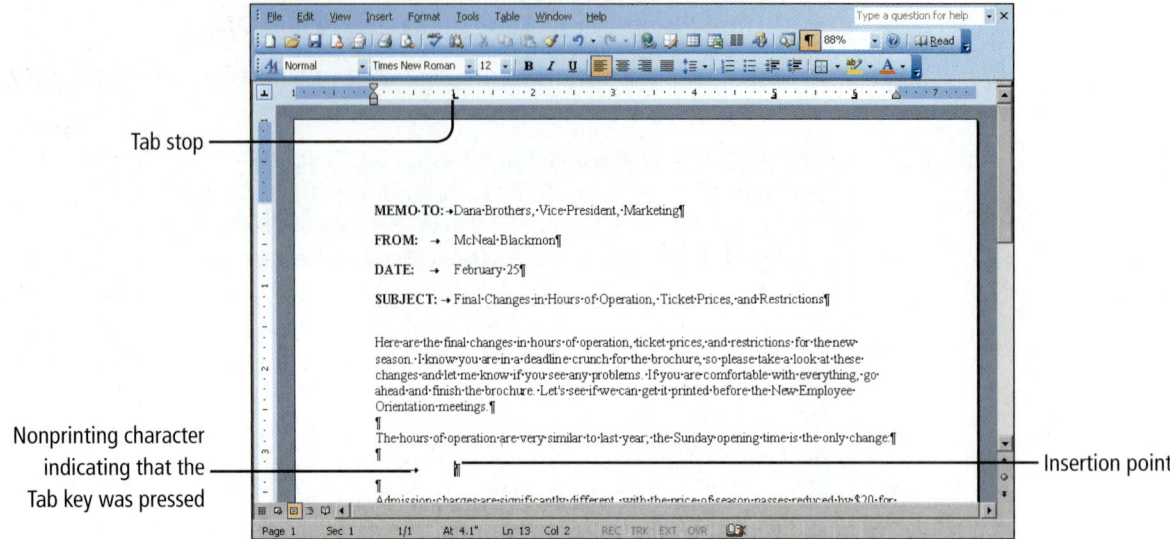

Figure 3.41

[2] Type **Monday-Thursday**

Notice that the left edge of the text stays aligned with the tab stop.

[3] Press Tab.

The insertion point moves to the tab stop at the 5 inch mark, and a dot leader is added, helping to draw your eye across the page to the next item. See Figure 3.42.

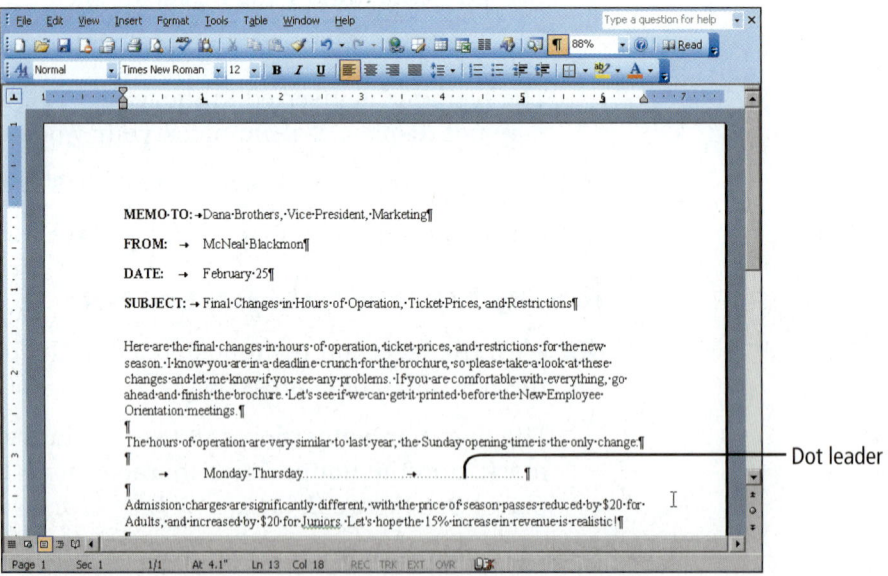

Figure 3.42

360 Word | Chapter 3: Using Graphics and Tables

> ### More Knowledge — Using Dot Leaders
>
> *A String of Periods Is Not the Same Thing*
>
> It is sometimes tempting to hold down the Period key on the keyboard to create a string of dots. This is not a good idea for several reasons. The periods, because of proportional spacing, may be spaced differently between rows, the periods will not line up, and, most importantly, the column on the right side of the string of periods may look lined up, but will be crooked when printed. If you need a string of dots, always use a tab with a dot leader.

4 Type **1 p.m.**

With a right tab, the right edge of the text stays aligned with the tab mark, and the text moves to the left. See Figure 3.43.

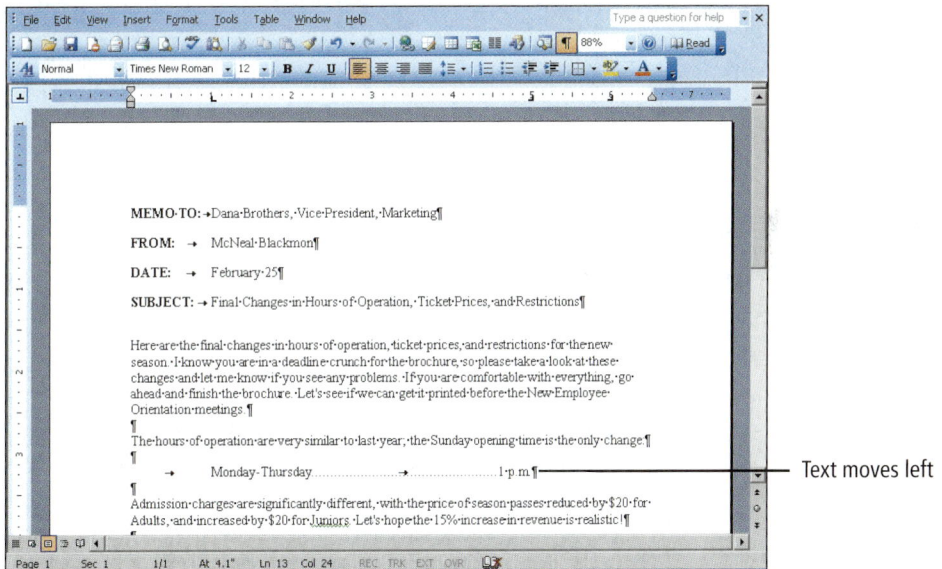

Figure 3.43

5 Press **Tab**. Type **10 p.m.**

The right edge of the text is aligned on the tab mark.

6 Press **Enter**.

Recall that when you press Enter, the formatting of the previous paragraph, including tab stops, is copied to the new paragraph. Tab stops are a form of paragraph formatting, and thus, the information about them is stored in the paragraph mark to which they were applied.

7 Type the following to complete the park schedule:

Friday	1 p.m.	11 p.m.
Saturday and Holidays	11 a.m.	11 p.m.
Sunday	NOON	11 p.m.

Compare your screen to Figure 3.44.

Project 3B: Park Changes | **Word** 361

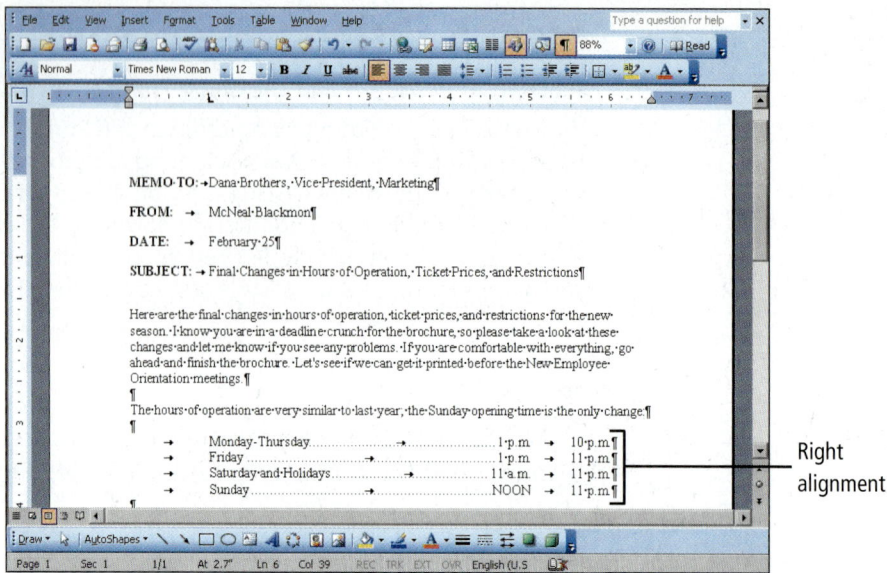

Figure 3.44

8 On the Standard toolbar, click the **Save** button.

Another Way

Indents versus Tabs

Using an Indent to Start a Tabbed List

If the items in the first column of a list are indented the same amount using a left-aligned tab, you can save keystrokes by indenting the paragraph instead. You can do this by using the Increase Indent button on the Formatting toolbar, or by using the Paragraph dialog box. You can also drag the Left Indent marker from the left side of the ruler and position it at the desired location. When you are finished typing the list, you can drag the marker back to the left margin position. When you use an indent at the beginning of the paragraph for a tabbed list, you do not have to press the Tab key before you type the first item in the list.

Activity 3.13 Moving Tab Stops

If you are not satisfied with the arrangement of your text after setting tab stops, it is easy to reposition the text by moving tab stops.

1 In the four lines of tabbed text, disregard any wavy green lines or right-click them and click **Ignore Once** to remove them. Move the pointer into the left margin area, to the left of the first line of tabbed text. When the pointer changes to a white arrow, drag down to select the four lines of text as shown in Figure 3.45.

By selecting all of the lines, changes you make to the tabs will be made to the tabs in all four rows simultaneously.

362 Word | Chapter 3: Using Graphics and Tables

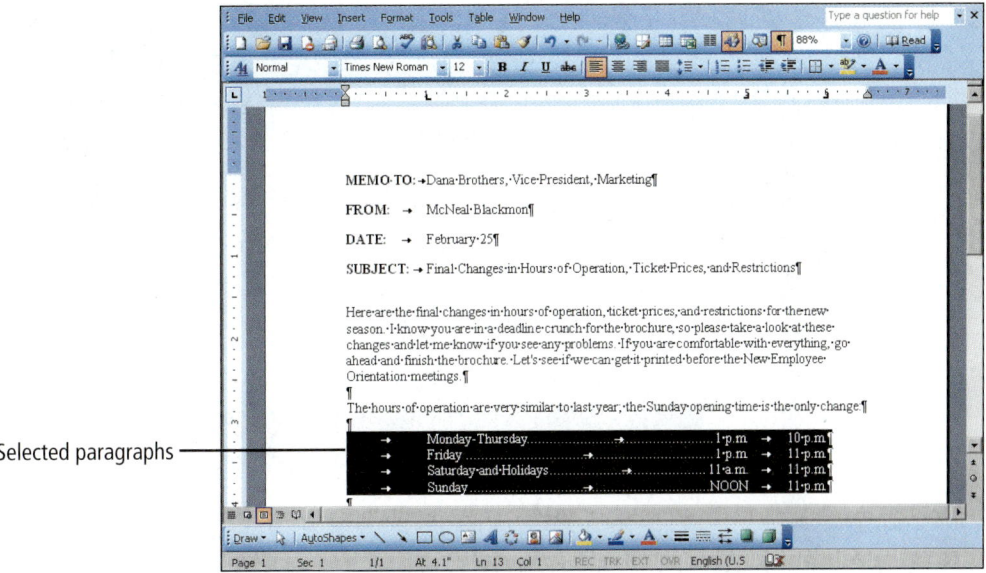

Selected paragraphs

Figure 3.45

2 With the four lines of tabbed text selected, move the pointer into the horizontal ruler and position it so the tip of the pointer arrow is touching the 1 inch tab stop mark.

3 When you see the ScreenTip *Left Tab*, drag the tab stop mark to the left to the **0.5 inch mark on the ruler** as shown in Figure 3.46 and then release the mouse button.

The first column of text is moved to the new location, as shown in Figure 3.46.

Note — Selecting Tab Stop Marks

Selecting and moving tab stop marks on the horizontal ruler requires fairly exact mouse movement. The tip of the pointer needs to touch the tab mark. If you miss it by even a little, you will probably insert another tab stop. One way to tell if you are in the right position to move a tab stop on the ruler is to look for a ScreenTip showing the tab type. To remove an accidental tab stop when you are trying to select an existing one, click the Undo button and try again. Alternatively, you can drag the unwanted tab stop marker below the ruler and release the mouse button.

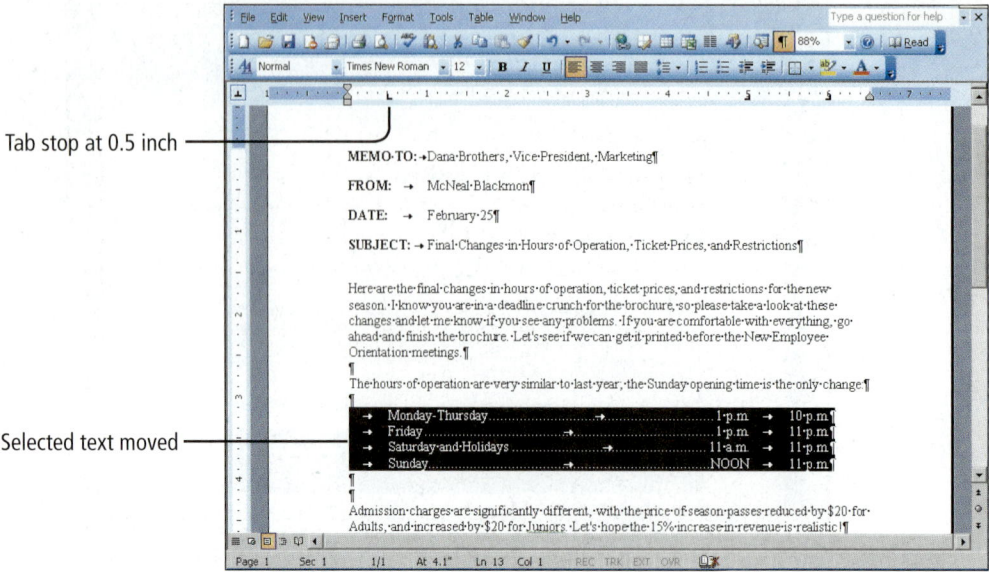

Figure 3.46

[4] Move the pointer into the ruler, and position it so the tip of the pointer arrow is touching the 5 inch tab stop mark and you see the ScreenTip *Right Tab*. Drag the tab stop mark to the left to the **4.5 inch mark on the ruler**.

Compare your screen to Figure 3.47.

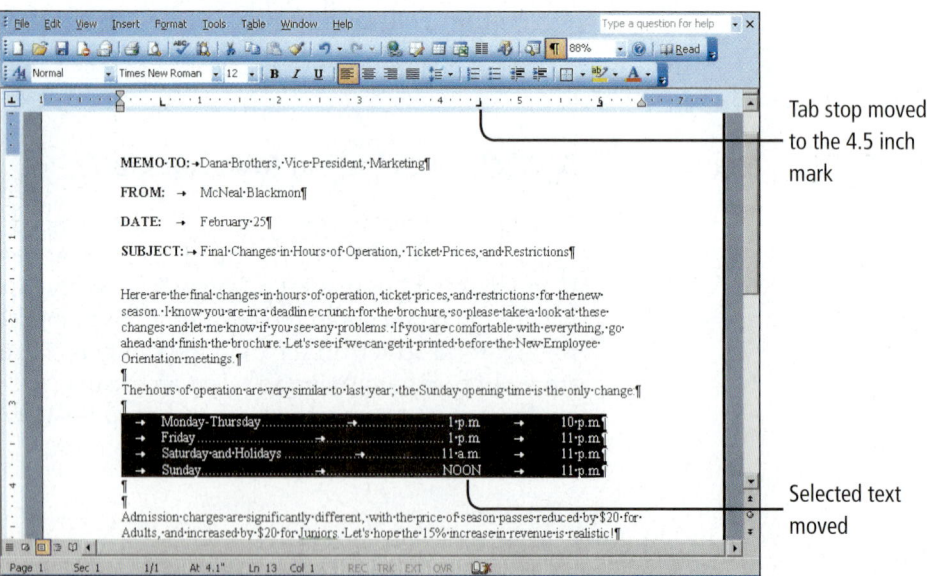

Figure 3.47

[5] Click anywhere to deselect and then, on the Standard toolbar, click the **Save** button.

364   Word | Chapter 3: Using Graphics and Tables

Objective 5
Create a Table

The table feature in Word processing programs has largely replaced the use of tabs because of its flexibility and ease of use. **Tables** consist of rows and columns and are used to organize data. You can create an empty table and then fill in the boxes, which are also called **cells**. You can also convert existing text into a table if the text is properly formatted.

If a table needs to be adjusted, you can add rows or columns and change the height of rows and the width of columns. The text and numbers in the cells can be formatted, as can the cell backgrounds and borders.

Activity 3.14 Creating a Table

1 In the paragraph beginning *Admission charges*, position the insertion point after the exclamation point at the end of the second sentence. Press [Enter] two times.

2 On the Standard toolbar, click the **Insert Table** button.

3 Move the pointer down to the cell in the third row and third column of the **Insert Table** menu.

The cells are highlighted, and the table size is displayed at the bottom of the menu, as shown in Figure 3.48.

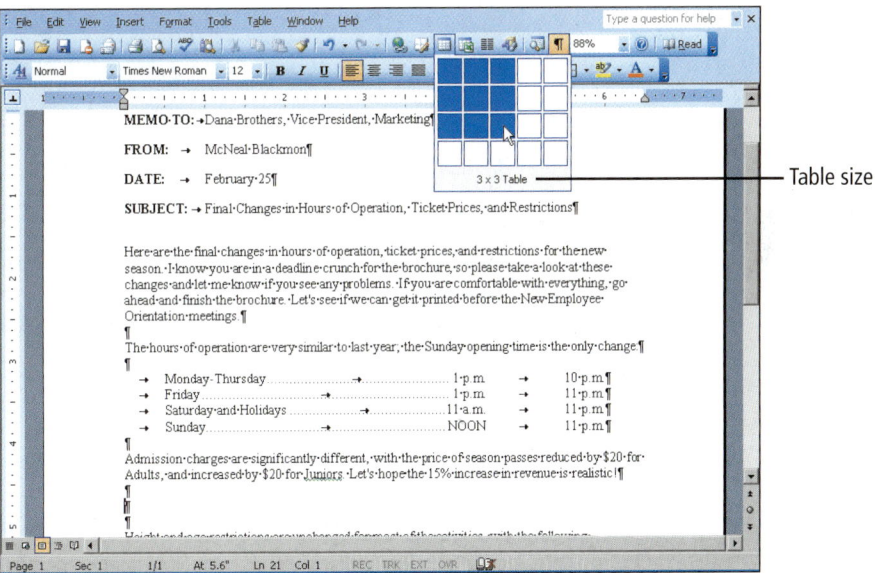

Figure 3.48

Project 3B: Park Changes | **Word** 365

4 Click the mouse button.

A table with three rows and three columns is created at the insertion point location and the insertion point is placed in the upper left cell. The table fills the width of the page, from the left margin to the right margin, as shown in Figure 3.49.

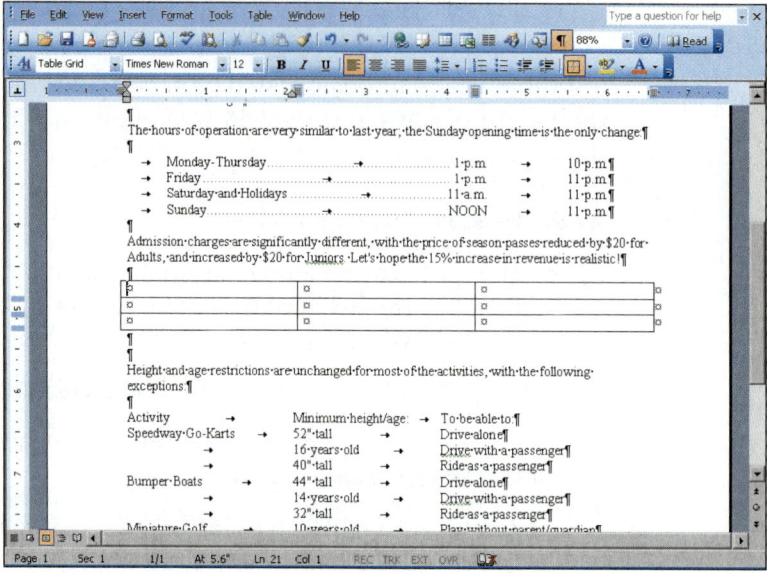

Figure 3.49

5 Press [Tab] to the second cell in the first row of the table.

> **Note — Moving Between Cells in a Table**
>
> *Using the Tab Key Rather than the Enter Key*
>
> The natural tendency is to press Enter to move from one cell to the next. In a table, however, pressing Enter creates another line in the same cell, similar to the way you add a new line in a document. If you press Enter by mistake, you can remove the extra line by pressing the Backspace key.

6 Type **Age** and press [Tab].

7 Type **One Day** and press [Tab].

The text displays in the top row, and the insertion point moves to the first cell in the second row, as shown in Figure 3.50.

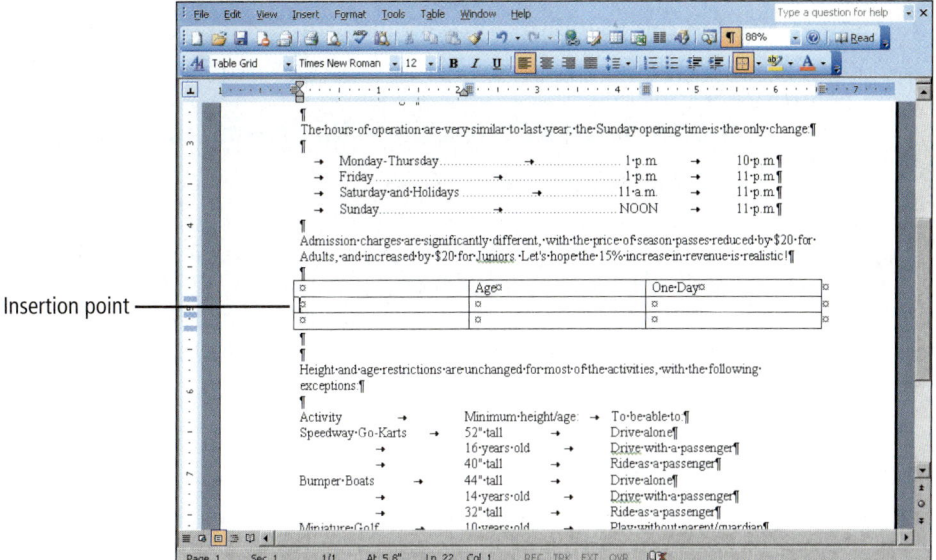

Figure 3.50

8. Type the following to complete the table (do not press Enter or Tab after the last item):

| **Toddler** | **3 & under** | **Free** |
| **Adult** | **12 to 59** | **$39** |

Compare your screen to Figure 3.51.

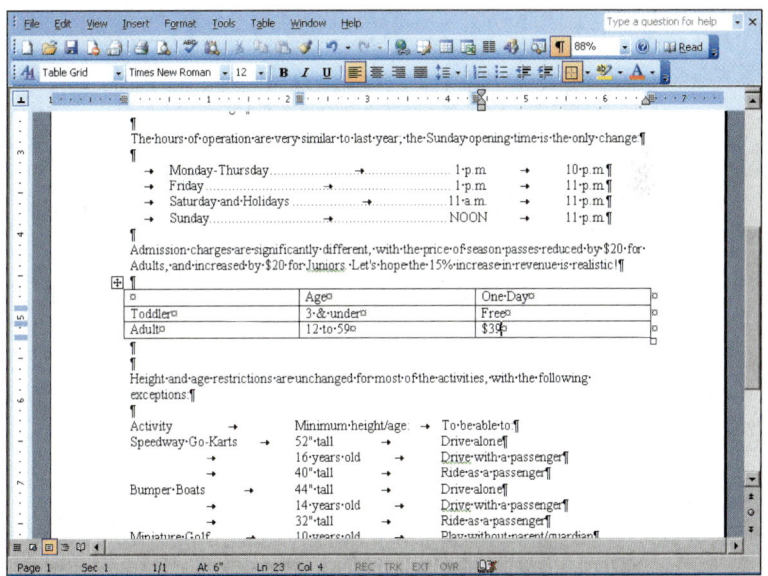

Figure 3.51

Project 3B: Park Changes | **Word** 367

9 On the Standard toolbar, click the **Save** button.

> ### More Knowledge — Navigating in a Table
> *Moving Between Cells in a Table*
> You can move to a previous cell in a table by pressing Shift + Tab. This action selects the contents of the previous cell. The selection moves back one cell at a time each time you press Tab while holding down Shift. You can also use the up or down arrow keys to move up or down a column. The left and right arrow keys, however, move the insertion point one character at a time within a cell.

Activity 3.15 Adding a Row to a Table

You can add rows to the beginning, middle, or end of a table.

1 With the insertion point in the last cell in the table, press Tab.

A new row is added to the bottom of the table. See Figure 3.52.

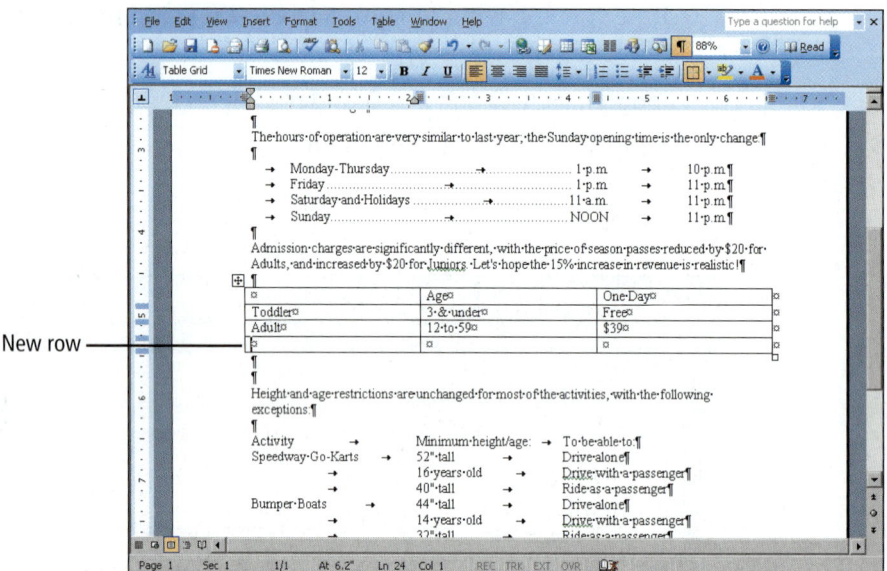

New row

Figure 3.52

2 In the first cell of the new row, type **Senior** and then press Tab.

3 Type **60+** and press Tab. Type **$29**

Compare your new row to Figure 3.53.

368 **Word** | Chapter 3: Using Graphics and Tables

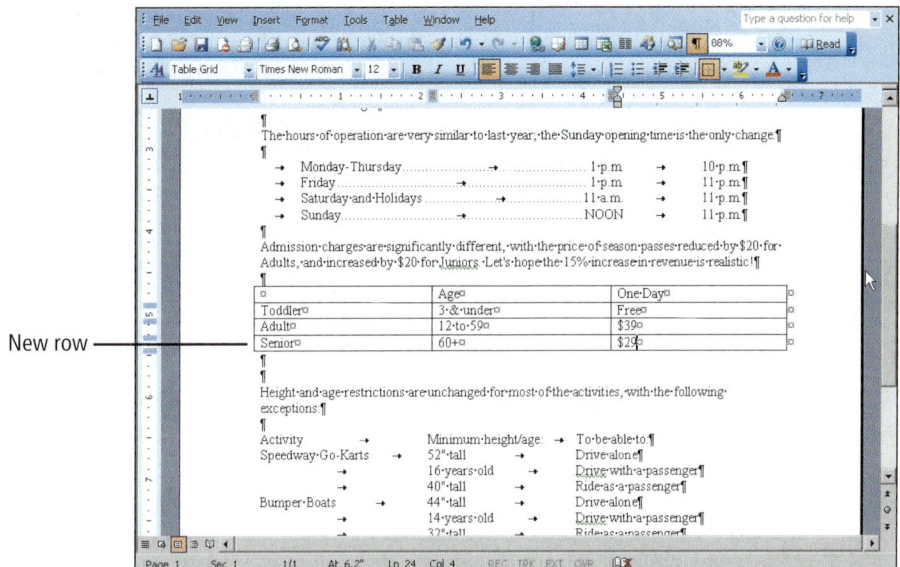

Figure 3.53

4 In the table row beginning *Adult*, click anywhere to place the insertion point.

5 From the **Table** menu, point to **Insert** and then click **Rows Above**.

A new row is added above the row containing the insertion point. See Figure 3.54.

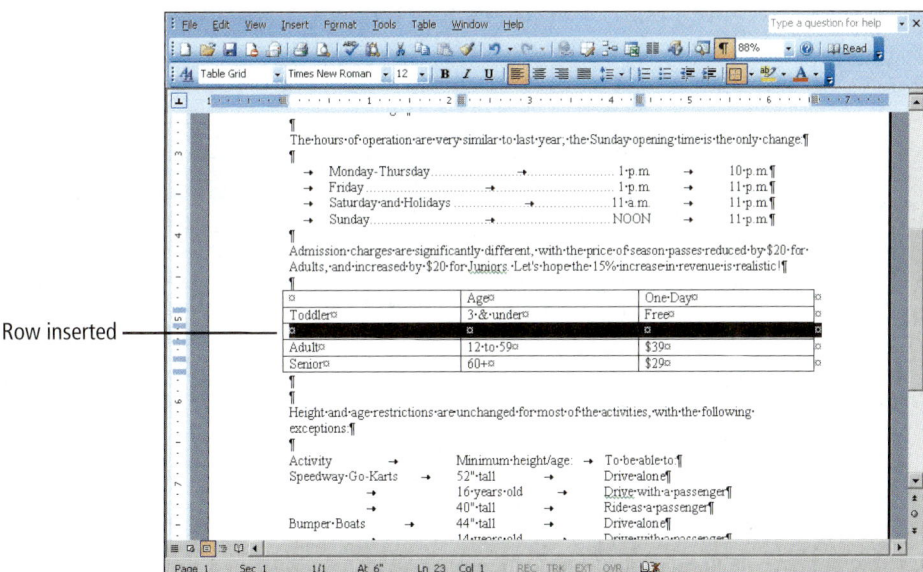

Figure 3.54

6 Type **Junior** and press Tab.

When the entire row is selected, text is automatically placed in the cell on the left.

7 Type **4 to 11** and press Tab. Type **$19**

Compare your table to Figure 3.55.

Project 3B: Park Changes | **Word** 369

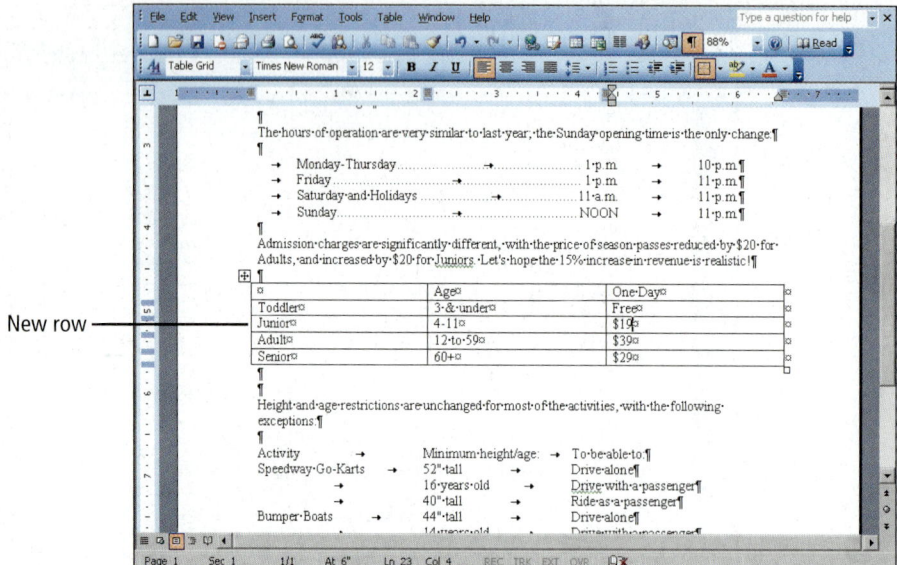

New row

Figure 3.55

8 On the Standard toolbar, click the **Save** button.

Activity 3.16 Changing the Width of a Table Column

In Word tables, you can change the column widths easily and quickly and adjust them as often as necessary to create a visually appealing table.

1 Move the pointer over the right boundary of the first column until the pointer changes to a left- and right-pointing resize arrow, as shown in Figure 3.56.

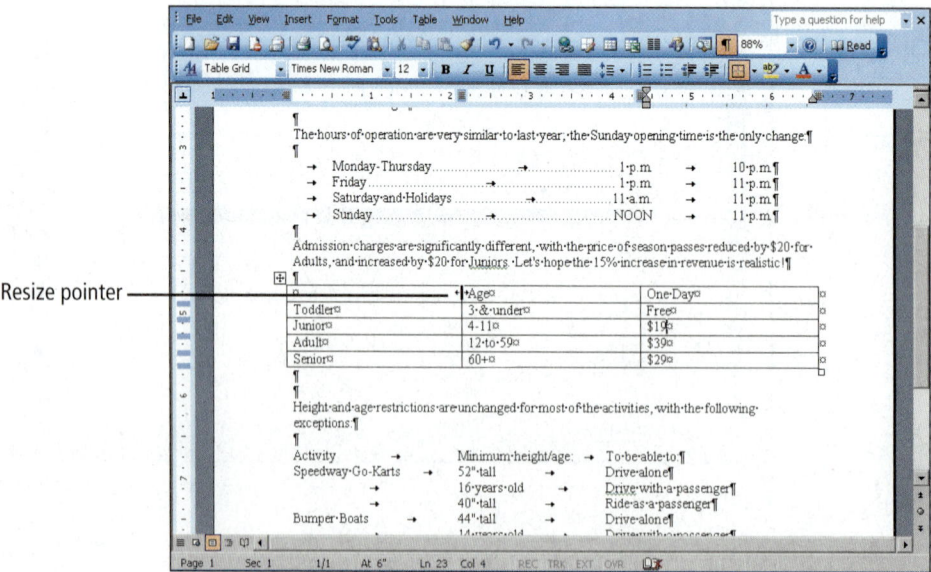

Resize pointer

Figure 3.56

370 Word | Chapter 3: Using Graphics and Tables

2 Drag the boundary to the left until the first column is about 1-inch wide, to approximately the **1 inch mark on the horizontal ruler**.

Use the horizontal ruler as a guide. If only one row resizes, click the Undo button and start again.

3 Drag the right boundary of the second column to the left until the column is about 1-inch wide, to approximately the **2 inch mark on the horizontal ruler**.

4 Drag the right boundary of the third column to the left until the column is about 1-inch wide, to approximately the **3 inch mark on the horizontal ruler**.

Compare your table to Figure 3.57.

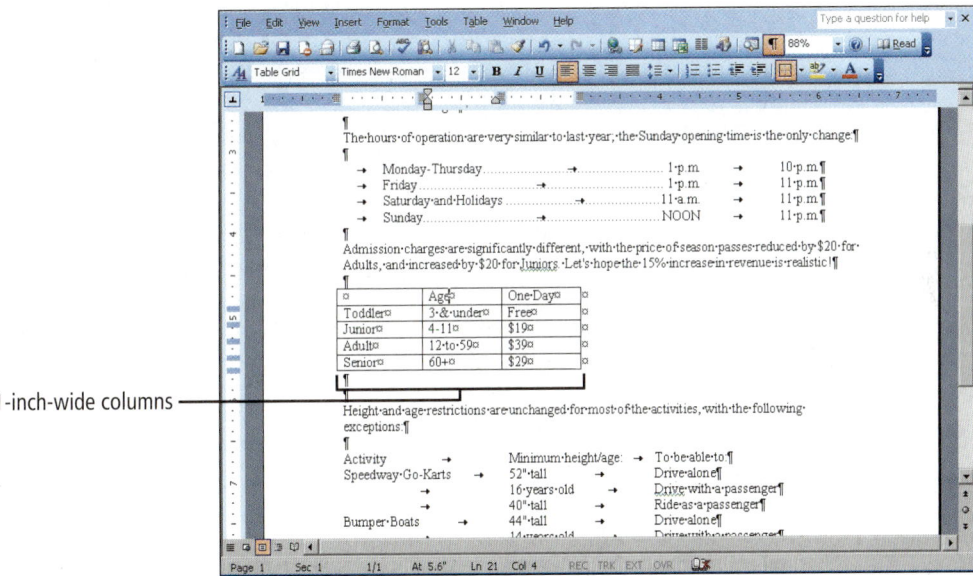

1-inch-wide columns

Figure 3.57

5 On the Standard toolbar, click the **Save** button.

Activity 3.17 Adding a Column to a Table

1 In the last column of the table, click anywhere in the column to position the insertion point.

2 From the **Table** menu, point to **Insert**, and then click **Columns to the Right**.

A new column is added to the right of the column containing the insertion point and is the same width as that column. See Figure 3.58.

Project 3B: Park Changes | **Word**   371

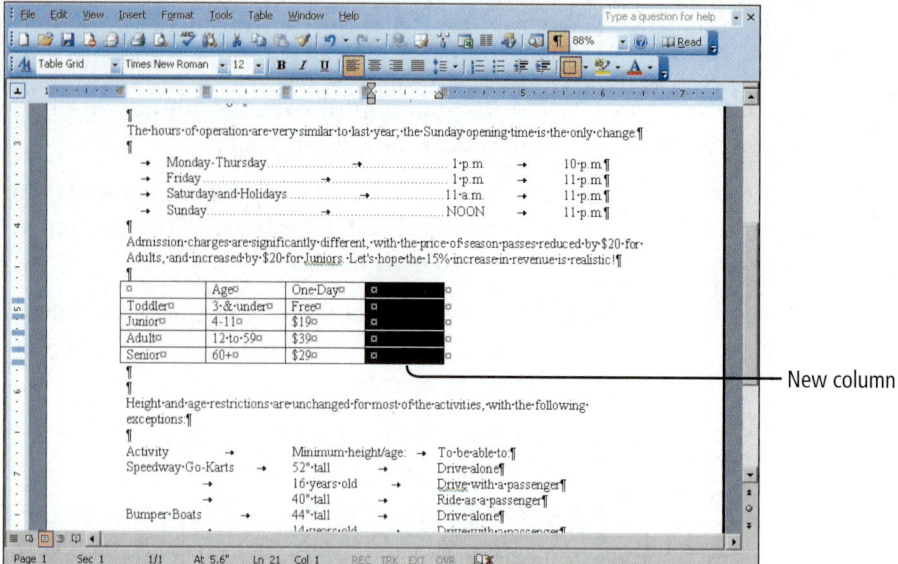

Figure 3.58

3 Type **Season Pass**

In a selected column, text is entered in the top cell when you type. If necessary, drag the column slightly to the right so that the text displays on one line.

4 Complete the column with the following information. Compare your table with Figure 3.59.

Toddler	**Free**
Junior	**$89**
Adult	**$129**
Senior	**$99**

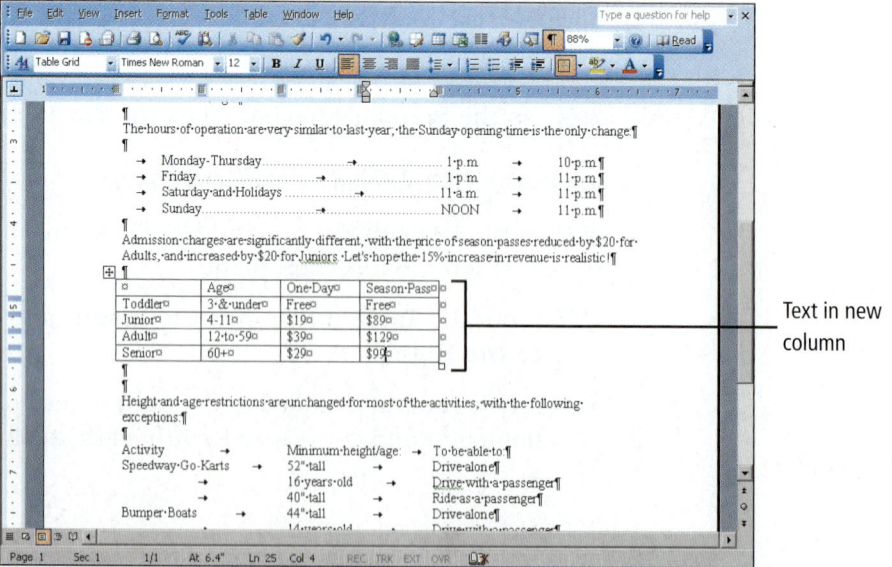

Figure 3.59

5 On the Standard toolbar, click the **Save** button.

372 Word | Chapter 3: Using Graphics and Tables

More Knowledge — Using Tabs in Tables

You can also add tabs to a table column so you can indent items within a table cell. The easiest way to add a tab is to click on the ruler to set the location within a column. Then you can drag the tab stop indicator to change the location of the tab within the column or add the hanging indent marker so multiple lines in a list are evenly indented. To move to the tabbed location within the cell, press Ctrl + Tab.

Objective 6
Format Tables

Formatted tables are more attractive and easier to read. When you type numbers, for example, they line up on the left of a column instead of on the right until you format them. With Word's formatting tools, you can shade cells, format the table borders and grid, and center the table between the document margins. All of these features make a table more inviting to the reader.

Activity 3.18 Formatting Text in Cells

In addition to aligning text in cells, you can also add emphasis to the text.

1 Click anywhere in the cell containing the word *Age*, hold down the left mouse button, and then drag to the right until the second, third, and fourth cells in the top row are selected. See Figure 3.60.

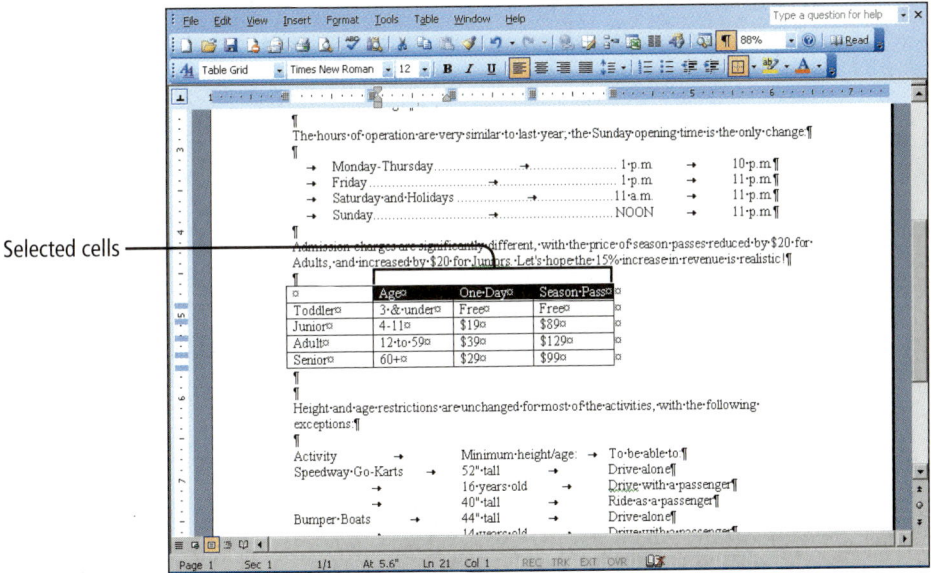

Figure 3.60

Project 3B: Park Changes | **Word** 373

2 On the Formatting toolbar, click the **Bold** button, and then click the **Center** button.

The text in the first row of cells is bold and centered, as shown in Figure 3.61.

Bold, centered text

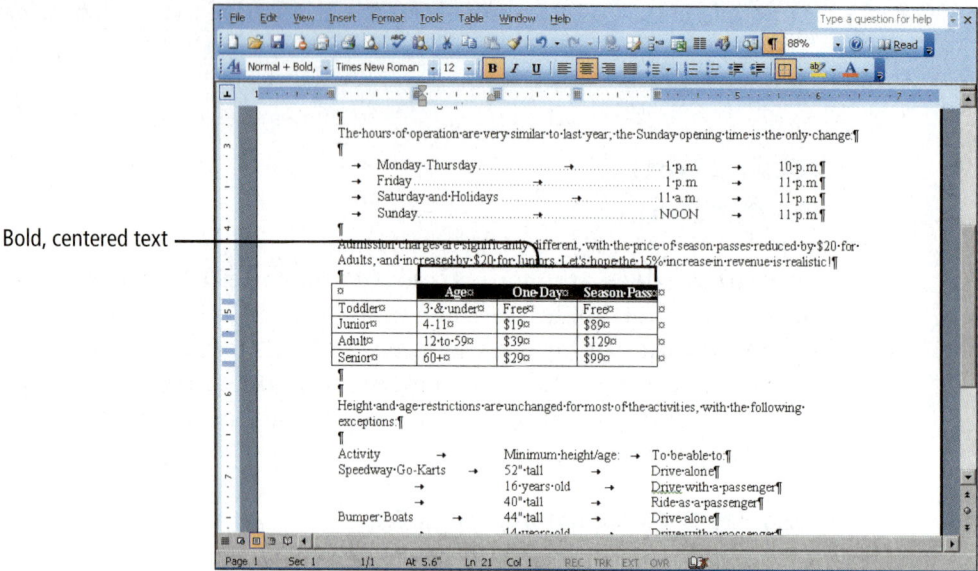

Figure 3.61

3 Click in the cell containing the word *Toddler* and then drag down to select the second, third, fourth, and fifth cells in the first column.

4 On the Formatting toolbar, click the **Bold** button.

5 In the third column, click in the cell containing *Free*, drag down and to the right until all of the cells in the last two columns, except the first row, are selected.

6 From the Formatting toolbar, click the **Align Right** button.

Compare your table to Figure 3.62.

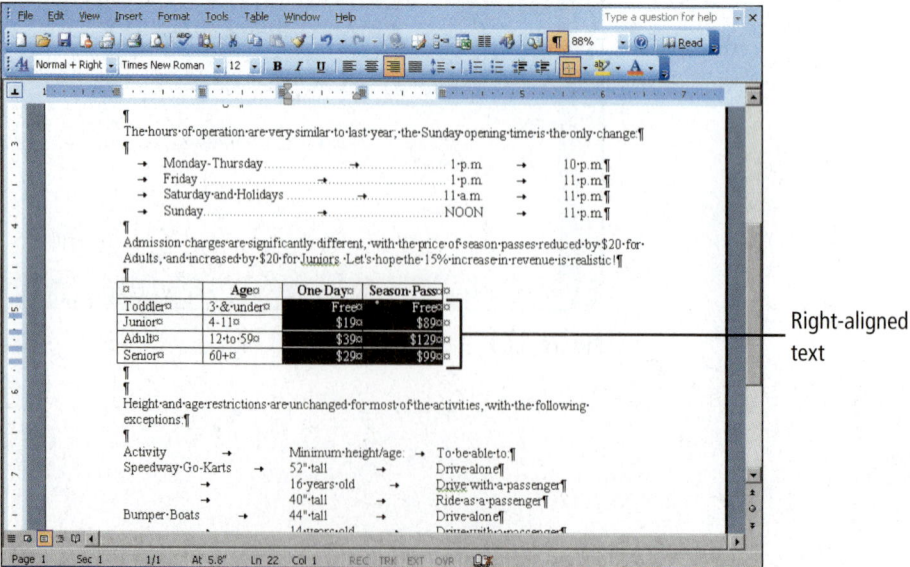

Right-aligned text

Figure 3.62

374 **Word** | Chapter 3: Using Graphics and Tables

7 Click anywhere to deselect, and then on the Standard toolbar, click the **Save** button.

Activity 3.19 Shading Cells

Backgrounds can be added to cells to differentiate them from other cells.

1 In the cell containing the word *Age*, drag to the right to select the second, third, and fourth cells in the top row.

2 From the **Format** menu, click **Borders and Shading**.

The Borders and Shading dialog box displays.

3 In the **Borders and Shading** dialog box click the **Shading tab**.

4 Under **Fill**, in the second row, click the third button as shown in Figure 3.63.

The name of the shading option—*Gray-10%*—displays to the right of the shading option buttons, and the Preview area shows what the shading will look like in the table.

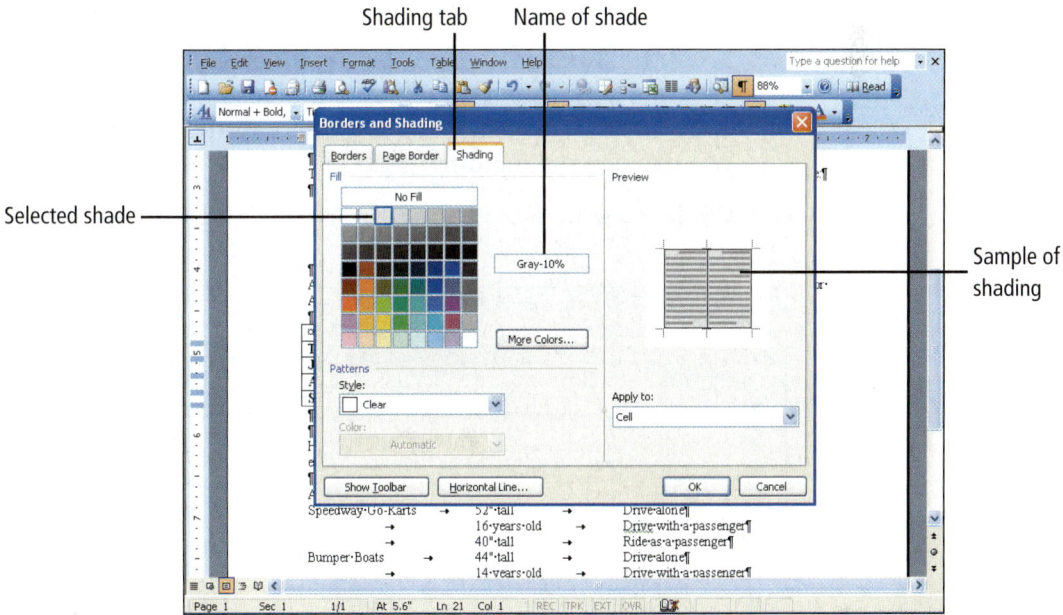

Figure 3.63

5 Click **OK**. Click anywhere in the document to deselect the text.

A light gray background is applied to the three column headings. See Figure 3.64.

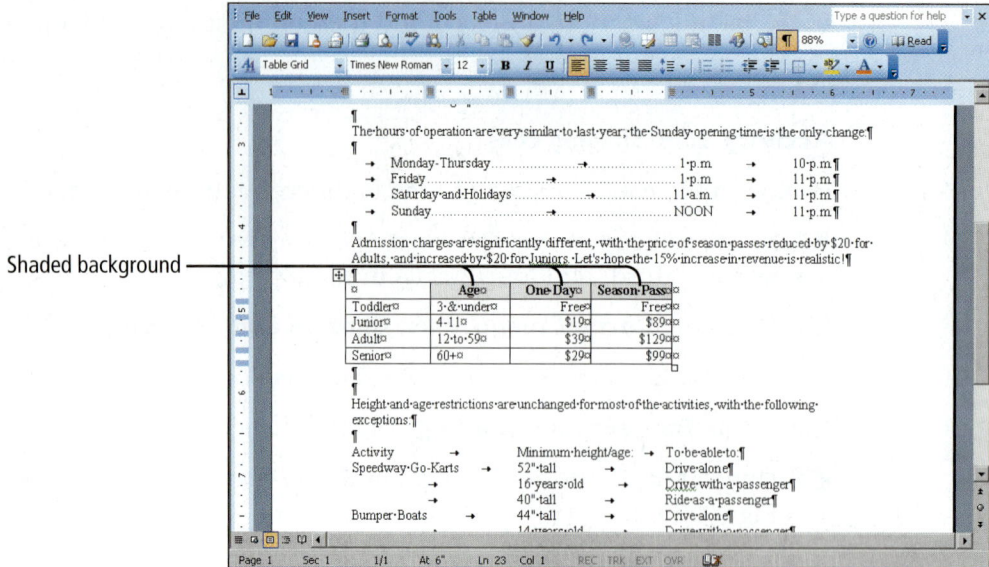

Shaded background

Figure 3.64

[6] Click in the cell containing the word *Toddler*, drag down until the second, third, fourth, and fifth cells in the first column are selected.

[7] From the **Format** menu, click **Borders and Shading**. Under **Fill**, click the same shading option you chose for the row headings—Gray-10%. Click **OK**. Click anywhere in the document to deselect so you can see the shading.

Compare your table to Figure 3.65.

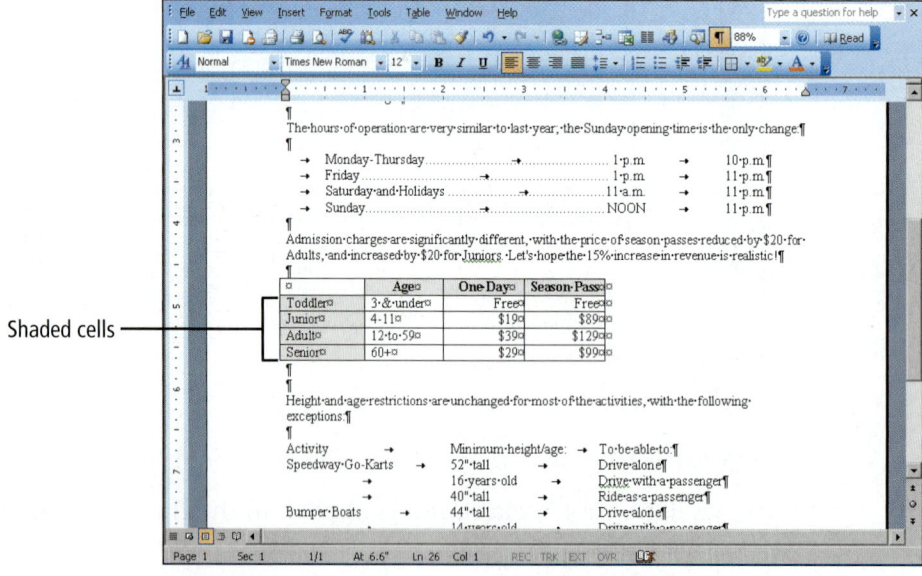

Shaded cells

Figure 3.65

[8] On the Standard toolbar, click the **Save** button.

376 **Word** | Chapter 3: Using Graphics and Tables

Activity 3.20 Changing the Table Border

You can modify or remove the border from the entire table, a selected cell, or individual boundaries of a cell.

1 Click in any cell in the table. From the **Format** menu, click **Borders and Shading**.

The Borders and Shading dialog box displays.

2 In the **Borders and Shading** dialog box, click the **Borders tab**.

3 Under **Setting**, click **Grid**.

The Preview area in the right portion of the dialog box displays the current border settings, and the line width is displayed in the Width box, as shown in Figure 3.66.

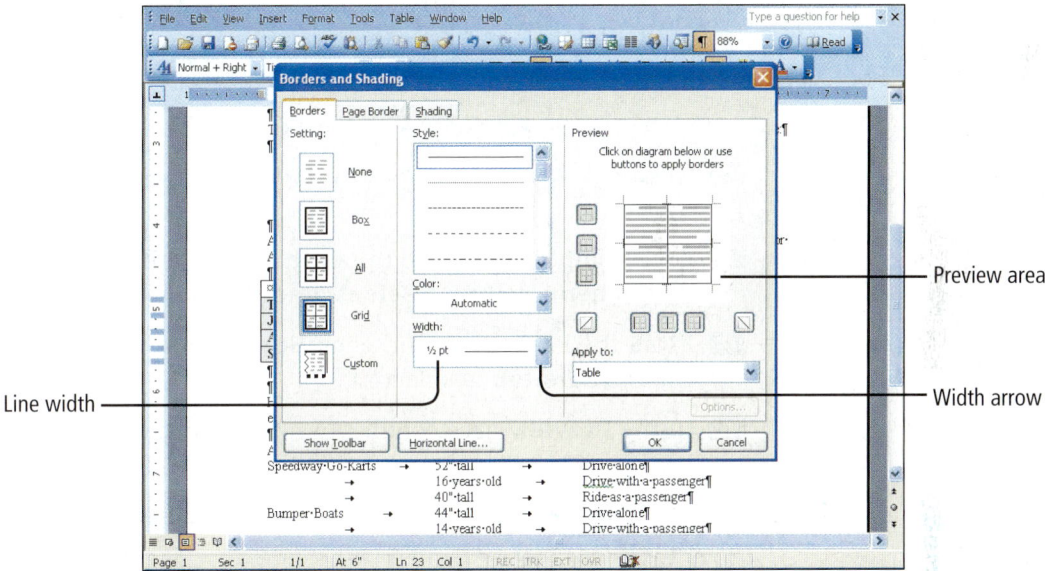

Figure 3.66

4 Click the **Width arrow**, and then from the displayed list, click **1½ pt**.

Notice, under Preview, the outside border is changed to a thicker 1½ point width, while the inner grid lines remain at ½ point width. See Figure 3.67.

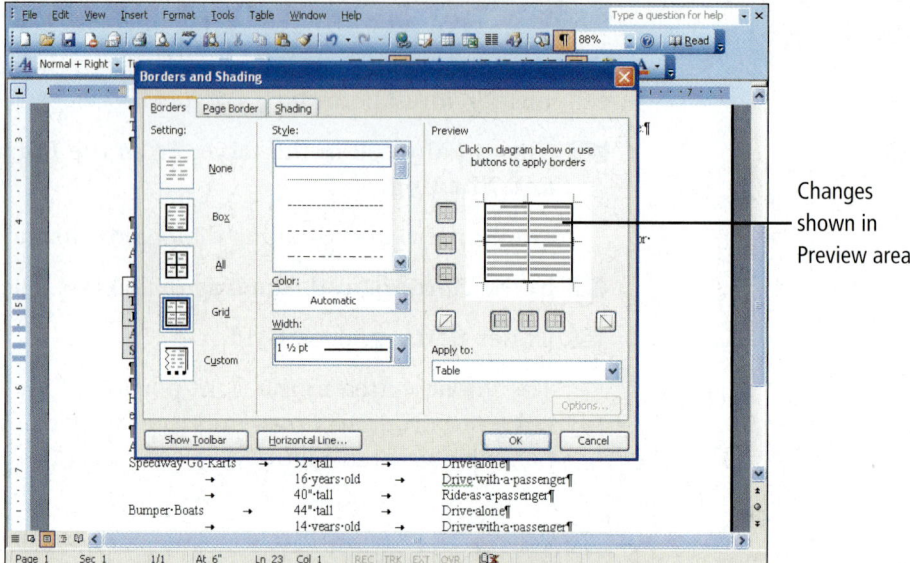

Figure 3.67

5. Click **OK**, and then click anywhere in the document to deselect the table.

6. In the empty cell at the upper left of the table, click once. From the **Table** menu, point to **Select**, and then click **Cell**.

7. From the **Format** menu, click **Borders and Shading**. Be sure that the **Borders tab** is selected.

8. In the **Preview** area, point to and then click the top border twice to remove all borders.

The first click returns the border to ½ point, the second click removes the border. See Figure 3.68.

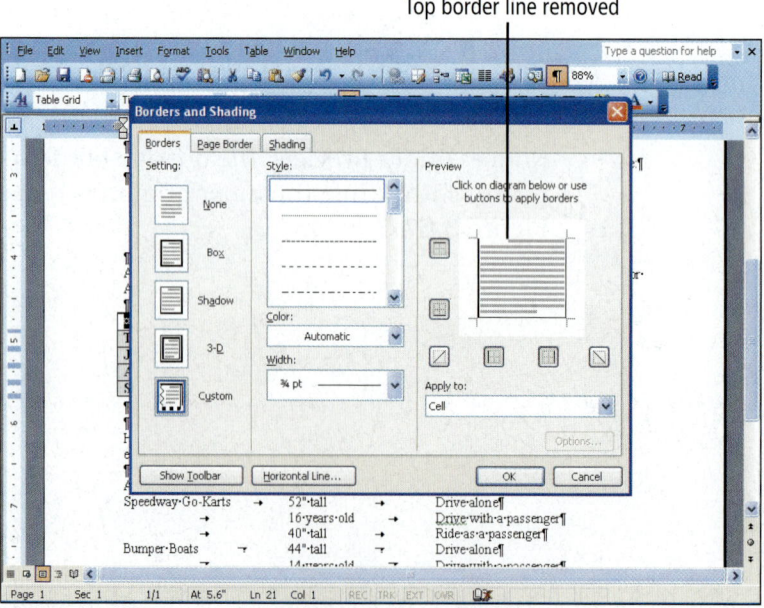

Figure 3.68

378   Word | Chapter 3: Using Graphics and Tables

9 In the **Preview** area, click the left border twice, until there is no border displayed.

The left border is removed.

10 Click the **Width arrow**, and from the displayed list, click **1½ pt**.

11 In the **Preview** area, click the bottom border once.

The bottom border is widened to 1½ point.

12 In the **Preview** area, click the right border once.

The right border is widened to 1½ point, as shown in Figure 3.69.

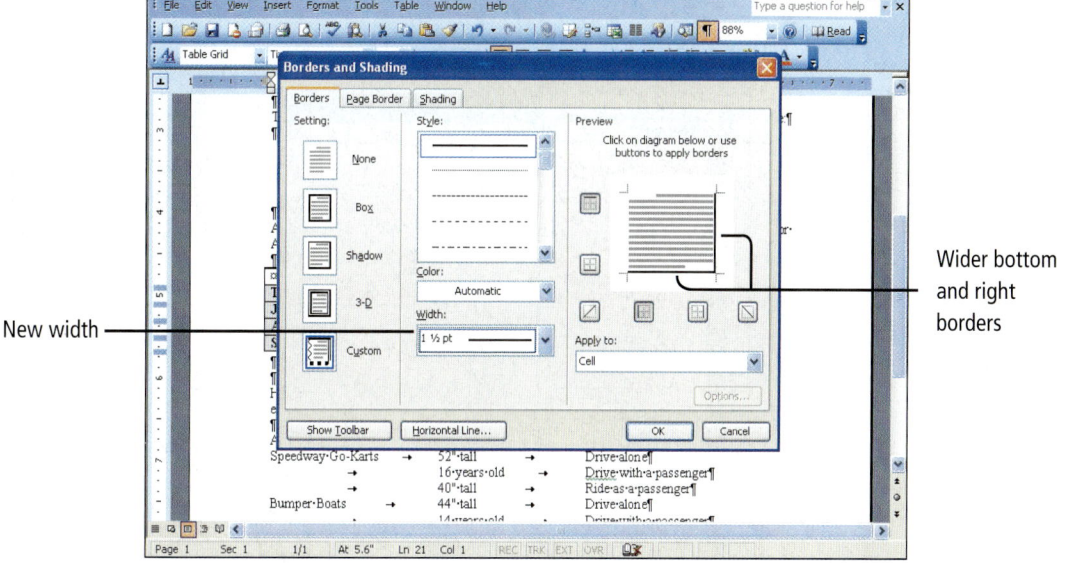

Figure 3.69

13 Click **OK**. Click anywhere in the document to deselect the table.

Compare your table to Figure 3.70.

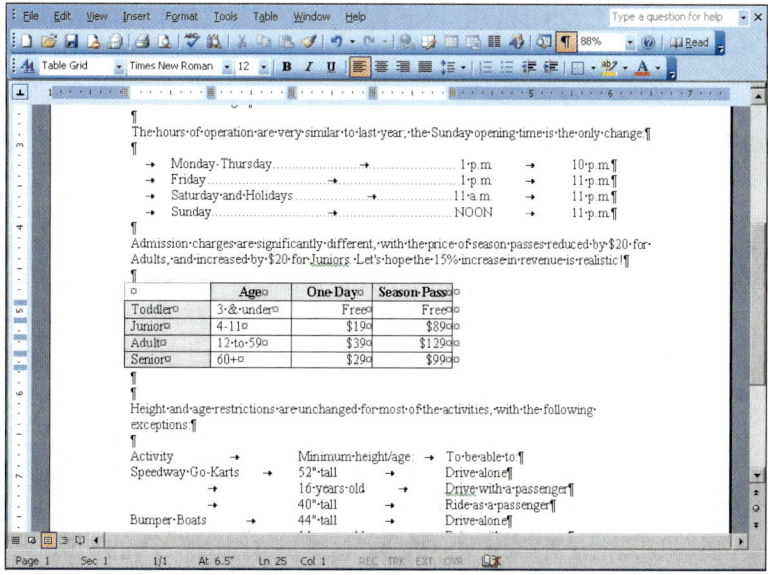

Figure 3.70

Project 3B: Park Changes | **Word** 379

14 On the Standard toolbar, click the **Save** button.

Activity 3.21 Centering a Table

1 Click anywhere in the table.

2 From the **Table** menu, click **Table Properties**.

The Table Properties dialog box displays.

3 In the **Table Properties** dialog box click the **Table tab**.

4 Under **Alignment**, click **Center**. See Figure 3.71.

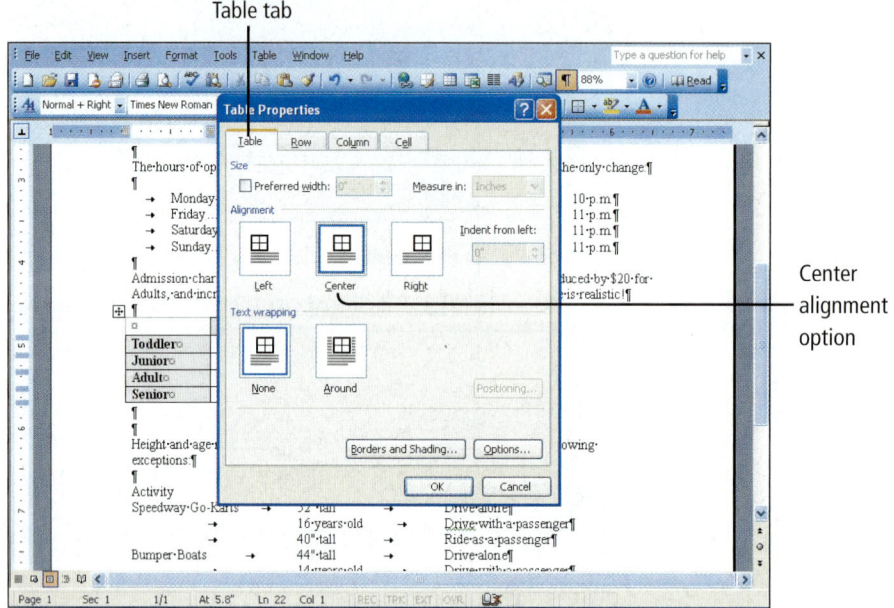

Figure 3.71

5 Click **OK**.

The table is centered horizontally between the left and right margins.

Another Way — Centering a Table

You can center a table by clicking the Center button on the Formatting toolbar. First you must select the entire table. To select a table, from the Table menu, point to Select and then click Table. Alternatively, in Print Layout view, rest the pointer on the upper left corner of the table until the table move handle appears, and then click the table move handle to select the table. After the table is selected, on the Formatting toolbar, click the Center button.

6 Place the insertion point in the blank line just below the table and press [Delete].

There should be only one empty paragraph before and one empty paragraph after the table.

7 Click the **Show/Hide ¶** button.

The nonprinting characters are hidden. Your table should look like Figure 3.72.

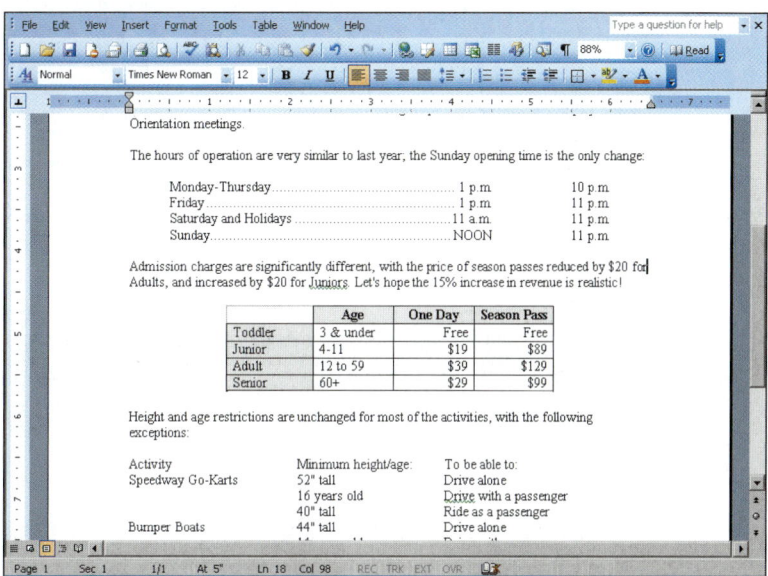

Figure 3.72

8 Click the **Show/Hide ¶** button to redisplay the nonprinting characters.

9 On the Standard toolbar, click the **Save** button.

Objective 7
Create a Table from Existing Text

The Insert Table feature is useful if you are beginning a new table, but Word also provides a tool that enables you to convert existing text into a table. The text needs to be marked using ***separator characters***—usually tabs or commas that separate the text in each line. When you convert text to a table, you can have Word optimize the column widths at the same time. You can also add blank rows or columns, if needed.

Activity 3.22 Converting Text to Tables

If text is separated with a recognized separator character, and the text is selected, converting text to a table is an easy process.

1 Scroll as necessary to view the lower portion of the document on your screen. In the block of text at the end of the document, beginning with *Activity* and continuing to the end of the document, notice the tab marks indicating where the [Tab] key was pressed.

The tab marks can act as separator characters for the purpose of converting text to a table. See Figure 3.73.

Project 3B: Park Changes | **Word**   381

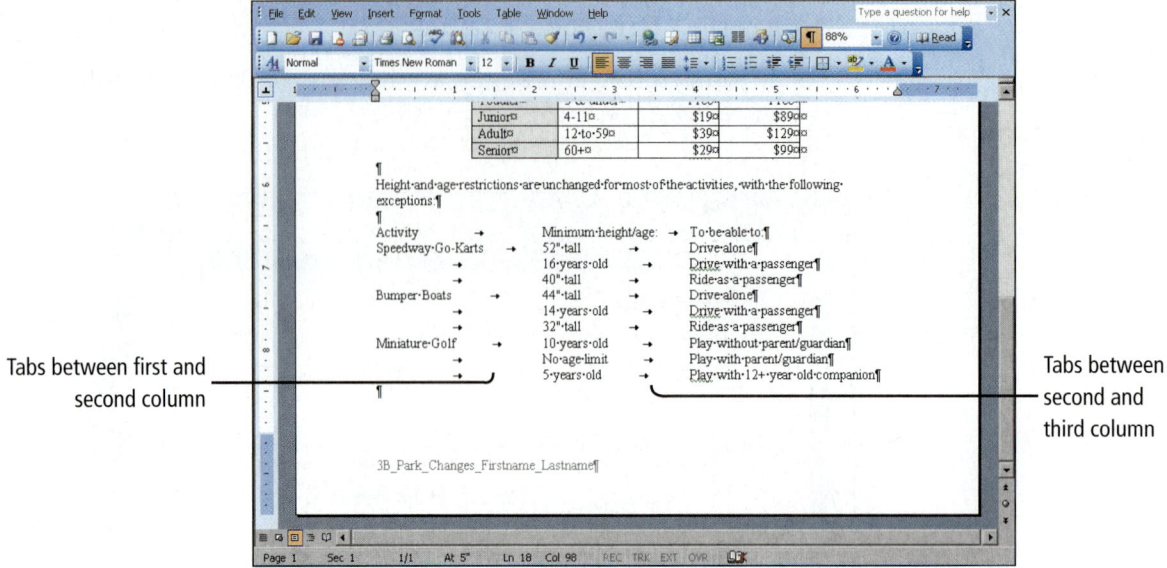

Figure 3.73

> **More Knowledge** — **Formatting Text to Convert to a Table**
>
> If you have text you would like to convert into a table, you will need to separate the columns using a separator character. Tabs and commas are the most commonly used separators, but you can specify a number of different marks, including dashes, dollar signs, or colons. You must be consistent, however. Word will not recognize a mixture of tabs and commas as separators in the same block of text.

2 Click to position the insertion point to the left of the word *Activity*, hold down **Shift**, and then click at the end of the last line, after the word *companion*.

3 With the text selected, from the **Table** menu, point to **Convert**, and then click **Text to Table**.

The Convert Text to Table dialog box displays. Under Table size, the Number of columns should be 3.

4 In the **Convert Text to Table** dialog box, under **AutoFit behavior**, click the **AutoFit to contents** option button.

5 Under **Separate text at**, click the **Tabs** option button, if necessary.

Compare your dialog box to Figure 3.74.

382   **Word** | Chapter 3: Using Graphics and Tables

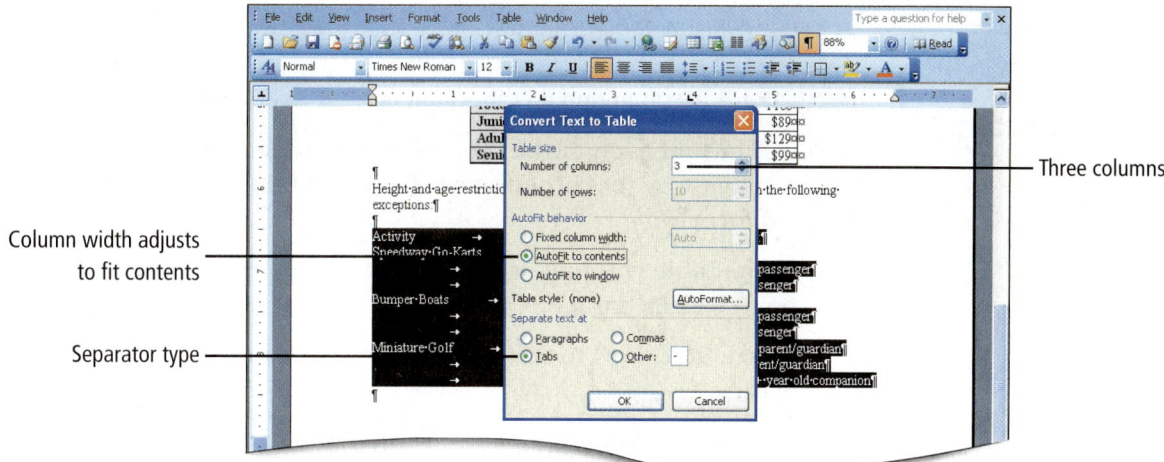

Figure 3.74

More Knowledge — Make Sure There Is Only One Separator Between Columns

Before you convert your text to a table, make sure there is only one separator between each column item. If you are using tabs, for example, each tab will move the subsequent item one more column to the right. An extra tab between items will mean that the item will eventually end up in the wrong column. There is an exception to this rule. If you have an empty cell, an extra tab will move the following item to the correct column. Always turn on the nonprinting characters in your document and visually scan the text for extra separators. Also, check the table once you have completed the conversion to make sure everything is in the right column.

6 At the bottom of the **Convert Text to Table** dialog box, click **OK**. Click anywhere in the document to deselect the table.

Compare your table to Figure 3.75.

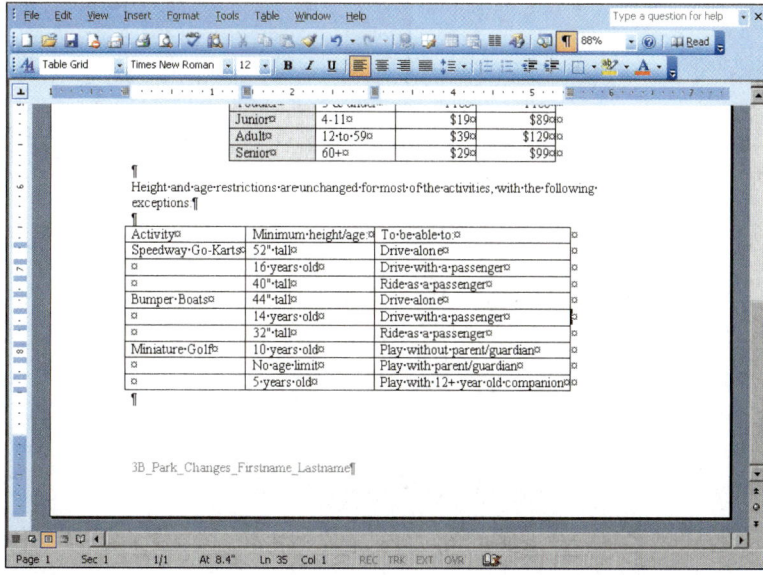

Figure 3.75

Project 3B: Park Changes | **Word** 383

7 On the Standard toolbar, click the **Save** button.

Activity 3.23 Applying a Predefined Format to a Table

You can format each of the table elements independently, but there is also a quick way to *AutoFormat* the whole table at one time, using predefined formats.

1 In the table you just created, click anywhere to position the insertion point within the table.

You do not need to select the entire table to use the AutoFormat feature.

2 From the **Table** menu, click **Table AutoFormat**.

3 In the displayed **Table AutoFormat** dialog box, under **Table styles**, click any of the table styles and, under **Preview**, notice the style. Click several of the AutoFormat styles to see what types of formatting are available.

4 Under **Table styles**, scroll toward the bottom of the list and click **Table Professional**. Under **Apply special formats to**, select the check boxes as necessary so that all four are selected, as shown in Figure 3.76.

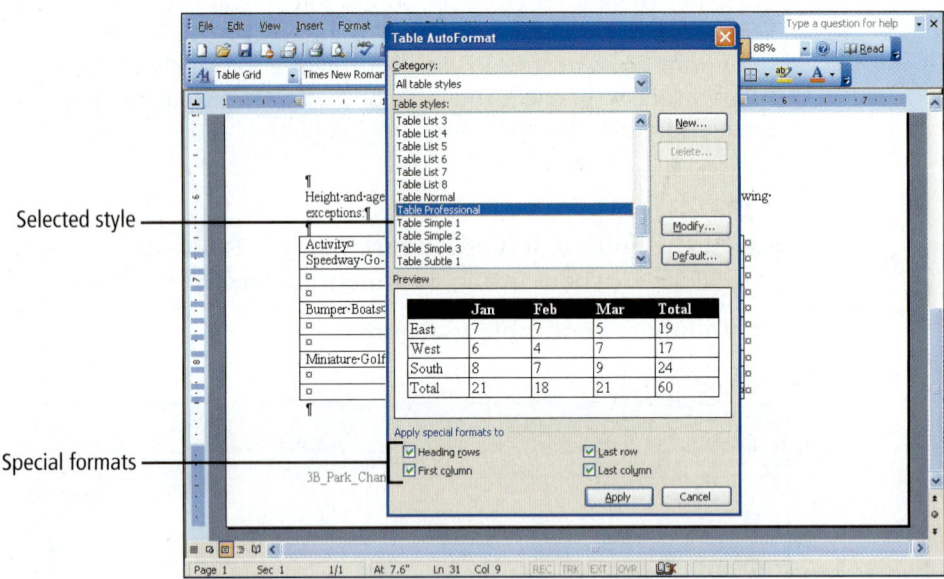

Figure 3.76

5 At the bottom of the **Table AutoFormat** dialog box, click **Apply**.

Compare your table to Figure 3.77.

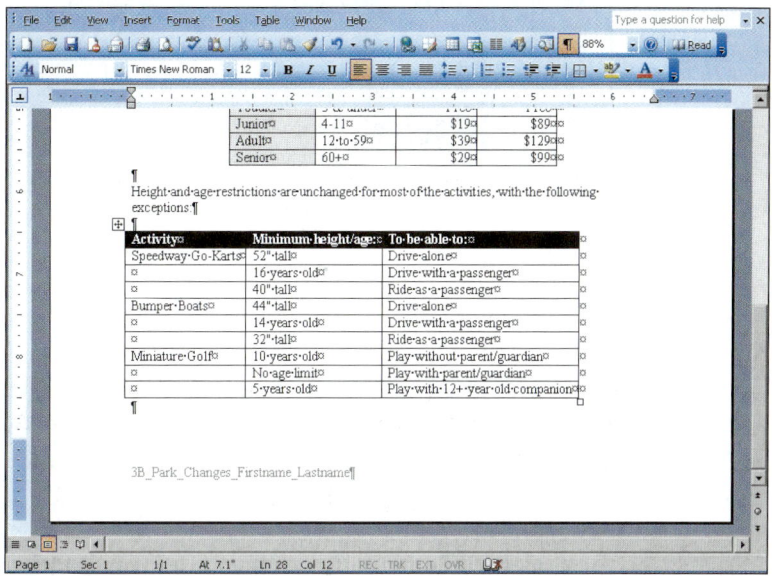

Figure 3.77

6 On the Standard toolbar, click the **Save** button.

Activity 3.24 Merging Cells and Aligning Text Vertically

Sometimes a title looks better if it spans two or more columns or rows. This can be accomplished by merging cells.

1 In the table you just formatted, position your pointer over the second cell in the first column—the *Speedway Go-Karts* cell—and then drag down to select the cell and the two empty cells below.

Because of the formatting in the first row, it will appear that four cells are selected, but if you look closely, you will see that the selection area is indented slightly. See Figure 3.78.

Project 3B: Park Changes | **Word**   385

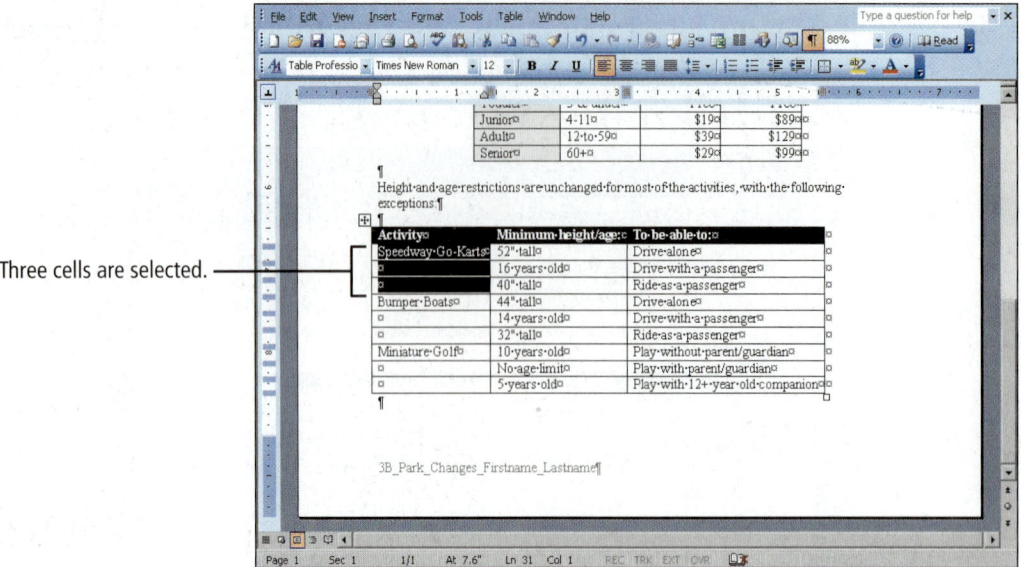

Three cells are selected.

Figure 3.78

2 On the Formatting toolbar, click the **Bold** button **B**. From the **Table** menu, click **Merge Cells**.

The cells are merged, and the cell borders are removed. Notice that making the text bold also increased the width of the cell. The widths of all of the cells in the first column increased slightly.

3 Repeat the procedure used in Steps 1 and 2 to bold and merge the three *Bumper Boats* cells and the three *Miniature Golf* cells.

Compare your table to Figure 3.79.

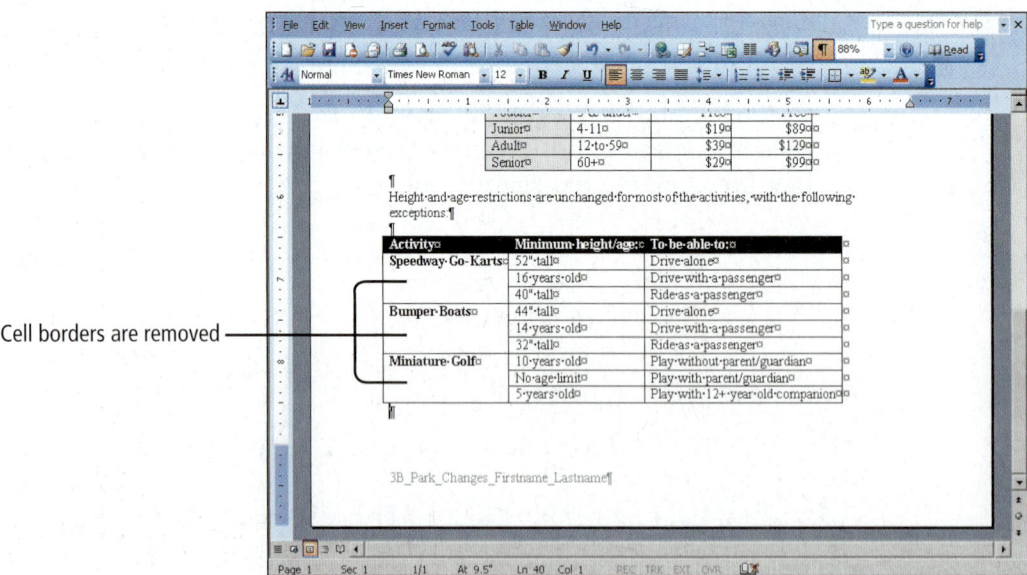

Cell borders are removed

Figure 3.79

386   Word | Chapter 3: Using Graphics and Tables

4. In the *Speedway Go-Karts* cell, click once to position the insertion point.

5. From the **Table** menu, click **Table Properties**.

   The Table Properties dialog box displays.

6. In the **Table Properties** dialog box, click the **Cell tab**. Under **Vertical alignment**, click **Center**. See Figure 3.80.

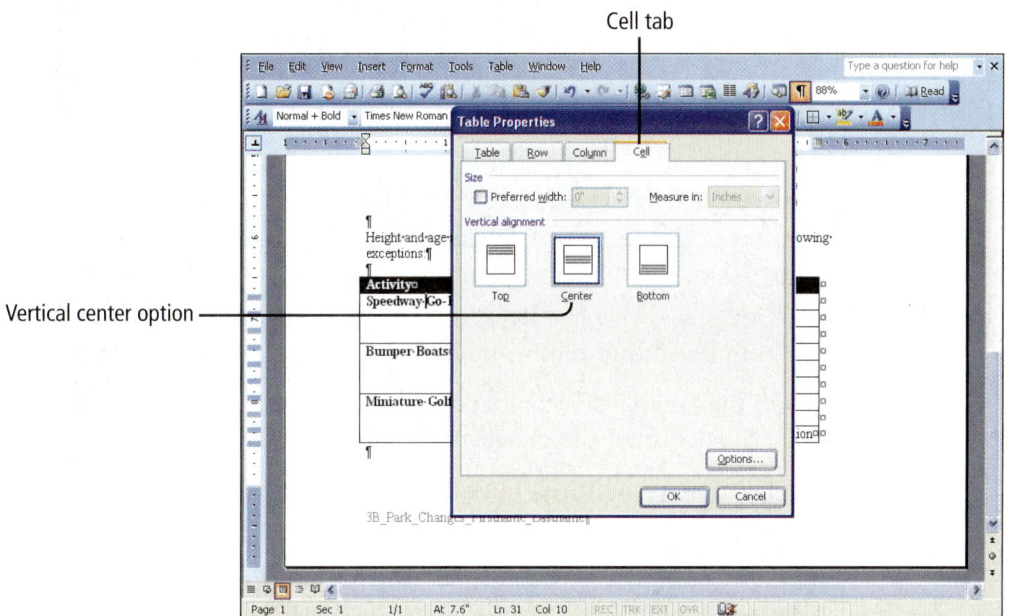

Figure 3.80

7. At the bottom of the **Table Properties** dialog box, click **OK**.

   The text is centered vertically.

Another Way

Aligning Text in a Table

Use the Shortcut Menu

You can use shortcut menus to align text in a table. Right-click the cell, point to Cell Alignment on the shortcut menu, and then click the alignment style you want from the Cell Alignment palette that displays. You can choose from both vertical and horizontal cell alignment options using the Cell Alignment palette.

8. Drag to select the *Bumper Boats* and the *Miniature Golf* cells, display the **Table** menu, click **Table Properties**, and on the **Cell tab** under **Vertical alignment**, click **Center**. Click **OK**. Click anywhere in the document to deselect the selected cells.

   Compare your table to Figure 3.81.

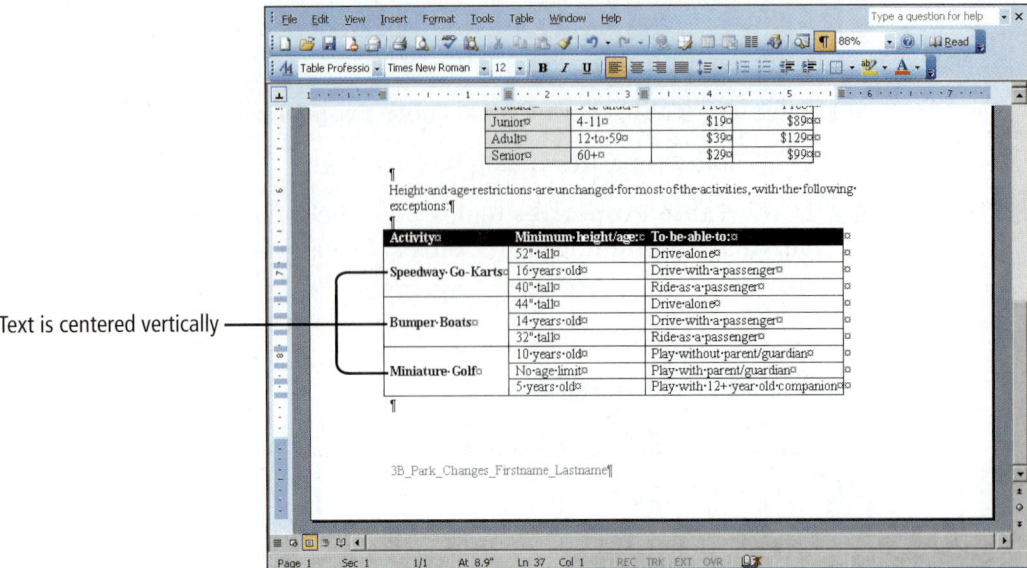

Text is centered vertically

Figure 3.81

9. From the **Table** menu, point to **Select** and then click **Table**.

10. On the Formatting toolbar, click the **Center** button. Click anywhere in the document to deselect the table.

    The table is centered horizontally on the page. Compare your finished table to Figure 3.82.

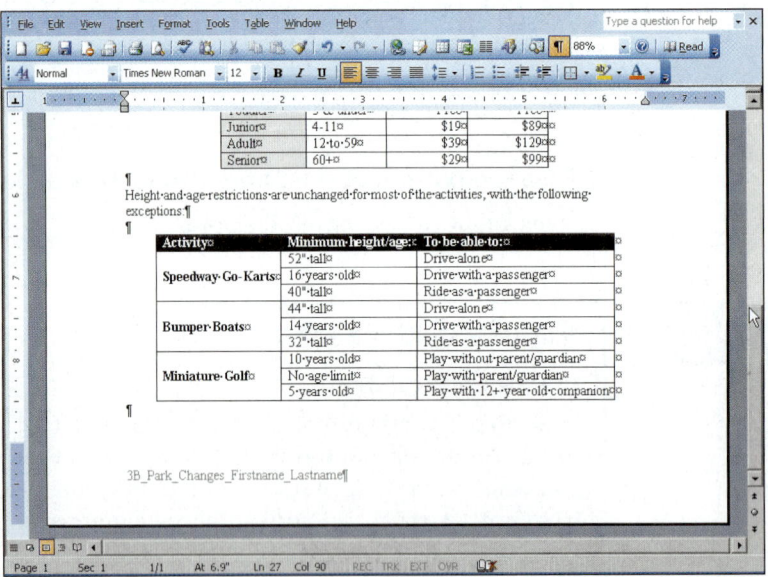

Figure 3.82

11. Press Ctrl + S to save your changes. On the Standard toolbar, click the **Print Preview** button to view your document.

12. On the Print Preview toolbar, click the **Print** button. Close Print Preview and close your document.

End You have completed Project 3B

Summary

Many graphical elements can be used with Word. In this chapter you practiced inserting, moving, and resizing clip art and pictures. You also worked with the Drawing toolbar and learned how to create basic shapes using the AutoShapes, line, and text box tools. You modified shapes by changing the size, shape, and background color.

An effective way to present information is with a tabbed list or a table. You have used tabs to display information in single rows with multiple columns. A variety of tabs can be used, such as dot-leader, decimal, centered, or right-aligned. You practiced setting, moving, and changing tabs, as well as entering text in a tabbed list.

Tables also have a row and column format, but have the advantage of displaying multiple lines of text in a cell and still maintaining a horizontal relationship with the other cells in the same row. Tables can be formatted to display the information in a manner that emphasizes certain parts of the table. You practiced how to format individual cells or an entire table, using both the Formatting toolbar and the AutoFormat with other commands found under the Table menu. Finally, you practiced how to convert text to a table.

In This Chapter You Practiced How To

- Insert Clip Art and Pictures
- Modify Clip Art and Pictures
- Work with the Drawing Toolbar
- Work with Tabs
- Create a Table
- Format Tables
- Create a Table from Existing Text

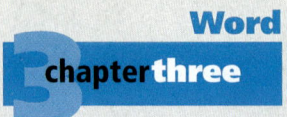

Concepts Assessments

Matching Match each term in the second column with its correct definition in the first column by writing the letter of the term on the blank line in front of the correct definition.

____ 1. A tool that is used to resize an image proportionally.

____ 2. Images that can be moved independently of the surrounding text.

____ 3. A tool that is used to move an image in a clockwise or counterclockwise direction.

____ 4. The term used to identify commas or tabs when they are used to separate text in a line so it can be converted into a table.

____ 5. The general term used for any media file such as art, sound, animation, or movies.

____ 6. A button on the Drawing toolbar that can be used to insert and to draw a variety of forms.

____ 7. A mark on the ruler that indicates the location where the insertion point will be placed when you press Tab.

____ 8. The symbol that indicates that an image is attached to the nearest paragraph.

____ 9. A group of cells organized in rows and columns.

____ 10. Images that behave just like characters in a sentence.

____ 11. This button can be used to change the type of tab stop that will be set, before clicking on the ruler.

____ 12. The term used to refer to the boxes in a table where information is typed.

____ 13. Before you can move an image on your screen you first need to change this property.

____ 14. To change the color of the outside border on a table you would open this dialog box.

____ 15. To move vertically down a column in a table you can use this key.

A Anchor
B AutoShapes
C Borders and Shading
D Cells
E Clip
F Corner sizing handles
G Down arrow
H Floating images
I Inline images
J Rotate handle
K Separator characters
L Tab Alignment button
M Tab stop
N Table
O Wrapping

Concepts Assessments (continued)

Fill in the Blank Write the correct answer in the space provided.

1. To create a table in Word, you can click on the _____ _____ button found on the Standard toolbar.

2. Predefined graphics such as those that come with the Word program or that can be downloaded from the Web are known as _____.

3. When a graphic image is selected, _____ _____ display around the edge of the image.

4. To align text to the contours of an irregularly shaped graphic, you would choose the _____ wrapping option.

5. A type of drawing object in which you can insert text, which can be placed outside of the document margin, is known as a _____ _____.

6. A series of dots following a tab that serve to guide the reader's eye is known as a dot _____.

7. A work area used for combining several graphic objects, known as the drawing _____, can also be turned off when adding simple shapes to a document.

8. To move from cell to cell across a table as you enter text, press _____.

9. To align a table on a page, you can use the _____ _____ dialog box.

10. A quick way to format a table is to use the _____ command found on the Table menu.

Concepts Assessments | **Word** 391

Word chapter three

Skill Assessments

Project 3C—Teacher Promotion

Objectives: *Create a Table, Format Tables, and Create a Table from Existing Text.*

In the following Skill Assessment, you will add a table to a planning meeting memo for the upcoming Teacher Appreciation Day at Sensation! Park. Your completed memo will look like the one shown in Figure 3.83. You will save your document as *3C_Teacher_Promotion_Firstname_Lastname*.

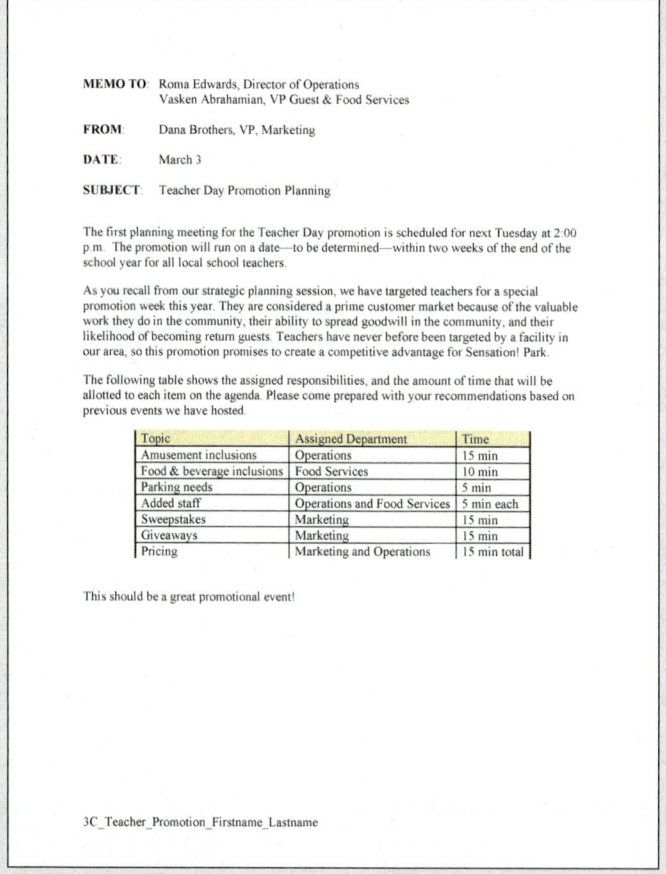

Figure 3.83

1. On the Standard toolbar, click the **Open** button. Navigate to the location where the student files for this textbook are stored. Locate and open **w03C_Teacher_Promotion**. On the Standard toolbar, click the **Show/Hide ¶** button if necessary to display the nonprinting characters.

2. From the **File** menu, click **Save As**. In the **Save As** dialog box, use the **Save in arrow** to navigate to the location where you are storing your files for this chapter. In the **File name** box, type 3C_Teacher_Promotion_Firstname_Lastname using your own name. Click the **Save** button.

(**Project 3C**–Teacher Promotion continues on the next page)

Skill Assessments (continued)

(Project 3C–Teacher Promotion continued)

3. Scroll down to the middle of the document and locate the tabbed list. Click to place the insertion point to the left of *Amusement inclusions* in the list. Move the mouse pointer to the right of *Marketing and Operations*, the last item in the tabbed list, hold down Shift, and then click to select the entire list.

4. Display the **Table** menu, point to **Convert**, and then click **Text to Table**.

5. In the **Convert Text to Table** dialog box, under **Table size**, be sure **2** displays in the **Number of columns** box. Under **AutoFit behavior**, click the **AutoFit to contents** option button. Under **Separate text at** be sure **Tabs** is selected. Click **OK**. The tabbed list is converted to a table.

6. Click anywhere in the second column of the table. Display the **Table** menu, point to **Insert**, and then click **Columns to the Right**. In the newly inserted column (which may be quite narrow), position the mouse pointer over the right border until the left-right arrow pointer displays, and then drag the border to the right to approximately **5.25 inches on the horizontal ruler**.

7. Click in the first cell of the third column and type **15 min** Press ↓ to move to the second cell in the third column and type **10 min** Continue to use the ↓ to move down the column and enter the remaining time blocks that have been allotted for each topic as follows:

Parking needs	5 min
Added Staff	5 min each
Sweepstakes	15 min
Giveaways	15 min
Pricing	15 min total

8. Click anywhere in the first row of the table, display the **Table** menu, point to **Insert**, and then click **Rows Above**. In the first cell of the new row, type **Topic** and then press Tab, type **Assigned Department** and then press Tab and then type **Time**

9. With the insertion point anywhere in the table, display the **Table** menu and then click **Table AutoFormat**. In the **Table AutoFormat** dialog box, scroll down and click the **Table Grid 4** format. In the lower portion of the dialog box, under **Apply special formats to**, be sure there is no check mark in the Last row and Last column check boxes. Clear them, if necessary. Click **Apply**. The table is formatted.

10. With the insertion point still in the table, display the **Table** menu, point to **AutoFit**, and then click **AutoFit to Contents**.

(Project 3C–Teacher Promotion continues on the next page)

Word

Skill Assessments (continued)

(Project 3C–Teacher Promotion continued)

11. Display the **Table** menu again and then click **Table Properties**. In the **Table Properties** dialog box, click the **Table tab** if necessary. Under **Alignment**, click the **Center** button and then click **OK**. The table is horizontally centered on the page.

12. Display the **View** menu and then click **Header and Footer**. On the Header and Footer toolbar, click the **Switch Between Header and Footer** button. With the insertion point positioned in the footer area, on the Header and Footer toolbar click the **Insert AutoText** button and then click **Filename**. Close the Header and Footer toolbar.

13. On the Standard toolbar, click the **Save** button and then click the **Print Preview** button to see the document as it will print. Click the **Print** button and then close Print Preview and close the file, saving changes if prompted to do so.

 You have completed Project 3C

Project 3D — Announcement Meeting

Objectives: *Insert Clip Art and Pictures, Modify Clip Art and Pictures, and Work with the Drawing Toolbar.*

In the following Skill Assessment, you will add graphics to an announcement for the upcoming Teacher Day promotion at Sensation! Park. Your completed announcement will look like the one shown in Figure 3.84. You will save your document as *3D_Announcement_Firstname_Lastname*.

1. On the Standard toolbar, click the **Open** button. Navigate to the location where the student files for this textbook are stored. Locate and open **w03D_Announcement**. The document opens at 75% zoom.

2. From the **File** menu, click **Save As**. In the Save As dialog box, use the **Save in arrow** to navigate to the location where you are storing your files for this chapter. In the **File name** box, type 3D_Announcement_Firstname_Lastname using your own name. Click the **Save** button.

3. From the **File** menu, display the **Page Setup** dialog box and click the **Margins tab**. Under **Orientation**, click **Landscape**. Under **Margins**, change the **Top** and **Bottom** boxes to **1.0** and then click **OK**.

4. From the **Tools** menu, click **Options**. Click the **General tab**. Under **General options**, locate the last check box—**Automatically create drawing canvas when inserting AutoShapes**—and be sure that it is unchecked. Clear the check box if necessary. Click **OK**. Recall that to use simple drawing tools, it is useful to turn off the drawing canvas.

(Project 3D–Announcement Meeting continues on the next page)

Skill Assessments (continued)

(Project 3D–Announcement Meeting continued)

Figure 3.84

5. Check to see if your Drawing toolbar is displayed at the bottom of your screen. If it is not, right-click on one of the toolbars and, from the displayed list, click Drawing. Click to place the insertion point to the left of the line that begins *It's been a LONG*. On the Drawing toolbar, click the **Line** button. Drawing a line is similar to drawing an arrow. Drag the crosshair pointer to draw a line under the text *Teacher Appreciation Day*. With the line still selected, on the Drawing toolbar, click the **Line Style** button and then click **2¼ pt**.

6. You can change the color of a line using the Line Color button, which is two buttons to the left of the Line Style button on the Drawing toolbar. With the line still selected, on the Drawing toolbar, locate the **Line Color** button and click its arrow to display a palette of colors. In the second row, click the **fourth color—green**.

7. Place the insertion point on the empty line under *And teachers deserve a break!* From the **Insert** menu, point to **Picture** and then click **Clip Art** from the submenu. In the **Clip Art** task pane, in the **Search for** box, type **teacher** In the **Search in** box, click the arrow and be sure **Everywhere** is selected. In the **Results should be box**, click the arrow and be sure **All media file types** are selected and then click the **Go** button. Locate the clip art image shown in Figure 3.84 and click the image to insert it. If you cannot locate that image, choose another image of a classroom teacher or insert the file **w03D_Teacher**. Close the Clip Art task pane.

(Project 3D–Announcement Meeting continues on the next page)

Skill Assessments (continued)

(Project 3D–Announcement Meeting continued)

8. Place the insertion point to the left of the line that begins *Come on June 22*. On the Drawing toolbar, click **AutoShapes**, point to **Stars and Banners** and then click the first shape—**Explosion 1**. Position the crosshair pointer at approximately **2.5 inches on the vertical ruler** and at the left margin in the horizontal ruler. Drag down so that one of the points is near the word *Come*, as shown in Figure 3.84. The size and placement need not be exact, but if you are not satisfied with your result, click Undo and begin again.

9. Right-click on the **Explosion 1 AutoShape** and, from the displayed shortcut menu, click **Add Text**. Type **Sweepstakes** and then select the text you typed. From the Formatting toolbar, change the font to **Comic Sans MS** and the font size to **16**. Point to a sizing handle and drag to expand the size of the shape until the text is displayed on one line.

10. With the Sweepstakes shape selected, locate the **Fill** button (paint can image) on the Drawing toolbar. Click the button's arrow and, on the displayed color palette, in the last row, click the **first color— Rose**. Click the arrow on the **Line Color** button and, from the displayed palette, click **Rose**. The line around the shape is the same color as the background color. Click the **Save** button.

11. Using the techniques you have just practiced, and using Figure 3.84 as a guide, create three more shapes as listed below. Use the Comic Sans MS 16-pt. font. Use the sizing handles to enlarge or to shrink your AutoShape, and recall that you can drag an AutoShape to a different position. Do not be concerned about exact placement.

AutoShape	Placement	Text	Fill Color	Line Color
24-point star	Lower left corner	**Door Prizes**	Light Yellow	Green
24-point star	Lower right corner	**BBQ Lunch**	Light Yellow	Green
Explosion 1	Right of date	**Discount Prices**	Bright Green	Bright Green

12. Select *Sweepstakes* and, on the Formatting toolbar, click the **Center** button. Repeat this process to center the text in each of the other three AutoShapes.

13. Click the **Sweepstakes shape**. Drag the **Rotate** button to the right until the shape is pointing to the date as shown in Figure 3.84. Adjust the position and sizes of the other shapes so they resemble the arrangement shown in the figure.

(Project 3D–Announcement Meeting continues on the next page)

Skill Assessments (continued)

(Project 3D–Announcement Meeting continued)

14. Display the **View** menu, and then click **Header and Footer**. On the Header and Footer toolbar, click the **Switch Between Header and Footer** button. With the insertion point positioned in the footer area, on the Header and Footer toolbar, click the **Insert AutoText button** and then click **Filename**. Close the Header and Footer toolbar.

15. On the Standard toolbar, click the **Save** button and then click the **Print Preview** button to see the document as it will print. Make sure none of the shapes are outside of the margin area. Click the **Print** button, close Print Preview, and then close the file saving changes if prompted to do so.

End You have completed Project 3D

Project 3E—Budget

Objectives: *Work with Tabs and Work with the Drawing Toolbar.*

In the following Skill Assessment, you will finish a memo by adding the results of the Teacher Promotion day at Sensation! Park. Your completed memo will look like the one shown in Figure 3.85. You will save your document as *3E_Budget_Firstname_Lastname*.

1. On the Standard toolbar, click the **Open** button. Navigate to the location where the student files for this textbook are stored. Locate and open **w03E_Budget**.

2. From the **File** menu, click **Save As**. In the **Save As** dialog box, use the **Save in arrow** to navigate to the location where you are storing your files for this chapter. In the **File name** box, using your own name, type **3E_Budget_Firstname_Lastname** Click the **Save** button.

3. If necessary, click the **Show/Hide ¶** button so you can see the non-printing characters as you complete this exercise. Place the insertion point at the end of the last paragraph—after the period following the word *below*—and press Enter. Spacing is added because spacing of 12 pt. after the paragraph has been set in this document.

4. On the Formatting toolbar, click the **Center** button and then click the **Underline** button. From the **Format** menu, click **Paragraph** and, under **Spacing**, use the spin box arrows to change **After** to **0 pt**. Click **OK**. Type **Attendance** and press Enter twice.

5. On the Formatting toolbar, click the **Align Left** button to change the alignment from Center, click the **Underline** button to turn off underline, and then click the **Increase Indent** button twice. This action indents the insertion point to the 1 inch mark—notice the indicator shown on the ruler.

(Project 3E–Budget continues on the next page)

Skill Assessments (continued)

(Project 3E–Budget continued)

[Figure 3.85 shows a memo document with the following content:

MEMO TO: McNeal Blackmon, President
FROM: Dana Brothers, VP, Marketing
DATE: July 1,
SUBJECT: Teacher Day Promotion Results

The Teacher Day Promotion was a great success with our expected attendance exceeding our plan by 300 people.

Although attendance was higher than expected, actual promotion costs were still very close to our original budget number. The purchasing staff was able to negotiate lower prices on some food and promotional giveaways by making bulk purchases. The marketing team negotiated extremely favorable contracts with the entertainment providers; and, the human resources staff was able to adjust staff schedules for the week to keep overtime hours required to staff this event to a minimum. The budget vs. actual numbers is outlined below.

Attendance

Teacher attendance: 200
Guests and families: 700
Total attendance for teacher promotion: 900

Total park attendance for day: 3,000

Budget Figures

Item	Budget	Actual
BBQ lunch	$7,200.00	$9,000.00
Refreshments/ice cream	1,800.00	1,875.00
Promotional giveaways	5,000.00	3,320.64
Additional parking shuttles	2,250.00	2,032.99
Additional park staff	10,885.00	12,864.98
Entertainment	5,000.00	4,000.00
Total	$32,135.00	$33,093.61

3E_Budget_Firstname_Lastname]

Figure 3.85

6. At the left end of the horizontal ruler, click the **Tab Alignment** button until the **Decimal Tab** marker displays and then click the ruler at the **5 inch** mark. Type the following lines; press [Tab] after typing the text to move to the decimal tab stop and then press [Enter] at the end of each line. Refer to Figure 3.85.

Teacher attendance: 200

Guests and families: 700

Total attendance for teacher promotion: 900

7. Select 700 and, on the Formatting toolbar, click the **Underline** button. Position the insertion point to the right of 900, press [Enter] twice, and then type the following line pressing [Tab] before typing the number:

Total park attendance for day: 3,000

8. Press [Enter] twice. On the Formatting toolbar, click the **Decrease Indent** button twice to move the Left Indent indicator back to the left margin. On the Formatting toolbar, click the **Center** button and then click the **Underline** button. Type **Budget Figures** and press [Enter] twice.

(Project 3E–Budget continues on the next page)

Skill Assessments (continued)

(Project 3E–Budget continued)

9. On the Formatting toolbar, click the **Align Left** button to return to left alignment, click the **Underline** button to turn it off, and then click the **Increase Indent** button once.

10. From the **Format** menu, click **Tabs**. In the lower portion of the **Tabs** dialog box, click the **Clear All** button to remove any tabs from this line. In the **Tab stop position** box, type **3.5** Under **Alignment**, click **Center** and then click the **Set** button. This sets the first tab. In the **Tab stop position** box, type **5.5** and, under **Alignment**, click **Center** and then click **Set**. Two tabs have been set for this line of text. Click **OK** to close the dialog box, and notice the two Center tab stops indicated on the horizontal ruler.

11. Type the following, pressing [Tab] between each word:

    Item   Budget   Actual

12. Press [Enter] twice. From the **Format** menu, click **Tabs**. With **3.5** in the **Tab stop position** box, under **Alignment**, click **Decimal** and then click **Set**. Click the **5.5" tab** to select it, under **Alignment**, click **Decimal** and then click **Set**. The alignment of the two tabs is changed to Decimal. In a decimal tab stop, text aligns around the decimal point. Click **OK** to close the dialog box.

13. Type the following on separate lines, pressing [Tab] between the items listed in the columns:

BBQ lunch	$7,200.00	$9,000.00
Refreshments/ice cream	1,800.00	1,875.00
Promotional giveaways	5,000.00	3,320.64
Additional parking shuttles	2,250.00	2,032.99
Additional park staff	10,885.00	12,864.98
Entertainment	5,000.00	4,000.00
Total	$32,135.00	$33,093.61

14. On the Standard toolbar, click the **Save** button. On the line beginning with *Entertainment*, select **5,000.00**, click the **Underline** button, and then select **4,000.00** and click the **Underline** button.

15. The words *Budget* and *Actual* need to be better aligned over the columns of figures. Click anywhere on the line of headings above the budget figures. On the ruler, drag the first center tab stop one tick-mark (the tiny vertical lines between the numbers on the horizontal ruler) to the left between the 3 and 3.5 inch marks, so the word *Budget* is centered over the column of figures. Drag the second center tab stop one tick-mark to the left between the 5 and 5.5 inch marks to center the word *Actual* over the column of figures. When dragging tab stops, you can place the insertion point anywhere in the line.

(Project 3E–Budget continues on the next page)

Skill Assessments (continued)

(Project 3E–Budget continued)

16. From the **Tools** menu, click **Options** and then click the **General tab**. Under **General options**, in the last check box, if necessary, clear the *Automatically* create drawing canvas when inserting AutoShapes check box. Click **OK**. Recall that it is easier to create simple drawing objects with the drawing canvas turned off.

17. Check to see if your Drawing toolbar is displayed. If necessary, right-click on one of the toolbars and then click Drawing to display the Drawing toolbar. Place the insertion point on the empty line under *Total park attendance for day* and press Enter once. On the Drawing toolbar, click the **Line** button and then position the crosshair pointer at the left margin at approximately **5 inches on the vertical ruler**. Hold Shift, and then drag to form a line from the left to the right margin. Holding down the Shift key ensures that your line will be straight, and not jagged. With the line selected, on the Drawing toolbar, click the **Line Style** button and click **1½ pt**.

18. With the line still selected, on the Standard toolbar, click the **Copy** button and then click the **Paste** button. A copy of the line is pasted under the first line. Drag the second line to a position under the budget as shown in Figure 3.85.

19. Display the **View** menu and then click **Header and Footer**. On the Header and Footer toolbar, click the **Switch Between Header and Footer** button. With the insertion point positioned in the footer area, on the Header and Footer toolbar, click the **Insert AutoText** button and then click **Filename**. Close the Header and Footer toolbar.

20. On the Standard toolbar, click the **Save** button and then click the **Print Preview** button to see the document as it will print. Click the **Print** button, close Print Preview, and then close the file saving changes if prompted to do so.

End You have completed Project 3E

Word
chapter three
Performance Assessments

Project 3F—Refreshments

Objectives: *Insert Clip Art and Pictures, Modify Clip Art and Pictures, Work with the Drawing Toolbar, and Work with Tabs.*

In the following Performance Assessment, you will create a poster for one of the refreshment stands at Sensation! Park. Your completed document will look like the one shown in Figure 3.86. You will save your publication as *3F_Refreshments_Firstname_Lastname*.

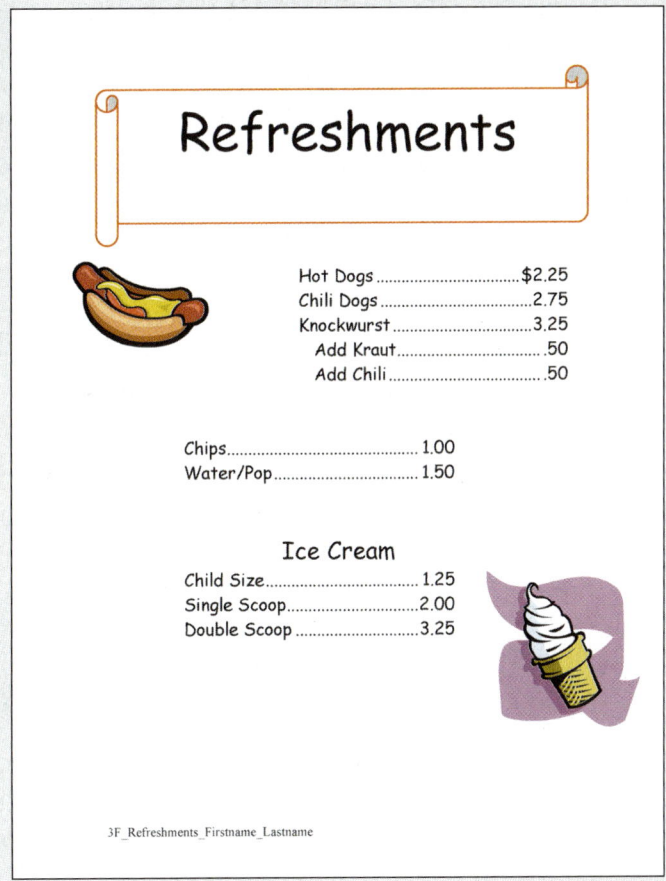

Figure 3.86

1. Start Word and display a blank document. If necessary, close the Getting Started task pane. Be sure that nonprinting characters are displayed; if necessary, click the **Show/Hide ¶** button. Make sure the document is in the **Print Layout** view. From the **Tools** menu, click **Options** and then click the **General tab**. Under General Options, if necessary, clear the check box next to Automatically create drawing canvas when inserting AutoShapes and then click **OK**. Recall that if you want to use a simple drawing object, it is best to turn off the drawing canvas. If necessary, right-click on one of the toolbars and click **Drawing** to display the Drawing toolbar.

(**Project 3F**–Refreshments continues on the next page)

Performance Assessments (continued)

(Project 3F–Refreshments continued)

2. On the Drawing toolbar, click **AutoShapes** and point to **Stars and Banners**. In the displayed menu, in the fourth row, click the second shape—**Horizontal Scroll**. Position the crosshair pointer at the paragraph mark and then drag down and to the right to approximately **2 inches on the vertical ruler** and **6 inches on the horizontal ruler**, as shown in Figure 3.86.

3. Right-click in the **Horizontal Scroll** shape and, from the displayed menu, click **Add Text**. On the Formatting toolbar, change the font to **Comic Sans MS**, the font size to **48**, and the alignment to **Center**. Type **Refreshments** The text is added to the banner in a large font that is centered in the banner. If necessary, drag a sizing handle to adjust the size of the banner so the text is displayed on one line.

4. With the banner shape selected, on the Drawing toolbar, click the arrow on the **Line Color** button. From the displayed palette, click **Red**. Click the **Line Style** button and then click **1½ pt**. The outline of the banner is changed to a thicker red border.

5. Click the **Save** button. In the **Save As** dialog box, navigate to the location where you are saving your files. In the **File name** box, using your own name, type **3F_Refreshments_Firstname_Lastname** and then click the **Save** button.

6. Move the I-beam pointer just below the banner's left edge and double-click to insert one or two paragraph marks and to place the insertion point under the banner. With the insertion point positioned in front of the final paragraph mark, change the font to **Comic Sans MS** and the font size to **16 pt**. Notice that the paragraph mark reflects the changes.

7. From the **Format** menu, click **Tabs**. In the **Tabs** dialog box, in the **Tab stop position** box, type **1** and then, under **Alignment**, click **Left**. Click the **Set** button. The first tab is set. Set a second **Left** tab at **1.3 inches** and a third tab at **4.5 inches** that is a **Right** tab with **Leader option 2**. Click **Set** and then click **OK**.

8. Press [Tab], type **Hot Dogs** press [Tab], type **$2.25** and then press [Enter]. Repeat this pattern to add the next two items shown below. Press [Enter] once after the last line.

    Chili Dogs   2.75

    Knockwurst   3.25

(Project 3F–Refreshments continues on the next page)

Word chapter three
Performance Assessments (continued)

(Project 3F–Refreshments continued)

Press [Tab] twice and type **Add Kraut** Press [Tab] again and type **.50** and then press [Enter]. This add-on is listed under Knockwurst. Press [Tab] twice and type **Add Chili** Press [Tab] again, type **.50** and then press [Enter] twice. Add the rest of the items listed below, pressing [Tab] once at the beginning of each line and again between the item and the price.

Chips	1.00
Water/Pop	1.50
Child Size	1.25
Single Scoop	2.00
Double Scoop	3.25

9. Click to the left of *Chips*, press [Enter] twice, and then press [Tab] once to restore the alignment of *Chips* in the listed items. Click to the left of *Child Size*, press [Enter] three times, and then press [Tab] once to restore the alignment. The prices for ice cream are moved down the page so you can add a subheading. Click the empty line above *Child Size*, change the font size to **22** and the alignment to **Center**, and then type **Ice Cream** Click the **Save** button.

10. Click to the left of *Hot Dogs*, to the left of the first tab mark. Display the **Insert** menu, point to **Picture**, and then click **Clip Art**. In the **Results should be** box, check that *All media file types* is displayed. In the **Search in box**, check that *All collections* is displayed. In the **Clip Art** task pane, in the **Search for** box, type **hot dog** and then click the **Go** button. Scroll down the list and locate the hot dog displayed in Figure 3.86. If you cannot find the hot dog shown in the figure, select another one of your choice or insert from your student files the file w03F_Hot_Dog. Click the image to insert it.

11. Click the inserted image to select it. Right-click to display the shortcut menu, and then click **Format Picture**. Click the **Layout tab**, click **Square**, and then click **OK**. In this case, you want the text to be aligned vertically in a list and not to wrap to the contour of the image. Drag the hot dog image as necessary to the left of the list of hot dog options as shown in Figure 3.86. Use the corner sizing handles to adjust the size of your image if needed. The size of the hot dog graphic used in Figure 3.86 was not changed.

12. Move your insertion point to the right of *1.25* on the *Child Size* row. In the **Clip Art** task pane, in the **Search for** box, replace *hot dog* with **ice cream cone** and then click the **Go** button. Scroll down the list and locate the ice cream cone displayed in Figure 3.86. If you cannot find the ice cream cone shown in the figure, select another one of your choice or, from your student files, insert w03F_Ice_Cream. Click the image to insert it.

(Project 3F–Refreshments continues on the next page)

Word chapter three

Performance Assessments (continued)

(Project 3F–Refreshments continued)

13. Click the inserted image. Display the **Format Picture** dialog box, click **Layout**, click **Square**, and then click **OK**. Position the ice cream cone image to the right of the list of ice cream cone choices as shown in Figure 3.86. Be sure the top of the image is anchored to the Child Size line and not to the Ice Cream heading. Use the corner sizing handles to adjust the size of the image if needed. The image used in Figure 3.86 was not resized. Close the Clip Art task pane.

14. Display the **View** menu and then click **Header and Footer**. Switch to the footer area, click the **Insert AutoText** button, and click **Filename**. Close the Header and Footer toolbar.

15. Click the **Save** button and then click the **Print Preview** button to see the document as it will print. Click the **Print** button, close Print Preview, and then close the file, saving changes if prompted to do so.

 End You have completed Project 3F ————————————————

Project 3G—Hours

Objectives: *Work with the Drawing Toolbar, Create a Table, and Format Tables.*

In the following Performance Assessment, you will create a poster listing the hours of operation at Sensation! Park. Your completed document will look like the one shown in Figure 3.87. You will save your document as *3G_Hours_Firstname_Lastname*.

1. On the Standard toolbar, click the **Open** button. Navigate to the location where the student files for this textbook are stored. Locate and open **w03G_Hours**.

2. From the File menu, open the **Save As** dialog box. Navigate to the location where you are storing your files for this chapter. In the **File name** box, type **3G_Hours_Firstname_Lastname** using your own name. Then click the **Save** button.

3. Click to the left of the first paragraph mark under *May Hours* to position your insertion point. On the Standard toolbar, click the **Insert Table** button, move the mouse pointer to select a table that is 3 columns wide by 4 rows high, and then click once to insert the table.

4. Enter the information in the table as shown below. Do not be concerned about the text alignment or formatting at this time.

Monday-Thursday	1 p.m.	10 p.m.
Friday	1 p.m.	11 p.m.
Saturday and holidays	11 a.m.	11 p.m.
Sunday	NOON	11 p.m.

(Project 3G–Hours continues on the next page)

404 Word | Chapter 3: Using Graphics and Tables

Performance Assessments (continued)

(Project 3G–Hours continued)

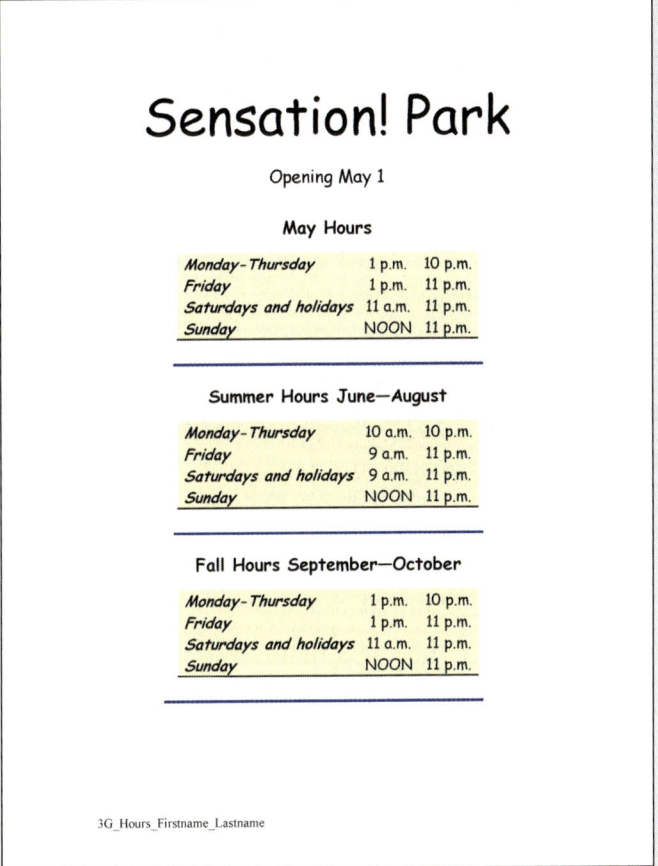

Figure 3.87

5. With your insertion point in the table, display the **Table** menu and then click **Table AutoFormat**. Under **Table styles**, scroll as necessary and then click **Table Colorful 2**. Under **Apply special formats to**, clear the **Heading rows** check box and, if necessary, clear the **Last column** check box. Click **Apply**.

6. Display the **Table** menu, point to **AutoFit**, and then click **AutoFit to Contents**.

7. Select the first column of the table. On the Formatting toolbar, click the **Align Left** button. From the **Table** menu, point to **Select** and then click **Table**. On the Formatting toolbar, click the **Center** button to center the table between the left and right margins.

8. With the table still selected, on the Standard toolbar, click the **Copy** button. Place the insertion point to the left of the first empty paragraph under *Summer Hours* and then click the **Paste** button. Click on the empty paragraph under *Fall Hours* and click the **Paste** button again. The table is copied to the two locations.

(Project 3G–Hours continues on the next page)

Word chapter three
Performance Assessments (continued)

(Project 3G–Hours continued)

9. Change the hours in the table under *Summer Hours* as shown below:

Monday-Thursday	10 a.m.	10 p.m.
Friday	9 a.m.	11 p.m.
Saturday and holidays	9 a.m.	11 p.m.
Sunday	NOON	11 p.m.

10. On the Standard toolbar, click the **Save** button and then, if necessary, display the Drawing toolbar. If necessary, turn off the Drawing Canvas (Tools, Options, General tab). Click the **Line** button and drag a line under the first table between the two empty paragraph marks. Refer to Figure 3.87 to see where to position the line and how long to make it. With the line selected, click the **Line Color** arrow and click **Blue** (second row, sixth from the left) and then click the **Line Style** button and click **2¼**. With the line selected, click **Copy** and then click **Paste** two times. Drag the lines into position under the remaining two tables, similar to the position for the May table. Compare your document to Figure 3.87.

11. Display the **View** menu and click Header and Footer. Switch to the footer area, click the **Insert AutoText** button, and click **Filename**. Close the Header and Footer toolbar.

12. Click the **Save** button and then click the **Print Preview** button to see the document as it will print. Click the **Print** button, close Print Preview, and then close the file, saving changes if prompted to do so.

 You have completed Project 3G

Project 3H—Prices

Objectives: *Create a Table from Existing Text and Format Tables.*

In the following Performance Assessment, you will create a poster with a list of prices for admission to Sensation! Park. Your completed document will look like the one shown in Figure 3.88. You will save your publication as *3H_Prices_Firstname_Lastname*.

1. On the Standard toolbar, click the **Open** button. Navigate to the location where the student files for this textbook are stored. Locate and open **w03H_Prices**.

2. From the **File** menu, open the **Save As** dialog box. Navigate to the location where you are storing your files for this Chapter. In the **File name** box, type **3H_Prices_Firstname_Lastname** using your own name. Then click the **Save** button.

(Project 3H–Prices continues on the next page)

406 Word | Chapter 3: Using Graphics and Tables

Word
chapter three
Performance Assessments (continued)

(Project 3H–Prices continued)

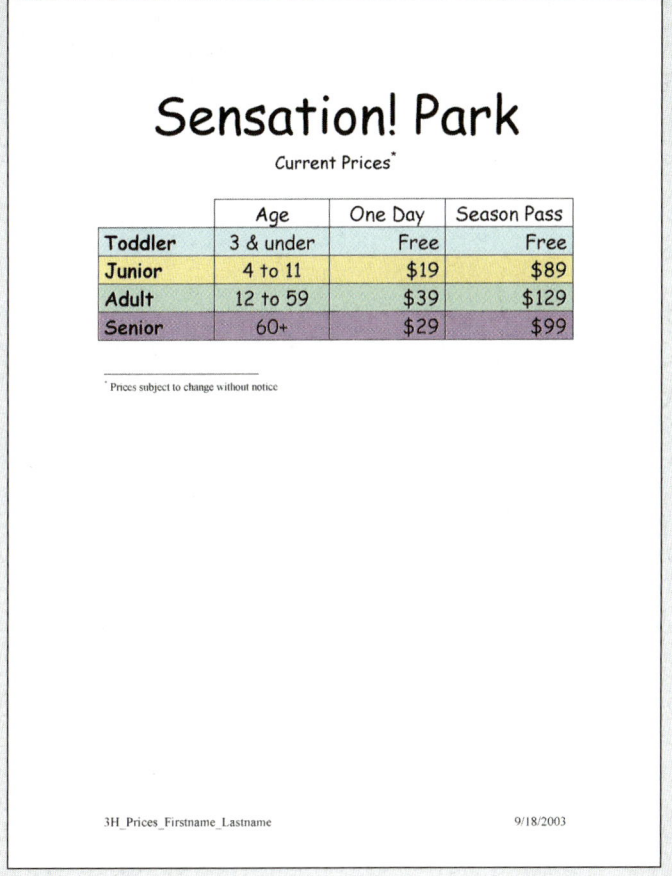

Figure 3.88

3. Click to the left of the first tab mark, left of *Age*, and select the five lines in the tabbed list. From the **Table** menu, point to **Convert** and then click **Text to Table**. In the **Convert Text to Table** dialog box, be sure **4** displays in the **Number of columns** box, and then click **OK**.

4. With the table still selected, using the Formatting toolbar, change the font to **Comic Sans MS** and the font size to **18**. Click anywhere to deselect the table.

5. Select the **first column** of the table and then click the **Bold** button. Select the **first row** of the table and then click the **Center** button. Select the four cells under *Age* and then click the **Center** button. In the last two columns, select the cells under the headings (do not select the headings) and click the **Align Right** button. Click the **Save** button.

(Project 3H–Prices continues on the next page)

Project 3H: Prices | **Word** 407

Performance Assessments (continued)

(Project 3H–Prices continued)

6. Click in the first cell of the table—the one that is empty. From the Format menu, click **Borders and Shading**. In the Borders and Shading dialog box, on the right side, click the **Apply to arrow** and then, from the displayed list, click **Cell**. In the **Preview** area, click the **top** and **left** borders to deselect them and then click **OK**. Click the **Print Preview** button to verify that the top and left borders on the first cell will not print. Close the Print Preview window.

7. Select the row beginning with *Toddler*. From the **Format** menu, click **Borders and Shading** and then click the **Shading tab**. Under **Fill**, in the last row of the color palette, click **Light Turquoise**—the fifth color from the left. The name of the color displays to the right of the color palette after it is selected. Click **OK**.

8. Repeat Step 7 to apply colors to the three remaining rows of the table as follows:

   Junior   Light Yellow

   Adult   Light Green

   Senior   Lavender

9. Place the insertion point to the right of *Current Prices*. From the **Insert** menu, point to **Reference** and then click **Footnote**. In the **Footnote and Endnote** dialog box, under **Location**, click the **Endnotes** option button. Under **Format**, click the **Number format arrow** and, from the displayed list, click the last item—symbols that begin with *. At the lower left of the dialog box, click **Insert**. In the new endnote box, type **Prices subject to change without notice**

10. Display the **View** menu and then click **Header and Footer**. Switch to the footer area, click the **Insert AutoText** button, and then click **Filename**. Press Tab twice and then, on the Header and Footer toolbar, click the **Insert Date** button. Close the Header and Footer toolbar.

11. Click the **Save** button and then click the **Print Preview** button to see the document as it will print. Click the **Print** button, close Print Preview, and then close the file, saving changes if prompted to do so.

End You have completed Project 3H

Mastery Assessments

Project 3I—Water Rides

Objectives: *Insert Clip Art and Pictures, Modify Clip Art and Pictures, Create a Table, Format Tables, and Create a Table from Existing Text.*

In the following Mastery Assessment, you will create a table announcing new water rides at Sensation! Park. Your completed document will look like the one shown in Figure 3.89. You will save your publication as *3I_Water_Rides_ Firstname_Lastname*.

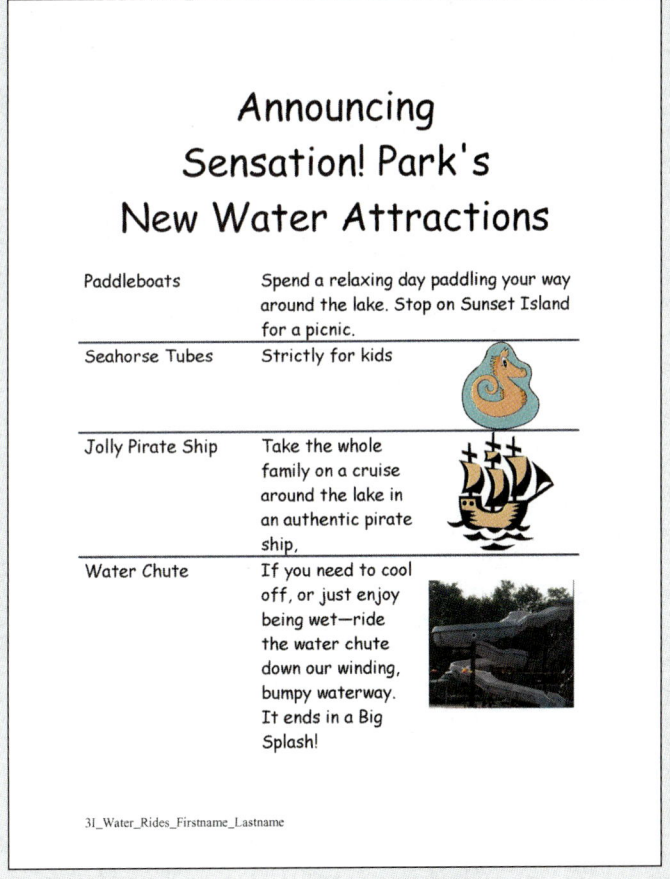

Figure 3.89

1. Start Word. From your student files, open **w03I_Water_Rides**. Save the file with the name **3I_Water_Rides_Firstname_Lastname** in the same location as your other files and using your own name. In the same manner as you have done in previous documents, display the footer and insert the AutoText filename.

2. Select the tabbed list, beginning with *Paddleboats* and ending with *Big Splash!* Convert this text to a two-column table.

3. Add a column to the right side of the table.

(Project 3I–Water Rides continues on the next page)

Word chapter three

Mastery Assessments (continued)

(Project 3I–Water Rides continued)

4. Drag to select the cell beginning with *Spend a relaxing day* and the empty cell to the right. Right-click the selected cells and click **Merge Cells** from the shortcut menu.

5. Click in the empty cell to the right of *Strictly for Kids*. Insert the file **w03I_Seahorse**. Use a corner sizing handle to resize the image to approximately 1 inch wide. With the image still selected, on the **Formatting** toolbar, click the **Center** button.

6. In the cell under the seahorse, insert file **03I_Pirate_Ship**. Resize the image so it is approximately 1 inch wide. With the image still selected, on the **Formatting** toolbar, click the **Center** button

7. Click in the empty cell in the last row. Press **Enter**, and then insert the **w03I_Waterride**.

8. Select the entire table and then display the **Borders and Shading** dialog box. Click the **Borders tab**. Under **Setting**, click **None** to remove all of the borders. In the lower middle of the dialog box, click the **Color arrow** and, from the displayed palette, in the second row, click the sixth color—**Blue**. Click the **Width arrow** and, from the displayed list, click **1½ pt**. In the Preview area, click the button that displays a **horizontal border line** between the rows. A horizontal border is added between the rows in the table preview graphic. Click **OK**.

9. Save the completed document. Preview the document and then print it.

 End You have completed Project 3I

Mastery Assessments (continued)

Project 3J—Events Memo

Objectives: *Create a Table, Format Tables, and Create a Table from Existing Text.*

In the following Mastery Assessment, you will add a table to a memo regarding the events that are planned for the upcoming season at Sensation! Park. In two columns in the memo, you will set tab stops and the hanging indent marker so you can create an indented list. Your completed document will look like the one shown in Figure 3.90. You will save your publication as *3J_Events_Memo_Firstname_Lastname*.

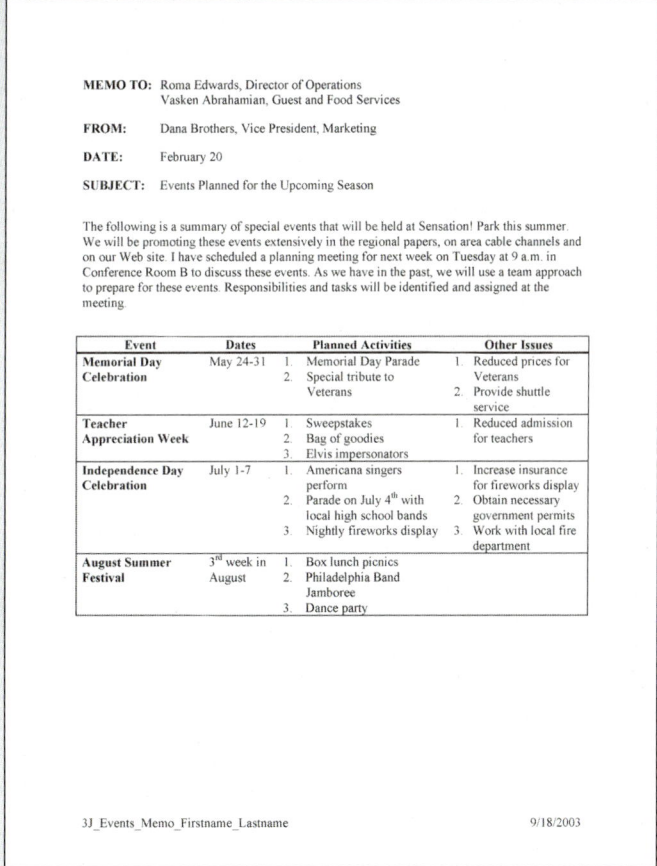

Figure 3.90

1. Start Word. From your student files, open **w03J_Events_Memo**. Save the file with the name **3J_Events_Memo_Firstname_Lastname** in the same location as your other files.

2. Click to position the insertion point to the left of the empty paragraph mark under the paragraph ending with *meeting* and insert a table that has four columns and four rows.

3. Be sure the ruler is displayed on your screen and the left tab indicator displays in the Tab Alignment button. Select the third

(**Project 3J**–Events Memo continues on the next page)

Mastery Assessments (continued)

(Project 3J–Events Memo continued)

column of the table and then click on the ruler at the **3⅝** inch mark (third tick mark to the left of the 4 inch mark) to add a left tab. Point to the gray indent markers on the ruler until the *Hanging Indent* ScreenTip displays and then drag the hanging indent marker for that column to the **3⅝** inch position.

4. Select the fourth column of the table, click to place a left tab stop at **5.25** inches, and then drag the hanging indent marker to that tab stop.

5. Refer to Figure 3.90, and then in the first row of the table, type the information shown below. In the third cell, type **1.** and press Ctrl + Tab to move to the tab stop you created and then continue typing. Press Enter to move to the second line in this cell. Type **2.** press Ctrl + Tab and finish typing the information for the third cell.

   Note that because numbers are used in this example, the AutoCorrect Options button may display to number the list for you. Click **Stop automatically creating numbered lists** from the displayed list. This will stop the AutoCorrect Options feature from creating a numbered list in each cell of the table.

| Memorial Day Celebration | May 24–31 | 1. Memorial Day Parade
2. Special tribute to Veterans | 1. Reduced prices for Veterans
2. Provide shuttle service |

   Press Tab to move to the fourth cell and use same process to type the information so it aligns on the tab stop.

6. Enter the remaining information as shown in the table below. Use the same technique in the third and forth column—type the number and the period and then press Ctrl + Tab before continuing to type the rest of the data. Be sure to press Enter when multiple items are listed in a cell.

Teacher Appreciation Week	June 12–19	1. Sweepstakes 2. Bag of goodies 3. Elvis impersonators	1. Reduced admission for teachers
Independence Day Celebration	July 1–7	1. Americana singers perform 2. Parade on July 4th with local high school bands 3. Nightly fireworks display	1. Increase insurance for fireworks display 2. Obtain necessary government permits 3. Work with local fire department
August Summer Festival	3rd week in August	1. Box lunch picnics 2. Philadelphia Band Jamboree 3. Dance party	

(Project 3J–Events Memo continues on the next page)

Word chapter three

Mastery Assessments (continued)

(Project 3J–Events Memo continued)

7. Click in the first row of the table and insert a new row above. Type the following headings in this new first row:

   Event   Dates   Planned Activities   Other Issues

8. Select the table and use the **AutoFormat** dialog box to apply the **Table List 5** format to the table. Use **AutoFit** to fit the table to the contents and then center the column headings.

9. In the same manner as you have done in previous documents, display the footer and insert the **AutoText filename**. Press to move to the right side of the footer. Notice that the right tab stop for the footer is not aligned with the right margin. On the ruler, drag the right tab stop to align with the right margin, and then click the **Insert Date** button.

10. Save the completed document. Preview the document and then print it.

End   You have completed Project 3J

Word chapter three — Problem Solving

Project 3K — Resume

Objectives: *Create a Table and Format Tables.*

The Table tool is convenient for creating resumes. In this Problem-Solving exercise, you will use a table to create your own resume. Your completed document will look similar to the one shown in Figure 3.91. You will save your resume as *3K_Resume_Firstname_Lastname*.

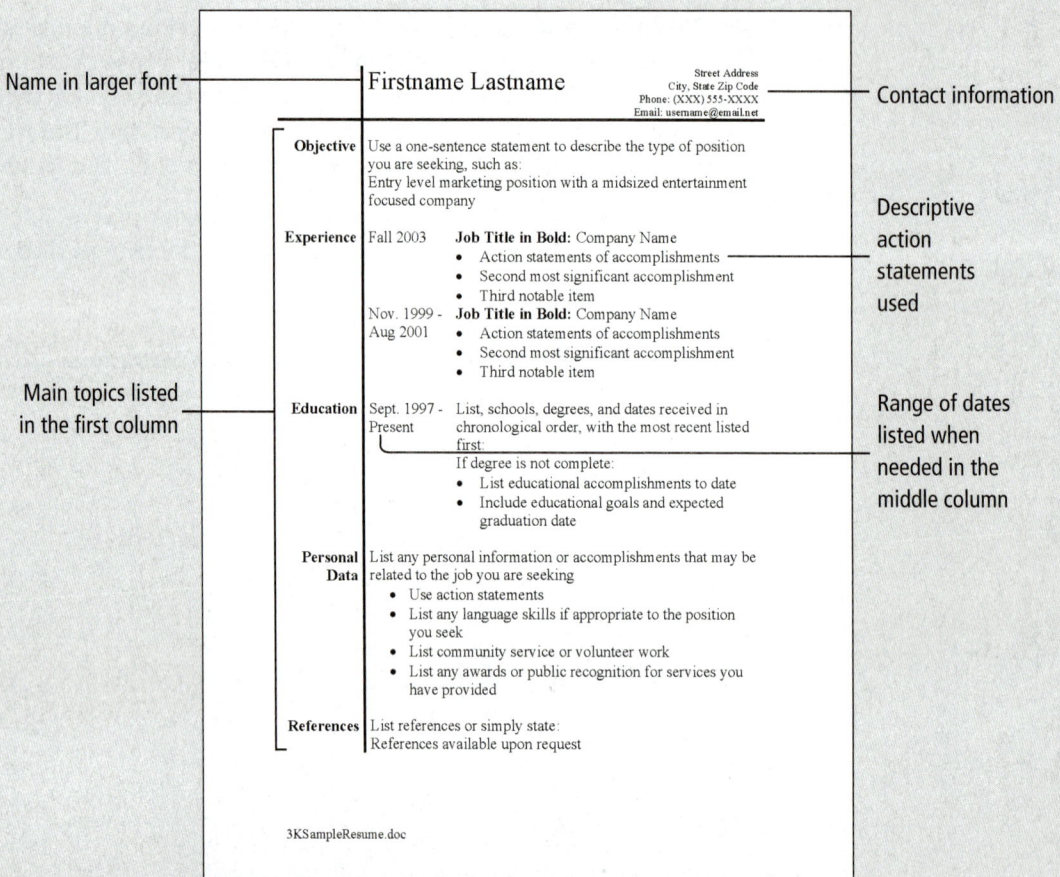

Figure 3.91

1. Examine Figure 3.91. This sample of a resume uses a three-column table with only a first column and first row border displayed. The middle column is used for dates when needed or merged with the third cell in the row to expand the text across a wider area.

2. Examine Figure 3.92, which displays the resume as it looks in Word. Notice the rows that have been added to increase space between major headings. The major topics in the left column have been aligned on the left and bold emphasis has been added.

(**Project 3K**–Resume continues on the next page)

414   **Word** | Chapter 3: Using Graphics and Tables

Word chapter three

Problem Solving (continued)

(Project 3K–Resume continued)

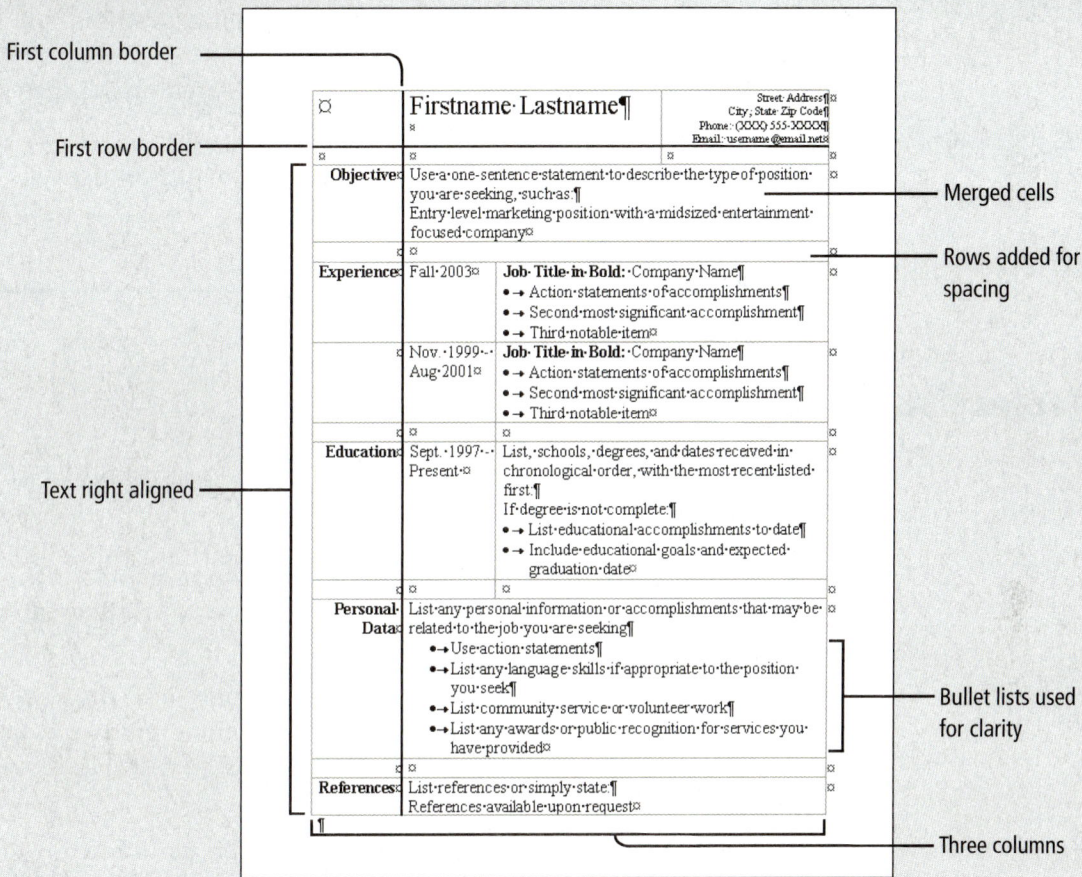

Figure 3.92

3. Create a three-column table with four rows to start—you can add more rows as needed. Remove all of the borders.

4. Select the top row and add a bottom border and then select the first column and add a right border. The bottom border of the first cell may be overwritten when you add the border to the right of the first column. Select the top left cell and re-apply the bottom border.

5. Fill in your name and personal information at the top of the table, formatting it appropriately.

6. The objective statement should be directed toward the job for which you are applying. You can write this as if applying for the job you already have, one you would like to have, or for a specific job posting.

7. Using the figures as a model, enter information for your own resume. The content of the figures provides tips on the type of information and format to use when writing a resume.

(Project 3K–Resume continues on the next page)

Problem Solving (continued)

(Project 3K–Resume continued)

8. Proofread your resume and remove any spelling, grammar, or typographical errors. Save the document as **3K_Resume_Firstname_Lastname** In the footer area, using the AutoText button, insert the file name.

9. Print the document and then close the file, saving changes if prompted to do so.

 You have completed Project 3K

Project 3L — July 4th

Objectives: *Insert Clip Art and Pictures, Modify Clip Art and Pictures, Work with Tab Stops, Work with the Drawing Toolbar*

Sensation! Park has several events that it needs to promote for the upcoming season. In this Problem Solving exercise, you will create a promotional poster for the July 4th Celebration.

1. Type the name of the park at the top of the page and then use an AutoShape to create a banner for the event name. Add an event title in the shape you selected and format the font to a size and style that will make it stand out.

2. Using the skills you have practiced in this chapter and your imagination, create and format a table listing four to five planned activities and the scheduled day and times during the week of July 4.

3. Add clip art, such as fireworks, picnics, or pictures of parades to call attention to the events that are planned for the week.

4. Add a text box or a callout shape and draw a line to point out a special event or time.

5. Add a tabbed list of discounts that are offered for special groups or large parties.

6. Preview the document. Make sure the font style is consistent throughout and the various components are balanced on the page.

7. Save the document as **3L_July_4th_Firstname_Lastname** In the footer area, using the AutoText button, insert the file name.

8. Print the document and then close the file, saving changes if prompted to do so.

 You have completed Project 3L

416   Word | Chapter 3: Using Graphics and Tables

On the Internet

Clip Art on the Internet

You do not have to limit your choice of clip art or pictures to those images that come with Microsoft Word. You can download clip art images or select pictures to use from the Web. You can also insert pictures from your own files into any Word document. If you use images from a proprietary Web site, such as National Geographic, you must provide proper credit and reference to the location where the images were found. In some cases, a Web site will state specifically that all content is copyrighted and cannot be used without written permission. Web sites offering free clip art images do not have that requirement.

1. Open your Web browser and go to a search engine such as www.google.com or www.yahoo.com. Type the key words **clip art** and **free** in the search box.

2. Look through the various sites for one you like that has a variety of interesting graphics. There are several that do not require that you sign up for advertising or provide your e-mail address.

3. Find a site you like and practice inserting images in a Word document. When you right-click on an image, you can either copy it or use the Save as option from the shortcut menu to save it to your disk.

4. Open a Word document and insert some new images you found on the Web. Try more than one site to sample the variety of Web sites available.

5. If you like a site you found, you can add it to your Favorite Sites list or bookmark it.

6. Close your browser and close Word.

GO! with Help

Changing Text Orientation

You may want to change the orientation of text in a Word document so it is vertical instead of horizontal. You can do this in a table or by using a text box. There are several tutorials in the Word Help program that provide instructions on how to change the orientation of text.

1. Start Word. In the Type a Question for Help box, type **Text Orientation** Scroll through the list of topics that displays in the Search Results task pane. From this list of help topics, click **Change the orientation of text**.

2. In a blank document, create a text box and type your name. Follow the directions to practice changing the orientation in a text box.

3. Create a 3-by-2 (three columns by two rows) table and type random words in the table. Try changing the orientation of the first column of text in your table. Use Word Help if necessary to provide instructions. This process also works in drawing objects.

4. Close the Help task pane and exit Word.

Word 2003

chapter four

Creating Documents with Multiple Columns and Special Formats

In this chapter, you will: complete these projects and practice these skills.

Project 4A
Creating a Newsletter

Objectives
- Create a Decorative Title
- Create Multicolumn Documents
- Add Special Paragraph Formatting
- Use Special Character Formats

Project 4B
Creating a Web Page

Objectives
- Insert Hyperlinks
- Preview and Save a Document as a Web Page

Project 4C
Creating a Memo

Objectives
- Locate Supporting Information
- Find Objects with the Select Browse Object Button

The City of Desert Park

Desert Park, Arizona, is a thriving city with a population of just under 1 million in an ideal location serving major markets in the western United States and Mexico. Desert Park's temperate year-round climate attracts both visitors and businesses, and it is one of the most popular vacation destinations in the world. The city expects and has plenty of space for long-term growth, and most of the undeveloped land already has a modern infrastructure and assured water supply in place.

© Getty Images, Inc.

Creating Documents with Multiple Columns and Special Formats

Creating a newsletter is usually a job reserved for ***desktop publishing*** programs, such as Microsoft Publisher. Word, however, has a number of tools that enable you to put together a simple, yet effective and attractive newsletter.

Newsletters consist of a number of elements, but nearly all have a title—called a ***masthead***—story headlines, articles, and graphics. The text is often split into two or three columns, making it easier to read than one-column articles. Column widths can be changed, text is usually justified, and lines can be inserted to separate columns.

Newsletters are often printed, but they can also be designed as Web pages. Links to other Web sites can be included and can be accessed by clicking words or graphics. Microsoft Word provides research tools to find information included in the Office package or information on the Web. These materials can be collected and then pasted into different parts of the document.

Project 4A Garden Newsletter

In this chapter, you will edit and format newsletters and add elements such as mastheads, borders, and shading. You will add links and save a document as a Web page. You will also use research tools to find information and place it in a document.

In Activities 4.1 through 4.10 you will edit a newsletter for the City of Desert Park Botanical Gardens. You will add a WordArt masthead and a decorative border line. You will also change the text of the articles from one column to two columns and then format the columns. Finally, you will use special text formatting features to change the font color and set off one of the paragraphs with a border and shading. Your completed document will look similar to Figure 4.1.
You will save your document as *4A_Garden_Newsletter_Firstname_Lastname*.

Figure 4.1
Project 4A—Garden Newsletter

Objective 1
Create a Decorative Title

The title at the top of a newsletter should be short and distinctive. Microsoft Word uses an Office program called **WordArt** to change text into a decorative graphic. WordArt can be formatted, even after the text has been changed to a graphic. Word also has attractive borders that can be used to separate the masthead from the articles.

Activity 4.1 Inserting WordArt

1 Start Word. On the Standard toolbar, click the **Open** button. Navigate to the location where the student files for this textbook are stored. Locate **w04A_Garden_Newsletter** and click once to select it. Then, in the lower right corner of the **Open** dialog box, click **Open**.

The w04A_Garden_Newsletter file opens.

2 From the **File** menu, click **Save As**. In the **Save As** dialog box, click the **Save in arrow** and navigate to the location in which you are storing your files for this chapter, creating a new folder for chapter 4 if you want to do so.

3 Type **4A_Garden_Newsletter_Firstname_Lastname** in the **File name** box, using your own name, and click **Save**. On the Standard toolbar, click the Zoom button arrow, and then click Page Width.

4 Be sure that you have the nonprinting characters displayed and notice the two blank lines at the top of the document. With the insertion point positioned to the left of the first blank paragraph mark, display the **Insert** menu, point to **Picture**, and then click **WordArt**.

The WordArt Gallery dialog box displays.

5 Under **Select a WordArt style**, in the second row, click the fifth option as shown in Figure 4.2.

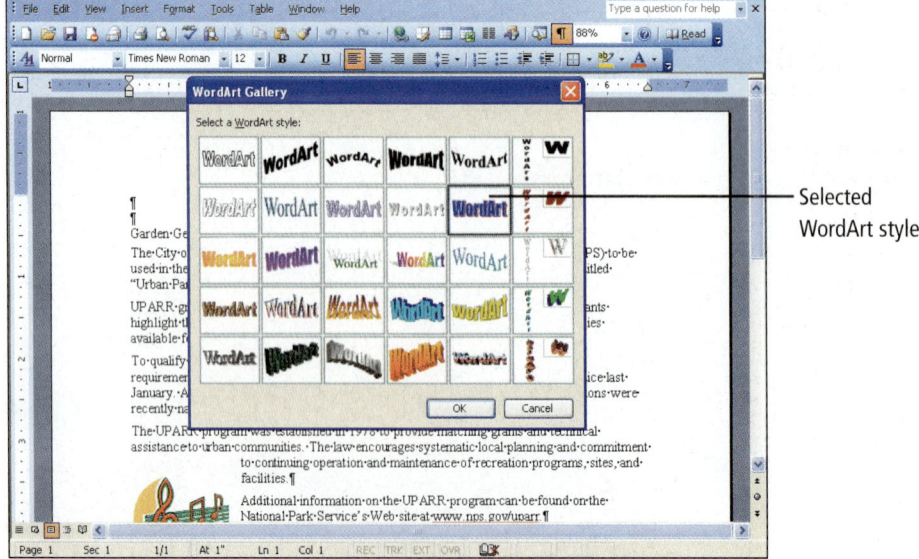

Figure 4.2

422 Word | Chapter 4: Creating Documents with Multiple Columns and Special Formats

6 At the bottom of the **WordArt Gallery** dialog box, click **OK**.

The Edit WordArt Text dialog box displays with placeholder text *Your Text Here*. As soon as you begin to type, the placeholder text will be replaced.

7 In the **Edit WordArt Text** dialog box, under **Text**, type **Botanical Notes**

The text you type displays. The default font size is 36 points, and the default font is Impact. Compare your Edit WordArt Text dialog box to Figure 4.3.

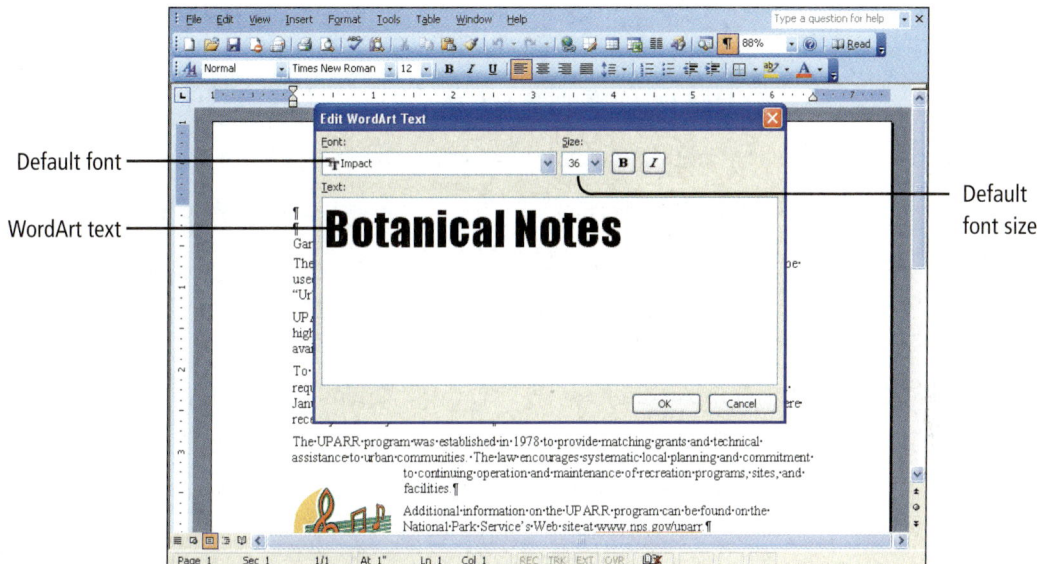

Figure 4.3

8 At the bottom of the **Edit WordArt Text** dialog box, click **OK**.

The WordArt graphic is inserted at the insertion point location, as shown in Figure 4.4.

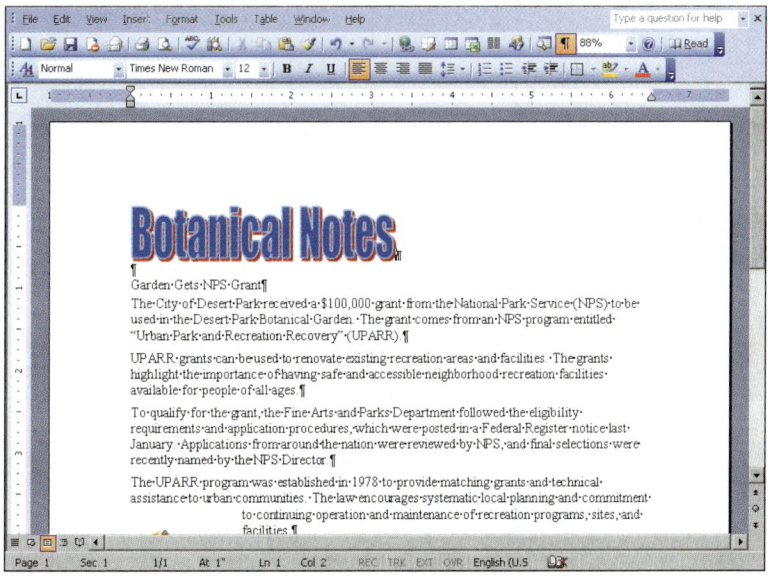

Figure 4.4

Project 4A: Garden Newsletter | **Word** 423

9 On the Standard toolbar, click the **Save** button.

Activity 4.2 Formatting WordArt

When you create a WordArt image, a good technique is to create the graphic at the default (36-point) font size and then adjust it after you see how it fits in the allotted space.

1 Click the **WordArt object** to select it, and notice that the WordArt toolbar displays, floating somewhere on your screen. Pause your mouse pointer over each button to display the ScreenTip and examine the description of each button in the table in Figure 4.5.

Buttons on the WordArt Toolbar

ScreenTip	Button	Description
Insert WordArt		Inserts a new WordArt object.
Edit Text	Edit Text...	Opens the Edit WordArt dialog box so that the text for an existing WordArt object can be modified.
WordArt Gallery		Opens the WordArt Gallery so that a new design can be applied to an existing WordArt object.
Format WordArt		Opens the Format WordArt dialog box so that fill colors, size, position, and layout can be modified.
WordArt Shape		Displays options for changing the shape of an existing WordArt object.
Text Wrapping		Displays the text wrapping menu.
WordArt Same Letter Heights		Changes the height of lowercase letters so that they are the same height as uppercase letters.
WordArt Vertical Text		Displays WordArt text vertically.
WordArt Alignment		Applies alignment options to a WordArt object.
WordArt Character Spacing		Adjusts the amount of spacing between WordArt characters.

Figure 4.5

2 On the WordArt toolbar, click the **Edit Text** button. Alternatively, move the pointer over the new WordArt graphic and double-click.

The Edit WordArt Text dialog box displays.

Note — If the WordArt Toolbar Disappears

If the WordArt toolbar has been turned off, you may have to turn it on using the menu. Display the View menu, point to Toolbars, and click WordArt from the Toolbar menu. If you click outside of the WordArt graphic, the toolbar will close. To reactivate the toolbar, click the WordArt graphic again.

3 In the **Edit WordArt Text** dialog box, click the **Size arrow** and then, from the displayed list, click **66**. Click **OK**.

The masthead of the newsletter you created using WordArt reaches nearly to the right margin.

4 Look at the horizontal ruler and locate the boundary of the right margin—the area at 6.5 inches where the shading changes. On the right edge of the masthead, drag the middle sizing handle to align approximately with the right margin. See Figure 4.6.

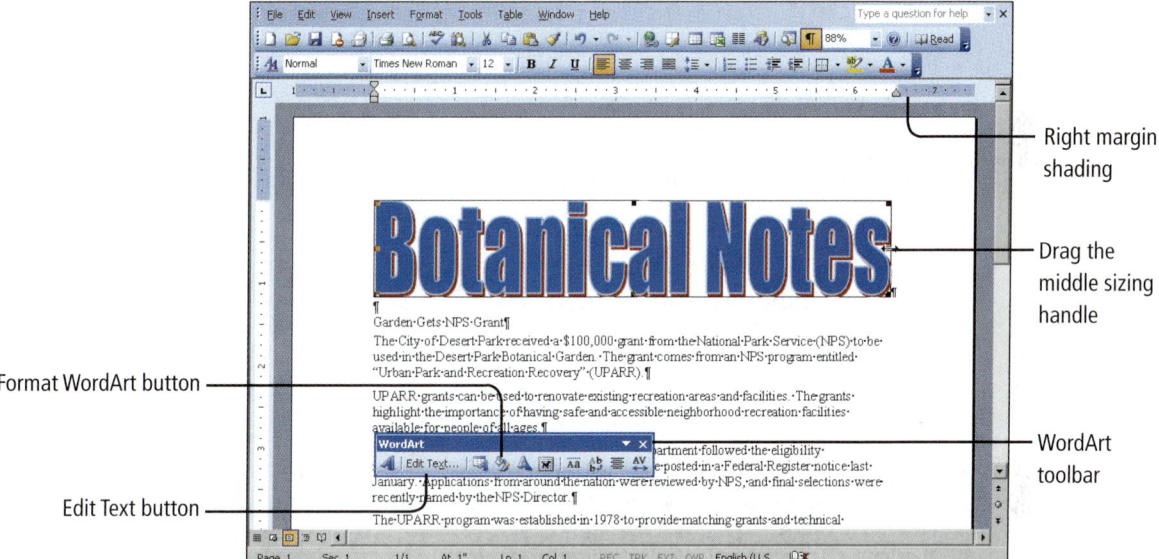

Figure 4.6

5 On the **WordArt** toolbar, click the **Format WordArt** button. If necessary, click the Colors and Lines tab.

Project 4A: Garden Newsletter | **Word** 425

6 Under **Fill**, click the **Color arrow**.

A color palette displays, as shown in Figure 4.7.

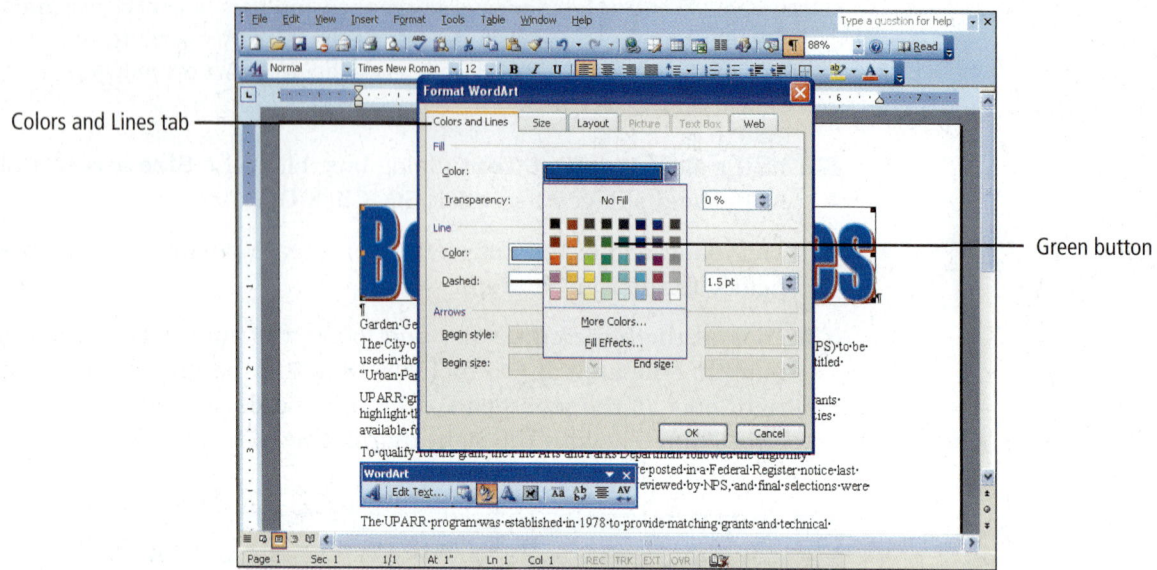

Figure 4.7

7 In the second row of color options, click the fourth color—**Green**. At the bottom of the **Format WordArt** dialog box, click **OK**.

The WordArt letters that form the newsletter's masthead letters change from blue to green.

8 On the Standard toolbar, click the **Save** button.

Activity 4.3 Adding a Border Line

A line between the masthead and the rest of the material makes the newsletter look more professional. Word provides many decorative line types that you can add to your document.

1 In the blank line below the masthead, click to position the insertion point.

2 From the **Format** menu, click **Borders and Shading**.

The Borders and Shading dialog box displays.

3 If necessary, click the Borders tab. Under **Setting**, click the **Custom** option.

4 Under **Style**, scroll down about halfway and click the double line with the heavy top and lighter bottom lines.

5 Under **Preview**, click the **Bottom Border** button.

Compare your dialog box to Figure 4.8.

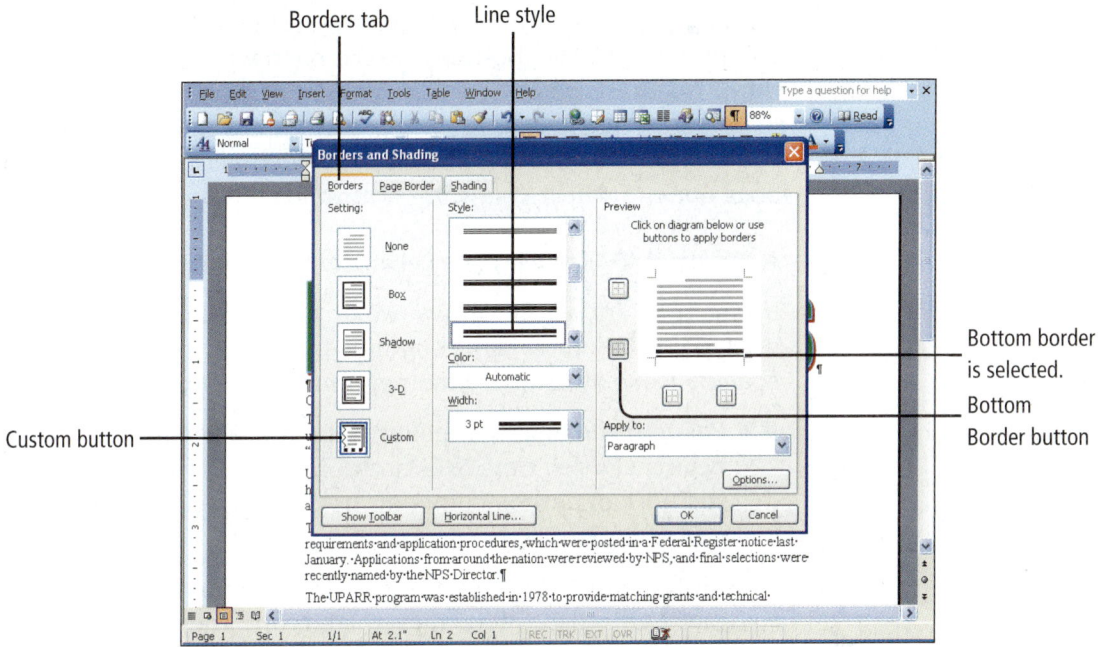

Figure 4.8

6 At the bottom of the **Borders and Shading** dialog box, click **OK**.

The double-line border is inserted at the bottom of the empty paragraph and stretches from the left margin to the right margin. See Figure 4.9.

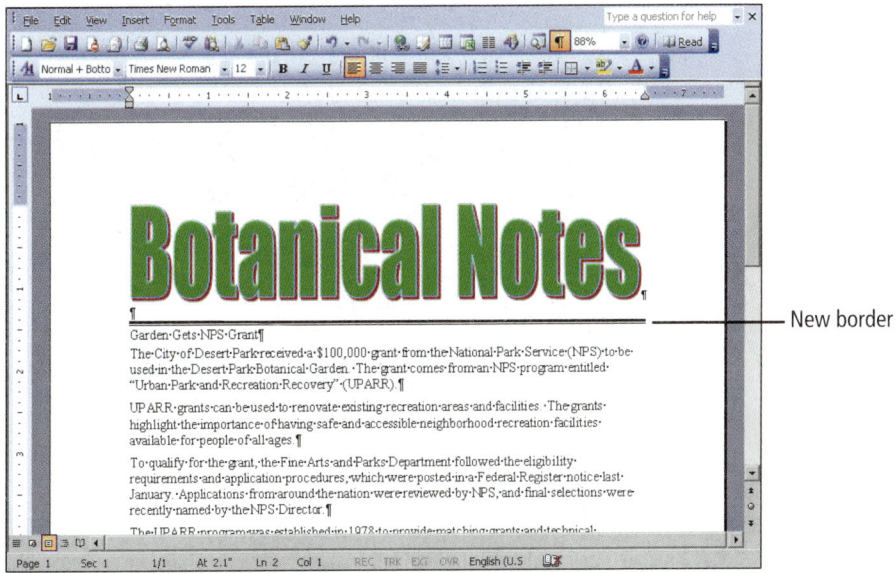

Figure 4.9

7 On the Standard toolbar, click the **Save** button.

Project 4A: Garden Newsletter | **Word** 427

Objective 2
Create Multicolumn Documents

All newspapers and most magazines and newsletters use multiple columns for articles because text in narrower columns is easier to read than text that stretches across a page. Word has a tool that enables you to change a single column of text into two or more columns. The columns can be formatted, and a line can be added between columns. If a column does not end where you want, a ***manual column break*** can be inserted.

Activity 4.4 Changing One Column to Two Columns

Newsletters are nearly always two or three columns wide. It is probably not wise to create four or more columns because they are so narrow that word spacing looks awkward, often resulting in one long word by itself on a line.

1 Position the insertion point to the left of the first line of text, which begins *Garden Gets NPS Grant*. Use the Scroll bar to scroll down to the bottom of the document, hold down [Shift], and then click at the end of the last line.

All the text is selected. Do not be concerned about selecting the two pictures—they will be moved later, and they are not affected by changing the number of columns.

2 On the Standard toolbar, click the **Columns** button .

A Columns menu displays, showing up to four possible columns.

3 Move the pointer over the second column.

Two columns are highlighted, and the bottom of the menu displays the number of columns, as shown in Figure 4.10.

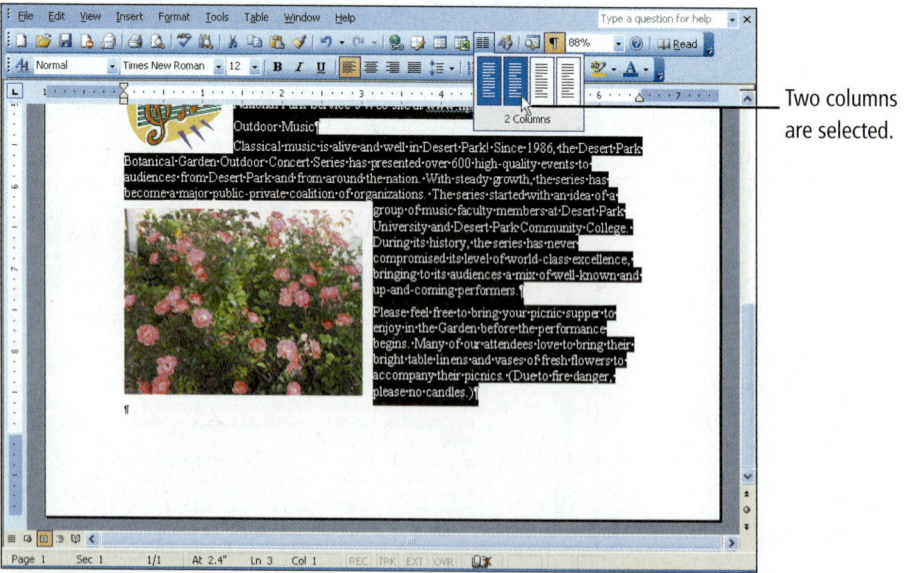

Two columns are selected.

Figure 4.10

428 **Word** | Chapter 4: Creating Documents with Multiple Columns and Special Formats

4 Click the mouse button and then scroll up as necessary to view the top of your document.

The text is divided into two columns, and a section break is inserted below the masthead, dividing the one-column section from the two-column section. Do not be concerned with the placement of the pictures—one may be displayed on top of the other, or one may display outside the document margin. See Figure 4.11.

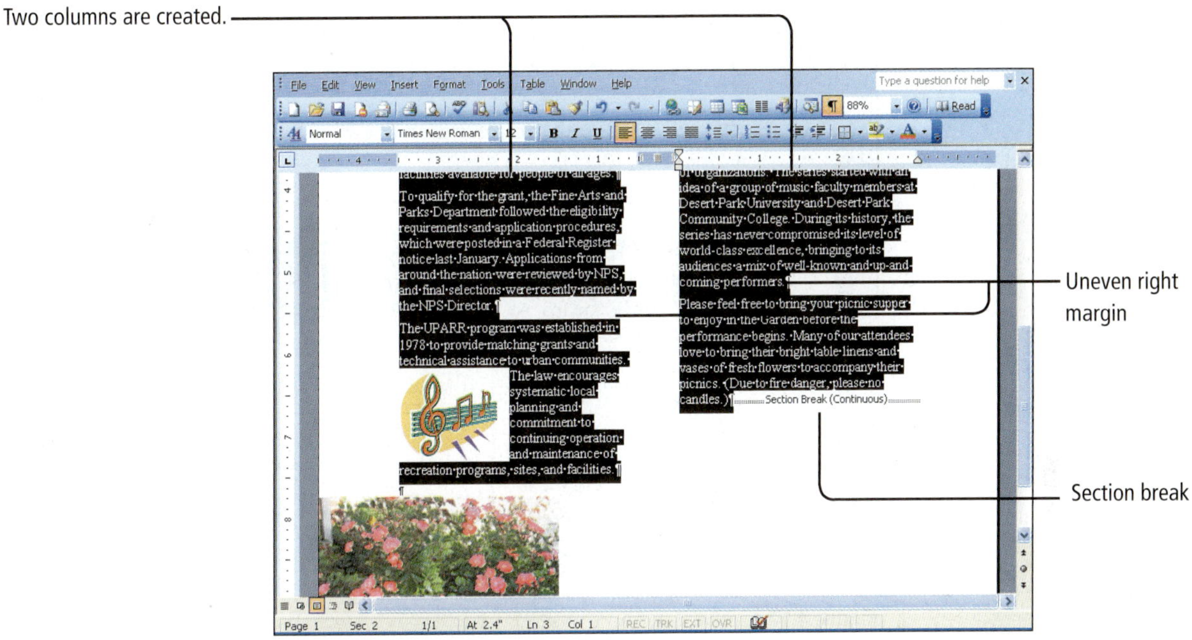

Two columns are created.

Uneven right margin

Section break

Figure 4.11

5 On the Standard toolbar, click the **Save** button.

Activity 4.5 Formatting Multiple Columns

The ragged right edge of a single page width column is readable. When you create narrow columns, justified text is preferable. The font you choose should also match the type of newsletter.

1 With the text still selected, on the Formatting toolbar, click the **Font button arrow** Times New Roman.

The Font menu displays.

2 From the **Font** menu, scroll to and click **Comic Sans MS**. Alternatively, you can press C to move to the first font beginning with that letter, and then scroll down to the desired font.

Because the Comic Sans MS font is larger than Times New Roman, the text expands to a second page.

3 On the Formatting toolbar, click the arrow **Font Size button arrow** 12 and then click **10**.

The document returns to a single page.

Project 4A: Garden Newsletter | **Word** 429

4 On the Formatting toolbar, click the **Justify** button. Scroll to the top of the document and click anywhere in the document to deselect the text.

The font is changed to 10-point Comic Sans MS, an informal, easy-to-read font, and the text is justified. See Figure 4.12. The text at the top of the second column may differ from the figure because of the displaced pictures. This will be adjusted later.

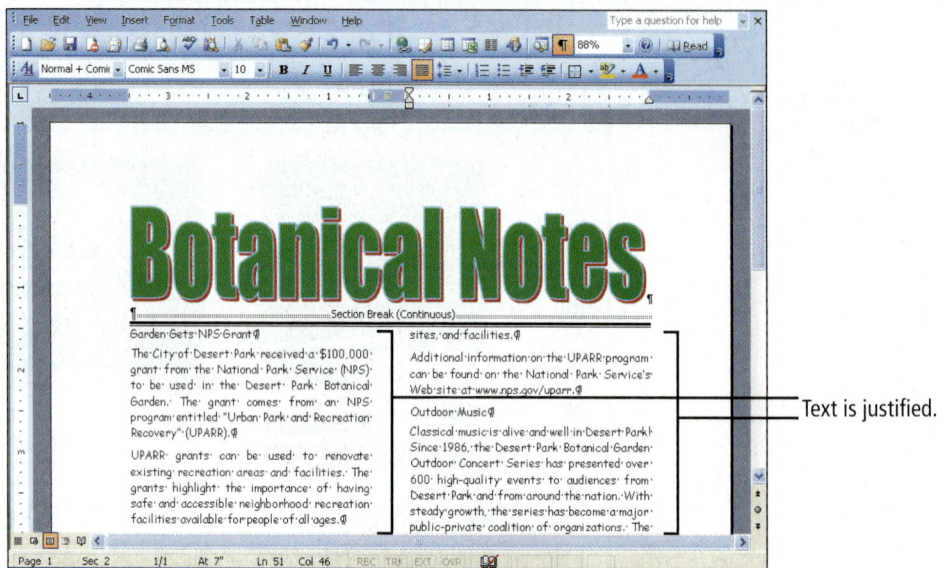

Text is justified.

Figure 4.12

5 From the **View** menu, click **Header and Footer**.

The Header and Footer toolbar displays.

6 On the Header and Footer toolbar, click the **Switch Between Header and Footer** button.

The insertion point is positioned in the footer box.

7 On the Header and Footer toolbar, click the **Insert AutoText** button, and then click **Filename**.

The file name is inserted in the footer. Do not be concerned if one of the pictures is covering your footer—this will be adjusted in a later activity.

8 On the Header and Footer toolbar, click the **Close** button.

9 On the Standard toolbar, click the **Save** button.

Activity 4.6 Inserting a Column Break

Manual column breaks can be inserted to adjust columns that end or begin awkwardly or to make space for graphics or text boxes.

1 On the Standard toolbar, click the **Print Preview** button.

If the newsletter was printed at this point, the ends of the columns would be uneven.

2 On the Print Preview toolbar, click the **Close** button. Position the insertion point to the left of the paragraph at the bottom of the first column that begins *The UPARR program was established*.

3 From the **Insert** menu, click **Break**.

The Break dialog box displays. See Figure 4.13. Here you can insert column breaks, page breaks, or text-wrapping breaks. You can also set four types of section breaks. The *Next page* break moves the text after the break to the next page of your document, whereas a *Continuous break* creates a section break on the same page. *Even page* and *Odd page* breaks are used when you need to have a different header or footer for odd and even pages in a manuscript, manual, or other long document that will be printed on two-sided paper.

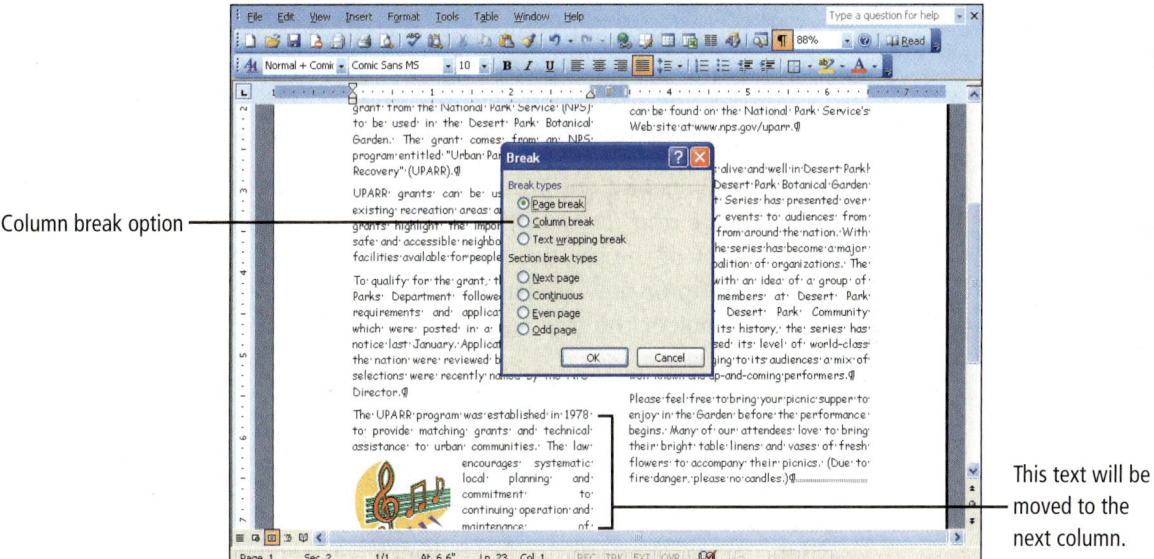

Figure 4.13

4 Under **Break types**, click the **Column break** option button.

5 At the bottom of the **Break** dialog box, click **OK**.

The column breaks at the insertion point, and the text following the insertion point moves to the top of the next column. See Figure 4.14.

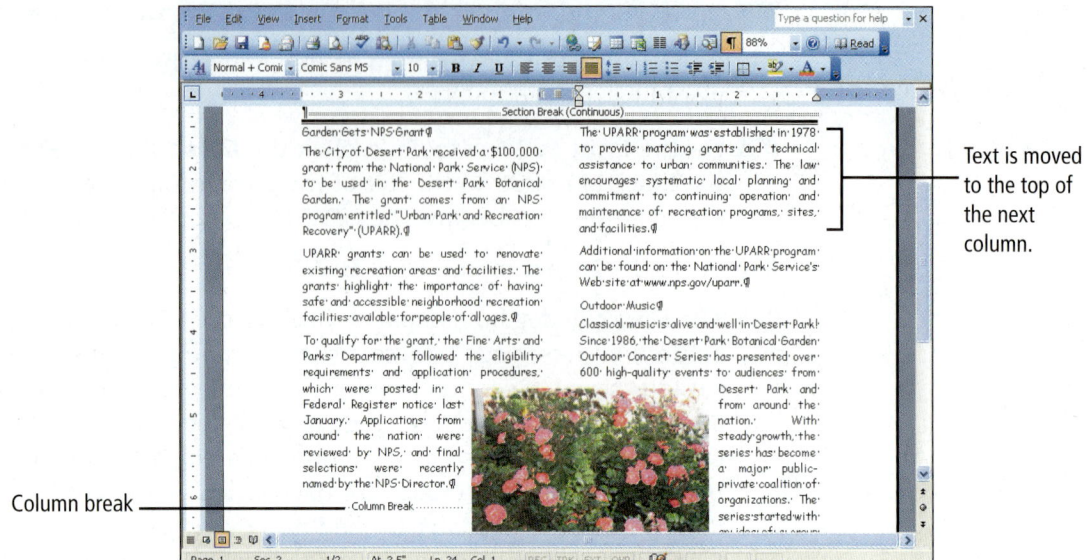

Figure 4.14

6 Position the document so that you can view the lower portion on your screen. Point to the picture of the flowers, hold down the left mouse button, and then drag the picture of the flowers slightly below the column break you just inserted at the bottom of the first column. Align the top edge of the picture at approximately **6 inches on the vertical ruler**.

7 In the second column, in the paragraph that begins *Classical music is alive and well*, drag the picture of the musical notes so the right border of the picture aligns with the right side of the column, then drag up or down as necessary to match Figure 4.15. Click anywhere to deselect the image.

Your newsletter should look similar to Figure 4.15.

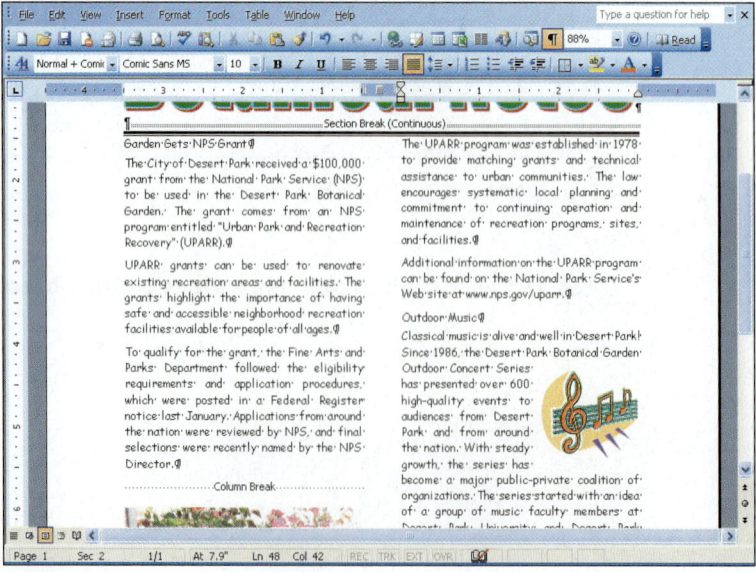

Figure 4.15

432 **Word** | Chapter 4: Creating Documents with Multiple Columns and Special Formats

8 On the Standard toolbar, click the **Save** button .

> **More Knowledge** — Balancing Column Breaks
>
> You can also insert a column break to help balance columns so that they end evenly. This is important when the end of the columns is not the end of the document. If you want to balance the columns in a document, switch to Print Layout view, if necessary, and click at the end of the last column. On the Insert menu, click Break and then click the Continuous section break option. This will cause the end of the columns to be approximately even.

Objective 3
Add Special Paragraph Formatting

Sometimes you will want to call attention to specific paragraphs of text. One way to do this is to place a border around the paragraph. You can also shade a paragraph, although use caution not to make the shade too dark, because it will be hard to read the text.

Activity 4.7 Adding a Border to a Paragraph

Paragraph borders provide strong visual cues to the reader.

1 At the top of the second column, in the second paragraph that begins *Additional information on the UPARR program*, triple-click in the paragraph to select it.

The paragraph is selected.

2 From the **Format** menu, click **Borders and Shading**.

The Borders and Shading dialog box displays.

> **Note** — Adding Borders to Text
>
> *Add Simple Borders Using the Outside Border Button*
>
> Simple borders, and border edges, can be added using the Outside Border button on the Formatting toolbar. This button offers very little control, however, because line thickness and color depends on the previous thickness and color chosen from the Borders and Shading dialog box.

3 Under **Setting**, click **Box**.

4 Under **Width**, click the arrow and then click **1½ pt**.

Compare your Borders and Shading dialog box to Figure 4.16. Notice that the Apply to box displays *Paragraph*. The Apply to box directs where the border will be applied—in this case, the border that has been set will be applied to the paragraph that is selected.

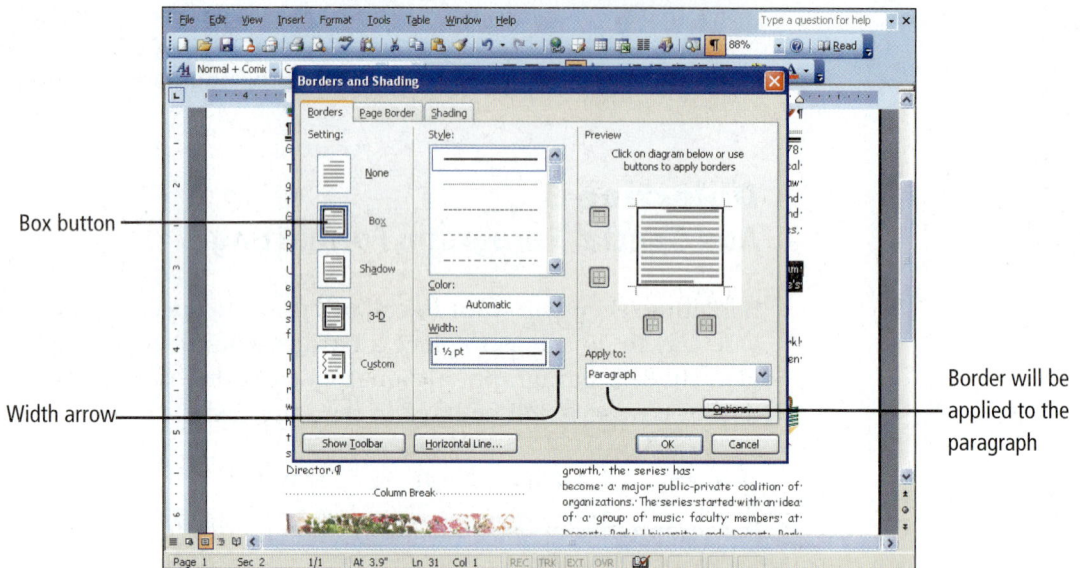

Figure 4.16

5 At the bottom of the **Borders and Shading** dialog box, click **OK**.

A border has been placed around the paragraph, as shown in Figure 4.17.

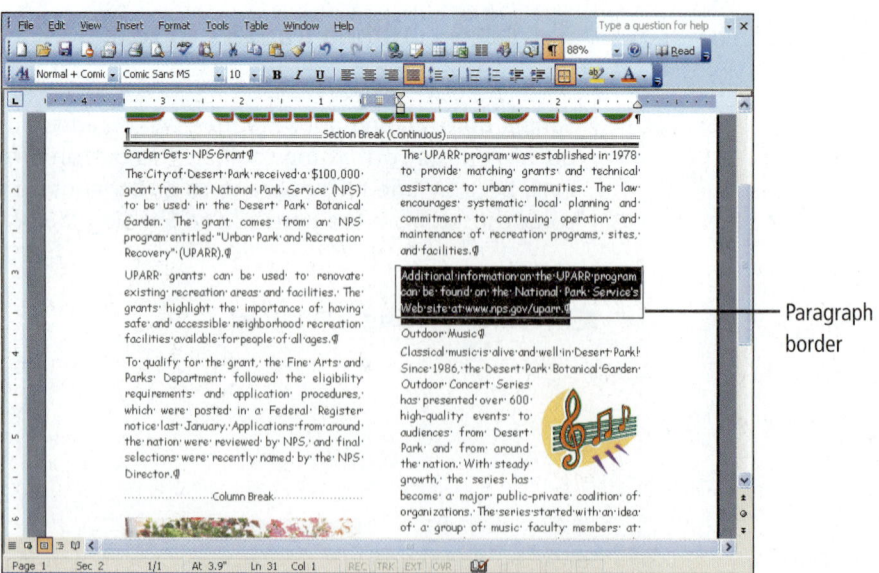

Figure 4.17

6 On the Standard toolbar, click the **Save** button.

434   Word | Chapter 4: Creating Documents with Multiple Columns and Special Formats

Activity 4.8 Shading a Paragraph

Shading can be used with or without borders. When used with a border, shading can be very effective.

1 With the paragraph still selected, from the **Format** menu, click **Borders and Shading**.

The Borders and Shading dialog box displays.

2 In the **Borders and Shading** dialog box, click the **Shading tab**.

3 Under **Fill**, in the first row of the color palette, click the third button.

A box to the right of the palette indicates *Gray-10%*. See Figure 4.18.

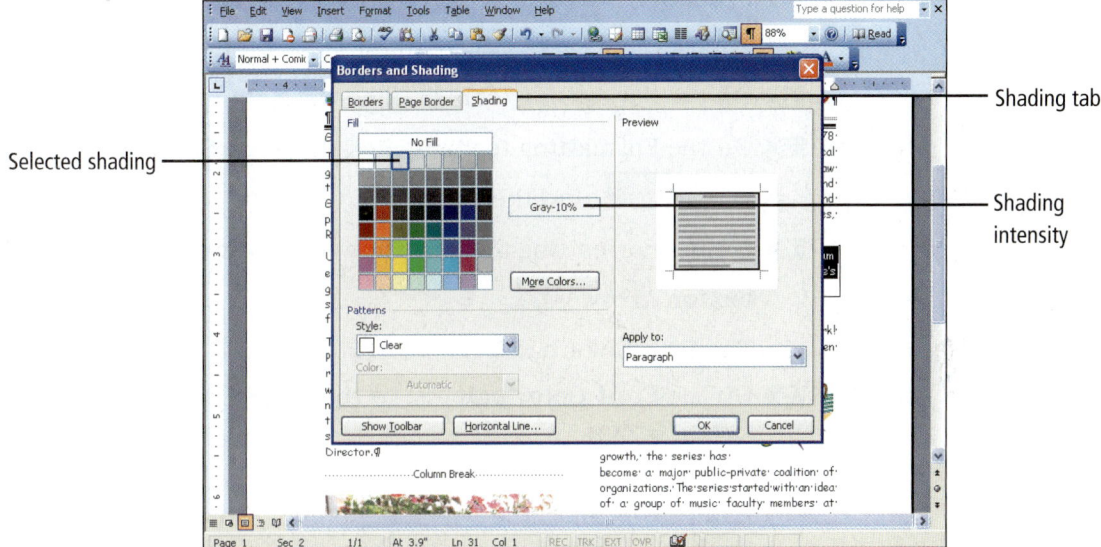

Figure 4.18

4 At the bottom of the **Borders and Shading** dialog box, click **OK**. Click anywhere in the document to deselect the text.

The paragraph is shaded and has a border, as shown in Figure 4.19.

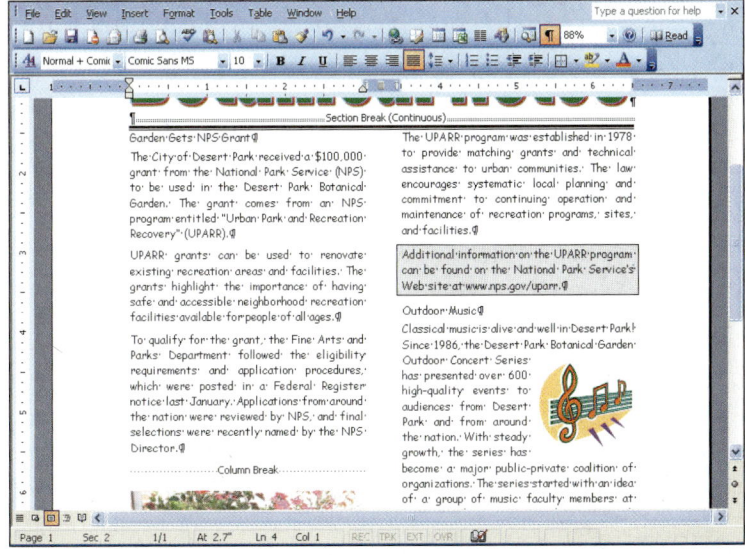

Figure 4.19

5 On the Standard toolbar, click the **Save** button.

Project 4A: Garden Newsletter | **Word** 435

Objective 4
Use Special Character Formats

Headlines and titles should be set off from the rest of the text in a distinctive manner. This is usually done by emphasizing the text with the use of bold or italics, different fonts, or increased font size. If you are going to use a color printer or post the document on the Web, changing the color is very effective.

Activity 4.9 Changing Font Color

1 At the top of the first column, select the *Garden Gets NPS Grant* headline.

This is the headline for the first story in the newsletter.

2 On the Formatting toolbar, click the **Bold** button.

3 On the Formatting toolbar, click the **Font Size button arrow**, and then click **18**.

4 On the Formatting toolbar, click the arrow click the **Font Color button arrow**.

The Font Color palette displays.

5 On the **Font Color palette**, in the second row, click the fourth color—**Green**.

The first headline is bold, 18 point, and green. The Font Color button retains the color that was just applied, which means that if you click the button, it will apply Green to whatever text has been selected.

6 Under the shaded paragraph, select the *Outdoor Music* headline. Repeat Steps 2 through 5 to apply the same format to the second headline. Alternatively, you could use the Format Painter to apply the format from the first headline to the second headline. Click anywhere in the document to deselect the text.

The second headline is formatted the same as the first, as shown in Figure 4.20.

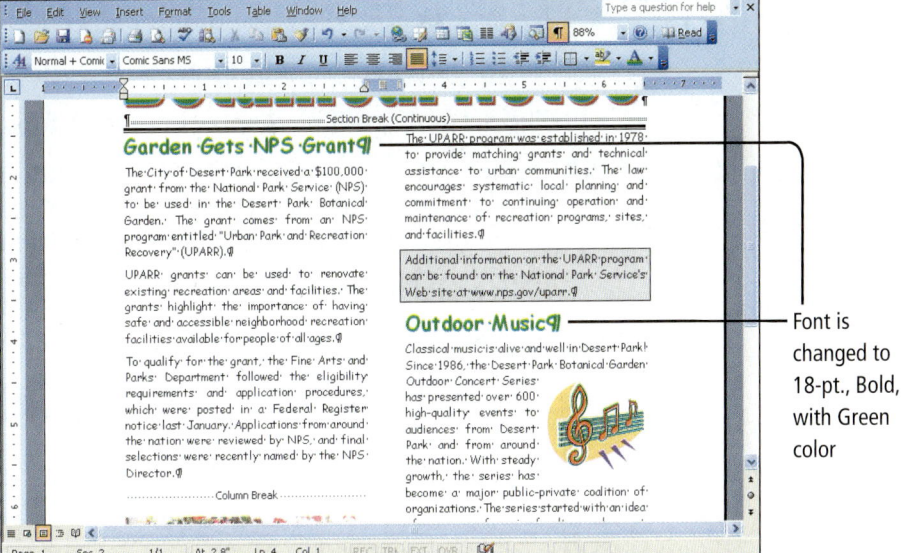
Font is changed to 18-pt., Bold, with Green color

Figure 4.20

7 On the Standard toolbar, click the **Save** button.

Activity 4.10 Using Small Caps

For headlines and titles, **small caps** is a useful font effect. Lower-case letters are changed to capital letters but remain the height of lower-case letters. Titles are often done in this style.

1 Select the *Outdoor Music* title again. From the **Format** menu, click **Font**.

The Font dialog box displays. See Figure 4.21. There are several special effects that can be applied to fonts using the Font dialog box.

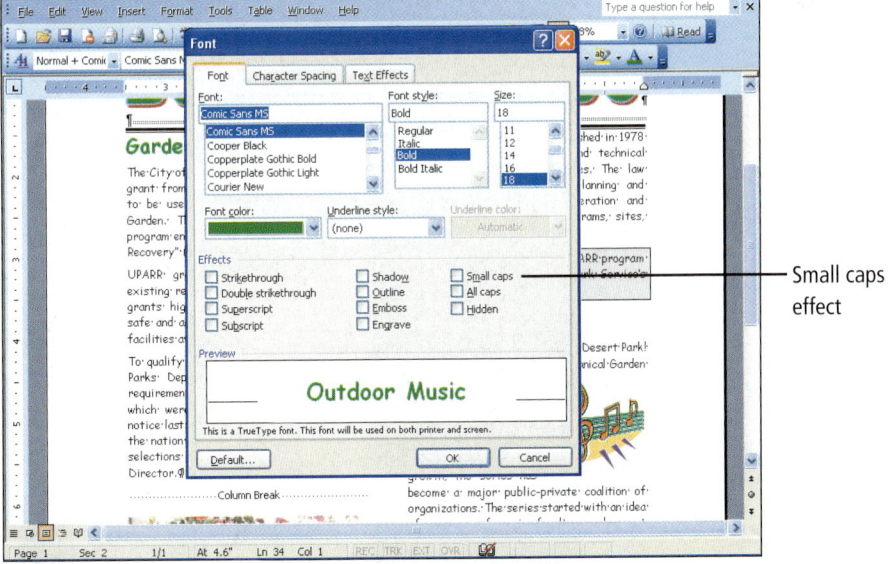
Small caps effect

Figure 4.21

Project 4A: Garden Newsletter | **Word** 437

2 Under **Effects**, select the **Small caps** check box.

3 At the bottom of the **Font** dialog box, click **OK**.

The second headline displays in small caps.

4 In the first title, *Garden Gets NPS Grant*, repeat Steps 1 through 3. Alternatively, use the Format Painter to apply the small caps effect to the first title. Click anywhere in the document to deselect the text.

Both headlines display in small caps, as shown in Figure 4.22.

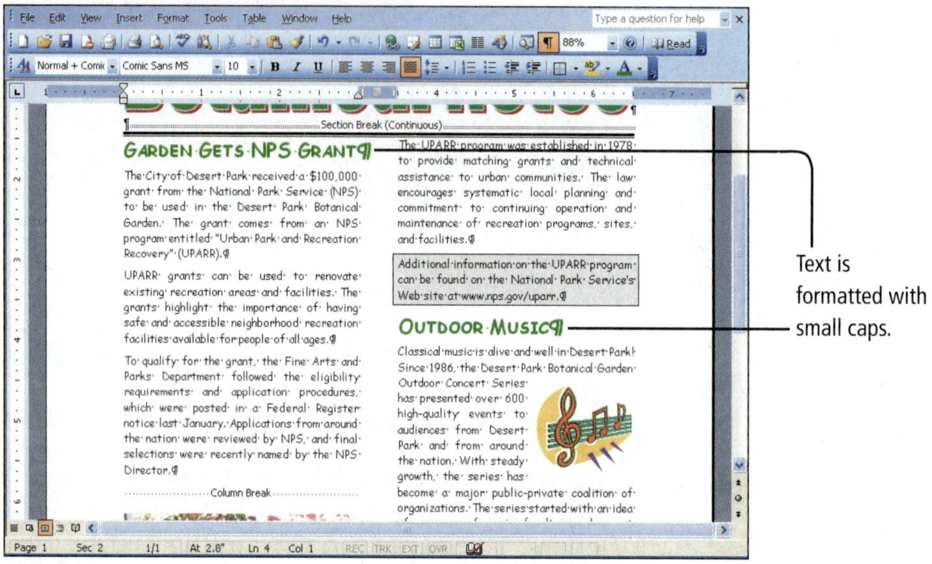

Figure 4.22

5 On the Standard toolbar, click the **Show/Hide ¶** button to turn off the nonprinting characters.

6 Click the **Zoom button arrow**, click the arrow and then click **Whole Page**.

The entire newsletter displays, as shown in Figure 4.23.

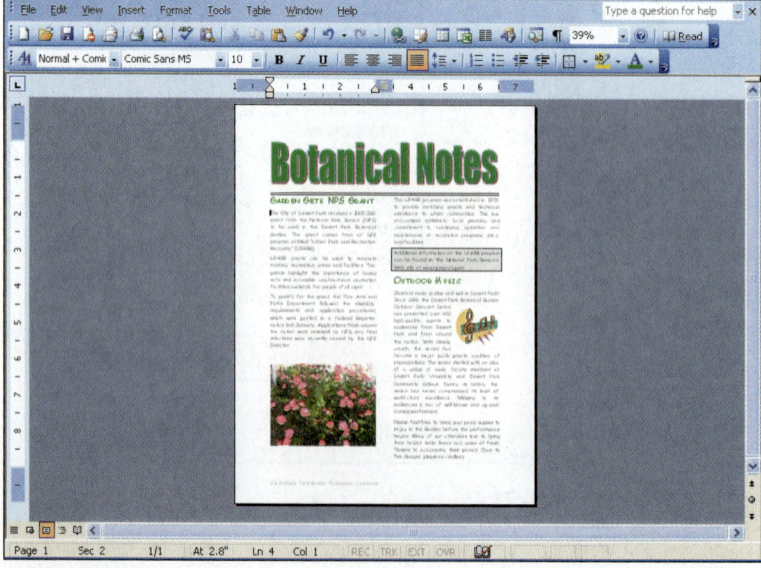

Figure 4.23

438   Word | Chapter 4: Creating Documents with Multiple Columns and Special Formats

> **More Knowledge** — Removing Blank Pages
>
> If you created empty paragraphs at the end of a document by pressing the Enter key too often, the result might be an extra blank page. To remove this page, click at the bottom of the document and press the Backspace key until the extra page is removed. It is best to use the Show/Hide ¶ button to show hidden characters so you can view the formatting marks that should be deleted.

7 If your document looks different, make the necessary adjustments.

8 On the Standard toolbar, click the **Show/Hide ¶** button to redisplay nonprinting characters.

9 Click the **Zoom button arrow** , click the arrow and then click **Page Width**.

Page Width displays the document at its maximum width while still displaying the margins. The percent displayed in the Zoom box is affected by your screen resolution, and whether you are in Print Layout View or Normal View.

10 On the Standard toolbar, click the **Print** button.

If you are using a black-and-white printer, the colors will print as shades of gray.

11 On the Standard toolbar, click the **Save** button. Close the document.

End You have completed Project 4A

Project 4B Water Matters

In Project 4A you created titles and worked with paragraph and character formatting. In the following project, 4B, you will insert hyperlinks and practice saving documents as Web pages.

In Activities 4.11 through 4.15 you will edit a document that deals with water issues in the City of Desert Park. You will add links to text and graphics and then save the document as a Web page. Your completed document will look similar to Figure 4.24. You will save your document as *4B_Water_Matters_Firstname_Lastname.*

City of Desert Park
Water Matters

Runoff Management—Residents can visit the City's Web site to view the Urban Runoff Management Plan. The Plan details the City's action to protect and improve water quality of the lakes, rivers, and creeks in the region, and achieve compliance with the State Municipal Storm Water Permit.

The Urban Runoff Management Plan has been posted to allow public access and understanding of the overall efforts of the City Manager's office to improve water quality in the City of Desert Park. Implementing the plan is one of the six objectives of the City's Storm Water Pollution Prevention Program to help improve water quality.

The City Council approved the plan last January, and is effective through February of 2006. At the City's Web site, click on "City Services," and choose "Storm Water Pollution Prevention." See the EPA Watershed site.

Drinking Water—Regulations from the State Public Health Services Drinking Water Program and the Environmental Protection Agency (EPA) require all community water systems to deliver an annual Consumer Confidence Report (water quality report) to customers. The City of Desert Park Water Bureau began sending this information to all postal customers in 1996, before these regulations went into effect in 1999.

The most interesting information for most consumers is this: our drinking water supply continues to meet all state and federal regulations, without exception. This report includes other information of interest to many consumers: water quality test results; definitions; information on our sources of water supply; how to reduce exposure to lead in drinking water; and special notice for immuno-compromised persons. Copies of the report may also be ordered in Braille by calling the City Manager's office at 626-555-1234.

4B_Water_Matters_Firstname_Lastname

Figure 4.24
Project 4B—Water Matters

Objective 5
Insert Hyperlinks

Cities, businesses, and other organizations are publishing their important documents on the Web with increasing frequency. Web pages are easy to create using Microsoft Word features that enable the creation of Web pages directly from word processing documents. One of the strengths of using Web pages is that hyperlinks can be added to take the user to related sites quickly and easily. **Hyperlinks** are text or graphics that you click to move to a file, another page in a Web site, or a page in a different Web site.

You can create a Web page in Word, add text, graphics, and hyperlinks, and then preview the document in a Web browser to see how it looks. You can adjust the page to your satisfaction and then save the document as a Web page.

Activity 4.11 Inserting Text Hyperlinks

The type of hyperlink used most frequently is one that is attached to text. Text hyperlinks usually appear underlined and in blue.

1. On the Standard toolbar, click the **Open** button. Navigate to the location where the student files for this textbook are stored. Locate **w04B_Water_Matters** and click once to select it. Then, in the lower right corner of the **Open** dialog box, click **Open**.

   The w04B_Water_Matters file opens.

2. From the **File** menu, click **Save As**. In the **Save As** dialog box, click the **Save in arrow** and navigate to the location in which you are storing your files for this chapter.

3. Type **4B_Water_Matters_Firstname_Lastname** in the **File name** box, using your own name, and click **Save**.

   The document is saved with a new name.

4. On the Standard toolbar, click the **Show/Hide ¶** button, if necessary, to display the nonprinting characters. On the Standard toolbar, click the Zoom button arrow, and then click Page Width.

5. Position the insertion point at the end of the paragraph beginning *The City Council approved*. Press Spacebar once and then type **See the EPA Watershed site.** In the sentence you just typed, select *EPA Watershed*.

6 From the **Insert** menu, click **Hyperlink**. Alternatively, right-click on the selected text and click Hyperlink from the shortcut menu or click the Insert Hyperlink button on the Standard toolbar.

The Insert Hyperlink dialog box displays, as shown in Figure 4.25.

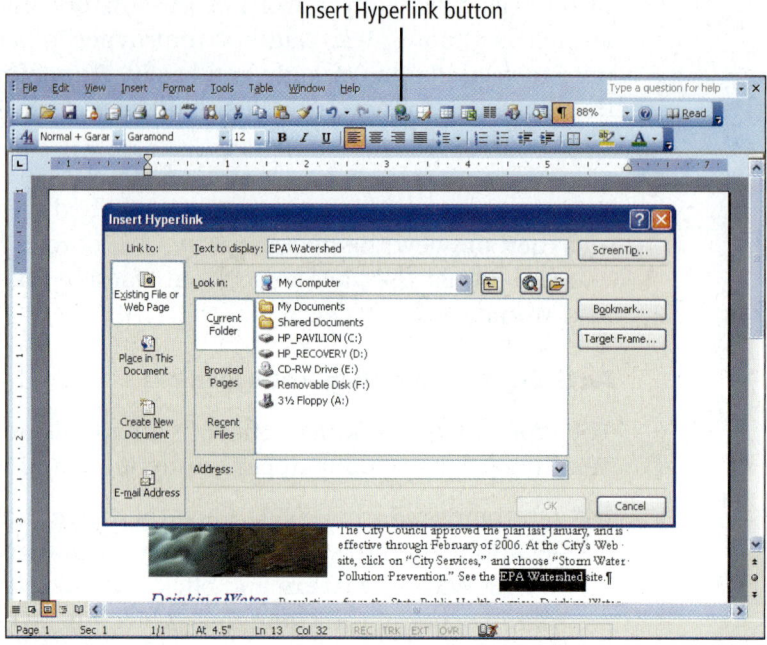

Figure 4.25

7 Under **Link to**, click **Existing File or Web Page**. In the **Address** box, type **http://cfpub.epa.gov/surf/locate/map2.cfm** If another address displays while you are typing, ignore it and continue typing.

An address may display in the Address box as you type. This is AutoComplete at work. It displays the most recently used Web address for your computer.

8 On the upper-right corner of the **Insert Hyperlink** dialog box, click **ScreenTip**.

The Set Hyperlink ScreenTip dialog box displays.

9 In the **Set Hyperlink ScreenTip** dialog box, type **Watershed Map**

This is the ScreenTip that will display when the pointer is placed over the hyperlink. See Figure 4.26.

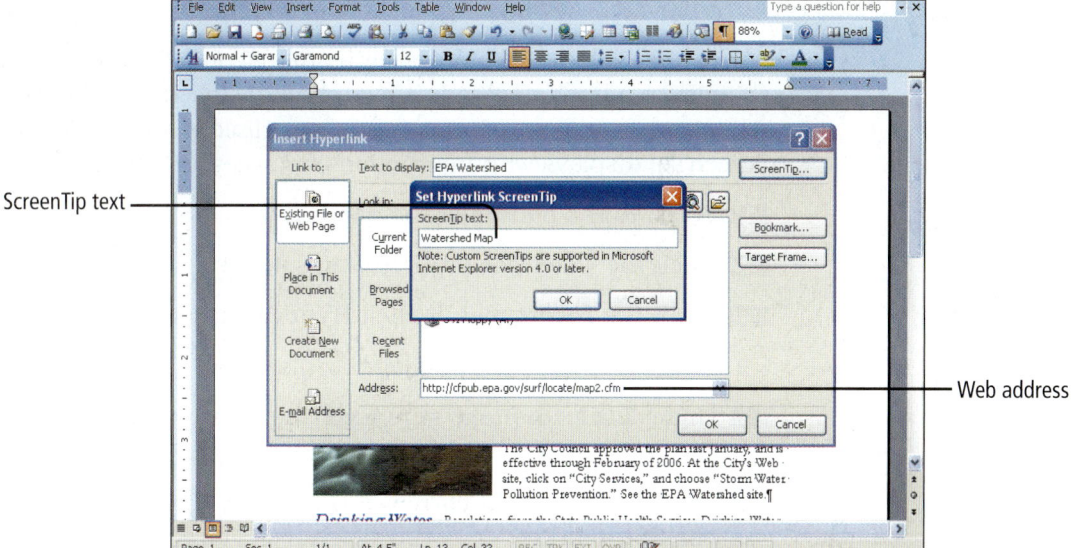

Figure 4.26

10. On the **Set Hyperlink ScreenTip** dialog box, click **OK**. At the bottom of the **Insert Hyperlink** dialog box, click **OK**.

    The hyperlink is recorded, and the selected text changes to blue and is underlined.

11. In the next paragraph, in the second line, select *Environmental Protection Agency (EPA)*. Repeat Steps 6 through 10 to create a hyperlink, but type **http://www.epa.gov** for the address and **EPA Home Page** for the ScreenTip.

    The hyperlink is recorded, and the selected text changes to blue and is underlined, as shown in Figure 4.27.

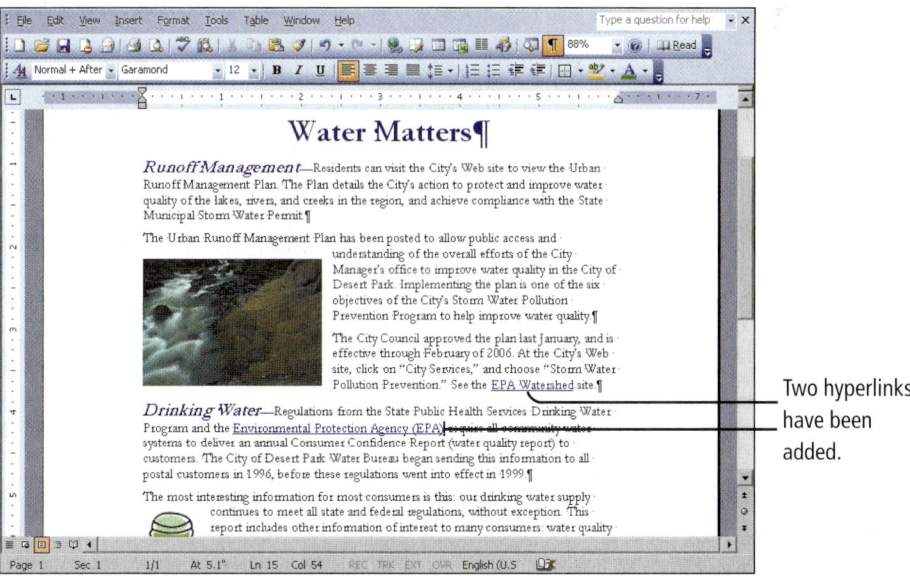

Figure 4.27

12. On the Standard toolbar, click the **Save** button.

Project 4B: Water Matters | **Word** 443

Activity 4.12 Adding a Hyperlink to a Graphic

When you move your pointer over a graphic on a Web page, and the pointer changes to a hand, it means a hyperlink has been added to the graphic. When you move your pointer over a hyperlink in a Word document, a ScreenTip displays with instructions for accessing the link.

1 Scroll to the bottom of the document.

2 Click the water cooler picture to select it.

3 From the **Insert** menu, click **Hyperlink**.

The Insert Hyperlink dialog box displays.

4 Under **Link to**, make sure **Existing File or Web Page** is selected. In the **Address** box, type **http://www.epa.gov**

5 On the upper-right corner of the **Insert Hyperlink** dialog box, click **ScreenTip**.

The Set Hyperlink ScreenTip dialog box displays.

6 In the **Set Hyperlink ScreenTip** dialog box, type **Drinking Water Standards**

Compare your dialog box with Figure 4.28.

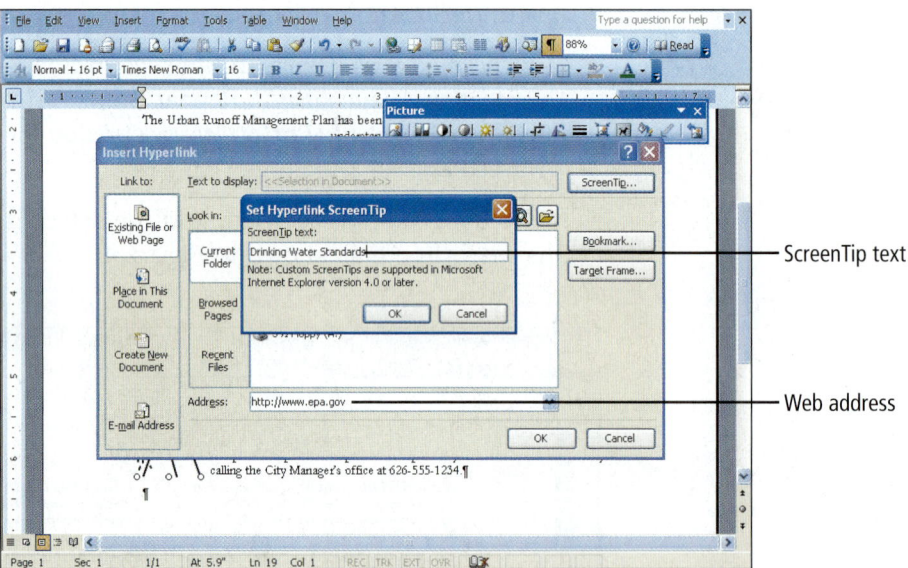

Figure 4.28

7 On the **Set Hyperlink ScreenTip** dialog box, click **OK**. At the bottom of the **Insert Hyperlink** dialog box, click **OK**.

The hyperlink is recorded, but there is no visual indication that the link has been added.

8 Move the pointer over the water cooler graphic.

The ScreenTip that you typed displays, as shown in Figure 4.29.

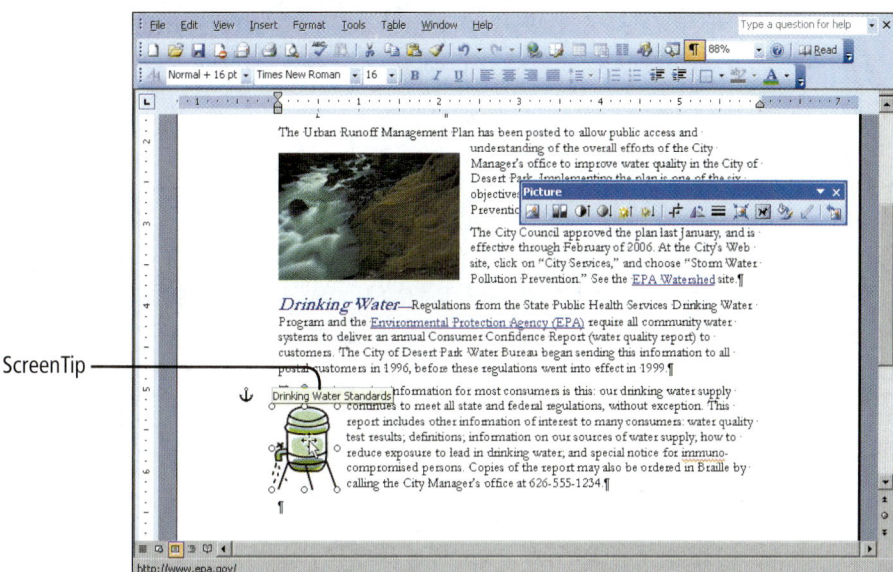

Figure 4.29

9 On the Standard toolbar, click the **Save** button.

Activity 4.13 Modifying Hyperlinks

If you need to change a hyperlink, you will use a dialog box similar to the one you used to create it.

1 Move the pointer over the water cooler and right-click.

A shortcut menu displays.

2 From the shortcut menu, click **Edit Hyperlink**.

The Edit Hyperlink dialog box displays. Its components are similar to those of the Insert Hyperlink dialog box.

3 At the bottom of the **Edit Hyperlink** dialog box, in the **Address** box, add **safewater** to the end of the Internet address.

Compare your dialog box to Figure 4.30.

> **Note** — If the Text Displays Automatically
>
> When you begin typing the text in the text boxes of the Edit Hyperlink dialog box, the complete text may display after only a few letters. This results from someone else using the same computer to do this exercise before you. The text is completed only if the AutoComplete feature is turned on.

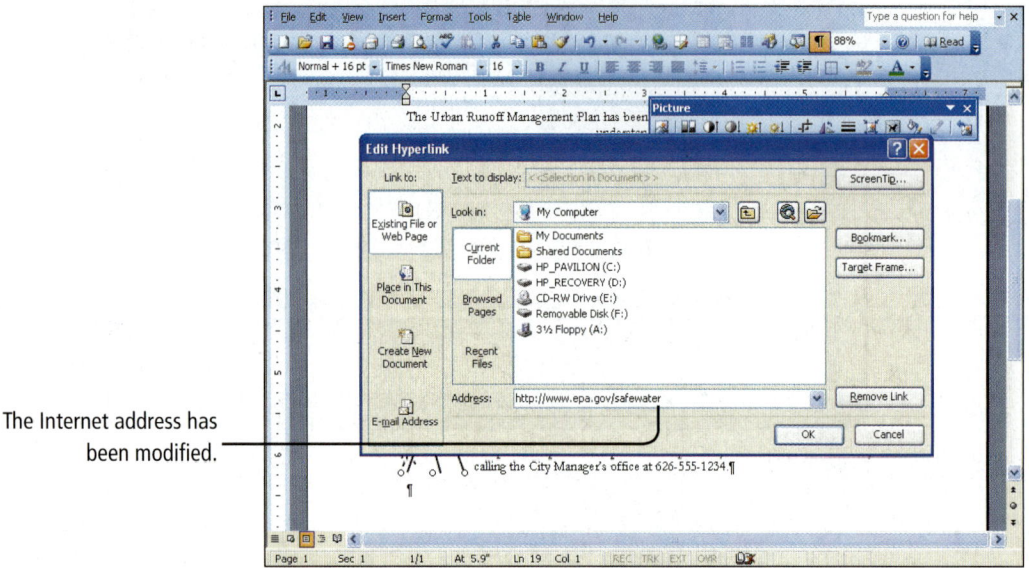

The Internet address has been modified.

Figure 4.30

4 At the bottom of the **Edit Hyperlink** dialog box, click **OK**.

The hyperlink address is changed.

5 From the **View** menu, click **Header and Footer**. On the Header and Footer toolbar, click the **Switch Between Header and Footer** button.

6 On the Header and Footer toolbar, click the **Insert AutoText** button, and then click **Filename**.

The file name is inserted in the footer.

7 On the Header and Footer toolbar, click the **Close** button.

8 On the Standard toolbar, click the **Save** button.

9 On the Standard toolbar, click the **Print Preview** button. Take a moment to check your work. On the **Print Preview** toolbar, click the **Close Preview** button.

10 On the Standard toolbar, click the **Print** button.

446 Word | Chapter 4: Creating Documents with Multiple Columns and Special Formats

Objective 6
Preview and Save a Document as a Web Page

After you have created a document to be used as a Web page, you can see what the page will look like when displayed in a **Web browser** such as Internet Explorer or Netscape. A Web browser is software that enables you to use the Web and navigate from page to page and site to site. You can adjust the image and preview it until you get it exactly right. Once you are satisfied with the way the document looks when displayed in a Web browser, you can save the document as a Web page.

Activity 4.14 Previewing a Document as a Web Page

1 From the **File** menu, click **Web Page Preview**.

Your Web browser opens, and your document displays as a Web page. Your screen may look different, depending on your screen size, screen resolution, and the Web browser you use.

2 Move your pointer over the *EPA Watershed* hyperlink.

The pointer changes to a hand, indicating that the text contains a link, as shown in Figure 4.31.

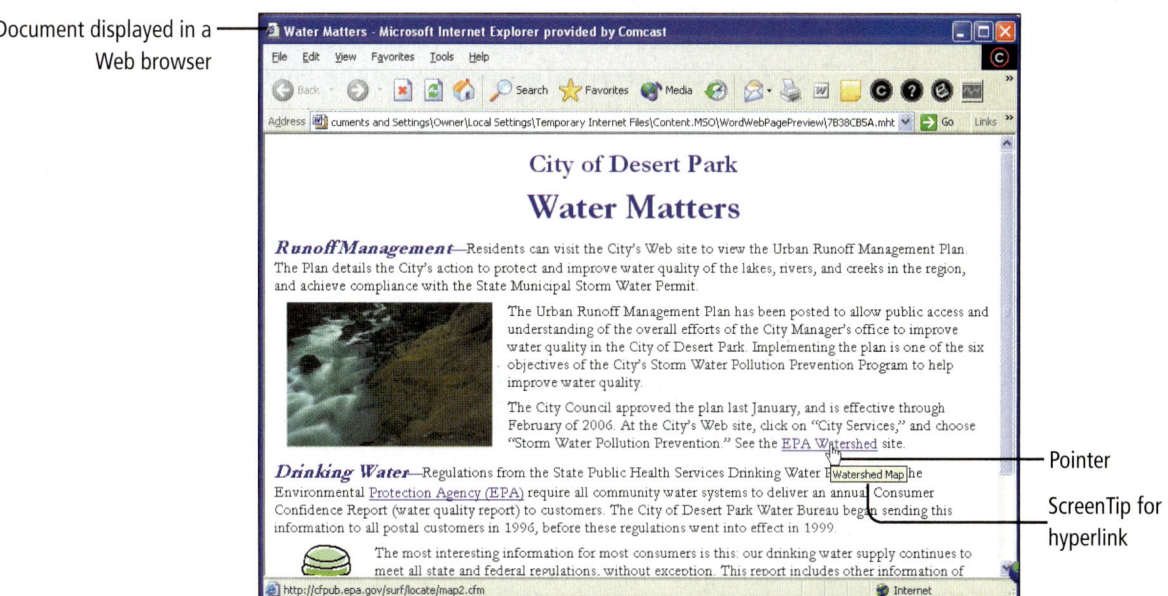

Document displayed in a Web browser

Pointer

ScreenTip for hyperlink

Figure 4.31

3 On the vertical scroll bar, click the down arrow to scroll down the page, if necessary.

On some high-resolution screens, you will not need to scroll down. Notice that the file name you placed in the footer does not display on the Web page.

4 Click the **water cooler image** to make sure your Web link works.

If you are connected to the Internet, you will see the *EPA Drinking Water* page.

Project 4B: Water Matters | **Word**   447

Alert!

If You Are Not Connected to the Internet
If you are not connected to the Internet, you will see a message box informing you that you are not connected, or the site could not be found. Click OK to acknowledge the message, and then resume with Step 6 of the instructions.

5 On the Browser title bar, click the **Close** button ⊠. Make any changes that you feel are necessary and preview your Web page again.

6 On the Standard toolbar, click the **Save** button 🖫.

Activity 4.15 Saving a Document as a Web Page

Once you are satisfied with your document, you can save it as a Web page.

1 From the **File** menu, click **Save as Web Page**.

The Save As dialog box displays.

2 In the **Save in** dialog box, navigate to the location in which you are saving your files.

Notice in the File name box that the file extension has changed from .doc to .mht. This is the extension of a single Web page. If file extensions have been turned off on your computer, you will not see the extension. The Save as type box displays *Single File Web Page*, and the document title displays as the Page title.

3 Near the bottom of the **Save As** dialog box, click **Change Title**.

The Set Page Title dialog box displays. What you type here will become the Web page title; this is the title that displays in the browser title bar and shows up in the Web browser's history list.

4 Type **City of Desert Park Water Issues** See Figure 4.32.

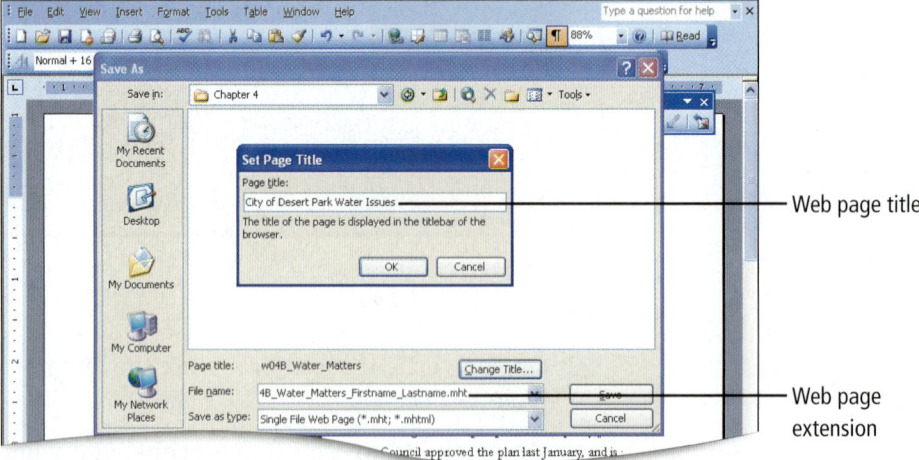

Figure 4.32

448 Word | Chapter 4: Creating Documents with Multiple Columns and Special Formats

5 Click **OK** to close the **Set Page Title** dialog box.

In the Save as dialog box, the new title for your Web page displays as the Page title. Accept the default File name for the Web page. When you save it, the Web page will have a different file extension and file type icon to distinguish it from the Word document by the same name.

5 At the bottom of the **Save As** dialog box, click **Save**.

A dialog box displays stating that some of the elements in this page will not display properly on very early versions of Web browsers. See Figure 4.33.

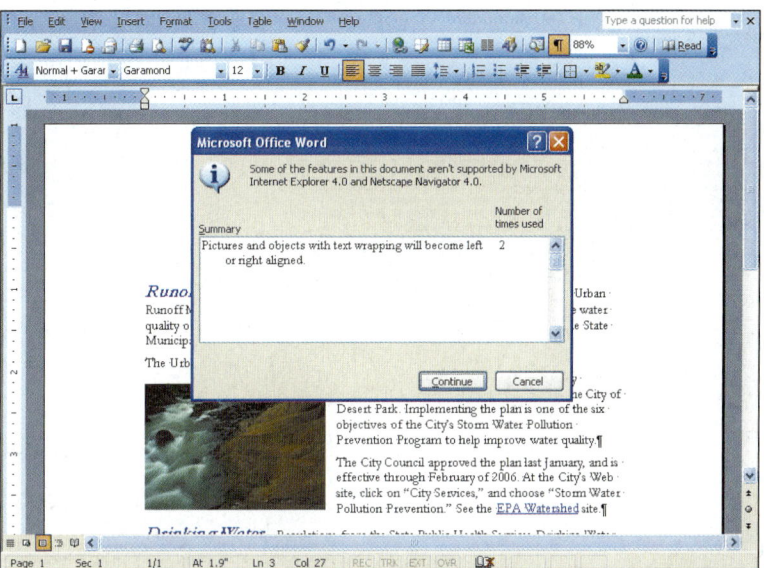

Figure 4.33

6 At the bottom of the dialog box, click **Continue**.

The file is saved and the document displays on your screen in the Web page format, with text across the full width of the screen—no margins, and both pictures displayed on the left side.

7 On the Standard toolbar, click the **Save** button . Close the document.

You have completed Project 4B

Project 4C Recreation Ideas

In Project 4B you practiced saving documents as Web pages. In Project 4C you will work with supporting information and objects.

In Activities 4.16 through 4.21, you will gather text and graphics that will be used in a Recreation Department newsletter. You will gather several documents and several pictures and then paste them from the Office Clipboard. You will use the ***Thesaurus***—a language tool for finding alternative words with similar meanings—and then you will use special tools to browse a document. You will save your document as *4C_Recreation_Ideas_Firstname_Lastname*.

MEMO TO: Jane Romano
FROM: Ray Hamilton
DATE: March 5, 2005
SUBJECT: Ideas for the June Recreation Notes Newsletter

Here are some ideas for the June *Recreation Notes* newsletter, which should include the rough drafts of articles on Golf and Bicycling. I've also included some information on the history of each sport that you might be able to use for the *Did You Know?* boxes. Finally, I've added an image you might be able to use.

GOLF

Draft of article:
The Desert Park Fine Arts and Parks Department is hosting a golf clinic and nighttime golf benefit at the North Park Golf Course on Friday, August 21 to benefit the city's Youth Golf Program.
A PGA Tour Professional, recognized as one of the most accomplished golfers to play the game, will be at the North Park Golf Course to offer a free Golf Clinic. The clinic will run from 9 a.m. – 10:30 a.m. It's open to the public and there is no charge for admission. Come on out and learn some valuable tips from a pro!
Want to see how a pro applies those clinic techniques to an actual round of golf? As a follow-up to the clinic, our pro will join tournament guests in an exhibition round beginning at 12 noon. Plan to follow this foursome to see how they perform.
The nighttime event begins at 8 p.m. Pre-registration is required. The cost is $25 per person. Registration includes greens fees, glow balls, prizes, soft drinks, and pull carts. The tournament is a four-person scramble with a shotgun start at 8:15 p.m.
The tournament, which is played on the nine-hole course, is limited to the first 12 teams (48 players). The Youth Golf Program provides free golf lessons to youth at six of Desert Park's municipal golf courses. Funding makes it possible to provide year-round instruction, golf clubs, balls and other equipment for use during the classes. For more information, call 626-555-1131.
"The Golf Benefit is a fun and informal way to support hundreds of young people in Desert Park and the surrounding county," said Fred Stein, president of the Youth Golf Program Foundation. "The golf clinic is a great opportunity for children to learn about the game and be exposed to business leaders who can have an influence on their lives."
Last year the Youth Golf Program Foundation helped 145 young men and women learn to play the value of good sportspersouship. The organization is a non-profit organization that provides golf events through structured, school-based golf programs.

Information for Did You Know? boxes:
Some historians believe that golf originated in the Netherlands (the Dutch word *kolf* n had a game played with a bent stick and a ball made of feathers that may have been th It has been fairly well established, however, that the game that is known today was ac the 14th or 15th century.
Image:

4C_Recreation_Ideas_Firstname_Lastname

BICYCLING

Draft of article:
The "Golden Age" of bicycling occurred during the development of Desert Park many years ago. Early photographs show street scenes with bicycles, horses, trolleys, and pedestrians. In fact, our first streets were arranged for these users. But Desert Park was ahead of its time, because this development pattern is actually an essential element of a livable community.
Desert Park is a city in which people can get around without cars, and the City hopes to make this a place where it is easier to ride a bicycle than to drive a car. Ideally, bicyclists should be able to circulate along city streets freely and safely. At the bicyclist's destination there should be safe, free, and accessible parking.
The City is working on a plan that identifies a network of bikeways that will connect bicycle riders to their destinations. The enhancements to the Agave Trail are an important part of this plan. The plan includes a list of other projects and programs, similar to the Agave Trail program, to be added to the Transportation Improvement Plan.

Information for Did You Know? boxes:
The bicycle was not invented by any one person. Rather, it is an outgrowth of ideas and inventions dating to the late 18th century. Some people claim the bicycle's history goes back even further, citing certain drawings by Leonardo da Vinci of a two-wheeled vehicle.
Image:

4C_Recreation_Ideas_Firstname_Lastname

Figure 4.34
Project 4C—Recreation Ideas

450 Word | Chapter 4: Creating Documents with Multiple Columns and Special Formats

Objective 7
Locate Supporting Information

When you are writing, you may want to refer to information related to your topic. This **supporting information** could be located in other documents or on the Web. As you collect information for a new document, you can store all of the pieces (text and pictures) on the Office Clipboard. When you have all of the information pieces gathered, you can go to your document and paste the information one piece at a time. This feature is called **collect and paste**.

Word has a Thesaurus tool that enables you to find exactly the right word. Also, a special button can be used to quickly locate various elements in a document. For example, you can navigate through a document by moving from one section to the next or from one image to the next. It is recommended that you do these activities on a computer with an Internet connection. You will not be able to complete Activity 4.18 without a connection.

Activity 4.16 Using Collect and Paste to Gather Images

Recall that the Office Clipboard is a temporary storage area maintained by your Windows operating system. When you perform the Copy command or the Cut command, the text that you select is placed on the Clipboard. From this Clipboard storage area, you can paste text into another location of your document, into another document, or into another Office program.

You can copy and then paste a single selection of text without displaying the Clipboard task pane. Displaying the Clipboard is essential, however, if you want to collect a group of selected text pieces or images and then paste them. The Clipboard can hold up to 24 items, and the Clipboard task pane displays a short representation of each item.

1 On the Standard toolbar, click the **Open** button. Locate and open the **w04C_Recreation_Ideas** file.

2 From the **File** menu, click **Save As**. Navigate to the location where you are storing your files for this chapter. In the **File name** box, type **4C_Recreation_Ideas_Firstname_Lastname** and click **Save**.

The document is saved with a new name. Be sure you substitute your name where indicated.

3 From the **Edit** menu, click **Office Clipboard**.

The Clipboard task pane displays, as shown in Figure 4.35.

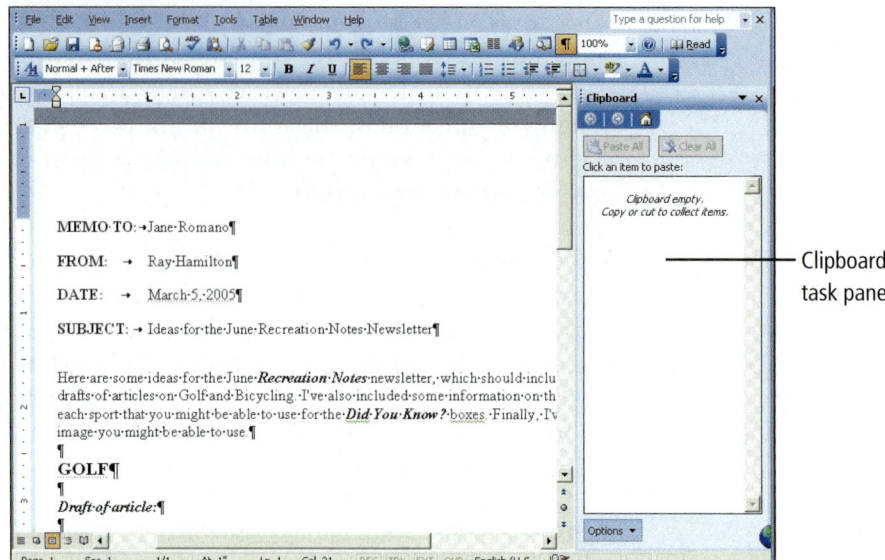

Clipboard task pane

Figure 4.35

Another Way

Other Ways to Display the Clipboard Task Pane

There are two other ways to display the Clipboard task pane:

- If a different task pane is displayed, click the Other Task Panes arrow and then click Clipboard.

- Select the first piece of text that you want to copy, hold down Ctrl, and then quickly press C two times.

4 If the Office Clipboard displays any entries, from the top of the Clipboard task pane, click the **Clear All** button. From the **Insert** menu, point to **Picture** and then click **Clip Art**.

The Clip Art task pane replaces the Clipboard task pane.

5 In the **Search for box**, type **golf** Click the **Search in arrow** and then select **Everywhere**. Click the **Results should be arrow**, be sure the **Clip Art** check box is selected, and then clear the other check boxes. Click **Go** twice.

6 In the **Clip Art** task pane, move the pointer over the image of a woman golfer.

If the image shown in Figure 4.36 is not available, choose another golf picture.

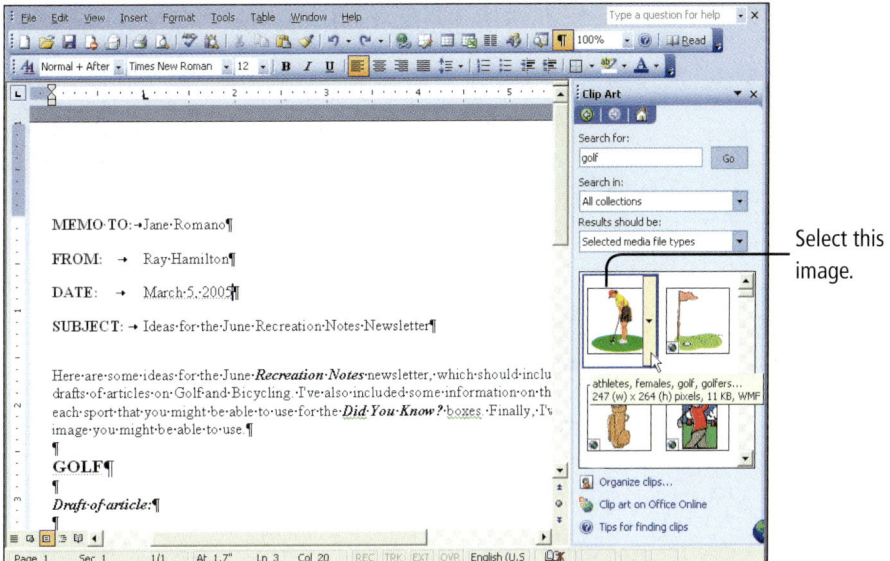

Select this image.

Figure 4.36

> **Note** — Inserting Clip Art Images from Your Student Files
>
> If you do not have an Internet connection, and if you have a minimum Office installation, you may not have any images of golf available. Both images used for this activity have been included with the files for this chapter. To access those files, from the bottom of the Clip Art task pane, click *Organize clips*. In the Favorites-Microsoft Clip Organizer dialog box, display the File menu, point to Add Clips to Organizer, and then click On My Own. Use the Look in arrow to navigate to the location of your student files and find *w04C_Golf*. Select it and then, in the lower right corner of the dialog box, click Add. When the image displays in the dialog box, move the pointer over the arrow on the right side of the image and then click Copy. Close the dialog box. When prompted, click the Yes button to copy the image to the Office Clipboard. Continue with Activity 4.16.

7 On the image of the woman golfer, click the arrow and then click **Copy**.

The image is copied to the Clipboard.

8 In the title bar of the **Clip Art** task pane, click the **Other Task Panes arrow**. From the task pane menu, click **Clipboard**.

The image you selected displays in the Clipboard task pane. When copying clip art, you need to redisplay the Clipboard after you copy an image; otherwise, the next image you copy will replace the current image.

9 In the title bar of the **Clipboard** task pane, click the **Other Task Panes arrow**. From the task pane menu, click **Clip Art**.

10 In the **Search for** box, type **cycling** and then click **Go**.

11 In the **Clip Art** task pane, move the pointer over the image of a cyclist on a trail.

If the image shown in Figure 4.37 is not available, choose another similar picture, or read the Note box for directions on how to find w04C_Cycling from your student files.

Project 4C: Recreation Ideas | **Word** 453

12 On the image of the cyclist, click the arrow and then click **Copy**.

The image is transferred to the Clipboard.

13 In the title bar of the **Clip Art** task pane, click the **Other Task Panes arrow**. From the task pane menu, click **Clipboard**.

Both images are displayed in the Clipboard task pane, with the most recently copied image on top. See Figure 4.37.

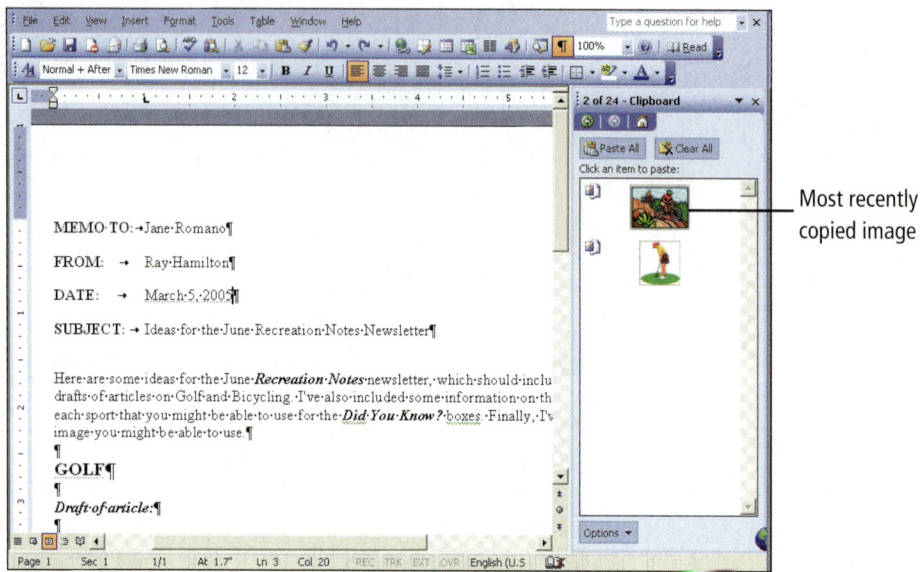

Figure 4.37

Activity 4.17 Collecting Information from Other Documents

If you need information from another document, you can open the source document, copy the text you need onto the Clipboard, and then paste it into your document later.

1 Be sure **4C_Recreation_Ideas** is still displayed on your screen, and the Clipboard task pane displays the two images you have copied.

On the Standard toolbar, click the **Open** button. Locate and open the **w04C_Golf** file.

2 In the **w04C_Golf** file, hold down Ctrl and press A.

All the text is selected.

3 On the Standard toolbar, click the **Copy** button.

The text is copied to the Clipboard, along with the two images.

4 On the Standard toolbar, click the **Open** button. Locate and open the **w04C_Bicycle** file.

454   Word | Chapter 4: Creating Documents with Multiple Columns and Special Formats

5. In the **w04C_Bicycle** file, hold down Ctrl and press A to select the document.

6. On the Standard toolbar, click the **Copy** button.

   The text is copied to the Clipboard along with the *Golf* text and the two images.

7. In the upper right corner of your screen, to the right of the *Type a question for help* box, click the **Close Window** button ☒ to close the **w04C_Bicycle** file.

8. Click the Close Window button ☒ to close the **w04C_Golf** file.

   Compare your clipboard to Figure 4.38. Notice that as new items are copied to the Office Clipboard, the most recent item moves to the top of the list.

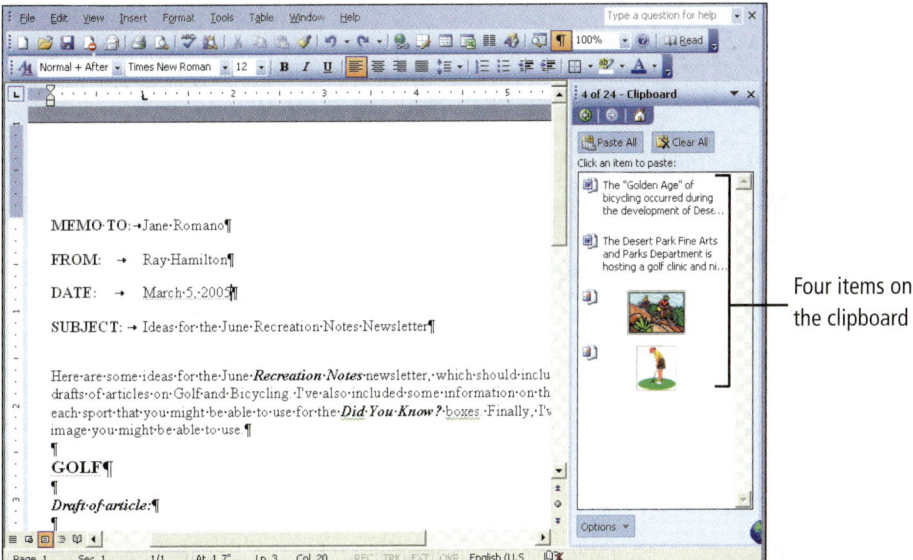

Four items on the clipboard

Figure 4.38

Activity 4.18 Finding Supporting Information Using the Research Tool

Word includes a research tool that enables you to search for information on a variety of topics. You will need an Internet connection to complete this activity.

1. On the Standard toolbar, click the **Research** button.

   The Research task pane displays.

2. In the **Search for** box, type **Golf**

Project 4C: Recreation Ideas | **Word** 455

3 Under the **Search for** box, in the second box, click the arrow, and then click **Encarta Encyclopedia**.

Your screen may indicate only *Encyclopedia* or it may display the language and version of the active encyclopedia. A list of golf topics displays. See Figure 4.39.

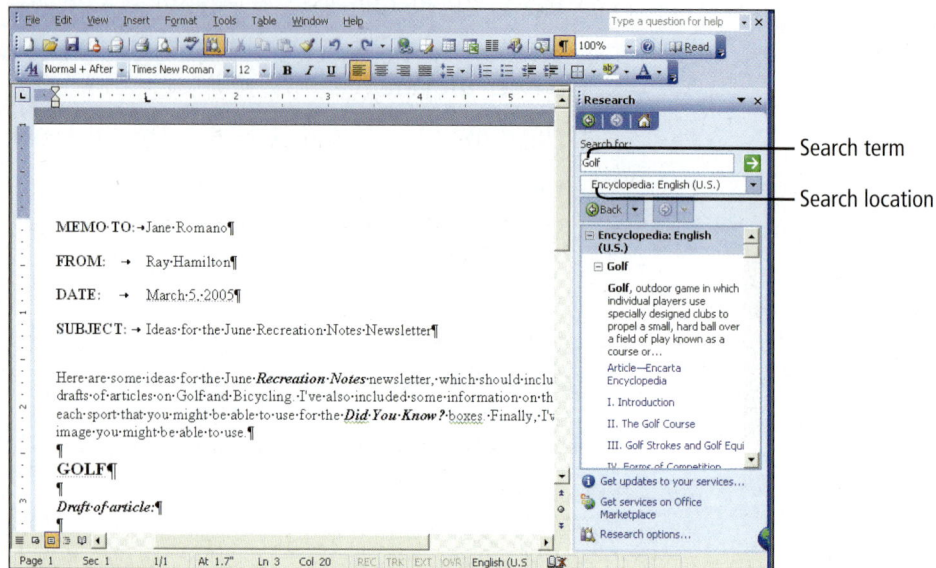

Figure 4.39

4 In the **Research** task pane list of topics, click **History**.

You may have to scroll down the list of topics. The program moves to the *MSN Learning & Research* site on the Web. The History section, which is in the middle of the document, displays at the top of the screen.

5 Move the pointer to the left of the top paragraph that begins *Some historians believe*. Drag to the end of the second sentence, which ends *the 14th or 15th century*.

Be sure you have only the two sentences selected. Your screen should look similar to Figure 4.40. Because the information on Web sites changes often, the information on your screen may look slightly different.

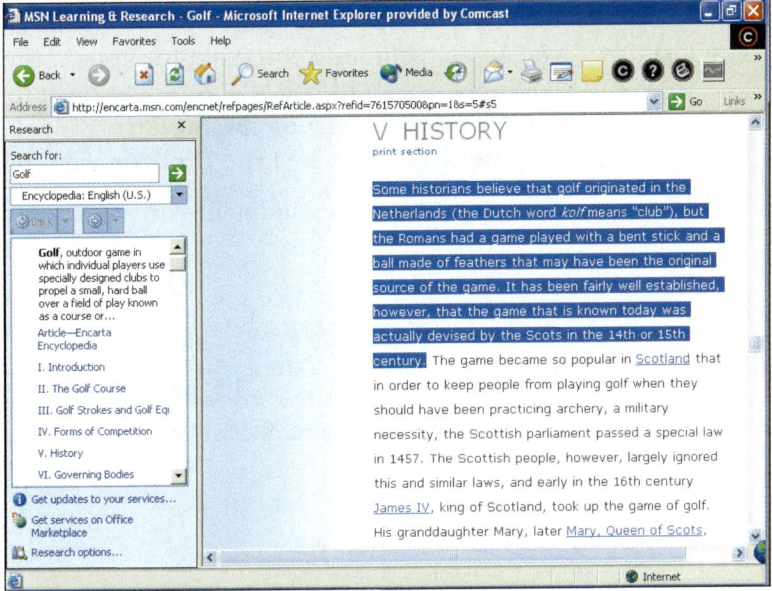

Figure 4.40

> ## More Knowledge — Being Careful of Copyright Issues
>
> Nearly everything you find on the Web is protected by copyright law, which protects authors of original works, including text, art, photographs, and music. If you want to use text or graphics that you find online, you will need to get permission. One of the exceptions to this law is the use of small amounts of information for educational purposes, which falls under Fair Use guidelines.
>
> Copyright laws in the United States are open to different interpretations, and copyright laws can be very different in other countries. As a general rule, if you want to use someone else's material, always get permission first.

6 From the **Edit** menu, click **Copy**. Alternatively, right-click the selected text and from the shortcut menu click Copy.

The text is added to the Clipboard.

7 Close the *MSN Learning & Research* window.

8 In the title bar of the **Research** task pane, click the **Other Task Panes arrow**. From the task pane menu, click **Clipboard**.

The text you copied displays in the Clipboard task pane.

Project 4C: Recreation Ideas | **Word** 457

9 Click the **Other Task Panes arrow** again and click **Research**. Use the same technique you used in Steps 2 through 7 for researching golf to research the **bicycle** You may have to scroll down the topics area to find **History of the Modern Bicycle**. Select and copy the first three sentences of the **History** area.

You should have six items in your Clipboard task pane, as shown in Figure 4.41.

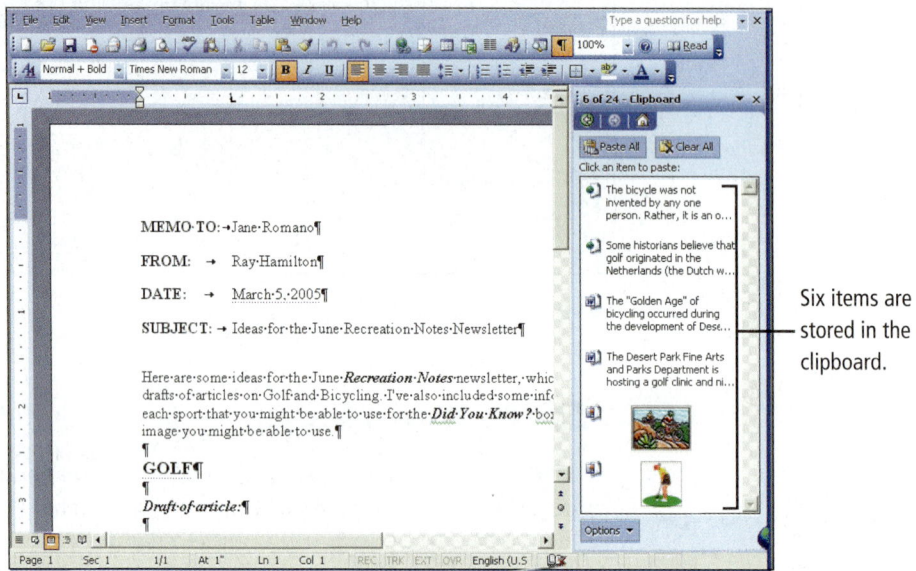

Six items are stored in the clipboard.

Figure 4.41

Activity 4.19 Pasting Information from the Clipboard Task Pane

Once you have collected text and images from other documents or sources, such as the Internet, you can paste them into your document.

1 With **4C_Recreation_Ideas_Firstname_Lastname** open, in the blank line under the **GOLF** *Draft of article*, click to position the insertion point.

2 On the Clipboard task pane, under **Click an item to paste**, click the fourth item in the item list, the one that begins *The Desert Park Fine Arts*.

The text is pasted into the document at the insertion point location, as shown in Figure 4.42.

458 Word | Chapter 4: Creating Documents with Multiple Columns and Special Formats

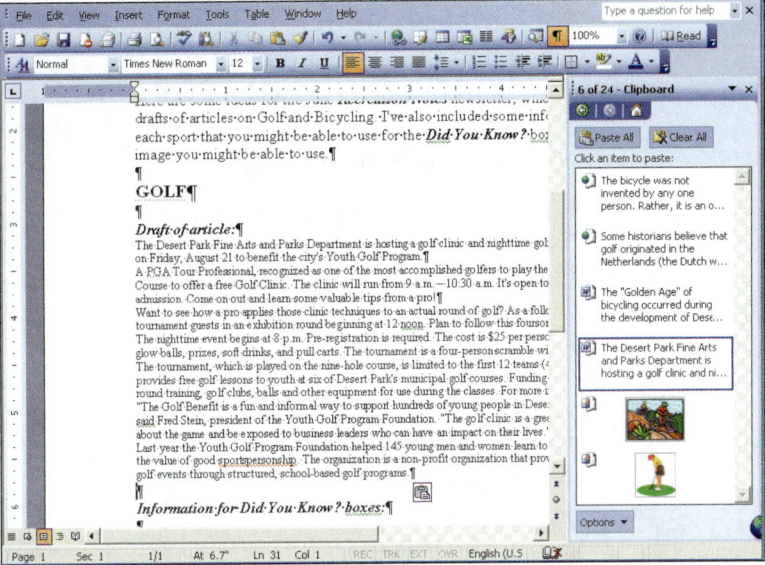

Figure 4.42

3. Position the insertion point in the blank line under the **GOLF** *Information for Did You Know? boxes*. From the **Click an item to paste** on the **Clipboard** task pane, click the second item in the item list, the one that begins *Some historians believe*.

   The text is placed at the insertion point.

4. Position the insertion point in the blank line under the **GOLF** *Image*. From the **Click an item to paste** on the **Clipboard** task pane, click the sixth item in the item list, the graphic of the golfer.

   The image is placed at the insertion point, as shown in Figure 4.43.

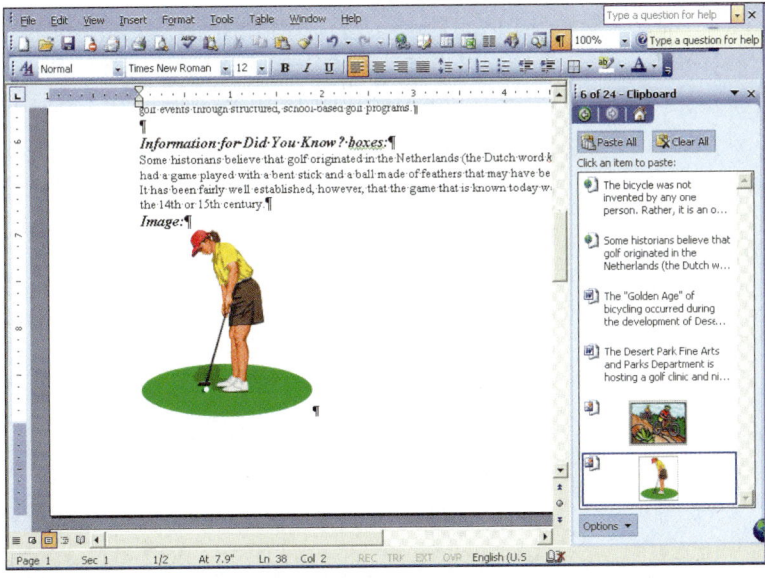

Figure 4.43

Project 4C: Recreation Ideas | **Word** 459

5 In the blank line under the BICYCLING Draft of article, click to position the insertion point. On the Clipboard task pane, under Click an item to paste, click the third item in the item list, the one that begins The "Golden Age" of bicycling. The text is pasted into the document at the insertion point location.

6 Position the insertion point in the blank line under the **BICYCLE** *Information for Did You Know? boxes*. From the **Click an item to paste** on the **Clipboard** task pane, click the text that begins *The bicycle was not invented*.

Compare your document to Figure 4.44.

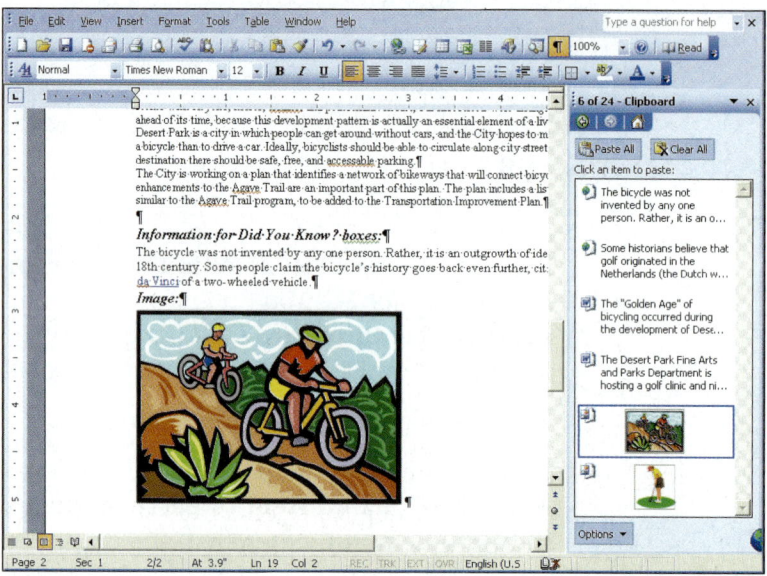

Figure 4.44

7 Position the insertion point in the blank line under the **Bicycling** *Image*. From the **Click an item to paste** on the **Clipboard** task pane, click the fifth item in the item list, the graphic of the bicyclists.

8 Under **Click an item to paste** on the **Clipboard** task pane, move the pointer over the first item in the list. Click the arrow.

9 From the menu, click **Delete**.

The item is removed from the list. You can remove one item from the Clipboard without disturbing the rest of the items stored there.

10 At the top of the **Clipboard** task pane, click **Clear All**.

All of the items are removed from the list.

11 In the title bar of the **Clipboard** task pane, click the Close button ⊠.

The Clipboard task pane closes.

12 On the Standard toolbar, click the **Save** button 🔲.

460   Word | Chapter 4: Creating Documents with Multiple Columns and Special Formats

Activity 4.20 Using the Thesaurus

The *thesaurus* is a language tool that assists in your writing by suggesting synonyms (words that have the same meaning) for words that you select.

1 From the **Edit** menu, click **Find**.

The Find and Replace dialog box displays.

2 In the **Find and Replace** dialog box, in the **Find what** box, type **training** and click **Find next**.

The word *training* in the Golf section is highlighted.

3 In the **Find and Replace** dialog box, click **Cancel**.

4 Right-click the selected word. From the shortcut menu, point to **Synonyms**.

A list of synonyms displays, as shown in Figure 4.45.

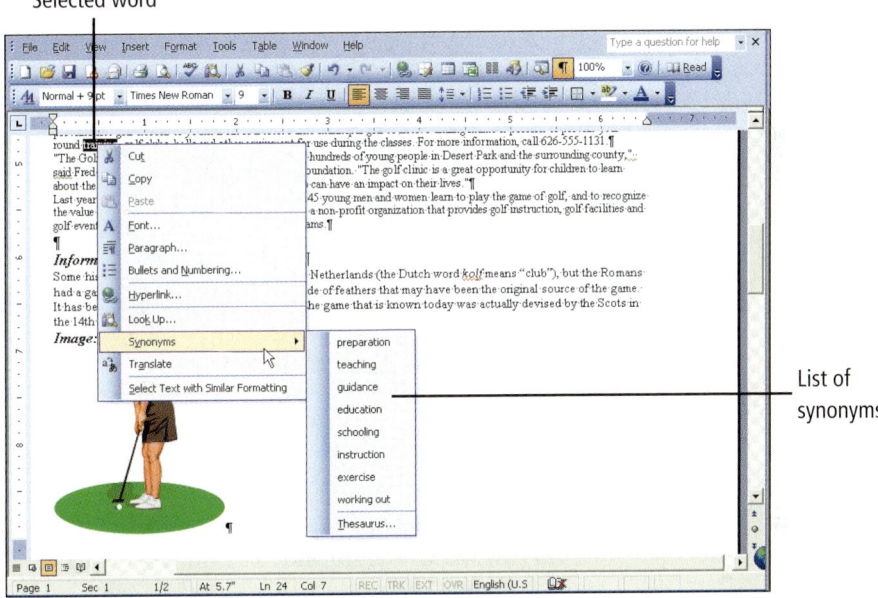

Figure 4.45

5 In the list of synonyms, click **instruction**.

Instruction replaces *training* in the document.

6 From the **Edit** menu, click **Find**. In the **Find and Replace** dialog box, in the **Find what** box, type **impact** and click **Find next**.

The word *impact* in the Golf section is highlighted.

Project 4C: Recreation Ideas | **Word**   461

7 In the **Find and Replace** dialog box, click **Cancel** to close the dialog box.

8 Right-click the selected word. From the shortcut menu, point to **Synonyms**.

A list of synonyms displays. Sometimes the best word is not included in the list of synonyms.

9 At the bottom of the synonym list, click **Thesaurus**.

The Research task pane displays and lists words from the English Thesaurus. Notice that there are more options available. See Figure 4.46.

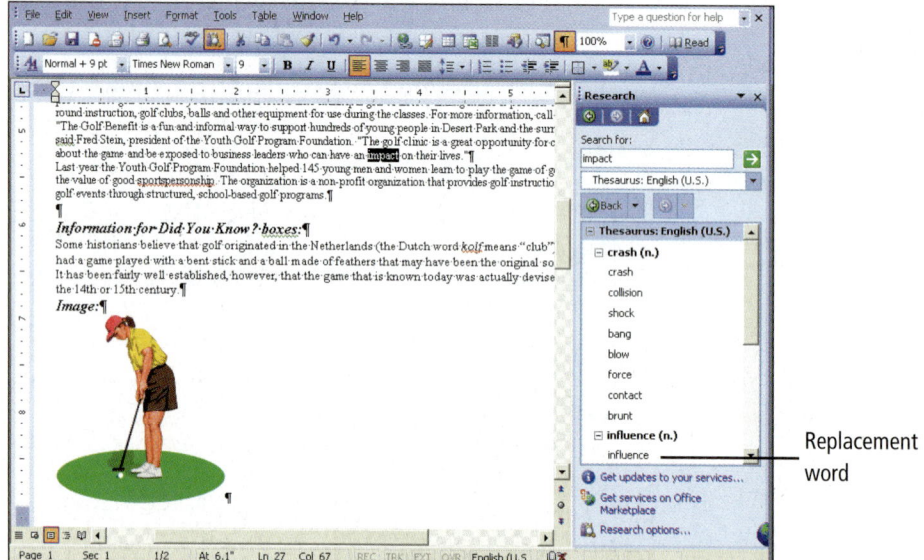

Figure 4.46

10 In the **Research** task pane, point to *influence*, click the down arrow on the right side of the word, and then, from the displayed list, click **Insert**.

Influence replaces *impact* in the document.

11 In the title bar of the **Research** task pane, click the **Close** button.

On the Standard toolbar, click the **Save** button.

Objective 8
Find Objects with the Select Browse Object Button

The Select Browse Object button is located at the bottom of the vertical scroll bar and can be used to navigate through a document by type of object. For example, you can move from one footnote to the next or from one section to the next. This feature can be used on short documents but is most effective when you are navigating long documents. You can navigate using several different object elements, by graphic, table, section, footnote, or page.

Activity 4.21 Using the Select Browse Object Menu to Find Document Elements

1 With the **4C_Recreation_Ideas_Firstname_Lastname** open, at the bottom of the vertical scroll bar, click the **Select Browse Object** button.

The Select Browse Object palette displays, as shown in Figure 4.47. The order of the buttons in the Select Browse Object palette on your computer may be different from what is shown in the figure. Examine the Object buttons on the palette and compare them to the ones shown in the table in Figure 4.48 to identify each button and its purpose.

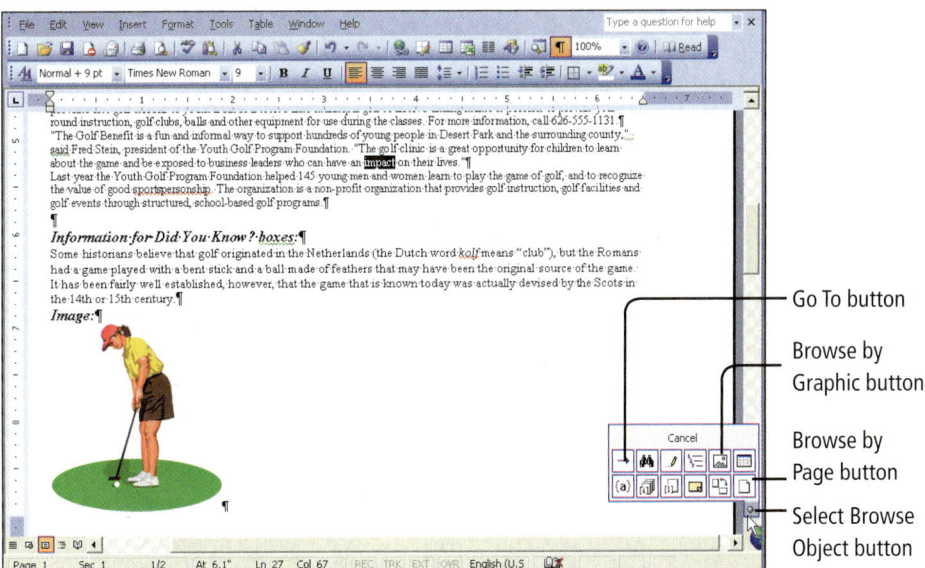

Figure 4.47

Buttons on the Select Browse Object Palette

ScreenTip	Button	Description
Browse by Field	{a}	Moves between objects in your document that have been defined as fields.
Browse by Endnote		Moves from one endnote to the next.
Browse by Footnote		Moves from one footnote to the next.
Browse by Comment		Moves between comments that have been inserted in your document.
Browse by Section		Moves from one section to the next.
Browse by Page		Moves by page in your document. This is the most common way to browse a document and is the default setting for the Select Browse Object button.
Go To	→	Moves to the next occurrence of an object as defined in the Go To page of the Find and Replace dialog box.
Find		Moves to the next word or phrase that has been entered in the Find and Replace dialog box.
Browse by Edits		Moves between Edits that have been made to your document using the Track Changes command.
Browse by Heading		Moves between Heading styles that have been applied to a document.
Browse by Graphic		Moves between graphic objects that have been inserted in your document.
Browse by Table		Moves between tables in your document.

Figure 4.48

2 On the **Select Browse Object** palette, click the **Browse by Page** button.

The insertion point moves to the top of the second page.

3 Click the **Select Browse Object** button again. On the **Select Browse Object** palette, click the **Go To** button →.

The Find and Replace dialog box displays. Notice that the Go To tab at the top of the Find and Replace dialog box is selected. This page of the dialog box enables you to go to a specific page, or navigate by various objects.

4 In the **Find and Replace** dialog box, under **Go to what**, scroll to the top of the list and click **Page**.

5 Under **Enter page number**, type **1**

Compare your Find and Replace dialog box to Figure 4.49.

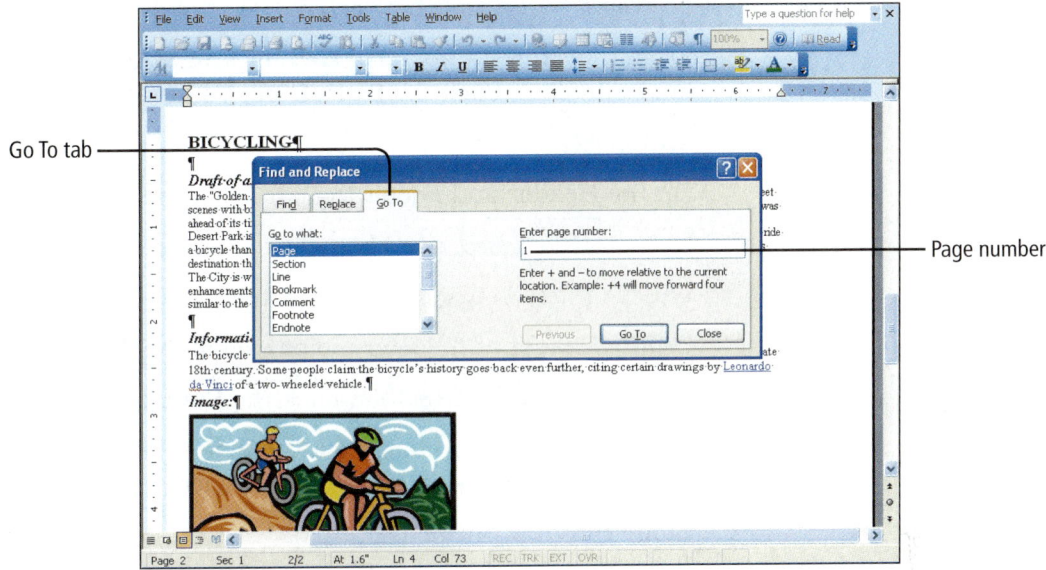

Figure 4.49

6 In the **Find and Replace** dialog box, click **Go To**.

The insertion point moves to the top of the first page of the document.

7 Close the **Find and Replace** dialog box. Click the **Select Browse Object** button. In the **Select Browse Object** palette, click the **Browse by Graphic** button.

The insertion point moves to the graphic of the golfer. The arrow buttons above and below the Select Browse Object button can be used to navigate to the next or previous object location. These buttons take on the name of the type of object that has been set with the Select Browse Object button.

8 Click the **Next Graphic arrow** below the **Select Browse Object** button.

The insertion point moves to the graphic of the bicyclists.

Project 4C: Recreation Ideas | **Word** 465

9 Click the **Select Browse Object** button . In the **Select Browse Object** palette, click the **Browse by Page** button .

This returns the Select Browse Object button to the Browse by Page function, which is the most common method for browsing a document. The Select Browse Object button retains the method of browsing that was last selected.

10 From the **View** menu, click **Header and Footer**. On the Header and Footer toolbar, click the **Switch Between Header and Footer** button .

11 On the Header and Footer toolbar, click the **Insert AutoText** button , and then click **Filename**.

The file name is inserted in the footer.

12 On the Header and Footer toolbar, click the **Close** button .

13 From the Standard toolbar, click the **Save** button .

14 On the Standard toolbar, click the **Print Preview** button . Take a moment to check your work. On the Print Preveiw toolbar, click the **Close Preview** button .

15 On the Standard toolbar, click the **Print** button . Close the document saving any changes.

End You have completed Project 4C

Summary

Microsoft Word includes many features that can be used to create a newsletter or a Web page, similar to those created by desktop publishing or Web design programs. In this chapter, you created a masthead by changing text into a graphic element with the WordArt program, added borders and shading to paragraphs for special effect, and used special character formats to create more distinctive headings. You learned how to change from a single- to a multiple-column document and to control where a column ends. You practiced adding hyperlinks to a Word document and saving it as a Web page.

Finally, you practiced gathering information from several resources to create a new document. This collect-and-paste process can involve using the Office Clipboard, the Microsoft Research tools to find supporting information, and such common but helpful tools as a thesaurus. The Select Browse Object button was introduced as a tool to help navigate within a document.

In This Chapter You Practiced How To

- Create a Decorative Title
- Create Multicolumn Documents
- Add Special Paragraph Formatting
- Use Special Character Formats
- Insert Hyperlinks
- Preview and Save a Document as a Web Page
- Locate Supporting Information
- Find Objects with the Select Browse Object Button

Word
Concepts Assessments

Matching   Match each term in the second column with its correct definition in the first column by writing the letter of the term on the blank line in front of the correct definition.

_____ 1. A Microsoft Office subprogram used to change text into a decorative graphic.

_____ 2. Text or graphic that you can click to move to a file, another page in a Web site, or a different Web site.

_____ 3. Laws that protect authors of original works, including text, art, photographs, and music.

_____ 4. The place where copied items are stored temporarily until they are pasted in another location.

_____ 5. The alignment used, especially in columns of text, to create a flush edge of text on both the left and right side of a column.

_____ 6. A button on the Standard toolbar that connects you to a group of resources for exploring information.

_____ 7. A special font effect where the lower-case letters are changed to capital letters but remain the height of lowercase letters.

_____ 8. The process of gathering various pieces of information together on the Office Clipboard for use in another document.

_____ 9. A dialog box used to add special formats to a paragraph so it stands out from the rest of the text.

_____ 10. A document that has been saved with a .mht extension so it can be viewed with a Web browser.

_____ 11. A dialog box used to change the appearance of a WordArt graphic.

_____ 12. The type of section break used when you want columns to end at approximately the same place on the page.

_____ 13. A dialog box used to create a Hyperlink.

_____ 14. An option used to expand a clip art search to include all possible locations.

_____ 15. A Word window that provides commonly used commands; useful for searching for clip art, researching information, or collecting items on the clipboard.

A Borders and Shading
B Collect and Paste
C Continuous
D Copyright
E Everywhere
F Format WordArt
G Hyperlink
H Insert Hyperlink
I Justified
J Office Clipboard
K Research
L Small caps
M Task pane
N Web page
O WordArt

Concepts Assessments (continued)

Fill in the Blank Write the correct answer in the space provided.

1. Netscape and Internet Explorer are examples of _____ _____.

2. To change the font size and style of a WordArt graphic, use the _____ _____ dialog box.

3. The title in a newsletter is known as a _____.

4. Microsoft Publisher is a _____ _____ program.

5. The Office Clipboard can store up to _____ items.

6. To artificially end a column and move the rest of the text in that column to the top of the next column, you can insert a _____ _____.

7. When you change from a two-column format to a one-column format, Word inserts a _____ _____.

8. To change one column of text into two columns, use the _____ button on the Standard toolbar.

9. To move in a document from one section to the next, or from one graphic to the next, use the _____ button.

10. If you want to substitute one word for another and need to look up a synonym, use the Word language tool called a _____.

Word chapter four

Skill Assessments

Project 4D — Council News

Objectives: *Create a Decorative Title, Create Multicolumn Documents, Add Special Paragraph Formatting, Use Special Character Formats, and Find Objects with the Select Browse Object Button.*

In the following Skill Assessment, you will create a newsletter for the Desert Park City Council. Your completed document will look similar to Figure 4.50. You will save your publication as *4D_Council_News_Firstname_Lastname*.

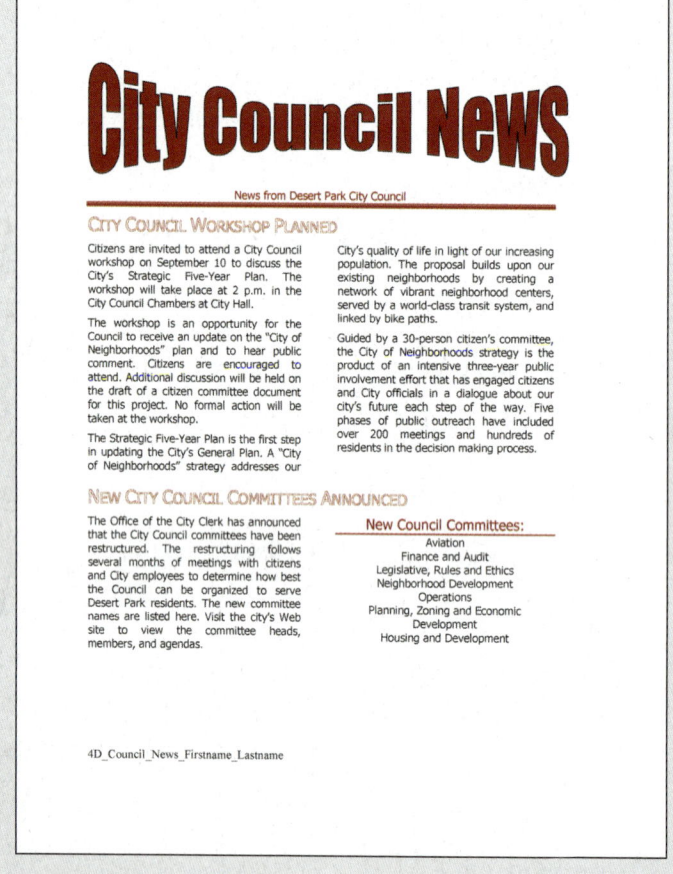

Figure 4.50

1. On the Standard toolbar, click the **Open** button and then navigate to the location where the student files for this textbook are stored. Locate **w04D_Council_News** and click once to select it. Then, in the lower right corner of the **Open** dialog box, click **Open**.

2. From the **File** menu, click **Save As**. In the **Save As** dialog box, click the **Save in arrow** and then navigate to the location in which you are storing your files for this chapter. In the **File name** box type **4D_Council_News_Firstname_Lastname** and click **Save**.

(Project 4D–Council News continues on the next page)

470　Word | Chapter 4: Creating Documents with Multiple Columns and Special Formats

Skill Assessments (continued)

(Project 4D–Council News continued)

3. Be sure that the nonprinting formatting marks are displayed and then be sure the insertion point is at the top of the document, to the left of the empty paragraph mark. From the **Insert** menu, point to **Picture** and then click **WordArt**. In the **WordArt Gallery** dialog box, in the first row, click the fourth style and then click **OK**.

4. In the **Edit WordArt Text** dialog box type **City Council News** and then change the **Size** box to **66** Click **OK**.

5. Click the WordArt graphic to select it, if necessary. On the floating WordArt toolbar, click the **Format WordArt** button. In the **Format WordArt** dialog box, under **Fill**, click the **Color arrow**. On the displayed color palette, in the second row, click the first color—**Dark Red**. Under **Line**, click the **Color arrow**, click **Dark Red**, and then click **OK**. Alternatively, under Line, click the Color arrow, click No Line, and then click OK. The letters will appear slightly narrower. The color of the WordArt graphic is changed. On the Standard toolbar, click the **Save** button.

6. On the line below your inserted WordArt, click to the left of *City Council Workshop Planned* and press Enter. Notice that when the WordArt is deselected, the WordArt toolbar is closed. Move the insertion point to the left of the empty line you just created and type **News from Desert Park City Council** Select the text you just typed, on the Formatting toolbar click the **Center** button, and then click the arrow on the **Font Color** button. From the displayed palette, click **Dark Red**.

7. With the line you typed still selected, from the **Format** menu, click **Borders and Shading**. In the **Borders and Shading** dialog box, click the **Borders tab**. Under **Setting**, click **Custom**. Under **Style**, scroll down and click the option with a thick bottom line and a thin line above it (refer to Figure 4.50). Click the **Color arrow** and then click **Dark Red**. In the **Preview** area, click the **bottom line** in the preview graphic and then click **OK**. On the Standard toolbar, click **Save** to save the changes you have made.

8. Select the text *City Council Workshop Planned* and, from the **Format** menu, click **Font**. In the **Font** dialog box, change the number in the **Size** box to **18**. Click the **Font Color arrow** and click **Dark Red**. Under **Effects**, select the **Outline** and **Small caps** check boxes and then click **OK**. Scroll down to view the lower half of the document and then repeat this process to apply the same font format to the headline *New City Council Committees Announced*. Alternatively, apply the font format by using the Format Painter.

(Project 4D–Council News continues on the next page)

Skill Assessments (continued)

(Project 4D–Council News continued)

9. Scroll to view the upper portion of your document. Beginning with *Citizens are invited*, select the text between the two headlines. (Hint: Click to the left of *Citizens*, hold down Shift, and then click to the right of the period following *process*.) Do not include the paragraph mark at the end of the selected text. On the Standard toolbar, click the **Columns** button, drag to select **two columns**, and then release the left mouse button. The selected text is arranged into two columns, and section breaks are inserted before and after the selected text. Repeat this process to format the text under *New City Council*, beginning with *The Office of the City Clerk*, to a two-column format. On the Standard toolbar, click the **Save** button.

10. Place the insertion point to the left of *Aviation*. Type **New Council Committees:** and press Enter. Select the heading you just typed and the list of committees listed under it, including those in the second column, and then, on the Formatting toolbar, click the **Center** button.

11. Select *New Council Committees:* and, on the Formatting toolbar, click the **Font Color arrow** and then click **Dark Red**. Click the **Font Size arrow** and then click **14**. From the **Format** menu, display the **Borders and Shading** dialog box and click the **Borders tab**. Under **Style**, be sure the single line at the top of the style list is selected. Click the **Color arrow** and then click **Dark Red**. Click the **Width arrow** and then click **1 pt**. In the **Preview** area, click the **bottom line** and then click **OK**.

12. At the lower end of the vertical scroll bar, click the **Select Browse Object** button to display the menu. Point to the buttons until you locate the **Browse by Section** button and then click it. This sets the browse object so you can move from section to section and moves the insertion point to the next section. Point to the arrow below the Select Browse Object button; the ScreenTip displays *Next Section*. Point to the arrow above the Select Browse Object button; the ScreenTip displays Previous Section. Click the **Previous Section arrow**. The insertion point moves up the document to the previous section. Continue clicking the **Previous section arrow** until the insertion point is at the WordArt Graphic at the top of the document.

13. Click the **WordArt** graphic to select it and then, from the WordArt toolbar, click the **Format WordArt** button. In the **Format WordArt** dialog box, under **Line**, click the **Color arrow** and then click **black**—the first color in the first row. A graphic like WordArt has two parts—its surrounding line, and its interior fill. This action will change the surrounding line color to black. Click **OK**. Click in the body of the document to deselect the graphic.

(Project 4D–Council News continues on the next page)

Skill Assessments (continued)

(Project 4D–Council News continued)

14. From the **View** menu, display the Header and Footer toolbar, switch to the footer, and then, on the Header and Footer toolbar, click **Insert AutoText**. From the displayed list, click **Filename**. Close the Header and Footer toolbar.

15. On the Standard toolbar, click the **Save** button and then click the **Print Preview** button to preview the document. Click the **Print** button. Close the Print Preview window and close the document, saving changes if prompted to do so.

End You have completed Project 4D

Project 4E—Public Safety

Objectives: *Insert Hyperlinks, Preview and Save a Document as a Web Page, and Locate Supporting Information.*

In the following Skill Assessment, you will create a Web page for the Desert Park Department of Public Safety. You will start with a file that contains the headings for the articles and then use the collect-and-paste technique to gather the necessary information for the article. You will add hyperlinks and save the document as a Web page. Your completed document will look similar to Figure 4.51. You will save your publication as *4E_Public_Safety_Firstname_Lastname*.

1. Be sure your computer is online and connected to the Internet. Start Word. On the Standard toolbar, click the **Open** button and navigate to the location where the student files for this textbook are stored. Locate **w04E_Public_Safety** and click once to select it. In the lower right corner of the **Open** dialog box, click **Open**.

2. From the **File** menu, click **Save As**. In the **Save As** dialog box, click the **Save in arrow** and navigate to the location in which you are storing your files for this chapter. In the **File name** box, type **4E_Public_Safety_Firstname_Lastname** and then click **Save**.

3. From the **Edit** menu, click **Office Clipboard**. If necessary, at the top of the Clipboard task pane, click the Clear All button to remove any items that display.

4. On the Standard toolbar, click the **Open** button. Locate and open the **w04E_Block_Clubs** file, and then press Ctrl + A to select all of the text. On the Standard toolbar, click the **Copy** button. The selected text is copied to the Office Clipboard. Close the w04E_Block_Clubs file.

5. Open and copy all of the text in the file **w04E_Fire**. Close the w04E_Fire file. The text is copied to the Clipboard.

(Project 4E–Public Safety continues on the next page)

Project 4E: Public Safety | **Word** 473

Word
chapter four
Skill Assessments (continued)

(Project 4E–Public Safety continued)

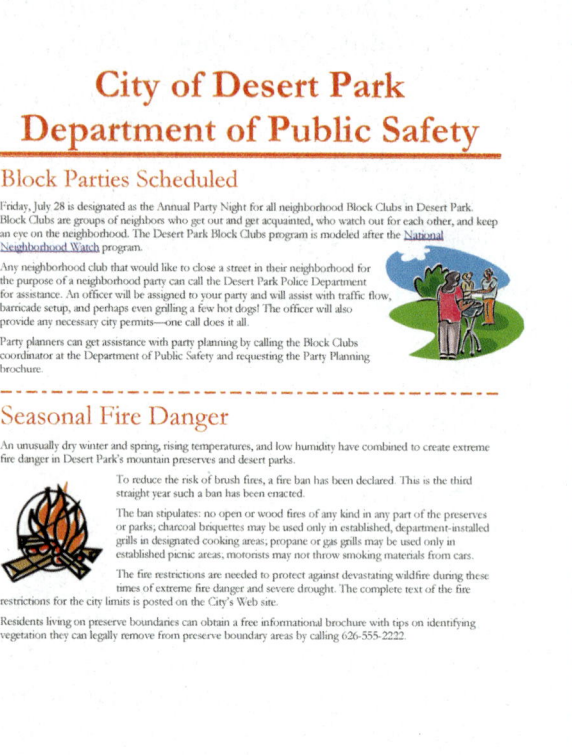

Figure 4.51

6. From the **Insert** menu, point to **Picture** and then click **Clip Art**. In the **Clip Art** task pane, in the **Search for** box, type **BBQ** If the **Search in** box does not display *All Collections*, click the **Search in arrow** and select **Everywhere**. Click the **Results should be arrow**, be sure only **Clip Art** is selected, and then click the **Go** button. Scroll the list of available images and locate the one shown in Figure 4.51. (If you cannot locate that image, choose one that is similar; alternatively, use the w04E_BBQ image that is with the student files for this book.) Copy the image to the Office Clipboard as described in Activity 4.16, step 11. On the image of the BBQ, click the arrow and then click Copy from the displayed menu.

7. In the title bar of the **Clip Art** task pane, click the **Other Task Panes arrow** and then click **Clipboard**. The image you copied is displayed at the top of the clipboard. Recall that as you copy items to the Clipboard, the most recent item moves to the top of the list.

(Project 4E–Public Safety continues on the next page)

Word chapter four
Skill Assessments (continued)

(Project 4E–Public Safety continued)

8. Place the insertion point to the left of the empty paragraph mark under *Block Parties Scheduled*. On the **Clipboard** task pane, click the block of text beginning with *Friday, July 28 is*. The text is pasted to the Public Safety document at the location of your insertion point.

9. Place the insertion point to the left of the empty paragraph mark under *Seasonal Fire Danger*. On the **Clipboard** task pane, click the block of text beginning with *An unusually dry winter*. The text is pasted to the Public Safety document. On the Standard toolbar, click the **Save** button.

10. In the Block Parties article, click to the left of the paragraph that begins *Any neighborhood club*. In the **Clipboard** task pane, click the **BBQ image** to insert it in the article. Click the inserted image to select it and, on the floating Picture toolbar, click the **Text Wrapping** button. From the displayed list, click **Tight**. Drag the image to the right, as shown in Figure 4.51, aligning the right sizing handles with the right margin and the top sizing handles at approximately **2.5 inches on the vertical ruler**. Do not be concerned if your text does not wrap exactly as shown in the figure. In the **Clipboard** task pane, click the **Clear All** button and then close the Clipboard task pane.

11. In the *Seasonal Fire* article, click to the left of the paragraph that begins *To reduce the risk*. From the **Insert** menu, point to **Picture** and then click **From File**. In the **Insert Picture** dialog box, navigate to the location where the student files for this textbook are stored and locate **w04E_No_Fire**. If you do not see the file, click the Files of type box arrow and then click All files from the displayed list. Click the file to select it and then click Insert.

12. Click the inserted image to select it and, on the floating Picture toolbar, click the **Text Wrapping** button. From the displayed list click **Square**. Compare your document to Figure 4.51.

13. Under the *Block Parties Scheduled* heading, at the end of the paragraph that begins *Friday, July 28*, select *National Neighborhood Watch* in the last sentence. (Hint: Double-click *National* to select it, hold down [Shift] and hold down [Ctrl], and then press [→] two times.) From the **Insert** menu click **Hyperlink**.

14. In the **Insert Hyperlink** dialog box, under **Link to**, click **Existing File or Web Page**. Under **Address**, type http://www.nnwi.org/

15. In the upper right corner of the **Insert Hyperlink** dialog box, click **ScreenTip**. In the **Set Hyperlink ScreenTip** dialog box, type **National Neighborhood Watch Institute** In the **Set Hyperlink ScreenTip** dialog box, click **OK**. At the bottom of the **Insert Hyperlink** dialog box, click **OK**. The hyperlink is recorded, and the selected text changes to blue and is underlined.

(Project 4E–Public Safety continues on the next page)

Skill Assessments (continued)

(Project 4E–Public Safety continued)

16. Right-click the **No Fire image** and then click **Hyperlink** from the shortcut menu. Repeat Steps 14 and 15, but type **http://www.smokeybear.com/** for the address and **Fire Safety Tips** for the ScreenTip.

17. From the **View** menu, display the Header and Footer toolbar, switch to the footer, and then, on the Header and Footer toolbar, click **Insert AutoText**. From the displayed list, click **Filename**. Close the Header and Footer toolbar. On the Standard toolbar, click the **Save** button.

18. From the **File** menu, click **Save as Web Page**. In the **Save As** dialog box, navigate to the location in which you are saving your files. In the lower portion of the **Save As** dialog box, click **Change Title**. The **Set Page Title** dialog box displays. Type **Public Safety** and then click **OK** to close the **Set Page Title** dialog box. In the lower right corner of the **Save As** dialog box, click **Save**. Click **Continue** to acknowledge the message box that displays. The Web page displays.

19. Point to the two hyperlinks you created to display the ScreenTips. Press and click to go to the related Web site(s). Close the site(s) to return to your Web page.

20. On the Standard toolbar, click the **Print Preview** button. Take a moment to check your work. On the **Print Preview** toolbar, click the **Close Preview** button.

21. Click the **Print** button to print the Public Safety Web page and then close the document.

End You have completed Project 4E

Project 4F—IT Volunteers

Objectives: *Add Special Paragraph Formatting, Use Special Character Formats, Insert Hyperlinks, Locate Supporting Information, and Preview and Save a Document as a Web Page.*

In the following Skill Assessment, you will create a Web page notifying the citizens of Desert Park about an opportunity to volunteer their computer skills. Your completed document will look similar to Figure 4.52. You will save your publication as *4F_IT_Volunteer_Firstname_Lastname*.

1. On the Standard toolbar, click the **Open** button and navigate to the location where the student files for this textbook are stored. Locate **w04F_IT_Volunteer** and click once to select it. In the lower right corner of the **Open** dialog box, click **Open**.

2. From the **File** menu, click **Save As**. In the **Save As** dialog box, click the **Save in arrow** and navigate to the location in which you are storing your files for this chapter. In the **File name** box type **4F_IT_Volunteer_Firstname_Lastname** and click **Save**.

(Project 4F—IT Volunteers continues on the next page)

Skill Assessments (continued)

(Project 4F–IT Volunteers continued)

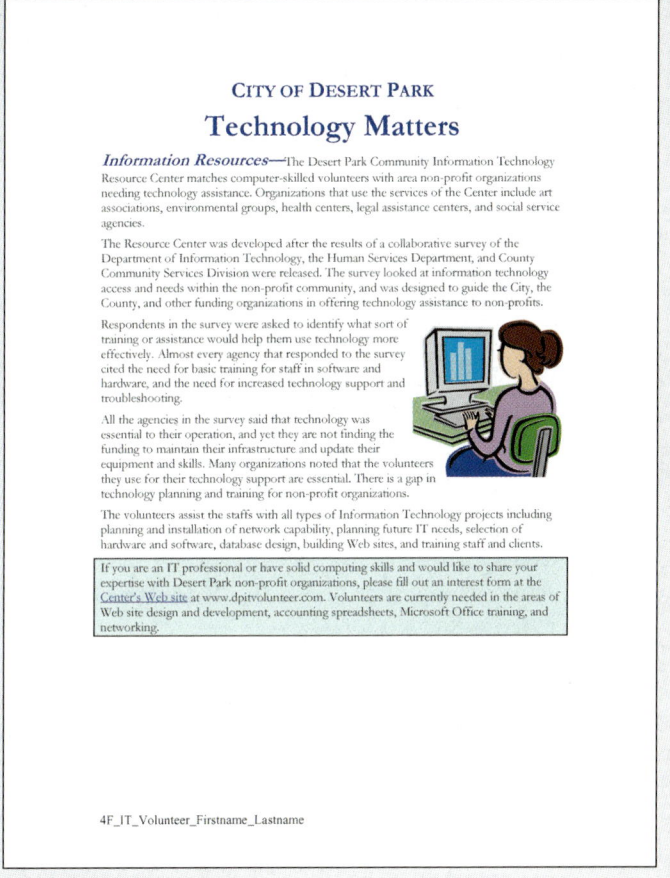

Figure 4.52

3. Press [Ctrl] + [A] to select all of the text in the document. Change the font to **Garamond 12 pt**. From the **Format** menu, display the **Paragraph** dialog box. Under **Spacing**, change the number in the **After** box to **6 pt**. and click **OK**.

4. Hold down [Ctrl] and press [Home] to place the insertion point at the top of the document. Press [Enter] to create an empty line preceding the text. Click to the left of the empty line and on two separate lines type

   City of Desert Park

   Technology Matters

5. Select *City of Desert Park* and, from the **Format** menu, click **Font**. In the **Font** dialog box, under **Font style**, click **Bold**. Under **Size**, click **20**. Click the **Font color arrow** and, in the second row, click the sixth color—**Blue**. Under **Effects**, select the **Small caps** check box and then click **OK**.

(Project 4F–IT Volunteers continues on the next page)

Project 4F: IT Volunteers | **Word** 477

Word chapter four
Skill Assessments (continued)

(Project 4F–IT Volunteers continued)

6. Select *Technology Matters* and, on the Formatting toolbar, use the **Font Size** button to change the font size to **28 pt**. Click the **Bold** button and then click the **Font Color arrow**. From the displayed palette, click **Blue**. Select the two title lines you just formatted and then, on the Formatting toolbar, click the **Center** button.

7. Under the two heading lines, click to the left of *The Desert Park Community* and type **Information Resources** From the **Insert** menu, click **Symbol**. Click the **Special Characters** tab, be sure **Em Dash** is selected, and then click **Insert**. Close the **Symbol** dialog box. Select *Information Resources* and the following dash and then, using the Formatting toolbar, change the font size to **16 pt**., change the font color to **Blue**, and add **Bold** and **Italic** for emphasis.

8. Place the insertion point at the start of the paragraph beginning *Respondents in the survey*. Display the **Insert** menu, point to **Picture**, and then click **Clip Art**. In the **Clip Art** task pane, in the **Search for** box, type **computer** Be sure the **Search in box** displays **All Collections**. Click the **Results should be arrow**, be sure only **Clip Art** is selected, and then click the **Go** button. Locate the image of a woman at a computer as shown in Figure 4.52. Click the figure to insert it in the document. Alternatively, insert the file w04F_Computer from your student files by displaying the insert menu, pointing to Picture, and then clicking From File.

9. Close the **Clip Art** task pane. Click the inserted image to select it and, on the floating Picture toolbar, click the **Text Wrapping** button. From the displayed list, click **Square**. Drag the image to the right of the paragraphs as shown in Figure 4.52, aligning its right edge with the right margin and the top edge at approximately **3 inches on the vertical ruler**. Do not be concerned if your text does not wrap exactly as shown in the Figure. On the Standard toolbar, click the **Save** button.

10. Scroll down the document until you can see the last paragraph, which begins *If you are*. Select the paragraph. From the **Format** menu, click **Borders and Shading**. In the **Borders and Shading** dialog box, click the **Shading tab**. Under **Fill**, in the last row, click the fifth color—**Light Turquoise**. Click the **Borders tab** and then, under **Settings**, click **Box**. Click the **Width** arrow and click **1 pt**. Click the **Color arrow** and click **Black**, if necessary, and then click **OK**. Click anywhere to deselect the paragraph and view your formatting. The special format is applied to the last paragraph.

11. In the same paragraph, select *Center's Web site* and then, from the **Insert** menu, click **Hyperlink**. In the **Insert Hyperlink** dialog box, under **Link to**, be sure **Existing File or Web Page** is selected. In the **Address** box, type **http://www.dpitvolunteer.com/**

(Project 4F–IT Volunteers continues on the next page)

Word | Chapter 4: Creating Documents with Multiple Columns and Special Formats

Skill Assessments (continued)

(Project 4F–IT Volunteers continued)

12. On the upper right corner of the **Insert Hyperlink** dialog box, click **ScreenTip**. In the **Set Hyperlink ScreenTip** dialog box, type **Click Here to Volunteer** and then click **OK**. At the bottom of the **Insert Hyperlink** dialog box, click **OK**. The hyperlink is recorded, and the selected text changes to blue and is underlined.

13. From the **Edit** menu, click **Find**. In the **Find and Replace** dialog box, in the **Find what** box, type **cooperative** and then click the **Find Next** button. If necessary, drag the dialog box away from the highlighted word. Leave the **Find and Replace** dialog box open and click the document to make it active. Right-click the highlighted word *cooperative* and point to **Synonyms** on the shortcut menu. To view additional synonyms for the word *cooperative*, click **Thesaurus**. The **Research** task pane displays. Under joint (adj.), point to *collaborative* and then click the arrow on *collaborative*. From the displayed list, click **Insert**; *cooperative* is replaced with *collaborative*.

14. Using the technique in step 13, from either the list of suggested synonymns or by opening the Thesaurus and finding additional synonymns, locate and replace *vital* with *essential* and *efficiently* with *effectively*. Close the **Find and Replace** dialog box and close the **Research** task pane.

15. From the **View** menu, display the Header and Footer toolbar, switch to the footer, and, on the Header and Footer toolbar, click **Insert AutoText**. From the displayed list, click **Filename**. Close the Header and Footer toolbar. On the Standard toolbar, click the **Save** button.

16. From the **File** menu, click **Save As Web Page**. In the **Save As** dialog box, navigate to the location in which you are saving your files. In the lower portion of the **Save As** dialog box, click **Change Title**. The **Set Page Title** dialog box displays. Type **IT Volunteer** and then click **OK** to close the **Set Page Title** dialog box. In the lower right corner of the **Save As** dialog box, click **Save**. Click **Continue** to acknowledge the message box that displays. The Web page is displayed in Word.

17. On the Standard toolbar, click the **Print Preview** button. Take a moment to check your work. On the **Print Preview** toolbar, click the **Close Preview** button.

18. Click the **Print** button and then close the document.

End You have completed Project 4F

chapter four — Word
Performance Assessments

Project 4G—Youth

Objectives: *Create a Decorative Title, Add Special Paragraph Formatting, Use Special Character Formats, Insert Hyperlinks, and Preview and Save a Document as a Web Page.*

In the following Performance Assessment, you will finish formatting a document for the Family Services Department of Desert Park. The document will then be saved as a Web page. Your completed document will look similar to Figure 4.53. You will save your document as *4G_Youth_Firstname_Lastname*.

Figure 4.53

1. Click the **Open** button and navigate to the location where the student files for this textbook are stored. Locate and open **w04G_Youth**. From the **File** menu, display the **Save As** dialog box. Navigate to the location in which you are storing your files for this chapter. In the **File name** box, type **4G_Youth_Firstname_Lastname** and click **Save**.

(**Project 4G**–Youth continues on the next page)

480 **Word** | Chapter 4: Creating Documents with Multiple Columns and Special Formats

Word chapter four

Performance Assessments (continued)

(Project 4G–Youth continued)

2. With the insertion point at the top of the document, click the **Insert** menu, point to **Picture**, and then click **WordArt**. In the third row, click the first style and then click **OK**. In the **Edit WordArt Text** dialog box, type **Desert Park Family Services** and click **OK**.

3. Click the **WordArt** graphic and, on the WordArt toolbar, click the **WordArt Shape** button. In the first row of the displayed palette, click the fifth style—the **Chevron Up** style. The WordArt graphic changes to the selected shape. Drag the right center sizing handle to the right margin—approximately **6.5 inches on the horizontal ruler**.

4. In the paragraph beginning with *The fair will focus*, select *dental care* at the end of the first line and then, from the **Insert** menu, display the **Insert Hyperlink** dialog box. Under **Link to**, be sure **Existing File or Web Page** is selected. In the **Address** box, type http://ada.org/public/topics/infants.html

5. In the upper right corner of the dialog box, click **ScreenTip**. Type **American Dental Association Tips** and then click **OK**. At the bottom of the **Insert Hyperlink** dialog box, click **OK**. The hyperlink is recorded, and the selected text changes to blue and is underlined.

6. In the same paragraph select *immunization*. Following the instructions in Steps 4 and 5, add a hyperlink to immunization, but for the address type **http://www.cdc.gov.nip/vfc/** and for the **ScreenTip** type **CDC Immunization Recommendations** and then click **OK** twice.

7. Scroll to the bottom of the page. In the paragraph beginning with *There's something*, click to place the insertion point to the left of *You* at the beginning of the second sentence. Press [Enter]. Select the paragraph you just created, beginning with *You can pick*, and, from the **Format** menu, display the **Borders and Shading** dialog box. Under **Setting**, click **Box**, change the **Width** of the border to **2¼ pt.**, and then change the **Color** to **Bright Green**—the fourth color in the fourth row. Click **OK**. Save your changes.

8. Select the text within the border and, from the **Format** menu, open the **Font** dialog box. Change the **Size** to **16**, the **Font style** to **Bold**, and the **Font color** to **Blue**. Under **Effects**, select the **Small caps** check box. Click **OK**. On the Formatting toolbar, click **Center** to center the text horizontally.

(Project 4G–Youth continues on the next page)

Word Chapter 4

Performance Assessments (continued)

(Project 4G–Youth continued)

9. Scroll to view the upper portion of your document. In the Child Health Fair article, in the paragraph beginning with *The Fair is part*, click to place the insertion point to the right of Desert Park Month. From the **Insert** menu, point to **Picture** and then click **Clip Art**. In the **Clip Art** task pane, search for **toothbrush** in the Clip Art collection. Locate the toothbrush image displayed in Figure 4.53. (If you cannot locate that image, select another image of a toothbrush; alternatively, use the w04G_Toothbrush image that is included the student files for this book.) Click the image to insert it. With the image selected, on the Picture toolbar, click the **Text Wrapping** button and then click **Tight**. Use the Rotate handle to rotate the image so it is on an angle as displayed in Figure 4.53 and then position it in the approximate location shown in the figure. Do not be concerned if your text wraps differently than shown in the figure. Close the **Clip Art** task pane.

10. From the **View** menu, display the Header and Footer toolbar, switch to the footer, click **Insert AutoText**, and then click **Filename**. Close the Header and Footer toolbar. Save your changes.

11. From the **File** menu, click **Web Page Preview**. The document displays as it will when you save it as a Web page. Notice that the toothbrush that you placed in the middle of the paragraph displays on the left side of the text. In the **Web Page** title bar, click the **Close** button to close your browser and return to your 4G_Youth Word file.

12. From the **File** menu, click **Save As Web Page**. Navigate to the location where you are saving your files. In the **Save As** dialog box, click **Change Title**, type **Youth Programs** and then click **OK** to close the **Set Page Title** dialog box. Save the Web page and click **Continue** to acknowledge the message box that displays.

13. **Print** the Web page view of your document and then close it.

 You have completed Project 4G

Project 4H — Cultural Affairs

Objectives: *Create a Decorative Title, Create Multicolumn Documents, Add Special Paragraph Formatting, and Locate Supporting Information.*

In the following Performance Assessment, you will gather information and create a newsletter concerning recent cultural activities in Desert Park. Your completed document will look similar to Figure 4.54. You will save your document as *4H_Cultural Affairs_Firstname_Lastname*.

(Project 4H–Cultural Affairs continues on the next page)

Word
chapter four
Performance Assessments (continued)

(Project 4H–Cultural Affairs continued)

Figure 4.54

1. Make sure you have an active Internet connection, which is required to complete this exercise. Click the **Open** button and navigate to the location where the student files for this textbook are stored. Locate and open **w04H_Cultural_Affairs**. From the **File** menu, display the **Save As** dialog box. Navigate to the location in which you are storing your files for this chapter. In the **File name** box, type **4H_Cultural_Affairs_Firstname_Lastname** and click **Save**.

2. With the insertion point at the top of the document, from the **Insert** menu, point to **Picture** and then click **WordArt**. In the fourth row, click the second style and then click **OK**. In the **Edit WordArt Text** dialog box, type **City of Desert Park** and press Enter. Type **Office of Cultural Affairs** and then click **OK**.

3. Click the **WordArt** graphic. Drag the right center sizing handle to approximately **6.5 inches on the horizontal ruler** to expand the shape and stretch it to the right margin. Click anywhere to deselect the **WordArt**.

(Project 4H–Cultural Affairs continues on the next page)

Project 4H: Cultural Affairs | **Word**   483

Word chapter four
Performance Assessments (continued)

(Project 4H–Cultural Affairs continued)

4. From the **Edit** menu, click **Office Clipboard**. At the top of the **Clipboard** task pane, click the **Clear All** button to remove any items that may be displayed. From your student files, open **w04H_Museum**, select all of the text, click the **Copy** button, and then close the document. The copied text displays as the first item on the Office Clipboard. Open **w04H_Artists**, select all of the text, click the **Copy** button, and then close the document. The text of both articles displays in the Clipboard task pane.

5. On the Standard toolbar, click the **Research** button. In the **Research** task pane, in the **Search for** box, type **museum** and then click the arrow on the second box. From the displayed list, click **Encyclopedia (or Encarta or Encarta Encyclopedia)**. Your system searches and then displays a list. Click the topic *Exhibitions*. In the Encyclopedia window, in the first paragraph starting with *An Exhibition*, select the first sentence and then press Ctrl + C to copy this sentence to the clipboard. Close the encyclopedia.

6. Now you will collect clip art and place it on the Office Clipboard. Click the **Other Task Panes arrow** on the title bar of the **Research** task pane and then click **Clip Art**. In the **Search for** box, type **artist** Be sure the **Search in** box displays **All collections**. Click the arrow on the **Results should be** box and be sure just **Clip Art** is selected. Click the **Go** button. Locate the image shown in Figure 4.54. Click the arrow on the image and then click **Copy**. (If you cannot locate the image shown, select another image of an artist. Alternatively, use the w04H_Artist_Picture that is with the student files for this book.)

7. Click the **Other Task Panes** arrow on the title bar of the **Clip Art** task pane and then click **Clipboard**. Place the insertion point on the empty line under *Museum of Art Relocated* and then click the Clipboard item beginning with *Thanks to a bond issue*. The article is inserted.

8. Place the insertion point on the empty line under *Call for Artists* and insert the article beginning with *The Desert Park Fine Arts*. The artist article is inserted.

9. Select all of the text in the document except the WordArt graphic and the line below the graphic. Click the **Columns** button and drag to select **two columns**. With the text selected, on the Formatting toolbar, click the **Justify** button. Click the **Save** button.

10. With the text still selected, on the **Format** menu, click **Columns**. The **Columns** dialog box displays. The Columns dialog box allows you to control the width of columns and offers some other formatting options. On the right side of the dialog box, select the **Line between** check box. Notice at the bottom of the dialog box, the **Applies to** box displays *Selected Text*. Click **OK**.

(Project 4H–Cultural Affairs continues on the next page)

Performance Assessments (continued)

(Project 4H–Cultural Affairs continued)

11. Position the insertion point to the left of the heading *Call for Artists*. From the **Insert** menu, click **Break** and, in the **Break** dialog box, click **Column break**. Click **OK**. The artist article moves to the top of the second column. On the Standard toolbar, click the **Print Preview** button to see the result of your work so far. On the Print Preview toolbar, click the **Close** button.

12. In the artist article, position the insertion point at the start of the paragraph that begins *A team can include*. From the **Clipboard**, click the artist image to insert it. Use the lower right corner sizing handle to reduce the size of the image to about one quarter of its original size. With the image selected, on the floating Picture toolbar, click the **Text Wrapping** button and then click **Square**. Position the image as shown in Figure 4.54. Do not be concerned if your text does not align exactly as shown in the figure. Click the **Save** button.

13. In the first column of text, position the insertion point to the left of the empty paragraph mark at the end of the museum article. Type **Did you know...** and then press Enter. From the **Clipboard**, click the Encarta information to insert it. Close the **Clipboard** task pane.

14. Select the *Did you know* heading and the inserted reference and change the font size to **11 pt**. From the **Format** menu, display the **Borders and Shading** dialog box. Under **Settings**, click **Shadow**, change the **Color** to **Plum**—the seventh color in the fourth row—and the **Width** to 2¼. Click the **Shading tab** and, in the first row under **No Fill**, click the second color—**5% gray** shading. Click **OK**.

15. Select the text *Did you know...* and add **Bold** emphasis. Then change the font size to **14** and the font color to **Plum** to match the other headings. Move to the top of the newsletter. Select the *Museum of Art Relocated* title and click **Center**. The selected text is centered over the column. Center the title *Call for Artists* over its column in the same manner.

16. Click the **Print Preview** button to see how the document will look when it is printed. Be sure you do not have a stray second page and that the columns are balanced—that is, their bottom edges align at approximately the same place. If you have an empty second page, remove any stray paragraph marks at the end of the document. Add the filename to the footer and save your changes. Print the newsletter and close the document.

End You have completed Project 4H

Word chapter four

Performance Assessments (continued)

Project 4I—Interns

Objectives: *Create a Decorative Title, Add Special Paragraph Formatting, Use Special Character Formats, and Preview and Save a Document as a Web Page.*

In the following Performance Assessment, you will create and format a document announcing the internship program for the city of Desert Park and then save the document as a Web page. Your completed document will look similar to Figure 4.55. You will save your document as 4I_Interns_Firstname_Lastname.

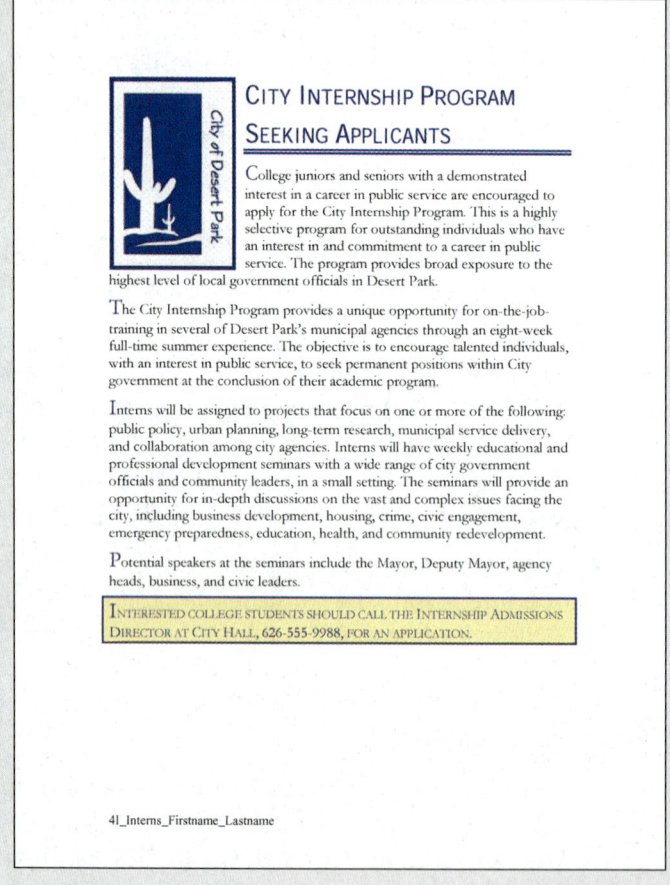

Figure 4.55

1. Click the **Open** button and navigate to the location where the student files for this textbook are stored. Locate and open **w04I_Interns**. From the **File** menu, display the **Save As** dialog box. Navigate to the location in which you are storing your files for this chapter. In the **File name** box type 4I_Interns_Firstname_Lastname and click **Save**.

(**Project 4I–Interns continues on the next page**)

Word
Performance Assessments (continued)

(Project 4I–Interns continued)

2. Select all of the text and change the font to **Garamond 14 pt**. From the **Format** menu, open the **Paragraph** dialog box and, under **Spacing**, increase the number in the **After** box to **6 pt**. Use the Spelling and Grammar Checker to correct the spelling errors in this document. Ignore grammar errors.

3. Select only the first letter in each paragraph and change the font size to **20** and the font color to **Dark Blue**—the sixth color in the first row. After you have formatted the first letter, use the **Format Painter** to copy the format to the first letter of each subsequent paragraph.

4. In the first paragraph, position the insertion point to the left of *College* and press [Enter] twice. Move the insertion point to the first empty line and type **City Internship Program** and press [Enter]. Type **Seeking Applicants**

5. Select the text you just typed and, from the **Format** menu, display the **Font** color dialog box. Change the **Font** to **Tahoma**, the **Size** to **24 pt.**, and the **Color** to **Dark Blue**. Under **Effects**, select the **Small caps** check box. Click **OK**.

6. With the title still selected, from the **Format** menu, display the **Borders and Shading** dialog box. Click the Borders tab if necessary. Under **Style**, scroll down and click the **double underline**, change the **Color** to **Dark Blue**, and then change the **Width** to **1½**. In the **Preview** area, be sure only the bottom line is displayed—click the left, right, and top lines to remove them from the preview if necessary. Check that **Paragraph** displays in the **Applies to** box and then click **OK**.

7. In the title, position the insertion point to the left of *City*. From the **Insert** menu, point to **Picture** and then click **From File**. Navigate to your student files and locate the **w04I_DPLogo** file. Click **Insert**. With the image selected, on the floating Picture toolbar, click the **Text Wrapping** button and then click **Square**. Remove the extra paragraph mark between the title and the first paragraph. The text moves up as shown in Figure 4.55. Save your changes.

8. Scroll to the bottom of the document and select the last paragraph. From the **Format** menu, display the **Borders and Shading** dialog box. Under **Setting**, click **Box**, change the **Color** to **Dark Blue** and the **Width** to **1½**. Be sure the preview area displays a dark blue border on all sides. Click the **Shading tab**. Under **Fill**, click **Light Yellow**—the third color in the last row. Click **OK**.

(Project 4I–Interns continues on the next page)

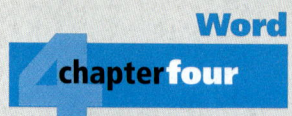

Performance Assessments (continued)

(Project 4I–Interns continued)

9. With the text still selected, open the **Font** dialog box. Change the **Font color** to **Dark Blue**. Under **Effects**, select the **Small caps** check box and then click **OK**.

10. From the **View** menu, display the Header and Footer toolbar, switch to the footer, click **Insert AutoText**, and then click **Filename**. Close the Header and Footer toolbar. Save your changes.

11. From the **File** menu, click **Save As Web Page**. Navigate to the location where you are saving your files. In the **Save As** dialog box, click **Change Title**, type **Intern Program** and then click **OK** to close the **Set Page Title** dialog box.

12. **Save** the Web page and click **Continue** to acknowledge the message box that displays. Print the Web page and then close it.

 You have completed Project 4I

488 Word | Chapter 4: Creating Documents with Multiple Columns and Special Formats

Mastery Assessments

Project 4J — Desert Oasis

Objectives: *Create a Decorative Title, Create Multicolumn Documents, Add Special Paragraph Formatting, Use Special Character Formats, and Locate Supporting Information.*

In the following Mastery Assessment, you will create a newsletter published by the Parks and Recreation Department in Desert Park. Your completed newsletter will look like Figure 4.56. You will save your document as *4J_Desert_Oasis_Firstname_Lastname*.

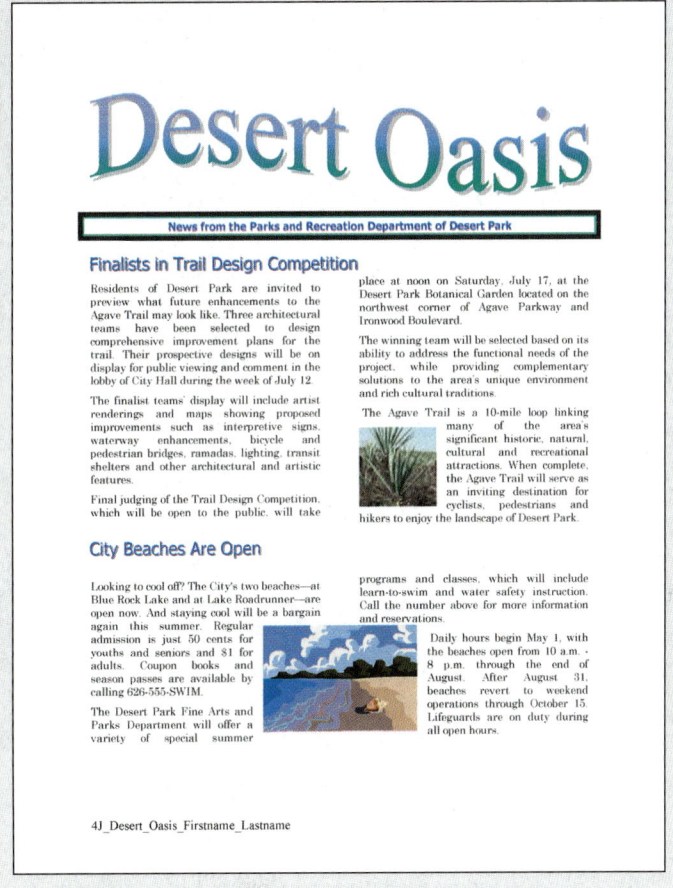

Figure 4.56

1. Start Word. In a blank document, open the **Page Setup** dialog box and change the left and right margins to 1 inch. Be sure you are in the **Print Layout View** and the nonprinting characters are displayed.

2. Display the **WordArt Gallery** dialog box and, in the third row, click the fifth style and click **OK**. In the **Edit WordArt Text** dialog box, type **Desert Oasis** Change the **Font Size** of the WordArt to **66** and then click **OK**.

(**Project 4J**–Desert Oasis continues on the next page)

Mastery Assessments (continued)

(Project 4J–Desert Oasis continued)

3. With the WordArt graphic selected, drag the side sizing handle so it stretches between the left and right margins. Use the horizontal ruler to see the margins.

4. On the right side of the WordArt graphic, click in the margin to deselect and then press [Enter] twice to insert two paragraph marks at the left margin. Click the **Center** button and then type **News from the Parks and Recreation Department of Desert Park**

5. Select the text you just typed and change the font to **Tahoma**, **10 pt.**, **Bold**, and **Blue**. Open the **Borders and Shading** dialog box, click the **Box** setting, and then, in the **Style** list box, click the style that is third from the bottom. Change the color to **Teal** and click **OK**. Compare your banner to Figure 4.56.

6. Save your work as you have previously with the file name **4J_Desert_Oasis_Firstname_Lastname**

7. Position your I-beam pointer slightly below the banner at the left margin and double-click to place the insertion point just below the banner. Adjust as necessary so that two paragraph marks display and then position your insertion point to the left of the second paragraph mark and type **Finalists in Trail Design Competition**

   Select the text and change the font to **16-point Tahoma**. Change the font color to **Blue**. Open the **Font** dialog box and select the **Emboss** check box. Deselect the text.

8. Press [Enter]. Recall that paragraph marks retain the formatting of the preceding paragraph. To change the formatting, select the paragraph mark and open the **Font** dialog box. Change the font to **10-point Century Schoolbook** and change the font color to **Black**. Under **Effects**, clear the check box next to **Emboss**. Click **OK**. Now you will collect and paste the articles that will be used for this newsletter.

9. Display the **Office Clipboard** and click the **Clear All** button. From your student files, locate and open **w04J_Agave_Trail**. Select and copy all of the text and then close the file. Locate and open **w04J_Beaches**. Copy all of the text and then close the file.

10. Display the **Clip Art** task pane and search for *beaches*. Locate the beach image displayed in Figure 4.56, click the arrow on the image, and then click **Copy** to copy it to the Clipboard. (If you cannot locate the image that is shown in the figure, select another beach image; alternatively, use the w04J_Beach_Picture that is included with the student files for this book. Use the technique you practiced in Activity 4.16, step 11, to copy the picture from your student files to the Office Clipboard.) On the **Clip Art** task pane, click the **Other Task Panes arrow** and click **Clipboard** to see the image you copied and the two articles.

(Project 4J–Desert Oasis continues on the next page)

Mastery Assessments (continued)

(Project 4J–Desert Oasis continued)

11. Display the **Research** task pane and type **Agave** and then select **Encyclopedia (or Encarta Encyclopedia)** as the research reference. In the list of choices displayed, under **Related items**, click *pictures of Agave plants*. In the MSN window that displays, locate the picture of a typical Agave type of plant. Right-click on the image and then click **Copy** to add the image to the Clipboard. Close the MSN window and then display the **Clipboard** task pane. Four items are displayed. Alternatively, insert the file w04J_Agave_Picture from your student files by displaying the Insert menu, pointing to Picture, and then clicking From File.

12. Position the insertion point in your document to the left of the last empty paragraph mark. From the **Clipboard** task pane, click the trail article that begins *Residents of Desert Park*. The article is inserted. Click the **Paste Options** button arrow that displays and click **Match Destination Formatting** to change the font to **Century Schoolbook, 10 pt**. Recall that the Paste Options button can be used to change the format of inserted text to match the formatting of the surrounding text.

13. Select the article text and change it to two columns, and then change the alignment to **Justify**. Display the **Paragraph** dialog box and add a **6-pt. Before** spacing to the article paragraphs. Save your changes.

14. To add the second article headline, click to the left of the empty paragraph mark on the left side of the screen, press Enter, and type **City Beaches Are Open**

    Press Enter twice. Select the new headline and change the font so it matches the *Finalists in Trail Design Competition* headline.

15. Click to the left of the second paragraph mark under the *Beaches* headline and, from the Clipboard task pane, paste the beach article that begins *Looking to cool off?* Click the **Paste Options** button that displays and click **Match Destination Formatting**. Change the article to two columns and the alignment to **Justify**. Display the **Paragraph** dialog box and add a **6-pt. Before** spacing to the paragraphs.

16. In the *Finalists in Trail Design Competition* article, in the second column, place the insertion point to the left of the paragraph that begins *The Agave Trail*.

    From the clipboard, paste the image of the Agave plant. Use a corner sizing handle to increase the size of the image until it is approximately 1 inch square. On the Picture toolbar, click the **Text Wrapping** button and click **Square**. Drag the image to position it in the article as shown in Figure 4.56. Do not be concerned if the text does not wrap around the image exactly as shown in the figure.

(Project 4J–Desert Oasis continues on the next page)

Word

Mastery Assessments (continued)

(Project 4J–Desert Oasis continued)

17. In the *City Beaches Are Open* article, place the insertion point at the beginning of the last paragraph that begins *Daily hours*. From the **Clipboard**, insert the beach picture. Set the **Text Wrapping** to **Square** and then position the image in the middle of the article as shown in Figure 4.56. If necessary, reposition the Agave plant image in the first article.

18. View the footer area and add the **AutoText file name** to the footer. Preview the document to be sure it is on one page. Make any necessary adjustments. Depending on your printer, the lines in the columns may be slightly different when compared to Figure 4.56. Print the newsletter, save your changes, and then close the document.

End You have completed Project 4J

Project 4K — Recreation Notes

Objectives: *Create a Decorative Title, Create Multicolumn Documents, Add Special Paragraph Formatting, Use Special Character Formats, Insert Hyperlinks, and Locate Supporting Information.*

In the following Mastery Assessment, you will create a newsletter about upcoming sports events in Desert Park. Your completed newsletter will look similar to Figure 4.57. You will save your document as 4K_Recreation_Notes_Firstname_Lastname.

1. Start Word. In a blank document open the **Page Setup** dialog box and set the left and right margins to 1 inch. Be sure you are in **Print Layout** view and that the nonprinting characters are displayed. If necessary, close the task pane.

2. Display the **WordArt Gallery** dialog box. In the fourth row, click the first style, click **OK**, and then type **Recreation Notes** Change the **Font Size** to **66** and then click **OK**. Select the **WordArt** graphic and open the **Format WordArt** dialog box. On the **Colors and Lines tab** of the dialog box, click the **Fill Color arrow** and then click **Fill Effects**. In the **Fill Effects** dialog box, click the **Texture tab** and then, in the first row, click the first texture—**Green marble**. Click **OK** twice.

3. On the right side of the **WordArt** graphic, click in the margin to deselect and then press twice to insert two paragraph marks at the left margin. Click the **Center** button and then type **Sports News from the Parks and Recreation Department of Desert Park**

Select the text you just typed and change the font to **Comic Sans MS**, **10 pt**., **Bold**. Change the font color to **Green**. Open the **Borders and Shading** dialog box, click the **3-D setting**, and then, in the **Style** list box, click the line style that displays a heavy top line and a narrow bottom line. Change the line color to **Green** and click **OK**. Compare your banner to Figure 4.57.

(Project 4K–Recreation Notes continues on the next page)

492 **Word** | Chapter 4: Creating Documents with Multiple Columns and Special Formats

Mastery Assessments (continued)

(Project 4K–Recreation Notes continued)

Figure 4.57

4. Save your work as you have previously with the file name **4K_Recreation_Notes_Firstname_Lastname**

5. Position your I-beam pointer at the left margin and slightly under the banner you just created and then double-click to place the insertion point below the banner. Adjust as necessary so that two paragraph marks display, and then position your insertion point to the left of the second paragraph mark. Type **Golf for a Cause**

   Select the text you just typed and change the font to **16 pt.**, **Bold**, and **Green**. Deselect the text.

(Project 4K–Recreation Notes continues on the next page)

Project 4K: Recreation Notes | Word   493

Mastery Assessments (continued)

(Project 4K–Recreation Notes continued)

6. Press [Enter] and drag to select the empty paragraph mark you just created. Change the font size to **11 pt.**, remove **Bold**, and change the font color to **Black**. Recall that paragraph marks retain the formatting of the preceding paragraph. You are ready to collect and paste the articles that will be used for this newsletter.

7. Display the **Office Clipboard** and, if necessary, click the **Clear All** button to clear the Clipboard. From the student files, locate and open **w04K_Recreation_Ideas**. This memo contains information that was gathered by the director of the Parks Department. You will copy each part separately so you can control the placement of the articles in the newsletter. Copy the golf article, starting with the paragraph that begins *The Desert Park*. Copy the first Did You Know paragraph, starting with *Some historians believe*. Copy the image of the woman golfer. Copy the bicycling article, starting at the paragraph that begins *The "Golden Age."* Copy the second Did You Know paragraph starting with *The bicycle was not*. Finally, copy the image of the bicyclers. Close the document.

8. Place the insertion point to the left of the last empty paragraph mark. From the **Clipboard** task pane, click the golf article that begins *The Desert Park*. The article is inserted. Point to the displayed **Paste Options** button and click the arrow. From the displayed list, click **Match Destination Formatting** to change the font to **Comic Sans, 11 pt.**

9. Press [Enter] and type **Did You Know?** Press [Enter] again and, from the Clipboard task pane, click the paragraph that begins *Some historians believe*. Click the **Paste Options button arrow** and then click **Match Destination Formatting**. Your newsletter expands to a second page.

10. On page 1, place the insertion point at the start of the paragraph that begins *"The Golf Benefit* and insert the woman golfer image. Select the image. From the displayed Picture toolbar, click the **Text Wrapping** button and then click **Top and Bottom**.

11. Hold down [Ctrl] and press [End] to move the insertion point to the end of the document. Press [Enter] and then type the headline for the next article: **Bicycling in Desert Park**

    Press [Enter] and then select the headline. Format the text the same as the *Golf for a Cause* headline—try using Format Painter to copy the format. Save your changes.

(Project 4K–Recreation Notes continues on the next page)

Mastery Assessments (continued)

(Project 4K–Recreation Notes continued)

12. Click to the left of the paragraph mark under the new headline and then paste the bicycle article, which begins The *"Golden Age."* Use the **Paste Options** button to match the destination formatting. Press Enter to add a blank line after the article and then paste the image of the bicyclers. Click to the right of the image, press Enter, and then type **Did You Know?** Press Enter again, paste the text beginning with *The bicycle was not*, and then use the **Paste Options** button to match the destination formatting. A third page may be created in your newsletter. Close the Clipboard.

13. Move to the top of the first page. Place the insertion point to the left of the *Golf for a Cause* headline. Select all of the text in the newsletter except the banner and the Word Art Graphic. Open the **Paragraph** dialog box, set the spacing after to **6 pt.**, and then click **OK**.

14. With the text still selected, change the columns to **two** and change the alignment to **Justify**. Deselect the text. The newsletter is now on two pages. On page 1, drag as necessary to visually center the image of the woman golfer horizontally within the column, between the two paragraphs. Compare the placement of the image to Figure 4.57.

15. On page 2, in the first column, select the *Did You Know?* heading. Change the font to **Comic Sans MS**, **12-pt.**, **Bold**, and center it. In the second column, below the bicycle image, do the same to the second Did You Know? heading.

16. Select the first *Did You Know?* heading and the paragraph that follows it. Open the **Borders and Shading** dialog box and add a **Shadow** style, **2¼ pt.**, **Green** border around the paragraph to draw the reader's eye to it. Do the same for the second *Did You Know?* heading and paragraph.

17. Select the *Golf for a Cause* headline, open the **Borders and Shading** dialog box, click the **Shading tab**, and then apply a **light green** shading to the paragraph. Open the **Font** dialog box, apply the **Small caps** effect, and then center the headline. On page 2, apply the same formatting to the *Bicycling in Desert Park* headline.

18. View the footer area and add the **AutoText file name** to the footer. Preview the document, pressing PgUp and PgDn to move between the pages—your newsletter should occupy two pages. Compare your document to Figure 4.57 and the print it. Save your changes and close the document.

End You have completed Project 4K

Word chapter four: Problem Solving

Project 4L — Tutoring Services

Objectives: *Create a Decorative Title, Add Special Paragraph Formatting, Use Special Character Formats, Insert Hyperlinks, and Preview and Save a Document as a Web Page.*

Use the skills you have learned in this and preceding chapters to create a one-page Word document to announce your services as a tutor for Microsoft Office applications. Save the document as a Web page with the file name *4L_Tutoring_Services_Firstname_Lastname*.

1. Start Word and create a headline to announce your services as a tutor. Use WordArt or any of the font characteristics you have practiced.

2. Write a paragraph or two to describe the skills you have acquired in Microsoft Word and other Microsoft programs. Include information about yourself that would make you qualified to be a tutor, such as patience or good listening skills. Think about the skills you would find helpful in a tutor. Format the text attractively so it is easy to read. When someone reads an announcement, they are usually seeking information about who, what, when, where, and why. Thus, be sure that your announcement describes who you are, what you do, when you are available to tutor, where tutoring can be held, and why you are qualified to be a tutor.

3. Add clip art or other pictures that are appropriate to the topic of tutoring using a computer.

4. Include a hyperlink to the Microsoft Web site—http://www.microsoft.com—or some other site appropriate to Microsoft Office programs.

5. Review your work and correct any errors. Be sure it is attractive and balanced on the page.

6. Save the document with the name **4L_Tutoring_Services_Firstname_Lastname** Add the filename to the footer area. Then save the document as a Web Page. Print your results.

End You have completed Project 4L

Problem Solving (continued)

Project 4M — Personal Newsletter

Objectives: *Create a Decorative Title, Create a Multicolumn Document, Add Special Paragraph Formatting, Use Special Character Formats, and Locate Supporting Information.*

Create a one-page personal newsletter to send to your friends and family. Save your document as *4M_Personal_Newsletter_Firstname Lastname*.

1. From a blank document, create a WordArt heading for your personal newsletter. Add a decorative banner line under the newsletter heading.

2. Write a few paragraphs to describe the significant events in your life over the last few months to share with your family or friends. Write about two or more significant topics for which you could create a headline; for example, Enrolled In a Computer Course!

3. Create headlines for the topics you have chosen and then format them appropriately.

4. Change the text of the articles to two columns.

5. Add appropriate clip art or pictures. Select a significant paragraph and format it to stand out from the rest of the text.

6. If necessary, insert a continuous break at the end of the newsletter so the columns are even.

7. Save the file as **4M_Newsletter_Firstname_Lastname** Add the file name to the footer area and then print the document.

End You have completed Project 4M

Word chapter four

On the Internet

Locating Supporting Information on the Web

In this chapter, you were introduced to the Research feature of Microsoft Word. The Research button connects you to resources that you can use as you write. This includes the thesaurus and encyclopedia, which you used in the chapter, as well as many other tools. You can translate a word or a whole document into another language. Some of the resources that are displayed require that you pay a fee. Open Word and click the Research button. Explore the options available to you. Discover which ones are free, and which ones require you to sign up for the service and pay a fee. Try the translation feature, which will require that you have a document open. Think about how this compares to using your favorite Internet search engine to locate information. Also, think about how much you would be willing to pay for the resources available through the Research button.

GO! with Help

Special Column Formats

In the exercises in this chapter you created a simple one- or two-page newsletter. While desktop publishing software offers many more features for newsletter creation, Word can still be used—an advantage if you do not own desktop publishing software. Some additional features of Word can be applied to columns in a newsletter.

1. Start Word. On the menu bar, in the **Type a question for help** box, type **Columns** and then press Enter.

2. Expand and review the topics that display. This information is a good review of the content in this chapter related to columns and also introduces some new information.

3. Open **w04D_Council_News**. From the **Format** menu, click **Columns**. In the **Columns** dialog box, experiment with the different preset column formats displayed. Use the Help pane to assist you as you experiment with different column formats.

4. Close your document without saving changes. Close Help and then close Word.

Excel 2003

chapter one

Getting Started with Excel 2003

In this chapter, you will: complete these projects and practice these skills.

Project 1A **Navigating a Workbook**	**Objectives** • Start Excel and Navigate a Workbook • Create Headers and Footers • Preview and Print a Workbook • Save and Close a Workbook and Exit Excel

Project 1B **Creating a New Workbook**	**Objectives** • Create a New Workbook • Enter and Edit Data in a Worksheet • Create Formulas • Use Zoom and the Spelling Checker Tool • Print a Worksheet Using the Print Dialog Box • Use Excel Help

The City of Desert Park

Desert Park, Arizona, is a thriving city with a population of just under 1 million in an ideal location serving major markets in the western United States and Mexico. Desert Park's temperate year-round climate attracts both visitors and businesses, and it is one of the most popular vacation destinations in the world. The city expects and has plenty of space for long-term growth, and most of the undeveloped land already has a modern infrastructure and assured water supply in place.

© Getty Images, Inc.

Working with Spreadsheets

Using Microsoft Office Excel 2003, you can create and analyze data organized into columns and rows. After the data is in place, you can perform calculations, analyze the data to make logical decisions, and create a visual representation of the data in the form of charts. In addition to its spreadsheet capability, Excel can manage your data, sort your data, and search for specific pieces of information within your data.

In this chapter you will learn to create and use an Excel workbook. You will learn the basics of spreadsheet design, how to create a footer, how to enter and edit data in a worksheet, how to navigate within a workbook, and how to save, preview, and print your work. You will create formulas to add and multiply numbers. You will use AutoComplete, Excel's spelling checker tool, and access Excel's Help feature.

1A

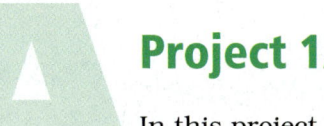

Project 1A Gas Usage

In this project, you will start the Excel program and practice moving around in a workbook. You will also create a footer with your name and print the four worksheets in the workbook.

In Activities 1.1 through 1.12, you will ***edit*** (update and make changes to) an existing Excel workbook for Dennis Johnson, Police Chief of Desert Park. The Desert Park Police Department has three 12-passenger vans—one at each of the three police stations in the city. Chief Johnson has asked all station captains to track the amount of gasoline and mileage for the vans by recording the number of miles traveled each time gasoline is purchased. The four worksheets of your completed workbook will look similar to Figure 1.1. You will save your workbook as *1A_Gas_Usage_Firstname_Lastname.*

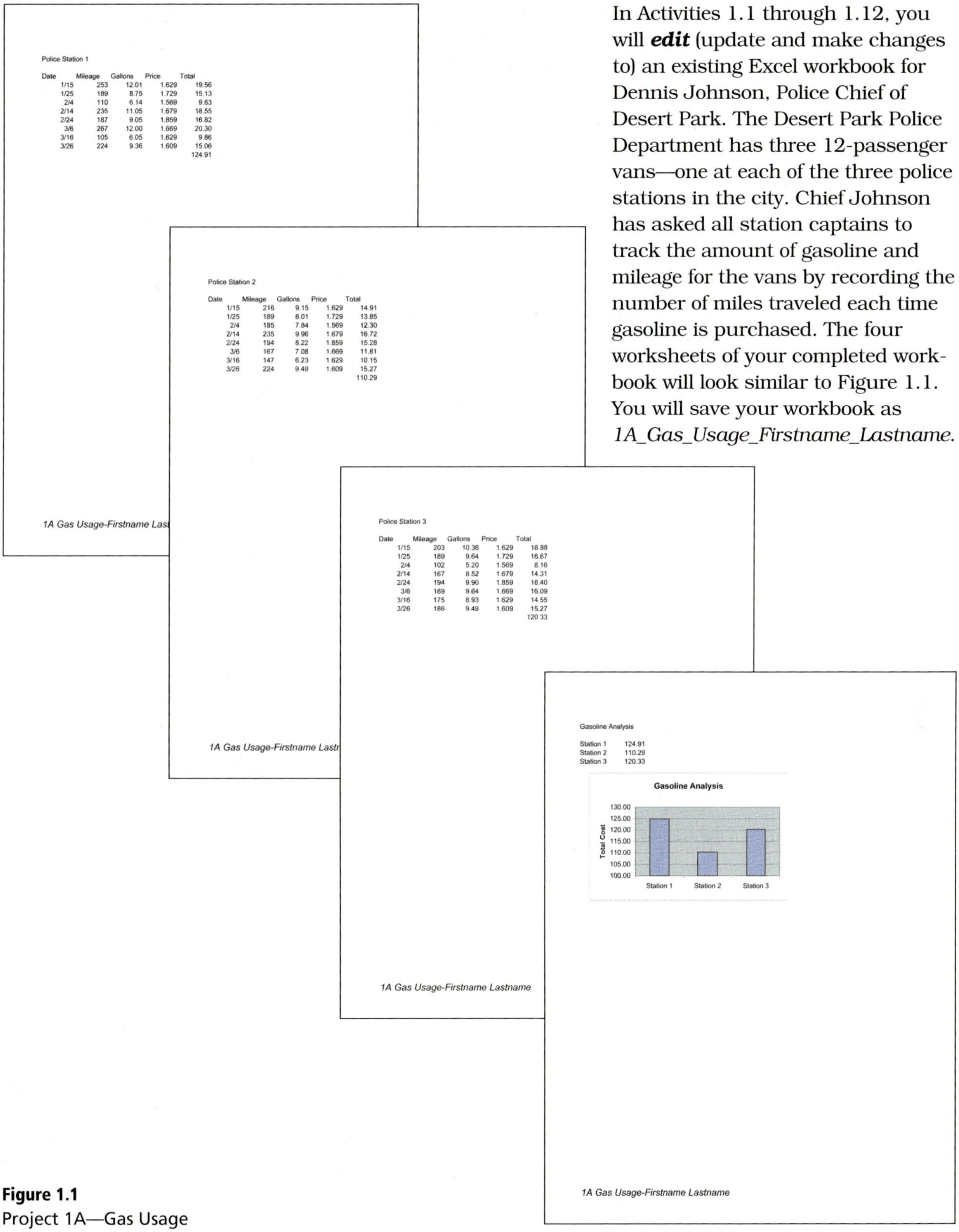

Police Station 1

Date	Mileage	Gallons	Price	Total
1/15	253	12.01	1.629	19.56
1/25	189	8.75	1.729	15.13
2/4	110	6.14	1.569	9.63
2/14	235	11.05	1.679	18.55
2/24	187	9.05	1.859	16.82
3/6	267	12.00	1.669	20.30
3/16	105	6.05	1.629	9.86
3/26	224	9.36	1.609	15.06
				124.91

1A Gas Usage-Firstname Las

Police Station 2

Date	Mileage	Gallons	Price	Total
1/15	216	9.15	1.629	14.91
1/25	189	8.01	1.729	13.85
2/4	185	7.84	1.569	12.30
2/14	235	9.96	1.679	16.72
2/24	194	8.22	1.859	15.28
3/6	167	7.08	1.669	11.81
3/16	147	6.23	1.629	10.15
3/26	224	9.49	1.609	15.27
				110.29

1A Gas Usage-Firstname Lastn

Police Station 3

Date	Mileage	Gallons	Price	Total
1/15	203	10.36	1.629	16.88
1/25	189	9.64	1.729	16.67
2/4	102	5.20	1.569	8.16
2/14	167	8.52	1.679	14.31
2/24	194	9.90	1.859	18.40
3/6	189	9.64	1.669	16.09
3/16	175	8.93	1.629	14.55
3/26	186	9.49	1.609	15.27
				120.33

1A Gas Usage-Firstname Lastname

Gasoline Analysis

Station 1	124.91
Station 2	110.29
Station 3	120.33

1A Gas Usage-Firstname Lastname

Figure 1.1
Project 1A—Gas Usage

Objective 1
Start Excel and Navigate a Workbook

When you start the Excel program, a new blank *workbook* displays. Within a workbook are one or more pages called *worksheets*. A worksheet is formatted as a pattern of uniformly spaced horizontal and vertical lines. This grid pattern of the worksheet forms vertical columns and horizontal rows. The intersection of a column and a row forms a small rectangular box referred to as a *cell*.

Activity 1.1 Starting Excel and Identifying the Parts of the Window

You start Excel in the same manner as you start other Microsoft Office System 2003 programs.

1 On the Windows taskbar, click the **Start** button .

The Start menu displays. Organizations and individuals store computer programs in a variety of ways. The Excel program might be installed under "All Programs" or "Microsoft Office" or some other arrangement. See Figure 1.2 for an example.

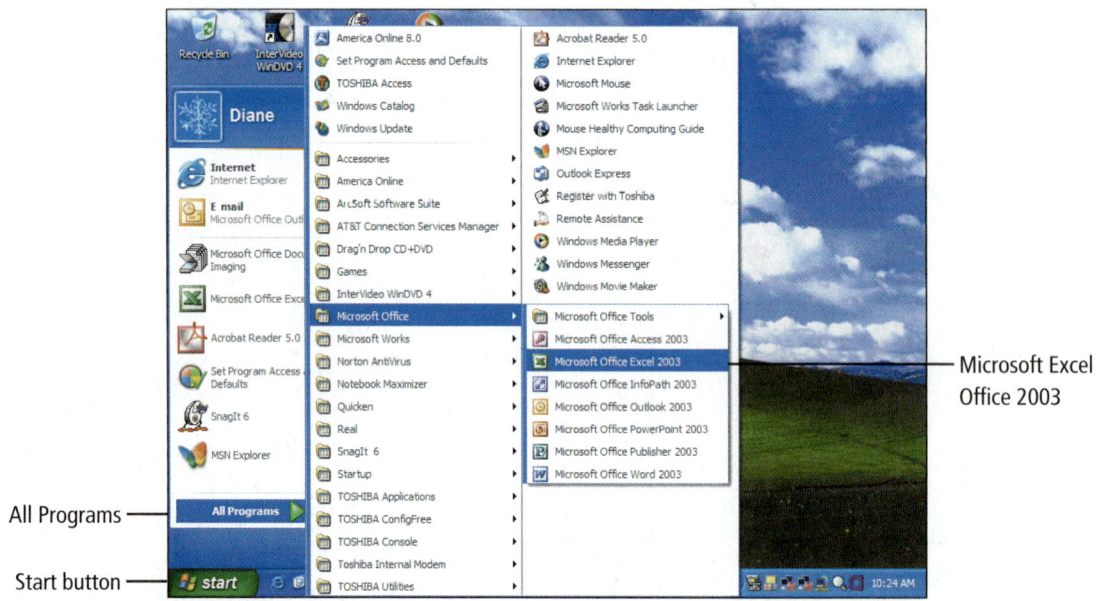

Figure 1.2

2 Point to **All Programs**, determine where the Excel program is located, point to **Microsoft Office Excel 2003**, and then click once to start the program.

Excel opens, and a blank workbook displays. The default Excel working environment consists of a menu bar, toolbars across the top of the window, and a main window divided into two sections—the *task pane* on the right and the worksheet on the left. The task pane is a window within a Microsoft Office application that displays commonly used commands. Its location and small size give you easy access to these commands while still working on your workbook. See Figure 1.3.

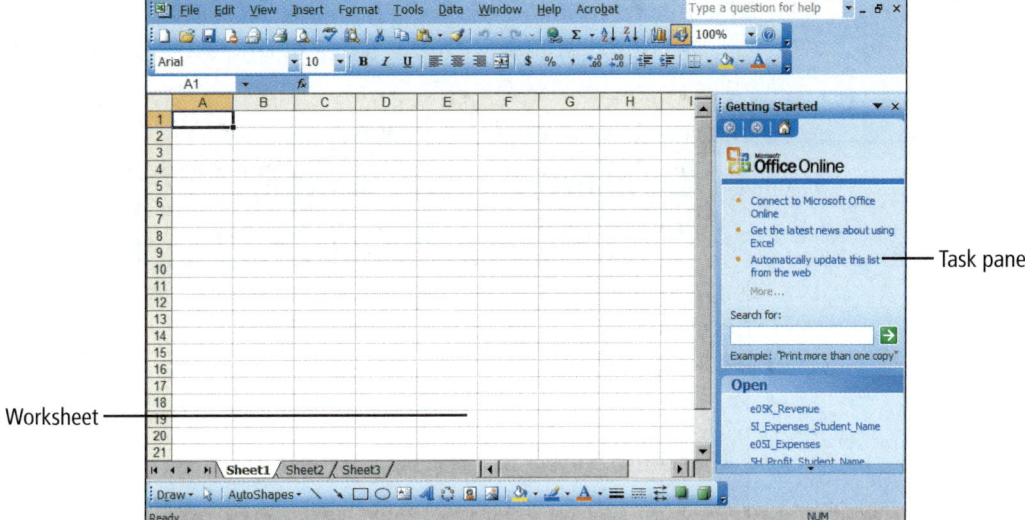

Figure 1.3

3 In the upper right corner of the task pane, click the **Close** button ⊠ to close the task pane.

The task pane closes. When not in use, you can close the task pane in this manner to allow the maximum amount of screen space for your worksheet. See Figure 1.4.

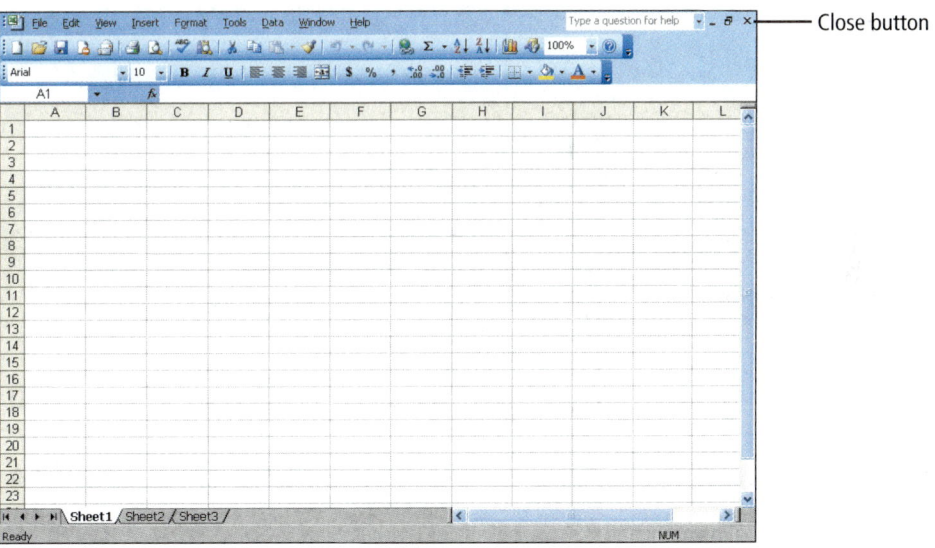

Figure 1.4

4 Take a moment to study Figure 1.5a-b and the table in Figure 1.6 to become familiar with the parts of the Excel window.

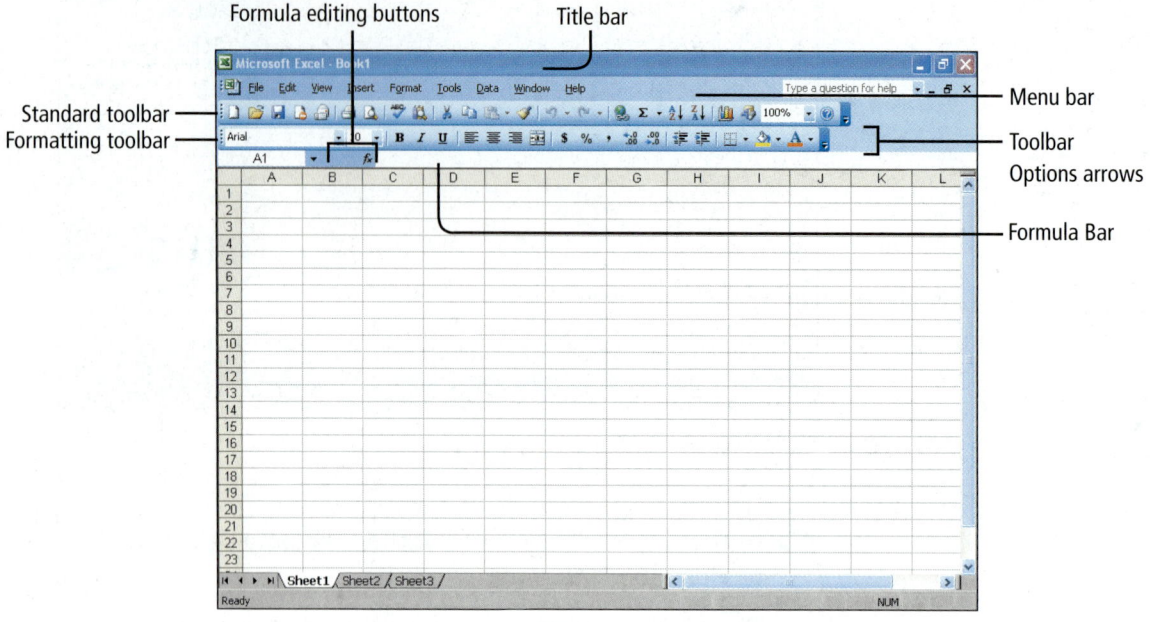

Figure 1.5a

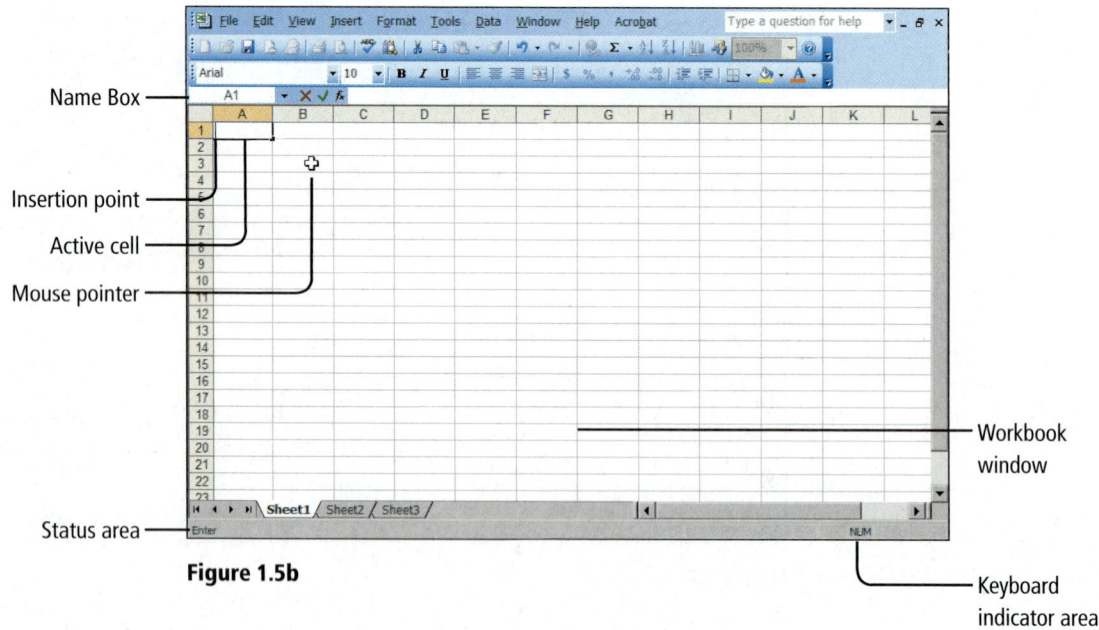

Figure 1.5b

504 Excel | Chapter 1: Getting Started with Excel 2003

Parts of the Excel Window

Excel Window Element	Description
Title bar	Displays the program icon, the program name, and the workbook name. The Minimize, Maximize or Restore, and Close buttons are at the extreme right edge of the title bar.
Menu bar	Contains the menus of commands. Display a menu by clicking on its name in the menu bar or by pressing [Alt] and pressing the underlined letter in the menu name.
Standard toolbar	Contains buttons for some of the most common commands in Excel, for example, Print and Save. It may occupy an entire row or share a row with the Formatting toolbar.
Formatting toolbar	Contains buttons for some of the most common formatting commands in Excel. It may occupy an entire row or share a row with the Standard toolbar.
Toolbar Options arrow	Displays additional buttons on the Formatting and Standard toolbars and also permits moving the toolbar to a separate or shared row.
Name Box	Identifies the selected cell, chart item, or drawing object. Also used to type a name for a cell or range of cells.
Formula editing buttons	Display when you are entering or editing data in a cell and assist in editing. The X button cancels the entry; the check mark button functions in the same manner as pressing [Enter]—it locks in your information; and the *fx* button displays the Insert Function dialog box to assist you in building a formula.
Formula Bar	Displays the value or formula contained in the active cell. Also permits entry or editing of values or formulas in cells or charts.
Insertion point	A blinking vertical bar that indicates where typed text or numbers will be inserted.
Active cell	The cell in which the next keystroke or command will take place. A black border surrounds the cell when it is active.
Mouse pointer	A graphic screen image controlled by your movement of the mouse.
Workbook window	The area of the Excel window containing the worksheets and the rows, columns, and cells of the active worksheet. The area of the workbook window ruled with horizontal and vertical lines makes up the worksheet's cells.
Status area	Displays information about the active cell.
Keyboard indicator area	Displays the current status of various keyboard functions such as the on or off status of [NumLock].

Figure 1.6

Activity 1.2 Using the Menu Bar, ScreenTips, and the Toolbars

1 On the menu bar, click **File**.

The File menu displays in either the full format, as shown in Figure 1.7, or in a short format, as shown in Figure 1.8. Excel's commands are organized in *menus*—lists of commands within a category. A short menu will display fully after a few seconds, or you can click the double arrows at the bottom to display the full menu. The File menu, when displayed in full, lists the last four to nine workbooks used on your computer. Whether your full menu displays immediately or is delayed by a few seconds depends on the options that are set for this software. Likewise, the number of previous workbook names displayed depends on how the software was set up. These default settings can be changed in the Options dialog box (displayed from the Tools menu) on systems where it is permissible to do so.

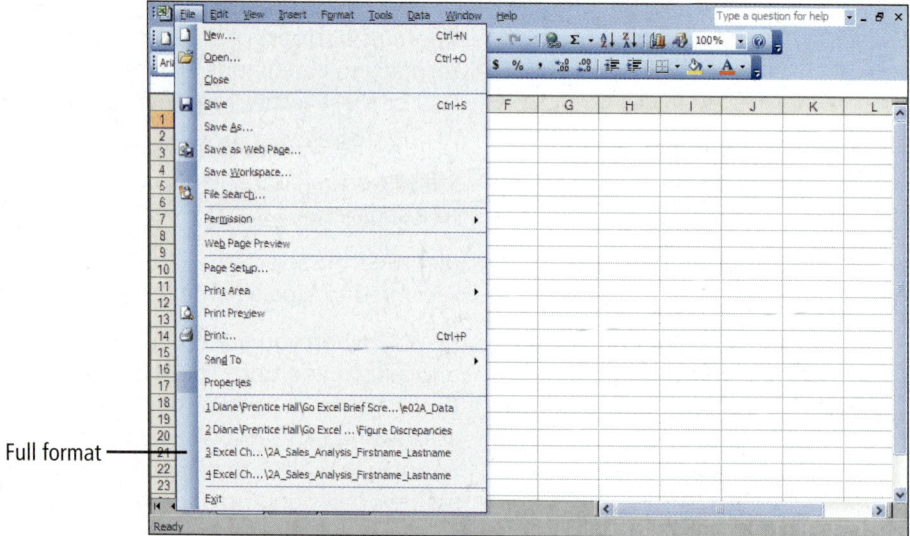

Full format

Figure 1.7

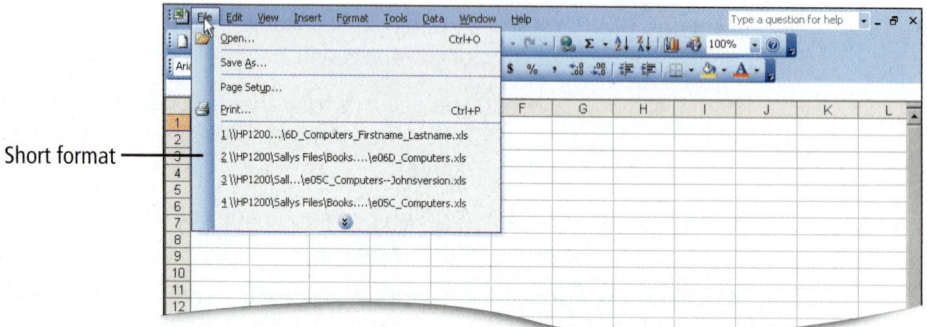

Short format

Figure 1.8

506 Excel | Chapter 1: Getting Started with Excel 2003

Note — Displaying Full Menus

Many Excel users prefer the automatic full menu display. To set a system to always display full menus, display the Tools menu, click Customize, and then click the Options tab. Under Personalized Menus and Toolbars, select the Always show full menus check box. Click the Reset menu and toolbar usage data button, click Yes, and then click Close.

2 If the full menu is not displayed, pause your mouse pointer over the **Expand arrows** to expand the **File** menu. See Figure 1.9.

On the left side of some command names is an image of the button that represents this command on a toolbar. This is a reminder that you can use the toolbar button to start the command with only one click. Likewise, to the right of some commands is a reminder that you can use a keyboard shortcut (holding down a combination of keys) to start the command.

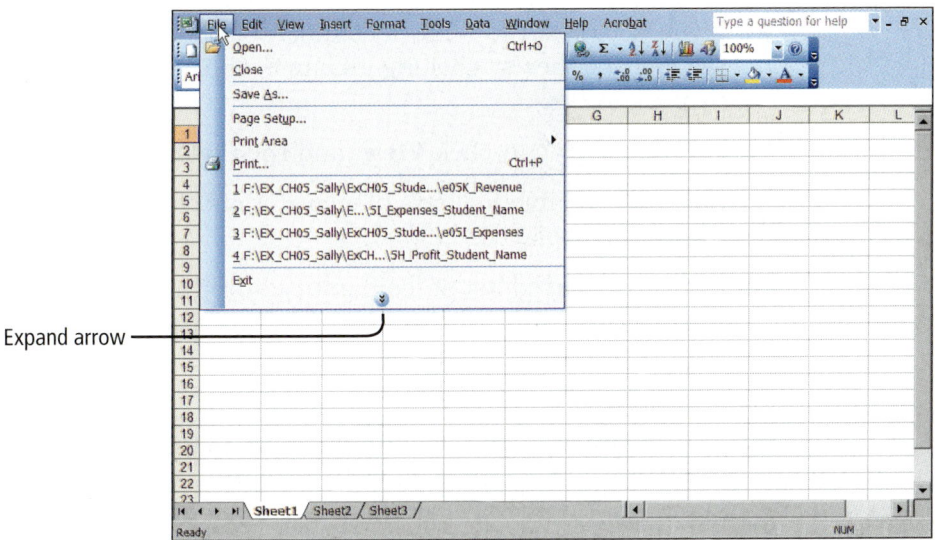

Expand arrow

Figure 1.9

3 Look at the full **File** menu on your screen.

Following or to the right of some menu commands, you will see various symbols, characters, or formatting, which are standard across all Microsoft products. The table in Figure 1.10 lists these characteristics and describes what will happen when you select the command.

Microsoft Menu Characteristics

Characteristic	Description	Example
... (ellipsis)	Indicates that a dialog box requesting more information will display.	Print...
▶ (triangle)	Indicates that a submenu—another menu of choices—will display.	Send to ▶
No symbol	Indicates that the command will perform immediately.	Exit
✓ (check mark)	Indicates that a command is turned on or active.	✓ Standard
Gray option name	Indicates that the command is currently unavailable (grayed out).	Properties

Figure 1.10

4 On the menu bar, click **File** again to close the menu.

If you decide not to select a command from a displayed menu, close the menu either by clicking its name, clicking outside the menu, or by pressing Esc.

5 On the menu bar, click **View**, and then point to **Toolbars**.

A list of available toolbars displays. A check mark indicates that the toolbar is displayed.

6 On the displayed list of toolbars, be sure that **Standard** and **Formatting** are both checked. Clear any other checked toolbar on the list by clicking its check mark to clear it, and then, if the list is still displayed, click outside the menu to close it.

7 Below the menu bar, be sure two rows of toolbars display, as shown in Figure 1.11. If, instead, your toolbars are sharing one row, as shown in Figure 1.12, at the end of the toolbar click the **Toolbar Options** button , and then click **Show Buttons on Two Rows**.

The toolbars will display on two rows, as shown in Figure 1.11. Alternatively, from the Tools menu, click Customize, click the Options tab, and then select the Show Standard and Formatting toolbars on two rows check box.

Toolbars on two rows —

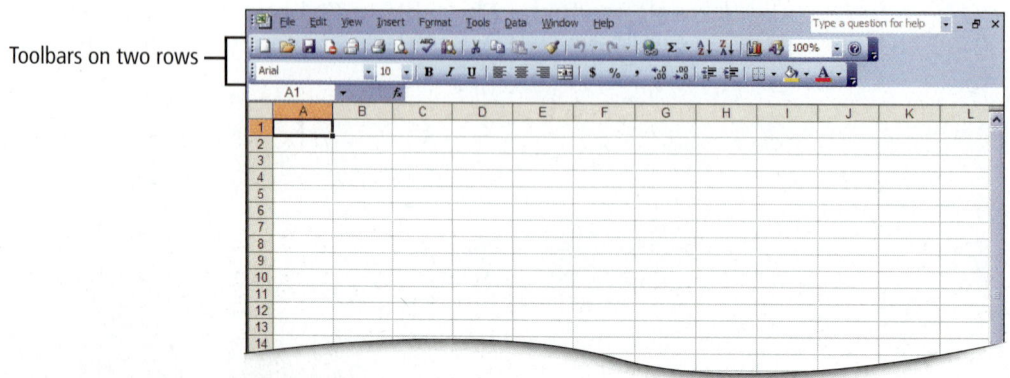

Figure 1.11

Toolbars on one row

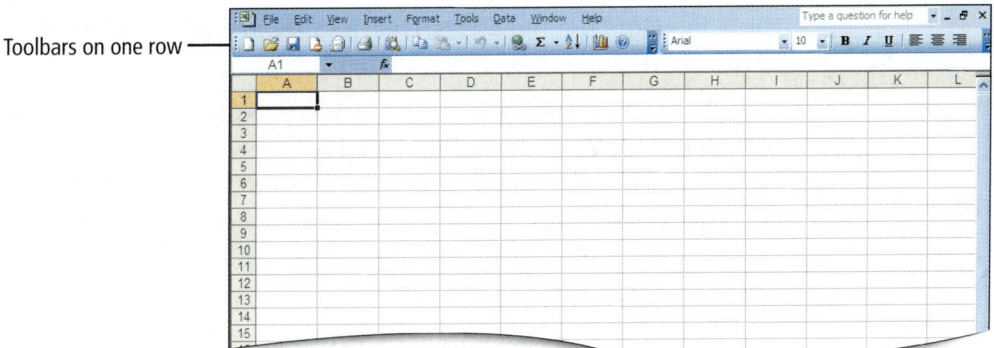

Figure 1.12

8 On the Standard toolbar, locate and pause your mouse pointer over the **New** button.

When you position the mouse pointer over a button, Excel displays the button's name in a **ScreenTip**. The ScreenTip *New* displays, indicating that clicking this button will activate the command to create a new workbook. See Figure 1.13.

New button
ScreenTip

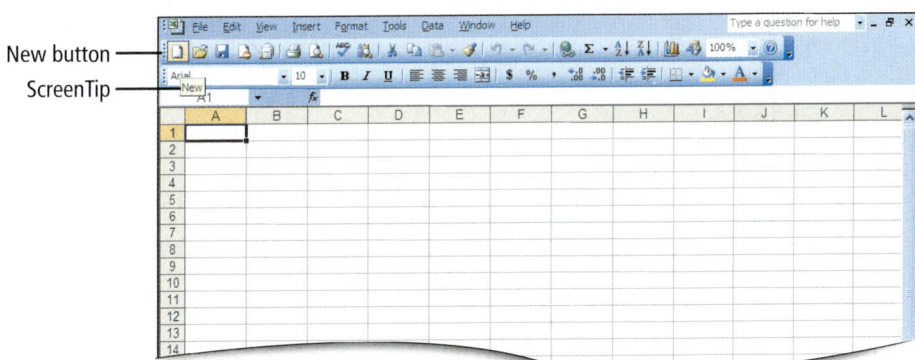

Figure 1.13

9 Pause your pointer over several buttons on both the Standard and Formatting toolbars to become familiar with the commands available to you. A toolbar button is a one-click method to activate frequently used commands that are also available from the menus. The ScreenTip describes the command that will be activated when you click the toolbar button.

Activity 1.3 Opening an Existing Workbook

1 From the menu bar, display the **File** menu, and then click **Open**.

Alternatively, click the Open button on the Standard toolbar.

The Open dialog box displays.

2 At the right side of the **Look in** box, click the **Look in arrow**, and then navigate to the student files that accompany this textbook.

Project 1A: Gas Usage | **Excel** 509

3. Click to select the file **e01A_Gas_Usage**, and then, in the lower right corner of the dialog box, click **Open**.

The workbook e01A_Gas_Usage displays. Alternatively, you can double-click a file name to open it. The workbook includes data already captured from gas slips, including the number of gallons purchased and the total amounts printed on the actual slips. Excel calculates the total of all slips by using a formula.

4. Take a moment to study Figures 1.14a and 1.14b and the table in Figure 1.15 to become familiar with the Excel workbook window.

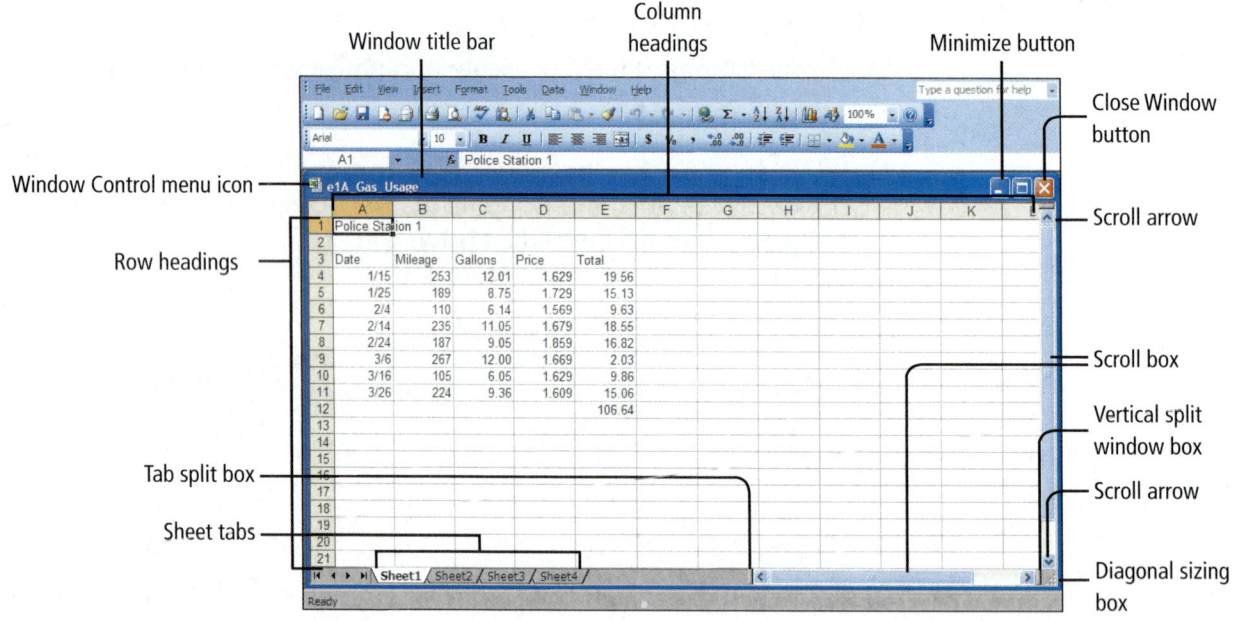

Figure 1.14a

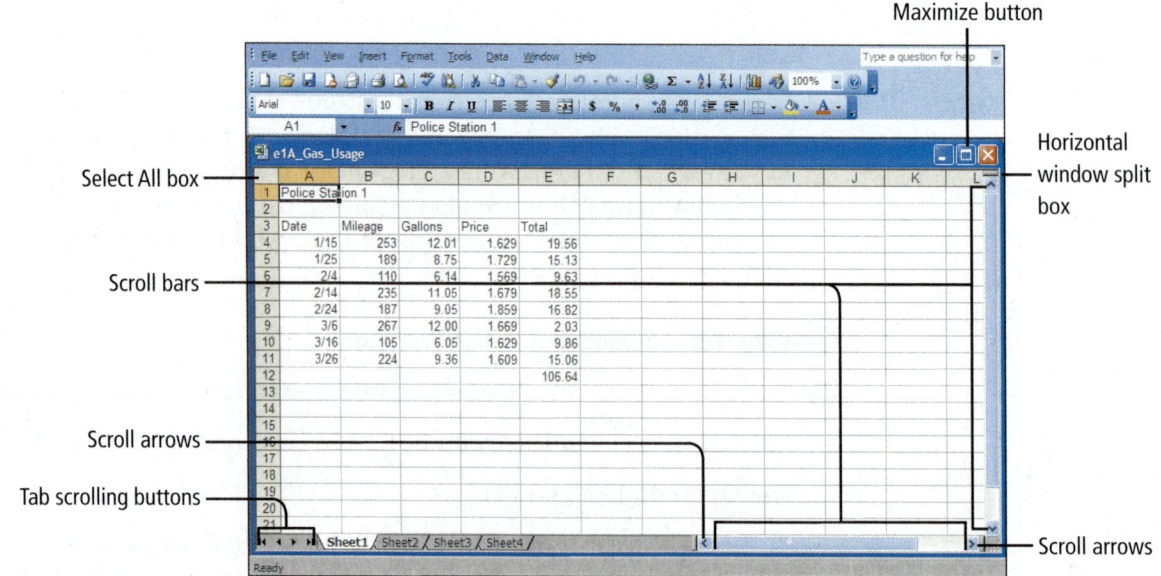

Figure 1.14b

510   Excel | Chapter 1: Getting Started with Excel 2003

Excel Workbook Elements

Workbook Element	Description
Close Window button	Closes the workbook.
Column headings	Indicate the column letter.
Diagonal sizing box	Indicates that the window can be resized; dragging this box changes the window size.
Horizontal window split box	Splits the worksheet into two vertical views of the same worksheet.
Maximize button	Displays the active window in its full size in the Excel workspace.
Minimize button	Collapses the active window to a button on the taskbar.
Row headings	Indicates the row number.
Scroll arrows	Scroll one column or row at a time.
Scroll bars	Scroll the Excel window up and down or left and right.
Scroll boxes	Used with the mouse to drag the position of a window up and down or left and right.
Select All box	Selects all cells in a worksheet.
Sheet tabs	Changes the active worksheet in a workbook.
Tab scrolling buttons	Display sheet tabs that are not in view; used when there are more sheet tabs than will display in the space provided.
Tab split box	Adjusts the space available for sheet tabs.
Vertical split window box	Splits the worksheet into two horizontal views of the same worksheet.
Window Control menu icon	Also known as the control program box. Allows keyboard access to move, resize, minimize, maximize, and close the worksheet window.
Window title bar	Displays the application name along with the name of the current workbook.

Figure 1.15

Activity 1.4 Selecting Columns, Rows, Cells, Ranges, and Worksheets

Recall that a *cell* is the rectangular box formed by the intersection of a column and a row. *Selecting* refers to highlighting, by clicking or dragging with your mouse, one or more cells so that the selected range of cells can be edited, formatted, copied, or moved. Excel treats the selected range of cells as a single unit; thus, you can make the same change, or combination of changes, to more than one cell at a time.

1 In the upper left corner of the displayed worksheet, position your mouse pointer over the letter **A** until the pointer ⬇ displays, as shown in Figure 1.16, and then click once.

Column A is selected (highlighted). A *column* is a vertical group of cells in a worksheet. Beginning with the first letter of the alphabet, A, a unique letter identifies each column—this is called the *column heading*. After using the entire alphabet from A to Z, Excel begins naming the columns AA, AB, AC, and so on.

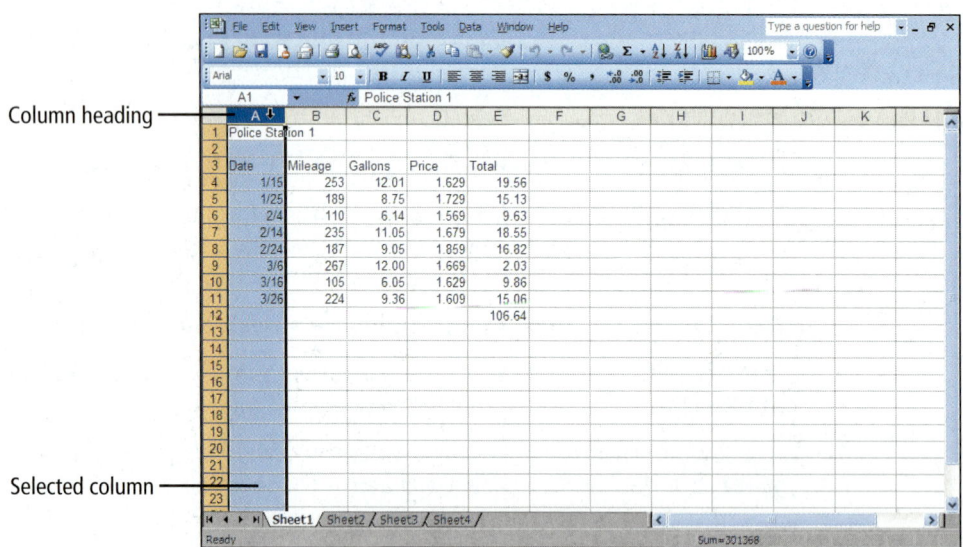

Figure 1.16

2 At the left edge of the workbook, position your mouse pointer over the number **3** until the pointer ➡ displays, as shown in Figure 1.17, and then click once.

Row 3 is selected. A *row* is a horizontal group of cells in a worksheet. Beginning with number 1, a unique number identifies each row—this is the *row heading*, located at the left side of the worksheet.

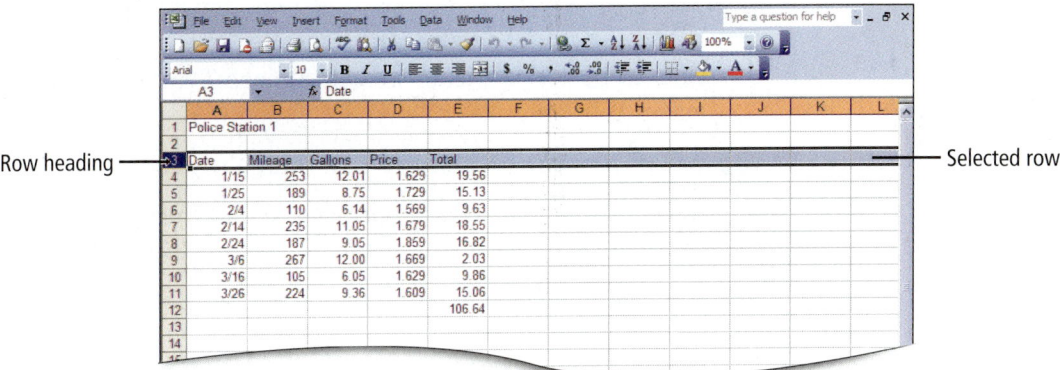

Figure 1.17

3 In the displayed worksheet, click the word **Date**. See Figure 1.18.

A black border surrounds the cell, indicating that it is the *active cell*. The active cell in a worksheet is the cell ready to receive data or be affected by the next Excel command. A cell is identified by the intersecting column letter and row number, which forms the *cell address*. A cell address is also referred to as a *cell reference*.

4 At the left end of the Formula Bar, look at the **Name Box**.

The cell address of the active cell, A3, displays.

5 Look at the Formula Bar.

The value of the cell—the word *Date*—displays. See Figure 1.18.

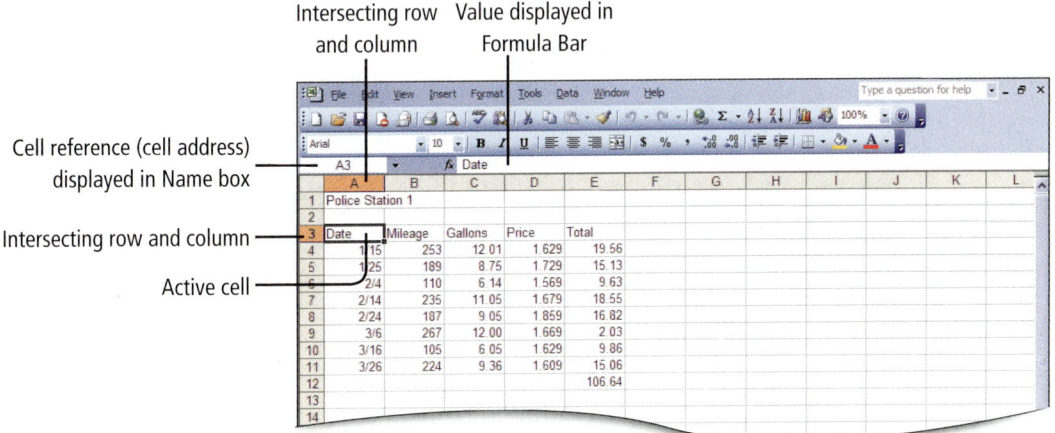

Figure 1.18

Project 1A: Gas Usage | **Excel** 513

6 On the keyboard, press ↓ three times.

Cell A6 becomes the active cell. Pressing an arrow key relocates the active cell.

7 With your mouse, point to and then click cell **B4**.

In the Name Box, notice that the cell address, *B4*, is indicated, and in the Formula Bar, the value of the cell, *253*, is indicated.

8 With the mouse pointer ⊕ over cell **B4**, hold down the left mouse button, drag down to select cells **B5**, **B6**, and **B7**, and then release the left mouse button.

The four cells, B4 through B7, are selected. This **range** (group) of cells is referred to as *B4:B7*. When you see a colon (:) between two cell references, the range includes all the cells between the two cell addresses—in this instance, all the cells from B4 through B7. Use this technique to select a range of cells adjacent (next) to one another in a worksheet. See Figure 1.19.

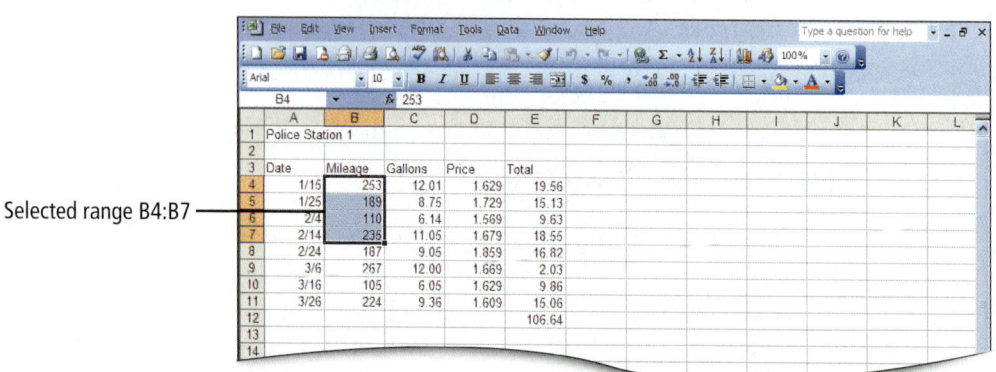

Selected range B4:B7

Figure 1.19

9 Point to and then click cell **B4** to make it the active cell.

10 Press and hold down Ctrl, click cell **B7**, and then click cell **C6**.

Cells B4, B7, and C6 are all selected. See Figure 1.20.

Use this technique to select cells that are nonadjacent (not next to one another). A range of cells can be adjacent or nonadjacent. A range of cells that is nonadjacent is separated with commas instead of a colon. In this instance, the range is referred to as *B4, B7, C6*.

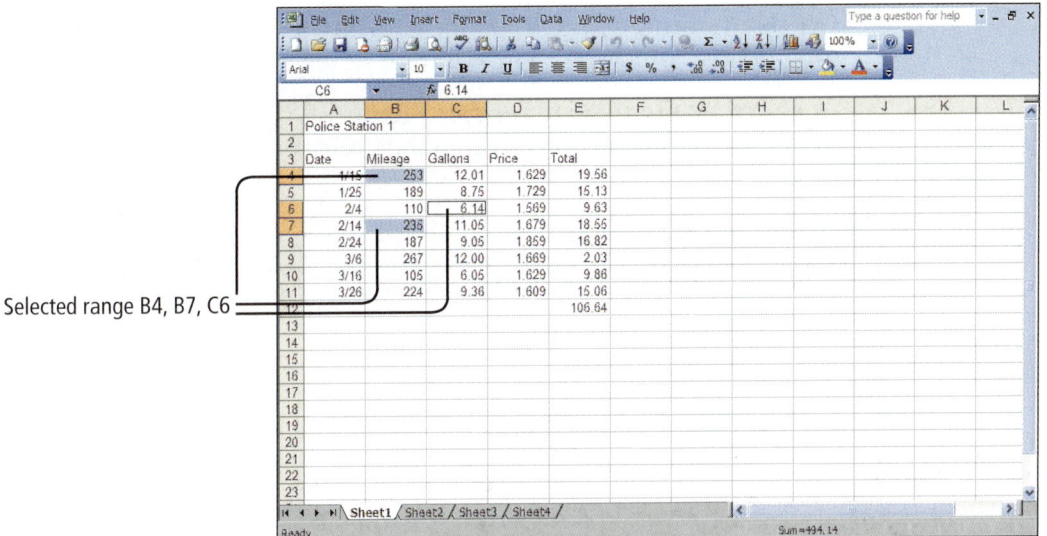

Selected range B4, B7, C6

Figure 1.20

11 Select **column C**.

Notice that when you select an entire column, the address of the first cell in the column displays in the Name Box. See Figure 1.21.

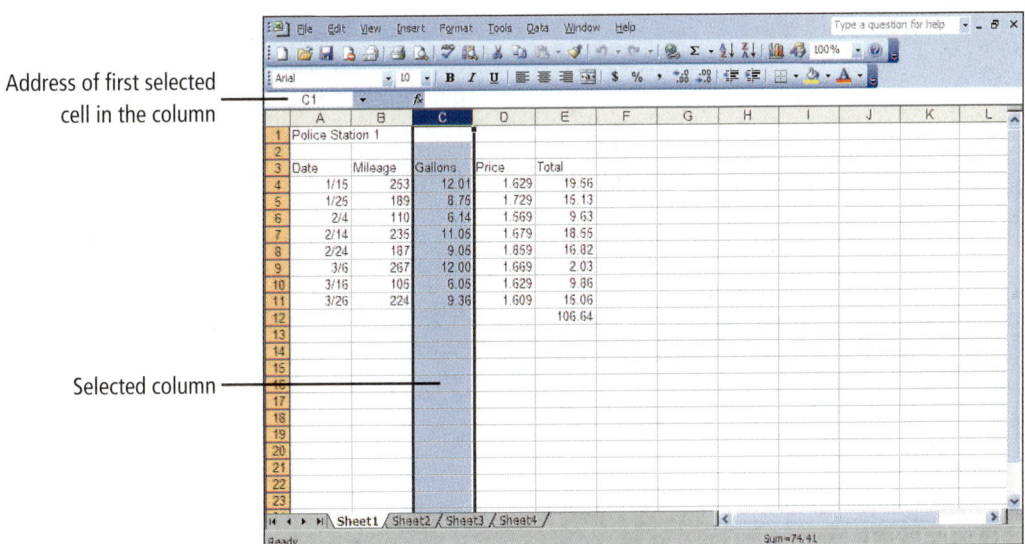

Address of first selected cell in the column

Selected column

Figure 1.21

Project 1A: Gas Usage | **Excel** 515

12 With **column C** selected, pause your mouse pointer anywhere in the highlighted area, and then **right-click** (click the right mouse button).

A **shortcut menu** displays. See Figure 1.22. A shortcut menu offers the most commonly used commands relevant to the selected area.

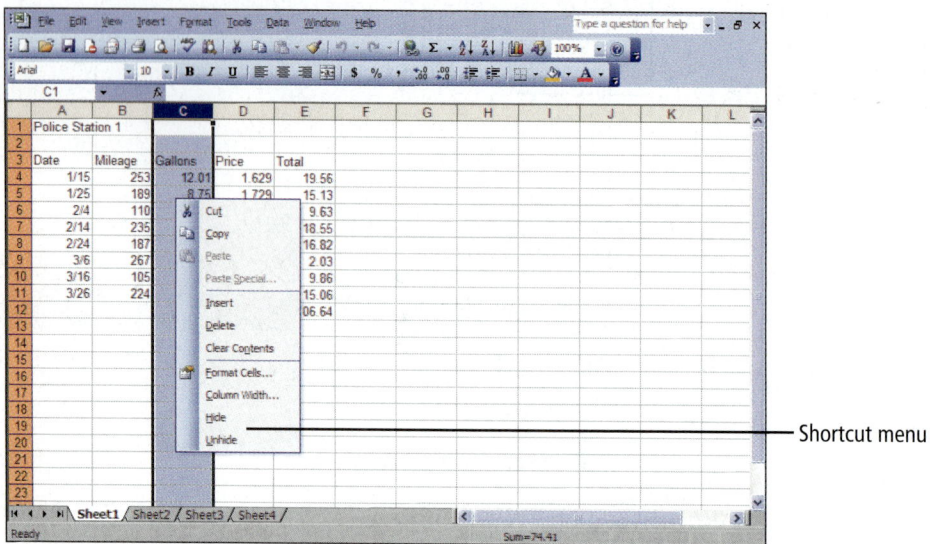

Figure 1.22

13 Move the pointer anywhere outside **column C** and away from the shortcut menu, and then click the left mouse button.

You have canceled the selection of—**deselected**—column C. The column is no longer highlighted, and the shortcut menu is closed.

14 At the left edge of the worksheet, move your mouse pointer over the **row 4** heading, and click to select the row.

When you select an entire row, the address of the first cell in the row displays in the Name Box. See Figure 1.23.

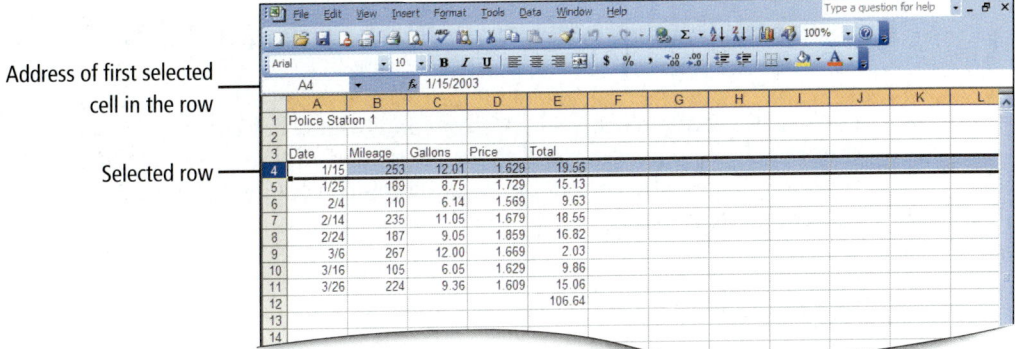

Address of first selected cell in the row

Selected row

Figure 1.23

15 With **row 4** selected, move the mouse pointer anywhere over the highlighted area, and right-click.

A shortcut menu displays the most commonly used row commands, as shown in Figure 1.24.

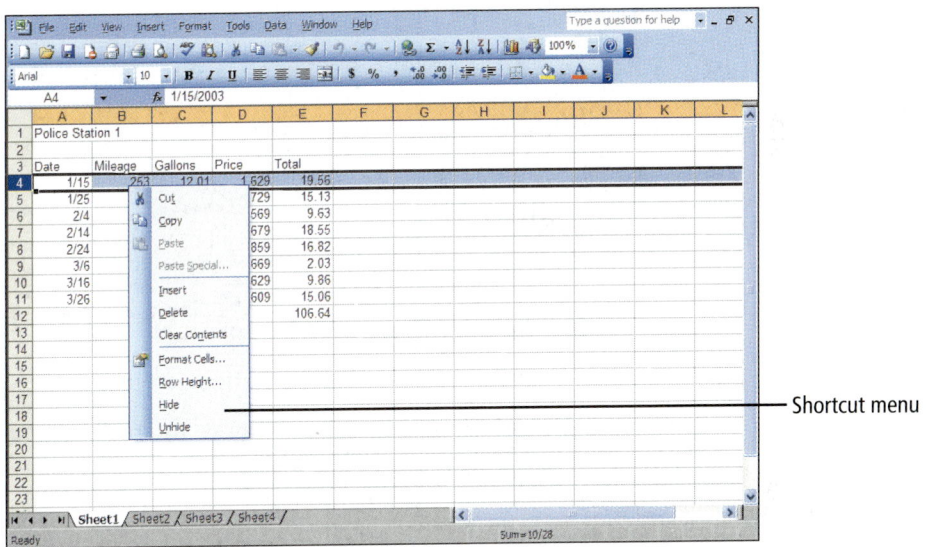

Shortcut menu

Figure 1.24

More Knowledge — Right-clicking to See the Shortcut Menu

You can simultaneously select a row and display the shortcut menu by pointing to the row heading and then clicking the right mouse button. In the same manner, you can simultaneously select a column and display its associated shortcut menu.

16 Click anywhere outside **row 4** to cancel the selection.

17 At the upper left corner of your worksheet, locate the **Select All** button—the small gray box above row heading 1 and to the left of column heading A—as shown in Figure 1.25.

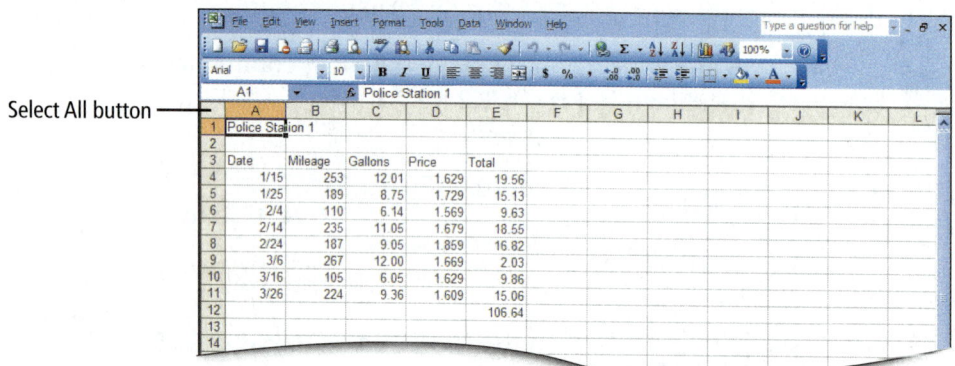

Select All button

Figure 1.25

18 Click the **Select All** button.

All the cells in the worksheet are selected.

19 Move your pointer anywhere in the worksheet and click once.

The selection is canceled.

Activity 1.5 Navigating Using the Scroll Bars

An Excel worksheet contains 256 columns and 65,536 rows. Of course, you cannot see that many rows and columns on your computer's screen all at the same time, so Excel provides scroll bars for you to display and view different parts of your worksheet. A scroll bar has a scroll box and two scroll arrows. *Scroll* is the action of moving the workbook window either vertically (up and down) or horizontally (side to side) to bring different areas of the worksheet into view on your screen. See Figure 1.26.

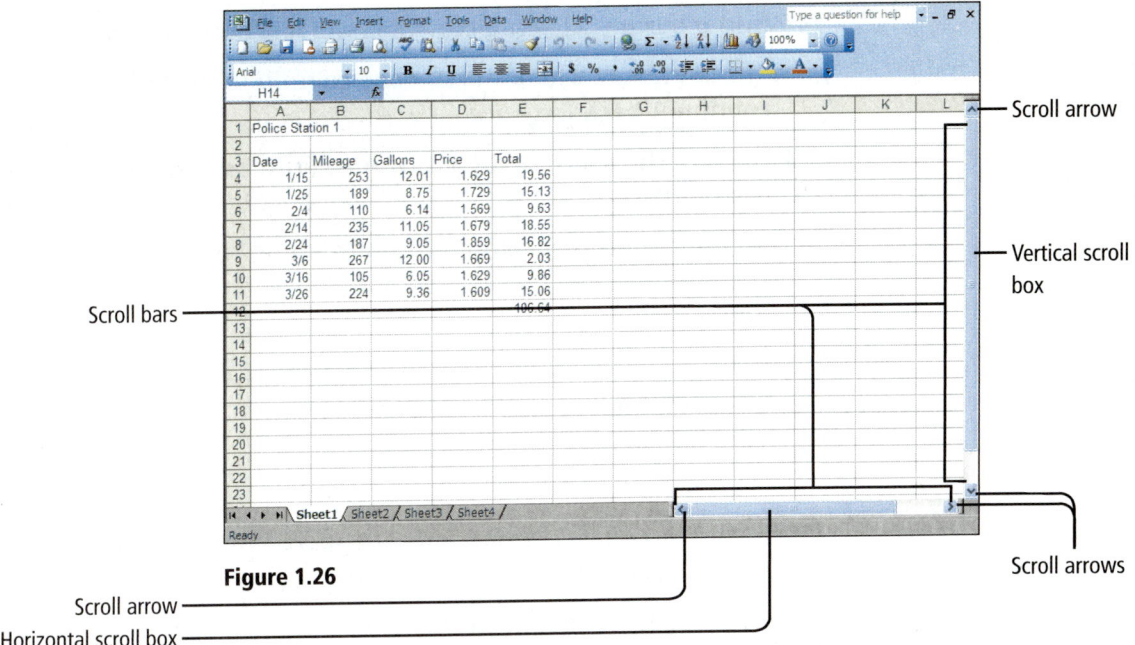

Figure 1.26

1. In the horizontal scroll bar, point to and then click the **right scroll arrow**.

   The workbook window moves one column to the right so that column A moves out of view, as shown in Figure 1.27. The number of times you click the arrows on the horizontal scroll bar determines the number of columns by which the window shifts—either to the left or to the right.

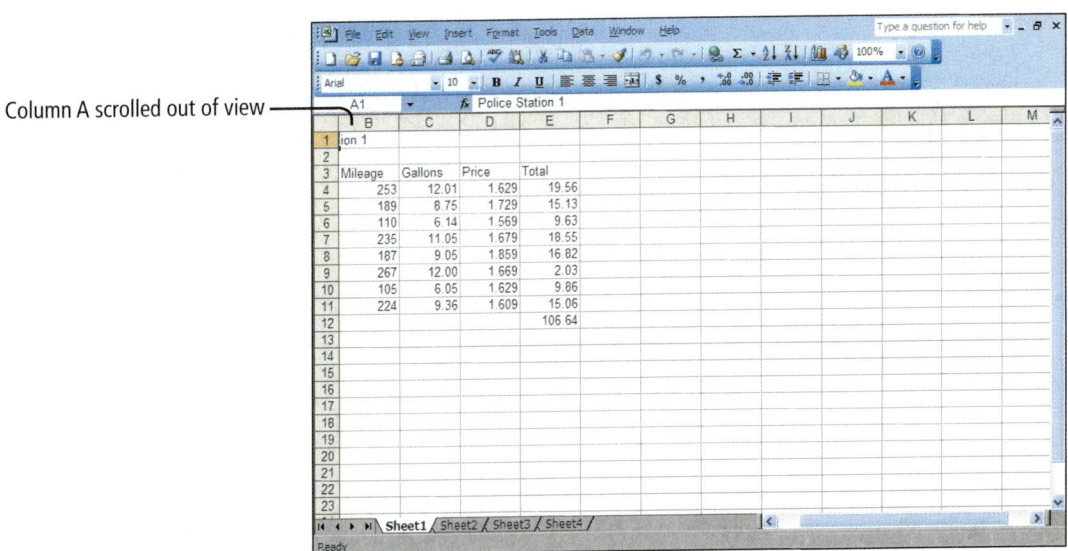

Figure 1.27

Project 1A: Gas Usage | **Excel** 519

2 In the horizontal scroll bar, click the **left scroll arrow**.

The workbook window shifts one column to the left, moving column A back into view.

3 Click in the space between the **horizontal scroll box** and the **right scroll arrow**.

An entire group of columns, equivalent to the number visible on your screen, scrolls to the left and out of view; in fact, the data has moved out of view.

4 Click in the space between the **horizontal scroll box** and the **left scroll arrow**.

The first group of columns, beginning with column A, moves back into view.

5 In the vertical scroll bar, point to and then click the **down scroll arrow**.

Row 1 is no longer in view. The number of times you click the arrows on the vertical scroll bar determines the number of rows shifted either up or down.

6 In the vertical scroll bar, point to and then click the **up scroll arrow**.

Row 1 comes back into view.

Activity 1.6 Navigating Using the Name Box

1 To the left of the Formula Bar, point to the **Name Box** to display the **I-beam** pointer, as shown in Figure 1.28, and then click once.

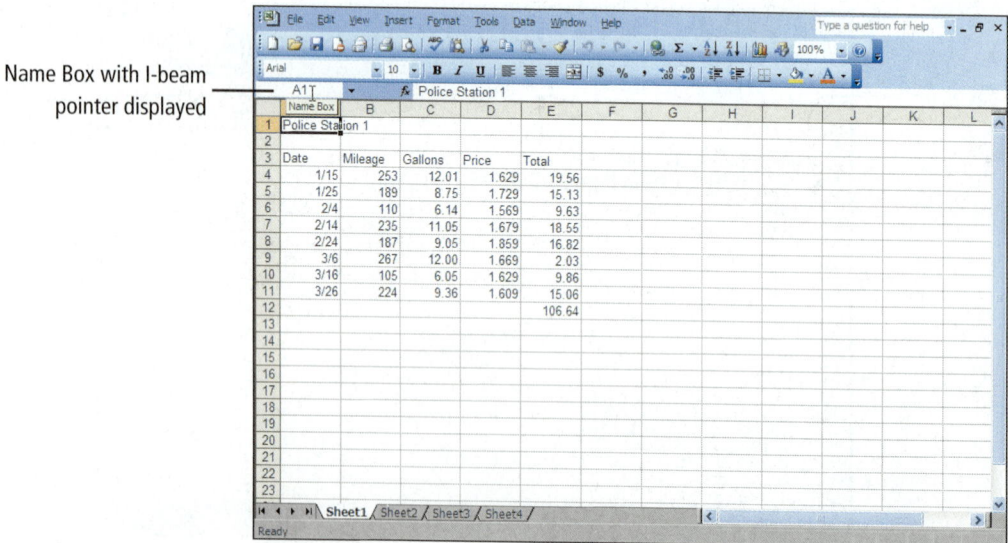

Name Box with I-beam pointer displayed

Figure 1.28

520   Excel | Chapter 1: Getting Started with Excel 2003

The cell reference that was displayed is highlighted in blue and aligned at the left. In Microsoft products, when text is highlighted in blue within a box, it is an indication that when you begin to type, the existing text will be deleted and replaced with your new keystrokes.

2 Using the keyboard, type **b6** and then press [Enter].

Cell B6 becomes the active cell. Typing a cell address in the Name Box is another way to select a cell and cause it to become the active cell. Notice that you do not have to use the capital letter B—typing in either uppercase or lowercase will result in *B6* displaying in the Name Box.

3 Selecting a cell to make it the active cell can also be accomplished using the keys on the keyboard. Take a moment to study the table shown in Figure 1.29 to become familiar with these keyboard commands.

Keyboard Commands

To Move the Location of the Active Cell:	Press:
Left, right, up, or down one cell	←, →, ↑, or ↓
Down one cell	[Enter]
Up one cell	[Shift] + [Enter]
Up one full screen	[Page Up]
Down one full screen	[PageDown]
Left one full screen	[Alt] + [Page Up]
Right one full screen	[Alt] + [PageDown]
To column A of the current row	[Home]
To the last cell in the last column of the *active area* (the rectangle formed by all the rows and columns in a worksheet that contain or contained entries.)	[Ctrl] + [End]
To cell A1	[Ctrl] + [Home]
Right one cell	[Tab]
Left one cell	[Shift] + [Tab]

Figure 1.29

Activity 1.7 Navigating Among the Worksheets in a Workbook

The default setting for the number of worksheets in a workbook is three. You can add worksheets or delete worksheets. Each worksheet has a total of 16,777,216 cells (256 columns × 65,536 rows). Sometimes a project may require that you enter data into more than one worksheet.

When you have more than one worksheet in a workbook, you can **navigate** (move) among worksheets by clicking the **sheet tab**. Sheet tabs identify each worksheet in a workbook. Sheet tabs are located along the lower border of the worksheet window. When you have more worksheets in the workbook than can be displayed in the sheet tab area, use the four tab scrolling buttons to move sheet tabs into and out of view. See Figure 1.30.

Notice that the background color for the Sheet1 tab displays in the same color as the background color for the worksheet and also displays as bold characters. See Figure 1.30. This indicates that *Sheet1* is the active worksheet within the current workbook.

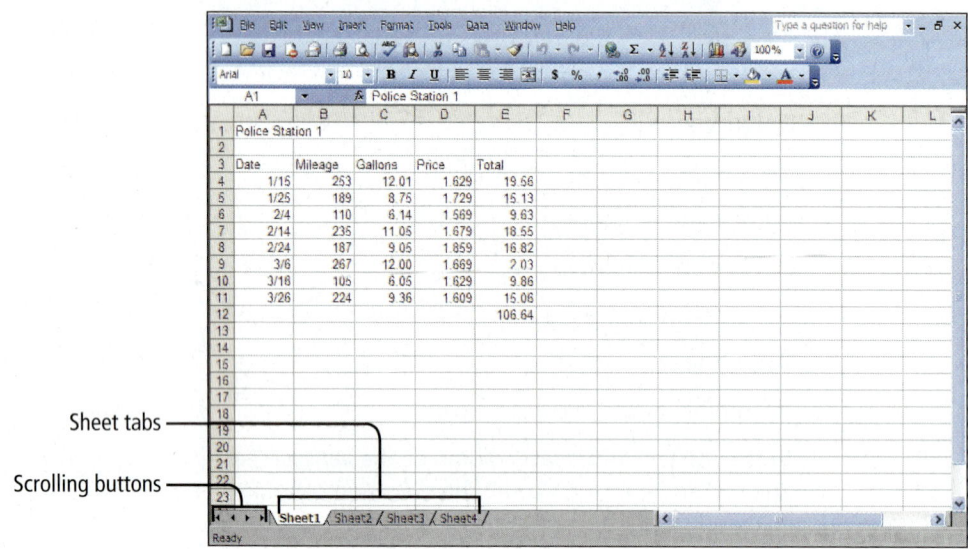

Figure 1.30

1 Point to and then click the **Sheet2 tab**.

The second worksheet in the workbook displays and becomes the active worksheet. Notice that cell A1 displays the text *Police Station 2* because the second worksheet of this workbook contains data for the 12-passenger van at Police Station 2.

2 Click the **Sheet1 tab**.

The first worksheet in the workbook becomes the active worksheet, and cell A1 displays *Police Station 1*.

Activity 1.8 Viewing a Chart

Excel can produce a graphical representation of your data. Data presented as a graph is easier to understand than rows and columns of numbers. Within Excel, a visual representation of your data using graphics is called a ***chart***.

1 In the row of sheet tabs, click the **Sheet4 tab**.

A worksheet containing a chart displays. See Figure 1.31. The chart represents the total gasoline expenses for the 12-passenger vans at each of the three police stations—graphically displaying the differences. The chart uses data gathered from the other three worksheets to generate the graphical representation. If you change the numbers in any of the worksheets, Excel automatically redraws the chart to reflect those changes.

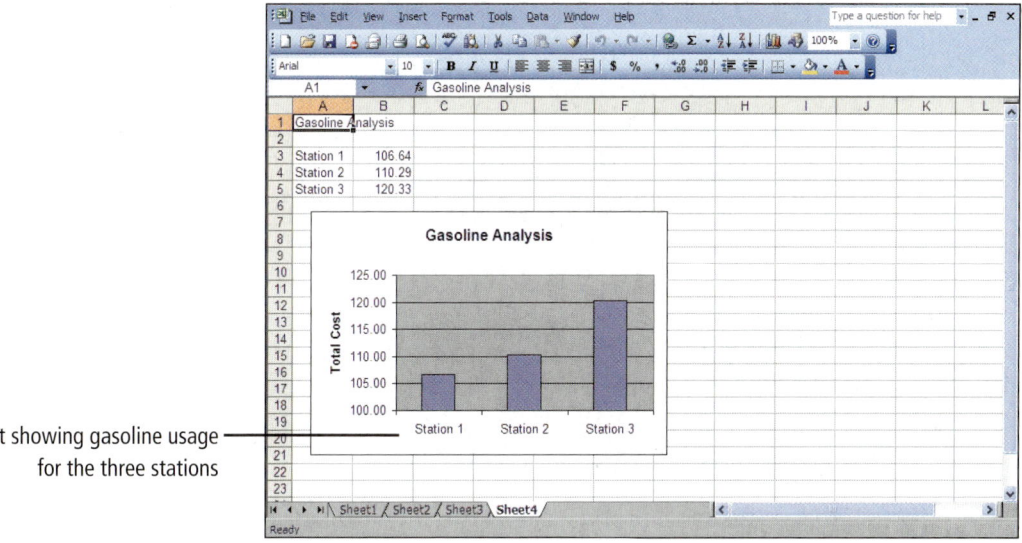

Chart showing gasoline usage for the three stations

Figure 1.31

2 Notice the height of the bar for Station 1. Then, click the **Sheet1 tab**, and click to select cell **E9**.

Project 1A: Gas Usage | **Excel** 523

3 Notice the column total of 106.64 in cell **E12**. In cell **E9**, replace the current value of *2.03* by typing **20.30** and then press [Enter].

When you type a value into a cell that already contains a value, the new value replaces the old. It is not necessary to delete the original contents of the cell first. With a new value in cell E9, pressing [Enter] caused Excel to recalculate the column total and display the new total, 124.91, in cell E12.

4 Click the **Sheet4 tab**.

The size of the bar representing Station 1 in the chart has changed to reflect the new total from the Station 1 worksheet as shown in Figure 1.32. This is an example of Excel's powerful ability to perform calculations and then update the visual representations of the data.

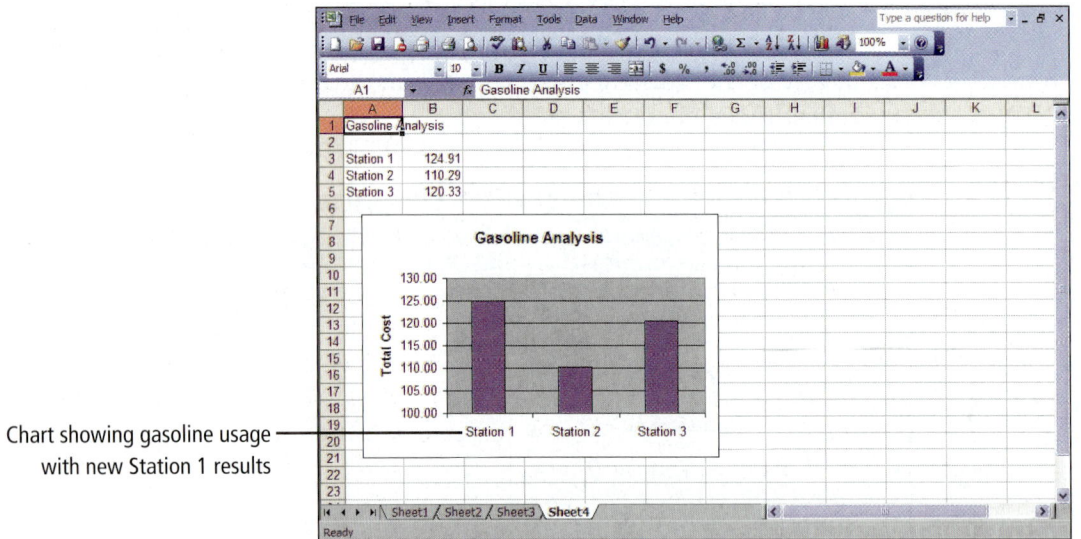

Chart showing gasoline usage with new Station 1 results

Figure 1.32

Activity 1.9 Renaming a Sheet Tab

Excel names the first worksheet in a workbook Sheet1 and each additional worksheet in order—Sheet2, Sheet3, and so on. Usually you will want to assign names to your worksheets that are more meaningful to you. Use either of two methods to rename a worksheet within a workbook:

- Right-click the sheet tab to display the shortcut menu, and then click the Rename command.

- Double-click the sheet tab, and then type a new name directly on the tab.

In this activity, you will rename the worksheets so that they are more descriptive.

1 Point to the **Sheet4 tab** and right-click. On the displayed shortcut menu, click **Rename**.

The Sheet tab name is selected.

524   Excel | Chapter 1: Getting Started with Excel 2003

2 Type **Chart** and then press Enter.

3 ***Double-click*** (click the left mouse button twice in rapid succession, keeping the mouse still between the clicks) the **Sheet1 tab** to select its name, and then type **Station 1**

4 Using either method, rename **Sheet2** to **Station 2** and **Sheet3** to **Station 3**

Objective 2
Create Headers and Footers

Headers and ***footers*** are text, page numbers, graphics, and formatting that print at the top (header) or bottom (footer) of every page.

Throughout this textbook, you will type the project name and your name on each of your worksheets by placing them in a footer. This will make it easier for you to identify your printed documents in a shared printer environment such as a lab or classroom.

Activity 1.10 Creating Headers and Footers

1 Point to the **Station 1 tab** and right-click. On the displayed shortcut menu, click **Select All Sheets**.

When a group of worksheets is selected, the word *Group* displays in the title bar to the right of the file name, as shown in Figure 1.33. By selecting all sheets, you will cause the Header and Footer information that you create to print on each worksheet in this workbook—not only on the active sheet.

Alert!

What Is "Read-Only"?
In addition to [Group], your title may display [Read-Only]. Workbook files provided by the textbook publisher frequently have this designation. It means that you cannot make permanent changes to the workbook. To make permanent changes, you will have to save the workbook with a new name, which you will be instructed to do.

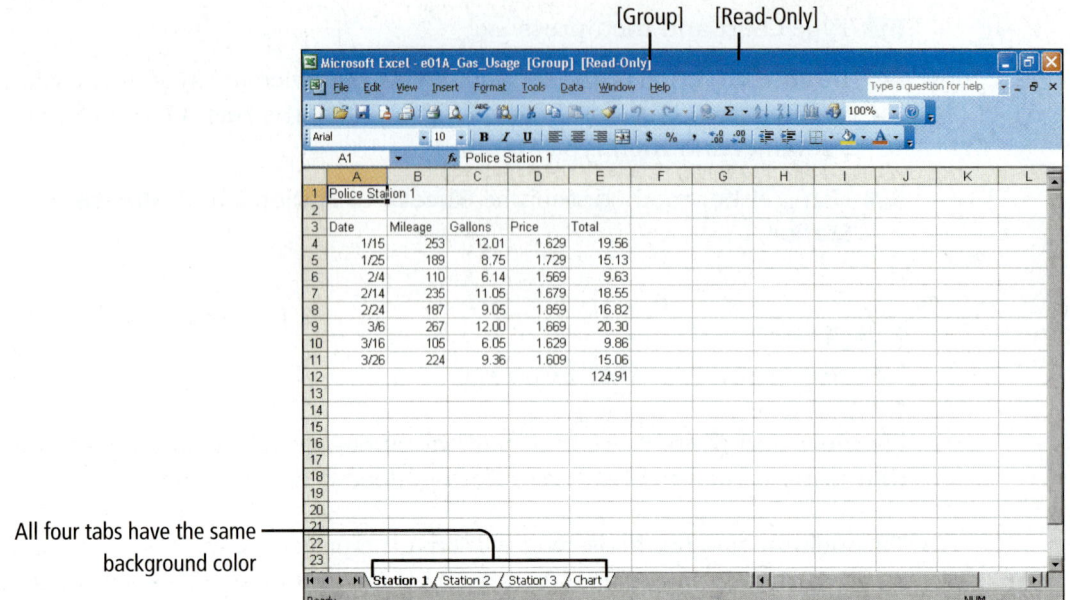

All four tabs have the same background color

Figure 1.33

2 On the menu bar, click **View**, and then click **Header and Footer**.

The Page Setup dialog box displays, as shown in Figure 1.34.

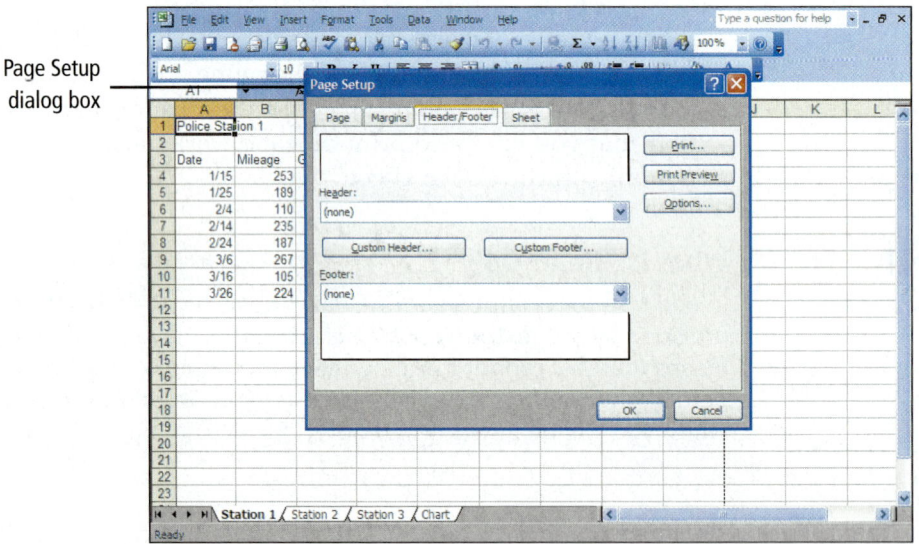

Page Setup dialog box

Figure 1.34

3 In the top portion of the **Page Setup** dialog box, click the **Header/Footer tab** once if necessary.

4 In the center of the dialog box, click the **Custom Footer** button.

The Footer dialog box displays, as shown in Figure 1.35. A flashing vertical line displays at the left edge of the *Left section* box. This is the ***insertion point***, the point at which anything you type will be inserted. The insertion point in this box is left-aligned—text you enter will begin at the left.

526   **Excel** | Chapter 1: Getting Started with Excel 2003

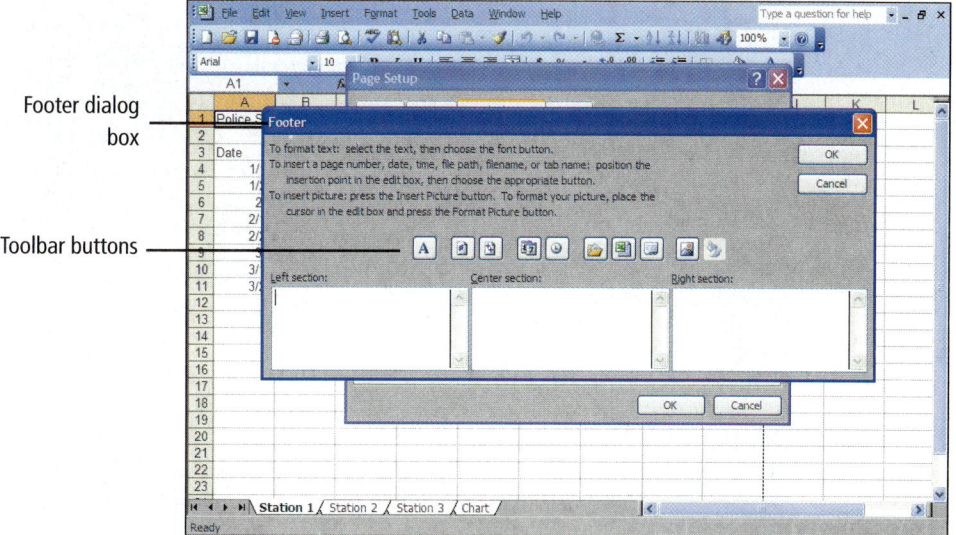

Figure 1.35

5 In the center of the **Footer** dialog box, locate the toolbar buttons shown in Figure 1.35, and then click the **Font** button. These toolbar buttons do not display ScreenTips.

The Font dialog box displays, as shown in Figure 1.36.

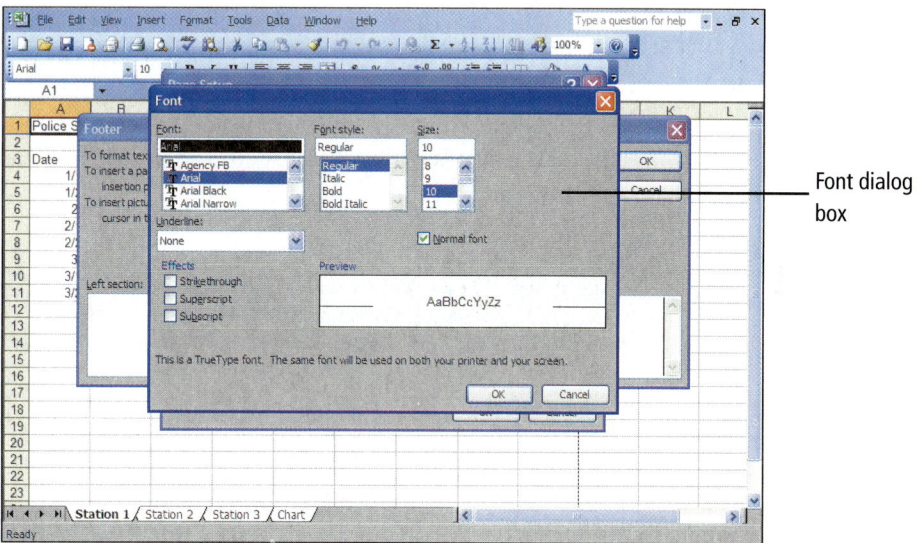

Figure 1.36

6 Under **Font**, click the **scroll bar arrows** as necessary, and then click **Arial**. Under **Font style**, scroll as necessary, and then click **Italic**. Under **Size**, scroll as necessary, and then click **14**. Then, in the lower right corner, click the **OK** button.

7 Using your own first and last name, type **1A Gas Usage-Firstname Lastname** and notice that as you type, Excel wraps the text to the next line in the box. When you print your workbook, the footer will print on one line.

Compare your screen with Figure 1.37.

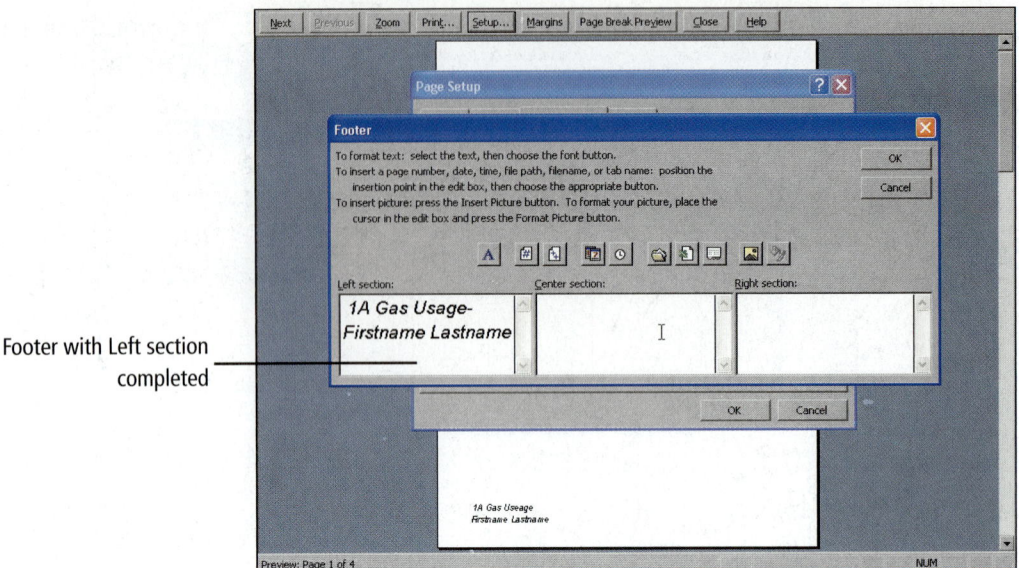

Footer with Left section completed

Figure 1.37

8 In the upper right of the **Footer** dialog box, click **OK**, and then at the lower right of the **Page Setup** dialog box, click **OK** to return to the workbook.

Headers and footers that you create do not display in the worksheet window; they display only on the page preview screen and on the printed page. The vertical dotted line between columns indicates that as currently arranged, only the columns to the left of the dotted line will print on the first page, as shown in Figure 1.38. The exact position of the dotted line will depend on the default printer settings. Yours may fall elsewhere.

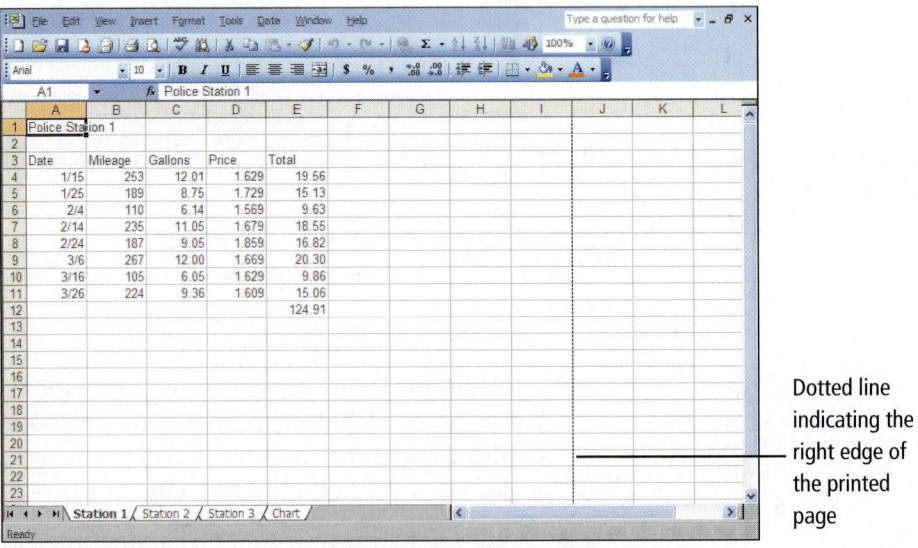

Dotted line indicating the right edge of the printed page

Figure 1.38

528 Excel | Chapter 1: Getting Started with Excel 2003

9 Right-click the **Station 1 tab**, and then click **Ungroup Sheets** to ungroup the sheets.

The word *Group* no longer displays in the worksheet title bar, indicating that the worksheet grouping has been removed.

> **More Knowledge** — Removing the [Group] Indicator on the Title Bar
>
> If sheets in a workbook are grouped, clicking any sheet tab other than that of the active sheet ungroups the sheets and removes the [Group] indicator from the title bar.

Objective 3
Preview and Print a Workbook

Before you print your worksheet or an entire workbook, you will want to check the formatting, placement, and layout. Excel's Print Preview feature lets you do this before printing your worksheets on paper.

From your instructor or lab coordinator, determine the default printer for the computer at which you are working, and check to see whether it is available for you to use.

Activity 1.11 Previewing and Printing a Workbook

1 Point to the **Station 1 tab** and right-click. On the displayed shortcut menu, click **Select All Sheets**.

The title bar shows [Group] indicating that multiple worksheets in the workbook are selected.

2 On the Standard toolbar, click the **Print Preview** button .

Your worksheet displays as an image of a piece of paper so that you can see how your worksheet will be placed on the page, including the footer. See Figure 1.39. Because more than one worksheet is being previewed, in the lower left of the preview window *Page 1 of 4* displays.

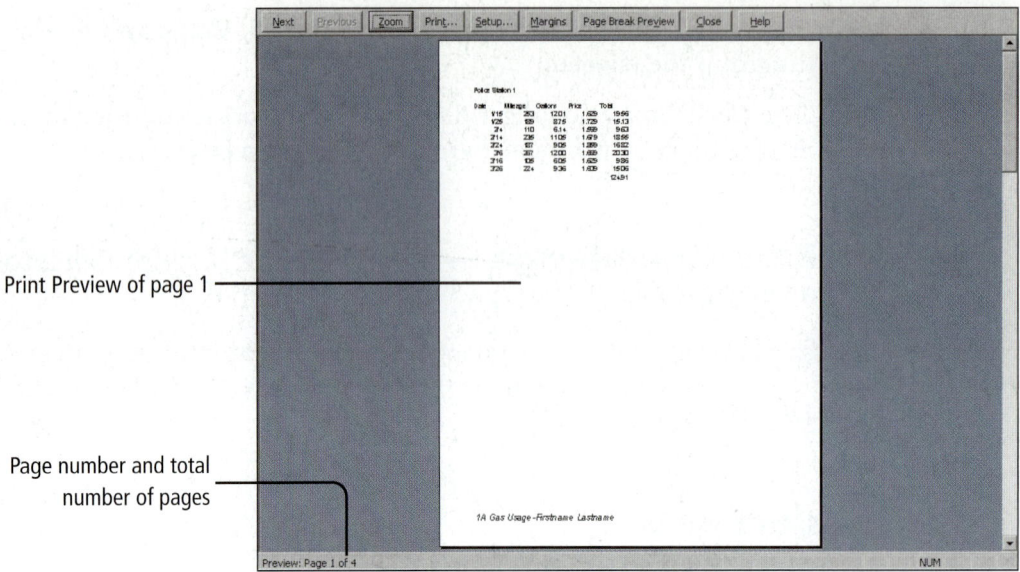

Print Preview of page 1

Page number and total number of pages

Figure 1.39

3 On the Print Preview toolbar, click the **Next** button to view page 2. Then, click the **Next** button two more times to view pages 3 and 4.

As you scroll forward and backward using the Next and Previous buttons, the words in the lower left of the Preview window change to indicate the page you are currently viewing—*Page 3 of 4* and so forth.

4 On the Print Preview toolbar, click the **Close** button to exit Print Preview.

5 On the Standard toolbar, click the **Print** button.

One copy of each worksheet in the workbook prints—a total of four sheets.

6 Right-click the **Station 1 tab**, and then click **Ungroup Sheets**.

The [Group] indication in the title bar is removed and the worksheets are no longer grouped together.

Objective 4
Save and Close a Workbook and Exit Excel

In the same way you use file folders to organize your paper documents, Windows uses a hierarchy of electronic folders to store and organize your electronic files (workbooks). In the following activities you will save the workbook with a name and in a location that will be easy for you to find.

Activity 1.12 Creating a New Folder and Saving a Workbook with a New Name

Creating a new folder in which to save your work will make finding the workbooks you create easier. Before saving, you will need to determine where you will be storing your workbooks, for example, on your own disk or on a network drive.

1 On the menu bar, click **File** to display the File menu, and then click **Save As**.

The Save As dialog box displays, as shown in Figure 1.40.

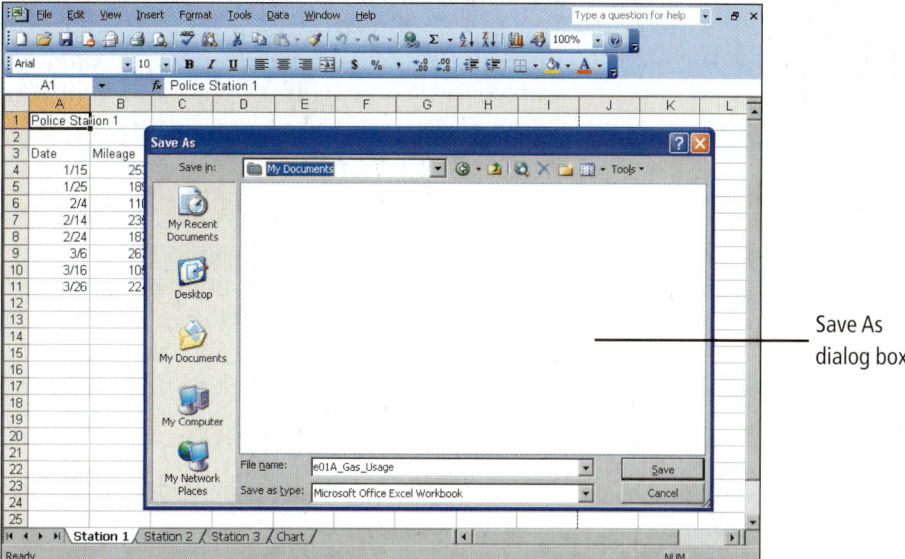

Save As dialog box

Figure 1.40

[2] Click the **Save in arrow** to view a list of the drives available to you, and then navigate to the drive on which you will be storing your folders and documents; for example, 3½ Floppy (A:).

[3] In the upper right of the dialog box, click the **Create New Folder** button .

The New Folder dialog box displays.

[4] In the displayed **New Folder** dialog box, in the **Name** box, type **Excel Chapter 1** as shown in Figure 1.41 and then click **OK**.

Windows creates the *Excel Chapter 1* folder and makes it the active folder in the Save As dialog box.

New Folder dialog box with folder name typed

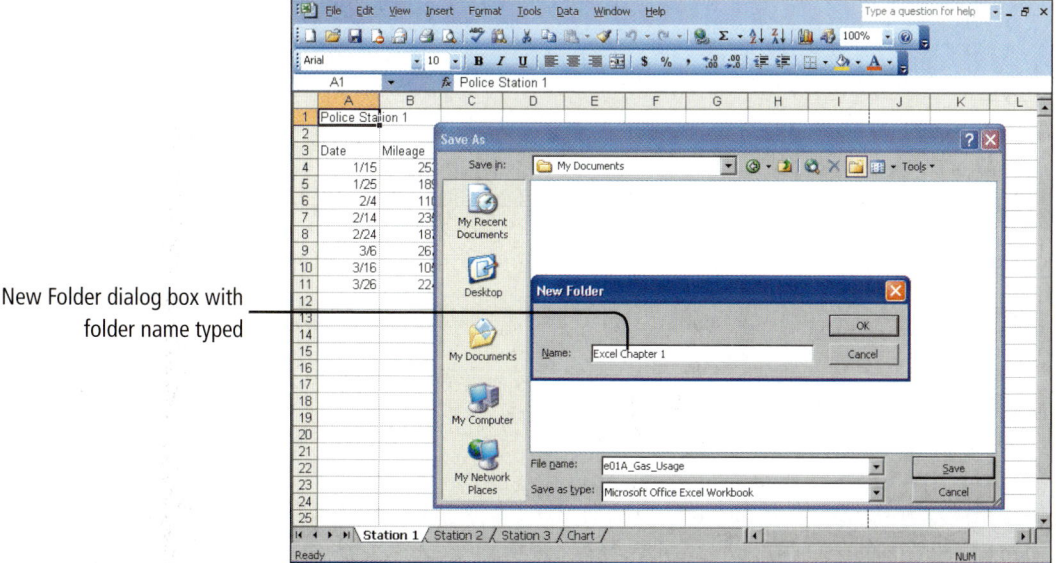

Figure 1.41

Project 1A: Gas Usage | **Excel** 531

5 In the **File name** box, delete any existing text by selecting it and pressing the ⌦ key, and type **1A_Gas_Usage_Firstname_Lastname** replacing *Firstname* with your first name and *Lastname* with your last name, being sure to include the underscore (⇧ + -) instead of spaces between words.

Windows recognizes file names that use spaces between words. However, many electronic file transfer programs do not. In this text, you will use underscores instead of spaces between words for your file names. In that manner, you can be assured that if you need to transfer files on the Web, for example, using Blackboard or WebCT for online courses, your files will move easily on the Internet.

6 In the lower right corner of the **Save As** dialog box, click **Save**.

The file is saved in the new folder with the new name. The workbook redisplays, and the new name displays in the title bar.

7 On the menu bar, click **File**, and then click **Close**.

Your workbook closes. The Excel program remains open, even when no workbooks are open.

8 At the extreme right of the title bar, click the **Close** button ⊠ to close Excel.

Note — Renaming Folders

You can rename folders by right-clicking a folder and selecting Rename from the shortcut menu. The folder name will display in an edit mode and you can type to rename the folder. You can also click once on the folder name, and then click a second time to invoke the edit mode, and then type a new folder name.

End You have completed Project 1A

Project 1B Salary Analysis

In this project, you will create a new workbook and enter data into it. Then you will create formulas to perform mathematical calculations and use the spelling checker to check for misspelled words in your spreadsheet.

In Activities 1.13 through 1.29, you will create a new workbook for Police Chief Johnson that contains an employee list showing the name, shift, date of hire, and current weekly salary of the police officers assigned to each police station. You will enter the data for Police Station 1. The resulting workbook will look similar to Figure 1.42. You will save your workbook as *1B_Salary_Analysis_Firstname_Lastname*.

```
Police Station 1 Weekly Salaries

Emp        Shift    Hired on     Salary    Annual
J Bryon    Day      5/13/1996      460     23920
T Cassidy  Day      6/11/1998      685     35620
L Shasta   Night    7/30/1998      550     28600
G Adams    Day      3/15/1999      526     27352
S Front    Day      4/17/2001      767     39884
M Pong     Night    5/17/2002      389     20228
Total                             3377    175604




1B Salary Analysis-Firstname Lastname
```

Figure 1.42
Project 1B—Salary Analysis

Project 1B: Salary Analysis | **Excel** 533

Objective 5
Create a New Workbook

When you save a file, the Windows operating system stores your workbook permanently on a storage medium—either a disk that you have inserted into the computer, the hard drive of your computer, or a network drive to which your computer system is connected. Changes that you make to existing workbooks, such as changing data or typing in new data, are not permanently saved until you perform a Save operation.

Save your workbooks frequently to avoid losing the data you have created in a new workbook or the changes you have made to an existing workbook. In rare instances, problems arise with your computer system or your electrical power source.

Activity 1.13 Creating a New Workbook

In the following activity, you will begin a new workbook and then save it in your Excel Chapter 1 folder.

1 If the Excel program is open, close it now.

2 **Start** the Excel program. If the **Getting Started** task pane is open, click its **Close** button ⊠. Notice that *Book1* displays in both the title bar and the taskbar. See Figure 1.43.

Excel displays the file name of a workbook in both the blue title bar at the top of the screen and on a button in the taskbar at the bottom of the screen—including new, unsaved workbooks. The unsaved workbook displays as *Book1* or *Book2*, depending on the number of times you have started a new workbook during your current Excel session.

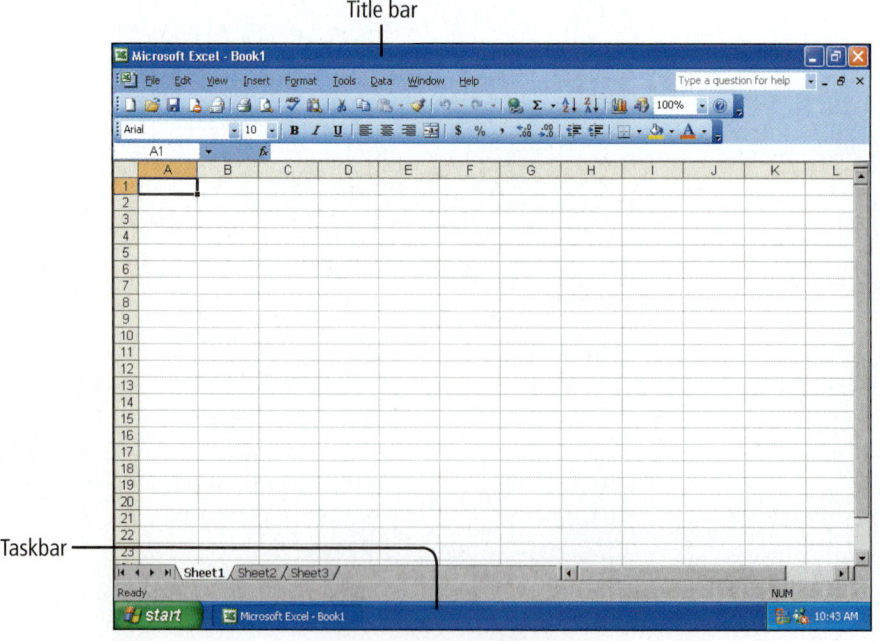

Figure 1.43

534   Excel | Chapter 1: Getting Started with Excel 2003

Alert! **The complete file name is not visible in the taskbar?**
The size of taskbar buttons varies, depending on your computer setup. To view the full file name in the taskbar, pause the mouse pointer over the button to display a ScreenTip containing the complete workbook name.

3 Display the **File** menu, and then click **Close**. Click **No** if you are prompted to save any changes to the workbook.

When all Excel workbooks are closed, most of the toolbar buttons display in gray, indicating that they are unavailable, and the workbook area displays in a darker shade. See Figure 1.44. Your screen will look like this when the Excel program is running but no workbooks are open.

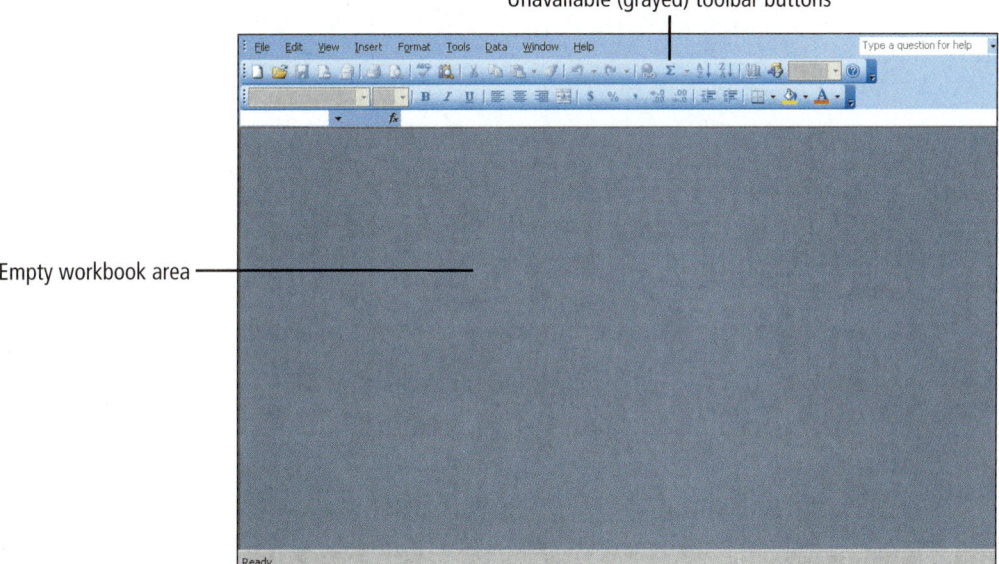

Figure 1.44

4 On the Standard toolbar, click the **New** button.

Recall that a toolbar button is a one-click method of performing a command. Alternatively, you could display the File menu and then click New, but this would require more than one click.

A new blank workbook displays, the toolbar buttons are reactivated, and *Book2* displays in the title bar and in the taskbar. Each time you open a new workbook during an Excel session, the number will increase by one. There is no limit to the number of blank workbooks. Each time you exit and then restart Excel, the numbering of blank workbooks begins again with the number 1.

Project 1B: Salary Analysis | **Excel** 535

Another Way — **Begin a New Workbook**

You can begin a new workbook in any of the following ways:

- Start Excel. The program opens with a new workbook displayed.
- From the File menu, click New.
- On the keyboard, press Ctrl + N.
- From the Getting Started task pane, click *Create a new workbook*.
- From the New Workbook task pane, click *Blank workbook*.

Activity 1.14 Saving and Naming a New Workbook

When Excel displays *Book* followed by a number, for example, *Book1*, *Book2*, and so forth, it indicates that this workbook has never been saved. To save the workbook, perform a Save As to specify a file name and the location where you want to store the workbook.

Your computer's memory stores changes you make to your workbook until you perform another Save operation. Get in the habit of saving changes you have made to an existing workbook by clicking the Save button on the Standard toolbar. The Save button saves any changes you have made to the file—without changing the file name or storage location.

1 On the Standard toolbar, click the **Save** button.

Because this workbook has never been saved with a name, the Save As dialog box displays. Alternatively, you can display the File menu and then click Save As.

2 In the **Save As** dialog box, click the **Save in arrow** to view a list of the drives available to you.

3 Navigate to the drive and folder in which you are storing your projects for this chapter; for example, 3½ Floppy (A:). Recall that you created an **Excel Chapter 1** folder previously for this purpose.

4 In the **File name** box, delete any existing text and type **1B_Salary_Analysis_Firstname_Lastname** as shown in Figure 1.45.

Recall that in this textbook, you will use underscores instead of spaces in your file names. This will make it easier to send files over the Internet if you need to do so.

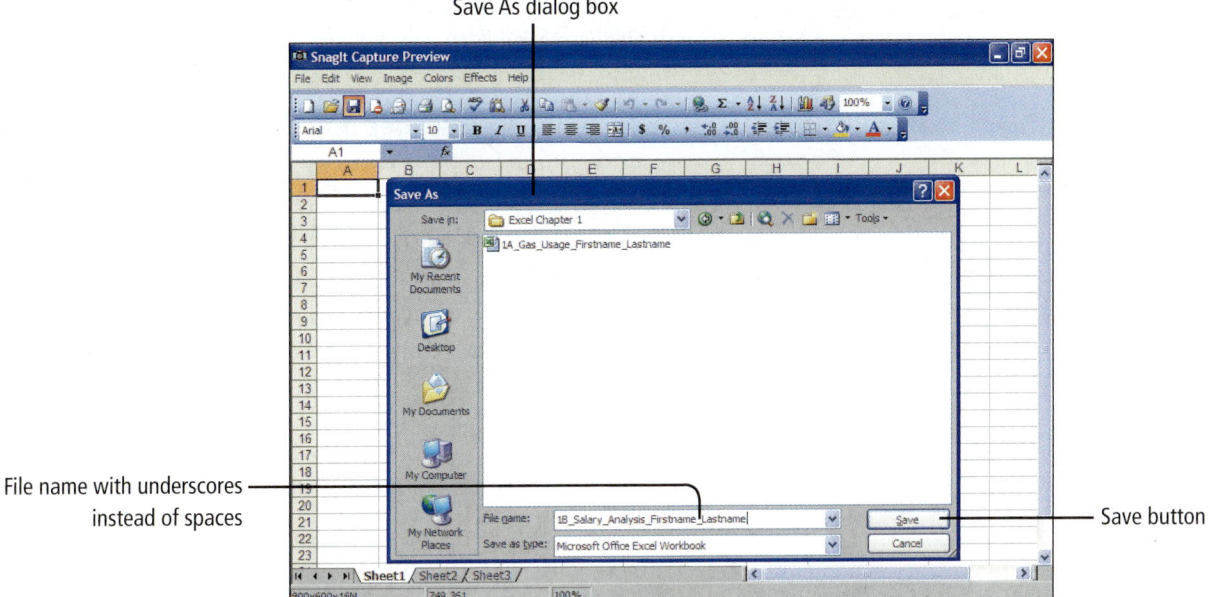

Figure 1.45

5 In the lower right corner of the **Save As** dialog box, click **Save**, or press Enter. The new workbook name displays in the title bar and on the taskbar.

Objective 6
Enter and Edit Data in a Worksheet

Every cell in a worksheet contains *formatting* information—information about how data typed into the cell will look. Formatting is easily changed, and as you progress in your study of Excel, you will practice applying various formats that will make your worksheets visually appealing.

Anything typed into a cell is referred to as *cell content*. Cell content can be one of only two things: a *constant value* or a *formula*. A constant value, also referred to simply as a *value*, can be numbers, text, dates, or times of day that you type into a cell. A formula, on the other hand, is an equation that you type into a cell. A formula acts as an instruction for Excel to perform mathematical calculations (such as adding and subtracting) on values in other cells.

In the next group of activities, you will enter various types of constant values. After you enter values into a cell, they can be edited (changed) or cleared from the cell.

Activity 1.15 Entering Text

Words (text) typed in a worksheet usually provide information about numbers in other worksheet cells. For example, *Police Station 1* gives the reader an indication that the data in this worksheet relates to information about Police Station 1. To enter text into a cell, activate the cell and type. Before entering text in this activity, you will create the footer with your name.

1 Point to the **Sheet1 tab** and right-click. On the displayed shortcut menu, click **Select All Sheets**.

[Group] displays in the title bar, indicating that the three worksheets are grouped. Recall that grouping the sheets in this manner will place your footer on all the sheets in the workbook—not only on the active sheet.

2 Display the **View** menu, click **Header and Footer**, click the **Custom Footer** button, and under **Left section**, type **1B Salary Analysis-Firstname Lastname** using your own first and last name. Do not change the font or font size—use the default font and font size.

3 In the upper right corner of the **Footer** dialog box, click **OK**. In the lower right corner of the **Page Setup** dialog box, click **OK**. Right-click the **Sheet2 tab**, and then click **Ungroup Sheets**.

The sheets are no longer grouped together, and [Group] no longer displays in the worksheet title bar.

4 On the Standard toolbar, click the **Save** button.

Recall that adding the footer causes the dotted line to display, indicating where the page would end if printed on the default printer. This may vary among printers.

5 Click the **Sheet1 tab** so that Sheet 1 is the active sheet. In cell **A1** type **Police Station 1 Weekly Salaries** and then press Enter.

After you type data into a cell, you must lock in the entry to store it in the cell. One way to do this is to press the Enter key, which makes another cell active and locks in the entry. You can use other keyboard movements, such as Tab, or one of the arrow keys on your keyboard to make another cell active and lock in the entry.

6 Look at the text you typed in cell **A1**.

Notice that the text is aligned at the left edge of the cell. Left alignment is the default for text entries and is an example of the formatting information stored in a cell. Cell A2 is the active cell, as indicated by the black border surrounding it.

7 Look at the **row 2 heading** and **column A heading**, as shown in Figure 1.46.

The shading indicates that the active cell is at the intersection of column A and row 2. In addition, the Name Box displays the cell reference, *A2*.

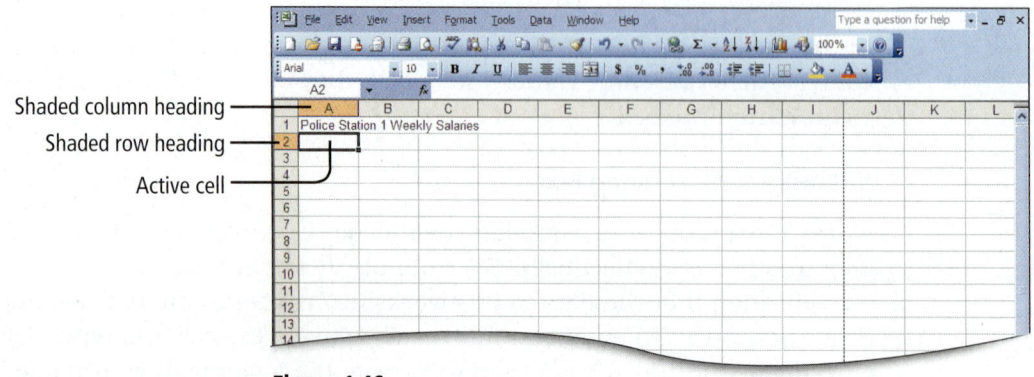

Figure 1.46

8 Press and hold down [Ctrl] and then press [Home] to make cell **A1** the active cell.

Recall that this keyboard shortcut is a quick way to move to cell A1 and make it the active cell.

9 Press [Enter] two times to move to cell **A3**. Type **Emp** and if you make a typing error press [Bksp]. Notice that as you type, a vertical line called the *insertion point* blinks, indicating where your keystrokes will be inserted. Press [Enter].

10 Click cell **A1** to make it the active cell, look at the Formula Bar, and notice that the words *Police Station 1 Weekly Salaries* display.

11 Click cell **B1** and look at the Formula Bar.

No text displays in the Formula Bar. Although the display of the value in cell A1 overlaps into cell B1, the value itself is contained within cell A1. When a value is too wide for its cell, Excel will display the value in the adjacent cell—if the adjacent cell is empty. If the adjacent cell is *not* empty, Excel displays only as much of the value as there is space to do so.

12 Click cell **A4**, and then type the remaining text into **column A** as shown in Figure 1.47. Press [Enter] after you type the text for each cell to lock in the entry and move down to the next cell. While typing in a cell, press [Bksp] to correct any errors.

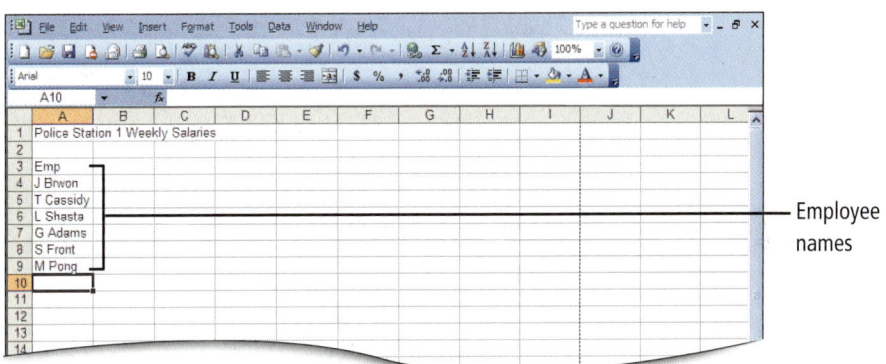

Figure 1.47

13 Click cell **B3** to make it the active cell, type **Shift** and then press [Tab] to move to cell **C3**.

> **More Knowledge** — More Ways to Use the Enter Key
>
> Pressing the Tab key makes the cell to the right the active cell. Pressing the Enter key makes the cell in the next row the active cell. If you prefer to have the Enter key make the cell to the right the active cell, select a group of horizontal cells, and then begin typing in the first cell. Then press Enter—the cell to the right will become the active cell. This is useful if you are entering data from the numeric keypad, where Enter is the only key available on the keypad to lock in the entry.

14 In cell **C3** type **Date** and then press Tab.

15 In cell **D3** type **Salary** and then press Enter.

B4 becomes the active cell. Because you used Tab to move the active cell to column C and then to column D, pressing Enter causes the active cell to return to the column in which you first pressed Tab.

16 Compare your screen with Figure 1.48.

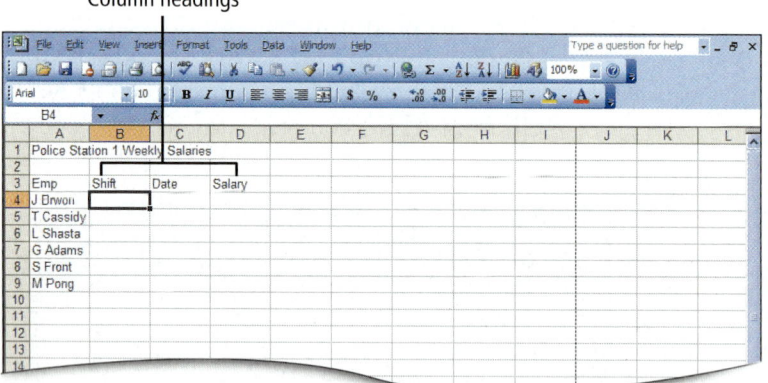

Figure 1.48

Activity 1.16 Using AutoComplete to Enter Data

Excel assists you in typing. If the first few characters you type in a cell match an existing entry in the column, Excel fills in the remaining characters for you. This feature, called ***AutoComplete***, speeds your typing. It is useful because, in a spreadsheet, you frequently type the same information over and over. AutoComplete assists only with alphabetic values; it does not assist with numeric values.

1 To check that the AutoComplete feature is available on your system, display the **Tools** menu, click **Options,** and then in the displayed **Options** dialog box, click the **Edit tab**. Under **Settings**, determine whether *Enable AutoComplete for cell values* is selected (checked) as shown in Figure 1.49. If a check mark appears, click **OK** to close the dialog box. If no check mark appears, click to select the option, and then click **OK**.

Options dialog box —
Edit tab —

Enable AutoComplete for cell values check box —

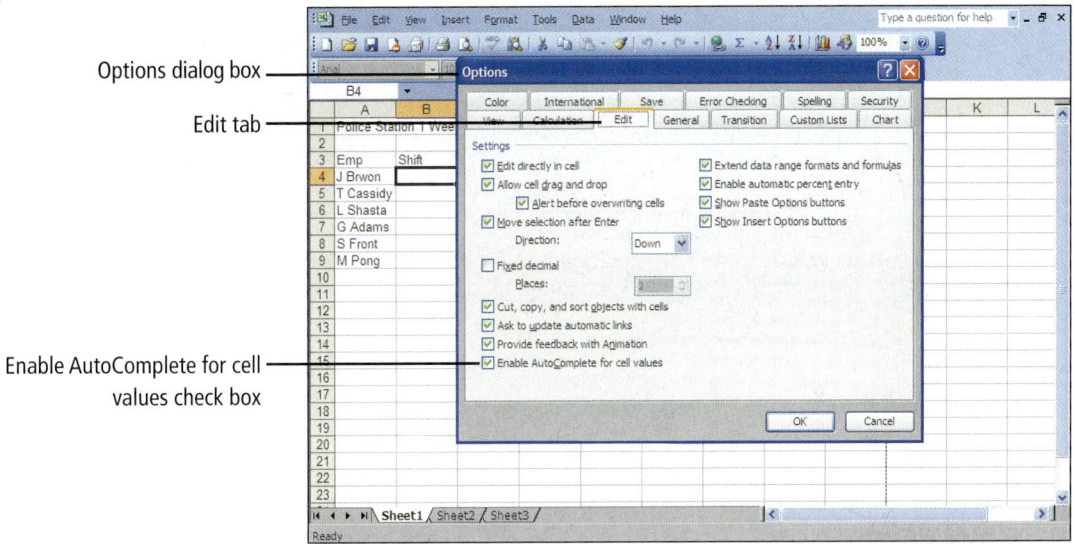

Figure 1.49

2 Be sure that cell **B4** is the active cell. Type **Day** and then press Enter.

3 In cell **B5**, type **D**

Excel completes the word *Day* because the first character matches an existing text entry in column B. See Figure 1.50.

AutoComplete fills in the *ay* of *Day*

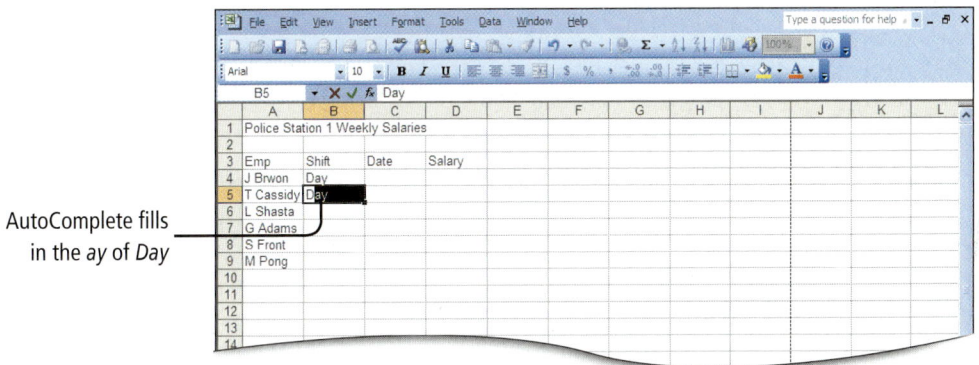

Figure 1.50

4 Press Enter to accept the entry.

Day is automatically entered in the cell, saving you from typing the entire word. The completed entry will match the pattern of uppercase and lowercase letters of the existing entry. If you do not want to accept an AutoComplete suggestion, press Bksp to delete the characters, or continue typing to replace the characters with your own typing.

5 Enter the remaining data in **column B** as shown in Figure 1.51, using **AutoComplete** when it is useful to complete the cell entry.

Project 1B: Salary Analysis | **Excel** 541

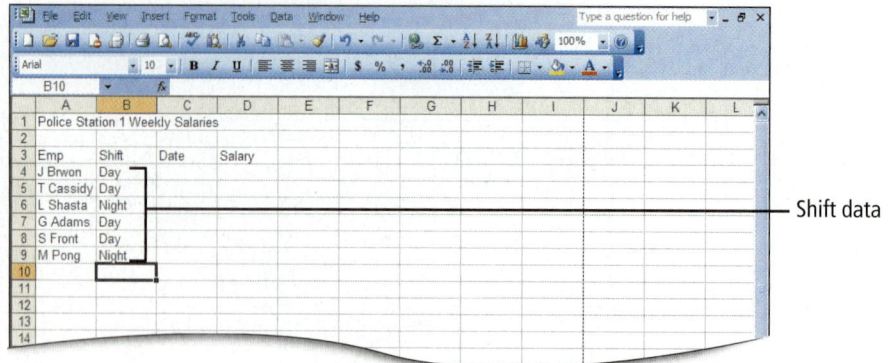

Figure 1.51

6 On the Standard toolbar, click the **Save** button to save the changes you have made to your worksheet.

The changes to your workbook are saved. Recall the importance of saving your work periodically.

Activity 1.17 Entering Numbers

When typing numbers, you can use either the number keys across the top of your keyboard or the number keys and [Enter] key on the numeric keypad. Try to develop some proficiency in touch control of the numeric keypad. On a desktop computer, the Num Lock light indicates that the numeric keypad is active. If necessary, press the Num Lock key to activate the numeric keypad.

1 In **column D**, under *Salary*, click cell **D4**, type **500** and then press [Esc] (located in the upper left corner of your keyboard).

Your typing is canceled, and D4 remains the active cell. If you change your mind about an entry while typing in a cell, press [Esc] or click the Cancel button on the Formula Bar.

2 With **D4** as the active cell, type **460** and then press [Enter].

The weekly salary of 460 is locked into cell D4, as shown in Figure 1.52. Notice that after you lock in the entry, the numbers align at the right edge of the cell. This is called **right alignment**. When you type a value consisting of numbers in a cell, the default alignment is right. Right alignment of numbers is another example of formatting information that is stored in a cell.

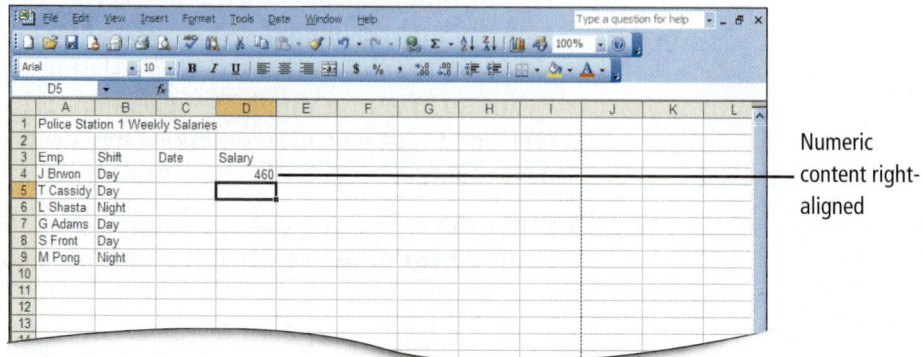

Figure 1.52

3 Click cell **D5**, type **685** and then press Enter. Continue entering the weekly salary amounts for **column D**, as shown in Figure 1.53.

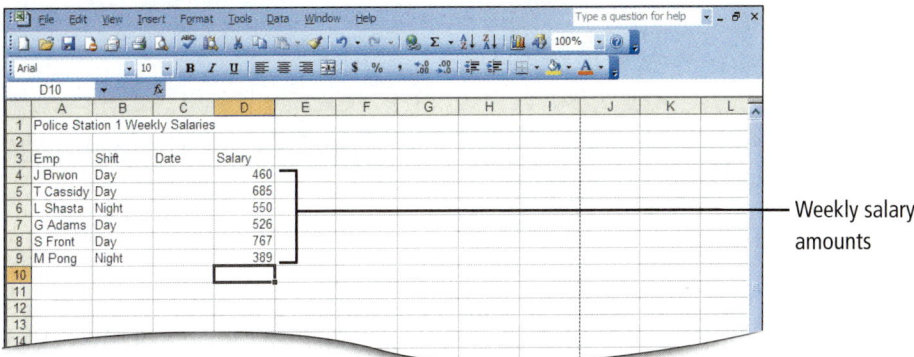
— Weekly salary amounts

Figure 1.53

4 These numbers will affect your final worksheet, so take a moment to check that you have typed accurately. To correct a cell, click it and type the data again. There is no need to delete the old value—typing a new value replaces any existing cell values.

5 On the Standard toolbar, click the **Save** button.

Activity 1.18 Typing Dates into a Worksheet

Date values are a type of content frequently typed into a worksheet. Date values entered in any of the following formats will be recognized by Excel as a date:

- m/d/yy   For example, 7/4/05
- d-mmm   For example, 4-Jul
- d-mmm-yy   For example, 4-Jul-05
- mmm-yy   For example, Jul-05

On your keyboard, - (the hyphen key) and / (the forward slash key) function identically in any of these formats and can be used interchangeably. You may abbreviate the month name to three characters or spell it out. You may enter the year as two digits, four digits, or even leave it off. When left off, the current year is assumed but does not display in the cell.

A two-digit year value of 30 through 99 is interpreted by the Windows operating system as the four-digit years of 1930 through 1999. All other two-digit year values are assumed to be in the 21st century. Get in the habit of typing year values as four digits, even though only two digits may display in the cell. In that manner, you can be sure that Excel interprets the year value as you intended. See the table in Figure 1.54 for examples.

Project 1B: Salary Analysis | **Excel** 543

How Excel Interprets Dates

Date Typed As:	Completed by Excel As:
7/4/05	7/4/2005
7-4-96	7/4/1996
7/4	4-Jul (current year assumed)
7-4	4-Jul (current year assumed)
July 4	4-Jul (current year assumed)
Jul 4	4-Jul (current year assumed)
Jul/4	4-Jul (current year assumed)
Jul-4	4-Jul (current year assumed)
July 4, 1996	4-Jul-96
July 2005	Jul-05
July 1996	Jul-96

Figure 1.54

1 In **column C**, under *Date*, click cell **C4** to make it the active cell, type **5/13/2004** and then press [Enter].

The date right-aligns in the cell and displays as 5/13/2004, using the m/d/yyyy format.

Alert!

The date does not display as 5/13/2004?

The Windows setting in the Control Panel under Regional and Language Options determines the default format for dates. If your result is different, it is likely that the formatting of the default date was adjusted on the computer at which you are working.

2 Click cell **C4** again to make it the active cell, press and hold down [Ctrl], and then press [;] (the semicolon key) on your keyboard. Press [Enter] to lock in the entry.

Excel enters the current date, obtained from your computer's internal calendar, into the selected cell using the m/d/yyyy formatting that was previously created in that cell. This is a convenient keyboard shortcut for entering the current date.

3 Click cell **C4** again, type **5/13/96** and press [Enter]. Then, enter the remaining dates as shown in Figure 1.55.

Because the year was between 30 and 99, Excel assumed a 20th century date and changed *96* to *1996* to complete the four-digit year.

4 On the Standard toolbar, click the **Save** button.

544 Excel | Chapter 1: Getting Started with Excel 2003

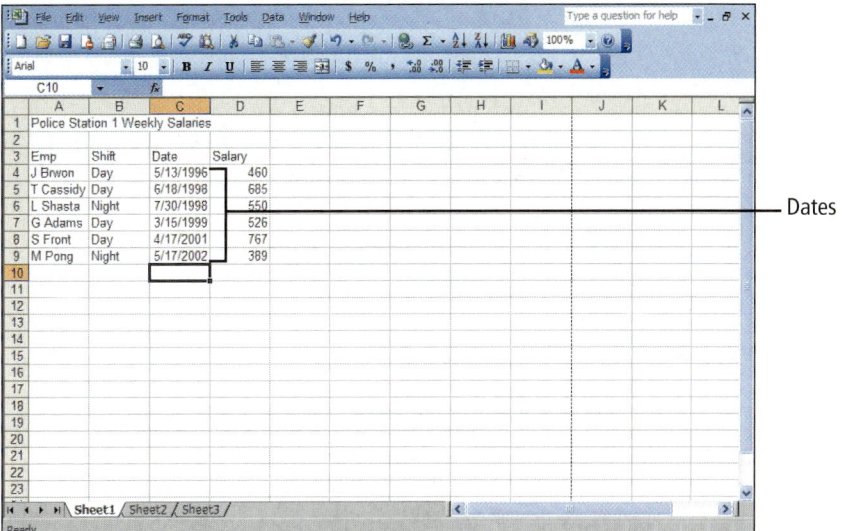

Figure 1.55

Activity 1.19 Editing Data in Cells

Before you lock in a cell entry by pressing [Enter] or by making another cell the active cell, you can correct typing errors in one of three ways:

- Press [Bksp] to delete characters to the left of the insertion point, one character at a time.
- Press [Esc] to cancel the entire entry.
- On the Formula Bar, click the Cancel button to cancel the entire entry.

Corrections can also be made after locking in the entry by either making the cell active and typing in new data, in which case the existing data will be replaced by your new keystrokes, or by activating Edit mode and editing a portion of the data in the cell. Once you activate Edit mode, you can perform editing directly in the cell or in the Formula Bar.

1 At the lower left corner of your screen, in the Status area, locate the word *Ready*.

Ready indicates that the active cell is ready to accept new data.

2 Point to cell **C4** and double-click to select the cell and simultaneously activate Edit mode. Alternatively, you can select the cell and then press [F2] to activate Edit mode.

The blinking vertical insertion point displays somewhere within the cell. The cell is active and ready to be edited (modified).

> **Note** — **Performing a Double-Click**
>
> Double-clicking may take some practice, but remember that it is not the speed of the two clicks that is important. What is important is that the mouse remain still between the two clicks. Mouse devices with an extra button on the side that functions as a double-click are available.

Project 1B: Salary Analysis | **Excel** 545

3 Look at the Status area and notice that *Ready* has been replaced with *Edit*.

This indicates that Edit mode is active. Now you can use the ← and → keys on the keyboard to reposition the insertion point and make changes. See Figure 1.56.

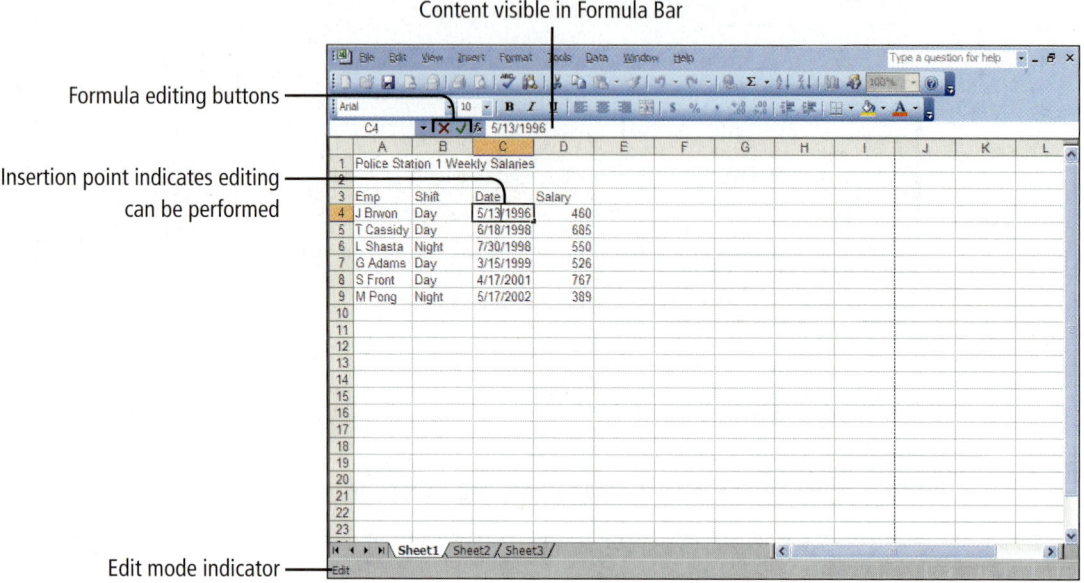

Figure 1.56

4 On the Formula Bar, locate the formula editing buttons. Refer to Figure 1.56.

The Cancel and Enter buttons are visible only when you are entering or editing data in a cell.

5 On the Formula Bar, click the **Cancel** button ❌ to exit Edit mode.

The cell remains active, but the insertion point no longer displays.

6 To activate Edit mode using the keyboard, click cell **C5** to make it the active cell, and then press F2. Move your mouse pointer away from the cell so you can see the insertion point.

Edit mode is activated, and the insertion point displays at the right edge of the cell. *Ready* is replaced with *Edit* in the Status area.

7 Using either ← or your mouse pointer, position the insertion point to the left of the number *8* in *18*. Press Delete to delete the number *8*.

The cell displays *6/1/998*. Recall that Bksp removes text to the left of the insertion point one character at a time, and Delete removes text to the right of the insertion point one character at a time.

8 Press Enter to lock in the entry.

9 Click cell **C5** again to make it the active cell. Pause the mouse pointer in the Formula Bar until the I-beam pointer displays.

Click to position the pointer before the *1* in *6/1* as shown in Figure 1.57.

Sometimes it is easier to perform your editing in the Formula Bar, where you have a better view of the cell contents.

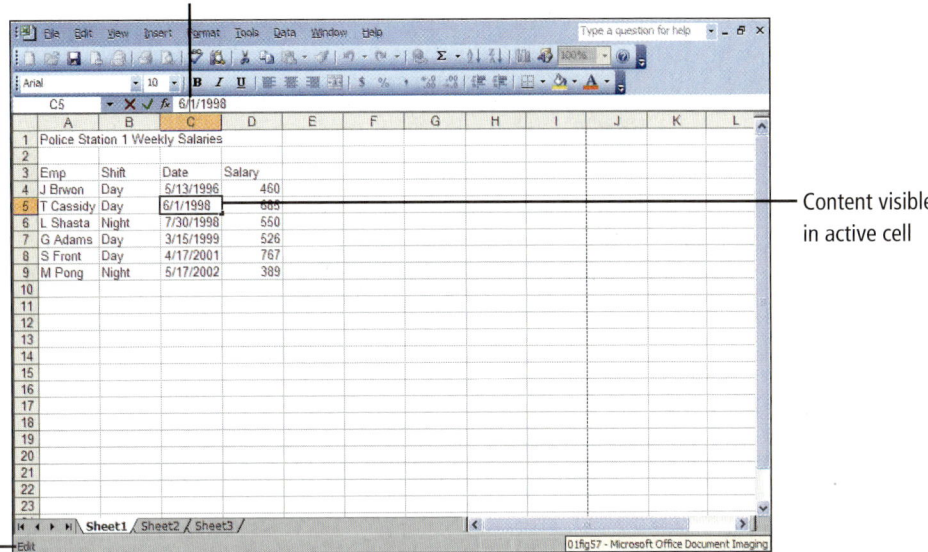

Figure 1.57

10 Type **1** and then click the **Enter** button on the Formula Bar.

The date changes to *6/11/1998* and C5 remains the active cell. Recall that clicking the Enter button on the Formula Bar locks in the entry while keeping the current cell active.

More Knowledge — Insert and Overtype Mode

The default for editing data in a worksheet is insert mode. Characters you type are inserted, and the existing characters move to the right to make space for your new typing. You can activate overtype mode, in which your typing replaces any existing characters, by pressing [Insert] when you are in *Edit* mode. In overtype mode, the letters *OVR* display in the status area, and the insertion point displays as a blinking block. Pressing [Insert] again turns off overtype mode, removes *OVR*, and reactivates insert mode.

Activity 1.20 Using Undo and Redo

You can reverse an action or a series of actions while entering data into an Excel worksheet by using the Undo command. You can Undo up to your past 16 keyboard actions. If you Undo something by mistake, the Redo command will reverse a previous Undo. Undo an action in any of the following ways:

- On the Standard toolbar, click the Undo button.
- Display the Edit menu, and then click Undo.
- From the keyboard, hold down the [Ctrl] key and press [Z].
- On the Standard toolbar, click the Undo arrow and choose one or more actions to undo.

1 Click cell **A3** to make it the active cell, type **Name** and then press [Enter].

The column heading *Emp* is replaced by your new entry, *Name*. Recall that typing a new value into a cell will delete the old value.

2 On the menu bar, click **Edit** to display the Edit menu.

The Undo command line describes the action that the Undo command will replace if you decide to do so. To the left is a reminder that a toolbar button can carry out this command, and to the right is a reminder that a keyboard shortcut can also carry out the command.

3 On the **Edit** menu, click **Undo Typing 'Name' in A3**.

The cell entry *Name* is deleted, and *Emp* displays again in cell A3.

4 Click cell **C3**, type **Hired on** and then press [Enter].

Date is replaced with *Hired on*.

5 On the Standard toolbar, click the **Undo** button. Alternatively, you can press [Ctrl] + [Z] on the keyboard to reverse the last action.

Date is restored and *Hired on* is deleted—your action was undone. Recall that a toolbar button is a one-click method of performing a command that would otherwise take several clicks to perform from the menu.

6 On the Standard toolbar, click the **Redo** button.

Hired on replaces *Date*.

7 Rename the **Sheet1 tab** to **Station 1** and then press [Enter].

8 On the Standard toolbar, click the **Save** button to save the changes you have made to your workbook.

Activity 1.21 Clearing a Cell

You can clear (delete) the contents of a selected cell in one of two ways:

- From the Edit menu, point to the Clear command, and then click Contents.
- Press the [Delete] key.

Recall that if you type anything into a cell, it is considered to have content—either a value or a formula. Recall also that every cell has some formatting instructions attached to it that determine how the content will display. As you progress in your study of Excel, you will learn to format cells with different looks, such as color or bold text, and to attach comments to a cell. Clearing the contents of a cell deletes the value or formula typed there, but it does *not* clear formatting and comments.

1 Click cell **A4** to make it the active cell. Display the **Edit** menu, point to **Clear**, and then on the displayed submenu, click **Contents**.

2 Click cell **A5,** display the **Edit** menu, and then point to **Clear**.

The displayed submenu indicates *Del* (the [Del] key) as the keyboard shortcut for the Clear Contents command.

3 Click any empty cell in the worksheet window to close the menu without activating a command.

4 Select cell **A5** again, press [Del] to clear the contents of the cell.

5 From the keyboard, hold down the [Ctrl] key and press [Z] twice to undo the last two actions, which will restore the contents of cells **A5** and then **A4**.

6 On the Standard toolbar, click the **Save** button to save your changes.

Objective 7
Create Formulas

Excel performs calculations on numbers. That is why people use Excel. You can arrange data in a format of columns and rows in other application programs—in a word processing program, for example—and even perform simple calculations. Only a spreadsheet program such as Excel, however, can perform complex calculations on numbers.

Recall that the content of a cell is either a constant value or a formula. Formulas contain instructions for Excel to perform mathematical calculations on values in other cells and then to place the result of the calculations in the cell containing the formula. You can create your own formulas, or you can use one of Excel's prebuilt formulas called a ***function***.

When you change values contained in any of the cells referred to by the formula, Excel recalculates and displays the new result immediately. This is one of the most powerful and valuable features of Excel.

Activity 1.22 Typing a Formula in a Cell

In this activity, you will sum the weekly salaries to calculate the total weekly payroll.

1 Click cell **A10** to make it the active cell, type **Total** and then press [Enter].

2 Click cell **D10** to make it the active cell, and press =.

The equal sign (=) displays in the cell with the insertion point blinking, ready to accept more data. All formulas begin with the = sign, which is the signal that directs Excel to begin a calculation. The Formula Bar shows the = sign, and the Formula Bar Cancel and Enter buttons are displayed.

3 At the insertion point, type **d4**

Cell D4 is surrounded by a blue border with small corner boxes, as shown in Figure 1.58. This indicates that the cell is part of an active formula. The color used in the box matches the color of the cell reference in the formula.

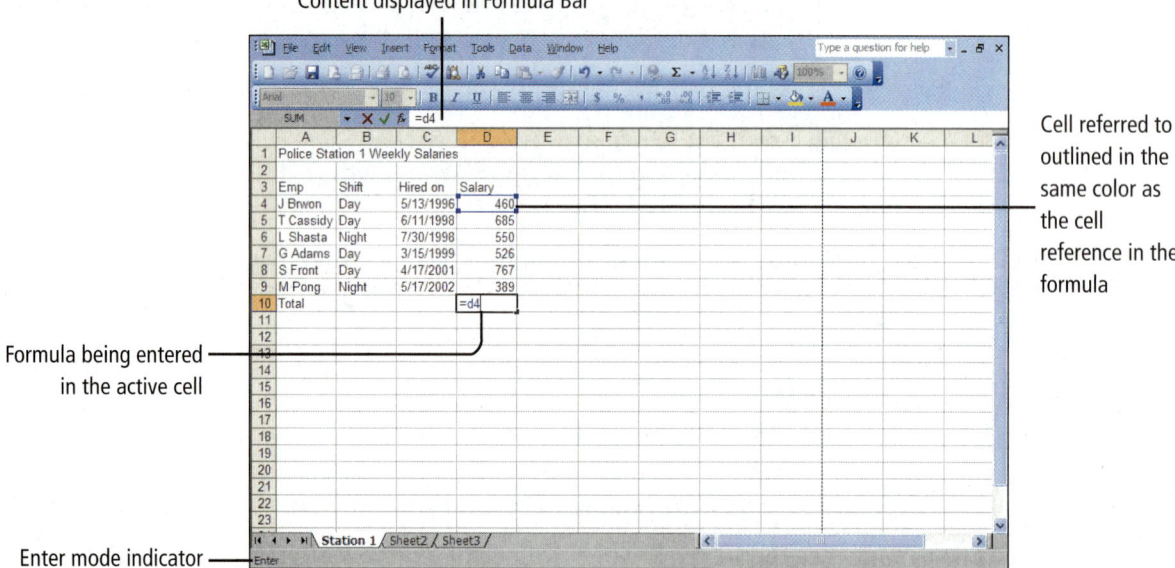

Figure 1.58

4 At the insertion point, press the + key (Shift + =) and then type **d5**

A border of another color surrounds cell D5, and the color matches the color of the cell address in the active formula. Recall that when typing cell references, it is not necessary to use uppercase letters.

5 At the insertion point, type **+d6+d7+d8+d9** and then press Enter.

The result of the calculation—*3377*—displays in the cell.

6 Click cell **D10** again to make it the active cell, and look at the Formula Bar, as shown in Figure 1.59.

You created a formula that added the values in cells D4 through D9, and the result of adding the values in those cells displays in cell D10. Although cell D10 displays the result of the formula, the formula itself is displayed in the Formula Bar. This is referred to as the **underlying formula**. Always view the Formula Bar to be sure of the exact content of a cell—a displayed number might actually be a formula.

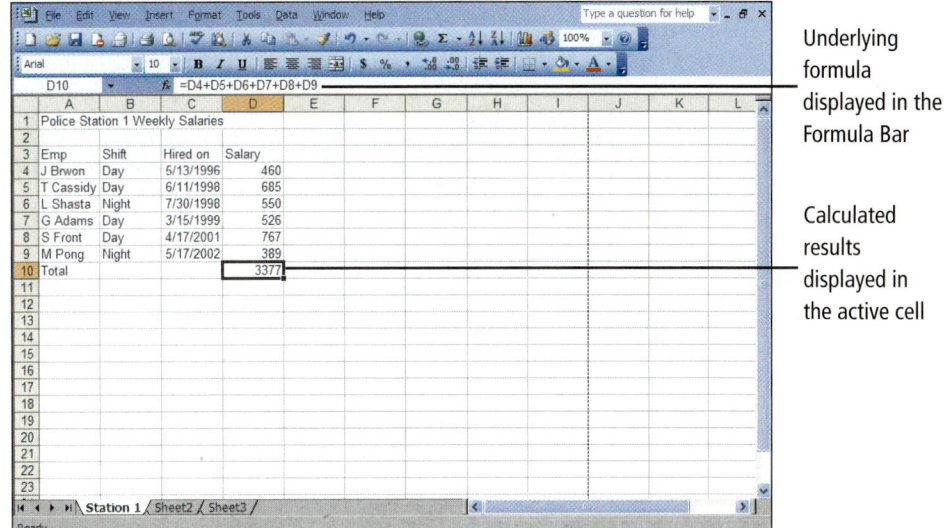

Figure 1.59

7 On the Standard toolbar, click the **Save** button to save the changes you have made to your workbook.

Activity 1.23 Using Point and Click to Enter Cell References in a Formula

In this activity, you will calculate the annual salary for each officer by multiplying the weekly salary by the number of pay periods in a year. So far, you have entered cell references into a formula by typing them. Another method is to point to the cell you want to refer to and click. The selected cell address is placed in the formula without any typing.

1 Click cell **E3** to make it the active cell, type **Annual** and then press Enter.

2 In cell **E4**, type = to signal the beginning of a formula.

3 With your mouse, point to cell **D4** and click once.

The reference to the cell, D4, is added to the active formula. A moving border surrounds the cell referred to, and the border color and the color of the cell reference in the formula are color coded to match. See Figure 1.60.

Project 1B: Salary Analysis | **Excel** 551

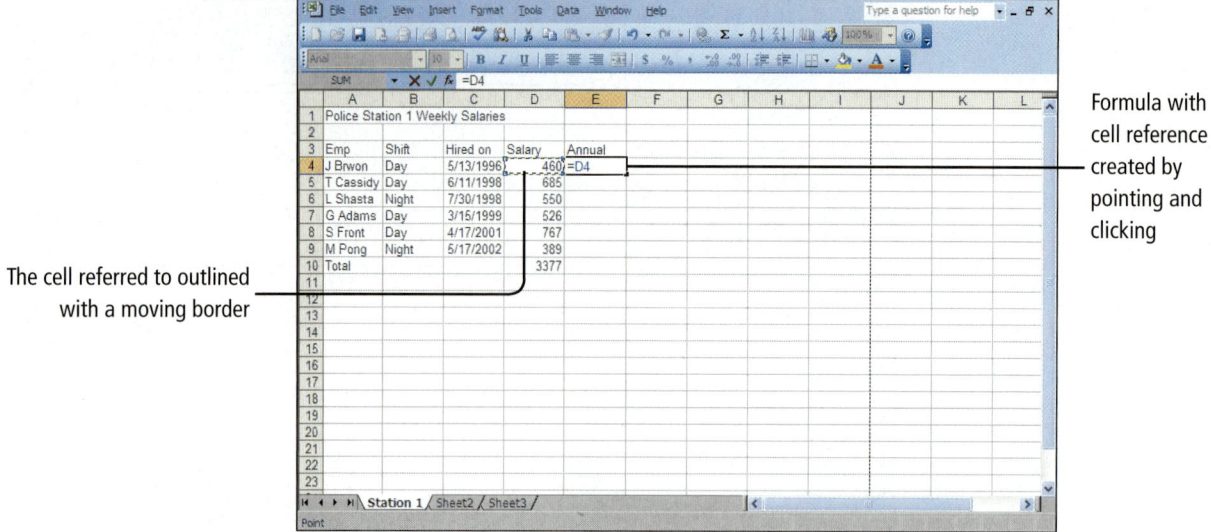

Figure 1.60

4 On your keyboard, locate the ⁎ key (Shift + 8), type **⁎52** and press Enter.

The calculated annual salary, *23920*, displays in cell E4. The ⁎ symbol, called an **asterisk**, functions in Excel as an **operator**. Operators are symbols that represent mathematical operations. The mathematical operation of multiplication is represented by the asterisk. Thus, you multiplied the weekly salary (the value in cell D4) by the constant value 52 (the number of weeks in a year) to calculate the annual salary—and placed the result in cell E4.

5 Take a moment to study the symbols you will use to perform mathematical operations in Excel, as shown in the table in Figure 1.61.

Mathematical Symbols Used in Excel

Operator Symbol	Operation
+	Addition
−	Subtraction
⁎	Multiplication
/	Division
^	Exponentiation

Figure 1.61

For reading ease, you may include spaces before and after the operators in a formula. Also, when you use more than one operator in a formula, Excel follows a mathematical rule called the **order of operations**. As you progress in your study of Excel and develop your own formulas, you will practice applying this rule, which has three basic parts:

552   Excel | Chapter 1: Getting Started with Excel 2003

- Expressions within parentheses are processed first.
- Exponentiation is performed before multiplication and division, which are performed before addition and subtraction.
- Consecutive operators with the same level of precedence are calculated from left to right.

6 In cell **E5**, type = to begin a formula.

7 With your mouse, point to cell **D5** and click once.

8 Type ***52** and then press [Enter].

The annual salary, *35620*, displays.

9 In cell **E6**, type **=d6*52** and press [Enter].

When constructing a formula, you can either type cell references or use the point-and-click method to insert the cell reference. The annual salary, *28600*, displays in cell E6.

10 In cells **E7**, **E8**, and **E9**, use either the point-and-click method or the typing method to construct a formula to multiply each officer's weekly salary by 52. Then compare your screen with Figure 1.62.

11 On the Standard toolbar, click the **Save** button to save the changes you have made to your worksheet.

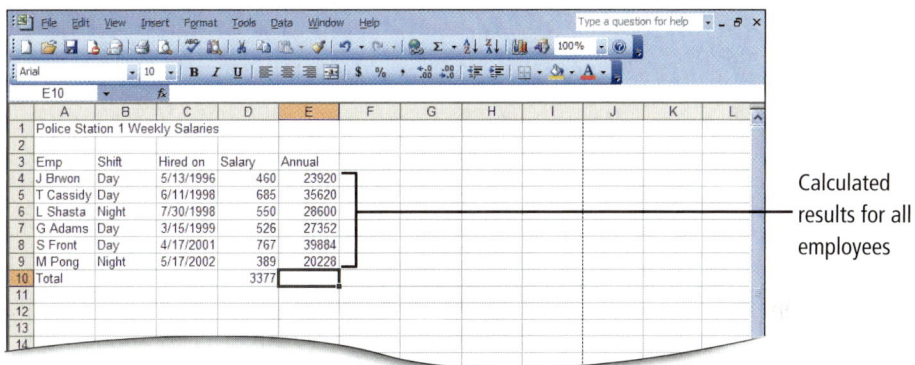

Figure 1.62

Activity 1.24 Summing a Column of Numbers with AutoSum

Excel has some prebuilt formulas, which are called *functions*. One function, *AutoSum*, is frequently used to add columns of numbers. Because it is used so frequently, a toolbar button was created for the AutoSum function. Other functions that are not so frequently used are available through the Insert Function dialog box.

1 Be sure **E10** is the active cell. On the Standard toolbar, click the **AutoSum** button.

As shown in Figure 1.63, cells E4:E9 are surrounded by a moving border, and =SUM(E4:E9) displays in cell E10. The = sign signals the beginning of a formula, SUM indicates the type of calculation that will take place (addition), and (E4:E9) indicates the range of cells on which the sum operation will be performed. A ScreenTip provides additional information about the action.

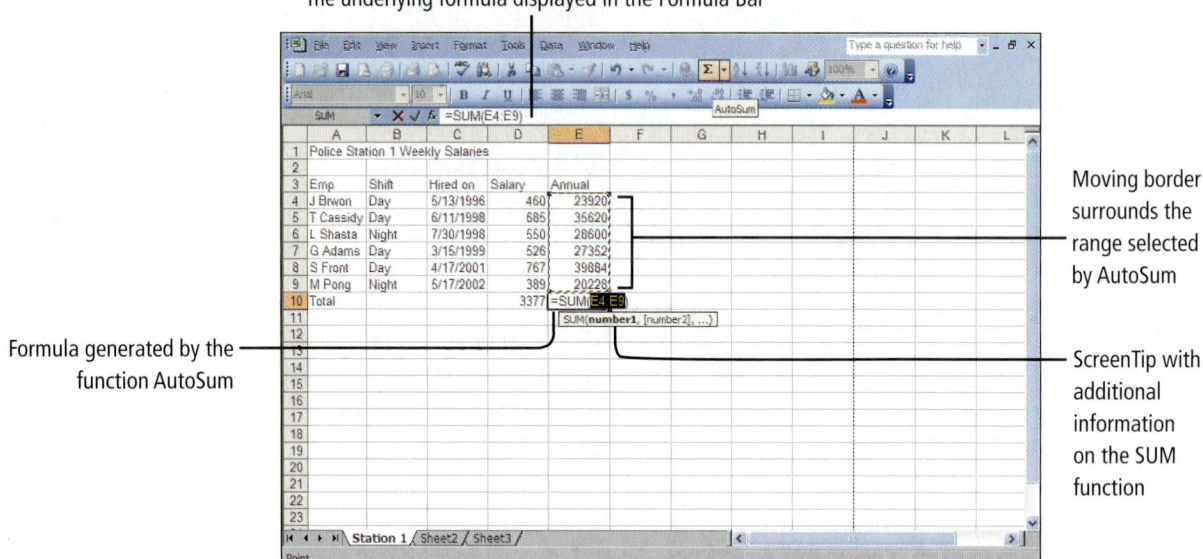

Figure 1.63

2. Look at the Formula Bar, and notice that the formula also displays there. Then, look again at the cells surrounded by a moving border.

When the AutoSum function is activated, Excel first looks above the active cell for a range of cells to sum. If no range is above the active cell, Excel will look to the left for a range of cells to sum. Regardless, Excel will propose a range of cells to sum, and if the proposed range is not what you had in mind, simply drag to select a different group of cells.

3. Press [Enter]. The total annual payroll amount of *175604* displays in cell E10.

4. On the Standard toolbar, click the **Save** button to save the changes you have made to your workbook.

Objective 8
Use Zoom and the Spelling Checker Tool

The Zoom command magnifies or shrinks the columns and rows of a worksheet to increase or decrease the number of cells displayed in the workbook window. Excel's default setting for the magnification size of a worksheet window is 100%, but you can increase the magnification to as much as 400% or decrease it to as little as 10%.

Excel's spelling checker tool checks for misspelled words in your workbook. A word that is not in Excel's dictionary is considered to be misspelled. For example, proper names of cities and people may be correctly spelled, but because Excel's dictionary does not include many of them, they will be flagged as misspelled words. Fortunately, you can add words to the dictionary or have Excel ignore words that are correctly spelled but that are not in Excel's dictionary.

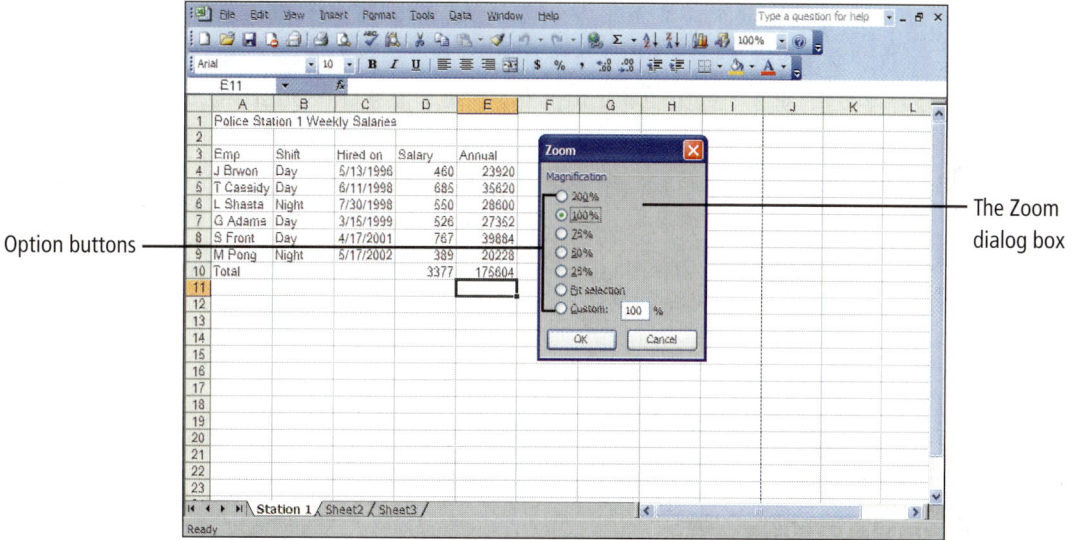

Figure 1.64

Activity 1.25 Zooming a Worksheet

1 Display the **View** menu, and then click **Zoom**.

The Zoom dialog box displays a list of Magnification options, as shown in Figure 1.64. The round buttons to the left of each option are referred to as ***option buttons***.

2 In the **Zoom** dialog box, click the **75%** option button, and then click **OK**.

As shown in Figure 1.65, the sizes of the columns and rows are reduced, and more cells are visible in the worksheet window.

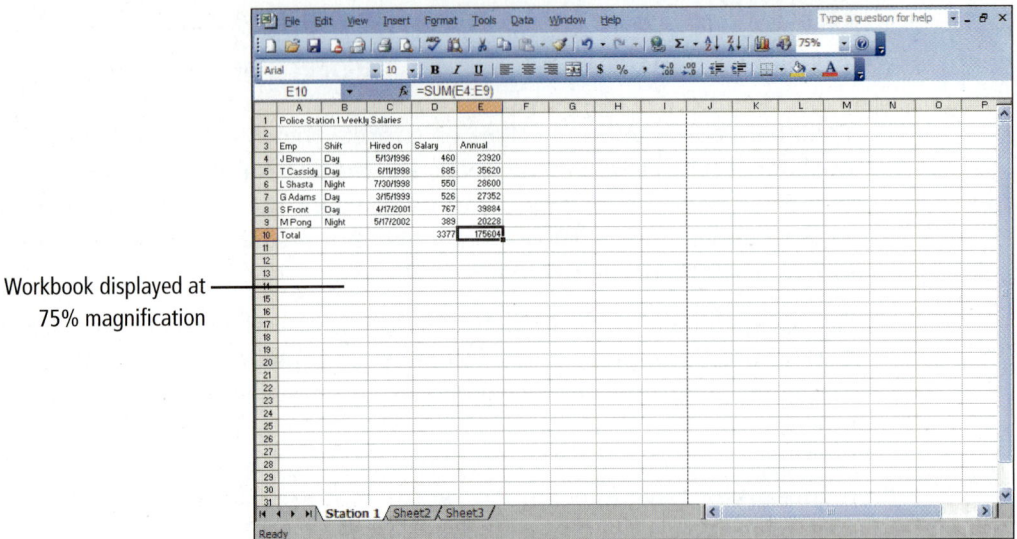

Workbook displayed at 75% magnification

Figure 1.65

3 From the **View** menu, click **Zoom**.

4 In the **Zoom** dialog box, click the **Custom** option button, type **150** in the box to right of *Custom*, and then click **OK**.

The columns and rows are much larger, and fewer cells are visible in the worksheet window.

5 On the Standard toolbar, click the **Zoom button arrow**, as shown in Figure 1.66.

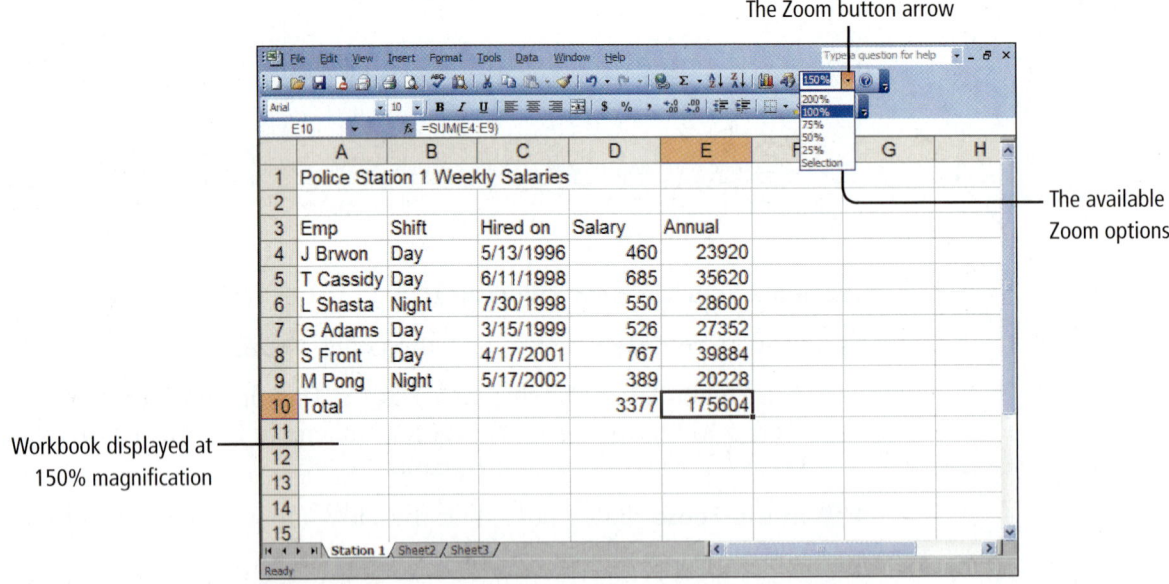

The Zoom button arrow

The available Zoom options

Workbook displayed at 150% magnification

Figure 1.66

6 In the displayed list, click **100%**.

The worksheet window returns to its default magnification size of 100%.

556   Excel | Chapter 1: Getting Started with Excel 2003

Activity 1.26 Checking for Spelling Errors in a Worksheet

1 Hold down Ctrl and press Home to make **A1** the active cell.

2 On the Standard toolbar, click the **Spelling** button.

The Spelling dialog box displays, as shown in Figure 1.67.

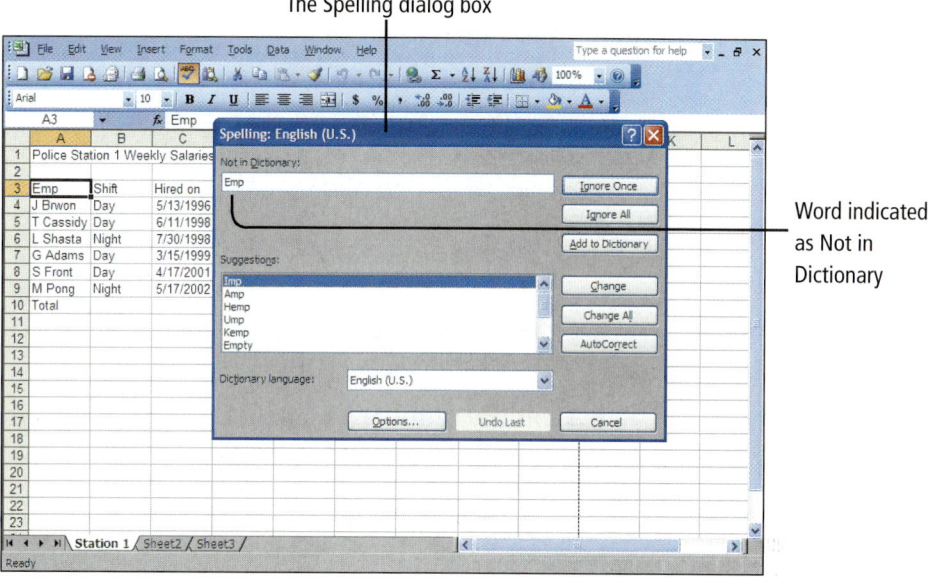

Figure 1.67

Alert!

Does Your Screen Differ?

Your first and last name, which are in the footer, may not be recognized by Excel. If your name displays under Not in Dictionary, click the Ignore Once button until Emp displays as shown in Figure 1.67. If the active cell was not A1, an informational dialog box displays, asking you whether you want to continue checking at the beginning of the sheet. Clicking Yes continues the spelling check from cell A1. Clicking No will end the spelling check command.

3 Under **Not in Dictionary**, notice the word *Emp*.

The spelling checker tool does not recognize the abbreviation you used for *Employee*. Under *Suggestions*, Excel provides a list of suggested spellings.

4 Under **Suggestions**, use the scroll bar to scroll through Excel's list of suggested spellings. Because *Emp* is an abbreviation that is useful in this worksheet but does not appear on the **Suggestions** list, click **Ignore All**.

Ignore All instructs Excel to ignore this particular spelling anywhere it is encountered in this worksheet. Excel stops at the next unrecognized word, *Brwon*.

5 Under **Suggestions**, click **Bryon** and then click the **Change** button.

Brwon, which was a typing error, is changed to Bryon. The spelling checker did not find *Brwon* in its dictionary. Although a number of proper names, such as *Brown* and *Bryon* are in the dictionary, many are not. Click Ignore All for those that are not contained in Excel's dictionary. You may want to add proper names that you expect to use often, such as your own last name, to the dictionary if you are permitted to do so.

> **Note** — Can't Add Names to the Dictionary?
>
> Some organizations prevent individuals from adding names to the dictionary to avoid overloading the server or disk drive where the software is located and also to avoid having misspellings inadvertently added to the dictionary.

6 On the displayed message, *The spelling check is complete for the entire sheet*, click **OK**.

7 On the Standard toolbar, click the **Save** button to save the changes you have made to your workbook.

Objective 9
Print a Worksheet Using the Print Dialog Box

Clicking the Print button on the Standard toolbar prints one complete copy of the active worksheet or all the selected sheets. To choose more options, such as printing additional copies or selecting a different printer, display the Print dialog box.

Activity 1.27 Previewing the Worksheet

1 With the Station 1 worksheet of your workbook **1B_Salary_Analysis** on your screen, display the **File** menu, and then click **Print Preview**.

The active worksheet displays as an image of a piece of paper so that you can see how the worksheet will be placed on the page.

2 On the Print Preview toolbar, click **Zoom**.

The worksheet zooms to 100%—you can read the contents of the page.

3 Click the **Zoom** button again to return to the full-page preview.

4 On the Print Preview toolbar, locate the **Print** button, and notice that the button name includes an ellipsis (...).

Recall that the ellipsis indicates that a dialog box will follow.

5 Click the **Print** button.

6 As shown in Figure 1.68, in the displayed **Print** dialog box, under **Print range** verify that the **All** option button is selected. Under **Print what** verify that **Active sheet(s)** is selected, under **Copies** verify that the Number of copies is **1**, and then click **OK**.

558   Excel | Chapter 1: Getting Started with Excel 2003

Print dialog box

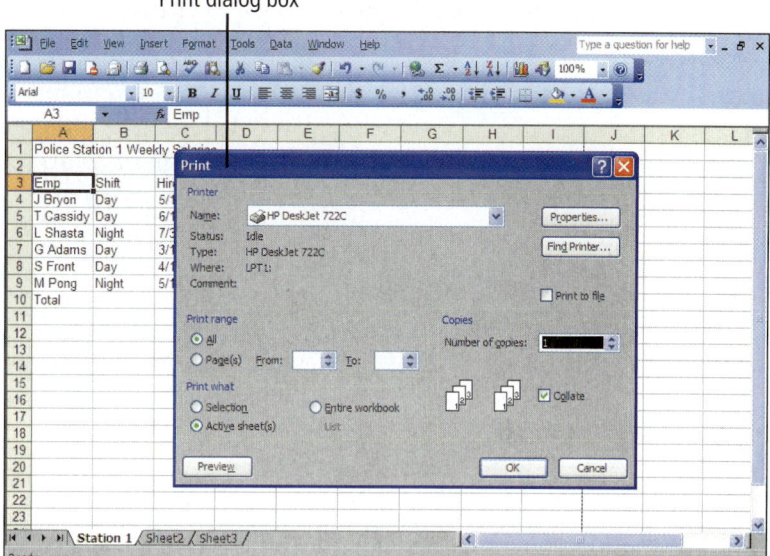

Figure 1.68

Activity 1.28 Closing a Workbook from the File Menu

When you have completed your work, save and close your workbook. Develop the habit of saving your workbook before closing it. If you forget to save it, however, Excel will display a reminder.

1 With your **1B_Salary_Analysis** worksheet still displayed, display the **File** menu, and then click **Close**, saving any changes if prompted to do so.

The workbook closes, leaving the workbook window empty and shaded in gray. Alternatively, close a workbook by clicking its

Close button.

Objective 10
Use Excel Help

Excel's Help feature provides information about all of Excel's features and displays step-by-step instructions for performing many tasks.

Activity 1.29 Using the Type a question for help Box

1 At the right side of the menu bar, locate the box containing the words *Type a question for help*. See Figure 1.69.

Figure 1.69

2 Click in the **Type a question for help** box. At the insertion point, type **How do I create a new workbook?** and then press Enter.

The Search Results task pane displays a list of Help topics with hyperlinks (blue text) listed. Clicking on these hyperlinks will link you to additional information about the topic. See Figure 1.70.

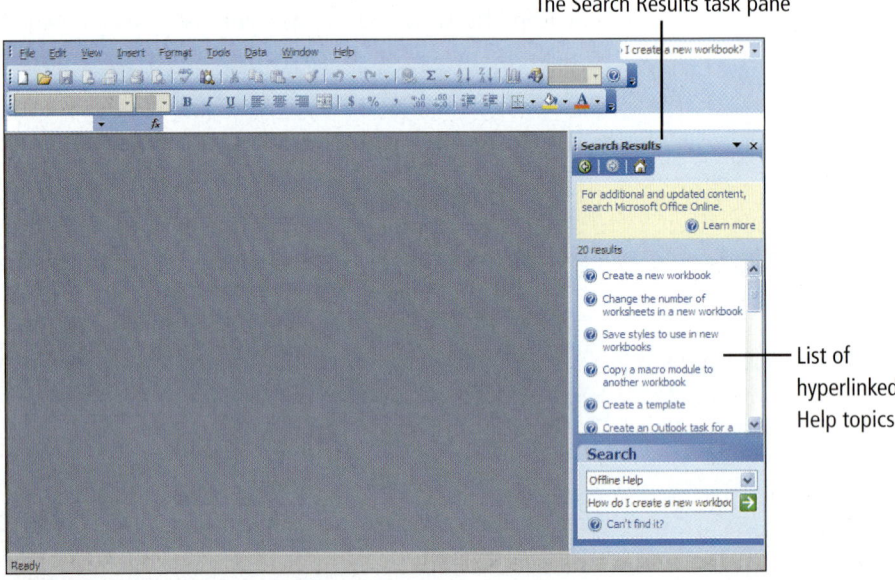

Figure 1.70

3 On the list of Help topics, click **Create a new workbook**.

4 Click the blue hyperlink **Create a new, blank workbook**.

The topic expands to display additional information.

5 In the upper right corner, click **Show All** to expand the information.

6 Locate and then click the word **task pane** that is displayed in blue.

A definition of the term *task pane* displays in green.

[7] Click the word **task pane** again to collapse (hide) the definition.

[8] Read the information about creating a new workbook.

[9] In the Excel Help window, on the toolbar, click the **Print** button 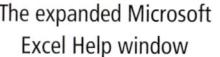. See Figure 1.71.

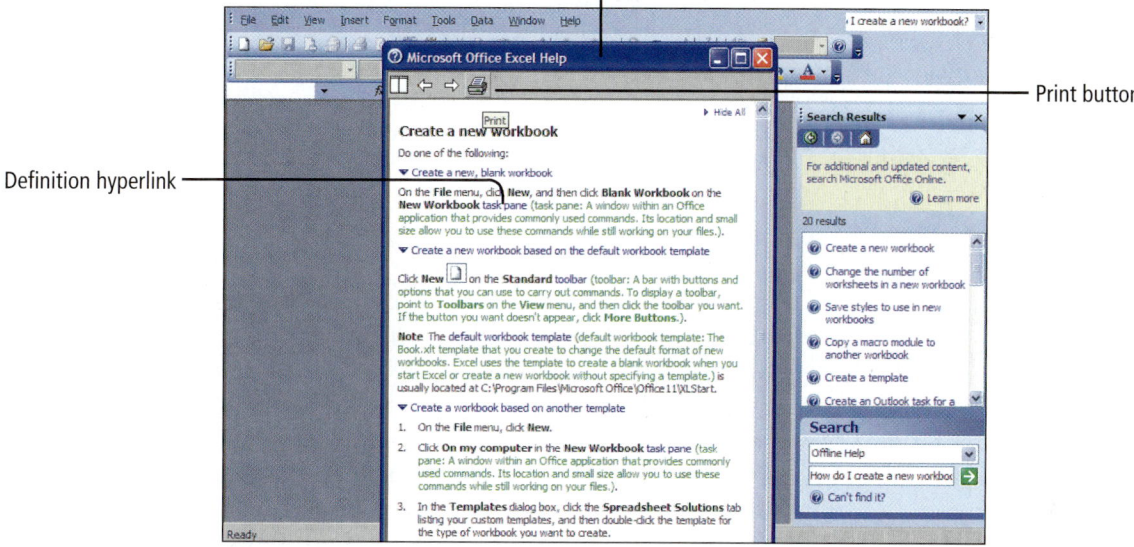

Figure 1.71

[10] In the **Print** dialog box, click **Print**.

The Help topic you have displayed is printed. Keep this document for your reference.

[11] On the Microsoft Excel Help title bar, click the **Close** button ⊠, and then on the task pane, click the **Close** button ⊠.

[12] On the right side of the title bar, click the **Close** button ⊠.

End You have completed Project 1B

Excel chapter one

Summary

Microsoft Excel 2003 is a spreadsheet application that can display and analyze data both numerically and graphically. Excel formulas are both powerful and easy to create.

In this chapter, you opened an existing workbook, added a footer, saved the file with a new name, and previewed and printed the file. The basics of using menus, toolbars and ScreenTips were reviewed. You practiced selecting cells, columns, rows and cell ranges. You navigated within a worksheet using the scroll bars and the name box, and among multiple worksheets in a workbook. You learned how to name a sheet tab so you can clearly label and identify information contained on each worksheet. You also examined an existing chart and saw how changing data also changes the chart.

In Project 6B a new workbook was created. You practiced entering and editing data in a worksheet. You edited text in the formula bar and in a cell, and used the Undo and Redo commands. The power of Excel lies in its ability to perform calculations on numbers. The basic techniques for creating formulas were introduced and then you created simple formulas by typing, by using the point-and-click method, and by using the AutoSum function. You changed the magnification of a worksheet with the Zoom button and used the Spelling Checker tool to ensure that the information was free of spelling mistakes. Finally, you asked a question of the Excel Help feature to explore this tool which is available to assist you as you work with the program.

In This Chapter You Practiced How To

- Start Excel and Navigate a Workbook
- Create Headers and Footers
- Preview and Print a Workbook
- Save and Close a Workbook and Exit Excel
- Create a New Workbook
- Enter and Edit Data in a Worksheet
- Create Formulas
- Use Zoom and the Spelling Checker Tool
- Print a Worksheet Using the Print Dialog Box
- Use Excel Help

Concepts Assessments

Matching Match each term in the second column with its correct definition in the first column by writing the letter of the term on the blank line in front of the correct definition.

____ 1. Located at the lower left of the Excel window, the identifier of individual worksheets within a workbook.

____ 2. The basic Excel document, consisting of one or more worksheets.

____ 3. The action of moving the workbook window horizontally or vertically to view areas of the worksheet.

____ 4. A symbol that represents a mathematical operation.

____ 5. A graphical representation of the values in a worksheet.

____ 6. A reference to a group of cells, for example, *A1:C18*.

____ 7. Data—numbers, text, dates, or times of day—that you type in a cell.

____ 8. The intersection of a column and a row.

____ 9. Text or graphics that print at the top or bottom of a worksheet.

____ 10. The cell bordered in black and ready to receive data or to be modified.

____ 11. Highlighting by clicking or dragging with your mouse.

____ 12. A window within a Microsoft Office application that displays commonly used commands.

____ 13. An instruction in Excel used to perform mathematical operations.

____ 14. An Excel feature that assists with your typing by automatically completing data entered in a cell based on similar values in the column.

____ 15. The column letter and row number that identify a specific cell.

A Active cell
B AutoComplete
C Cell
D Cell address
E Chart
F Constant value
G Formula
H Headers and footers
I Operator
J Range
K Scrolling
L Selecting
M Sheet tabs
N Task pane
O Workbook

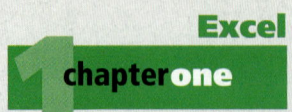

Concepts Assessments (continued)

Fill in the Blank Write the correct answers in the space provided.

1. The two most frequently used toolbars are the _____ and the _____ toolbars.

2. To reduce the magnification and thus view more columns and rows on one screen, use the _____ feature.

3. When viewing a menu, an _____ following a command name indicates that a dialog box will display.

4. If a workbook has never been saved, clicking the Save button causes the _____ dialog box to open.

5. To group worksheets for the purpose of applying a header or footer, from the sheet tab shortcut menu click _____.

6. Nonadjacent cells can be selected by holding down the _____ key while clicking the desired cells.

7. The address of the active cell is always displayed in the _____.

8. Switch to another worksheet in the workbook by clicking on the _____.

9. Editing can be performed either in the cell or in the _____.

10. To select all the cells in the worksheet, click the _____ button.

564 Excel | Chapter 1: Getting Started with Excel 2003

Skill Assessments

Project 1C—Computer Passwords

Objectives: *Start Excel and Navigate a Workbook, Create Headers and Footers, Preview and Print a Workbook, Save and Close a Workbook and Exit Excel, Enter and Edit Data in a Worksheet, and Use Zoom and the Spelling Checker Tool.*

In the following Skill Assessment, you will complete a workbook for the Desert Park Police Department listing the assigned computer system passwords for the officers. Your completed workbook will look similar to Figure 1.72. You will save the workbook as *1C_Computer_Passwords_Firstname_Lastname*.

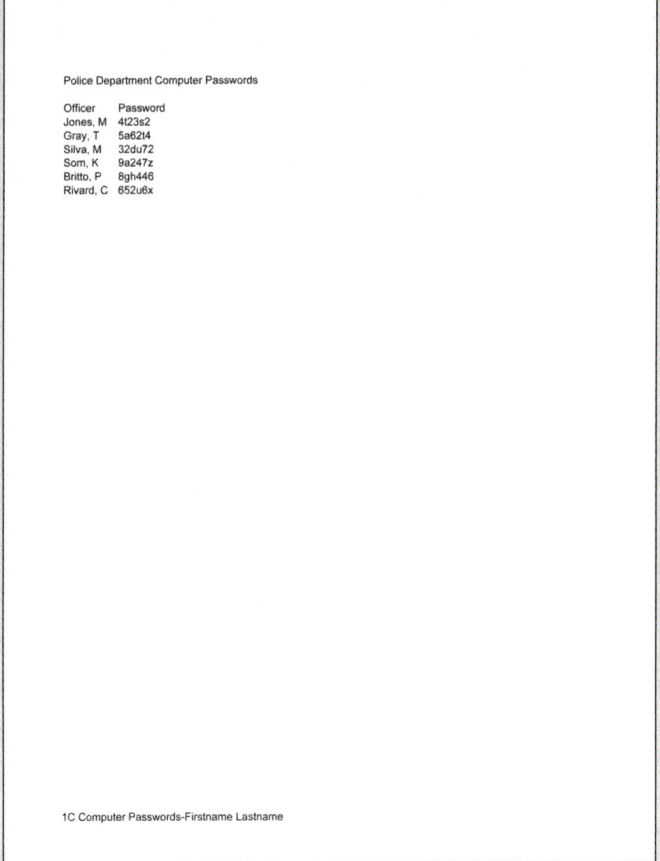

Figure 1.72

1. Start Excel. Display the **File** menu, and then click **Open**.
2. Navigate to the student files that accompany this textbook, and then open the workbook *e01C_Computer_Passwords*.
3. Display the **View** menu, click **Header and Footer**, click the **Custom Footer** button, and in the **Left section**, type **1C Computer Passwords-Firstname Lastname** using your own first and last name. Use the default font and font size.

(**Project 1C**–Computer Passwords continues on the next page)

Excel chapter one
Skill Assessments (continued)

(Project 1C–Computer Passwords continued)

4. In the upper right corner of the **Footer** dialog box, click **OK**. In the lower right corner of the **Page Setup** dialog box, click **OK**. Recall that the dotted line indicates the number of columns that will print on the page as the page is currently set up.

5. From the **File** menu, click **Save As**, and then navigate to the location where you are storing your projects for this chapter. In the **File name** box, type **1C_Computer_Passwords_Firstname_Lastname** and then click the **Save** button.

6. In cell **A4**, type **Jones, M** and then press [Enter] to lock in the entry.

7. Display the **View** menu, and then click **Zoom**. In the **Zoom** dialog box, click the **200%** option button, and then click **OK**. This gives you an enlarged view, which is helpful when you are entering complex statistical data such as passwords.

8. Beginning in cell **A5**, add the following names to column A. Recall that pressing [Enter] after each entry relocates the active cell to the next row.

   Gray, T
   Silva, M
   Som, K
   Britto, P
   Rivard, C

9. In cell **B4**, type **4t23s2** and then press [Enter].

10. Beginning in cell **B5**, add the remaining passwords to column B:

    5a62t4
    32du72
    9a347z
    8gh446
    652u6x

11. Point to cell **B7** and double-click to select the cell and simultaneously activate Edit mode. Using the arrow keys on the keyboard, place the insertion point before the *3*. Press [Delete], type **2** and then press [Enter] to display the corrected password, *9a247z*.

12. On the Standard toolbar, click in the **Zoom** box so that *200%* is highlighted, type **100** and then press [Enter]. This is another method for changing the Zoom setting.

13. On the Standard toolbar, click the **Save** button to save your changes, and then click the **Print Preview** button.

14. On the Print Preview toolbar, click the **Print** button. In the displayed **Print** dialog box, click **OK** to print one complete copy of your worksheet on the default printer. From the **File** menu, click **Close** to close the workbook. Display the **File** menu again, and click **Exit** to close Excel.

 You have completed Project 1C

Excel chapter one

Skill Assessments (continued)

Project 1D — Crossing Guards

Objectives: *Start Excel and Navigate a Workbook, Create Headers and Footers, Preview and Print a Workbook, Save and Close a Workbook and Exit Excel, Enter and Edit Data in a Worksheet, Create Formulas, and Use Zoom and the Spelling Checker Tool.*

In the following Skill Assessment, you will complete a Crossing Guard report for the month of January for the Desert Park Police Department, whose officers volunteer as school crossing guards. Your completed workbook will look similar to the one shown in Figures 1.73a and 1.73b. You will save the workbook as *1D_Crossing_Guards_Firstname_Lastname*.

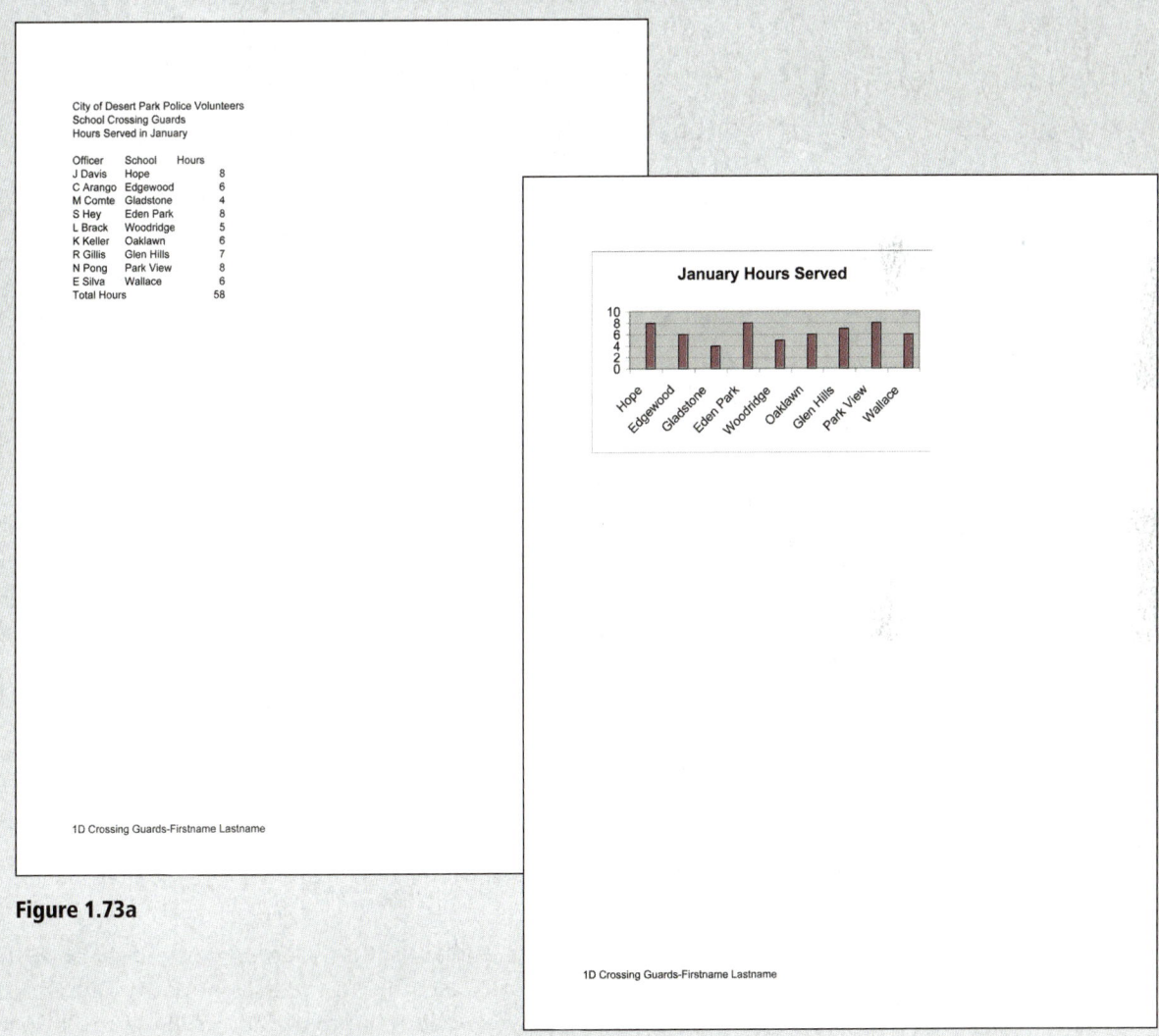

Figure 1.73a

Figure 1.73b

1. Start Excel. On the Standard toolbar, click **Open**.
2. Navigate to the student files that accompany this textbook, and then open the workbook **e01D_Crossing_Guards**.

(**Project 1D**–Crossing Guards continues on the next page)

Project 1D: Crossing Guards | **Excel** 567

Skill Assessments (continued)

(Project 1D–Crossing Guards continued)

3. Right-click the **Sheet1 tab**, and on the displayed shortcut menu, click **Select All Sheets**.

4. Display the **View** menu, click **Header and Footer**, click the **Custom Footer** button, and in the **Left section**, type **1D Crossing Guards-Firstname Lastname** using your own first and last name. Use the default font and font size.

5. In the upper right corner of the **Footer** dialog box, click **OK**. In the lower right corner of the **Page Setup** dialog box, click **OK**. Recall that the dotted line indicates the number of columns that will print on the page as the page is currently set up.

6. Right-click the **Sheet1 tab**, and click **Ungroup Sheets**.

7. From the **File** menu, click **Save As**, and then navigate to the location where you are storing your projects for this chapter. In the **File name** box, type **1D_Crossing_Guards_Firstname_Lastname** and then click the **Save** button.

8. In cells **A6** through **A14**, type the following list of volunteer crossing guards:

    J Davis
    C Arango
    M Comte
    S Hey
    L Brack
    K Keller
    R Gillis
    N Pong
    E Silva

9. In cells **B6** through **B11**, enter the following list of school names:

    Hope
    Park View
    Gladstone
    Eden Park
    Woodbridge
    Oaklawn

10. In cell **B12**, type **G** and notice that as soon as you enter the *G*, the AutoComplete feature of Excel fills in the school name *Gladstone*. Type **len Hills** to enter the school name of *Glen Hills* and to overwrite the AutoComplete entry. Press Enter.

11. In cells **B13** and **B14**, type the remaining two school names, **Edgewood** and **Wallace** overwriting the AutoComplete entries as you type.

12. Click cell **B10** to make it the active cell. Pause the mouse pointer in the Formula Bar until the **I-beam** pointer displays. Click to position

(Project 1D–Crossing Guards continues on the next page)

Skill Assessments (continued)

(Project 1D–Crossing Guards continued)

the pointer before the *b* in *Woodbridge*, press [Delete] to remove the *b* and correct the school name to *Woodridge*. Click the **Enter** button on the Formula toolbar to lock in the change.

13. In cells **C6** through **C14**, enter the following list of hours that each volunteer worked. Because these are numeric values, as you lock them in by pressing [Enter], they are right-aligned in each cell.

    8
    6
    4
    6
    5
    6
    7
    8
    6

14. In cell **A15**, type **Total Hours** and then press the [Tab] key twice to make **C15** the active cell.

15. With **C15** as the active cell, move to the Standard toolbar and click the **AutoSum** button. AutoSum borders the cells above and proposes a formula. Press [Enter] to accept the formula. The total in C15 is *56*.

16. Click cell **C15** again. Compare what is displayed in the cell, *56*, with what is displayed in the Formula Bar, *=SUM(C6:C14)*. Recall that this is called the underlying formula. The formula indicates that the contents of the cells in the range C6:C14 are summed.

17. Right-click the **Sheet1 tab**, click **Rename**, type **Hours** and then press [Enter]. Rename Sheet2 as **Chart** and then be sure that the Chart sheet is displayed.

18. View the graphical chart of the schools and number of hours worked. Notice the height of the Eden Park entry—6 hours. Click the **Hours tab** to return to the previous worksheet.

19. Change the number of hours for Officer *Hey* to **8** and press [Enter]. The calculated result in C15 changes to *58*. Click the **Chart tab** and notice the new height of the Eden Park entry. When you changed the number of hours worked on the Hours worksheet, the entry in the chart was also updated by Excel. Return to the Hours worksheet by clicking the **Hours sheet tab**.

20. On the Hours worksheet, click cell **B13**. Type **P** and notice that the existing value is deleted and that AutoComplete assists with your typing. With *Park View* in the cell, press [Enter] to accept it. Recall that when you type a new value in a cell, the existing value is deleted and replaced by your typing.

(Project 1D–Crossing Guards continues on the next page)

Skill Assessments (continued)

(Project 1D–Crossing Guards continued)

21. Change the school name for Officer *Davis* to **Edgewood** overriding AutoComplete, and then press Enter. On the Standard toolbar, click **Undo** to restore the original value of *Hope*. Change the school name for Officer *Arango* to **Edgewood** and press Enter.

22. Click in the **Name Box**, type **a1** and then press Enter to make **A1** the active cell. Recall that you can navigate to a cell address by typing it in the Name Box and that you may type the column reference as either lower- or uppercase.

23. On the Standard toolbar, click the **Spelling** button. If necessary, click the Ignore All button as necessary to ignore the spelling of your name. The first word interpreted by Excel to be misspelled is *Crosing*. Under **Suggestions**, be sure that *Crossing* is selected, and then click the **Change** button. Correct the spelling for *January* and *School*.

24. Click **Ignore All** for the proper names that Excel does not have in its dictionary. Click **OK** when the spelling complete message displays.

25. From the **File** menu, click **Save** to save the changes you have made to your workbook since the last Save operation. Then, display the **File** menu again and click **Print Preview** to view the worksheet page as it will print on paper. Close Print Preview, click the **Chart** worksheet, and then click the **Print Preview** button.

26. On the Print Preview toolbar, click the **Print** button. On the displayed **Print** dialog box, under **Print what**, click the **Entire workbook** option button, and then click **OK** to print one copy of the workbook. Two sheets will print. From the **File** menu, click **Close**, and then exit Excel.

End You have completed Project 1D

Excel chapter one

Skill Assessments (continued)

Project 1E—AV Equipment

Objectives: *Start Excel and Navigate a Workbook, Create Headers and Footers, Preview and Print a Workbook, Save and Close a Workbook and Exit Excel, Create a New Workbook, Enter and Edit Data in a Worksheet, and Create Formulas.*

In the following Skill Assessment, you will create a new workbook to generate an inventory report for the audiovisual equipment at the Desert Park Public Library. Your completed workbook will look similar to the one shown in Figure 1.74. You will save the workbook as *1E_AV_Equipment_Firstname_Lastname*.

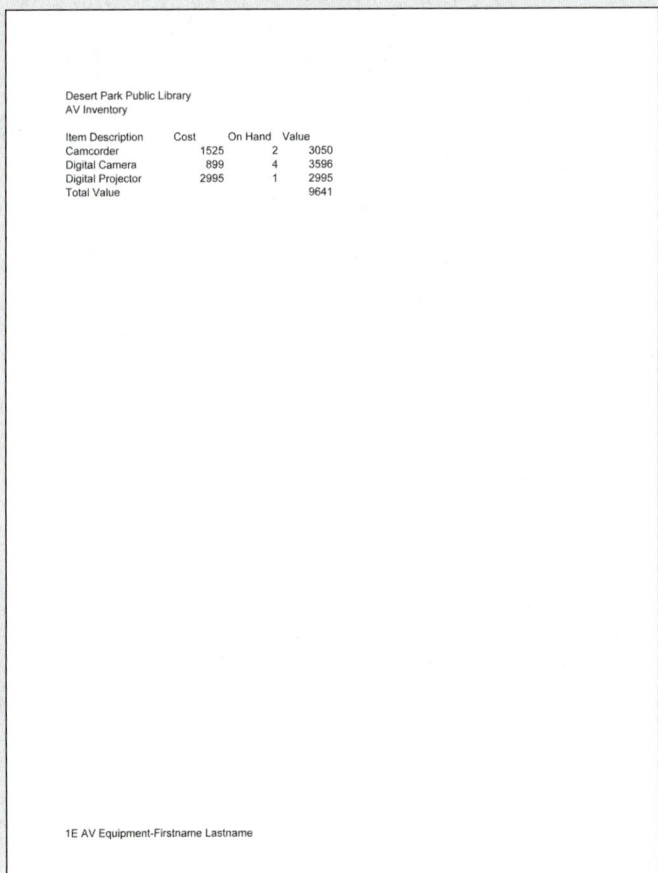

Figure 1.74

1. Start the Excel program. *Book1* displays in both the title bar and the taskbar, indicating a new, unnamed workbook.

2. Display the **View** menu, click **Header and Footer**, click the **Custom Footer** button, and in the **Left section**, type **1E AV Equipment-Firstname Lastname** using your own first and last name. Use the default font and font size.

(Project 1E–AV Equipment continues on the next page)

Skill Assessments (continued)

(Project 1E–AV Equipment continued)

3. In the upper right corner of the **Footer** dialog box, click **OK**. In the lower right corner of the **Page Setup** dialog box, click **OK**. Recall that the dotted line indicates the number of columns that will print on the page as the page is currently set up.

4. If necessary, close the Getting Started task pane by clicking its small black **Close** button. From the **File** menu, click **Save As**, and then navigate to the location where you are storing your projects for this chapter. In the **File name** box, delete the existing text, type **1E_AV_Equipment_Firstname_Lastname** and then click **Save**.

5. In cell **A1**, type **Desert Park Public Library** and press Enter. Because cells B1 and C1 are empty, the content of cell A1 can display into the adjacent cells. Recall, however, that the text is contained entirely within cell A1. In cell A2, type **AV Inventory** and press Enter.

6. Right-click the **Sheet1 tab**, click **Rename**, type **AV Equipment** and notice that the tab expands to accommodate the name. Press Enter.

7. Move to cell **A4**, type **Item Description** and then press Tab twice. In cell **C4**, type **Cost** and then press Tab once. In cell **D4**, type **On Hand** and in cell **E4**, type **Value** and press Enter. Recall that when you use Tab, the cell entry is locked in and the cell to the right becomes the active cell. When Enter is pressed, the active cell becomes the cell below the first cell in which Tab was pressed. A5 is the active cell.

8. Beginning in the active cell, **A5**, enter the following descriptions in cells **A5:A7**:

    Camcorder
    Digital Camera
    Digital Projector

9. Beginning in cell **C5**, enter the following costs in the Cost column:

    1525
    899
    2995

10. Beginning in cell **D5**, enter the following On Hand quantities.

    2
    4
    1

11. Click in cell **E5** and type = to begin a formula. Click cell **C5** to insert it in the formula, type * (the operator for multiplication), and then click cell **D5**. This will multiply the camcorder cost in cell C5 by the number on hand in cell D5. Press Enter to display the result of *3050*.

(Project 1E–AV Equipment continues on the next page)

Skill Assessments (continued)

(Project 1E–AV Equipment continued)

12. Click cell **E5** again, and compare what is displayed in the cell (3050) with what is displayed in the Formula Bar (=C5*D5). Recall that this is called the underlying formula and that to determine the exact content of a cell, check the Formula Bar.

13. In cells **E6** and **E7**, use the point-and-click method to construct similar formulas to multiply the cost of the item by the number on hand. Compare your results with Figure 1.74. Click **Save** to save your changes.

14. In cell **A8**, type **Total Value** and then click cell **E8**. Using the point-and-click method to add the column, type = to begin a formula, click cell **E5**, press +, click cell **E6**, press +, and click cell **E7** and press . The result, *9641*, displays in cell E8.

15. On the Standard toolbar, click **Save** to save the changes to your workbook.

16. On the Standard toolbar, click the **Print Preview** button to view the worksheet page. On the Print Preview toolbar, click the **Print** button. In the displayed dialog box, click **OK** to print one copy of your worksheet. Close the workbook, saving any changes if prompted, and then exit Excel.

End You have completed Project 1E

Excel chapter one

Performance Assessments

Project 1F — Phone Charges

Objectives: *Start Excel and Navigate a Workbook, Create Headers and Footers, Preview and Print a Workbook, Save and Close a Workbook and Exit Excel, Enter and Edit Data in a Worksheet, Create Formulas, Use Zoom and the Spelling Checker Tool, and Use Excel Help.*

In the following Performance Assessment, you will complete a list of phone charges for Desert Park's City Manager, Madison Romero. Your completed workbook will look similar to the one shown in Figure 1.75. You will save the workbook as *1F_Phone_Charges_Firstname_Lastname*.

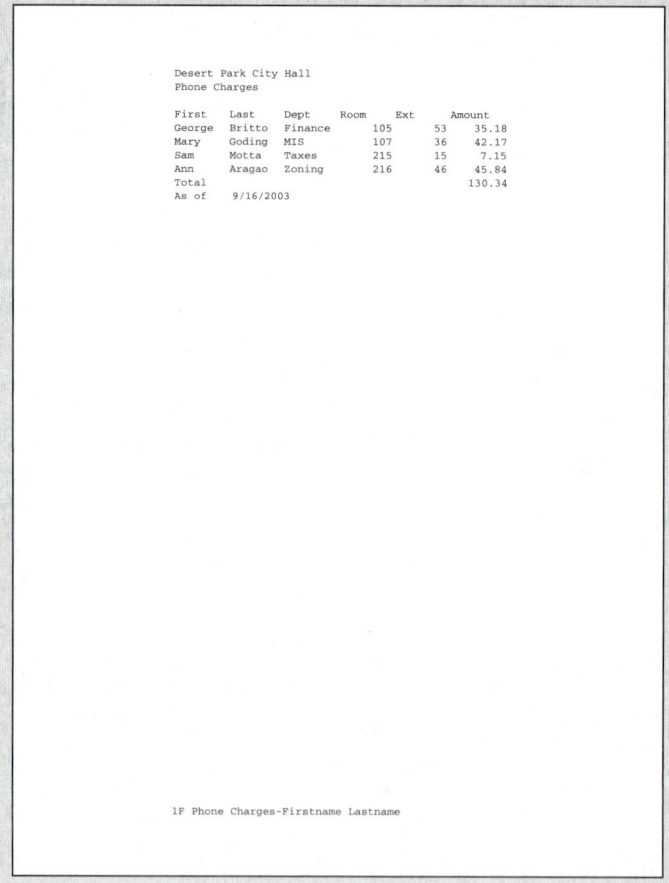

Figure 1.75

(**Project 1F**–Phone Charges continues on the next page)

574 Excel | Chapter 1: Getting Started with Excel 2003

Performance Assessments (continued)

(Project 1F–Phone Charges continued)

1. Start Excel, navigate to the location where the student files for this textbook are stored, and then open workbook **e01F_Phone_Charges**. Display the **View** menu, click **Header and Footer**, click the **Custom Footer** button, and in the **Left section**, type **1F Phone Charges-Firstname Lastname** using your own first and last name. Use the default font and font size. In the upper right corner of the **Footer** dialog box, click **OK**. In the lower right corner of the **Page Setup** dialog box, click **OK**.

2. From the **File** menu, click **Save As**, and then navigate to the location in which you are storing your projects for this chapter. In the **File name** box, type **1F_Phone_Charges_Firstname_Lastname** and then click **Save**.

3. Beginning in cell **A4**, type the following, using the [Tab] key to move across each row:

First	Last	Dept	Room	Ext	Amount
George	Britto	Finance	105	53	35.18
Mary	Goding	MIS	107	36	16.05
Sam	Motta	Taxes	215	15	7.15
Ann	Aragao	Zoning	216	46	45.84

4. In cell **A9**, type **Total** and then press [Enter]. In cell **F9**, using the point-and-click method to create a formula to add up the total phone charges, type = to start the formula, click cell **F5**, press [+], and then continue in the same manner for the remaining cells. Alternatively, click the **AutoSum** button. The total charges add up to *104.22*.

5. In cell **A10**, type **As of** and then press [Tab]. In cell **B10**, hold down [Ctrl] and then press [;] to insert today's date.

6. Change the amount for the MIS department to 42.17 and press [Enter] to recalculate the total—130.34.

7. Press [Ctrl] + [Home] to move to cell **A1**, and then on the Standard toolbar, click the **Spelling** button. For proper names, including your own, click Ignore All as necessary. Correct the word *Charges* and then click **Ignore All** for the proper names.

8. Save your changes, and then preview and print the worksheet. Close the file and exit Excel.

End You have completed Project 1F

Excel chapter one

Performance Assessments (continued)

Project 1G — Building Permits

Objectives: *Start Excel and Navigate a Workbook, Create Headers and Footers, Preview and Print a Workbook, Save and Close a Workbook and Exit Excel, Enter and Edit Data in a Worksheet, Create Formulas, and Use Zoom and the Spelling Checker Tool.*

In the following Performance Assessment, you will complete a workbook for the Desert Park Deputy Mayor, Andrew Gore, that summarizes the number of building permits issued for the second quarter. Your completed workbook will look similar to Figure 1.76. You will save the workbook as *1G_Building_Permits_Firstname_Lastname*.

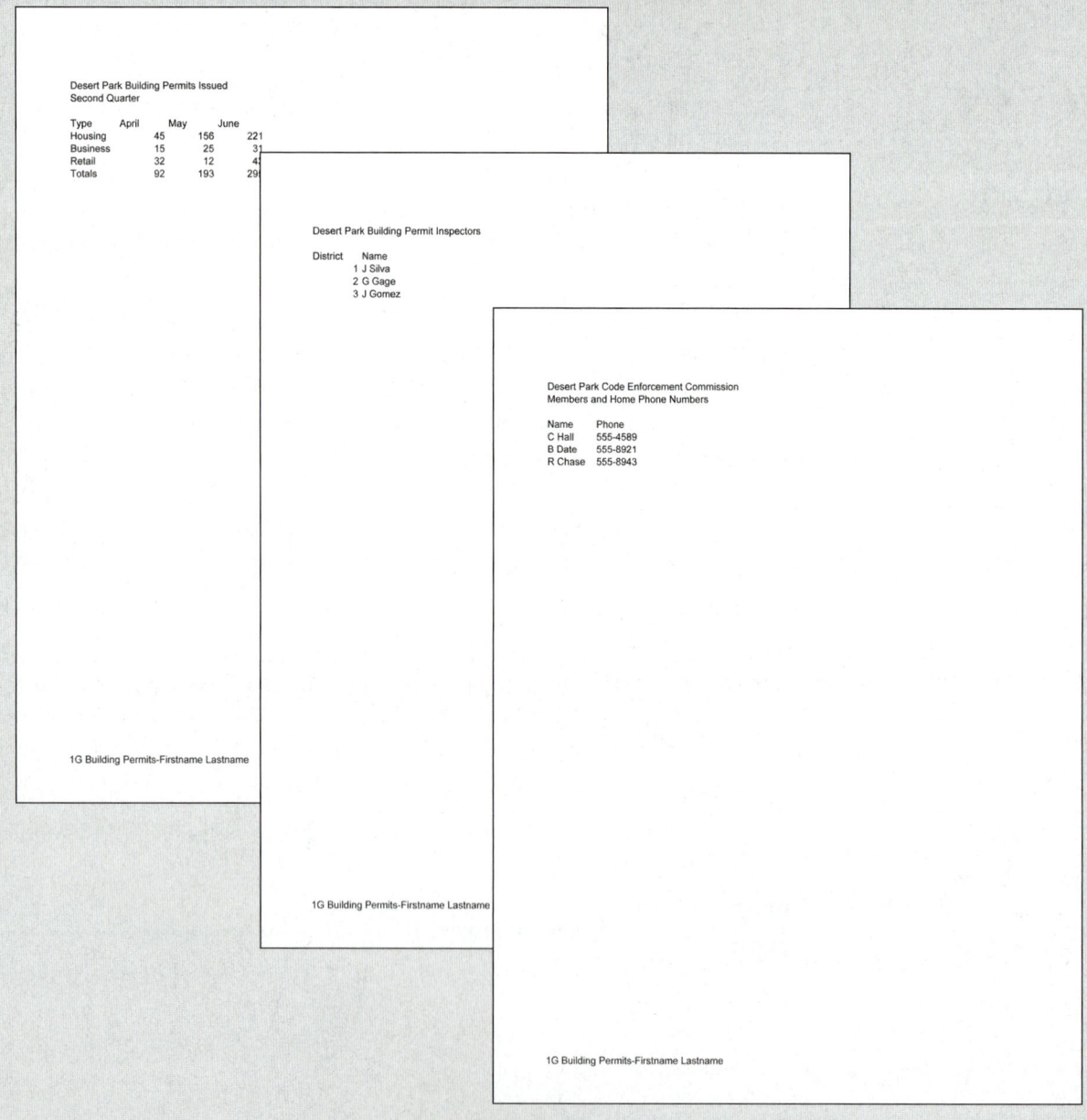

Figure 1.76

(**Project 1G**–Building Permits continues on the next page)

576   Excel | Chapter 1: Getting Started with Excel 2003

Excel chapter one
Performance Assessments (continued)

(Project 1G–Building Permits continued)

1. Start Excel, navigate to your student files, and then open the workbook **e01G_Building_Permits**. Right-click the **Sheet1 tab** and click **Select All Sheets**.

2. From the **View** menu, click **Header and Footer**, click the **Custom Footer** button, and in the **Left section**, type **1G Building Permits-Firstname Lastname** using your own first and last name. Use the default font and font size. In the upper right corner of the **Footer** dialog box, click **OK**. In the lower right corner of the **Page Setup** dialog box, click **OK**. Right-click the **Sheet1 tab**, and click **Ungroup Sheets**.

3. From the **File** menu, click **Save As**, and then navigate to the location where you are storing your projects for this chapter. In the **File name** box, type **1G_Building_Permits_Firstname_Lastname** and then click **Save**.

4. In **Sheet1**, be sure that cell **A1** is the active cell. Click in the **Formula Bar** so that you can edit the text. Click to the left of the *P* in *Permits*, insert the word **Building** followed by a space, and then press Enter.

5. Double-click cell **A2** to display the insertion point within the cell. Alternatively, select the cell and press F2. Edit the text by changing the word *First* to **Second** and then press Enter.

6. In cells **A4:D7**, enter the following data. Use Tab to move across the row and Enter to move down to a new row:

Type	April	May	June
Housing	45	156	221
Business	15	25	31
Retail	32	12	43

7. In cell **A8**, type **Totals** and then, using either the **AutoSum function** button or the point-and-click method, create formulas to sum each month's permits. Your results should be 92, 193, and 295. Rename Sheet1 **2nd Quarter**

8. Select **Sheet2**. Rename the sheet **Inspectors** and then enter the following data in cells **A3:B6**:

District	Name
1	J Silva
2	G Gage
3	J Gomez

(Project 1G–Building Permits continues on the next page)

Performance Assessments (continued)

(Project 1G–Building Permits continued)

9. Select **Sheet3**, rename the sheet **Commission Members** and then in cells **A4:B7**, enter the following data:

Name	Phone
C Hall	555-4589
B Date	555-8921
R Chase	555-8943

10. For each worksheet, make **A1** the active cell and then check the spelling. (Hint: Each worksheet contains one spelling error.) Save your changes. Right-click the **2nd Quarter Sheet** tab, and then click **Select All Sheets** so that all three sheets display in Print Preview.

11. Use Print Preview to review the overall look of your workbook. Display the **Print** dialog box. Because the sheets are still grouped, all are active and will print; thus you need not select the Entire workbook option. Print, close the file, saving any changes, and close Excel.

End You have completed Project 1G

Performance Assessments (continued)

Project 1H — Public Service

Objectives: *Create Headers and Footers, Preview and Print a Workbook, Save and Close a Workbook and Exit Excel, Create a New Workbook, Enter and Edit Data in a Worksheet, Create Formulas, Use Zoom and the Spelling Checker Tool, Print a Worksheet Using the Print Dialog Box, and Use Excel Help.*

In the following Performance Assessment, you will create a new workbook for the Desert Park Deputy Mayor, Andrew Gore, that reports the number of students that attended a public service presentation at their school. Your completed workbook will look similar to the one shown in Figure 1.77. You will save the workbook as *1H_Public_Service_Firstname_Lastname*.

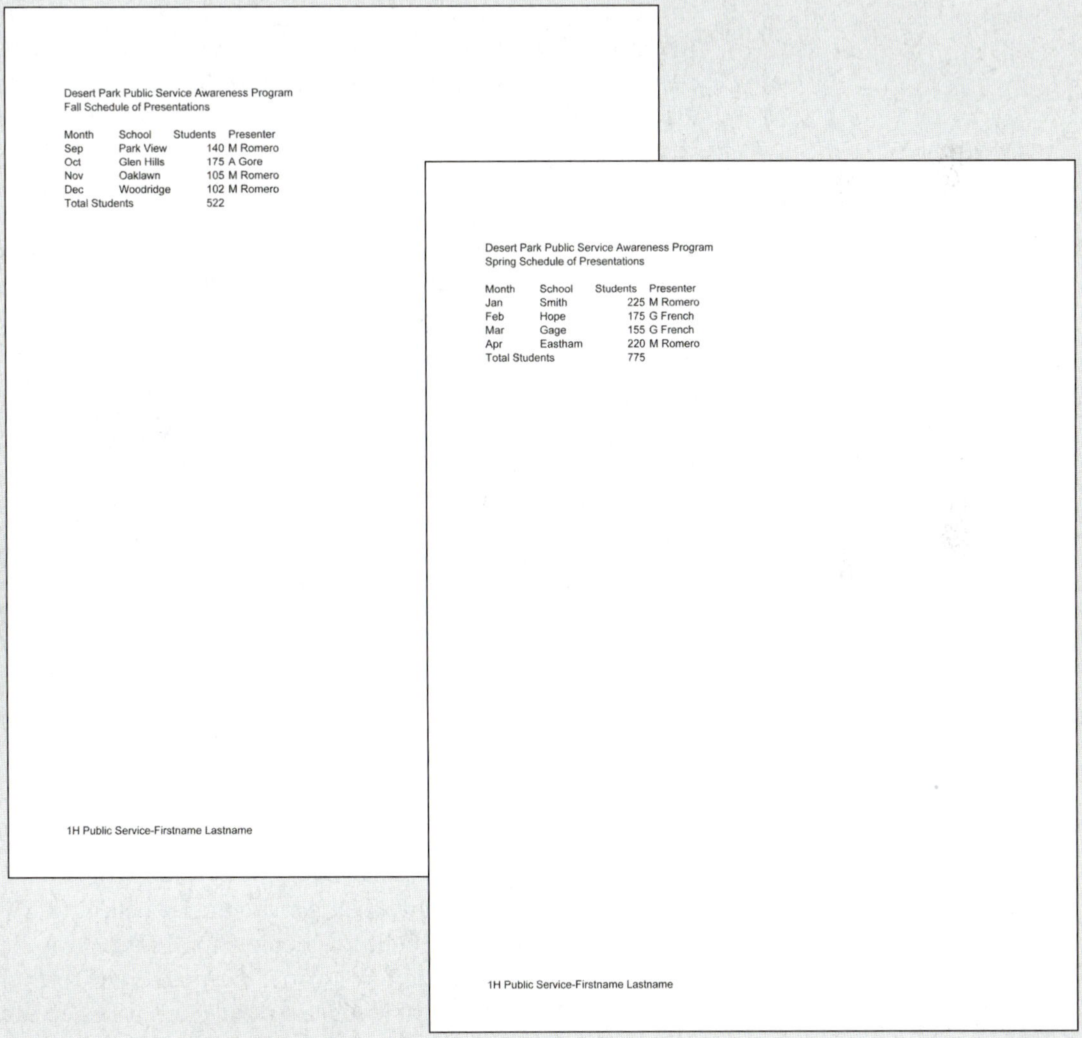

Desert Park Public Service Awareness Program
Fall Schedule of Presentations

Month	School	Students	Presenter
Sep	Park View	140	M Romero
Oct	Glen Hills	175	A Gore
Nov	Oaklawn	105	M Romero
Dec	Woodridge	102	M Romero
Total Students		522	

Desert Park Public Service Awareness Program
Spring Schedule of Presentations

Month	School	Students	Presenter
Jan	Smith	225	M Romero
Feb	Hope	175	G French
Mar	Gage	155	G French
Apr	Eastham	220	M Romero
Total Students		775	

1H Public Service-Firstname Lastname

Figure 1.77

(**Project 1H**–Public Service continues on the next page)

Excel chapter one
Performance Assessments (continued)

(Project 1H–Public Service continued)

1. Start Excel. On the new blank workbook, right-click the **Sheet1 tab** and click **Select All Sheets**. From the **View** menu, click **Header and Footer**, click the **Custom Footer** button, and in the **Left section**, type **1H Public Service-Firstname Lastname**. Use the default font and font size. In the upper right corner of the **Footer** dialog box, click **OK**. In the lower right corner of the **Page Setup** dialog box, click **OK**. Right-click the **Sheet1 tab**, and click **Ungroup Sheets**.

2. From the **File** menu, click **Save As**, navigate to the location where you are storing your projects for this chapter, and in the **File name** box, type **1H_Public_Service_Firstname_Lastname** and then click **Save**. If necessary, close the task pane.

3. On Sheet1, select cell **A1** and type **Desert Park Public Service Awareness Program** and in cell **A2**, type **Fall Schedule of Presentations** Select **Sheet2**. In cell **A1**, type **Desert Park Public Service Awareness Program** and in cell **A2**, type **Spring Schedule of Presentations**

4. Select **Sheet1**. In cells **A4:D8**, enter the following data:

Month	School	Students	Presenter
Sep	Park View	140	M Romero
Oct	Glen Hills	175	A Gore
Nov	Oaklawn	105	M Romero
Dec	Woodridge	102	M Romero

5. In cell **A9**, type **Total Students** and then, in cell **C9**, use any method (typing, point-and-click, or AutoSum) to construct a formula to sum the total number of students. The total should be 522. Rename the Sheet1 tab to **Fall**

6. Select Sheet2 and enter the following data in cells **A4:D8**:

Month	School	Students	Presenter
Jan	Smith	225	M Romero
Feb	Hope	175	G French
Mar	Gage	155	G French
Apr	Eastham	220	M Romero

7. In cell **A9**, type **Total Students** and then, in cell **C9**, construct a formula to add the total number of students. The total should be *775*. Rename Sheet2 as **Spring**

8. On each worksheet, make cell **A1** the active cell, and then check the spelling by using the Spelling Checker tool; make any necessary corrections. If necessary, ignore proper names. Save your changes. To view both sheets in Print Preview, right-click a **sheet tab**, and click **Select All Sheets**. Click **Print Preview** to review both sheets, and then close Print Preview. From the **File** menu, click **Print**, and in the **Print** dialog box, under **Print what**, click the **Entire workbook** option button. Two sheets will print. Close the workbook, and exit Excel.

End You have completed Project 1H

Mastery Assessments

Project 1I — Police Cars

Objectives: *Start Excel and Navigate a Workbook, Create Headers and Footers, Preview and Print a Workbook, Enter and Edit Data in a Worksheet, Create Formulas, and Use Zoom and the Spelling Checker Tool.*

In the following Mastery Assessment, you will create a workbook for the Desert Park Police Department with an inventory of the police cars, including license tag number, date placed in service, and total number of miles driven. Your completed workbook will look similar to the one shown in Figure 1.78. You will save the workbook as *1I_Police_Cars_Firstname_Lastname*.

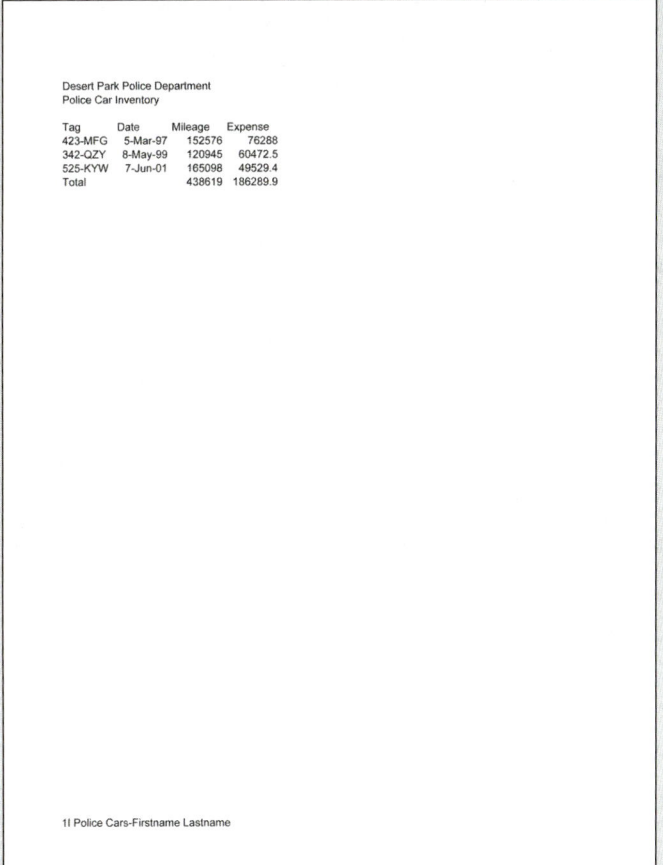

Figure 1.78

1. Start Excel. In a new workbook, create a custom footer, and in the **Left section**, type **1I Police Cars-Firstname Lastname**

2. Save the file in your storage location for this chapter as **1I_Police_Cars_Firstname_Lastname**

(**Project 1I**–Police Cars continues on the next page)

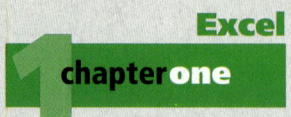

Mastery Assessments (continued)

(Project 1I–Police Cars continued)

3. On **Sheet1**, in cell **A1**, type **Desert Park Police Department** and, in cell **A2**, type **Police Car Inventory**

4. In cells **A4:C7**, enter the following data:

Tag	Date	Mileage
423-MFG	5-Mar-97	152576
342-QZY	8-May-99	120945
525-KYW	7-Jun-01	65098

5. Type **Total** in column A in the cell below the last car's data. In the appropriate cell, construct a formula to sum the total miles driven. The result should be 338619.

6. Rename the **Sheet1 tab Police Cars**

7. In cell **D4**, type **Expense** and then, using the following rules, create a formula in cells **D5**, **D6**, and **D7** to compute the expenses for each car:

   Rule 1: Cars placed in service before the year 2000 have an expense value of 50 cents per mile.

   Rule 2: Cars placed in service after January of 2000 have an expense value of 30 cents per mile.

8. Change the mileage for **525-KYW** to **165098** and press Enter to recalculate. Create a formula to sum the total expenses. The result should be 186289.9.

9. Click cell **A1**, and then check the spelling. Save your changes. Use Print Preview to review the overall look of your worksheet. Print the worksheet, close the workbook, and exit Excel.

End You have completed Project 1I

Mastery Assessments (continued)

Project 1J — Cell Phones

Objectives: *Start Excel and Navigate a Workbook, Create Headers and Footers, Preview and Print a Workbook, Enter and Edit Data in a Worksheet, Create Formulas, and Use Zoom and the Spelling Checker Tool.*

The Desert Park Police Department uses cell phones to communicate with the officers. Chief Dennis Johnson wants an analysis of the cell phones that shows the number of minutes per phone used last month and the total cost of each phone. Your completed workbook will look similar to the one shown in Figure 1.79. You will save the workbook as *1J_Cell_Phones_Firstname_Lastname*.

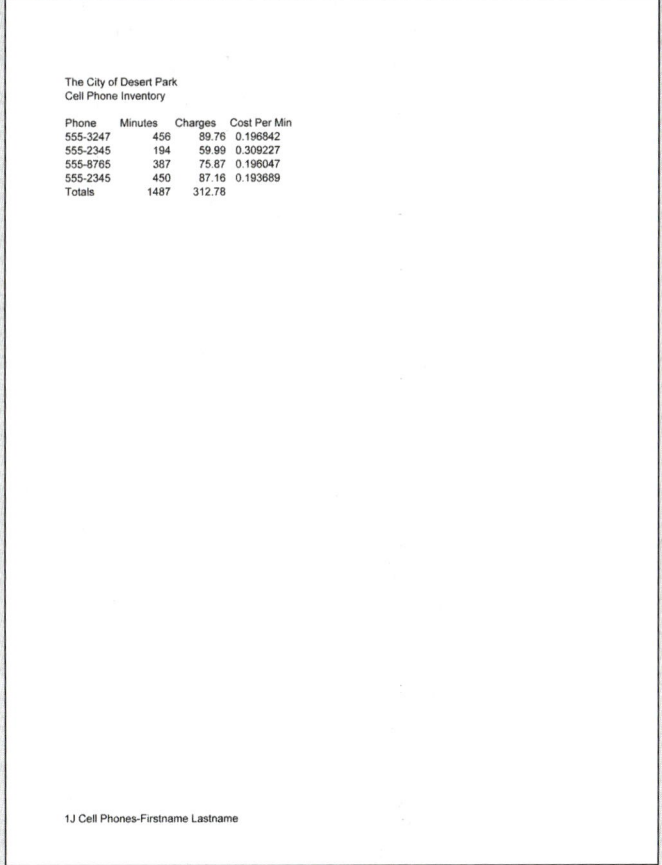

Figure 1.79

1. Start Excel, navigate to your student files, and then open the workbook **e01J_Cell_Phones**. Create a custom footer, and in the **Left section** type 1J_Cell_Phones_Firstname_Lastname

2. Save the file in your storage location for this chapter as **1J Cell Phones-Firstname Lastname**

(**Project 1J**–Cell Phones continues on the next page)

Mastery Assessments (continued)

(Project 1J–Cell Phones continued)

3. Beginning in cell **A4**, enter the following data:

Phone	Minutes	Charges
555-3247	456	89.76
555-2345	194	59.99
555-8765	387	75.87
555-3356	450	87.16

4. In cell **A9**, enter **Totals** and construct a formula to sum the total Minutes used and the total Charges. Your results should be 1487 and 312.78.

5. In cell **D4**, enter **Cost Per Min** and then, in cell **D5**, type = to begin a formula. Click cell **C5** and then type , which is the operator for division. (This key is next to the Right Shift on most keyboards.) Click cell **B5**, and press Enter. Your result, 0.196842, indicates the *per minute charge* for this phone (charges divided by minutes). Construct similar formulas for the remaining phones, and then compare your results with Figure 1.79.

6. Rename the **Sheet1 tab Cell Phones**

7. Check for and correct spelling errors. (Hint: There are at least three spelling errors.) Save your changes. Use Print Preview to review the overall look of your worksheet. Print the worksheet, close the workbook, and exit Excel.

End You have completed Project 1J

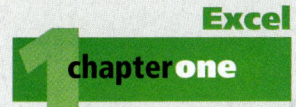

Problem Solving

Project 1K — Permit List

Objectives: *Start Excel and Navigate a Workbook, Create Headers and Footers, Preview and Print a Workbook, Save and Close a Workbook and Exit Excel, Create a New Workbook, Enter and Edit Data in a Worksheet, and Create Formulas.*

The Director of Arts and Parks, Roy Hamilton, wants to compile a list of all community organizations that have requested a summer picnic permit. Additionally, he would like to know the approximate number of people who will be attending each organization's picnic. This will help the department plan for park maintenance and trash collection. Three parks have picnic shelters: North Park, South Park, and Mariposa Park.

Create a workbook that has three worksheets, one for each of the three parks. For each park, create the name of at least three community organizations, the dates of their picnics, and the approximate number of people who will attend each. You might visit your community's Web site to get ideas of various community organizations. Total the number of picnic attendees for each park. Create a footer that includes your name as you have in the past, and save the file as **1K_Permit_List_Firstname_Lastname**.

 You have completed Project 1K

Project 1L — Museum Visits

Objectives: *Start Excel and Navigate a Workbook, Create Headers and Footers, Preview and Print a Workbook, Enter and Edit Data in a Worksheet, and Create Formulas.*

Gloria French, Public Information Officer for Desert Park, wants to report the number of students who have visited the city's museum over the past year. Create a workbook with one worksheet that lists the names of at least six schools. For each school, list the number of students that visited the museum for both the fall semester and the spring semester. Include totals by school and by semester. For school names, use school names from your local area. Create a footer that includes your name as you have in the past, and save the file as
1L_Museum_Visits_Firstname_Lastname.

 You have completed Project 1L

On the Internet

Learning More About Excel 2003

Additional information about using Microsoft Office 2003 Excel is available on the official Microsoft Web site. Take a look at the Top 10 Questions about Excel found at the following URL: **www.microsoft.com/office/excel/using/**

Many additional pages at this site have tips, help, downloads, and more. Plan to visit this site on a regular basis.

GO! with Help

Becoming Familiar with Excel Help

The easiest way to become successful with Microsoft Excel is to get in the habit of using the Help feature. In this exercise, you will access tips from Microsoft Help.

1. If necessary, start Excel to open a new workbook.

2. At the right edge of the menu bar, click in the **Type a question for help** box, type **How do I get Help?** and then press Enter.

   The Search Results task pane displays a list of results.

3. Click **About getting help while you work**.

   A Microsoft Excel Help window displays with a detailed list of various ways to access Help for Excel.

4. Using the **Print** button at the top of the Help window, print the contents of the Help window. Recall that your printed document will not contain any document identifier containing your name.

5. Close the Help window, and close the task pane.

chapter two

Excel 2003

Editing Workbooks, Formulas, and Cells

In this chapter, you will: complete these projects and practice these skills.

Project 2A
Creating a Quarterly Sales Analysis

Objectives
- Enter Constant Values with AutoFill and the Fill Handle
- Insert, Delete, and Adjust Rows and Columns
- Align Cell Contents Horizontally
- Copy and Move Cell Contents

Project 2B
Calculating Annual Sales

Objectives
- Format Numbers Using the Toolbar
- Edit Formulas
- Copy Formulas
- Conduct a What-if Analysis
- Display and Print Underlying Formulas
- Change Page Orientation

The Perfect Party

The Perfect Party store, owned by two partners, provides a wide variety of party accessories including invitations, favors, banners and flags, balloons, piñatas, etc. Party-planning services include both custom parties with pre-filled custom "goodie bags" and "parties in a box" that include everything needed to throw a theme party. Big sellers in this category are the Football and Luau themes. The owners are planning to open a second store and expand their party-planning services to include catering.

© Getty Images, Inc.

Editing Workbooks, Formulas, and Cells

In this chapter you will expand your knowledge of Excel by copying formulas and conducting a what-if analysis. You will enhance the appearance of workbooks by centering headings and adjusting the size of rows and columns and discover how easy it is to create a series of numbers without typing.

While working with the formulas in this chapter, you will discover how Excel can easily replicate formulas without having to retype them. You will also move and copy the contents of cells within a worksheet, within worksheets in the same workbook, and between worksheets from one workbook to another workbook.

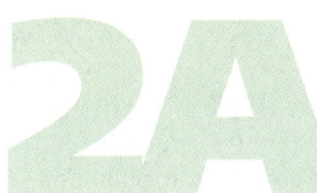

Project 2A Sales Analysis

In this project, you will use a quick method to enter constant values in a spreadsheet. You will also insert, delete, and adjust columns and rows and copy and move cell contents.

In Activities 2.1 through 2.13, you will create a workbook for Angie Nguyen and Gabriela Quinones, owners of The Perfect Party, that shows the sales totals for each quarter for the previous fiscal year. You will import data for last year from another workbook. The resulting workbook will look similar to Figure 2.1. You will save your workbook as *2A_Sales_Analysis_Firstname_Lastname.*

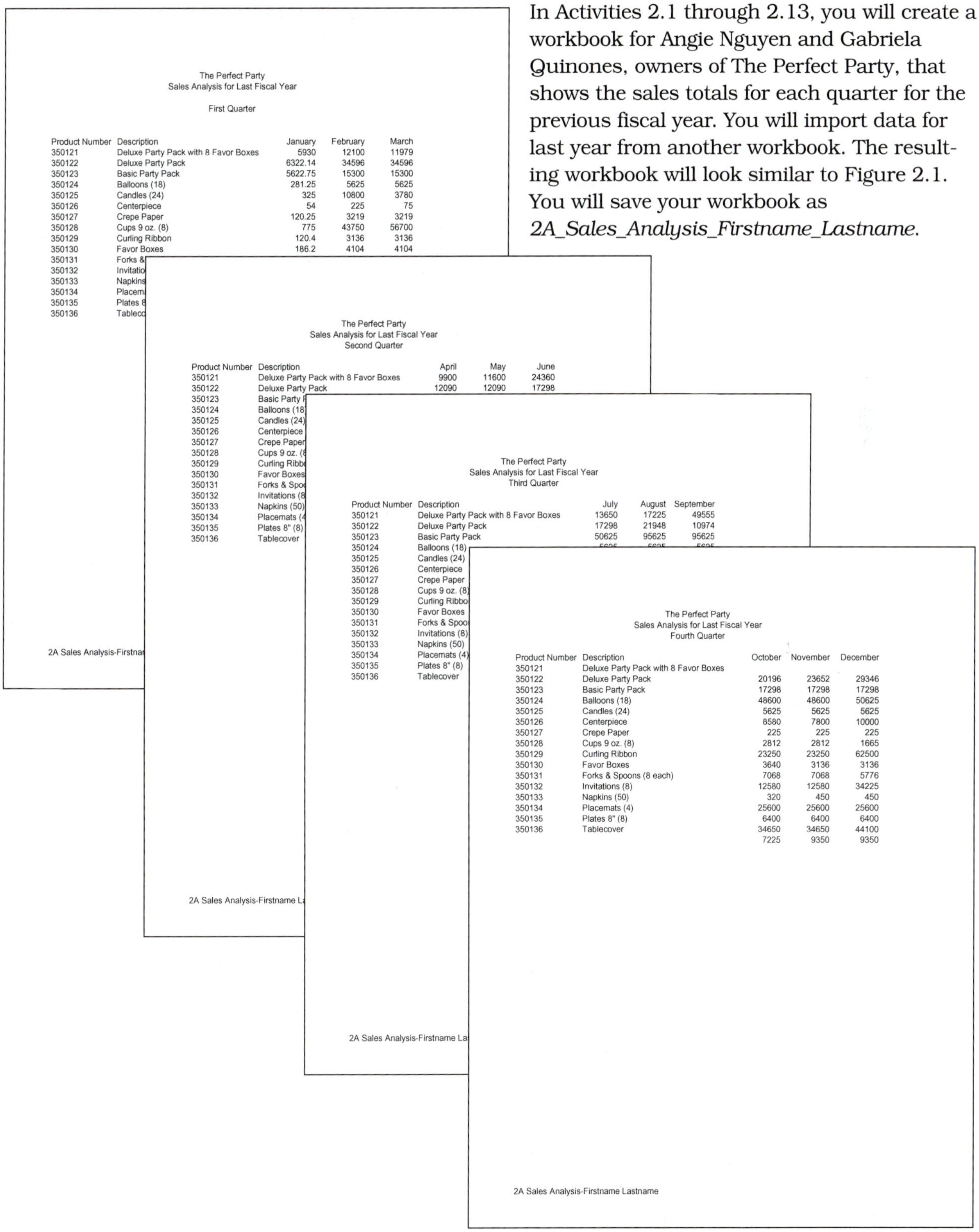

The Perfect Party
Sales Analysis for Last Fiscal Year
First Quarter

Product Number	Description	January	February	March
350121	Deluxe Party Pack with 8 Favor Boxes	5930	12100	11979
350122	Deluxe Party Pack	6322.14	34596	34596
350123	Basic Party Pack	5622.75	15300	15300
350124	Balloons (18)	281.25	5625	5625
350125	Candles (24)	325	10800	3780
350126	Centerpiece	54	225	75
350127	Crepe Paper	120.25	3219	3219
350128	Cups 9 oz. (8)	775	43750	56700
350129	Curling Ribbon	120.4	3136	3136
350130	Favor Boxes	186.2	4104	4104
350131	Forks &			
350132	Invitatio			
350133	Napkins			
350134	Placem			
350135	Plates 8			
350136	Tablecc			

2A Sales Analysis-Firstna

The Perfect Party
Sales Analysis for Last Fiscal Year
Second Quarter

Product Number	Description	April	May	June
350121	Deluxe Party Pack with 8 Favor Boxes	9900	11600	24360
350122	Deluxe Party Pack	12090	12090	17298
350123	Basic Party F			
350124	Balloons (18			
350125	Candles (24)			
350126	Centerpiece			
350127	Crepe Paper			
350128	Cups 9 oz. (8			
350129	Curling Ribb			
350130	Favor Boxes			
350131	Forks & Spo			
350132	Invitations (8			
350133	Napkins (50)			
350134	Placemats (4			
350135	Plates 8" (8)			
350136	Tablecover			

2A Sales Analysis-Firstname L

The Perfect Party
Sales Analysis for Last Fiscal Year
Third Quarter

Product Number	Description	July	August	September
350121	Deluxe Party Pack with 8 Favor Boxes	13650	17225	49555
350122	Deluxe Party Pack	17298	21948	10974
350123	Basic Party Pack	50625	95625	95625
350124	Balloons (18)			
350125	Candles (24)			
350126	Centerpiece			
350127	Crepe Paper			
350128	Cups 9 oz. (8)			
350129	Curling Ribbo			
350130	Favor Boxes			
350131	Forks & Spoo			
350132	Invitations (8)			
350133	Napkins (50)			
350134	Placemats (4)			
350135	Plates 8" (8)			
350136	Tablecover			

2A Sales Analysis-Firstname La

The Perfect Party
Sales Analysis for Last Fiscal Year
Fourth Quarter

Product Number	Description	October	November	December
350121	Deluxe Party Pack with 8 Favor Boxes			
350122	Deluxe Party Pack	20196	23652	29346
350123	Basic Party Pack	17298	17298	17298
350124	Balloons (18)	48600	48600	50625
350125	Candles (24)	5625	5625	5625
350126	Centerpiece	8580	7800	10000
350127	Crepe Paper	225	225	225
350128	Cups 9 oz. (8)	2812	2812	1665
350129	Curling Ribbon	23250	23250	62500
350130	Favor Boxes	3640	3136	3136
350131	Forks & Spoons (8 each)	7068	7068	5776
350132	Invitations (8)	12580	12580	34225
350133	Napkins (50)	320	450	450
350134	Placemats (4)	25600	25600	25600
350135	Plates 8" (8)	6400	6400	6400
350136	Tablecover	34650	34650	44100
		7225	9350	9350

2A Sales Analysis-Firstname Lastname

Figure 2.1—Sales Analysis

Objective 1
Enter Constant Values with AutoFill and the Fill Handle

Excel provides shortcuts for entering and editing data within cells. For example, AutoComplete, which you practiced in Chapter 1, assists you in typing duplicate entries in the same column. Shortcuts are designed to reduce typing. Excel has a shortcut called **AutoFill** that generates a series of constant values such as the months of the year in order or the days of the week in order. The table in Figure 2.2 lists some of the series that Excel can generate.

AutoFill Series

Start with:	AutoFill generates this series:
Jan	Feb, Mar, Apr...
January	February, March, April...
Mon	Tue, Wed, Thu...
Monday	Tuesday, Wednesday, Thursday...
Qtr 1	Qtr 2, Qtr 3, Qtr 4...
Quarter 1	Quarter 2, Quarter 3, Quarter 4...
Oct-99	Nov-99, Dec-99, Jan-00...
15-Jan	16-Jan, 17-Jan, 18-Jan...
1st Period	2nd Period, 3rd Period, 4th Period...
Product 1	Product 2, Product 3, Product 4...
Text 1	Text 2, Text 3, Text 4...
10:00 AM	11:00 AM, 12:00 PM, 1:00 PM...

Figure 2.2

Activity 2.1 Inserting Titles and Headings

In a new worksheet, the first information you enter is usually a title and perhaps one or more subtitles that describe the purpose of the worksheet. Additionally, each column of data normally has a column heading describing the type of information in the column. Likewise, each row may have a description in the left column that describes the data in the row.

1 Start Excel and, if necessary, close ☒ the **Getting Started** task pane.

Excel displays a new workbook named *Book1*.

2 Right-click the **Sheet1 tab**, and then click **Select All Sheets**.

In the blue title bar, *[Group]* displays, indicating that the three sheets are grouped. When worksheets are grouped, information such as a header or footer is placed on all the sheets in the workbook.

3 From the **View** menu, click **Header and Footer**. In the displayed **Page Setup** dialog box, click the **Header/Footer tab**, and then click the **Custom Footer** button.

4 In the displayed **Footer** dialog box, under **Left section**, type **2A Sales Analysis-Firstname Lastname** using your own first and last name, and then in the upper right corner, click **OK** to close the **Footer** dialog box. Click **OK** again to close the **Page Setup** dialog box.

A dotted vertical line may display on the worksheet, indicating the right edge of the page as currently formatted. Recall that headers and footers do not display in the worksheet on your screen. They display only in the Print Preview and on the printed worksheets. Because you grouped the sheets, your footer will print on all the sheets in the workbook.

5 Right-click the **Sheet1 tab**, and then click **Ungroup Sheets**.

[Group] no longer displays in the blue title bar.

6 In cell **A1**, type **The Perfect Party** as the title of the worksheet, and then press Enter.

7 In cell **A2**, type **Sales Analysis for Last Fiscal Year** as the first subtitle, and then press Enter two times.

8 Be sure cell **A4** is the active cell, type **Product Number** as the column heading for this column of data, and then press Enter. Compare your screen with Figure 2.3.

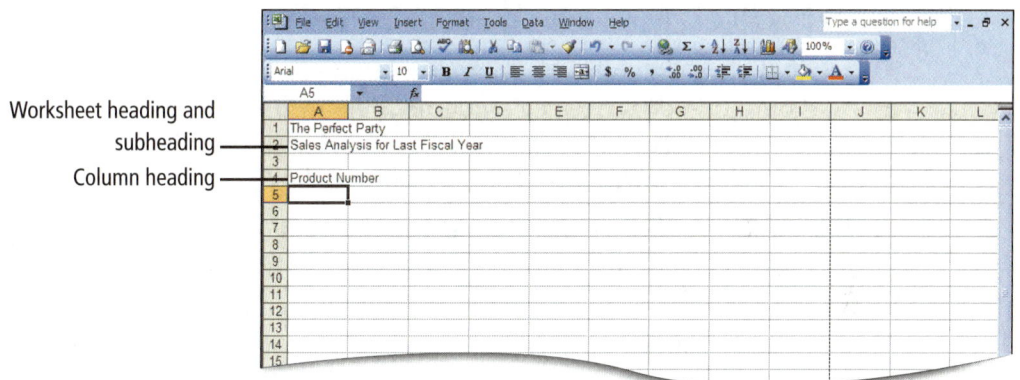

Worksheet heading and subheading
Column heading

Figure 2.3

9 Display the **File** menu, and then click **Save As**.

10 In the displayed **Save As** dialog box, click the **Save in arrow**. Navigate to the drive and folder where you are storing your projects for this chapter, creating a new folder for Chapter 2 if you want to do so.

11 In the **File name** box, delete **Book 1**, type **2A_Sales_Analysis_Firstname_Lastname** and then in the lower right corner, click **Save** or press Enter.

The workbook name displays in both the title bar and the taskbar. Recall that when saving files, using the underscore character instead of spaces will facilitate sending your files over the Internet.

Activity 2.2 Creating a Series Using AutoFill

A *series* is a group of things that come one after another in succession. For example, January, February, March, April, and so on, is a series. The days of the week form a series. Quarter 1, Quarter 2, Quarter 3, and Quarter 4 form a series. The numbers 1, 2, 3, 4, 5 and 10, 15, 20, 25 are series. Excel's **AutoFill** feature completes a series so that you do not have to type every value. AutoFill is the ability to extend a series of values into adjacent cells, based on the value of other cells.

1 With your workbook **2A_Sales_Analysis** displayed, click cell **B4**.

Although text displays in cell B4, the text *Product Number* is contained within cell A4. Recall that if a cell is not wide enough to accommodate a text value, its display will spill over to the next cell, provided the cell is empty. If you look at the Formula Bar, you can see that cell B4 does not contain a value.

2 In cell **B4** type **January** and then press Tab to make cell **C4** the active cell.

January will form the heading for its column, which will contain January sales amounts. *Product Number* no longer overlaps into cell B4. Now that cell B4 contains a value, the value in cell A4 is *truncated*—cut off. Although not completely visible, the underlying value of cell A4 remains unchanged.

3 In cell **C4**, type **February** and then press Tab.

February will form the column heading for this column, which will contain February sales amounts. One by one you could enter the months from March through December, but AutoFill will complete the series for you without additional typing.

4 Click cell **C4** to make it the active cell, and then notice the small black square in the lower right corner of the cell, as shown in Figure 2.4.

This is the *fill handle*. You can drag the fill handle to adjacent cells to fill them with values based on the first cell in the series.

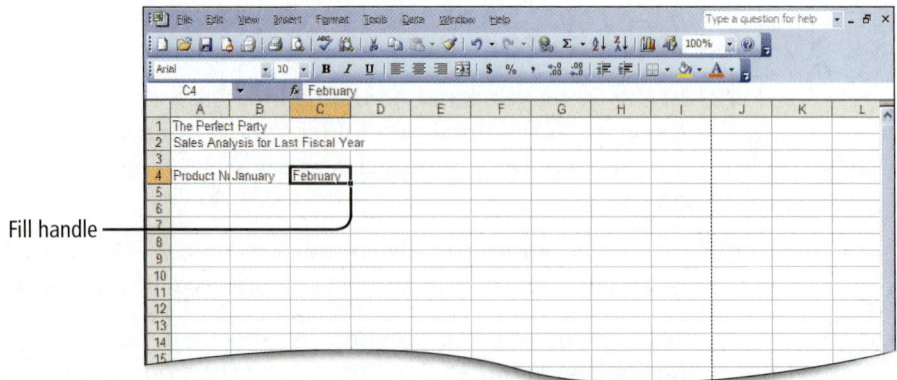

Figure 2.4

5 Point to the **fill handle** until your mouse pointer changes from a white cross to a black cross, hold down the left mouse button, drag to the right through cell **M4**, and as you do so, notice that a ScreenTip displays for each month, as shown in Figure 2.5. Release the left mouse button.

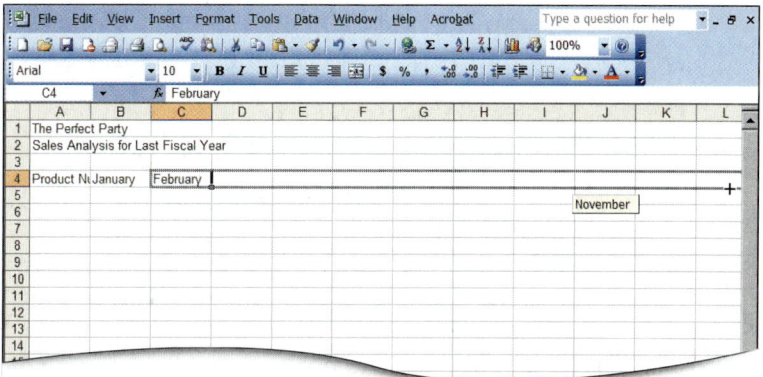

Figure 2.5

6 After you release the mouse button, the months March through December are filled in. On your screen, locate and then point to the **Auto Fill Options button** to display its ScreenTip, as shown in Figure 2.6.

The Auto Fill Options button is a type of **smart tag**. When Excel recognizes certain types of data, Excel labels the data with a smart tag. Some smart tags, for example, the Auto Fill Options button, provide a menu of options related to the current task. Because the options are related to the current task, the tag or button is referred to as being **context-sensitive**.

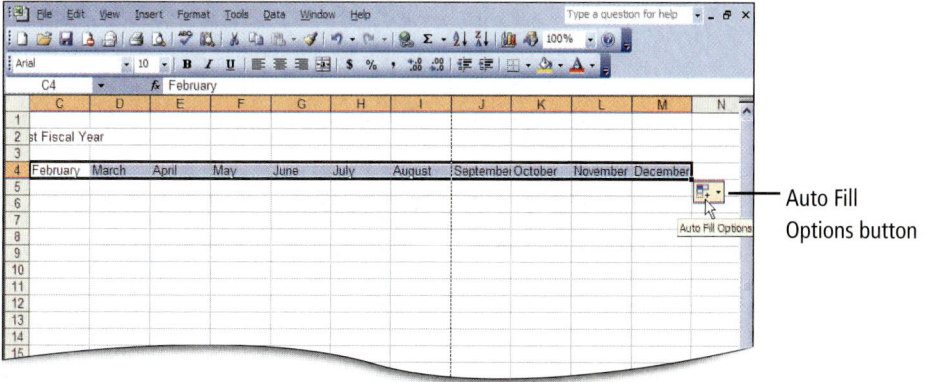

Figure 2.6

7 Point to and then click the **Auto Fill Options button arrow** to display a menu, as shown in Figure 2.7.

The menu offers options about how to fill the selected cells. On the displayed menu, *Fill Series* is selected, indicating the action that was taken. From the displayed menu, you could also select other actions. For example, if you clicked Copy Cells, February would fill each of the selected cells because February was the selected cell when you began to drag the mouse. As you progress in your study of Excel, you will encounter additional smart tags.

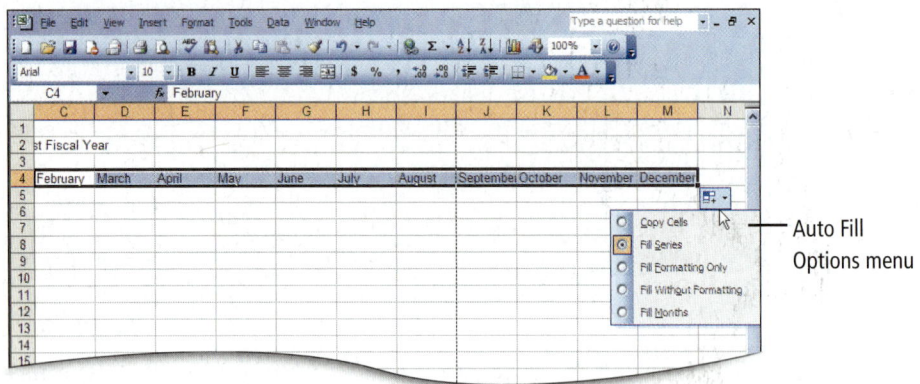

Figure 2.7

8 Click any empty cell to close the **Auto Fill Options** menu without changing the selection.

The smart tag will remain visible until you perform another screen action.

9 On the Standard toolbar, click the **Save** button.

More Knowledge — Smart Tags

Smart tags were first introduced in Microsoft Office XP. In Microsoft Office System 2003, smart tags have been made even smarter. Using various types of software, organizations can develop their own custom smart tags, and smart tags can automatically search for information on the Web.

Activity 2.3 Duplicating Data Using AutoFill

AutoFill not only extends a series of values, but it also duplicates data into adjacent cells. This is another way that Excel helps to reduce your typing.

1 Click cell **A5**, type **350121** and then press Enter.

Product Number 350121 displays in cell A5.

2 Click cell **A5** again, position your pointer over the **fill handle** in the lower right corner of the cell to display the pointer ✥, and then drag downward through cell **A10**.

The value 350121 is duplicated in all the cells, and the Auto Fill Options button displays.

3 Point to and then click the **Auto Fill Options button arrow** to display the menu, as shown in Figure 2.8.$I~AutoFill;duplicating data with>

The default option *Copy Cells* is selected. Because Excel did not interpret the single value of 350121 to be part of a series, it copied (duplicated) the value in the selected cells.

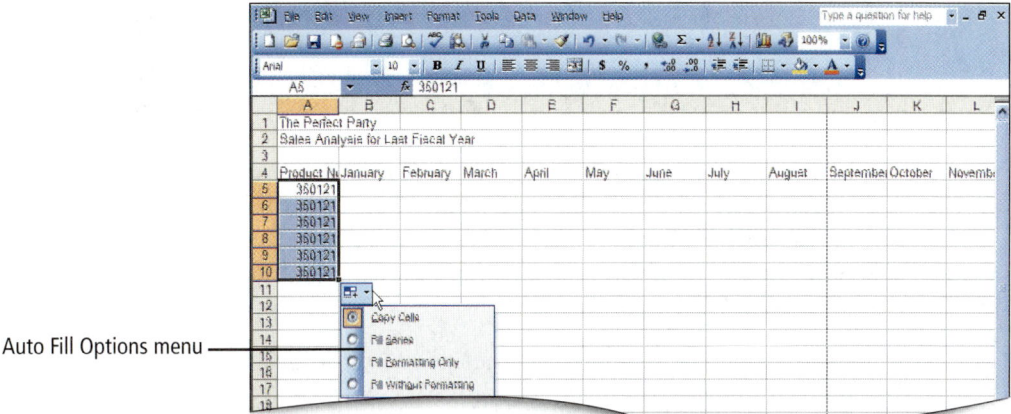

Auto Fill Options menu

Figure 2.8

4 From the displayed menu, click **Fill Series**.

A series of numbers, 350121–350126, replaces the duplicate numbers. You can use AutoFill to create a series or to duplicate data in adjacent cells. Compare your screen with Figure 2.9.

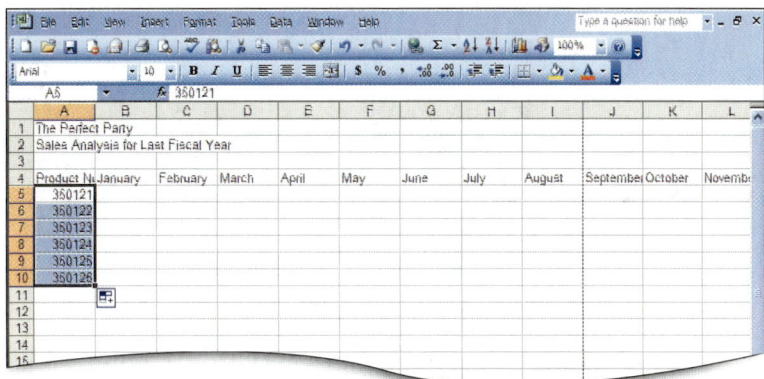

Figure 2.9

5 Click in any empty cell to cancel the selection. On the Standard toolbar, click the **Save** button to save the changes you have made to your worksheet.

Recall that the Auto Fill Options button will remain visible until you perform another screen action. This is characteristic of the various smart tags in Excel.

Project 2A: Sales Analysis | **Excel** 595

Objective 2
Insert, Delete, and Adjust Rows and Columns

Within the spreadsheet grid you can control the size of cells in various ways. For example, you can change the width of columns and the height of rows to accommodate your data. You can also insert new columns and rows and delete existing columns and rows—even after data has been typed into them. You also have the ability to merge several cells into one cell.

Activity 2.4 Adjusting Column Width and Row Height

The size of cells is controlled by either adjusting the width of a column or by increasing the height of a row. The cell size you need is determined by the amount of data you type into the cell and by the *font* and *font size* of the data. A font is a set of characters with the same design and shape. Font size is measured in *points*, with one point equal to ½ of an inch, and abbreviated as *pt*.

1 Click **A4** to make it the active cell.

2 In the **column heading area**, position the pointer over the vertical line between **column A** and **column B** until the white cross changes to a double-headed arrow, and then hold down the left mouse button. See Figure 2.10.

A ScreenTip displays information about the width of the column. The default width of a column is 64 pixels, or 8.43 characters, which is the average number of digits that will fit in a cell using the default font. The default font in Excel is Arial, and the default font size is 10 pt.

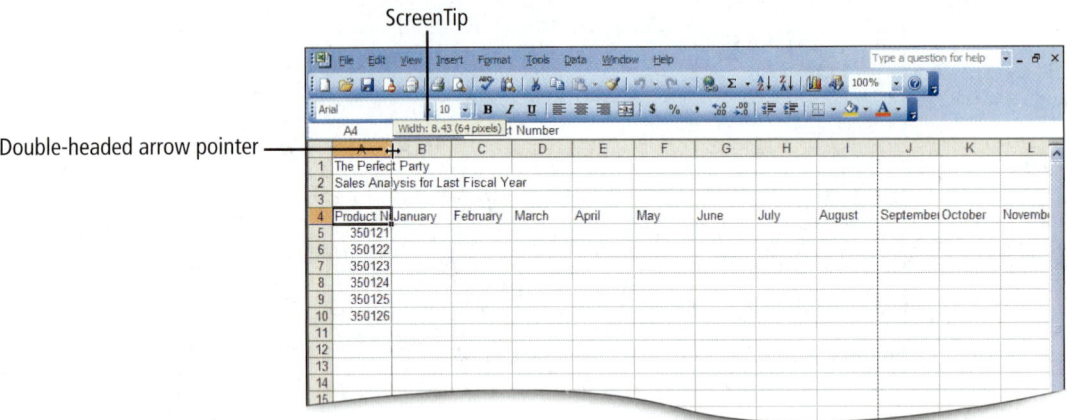

Figure 2.10

3 Drag to the right until the number of pixels indicated in the ScreenTip reaches **200 pixels**, as shown in Figure 2.11, and then release the mouse button. If you are not satisfied with your result, click the **Undo** button and begin again.

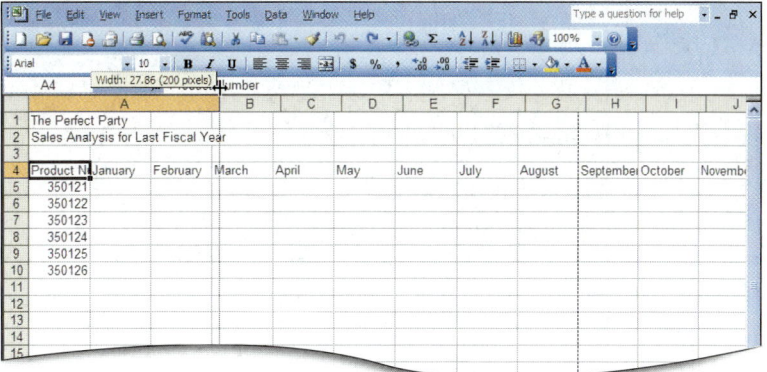

Figure 2.11

4 Using the technique you just practiced, decrease the width of **column A** to **40 pixels**.

A pattern, #####, displays in cells A5:A10. When a column is too narrow to display the entire numeric value in a cell, the cell displays as a series of number signs (also called pound signs), as shown in Figure 2.12.

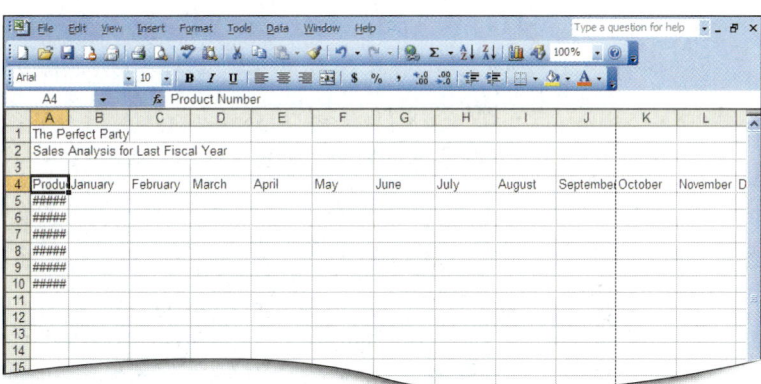

Figure 2.12

5 Click cell **A5**, and then look at the value in the Formula Bar.

Although the cell displays #####, the underlying value is unchanged; it is still 350121.

6 Click cell **A4**, display the **Format** menu, point to **Column**, and then click **AutoFit Selection**.

This command adjusts the width of a column to accommodate the value in the selected cell, cell A4 in this instance.

7 Click cell **A2**, and notice that the text in cell **A2** still overlaps into **columns B** and **C**. See Figure 2.13.

Project 2A: Sales Analysis | **Excel** 597

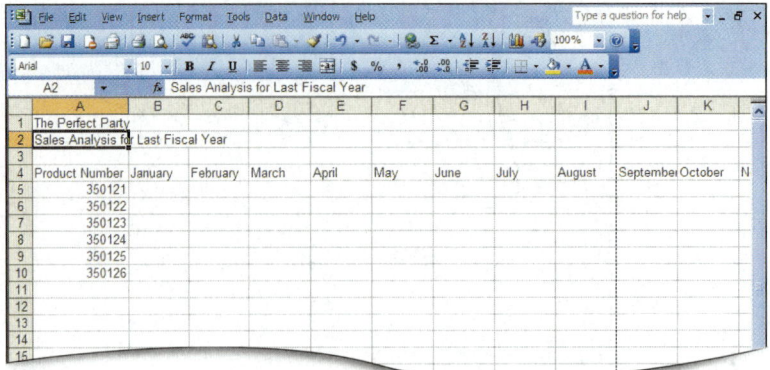

Figure 2.13

8 In the **column heading area**, position your pointer over the **column B** heading until the pointer changes to a black down arrow ⬇, hold down the left mouse button, and then drag to the right through **column M**.

Columns B though M are selected, as shown in Figure 2.14.

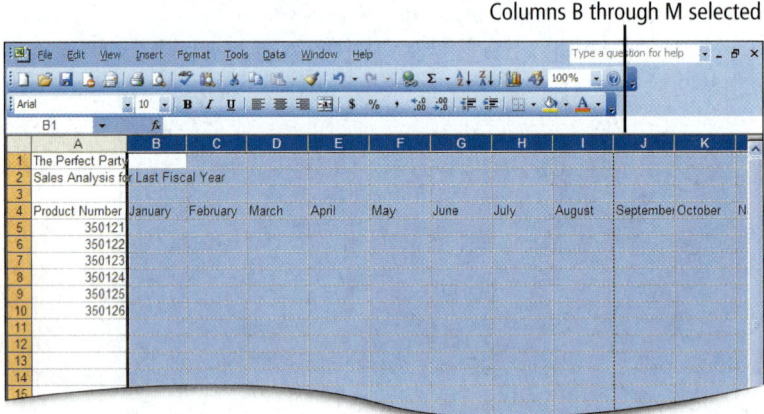

Figure 2.14

9 With the columns still selected, in the **column heading area**, position the pointer over the vertical line between **column B** and **column C** to display the double-headed arrow pointer, and then drag to the right until **75 pixels** displays in the ScreenTip. Release the mouse. If you are not satisfied with your result, click Undo and begin again. Alternatively, from the Format menu, point to Column, click Width, and type **75**

All the selected columns are increased in width to 75 pixels.

10 Click anywhere to cancel the selection. In the **row heading area**, position the pointer over the horizontal line between **row 3** and **row 4** until the double-headed arrow pointer displays, as shown in Figure 2.15.

598   **Excel** | Chapter 2: Editing Workbooks, Formulas, and Cells

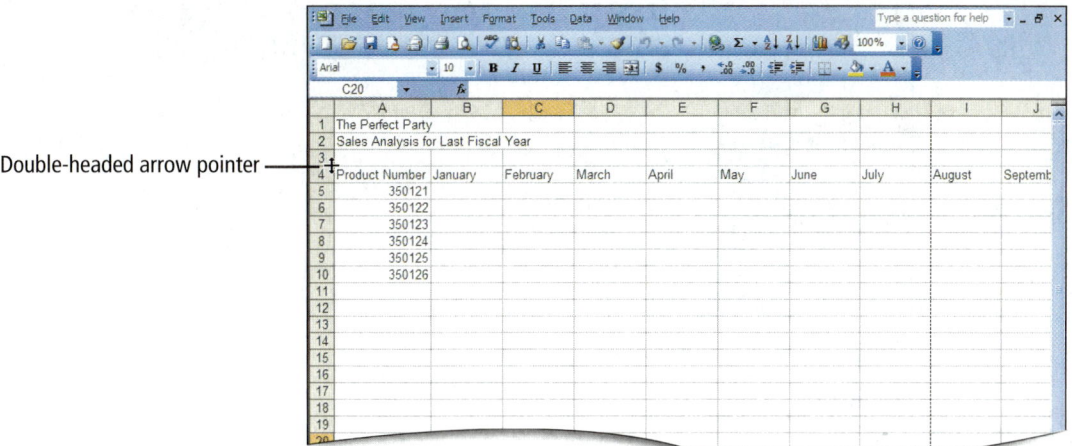

Double-headed arrow pointer

Figure 2.15

11 Hold down the left mouse button, and then watch the ScreenTip while dragging downward until the height is **27 pixels**. If you are not satisfied with your result, click **Undo** and begin again.

The height of the row is increased. The height of rows is measured in points. Recall that one point equals ½₂ of an inch. The default height of a row is 12.75 points.

More Knowledge — Adjusting Cell Height

Excel adjusts the height of a row to accommodate the largest font used in that particular row. Thus, you need not be concerned that your characters are too tall for the row.

Activity 2.5 Inserting and Deleting Rows and Columns

You can insert columns or rows in the following ways:

- From the Insert menu, click Rows or click Columns.

- In the column heading or the row heading, right-click to simultaneously select the column or row and display a shortcut menu. From the displayed shortcut menu, click Insert.

You can delete columns or rows in the following ways:

- Select the column or row, and then from the Edit menu, click Delete.

- In the column heading or the row heading, right-click to simultaneously select the column or row and display a shortcut menu. From the displayed shortcut menu, click Delete.

1 Right-click the **column B** heading to simultaneously select the column and display the shortcut menu, as shown in Figure 2.16.

Project 2A: Sales Analysis | **Excel** 599

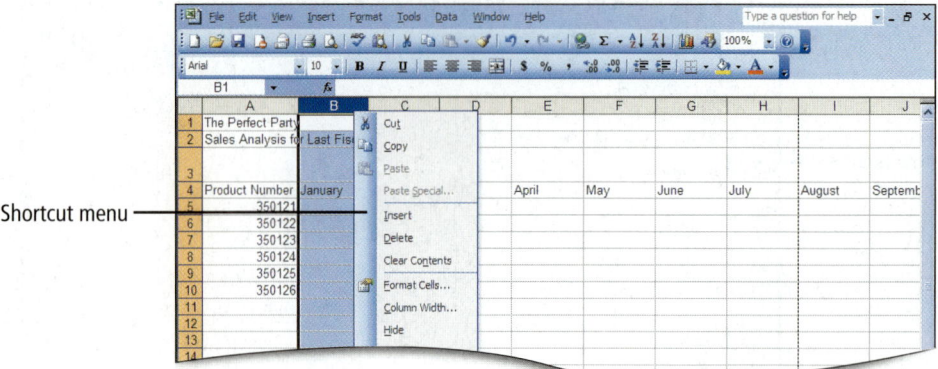

Shortcut menu

Figure 2.16

2 From the displayed shortcut menu, click **Insert**.

A new column B is inserted to the left of the selected column, and the existing columns are shifted to the right. Additionally, the Insert Options button displays.

3 Point to the **Insert Options** button to display its ScreenTip and its arrow, and then click the arrow to display the menu, as shown in Figure 2.17.

From this menu, you can format the new column like the column to the left or the column to the right, or you can leave it unformatted. The default is *Format Same As Left*.

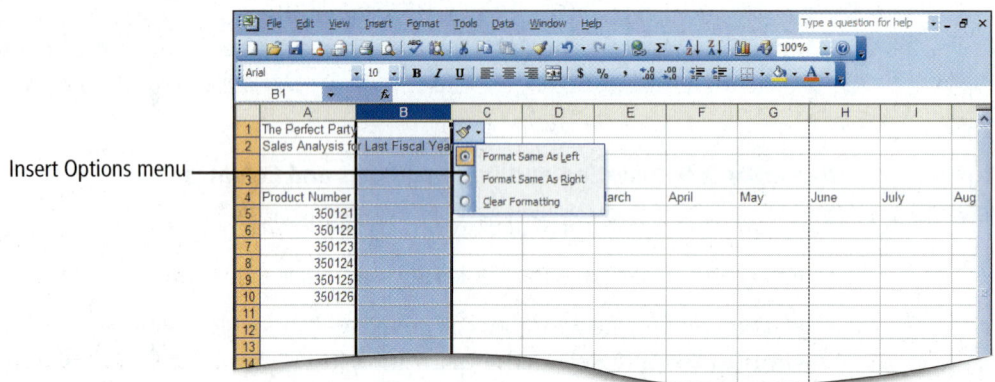

Insert Options menu

Figure 2.17

More Knowledge — Inserting and Deleting Cells

You can also insert or delete individual cells in a worksheet using a similar technique. Right-click the cell position where you want to add a cell, and from the shortcut menu click Insert. In the Insert dialog box click the option button for the direction you wish to shift the existing cells—down or to the right. All the cells in the column are shifted down one, or the cells in the row are shifted to the right one cell. Similarly, when you delete a cell, the delete dialog box will display so you can choose to shift the remaining cells up or to the left.

4 Click anywhere outside the selected column to cancel the selection and accept the default value.

The new column is formatted in the same width as column A to the left. The Insert Options button remains visible until you perform another screen action.

5 Click cell **B4**, type **Description** and then press [Enter].

6 Right-click the **row 4 heading** to simultaneously select the row and display the shortcut menu, and then from the displayed menu, click **Insert**.

A new row 4 is inserted, formatted in the same height as the row above it. The Insert Options button displays. New rows are inserted above the selected row.

7 Select cell **A3**, type **First Quarter** and then press [Enter].

Businesses frequently track their yearly financial information by dividing a year into four equal parts called **quarters**. Thus, *First Quarter* refers to the period from January through March, *Second Quarter* refers to April through June, *Third Quarter* refers to July through September, and *Fourth Quarter* refers to October through December.

8 Right-click the **column F heading**, and then from the displayed shortcut menu, click **Delete**.

Column F is deleted from the worksheet, and the columns to the right shift one letter to the left. Thus, the former column G becomes column F.

9 In the **column heading area**, hold down the left mouse button and drag to select **columns F through M**. Pause your pointer anywhere over the selected area, right-click, and from the shortcut menu, click **Delete**. Click anywhere to cancel the selection.

The selected range of columns is deleted. Both columns and rows can be deleted in this manner—individually or as a range (group).

10 Hold down [Ctrl] and press [Home] to make cell **A1** the active cell and bring the left side of the worksheet into view. On the Standard toolbar, click the **Save** button to save the changes you have made to your workbook. Compare your screen with Figure 2.18.

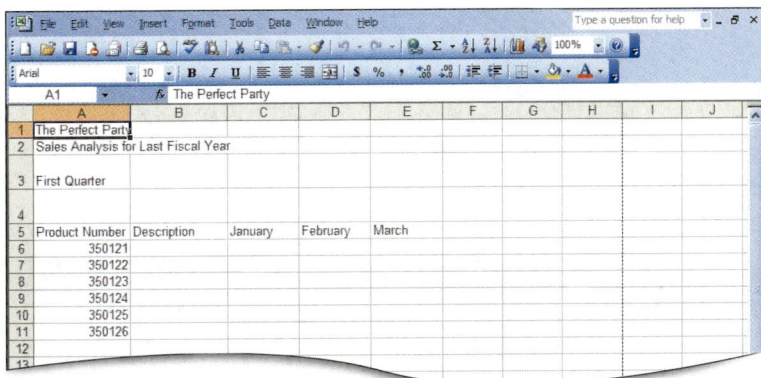

Figure 2.18

Objective 3
Align Cell Contents Horizontally

Within cells, data can be aligned at the left edge of the cell—*left-aligned*—or at the right edge of the cell—*right-aligned*. Within a cell, data can also be centered, or data can be centered across a group of cells using a feature called *Merge and Center*.

Activity 2.6 Aligning Cell Contents

By default, Excel aligns numeric values at the right edge of a cell and aligns text values at the left edge of the cell. These default settings can be changed as needed.

1 Look at the data in cells **A3:A11**, and notice that text values, for example, *First Quarter*, are aligned at the left edge of the cell and that the numeric product numbers are aligned at the right edge of the cell.

2 Click cell **A6**, and then on the Formatting toolbar, click the **Center** button .

Product Number *350121* is aligned in the center of the cell.

3 With **A6** still the active cell, on the Formatting toolbar click the **Align Left** button .

Product Number *350121* is aligned at the left of the cell. Because this numeric value is used for reference and not in a mathematical calculation, it can be aligned at the left. Numeric values that are not used for calculations, such as phone numbers, postal codes, and taxpayer identification numbers, are commonly left-aligned so that it is obvious that they are not numbers to be used in calculations.

4 Select the range **A7:A11**, and then click **Align Left** .

The entire group of cells is left-aligned. Compare your screen with Figure 2.19.

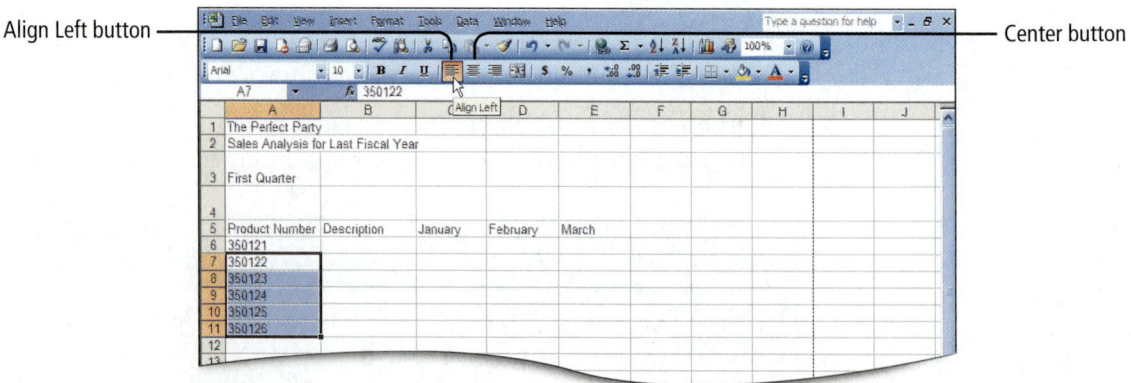

Figure 2.19

5 Select cell **A12**, type **350127** and press Enter.

Notice that although this is a number, Excel did not apply the default right-alignment. This happened because when three or more adjacent cells are formatted differently from the default, Excel applies the same formatting to the next three adjacent cells.

602   Excel | Chapter 2: Editing Workbooks, Formulas, and Cells

6 Select cell **A16**, which is more than three cells away from the previous entry, type **350128** and press Enter. Notice the alignment.

Because this cell was more than three cells down from the last active cell containing the left-align format, Excel used its default alignment for numeric values, which is right-align.

7 Select **column A**, on the Formatting toolbar click **Align Left**, and then click outside the selected area to cancel the selection.

All the cells in column A are formatted with left alignment. You can format entire rows and columns in this manner. Now that left alignment has been applied to all the cells in the column, any new numeric entries in column A will be left-aligned.

8 Right-click cell **A16**, and on the shortcut menu, click **Clear Contents** to remove *350128*.

9 Select the range **C5:E5**. On the Formatting toolbar click **Align Right**, and then click outside the selected area to cancel the selection. Click **Save**.

The column headings for January through March are right-aligned. When entered, the data in these columns will be numeric values that are right-aligned. Visually, it is useful if the heading for a numeric column lines up with the data it describes.

Activity 2.7 Using Merge and Center

In addition to widening columns and making rows taller, you can control the size of cells in another way. Several cells can be merged into one large cell. When you merge cells, the result is a single cell that comprises all the original cells.

Because the title information in a worksheet is so frequently centered across the columns of the worksheet, Excel provides a command that combines the merging of cells with center alignment. This command is *Merge and Center*.

1 Select the range **A1:E1**, and then, on the Formatting toolbar, click the **Merge and Center** button. Click outside the selected area to cancel the selection.

Cells A1:E1 are merged into one cell, and the heading, *The Perfect Party*, is centered across the columns in the newly formed cell. Cells B1:E1 cease to exist because they are contained with cell A1.

2 Select the range **A2:E2**, and then, on the Formatting toolbar, click the **Merge and Center** button.

Cells A2:E2 are merged into one cell, and the data is centered in the cell.

3 Click the **Merge and Center** button again.

The text value returns to cell A2, and the merged cells are changed back to their individual cells. In this manner, you can reverse the Merge and Center command.

Project 2A: Sales Analysis | **Excel** 603

4 With cells **A2:E2** still selected, click the **Merge and Center** button again to merge and center the data.

5 Using the technique you have just practiced, in **row 3**, merge and center the subtitle *First Quarter* across the range **A3:E3**. Compare your results with Figure 2.20.

6 On the Standard toolbar, click the **Save** button.

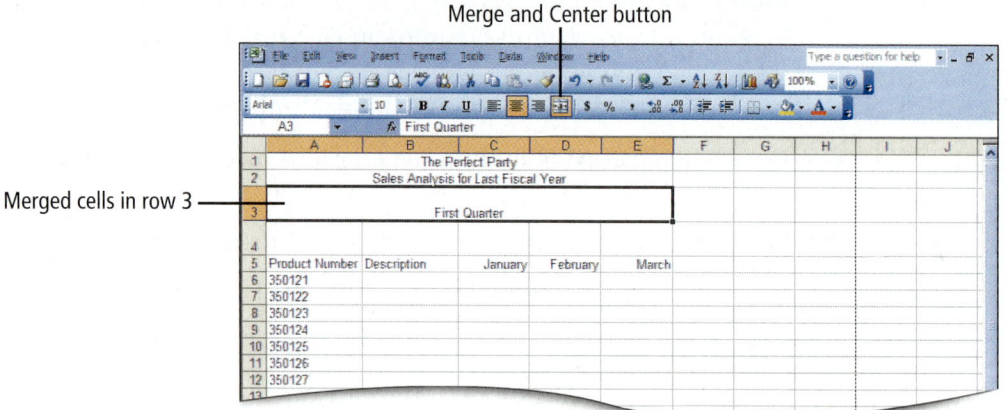

Figure 2.20

Objective 4
Copy and Move Cell Contents

Data from individual cells and groups of cells can be copied to other cells in the same worksheet, to other sheets in the same workbook, or to sheets in another workbook. Likewise, data can be moved (*cut*) from one place to another. The action of placing cell contents that have been copied or moved from one location to another location is called *paste*.

Data from other sources can also be copied into a worksheet. For example, if your instructor uses a course management program such as BlackBoard or WebCT, data from the program can be copied into an Excel worksheet. In the following activities, you will use various methods to copy and move cell contents.

Activity 2.8 Copying Cell Contents

The *Office Clipboard* is a temporary storage area maintained by your Windows operating system. When you perform the Copy command or the Cut command, the data you select is placed on the Clipboard. From this Clipboard storage area, the data is available for pasting into other cells, worksheets, workbooks, and even other Office programs.

1 From the **Edit** menu, click **Office Clipboard**.

2 The **Clipboard** task pane displays.

3 Check to see whether the top of the Clipboard indicates *Clipboard empty*, and if it does not, at the top of the task pane click the **Clear All** button.

4 Click cell **A1**, the merged and centered cell, and then on the Standard toolbar, click the **Copy** button.

A moving border surrounds the merged cell, and the contents of cell A1, including its formatting, are copied to the Clipboard, as shown in Figure 2.21. A moving border indicates cells that have been copied, and the border will remain until you perform another screen action.

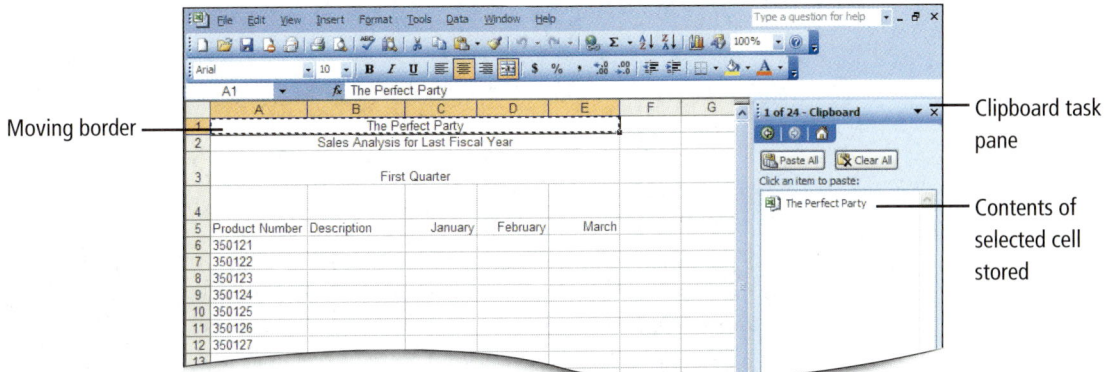

Moving border

Clipboard task pane

Contents of selected cell stored

Figure 2.21

5 In the lower left of the grid area, click the **Sheet2 tab**, and be sure that cell **A1** is the active cell.

6 On the Standard toolbar, click the **Paste** button.

The Clipboard entry is pasted into cell A1, with the identical formatting, and the Paste Options button displays, as shown in Figure 2.22.

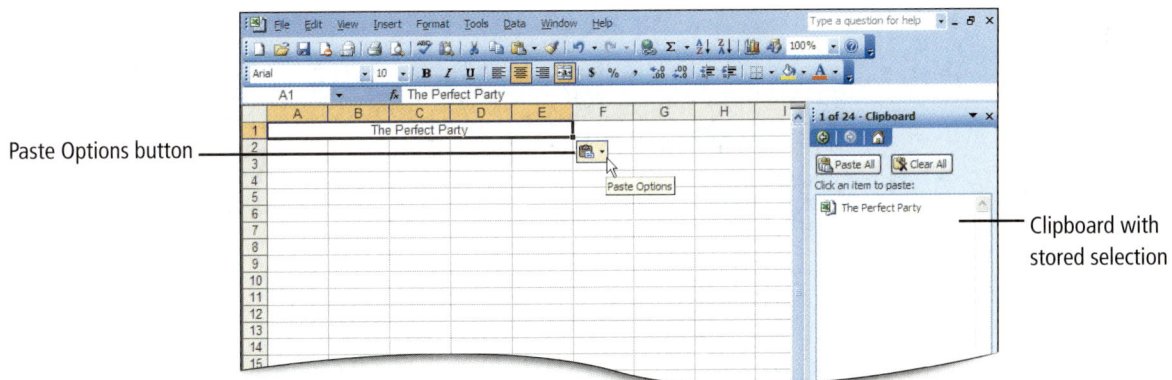

Paste Options button

Clipboard with stored selection

Figure 2.22

7 Point to the **Paste Options** button, and then click its **arrow** to display a menu of options.

The Paste Options menu displays, as shown in Figure 2.23. Notice that *Keep Source Formatting* is the default. You can see that the original formatting, merge and center, was retained.

Project 2A: Sales Analysis | **Excel** 605

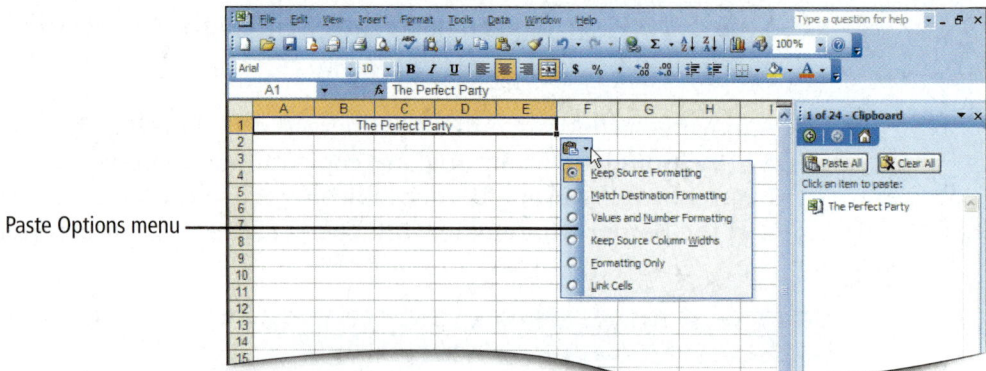

Paste Options menu

Figure 2.23

> **Note — Paste Options**
>
> When pasting items you can also choose the Paste Special command from the Edit menu or from the shortcut menu. This gives you even greater control over what is pasted. Using the Paste Special command you can choose the values, formulas, formats or other specific characteristics of the cell that has been cut or copied.

8 Click outside the menu to close it without changing the selection. Navigate back to **Sheet1**, select the range **A2:A3**, and then hold down Ctrl and press C.

Ctrl + C is the keyboard shortcut for the Copy command. The contents of the two cells are copied to the top of the Clipboard, as shown in Figure 2.24, and the first copied item on the Clipboard moves down. A moving border surrounds the copied cells.

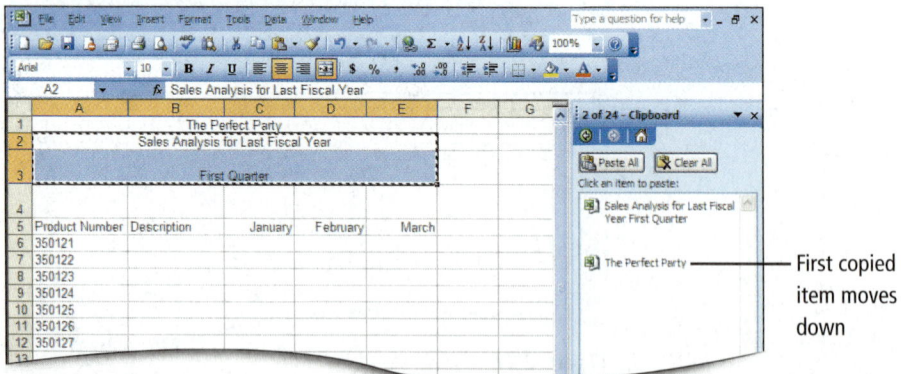

First copied item moves down

Figure 2.24

9 Navigate to **Sheet2**, select cell **A2**, and then press Ctrl + V.

The content of the copied cells is copied to the same cells in Sheet2. Notice that you did not have to select both cells A2 and A3. You need only select the top left cell of the paste range before performing the paste. Excel will select the correct cells for the remaining data.

10 In the upper left corner of your keyboard, press (Esc) to remove the **Paste Options** button.

Because you want to retain the source formatting, it is not necessary to display the Paste Options menu.

11 Using one of the copy techniques you have just practiced, navigate to **Sheet1**, select the range **A5:E5**, and then copy it. Navigate to **Sheet2**, and then paste to cell **A5**.

Notice that the widths of the columns on Sheet2 are not the same as those you have formatted on Sheet1.

12 Click the **Paste Options button arrow**, and then click **Keep Source Column Widths**.

The columns are adjusted to the same widths as those on Sheet1. This is a good example of the usefulness of smart tags in Excel.

13 On **Sheet2**, select **C5:E5**, and then press (Delete). Select cell **C5**, type **April** and press (Enter).

14 Click cell **C5**, and then drag the **fill handle** to the right to fill in *May* and *June* in cells **D5** and **E5**.

15 Select cell **A3**, click to place the insertion point in the Formula Bar, and then edit the heading as necessary to read **Second Quarter** Press (Enter), and then compare your screen with Figure 2.25.

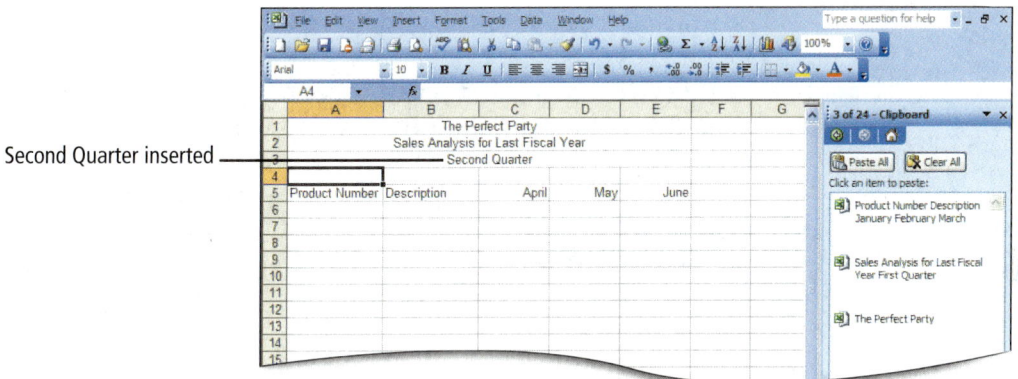

Second Quarter inserted

Figure 2.25

16 **Save** the changes you have made to your workbook.

> ### Note — Copying and Pasting a Single Item
> When copying and then pasting one item at a time, as you have done in the previous steps, it is not necessary to display the Clipboard task pane. The Paste command always takes its data from the top of the Clipboard, and as new items are stored on the Clipboard, they occupy the top position. It was useful to display the Clipboard here, however, so that you could have a visual indication of how the Clipboard works.

Activity 2.9 Copying Multiple Selections Using Collect and Paste

When copying and then pasting a single item, you can do so without displaying the Clipboard task pane. As you saw in the previous activity, each time you perform the Copy command, the selected cells move to the top of the Clipboard list, and each time you perform the Paste command, the item at the top of the list is pasted to the desired location.

Displaying the Clipboard is essential, however, if you want to collect a group of items and then paste them where you want them. The Clipboard can hold up to 24 items, and as you have seen, the Clipboard task pane displays a short representation of each item.

You can display the Clipboard task pane in one of three ways:

- If a different task pane is displayed, click the Other Task Panes arrow, and then click Clipboard.
- From the Edit menu, click Office Clipboard.
- Select the first cell or cells that you want to copy, hold down [Ctrl], and then quickly press [C] two times.

1 Navigate to **Sheet3**, click cell **A1**, and then at the top of the **Clipboard** task pane, click the **Paste All** button.

The three copied entries are all pasted into Sheet3, beginning in cell A1. The empty row above the monthly column headings was not copied, so it is not included. Compare your screen with Figure 2.26.

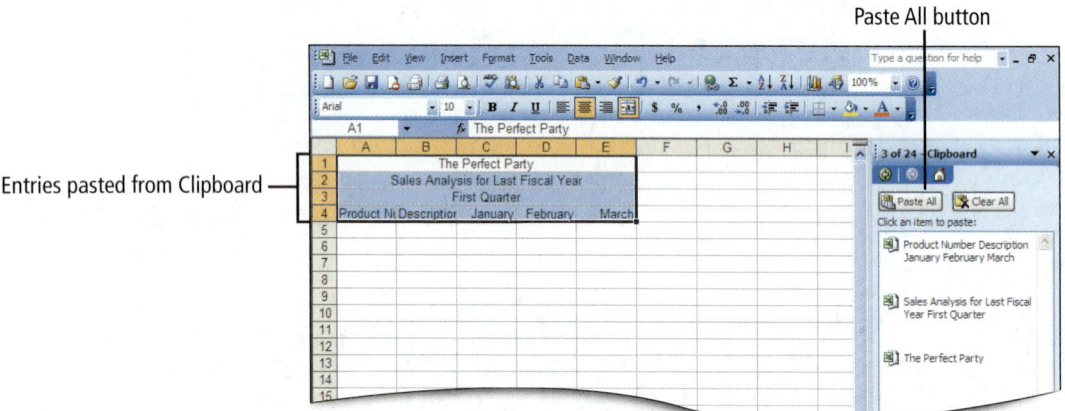

Figure 2.26

2 In the **row heading area**, right-click to simultaneously select **row 4** and display a shortcut menu. From the displayed menu, click **Insert**.

A blank row is inserted above the selected rows, and the rows are renumbered accordingly.

3 Select **columns A** and **B**, and then drag to increase the width to **102 pixels**. Use the same technique to widen **columns C** through **E** to **75 pixels**.

4 Delete *January*, *February*, and *March*, and then use **AutoFill** to change the months to *July*, *August*, and *September*.

[5] Edit cell **A3** to read **Third Quarter** and then compare your results with Figure 2.27.

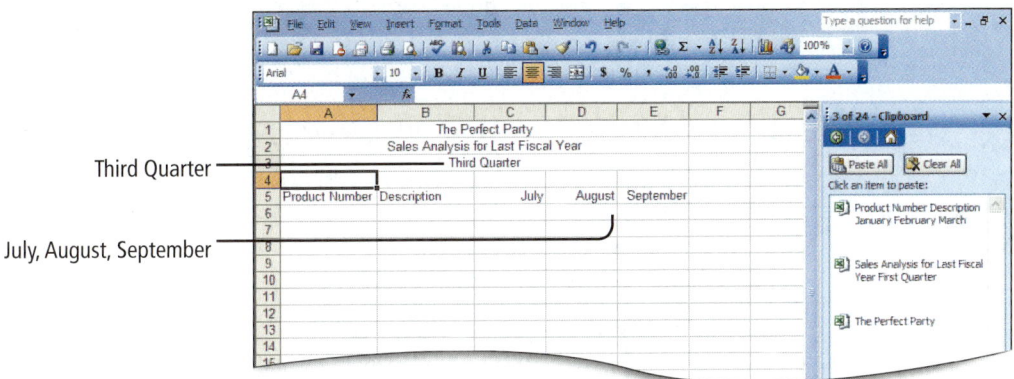

Figure 2.27

[6] On the **Clipboard**, click the **Clear All** button [Clear All], and **Close** [X] the **Clipboard** task pane. **Save** [icon] your workbook.

The collection of copied items is removed from the Clipboard.

Activity 2.10 Copying an Entire Worksheet to a New Worksheet

You can copy an entire worksheet to another worksheet in the same workbook.

[1] Be sure that **Sheet3** is displayed. From the **Edit** menu, click **Move or Copy Sheet**.

The Move or Copy dialog box displays.

[2] In the **Move or Copy** dialog box, under **Before sheet**, click **(move to end)**, and then select the **Create a copy** check box. Click **OK**.

A fourth worksheet named *Sheet3 (2)* displays, as shown in Figure 2.28. It contains a duplicate of all the data and formatting from Sheet3, from which it was copied.

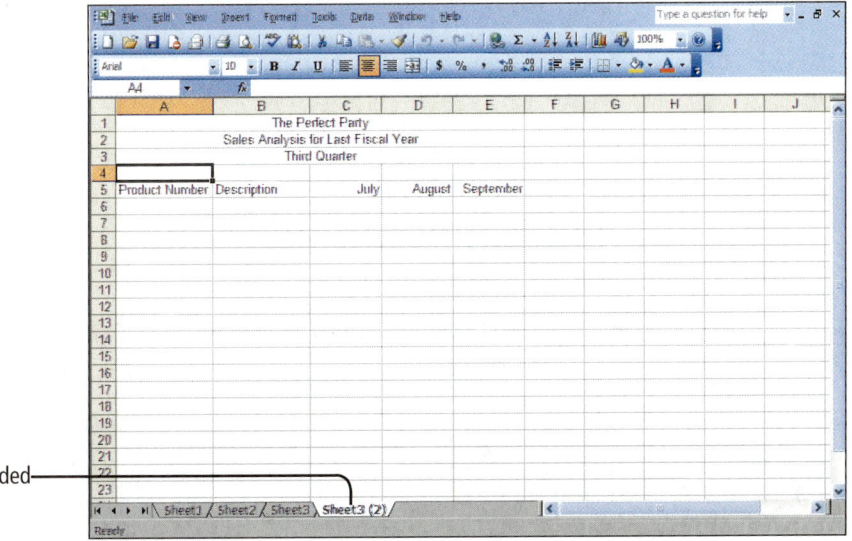

Figure 2.28

Project 2A: Sales Analysis | **Excel** 609

3 Right-click the **Sheet1 tab**, click **Rename**, type **First Qtr** and then rename the remaining sheets as **Second Qtr** and **Third Qtr** and **Fourth Qtr**

4 Display the **Fourth Qtr** sheet. Use **AutoFill** to change the months to *October*, *November*, and *December*.

5 Edit cell **A3** to read **Fourth Quarter** and compare your screen with Figure 2.29. Click **Save** to save the changes you have made to your workbook.

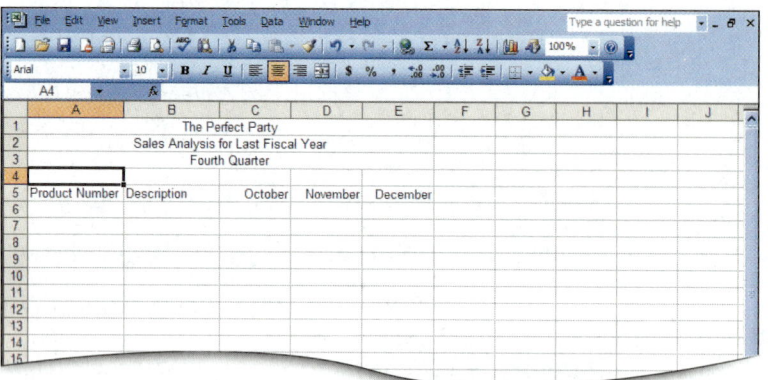

Figure 2.29

Activity 2.11 Pasting Data from Another Workbook

You can paste data from one workbook into another workbook.

1 From the **File** menu, click **Open**, click the **Look in arrow**, and then navigate to the student files that accompany this textbook. Click to select the file **e02A_Data**, and then click **Open**.

The workbook e02A_Data displays. This workbook contains a year of sales data for The Perfect Party.

2 From the **Edit** menu, click **Office Clipboard**. If necessary, click the **Clear All** button to clear any items from the Clipboard. Click cell **A2**, hold down Shift, and then click cell **B17**.

The range A2:B17 is selected. You can select a range of consecutive cells by clicking the first cell in the range, holding down Shift, and then clicking the last cell in the range. Alternatively, you can drag from the first to the last cell in the range.

3 On the Standard toolbar, click the **Copy** button.

The selected range is surrounded by a moving border, and the range is copied to the Clipboard, as shown in Figure 2.30.

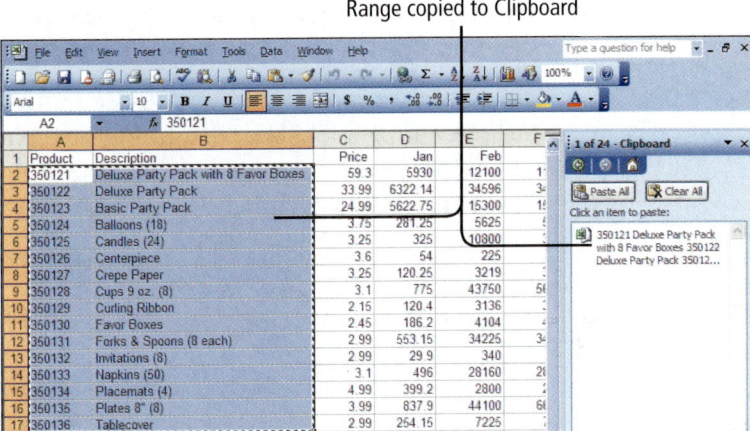

Figure 2.30

4 Click cell **D2**, hold down Shift, and then click cell **F17** to select the range. Click the **Copy** button.

The dollar amounts for the first quarter, January through March, are copied to the Clipboard. Compare your screen with Figure 2.31.

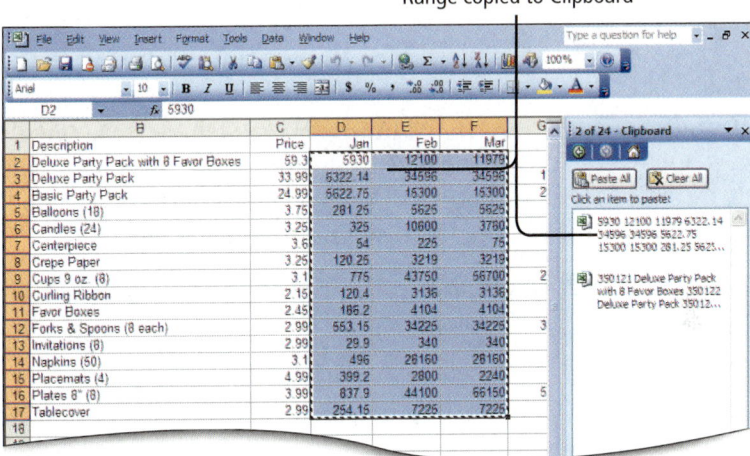

Figure 2.31

5 On the menu bar, click **Window**, and then at the bottom of the menu, click the **2A_Sales_Analysis** workbook containing your name. Alternatively, click the name of your workbook on the taskbar.

6 Display the **First Qtr** worksheet. Click cell **A6** to set the active cell, and then on the task pane, click the second entry, which begins *350121 Deluxe Party Pack*.

The product numbers and descriptions are copied from the Clipboard to the active worksheet beginning at the active cell. Data in cells A2:A12 was overwritten by the paste operation. It was not necessary to clear the cells first.

Project 2A: Sales Analysis | **Excel** 611

7 Click cell **C6** to set the active cell, and then on the task pane, click the entry beginning *5930*.

The sales amounts for the first three months of the year are copied into the active worksheet beginning at the active cell. This process of copying multiple pieces of data to the Clipboard and then pasting the data into another location is called **collect and paste**. Compare your screen with Figure 2.32.

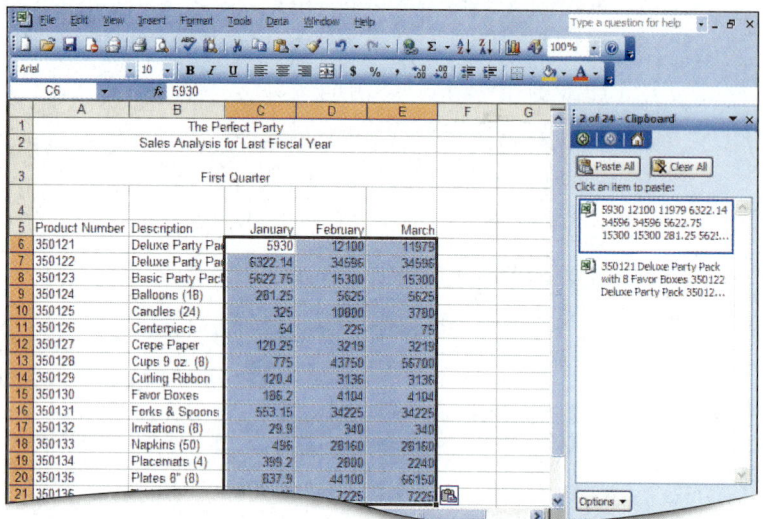

Figure 2.32

8 From the **Window** menu, click **e02A_Data** to return to the worksheet with the sales amounts. Scroll as necessary to view **columns G through I**. To select the second quarter dollar amounts, click cell **G2**, hold down Shift, and then click cell **I17**.

9 Right-click in the selected area, and then from the shortcut menu, click **Copy**.

The second quarter's data is copied and moves to the top of the Clipboard.

10 On the taskbar, click your workbook **2A_Sales_Analysis**.

Recall that the taskbar can also be used to switch between open workbooks.

11 Display the **Second Qtr** worksheet. Click **A6** to set the active cell, and then on the Clipboard, click the entry beginning with *350121 Deluxe Party Pack*.

The product numbers and descriptions are copied from the Clipboard and pasted to the active worksheet beginning at the active cell in the second quarter's sheet. Items collected on the Clipboard can be pasted as many times as needed.

12 Click **C6** to set the active cell, and then on the Clipboard click the entry beginning with *9900*.

The sales amounts for the second three-month quarter of the year are copied into the active worksheet beginning at the active cell.

13 Navigate to the **e02A_Data** workbook, select the range **J2:L17**, and copy the range to the Clipboard. Then, display your **2A_Sales_Analysis** workbook and click the sheet tab for the **Third Qtr**.

14 Click cell **A6**, and then from the Clipboard, paste the last item, which begins *350121 Deluxe Party Pack*. Then click cell **C6**, and from the Clipboard, paste the first item, which begins *13650*.

The sales amounts for the third quarter are pasted into the Third Qtr worksheet. Compare your screen with Figure 2.33.

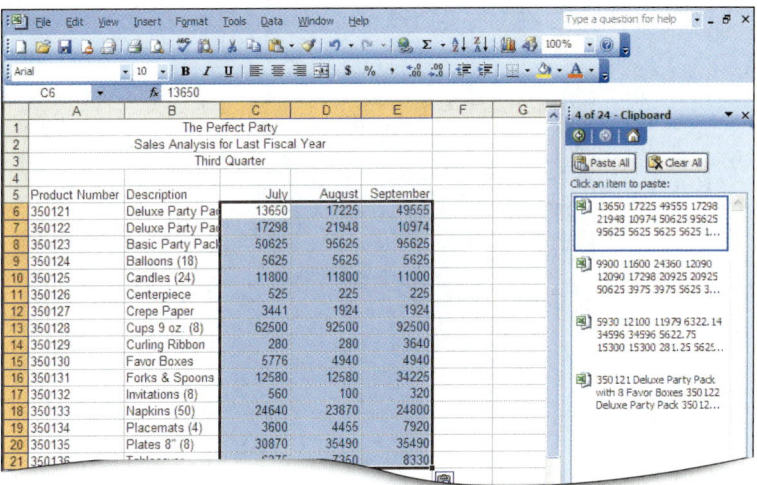

Figure 2.33

15 From the **e02A_Data** workbook, copy the range **M2:O17** to the Clipboard. Then display the **Fourth Qtr** worksheet of your **2A_Sales_Analysis** workbook. In cell **A6**, paste the last item on the Clipboard—the product numbers and descriptions. In cell **C6**, paste the first item on the Clipboard, which begins *20196*.

The sales amounts for the fourth quarter are pasted into the Fourth Qtr worksheet. Compare your screen with Figure 2.34.

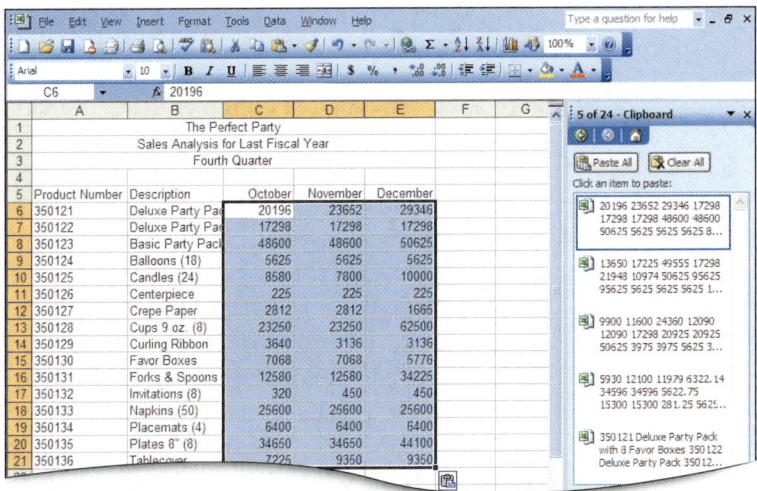

Figure 2.34

16 Right-click on the **First Qtr tab**, and then click **Select All Sheets**.

[Group] displays in the title bar.

Project 2A: Sales Analysis | **Excel** 613

17 Select **column B**, display the **Format** menu, point to **Column**, and then click **AutoFit Selection**.

Column B is widened to accommodate the longest entry in the column. Because you selected all sheets, this action is applied to all four sheets in the workbook. Compare your screen with Figure 2.35.

Column B widened

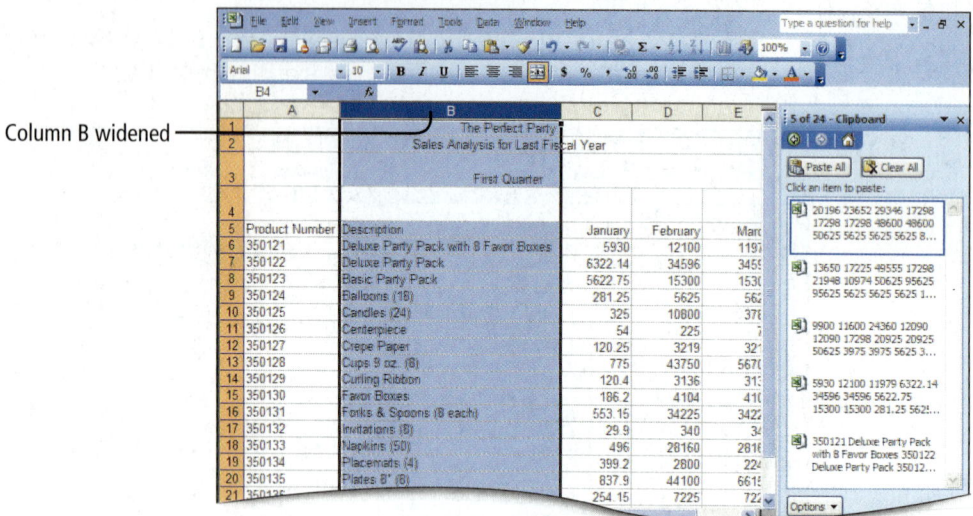

Figure 2.35

18 Display the **Second Qtr**, **Third Qtr**, and **Fourth Qtr** worksheets to verify that **column B** was widened on each.

By displaying other worksheets, the sheets are automatically ungrouped, and the word *[Group]* is removed from the title bar.

19 With your **2A_Sales_Analysis** workbook displayed, on the Standard toolbar, click the **Save** button.

20 On the taskbar, click the **e02A_Data** button to display the workbook. From the **File** menu, click **Close**. If prompted to save the changes, click **No**.

21 On the **Clipboard** task pane, click the **Close** button.

Activity 2.12 Moving Cell Contents Using the Cut Command

1 Be sure that your **2A_Sales_Analysis** workbook is open, and then display the **First Qtr** worksheet. If necessary, close the task pane.

2 Click cell **E21**, and then on the Standard toolbar, click the **Cut** button.

A moving border surrounds the cell that has been cut, and a copy of the contents of the cell is moved to the Clipboard. Because you are not going to collect or paste multiple items, it is not necessary to view the Clipboard. As you have seen, the most recent Clipboard item goes to the top of the Clipboard list.

3 Pause your mouse pointer over cell **F21**, right-click, and then from the displayed shortcut menu, click **Paste**.

The content of cell E21 is moved from the Clipboard to cell F21. The

614   Excel | Chapter 2: Editing Workbooks, Formulas, and Cells

Cut command removes text from one location and lets you paste it to another location. The Paste operation automatically uses the first Clipboard item. Thus, unless you need to choose some other pasted item, it is not necessary to display the Clipboard.

4 Select the range **E6:E20**. Pause the pointer over the selection, and right-click. From the displayed shortcut menu, click **Cut**.

A moving border surrounds the selection, and a copy of the cell content is moved to the top of the Clipboard list. Compare your screen with Figure 2.36.

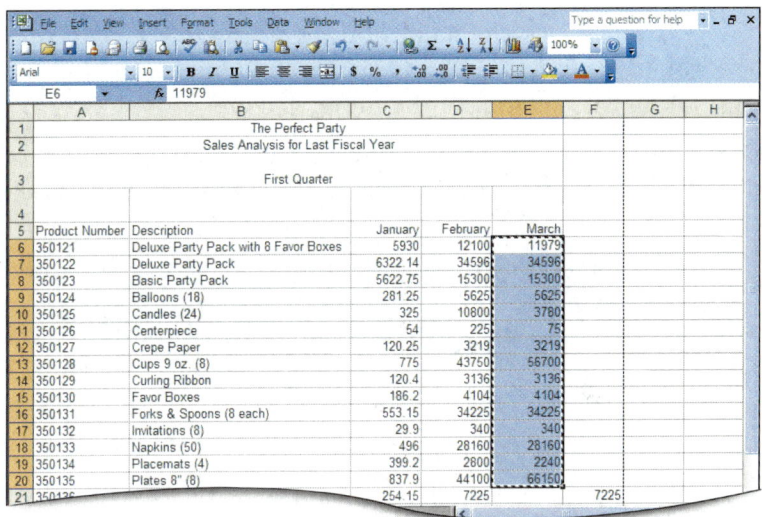

Figure 2.36

5 Select cell **F6**, hold down Ctrl, and press V.

Ctrl + V is the keyboard shortcut for the Paste command. The range of cells cut from E6:E21 is moved from the Clipboard and pasted into a similar range beginning in cell F6. When pasting a range of cells, it is necessary only to select the starting cell.

6 On the Standard toolbar, click **Undo** two times to restore the contents of cells **E6:E21**, and then press Esc to clear the moving border surrounding cell **E21**. Compare your screen with Figure 2.37.

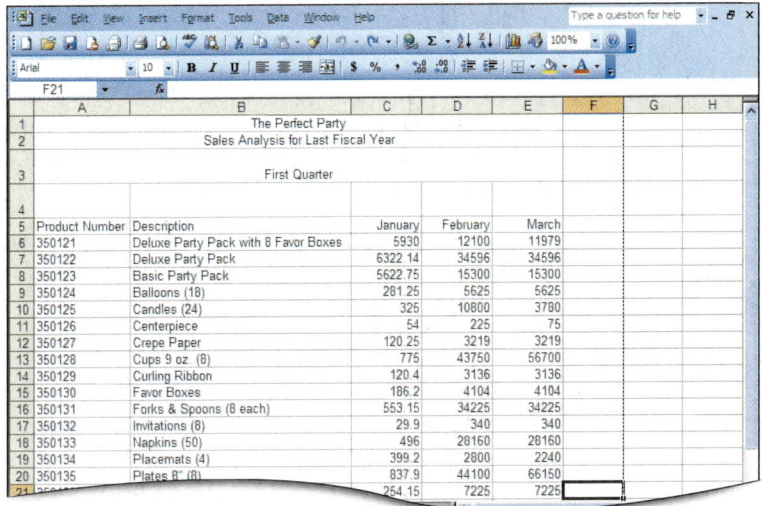

Figure 2.37

Project 2A: Sales Analysis | **Excel** 615

7 Click **Save**.

Activity 2.13 Moving Cell Contents Using Drag-and-Drop

The Cut command is one way to move the contents of one or more cells from one location to another. In this activity, you will use the mouse to move the contents of a cell.

1 With your **2A_Sales_Analysis** workbook open and the **First Qtr** worksheet displayed, select the range **E17:E21**.

2 Pause your mouse over the black cell border until the **move** pointer displays, and then drag to the right until the ScreenTip displays **G17:G21**, as shown in Figure 2.38, and then release the mouse to complete the move.

Using this technique, cell contents can be moved from one location to another. This is referred to as ***drag-and-drop***.

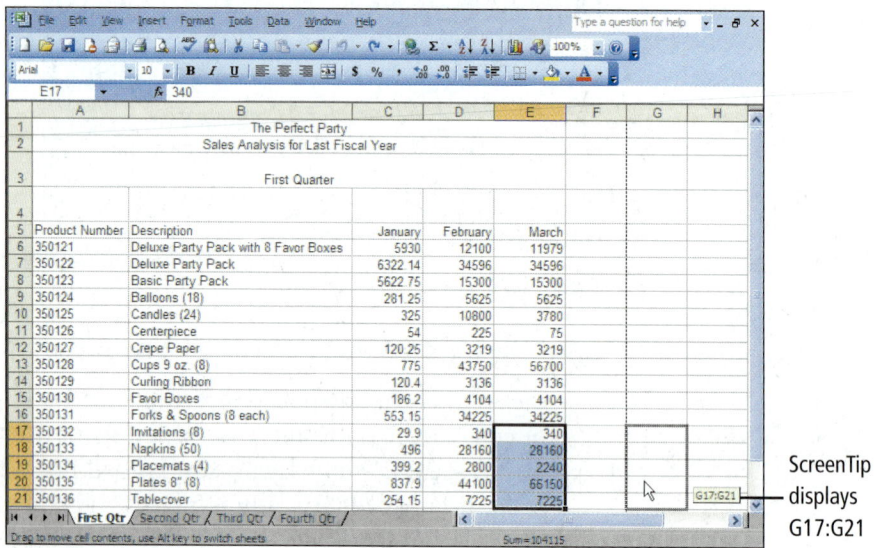

Figure 2.38

3 With the range **G17:G21** still selected, use the same technique to drag and then drop the range back to its original location, **E17:E21**.

4 On the Standard toolbar, click the **Save** button. From the **File** menu, click **Print**. Under **Print what**, click the **Entire workbook** option button. Click **OK** to print the four worksheets in the workbook. Close the file, and then close Excel.

End You have completed Project 2A

Project 2B Annual Sales

In this project, you will edit numbers from the Formatting toolbar and copy and edit formulas. You will also conduct a what-if analysis—a business technique in which you determine what will happen if you change values in one or more cells.

In Activities 2.14 through 2.25, you will edit a workbook for Angie Nguyen and Gabriela Quinones, owners of The Perfect Party, that shows the sales totals and product percentages for the previous fiscal year. The resulting workbook will look similar to Figure 2.39. You will save your workbook as *2B_Annual_Sales_ Firstname_Lastname*.

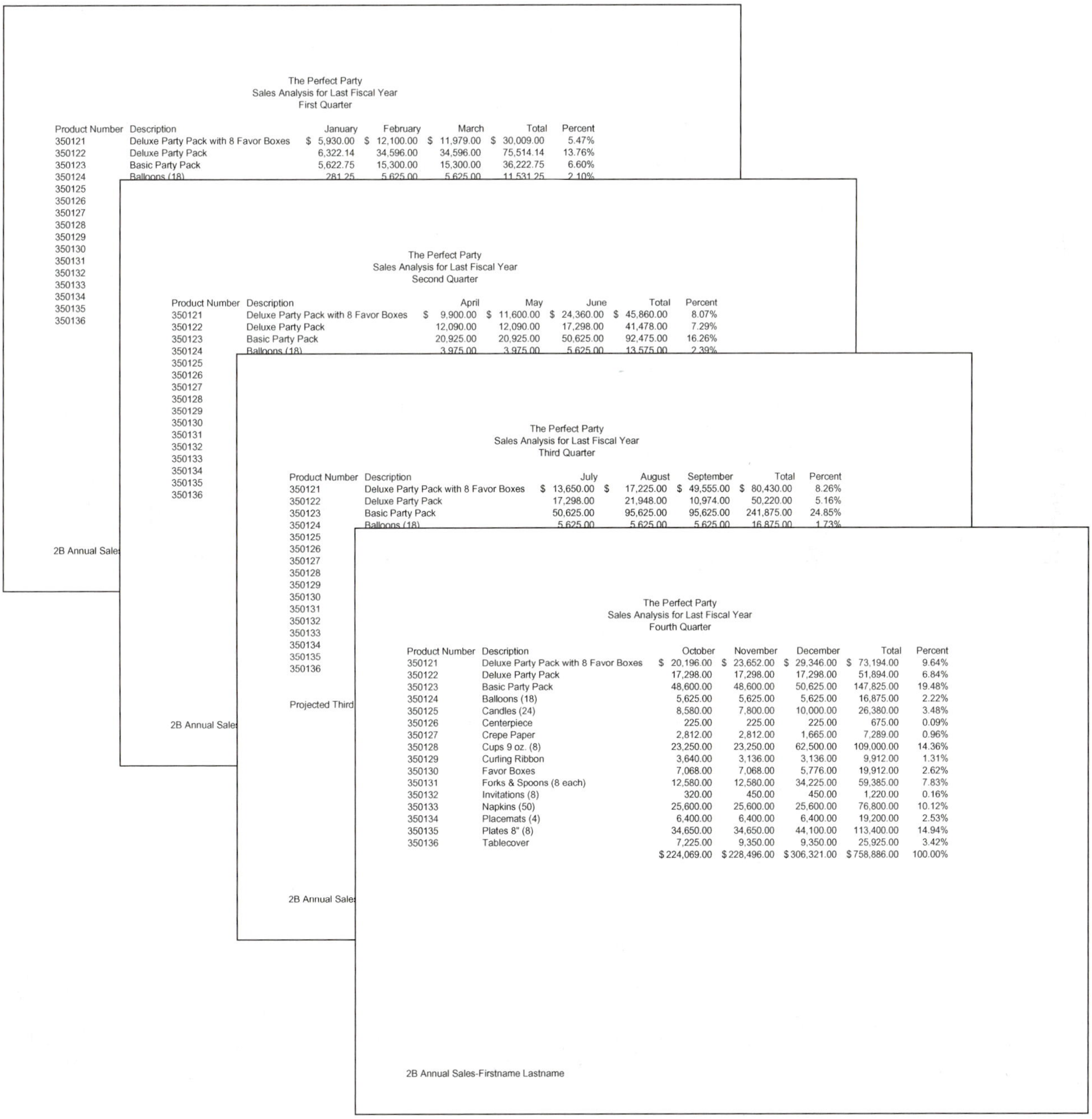

Figure 2.39

Objective 5
Format Numbers Using the Toolbar

Financial data is formatted with thousand comma separators, decimals, and dollar signs ($). By default, numbers in Excel are right-aligned in the cell and have no formats applied. To apply formats, you must either type them or use Excel features to apply them.

Dollar amounts such as sales figures are usually shown with two decimal places and commas inserted to separate values into thousands, millions, and so forth. Additionally, the first row of dollar amounts and the total row of dollar amounts usually display the dollar sign.

Activity 2.14 Formatting Cells with the Currency Style Button

The Currency Style button on the Formatting toolbar applies several cell formatting attributes in a single mouse click, including the dollar sign ($), thousand commas, separator and two decimal places to the selected cell. This is the style used for *currency* (monetary values) displayed in dollars and cents.

1 **Start** Excel. Display the **File** menu, and then click **Open**. Navigate to the student files that accompany this textbook, and then open the workbook **e02B_Annual_Sales**.

2 From the **File** menu, click **Save As**. In the displayed **Save As** dialog box, use the **Look in arrow** to navigate to the location where you are storing your projects for this chapter. In the **File name** box, type **2B_Annual_Sales_Firstname_Lastname** and press [Enter].

3 Right-click the **First Qtr sheet tab**, and then click **Select All Sheets**.

4 Display the **View** menu, click **Header and Footer**, click the **Custom Footer** button, and under **Left section**, type **2B Annual Sales-Firstname Lastname** using your own first and last name.

5 Click **OK** to close the **Footer** dialog box, and then click **OK** again to close the **Page Setup** dialog box.

A dotted vertical line displays, indicating how many columns will print on the page as the page is currently set up. Do not be concerned if it appears that the columns will not fit on a single page—you will have an opportunity to adjust this before you complete the project.

6 Click the **Second Qtr sheet tab**, and then click the **First Qtr sheet** tab again.

Notice that *[Group]* no longer displays in the title bar. Displaying another worksheet automatically ungroups the sheets.

7 With the **First Qtr** worksheet displayed, select the range **C6:F6**, and then on the Formatting toolbar, click the **Currency Style** button [$].

As shown in Figure 2.40, some cells display ########, indicating that the cell is not wide enough to accommodate the newly formatted numeric data.

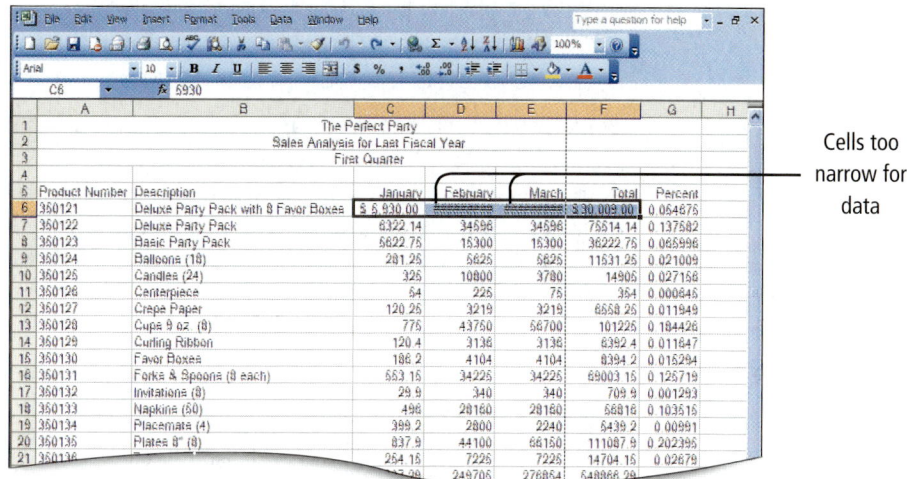

Figure 2.40

8 Select the range **C22:F22**, and then on the Formatting toolbar, click the **Currency Style** button.

The overall total, $548,866.29, is properly formatted, but the column width is not large enough to accommodate the monthly totals—they display as ##########.

9 From the **column heading area**, drag to select **columns C, D, E, and F**.

Recall that when multiple columns are selected, any changes you make are applied to all the selected columns.

10 In the **column heading area**, move the pointer over the vertical line that separates **columns C** and **D** until the double-headed arrow pointer displays, as shown in Figure 2.41, and then double-click.

This is the mouse shortcut to AutoFit selected columns to accommodate their longest entry. Alternatively, from the Format menu, point to Column and then click AutoFit selection. Each column now accommodates the totals with the currency format applied.

Figure 2.41

Project 2B: Annual Sales | **Excel** 619

11 Click outside the selected area to cancel the selection, and then, on the Standard toolbar, click the **Save** button . Compare your screen with Figure 2.42.

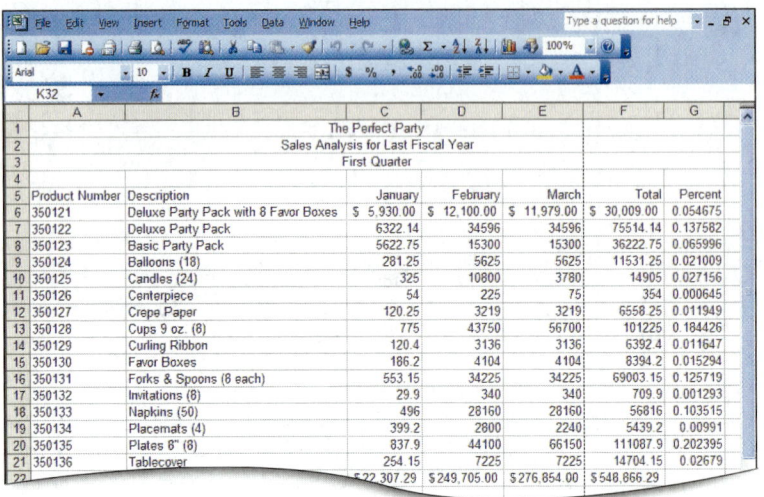

Figure 2.42

Activity 2.15 Formatting Cells with the Percent Style Button

A percentage is a part of a whole expressed in hundredths. For example, .75 is the same as 75% percent of one dollar. The Percent Style button on the Formatting toolbar formats the selected cell as a percentage rounded to the nearest hundredth.

1 Click cell **G6**, and notice the number *0.054675*.

This number is the result of dividing the value in F6 (total quarterly sales for Product Number 350121) by the total in cell F22 (total quarterly sales for all products combined). Applying the Percent Style to 0.054675 will result in 5%—0.0545675 rounded up to the nearest hundredth and expressed as a percentage.

2 With cell **G6** selected, on the Formatting toolbar, click the **Percent Style** button .

The result, 5%, indicates that 5 percent of the total sales for the first quarter of the fiscal year resulted from selling the *Deluxe Party Pack with 8 Favor Boxes* product.

3 Select the range **G7:G21**, click the **Percent Style** button to format the remaining cells, and then click outside the selected area to cancel the selection. Compare your screen with Figure 2.43.

4 **Save** your workbook.

620   Excel | Chapter 2: Editing Workbooks, Formulas, and Cells

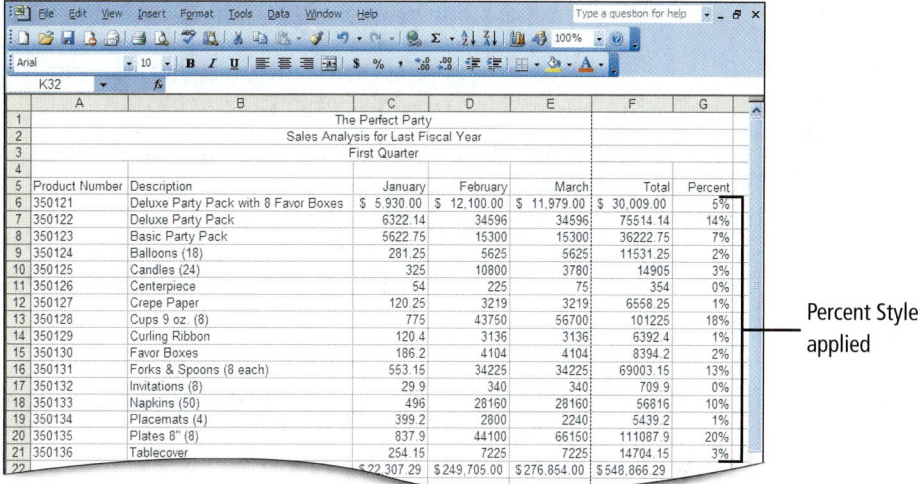

Figure 2.43

Activity 2.16 Increasing and Decreasing Decimal Places

Rounding percentages to the nearest hundredth may not offer a percentage precise enough to analyze important financial information such as sales data. For example, on your displayed worksheet, some product percentages indicate 0%. To make data more precise, Excel can add additional decimal places.

1 With your **2B_Sales_Analysis** workbook open and the **First Qtr** worksheet displayed, locate the percentages for the products in **row 11** and **row 17**.

Obviously, there were sales of these two products, but the sales were less than 1%; thus, the percentage, as currently expressed, indicates 0%.

2 Select the range **G6:G21**, and then on the Formatting toolbar, click the **Increase Decimal** button three times.

The percentages display with three decimal places, as shown in Figure 2.44. The cells that displayed 0% now contain a more meaningful value. The Increase Decimal command increases the display by one decimal position each time it is clicked.

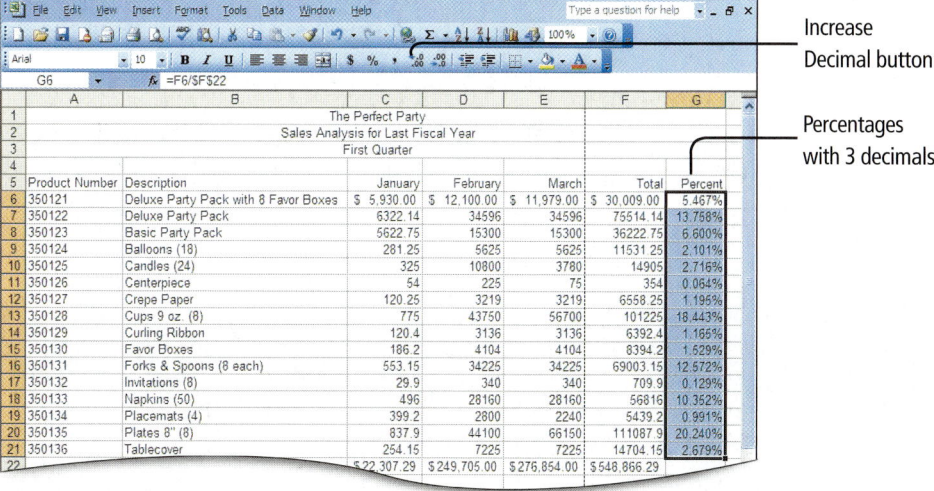

Figure 2.44

Project 2B: Annual Sales | Excel 621

3 With cells **G6:G21** selected, on the Formatting toolbar click the **Decrease Decimal** button once, and then click outside the selected area to cancel the selection.

The percentages display with two decimal places. The Decrease Decimal command decreases one decimal position each time it is clicked.

4 Compare your screen with Figure 2.45. Click **Save**.

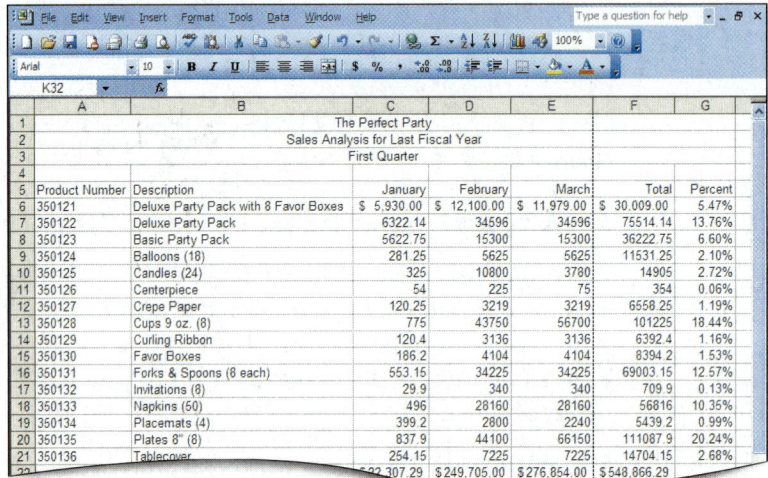

Figure 2.45

Activity 2.17 Formatting Cells with the Comma Style Button

When preparing spreadsheets with financial information, the first row of dollar amounts and the total rows of dollar amounts are formatted in the Currency Style; that is, with thousand comma separators, dollar signs, and two decimal places.

All other dollar amounts in the worksheet are usually formatted only with thousand comma separators and two decimal places. This format, referred to as *Comma Style*, is easily applied with the Comma Style button on the Formatting toolbar.

1 Be sure your **First Qtr** worksheet is displayed. Select the range **C7:F21**, and then on the Formatting toolbar, click the **Comma Style** button. Click outside the selected area to cancel the selection.

The selected cells are formatted with two decimals and thousand comma separators, as shown in Figure 2.46.

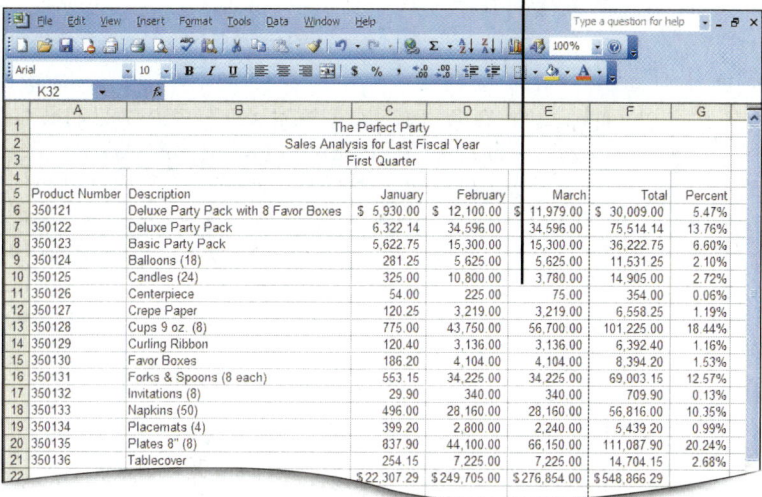

Figure 2.46

2 On the Standard toolbar, click the **Save** button.

Objective 6
Edit Formulas

Recall that data in a cell can be only one of two things—either a formula, which is an instruction for a mathematical calculation, or a constant value. Constant values fall into three main categories:

- Numeric values (numbers)
- Text values (text or a combination of text and numbers such as a street address)
- Date and time values

Activity 2.18 Selecting Ranges Using the AutoSum Function

Recall that AutoSum is one of many *functions*—formulas that Excel has already built for you. AutoSum is frequently used, and thus has its own button on the Standard toolbar. When you initiate the AutoSum command, Excel first looks *above* the cell to propose a group of numbers to add. In this activity, you will discover that there is additional versatility in the AutoSum function.

1 Be sure that your **2B_Annual_Sales** workbook is open. Then, click the **Second Qtr sheet tab**.

2 In cell **F5** type **Total** and in cell **G5** type **Percent**

3 Click cell **A1** and notice that this is a merged cell encompassing the range **A1:E1**.

Now that you have added two additional columns, it will be necessary to adjust the centering of the title and the two subtitles.

Project 2B: Annual Sales | **Excel** 623

4 Select the range **A1:G1** as shown in Figure 2.47.

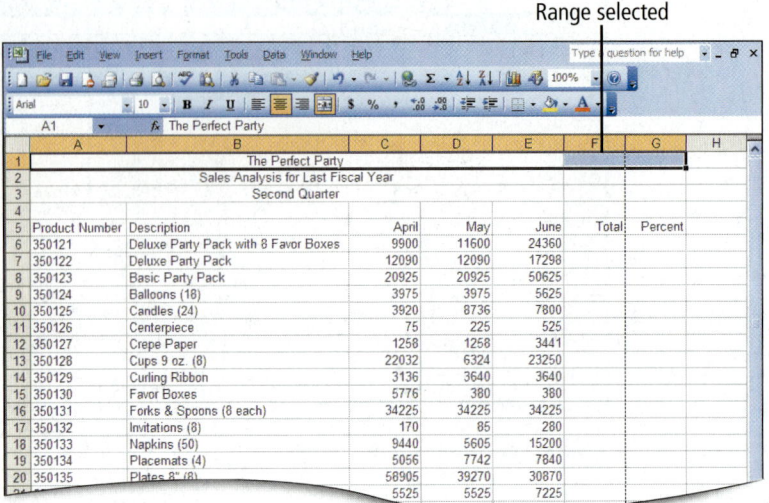

Figure 2.47

5 On the Formatting toolbar, click the **Merge and Center** button once.

Recall that if a cell has been merged and centered, clicking the Merge and Center button again reverses the action, as shown in Figure 2.48.

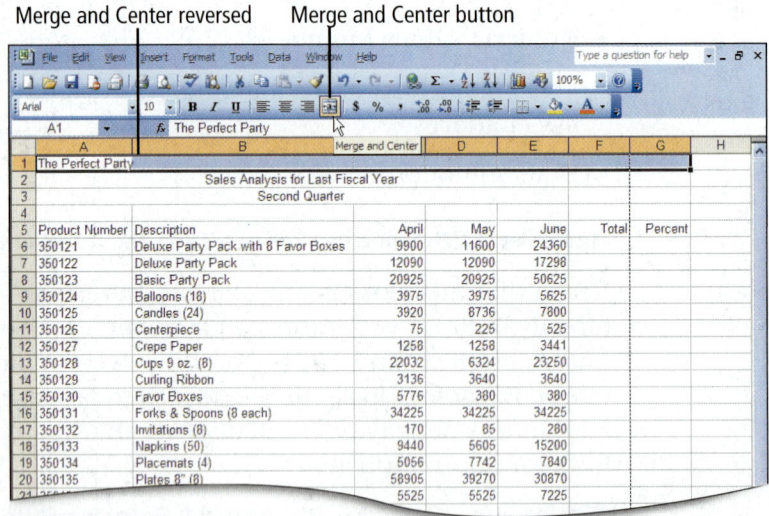

Figure 2.48

6 With the range still selected, click **Merge and Center** again.

Cells A1:G1 are merged into one cell, and the text is centered in the cell.

7 Use the technique you just practiced to merge and center the subtitle *Sales Analysis for Last Fiscal Year* across the range **A2:G2**, and then repeat the process for the subtitle *Second Quarter* across the range **A3:G3**. Compare your screen with Figure 2.49.

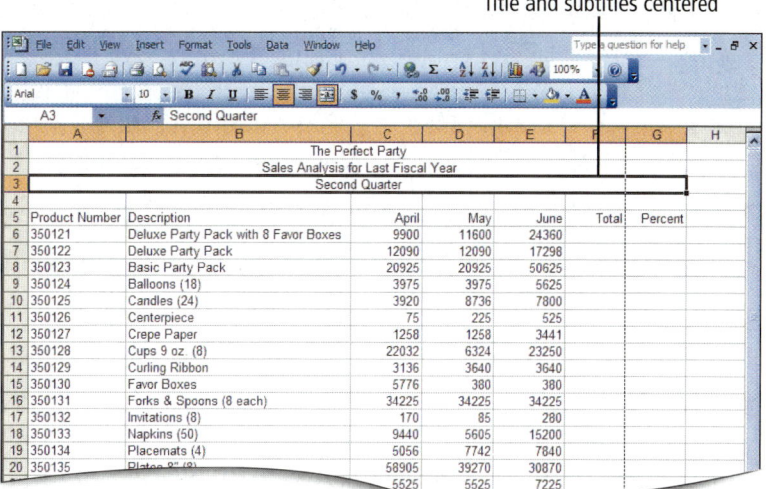

Figure 2.49

8 Click **C22** to make it the active cell, and then on the Standard toolbar, click the **AutoSum** button .

A moving border surrounds the April sales numbers, as shown in Figure 2.50.

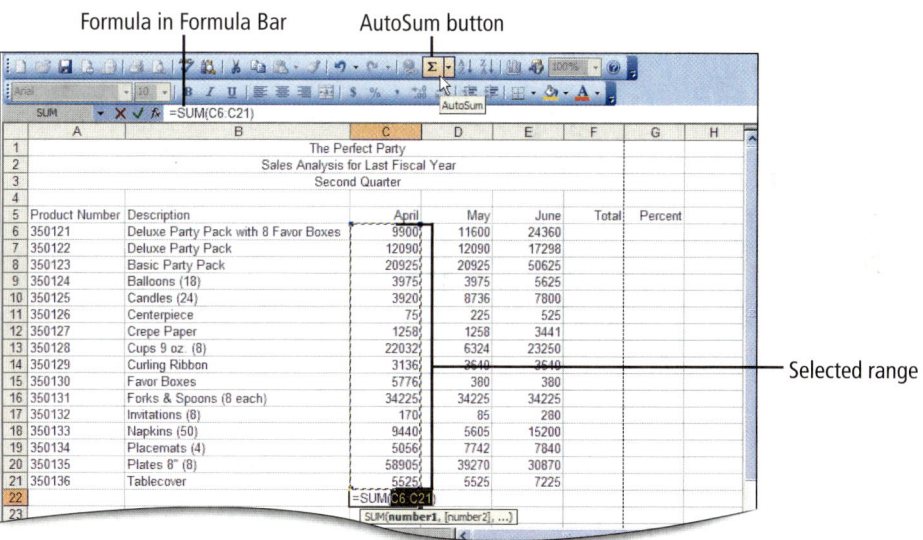

Figure 2.50

9 Look at the Formula Bar.

The word *SUM*, the function name, indicates that Excel will add (sum) the values contained in the cells referenced in the range *(C6:C21)*. See Figure 2.50.

10 Press Enter to accept the formula created by AutoSum.

The sum *196408* displays in cell C22.

Project 2B: Annual Sales | **Excel** 625

11 Click cell **C13**, type **483** and then press Enter.

483 displays in cell C13, and Excel recalculates the sum in cell C22 as *174859*. Recall that this is Excel's great strength. After formulas are in place, Excel recalculates the formula each time a value changes in any of the cells referenced in the formula.

12 Select the range **D6:D21**—the May sales amounts.

13 On the Standard toolbar, click the **AutoSum** button Σ.

The result, *161605*, displays in cell D22. This is another way that you can use AutoSum. Using this method, Excel places the formula in the first empty cell following the selected range.

14 Click cell **D22** and look at the Formula Bar.

The underlying formula, inserted by AutoSum, displays, as shown in Figure 2.51.

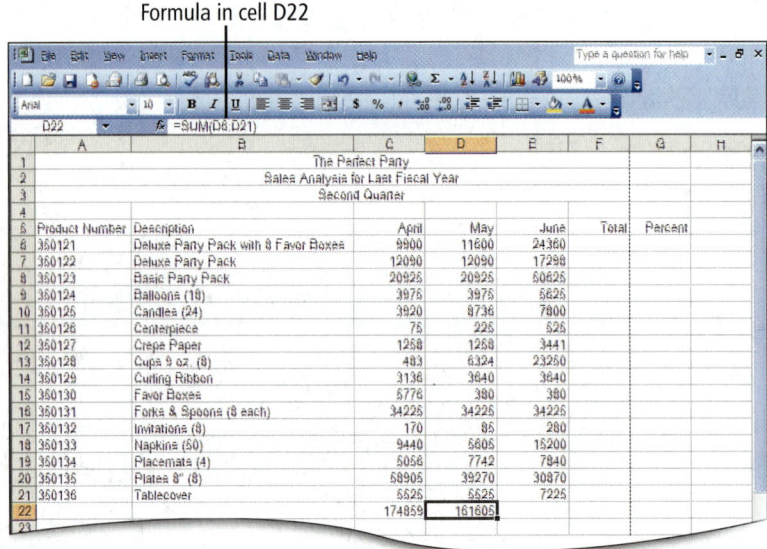

Formula in cell D22

Figure 2.51

15 Click **E11**, and then press Delete to clear the value from the cell.

16 Click cell **E22**, and then on the Standard toolbar, click **AutoSum** Σ.

As shown in Figure 2.52, Excel selects only the range E12:E21 because E11 does not contain a value.

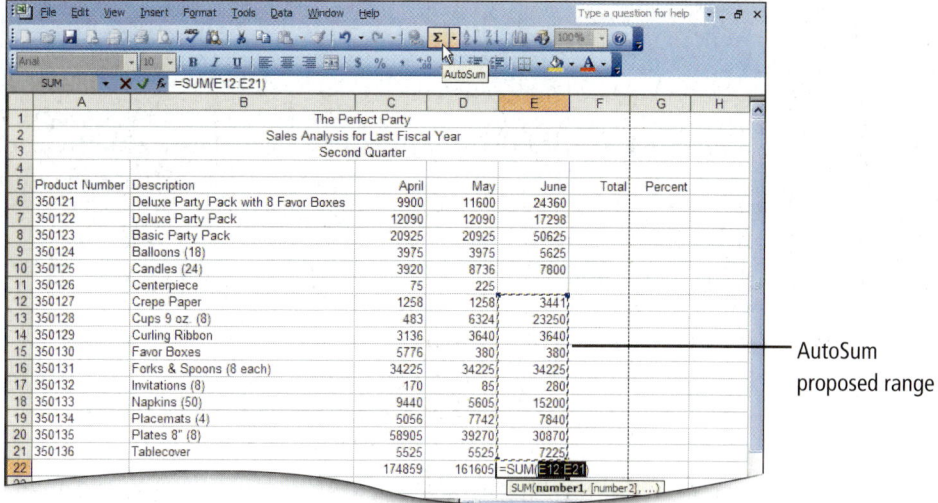

Figure 2.52

17 With the moving border still displayed, drag to select the range **E6:E21**.

Excel changes the selection and displays the new range of referenced cells in the formula. Because AutoSum will not automatically include an empty cell in a range, use this method to select a range containing an empty cell. In this manner, you can still take advantage of the ease with which AutoSum creates a formula.

18 Press [Enter] to insert the formula and calculate the total. In cell **E11**, type **75** and press [Enter] again to recalculate the formula.

The result, *232134*, displays. Compare your screen with Figure 2.53.

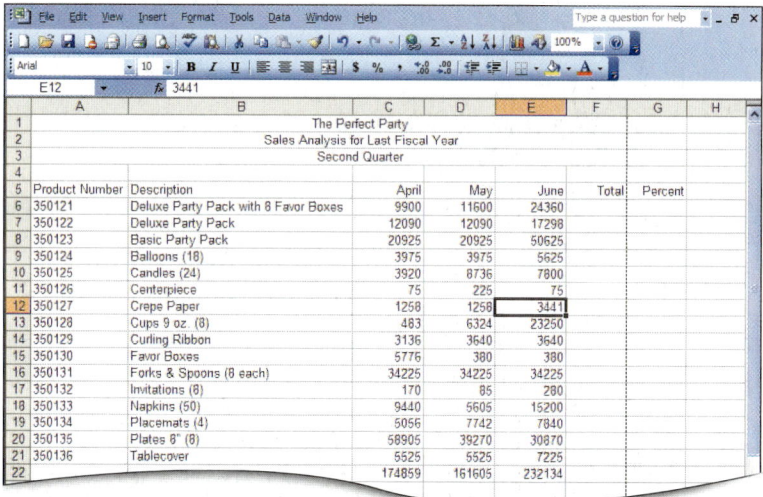

Figure 2.53

19 Select the range **C22:E22** and apply the **Currency Style**. Then, display the **Format** menu, point to **Column**, and click **AutoFit Selection**.

Recall that AutoFit Selection widens the column to accommodate the data in the selected cell or, if the entire column is selected, for the widest entry in the column.

20 Select the range **C6:E6** and apply the **Currency Style**. Select the range **C7:E21** and apply the **Comma Style**. On the Standard toolbar, click **Save**. Click outside the selection to deselect it, and compare your screen with Figure 2.54.

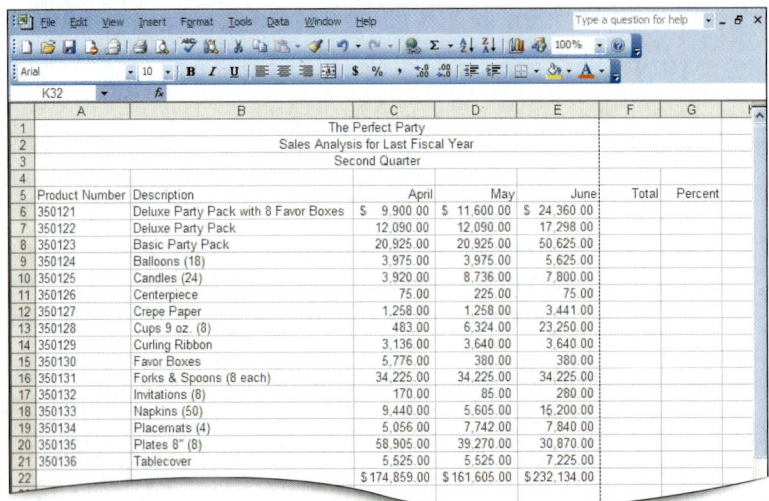

Figure 2.54

21 Click the **Third Qtr sheet tab**. In cell **F5** type **Total** and in cell **G5** type **Percent**

22 Select the range **A1:G1** and click the **Merge and Center** button two times to merge the cells and recenter the title. Repeat the process for the range **A2:G2** and for **A3:G3**.

23 In row 22, use **AutoSum** to total the columns for each of the three months in the quarter. Select the range **C6:E6**, hold down Ctrl and select the range **C22:E22**, and then apply the **Currency Style**. To make the columns wide enough to accommodate their newly formatted data, select **columns C**, **D**, and **E**, and use either the double-click method between two of the column headings, or display the Format menu to apply AutoFit Selection to the selected columns.

24 Select the range **C7:E21** and apply the **Comma Style**. Click anywhere to deselect the range, and compare your screen with Figure 2.55.

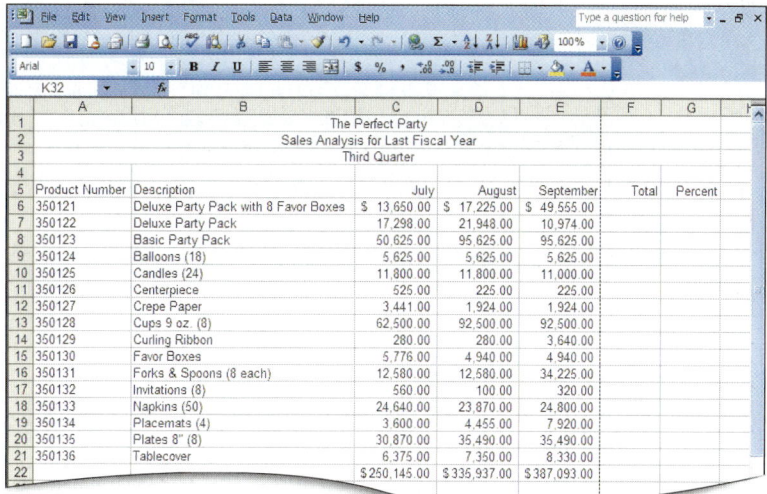

Figure 2.55

25 Select the **Fourth Qtr sheet tab**. In cell **F5** type **Total** and in cell **G5** type **Percent** and then repeat Steps 22–24. Compare your result with Figure 2.56.

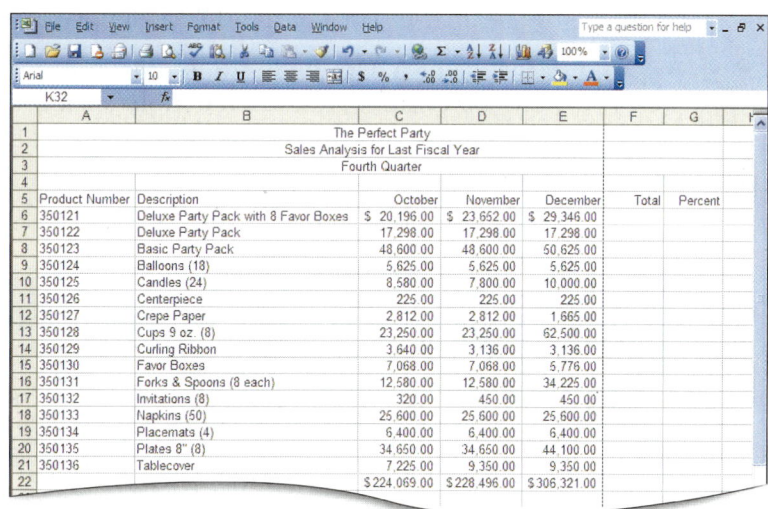

Figure 2.56

26 On the Standard toolbar, click **Save** to save your workbook.

Activity 2.19 Editing Within the Formula Bar

1 In your **2B_Annual_Sales** workbook, display the **Second Qtr** worksheet.

2 Click cell **F6**, click the **AutoSum** button, and compare your screen with Figure 2.57.

Recall that AutoSum first looks above the selected cell, and then, if no values are present, looks to the left for a proposed range of values to sum.

Project 2B: Annual Sales | **Excel**   629

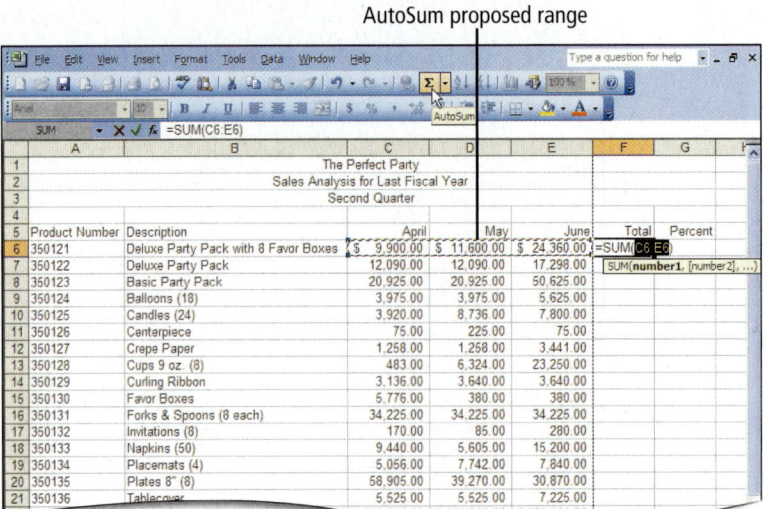

Figure 2.57

3 Press Enter.

The total, *$45,860.00*, displays in cell F6 and is formatted in the Currency Style. Recall that if adjacent cells have formatting applied, the next three cells to the right will have the same formatting applied.

4 Select cell **F6**. On the Formula Bar, position the **I-beam** pointer between *C* and *6*, and then double-click to select the cell reference **C6**. Point to cell **D6**, as shown in Figure 2.58.

Figure 2.58

5 Click once to border cells **D6:E6** in blue, and then press Enter to accept this change to the formula. In cell **F6**, locate the small green triangle in the upper left corner, as shown in Figure 2.59.

The green triangle is the ***Trace Error*** smart tag, which indicates a potential error in a formula.

630   Excel | Chapter 2: Editing Workbooks, Formulas, and Cells

Green triangle in cell

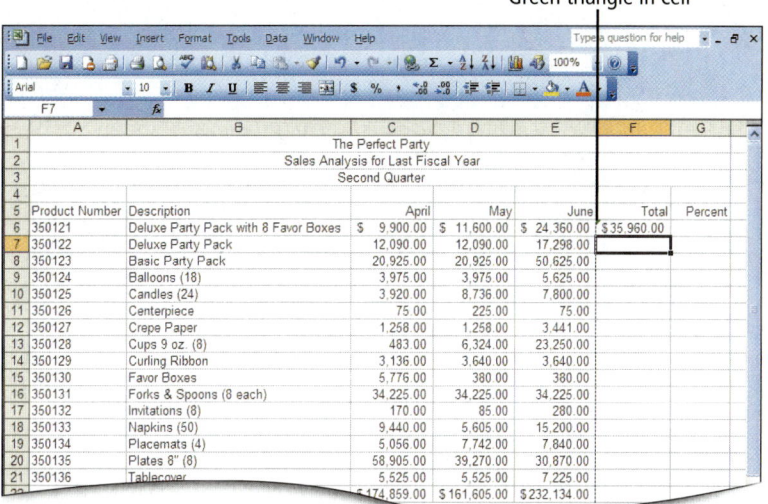

Figure 2.59

6 Select cell **F6** and then point to the displayed **Trace Error** button, as shown in Figure 2.60.

The ScreenTip indicates *The formula in this cell refers to a range that has additional numbers adjacent to it.* This is Excel's method for alerting you that, logically, it would appear that you want to total all three cells.

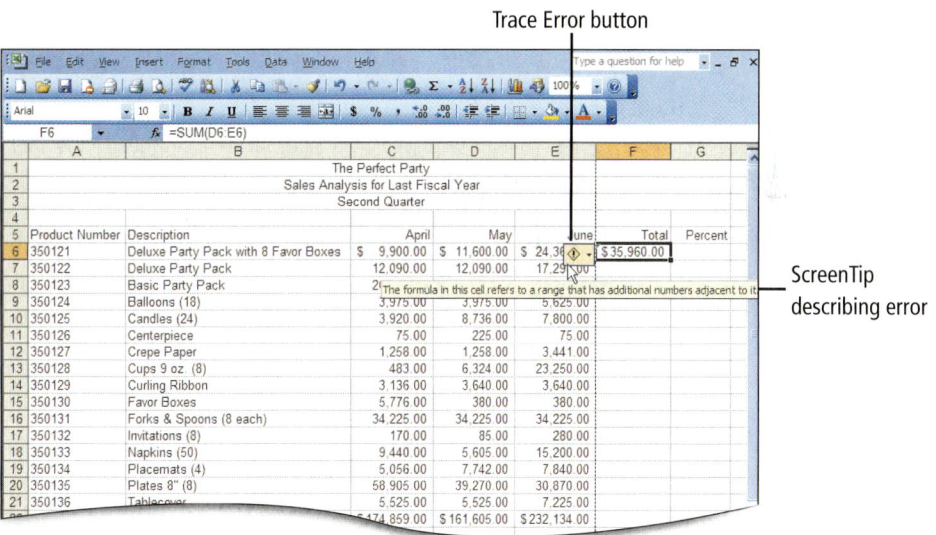

Figure 2.60

7 On the displayed button, click the **arrow** to display the list of options, as shown in Figure 2.61.

Project 2B: Annual Sales | **Excel** 631

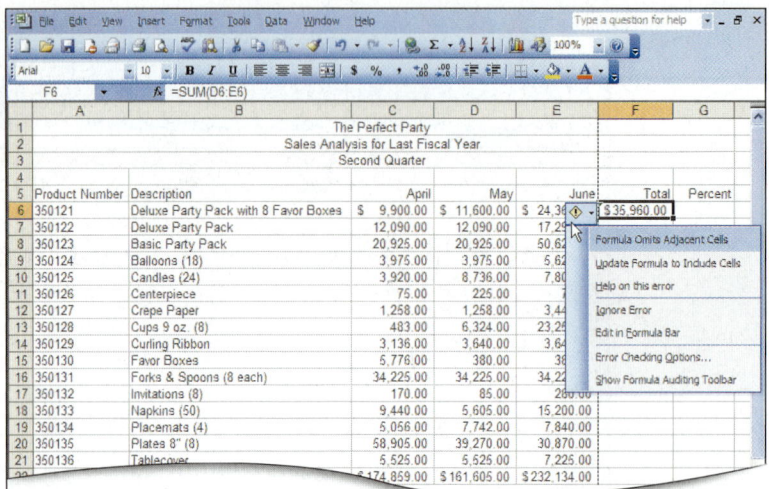

Figure 2.61

8 From the displayed menu, click **Ignore Error**, and click **Save**.

The Trace Error option button and the green triangle are both removed. In this manner, you can override Excel's suggested formula.

Activity 2.20 Editing Within a Cell Using Edit Mode

1 Double-click cell **F6**.

Double-clicking a cell that contains a formula causes the result of the calculation to be replaced with the underlying formula in the cell. The Formula Bar also displays the formula for editing, as shown in Figure 2.62.

Figure 2.62

2 Move your mouse pointer away from the cell so that you have a clear view. Then, click to position the insertion point within the cell to the left of *D6*, as shown in Figure 2.63.

632   **Excel** | Chapter 2: Editing Workbooks, Formulas, and Cells

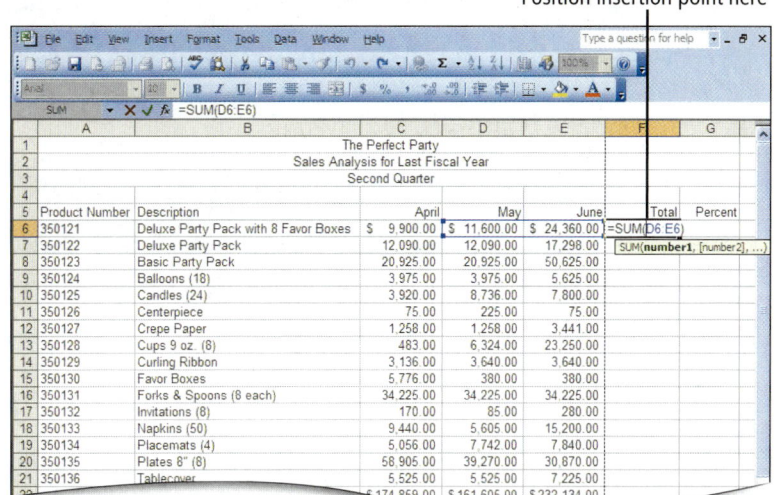

Figure 2.63

3. Press Delete, and then type **c** so that the formula indicates *=SUM(c6:E6)*.

    The cell range C6:E6 is surrounded in blue, indicating the new range in the formula. Recall that although cell references are converted to uppercase letters, it is not necessary to type uppercase letters. You can edit a formula either in the Formula Bar or directly in the cell as you have done here.

4. Press Enter to display the three-month total *$45,860.00* in the cell, and on the Standard toolbar, click the **Save** button.

Objective 7
Copy Formulas

Excel provides a quick method to create formulas without typing them and without clicking a toolbar button. This method is known as ***copying formulas***. For example, you have a quarterly total of $45,860.00 for the product *Deluxe Party Pack with 8 Favor Boxes*. Obviously, you would like to calculate similar totals for each of the remaining products in rows 7 through 22.

When a formula is copied from one cell to another, Excel adjusts the cell references to fit the new location of the formula. This is known as a ***relative cell reference***.

Activity 2.21 Copying a Formula with Relative Cell References Using the Fill Handle

1. With your **2B_Annual_Sales** workbook open and the **Second Qtr** worksheet displayed, click cell **F6**.

    You can see that in cells F7:F22, you need a formula similar to the one in F6, but one that properly refers to the cells in row 7, row 8, and so forth.

Project 2B: Annual Sales | **Excel** 633

2 Position your mouse pointer over the **fill handle** in the lower right corner of cell **F6** until the pointer ⊞ displays. Then, drag downward through cell **F22** and release the left mouse button. Compare your screen with Figure 2.64.

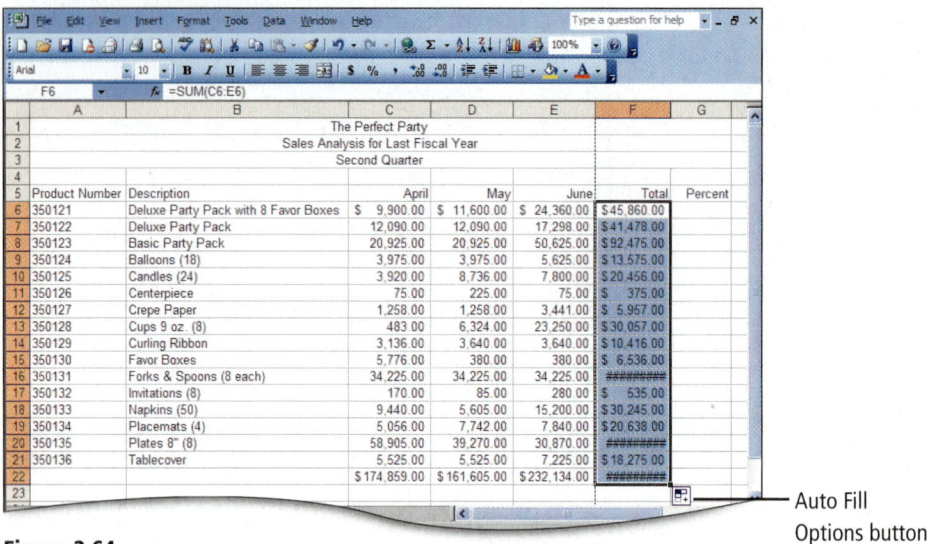

Auto Fill Options button

Figure 2.64

Totals display in the selected cells, formatted with Currency Style because the formula you copied was formatted in Currency Style. Also, several values are now too wide for the column and display ######. The Auto Fill Options button displays.

3 **Point** to the **Auto Fill Options** button, click the **arrow**, and from the displayed menu, click **Fill Without Formatting**.

All formatting is removed from the selected cells so that you can apply the formatting of your choice.

4 Select the range **F7:F21** and apply the **Comma Style**. Click cell **F22** and apply the **Currency Style**. If any cells still display #####, select column F, display the Format menu, point to Column, and then click AutoFit Selection.

5 Click cell **F7**, look at the Formula Bar, and notice the formula =SUM(C7:E7). Click cell **F8**, look at the Formula Bar, and notice the formula =SUM(C8:E8).

In each row, Excel copied the formula but adjusted the cell references *relative to* the row number. This is called a relative cell reference. The calculation is the same, but it is performed on the cells in that particular row. This is a quick method to insert numerous formulas into large spreadsheets.

6 Click the **Third Qtr sheet tab**.

7 Click cell **F6**. On the Standard toolbar, click **AutoSum**, and then move up to the Formula Bar and click the **Enter** button.

Recall that clicking the Enter button on the Formula Bar retains the cell in which you are working as the active cell.

634 Excel | Chapter 2: Editing Workbooks, Formulas, and Cells

8 Position your pointer over the **fill handle** of cell **F6**, display the pointer ➕, and then drag downward through cell **F22** to copy the formula to the remaining rows.

9 Point to the **Auto Fill Options** button, click the **arrow**, and from the displayed menu, click **Fill Without Formatting**.

10 Select the range **F7:F21** and apply the **Comma Style** 』. Click cell **F22** and apply the **Currency Style** ⓢ. If any cells display ######, select column F, display the Format menu, point to Column, and then click AutoFit Selection.

11 Click the **Fourth Qtr sheet tab**, repeat Steps 7–10, and then click **Save** 💾.

You can see how fast it is to insert formulas using the copy method and how helpful Excel is because it adjusts the cell references for you as you copy the formula.

More Knowledge — Copy Formulas with the Copy and Paste Command

You can also copy formulas with relative cell references using the Copy and Paste commands. Click the cell containing the first formula, and then click the Copy button. Select the range to which you want to copy formulas, and then click the Paste button. The formula will be copied and the relative cell references adjusted accordingly. Recall that the Copy and Paste commands can also be initiated from the Edit menu or with the keyboard shortcuts [Ctrl] + [C] and [Ctrl] + [V], respectively.

Activity 2.22 Copying Formulas Containing Absolute Cell References

You have seen that a relative cell reference refers to cells by their position in relation to the cell that contains the formula. **Absolute references**, on the other hand, refer to cells by their fixed position in the worksheet, for example, the cell at the intersection of column F and row 22.

A relative cell reference automatically adjusts when a formula is copied. An absolute cell reference does *not* adjust; rather, it remains the same when the formula is copied—and there are times when you will want to do this. To make a cell reference absolute, dollar signs are inserted into the cell reference. The use of dollar signs to denote an absolute reference is not related in any way to whether or not the values you are working with are currency values. It is simply the symbol used by Excel to denote an absolute cell reference.

1 In your **2B_Annual_Sales** workbook, click the **Second Qtr sheet tab**.

2 In cell **G6** type = to begin a formula, click cell **F6** to insert its reference into the formula, type / (on your keyboard, next to the right Shift key) to insert the division operator, click cell **F22**, and then on the Formula Bar click the **Enter** button ✓.

The formula created, =F6/F22, indicates that the value in cell F6 will be divided by the value in cell F22. Why? Because the owners of The Perfect Party want to know the percentage by which each product contributes to total sales. Arithmetically, the percentage is computed by dividing the sales for the specific product by the total sales, and that is accomplished with this formula.

3 Be sure cell **G6** is selected. Position your pointer over the **fill handle**, and then drag down to cell **G21**.

As shown in Figure 2.65, each cell displays an error message; each cell displays a Trace Error triangle in the upper left corner, and the Auto Fill Options button displays.

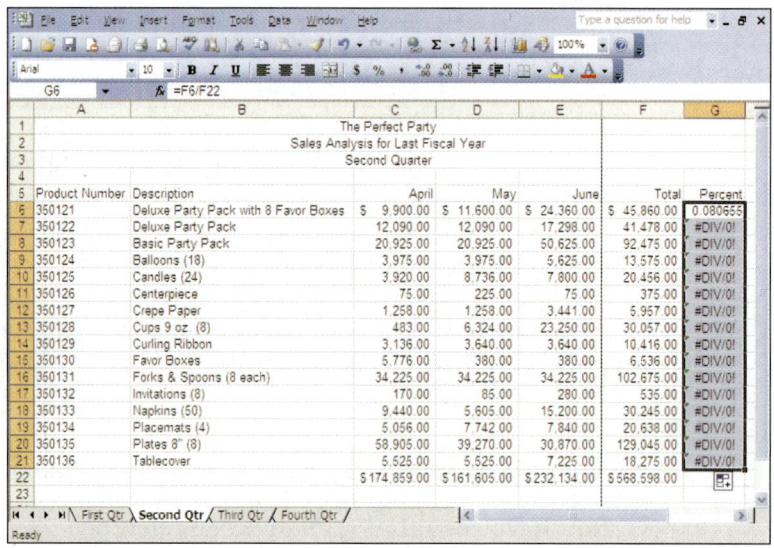

Figure 2.65

4 Click cell **G7**, and then point to the **Trace Error** button.

As shown in Figure 2.66, the ScreenTip displays *The formula or function used is dividing by zero or empty cells.*

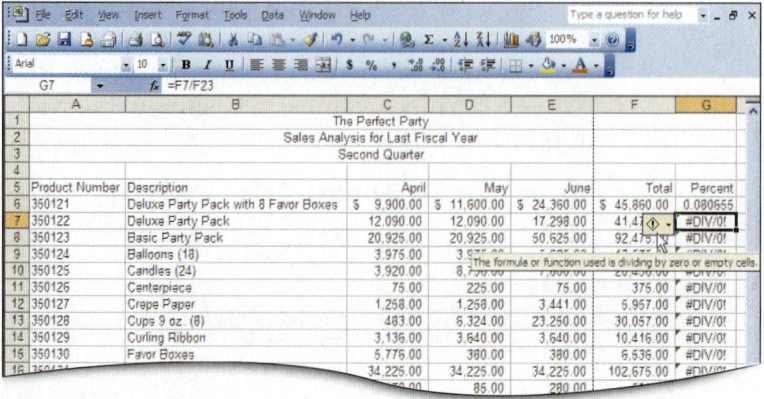

Figure 2.66

5 Look at the Formula Bar to examine the formula.

Indeed, the cell reference following the divisor operator (/) is F23, and F23 is an empty cell.

6 Click cell **G8**, and in the Formula Bar, notice the cell reference following the divisor operator is **F24**, also an empty cell.

Because the cell references are relative, Excel attempts to build the formula by increasing the row number for each equation. In this particular calculation, however, the divisor must always be the value in cell F22—the total sales.

7 Click cell **G6**. In the Formula Bar, edit the formula so that it indicates **=F6/$F$22** as shown in Figure 2.67, and then click the **Enter** button on the Formula Bar to finish editing the formula.

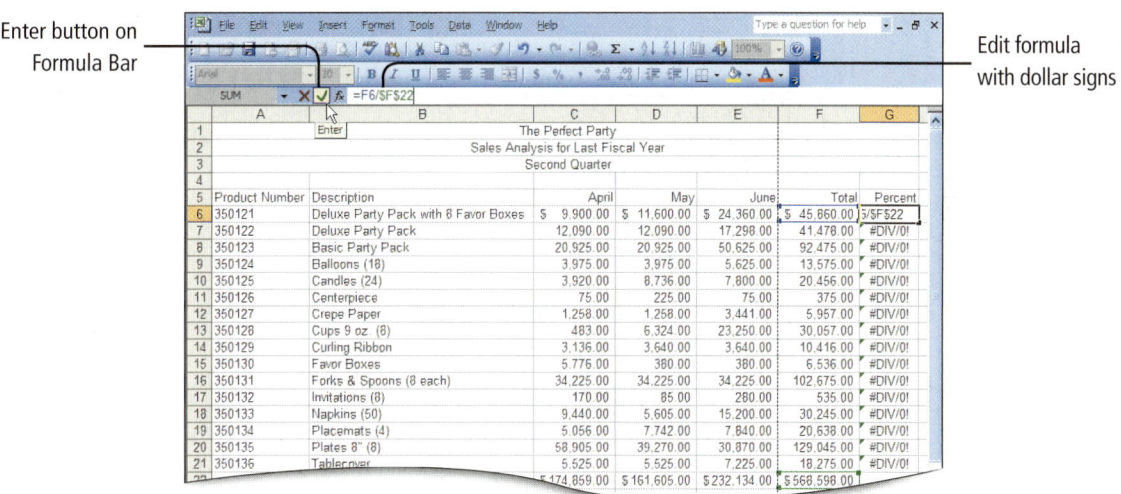

Figure 2.67

8 Using the **fill handle** in cell **G6**, copy the formula down through cell **G21**, and then compare your screen with Figure 2.68.

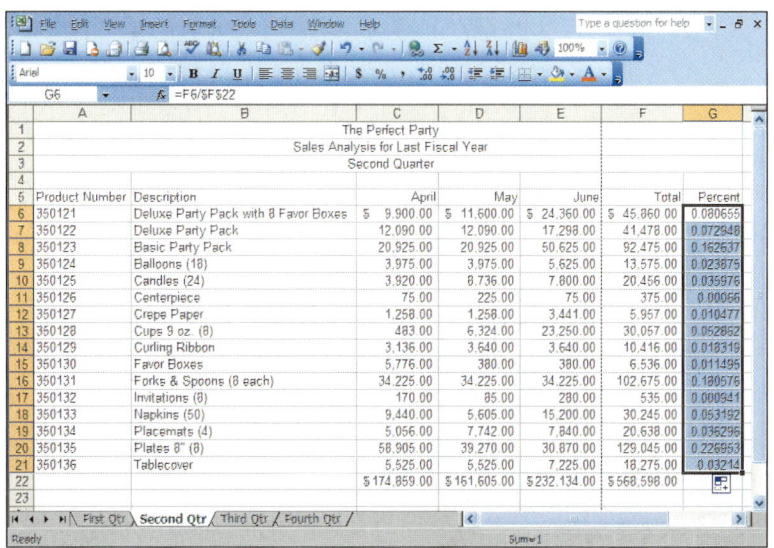

Figure 2.68

9. Click in several of the copied cells, and observe the formula in the Formula Bar. You can see that for each formula, the cell reference for the product's total sales changed relative to its row, but the value used as the divisor—total sales—the value in cell F22, remained absolute. Thus, using either relative or absolute cell references, it is easy to duplicate formulas without typing them.

10. Select the range **G6:G21**, apply the **Percent Style** %, and then click **Increase Decimal** two times. Compare your screen with Figure 2.69.

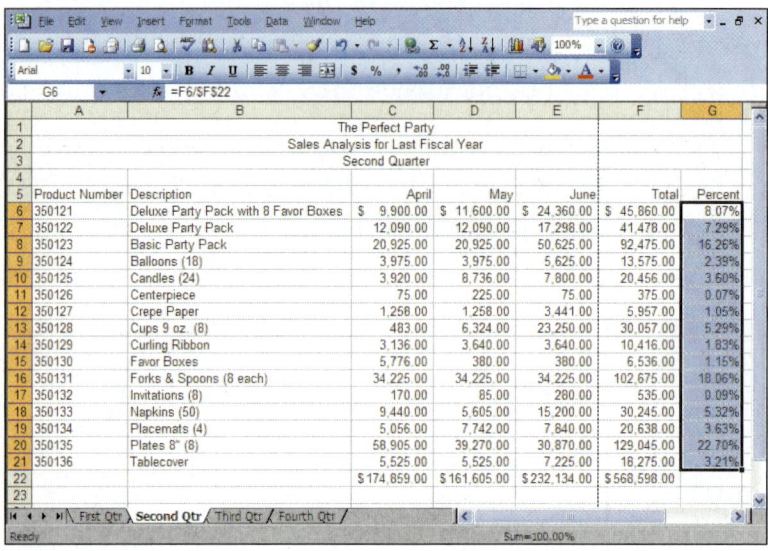

Figure 2.69

11. Click the sheet tab for **Third Qtr**.

12. Click cell **G6**, construct the formula =F6/$F$22 and then click the **Enter** button on the Formula Bar. Copy the formula to cells **G7:G21**. Apply the **Percent Style** % to the range **G6:G21**, and then click **Increase Decimal** two times on the selected range.

13. Repeat Step 12 above on the **Fourth Qtr** worksheet.

14. On the Standard toolbar, click **Save** to save the changes to your workbook.

More Knowledge — Make a Cell Reference Absolute While Creating a Formula

To make a cell reference absolute while creating a formula, click to select the cell to which you want to refer, press F4, and then continue creating the formula. Excel will insert the dollar signs for you.

Objective 8
Conduct a What-if Analysis

A ***what-if analysis*** is a business management technique in which you ask *what* happens *if* something else happens. For example, the owners of The Perfect Party plan to increase their marketing efforts in the third quarter of next year for the major events that people celebrate during those months—specifically, Independence Day parties in July and the increasingly popular wedding month of September. They estimate that the increased marketing will result in a 20% increase in third quarter sales.

Activity 2.23 Conducting a What-if Analysis

1 Display the **Third Qtr** worksheet. In cell **A24**, type **Projected Third Quarter Revenue With a 20% Increase in Sales**

2 In cell **D24**, type the formula **=F22*1.20** and then compare your screen with Figure 2.70.

Cell F22 is the total sales for the third quarter just finished, the asterisk (*) represents the multiplication operator, and *1.20* represents the current total sales plus 20%.

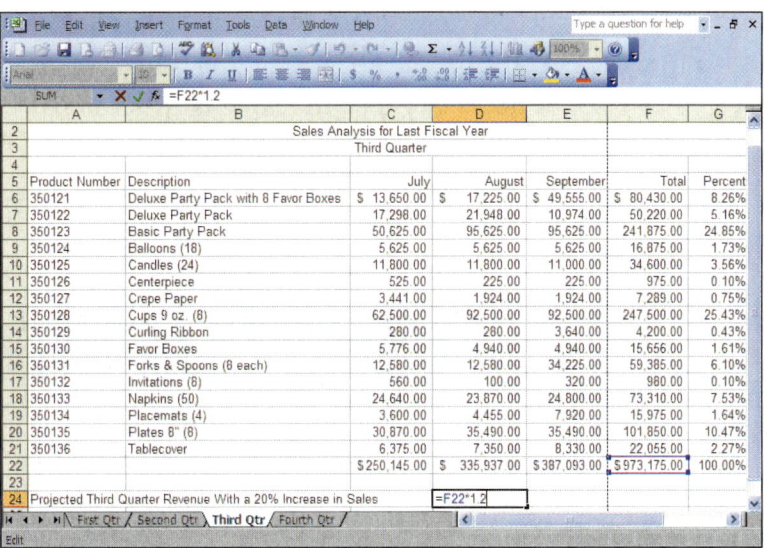

Figure 2.70

3 Press **Enter** to view the result.

If next year's sales for the third quarter are increased by 20% over the last year, the total sales for the quarter will be $1,167,810.

4 On the Standard toolbar, click the **Save** button to save the changes you have made to your workbook.

Objective 9
Display and Print Underlying Formulas

When you have a formula in a cell, the cell displays the results of the formula. Recall that this value is called the ***displayed value***. To see the actual formula—the ***underlying formula***—you must activate the cell and look at the Formula Bar.

There are two ways to display all the underlying formulas in your worksheet:

- From the Tools menu, click Options, display the View tab, and select the Formulas check box.

- Press Ctrl + ` to display the formulas, and then activate the same keyboard shortcut to toggle back to the displayed values. The ` is called the ***grave accent*** and is located below the Esc key on most keyboards.

Activity 2.24 Displaying and Printing Underlying Formulas

1 Be sure that your **2B_Annual_Sales** workbook is open, and then click the **First Qtr sheet tab**.

2 Hold down Ctrl and press ` (below Esc). If the Formula Auditing tool bar displays, click the **close** button ⊠ on the toolbar.

3 If necessary, use the horizontal scroll bar to view the formulas in **columns F** and **G**, as shown in Figure 2.71.

It is frequently useful to view the formulas in all the cells, especially if you are trying to locate an error in your worksheet.

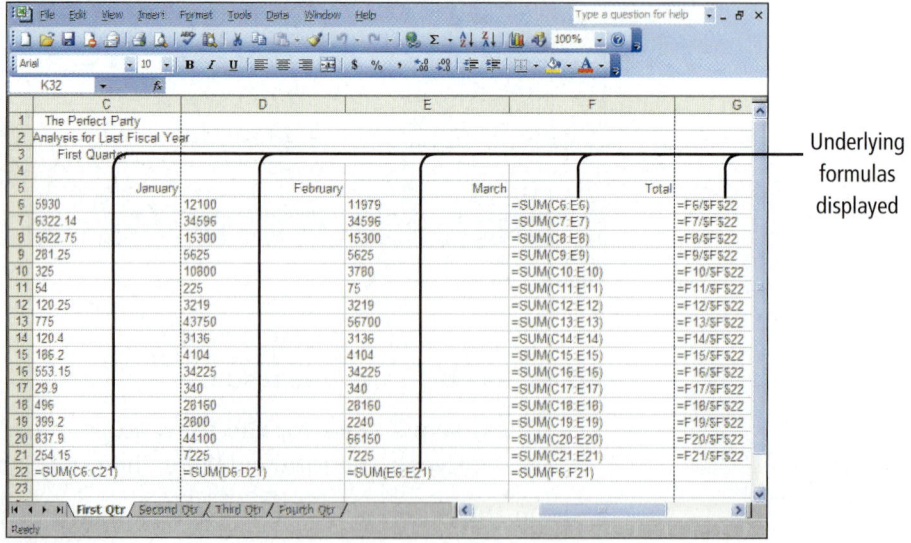

Figure 2.71

640   Excel | Chapter 2: Editing Workbooks, Formulas, and Cells

4 Hold down [Ctrl] and press [`] again.

The normal view of your worksheet redisplays.

5 Click **Save**.

Objective 10
Change Page Orientation

Thus far you have printed your worksheets in **Portrait orientation**. In this orientation, the paper is taller than it is wide. Excel can also print in **Landscape orientation**, in which the paper is wider than it is tall. Landscape orientation is frequently used in Excel because worksheets tend to have numerous columns.

Activity 2.25 Changing Page Orientation

1 With your **2B_Annual_Sales** workbook open, if necessary, display the **First Qtr** worksheet.

2 Press [Ctrl] + [Home] to move to the top left corner of the worksheet. A vertical dotted line may display. If it does not, click **Print Preview**, and then close **Print Preview**.

This line indicates where the first page would end and the second page would begin if you printed your worksheet. It is likely that columns F and G would fall onto another page if printed in the current setup.

3 Right-click the **First Qtr sheet tab**, and click **Select All Sheets**.

[Group] displays in the title bar. For the purpose of changing the orientation, select all the sheets in the workbook so that you have to make the change only once.

4 From the **File** menu, click **Page Setup**.

The Page Setup dialog box displays.

5 In the displayed **Page Setup** dialog box, if necessary, click the **Page tab**. Under **Orientation**, click the **Landscape** option button. See Figure 2.72.

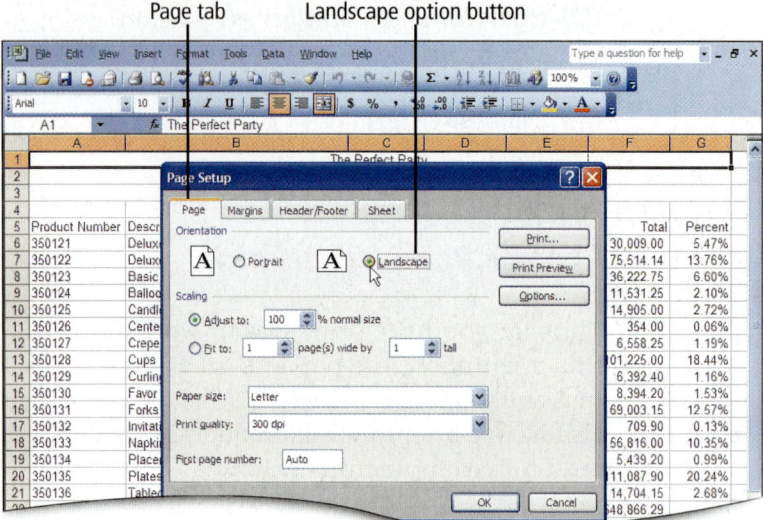

Figure 2.72

6 In the upper right corner of the **Page Setup** dialog box, click the **Print Preview** button and compare your screen with Figure 2.73.

Notice the landscape orientation. In the lower left corner, notice that there are 4 sheets. This is the result of grouping the sheets.

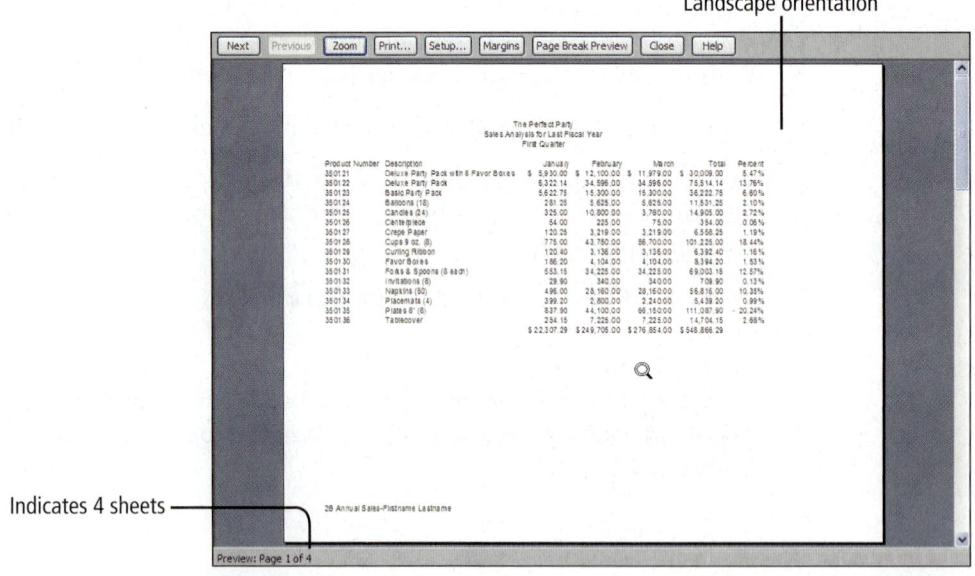

Figure 2.73

7 Press PageDown as many times as necessary to view each of the four worksheets in the workbook. Then, on the Print Preview toolbar, click the **Print** button.

Because you selected all sheets, all four sheets will print, and thus it is not necessary to select the Entire Workbook option button.

8 **Save** your workbook. Close the file and close Excel.

End You have completed Project 2B

Excel chapter two

Summary

With Excel, it is easy to create complex, multipage workbooks to analyze financial information such as quarterly sales. You can create formulas and copy them easily within a single spreadsheet and among spreadsheets in the same workbook. Numeric data can be formatted in a way that is meaningful to the reader. Flexibility in the layout of a spreadsheet is accomplished by controlling the size of columns, rows, and cells. Finally, Excel helps with your typing by completing a series, such as the days of the week or the months of the year.

In This Chapter You Practiced How To

- Enter Constant Values with AutoFill and the Fill Handle
- Insert, Delete, and Adjust Rows and Columns
- Align Cell Contents Horizontally
- Copy and Move Cell Contents
- Format Numbers Using the Toolbar
- Edit Formulas
- Copy Formulas
- Conduct a What-if Analysis
- Display and Print Underlying Formulas
- Change Page Orientation

Concepts Assessments

Matching Match each term in the second column with its correct definition in the first column. Write the letter of the term on the blank line to the left of the correct definition.

_____ 1. A cell reference with a fixed position in the worksheet that does not automatically change based on its location.

_____ 2. The process of copying multiple pieces of data to the Office Clipboard and then pasting the data into another location.

_____ 3. A small black box in the lower right corner of a selected cell that can be used to complete a series with AutoFill.

_____ 4. A temporary storage area maintained by your Windows operating system where data is stored for the Cut and Paste commands.

_____ 5. The ability to extend a series of values into adjacent cells based on the value of other cells.

_____ 6. During the formula copying process, the automatic adjustment of cell references to fit the new location of the formula.

_____ 7. The style of data formatted with thousand comma separators and two decimal places, but with no dollar sign.

_____ 8. A button or other screen indication that displays when Excel recognizes certain types of data and that offers a list of commands related to the data.

_____ 9. A page orientation in which the paper is wider than it is tall.

_____ 10. A group of things that come one after another in succession.

_____ 11. A set of characters with the same size and shape.

_____ 12. A business management technique in which one asks *what* happens *if* something else happens.

_____ 13. Monetary values.

_____ 14. A small green triangle in the upper left corner of a cell that indicates a potential error in a formula.

_____ 15. The term used to refer to data that is aligned at the left edge of a cell.

A Absolute cell reference

B AutoFill

C Collect and paste

D Comma style

E Currency

F Fill handle

G Font

H Landscape orientation

I Left-aligned

J Office Clipboard

K Relative cell reference

L Series

M Smart tag

N Trace Error

O What-if analysis

Concepts Assessments (continued)

Fill in the Blank Write the correct answers in the space provided.

1. In the formula =B6/$C$52, the absolute cell reference is
   _____.

2. AutoSum is a _____, predefined by Excel, which generates a formula.

3. Font size is measured in _____, one being equal to 1/72 of an inch.

4. A pattern of number signs (#######) displays in a cell when the data is too _____ for the existing size of the column.

5. Using the keyboard, you can copy a selected range of cells to the Clipboard by pressing _____.

6. Right-clicking on a column heading letter or row heading number will display a _____.

7. In the series JAN, APR. . . the next month in the series is
   _____.

8. Data aligned at the right edge of a cell is said to be
   _____.

9. The _____ Style button is used to format the numbers in a cell to display commas, two decimal places, and a dollar sign.

10. The [`] key is called the _____ accent.

Excel chapter two
Skill Assessments

Project 2C — Bonuses

Objectives: *Enter Constant Values with Autofill and the Fill Handle; Insert, Delete, and Adjust Rows and Columns; Align Cell Contents Horizontally; and Format Numbers Using the Toolbar.*

In the following Skill Assessment, you will edit a workbook for the owners of The Perfect Party that tracks monthly sales and the bonuses paid on monthly sales to sales associates. Bonuses are paid at the end of each year. Your completed workbook will look similar to the one shown in Figure 2.74. You will save the workbook as 2C_Bonuses_Firstname_Lastname.

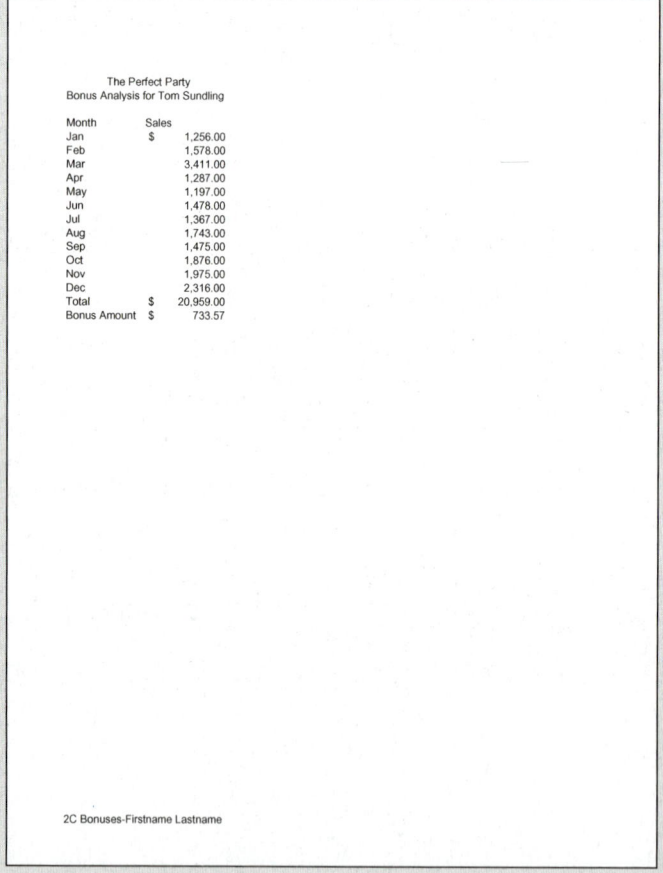

Figure 2.74

1. Start Excel. On the **File** menu, click **Open**. In the **Open** dialog box, navigate to the student files that accompany this textbook, and open the file **e02C_Bonuses**. Display the **View** menu, click **Header and Footer**, and then click the **Custom Footer** button. In the **Left section** type **2C Bonuses-Firstname Lastname** and then click OK to close the dialog boxes.

(**Project 2C**–Bonuses continues on the next page)

Excel | Chapter 2: Editing Workbooks, Formulas, and Cells

Skill Assessments (continued)

(Project 2C–Bonuses continued)

2. From the **File** menu, click **Save As**. In the **Save As** dialog box, navigate to the location where you are storing your projects for this chapter. In the **File name** box, type **2C_Bonuses_Firstname_Lastname** and then click **Save** or press Enter.

3. Click cell **A5**, type **Jan** and press Enter. Select cell **A5** again, point to the **fill handle**, and then drag downward through cell **A16** to create a series containing the months from Jan through Dec. In cell **A17**, type **Total** and in cell **A18**, type **Bonus Amount**

4. Click cell **A18**, display the **Format** menu, point to **Column**, and then click **AutoFit Selection**. Rename Sheet1 as **Bonus**

5. Select **column B**, point to the vertical line between **columns B** and **C** to display the double-headed arrow pointer, and then drag to the right until the width of the column is **105 pixels**. Select the range **A1:B1** and then click the **Merge and Center** button.

6. Click cell **B17**, on the Standard toolbar click **AutoSum**, and then press Enter to accept the formula and display the total, *20959*.

7. Click cell **B5**, hold down Ctrl and click cell B17, and then apply **Currency Style**. Select the range **B6:B16** and apply **Comma Style**.

8. The total sales generated by Mr. Sundling for the year is $20,959. Sales associates are paid a bonus of 3.5% of total annual sales. Click cell **B18** and enter the formula **=B17*.035** to multiply the total in cell B17 by the bonus rate of 3.5%. The bonus will be $733.57. Cell B18 displays Currency Style formatting because the referenced cell used Currency Style.

9. On the Standard toolbar, click **Save** to save the changes you have made to your workbook. Then, on the Standard toolbar, click the **Print Preview** button to view your worksheet. On the Print Preview toolbar, click the **Print** button.

10. Close your file, and close Excel.

End You have completed Project 2C

Project 2C: Bonuses | **Excel** 647

Skill Assessments (continued)

Project 2D—Expense Report

Objectives: *Enter Constant Values with AutoFill and the Fill Handle; Insert, Delete, and Adjust Rows and Columns; Align Cell Contents Horizontally; Format Numbers Using the Toolbar; Edit Formulas; Copy Formulas; and Change Page Orientation.*

In the following Skill Assessment, you will edit a workbook that details business travel expenses for the owners of The Perfect Party. Your completed workbook will look similar to the one shown in Figure 2.75. You will save the workbook as *2D_Expense_Report_Firstname_Lastname*.

The Perfect Party
Weekly Expense Report

Traveler	Gabriela Quinones
Report Date	5/21/2005
Destination	Boston
Purpose of Trip	Meet with new vendor

	Monday 5/19/2005	Tuesday 5/20/2005	Wednesday 5/21/2005	Thursday 5/22/2005	Friday 5/23/2005	Saturday 5/24/2005	Sunday 5/25/2005	Total
Airfare			$ 369.00					$ 369.00
Hotel					289.72			289.72
Breakfast				12.95	15.56			28.51
Lunch				17.50				17.50
Dinner			37.85	42.95				80.80
Bus								-
Train								-
Taxi			20.00	10.00	20.00			50.00
Gratuity								-
Auto Rental								-
Gasoline								-
Parking					60.00			60.00
Telephone & Fax								-
Tolls								-
Other								-
Total	$ -	$ -	$ 426.85	$ 83.40	$ 385.28	$ -	$ -	$ 895.53

2D Expense Report-Firstname Lastname

Figure 2.75

1. Start Excel. On the **File** menu, click **Open**. In the **Open** dialog box, navigate to the student files that accompany this textbook, and then open the file **e02D_Expense_Report**. Display the **View** menu, click **Header and Footer**, and then click the **Custom Footer** button. In the **Left section**, type **2D Expense Report-Firstname Lastname** and then click **OK** to close the dialog boxes.
2. From the **File** menu, click **Save As**. In the **Save As** dialog box, navigate to the location where you are storing your projects for this chapter. In the **File name** box, type **2D_Expense_Report_Firstname_Lastname** and then click **Save** or press Enter.

(**Project 2D**–Expense Report continues on the next page)

Skill Assessments (continued)

(Project 2D–Expense Report continued)

3. Click cell **B8**, type **Monday** and press Enter. Select cell **B8** again, and then using the fill handle, drag to the right to create a series containing the days of the week from Monday through Sunday. Click cell **I8**, type **Total** and then rename Sheet1 as **Expense Report**.

4. Select the range **A1:I1**, and then on the Formatting toolbar, click **Merge and Center**. Merge and center the range **A2:I2**.

5. Right-click the **row 8 heading**, and on the displayed shortcut menu, click **Insert** to insert a blank row. Select **row 9**, and on the Formatting toolbar, click the **Align Right** button.

6. Select **columns B** through **I**. Position the mouse pointer between any two of the selected column headings until the double-headed pointer displays, and then drag right until the ScreenTip indicates **80 pixels**. This will increase the width of all the selected columns to 80 pixels.

7. Right-click the **row 10 heading**, and then on the displayed shortcut menu, click **Insert**. Point to the displayed **Insert Options** button, click the **arrow** to display the menu, and then click **Format Same As Above**. In your newly created **row 10**, you will enter dates, and they will be right-aligned, the same as the row above.

8. Position your pointer in the column heading area between **columns A** and **B** until the double-headed arrow displays, and then double-click. The width of column A adjusts to accommodate its longest entry.

9. Select the range **B11:I11**, and then on the Formatting toolbar, click the **Currency Style** button. Select the range **B27:I27** and click the **Currency Style** button. Values in this row will be formatted with the Currency Style. Select the range **B12:I26**, and on the Formatting toolbar, click the **Comma Style** button.

10. Click cell **B27**, on the Standard toolbar click the **AutoSum** button, and then select the range **B11:B25** to select the cell references for the formula. Press Enter. Recall that to include empty cells in an AutoSum formula, you must manually select the cells. In cell B27, only the dollar sign and a small line display because there are no values in the range to sum.

11. Click cell **B27**, and then drag the fill handle to the right through cell **I27** to copy the formula. For the days that have expenses reported, totals display. For the days that have no expenses reported, only the dollar sign and a small line display. Recall that because the cell references are relative, Excel adjusts the cell references relative to their location in the worksheet.

(Project 2D–Expense Report continues on the next page)

Skill Assessments (continued)

(Project 2D–Expense Report continued)

12. Click cell **I11**, click the **AutoSum** button, and then select the range **B11:H11** to select the cell references to be included in the formula. This technique will include the empty cells of B11 and C11 in the formula. Press [Enter]. The total Airfare for the week, $369.00, displays in cell I11.

13. Select cell **I11**, and then from the **Edit** menu, click **Copy**. Select the range **I12:I25** and then, from the **Edit** menu, click **Paste**. The formula in I11 is copied to the selected range of cells, and the relative cell references are changed to fit the receiving cells. Because the copied formula was formatted with Currency Style, the resulting formulas also retain the Currency Style. With the range **I12:I25** still selected, click the **Comma Style** button.

14. Press [Ctrl] + [Home] to return to cell **A1**. On the Standard toolbar, click the **Spelling** button, and correct any spelling errors. (Hint: You should discover three misspelled words. Click Ignore All to Ignore proper names.) On the Standard toolbar, click **Save** to save your work.

15. In cells **B4:B7** enter the following values regarding this two-day trip Gabriela Quinones made to Boston:

Traveler	**Gabriela Quinones**
Report Date	**5/21/2005**
Destination	**Boston**
Purpose of Trip	**Meet with new vendor**

16. In cell **B10**, type **5/19/2005** and press [Enter]. Select cell **B10** again, and then using the fill handle, drag to the right through cell **H10** to extend the dates in the series.

    In **row 27**, the totals display the Trace Error smart tags (green triangles) that indicate a potential formula error. These appear because not all the cells contain values; in this instance, that is acceptable because Gabriela did not travel on all days, and she did not incur every type of expense allowable on any of the days. Thus, the worksheet will contain blank cells.

17. Click anywhere to cancel the selection in row 10. In cell **I27**, verify that Gabriela spent a total of $895.53 on this trip.

18. On the Standard toolbar, click the **Save** button. If you see the vertical dotted line on your screen, this indicates that, as currently set up, the entire worksheet will not print on one page. From the **File** menu, click **Page Setup**. On the **Page tab**, click the **Landscape** option button, and then click **OK**. The vertical dotted line moves to the right, indicating that all the columns will now print on one page.

(Project 2D–Expense Report continues on the next page)

Skill Assessments (continued)

(Project 2D–Expense Report continued)

19. On the Standard toolbar, click the **Print Preview** button, visually check your worksheet, and then, on the Print Preview toolbar, click **Print**.

20. Close the file, saving any changes, and then close Excel.

 You have completed Project 2D

Project 2E—Profit Loss

Objectives: *Insert, Delete, and Adjust Rows and Columns; Align Cell Contents Horizontally; Format Numbers Using the Toolbar; Edit Formulas; and Copy Formulas.*

In the following Skill Assessment, you will edit a workbook that contains a Profit & Loss Statement for The Perfect Party for the month of June. Your completed workbook will look similar to the one shown in Figure 2.76. You will save the workbook as *2E_Profit_Loss_Firstname_Lastname*.

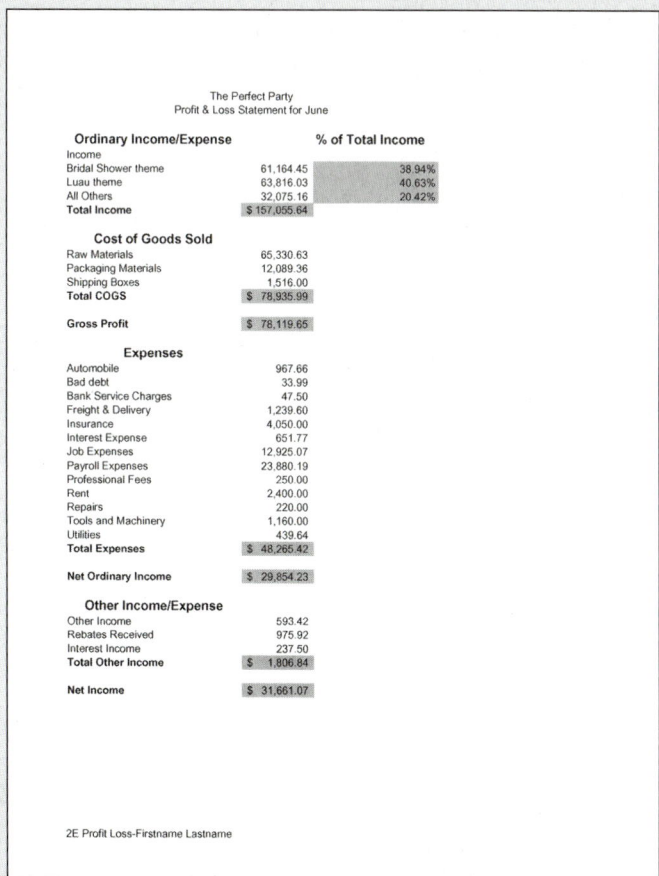

Figure 2.76

(Project 2E–Profit Loss continues on the next page)

Project 2E: Profit Loss | **Excel** 651

Excel chapter two
Skill Assessments (continued)

(Project 2E–Profit Loss continued)

1. Start Excel. On the **File** menu, click **Open**. In the **Open** dialog box, navigate to the student files that accompany this textbook, and then open the file **e02E_Profit_Loss**. Display the **View** menu, click **Header and Footer**, and then click the **Custom Footer** button. In the **Left section**, type **2E Profit Loss-Firstname Lastname** and then click **OK** to close the dialog boxes.

2. From the **File** menu, click **Save As**. In the **Save As** dialog box, navigate to the location where you are storing your projects for this chapter. In the **File name** box, type **2E_Profit_Loss_Firstname_Lastname** and then click **Save** or press Enter.

3. Click cell **A2**. Move your pointer to the Formula Bar, click to position the insertion point following the word *Statement*, edit as necessary to add **for June** and then press Enter. Rename Sheet1 to **P&L for June**

4. Select the range **A1:C1**, and then, on the Formatting toolbar, click the **Merge and Center** button. Select the range **A2:C2** and click **Merge and Center**. Select **column B**, and then, on the Formatting toolbar, click the **Comma Style** button.

5. In cell **B9** you will add the three items that make up Total Income. Click cell **B9**, on the Standard toolbar, click the **AutoSum** button, and then press Enter to display a Total Income of *157,055.64*.

6. In cell **B15** you will add the three items that make up the Cost of Goods Sold. Click **B15**, click **AutoSum**, and then press Enter to display Total COGS (Cost Of Goods Sold) of *78,935.99*.

7. The accounting formula for calculating Gross Profit is TOTAL INCOME MINUS COST OF GOODS SOLD.

    Click cell **B17** and type **=** to begin a formula. Click cell **B9** to enter the cell reference using the point-and-click method, type **–** (the subtraction operator), click cell **B15** to insert the cell reference, and then press Enter. The Gross Profit is *78,119.65*.

8. In cell **B33**, use **AutoSum** to add the items that make up Total Expenses. The Total Expenses are *48,265.42*.

9. The accounting formula for calculating Net Ordinary Income is GROSS PROFIT MINUS TOTAL EXPENSES.

    In cell **B35**, construct a formula that calculates the value in cell B17 (Gross Profit) minus the value in cell B33 (Total Expenses). The Net Ordinary Income should be 29,854.23. If necessary, edit your formula to get the correct result.

10. In cell **B41**, use **AutoSum** to add the three items that make up Total Other Income. Your result should be *1,806.84*.

(Project 2E–Profit Loss continues on the next page)

Excel chapter two
Skill Assessments (continued)

(Project 2E–Profit Loss continued)

11. The accounting formula for calculating Net Income is *NET ORDINARY INCOME PLUS TOTAL OTHER INCOME*.

    In cell **B43**, construct a formula to calculate Net Income. Your result should be 31,661.07. Click **Save**.

12. In **column B**, apply the **Currency Style** to all the cells that are gray. (Hint: Hold down [Ctrl] to select all the nonadjacent cells.) Widen the column by selecting the column and then applying the **AutoFit Selection** command from the **Format** menu.

13. The Luau and Bridal Shower themes are big sellers in June, and Angie and Gabriela want to compute the percentage of their Total Income that comes from these two party packages. In cell **C6**, type **=b6/b9** and press [Enter]. Apply the **Percent Style** to the result, and click **Increase Decimal** two times. Almost 39% of income in June was derived from the Bridal Shower theme packages.

14. Click cell **C6** again. In the Formula Bar, position the I-beam pointer over *B9*, and double-click. The entire Formula Bar from *B9* on will be selected. Press [F4]. Recall that this is a keyboard shortcut for making a cell an absolute reference by inserting dollar signs. On the Formula Bar, click the **Enter** button, and then use the fill handle to copy this formula to cells **C7** and **C8**. Cell C7 will contain 40.63%. Cell C8 will contain 20.42%.

15. Press [Ctrl] + [Home] to move to cell **A1**. On the Standard toolbar, click the **Spelling** button, and correct any spelling errors in the worksheet. (Hint: There are two spelling errors.) Click **Save**.

16. On the Standard toolbar, click the **Print Preview** button, visually check your worksheet, and then on the Print Preview toolbar, click **Print**.

17. Close the file, saving any changes, and then close Excel.

 You have completed Project 2E

Excel chapter two

Performance Assessments

Project 2F—Product Inventory

Objectives: *Align Cell Contents Horizontally; Copy and Move Cell Contents; Format Numbers Using the Toolbar; and Copy Formulas.*

At the end of each month, the owners of The Perfect Party count the number of products on hand to determine what to order for next month. In the following Performance Assessment, you will create a new workbook to display the results of this physical inventory. Your completed workbook will look similar to the one shown in Figure 2.77. You will save the workbook as *2F_Product_Inventory_Firstname_Lastname*.

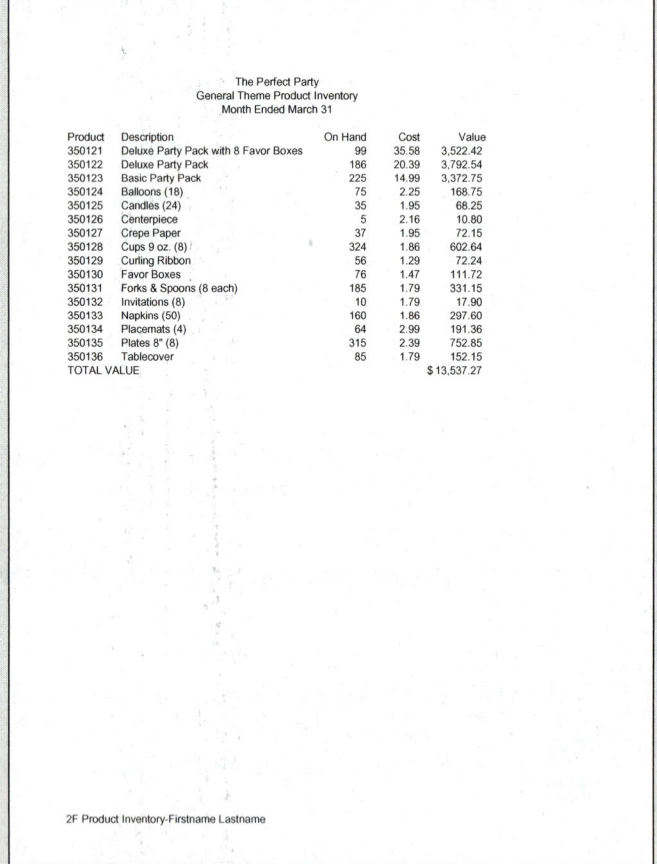

Figure 2.77

1. Start Excel and display a new, blank workbook. Display the **View** menu, click **Header and Footer**, and then click the **Custom Footer** button. In the **Left section**, type **2F Product Inventory-Firstname Lastname** and then click **OK** to close the dialog boxes.

2. From the **File** menu, click **Save As**. In the **Save As** dialog box, navigate to the location where you are storing your projects for this chapter. In the **File name** box, type **2F_Product_Inventory_Firstname_Lastname** and then click **Save** or press Enter.

(**Project 2F**–Product Inventory continues on the next page)

654   Excel | Chapter 2: Editing Workbooks, Formulas, and Cells

Excel chapter two

Performance Assessments (continued)

(Project 2F–Product Inventory continued)

3. Rename Sheet1 to **March Inventory** and then, in cells **A1** through **A3**, enter the following titles:

   The Perfect Party
   General Theme Product Inventory
   Month Ended March 31

4. On the **File** menu, click **Open**. Navigate to the student files that accompany this textbook, click to select the file **e02F_Data**, and then click **Open**.

5. Click cell **A1**, hold down Shift, and then click cell **B17**. On the Standard toolbar, click the **Copy** button to copy the product numbers and descriptions to the Office Clipboard.

6. On the taskbar, click the button to return to your **2F_Product_Inventory** workbook. Click cell **A5**, and then on the Standard toolbar, click the **Paste** button. Excel pastes the range of cells, beginning with the selected destination cell.

7. Change the width of **column B** to fit all the entries in column B. Merge and Center each of the three titles in **A1** through **A3** across **columns A:E**.

8. In cell **C5**, type **On Hand** in cell **D5**, type **Cost** and in cell **E5**, type **Value**

9. From the taskbar, return to the **e02F_Data** workbook. From the **Edit** menu, click **Office Clipboard**. If the Clipboard is not empty, at the top of the **Clipboard** task pane, click the **Clear All** button.

10. Select the range **C2:C17**, pause the pointer over the selection, right-click to display the shortcut menu, and then click **Copy**. The selection is copied to the Office Clipboard.

11. Select the range **D2:D17**, and copy the range to the Office Clipboard. From the **File** menu, click **Close**. The **e02F_Data** workbook closes, your 2F_Product_Inventory workbook displays, and the **Office Clipboard** task pane remains open.

12. Click cell **C6**. Point to the first item on the Clipboard, which begins *99 186*, and click to paste the selection into column C. Click cell **D6**, point to the **Clipboard**, and paste the second selection, which begins *35.38 20.39*. Close the task pane.

13. Using the Align Right command, align the column titles in **C5:E5**.

14. In cell **E6**, construct a formula to multiply the number On Hand (C6) by the Cost per item (D6). Then, using the fill handle, copy the formula in cell **E6** through cell **E21**.

15. In cell **E22**, using **AutoSum**, create a formula to add the total value of all products, and then apply the **Currency Style** to cell **E22**. Widen the column if necessary. The total value is $13,537.27. Select the range **E6:E21**, and apply the comma style.

(Project 2F–Product Inventory continues on the next page)

Excel chapter two
Performance Assessments (continued)

(Project 2F–Product Inventory continued)

16. In cell **A22**, type **TOTAL VALUE** and then save your workbook. Click the **Print Preview** button to view the worksheet page. Print your worksheet. Close the workbook and close Excel.

 End You have completed Project 2F

Project 2G — Profit Analysis

Objectives: *Enter Constant Values with AutoFill and the Fill Handle; Insert, Delete, and Adjust Rows and Columns; Align Cell Contents Horizontally; Copy and Move Cell Contents; Format Numbers Using the Toolbar; Edit Formulas; Copy Formulas; and Display and Print Underlying Formulas.*

At the end of each quarter, the owners of The Perfect Party analyze profit by product. In the following Performance Assessment, you will complete a workbook that calculates the total profit for the quarter for each of the products in one theme. Your completed workbook will look similar to the one shown in Figure 2.78. You will save the workbook as *2G_Profit_Analysis_Firstname_Lastname*.

The Perfect Party
Profit Analysis for First Quarter

Product	Qty Sold	Cost	Selling Price	Profit Per Unit
350121	1,724	35.58	59.30	23.72
350122	1,764	20.39	33.99	13.60
350123	2,602	14.99	24.99	10.00
350124	878	2.25	3.75	1.50
350125	1,139	1.95	3.25	1.30
350126	190	2.16	3.60	1.44
350127	609	1.95	3.25	1.30
350128	2,623	1.86	3.10	1.24
350129	639	1.29	2.15	0.86
350130	825	1.47	2.45	0.98
350131	1,986	1.79	2.99	1.20
350132	249	1.79	2.99	1.20
350133	1,759	1.86	3.10	1.24
350134	900	2.99	4.99	2.00
350135	2,453	2.39	3.99	1.60
350136	1,028	1.79	2.99	1.20
	21,368			

2G Profit Analysis-Firstname Lastname

Figure 2.78

(**Project 2G**–Profit Analysis continues on the next page)

Performance Assessments (continued)

(Project 2H–Sales Tax continued)

3. Select **rows 1**, **2**, and **3**. From the **Insert** menu, click **Rows**. Excel inserts as many new rows as you selected—three. In cell **A1**, type **The Perfect Party** and in cell **A2**, type **Sales Tax Due for 2nd Quarter** Click cell **A21**, and type **Total Quarterly Sales Tax Due** Rename Sheet1 as **2nd Quarter**

4. Select **column B**, display the **Format** menu, point to **Column**, and then click **AutoFit Selection**. **Merge and Center** the titles in **row 1** and **row 2** across columns **A:D**.

5. In cell **B22**, type **.07** as the sales tax rate. Select **B22**, click the **Align Left** button, and apply the **Percent Style**. Insert a blank row above **row 22**, moving the Tax Rate down to **row 23**. Select the range **C5:C20**, and apply the **Comma Style**.

6. For each item, the sales tax due will be calculated by multiplying the Sales amount in column C by the tax rate in cell B23. Thus, the formula will require a relative cell reference for sales and an absolute cell reference for the tax rate, which is fixed in cell B23. In cell **D5**, construct the formula to multiply cell **C5** by cell **B23**. Edit as necessary to make cell **B23** an absolute cell reference. The sales tax amount for the first product should be *3,210.20*.

7. Copy the formula down through cell **D20**. With the range **D5:D20** selected, click **AutoSum**, and then widen the column as necessary. To cell **D21**, apply the **Currency Style**. The total sales tax due is $41,341.79.

8. Double-click cell **C14**, and edit as necessary to change the value to **6236.00** The new calculated tax for Favor Boxes is *436.52*.

9. To find out what would happen if the sales tax rate changed from 7% to 8%, click cell **B23**, and in the Formula Bar, edit as necessary to change the number to 8%, and then press [Enter]. The tax rate displays as 8% and the new tax due amount is *$47,223.76*.

10. Change the tax rate back to 7%. Your result is $41,320.79.

11. Press [Ctrl] + [`] to view the underlying formulas, and then use the same keyboard shortcut to return to normal view. Save your workbook, and then click the **Print Preview** button to view the worksheet page. Print the worksheet, and then close the file and close Excel.

End You have completed Project 2H

Mastery Assessments

Project 2I — Open Invoices

Objectives: *Enter Constant Values with AutoFill and the Fill Handle; Insert, Delete, and Adjust Rows and Columns; Align Cell Contents Horizontally; Format Numbers Using the Toolbar; and Copy Formulas.*

Most customers of The Perfect Party pay when their orders are received. A few larger customers have open accounts, and it is necessary to track how much they owe. In the following Mastery Assessment, you will complete a workbook that lists all open invoices. Your completed workbook will look similar to the one shown in Figure 2.80. You will save the workbook as *2I_Open_Invoices_Firstname_Lastname*.

The Perfect Party
Open Invoices

Count	Customer No.	Invoice No.	Invoice Date	Invoice Amount	Paid	Open
1	5551268	875342	1/16/2005	4,324.50		4,324.50
2	5551292	875344	1/18/2005	703.12		703.12
3	5551304	875346	1/19/2005	472.50		472.50
4	5551316	875341	1/15/2005	497.37		497.37
5	5551316	875347	1/20/2005	9.37		9.37
6	5551316	875355	1/24/2005	513.00		513.00
7	5551316	875362	1/31/2005	1,237.50		1,237.50
8	5551316	875371	2/15/2005	157.25	100.00	57.25
9	5551316	875379	2/21/2005	632.00		632.00
10	5551316	875380	2/22/2005	363.12	300.00	63.12
11	5551328	875348	1/21/2005	402.37	200.00	202.37
12	5551352	875354	1/23/2005	392.00		392.00
13	5551376	875356	1/25/2005	278.12		278.12
14	5551388	875343	1/17/2005	1,912.50		1,912.50
15	5551532	875373	2/16/2005	2,754.00		2,754.00
16	5551568	875376	2/18/2005	278.12		278.12
17	5551580	875377	2/19/2005	21.25		21.25
18	5551592	875378	2/20/2005	1,180.00		1,180.00
						$ 15,528.09

2I Open Invoices-Firstname Lastname

Figure 2.80

1. Start Excel. On the **File** menu, click **Open**. In the **Open** dialog box, navigate to the student files that accompany this textbook, and open the file **e02I_Open_Invoices**. Display the **View** menu, click **Header and Footer**, and then click the **Custom Footer** button. In the **Left section**, type **2I Open Invoices-Firstname Lastname** and then click **OK** to close the dialog boxes.

(Project 2I–Open Invoices continues on the next page)

Mastery Assessments (continued)

(Project 2I–Open Invoices continued)

2. From the **File** menu, click **Save As**. In the **Save As** dialog box, navigate to the location where you are storing your projects for this chapter. In the **File name** box, type **2I_Open_Invoices_Firstname_Lastname** and then click **Save** or press Enter.

3. Rename Sheet1 as **Open Invoices** Select **rows 1** through **4**, display the **Insert** menu, and then click **Rows** to insert four empty rows above row 1. In cell **A1**, type **The Perfect Party** and in cell **A2**, type **Open Invoices** In cells **A4** through **D4**, type the following column headings:

   Customer No.
   Invoice No.
   Invoice Date
   Invoice Amount

4. Merge and center the title and subtitle in **row 1** and **row 2** across **columns A:F**. Select **Columns A:D** and then, using either the **Format** menu or the double-click method, AutoFit to set the width to display the longest entry in each column. In cell **E4**, type **Paid** and then, in cell **F4**, type **Open** Select the range **A4:F4** and right-align.

5. Select the range **D5:F25** and apply **Comma Style**. Enter the following paid amounts, being careful to locate the correct invoice number. The invoice numbers are not in numerical order.

Invoice No.	Amount Paid
875348	200.00
875349	87.50
875370	9.37
875371	100.00
875375	722.00
875380	300.00

6. The accounting formula to calculate the Open amount is *INVOICE AMOUNT MINUS PAID*.

   In cell **F5**, create a formula to calculate the amount Open, also referred to as the open balance. For some customers, the invoice amount has been paid in full; thus, some customers will have no open balance.

7. Using the fill handle, copy the formula in cell **F5** down through cell **F25**. With the range **F5:F25** still selected, click **AutoSum** to calculate the total in the empty cell following the range. Widen the column as necessary, and apply **Currency Style** to cell **F26**. The total Open amount is $15,528.09.

8. Hold down Ctrl and then select each row that shows no open amount. (Hint: There are three rows with no open amount.) With the three rows selected, display the **Edit** menu, and then click **Delete**. Click anywhere to cancel the selection.

(Project 2I–Open Invoices continues on the next page)

Mastery Assessments (continued)

(Project 2I–Open Invoices continued)

9. Select **column A**, and then insert a new column to the left of **column A**. Adjust the two titles in **rows 1–2** to **Merge and Center**, starting with the new column A. Type **Count** in cell **A4**, and then type **1** in cell **A5**. Using AutoFill, select cell **A5**, and drag the fill handle down through cell **A22**. On the **Auto Fill Options** button, click the **arrow** to display the menu, and then click **Fill Series**. This will assign a sequential number to each invoice entry by creating a series in **A5:A21**. See Figure 2.80. This is an easy way to determine the number of invoices that are open.

10. Save your workbook, view it in Print Preview, and then print it. Close the file, and then close Excel.

 End You have completed Project 2I

Project 2J — Product Order

Objectives: *Enter Constant Values with AutoFill and the Fill Handle; Insert, Delete, and Adjust Rows and Columns; Align Cell Contents Horizontally; Copy and Move Cell Contents; Format Numbers Using the Toolbar; Copy Formulas; and Conduct a What-if Analysis.*

In the following Mastery Assessment, you will edit a workbook that lists all products in the general theme category, the current inventory levels, and average monthly sales by quantity. You will calculate a quantity to order for each product. Your completed workbook will look similar to the one shown in Figure 2.81. You will save the workbook as *2J_Product_Order_Firstname_Lastname*.

1. Start Excel. On the **File** menu, click **Open**. In the **Open** dialog box, navigate to the student files that accompany this textbook, and open the file **e02J_Product_Order**.

2. Right-click the **Sheet1 tab**, and then click **Select All Sheets**. Display the **View** menu, click **Header and Footer**, and then click the **Custom Footer** button. In the **Left section**, type **2J Product Order-Firstname Lastname** and then click **OK** to close the dialog boxes. Right-click the **Sheet 1 tab**, and click **Ungroup Sheets**.

3. From the **File** menu, click **Save As**. In the **Save As** dialog box, navigate to the location where you are storing your projects for this chapter. In the **File name** box, type **2J_Product_Order_Firstname_Lastname** and then click **Save** or press Enter.

4. Select **rows 1–3**, display the **Insert** menu, and then click **Rows** to insert three new blank rows. In cell **A1**, type **The Perfect Party** and in cell **A2**, type **Product Order Report** Rename Sheet1 to **Order** and then **Merge and Center** the titles in **rows 1 and 2** across **columns A:E**.

(Project 2J–Product Order continues on the next page)

Mastery Assessments (continued)

(Project 2J–Product Order continued)

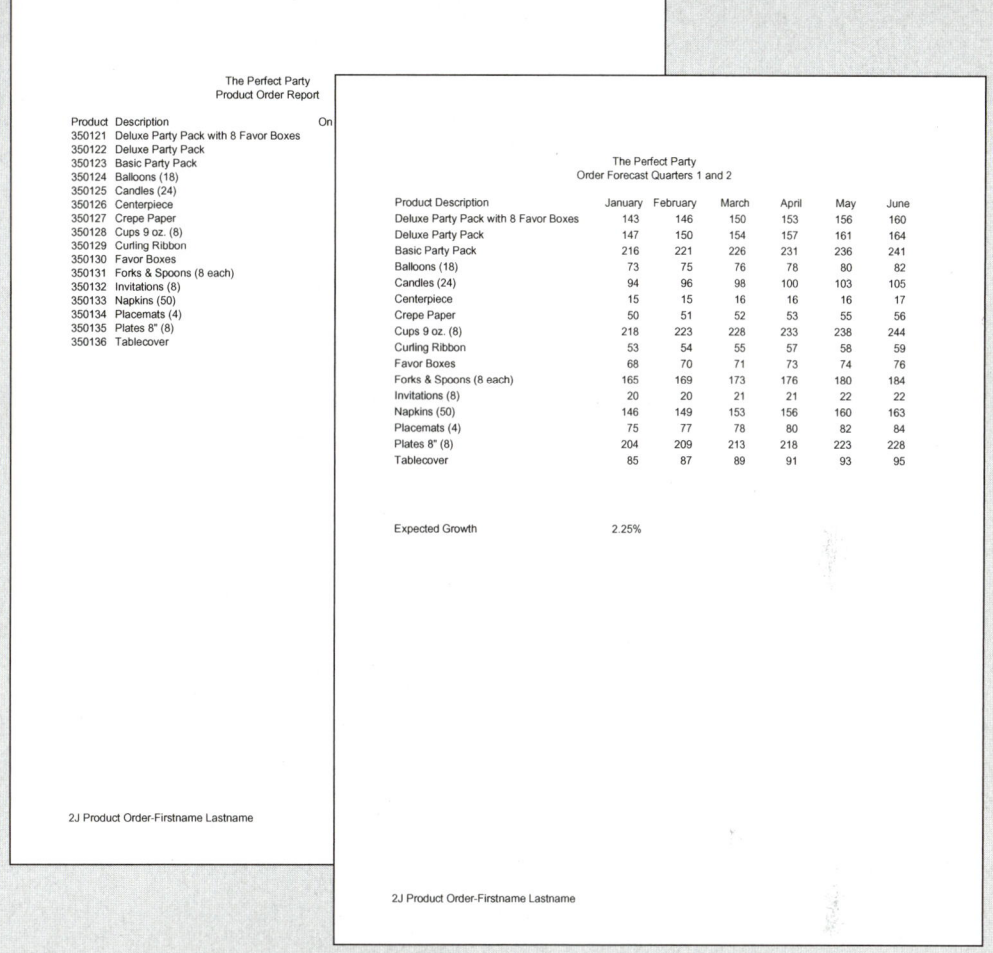

Figure 2.81

5. Select **columns A:B** and AutoFit the width to display the longest entry in each column. Select **columns C:E**, adjust the width to **60 pixels** wide, and then click the **Align Right** button so that all cells in these columns will be right-aligned.

6. Column D contains the average quantity sold of each product number, each month. The owners like to maintain a two-month average supply of products. In cell **E5**, create a formula to calculate the quantity that should be ordered to maintain a two-month supply, taking into account the number currently on hand. (Hint: Average multiplied by 2 months minus On Hand.) Recall that the **Average column** contains the average monthly sales quantities. The Order quantity for the first product should be *214*.

7. Using the fill handle, copy the formula in cell **E5** down through the remaining rows. Select the range **C5:E20**, apply **Comma Style**, and then click **Decrease Decimal** two times. Click anywhere to cancel the selection, and then, on the Standard toolbar, click **Save**.

(Project 2J–Product Order continues on the next page)

Excel chapter two

Mastery Assessments (continued)

(Project 2J–Product Order continued)

8. Select **Sheet2**, and then rename the sheet as **Forecast** Display the **Order** sheet, copy the title in cell **A1**, and paste it to cell **A1** on the **Forecast** sheet.

9. In cell **A2** of the **Forecast** sheet, type **Order Forecast Quarters 1 and 2** In cell **A4** of the **Forecast** sheet, type **Product Description** Display the **Order** sheet, copy the range **B5:B20**, and then return to the **Forecast** sheet.

10. On the **Forecast** sheet, click cell **A5**, and then click the **Paste** button. Adjust **column A** on the **Forecast** sheet so that it is wide enough to accommodate the longest product description.

11. On the **Forecast** sheet, change the height of **rows 5 through 20** to **20** pixels. This taller row size will make it easier to view the entries in each row.

12. Beginning in cell **B4** on the Forecast sheet, create a series of month names for the first and second quarters, beginning with January and ending with June, and then apply right alignment to the month names.

13. Display the **Order** sheet. Copy the range **D5:D20**, display the **Forecast** sheet, and paste the range beginning in cell **B5** under *January*.

14. **Merge and Center** the two titles on the **Forecast** sheet across all the active columns. Select the range **B5:G20** and apply **Comma Style**. Decrease the number of decimals showing to none.

15. The expected growth per month is expressed as a percentage. In cell **A25**, type **Expected Growth** Then, in cell **B25**, type **.0156** and format it as a percentage with two decimals.

16. Sales of products in February are expected to grow by 1.56% over January sales. Likewise, March sales are expected to grow 1.56% over February sales, and so forth through June. Create a formula in cell **C5** to compute the February forecast for the first product. The result, *145*, is the January usage plus the increase.

17. Copy the formula down for all products. With the range selected, copy the entire range across all months through June. The June total for *Tablecover* should be *92*.

18. Conduct a what-if analysis by proposing a growth percentage of 2.25% rather than 1.56%. On the Standard toolbar, click **Save**.

19. Right-click the **Forecast sheet tab**, and then click **Select All Sheets**. Click the **Print Preview** button to view the two worksheet pages (use PageDown to view the second sheet). On the Print Preview toolbar, click the **Print** button. Because you have selected all sheets, both sheets will print. Close the file and close Excel.

End You have completed Project 2J

Problem Solving

Project 2K — Sales Forecast

Objectives: *Enter Constant Values with AutoFill and the Fill Handle; Conduct a What-if Analysis; Insert, Delete, and Adjust Rows and Columns; Edit Formulas; and Copy Formulas.*

Using the data found in *e2K_Data*, create a workbook that computes a sales forecast for the next year assuming an increase in sales of 5 percent. List each month from January through December with a total forecast for each month and for the year. Include a footer with your first and last name. Select a company name of your choice, and create appropriate worksheet titles. Place the percentage in an assumption area below column A in your workbook. Save the workbook as *2K_Sales_Forecast_Firstname_Lastname*.

 You have completed Project 2K

Project 2L — Gross Payroll

Objectives: *Enter Constant Values with AutoFill and the Fill Handle; Conduct a What-if Analysis; Insert, Delete, and Adjust Rows and Columns; Edit Formulas; and Copy Formulas.*

Create a weekly payroll report for The Perfect Party. The owners, Angie Nguyen and Gabriela Quinones, receive an annual salary of $40,000 each, paid weekly. The other employees, Tom Sundling, Corey Finstad, and Christina Stevens, each receive $20 per hour. Create a workbook that will enable the owners to enter the number of hours worked in one week for each of the hourly employees. Include formulas that will calculate the total gross pay for each employee, including the owners. The total gross payroll amount should also be displayed. Include a footer that contains your first and last name. Create appropriate worksheet titles. Save the workbook as *2L_Gross_Payroll_Firstname_Lastname*.

 You have completed Project 2L

On the Internet

Excel Help on the Web

Microsoft is not the only source for additional information about Excel. Using Internet Explorer, type **Excel absolute cell reference** in the address bar, and press Enter.

MSN Search finds over 9,000 sites that refer to those search words. Review a few of those pages to see whether you can pick up some new information about using cell references in Excel. You might also want to try the same search in your favorite search engine to see whether you can find additional information on the Web.

GO! with Help

Using Excel Help

In this exercise, you will use Microsoft Help to get help with absolute cell references.

1. If necessary, start Excel to open a new workbook.//
2. At the right edge of the menu bar, click in the *Type a question for help* box, type **absolute reference** and then press the Enter key.

   The task pane opens, showing Search Results. Notice that you typed *absolute reference* as the question instead of *What is an absolute reference?* It is not actually necessary to ask the question *as* a question.
3. Click the link **Switch between relative, absolute, and mixed references**.

   A Microsoft Excel Help window displays with Help for the topic.
4. In the upper right corner of the Help window, click **Show All**.

   Detailed descriptions of the terms included on the help screen are displayed. Alternatively, you can click on the individual links associated with each term to display them as needed.
5. Review the information provided in the Help window.
6. Print the contents of the Help window with the expanded material.
7. Close the Help Window, and close the task pane.

Excel 2003

chapter three

Formatting a Worksheet

In this chapter, you will: **complete these projects** and **practice these skills.**

Project 3A
Format Numbers and Cells

Objectives
- Change Number Format
- Change Alignment of Cell Contents
- Apply Cell Formatting

Project 3B
Apply Workbook Formatting

Objective
- Apply Workbook Formatting

Project 3C
Print Gridlines and Insert Comments

Objectives
- Print Gridlines, Print Row and Column Headings, and Set Print Quality
- View and Insert Comments in a Cell

Oceana Palm Grill

Oceana Palm Grill is a chain of 25 upscale, casual, full-service restaurants based in Austin, Texas. The company opened its first restaurant in 1975 and now operates 25 outlets in the Austin and Dallas areas. Plans call for 15 additional restaurants to be opened in North Carolina and Florida by 2008. These ambitious plans will require the company to bring in new investors, develop new menus and recruit new employees, all while adhering to the company's strict quality guidelines and maintaining its reputation for excellent service.

© Getty Images, Inc.

Formatting a Worksheet

In this chapter, you will learn how to change the format of numbers and decimals. You will change the alignment of text and numbers, indent text, rotate text, wrap text, and merge cells. You will change the appearance of cells by changing fonts and font size and by creating cell borders and shading. Additionally, you will format your worksheet for printing by creating headers and footers and changing the placement of your worksheet on the printed page.

Project 3A Tableware

In this project, you will use various methods to format numbers and the appearance of cells. Cell formatting includes adding color or patterns to a cell. You will also practice how to change the horizontal and vertical alignment of data in a cell.

In Activities 3.1 through 3.14, you will edit a workbook for Donna Rohan Kurian, Executive Chef for the Oceana Palm Grill, detailing tableware purchases for the Dallas location. Your workbook will look similar to Figure 3.1. You will save the workbook as 3A_Tableware_Firstname_Lastname.

Figure 3.1
Project 3A—Tableware

Project 3A: Tableware | **Excel** 669

Objective 1
Change Number Format

Excel's power lies in its ability to perform calculations on numbers. Because there are many ways to write numbers—think of percentages, fractions, money—Excel has a variety of ways to help you enter numbers so that you get the results you want. Excel refers to the various ways to write numbers as ***number formats***.

Activity 3.1 Using the Format Cells Dialog Box to Format Numbers

Formatting is the process of determining the appearance of cells and the overall layout of a worksheet. Formatting of cells is accomplished through the Format Cells dialog box. Additionally, the Formatting toolbar has some buttons that provide a one-click method of performing commonly used cell formatting without displaying the Format Cells dialog box.

Once applied, cell formats stay with the cell, even if you delete the contents of the cell. To delete the format from a cell, you must purposely clear the format using either the Clear Formats command or the Clear All command from the Edit menu.

The table in Figure 3.2 details the many ways Excel can format numbers for you.

Excel Number Formats

Number Format	Description
General	The General format is the default format for a number that you type in a cell. The General format displays a number exactly as you type it—with three exceptions: 1. Extremely long numbers may be abbreviated to a shorthand version of numbers called scientific notation, and long decimal values may be rounded up. Even if this happens, Excel will still use the underlying value, not the displayed value, in any calculations. 2. Trailing zeros will not display in the General format. For example, if you type the number *456.0* the cell will display 456 with no zero or decimal point. 3. A decimal fraction entered without a number to the left of the decimal point will display with a zero. For example, if you type *.456* you will see 0.456 displayed in the cell.
Number	Number format is used for the general display of noncurrency numbers. The default format has two decimal places, and you may choose to check the option for using a comma as a thousand separator. Negative numbers can display in red, be preceded by a minus sign, be enclosed in parentheses, or display both in red and in parentheses.
Currency	Currency format is used for general monetary values, and you can select from a list of worldwide currency symbols—the U.S. dollar sign is the default symbol. When you click the Currency Style button on the Formatting toolbar, you apply a two-decimal-place Accounting format.
Accounting	Accounting format is similar to Currency format with two differences—the dollar sign (or other currency symbol) always displays at the left edge of the cell, rather than flush against the first number. Thus, both dollar signs and numbers are vertically aligned in the same column. Also, Accounting formats add a blank space equal to the width of a close parenthesis on the right side of positive values to ensure that decimal points align if a column has both positive and negative numbers.
Date	Date format provides many common ways to display dates. The default format in the Format Cells dialog box is month, day, and year, separated by a slash. The year displays as four digits by default, but may be changed in the Control Panel to a four-digit display.
Time	Time format provides many common ways to display time. The default format in the Format Cells dialog box is the hour and minute.
Percentage	Percentage format multiplies the cell value by 100 and displays the result with a percent sign. The default is two decimal places.
Fraction	Fraction format displays fractional amounts as actual fractions rather than as decimal values. The first three formats use single-digit, double-digit, and triple-digit numerators and denominators. For example, the single-digit format rounds up to the nearest value that can be represented as a single-digit fraction.
Scientific	Scientific format displays numbers in scientific (exponential) notation. This is useful for extremely large numbers.
Text	Text format treats a number as if it were text. The number is left-aligned like text.
Special	Special formats are used primarily with database functions. You can type postal codes, telephone numbers, and taxpayer ID numbers quickly without having to enter the punctuation.
Custom	Custom format is used to create your own number format. For example, perhaps your organization has a special format for invoice numbers.

Figure 3.2

1 Start Excel. On the **File** menu, click **Open**. In the **Open** dialog box, navigate to the student files that accompany this textbook, and open the file **e03A_Tableware**. Display the **View** menu, click **Header and Footer**, and then click the **Custom Footer** button. In the **Left section**, using your own name, type **3A Tableware-Firstname Lastname** and then click **OK** to close the dialog boxes.

2 From the **File** menu, click **Save As**. In the **Save As** dialog box, navigate to the location where you are storing your projects for this chapter, creating a new Chapter 3 folder if you want to do so. In the **File name** box, type **3A_Tableware_Firstname_Lastname** and then click **Save** or press Enter.

3 Click the **Format Cells Practice sheet tab**.

4 In cell **A1** type **52350** and press Enter. Click cell **A1** again to make it the active cell.

The default format for numbers is no commas, no decimal points, and aligned at the right boundary of the cell.

5 Display the **Format** menu, and then click **Cells**. If necessary, click the **Number tab**.

The Format Cells dialog box displays, as shown in Figure 3.3. Under Category, all of Excel's Number formats are listed. The first format, General, is highlighted. The **General format** is the default format for a number that you type in a cell. Unless you apply a different number format to a cell, Excel will use the General format. The General format displays a number exactly as you type it—with three exceptions, as noted in the table in Figure 3.2.

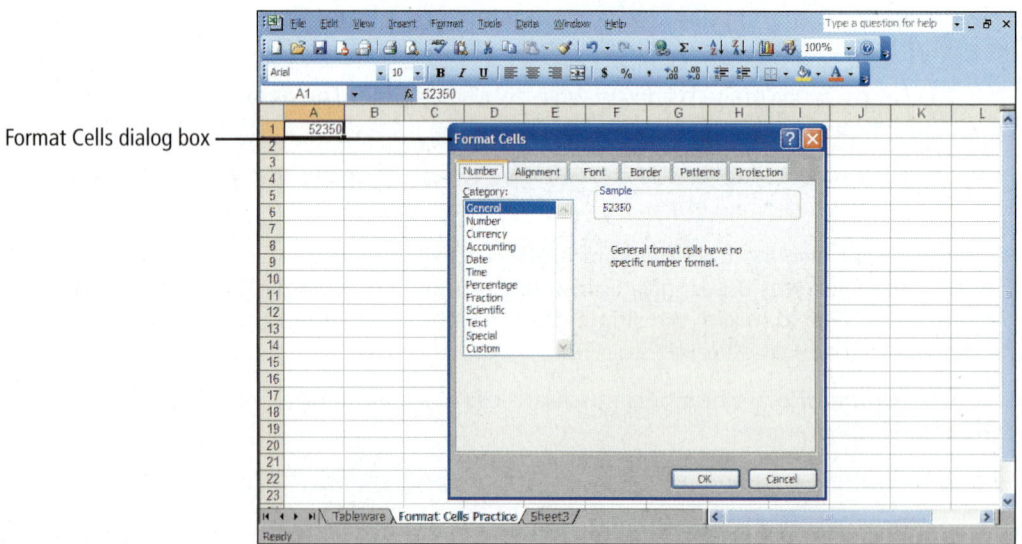

Format Cells dialog box

Figure 3.3

672   Excel | Chapter 3: Formatting a Worksheet

6 In the **Format Cells** dialog box, under **Category**, click **Number**, and then look at the right side of the dialog box under **Sample**.

Assuming the selected cell contains numbers, the Format Cells dialog box ***Sample area*** will always show you how the format will look with the numbers you have typed into the cell. The default number of decimal places for the Number format is two decimal places.

7 In the middle of the dialog box, click to select (place a check mark in) the **Use 1000 Separator (,)** check box, and then look again at the **Sample** area.

Excel demonstrates how your number will look if you apply this format.

8 In the **Decimal places** box, click once on the **up arrow** in the spin box to change the number of decimal places to **3**. Look at the **Sample** area to see the effect that three decimal places will have on your cell.

> **Note**
>
> A spin box enables you to move through a set of fixed values. A spin box is found in many dialog boxes throughout Windows-based applications. You can also type a valid value in the box if you prefer.

9 At the lower right corner of the dialog box, click the **Cancel** button to close the dialog box and reject any of the number formats that you examined.

Another Way

Display the Format Cells Dialog Box

There are three ways to display the Format Cells dialog box:

- From the menu bar, click Format, and then click Cells.
- Use the keyboard shortcut by holding down [Ctrl] and pressing [1] on the alphanumeric keyboard.
- Select a range of cells, right-click to display a shortcut menu, and then click Format Cells.

10 With **A1** as the active cell, press and hold down [Ctrl] and then press [1] at the top left of your keyboard.

The Format Cells dialog box displays. This is the keyboard shortcut for displaying the Format Cells dialog box. You cannot use the numeric keypad for this keyboard shortcut.

11 In the displayed **Format Cells** dialog box, under **Category**, click **Currency**, and then observe the **Sample** area. Click **Accounting** and observe the **Sample** area.

The Currency and Accounting formats always include the thousand comma separator where necessary. These two number formats are similar—there is only a slight difference in the way dollar signs are aligned and the way negative numbers are formatted. In the **Currency format**, the dollar sign is always flush against the first number. In the **Accounting format**, the dollar sign is always flush with the left cell boundary. See the examples shown in Figure 3.4.

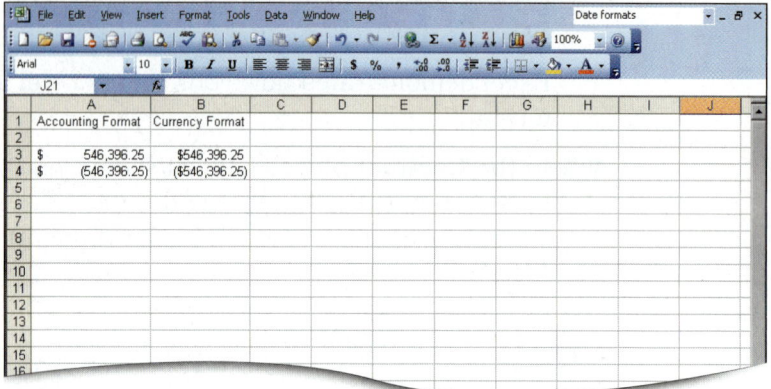

Figure 3.4

12 Under **Category**, click **Percentage**. At the bottom of the dialog box, read how percentage formats are handled and displayed. Then, at the lower right corner of the dialog box, click the **Cancel** button.

13 With cell **A1** as the active cell, press [Delete] to delete the contents of the cell.

More Knowledge

When you click the Comma Style button on the Formatting toolbar, Excel applies a two-decimal place Accounting format *without* currency symbols. When you click the Percent Style button on the Formatting toolbar, Excel applies a Percentage format *without* decimals.

Activity 3.2 Selecting and Applying the Currency Format

1 Click the **Tableware sheet tab**. Select the range **B3:H3**. Press and hold down [Ctrl] and select the range **B12:H12**. Recall that this is the technique to select nonadjacent ranges. With the two ranges selected, display the **Format** menu, and then click **Cells**.

2 If necessary, click the **Number tab**, and then, under **Category**, click **Currency**. Click the **Symbol arrow** to display the list of symbols, and from the displayed list, click **$**. In the **Decimal places** spin box, click the **down arrow** twice to set **0** decimal places. Click **OK**.

Recall that it is common practice to include the dollar sign ($) symbol in the first line of a worksheet and in the Total line of a worksheet. When you add totals to row 12, they will display with this format.

674   Excel | Chapter 3: Formatting a Worksheet

3 Select the range **B4:H11**, and then right-click to display the shortcut menu, as shown in Figure 3.5.

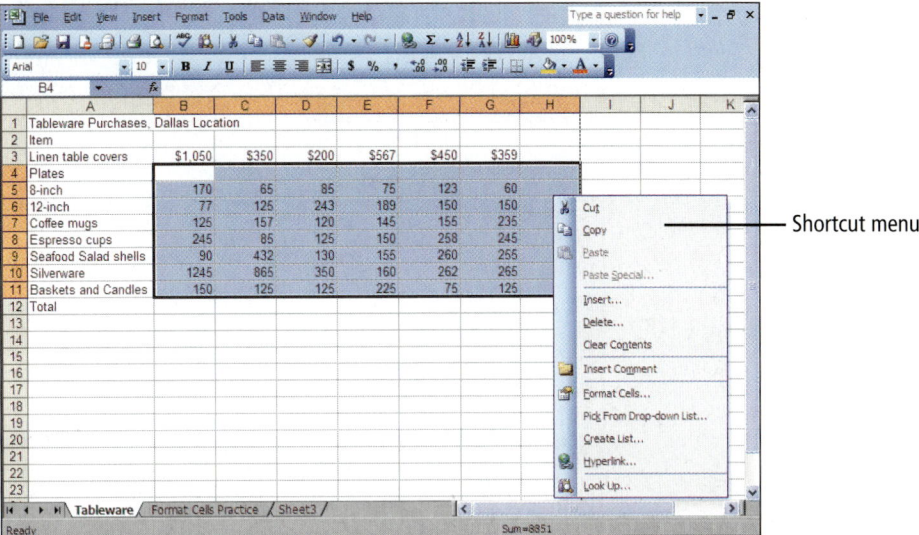

Figure 3.5

4 On the displayed shortcut menu, click **Format Cells**.

This is another way to display the Format Cells dialog box.

5 If necessary, click the **Number tab**. Under **Category**, click **Currency**. In the **Decimal places** box, click the **spin box arrows** as necessary to set **0** decimal places. Click the **Symbol arrow** and click **None**. Click **OK**. Click anywhere to cancel the selection.

The Currency format automatically includes the thousand comma separator where appropriate.

6 On the Standard toolbar, click the **Save** button.

Objective 2
Change Alignment of Cell Contents

Alignment refers to the position of text or numbers within a cell. You have already used the alignment options on the toolbar, for example, Align Left, Center, and Align Right.

Options for more complex alignment, such as rotating cell contents, aligning the contents vertically and horizontally, and increasing or decreasing indentation, are available from the Format Cells dialog box.

Activity 3.3 Changing Horizontal Alignment Using the Format Cells Dialog Box

Within a cell, you can align data horizontally in a number of ways. ***Horizontal alignment*** is the positioning of data between the left and right boundaries of a cell. Recall that Excel's default horizontal alignment for numbers, dates, and times is right-aligned. Excel's default horizontal alignment for text is left-aligned. Other horizontal alignments include Center, General, Indent, Fill, Justify, and Center Across Selection. See Figure 3.6.

Project 3A: Tableware | **Excel**

Examples of horizontal alignments

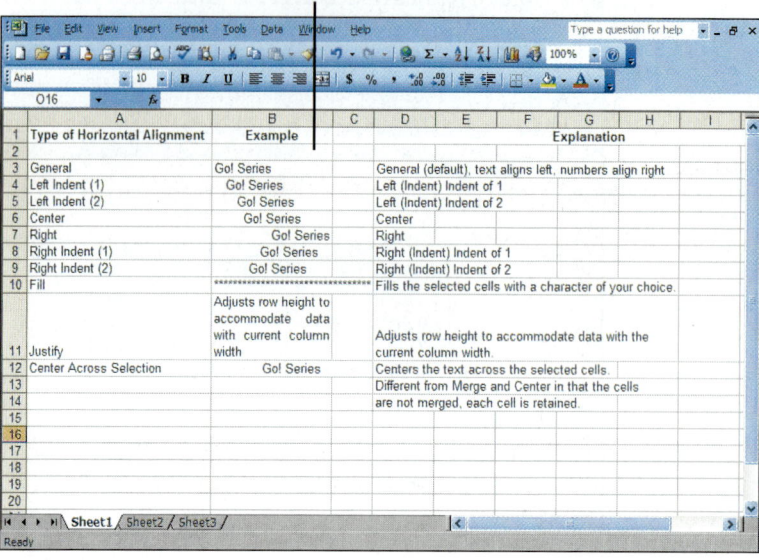

Figure 3.6

1. If necessary, **Open** your file **3A Tableware**. Click cell **A12**. On the Formatting toolbar, click the **Center** button. The text is centered horizontally within the cell.

2. In cell **B2**, type **Jan** and then press Enter. Click in cell **B2** again, position your pointer over the **fill handle**, and drag to the right to cell **G2** to fill in the series of month abbreviations *Jan* through *Jun*.

3. In cell **H2**, type **Total** and press Enter.

4. Select the range **B2:G2**, position your pointer over the selected area, and then right-click to display the shortcut menu. Click **Format Cells**.

5. In the **Format Cells** dialog box, click the **Alignment tab**. Under **Text alignment**, click the **Horizontal arrow**, and then click **Center**, as shown in Figure 3.7.

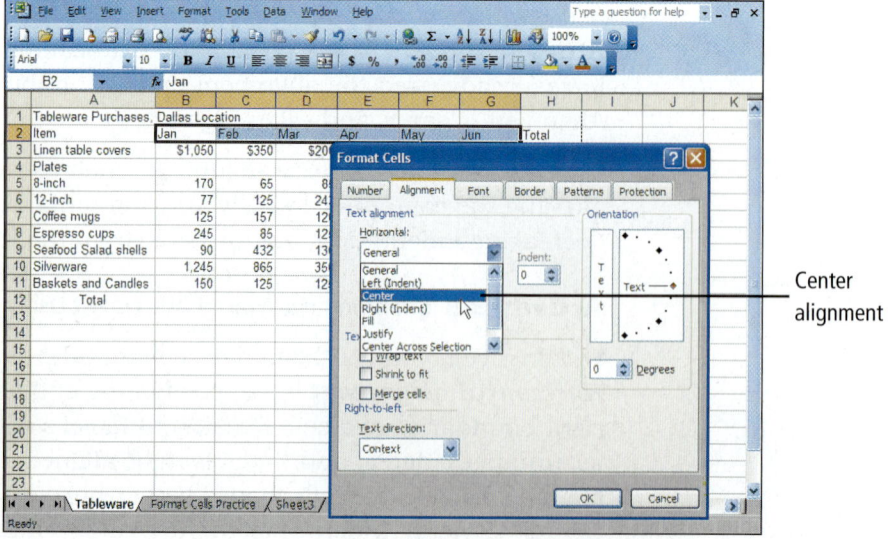

Center alignment

Figure 3.7

676   Excel | Chapter 3: Formatting a Worksheet

6 Click **OK**.

The text in each of the selected cells is centered horizontally between the left and right boundaries of the cell. You can accomplish horizontal centering either by clicking the Center button on the Formatting toolbar or, as you just did, from the Format Cells dialog box. This is another example of the convenience and speed of toolbar buttons.

7 In cell **H3**, click **AutoSum** and press Enter to sum the cost of linen table covers for the six-month period.

Notice that the Currency format with no decimal places is applied because earlier, you applied that format to the empty cell. Also, it is the format of the adjacent cells.

8 Click cell **H3** again, and then drag the **fill handle** downward to copy the formula through cell **H11**. Click cell **H4** and press Delete.

Because this row functions as a subheading for the two plate types, this cell needs no formula.

9 Click cell **B12**, click **AutoSum**, press Enter, and then copy the formula across through cell **H12**. Click anywhere to cancel the selection, and compare your screen with Figure 3.8.

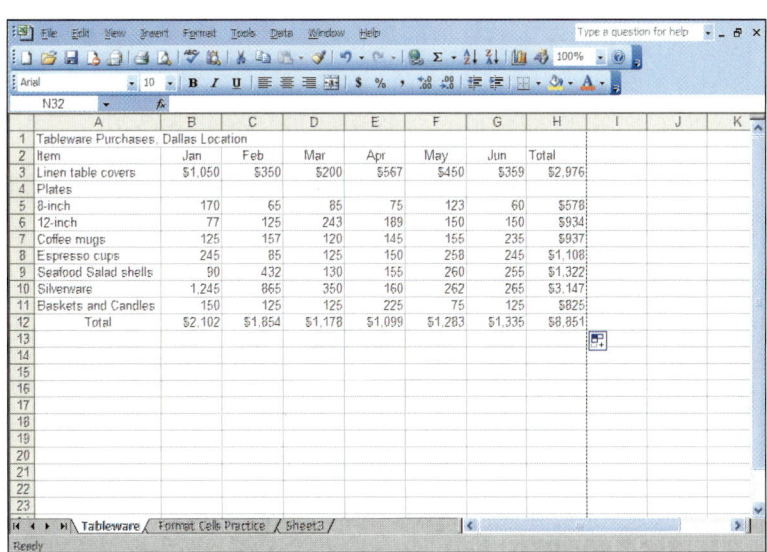

Figure 3.8

10 Click **Save**.

Activity 3.4 Indenting Cell Contents

Indenting increases the distance of the cell contents from either the left cell boundary (***left indent***) or the right cell boundary (***right indent***). Each time you increase the left indent by 1, the data in the cell begins one character width farther to the right. A character width in Excel is an approximate measurement equivalent to the width of an uppercase W. Zero is the default number of indents.

1 Click cell **A5**. From the **Format** menu, click **Cells**.

2 If necessary, click the **Alignment tab**. Under **Text alignment**, click the **Horizontal arrow**, and then click **Left (Indent)**. In the **Indent spin box**, click the **up arrow** to indent by **2**. See Figure 3.9. Click **OK**.

The cell contents are indented by two character widths. Recall that a character width is an approximate measurement equivalent to the width of an uppercase W, and thus it may appear that the indent is more than 2 characters because the characters above are much narrower than an uppercase W.

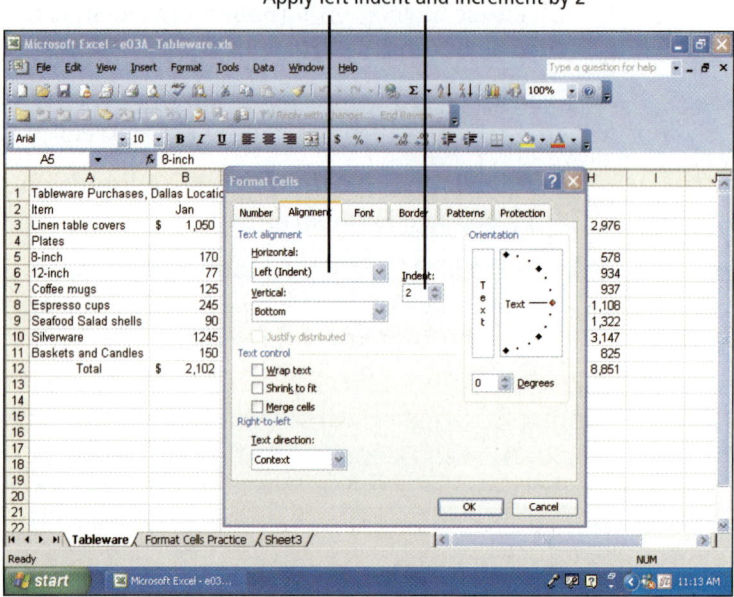

Figure 3.9

3 Click cell **A6**. On the Formatting toolbar, click the **Increase Indent** button once. Notice how the data indents to the right. Click the **Increase Indent** button again to align the data by two character widths—the same as the data in the cell above.

As you have just practiced, Right Indent can be applied from either the Format Cells dialog box or from the Formatting toolbar.

Activity 3.5 Filling a Cell

The *Fill* alignment repeats any character you type into a cell to fill the width of the cell or to fill a group of selected cells across two or more columns.

1 In cell **A13**, type * and then press Enter. Select the range **A13:H13**. With your mouse pointer positioned over the selection, right-click to display the shortcut menu, and then click **Format Cells**.

2 If necessary, click the **Alignment tab**. Under **Text alignment**, click the **Horizontal arrow**, and then click **Fill**. Click **OK**, and then click in a blank cell to cancel the selection. Compare your worksheet with Figure 3.10.

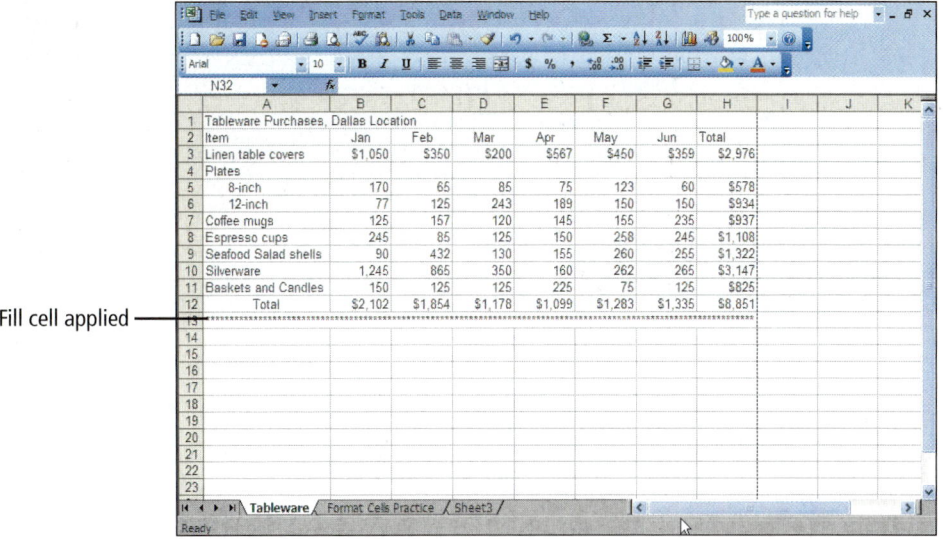

Fill cell applied

Figure 3.10

3 Select the range **A1:H1**. Press and hold down Ctrl and press 1 at the top left of your keyboard—recall that this is another way to display the **Format Cells** dialog box.

4 On the **Alignment tab** of the displayed **Format Cells** dialog box, click the **Horizontal arrow**, and then click **Center Across Selection**. Click **OK**.

The Center Across Selection alignment looks similar to the result you get when you use the Merge and Center button; however, the two features work differently. Merge and Center merges the selected cells and replaces them with a single cell. Thus, the first selected cell remains, but the other selected cells no longer exist. You cannot select them.

The Center Across Selection feature centers the text in one cell across all selected blank cells to the right. The cell contents remain in the first cell, and the remaining cells continue to exist as empty cells.

5 Click **Save** to save the changes you have made to your workbook.

Activity 3.6 Aligning Cell Contents Vertically

Vertical alignment is the positioning of data between the top and bottom boundaries of a cell. Vertical alignment has four positions from which you can choose: top, bottom, center, and justify. The default vertical alignment for all data is bottom—aligned along the lower boundary of the cell.

1 Position your mouse pointer over the **row 1 heading**, and right-click to simultaneously select the row and display the shortcut menu. On the shortcut menu, click **Row Height**.

The Row Height dialog box displays, as shown in Figure 3.11.

Project 3A: Tableware | **Excel** 679

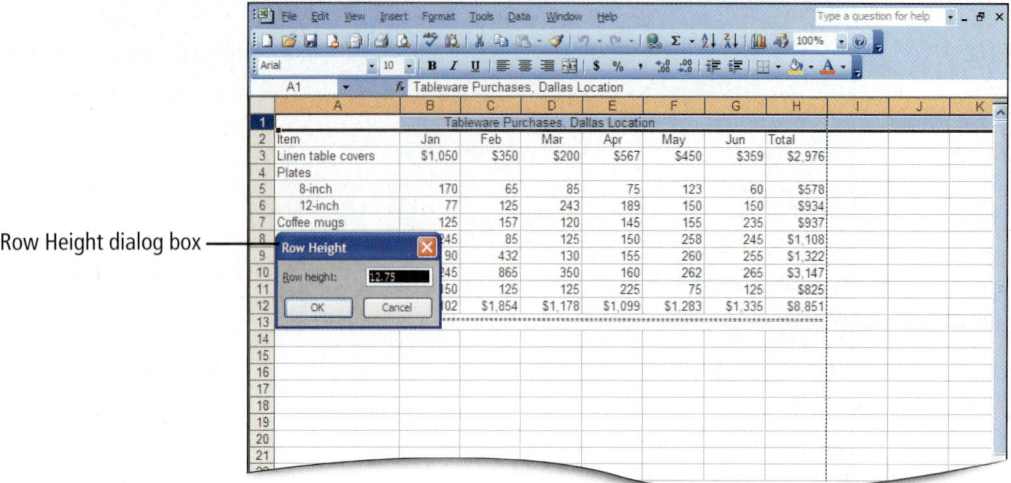

Figure 3.11

[2] With 12.75 highlighted, type **30** and then click **OK**.

Your new typing replaces the highlighted text, and the height of row 1 is changed to 30 pts. Recall that a pt. is ½₂ of an inch.

[3] Select the range **A1:H1**, position your pointer over the selected area, and then right-click to display the shortcut menu. Click **Format Cells**.

[4] In the **Format Cells** dialog box, click the **Alignment tab**. Under **Text alignment**, click the **Vertical arrow**, scroll this small box as necessary, and then click **Top**. Click **OK**.

The data is vertically aligned with the top boundary of the cell, as shown in Figure 3.12.

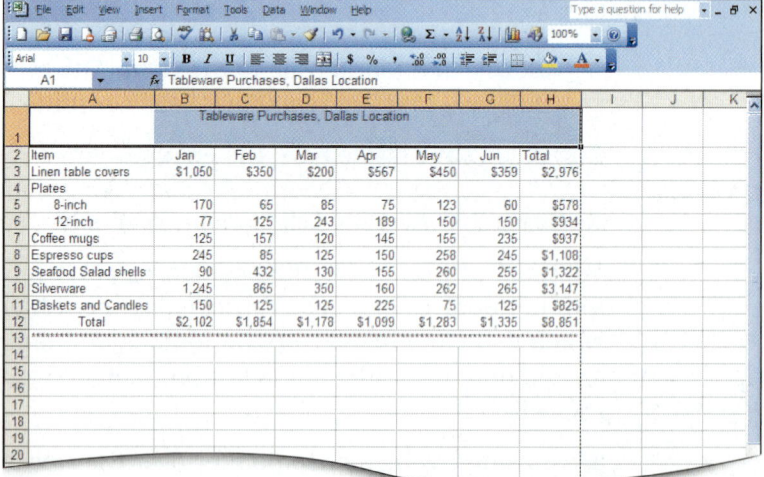

Figure 3.12

680 Excel | Chapter 3: Formatting a Worksheet

5 With the range **A1:H1** still selected, press and hold down Ctrl and press 1 at the upper left corner of your keyboard. In the **Alignment tab** of the **Format Cells** dialog box, click the **Vertical arrow**, and then click **Center**. Click **OK**, and then click anywhere to cancel the selection.

The data in the cells is vertically centered. Compare your screen with Figure 3.13.

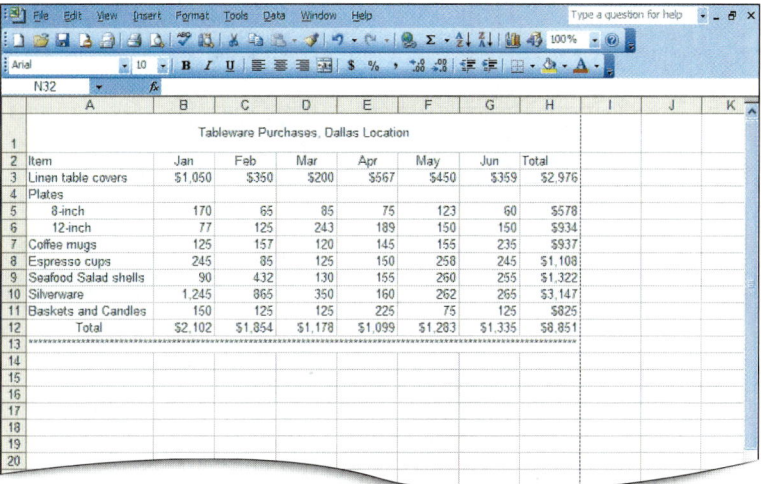

Figure 3.13

Activity 3.7 Rotating Text

The Orientation section of the Alignment tab in the Format Cells dialog box lets you change the angle of cell contents to read vertically from top to bottom (*stacked*), or at an angle of your choice—from 90 degrees counterclockwise to 90 degrees clockwise—for a total of 180 degrees. See Figure 3.14.

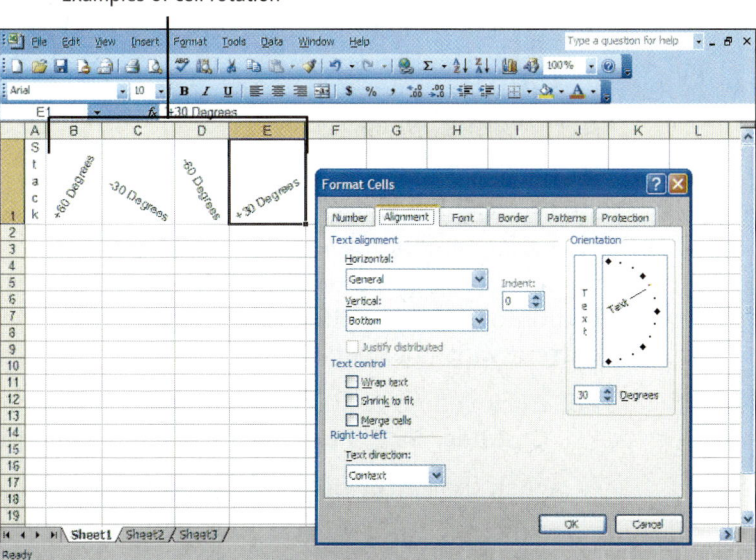

Figure 3.14

Project 3A: Tableware | **Excel** 681

1 Select the range **B2:G2**, and then use any method to display the **Format Cells** dialog box. (Hint: When you have a group of cells selected, right-clicking is probably the quickest way to display the **Format Cells** dialog box. Remember that your mouse pointer must be over the selection when you right-click.)

2 If necessary, click the **Alignment tab**. Under **Orientation**, point to the **small red diamond** to the right of the word *Text*. Hold down the left mouse button, and drag the diamond upward until the **Degrees** spin box indicates *30*. Alternatively, click the up spin box arrow until *30* displays, or type **30** directly into the spin box. See Figure 3.15.

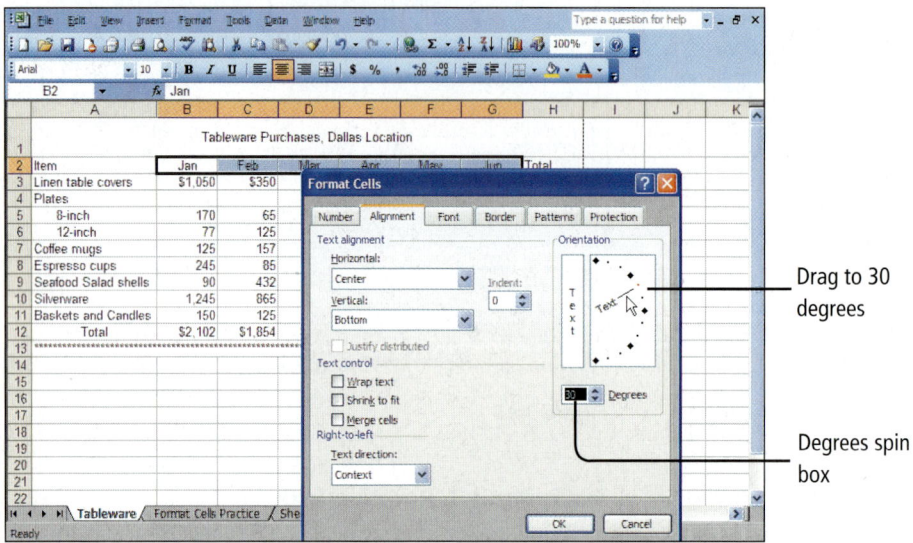

Figure 3.15

3 Click **OK**.

The text in the selected cells is rotated 30 degrees, and the row height is automatically adjusted to accommodate the rotated text.

4 On the Standard toolbar, click **Save** to save the changes you have made to your workbook.

Activity 3.8 Wrapping Text in a Cell

Recall that when you type text that is too long for the active cell, Excel lets the text spill over into adjacent cells—if they are empty. Using the Text control option **Wrap text**, Excel displays your text entirely within the active cell by increasing the *height* of the row and then wrapping the text onto additional lines in the same cell. Thus, Wrap text maintains the current width of the cell.

1 Click cell **A11**, and then edit the cell so that it indicates **Baskets and Candles, Salt, Pepper, Butter** as shown in Figure 3.16, and then click the **Enter** button on the Formula Bar.

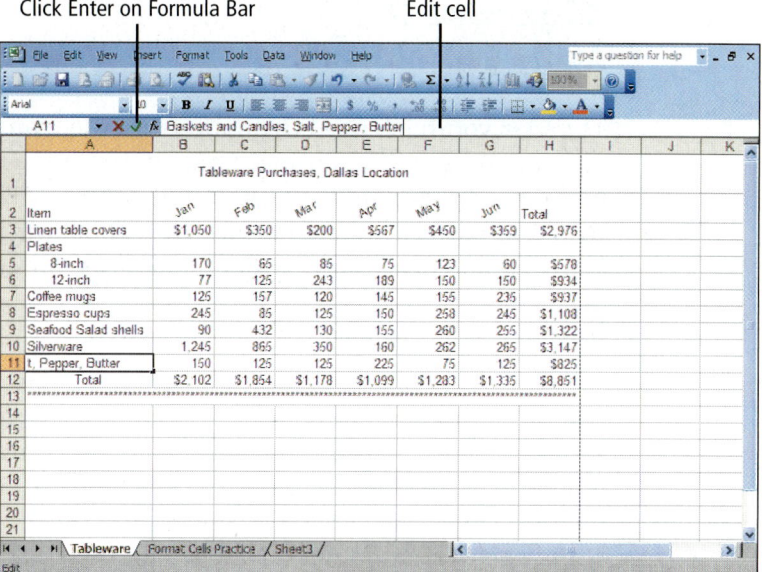

Figure 3.16

2 With **A11** as the active cell, use any method to display the **Format Cells** dialog box.

3 If necessary, click the **Alignment tab**. Under **Text control**, click to place a check mark in the **Wrap text** check box, as shown in Figure 3.17.

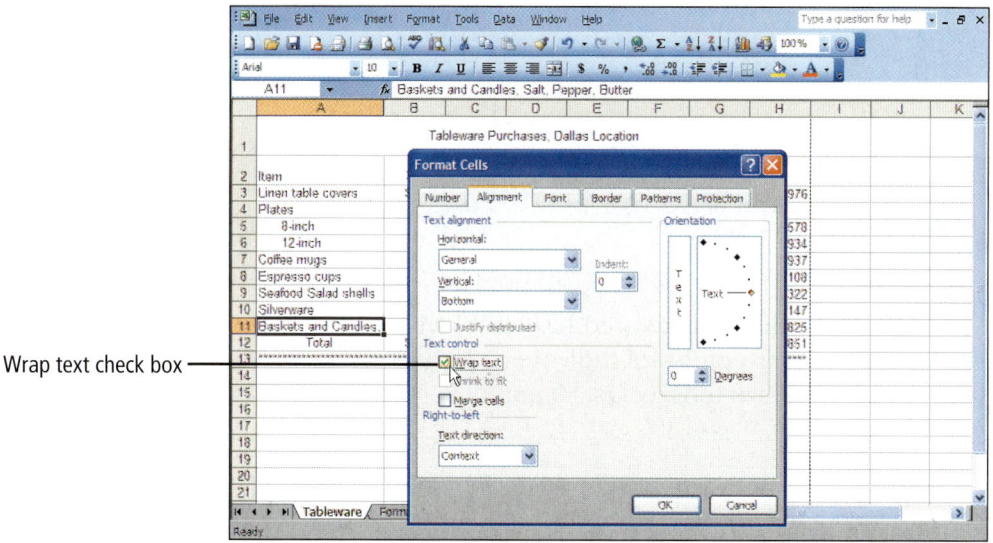

Figure 3.17

4 Click **OK**. On the Standard toolbar, click **Save** to save the changes you have made to your workbook.

Project 3A: Tableware | **Excel** 683

Objective 3
Apply Cell Formatting

Thus far you have used the options on the Number tab and the Alignment tab of the Format Cells dialog box. Additional tabs provide options for changing the font of data within cells and also for adding borders and pattern effects to cells. In the following activities, you will change fonts and apply borders and patterns to cells in your worksheet.

Activity 3.9 Changing the Font and Font Size

A *font* is a set of characters with the same design and shape. There are two basic types of fonts—serif and sans serif. **Serif fonts** have extensions, or lines, on the ends of the characters and are good for large amounts of text because they are easy to read. Examples of serif fonts include Times New Roman, Copperplate Gothic Light, and Garamond. **Sans serif fonts** do not have lines on the ends of characters. Sans serif fonts are good for worksheets because worksheets normally contain more numbers than text. The default font for an Excel worksheet is Arial—a commonly used sans serif font. Other sans serif fonts include Impact and Comic Sans MS. See Figure 3.18.

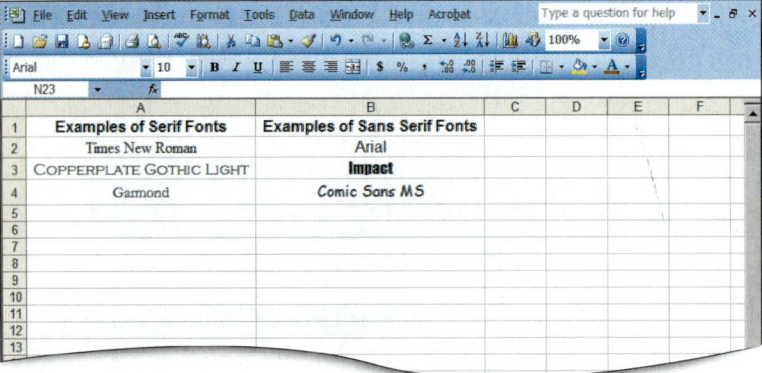

Figure 3.18

Fonts are measured in points, with one point equal to 1/72 of an inch. A higher point size indicates a larger font size. See Figure 3.19. The default font size in Excel is 10 points.

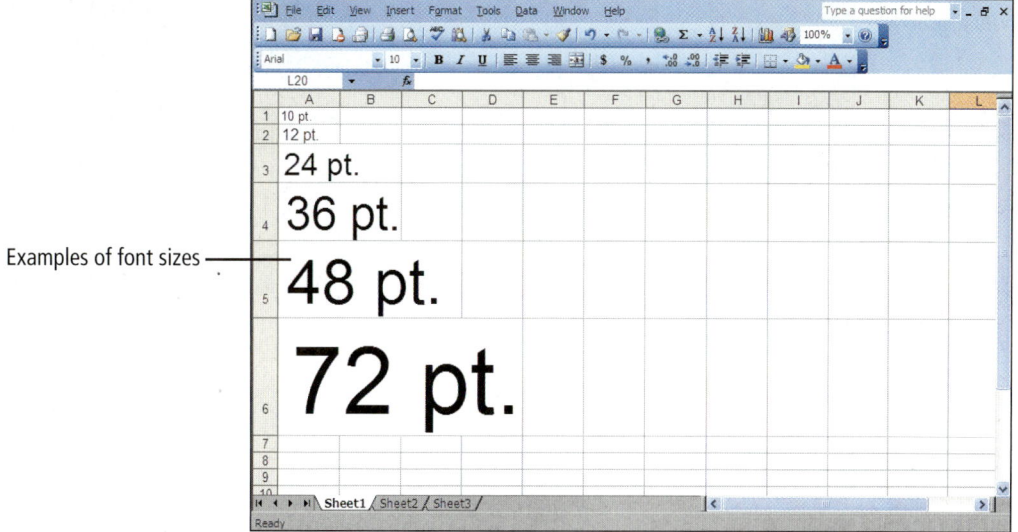

Examples of font sizes

Figure 3.19

You can apply a new font to cells in a worksheet from either of two places:

- The Font list on the Formatting toolbar
- The Font tab on the Format Cells dialog box

Font styles are used to emphasize text using bold, italic, and underline. You can apply font styles in three ways:

- On the Formatting toolbar, click the Bold, Italic, or Underline buttons.
- Select the font style from the Font tab of the Format Cells dialog box.
- Use the keyboard shortcuts Ctrl + B (Bold), Ctrl + I (Italic), or Ctrl + U (Underline).

1 If necessary, **Open** your file **3A_Tableware**.

2 Click cell **A1**, which contains the centered text *Tableware Purchases, Dallas Location*. On the Formatting toolbar, click the **Font button arrow** [Arial], as shown in Figure 3.20.

The Font list displays the fonts available on your system. Each font name displays in its actual design so that you have an immediate indication of the way the font will appear on your screen and on your printed page.

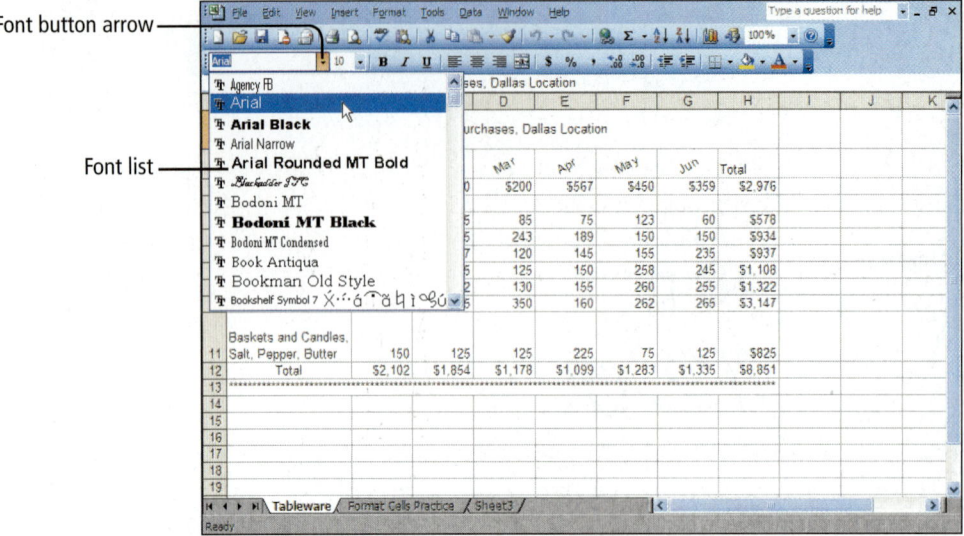

Figure 3.20

Note

Many fonts are TrueType, indicated by the two overlapping *T*s to the left of the font name in the font list. Text formatted in a TrueType font prints exactly as it appears on your screen, provided that the font is installed on the system from which you are printing.

3 In the **Font** list, scroll down to find, and then click, **Century Schoolbook**. If Century Schoolbook is not available on the Font list, select Times New Roman.

The text *Tableware Purchases, Dallas Location* is formatted in the Century Schoolbook font. Century Schoolbook is a serif font—it has small line extensions on the ends of the letters.

4 With cell **A1** still selected, move to the Formatting toolbar and click the **Font Size arrow** 10, as shown in Figure 3.21, and from the displayed list, click **18**.

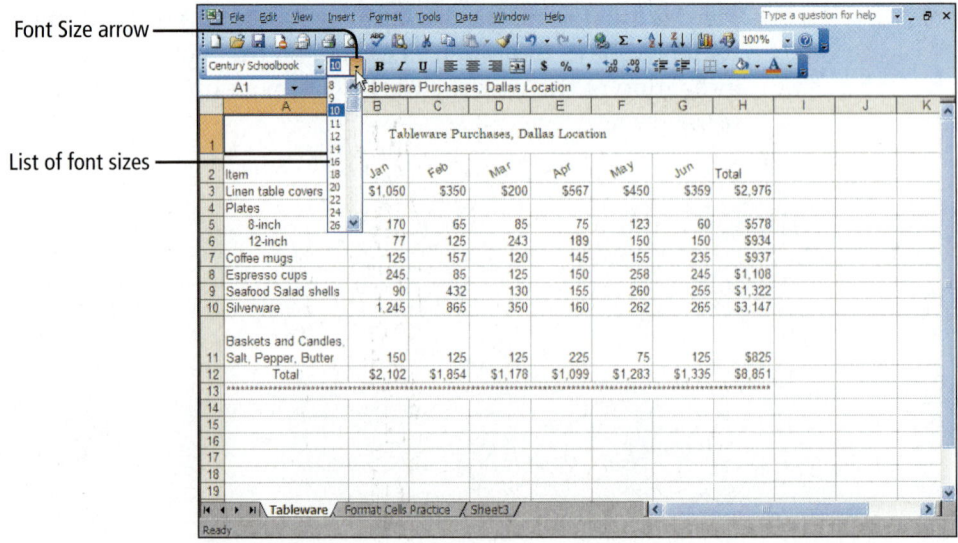

Figure 3.21

5 With cell **A1** selected, move to the Formatting toolbar and click the **Bold** button **B**.

The Bold style is applied to your text.

6 With cell **A1** still selected, display the **Format** menu, and then click **Cells** to display the **Format Cells** dialog box. Click the **Font tab**. Under **Font**, notice that *Century Schoolbook* is selected and that a preview of the font is also displayed under **Preview**.

7 Under **Font style**, click **Italic**, and notice that the Preview changes to reflect your selection. Click **OK**.

8 With cell **A1** still selected, move to the Formatting toolbar, and then click the **Underline** button **U**. The **Underline** button places a single underline under the contents of a cell.

The Bold, Italic, and Underline buttons on the Formatting toolbar are ***toggle buttons***, which means that you can click once to turn the formatting on and click again to turn it off.

9 With cell **A1** selected, move to the Formatting toolbar and click the **Underline** button **U** again.

The Underline font style is removed from the text, but the Bold and Italic styles remain.

10 Click cell **A2**. On the Formatting toolbar, click the **Bold** button **B** and click the **Center** button. Click the **Font Size arrow** `10`, and from the displayed list, click **12**.

11 Click cell **H2**. On the Formatting toolbar, click the **Bold** button **B** and click the **Align Right** button. Click in an empty cell, and then compare your worksheet with Figure 3.22.

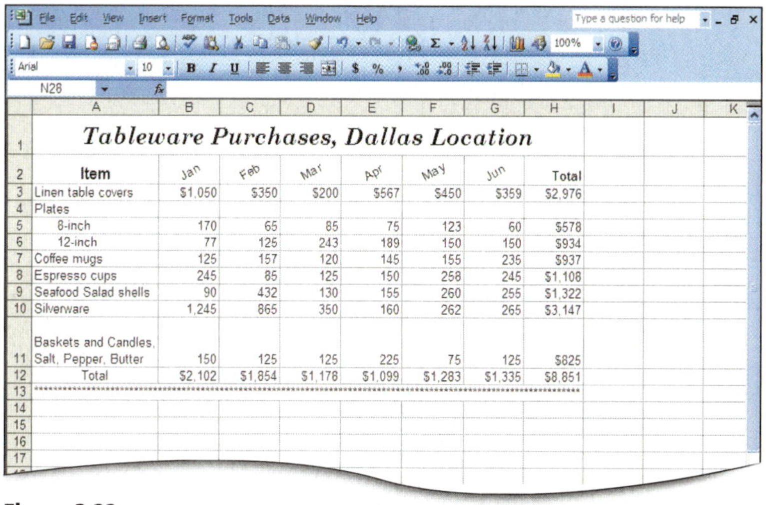

Figure 3.22

Project 3A: Tableware | **Excel** 687

12 Click cell **A3**, press F2 to turn on Edit mode, and with the insertion point positioned following *s* type ***** and then press Enter.

13 Select cell **A14**. Type ***Order only in white or cream** and press Enter.

Because the adjacent cell is empty, the text spills into cell B14. To avoid having to adjust the column width, you can *shrink* the size of a font in a cell.

14 Click to select cell **A14**, display the **Format Cells** dialog box, and then click the **Alignment tab**. Under **Text control**, select the **Shrink to fit** check box, as shown in Figure 3.23, and then click **OK**.

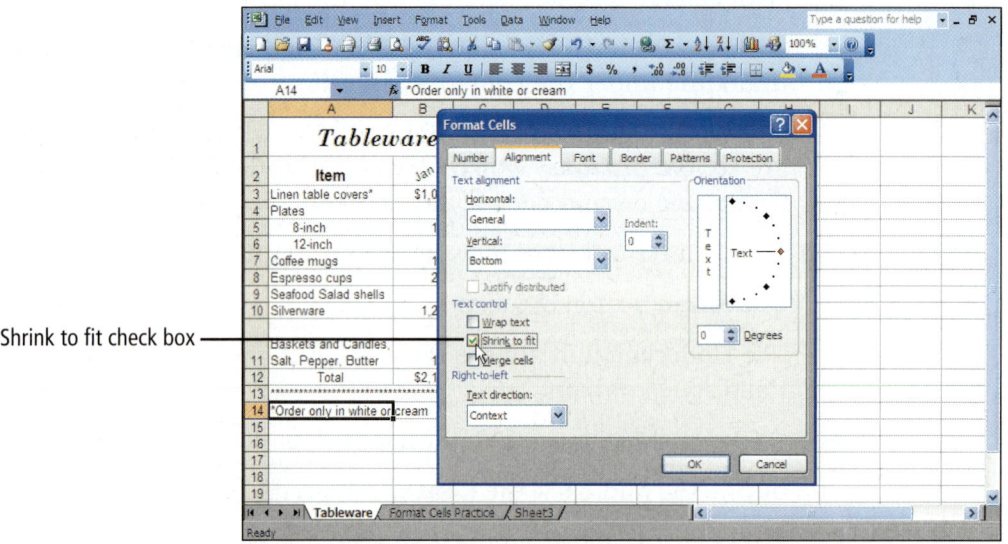

Shrink to fit check box

Figure 3.23

15 **Save** your workbook and compare your screen with Figure 3.24.

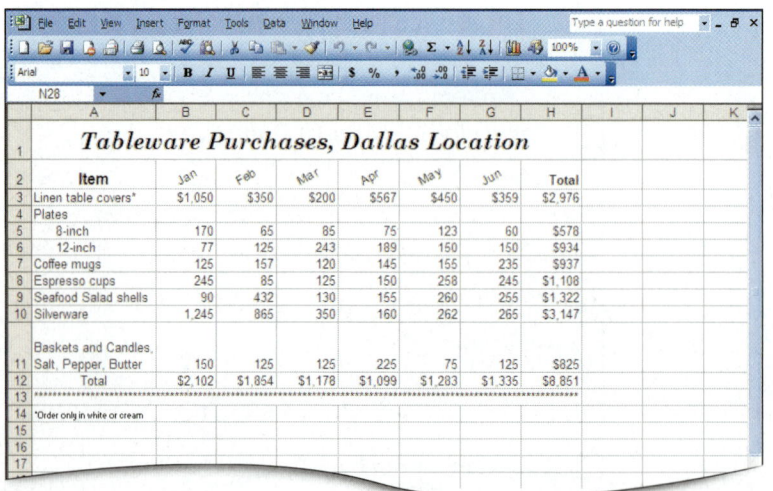

Figure 3.24

688 **Excel** | Chapter 3: Formatting a Worksheet

Activity 3.10 Merging Cells

Recall that an Excel worksheet is a *grid*—a network of uniformly spaced vertical and horizontal lines. Occasionally, it is desirable to have non-uniform cells. In those instances you can merge cells together.

After you merge a group of cells to form one large cell, the new, larger cell uses the address of the cell that was in the upper left corner of the selected group.

1 Select the range **I3:I11**. Use the shortcut menu to display the **Format Cells** dialog box. If necessary, click the **Alignment tab**. Under **Text control**, click to place a check mark in the **Merge cells** check box. Click **OK**. See Figure 3.25.

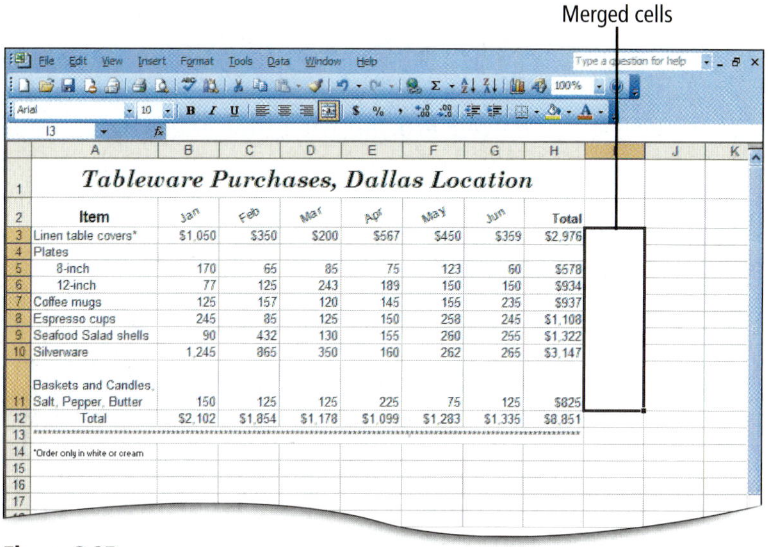

Figure 3.25

2 Click anywhere outside the selected cell. Click cell **I12** and look at the Name Box to the left of the Formula Bar. Notice that *I12* displays. Click in the **large merged cell above cell I12** and notice that *I3* displays in the name box.

When a group of cells are merged, the first cell in the selection becomes the cell address of the new, larger cell. The other cells cease to exist.

3 With cell **I3** still selected, type **First Half** and press Enter. Select cell **I3** again, display the **Format Cells** dialog box, and click the **Alignment tab**. Click the **Vertical arrow**, and then click **Center**. Click **OK**.

The text is vertically centered within the cell.

4 To separate the merged cells, select cell **I3**. Display the **Format Cells** dialog box, and then display the **Alignment tab**. Under **Text control**, clear (click to remove the check mark) the **Merge cells** check box. Click **OK**.

The cells are separated, and the text displays in cell I3.

5 Click cell **I3** and press Delete to delete the cell contents.

6 On the Standard toolbar, click **Save** to save the changes you have made to your workbook.

Activity 3.11 Applying Cell Borders

Apply cell borders to visually differentiate one part of a worksheet from another and to draw the reader's eye to specific data. Use cell borders to add the type of underline and double underline that is often found in an accounting-style worksheet. You can customize borders by adjusting color and width. You can apply cell borders in two ways:

- On the Formatting toolbar, click the Borders button.
- Select the border from the Border tab of the Format Cells dialog box.

1 Select the range **A1:H1**. Display the **Format Cells** dialog box, and then click the **Border tab**.

Here you can specify where you want the border and select the style and color of the line that will be used for the border.

2 Under **Presets**, click **Outline**.

Under Border, your selection is previewed. The Outline preset places a border around the outer edges of the selected group of cells. Additionally, under Line, in the Style list, the default line style—a single line—is selected and blinking, as shown in Figure 3.26.

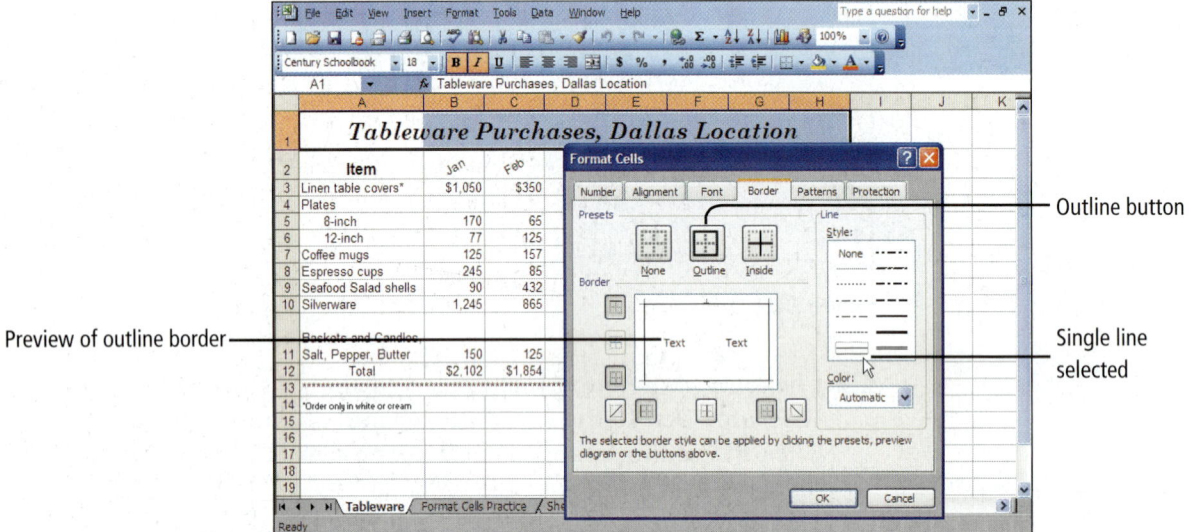

Figure 3.26

3 Under **Line**, in the **Style** list, click the **fifth line style in the second column**—a medium-thick solid line. Under **Presets**, click the **Outline** button again to apply the new line style to the outline of the selected cells.

Your selected line style is surrounded by dots, indicating that it is the selected line style, and a line blinks beneath it. After you select a new line style, you have to reapply the border to the selected areas. You can do this by clicking the Outline button, or by clicking the Border buttons that surround the border preview area.

4 Click **OK**. Click in an empty cell so you can see the border that has been applied.

On some computer screens, the applied border is not as readily visible as on others.

5 To visualize how your bordered cells will look, on the Formatting toolbar click the **Print Preview** button. Compare your screen with Figure 3.27.

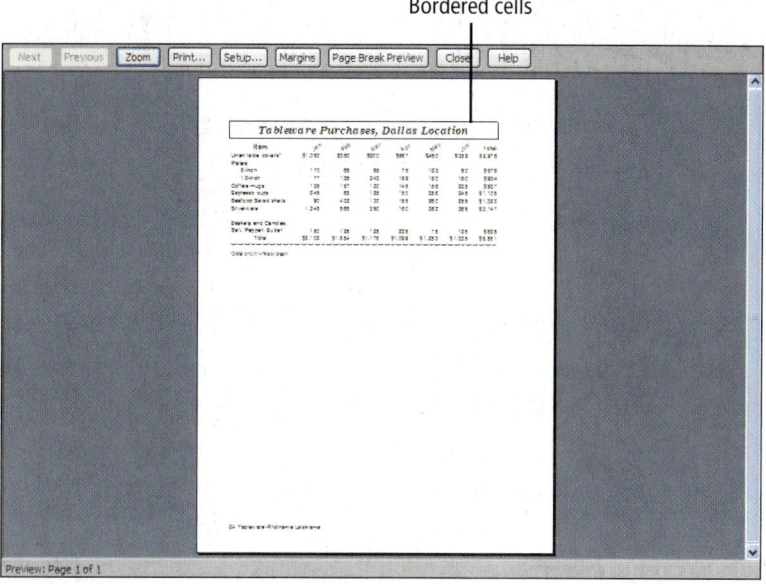

Figure 3.27

6 On the Print Preview toolbar, click the **Close** button.

7 Select the range **A11:H11** and display the **Format Cells** dialog box. If necessary, click the **Border tab**.

8 Under **Border**, move your mouse pointer into the white area. Point to the lower edge of the white preview area, and click the left mouse button once.

A line displays, and the **Bottom border** button appears "pressed." See Figure 3.28.

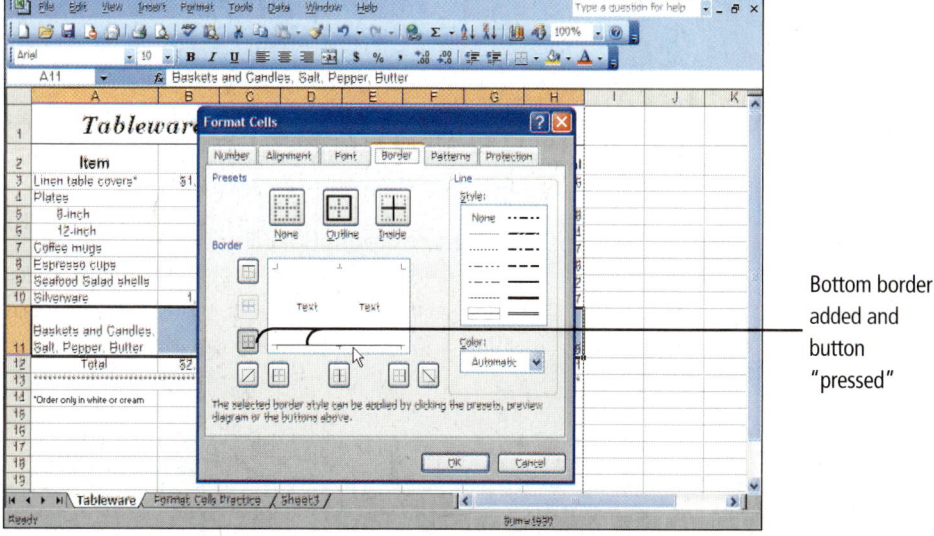

Figure 3.28

Project 3A: Tableware | **Excel** 691

> **Note**
>
> To apply color to cell borders, click the **Color arrow** on the **Border tab** of the **Format Cells** dialog box.

9 Click **OK** to close the dialog box.

10 Select the range **A2:H12**. On the Formatting toolbar, click the **Borders arrow** to display the Border palette, as shown in Figure 3.29.

The content of and ScreenTip for the Border button reflect its most recent use and thus can vary. Clicking the button will apply the border indicated on the button. Clicking the Border arrow, however, will always display the Border palette, from which you can choose any of the border styles.

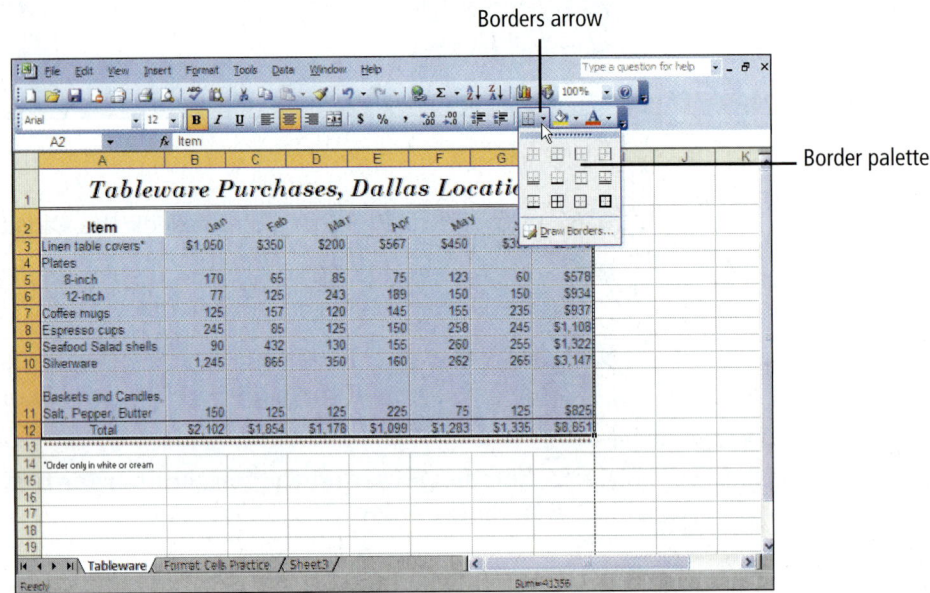

Figure 3.29

11 On the displayed Border palette, in the last row, click the second button, **All Borders**, as shown in Figure 3.30, and then click anywhere to cancel the selection.

Borders are applied to the top, bottom, left, and right of each *cell* in the selection. In Figure 3.31, notice that in row 2, the borders are applied diagonally. Row 2 contains rotated text, and the borders are applied using the same rotation.

> **Note** — Applying Borders
>
> The border applied in this step overrides the outline border applied to the lower edge of cells A1:H1.

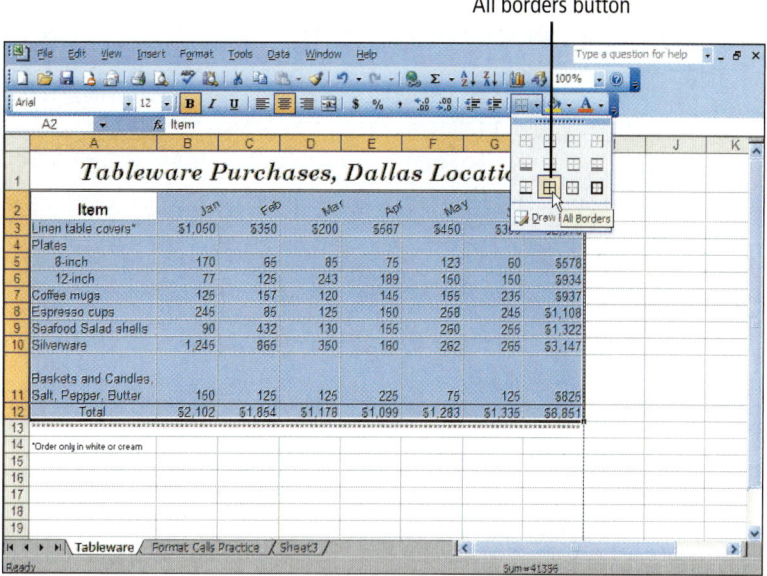

All borders button

Figure 3.30

12 Click **Save**. Compare your screen with Figure 3.31.

Borders applied diagonally to the cells in row 2

Figure 3.31

Activity 3.12 Applying Cell Shading

Applying shading to cells is another way to visually differentiate one part of a worksheet from another and to draw the reader's eye to specific data or to a group of cells. You can select colors and patterns for shading. You can apply shading to cells in two ways:

- Click the Fill Color button on the Formatting toolbar.
- Select the shading from the Patterns tab of the Format Cells dialog box.

1 Select the range **A1:H1**. On the Formatting toolbar, click the **Fill Color arrow** to display the color palette, as shown in Figure 3.32.

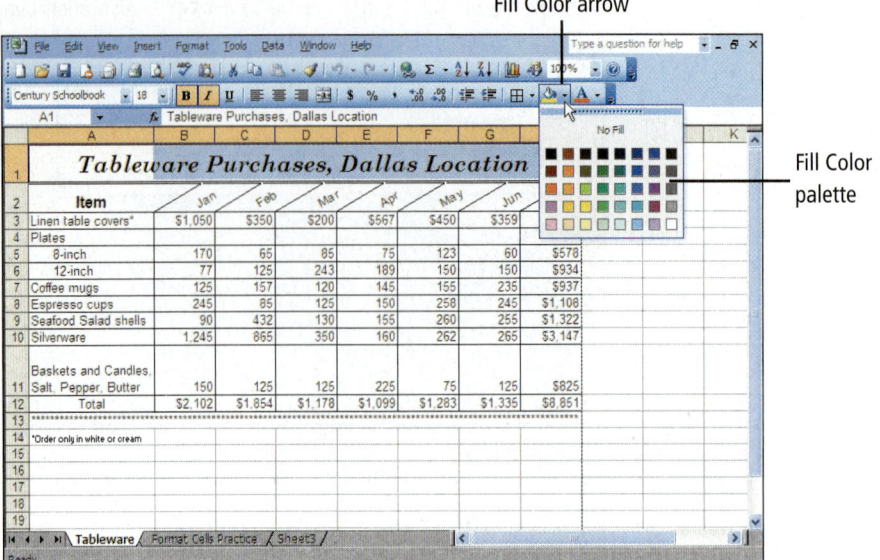

Figure 3.32

[2] On the displayed color palette, in the last row, click the sixth color—**Pale Blue**.

[3] Select the range **A12:H12**. Display the **Format Cells** dialog box, and then click the **Patterns tab**.

[4] In the lower portion of the dialog box, click the **Pattern arrow**, and then in the first row of the displayed palette, click the fifth pattern—**12.5% Gray**—as shown in Figure 3.33.

You can see a preview of the pattern in the Sample area after the pattern is selected.

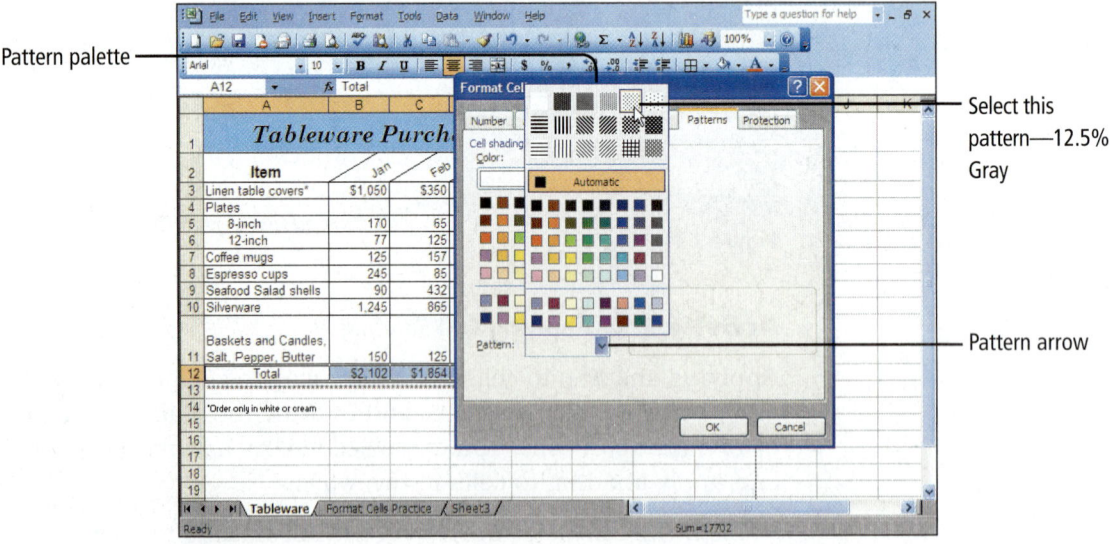

Figure 3.33

[5] Click **OK**, and then click anywhere to cancel the selection. On the Standard toolbar, click **Save** to save the changes you have made to your workbook.

694   Excel | Chapter 3: Formatting a Worksheet

Activity 3.13 Using Format Painter

Format Painter copies all formatting from one selection of cells to another selection of cells. This differs from copy and paste because the cell contents are not copied. Instead, only the formatting of the cell is copied. Any type of formatting applied to the selected cells—number format, alignment, font, font style, borders, or patterns—is copied.

1 Click cell **A3** to make it the active cell. On the Formatting toolbar, click the **Font button arrow** `Arial`, scroll the displayed list as necessary, and change the font to **Comic Sans MS**. Then, on the Formatting toolbar, click the **Italic** button, and then click the **Center** button to apply Italic style and Center alignment to the cell.

2 With cell **A3** still selected, move to the Standard toolbar and click the **Format Painter** button. Move the pointer into the grid area, and notice that the Format Painter button is highlighted. Also, cell A3 displays a moving border, and the mouse pointer displays with a small paintbrush attached to it, as shown in Figure 3.34.

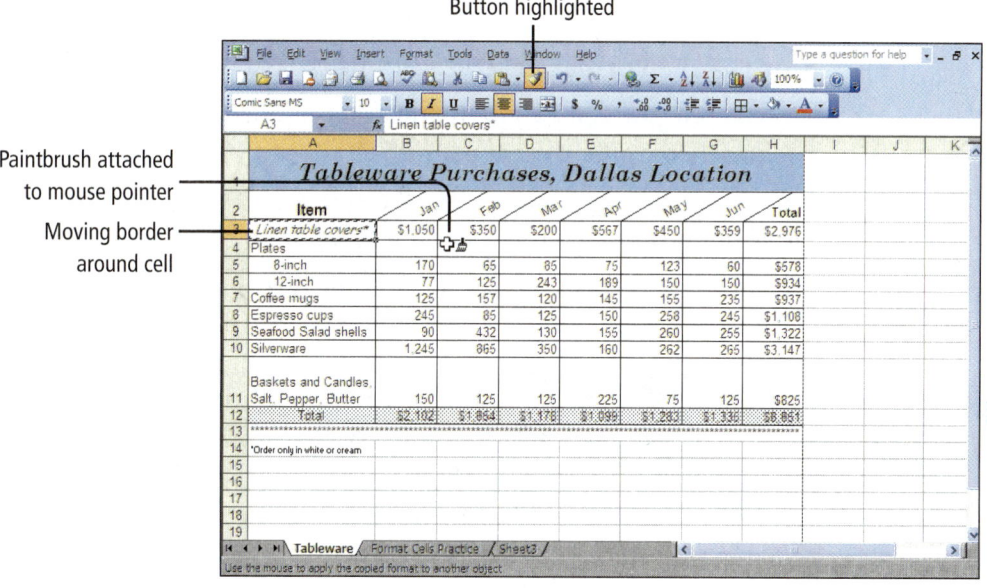

Figure 3.34

3 Select the range **A4:A11**.

As you release the left mouse button, notice that the range of cells has acquired the same formatting—font style of Comic Sans MS, Italic, and Centering—as cell A3. The paintbrush is no longer attached to the mouse pointer, and the Format Painter button is no longer highlighted. This is a convenient way to copy *formats* to other cells without having to reapply each format individually.

4 Select cell **A3**. On the Formatting toolbar, change the font to **Century Schoolbook**, be sure the **Font Size** is **10**, and change the alignment to **Align Left**.

Project 3A: Tableware | **Excel** 695

5 On the Standard toolbar, *double-click* the **Format Painter** button.

Double-clicking the Format Painter button causes it to remain active until you click the button again to turn it off.

6 Click cell **A10**.

The format from cell A3—Century Schoolbook, 10 pt, left aligned—is copied to cell A10.

7 Move your mouse pointer anywhere into the grid area of your worksheet and verify that the paintbrush is still attached to the pointer. This indicates that Format Painter is still active.

If you do not see the paintbrush, it is likely that your hand moved slightly when you attempted your double-click of the Format Painter button, and it was interpreted as a single click. Double-click the Format Painter button again.

8 Click cell **A4**.

The format from cell A3 is copied to cell A4.

9 Drag to select the range **A7:A11**.

The format from cell A3 is copied to the selected range.

10 Click the **Format Painter** button once to turn it off.

The button is no longer highlighted, and the paintbrush is no longer attached to the mouse pointer.

11 Select cell **A11**, display the **Format Cells** dialog box, click the **Alignment tab**, and select the **Wrap text** check box. Click **OK**.

12 On the Standard toolbar, click **Save** to save the changes you have made to your workbook. Compare your screen with Figure 3.35.

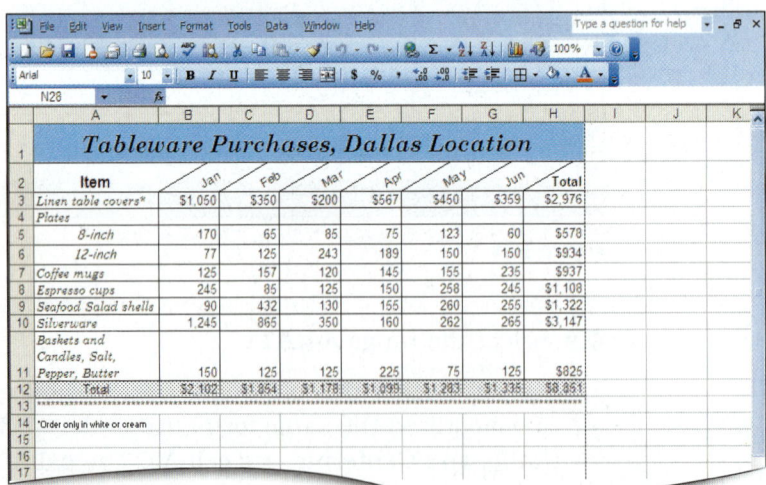

Figure 3.35

Note

You can apply formatting to individual characters in a text entry (but not a numeric entry) by first selecting only the characters and then applying any of the cell formats.

Activity 3.14 Clearing Cell Formats

Once applied, cell formats stay with the cell, even if you delete the contents of the cell. To delete the *format* from a cell, you must purposely clear the format using the Clear Formats or Clear All commands from the Edit menu.

1 If necessary, **Open** your file **3A_Tableware**.

2 Click to make cell **A5** the active cell. On the menu bar, click **Edit**, point to **Clear**, and then click **Formats**.

All the formatting for the cell—the Comic Sans font, Italic, and Centering—are removed from the cell, and the default font (Arial) and alignment for text (left) are applied to the cell.

3 Click to make cell **A6** the active cell. Press [Delete] to delete the contents of the cell. Type **13-inch** and then press [Enter].

Notice that deleting the contents of the cell does not delete the formatting.

4 Click cell **A6** again. To delete the cell contents and the cell formats at the same time, display the **Edit** menu, point to **Clear**, and then click **All**.

This command deletes the cell contents and removes all cell formatting—all at the same time.

5 Type **12-inch** and then press [Enter].

6 To reapply the original formatting, click cell **A4**, and then click the **Format Painter** button. With the Format Painter paintbrush attached to the mouse pointer, drag to select the range **A5:A6**. With the range **A5:A6** still selected, click the **Increase Indent** button two times.

7 Select the range **A14:H14**. Display the **Format Cells** dialog box, click the **Alignment tab**, and then click the **Horizontal arrow**. Click **Center Across Selection**, and then click **OK**.

8 On the Standard toolbar, click **Save** to save the changes you have made to this workbook since your last Save operation.

9 View your worksheet in **Print Preview**, and then on the Print Preview toolbar, click **Print**, in the **Print** dialog box click **OK**. On the menu bar, click **File**, and then click **Close** to close the workbook.

End You have completed Project 3A

Project 3B Suppliers

In this project, you will change the appearance of your printed workbook by changing the page orientation, the scale of the worksheet, and the paper size. You will also set margins and center the worksheet on the printed page, and insert a picture within a header or footer.

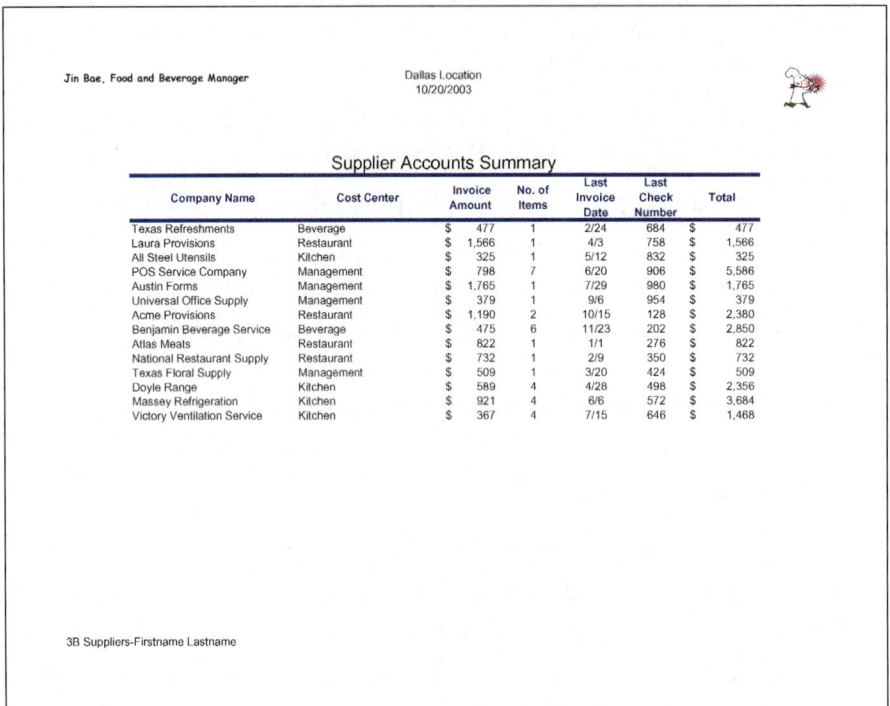

In Activities 3.15 through 3.18, you will edit a workbook for Jin Bae, Food and Beverage Manager for the Oceana Palm Grill, listing recent payments to suppliers. You will save the file as *3B_Suppliers_Firstname_Lastname*. Your completed worksheet will look similar to Figure 3.36.

Figure 3.36
Project 3B—Suppliers

Objective 4
Apply Workbook Formatting

In the remainder of the chapter, you will practice methods to format the printed worksheet using the **Page Setup** command. Settings that you adjust in the Page Setup dialog box affect only the active worksheet, not the entire workbook. To adjust settings for the entire workbook, use the Select All Sheets command before displaying the Page Setup dialog box. To select two or more adjacent sheets, use the [Shift] plus click technique to select sheets before displaying the Page Setup dialog box. Use the [Ctrl] plus click technique to select nonadjacent sheets.

Activity 3.15 Selecting Page Orientation, Scaling, and Paper Size

The default page orientation in Excel is *portrait* orientation. In portrait orientation, the paper is taller than it is wide. You can also select a *landscape* orientation in which the paper is wider than it is tall. The default paper size in Excel is 8½-inches by 11 inches—standard business letter-size paper.

1 Start Excel. On the **File** menu, click **Open**. In the **Open** dialog box, navigate to the student files that accompany this textbook, and then open the file **e03B_Suppliers**. Display the **View** menu, click **Header and Footer**, and then click the **Custom Footer** button. In the **Left section**, type **3B Suppliers-Firstname Lastname** and then click **OK** to close the dialog boxes.

2 From the **File** menu, click **Save As**. In the **Save As** dialog box, navigate to the location where you are storing your projects for this chapter. In the **File name** box, type **3B_Suppliers_Firstname_Lastname** and then click **Save** or press [Enter].

3 On the Standard toolbar, click the **Print Preview** button. In the **Print Preview** window, notice at the lower left corner *Preview: Page 1 of 2*, as shown in Figure 3.37.

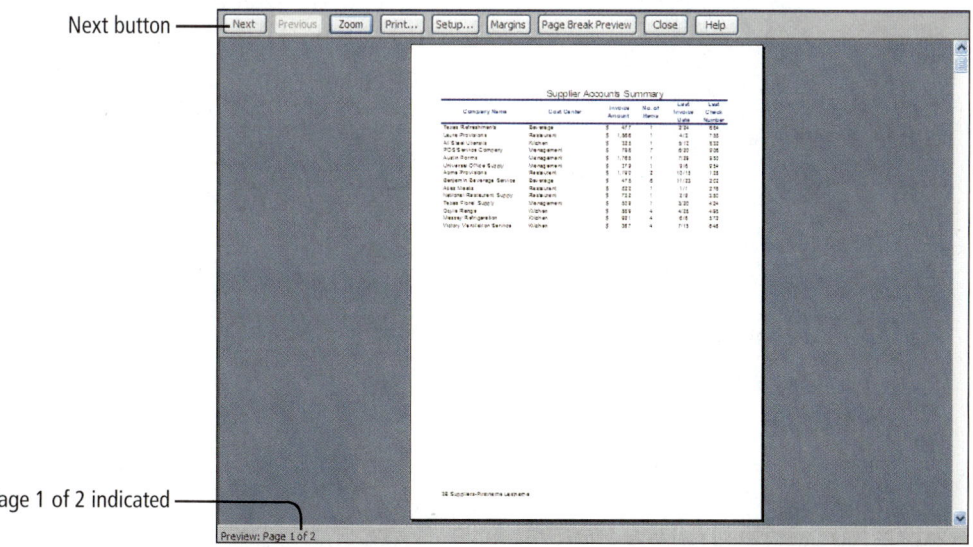

Figure 3.37

4 On the Print Preview toolbar, click the **Next** button.

Page 2 of the worksheet displays in the Print Preview window. Because all the columns on this worksheet cannot print on one page as the page is currently set up, the Print Preview displays the worksheet as two pages.

5 On the Print Preview toolbar, click the **Previous** button to redisplay Page 1 of the worksheet.

The preview is shown in portrait orientation—the paper is taller than it is wide.

6 On the Print Preview toolbar, click the **Close** button to close Print Preview.

The boundary between columns F and G displays as a dotted line. As you saw in the Print Preview, columns to the right of the dotted line will print on the second page as the page is currently set up.

7 From the **File** menu, click **Page Setup**. In the displayed **Page Setup** dialog box, click the **Page tab**. Under **Scaling**, click the **Fit to** option button with the default of *1 page(s) wide by 1 tall*.

8 In the upper right portion of the dialog box, click **Print Preview**.

Excel has **scaled** (shrunk) the data to fit on one page in the portrait orientation, as shown in Figure 3.38. Scaling is a good choice when the data is slightly too wide to display on one page, or if you need to keep the worksheet in a portrait orientation.

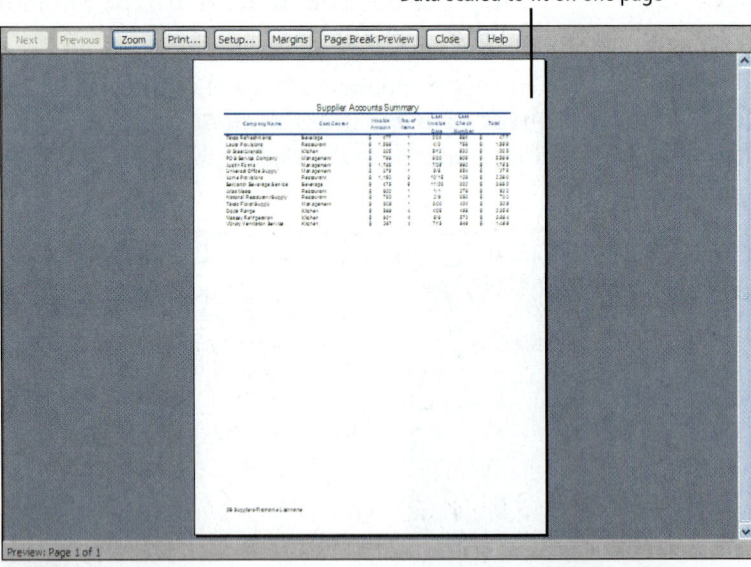

Figure 3.38

9 On the Print Preview toolbar, click **Setup** to return to the **Page Setup** dialog box.

Under Scaling, your print has been scaled to 88% (or a number close to 88%). The two options under *Scaling* on the Page tab of the Page Setup dialog box enable you to override the default size of your printout by specifying a scaling factor of 10% to 400%, or by automatically fitting the data to a specified number of pages—as you did here. Use caution with this feature, because Excel will scale the print both horizontally and vertically, so some distortion is possible. Always use Print Preview to view your results before printing.

10 Under **Scaling**, click the **Adjust to** option button, and then, in the **Adjust to** spin box, click the **up arrow** until **100** displays. This will return the data to a full-size printout. Click **OK**, and then, on the Print Preview toolbar, click the **Close** button to close Print Preview.

11 From the **File** menu, click **Page Setup**. On the **Page tab**, under **Orientation**, click the **Landscape** option button. In the lower portion of the dialog box, click the **Paper size arrow**.

It is likely that the default paper size, Letter, is already selected, but here you can view the different sizes available.

12 Scroll through the list, and then click **Letter**.

As you make changes to the setup of your worksheet, you will want to look at it in Print Preview; thus, a Print Preview button is conveniently placed at the upper right of this dialog box.

13 Click the **Print Preview** button in the dialog box to view your worksheet in landscape orientation as it would print on letter-size paper.

In this orientation, all the columns will print on one sheet. If necessary, you can return to the Page Setup dialog box from this screen by clicking the *Setup* button on the toolbar of the Print Preview window.

14 On the Print Preview window's toolbar, click **Close**. On the Standard toolbar, click **Save**.

Activity 3.16 Setting Margins and Centering the Worksheet

The default margins in Excel are 1 inch for the top and bottom margins and ¾ (.75) inch for the left and right margins.

1 From the **File** menu, click **Page Setup**, and in the displayed **Page Setup** dialog box, click the **Margins tab**.

As shown in the small preview picture on the dialog box, Excel will begin the print starting at the top and left margins—within the settings that you select. See Figure 3.39.

Preview of margins and centering

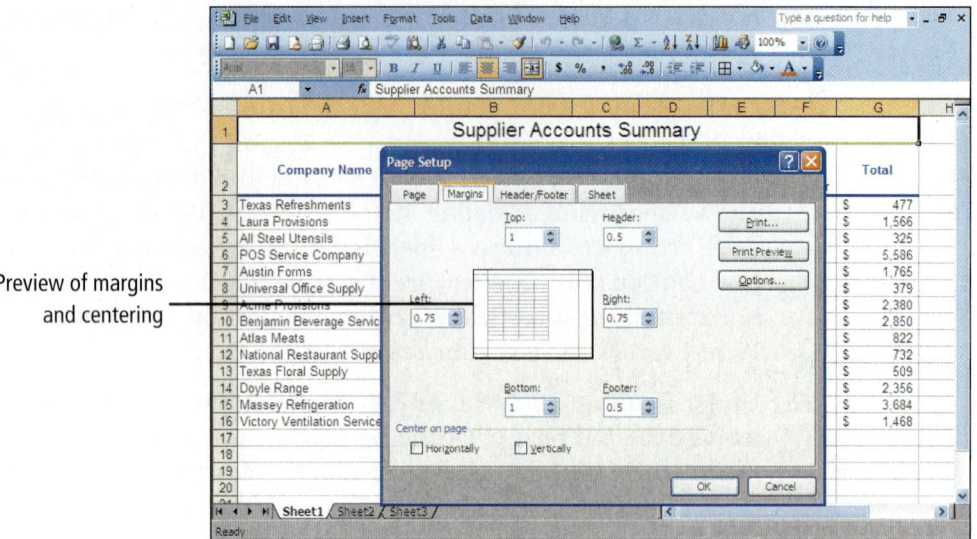

Figure 3.39

2 Click to position the insertion point within the **Right** box.

On the small picture in the middle of the dialog box, a black line displays to give you a visual indication that you are working with the right margin of the worksheet.

3 Click in the **Top** box.

The black line moves to indicate that you are working with the top margin.

4 In the **Top** box, click the **up arrow** in the spin box so that the top margin is **1.75** inches.

5 At the bottom of the dialog box, under **Center on page**, click to select the **Horizontally** check box.

The preview changes to give a visual indication of the horizontal centering you have chosen. If you center your printout horizontally on the page, you need not be concerned with left and right margins. If you center your printout vertically on the page, you need not be concerned with top and bottom margins.

6 In the **Page Setup** dialog box, click the **Print Preview** button to view the changes you have made to your workbook. Then, on the Print Preview toolbar, click the **Close** button.

7 On the Standard toolbar, click **Save** to save the changes you have made to your workbook.

More Knowledge

From the Print Preview toolbar's Margins button, you can change margins visually by dragging the margin boundaries with the mouse.

702 Excel | Chapter 3: Formatting a Worksheet

Activity 3.17 Creating Headers and Footers with Inserted Pictures

Headers and *footers* refer to text and graphics that appear at the top (headers) or bottom (footers) of a worksheet in a workbook. For example, a header might contain the company or department name and a company logo. A footer might contain the page number and the time and date the worksheet was printed. You are already familiar with creating a custom footer containing your name and the project name.

Headers and footers can display character formatting such as bold and italic. You can also align the characters, apply borders and shading, and insert pictures. Excel's default setting is to display no header and no footer.

You can create headers and footers in Excel in two ways:

- Use one of Excel's predefined headers and footers.
- Create your own custom header or footer.

In this activity, you will use both methods to place a header and footer in your worksheet.

1 From the **View** menu, click **Header and Footer**. Alternatively, on the menu bar, click File, Page Setup, and then click the Header/Footer tab.

The Header/Footer tab of the Page Setup dialog box displays. Notice that under Header, *(none)* displays, and under Footer, the custom footer that you already created for this project displays. See Figure 3.40.

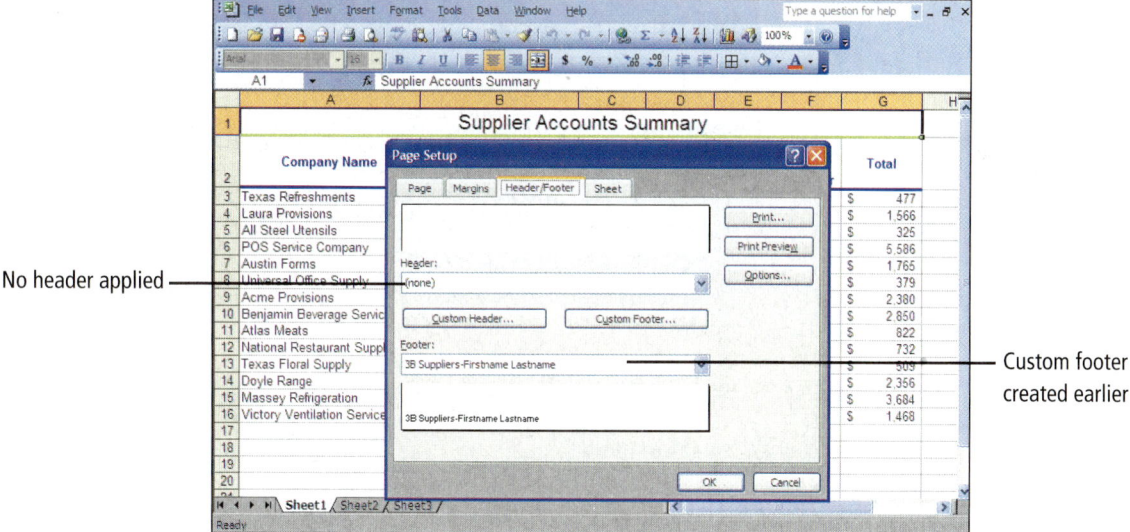

Figure 3.40

Project 3B: Suppliers | **Excel** 703

2 Click the **Header arrow** to view a list of predefined headers. Scroll down the list, and notice that Excel has included several variations of the file name as one of the predefined headings.

Excel always displays the file name as a possible header or footer as well as other variations of possible headers that include the file name.

3 In the displayed list, click **(none)**. Click the **Custom Header** button. The **Header** dialog box displays. Click in the **Left section**, and then type **Jin Bae, Food and Beverage Manager**

Text in the Left section is aligned at the left, and as you type, the text wraps to a second line.

4 Click in the **Center section**, and then type **Dallas Location** Text in the **Center section** is centered. Press [Enter]. On the **Header** dialog box toolbar, click the **Date** button to insert today's date. Compare your screen with Figure 3.41.

Although a code displays, the current date will display and print in your worksheet. Excel has codes that begin with an ampersand and are enclosed in brackets to represent things you might want to insert into a header or footer—such as the current time, current date, and page number. You do not have to know the codes; they are automatically inserted using one of the buttons on the dialog box's toolbar.

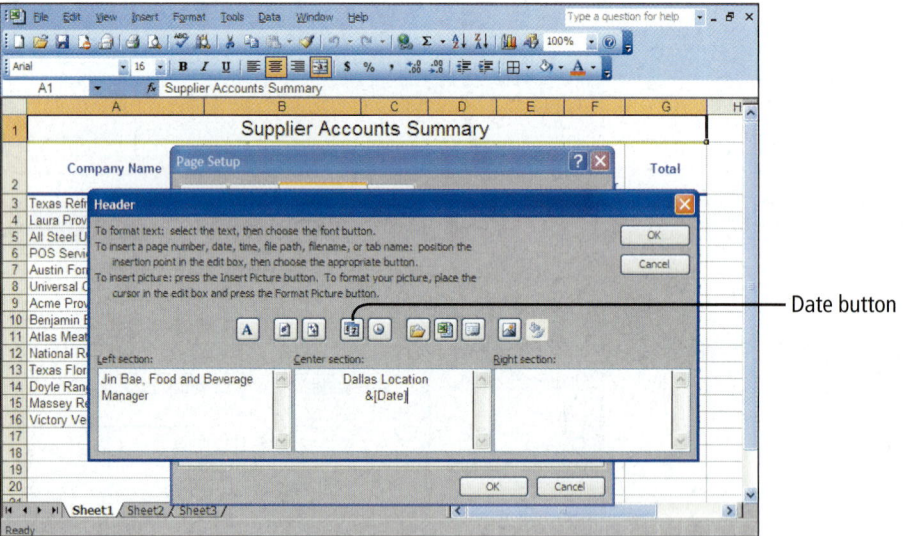

Figure 3.41

5 Take a moment to review the table in Figure 3.42 that describes the buttons on the Header (and Footer) dialog box toolbar.

Header and Footer Toolbar Buttons

Button	Action
A	Opens the Font dialog box in which you can change the font, font style, font size, underline, or effects.
	Inserts the page number.
	Inserts the total number of pages in a worksheet.
	Inserts the current date.
	Inserts the current time.
	Inserts the directory path and file name.
	Inserts the name of the Excel file.
	Inserts the name on the sheet tab.
	Displays the Insert Picture dialog box, from which you can insert a picture.
	Displays the Format Picture dialog box, from which you can format an inserted picture.

Figure 3.42

Note

To print header or footer text on more than one line, press Enter at the end of the line.

6 Click in the **Right section**, and then on the **Header** dialog box toolbar, click the **Insert Picture** button, as shown in Figure 3.43.

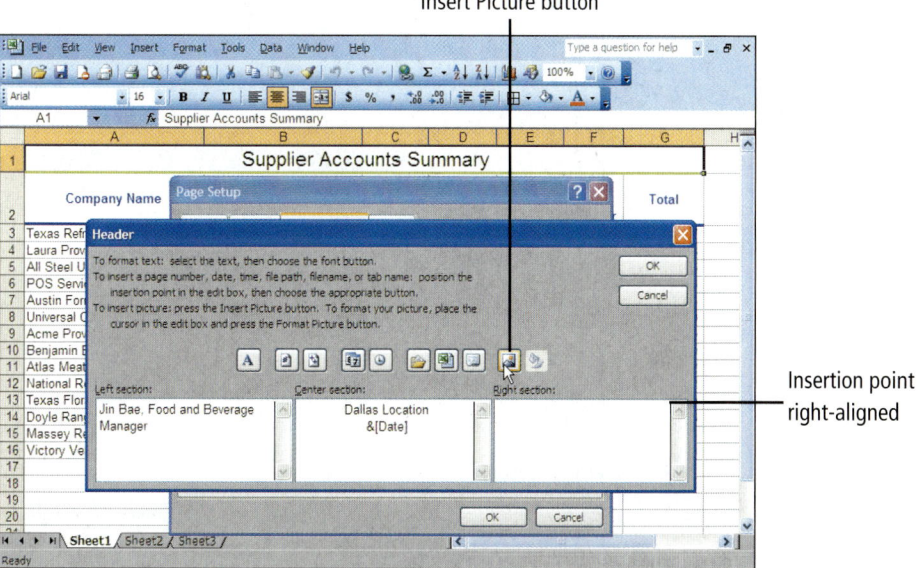

Figure 3.43

7 In the displayed **Insert Picture** dialog box, click the **Look in arrow**, and then navigate to the student files that accompany this textbook. Click to select the file **03B_Chef**, and then, in the lower right corner, click the **Insert** button.

&[Picture] displays, and the Format Picture button becomes active, as shown in Figure 3.44.

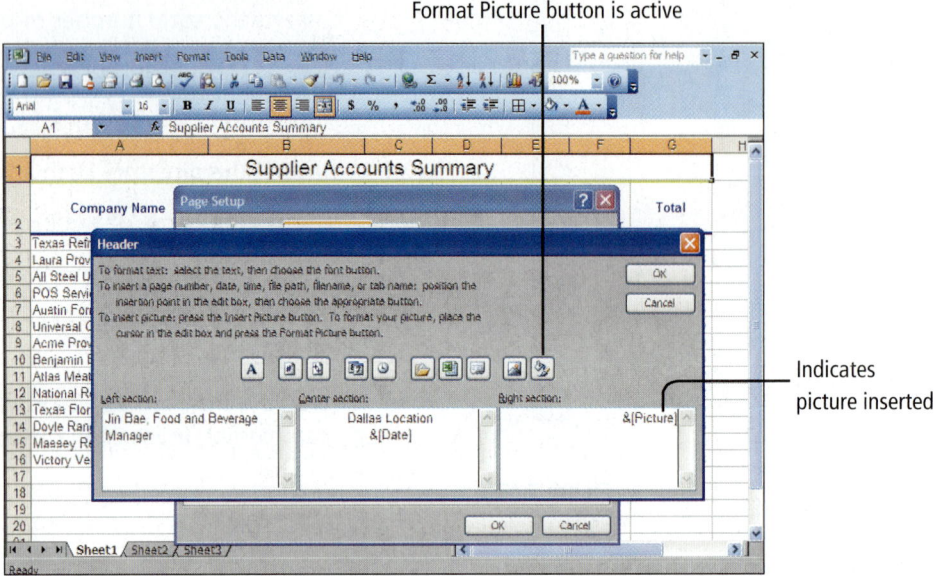

Figure 3.44

8 Click the **Format Picture** button on the toolbar, located to the right of the Insert Picture button.

9 In the displayed **Format Picture** dialog box, under **Size and rotate**, in the **Height** spin box, click the **down arrow** until **0.5** displays in both the **Height** and **Width** spin box, as shown in Figure 3.45.

This will reduce the size of the chef picture to fit within the header.

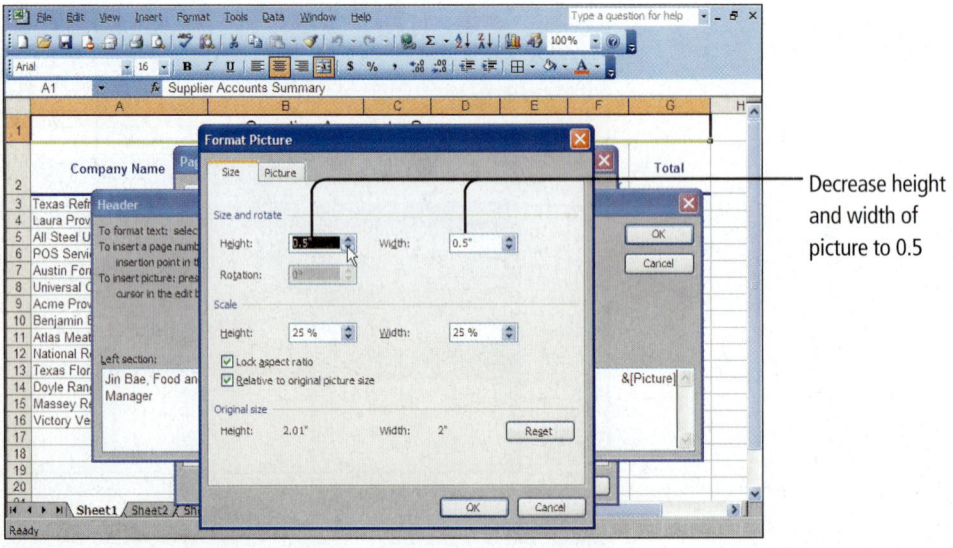

Figure 3.45

706   Excel | Chapter 3: Formatting a Worksheet

10 In the lower right corner of the dialog box, click **OK**. In the upper right corner of the **Header** dialog box, click **OK**.

Do not be concerned if, in the Page Setup dialog box, it appears that your header elements are layered on top of one another.

11 In the **Page Setup** dialog box, click the **Print Preview** button. Compare your screen with Figure 3.46.

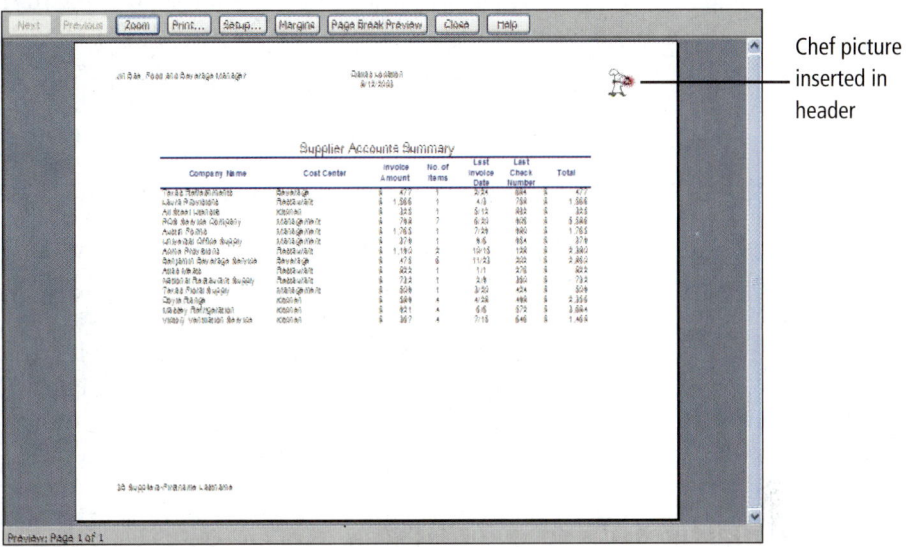

Chef picture inserted in header

Figure 3.46

12 On the Print Preview toolbar, click the **Setup** button to return to the **Header/Footer tab** of the **Page Setup** dialog box, and then click the **Custom Header** button.

13 In the **Left section**, select the entire text if it is not already selected, and then click the **Font** button to display the **Font** dialog box. Under **Font**, scroll as necessary, and click **Comic San MS**. Change the **Font style** to **Bold** and the **Size** to **9**, as shown in Figure 3.47, and then click **OK**.

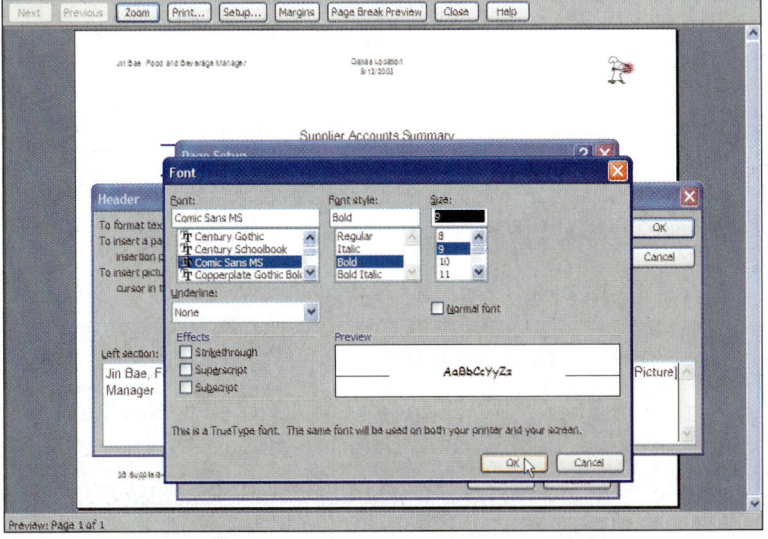

Figure 3.47

Project 3B: Suppliers | **Excel** 707

14 Click **OK** to close the **Header** dialog box. Click **OK** to close the **Page Setup** dialog box.

To edit (make changes to) headers or footers, display the dialog box and make changes directly within a section.

15 Examine the Print Preview on your screen.

Your worksheet data is centered horizontally on the page, and the header and footer use the left and right margins as set on the Margins tab of the Page Setup dialog box.

16 On the Print Preview toolbar, click the **Close** button.

17 Save the changes you have made to your workbook.

Activity 3.18 Setting Header and Footer Margins

Use the Margins tab of the Page Setup dialog box to adjust the distance between the header and the top of the page or to adjust the distance between the footer and the bottom of the page. This setting should always be less than the setting for the corresponding top or bottom margin. Otherwise, the text from the header or footer will overlap into the worksheet data.

1 On the menu bar, click **File** and then click **Page Setup**. If necessary, click the **Margins tab**.

2 Using the spin box arrows, increase the **Header** margin to **0.75**. Then, increase the **Footer** margin to **0.75**. Compare your screen with Figure 3.48.

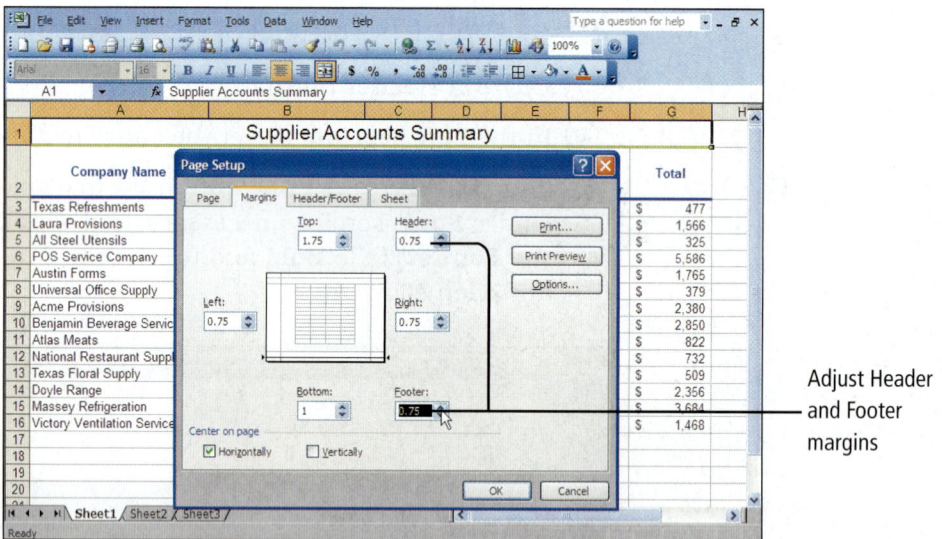

Figure 3.48

3 In the upper right corner of the dialog box, click the **Print Preview** button, and then, on the **Print Preview** toolbar, click **Print**, and then click **OK**.

4 On the Standard toolbar, click **Save** to save the changes you have made to your workbook.

5 Close the workbook, and close Excel.

End You have completed Project 3B

708   Excel | Chapter 3: Formatting a Worksheet

Project 3C Totals

In this project, you will practice how to print a worksheet with the gridlines, row headings, and column headings that you see on your screen. You will also insert a comment in a cell, and view and edit a comment in a cell.

In Activities 3.19 through 3.20, you will edit a workbook for Jin Bae, Food and Beverage Manager. You will save your file as *3C_Totals_Firstname_Lastname*. Your completed worksheet will look similar to Figure 3.49.

Figure 3.49
Project 3C—Totals

Objective 5
Print Gridlines, Print Row and Column Headings, and Set Print Quality

When you work in Excel, you see the row headings (numbers 1, 2, 3, and so on), the column headings (letters A, B, C, and so on) and the gridlines (the vertical and horizontal lines that define cells). By default, row headings, column headings, and gridlines do not print, but if you want to print them, you can do so by displaying the Page Setup dialog box and adjusting the settings.

Activity 3.19 Printing Gridlines, Printing Row and Column Headings, and Setting Print Quality

1 Start Excel. On the **File** menu, click **Open**. In the **Open** dialog box, navigate to the student files that accompany this textbook, and then open the file **e03C_Totals**. Display the **View** menu, click **Header and Footer**, and then click the **Custom Footer** button. In the **Left section**, type 3C Totals-Firstname Lastname and then click **OK** to close the dialog boxes.

2 From the **File** menu, click **Save As**. In the **Save As** dialog box, navigate to the location where you are storing your projects for this chapter. In the **File name** box, type 3C_Totals_Firstname_Lastname and then click **Save** or press Enter.

3 From the **File** menu, click **Page Setup**. In the **Page Setup** dialog box, click the **Sheet tab**.

4 Under **Print**, select the **Gridlines** check box and the **Row and column headings** check box. In the upper right corner of the dialog box, click the **Print Preview** button. Compare your screen with Figure 3.50.

Notice that gridlines, column headings, and row headings are displayed and will print.

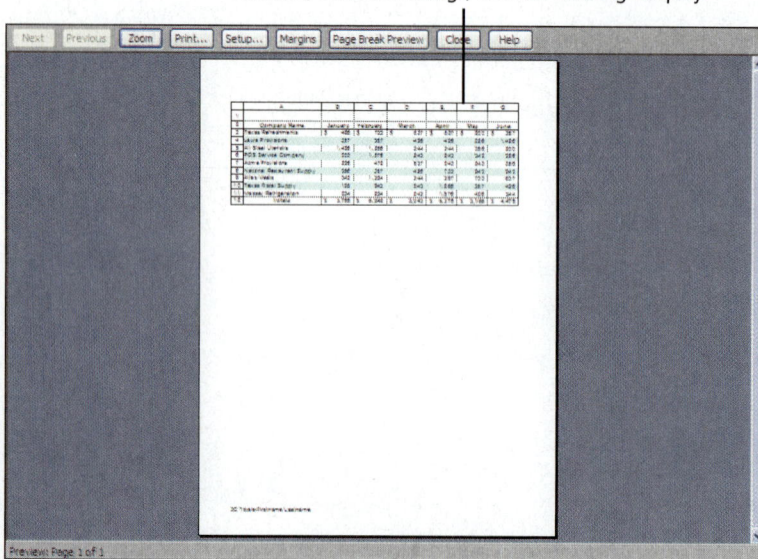

Figure 3.50

5 On the Print Preview toolbar, click the **Setup** button to return to the **Page Setup** dialog box.

6 Under **Print**, select the **Black and white** check box, as shown in Figure 3.51.

If background colors and patterns have been applied to your worksheet, as they are in this worksheet, but you are using a black-and-white printer (most laser printers are black and white), selecting this option signals Excel to use only black and white when printing. The result is that the printer will *not* use shades of gray for the areas that are in color.

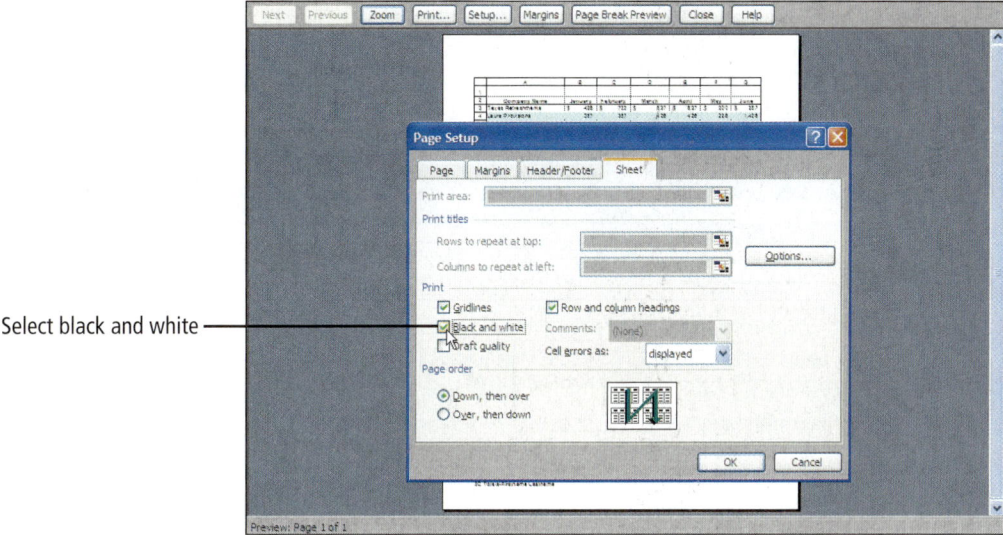

Select black and white

Figure 3.51

7 Click **OK** to close the dialog box, and then, on the Print Preview toolbar, click **Close** to close the Print Preview screen.

8 On the menu bar, click **View**, and then click **Header and Footer**. Click the **Custom Footer** button. In the **Center section**, click the **Date** button. In the **Footer** dialog box, click the **OK** button, and then, in the **Page Setup** dialog box, click **OK** again.

9 On the Standard toolbar, click the **Print Preview** button. Notice that the date is displayed (and will print) at the bottom center of your worksheet.

10 **Close** the Print Preview, and then, on the Standard toolbar, click **Save** to save the changes you have made to your workbook.

Objective 6
View and Insert Comments in a Cell

Comments provide reminders, document work, or provide clarifying information about data within a cell. You can attach one comment to a cell. When you move the mouse pointer over the cell, the comment and the name of the computer user who created the comment display.

Activity 3.20 Viewing and Inserting Comments in a Cell

1 Look at cell **A6** and notice the small red triangle in upper right corner of the cell.

The red triangle indicates that a comment is applied to the cell.

2 Move your mouse pointer over cell **A6**, and notice the comment that displays, as shown in Figure 3.52.

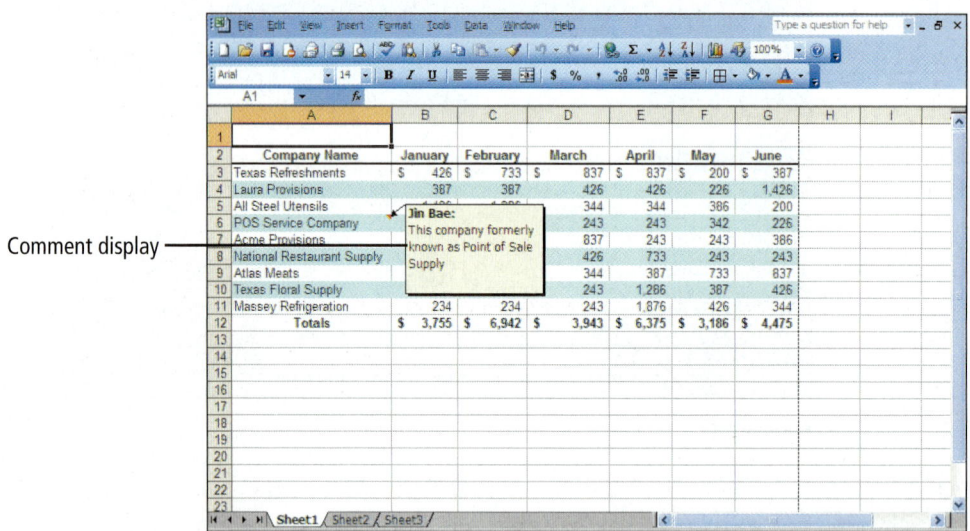

Figure 3.52

3 Right-click cell **A9** to simultaneously select it and display the shortcut menu.

4 From the displayed shortcut menu, click **Insert Comment**.

The name that displays is the name of the person or organization to whom your computer is registered, derived from your computer system's information.

5 Replace the name with your name, position your insertion point after the colon, and press Enter. Turn off bold if necessary, and then type **Atlas Meats supplies only beef products.** Compare your screen with Figure 3.53.

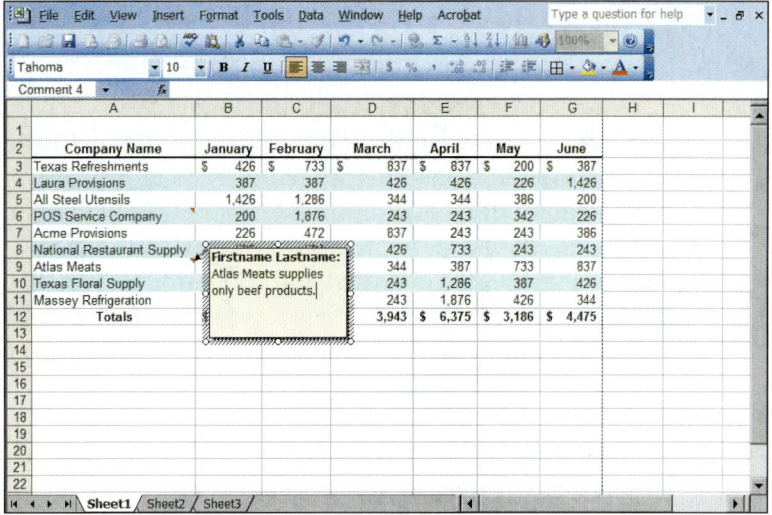

Figure 3.53

6 Click in any empty cell, and then move your mouse pointer over cell **A9** to view your comment.

Alert! — **Hiding and Unhiding Comments**

If your comment does not close when you click an empty cell, the Show/Hide Comments feature may be turned on. To turn this off and hide the comments, right-click on the cell containing the comment and from the shortcut menu click Hide Comments.

7 On the Standard toolbar, click the **Save** button. Print your worksheet, and then close the file and close Excel. Your worksheet will print with the column heading letters, the row heading letters, and the gridlines.

Note

Comments do not automatically print. To print comments, access the **Sheet tab** of the **Page Setup** dialog box, and select the appropriate check box.

End You have completed Project 3C

Project 3C: Totals | **Excel** 713

Summary

You can change the look of your worksheet in two primary ways. First, you can format the individual cells or groups of cells on your worksheet by changing cell alignment, applying cell borders, and shading cells. Second, you can format the worksheet itself by changing margins, centering the data vertically and horizontally on the page, and adding headers and footers. Graphics can be inserted in a header or footer to display, for example, a company logo. Cell formatting can be accomplished by using buttons on the Formatting toolbar, or by using the Format Cells dialog box. The dialog box offers more options and control, while the toolbar buttons are quicker to use. You can copy the format from one cell or group of cells to another by using the Format Painter. Worksheet formatting is accomplished using the Page Setup dialog box. Here you have control over the page orientation, margin settings, placement of the worksheet on the page, as well as the header and footer area.

Comments can be viewed and inserted in a cell to assist you in documenting your worksheets. Comments can also be printed. If desired, the gridlines and the row and column headings of a worksheet can be printed.

In This Chapter You Practiced How To

- Change Number Format
- Change Alignment of Cell Contents
- Apply Cell Formatting
- Apply Workbook Formatting
- Print Gridlines, Print Row and Column Headings, and Set Print Quality
- View and Insert Comments in a Cell

Concepts Assessments

Matching Match each term in the second column with its correct definition in the first column by writing the letter of the term on the blank line in front of the correct definition.

____ 1. The various ways to display numbers in Excel.

____ 2. The process of determining the overall appearance of a worksheet.

____ 3. The default format for a number that you type in a cell.

____ 4. The position of text or numbers in a cell.

____ 5. The positioning of data between the left and right boundaries of a cell.

____ 6. The positioning of data between the top and bottom boundaries of a cell.

____ 7. An arrangement of cell contents that reads vertically from the top of the cell to the bottom of the cell.

____ 8. Fonts that have extensions or lines on the ends of the characters and that are good for large amounts of text because they are easy to read.

____ 9. A feature to emphasize text using bold, italic, and underline.

____ 10. A feature that copies all formatting from one selection of cells to another selection of cells.

____ 11. A page orientation in which the paper is wider than it is tall.

____ 12. The default page orientation in Excel, in which the paper is taller than it is wide.

____ 13. A text control option that displays text entirely within the active cell by increasing the height of the row and then wrapping the text onto additional lines in the same cell—thus maintaining the current width of the cell.

____ 14. A feature that repeats your cell entry to occupy the entire width of the cell.

____ 15. A set of characters with the same design and shape.

A Alignment

B Fill

C Font

D Font styles

E Format Painter

F Formatting

G General format

H Horizontal alignment

I Landscape

J Number formats

K Portrait

L Serif fonts

M Stacked

N Vertical alignment

O Wrap text

Concepts Assessments | **Excel** 715

Concepts Assessments (continued)

Fill in the Blank Write the correct answer in the space provided.

1. In addition to formatting individual cells, Excel also enables you to format the overall layout of the _____.

2. Once applied, cell formats stay with the _____, even if you delete the contents of the cell.

3. Unless you apply a different number format to a cell, Excel will use the _____ format.

4. The General number format displays a number exactly as you type it—with _____ exceptions.

5. The default number of decimal places for the Number format is _____.

6. Excel's default horizontal alignment for text is _____ aligned.

7. The default vertical alignment for all data in a cell is _____.

8. Because worksheets usually contain more numbers than text, a _____ type of font is a good choice.

9. The default font for an Excel worksheet is _____.

10. After merging a group of cells to form one large cell, the new, larger cell uses the address of the cell that was in the _____ corner of the selected group.

716 Excel | Chapter 3: Formatting a Worksheet

Excel chapter three
Skill Assessments

Project 3D — Costs

Objectives: *Change Number Format, Change Alignment of Cell Contents, Apply Cell Formatting, and Apply Workbook Formatting.*

In the following Skill Assessment, you will edit a workbook for Felicia Mabry, President of the Oceana Palm Grill, which details the operating costs at the various restaurant locations. Your completed workbook will look similar to the one shown in Figure 3.54. You will save the workbook as *3D_Costs_Firstname_Lastname*.

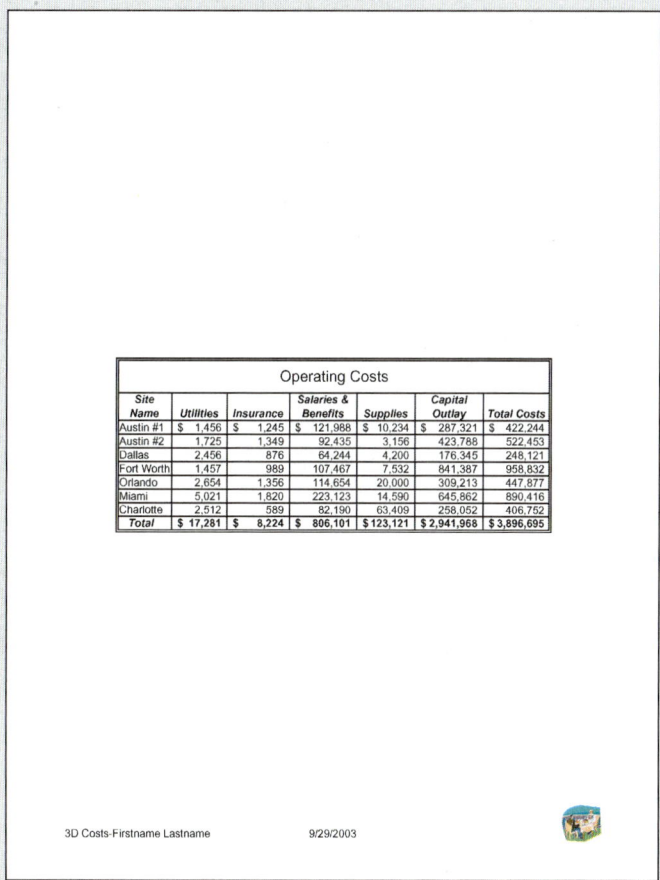

Figure 3.54

1. Start Excel. From the **File** menu, click **Open**. In the **Open** dialog box, navigate to the student files that accompany this textbook, and open the file **e03D_Costs**. Display the **View** menu, click **Header and Footer**, and then click the **Custom Footer** button. In the **Left section**, type **3D Costs-Firstname Lastname** and then close the dialog boxes.

2. From the **File** menu, click **Save As**. In the **Save As** dialog box, navigate to the location where you are storing your projects for this chapter. In the **File name** box, type **3D_Costs_Firstname_Lastname** and then click **Save** or press Enter.

(**Project 3D–Costs** continues on the next page)

Project 3D: Costs | **Excel** 717

Excel chapter three
Skill Assessments (continued)

(Project 3D–Costs continued)

3. Select the range **A2:G2**. From the **Format** menu, click **Cells**, and then click the **Alignment tab**. Under **Text control**, select the **Wrap text** check box so that the headings that do not fit within the cell margins display on two lines.

4. Under **Text alignment**, click the **Horizontal arrow**, and then click **Center** to center the text between the left and right boundaries of each cell. Click **OK**. Notice that the text in cells **A2**, **D2**, **F2**, and **G2** has wrapped to two lines. The rows were made taller to accommodate the wrapped text.

5. With the range **A2:G2** still selected, move to the Formatting toolbar, and then click **Bold** and **Italic**. Select **column C**, and then from the column heading area, drag its right edge to the right slightly to accommodate the entire word *Insurance*.

6. Click cell **A1**. On the Formatting toolbar, click the **Font Size arrow**, and then click **14** to enlarge the worksheet title. From the **Format** menu, point to **Row**, and then click **Height**. Change the height of the row to **31.5** and then click **OK**.

7. Select the range **A1:G1**. Press and hold down Ctrl, and then press 1 to display the **Format Cells** dialog box. Click the **Alignment tab**. Under **Text alignment**, click the **Horizontal arrow**, and then click **Center Across Selection**. Click the **Vertical arrow**, click **Center**, and then click **OK**.

8. Click cell **G3**, and then on the Standard toolbar, click **AutoSum** and press Enter. This totals the operating costs for the Austin #1 location. Copy the formula down through cell **G9** to total the costs for each location. Click cell **B10**, click **AutoSum** and press Enter. Copy the formula across through cell **G10** to total the costs in each category and the total for all locations.

9. Select the range **B3:G3**. Point to the selection, right-click, and from the displayed shortcut menu, click **Format Cells**. Click the **Number tab**, and then under **Category**, click **Accounting**. Change the number of **Decimal places** to zero (0), and verify that under **Symbol**, a $ displays. Click **OK**.

10. With the range **B3:G3** still selected, move to the Standard toolbar, and then click **Format Painter**. Point to cell **B10**, and then press and hold down the left mouse button and drag the **Format Painter** pointer across cells **B10:G10**. Release the left mouse button to apply the Accounting format to the selection. Select the columns that are now too narrow, display the **Format** menu, point to **Column**, and then click **AutoFit Selection**.

(Project 3D–Costs continues on the next page)

Skill Assessments (continued)

(Project 3D–Costs continued)

11. Select the range **B4:G9**. Press Ctrl + 1 to display the **Format Cells** dialog box. On the **Number tab**, under **Category**, click **Number**. Change the number of **Decimal places** to 0, and then select the **Use 1000 Separator (,)** check box.

12. Under **Negative numbers**, click the third option—**(1,234)**. Recall that the Accounting format automatically displays negative numbers with parentheses. In the event that you have negative numbers, to align the digits correctly, you must choose the option that includes the parentheses. Click **OK**.

13. Select the range **A10:G10**. On the Formatting toolbar, click **Bold**. Click cell **A10**. On the Formatting toolbar, click **Increase Indent**, and then on the Formatting toolbar, click **Italic**.

14. Select the range **A2:G10**. On the Formatting toolbar, click the **Borders arrow** to display the **Border palette**. In the last row, click the second button, **All Borders**.

15. Select the range **A1:G10**. From the **Format** menu, click **Cells**, and then click the **Border tab**. Under **Line**, in the **Style** list, click the **last style in the second column**—the double line. Under **Presets**, click **Outline**, and then click **OK**.

16. On the Standard toolbar, click **Print Preview** to view the borders you have applied. **Close** Print Preview.

17. From the **File** menu, click **Page Setup**, and then click the **Margins tab**. Under **Center on page**, select the **Horizontally** and **Vertically** check boxes. Click the **Header/Footer tab**, and then click **Custom Footer**. Click in the **Center section**, and then click the **Date** button. Press Tab once to move the insertion point to the **Right section**, and then, on the **Footer** dialog box toolbar, click the **Insert Picture** button.

18. In the displayed **Insert Picture** dialog box, click the **Look in arrow**, and navigate to the student files for this textbook. Select **e03D_Dining** and then click the **Insert** button.

19. On the **Footer** dialog box toolbar, click the **Format Picture** button. In the displayed **Format Picture** dialog box, decrease the height and width of the picture to **0.5** either by using the spin box arrows or by typing directly in the box. Click **OK**.

20. Click **OK** to close the **Footer** dialog box, and then, in the **Page Setup** dialog box, click **Print Preview**. On the **Print Preview** dialog box, click **Print**. In the **Print** dialog box, click **OK**.

21. On the Standard toolbar, click **Save**, close your file, and close Excel.

End You have completed Project 3D

Excel chapter three
Skill Assessments (continued)

Project 3E—POS

Objectives: *Change Alignment of Cell Contents, Apply Cell Formatting, and Apply Workbook Formatting.*

In the following Skill Assessment, you will edit a workbook for Laura Mabry Hernandez, Director of Point of Sale (POS) Systems for the Oceana Palm Grill, that lists the point of sale equipment at the restaurant locations. Your completed workbook will look similar to the one shown in Figure 3.55. You will save the workbook as *3E_POS_Firstname_Lastname*.

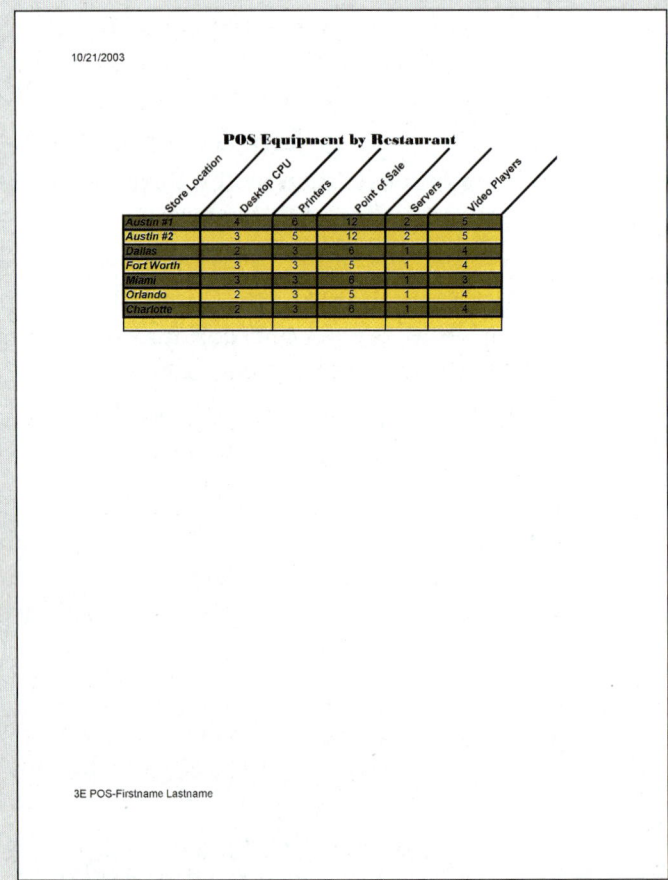

Figure 3.55

(**Project 3E–POS** continues on the next page)

Skill Assessments (continued)

(Project 3E–POS continued)

1. Start Excel. From the **File** menu, click **Open**. In the **Open** dialog box, navigate to the student files that accompany this textbook, and open the file **e03E_POS**. Display the **View** menu, click **Header and Footer**, and then click the **Custom Footer** button. In the **Left section**, type **3E POS-Firstname Lastname** and then close the dialog boxes.

2. From the **File** menu, click **Save As**. In the **Save As** dialog box, navigate to the location where you are storing your projects for this chapter. In the **File name** box, type **3E_POS_Firstname_Lastname** and then click **Save** or press Enter.

3. Select the range **A2:F10**. From the **Edit** menu, point to **Clear**, and then click **Formats** to clear all formatting from the selected range. Click anywhere to cancel the selection, and notice that the shading format is removed from the selected cells.

4. Click cell **A1**. On the Formatting toolbar, click the **Font arrow**, and then click **Britannic Bold**. If this font is not available on your system, choose another serif font. Recall that a serif font contains extensions (lines) on the ends of the characters. Click the **Font Size arrow**, and then click **14**.

5. Select the range **A2:F2**. On the Formatting toolbar, click **Bold**. Point to the selection, and then click the right mouse button to display the shortcut menu. Click **Format Cells**. Click the **Alignment tab**. Under **Orientation**, point to the **red diamond**, press and hold down the left mouse button, and then drag upward so that **45** displays in the **Degrees** box. Alternatively, you can type **45** in the degrees box or click the spin box arrows. Under **Text alignment**, click the **Horizontal arrow**, and then click **Center**. Click **OK**.

6. Select the range **A1:G1**. Display the **Format Cells** dialog box. On the **Alignment tab**, click the **Horizontal arrow**, and then click **Center Across Selection**. Recall that when you use this method, all the cells remain intact—none is merged into the first cell in the selection, as is the case with the Merge and Center button. Click **OK**.

7. Select the range **A3:A9**. On the Formatting toolbar, click **Italic**, and then click **Bold**.

8. Select the range **A3:F9**. On the Formatting toolbar, click the **Borders arrow** to display the **Borders palette**. In the last row, click the second button, **All Borders**. From the **Format** menu, click **Cells**, click the **Border tab**, and then under **Line**, in the **Style** list, click the **fifth line style** in the second column. In the **Presets** area click the **Outline** and the **Inside** buttons to apply the new line style to the borders. Click **OK**.

(Project 3E–POS continues on the next page)

Skill Assessments (continued)

(Project 3E–POS continued)

9. Select the range **A2:F2**. When you select this range, a portion of the word *Players* may not appear to be included in the selection. Because the text is formatted at a 45-degree angle, it may not display within the selection. From the **Format** menu, click **Cells**. Under **Border**, in the white preview area, click to apply a **Right** border and a **Center** border—the button with the vertical line displayed in the center. Notice that in the white preview area, the left and top edges of the sample cells do not contain a border. Click **OK**.

10. Select the range **B3:F9** (all of the cells with numbers). On the Formatting toolbar, click the **Center** button. On the Standard toolbar, click **Save**. Then, on the Standard toolbar, click the **Print Preview** button to see the changes you have made. On the Print Preview toolbar, click **Close** to return to the worksheet.

11. From the **File** menu, click **Page Setup**, and then click the **Margins tab**. Change the **Top** margin to **1.5**, and then change the **Footer** margin to **1**. Under **Center on page**, select the **Horizontally** check box.

12. Click the **Header/Footer tab**, and then click **Custom Header**. With the insertion point positioned in the **Left section**, click the **Date** button. Click **OK**.

13. In the displayed **Page Setup** dialog box, click the **Print Preview** button to view your worksheet. On the Print Preview toolbar, click **Print**, and then click **OK**. Save the changes you have made to your worksheet since the last Save operation, and then close the file and close Excel.

 You have completed Project 3E

Skill Assessments (continued)

Project 3F—Time Sheets

Objectives: *Change Number Format, Change Alignment of Cell Contents, Apply Cell Formatting, Apply Workbook Formatting, and View and Insert Comments in a Cell.*

In the following Skill Assessment, you will edit a workbook for Seth Weddel, Controller for the Oceana Palm Grill, that lists the time sheets and weekly salaries for the Austin #1 location. Your completed workbook will look similar to the one shown in Figure 3.56. You will save the workbook as *3F_Time_Sheets_Firstname_Lastname*.

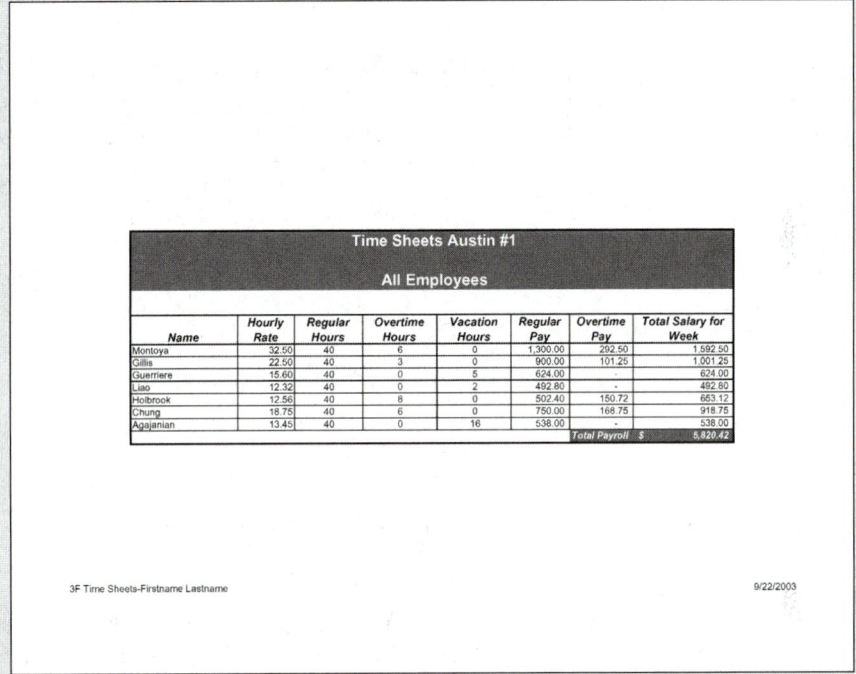

Figure 3.56

1. Start Excel. From the **File** menu, click **Open**. In the **Open** dialog box, navigate to the student files that accompany this textbook, and open the file **e03F_Time_Sheets**. Display the **View** menu, click **Header and Footer**, and then click the **Custom Footer** button. In the **Left section**, type **3F Time Sheets-Firstname Lastname** and then close the dialog boxes.

2. From the **File** menu, click **Save As**. In the **Save As** dialog box, navigate to the location where you are storing your projects for this chapter. In the **File name** box, type **3F_Time_Sheets_Firstname_Lastname** and then click **Save** or press Enter.

(**Project 3F**–Time Sheets continues on the next page)

Excel Chapter 3

Skill Assessments (continued)

(Project 3F–Time Sheets continued)

3. Select the range **A1:H3**. Press and hold down Ctrl and press 1 to display the **Format Cells** dialog box. Click the **Alignment tab**, and then click the **Horizontal arrow**. Click **Center Across Selection**. Click the **Patterns tab**. Under **Cell shading**, in the second row of the palette, click the last color—**Dark Gray**. Click the **Font tab**, and then under **Font style**, click **Bold**, and under **Size**, click **16**. Click the **Color arrow**, and in the fifth row of the palette, click the last color—**White**. Click **OK**.

4. Select the range **A6:H6**. Right-click the selection to display the shortcut menu, and then click **Format Cells**. Click the **Alignment tab**, and then, under **Text control**, select the **Wrap text** check box. Under **Text alignment**, click the **Horizontal arrow**, and then click **Center**. Click the **Font tab**. Change the **Size** to **12** and change the **Font style** to **Bold Italic**. Click **OK**.

5. Select the range **B7:B13**. Display the **Format** menu, click **Cells**, and then click the **Number tab**. Under **Category**, click **Number**. Verify that **2 Decimal places** display. Click **OK**.

6. Select the range **F7:H13**. On the Formatting toolbar, click the **Comma Style** button. Click cell **H14**, and then, on the Formatting toolbar, click the **Currency Style** button.

7. Click cell **H7**, and on the Standard toolbar, click the **AutoSum** button. Because you need only add the regular pay to the overtime pay to compute the total weekly salary, drag to select **F7:G7** so that the formula indicates =SUM(F7:G7) and then press Enter. Copy the formula down through cell **H13**.

8. In cell **H14**, click **AutoSum** to total the column—your result should be $5,820.42. Select the range **C7:E13**, and then, on the Formatting toolbar, click **Center**. Click cell **G14** and type **Total Payroll**

9. Select the range **G14:H14**. Press and hold down Ctrl and press 1 to display the **Format Cells** dialog box. Click the **Patterns tab**. Under **Cell shading**, in the second row of the palette, click the last color—**Dark gray**. Click the **Font tab**, and then click the **Color arrow**. In the fifth row of the palette, click the last color—**White**. Under **Font style**, click **Bold Italic**. Click **OK**.

10. Select the range **A6:H13**. On the Formatting toolbar, click the **Borders arrow** and then, in the third row, click the second button—**All Borders**. On the Standard toolbar, click **Save**. Recall that it is good practice to save your work periodically.

(Project 3F–Time Sheets continues on the next page)

Skill Assessments (continued)

(Project 3F–Time Sheets continued)

11. Select the range **A1:H14**. On the Formatting toolbar, click the **Borders arrow**. In the last row, click the last button—**Thick Box Border**. Click cell **D6**, right-click, and from the displayed shortcut menu, click **Insert Comment**. In the comment box, type **Overtime paid at 1.5 times hourly rate** and then change the inserted name to your name. Click in any empty cell to close the comment box. If necessary, right-click cell D6 and click Hide Comments from the shortcut menu.

12. On the menu bar, click **File**, and then click **Page Setup**. Click the **Margins tab**, and then under **Center on page**, select the **Horizontally** and **Vertically** check boxes. Change the **Footer margin** to **1**.

13. Click the **Header/Footer tab**, and then click **Custom Footer**. Press twice to position the insertion point in the **Right section**. On the **Footer** dialog box toolbar, click the **Date** button, and then click **OK**.

14. Click the **Page tab**. Under **Orientation**, click **Landscape**. Under **Scaling**, adjust the worksheet to **90%** of its normal size. Click **OK**.

15. On the Standard toolbar, click the **Save** button, and then click the **Print Preview** button. On the **Print Preview** toolbar, click **Print** and then click **OK**. Close your file, and then close Excel.

End You have completed Project 3F

Excel chapter three
Performance Assessments

Project 3G — Category Sales

Objectives: *Change Number Format, Change Alignment of Cell Contents, Apply Cell Formatting, and Apply Workbook Formatting.*

In the following Performance Assessment, you will edit a workbook for Donna Rohan Kurian, Executive Chef for the Oceana Palm Grill, that lists category sales for a recent Saturday. Your completed workbook will look similar to the one shown in Figure 3.57. You will save the workbook as *3G_Category_Sales_Firstname_Lastname*.

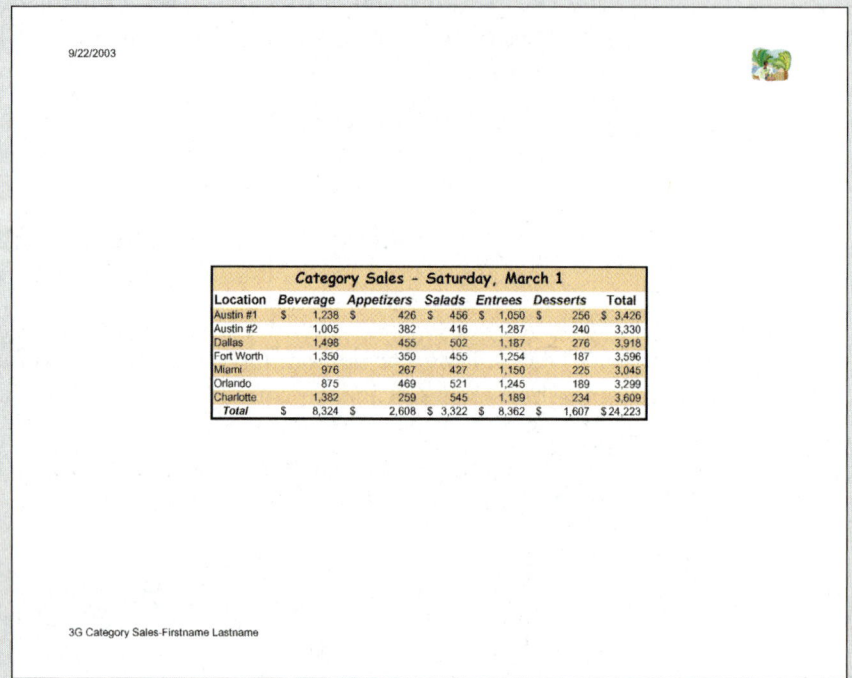

Figure 3.57

1. Start Excel. From the **File** menu, click **Open**. In the **Open** dialog box, navigate to the student files that accompany this textbook, and open the file **e03G_Category_Sales**. Display the **View** menu, click **Header and Footer**, and then click the **Custom Footer** button. In the **Left section**, type **3G Category Sales-Firstname Lastname** and then close the dialog boxes.

2. From the **File** menu, click **Save As**. In the **Save As** dialog box, navigate to the location where you are storing your projects for this chapter. In the **File name** box, type **3G_Category_Sales_Firstname_Lastname** and then click **Save** or press Enter.

(**Project 3G**–Category Sales continues on the next page)

Performance Assessments (continued)

(Project 3G–Category Sales continued)

3. Select the range **A1:G1**. Display the **Format Cells** dialog box, and click the **Font tab**. Change the **Font** to **Comic Sans MS**, change the **Font style** to **Bold**, and change the **Font Size** to **14 pt**. Click the **Alignment tab**, and apply the **Center Across Selection** horizontal alignment. Click **OK** to close the **Format Cells** dialog box.

4. In cell **B10**, use the **AutoSum** button to create a total for the Beverage category. Use the **fill handle** to copy the formula across through cell **F10**.

5. In cell **G3**, use the **AutoSum** button to create a total for the Austin #1 location. Use the **fill handle** to copy the formula through cell **G9**. Click cell **G10**, and total the column.

6. Select the range **B4:G9**, apply the **Comma Style**, and then click **Decrease Decimal** two times so that there are no decimal places. Select the range **B3:G3**, hold down Ctrl, and select **B10:G10**. Then, with the two nonadjacent ranges selected, apply **Currency Style**, and click **Decrease Decimal** two times. The total sales for all categories in cell **G10** should be $24,223.

7. Select the range **A2:G2**, change the **Font Size** to **12**, and then apply **Bold** to the selection. Select **columns A:G** and **AutoFit** the columns.

8. Apply **Italic** to the names of each of the categories. Click in cell **A10** and apply **Bold** and **Italic**, and then **Increase Indent** one time.

9. Select the range **A1:G1**. Display the **Format Cells** dialog box, click the **Patterns tab**, and under **Color**, in the fifth row of the palette, click the second color box—**Tan**. Click **OK**.

10. Select the range **A3:G3**. On the Formatting toolbar, click the **Fill Color arrow** (to the right of the **Borders** button) to display the color palette. In the last row, click the second color—**Tan**—to apply tan shading across the row. Notice that you can apply shading to cells either from the **Format Cells** dialog box or from the **Fill Color** button.

11. Repeat this shading for the data in rows **5**, **7**, and **9**. (Hint: After formatting the color for a row, you can select the next row's data and then press the Repeat key, F4. Do not use the Format Painter because this would apply the Currency style to rows where it is not appropriate.)

12. Select the range **A1:G10**. Apply a **Thick Box** border to the selection. Display the **Page Setup** dialog box, change the worksheet orientation to **Landscape**, and then center the worksheet on the page **horizontally** and **vertically**. Create a **Custom Header** that includes the **date** in the **Left section** and the picture **e03G_Waiter** in the **Right section**. Format the picture to a height and width of **0.5 inches**.

13. Save your worksheet, and then view it in **Print Preview**. Print the worksheet, close your file, and then close Excel.

End You have completed Project 3G

Excel chapter three

Performance Assessments (continued)

Project 3H—Restaurant Sales

Objectives: *Change Number Format, Change Alignment of Cell Contents, Apply Cell Formatting, Apply Workbook Formatting, and View and Insert Comments in a Cell.*

In the following Performance Assessment, you will edit a workbook for Felicia Mabry, President of the Oceana Palm Grill, that details restaurant sales for the first half of the year. Your completed workbook will look similar to the one shown in Figure 3.58. You will save the workbook as *3H_Restaurant_Sales_Firstname_Lastname*.

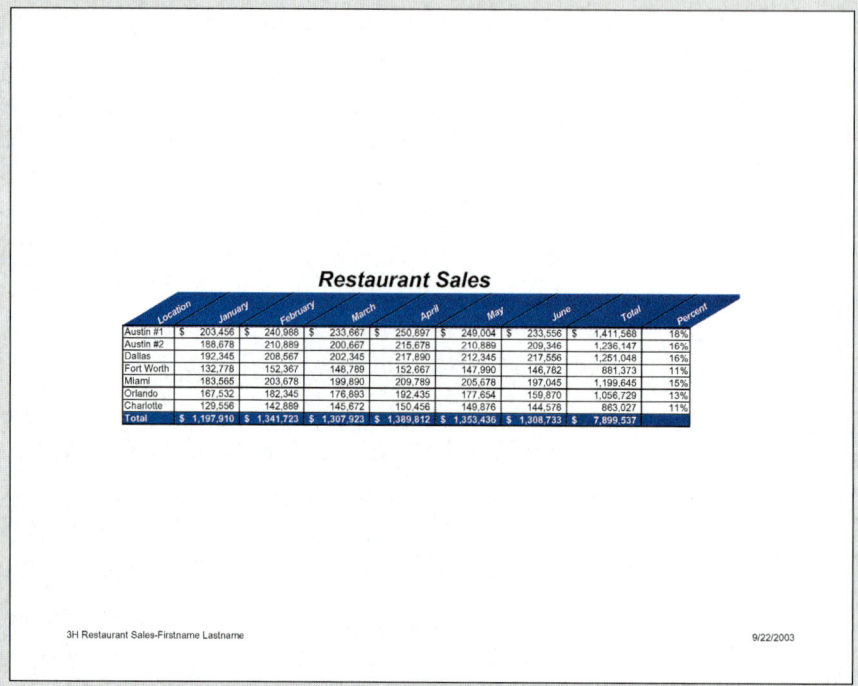

Figure 3.58

1. Start Excel. From the **File** menu, click **Open**. In the **Open** dialog box, navigate to the student files that accompany this textbook, and open the file **e03H_Restaurant_Sales**. Display the **View** menu, click **Header and Footer**, and then click the **Custom Footer** button. In the **Left section**, type 3H Restaurant Sales-Firstname Lastname and then close the dialog boxes.

2. From the **File** menu, click **Save As**. In the **Save As** dialog box, navigate to the location where you are storing your projects for this chapter. In the **File name** box, type 3H_Restaurant_Sales_Firstname_Lastname and then click **Save** or press [Enter].

(**Project 3H**–Restaurant Sales continues on the next page)

Performance Assessments (continued)

(Project 3H–Restaurant Sales continued)

3. In cell **A1**, change the **Font Size** to **22**, and apply **Bold** and **Italic**. Select the range **A1:I1**. Display the **Format Cells** dialog box, and from the **Alignment tab**, apply the **Center Across Selection** horizontal alignment.

4. In cell **B2**, type **January** and then use the **fill handle** to complete the series across through June.

5. Select the range **A2:I2**. Using the Formatting toolbar buttons, apply **Bold** and **Italic**, and then **Center** the text. From the **Alignment tab** of the **Format Cells** dialog box, change the orientation to **30 Degrees**, and change the **Vertical alignment** to **Center**.

6. In cell **H3**, use the **AutoSum** button to create a formula that calculates the January through June total for the Austin #1 location. Use **AutoFill** to copy the formula for the remaining locations. In cell **H2**, type **Total**

7. In cell **A10**, type **Total** In cell **B10**, use the **AutoSum** button to create a formula that calculates the January total. Use **AutoFill** to copy the formula for each month and the Total column.

8. Select the range **B3:H3**. Using the Formatting toolbar button, apply the **Currency Style**. Use the **Decrease Decimal** button to decrease the number of decimals to zero (0). Click **Format Painter**, and copy the formatting to the Total row—cells **B10:H10**.

9. Select the range **B4:H9**. Using the Formatting toolbar button, apply the **Comma Style**. Use the **Decrease Decimal** button to decrease the number of decimals to zero (0). **AutoFit** any columns if necessary.

10. Click cell **I2** and type **Percent** Click in cell **I3**. Create a formula that calculates the percent that each location's total is of the total income. (To create this formula, divide the total for Austin #1 location, cell **H3**, by the total in cell **H10**. Be sure to make the cell reference to cell **H10** absolute—**$H$10**.) Copy the formula down through cell **I9**. Select the range **I3:I9**, and using the Formatting toolbar button, apply the **Percent Style**. Click **Save**.

11. Select the range **A2:I2**. Use the **Fill Color** button to apply the **Blue** fill color to the range—the sixth color in the second row of the color palette. To provide better contrast of the text on the blue background, display the **Format Cells** dialog box, and from the **Font tab**, change the **Font Color** to **White**—the last color in the fifth row. Select the range **A10:I10**, and apply the same **Fill Color** and **Font Color** as you did in **row 3**. (Hint: The Fill Color button is now the same color—Blue—and you can click the arrow on the Font Color button and click White from the displayed palette.) Apply **Bold**. Widen columns if necessary.

(Project 3H–Restaurant Sales continues on the next page)

Performance Assessments (continued)

(Project 3H–Restaurant Sales continued)

12. Select the range **A3:I10**. Using the Formatting toolbar button, apply the **All Borders** border style to the selection.

13. Select the range **A2:I2**. Display the **Format Cells** dialog box, and click the **Border tab**. Apply a single line border style to the bottom and to the center of the selection.

14. Display the **Page Setup** dialog box. Change the worksheet orientation to **Landscape** and then, under **Scaling**, scale the worksheet to **90%**. Center the worksheet on the page **horizontally** and **vertically**. Create a **custom footer** that includes the **date** in the **Right section**.

15. In cell **I3**, add the following comment, using your own name: **Same percentage as last year**

16. Save your worksheet, and then view it in **Print Preview**. Print the worksheet, close your file, and then close Excel.

End You have completed Project 3H

Excel chapter three
Performance Assessments (continued)

Project 3I—Employee Sales

Objectives: *Change Number Format, Change Alignment of Cell Contents, Apply Cell Formatting, and Apply Workbook Formatting.*

In the following Performance Assessment, you will edit a workbook for Seth Weddel, Controller for the Oceana Palm Grill, that details restaurant sales by employee. Your completed workbook will look similar to the one shown in Figure 3.59. You will save the workbook as *3I_Employee_Sales_Firstname_Lastname*.

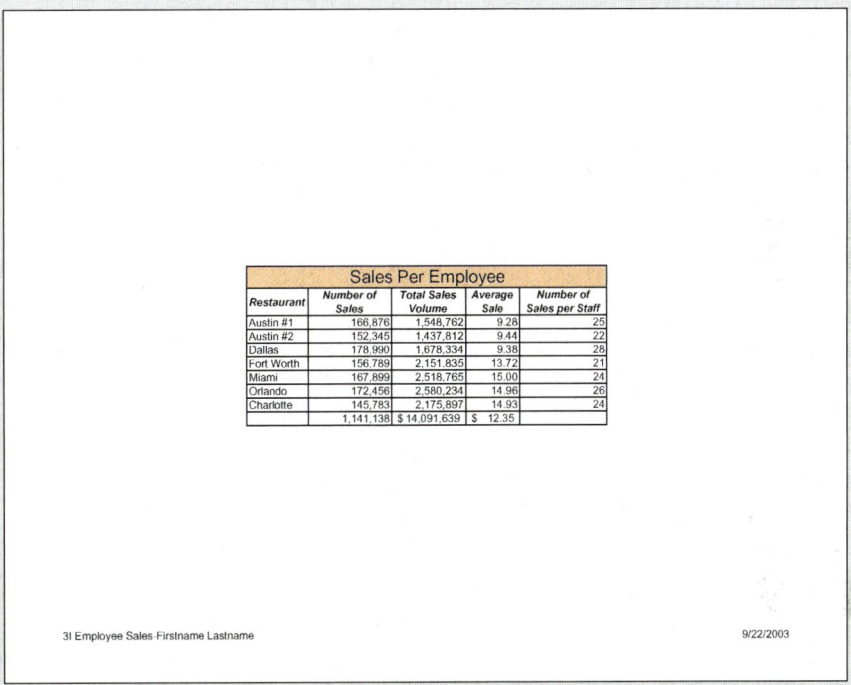

Figure 3.59

1. Start Excel. From the **File** menu, click **Open**. In the **Open** dialog box, navigate to the student files that accompany this textbook, and open the file **e03I_Employee_Sales**. Display the **View** menu, click **Header and Footer**, and then click the **Custom Footer** button. In the **Left section**, type **3I Employee Sales-Firstname Lastname** and then close the dialog boxes.

2. From the **File** menu, click **Save As**. In the **Save As** dialog box, navigate to the location where you are storing your projects for this chapter. In the **File name** box, type **3I_Employee_Sales_Firstname_Lastname** and then click **Save** or press Enter.

(**Project 3I**–Employee Sales continues on the next page)

Project 3I: Employee Sales | **Excel** 731

Performance Assessments (continued)

(Project 3I–Employee Sales continued)

3. Select the range **A2:E2**, and then display the **Format Cells** dialog box. Use the appropriate tabs in the dialog box to activate **Wrap text**, and center the text in the cells both **horizontally** and **vertically**. Apply **Bold** and **Italic**. Drag to adjust the width of each column so that the column titles make sense, display on no more than two lines, and look attractive. See Figure 3.59.

4. Create totals in **row 10** for the **Number of Sales** and the **Total Sales Volume**.

5. To create the Average Sale formula for each location, click in cell **D3**, divide the Total Sales Volume (cell **C3**) by the Number of Sales (cell **B3**). Fill the formula down through row 10.

6. To format the title, change the font to **Berlin Sans FB** or some other sans sarif font, **16 pt**, and then **center** the title over the worksheet columns.

7. Select the nonadjacent ranges **B3:B10** and **E3:E9**. Display the **Format Cells** dialog box. Apply the **Number** format with the **1000 separator** and **zero (0)** decimal places.

8. Select the range **C3:C9**, and use the **Format Cells** dialog box (not the toolbar button) to apply the **Currency** format with **zero (0)** decimal places and **no dollar sign**. Select the range **D3:D9** and apply the **Currency** format with **2 decimal places** and **no dollar sign**.

9. Select cell **C10**, click the **Currency Style** button, and then click **Decrease Decimal** twice. If necessary, **AutoFit** to display results. Select cell **D10**, and click the **Currency Style** button.

10. Select the range **A1:E10**, click the **Borders button arrow**, and apply **All Borders**. To the range **A1:E1**, apply **Tan** cell shading from the **Fill Color** button palette.

11. Use the **Page Setup** dialog box to change the worksheet orientation to **Landscape**. Center the worksheet on the page **horizontally** and **vertically**. Create a **custom footer** that includes the **date** in the **Right section**.

12. Save your worksheet, and then view it in **Print Preview**. Print the worksheet, close your file, and then close Excel.

End You have completed Project 3I

Excel chapter three
Mastery Assessments

Project 3J — Seafood Sales

Objectives: *Change Number Format, Change Alignment of Cell Contents, Apply Cell Formatting, and Apply Workbook Formatting.*

In the following Mastery assessment, you will edit a workbook for Donna Rohan Kurian, Executive Chef for the Oceana Palm Grill, that details the sales of seafood specials during a one-week period in July at the two Austin restaurants. Your completed workbook will look similar to the one shown in Figure 3.60. You will save the workbook as *3J_Seafood_Sales_Firstname_Lastname*.

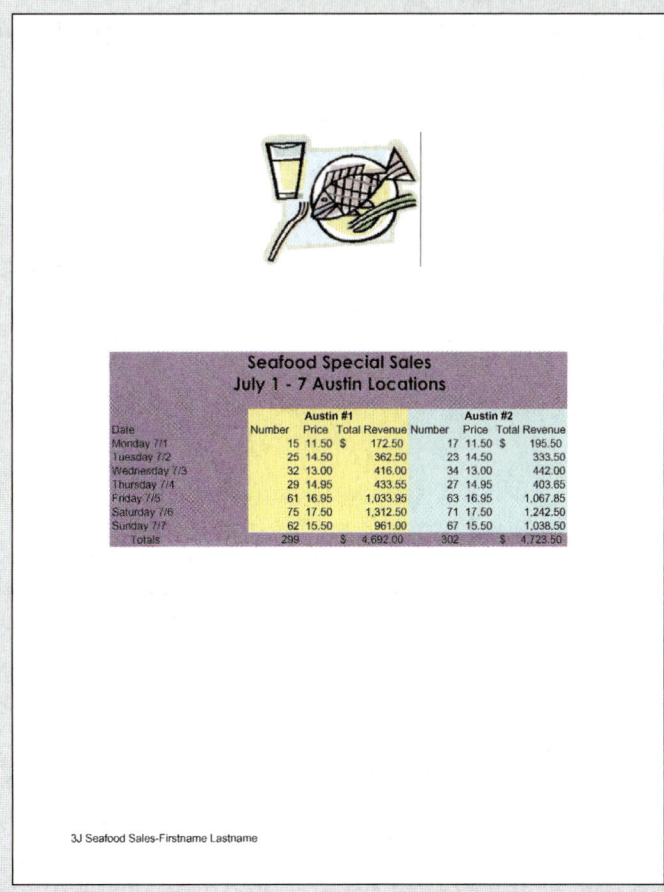

Figure 3.60

(**Project 3J**–Seafood Sales continues on the next page)

Excel chapter three

Mastery Assessments (continued)

(Project 3J–Seafood Sales continued)

1. Start Excel. On the **File** menu, click **Open**. In the **Open** dialog box, navigate to the student files that accompany this textbook, and open the file **e03J_Seafood_Sales**. Display the **View** menu, click **Header and Footer**, and then click the **Custom Footer** button. In the **Left section** type 3J Seafood Sales-Firstname Lastname and then click **OK** to close the dialog boxes.

2. From the **File** menu, click **Save As**. In the **Save As** dialog box, navigate to the location where you are storing your projects for this chapter. In the **File name** box, type 3J_Seafood_Sales_Firstname_Lastname and then click **Save** or press Enter.

3. Select **columns A:G**, and from the **Format** menu, point to **Column** and **AutoFit Selection**.

4. Select the range **A1:G2** and display the **Format Cells** dialog box. Change the font to **Century Gothic**, change the font style to **Bold**, change the font size to **16**, and then change the horizontal alignment to **Center Across Selection**.

5. Select the range **B4:D4**, change the font style to **Bold**, and change the horizontal alignment to **Center Across Selection**. Repeat for the range **E4:G4**. Select the range **B4:D12** and from the **Fill Color arrow**, apply **Light Yellow** shading. Select the range **E4:G12** and apply **Light Turquoise** shading. To the ranges **A1:G3** and **A4:A12**, apply **Lavender** shading.

6. In cell **D6**, create a formula to calculate the total revenue for the seafood specials sold at the Austin #1 location for Monday, July 1. Copy the formula down through cell **D12**. In cells **D7:D12**, use the **Format Cells** dialog box to format the numbers as **Currency** with **two decimal places** and **no symbol**. To cell **D6**, use the **Format Cells** dialog box to apply the **Currency** style with the **$** symbol. Repeat the calculation and the formatting for the Austin #2 location.

7. In cell **A13**, type Totals and **Increase Indent** twice. In cells **D13** and **G13**, compute total revenue for each location. If necessary, apply currency formatting with two decimal places to the two cells. In cells **B13** and **E13**, compute the total number of seafood specials sold for each location. Select the range **B13:G13**, and apply **Lavender** shading. Save your worksheet.

8. Create a custom header, and in the center section, insert the picture **e03J_Seafood**. Format the picture as **2 inches high** and **2 inches wide**. Change the **header margin** to **1.5**, and center the worksheet both **horizontally** and **vertically** on the page.

9. Save your workbook, view it in **Print Preview**, and then print it. Close the file, and then close Excel.

End You have completed Project 3J

Excel chapter three

Mastery Assessments (continued)

Project 3K — Chef Expenses

Objectives: *Change Number Format, Change Alignment of Cell Contents, Apply Cell Formatting, Apply Workbook Formatting, and View and Insert Comments in a Cell.*

In the following Mastery assessment, you will edit a workbook that details chef expenses for all locations of the Oceana Palm Grill. Your completed workbook will look similar to the one shown in Figure 3.61. You will save the workbook as *3K_Chef_Expenses_Firstname_Lastname*.

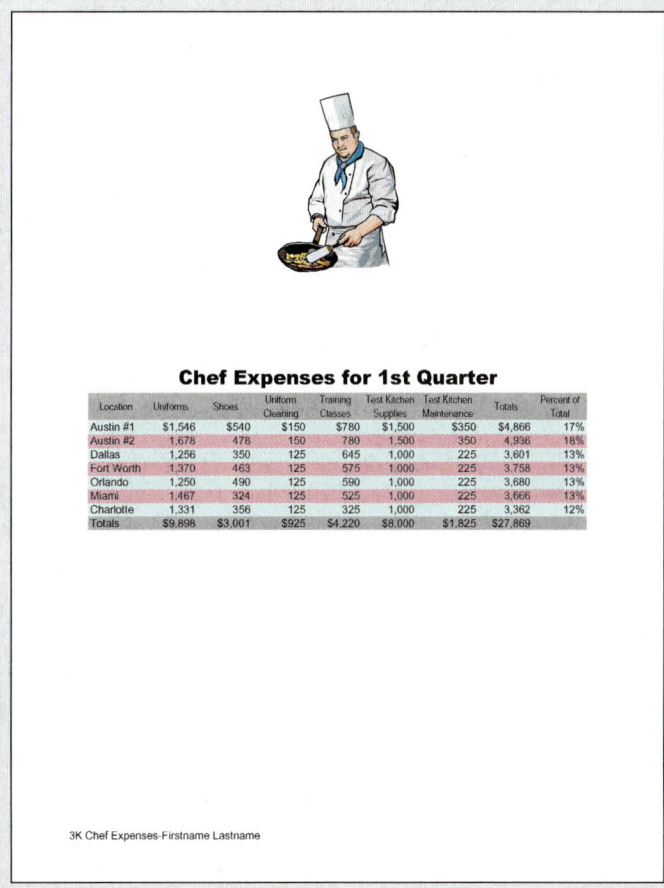

Figure 3.61

(**Project 3K**–Chef Expenses continues on the next page)

Excel chapter three
Mastery Assessments (continued)

(Project 3K–Chef Expenses continued)

1. Start Excel. On the **File** menu, click **Open**. In the **Open** dialog box, navigate to the student files that accompany this textbook, and open the file **e03K_Chef_Expenses**. Display the **View** menu, click **Header and Footer**, and then click the **Custom Footer** button. In the **Left section** type **3K Chef Expenses-Firstname Lastname** and then click **OK** to close the dialog boxes. Save the file in your storage location for this chapter as **3K_Chef_Expenses_Firstname_Lastname**

2. Select cell **A1**. Center the contents across cells **A1:I1**, change the font to **Arial Black**, and change the font size to **18**. Select the range **A2:G2**, wrap the text, center the text in the cells **horizontally** and **vertically**, and change the font to **Arial Narrow**. If necessary, adjust any columns so that the text displays attractively on no more than two lines.

3. In cell **A10**, type **Totals** and then in cells **B10:G10**, compute the totals in each category. Select the nonadjacent ranges **B3:G3** and **B10:G10** and use the **Format Cells** dialog box to apply the **Currency Style** with no decimal places and the $ symbol. To the range **B4:G9**, use the **Format Cells** dialog box to apply the **Currency Style** with no symbol and no decimal places.

4. In cell **H2**, type **Totals** and in cell **I2**, type **Percent of Total** In cell **H3**, total the expenses for the Austin #1 location, and then copy the formula to the remaining locations. Click cell **G4**, click the **Format Painter** button, and then format the range **H4:H9**.

5. In cell **H10**, compute the grand total for all expenses at all locations. In cell **I3**, construct a formula to compute the percentage that this location represents of the total expenses. Be sure to make your reference to cell **H10** absolute. Copy the formula down for each location, and apply the **Percent Style**. Save your workbook.

6. Shade the data in **rows 3**, **5**, **7**, and **9** in **Light Turquoise**. Shade the data in **rows 4**, **6**, and **8** in **Rose**. Select the nonadjacent ranges **A2:I2** and **A10:I10**, and apply **25 percent Gray** shading. In cell **D2**, insert the following comment, and use your own name: **New cleaning service, Kitchen Pro Cleaners, being tested this quarter.**

7. Center the page **horizontally** and **vertically**, and set the header margin to **1 inch**. Create a custom header, and in the center section, insert the picture **03K_Chef_at_Work**. Format the size of the picture to **2.5 inches high** and **1.5 inches wide**.

8. Save your workbook. View the workbook in **Print Preview**, print it, close the workbook, and close Excel.

End You have completed Project 3K

Problem Solving

Project 3L — Budget

Objectives: *Change Number Format, Change Alignment of Cell Contents, Apply Cell Formatting, and Apply Workbook Formatting.*

Using the data found in e03L_Budget, use the techniques you have learned in this chapter to attractively format the data in the workbook. Compute totals where appropriate. Use each of the following at least once: apply currency format, indent cell contents, rotate text, change font and font size, apply cell borders, apply cell shading, insert a picture in a header or footer (use e03L_Table), and center the worksheet horizontally and vertically. Insert your name in the footer, print the worksheet, and save the workbook as *3L_Budget_Firstname_Lastname*.

End You have completed Project 3L ─────────────────

Project 3M — Schedule

Objectives: *Change Number Format, Change Alignment of Cell Contents, Apply Cell Formatting, and Apply Workbook Formatting.*

Select three of the restaurant locations for the Oceana Palm Grill, and create a weekly schedule for the hours when various chefs will be supervising the kitchen. At each location, a supervising chef is in the kitchen every day between 8 a.m. and 12 midnight. Chefs work an eight-hour shift in the kitchen—either 8 a.m.–4 p.m. or 4 p.m.–midnight. Use the techniques you have practiced in this chapter to format the worksheet attractively. Use each of the following at least once: indent cell contents, rotate text, change font and font size, apply cell borders, apply cell shading, insert a picture in a header or footer (use e03M_Chef), and center the worksheet horizontally and vertically. Insert your name in the footer, print the worksheet, and save the workbook as *3M_Schedule_Firstname_Lastname*.

End You have completed Project 3M ─────────────────

On the Internet

Locate Corporate Financial Information

Go to the Web site **http://www.thecheesecakefactory.com/financial.html** and look at the various types of financial information that is generated for a restaurant. Then, use a search engine to locate financial information about a restaurant chain about which you think you might like to learn more or in which you might possibly invest in some stock.

GO! with Help

Print Comments in a Worksheet

In this exercise, you will use Microsoft Help to get help with printing comments.

1. If necessary, start Excel to open a new workbook.

2. At the right edge of the menu bar, click in the **Type a question for help** box, type **print comments** and then press the [Enter] key.

    The task pane opens, showing Search Results. Notice that you typed *print comments* as the question instead of *How do I print comments?* It is not actually necessary to ask the question *as* a question.

3. Click the link **Print comments**.

    A Microsoft Excel Help window displays with Help for the topic.

4. In the upper right corner of the Help window, click **Show All**.

5. Review the information provided in the Help window. Notice that there are two ways to format comments on your printed worksheet.

6. Print the contents of the Help window with the expanded material.

7. Close the Help Window, and then close the task pane.

Access 2003

chapter one

Getting Started with Access Databases and Tables

In this chapter, you will: complete these projects and practice these skills.

Project 1A
Opening and Viewing a Database

Objectives
- Rename a Database
- Start Access, Open an Existing Database, and View Database Objects

Project 1B
Creating a Database

Objectives
- Create a New Database
- Create a New Table
- Create a Primary Key and Add Records to a Table
- Close and Save a Table
- Open a Table
- Modify the Table Design
- Print a Table
- Edit Records in a Table
- Sort Records
- Navigate to Records in a Table
- Close and Save a Database
- Use the Access Help System

Lake Michigan City College

Lake Michigan City College is located along the lakefront of Chicago—one of the nation's most exciting cities. The college serves its large and diverse student body and makes positive contributions to the community through relevant curricula, partnerships with businesses and nonprofit organizations, and learning experiences that allow students to be full participants in the global community. The college offers three associate degrees in 20 academic areas, adult education programs, and continuing education offerings on campus, at satellite locations, and online.

© Getty Images, Inc.

Getting Started with Access Databases and Tables

Do you have a collection of things that you like, such as a coin collection, stamp collection, recipe collection, or collection of your favorite music CDs? Do you have an address book with the names, addresses, and phone numbers of your friends, business associates, and family members? If you collect something, chances are you have made an attempt to keep track of and organize the items in your collection. If you have an address book, you have probably wished it were better organized. A computer program like Microsoft Access can help you organize and keep track of information.

For example, assume you have a large collection of music CDs. You could organize your CDs into a database because your CDs are a collection of related items. By organizing your CDs in a database, you would be able to find the CDs by various categories that you define. If the information in your address book were placed in a database, you could produce a list of all your friends and family members who have birthdays in the month of April. In this chapter, you will see how useful a database program like Access can be.

Project 1A Computer Club

Data refers to facts about people, events, things, or ideas. A ***database*** is a collection of data related to a particular topic or purpose. Data that has been organized in a useful manner is referred to as ***information***. Examples of data that could be in a database include the titles and artists of all the CDs in a collection or the names and addresses of all the students in an organization. Microsoft Office Access 2003 is a database program that you can use to create and work with information in databases. Databases, like the ones you will work with in Access, include not only the data, but also tools for organizing the data in a way that is useful to you.

In Activities 1.1 through 1.8, you will create a new folder where you will store your projects. Then you will copy a database to your folder and rename the database so you can use it to complete the steps in this project. In this project, you will open a database and view information about the Club Events sponsored by the Computer Club at Lake Michigan City College. See Figure 1.1. In addition to the Event Name and the date of the event, the information includes the name of the Event Coordinator and the type of event.

Club Events

Event#	Event Name	Date	Event Type	Coordinator
01	New Member Social	08/15	Social	Jordan Williams
02	Bi-Monthly Meeting	08/15	Meeting	Annette Jacobson
03	Bi-Monthly Meeting	09/1	Meeting	Annette Jacobson
04	Making Access work for	09/10	Training	Mike Franklin
05	Introduction to Outlook	09/16	Training	Mike Franklin
06	Bi-Monthly Meeting	09/15	Meeting	Annette Jacobson
07	Bi-Monthly Meeting	10/1	Meeting	Annette Jacobson
08	Bi-Monthly Meeting	10/15	Meeting	Annette Jacobson
09	Bi-Monthly Meeting	11/1	Meeting	Annette Jacobson
10	Bi-Monthly Meeting	11/15	Meeting	Annette Jacobson
11	Bi-Monthly Meeting	12/1	Meeting	Annette Jacobson
12	Annual Party	12/10	Social	Linda Turpen
13	Project 1A	11/18	Training	Firstname Lastname

Thursday, October 16, 2003   *Page 1 of 1*

Figure 1.1
Project 1A—Computer Club

Objective 1
Rename a Database

To complete the projects in the chapters, you will locate the student files that accompany this textbook and copy them to the drive and folder where you are storing your projects. Databases that you copy to your storage location must be renamed so you can differentiate them from the data files that accompany this book. In this activity, you will learn how to do this.

Activity 1.1 Renaming a Database

1 Using the **My Computer** feature of your Windows operating system, navigate to the drive where you will be storing your projects for this book, for example, Removable Disk (D:) drive.

2 On the menu bar, click **File**, point to **New**, and then click **Folder**.

A new folder is created, the words *New Folder* display highlighted in the folder's name box, and the insertion point is blinking. Recall that within Windows, highlighted text will be replaced by your typing.

3 Type **Chapter 1** and then press [Enter].

4 Navigate to the location where the student files that accompany this textbook are located, and then click once to select the file **a01A_ComputerClub**.

> **Note** — Using File Extensions
>
> *Access databases use a .mdb extension.*
>
> The computer that you are using may be set such that file extensions display. If so, this file name will display as a01A_ComputerClub.mdb. The .mdb extension indicates that this file is a Microsoft database file.

5 Move the mouse pointer over the selected file name and then right-click to display a shortcut menu. On the displayed shortcut menu, click **Copy**.

6 Navigate to and open the **Chapter 1** folder you created in Step 3. Right-click to display a shortcut menu and then click **Paste**.

The database file is copied to your folder and is selected.

7 Move your mouse pointer over the selected file name, right-click to display the shortcut menu, and then on the shortcut menu, click **Rename**. As shown in Figure 1.2, and using your own first and last name, type **1A_ComputerClub_Firstname_Lastname**

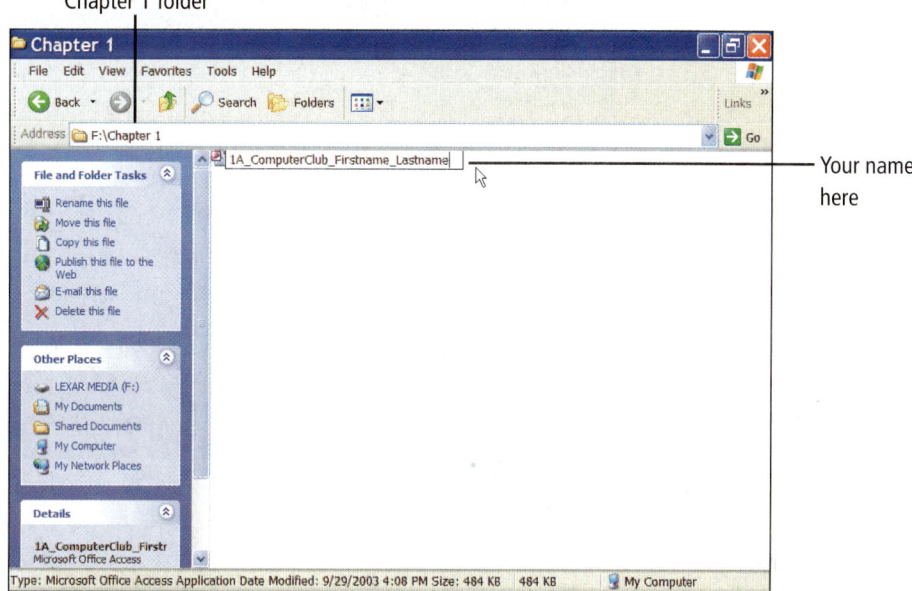

Figure 1.2

8 Press [Enter] to save the new file name. If the *Confirm File Rename* message displays, click **Yes**. Be sure that the file name is still selected (highlighted), pause your mouse pointer over the selected name, and then right-click to display the shortcut menu.

Note — Naming Files

Use underscores instead of spaces.

The Microsoft Windows operating system recognizes file names with spaces. However, some Internet file transfer programs do not. To facilitate sending your files over the Internet using a course management system, in this textbook you will be instructed to save files using an underscore rather than a space. On your keyboard, the underscore key is the shift of the hyphen key, to the right of the zero key.

9 On the displayed shortcut menu, click **Properties**.

The Properties dialog box with the database name in the title bar displays. The databases provided with this book have a Read-only attribute that protects them from being altered. To use a database, you must first save the database to the location where you are storing your files, rename the database, and then remove the Read-only attribute so you can make changes to the database.

10 At the bottom of the dialog box, click to clear the check mark next to **Read-only**. See Figure 1.3.

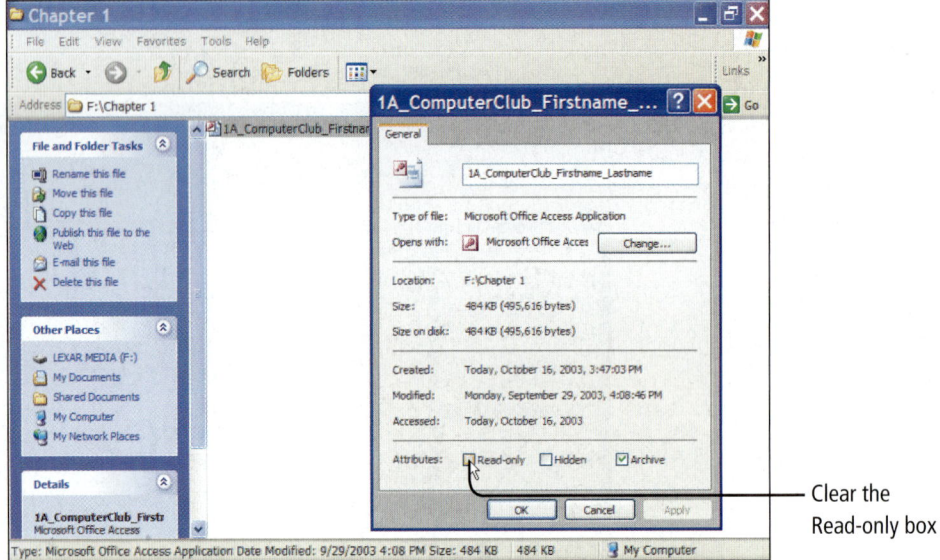
Clear the Read-only box

Figure 1.3

11 Click **OK** to close the dialog box.

12 Close the **My Computer** window.

You may want to mark or otherwise make a note of this section for future reference when you need to retrieve, copy, and rename additional databases for use in this textbook.

Objective 2
Start Access, Open an Existing Database, and View Database Objects

Activity 1.2 Starting Access and Opening an Existing Database

Data that is organized in a format of horizontal rows and vertical columns is called a *table*. A table is the foundation on which an Access database is built. In the following activity, you will view a table within a database.

1 On the left side of the Windows taskbar, click the **Start** button start.

The Start menu displays.

2 On the computer you are using, determine where the Access program is located and point to **Microsoft Office Access 2003**.

Organizations and individuals store computer programs in a variety of ways. The Access program might be located under All Programs or Microsoft Office or some other arrangement. See Figure 1.4 for an example.

744   Access | Chapter 1: Getting Started with Access Databases and Tables

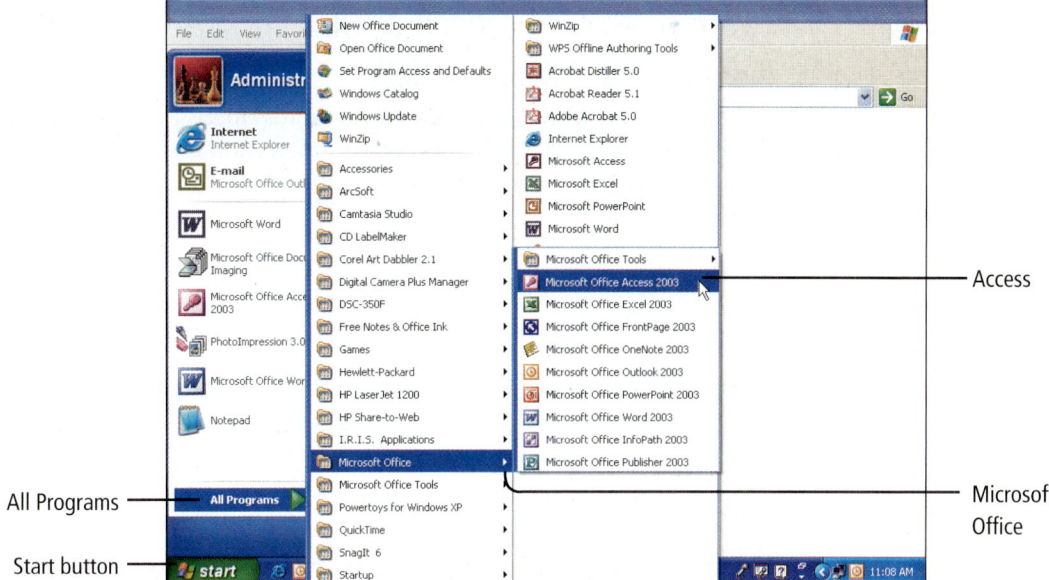

Figure 1.4

3. Click once to open the **Access** program.

The Access program opens. Across the upper portion of the Access window is the title bar, a menu bar, and the Database toolbar. The main window is divided into two sections—the **task pane** on the right and a blank gray area on the left. The task pane is a window within a Microsoft Office application that provides commonly used commands. Its location and small size allow you to use these commands while working in your database. A database, when opened, will display in the gray area. See Figure 1.5.

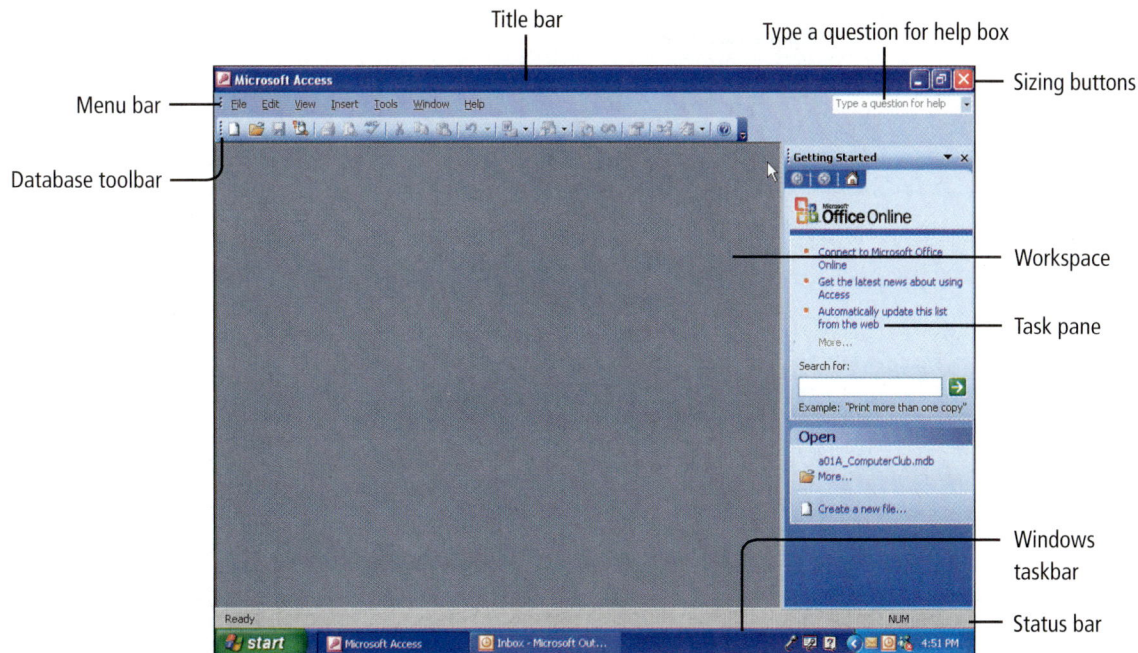

Figure 1.5

Project 1A: Computer Club | **Access** 745

> **Note** — **Comparing Programs**
>
> *Access opens the program only.*
>
> You may have used Microsoft Word, which opens and displays a blank document, or Microsoft Excel, which opens and displays a blank workbook. Access, however, does not open a blank database—it opens the program only.

4 Take a moment to study the elements of the Access window as shown in Figure 1.5 and as described in the table in Figure 1.6.

Elements of the Access Window

Element	Description
Title bar	Displays the name of the program.
Sizing buttons	Enable you to minimize, maximize, restore, and close the Access window.
Type a question for help box	Allows you to access the Microsoft Access Help feature by typing a question.
Menu bar	Contains the menus of Access commands. Display a menu by clicking on its name in the menu bar.
Database toolbar	Contains a row of buttons that provide a one-click method to perform the most common commands in Access.
Task pane	Displays commonly used commands.
Status bar	Displays information about the task you are working on.
Windows taskbar	Displays the Start button and buttons indicating active windows.
Workspace	Gray area where an open database displays.

Figure 1.6

5 On the Database toolbar, pause your mouse pointer over the **Open** button.

When you position the mouse pointer over a button, Access displays the button's name in a box called a **ScreenTip**. You should see the ScreenTip *Open*.

6 On the menu bar, click **File**.

The File menu displays. When you display a menu in Access, either the short menu, shown in Figure 1.7, or the full menu, shown in Figure 1.8, displays.

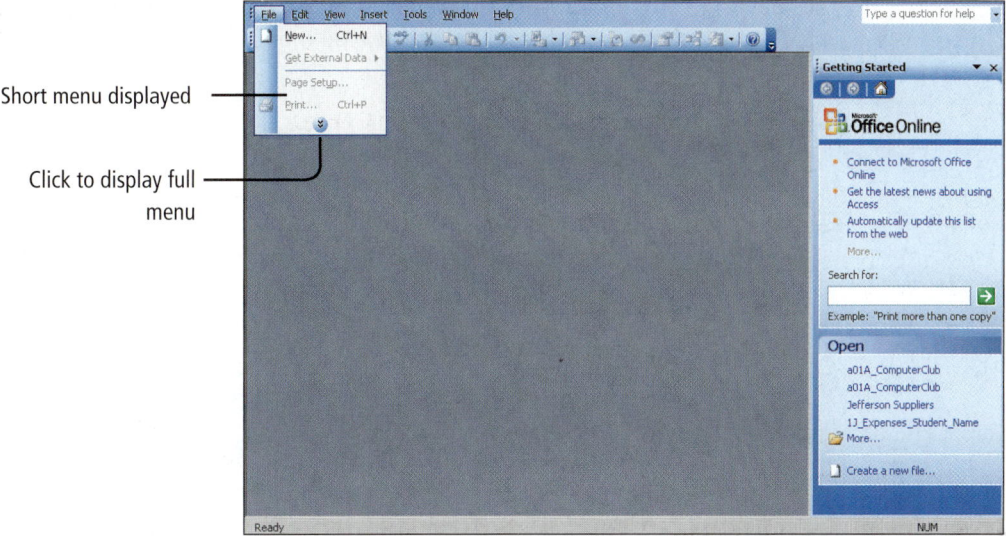

Short menu displayed

Click to display full menu

Figure 1.7

The short menu will display fully after a few seconds. Alternatively, you can click the small double arrow at the bottom of the short menu to display the full menu.

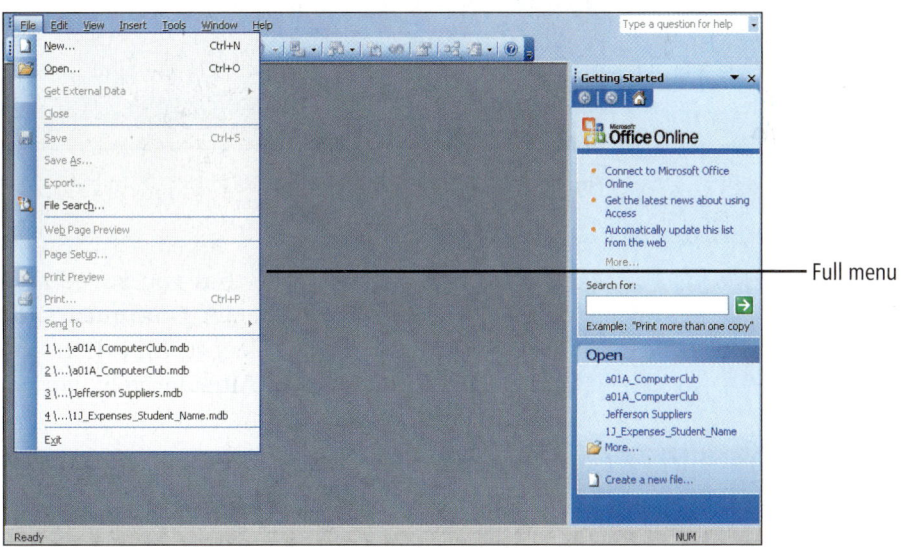

Full menu

Figure 1.8

Project 1A: Computer Club | **Access** 747

More Knowledge — Displaying the Full Menu

Select the Always show full menus *option.*

If you do not see the short version of the File menu as shown in Figure 1.7, your system has been set so that full menus always display. Many individuals prefer the full menu display. To set a system to always display the full menu, display the Tools menu, click Customize, and then click the Options tab. Select (place a check mark in) the Always show full menus check box. Click Close.

7 On the displayed **File** menu, click **Open**.

The Open dialog box displays.

8 Click the **Look in arrow** shown in Figure 1.9 and then navigate to the location where you are storing your projects for this chapter.

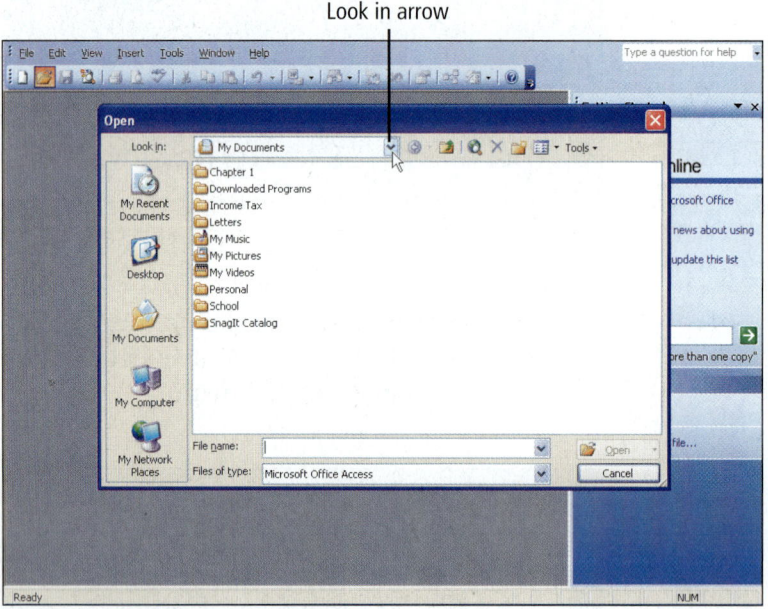

Figure 1.9

9 Locate the database file that you saved and renamed with your name in Activity 1.1. Click the **1A_ComputerClub_Firstname_Lastname** database file once to select it, and then, in the lower right corner, click the **Open** button. Alternatively, you can double-click the name of the database.

748   Access | Chapter 1: Getting Started with Access Databases and Tables

10 If the message in Figure 1.10, or similar message, displays on your screen, click **Yes**.

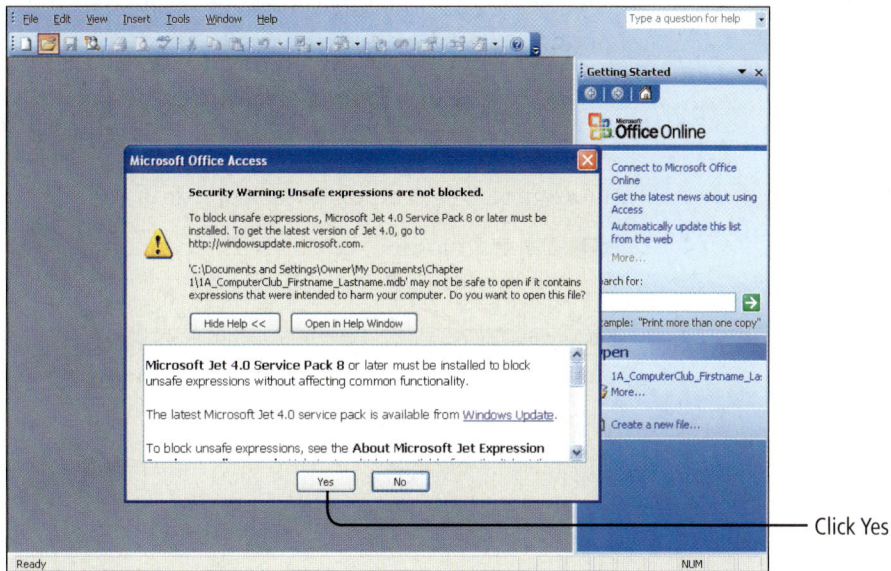

Figure 1.10

11 If another Security Warning message displays, click **Open**.

The ComputerClub Database window opens, as shown in Figure 1.11.

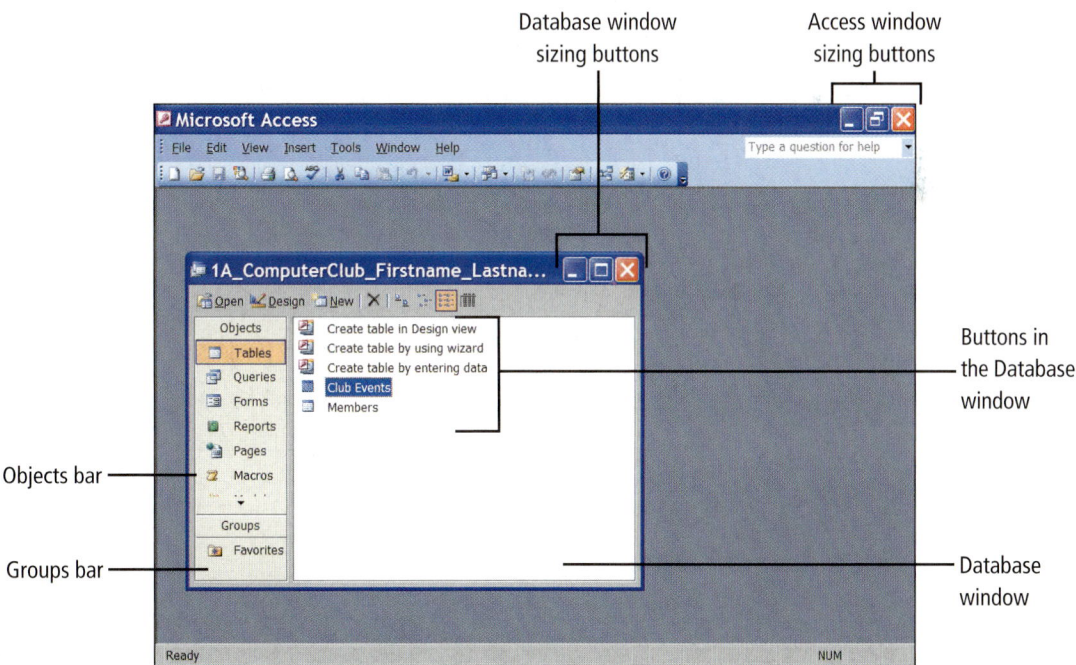

Figure 1.11

Project 1A: Computer Club | **Access** 749

Activity 1.3 Viewing the Database Window

The ***Database window*** displays when a database is open. The ***Objects bar*** on the left side of the Database window has buttons—called ***objects***—that you can work with in Access. Objects are the primary components of an Access database.

Just one object—***Tables***—actually *stores* your data; the other objects are used to organize, manage, and manipulate the data. Recall that a table is a collection of data organized in a format of columns and rows. One or more tables can be used to store data in a database.

1 Take a moment to study the elements of the Database window shown in Figure 1.11 and described in the table in Figure 1.12.

Elements of the Database Window

Element	Description
Database window	Displays when a database is open and allows you to access all the database objects.
Objects bar	Contains buttons that activate the objects (tools) of a database.
Groups bar	Contains shortcuts to different types of database objects.
Database window sizing buttons	Enables you to minimize, maximize, and close the Database window.
Buttons in the Database window	Activate commands related to the selected database object.

Figure 1.12

2 In the extreme upper right corner of your screen, locate the **Type a question for help** box. Just above that box, click the Access window's **Minimize** button . See Figure 1.11.

The Access window is minimized and displays as a button on the Windows taskbar at the lower edge of your screen. See Figure 1.13.

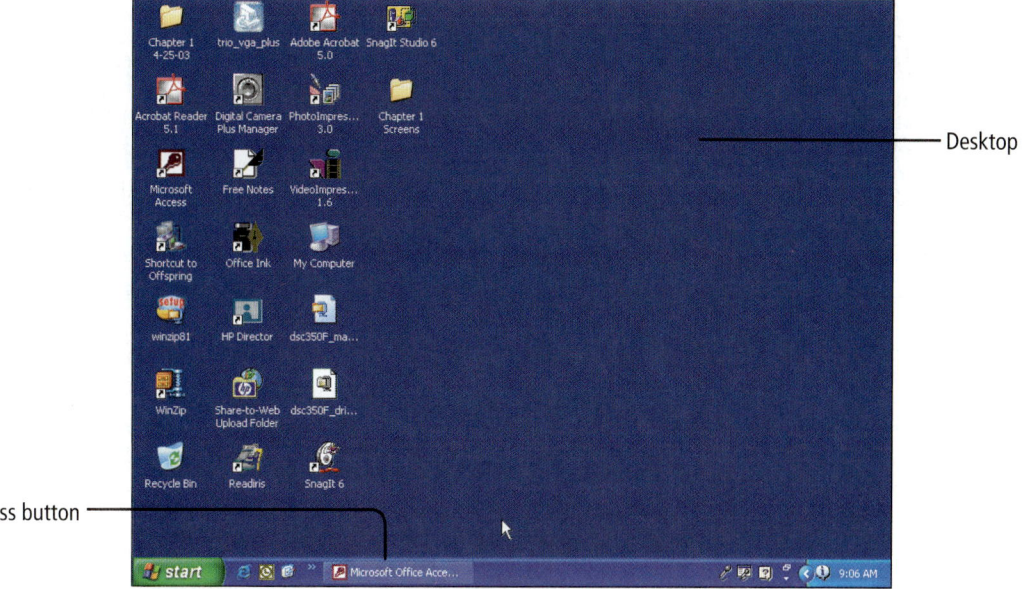

Figure 1.13

3 On the Windows taskbar, click **Microsoft Access**.

The Access window and Database window are restored. Minimizing windows in this manner enables you to view your Desktop.

4 Look at the Database window (the smaller window) and notice that it also has a set of sizing buttons at the right edge of its title bar. Click its **Maximize** button.

The Database window fills the entire gray workspace within the Access window. The Database window's title bar no longer displays—the name of the database displays instead on the main title bar enclosed in square brackets. See Figure 1.14.

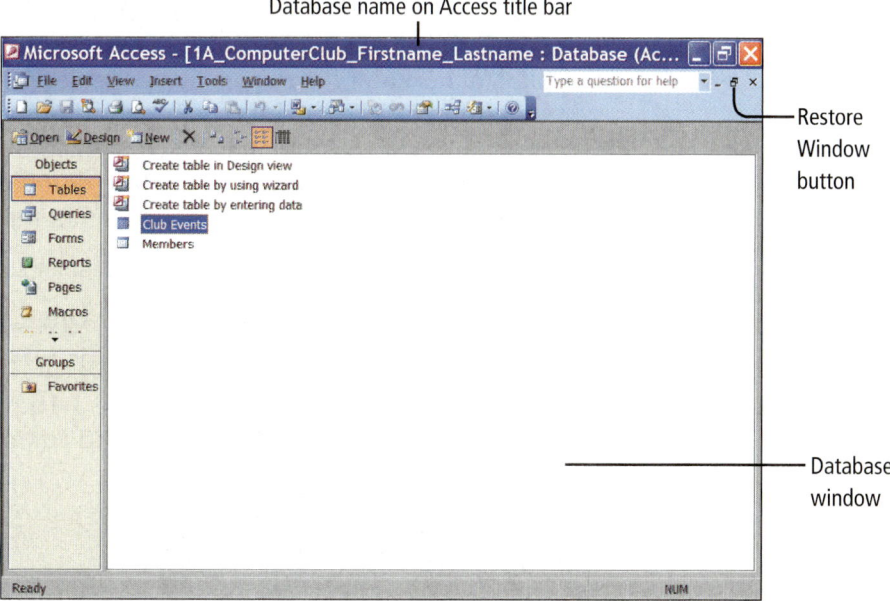

Figure 1.14

Project 1A: Computer Club | **Access** 751

5 To the right of the **Type a question for help** box, click the small **Restore Window** button . See Figure 1.14.

The Database window is restored to its original size and position, as shown in Figure 1.11. You can see that the Database window is a separate window that can be manipulated like other windows.

> **Note** — Sizing the Database Window
>
> *Maximize to fill the gray area.*
>
> You have seen that the Database window can be maximized to fill the gray area, or left in its original size, which is smaller and contained within the gray area. Many Access users prefer keeping the Database window smaller than the gray area of the Access window. This visually separates the Objects bar and the other parts of the Database window from features that are part of the larger Access window.

6 On the Objects bar, notice that *Tables* is selected. With the Tables object selected, point to, but do not click, each of the remaining objects one by one.

The Computer Club Database window displays seven objects: Tables, Queries, Forms, Reports, Pages, Macros, and Modules. Each of these objects is used by Access to manage the information stored in the Computer Club database. As you progress in your study of Access, you will learn more about each of these objects.

Activity 1.4 Opening a Table

Recall that tables are the foundation of your Access database because that is where the data is stored. Each table in an Access database stores data about only one subject. For example, in the Computer Club database, the Club Events table stores data about individual club events and the Members table stores data about the Club's members.

1 On the Objects bar, if necessary, click **Tables** to select it.

Notice that to the right of the Objects bar, three command icons display followed by the names of two tables. The command icons provide three different methods for creating a new table. Following the command icons, the names of the tables that have been created and saved as part of the Computer Club database display. There are two tables in this database, the *Club Events* table and the *Members* table.

2 Click the **Club Events** table once to select it if necessary, and then, just above the Objects bar, click the **Open** button . Alternatively, you can double-click the table name to open it.

The table opens, as shown in Figure 1.15. Here you can see the data organized in a format of columns and rows.

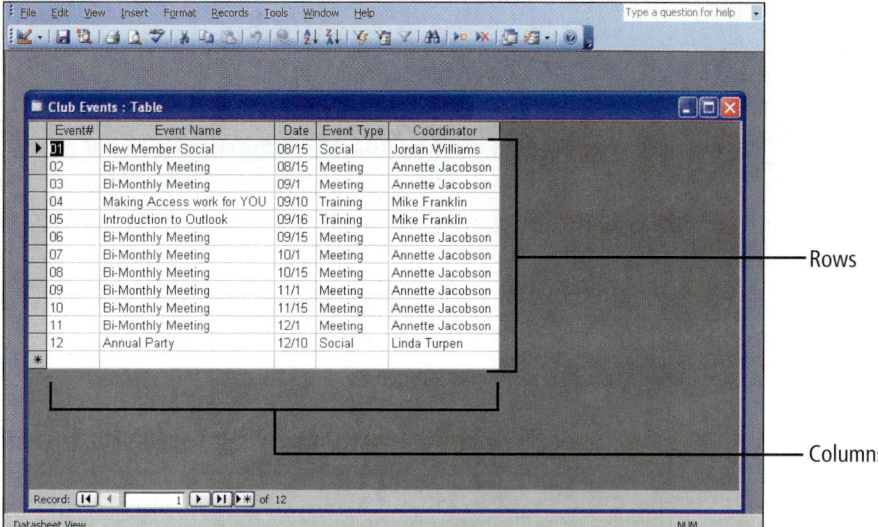

Figure 1.15

3. Along the left side of the open table, move your mouse pointer until it displays as a right-pointing arrow, as shown in Figure 1.16.

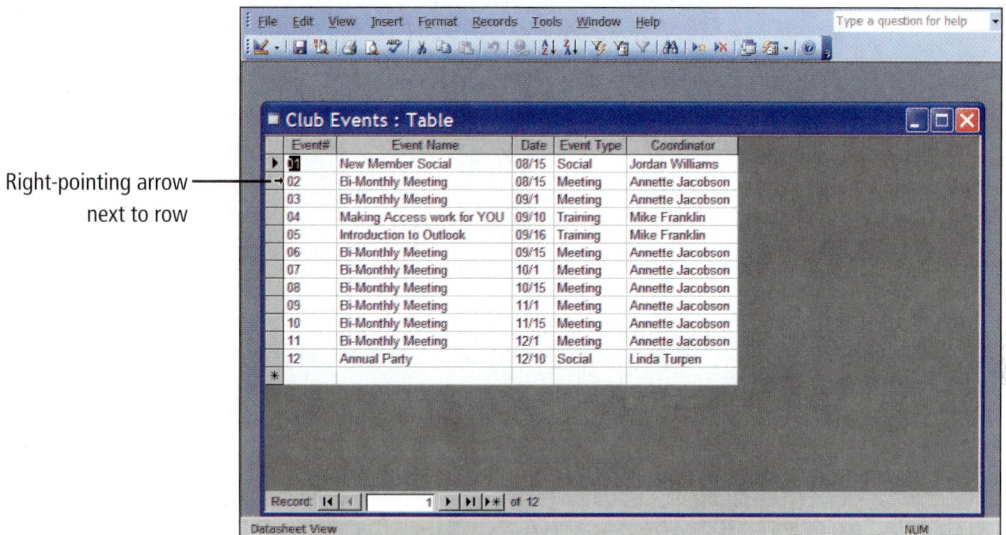

Figure 1.16

Project 1A: Computer Club | **Access** 753

4 Pause the arrow pointer at the row containing the event *Annual Party* and click once.

The row containing the information for the Annual Party is highlighted in black. Each horizontal row of a table stores all of the information about one database item. You can see that, in the Club Events table, each event has a separate row in the database table. The information in a row is referred to as a **record**.

5 Use the technique you just used in Step 4 to find and select the record for the training event **Introduction to Outlook**.

6 Across the top of the table, move your mouse pointer over the words *Event Type* until it becomes a down arrow, and then click once to select the column. See Figure 1.17.

Each record contains information located in vertical columns, called **fields**, which describe the record. For example, in the Club Events table, each event (record) has the following fields: Event#, Event Name, Date, Event Type, and Coordinator.

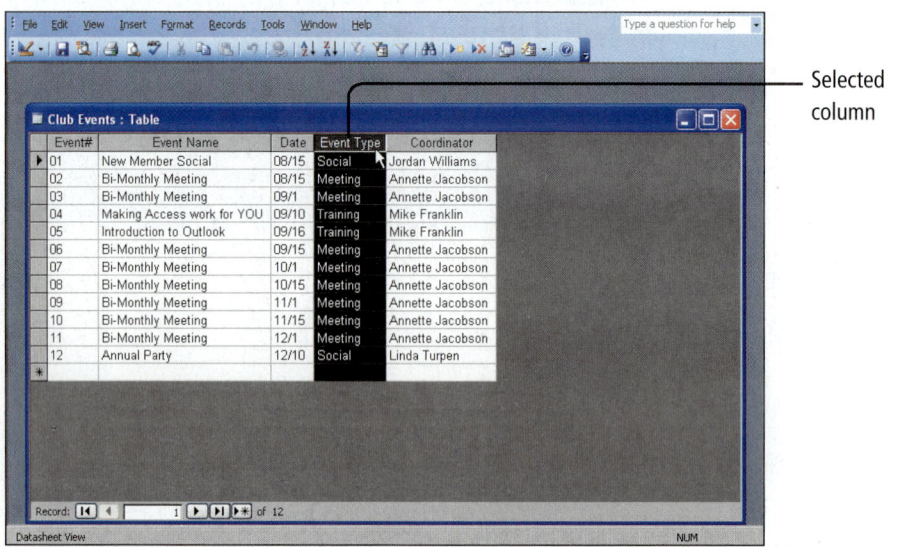

Figure 1.17

7 Use your mouse pointer to select the column representing the **Coordinator** field. Take a moment to look at the other column names in the table to familiarize yourself with these *fields*.

8 In the last row of the table, click once in the **Event#** field under the last record in the table. See Figure 1.18.

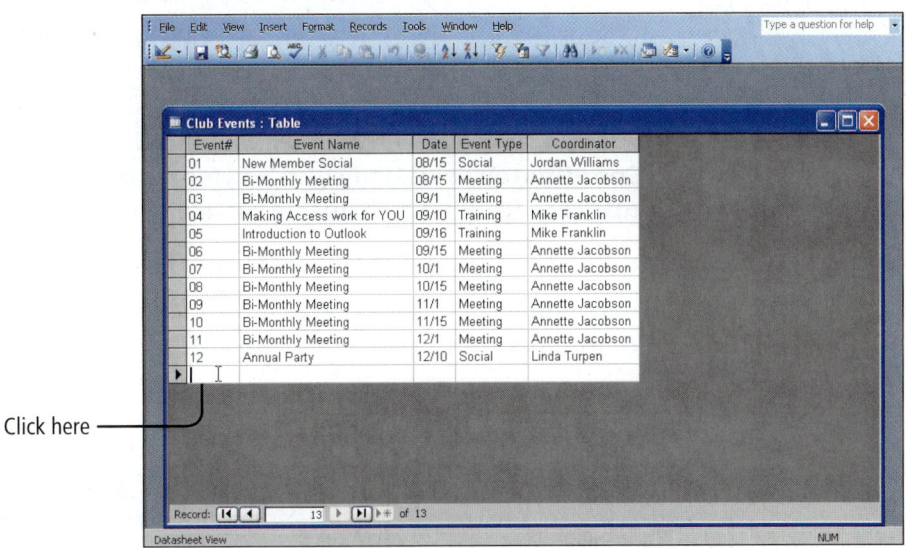

Click here

Figure 1.18

9 In the **Event#** field type **13**

10 Notice the pencil image in the gray box to the left. See Figure 1.19.

In the ***row selector***—the small gray box at the left end of a row—a small pencil image displays in the row in which a new record is being entered. The pencil image in the row selector indicates that the information in this record is in the process of being entered and has not yet been saved.

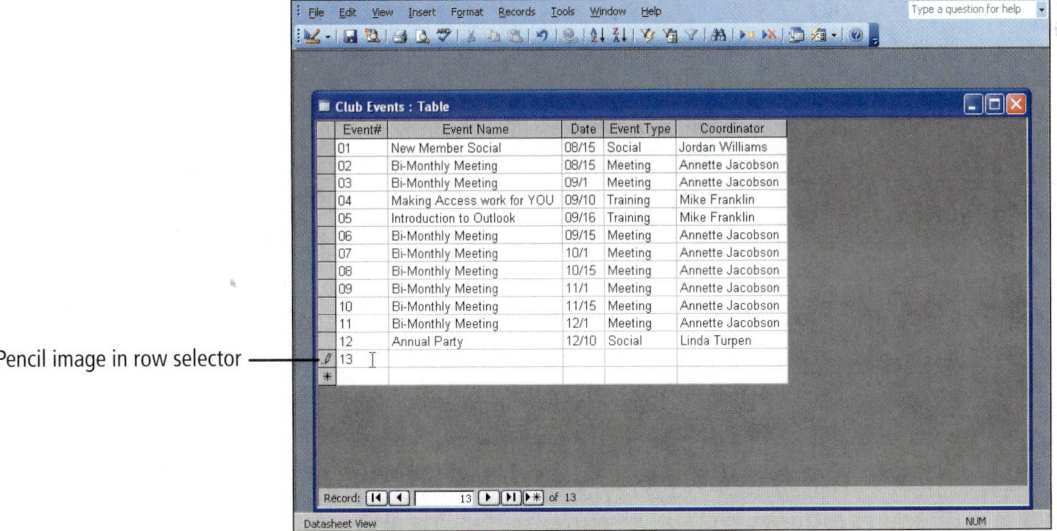

Pencil image in row selector

Figure 1.19

11 Press Tab once.

The insertion point is blinking in the next field to the right, which is the *Event Name* field.

12 In the **Event Name** field, type **Project 1A** and then press Tab.

13 In the **Date** field, type **11/18** and then press Tab.

14 In the **Event Type** field, type **Training** and then press Tab to move to the **Coordinator** field. Using your own first and last name, in the **Coordinator** field, type **Firstname Lastname**

15 Press either Enter or Tab on your keyboard to save the record.

The pencil image no longer displays, indicating that the record is saved. Compare your screen to Figure 1.20.

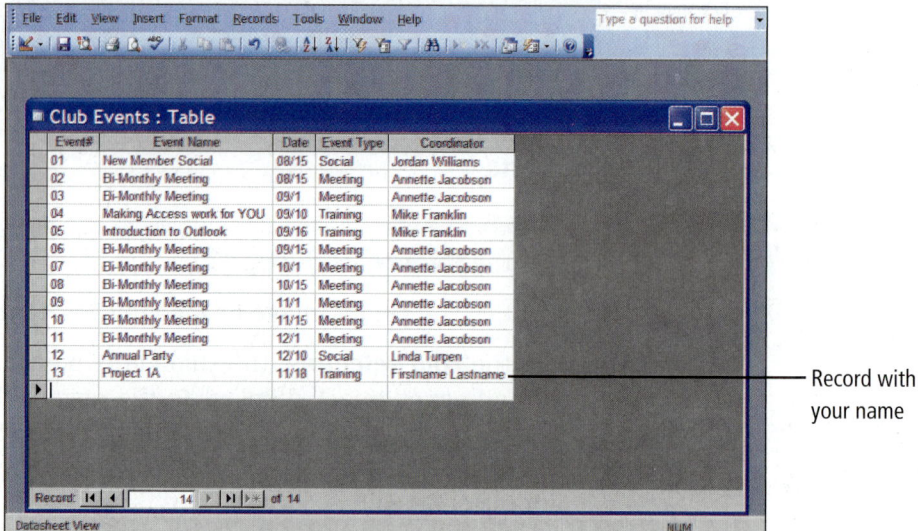

Figure 1.20

Activity 1.5 Viewing a Table

The Tables database object has four ***views***. A view is a way of looking at something such as a table or form. As you work with tables of data, there are two ways to look at tables that are particularly useful—the Datasheet view, which is currently displayed on your screen, and the Design view.

In the previous activity, you opened the Club Events table in the Datasheet view. The Datasheet view displays all the records in a table in a format of columns (fields) and rows (records).

1 On the Table Datasheet toolbar, locate the **View** button, as shown in Figure 1.21.

Its picture, displaying a ruler, a pencil, and a protractor, indicates that clicking the button will switch the display to the Design view of the table. This button will change depending on the current view to allow you to switch back and forth between ***Design view*** and ***Datasheet view***.

756 Access | Chapter 1: Getting Started with Access Databases and Tables

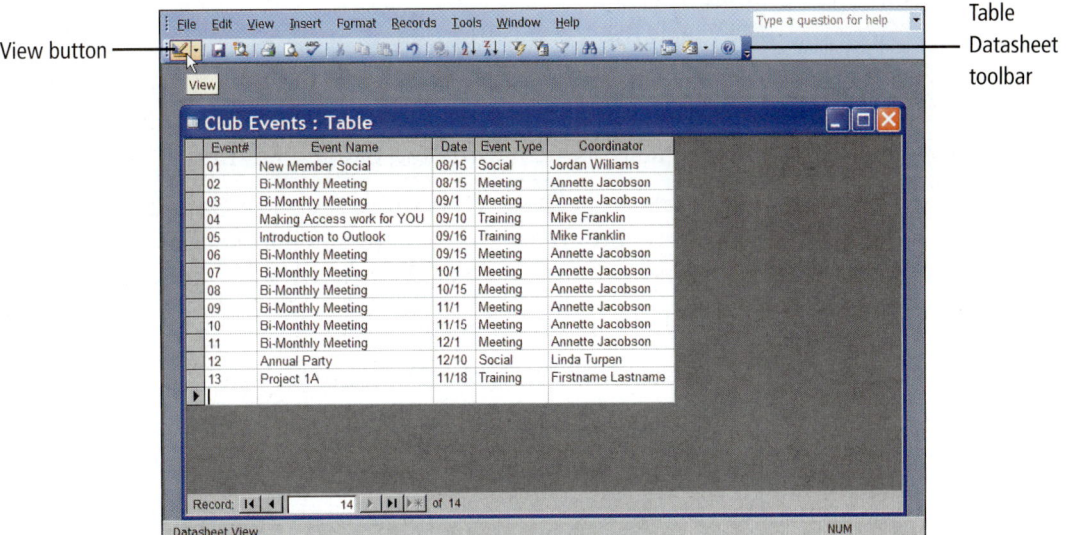

Figure 1.21

2 Click the **View** button.

The Design view of the table displays. Notice that in Design view, you do not see the names of the club events—or other information contained in the records. You see only the names of the fields, such as *Event Name* and *Coordinator*. In this view, you can change the design of the table—that is, the way each field displays its associated data.

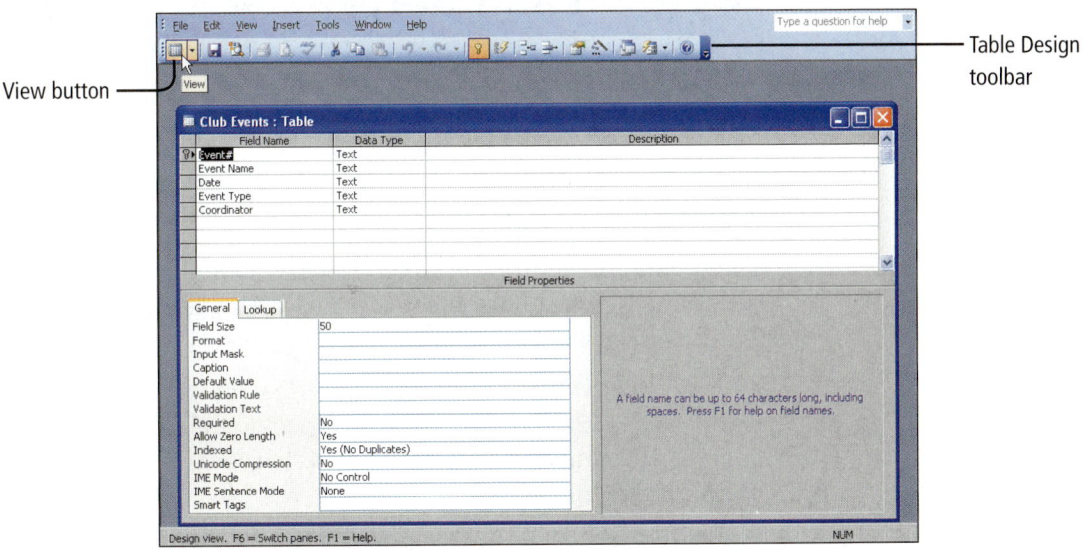

Figure 1.22

3 On the Table Design toolbar, locate the **View** button. See Figure 1.22.

Now the View button displays as a small table—or datasheet. This picture on the View button indicates that clicking the button will return you to the Datasheet (table) view.

Project 1A: Computer Club | **Access** 757

4 Click the **View** button.

The table redisplays in Datasheet view. Recall that the Datasheet view of a table displays the individual records in horizontal rows and the field names at the top of each column. Thus, the View button displays as when you are in the Datasheet view and as when you are in the Design view—indicating which view will be displayed when you click the button.

5 In the upper right corner of the Table window, click the **Close** button to close the table. See Figure 1.23.

The Database window displays.

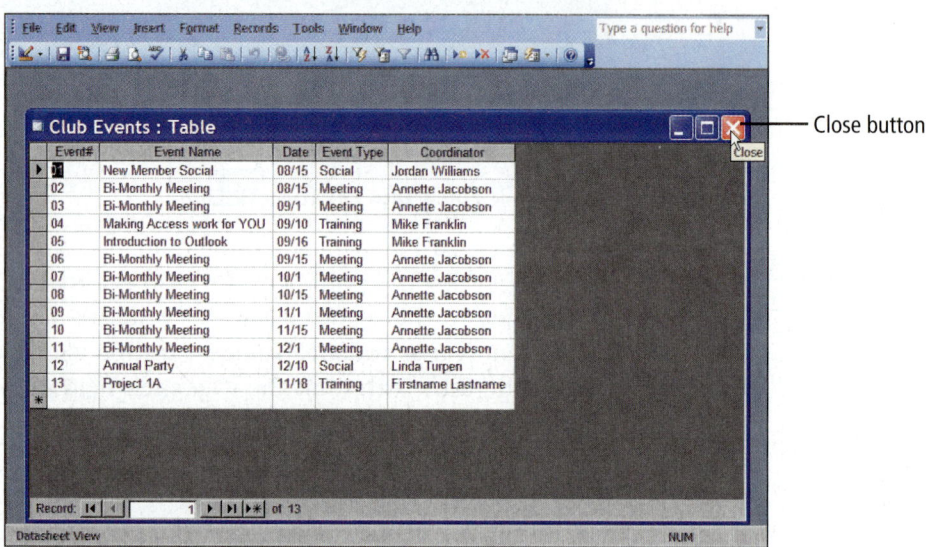

Figure 1.23

Activity 1.6 Viewing a Query

The second object on the Objects bar is *Queries*. To *query* is to ask a question. The Queries object is a tool with which you can ask questions about the data stored in the Tables objects.

For example, you could use the Queries object to ask how many Club Events are social events. Locating specific information in a database, such as the number of social events, is referred to as ***extracting*** information from the database.

1 On the Objects bar, click **Queries**.

The Database window displays two command icons that can be used to create a new query. They are followed by one query that has been created and saved as part of the Computer Club database. Later, you will create and save your own queries.

2 Double-click the **Social Events Query**. Alternatively, you can right-click the query name, and then click Open on the displayed shortcut menu, or click once to select the query and then click the Open button [Open] in the Database window.

When a query is opened, Access *runs*—processes—the query and displays the results. The results of the query will display only selected information from the table.

3 Look at the records that display as a result of this query.

The number of records in the query result is less that the number of records in the original table because certain **criteria**—specifications that determine what records will be displayed—were entered as part of the query. For example, this query was created to locate the names of all the events in the table that are Social Events. Notice that two records display—New Member Social and Annual Party. See Figure 1.24.

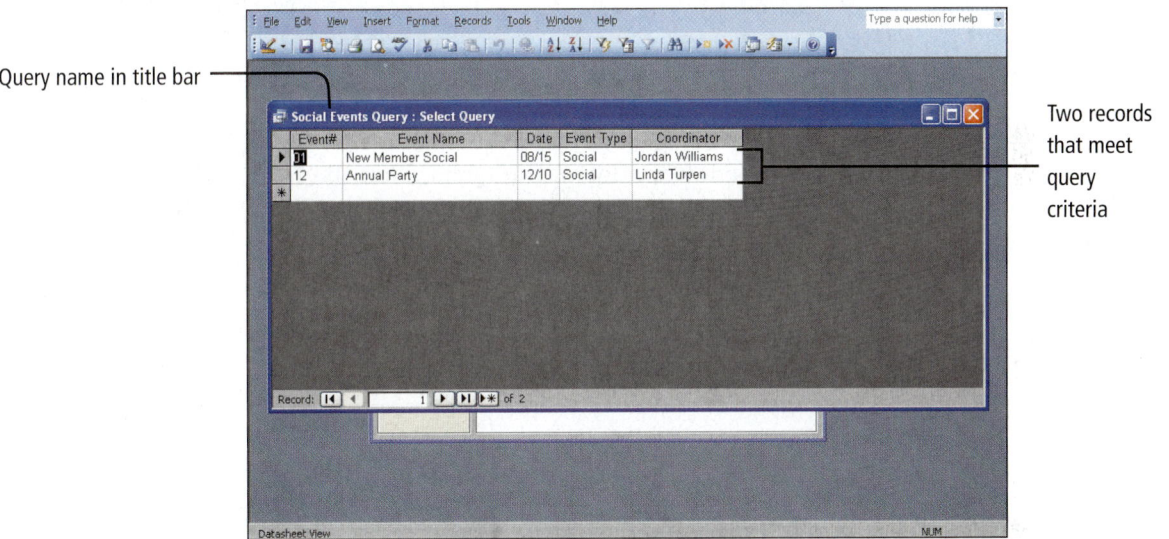

Figure 1.24

4 In the upper right corner of the query window, click the **Close** button [X].

The Database window displays.

Activity 1.7 Viewing a Form

Forms, the third object on the Objects bar, provides an alternative method to both enter and display data in the Tables object. The records that display in a form are the same records that are in the table, with one difference: forms can be designed to display only one record at a time.

1 On the Objects bar, click **Forms**.

To the right of the Objects bar, two command icons for creating a new form display, followed by a form that has been created and saved as part of the Computer Club database. Thus far, only one form, the Club Events form, has been created for this database.

Project 1A: Computer Club | **Access** 759

2 Double-click the **Club Events** form.

The Club Events form displays with fields filled in with the data representing the first record in the database. See Figure 1.25.

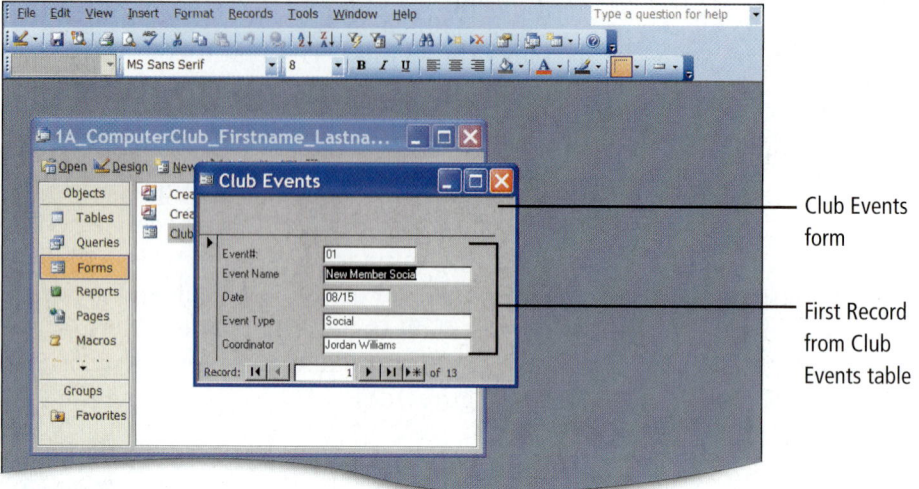

Figure 1.25

3 At the lower edge of the form, click the **Next Record** button until you see the 12th record—the Annual Party event—displayed in the form. See Figure 1.26.

As you click the Next Record button, notice how each individual record in the table of Club Events displays in the window.

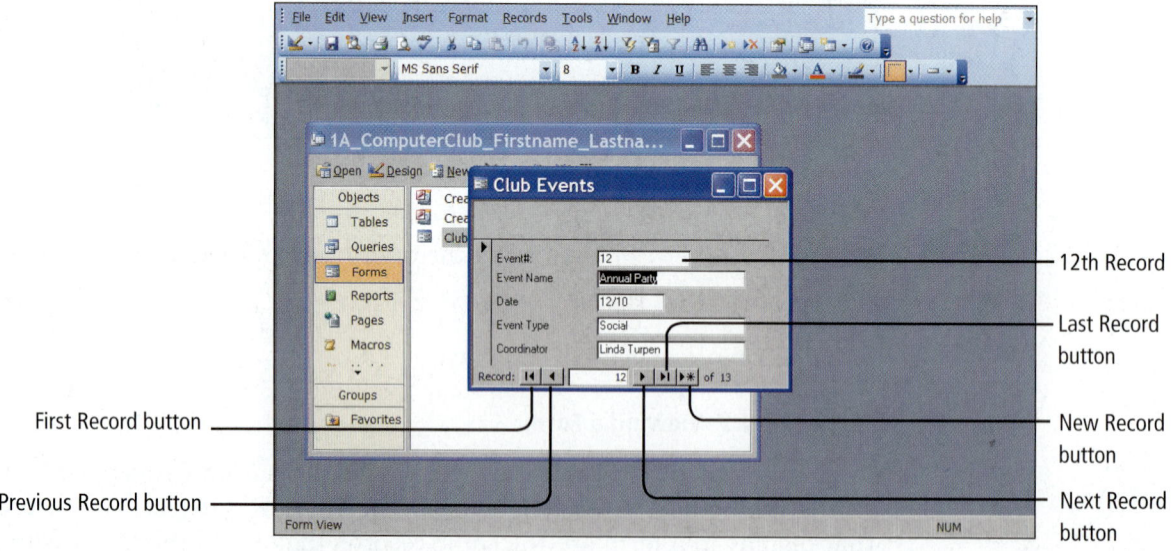

Figure 1.26

4 In the upper right corner of the Club Events form window, click the **Close** button to close the form. The Database window displays.

760   Access | Chapter 1: Getting Started with Access Databases and Tables

Activity 1.8 Viewing and Printing a Report

The fourth button on the Objects bar is *Reports*. A **report** is a database object that displays the fields and records from the table (or query) in an easy-to-read format suitable for printing. Reports are created to summarize information in a database in a professional-looking manner.

1 On the Objects bar, click **Reports**. See Figure 1.27.

To the right of the Objects bar, command icons for creating a new report display, followed by a report that has been created and saved as part of the Computer Club database. Thus far, only one report, the Club Events report, has been created for this database.

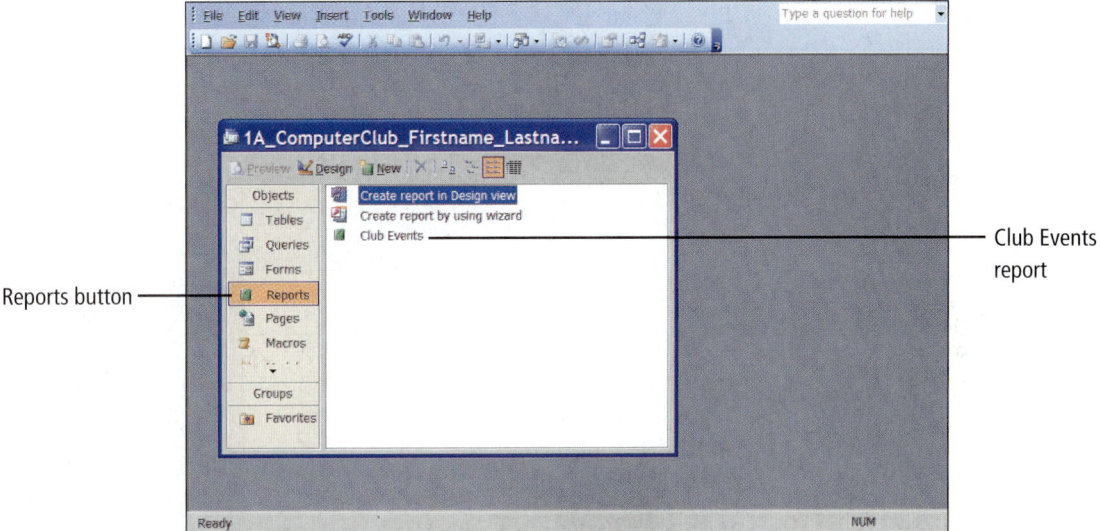

Figure 1.27

2 Double-click the **Club Events** report.

The Club Events report displays, as shown in Figure 1.28.

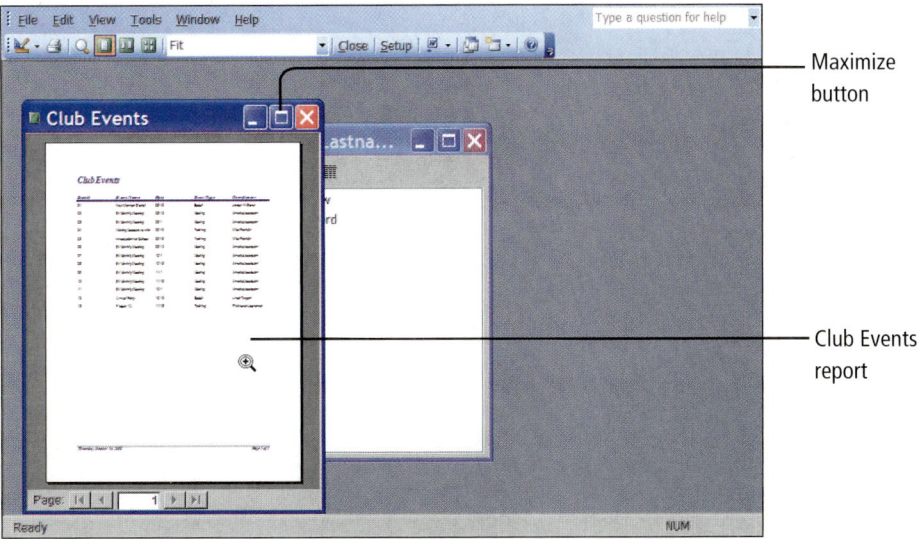

Figure 1.28

Project 1A: Computer Club | **Access** 761

3 In the upper right corner of the Club Events report window, click the **Maximize** button.

The window is maximized on your screen.

4 On the toolbar, pause the mouse pointer over the word *Fit* and see the ScreenTip *Zoom*.

To **zoom** means to make the page view larger or smaller. **Fit** means that an entire page of the report will display on your screen at one time giving you an overall view of what the printed pages will look like.

5 On the toolbar, click the **Zoom arrow** and then, from the displayed list, click **100%**. See Figure 1.29.

Zooming to 100% displays the report in the approximate size it will be when it is printed.

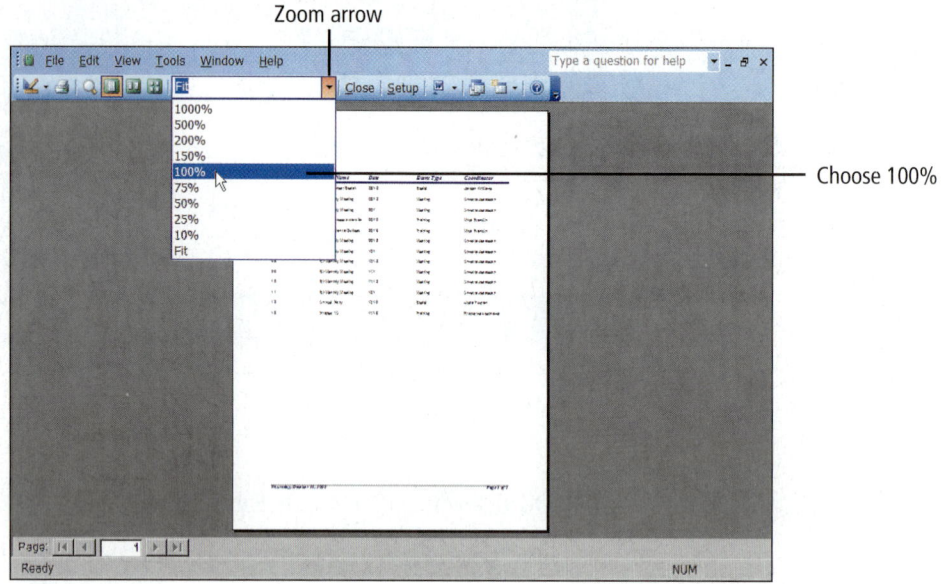

Figure 1.29

762 Access | Chapter 1: Getting Started with Access Databases and Tables

6 In the displayed report page, locate the record **Project 1A**. You may need to use the vertical scroll bar in the window to see this record. See Figure 1.30.

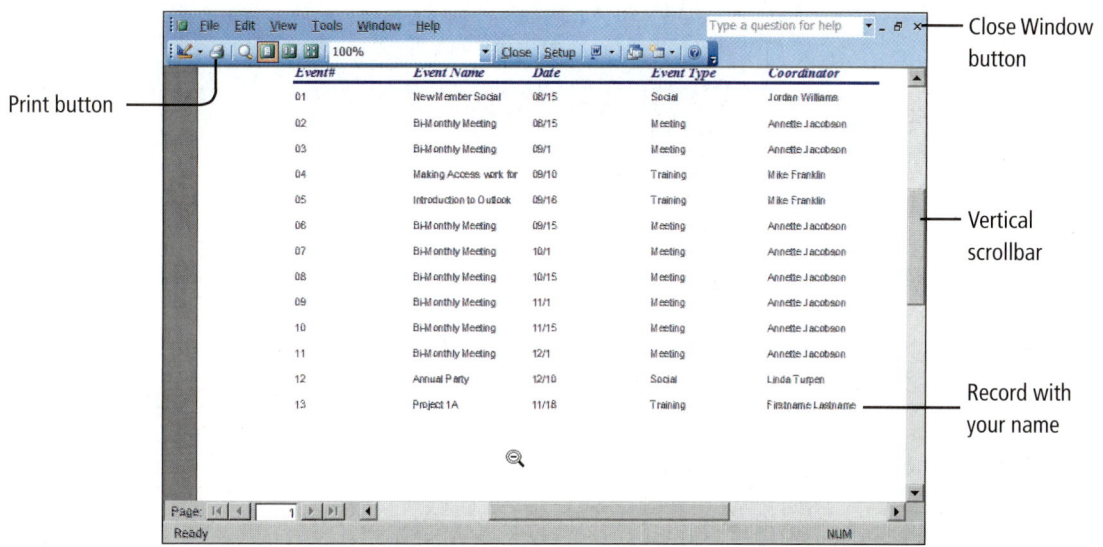

Figure 1.30

Notice that on your screen, the report displays as if it were printed on a piece of paper. A report is designed to be a professional-looking document that you can print.

A report is generated each time you open it and displays up-to-date information. For example, this report was created before you opened the database, but the record you added with your name now displays in the report.

7 On the toolbar, click the **Print** button . See Figure 1.30.

The Club Events report prints.

8 In the upper right corner of the report window, click the **Close Window** button to close the report.

The Database window displays.

Project 1A: Computer Club | **Access** 763

9 To the right of the **Type a question for help** box, click the small **Restore Window** button to restore the Database window to its previous size. See Figure 1.31.

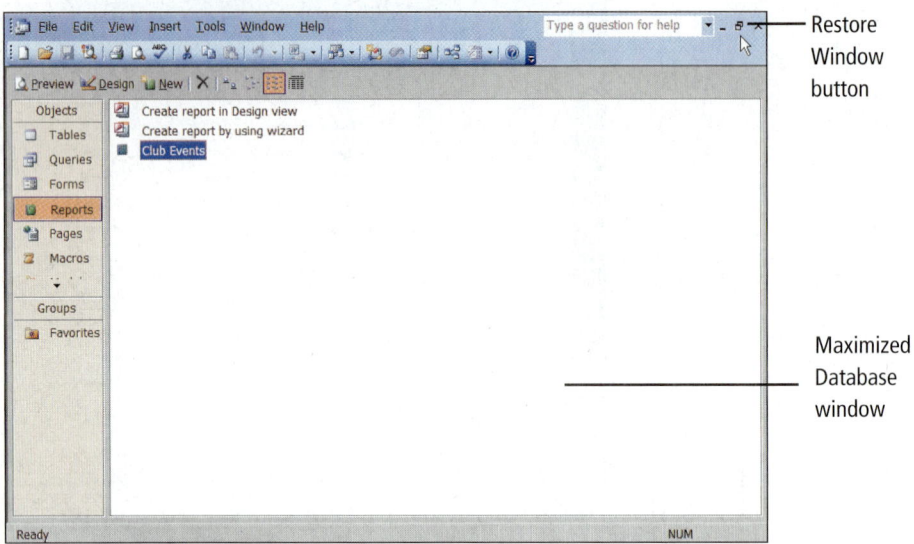

Figure 1.31

10 In the Database window, click the **Close** button to close the Computer Club database. See Figure 1.32.

The Computer Club database closes. The Access program remains open. As you advance in your studies of Access, you will learn about the remaining objects on the Objects bar: Pages, Macros, and Modules.

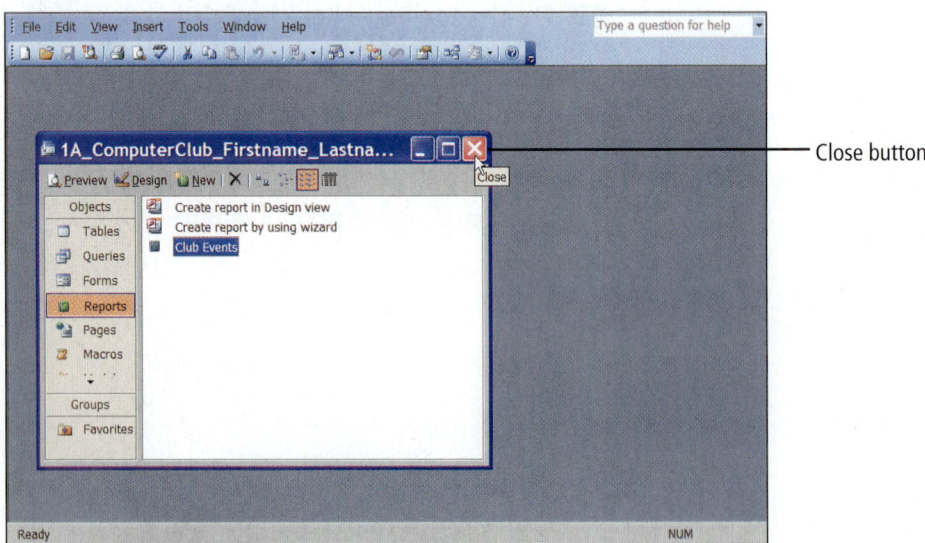

Figure 1.32

End You have completed Project 1A

Project 1B School

In the previous project, you opened an existing database. The Tables object and some of the other object tools used for viewing and manipulating the database were already created. In this project, you will begin a new database and create the table yourself.

In Activities 1.9 through 1.27 you will create a new database for the Distance Learning Department at Lake Michigan City College. The database will have one table that will store student records. Your student table object will look like Figure 1.33. You will save the database as *1B_School_Firstname_Lastname*.

Student#	Last Name	First Name	Address	City	Postal Code	Balance	First Term Attend
23895	Jackson	Robert	2320 Aldrich Circle	Chicago	60605	$46.00	SP01
45689	Jackson	Laura	1967 Arizona St.	Chicago	60605	$65.00	FA02
54783	Williams	Pat	62 Cockatiel Lane	Chicago	60605	$42.00	SP03
63257	Apodaca	Allen	679 Martinique Pl.	Chicago	60605	$32.00	SU03
64589	Metheny	Elizabeth	10225 Fairview	Chicago	60605	$15.00	FA02
95140	Vaughn	Sydney	2105 Waldo Ave.	Chicago	60605	$56.00	FA03
95874	Van Wegan	Michaela	100 Quantico Ave.	Chicago	60605	$25.00	FA99
96312	Berstein	Krista	136 South Street	Chicago	60605	$12.00	FA00

Figure 1.33

Objective 3
Create a New Database

Activity 1.9 Creating a New Database

In this activity you will create a new database. There are two methods to create a new Access database:

- Create a new database using a wizard (an Access tool that walks you step-by-step through a process).
- Create a new blank database—which is more flexible because you can add each object separately.

Regardless of which method you use, you will have to name and save the database before you can create any objects such as tables, queries, forms, or reports. Think of a database file as a container that stores the database objects—tables, queries, forms, reports, and so forth—that you create and add to the database.

1 If necessary, start Access and close any open databases.

2 On the Database toolbar, click the **New** button.

The New File task pane displays on the right. See Figure 1.34. Recall that the task pane is a window within a Microsoft Office application that provides commonly used commands related to the current task.

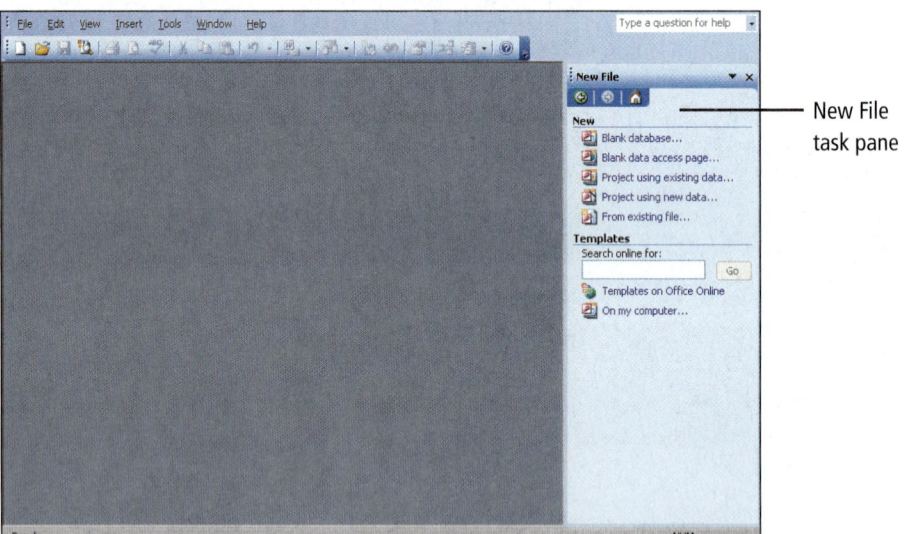

Figure 1.34

3 In the task pane, under **New**, click **Blank database**.

The File New Database dialog box displays.

4 In the **Save in** box, click the **Save in arrow** (the arrow at the right edge of the Save in box) to view a list of the drives available to you.

5 If necessary, navigate to your Chapter 1 folder where you are storing your projects.

6 Clear any text in the **File name** box and then, using your own information, type **1B_School_Firstname_Lastname**

7 In the lower right corner of the dialog box, click **Create**.

The School database is created and the Database window displays with the new database name indicated in the title bar of the Database window.

Objective 4
Create a New Table

When you buy a new address book, it is not very useful until you fill it with names, addresses, and phone numbers. Likewise, a new database is not useful until you *populate*, or fill, a table with data.

In the next activity, you will create a table in Design view and then add the table's fields.

Activity 1.10 Adding Fields to a Table

Recall that fields, located in columns, contain the information that describes each record in your database. The columnar fields describe the records in a table. For example, in the Club Events table you viewed earlier in Project 1A, there were fields for the *Event Name*, *Event Type*, and so forth. These fields provided information about the records in the table.

1 In the Database window, double-click the command icon **Create table in Design view**. See Figure 1.35. Alternatively, right-click the command icon and click Open on the displayed shortcut menu.

The Design view of the new table displays and the title bar indicates *Table1*: Because you have not yet named or saved this table, it has the default name *Table1*. The word *Table* after the colon indicates that this database object is a table. The insertion point is blinking in the first Field Name box, indicating that Access is ready for you to type the first field name. See Figure 1.36.

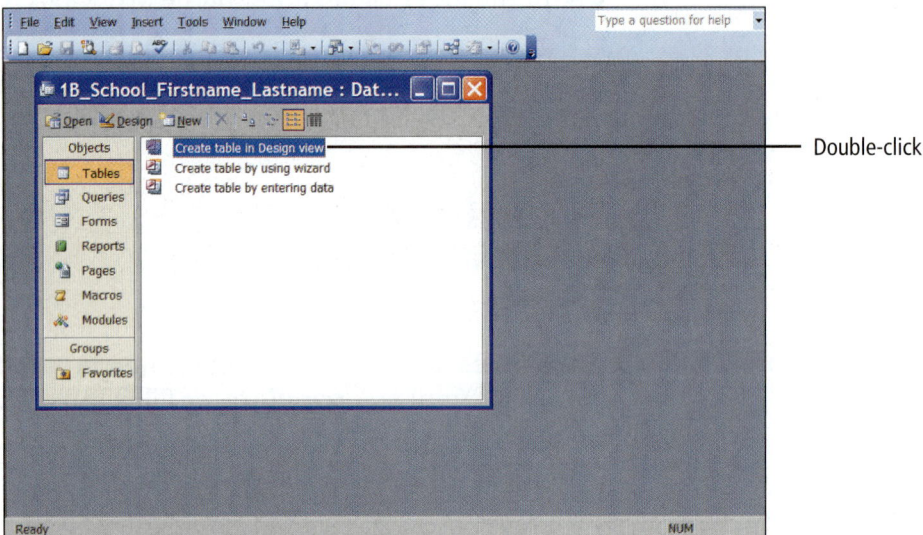

Figure 1.35

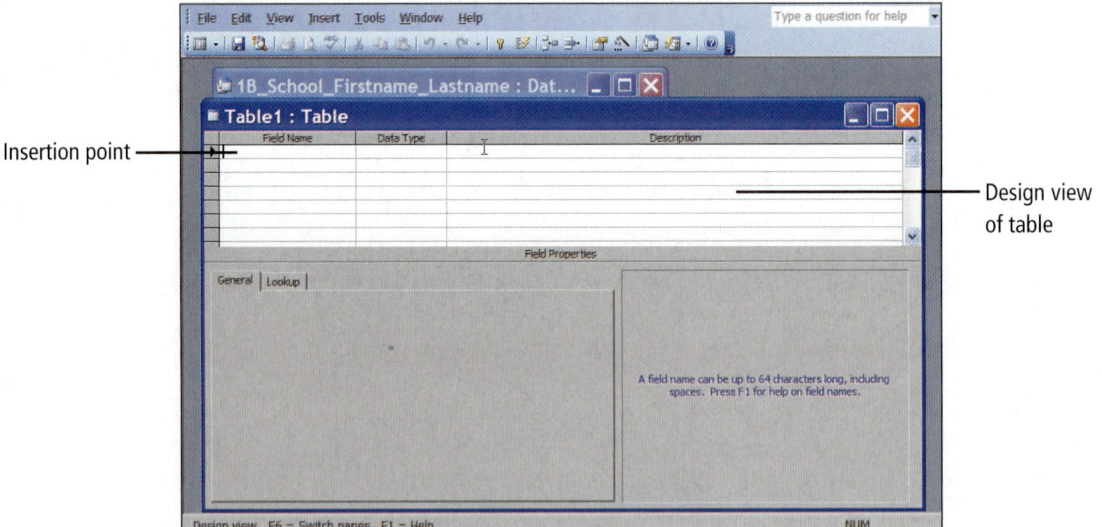

Figure 1.36

2 In the first **Field Name** box, refer to Figure 1.37 and then type **Student#**

Type first field name here

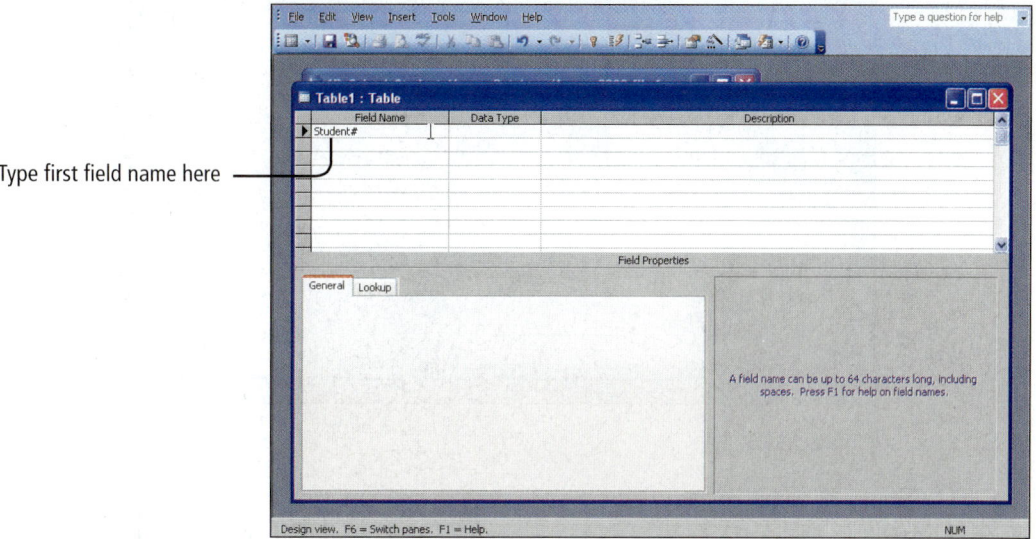

Figure 1.37

3 Press Tab to move the insertion point to the **Data Type** column.

The insertion point is blinking in the Data Type column and *Text* displays and is selected. At the right end of the box, an arrow displays. Notice that this arrow does not display until you click in this box. Some Access features become available in this manner—when a specific location is selected.

Data type specifies how Access organizes and stores data in a field. For example, if you define a field's data type as *Text*, any character can be typed as data in the field. If you define a field's data type as *Number*, only numbers can be typed as data in the field.

4 Click the **Data Type arrow** to display a list of data types. From the displayed list, click **Text** to accept the default data type. See Figure 1.38.

This field will contain a student number for each individual record. Although the student number contains only numbers—no letters or characters—it is customary to define such a number as *Text* rather than *Number*. Because the numbers are used only as a way to identify students—and not used for mathematical calculations—they function more like text.

Project 1B: School | **Access** 769

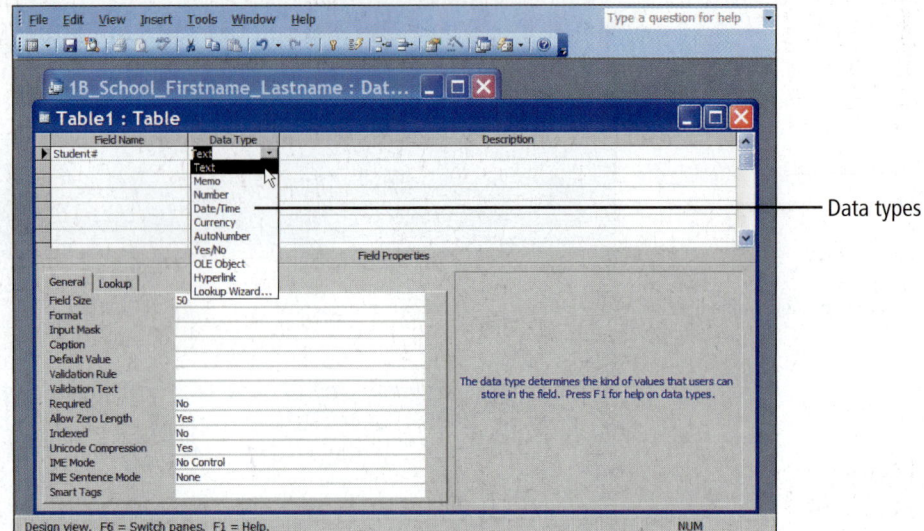

Figure 1.38

5 Press Tab to move the insertion point to the **Description** column.

Descriptions for fields in a table are not required. Include a description if the Field Name does not provide an obvious description of the field. In this instance, the field name *Student#* is self-explanatory, so no additional description is necessary.

6 Press Tab again to move the insertion point down and prepare to enter the next field name.

7 Using the technique you just practiced, add the fields shown in the Figure 1.39.

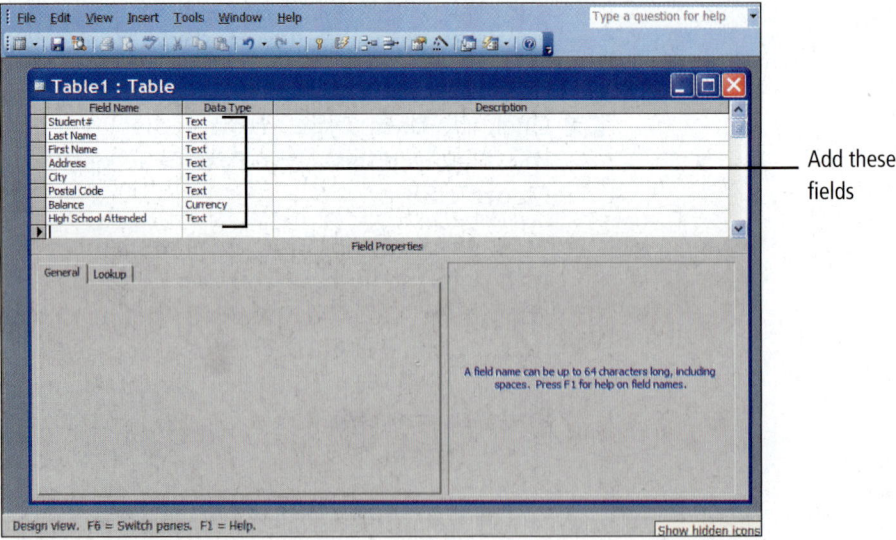

Figure 1.39

Another Way

Creating a New Table in a Database

There are three ways to create a new table in a database:

- Create a table in Design view by creating and naming the fields (columns).
- Create a table using a wizard, a process that helps you, step-by-step, to create the table.
- Create a table by typing data directly into an empty table in the Datasheet view, creating the column (field) names as you do so.

Activity 1.11 Switching Between Views

By naming and defining the data types for the fields, you have determined the number and type of pieces of information that you will have for each student's record in your database. In this activity, you will add the student records to the database. You will use the method of typing records directly into the Datasheet view of the table. You will learn other ways to enter records as your study of Access progresses.

1 On the Table Design toolbar, click the **View** button , as shown in Figure 1.40.

A message displays indicating that you must save the table before this action can be completed. See Figure 1.41.

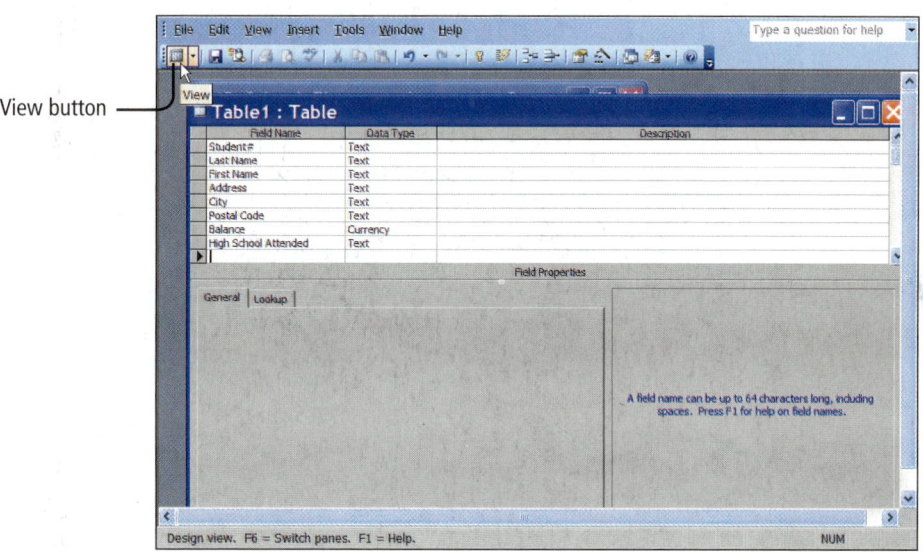

View button

Figure 1.40

Project 1B: School | **Access** 771

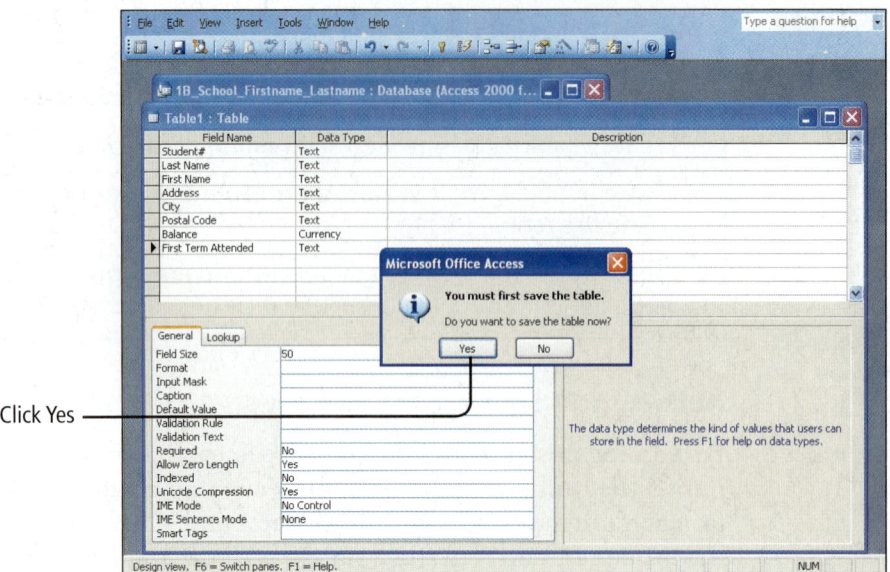

Click Yes

Figure 1.41

2 Click **Yes**.

3 In the displayed **Save As** dialog box, in the **Table Name** box, use your own first and last name and type **1B Students Firstname Lastname** and then click **OK**.

The message *There is no primary key defined* displays.

4 Click **No**.

The Datasheet view displays. You will add a primary key to the table in the next activity.

> **Note — Varying Toolbar Names**
>
> *Toolbar name changes depending on view.*
>
> In Access, the name used to refer to the toolbar changes, depending on the current view of the database object. When a table is displayed in the Design view, the toolbar below the menu bar is referred to as the Table Design toolbar.

Objective 5
Create a Primary Key and Add Records to a Table

A *primary key* is a field that uniquely identifies a record in a table. For example, in a college registration system, your student number uniquely identifies you—no other student at the college has your exact student number. Two students at your college could have the exact same name, for example, *David Michaels*, but each would have a different and unique student number. Designating a field as a primary key ensures that you do not enter the same record more than once, because primary keys do not permit duplicate entries within the database.

Activity 1.12 Creating a Primary Key in a Table

If Access creates a primary key for you, as it prompted you to do in the previous activity, Access will add an additional field with a Data Type of

AutoNumber. AutoNumber assigns a number to each record as it is entered into the database. AutoNumber fields are convenient as a primary key for a database where the records have no unique field—such as the CDs in your CD collection. When each record in your table already has a unique number, such as a Student#, you will want to define that as your primary key.

1 On the Table Datasheet toolbar, click the **View** button to switch to the Design view of your Students table.

When a table is displayed in the Datasheet view, the toolbar is referred to as the *Table Datasheet toolbar*.

2 Click to position the insertion point anywhere in the Field Name for **Student#**.

3 On the toolbar, click the **Primary Key** button , as shown in Figure 1.42.

The Primary Key image displays to the left of the Student# field.

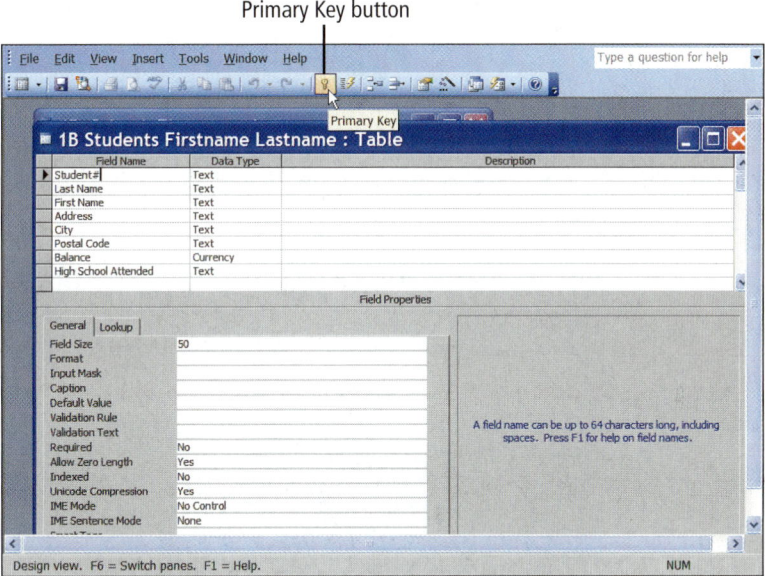

Figure 1.42

Alert!

Does Your Screen Differ?

If you attached the Primary Key to the wrong Field Name, move to the toolbar and then click the Primary Key button again. The Primary Key image will be removed and you can click the correct field name.

4 On the toolbar, click the **View** button to switch back to the Datasheet view. When prompted, click **Yes** to save the change you have made to the table.

Project 1B: School | **Access** 773

Activity 1.13 Adding Records to a Table

1 With your table in Datasheet view, make sure your insertion point is in the **Student#** column and then type **54783**

2 Press [Tab] to move to the **Last Name** column and then type **Williams**

3 Press [Tab], and then, in the **First Name** column, type **Pat**

4 Continue in this manner until the remainder of the information for Pat Williams is entered as the first record in the Students table shown in Figure 1.43. Press [Tab] after you enter the information for each column.

> **Note — Entering Currency Data**
>
> *Type only the whole number.*
>
> When you enter the information in the Balance column, you only need to type in the whole number, for example, 42, for the Balance in the Pat Williams record. After you press [Tab], Access will add the dollar sign, decimal point, and two decimal places to the entry in that column. The reason for this is that the Balance field has a data type of Currency.

As you type, do not be alarmed if it appears that your entries will not fit into the columns in the table. The widths of the columns in the figure have been adjusted so that you can view the data that is to be entered.

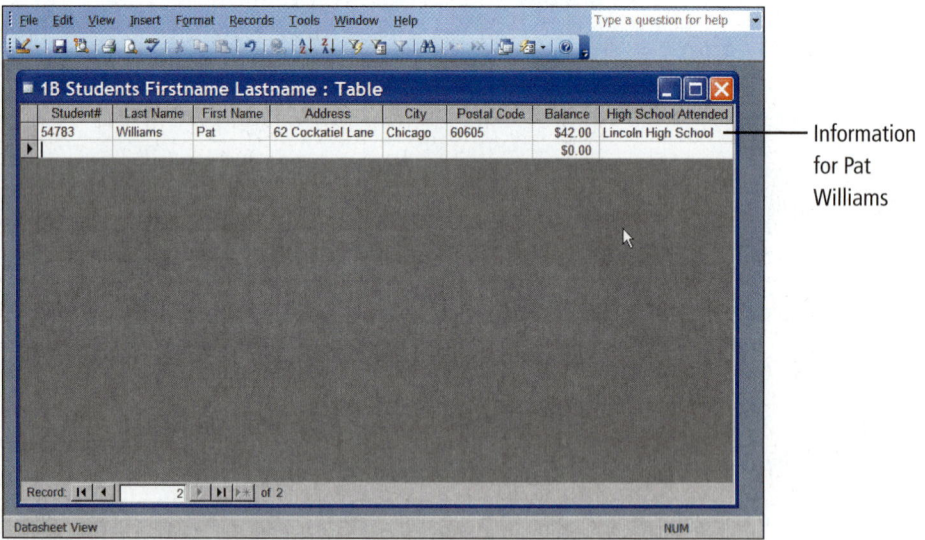

— Information for Pat Williams

Figure 1.43

5 Continue entering the remaining seven records shown in Figure 1.44.

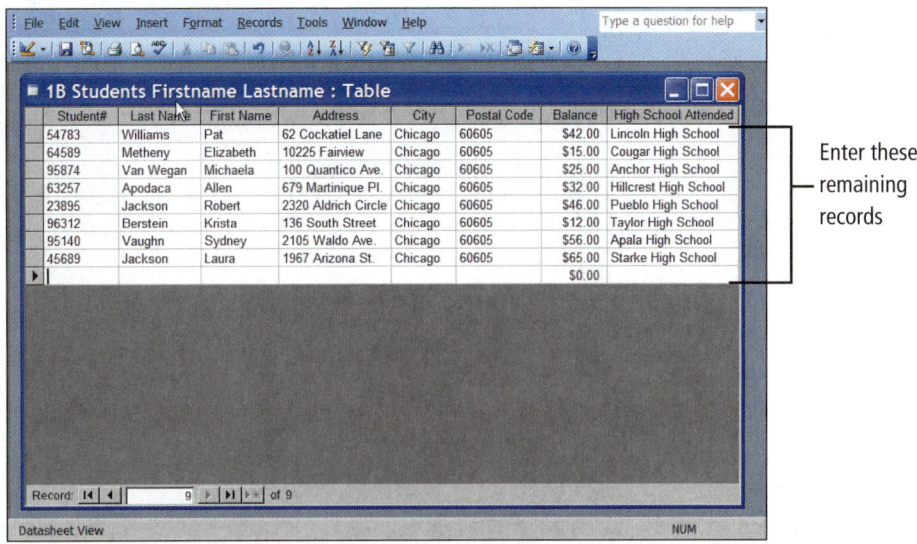

Figure 1.44

Objective 6
Close and Save a Table

When you close a table object, Access saves any additions or changes you made to the records or fields. You do not have to initiate a Save operation.

Activity 1.14 Closing and Saving a Table

1 In the upper right corner of the Table window, click the **Close** button. See Figure 1.45.

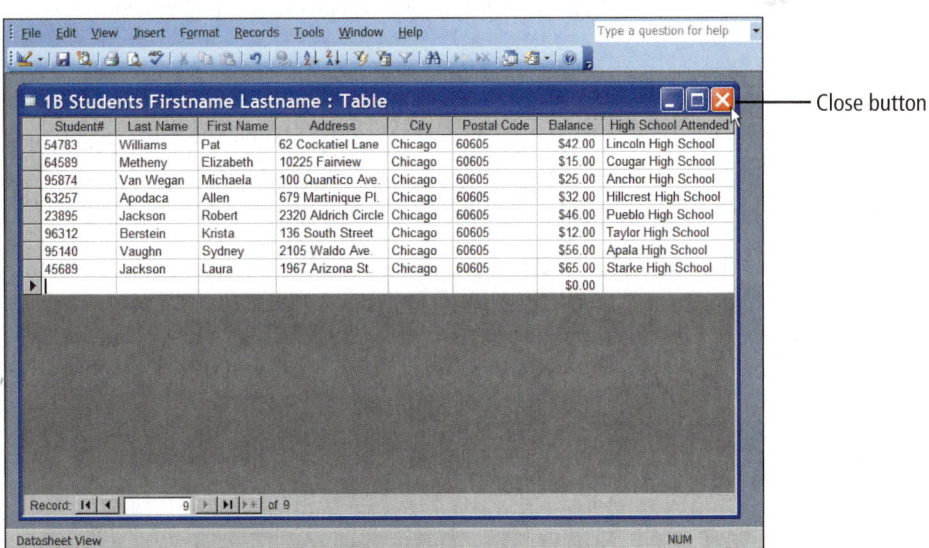

Figure 1.45

The table is closed and the records you entered are saved. Your Students table displays in the Database window. See Figure 1.46.

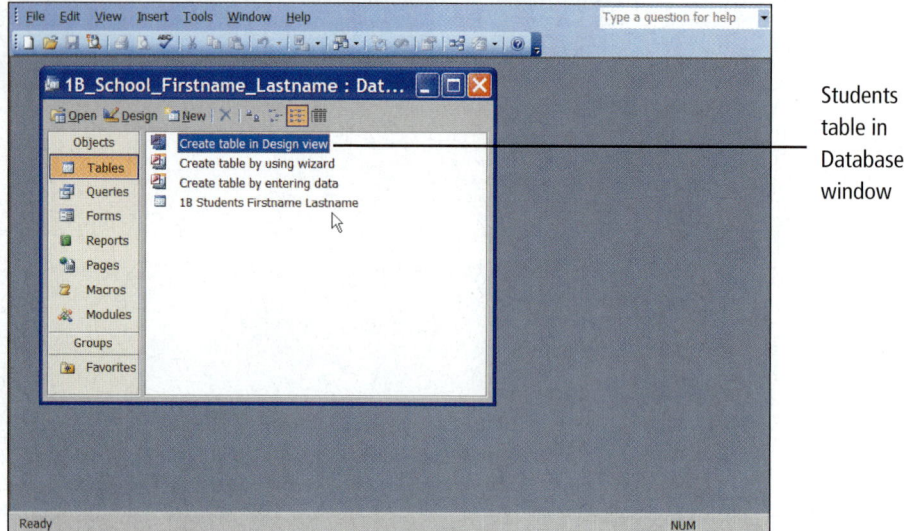

Figure 1.46

Objective 7
Open a Table

There are multiple ways to perform tasks in Access. You can open a table in Design view or Datasheet view, depending on what action you want to perform on the table. For example, if you want to view, add, delete, or modify records, use the Datasheet view. If you want to view, add, delete, or modify the field information (such as field name), use the Design view.

Activity 1.15 Opening a Table

1 In the Database window, double-click your **1B Students** table.

The table opens in Datasheet view, but the records do not display in the same order in which you entered them. Rather, Access has placed the records in sequential order according to the Primary key field.

2 Click the **Close** button in the upper right corner of the table window to close the table.

The Database window displays.

3 If necessary, click your **1B Students** table once to select it, and then just above the Objects bar, click the **Open** button in the Database window.

The table opens again in Datasheet view. This is another method to open a table in the Datasheet view.

4 In the upper right corner of the table window, click the **Close** button to close the table and display the Database window.

5 Open the table in Design view by clicking your **1B Students** table once (it may already be selected), and then clicking the **Design** button ![Design] in the area above the Objects bar. See Figure 1.47. Alternatively, you can right-click the table name and then click Design View from the displayed shortcut menu.

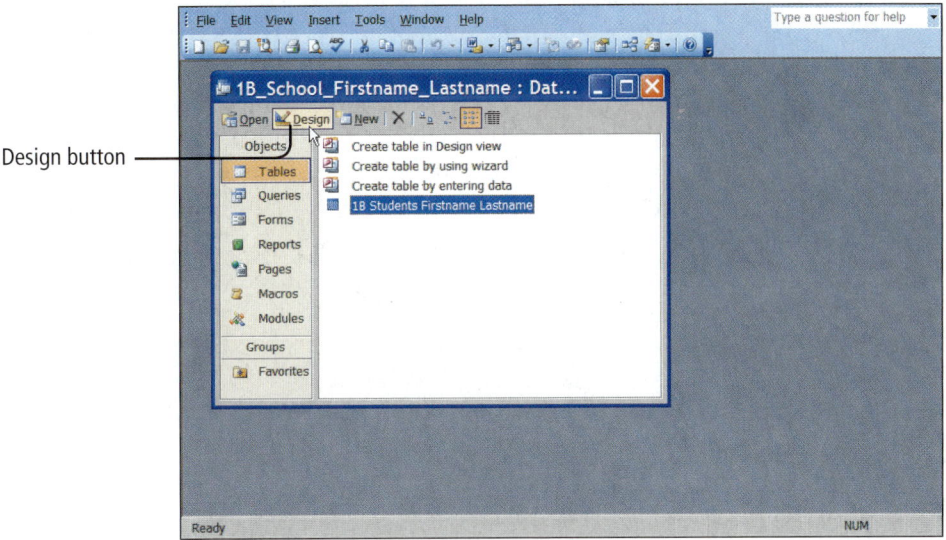

Figure 1.47

6 Leave the table open in Design view for the next activity.

Objective 8
Modify the Table Design

An early consideration when creating a new table is the number and content of the fields in the table. This is referred to as the table's *design*. For example, when setting up an address book database, you will want to have fields for name, address, home phone number, and so forth. After you begin entering records, you might realize that you should have included a field for a cell phone number, too. Fortunately, Access lets you add or delete fields at any time.

Activity 1.16 Deleting Fields

If you decide that a field in your database is no longer useful to you, you can delete that field from the table.

1 In the Design view of your **1B Students** table, position your mouse pointer in the row selector at the far left, next to **High School Attended** field.

The pointer changes to a right-pointing arrow. See Figure 1.48.

Arrow in row selector

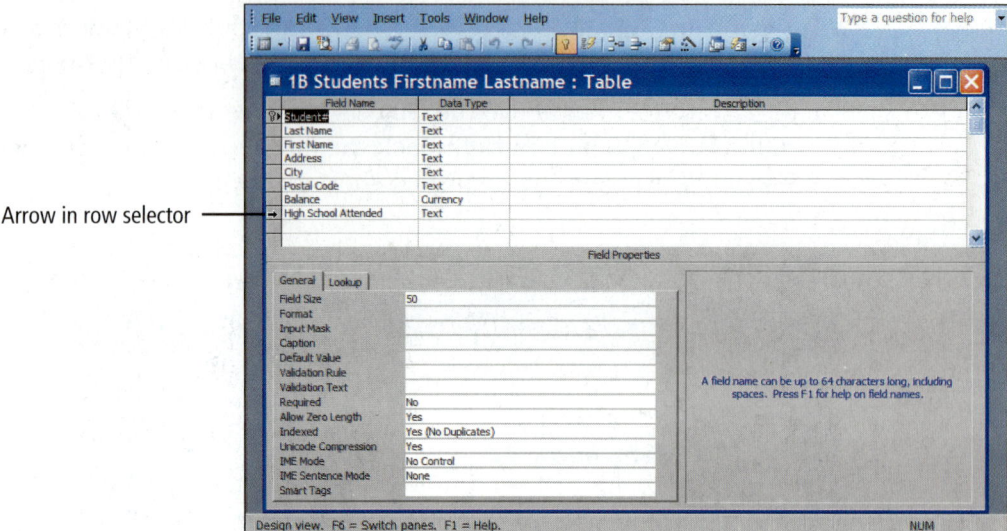

Figure 1.48

2 Click to select the row **High School Attended** and then press Delete.

A message displays asking whether or not you want to permanently delete the field. See Figure 1.49.

Click Yes

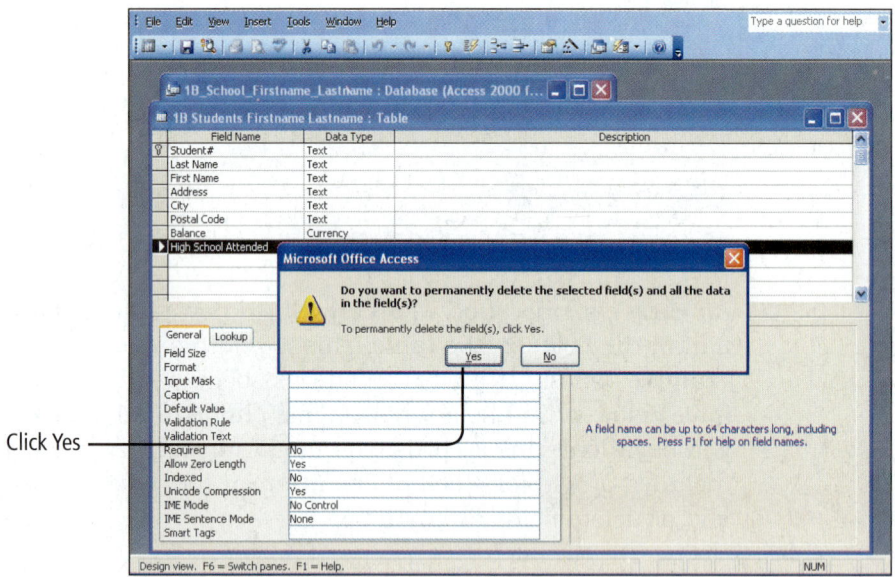

Figure 1.49

3 Click **Yes** to delete the field.

The High School Attended field is deleted. Deleting the field also deletes any data in the field of each record. Later, you could add the field back if you decide to do so, but you would have to re-enter the field's data for each record.

4. Pause your mouse pointer in the title bar area of the table and right-click. On the displayed shortcut menu, click **Datasheet view**, and when prompted, click **Yes** to save the table. This is another way to switch back to Datasheet view.

The High School Attended field no longer displays in the Datasheet view of the table.

5. On the toolbar, click the **View** button to switch back to Design view.

Activity 1.17 Adding Fields

If you decide to add a field to the table, you can add the field and then, for each record, enter data into the field.

1. At the bottom of the list of fields, click in the next available **Field Name** box, type **First Term Attended** and then press Tab two times.

The default text data type is accepted and the description column is left empty.

2. Use any method to switch back to Datasheet view, and when prompted, click **Yes** to save the table. Notice the new column for the field you just added.

3. For each record, enter the information shown in Figure 1.50 for the **First Term Attended** field.

> **Note** — Using Long Column Headings
>
> *Adjust them later.*
>
> The column heading for the First Term Attended field may not display entirely. You will adjust this in a later step.

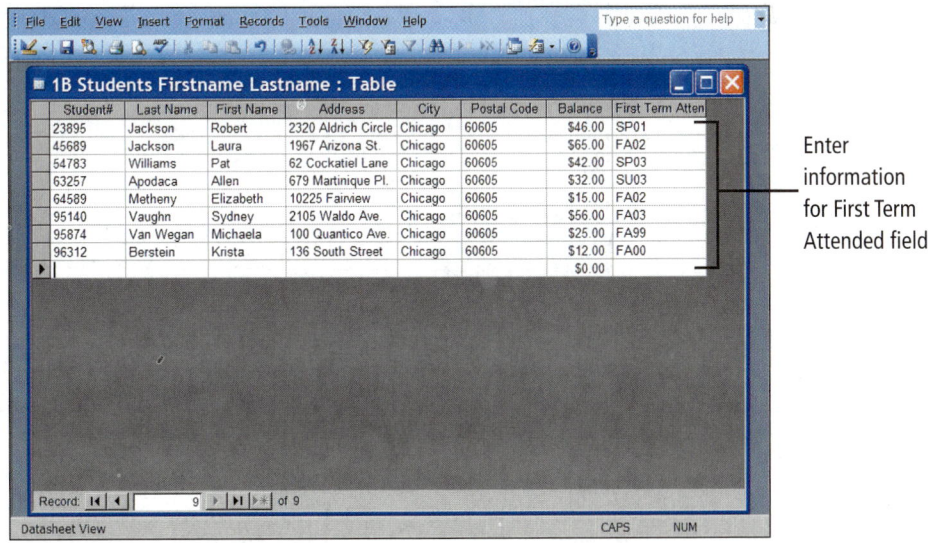

Enter information for First Term Attended field

Figure 1.50

Objective 9
Print a Table

There are multiple ways to print objects in Access. The quickest way to print a database table is to click the Print button on the Database toolbar. This will print one complete copy of the table on the default printer. If you want to print anything other than one complete copy, for example, multiple copies or only selected pages, or to select a different printer, you must initiate the Print command from the File menu.

Activity 1.18 Printing a Table

Although a printed table is not as professional or formal looking as a report, there are times when you may want to print your table in this manner as a quick reference or for proofreading.

1 If necessary, open your **1B Students** table in the Datasheet view.

2 On the toolbar, locate but do not click the **Print** button.

You could print the table without opening the table by selecting the table from the Database window, and then clicking the Print button on the toolbar. This method does not offer you an opportunity to change anything about the way the table prints.

3 With your **1B Students** table still open, display the **File** menu and then click **Print**.

The Print dialog box displays. Here you can make changes to your print settings. See Figure 1.51.

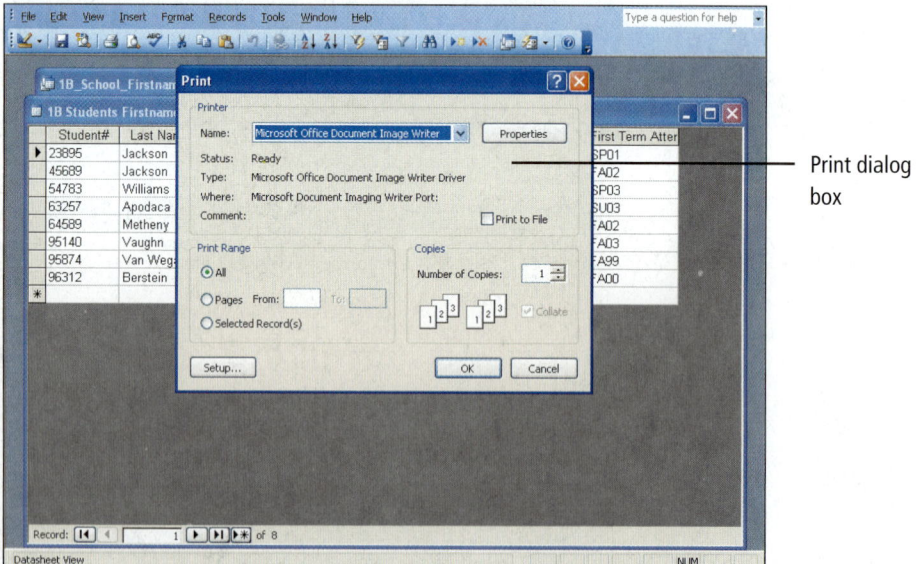

Figure 1.51

4 In the upper right corner next to the printer name, click the **Properties** button.

The Properties dialog box displays. See Figure 1.52. Because the settings for printer models vary, your Properties box may display differently than that shown in the figure.

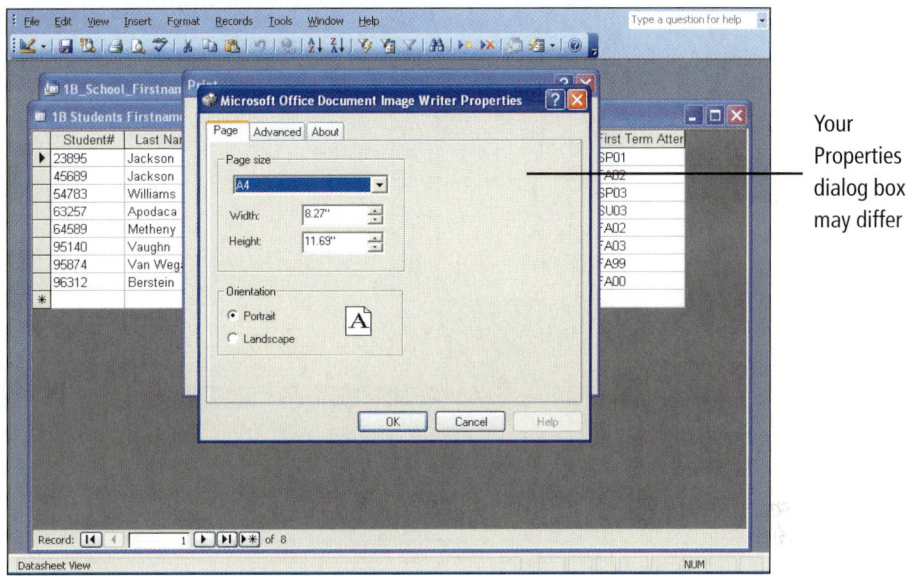

Figure 1.52

By default, Access prints in **Portrait orientation**—the printed page is taller than it is high. An alternate orientation is **Landscape orientation**—the printed page is wider than it is tall.

5 Locate and then click **Landscape**. See Figure 1.53. The properties for printer models vary somewhat. You may have to locate the Landscape orientation on a different tab of your printer Properties dialog box, and thus your screen will differ from the figure shown.

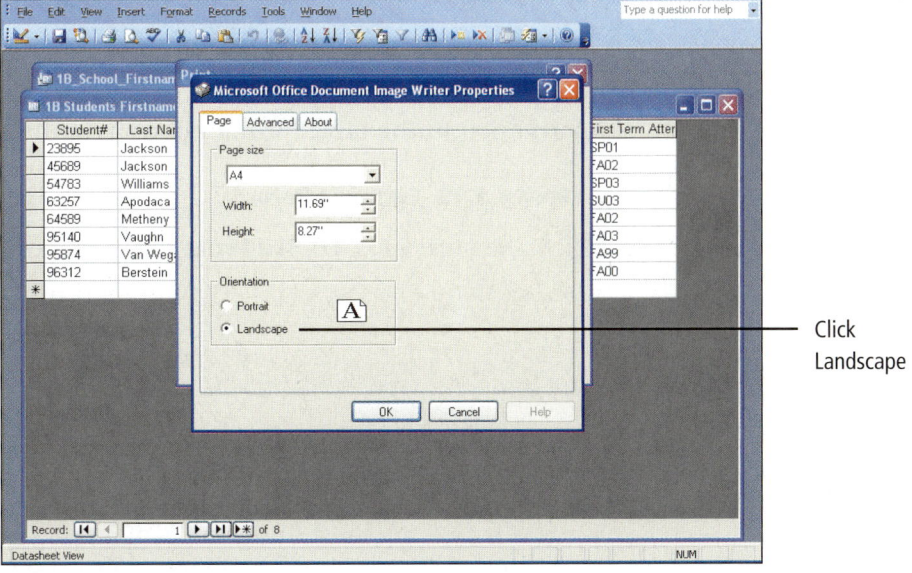

Figure 1.53

Project 1B: School | **Access** 781

6 Click the **OK** button.

7 In the lower left corner of the **Print** dialog box, click the **Setup** button.

The Page Setup dialog box displays with margins set to 1 inch on the Top, Bottom, Left, and Right of the page. See Figure 1.54.

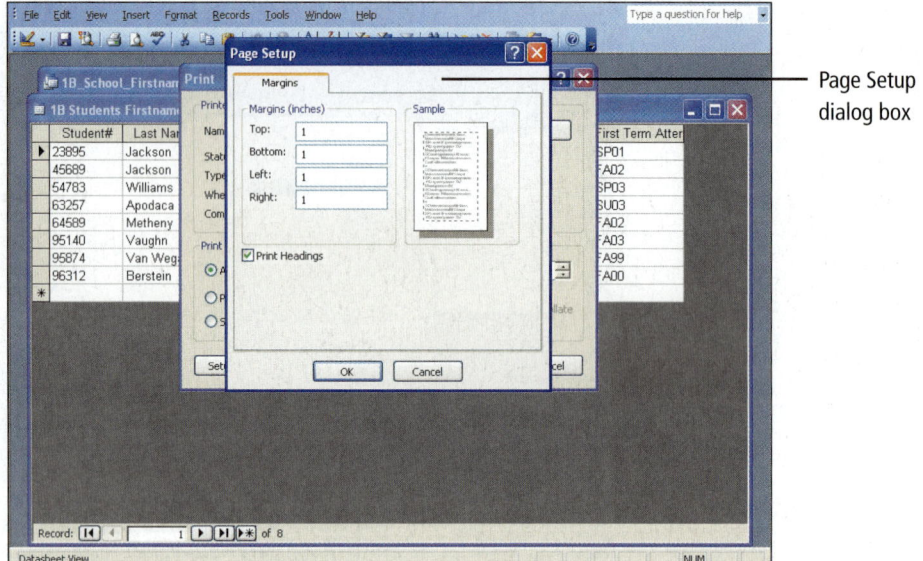
Page Setup dialog box

Figure 1.54

8 Click **OK** to accept the default settings.

9 In the Print dialog box, click **OK**.

Your table prints, and your name is printed at the top of the page in the table name.

Objective 10
Edit Records in a Table

When necessary, you will edit (change) the information in a record. For example, you may realize that you made an error when you entered the information in the table, or the information has changed.

Activity 1.19 Editing a Record

1 Make sure your **1B Students** table is open in Datasheet view.

2 Locate the record for **Pat Williams**. In the **Address** field, click to position the insertion point to the right of 62. See Figure 1.55.

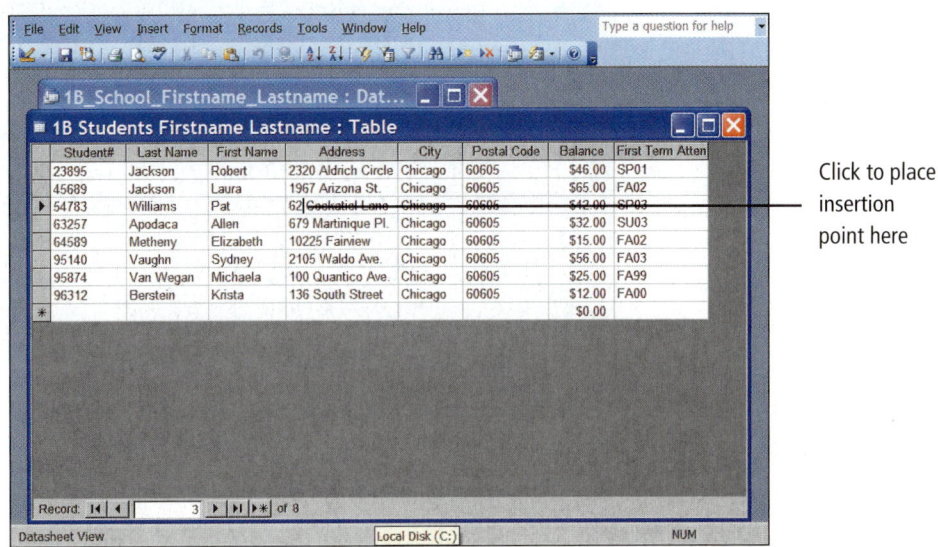

Click to place insertion point here

Figure 1.55

3 Type **5** and then press Tab.

The address for Pat Williams is changed to *625 Cockatiel Lane*. Leave the Students table open.

Activity 1.20 Deleting a Record

Keeping a database up to date means that you may have to delete records when they are no longer needed. In this activity, you will delete the record for Sydney Vaughn, which was mistakenly included in the Students table—she is not a student.

1 Be sure your **1B Students** table is open in Datasheet view.

2 Locate the record for **Sydney Vaughn**, position the mouse pointer in the row selector for Sydney Vaughn's record until it takes the shape of a right-pointing arrow, and then click to select the row.

The entire record is selected. See Figure 1.56.

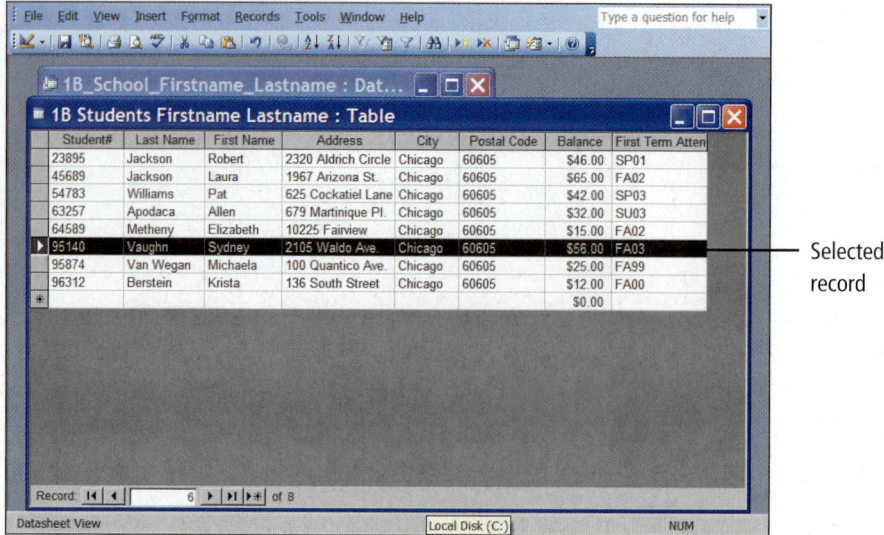

Figure 1.56

[3] On the toolbar click the **Delete Record** button . Alternatively, you could press [Delete] on the keyboard.

A message displays alerting you that you are about to delete a record. If you click Yes and delete the record, you cannot use the Undo button to reverse the action. If you delete a record by mistake, you will have to re-create the record.

[4] Click **Yes** to delete the record.

The record is deleted from the 1B Students table.

Activity 1.21 Resizing Columns and Rows

You can adjust the size of columns and rows in a table. Sometimes this is necessary to get a better view of the data. Column widths and row heights are adjusted by dragging the borders between the columns or rows. Reducing the column width allows you to display more fields on your screen at one time. Increasing the width of a column allows you to view data that is too long to display in the column.

Adjusting the size of columns and rows does not change the data contained in the table's records. It changes only your *view* of the data.

[1] Be sure your **1B Students** table is open in Datasheet view.

[2] In the gray row of column headings, pause your mouse pointer over the vertical line between the **Address** column and the **City** column until it becomes a double-headed arrow, as shown in Figure 1.57.

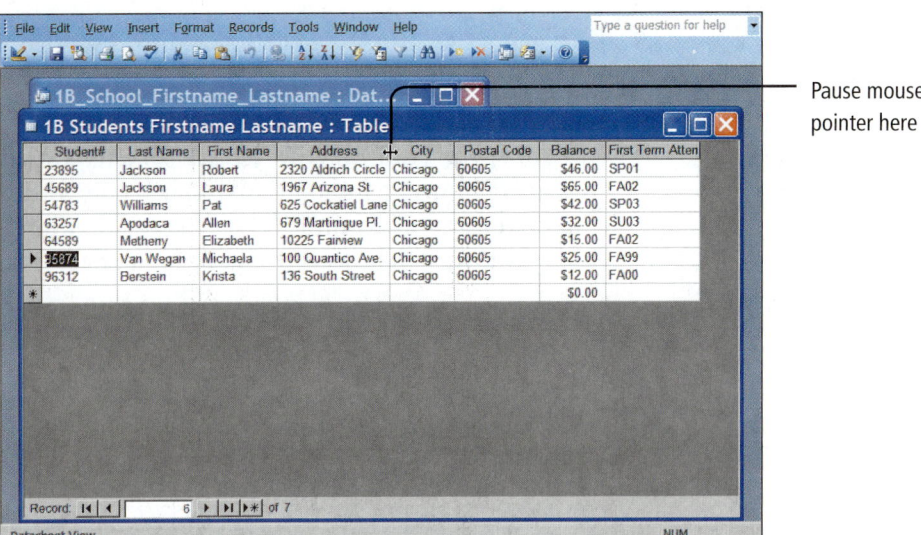

Figure 1.57

3 Press and hold the left mouse button and drag the line in between the columns to the right approximately 0.5 inch. The measurement need not be precise; use your eye to judge this. Release the mouse button.

The column's width is increased.

4 In the gray column headings, point to the vertical bar between the **Address** column heading and the **City** column heading until the double-headed arrow displays, and then double-click.

Access adjusts the width of the Address column to accommodate the widest entry in the column. Use this as a quick method to adjust columns to accommodate the widest entry in a column.

5 In the row of column headings, pause the mouse pointer over the **Student#** column heading until the mouse pointer becomes a downward-pointing black arrow. Then drag to the right until all of the columns are selected. See Figure 1.58.

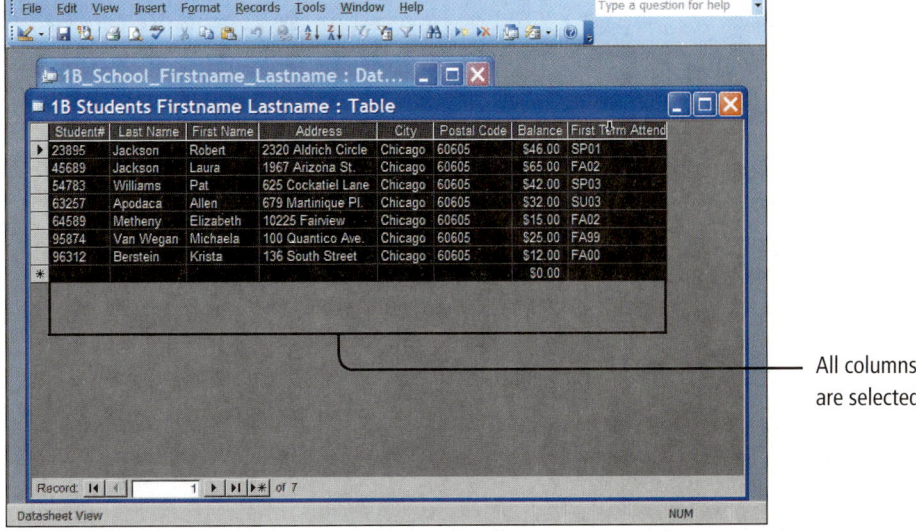

Figure 1.58

Project 1B: School | **Access**   785

6 With the columns selected, pause your mouse pointer over the vertical line between any of the column headings until the mouse pointer takes the shape of a double-headed arrow, and then double-click.

All of the columns are resized to accommodate the widest entry in each column. In some instances, the widest entry is the column heading, for example, *First Term Attended*. Use this method as a quick way to adjust the widths of several columns at once.

7 Click anywhere in the table to deselect the table.

8 To adjust row height, point to the horizontal line between the second and third record until the double-headed arrow displays. See Figure 1.59.

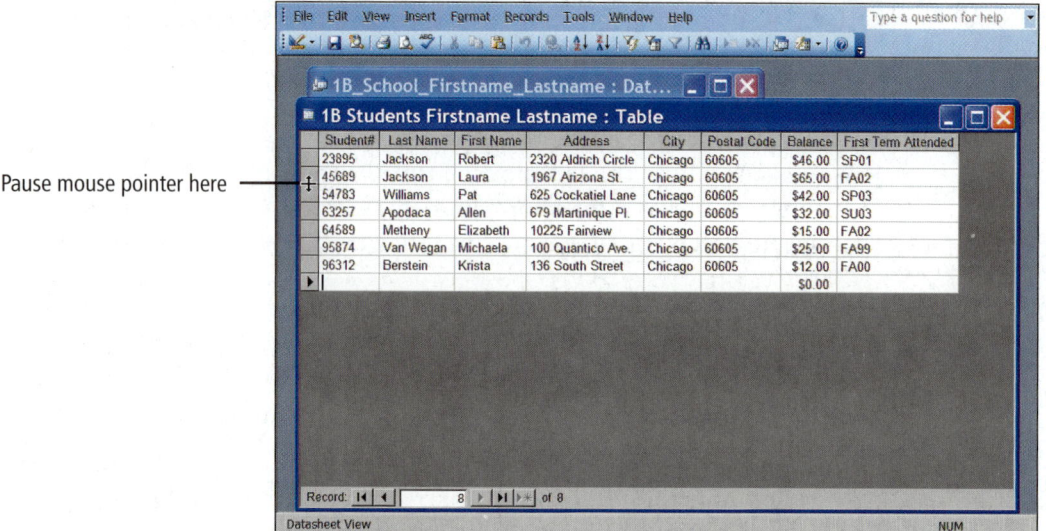

Pause mouse pointer here

Figure 1.59

9 Drag the horizontal line down approximately 0.5 inch. The exact measurement is not important. Use your eye to judge the distance. Release the mouse button.

The height of all of the rows is increased by the same amount. Adjusting the row height enables you to see long names that may have wrapped to two lines in a column—and still have many columns visible on the screen.

10 On the menu bar, click **Format** and then click **Row Height**.

The Row Height dialog box displays. Here you can return row heights to their default setting or enter a precise number for the height of the row.

11 Select the **Standard Height** check box and then click **OK**. See Figure 1.60.

The height of all rows is restored to the default setting. Use this dialog box to set the rows to any height.

Standard Height check box

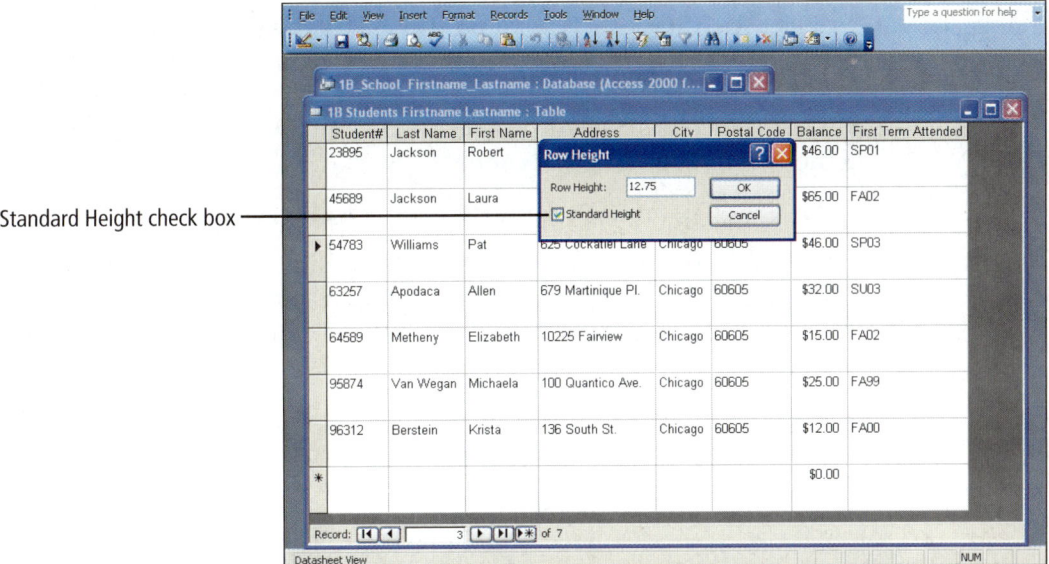

Figure 1.60

Activity 1.22 Hiding Columns

When a table contains many fields (columns), you can temporarily hide one or more columns so that you can get a better view of other columns.

1 Click to position your insertion point anywhere in the **City** column, display the **Format** menu, and then click **Hide Columns**.

The City column is hidden from view, and the columns to the right of the City column shift to the left. Hidden columns and the data that they contain are not deleted—they are merely hidden from view.

2 From the **Format** menu, click **Unhide Columns**. See Figure 1.61.

The Unhide Columns dialog box displays. All of the columns except the City column are checked, indicating that they are in view.

Unhide Columns option on Format menu

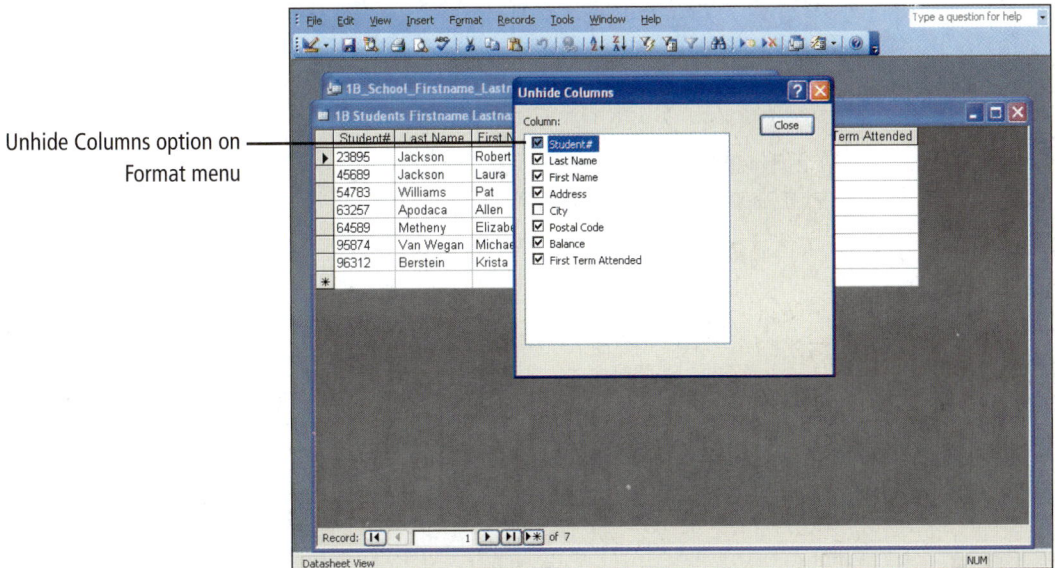

Figure 1.61

Project 1B: School | **Access** 787

3 Select the **City** check box and then click the **Close** button.

The City column returns to view.

4 Click the column heading **City**, press and hold Shift, and then click the column heading **Balance**.

The City, Postal Code, and Balance columns are selected.

You can hide two or more *adjacent* columns (columns that are next to each other) at one time. If you select a column and then select another column while holding Shift, those columns are selected in addition to any columns between them.

5 With the three columns selected, display the **Format** menu, and then click **Hide Columns**. See Figure 1.62.

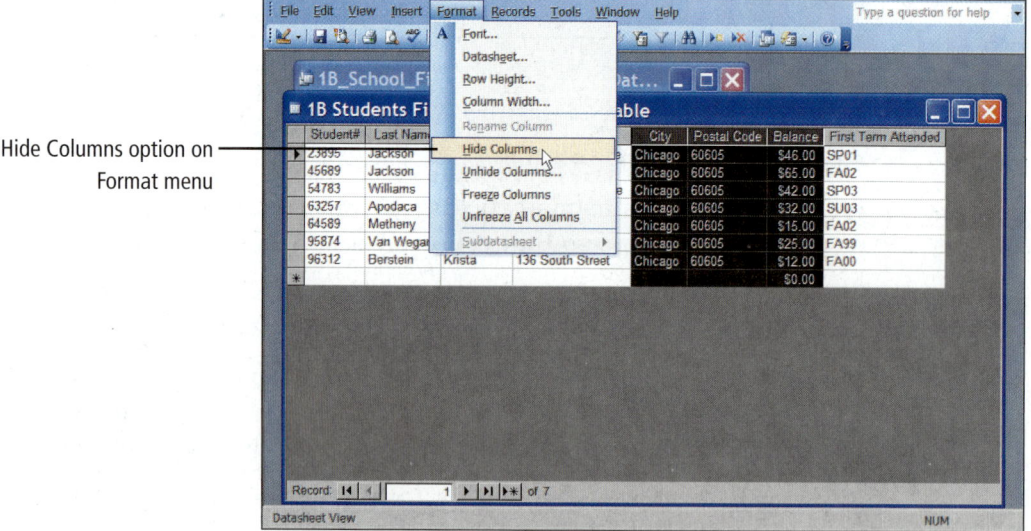

Hide Columns option on Format menu

Figure 1.62

The City, Postal Code, and Balance columns are hidden.

6 To unhide the columns, display the **Format** menu, click **Unhide Columns**, and then select the **City**, **Postal Code**, and the **Balance** check boxes. Click the **Close** button.

The three columns are returned to view in your 1B Students table.

Objective 11
Sort Records

Sorting records in a table is the process of rearranging records in a specific order. For example, you could sort the names in your address book database alphabetically by each person's last name, or you could sort your CD collection database by the date of purchase.

Activity 1.23 Sorting Records in a Table

Information stored in an Access table can be sorted in either ***ascending order*** or ***descending order***. Ascending order sorts text alphabetically (A to Z) and sorts numbers from the lowest number to the highest number. Descending order sorts text in reverse alphabetic order (Z to A) and sorts numbers from the highest number to the lowest.

1 Be sure your **1B Students** table is open in the Datasheet view.

2 Click anywhere in the **Last Name** column and then on the toolbar click the **Sort Ascending** button. See Figure 1.63.

The records are sorted in ascending order according to each Student's Last Name.

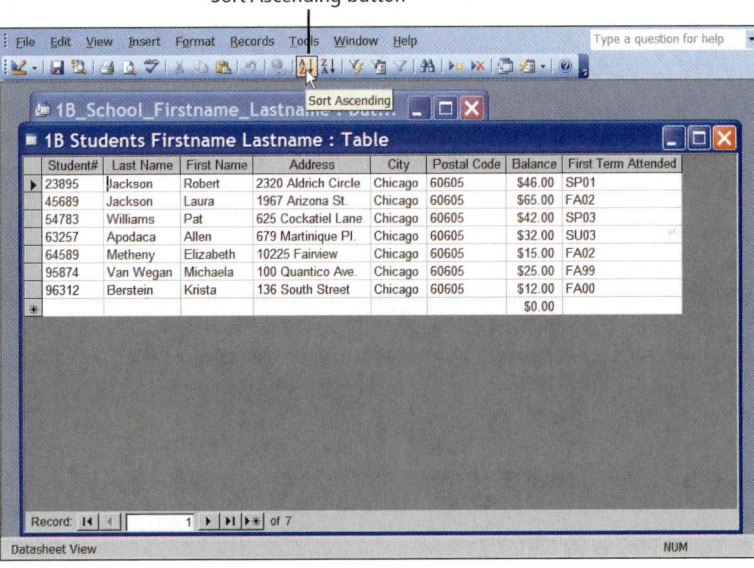

Figure 1.63

3 Click anywhere in the **First Name** column and then on the toolbar click the **Sort Ascending** button.

The records are sorted in ascending order according to each student's First Name.

4 Click the column heading **Last Name**, press and hold Shift, and then click the column heading **First Name**.

Both the Last Name column and the First Name column are selected.

Information in an Access table can be sorted using more than one field. For example, data can be sorted by the *primary sort field*—the field that Access sorts by initially—and then, for any records having an identical primary sort field, records are sorted further by the *secondary sort field*—the field that Access uses to sort records that have matching primary sort fields.

5 On the toolbar, click the **Sort Ascending** button.

The records are sorted alphabetically by Last Name. Within records that have identical last names, for example, *Jackson*, the records are sorted alphabetically by First Name.

Access sorts the records consecutively from left to right, meaning any fields that you want to sort *must* be adjacent to each other, and your primary sort field (*Last Name* in this example) must be to the left of the secondary sort field (*First Name* in this example).

6 Look at the two records for which the last name is **Jackson**.

Notice that those two records are also sorted alphabetically by First Name—Laura comes before Robert.

7 On the menu bar, click **Records** and then click **Remove Filter/Sort**.

You can return your records to the original sort order at any time by selecting Remove Filter/Sort from the Records menu. In this instance, the original sort order is by primary key.

8 Leave your **1B Students** table open for the next activity.

Objective 12
Navigate to Records in a Table

The Students table that you created has only seven records, and you can see all of them on the screen. Most Access tables, however, contain many records—more than you can see on the screen at one time. Access provides several tools to help you navigate (move) among records in a table. For example, you can move the insertion point to the last record in a table or to the first record in a table, or move up one record at a time or down one record at a time.

Activity 1.24 Navigating Among Records Using the Navigation Area

Figure 1.64 illustrates the navigation functions in the navigation area of a table.

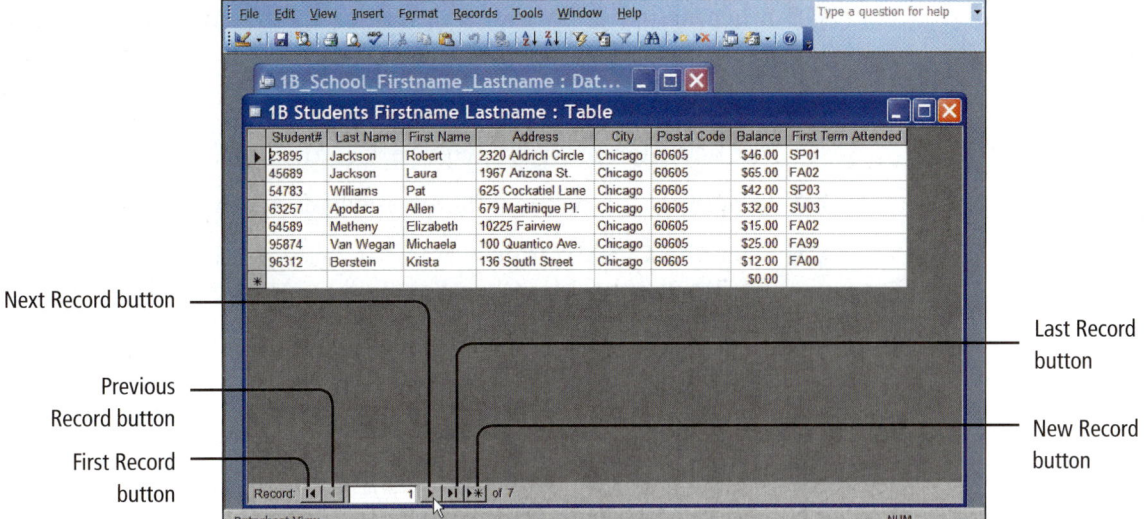

Figure 1.64

1. If necessary, open your **1B Students** table in Datasheet view.

2. Click anywhere in the first record of the table.

3. In the navigation area, click the **Next Record** button. See Figure 1.64.

    Depending on the field in which your insertion point was located, the next record in the table is selected, in the same field.

4. In the navigation area, click the **Last Record** button. See Figure 1.64.

    The last record in the table is selected.

5. Experiment with the different navigation buttons as shown in Figure 1.64.

Activity 1.25 Navigating Among Records Using the Keyboard

You can also navigate among records in a table using the keyboard. Figure 1.65 lists the keystrokes and the resulting movement.

Key Combinations for Navigating a Table

Keystroke	Movement
↑	Moves the selection up one record at a time.
↓	Moves the selection down one record at a time.
Page Up	Moves the selection up one screen at a time.
PageDown	Moves the selection down one screen at a time.
Ctrl + Home	Moves the selection to the first field in the table.
Ctrl + End	Moves the selection to the last field in the table.

Figure 1.65

Project 1B: School | **Access** 791

1 If necessary, open your **1B Students** table in Datasheet view and click anywhere in any record except the last record.

2 Press ↓.

The selection moves down one record.

3 Experiment with the different navigation keystrokes.

4 Click the **Close** button ⊠ in the table window to close the **1B Students** table. Click **Yes** if you are prompted to save changes to the design of your table.

The Database window displays.

Objective 13
Close and Save a Database

When you close an Access table, any changes are saved automatically. At the end of your Access session, close your database and then close Access.

Activity 1.26 Closing and Saving a Database

1 In the smaller Database window, click the **Close** button ⊠.

The database closes. The Access program remains open. See Figure 1.66.

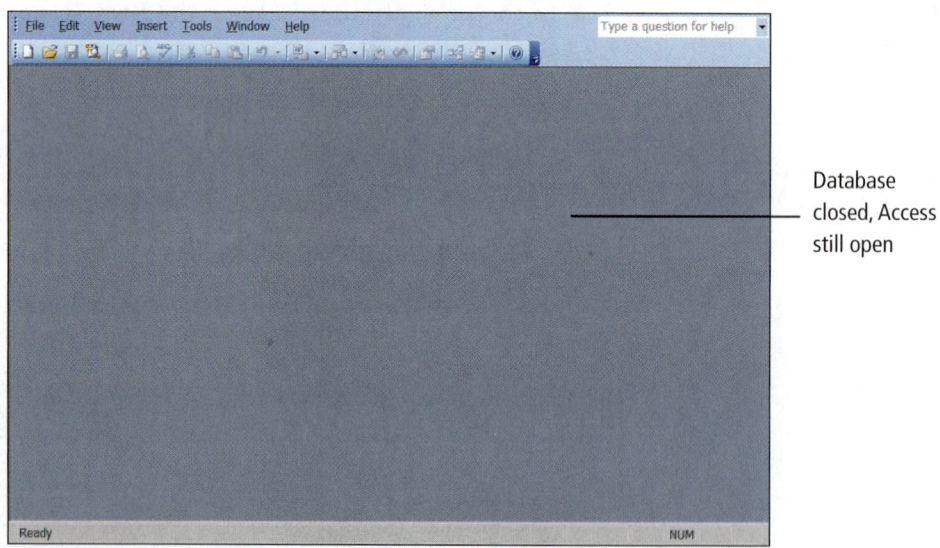

Database closed, Access still open

Figure 1.66

2 On the title bar of the Access window, click the **Close** button ⊠ to close the Access program.

Objective 14
Use the Access Help System

Access contains a Help feature designed to assist you when performing a task in Access or if you would like more information about a particular topic in Access. There are multiple ways to use the Help feature in Access, including the Office Assistant, and the Type a question for help box.

Activity 1.27 Using the Access Help System

The Office Assistant is an animated figure that displays to assist you with a task.

1. Start Access. On the menu bar, click **Help** and then click **Show the Office Assistant**.

   The Office Assistant character displays. The animated character may be a paperclip, or some other character.

2. Double-click the Office Assistant to display the **What would you like to do?** box.

3. With *Type your question here and then click Search* highlighted, type **How do I get help?** and then click **Search**.

4. In the **Search Results** task pane, click **About getting help while you work**. You may have to use the vertical scroll bar to see this topic.

   The Microsoft Access Help window displays with hyperlinks (usually in blue text) listed. Clicking on these hyperlinks will link you to additional information about the topic.

5. Click on the links that display and you will see the description of each of these expanded in the area below the link. For example, click **Microsoft Press** to expand the topic and then click it again to collapse it.

6 After viewing the Help topics, click the **Close** button ☒ to close the Help window. See Figure 1.67.

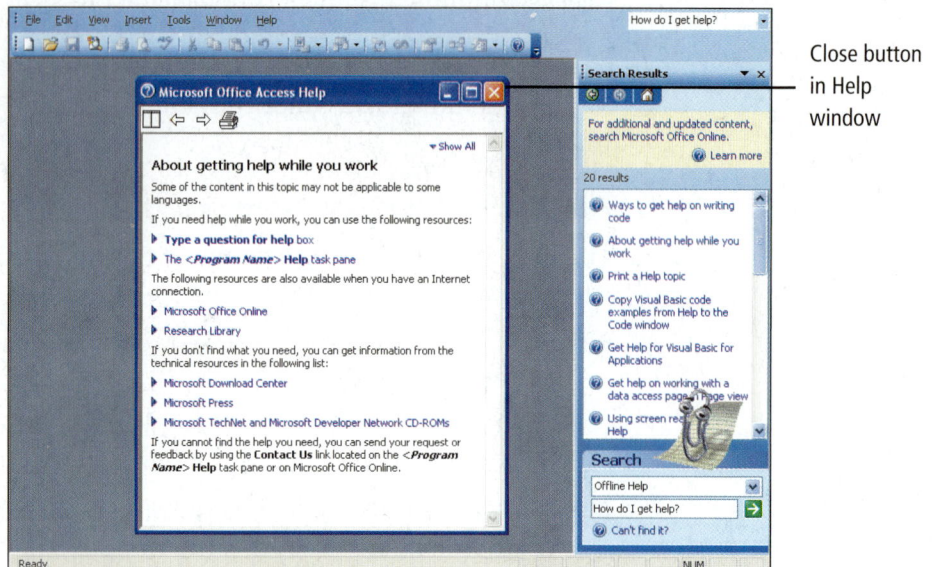

Figure 1.67

7 In the upper right corner of the Access window, locate the **Type a question for help** box and click it. See Figure 1.68.

The text in the box is selected.

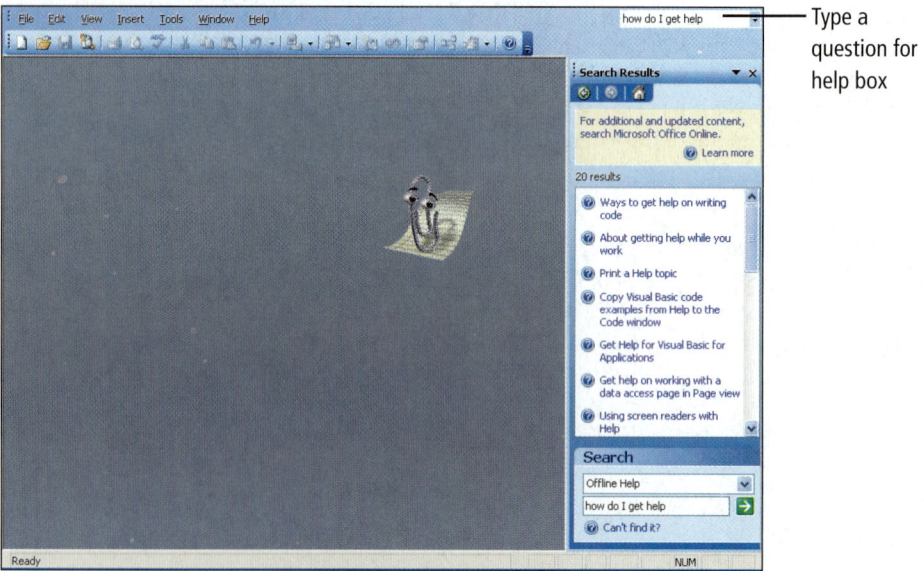

Figure 1.68

8 In the **Type a question for help** box, type **table**

9 Press Enter and click **About creating a table (MDB)**.

A window containing information about creating a table displays. See Figure 1.69. Keywords, identified in a different color, display additional information when they are clicked.

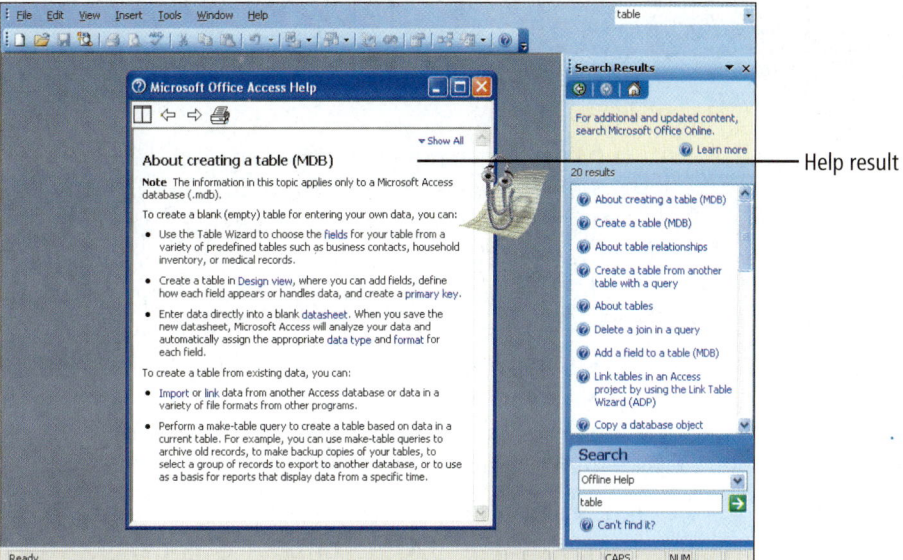

Figure 1.69

10 In the second bullet, click on the words **Design view**. Scroll down if necessary to view this description.

An explanation of Design View displays in green within the paragraph.

11 In the Microsoft Access Help window, on the toolbar, click the **Print** button . See Figure 1.70.

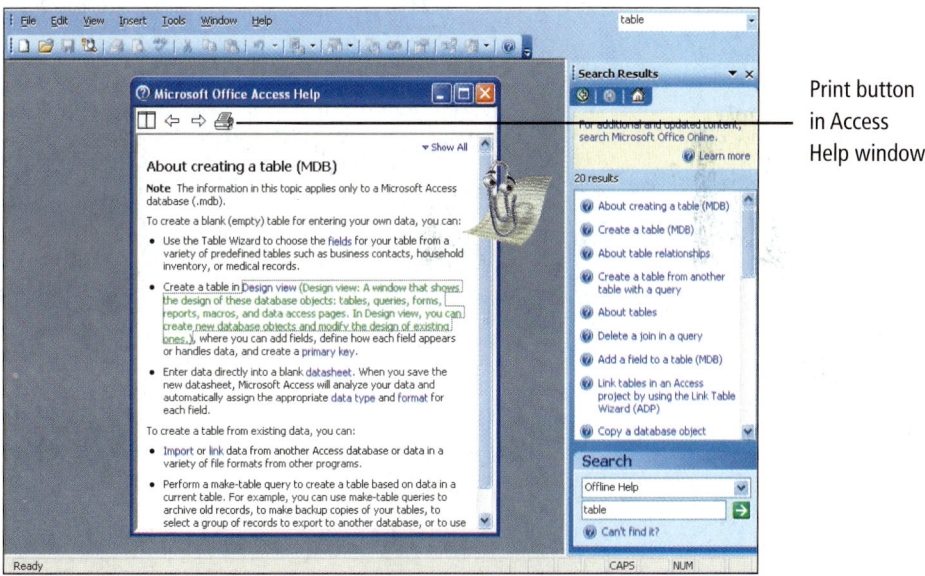

Figure 1.70

12 In the **Print** dialog box, click **Print** (or **OK**).

The Help topic you have displayed is printed. Keep this document for your reference.

13 Close the Microsoft Access Help window.

14 On the title bar of the Access window, click the **Close** button to close Access.

End You have completed Project 1B

Access chapter one

Summary

Microsoft Access 2003 is a database management system. Databases help you organize information, such as the names and addresses in your address book, a CD collection, or a list of students at a college.

In an existing database, you can either view the information in the database or edit the information. Access contains tools, called objects, which enable you to enter information into a database, and then organize, manipulate, and analyze the information. Information in a database is stored in tables. The data in a table is organized by rows, called records, and columns, called fields. Each record in a table stores information about one database item.

Queries extract information from a table according to the criteria set for the query. Forms are another tool that you can use to either enter or view records—one record at a time. Reports are professional-looking documents that summarize the information in a table.

Information stored in a table can be edited and sorted. Access contains navigation tools to assist you in locating specific records.

In This Chapter You Practiced How To

- Rename a Database
- Start Access, Open an Existing Database, and View Database Objects
- Create a New Database
- Create a New Table
- Create a Primary Key and Add Records to a Table
- Close and Save a Table
- Open a Table
- Modify the Table Design
- Print a Table
- Edit Records in a Table
- Sort Records
- Navigate to Records in a Table
- Close and Save a Database
- Use the Access Help System

Concepts Assessments

Matching Match each term in the second column with its correct definition in the first column by writing the letter of the term on the blank line in front of the correct definition.

___ 1. A printing orientation in which the printed page is taller than it is high.

___ 2. The field that serves as a unique identifier for records in a table.

___ 3. The Access object that stores the information in a database.

___ 4. The process of rearranging items in a specific order.

___ 5. The Access object that displays records one at a time.

___ 6. A sorting order in which records are sorted alphabetically from A to Z.

___ 7. The process of pulling out information from a database according to specified criteria.

___ 8. The Access object that displays selected fields and records in an easy-to-read format.

___ 9. A printing orientation in which the printed page is wider than it is tall.

___ 10. A window within a Microsoft Office application that provides commonly used commands.

___ 11. The Access object that assists you in asking a question about the data.

___ 12. A sorting order in which records are sorted alphabetically from Z to A.

___ 13. Data that has been organized in a useful manner.

___ 14. A collection of data related to a particular topic.

___ 15. The collection of tools in Access used to enter and manipulate the data in a database.

A Ascending

B Database

C Descending

D Extracting

E Form

F Information

G Landscape

H Objects

I Portrait

J Primary key

K Query

L Report

M Sorting

N Table

O Task pane

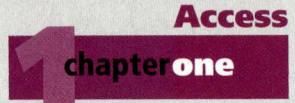

Concepts Assessments (continued)

Fill in the Blank Write the correct answer in the space provided.

1. Tables are the foundation of an Access database, because that is where the data is _____.

2. Each table in an Access database stores data about only _____ subject.

3. The _____ window displays when a database is open.

4. Each horizontal _____ of a table stores all the information about one database record.

5. Each vertical _____ of a table has a name that describes one category of information contained within each record.

6. The small gray box at the left end of a row in a table is the _____.

7. In the _____ view of a table, only the names of the fields, and not the records, display.

8. Specifications that determine what records will be displayed as a result of a query are called _____.

9. Filling a table with data is referred to as _____ the table.

10. A rule that you define for data within a field is referred to as the _____.

Access chapter one
Skill Assessments

Project 1C — Departments

Objectives: *Rename a Database; Start Access, Open an Existing Database, and View Database Objects; Close and Save a Table; Open a Table; Print a Table; Sort Records; and Close and Save a Database.*

In the following Skill Assessment, you will open an existing database, view the database objects, and add two records to the database table. This database is used by the administration offices at Lake Michigan City College to store information regarding the various departments at the College. Your completed database objects will look like the ones shown in Figures 1.71 and 1.72. You will rename and save the database as *1C_LMccDept_Firstname_Lastname*.

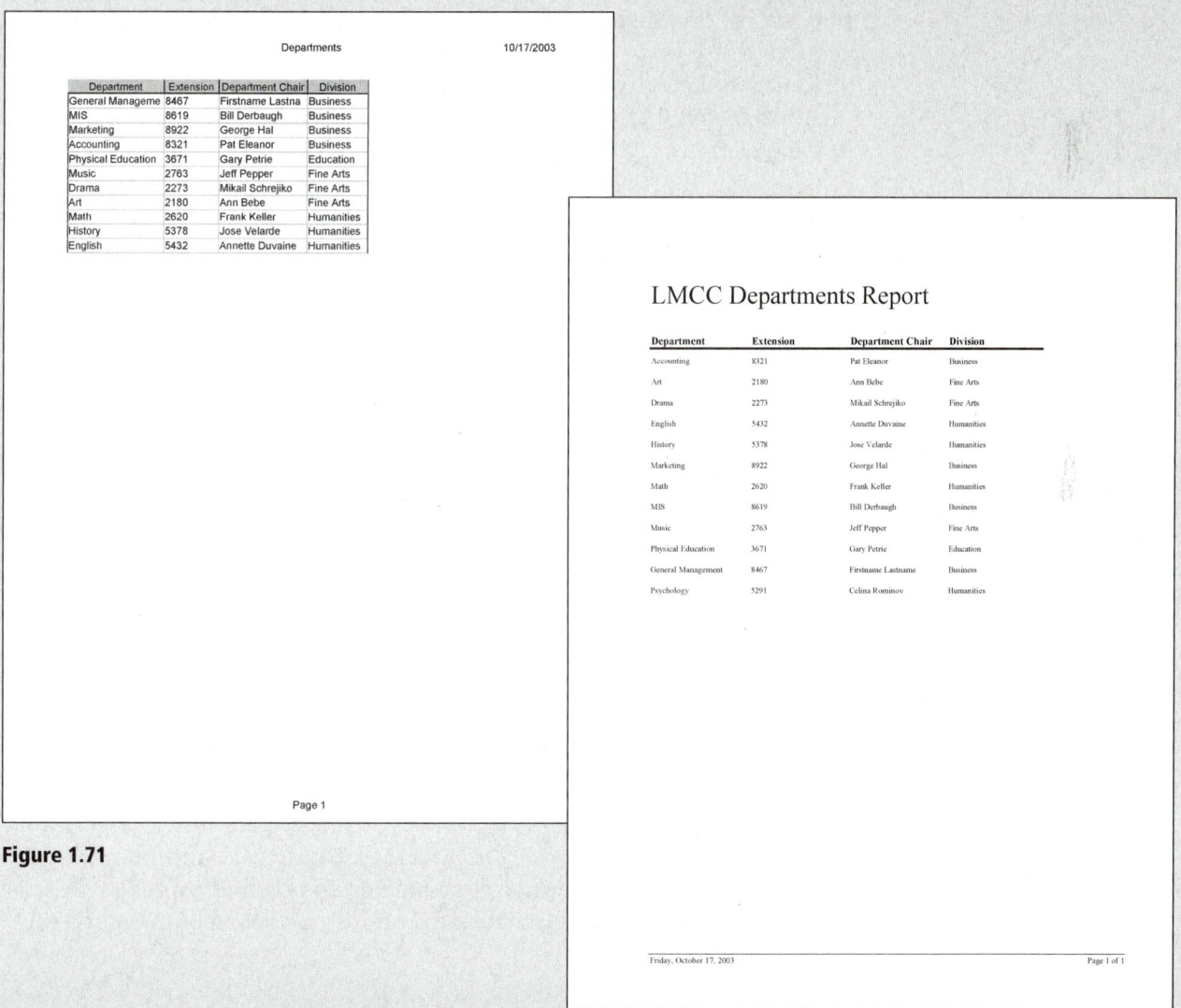

Figure 1.71

Figure 1.72

(Project 1C–Departments continues on the next page)

Project 1C: Departments | Access 799

Skill Assessments (continued)

(Project 1C–Departments continued)

1. On your Windows desktop, open **My Computer** and navigate to the student files that accompany this textbook. Locate and then click once to select the file **a01C_LMccDept**.

2. Move the mouse pointer over the selected file name and then right-click to display a shortcut menu. On the displayed shortcut menu, click **Copy**. Navigate to the drive and folder where you are storing your projects for this chapter. On the menu bar, click **Edit** and then click **Paste**. The database file is copied to your folder and is selected (highlighted).

3. Move your mouse pointer over the selected file name, right-click to display the shortcut menu, and then on the shortcut menu, click **Rename**. In the **File name** box, clear any existing text. Using your own first and last name, type **1C_LMccDept_Firstname_Lastname** and then press Enter to save the new file name. If the **Confirm File Rename** dialog box displays, click **Yes**. Be sure that the file name is still selected (highlighted) and then right-click to display the shortcut menu.

4. On the displayed shortcut menu, click **Properties**. At the lower part of the displayed dialog box, click to clear the check mark next to **Read-only**, and then click **OK** to close the dialog box. Close **My Computer**.

5. Start Access. On the menu bar, click **File** and then click **Open**. Click the **Look in arrow** and then navigate to the location where you are storing your projects for this chapter. Locate the database file that you renamed and saved with your name in Step 3. Click the database file once to select it, and then, in the lower right corner, click the **Open** button. Alternatively, you can double-click the name of the database, and it will open. If the security warning message displays, click **Yes and/or Open**.

6. In the Database window, on the Objects bar, click **Tables** once to display a list of tables in this database. To the right of the Objects bar, double-click the **Departments** table to open the table in Datasheet view. Notice that the table includes fields for Department, Extension, Department Chair, and Division.

7. In the **Department** column, click in the blank record at the bottom of the table and type **General Management** as the department name for the new record. Press Tab once. In the **Extension** field type **8467** and press Tab once. In the **Department Chair** field and using your own information, type your **Firstname Lastname** and press Tab once. In the **Division** field, type **Business** and then press Enter to complete the record.

(Project 1C–Departments continues on the next page)

Skill Assessments (continued)

(Project 1C–Departments continued)

8. On the Table Datasheet toolbar, click the **View** button to switch to the Design view and notice that the **Department** field is the primary key. Recall that one field in a table is designated as the primary key so that each record has a unique identifier. In this case, each department has a different name—no two departments at the college have the same name.

9. On the Table Design toolbar, click the **View** button to return to the Datasheet view. Click anywhere in the **Division** column, and then, on the Table Datasheet toolbar, click the **Sort Ascending** button. Notice that the records are now sorted in alphabetical order by Division.

10. On the Table Datasheet toolbar, click the **Print** button. In the upper right corner of the table window, click the **Close** button to close the table. A copy of the table is printed, and your name is printed as the Chair of the General Management Department. Save any changes if prompted to do so.

11. On the Objects bar, click **Queries** to display a list of available queries in the database. Double-click the **Business Division** query to open the query. Notice that each entry in the *Business Division* query has *Business* in the **Division** field. Recall that a query locates records from a table that meet specific criteria and then displays the result. In this case, the Business Division query was designed to locate all of the records that have *Business* as the Division. You can see that there are four Departments within the Business Division. In the upper right corner of the table window, click the **Close** button to close the query.

12. On the Objects bar, click **Forms** to display a list of available forms in the database. Recall that forms are another database object, in addition to tables, that allow you to view and enter new records into a table—one record at a time. To the right of the Objects bar, double-click the **Departments Form** to open the form. The Departments Form opens and the first record in the table displays.

13. At the bottom of the Department Form, locate the **New Record** button (the button at the bottom of the form with the *) and click it. With the insertion point blinking in the **Department** box, type **Psychology** and then press [Tab] once. Use the information below to fill in the remaining information for this record.

Department	Extension	Department Chair	Division
Psychology	5291	Celina Rominov	Humanities

14. In the Form window, click the **Close** button to close the form.

(Project 1C–Departments continues on the next page)

Access chapter one

Skill Assessments (continued)

(Project 1C–Departments continued)

15. On the Objects bar, click **Reports** to display a list of available reports that have been created for this database. Recall that a report is a professional-looking document that summarizes information from a table in an easy-to-read format. To the right of the Objects bar, double-click the **LMCC Departments Report** to open the report in Print Preview.

16. In the upper right corner of the report title bar, click the **Maximize** button and then on the Print Preview toolbar, click the **Zoom arrow**. Zoom to **100%**. On the Print Preview toolbar, click the **Print** button to print the report. On the Print Preview toolbar, click the **Close** button to close the report. In the Access window, click the **Close** button to close Access.

End You have completed Project 1C

Project 1D — Office Supplies

Objectives: *Create a New Database, Create a New Table, Create a Primary Key and Add Records to a Table, Close and Save a Table, Modify the Table Design, Print a Table, and Close and Save a Database.*

In the following Skill Assessment, you will create a new database to track office supplies for the Distance Learning Department at Lake Michigan City College. The database table will look like the one shown in Figure 1.73. You will save your database as *1D_Office_Supplies_Firstname_Lastname*.

1. Start Access. From the **File** menu, click **New**. In the **New File** task pane, under **New**, click **Blank database**.

2. In the displayed **File New Database** dialog box, click the **Save in arrow**, and then navigate to the folder in which you are storing your projects for this chapter. In the **File name** box, delete any existing text, type **1D_Office_Supplies_Firstname_Lastname** and then in the lower right corner click **Create**. The Office Supplies database is created and the Database window displays with the new database name indicated in the title bar.

3. In the Database window, double-click the command icon **Create table in Design view**. Because you have not yet named or saved this table, the title bar indicates the default name of *Table1*. The insertion point is blinking in the first **Field Name** box.

4. In the first **Field Name** box, type **Inventory #** and then press  to move the insertion point to the **Data Type** column. Recall that Data Type refers to the rules that you can define for data within a field.

5. Press Tab to accept the default Data Type of **Text**. Press Tab again to move to the next **Field Name** box.

(Project 1D–Office Supplies continues on the next page)

Skill Assessments (continued)

(Project 1D–Office Supplies continued)

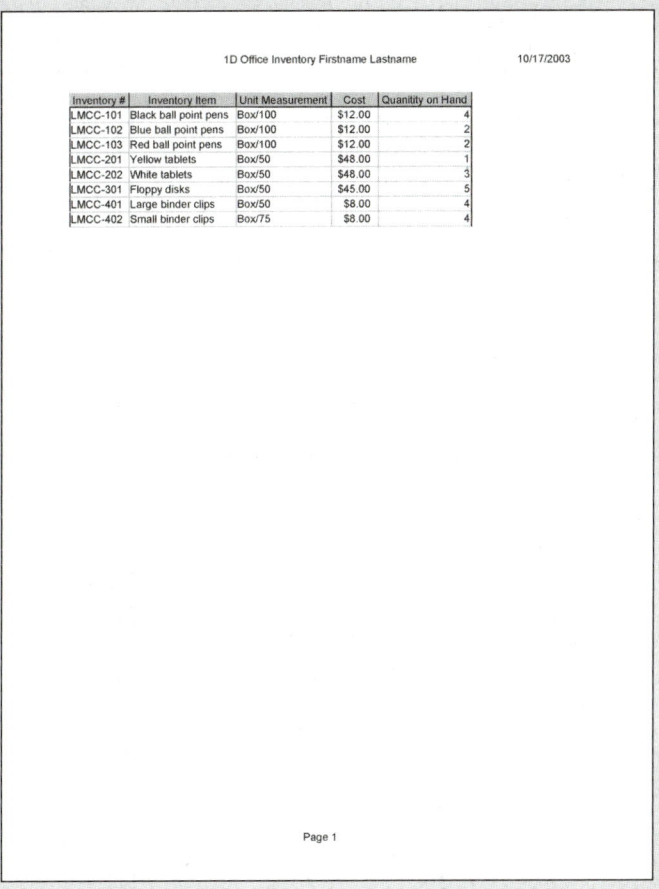

Figure 1.73

6. Use the following information to add the remaining fields to your table. Recall that a description for a field is optional. The descriptions for this table describe the purpose of the corresponding field.

Field Name	Data Type	Description
Inventory Item	Text	
Unit Measurement	Text	Identifies the number of items in a unit
Cost	Currency	Cost per unit
Quantity on Hand	Number	Current number of items available

7. Click in the field name for **Inventory #**. On the toolbar, click the **Primary Key** button to set the **Inventory #** field as the primary key for this table. Within this table, no two items will have the same Inventory number—the Inventory number is a unique identifier. On the Table Design toolbar, click the **View** button to switch to the Datasheet view. When prompted, click **Yes** to save the table.

(Project 1D–Office Supplies continues on the next page)

Skill Assessments (continued)

(Project 1D–Office Supplies continued)

8. In the displayed **Save As** dialog box, in the **Table Name** box, use your own first and last name to type **1D Office Inventory Firstname Lastname** and then click **OK**. The table displays and you can begin to enter records into it.

9. With the table in Datasheet view, be sure your insertion point is in the **Inventory #** column. Type **LMCC-101** and press Tab. Type **Black ball point pens** and press Tab. Type **Box/100** and press Tab. Type **12** in the **Cost** column and press Tab. The dollar sign and the decimal point are inserted for you because a data type of Currency was specified for the Cost field. Type **4** in the Quantity on Hand column and press Enter.

10. Use the following information to add the remaining records to the Inventory table. Press Enter after entering the last record.

Inventory #	Inventory Item	Unit Measurement	Cost	Quantity on Hand
LMCC-102	Blue ball point pens	Box /100	12.00	2
LMCC-103	Red ball point pens	Box/100	12.00	2
LMCC-201	Yellow tablets	Box/50	48.00	1
LMCC-202	White tablets	Box/50	48.00	3
LMCC-301	Floppy disks	Box/50	45.00	5
LMCC-401	Large binder clips	Box/50	8.00	4
LMCC-402	Small binder clips	Box/75	8.00	4

11. Pause the mouse pointer over the gray **Inventory #** column heading, and then click and hold the left mouse button while dragging to the right until all of the columns are selected. With the columns selected, pause your mouse pointer over the vertical line between any of the column headings until the mouse takes the shape of a double-headed arrow, and then double-click. All of the columns are resized to accommodate the widest entry in each column. Recall that you can use this method as a quick way to adjust the widths of several columns at once. Recall also that adjusting the size of columns and rows does not change the data contained in the table's records. It changes only your *view* of the data.

12. Click anywhere in the table to deselect the table. On the Table Datasheet toolbar, click the **Print** button. Because you inserted your name in the table name, it prints in the heading. In the upper right corner of the table window, click the **Close** button to close the table. Click **Yes** to save changes to the layout of the table.

(Project 1D–Office Supplies continues on the next page)

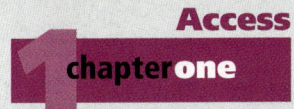

Skill Assessments (continued)

(Project 1D–Office Supplies continued)

13. In the Database window, click the **Close** button to close the Office Supplies database. In the Access window, click the **Close** button to close Access.

End You have completed Project 1D

Project 1E — Recipes

Objectives: *Rename a Database; Start Access, Open an Existing Database, and View Database Objects; Open a Table; Print a Table; Edit Records in a Table; Navigate to Records in a Table; and Close and Save a Database.*

In the following Skill Assessment, you will open and edit an existing database that stores information about the recipes that the Computer Club at Lake Michigan City College prepares for social events. Your completed database objects will look like the ones shown in Figure 1.74. You will save the database as *1E_Recipes_Firstname_Lastname* in the folder designated for this chapter.

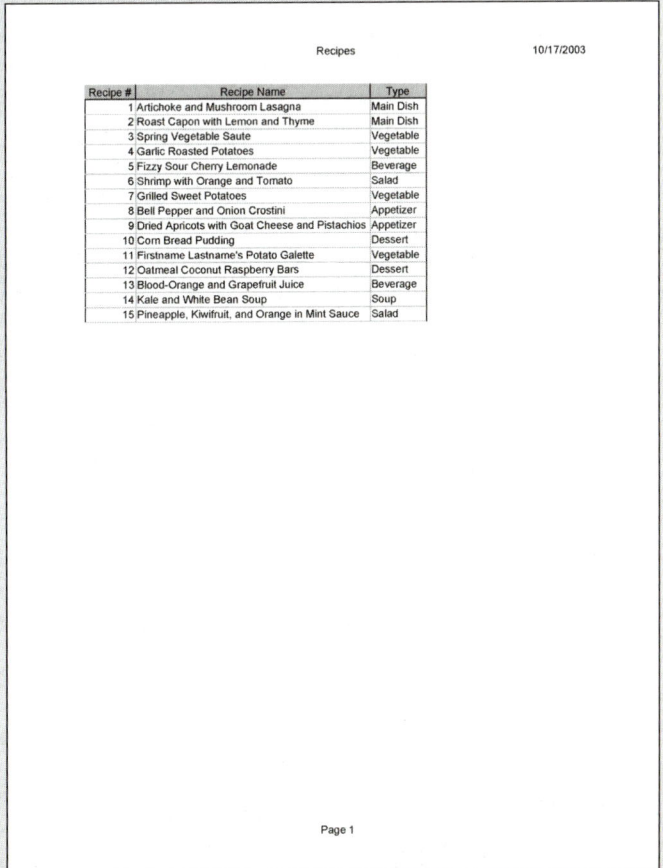

Figure 1.74

(Project 1E–Recipes continues on the next page)

Project 1E: Recipes | **Access** 805

Skill Assessments (continued)

(Project 1E–Recipes continued)

1. Open **My Computer** and navigate to the student files that accompany this textbook. Click once to select the file **a01E_recipes**. Move the mouse pointer over the selected file name, right-click, and on the displayed shortcut menu, click **Copy**.

2. Navigate to the drive and folder where you will be storing your projects for this chapter. On the menu bar, click **Edit** and then click **Paste**. The database file is copied to your folder and is selected. Move your mouse pointer over the selected file name, right-click to display the shortcut menu, and then click **Rename**. Using your own first and last name, type **1E_Recipes_Firstname_Lastname**

3. Press [Enter] to save the new file name. If the Confirm File Rename message displays, click **Yes**. Be sure that the file name is still selected (highlighted), point to the file name, and right-click to display the shortcut menu. On the displayed shortcut menu, click **Properties**.

4. In the lower portion of the displayed dialog box, click to clear the check mark from the **Read-only** check box. Click **OK** to close the dialog box. Close **My Computer** and start Access.

5. On the menu bar, click **File** and then click **Open**. In the displayed dialog box, click the **Look in arrow**, and then navigate to the location where you are storing your projects for this chapter. Locate the database file that you saved and renamed with your name in Step 2. Click the database file once to select it, and then, in the lower right corner, click the **Open** button. Alternatively, you can double-click the name of the database, and it will open.

6. If necessary, in the Database window on the Objects bar, click **Tables** to display a list of tables in this database. To the right of the Objects bar, double-click the **Recipes** table to open the table in Datasheet view.

7. In **record #5**, click in the **Type** field and delete the existing text. Type **Beverage** and then press [Enter]. In **record #11**, click to place the insertion point in front of *Potato*. Use your own information to type **Firstname Lastname's** and then press [Spacebar] once.

8. On the Table Datasheet toolbar, click the **Print** button. In the upper right corner of the table window, click the **Close** button to close the table. On the title bar of the Access window, click the **Close** button to close Access.

 You have completed Project 1E

Performance Assessments

Project 1F — CD Log

Objectives: *Create a New Database, Create a New Table, Create a Primary Key and Add Records to a Table, Close and Save a Table, Sort Records, Print a Table, and Close and Save a Database.*

In the following Performance Assessment, you will create a new database and a new table to store information about the CD collection for the Music Department at Lake Michigan City College. Your completed table will look like the one shown in Figure 1.75. You will save your database as *1F_CDlog_Firstname_Lastname*.

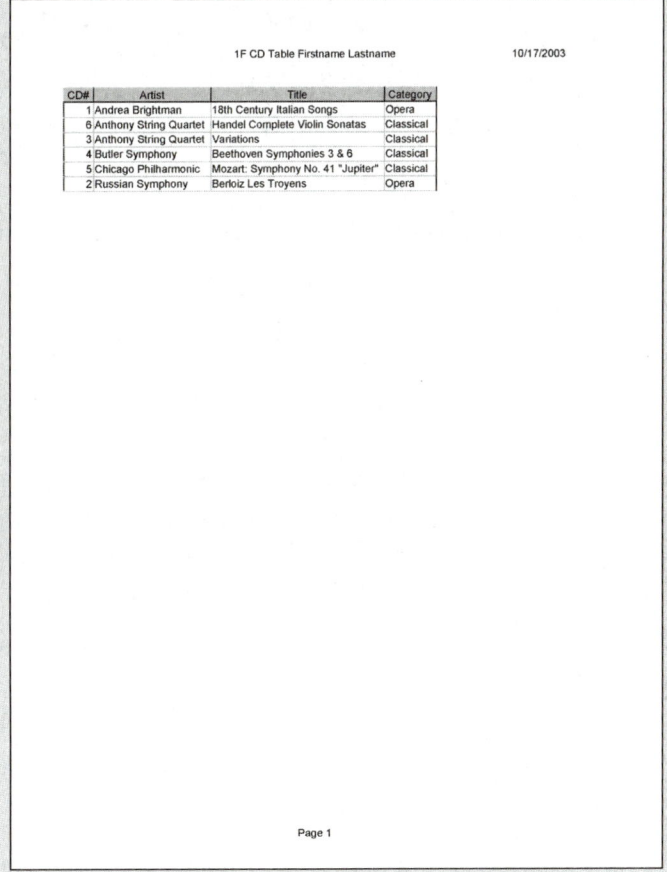

Figure 1.75

(Project 1F–CD Log continues on the next page)

Performance Assessments (continued)

(Project 1F–CD Log continued)

1. Start Access. Display the **New File** task pane and click **Blank database**. In the **File New Database** dialog box, navigate to the drive and folder where you are storing your projects for this chapter. Name the file **1F_CDlog_Firstname_Lastname**

2. In the Database window, double-click the command icon **Create table in Design view**. Use the following information to create the fields for the table.

Field Name	Data Type	Description
CD#	AutoNumber	
Artist	Text	
Title	Text	
Category	Text	Music Classification

3. Because two CDs could have the same title, you will use the **AutoNumber** field that you created as the primary key. Click in the field name for **CD#** and then click the **Primary Key** button. Click the **View** button to switch to the Datasheet view of the table.

4. When prompted, save the table by typing **1F CD Table Firstname Lastname** in the **Save As** dialog box and then click **OK**.

5. With the table open in the Datasheet view, press Tab to move to the **Artist** field and type the first artist in the following table. As you type in the **Artist** field, Access fills in the AutoNumber to assign a unique number to each CD. You do not need to type the numbers. Use the following information to create the records.

CD#	Artist	Title	Category
1	Andrea Brightman	18th Century Italian Songs	Opera
2	Russian Symphony	Berlioz Les Troyens	Opera
3	Anthony String Quartet	Variations	Classical
4	Butler Symphony	Beethoven Symphonies 3 & 6	Classical
5	Chicago Philharmonic	Mozart: Symphony No. 41 "Jupiter"	Classical
6	Anthony String Quartet	Handel Complete Violin Sonatas	Classical

(Project 1F–CD Log continues on the next page)

Access chapter one

Performance Assessments (continued)

(Project 1F–CD Log continued)

6. Select all of the columns in the table. Display the **Format** menu, click **Column Width**, and in the displayed **Column Width** dialog box, click **Best Fit**. All of the columns are resized to accommodate the widest entry in each column.

7. Click anywhere in the table to deselect it. Click the **Artist** column heading to select the column, press and hold , and then click the **Title** column heading. On the toolbar, click the **Sort Ascending** button. The table is sorted by Artist, and within Artist, it is further sorted by title.

8. On the Table Datasheet toolbar, click the **Print** button. Close the table, save any changes, and then close Access.

End You have completed Project 1F

Project 1G — Employees

Objectives: *Rename a Database; Start Access, Open an Existing Database, and View Database Objects; Create a Primary Key and Add Records to a Table; Close and Save a Table; Open a Table; Modify the Table Design; and Print a Table.*

In the following Performance Assessment, you will open an existing database that stores employee information for Lake Michigan City College, add a record, and then work with other objects in the database. The first page of your completed database object will look similar to Figure 1.76. You will rename the database as *1G_Employees_Firstname_Lastname*.

1. Use the Windows My Computer tool to navigate to your student files and then select the file **a01G_Employees**. Copy the file to the drive and folder where you are storing your projects for this chapter. Using your own information, rename the file
1G_Employees_Firstname_Lastname

2. Remove the Read-only attribute from the renamed file so that you can make changes to the database. Start Access.

3. Open your **1G_Employees** database that you renamed in Step 1. Open the **Employees** table and switch to Design view. Set the primary key for this table to **ID**. This is the employee ID number, which uniquely identifies each employee.

(Project 1G–Employees continues on the next page)

Project 1G: Employees | **Access** 809

Access chapter one

Performance Assessments (continued)

(Project 1G–Employees continued)

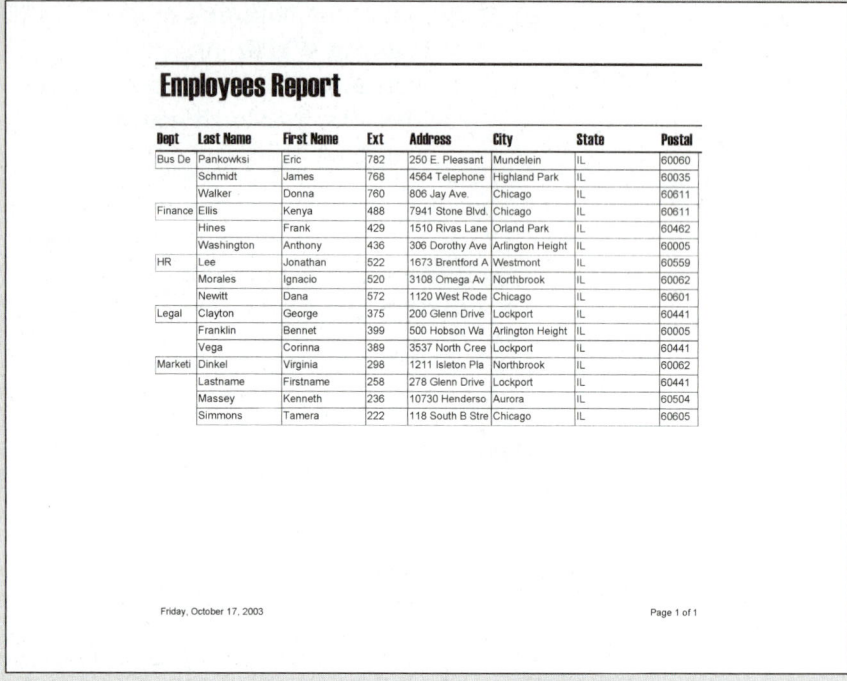

Figure 1.76

4. Switch to the Datasheet view of the table and save changes to the table when prompted to do so. Add the following record to the table, using your own first and last name.

ID	5588
First Name	Your First Name
Last Name	Your Last Name
Dept	Marketing
Ext	258
Address	278 Glenn Drive
City	Lockport
State	IL
Postal Code	60441
Phone	815-555-0365

5. Use any method to resize all of the columns to accommodate their data and then close the table. On the Objects bar, click **Queries** and open the **Marketing Query**. Because you added your name as a member of the Marketing Department, you should see your record among the other employees in the Marketing Department.

(Project 1G–Employees continues on the next page)

Access chapter one
Performance Assessments (continued)

(Project 1G–Employees continued)

6. Close the query. On the Objects bar, click the **Reports** button and open the **Employees Report**. Display the **File** menu, and then click **Page Setup**. In the **Page Setup** dialog box, click the **Page tab**, and then click the **Landscape** option button so that the report prints in Landscape orientation. Print the report. Notice that your name will print as one of the employees in the Marketing Department. Close the report and then close the database. Close Access.

 End You have completed Project 1G

Project 1H — DL Courses

Objectives: *Create a New Database, Create a New Table, Create a Primary Key and Add Records to a Table, Modify the Table Design, Close and Save a Table, Print a Table, and Close and Save a Database.*

In the following Performance Assessment, you will create a new database and a new table to store information about Distance Learning courses at Lake Michigan City College. Your completed table will look similar to the one shown in Figure 1.77. You will save your database as 1H_DLcourses_Firstname_Lastname.

1. Start Access and display the **New File** task pane. Click **Blank database**. Navigate to the drive and folder where you are storing your projects for this chapter. In the **File name** box, type **1H_DLcourses_Firstname_Lastname** as the name for your database, and then click **Create**.

2. Use the following information to create a table in Design view and to add fields to the table.

Field Name	Data Type	Description
Course Number	Text	
Course Name	Text	
Credit Hours	Number	Credit hours for this course

3. Switch to the Datasheet view of the table. Using your own first and last name, save the table as **1H DLcourses Firstname Lastname** and then click **OK**. When prompted if you would like to add a primary key now, click **No**.

(Project 1H–DL Courses continues on the next page)

Project 1H: DL Courses | **Access** 811

Performance Assessments (continued)

(Project 1H–DL Courses continued)

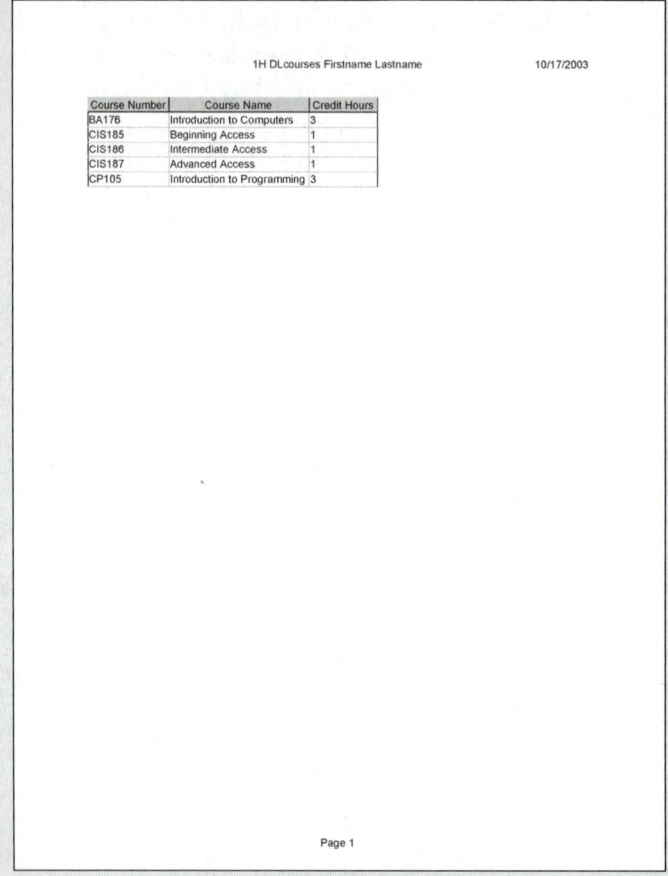

Figure 1.77

4. Using the following information, fill in the records for the DLcourses table.

Course Number	Course Name	Credit Hours
BA176	Introduction to Computers	3
CP105	Introduction to Programming	3
CIS185	Beginning Access	1
CIS186	Intermediate Access	1
CIS187	Advanced Access	1

5. Switch to the Design view of the table. Set the **Course Number** field as the primary key for this table. Click the **View** button to switch to the Datasheet view of the table. Save the table when prompted. Verify that the records are sorted by the primary key.

6. Use any method to resize the column widths to accommodate their data. Print and then close the table, saving any changes if prompted to do so. Close the database and close Access.

 You have completed Project 1H

Mastery Assessments

Project 1I—Suppliers

Objectives: *Create a New Database, Create a New Table, Create a Primary Key and Add Records to a Table, Close and Save a Table, Modify the Table Design, Sort Records, Navigate to Records in a Table, and Close and Save a Database.*

In the following Mastery Assessment, you will create a new database and a new table to store supplier information for Lake Michigan City College. Your completed table will look like the one shown in Figure 1.78. You will save your database as *1I_LMCCsuppliers_Firstname_Lastname*.

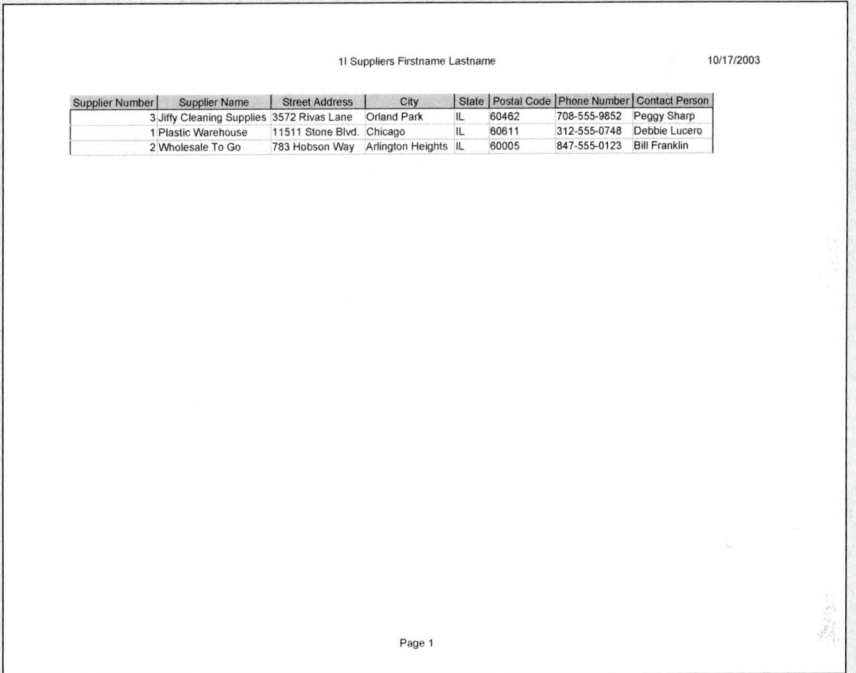

Figure 1.78

(**Project 1I**–Suppliers continues on the next page)

Mastery Assessments (continued)

Project 1I–Suppliers continued)

1. Start Access. In your Project folder, create a new database and name it **1I_LMCCsuppliers_Firstname_Lastname**

2. Use the following information to create a new table.

Field Name	Data Type	Description
Supplier Number	AutoNumber	
Supplier Name	Text	
Street Address	Text	
City	Text	
State	Text	
Postal Code	Text	
Phone Number	Text	
Contact Person	Text	Main contact

3. Choose the **Supplier Number** as the primary key for this table. Switch to Datasheet view, and then, using your own information, save the table as **1I Suppliers Firstname Lastname** and then add the following records to the table.

Supplier Number	Supplier Name	Street Address	City	State	Postal Code	Phone Number	Contact Person
1	Plastic Warehouse	11511 Stone Blvd.	Chicago	IL	60611	312-555-0748	Debbie Lucero
2	Wholesale To Go	783 Hobson Way	Arlington Heights	IL	60005	847-555-0123	Bill Franklin
3	Jiffy Cleaning Supplies	3572 Rivas Lane	Orland Park	IL	60462	708-555-9852	Peggy Sharp

4. Resize all of the columns to accommodate their data. Sort the table alphabetically by Supplier Name. Display the **Page Setup** dialog box and change the page orientation to **Landscape**. Print and then close the table. Close the database and then close Access.

End You have completed Project 1I

Mastery Assessments (continued)

Project 1J — Expenses

Objectives: *Rename a Database; Start Access, Open an Existing Database, and View Database Objects; Modify the Table Design; Print a Table; Edit Records in a Table; Navigate to Records in a Table; and Close and Save a Database.*

In the following Mastery Assessment, you will open an existing database and modify items in the database that stores information about the expenses of the Computer Club at Lake Michigan City College. Your completed database object will look similar to the one shown in Figure 1.79. You will rename the database as *1J_Expenses_Firstname_Lastname*.

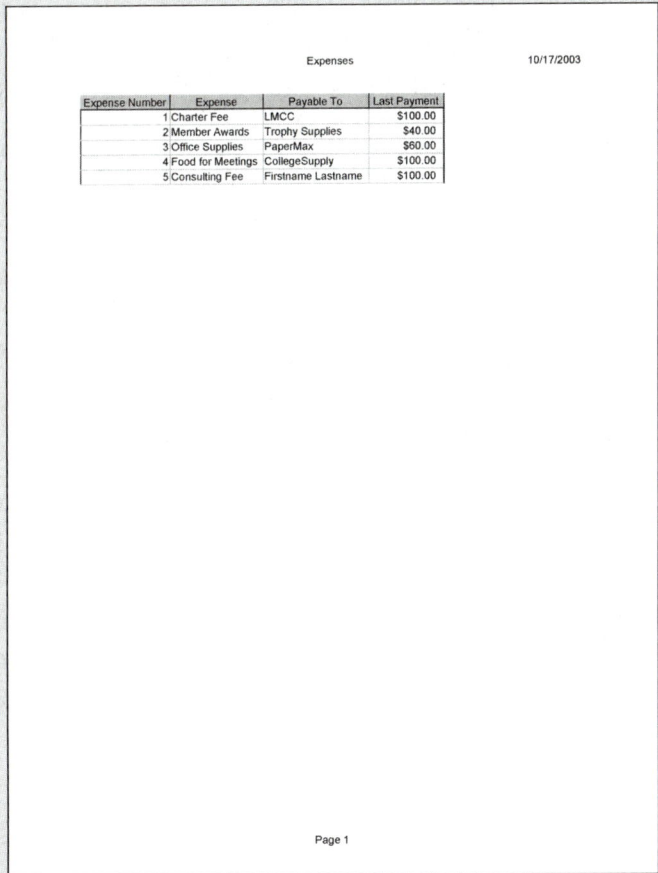

Figure 1.79

(**Project 1J**–Expenses continues on the next page)

Mastery Assessments (continued)

Project 1J–Expenses continued)

1. Copy the student file **a01J_Expenses** to the drive and folder where you are storing your projects for this chapter. Rename the database as **1J_Expenses_Firstname_Lastname** and remove the Read-only attribute.

2. Start Access and open the database you renamed in Step 1. Open the **Expenses** table and make the following changes to the table:

   Change the *Expense ID* field to **Expense Number**

   Change the primary key for the table to **Expense Number**

   For the *Member Awards* expense record, change the information in the Payable To column from *LMCC* to **Trophy Supplies**

3. Add the following record using your own name:

Expense Number	Expense	Payable To	Last Payment
AutoNumber	Consulting Fee	Firstname Lastname	100

4. Resize the fields in the table to accommodate their data. Print and then close the table, saving any changes if prompted to do so. Close the database and close Access.

End You have completed Project 1J

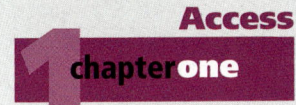

Problem Solving

Project 1K — Video Store

Objectives: *Create a New Database, Create a New Table, Create a Primary Key and Add Records to a Table, Modify the Table Design, Close and Save a Table, Print a Table, and Close and Save a Database.*

Lake Michigan City College has a small video rental shop on campus that rents videos and DVDs to students, staff, and faculty of the college. Create a database that will store information about the movie rentals such as customer names and the names of movies in the inventory. This database should have at least two tables: one for customers and another for the inventory of videos that are available to rent. Create a new database with an appropriate name for the video rental store and add two tables as described above to the database. In each of the tables, add the fields that you think should be included in each of these tables. Designate one field in each table as the primary key. Print your tables.

 You have completed Project 1K

Project 1L — Fix It

Objectives: *Rename a Database; Start Access, Open an Existing Database, and View Database Objects; Create a Primary Key and Add Records to a Table; Open a Table; Modify the Table Design; and Close and Save a Database.*

The Business Division at Lake Michigan City College needs to correct some errors in a student database. Copy the student file a01L_FixIt to your storage location and rename it **1L_FixIt_Firstname_Lastname**. Clear the Read-only property and then open the database. View the FixIt table in this database. Think about the way the data is arranged in the table. Based on the databases you have worked with in this chapter, identify at least four ways this table could be improved. Then make your suggested changes to this database.

 You have completed Project 1L

Project 1L: Fix It | **Access**   817

On the Internet

Databases and Today's Industries

Most of the world's information is stored in some type of database. Databases play a large role in industries today. Their expansive applications have made databases an integral part of business in the current marketplace.

Go online and perform a search to identify the current trends involving databases and the different career paths that include database training as part of their job descriptions.

GO! with Help

Searching Access Help

The Access Help system is extensive and can help you as you work. In this exercise, you will view information about getting help as you work in Access.

1. Start Access. In the **Type a question for help** box, type **Printing a table** and then press Enter.

2. In the displayed **Search Results** task pane, click the result—**Print a record, datasheet, or database object**. Maximize the displayed window, and at the top of the window, click the **Show All** button. Scroll through and read about printing database objects in Access.

3. If you want, print a copy of the information by clicking the printer button at the top of the window.

4. Close the Microsoft Access Help window, then close Access.

Access 2003

chapter two

Forms and Reports

In this chapter you will: complete these projects and practice these skills.

Project 2A
Creating Forms

Objectives
- View and Navigate to Records with a Form
- Create an AutoForm
- Save and Close an AutoForm
- Use a Form to Add Records to and Delete Records from a Table

Project 2B
Creating Forms and Reports

Objectives
- Create a Form with the Form Wizard
- Modify a Form
- Create a Report with the Report Wizard
- Save a Report
- Modify the Design of a Report
- Print a Report

Lake Michigan City College

Lake Michigan City College is located along the lakefront of Chicago—one of the nation's most exciting cities. The college serves its large and diverse student body and makes positive contributions to the community through relevant curricula, partnerships with businesses and nonprofit organizations, and learning experiences that allow students to be full participants in the global community. The college offers three associate degrees in 20 academic areas, adult education programs, and continuing education offerings on campus, at satellite locations, and online.

© Getty Images, Inc.

Forms and Reports

You can both enter and view database information in the database table itself. However, for entering and viewing information, it is usually easier to use an Access form.

Think about having to enter the information from hundreds of paper forms into a database. If the form on the screen matches the pattern of information on the paper form, it will be much easier to enter the new information. Additionally, when using a form, only one record is visible at a time, making data entry easier.

When viewing information, it is also easier to view just one record at a time. For example, your college counselor can look at your college transcript in a nicely laid out form on the screen without seeing the records for dozens of other students at the same time.

Reports in Access summarize the data in a database in a professional-looking manner suitable for printing. The design of a report can be modified so that the final report is laid out in a format that is useful for the person reading it.

In this chapter, you will create and modify both forms and reports for Access databases.

Project 2A Computer Club

In Chapter 1, you saw that two database objects can be used to enter data into a database. You can type data directly into a table in Datasheet view. Recall that tables are the place where the data is stored. You can also type data into a form. A *form* is an organized view of the fields in one or more database tables or queries laid out in a visually appealing format on the screen. For the purpose of entering new records or viewing existing records, forms are generally easier to use than the table itself.

The Computer Club at Lake Michigan City College maintains a database with two tables—the Members table and the Club Events table. In Activities 2.1 through 2.5 you will use an Access form to view and navigate to the records in the Members table. Then, using AutoForm, you will create and save a new form to view and navigate to the records in the Club Events table. Your completed database objects will look similar to Figure 2.1. In addition, you will use the new form to add and delete records in the Club Events table.

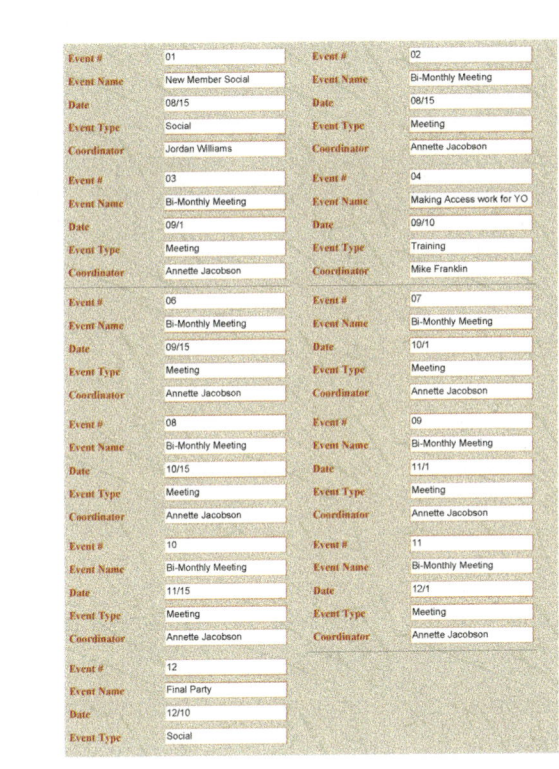

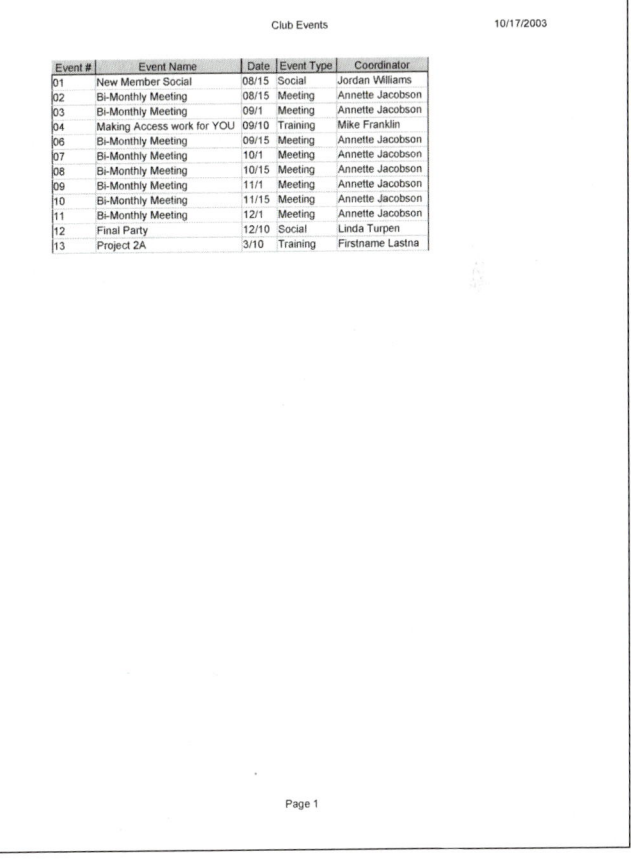

Figure 2.1
Project 2A—Computer Club

Project 2A: Computer Club | **Access** 821

Objective 1
View and Navigate to Records with a Form

Your personal address book would not be useful to you if the addresses or phone numbers in it contained errors. Likewise, a database is useful only if the data in it is accurate. You can see that the process of getting the information into a database is an important one. The individual who performs the *data entry*—typing in the actual data—has a better chance of entering the data accurately if he or she is provided with a data entry tool that assists in preventing data entry errors. Access forms are an example of such a tool.

Because a form can be set to display only one record in the database at a time, a form is also useful to anyone who has the job of viewing information in a database. For example, when you visit the Records office at your college to obtain a transcript, someone displays your record on a screen. For the viewer, it is much easier to look at one record at a time, using a form, than to look at all the student records in the database table.

Activity 2.1 Viewing and Navigating to Records Using a Form

1. Using the skills you practiced in Chapter 1, and using either My Computer or Windows Explorer, create a new folder named Chapter 2 in the location where you will be storing your projects for this chapter.

2. Locate the file **a02A_ComputerClub** from the student files that accompany this text. Copy and paste the file to the Chapter 2 folder you created in Step 1.

3. Using the technique you practiced in Activity 1.1 of Chapter 1, rename the file as **2A_ComputerClub_Firstname_Lastname** and remove the Read-only property from the file if necessary.

4. Close the Windows accessory you are using, either My Computer or Windows Explorer. Start Access and open your **2A_ComputerClub** database.

5. On the Objects bar, click **Forms**.

    To the right of the Objects bar, two command icons for creating a new form display, followed by the Members form that has been created and saved as part of the Computer Club database.

6. Click to select the **Members** form if necessary, and then on the toolbar above the Objects bar, click the **Open** button . Alternatively, double-click the Members form to open it.

    The Members form, in *Form view*, displays the first record in the Members table—the record for *Annette Jacobson*. In Form view, you can modify the information in a record or add a new record, one record at a time.

7 At the lower edge of the form, in the navigation area, click the **Last Record** button. See Figure 2.2.

Record 15—*Ceara Thibodeaux*—displays.

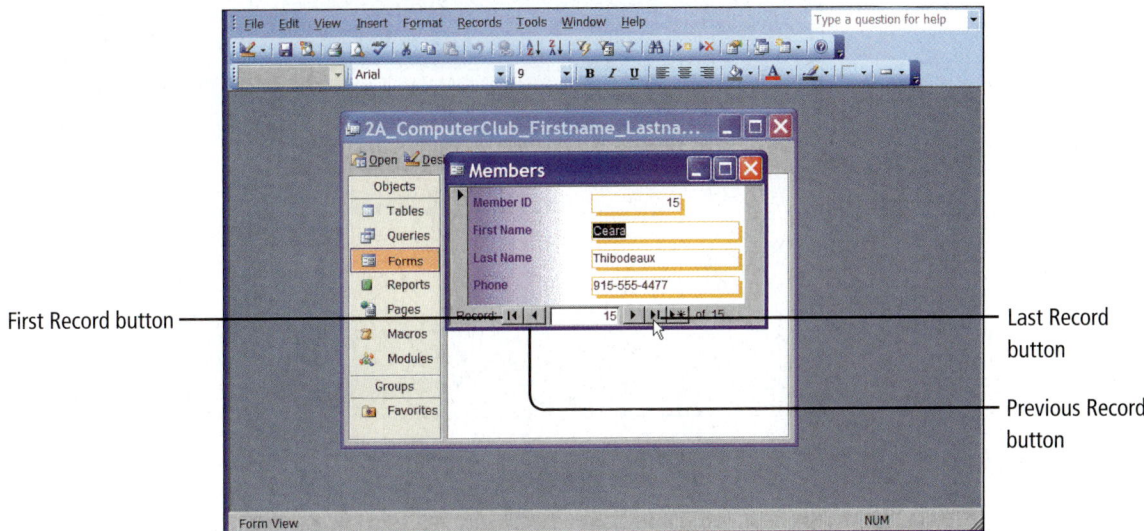

First Record button — Last Record button — Previous Record button

Figure 2.2

8 In the navigation area, click the **Previous Record** button once.

Record 14, the previous record—*Debbie Greggs*—displays.

9 In the navigation area, click the **First Record** button.

Record 1—*Annette Jacobson*—displays.

10 Position your mouse pointer in the navigation area over the number of the current record until the pointer takes the shape of an I-beam. See Figure 2.3.

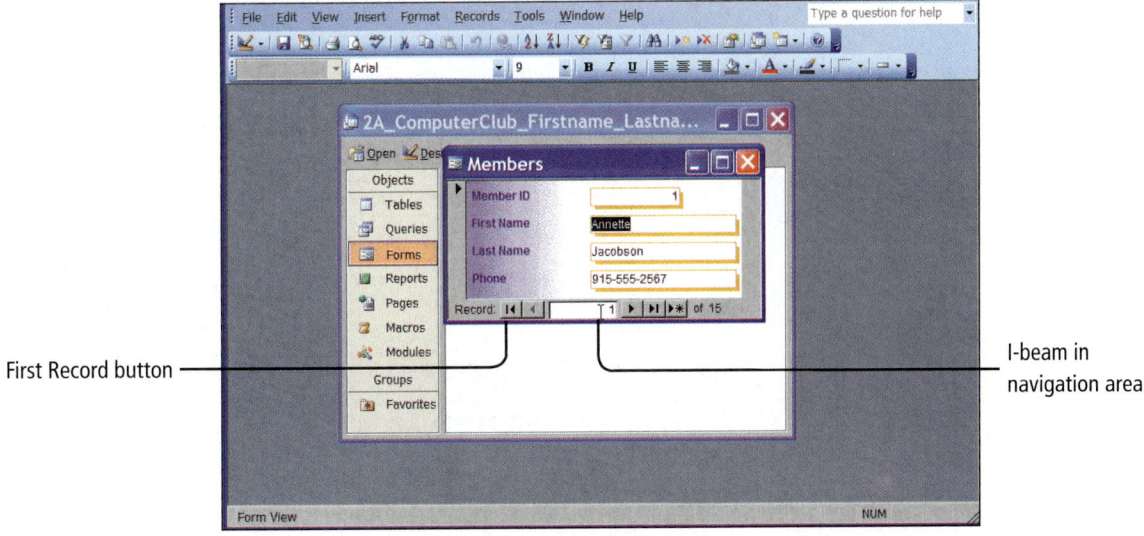

First Record button — I-beam in navigation area

Figure 2.3

Project 2A: Computer Club | **Access** 823

11 Drag your mouse over the number **1** to select it. See Figure 2.4.

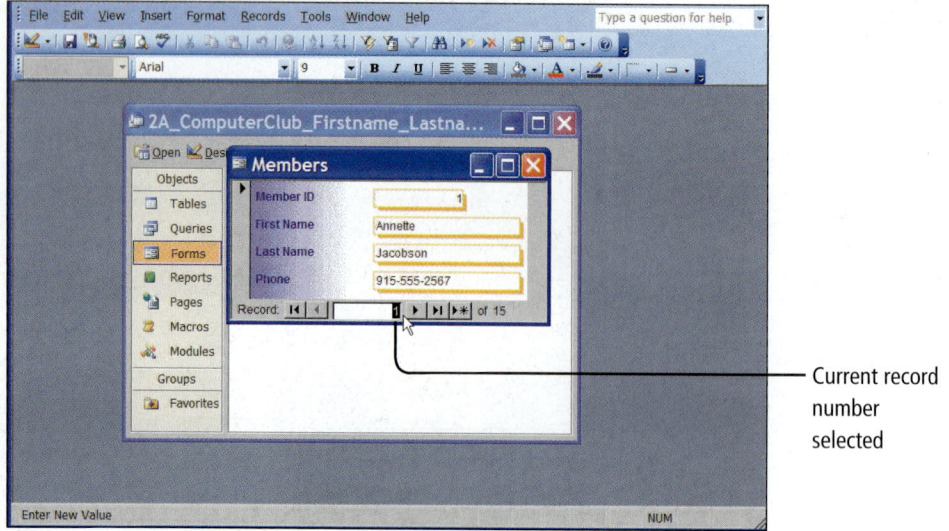

Figure 2.4

12 With the number 1 selected, type **8** and then press Enter.

Record 8 in the Members table—*Kathleen Lightfoot*—displays, as shown in Figure 2.5.

Assuming you know the exact number of the record you want to view, this is a useful method of navigating to a record when there is a large number of records to navigate through.

Use the navigation buttons—Next Record, Last Record, Previous Record, First Record—to jump to specific records in a database table. Use the New Record button to move to the end of the database table for the purpose of entering a new record. You will do this in a later activity.

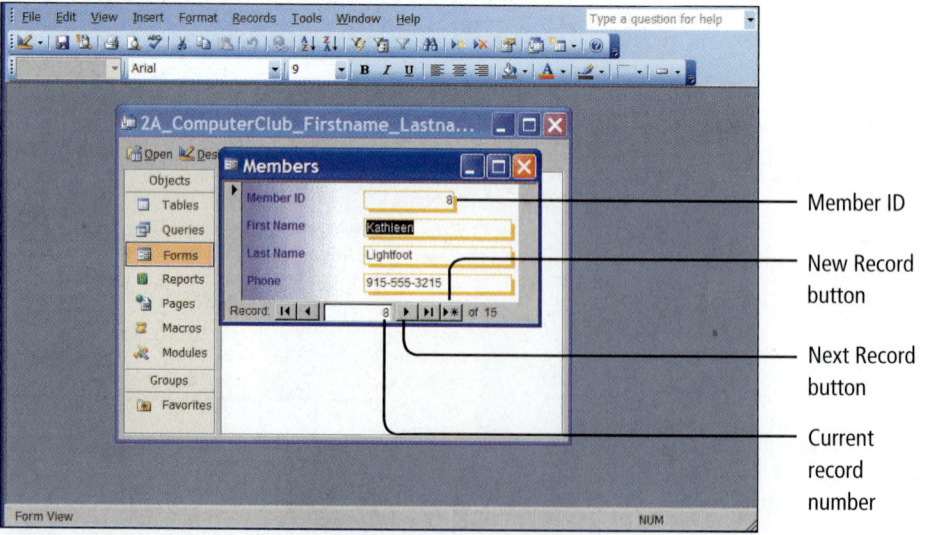

Figure 2.5

13 In the upper right corner of the **Members** form, click the **Close** button to close the form.

824 Access | Chapter 2: Forms and Reports

Objective 2
Create an AutoForm

AutoForm is a feature that creates a form for an existing database table. AutoForm incorporates all the information, both the field names and the individual records, from an existing table and then creates the form for you.

Activity 2.2 Creating an AutoForm

1 On the Objects bar, verify that **Forms** is selected. Above the Objects bar, locate and then click the **New** button.

The New Form dialog box displays as shown in Figure 2.6. The dialog box lists a variety of form types that can be created with a ***wizard***, an Access feature that walks you step by step through a process by having you answer questions.

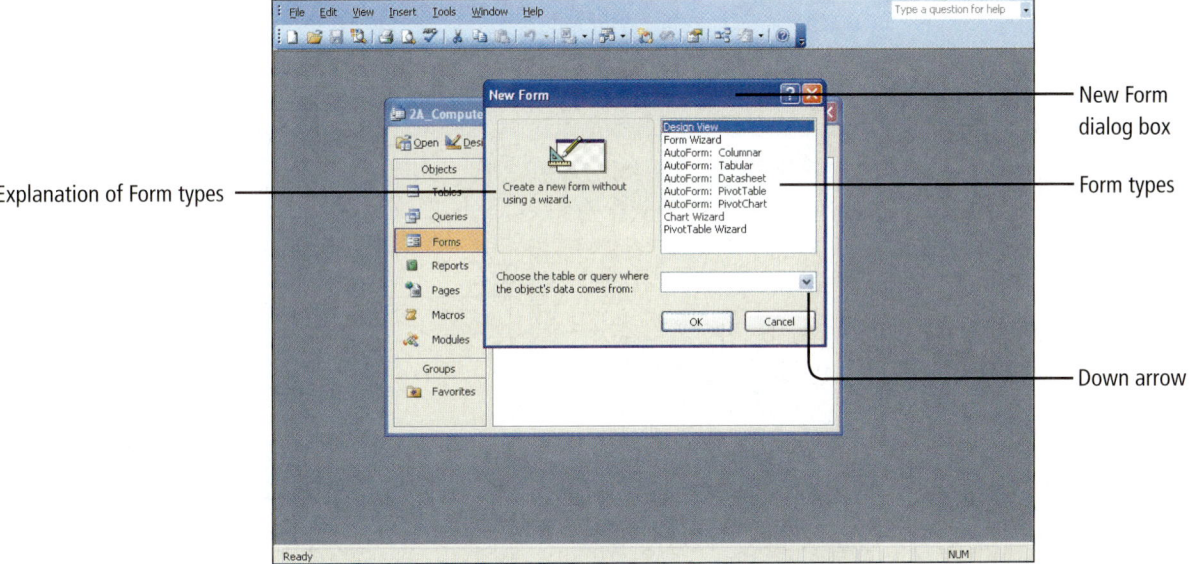

Figure 2.6

2 On the right side of the displayed dialog box, click **AutoForm: Datasheet** and then read the explanation in the box to the left. Then, on the displayed list, click **Chart Wizard** and read the explanation in the box to the left.

As you progress in your study of Access, you will use many of the New Form wizards, and you can see that Access provides explanations for each one.

3 On the displayed list, click **AutoForm: Columnar** and then read the explanation to the left.

The Columnar format displays records in a form one at a time in a column format.

Project 2A: Computer Club | **Access** 825

4 In the text box to the right of *Choose the table or query where the object's data comes from:* click the **down arrow**.

A list of available tables and queries for this database displays. An AutoForm can be created using the information in either a table or a query. Recall that a query contains only those records that meet specified criteria.

5 From the displayed list, click **Club Events** and then click **OK**. Compare your screen to Figure 2.7.

A new form, based on the fields and records in the Club Events table, is created and displays on your screen. Notice that all five field names in the table are shown and the first record, Event #01, is displayed.

Depending on previous use of the computer at which you are working, your form may have a different background color. The various Form Wizards apply different backgrounds, and Access will apply the most recently used background. The background color will not affect the way the form works.

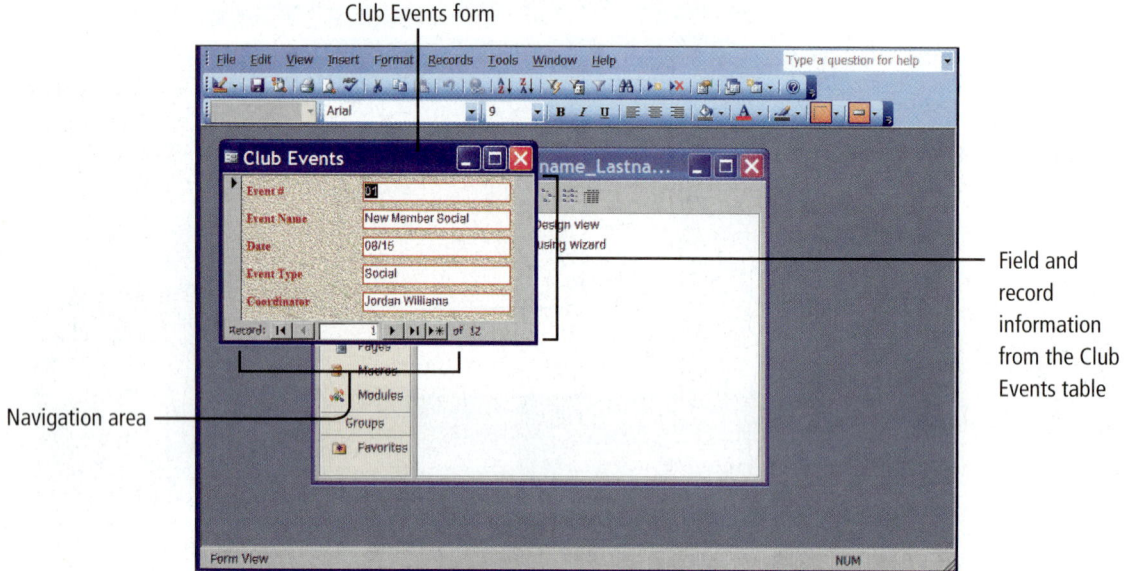

Figure 2.7

6 Click several of the navigation buttons to view the records in the form. All of the records in the Club Events table are available for viewing.

826   Access | Chapter 2: Forms and Reports

Objective 3
Save and Close an AutoForm

Because this form will be convenient for people who need to enter new data into the Club Events table, and for people who need to look up information about various club events, you will want to save the form for future use. When you close a form, you will be asked to save the changes.

Activity 2.3 Saving and Closing an AutoForm

1 In the upper right corner of the **Club Events** form, click the **Close** button ⊠.

Because you have not previously named or saved this form, a message displays asking you if you want to save the changes to the design of form "Form1."

2 Click **Yes**.

The Save As dialog box displays.

3 In the **Form Name** box, accept the default form name of *Club Events* by clicking **OK**.

The form is saved and closed. The new form name, *Club Events*, displays in the Database window. See Figure 2.8. The default name of a form created in this manner is the name of the table upon which the form was based.

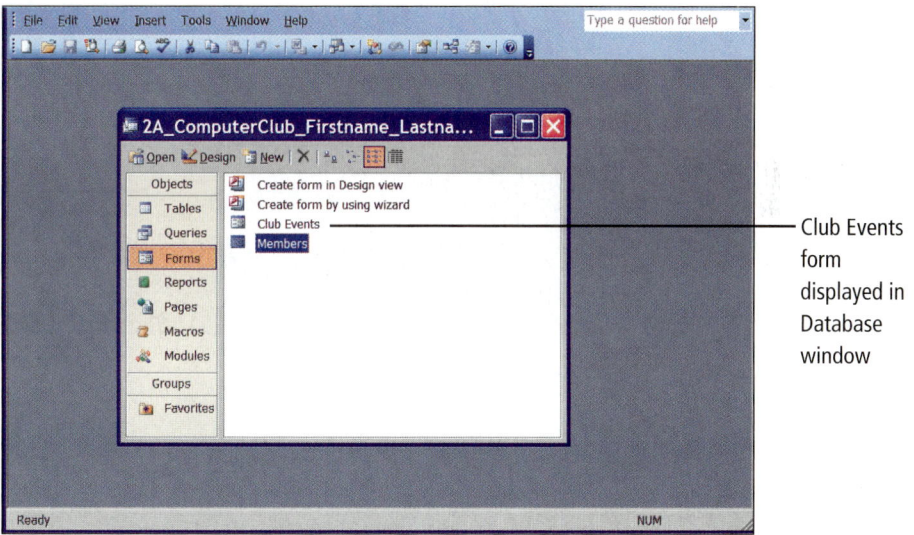

Club Events form displayed in Database window

Figure 2.8

Another Way — Using the Database Toolbar to Create an AutoForm

Use the New Object: AutoForm button.

Access can create an AutoForm directly from the Database toolbar. On the Objects bar, click Tables. Click once on the table that contains the fields and records you would like in your form, then click the New Object: AutoForm button on the Database toolbar.

Objective 4
Use a Form to Add Records to and Delete Records from a Table

Forms and tables are interactive objects in an Access database. That is, when a record is added to a table using a form, the new record is inserted into the corresponding table. The reverse is also true—when a record is added to a table, the new record can be viewed in the corresponding form.

Activity 2.4 Adding Records to a Table Using a Form

1 On the Objects bar, verify that **Forms** is selected and then open the **Club Events** form.

The Club Events form opens in the Form view.

2 In the navigation area of the form, click the **New Record** button.

The fields are cleared and ready to accept a new entry. The record number advances to 13, indicating that this will be the 13th record. See Figure 2.9.

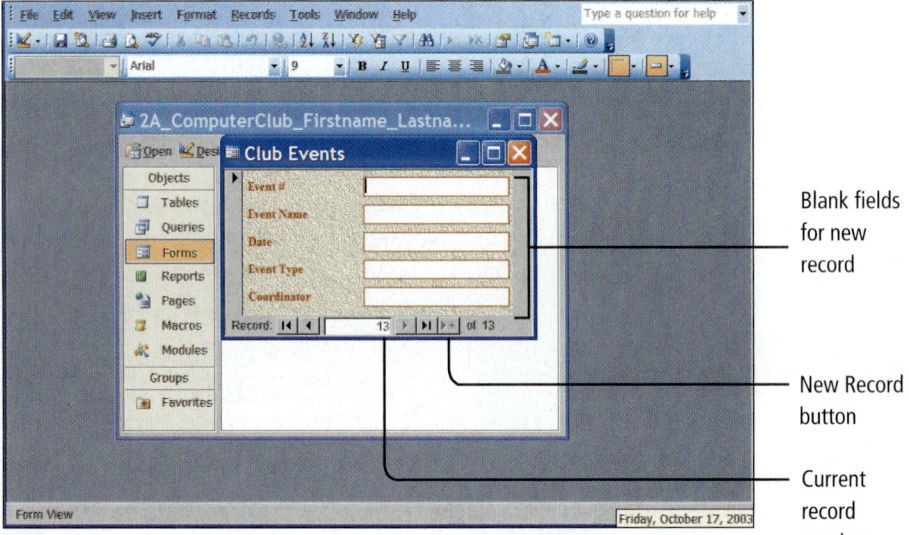

Figure 2.9

3 With the insertion point blinking in the **Event #** box, type **13** and then press Tab. After you start typing, notice that the pencil image displays in the gray bar to the left.

4 In the **Event Name** box, type **Project 2A** and then press Tab.

5 In the **Date** box type **3/10** and then press Tab.

6 In the **Event Type** box, type **Training** and then press Tab.

7 In the **Coordinator** box, using your own information, type **Firstname Lastname**

8 On the title bar of the **Club Events** form, click the **Close** button.

The form closes and the new record is saved and added to the Club Events table.

9 On the Objects bar, click **Tables** and then double-click the **Club Events** table to open it in Datasheet view. Alternatively, select the table name and click the Open button just above the Objects bar.

10 Verify that record 13, the record you just added using the form, displays in the table and that your name is listed as the coordinator.

Recall that tables and forms are interactive objects—the record you added by using the Club Events *form* displays in the Club Events *table*.

11 On the title bar of the table, click the **Close** button to close the table.

12 On the Objects bar, click **Forms**. Right-click the **Club Events** form and then click **Open**.

13 Using the navigation method of your choice (the **Next Record** button, the **Last Record** button, or by typing the record number in the Record box), navigate to record **13**.

Record 13 displays and your name displays in the Coordinator field.

Activity 2.5 Deleting Records from a Table Using a Form

Using a form, you can also delete records from a database table. You should delete records when they are no longer needed in your database. In this activity, you will delete a record in the Club Events table—the record for the Introduction to Outlook event.

1 With the **Club Events** form displayed, navigate to **Event #5**, *Introduction to Outlook*. Then, on the left side of the form, locate the gray bar that contains a right-pointing arrow, as shown in Figure 2.10.

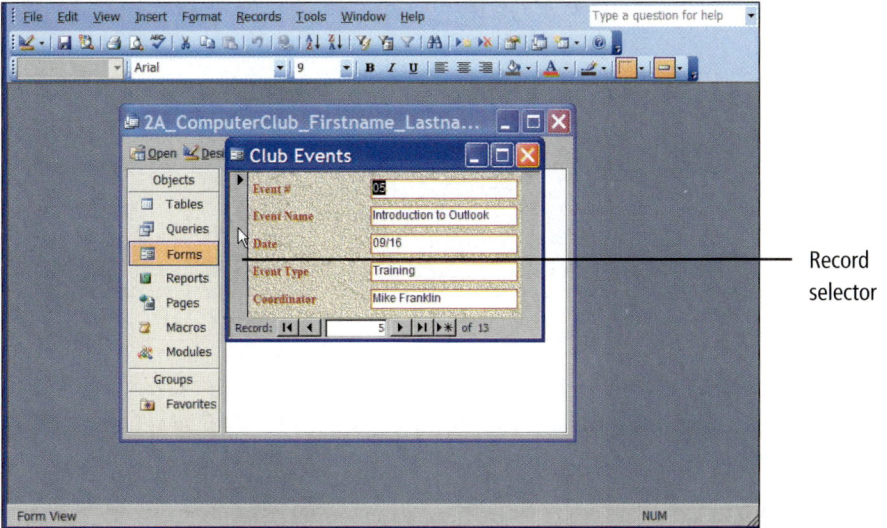

Record selector

Figure 2.10

Project 2A: Computer Club | **Access** 829

2 Click anywhere in the gray bar area.

The gray bar is selected; this area is known as the *record selector*. The record selector in the form is similar to the record selector in a table. The record selector selects an entire record in a form, just as the record selector in a table allows you to select the entire row (record) in the table. When the record selector is highlighted in black—selected—all the fields in the displayed record are selected.

3 On the Form View toolbar, click the **Delete Record** button . Alternatively, press Delete on the keyboard.

A message displays alerting you that you are about to delete a record. If you click Yes and delete the record, you cannot use the Undo button to reverse the action. If you delete a record by mistake, you will have to re-create the record.

4 Click **Yes** to delete the record.

The record is deleted from the Club Events table, reducing the number of records in the table to 12.

5 On the title bar of the **Club Events** form, click the **Close** button to close the form.

6 Be sure the **Club Events** form is selected in the Database window. Display the **File** menu, click **Page Setup**, and in the displayed **Page Setup** dialog box, click the **Columns tab**. See Figure 2.11.

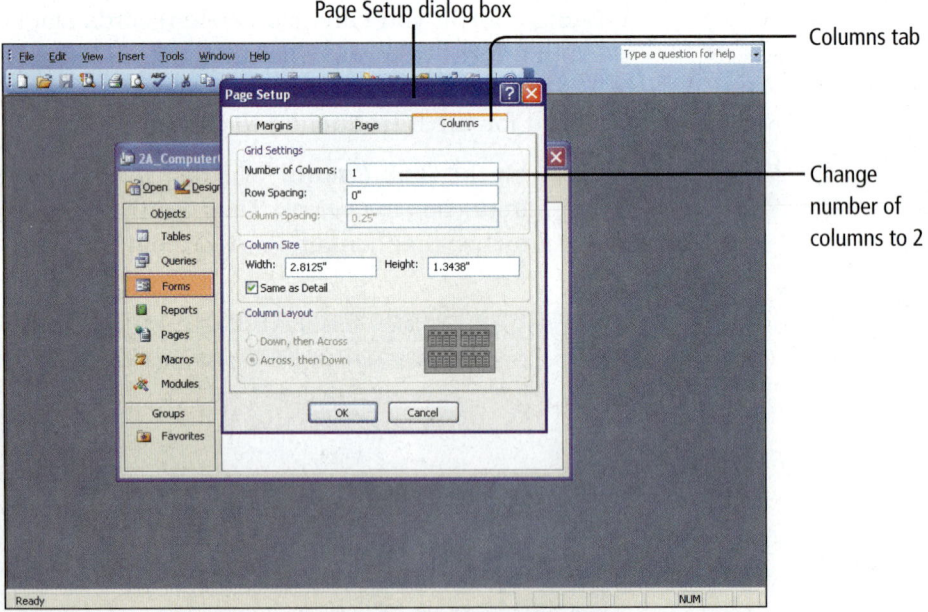

Figure 2.11

7 Under **Grid Settings**, change the **Number of Columns** to **2** and then click **OK**. On the Database toolbar, click the **Print** button.

Each record in the table will print in a newspaper column format. By selecting 2 columns, all the records will print on a single sheet. Recall that record 13 contains your name and that record 5 was deleted. Depending upon previous usage of your computer, your printed format may vary slightly from the one shown in Figure 2.1.

8 On the Objects bar, click **Tables** and then click the **Club Events** table. On the Database toolbar, click the **Print** button. Compare this printout to your forms printout.

You can see that all of the records are contained within both printouts. In the printed table, each record occupies a single row. In the Forms view, each record displays in its own individual form. The current date will print on the table printout.

9 On the title bar of the Database window, click the **Close** button to close the database. On the title bar of the Access window, click the **Close** button to close Access.

End **You have completed Project 2A**

2B Project 2B School

In Project 2A, you used AutoForm to create a form that incorporated all the fields from the table on which it was based. AutoForm creates a form in a simple top-to-bottom layout, with all the fields lined up in a single column. For the individual who is typing in the records, this layout is efficient and easy to use. Whereas AutoForm creates a form using all the fields in the table, and lays them out in a simple column, the **Form Wizard** creates a form in a manner that gives you much more flexibility in the design, layout, and number of fields included.

In Activities 2.6 through 2.15, you will use the Form Wizard to create a form for the Students database at Lake Michigan City College. Then you will modify the form and add a Page Footer to the form. You will also create a report for the Students database. See Figure 2.12.

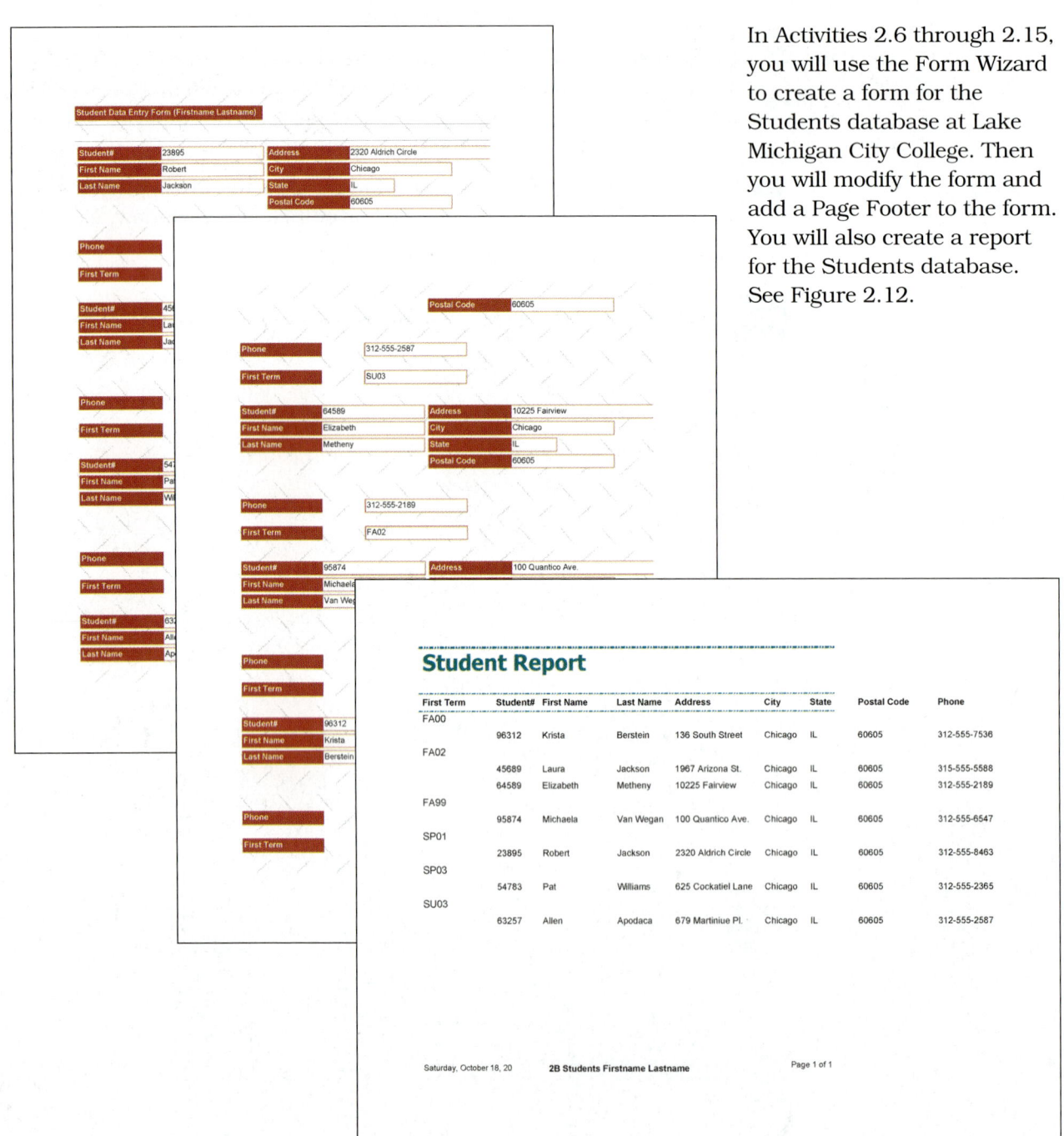

Figure 2.12
Project 2B—School

832 Access | Chapter 2: Forms and Reports

Objective 5
Create a Form with the Form Wizard

Different form layouts are useful for individuals who both view database information with a form and enter information into a database using a form. For example, when the admissions representative at your college displays your information to answer a question for you, it is easier to view the information spread out in a logical pattern across the screen rather than in one long column.

Activity 2.6 Creating a Form Using the Form Wizard

Recall that a wizard is an Access feature that walks you step by step through a process by asking you questions.

1 Using either **My Computer** or **Windows Explorer**, locate the file **a02B_School** from your student files. Copy the file and then paste it into your Chapter 2 folder. Rename the file as **2B_School_Firstname_Lastname** and remove the Read-only attribute. Close the Windows accessory you are using.

2 Start Access and open your **2B_School** database. On the Objects bar, click **Forms**.

3 To the right of the Objects bar, double-click the command icon **Create form by using wizard**. Alternatively, right-click the command icon and click Open on the displayed shortcut menu.

The Form Wizard dialog box displays, as shown in Figure 2.13. The first step is to indicate the table for which you want the wizard to design a form, and then indicate what fields from the table that you want to include in the form.

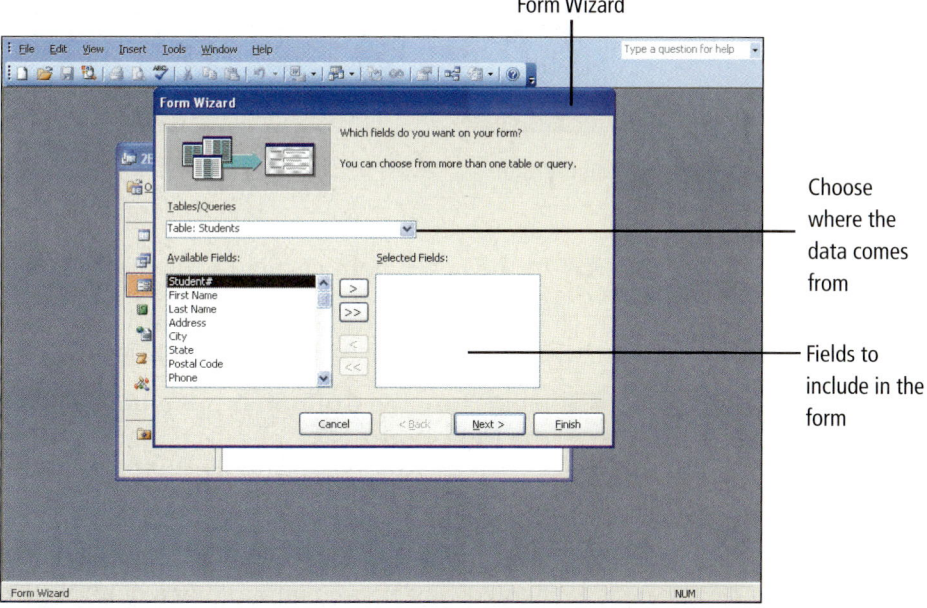

Figure 2.13

4 Under **Tables/Queries**, click the **down arrow**.

A list of tables and queries available for this database displays. Currently, only one object, the Students table, has been created in this database.

5 Click **Table: Students**.

Under Available Fields, a list of the fields in the Students table displays.

6 To the right of the **Available Fields** list, click the **All Fields** button to select all of the fields from the Students table and move them into the Selected Fields column. See Figure 2.14.

This action will place *all* of the fields from the table into the new form. It is also possible to use the **One Field** button to select fields one at a time so that you can select only those fields you want to include in the form.

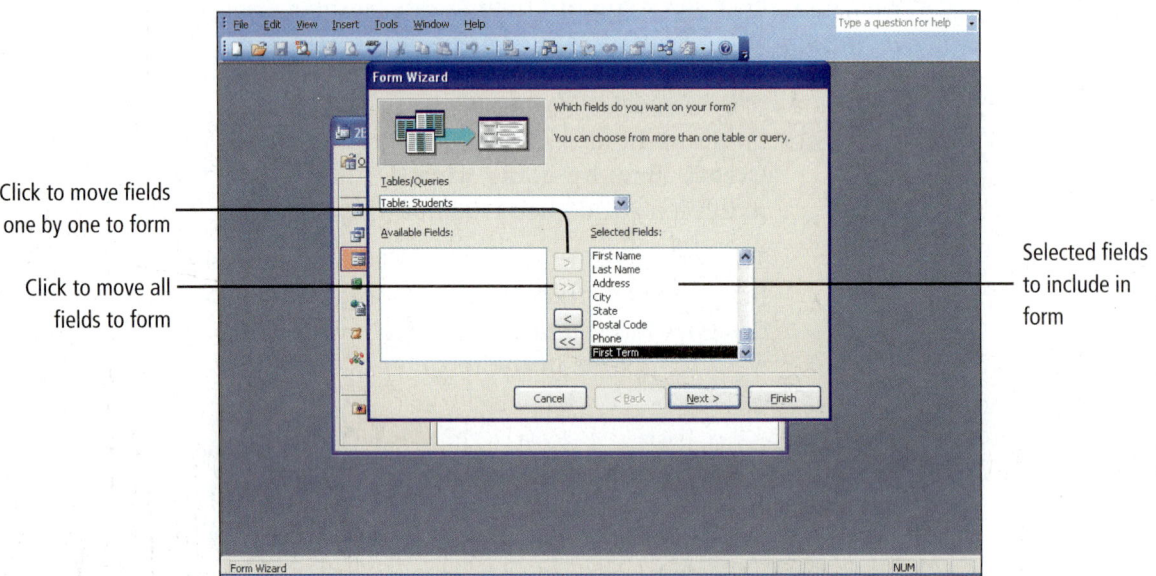

Click to move fields one by one to form

Click to move all fields to form

Selected fields to include in form

Figure 2.14

7 In the lower right corner of the dialog box, click the **Next** button.

The next step in the Form Wizard displays requesting information about the desired layout of your form.

8 Make sure the **Columnar** option button is selected and then click the **Next** button.

The next step in the Form Wizard displays requesting information about the desired style of your form, similar to Figure 2.15. Depending on previous use of your computer, a different style might be highlighted. Styles are combinations of attractive colors and graphics that are applied to the form to make it more visually appealing.

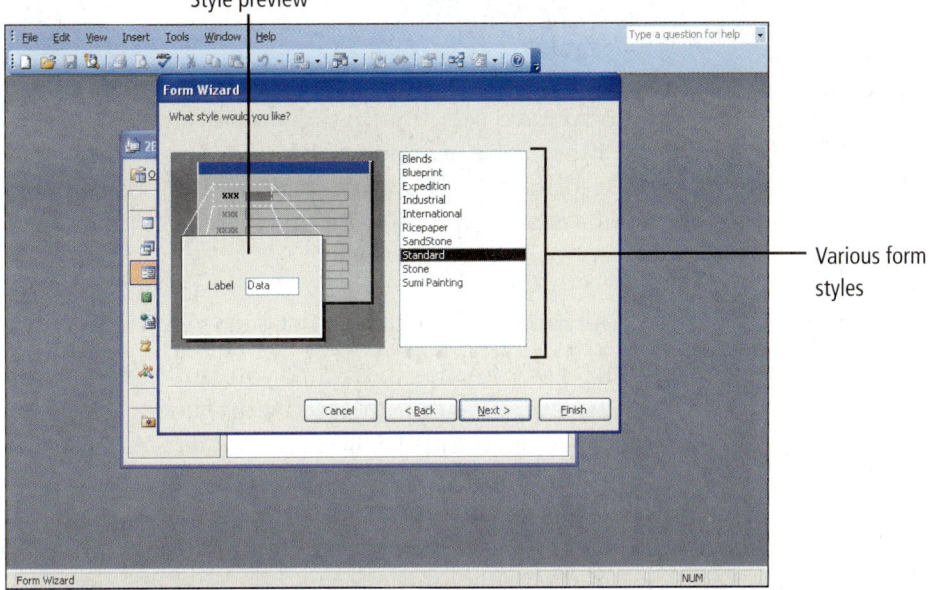

Figure 2.15

9. Click the **Industrial** style, notice the small preview of the style on the left, and then click the **Next** button.

   The final step in the Form Wizard displays, and the default name for the form—*Students*—displays and is highlighted. Access always uses the table name as the default name for the form.

10. With the default name highlighted, press Delete and then, using your own first and last name, type **Students Firstname Lastname**

11. Click the **Finish** button.

    Access creates the form using the responses you provided in the Wizard. The completed form displays in Form view. See Figure 2.16. Leave the form open for the next activity.

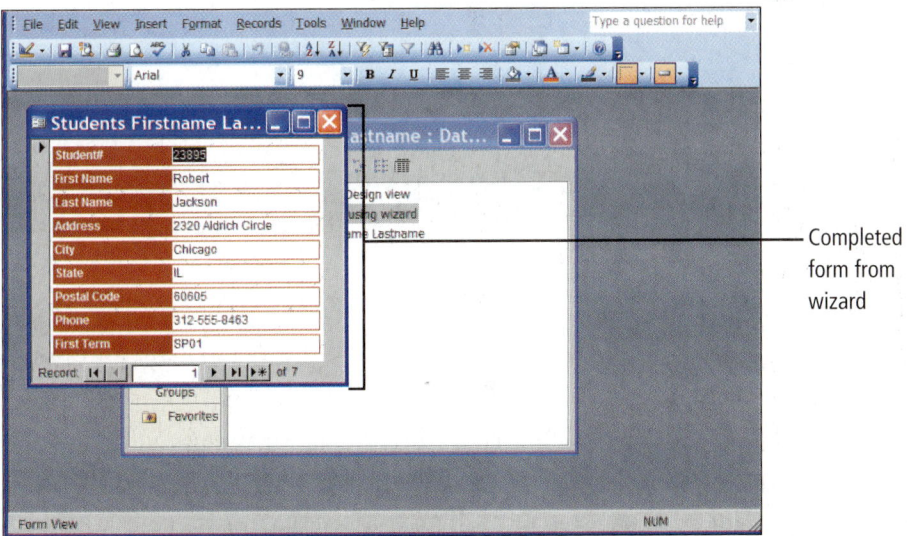

Figure 2.16

Project 2B: School | **Access** 835

Objective 6
Modify a Form

You have seen that it is a quick and easy process to create a form using either the AutoForm method or the Form Wizard. After you have created a form, you may want to change the placement of the fields on the form for easier viewing or more efficient data entry. In the following activities, you will modify a form.

Activity 2.7 Switching Between Views in a Form and Adding a Form Header

Access provides tools that you can use to modify the layout of a form. These tools are available by displaying the form in its Design view. You can open a form in Design view or Form view, depending on what action you want to perform on the form. For example, if you want to view, add, delete, or modify records using a form, use the Form view. If you want to view, add, delete, or modify the field information (such as the placement of the fields on the form), use the Design view.

1 With your **Students** form displayed, on the Form View toolbar, click the **View** button. See Figure 2.17. In a manner similar to viewing tables, the View button will change depending on the current view to allow you to switch back and forth between *Design view* and *Form view*.

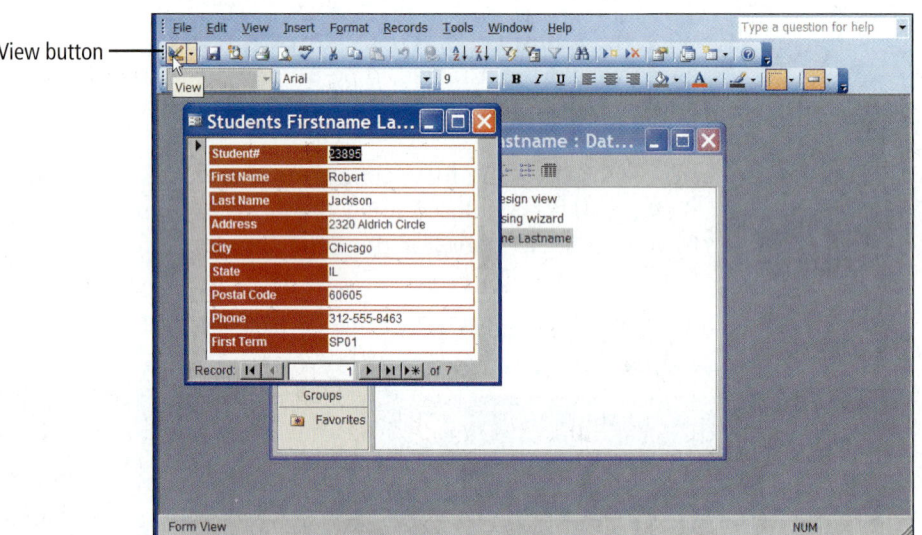

Figure 2.17

The form displays in Design view and the Toolbox toolbar displays, floating on your screen.

Notice that in Design view, you do not see the names of the students—or other information contained in the records. You see only the names of the fields. In this view, you can change the design of the form, such as the location of the fields on the form.

2 If necessary, drag the Toolbox by its title bar into the gray area of your screen. On the form's title bar, click the **Maximize** button.

The Design view of the form is maximized on your screen. This larger view is helpful to view the various sections of the form. See Figure 2.18.

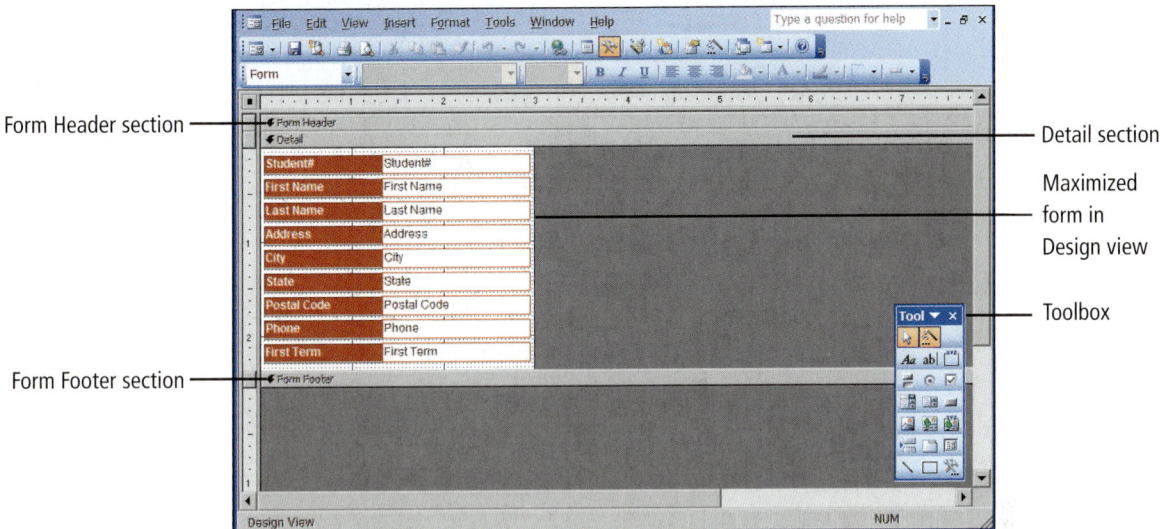

Figure 2.18

3 On your screen, locate the following three sections of the form, as shown in Figure 2.18: the Form Header section, the Detail section, and the Form Footer section.

Information typed into the **Form Header** or **Form Footer** sections displays at the top (header) or bottom (footer) of the form when it is viewed in Form view or when the form is printed. For example, on a form that displays transcript information for students, the form header could indicate *Official Transcript* and the form footer could indicate the name of the college. The **Detail** section contains the fields and records that display in the form. The small dots behind the Detail section create a grid to guide your eye in rearranging the layout of the form if you decide to do so.

Project 2B: School | **Access** 837

Double arrow between Form Header and Detail sections

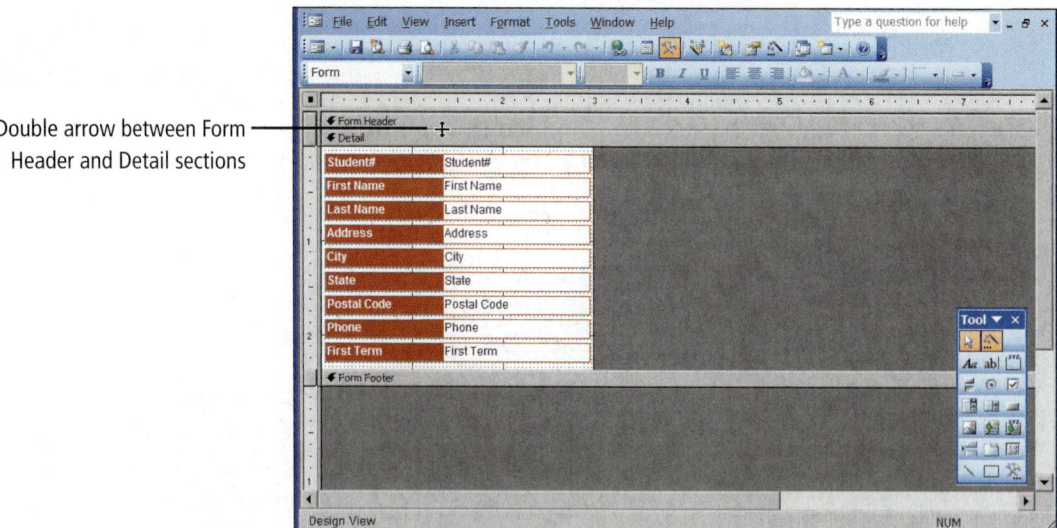

Figure 2.19

4 Position your pointer on the horizontal line between the **Form Header** section and the **Detail** section until the pointer changes to a large double arrow, as shown in Figure 2.19.

5 Drag downward approximately 0.5 inch. Use your eye or the vertical ruler to determine this distance; it need not be exact. Release the mouse button.

The Form Header section expands and a grid pattern of dots displays.

6 On the Toolbox toolbar floating on your screen, click the **Label** button , as shown in Figure 2.20.

The **Toolbox** toolbar has various **controls** that can be added to forms in Access. Controls are the objects in a form, such as the brown labels and white text boxes currently displayed on your screen, with which you view or manipulate information stored in tables or queries.

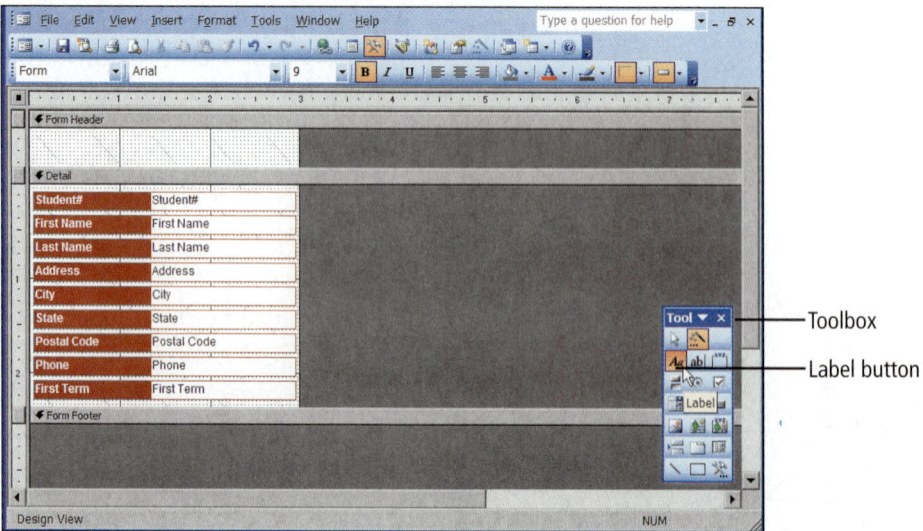

Toolbox
Label button

Figure 2.20

838   Access | Chapter 2: Forms and Reports

Alert! **Is your Toolbox missing?**
If the toolbox is not displayed, click the Toolbox button on the Form Design toolbar. Alternatively, from the View menu, click Toolbox.

7 Move your pointer into the **Form Header section** and notice that the pointer shape is a plus sign and the letter A. See Figure 2.21.

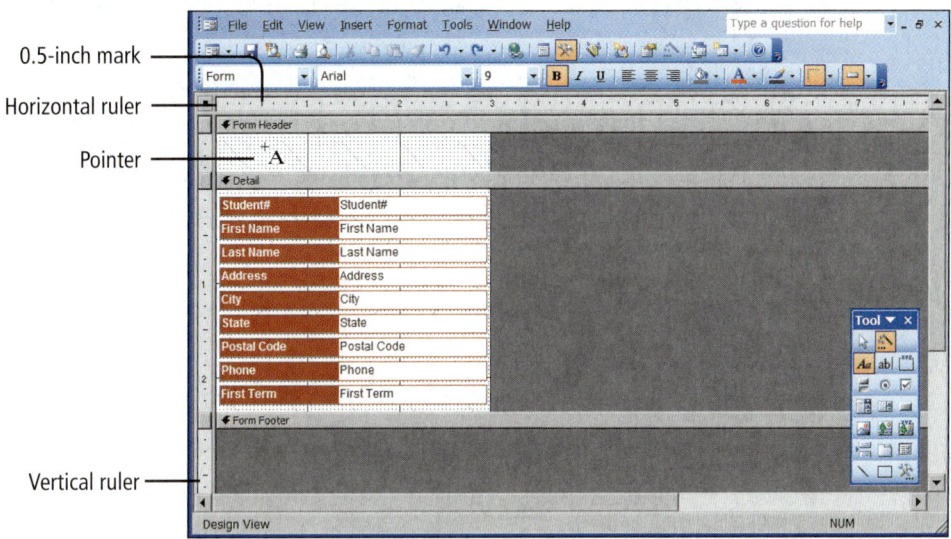

Figure 2.21

8 On your screen, locate the horizontal and vertical rulers as shown in Figure 2.21 and then locate the 0.5-inch mark on the horizontal ruler.

Note — Displaying Rulers in Form Design View

Click Ruler on the View menu.

If the rulers are not displayed in the Design view of your form, display the View menu and then click Ruler.

9 With the plus sign of your mouse pointer positioned at the left edge of the **Form Header section**, drag down about 0.25 of an inch and to the right to **2.5 inches on the horizontal ruler**. Release the mouse button and compare your result to Figure 2.22.

If you are not satisfied with your result, click the Undo button and begin again. A new label control is created in the Form Header section and the insertion point is blinking in the control.

Project 2B: School | **Access** 839

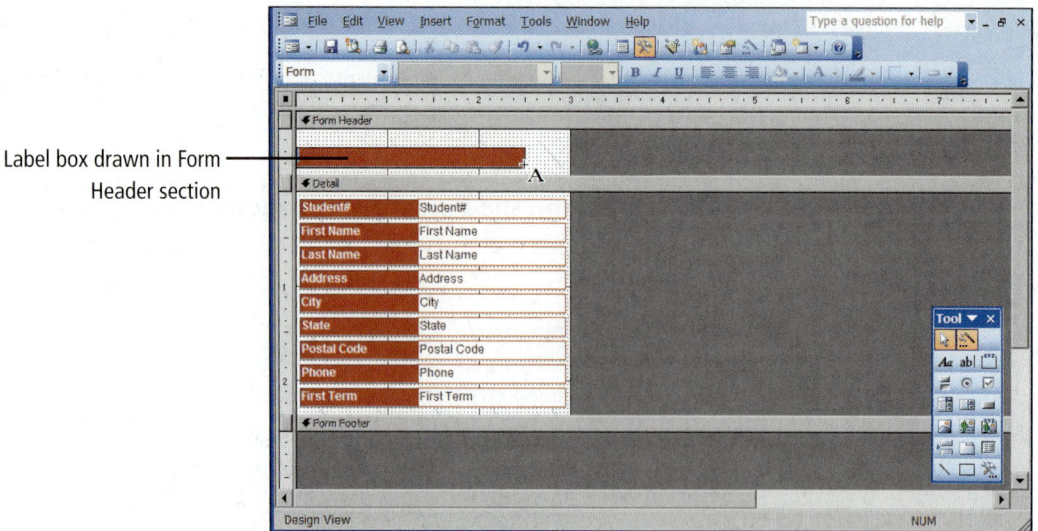

Label box drawn in Form Header section

Figure 2.22

10 In the label control that you just created, using your own first and last name, type **Student Data Entry Form (Firstname Lastname)**

The label expands to accommodate your typing.

11 Press Enter and then notice that the label is surrounded by small squares.

The small squares surrounding the label are *sizing handles* that indicate that the label control is selected.

12 On the Form View toolbar, click the **View** button to switch to the Form view.

The form header displays with the information you inserted. See Figure 2.23. By placing a form header on the form, you have created information that will display at the top of the form when it is viewed, and also print at the top of the form when it is printed.

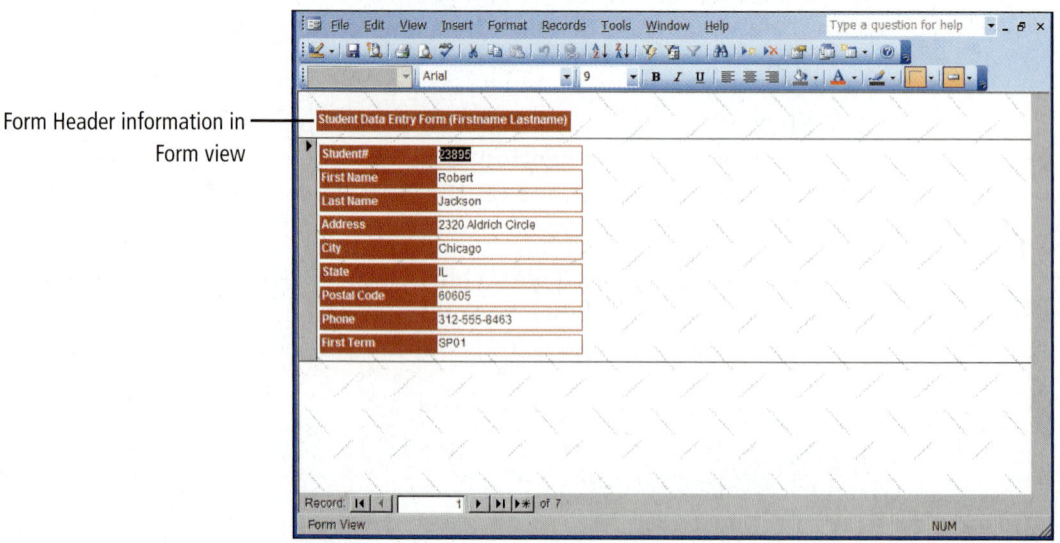

Form Header information in Form view

Figure 2.23

13 Click the **View** button again to return to the Design view of the form for the next activity.

Activity 2.8 Moving and Resizing Fields in a Form

The Design view of any database object is the view that is used to change the layout—the design—of the object. The reason for changing the layout of a form is usually to make it easier for the people using it to view and enter data. Sometimes forms are modified to match an existing paper form already in use by an organization. For example, the Student Registration Department at your college may have an existing paper form that you fill out when registering for courses. Transferring or entering this information from the paper form is easier if the Access form on the screen matches the pattern on the paper form.

1 With your form displayed in Design view, locate the horizontal and vertical rulers on your screen. Notice that the form is 3 inches wide.

2 As shown in Figure 2.24, position your mouse pointer on the right edge of the form until your pointer changes to a large, double arrow. Then, drag the right edge of the form to **6.5 inches on the horizontal ruler**.

By increasing the width of the form area, you have more space in which to rearrange the various form controls.

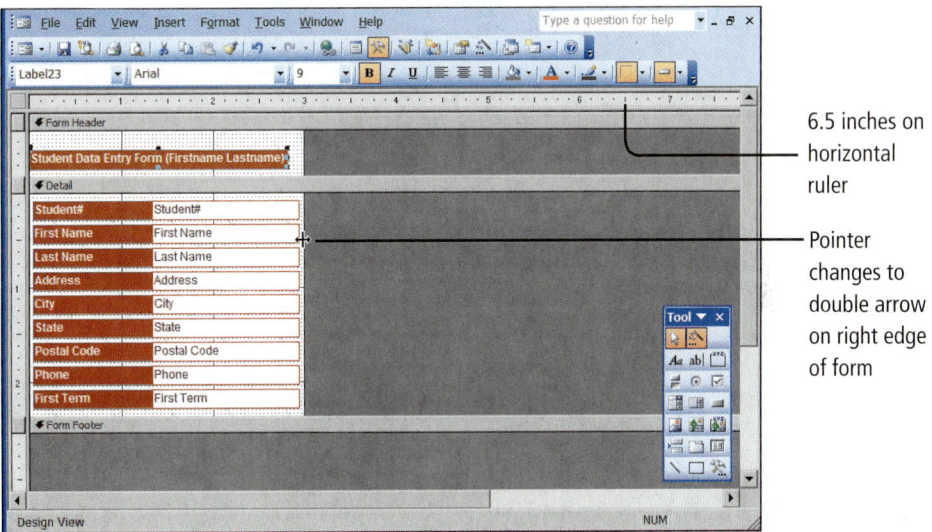

6.5 inches on horizontal ruler

Pointer changes to double arrow on right edge of form

Figure 2.24

3 Click once in the white **Address text box control**. See Figure 2.25.

The Address *text box control* is selected and handles surround the selected object. A text box control on a form is where data from the corresponding table is displayed when the form is viewed.

Project 2B: School | **Access** 841

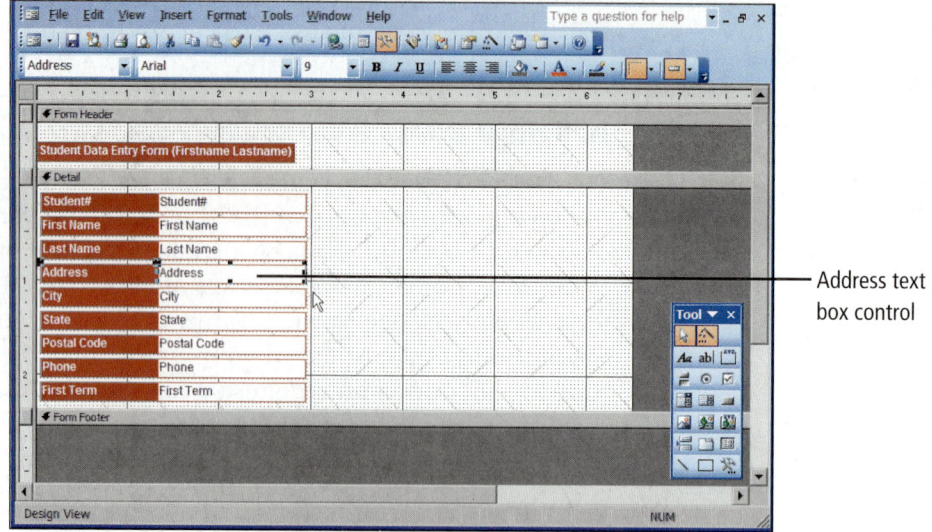

Figure 2.25

4 Position your mouse pointer over any border of the selected text box control until the **hand** pointer displays. See Figure 2.26. The hand pointer displays when the mouse pointer is positioned on the border of a control.

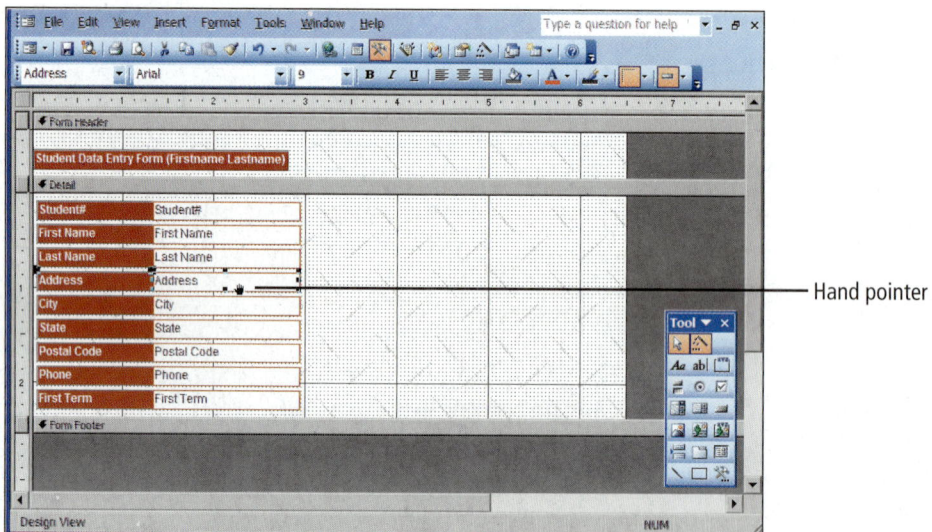

Figure 2.26

5 With the **hand** pointer displayed, drag the text box up and to the right of the Student# field as shown in Figure 2.27. Make sure that the left edge is positioned at approximately **3 inches on the horizontal ruler**.

Notice that both the *label* control—the brown box that, when viewed in Form view, contains the field name—and the *text box* control—the white box that, when viewed in Form view, contains the actual data—move together to the new location. Dragging with the hand pointer on the border of a control allows you to reposition both the label control and the text box control as one unit.

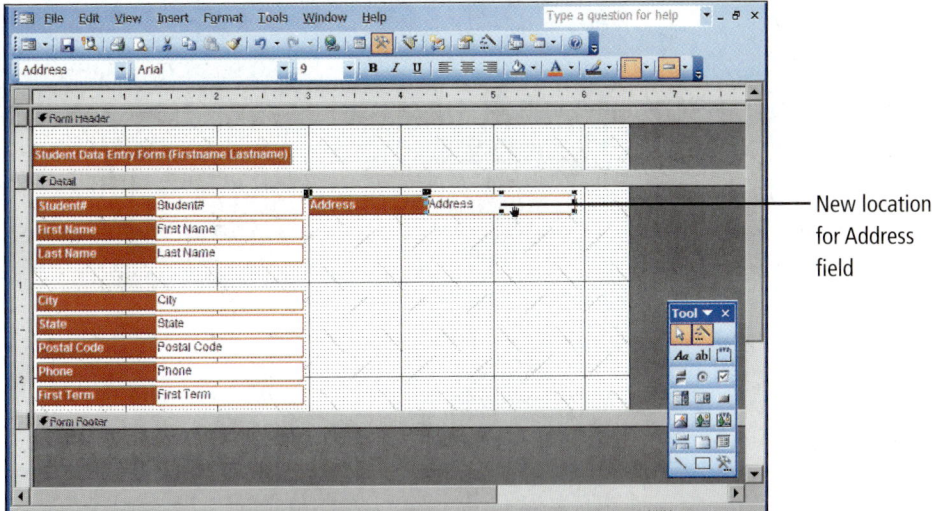

Figure 2.27

6 Click once in the white **City text box control** to select it, then position your pointer over any border of the text box to display the **hand pointer**.

7 Drag to position the **City controls** directly under the **Address controls**, to the right of the First Name controls, as shown in Figure 2.28.

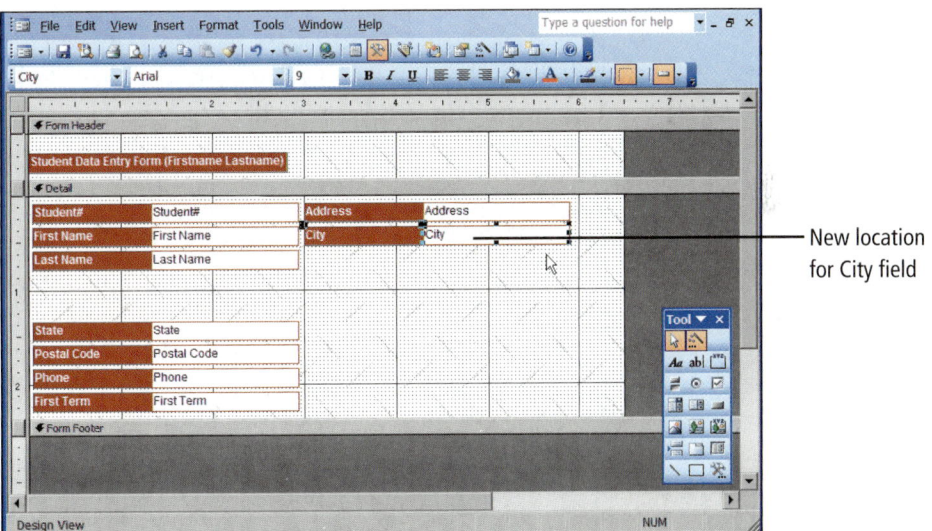

Figure 2.28

8 Using the technique you just practiced, move the **State controls** and the **Postal Code controls**, as shown in Figure 2.29.

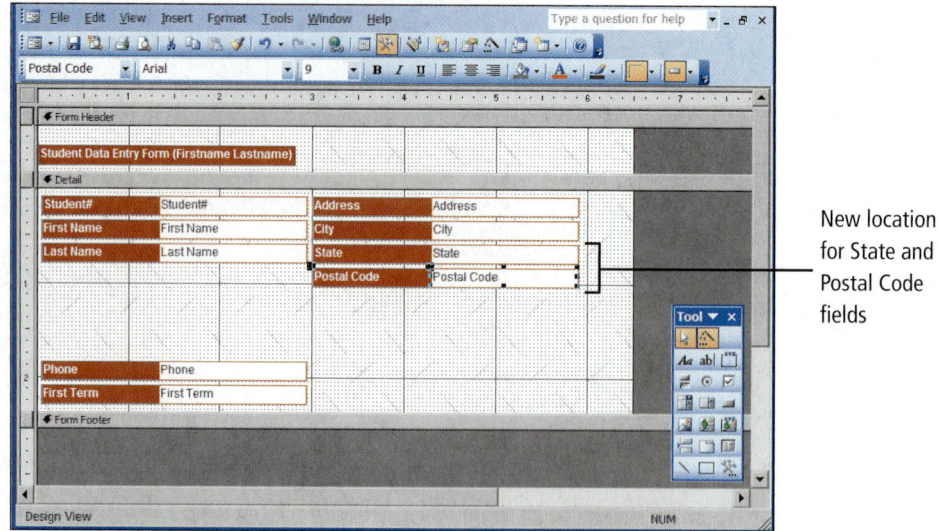

Figure 2.29

9. Click once in the **Phone text box control** to select it. Position your pointer over the large black handle that is between the Phone label control and the Phone text box control until the **pointing hand** pointer displays. See Figure 2.30.

The pointing hand displays when your mouse pointer is positioned on the larger, upper left handle. With this pointer shape, you can move the text box control separately from the label control.

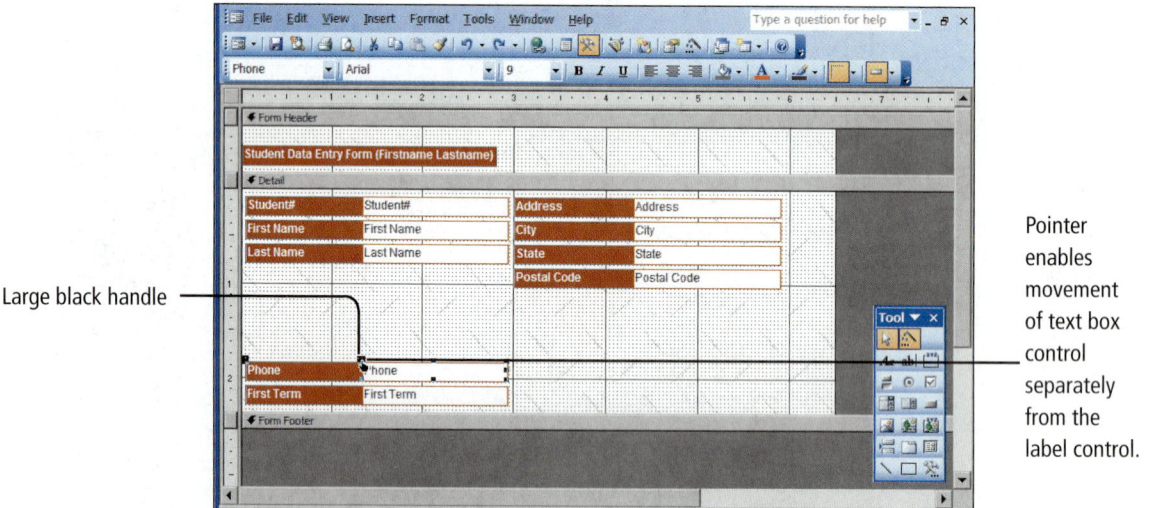

Figure 2.30

10 With the **pointing hand** pointer displayed, drag the white **Phone text box control** to the position shown in Figure 2.31—positioning its left edge at **2 inches on the horizontal ruler** and its top edge at **1.5 inches on the vertical ruler**.

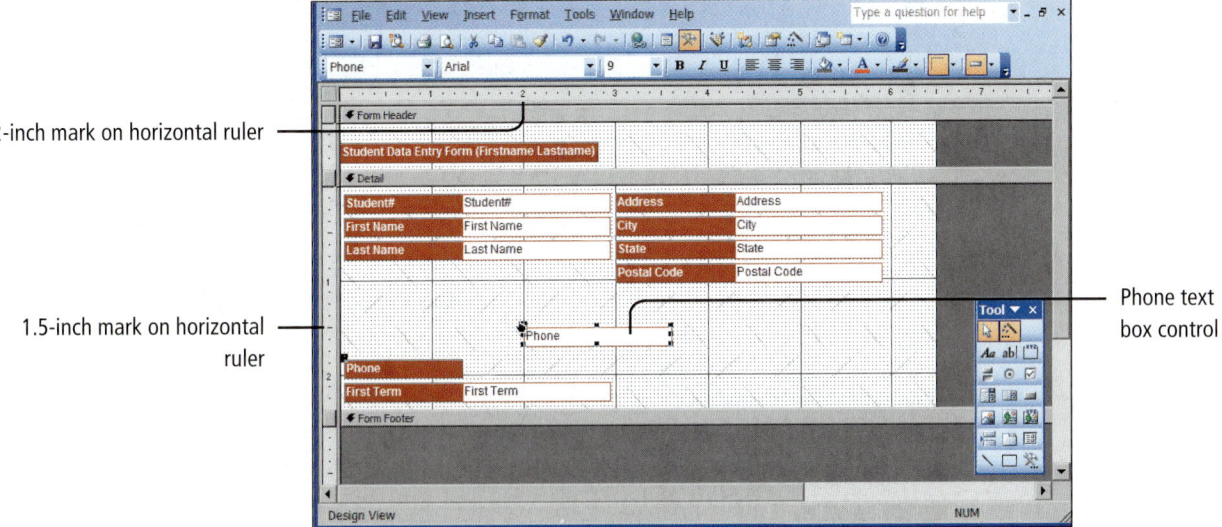

Figure 2.31

11 Select the brown **Phone label control**, point to the large black handle at the upper left corner to display the **pointing hand** pointer, and then drag to position it as shown in Figure 2.32.

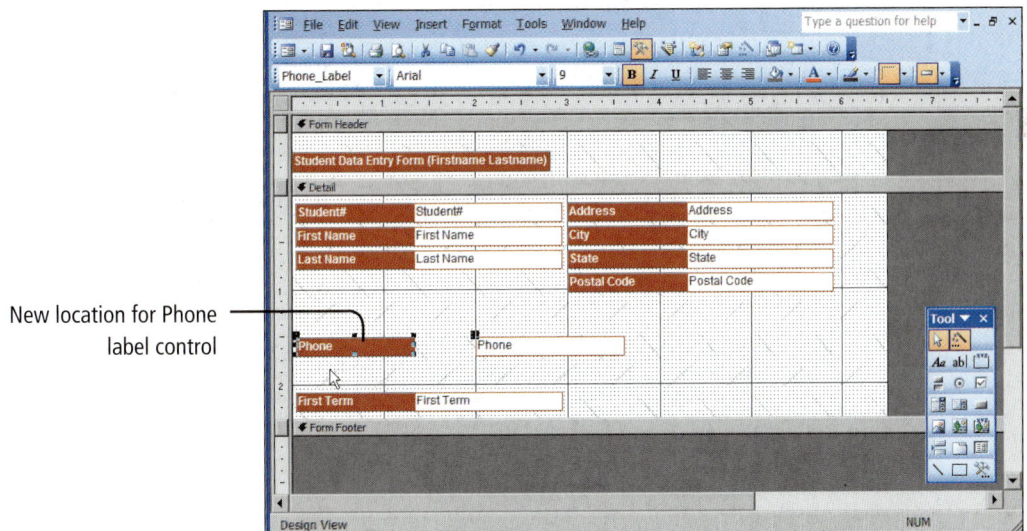

Figure 2.32

Project 2B: School | **Access**   845

12 Move the white **First Term text box control** directly under the Phone text box control aligning its left edge at **2 inches on the horizontal ruler** and its top edge **at 1⅞ inches on the vertical ruler**, as shown in Figure 2.33.

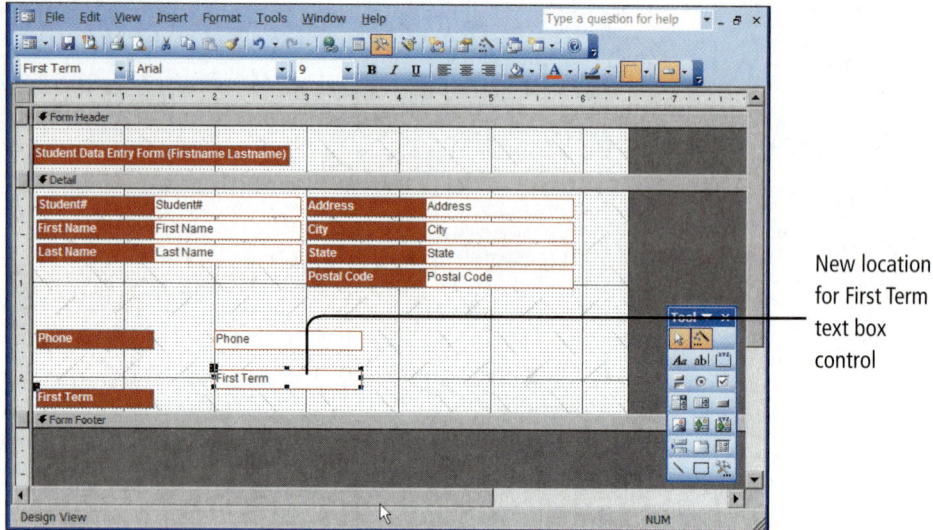

New location for First Term text box control

Figure 2.33

13 Move the brown **First Term label control** as shown in Figure 2.34.

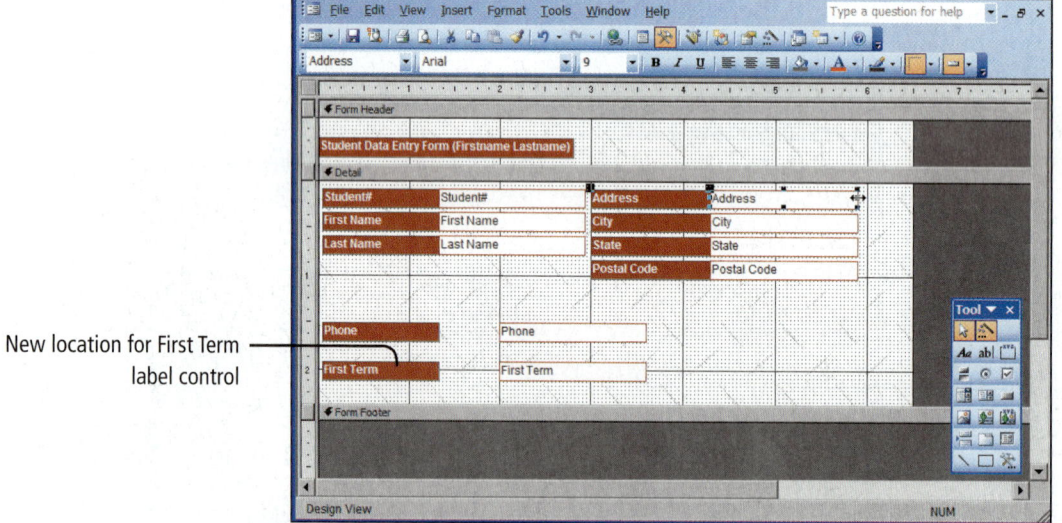

New location for First Term label control

Figure 2.34

14 Click to select the white **Address text box control**, then position your pointer over the right center handle until the pointer changes to a horizontal double arrow, as shown in Figure 2.35.

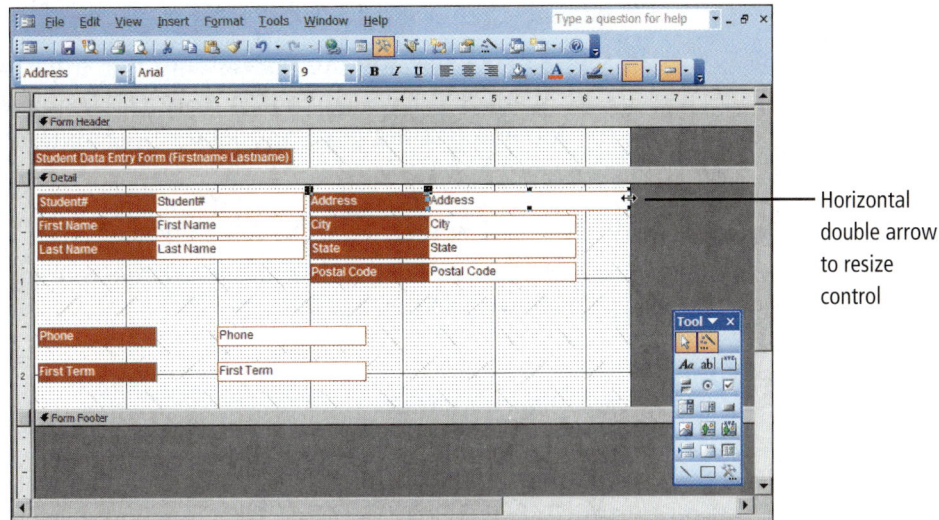

Figure 2.35

15 Drag the center right handle to **6.5 inches on the horizontal ruler**.

The width of the Address text box control is increased. This is a good idea because addresses are typically longer than the data in a City or State field.

16 Use the technique you just practiced to *decrease* the width of the **State text box control**, as shown in Figure 2.36.

You can see how the grid pattern provides a visual guide in placing the controls exactly where you want them.

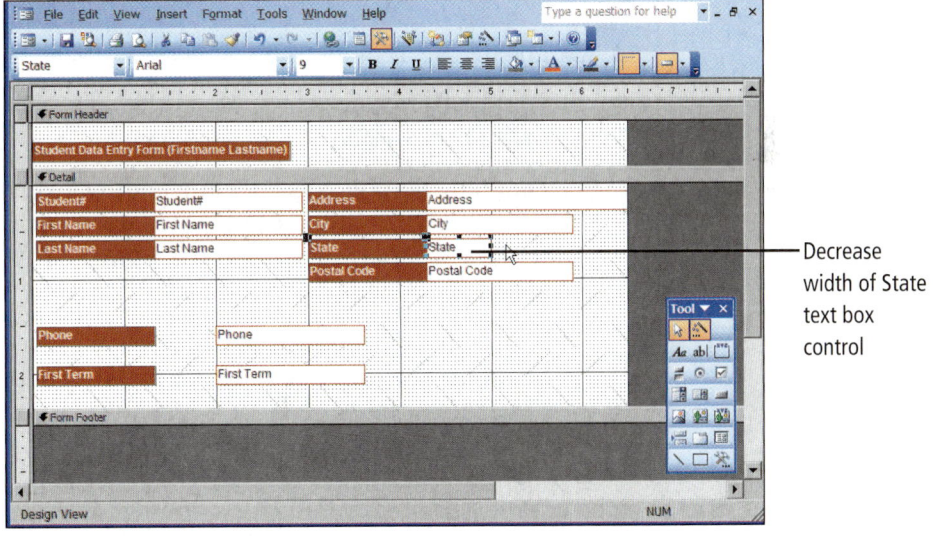

Figure 2.36

17 On the Form Design toolbar, click the **View** button to switch to the Form view and notice the changes you have made to the layout of the form.

18 Click the **View** button again to return to the Design view of the form for the next activity.

Activity 2.9 Adding a Page Footer to a Form

A *Page Header* or *Page Footer* contains information that displays on every page of a form when it is printed. Header information displays at the top of a printed page and footer information displays at the bottom of a printed page.

1 On the menu bar, click **View** and then click **Page Header/Footer**.

Page Header and Page Footer sections are added to your form, as shown in Figure 2.37.

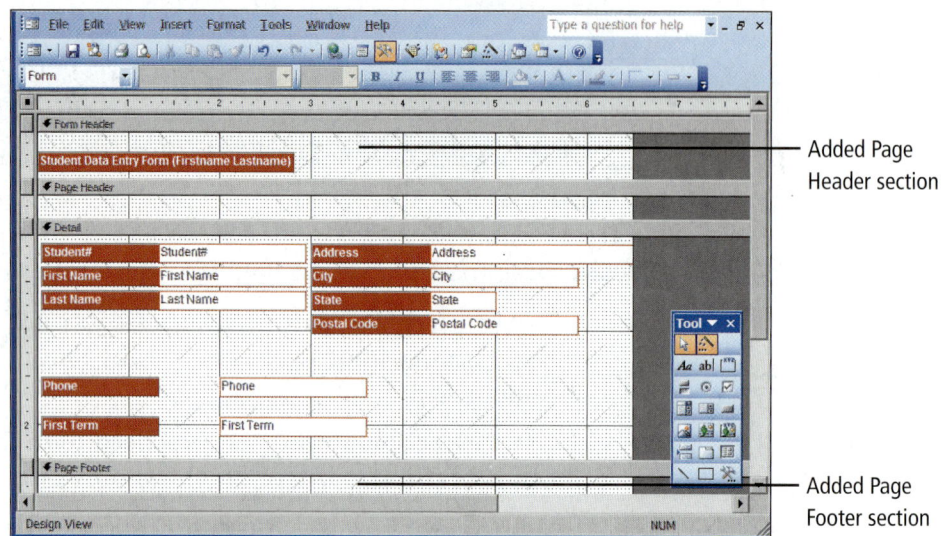

Figure 2.37

2 Locate the Toolbox toolbar floating on your screen. If it is not visible, display the View menu and click **Toolbox**. On the Toolbox, click the **Label** button.

3 Position the plus sign of your pointer just below the Page Footer separator at **2 inches on the horizontal ruler**, and then drag down to the lower separator and to the right to **4.5 inches on the horizontal ruler**, as shown in Figure 2.38.

If you are not satisfied with your result, recall that you can click the Undo button and begin again. An insertion point is blinking at the left edge of the control.

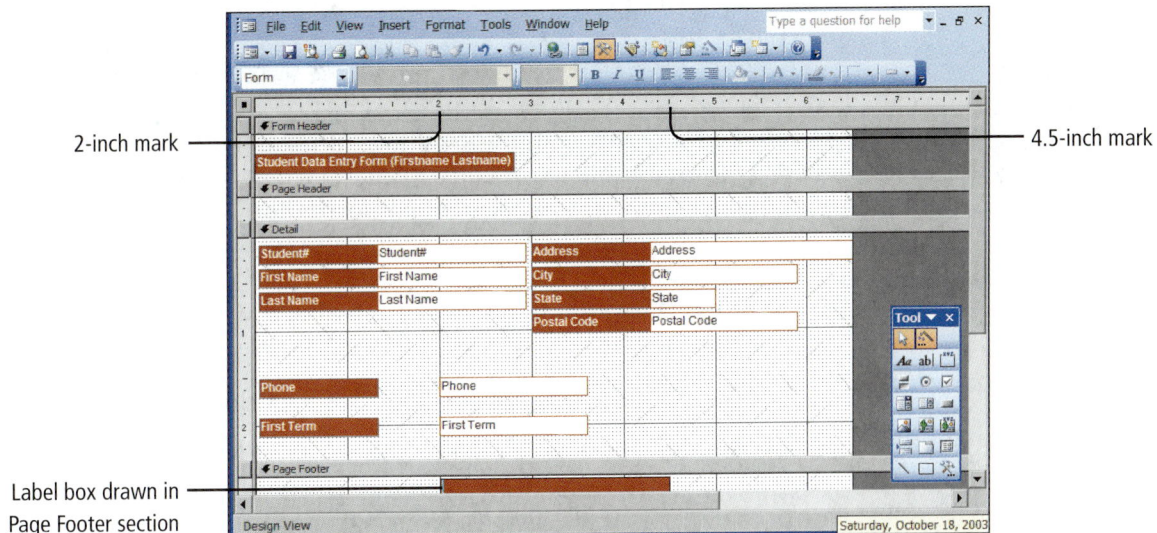

Figure 2.38

4. In the label control you just created, using your own first and last name, type **2B Students Firstname Lastname** and then press Enter.

   Label controls, when placed in headers or footers, function as descriptors to either clarify the contents of a text box control, or to add additional information—such as a title or your name—to a form.

5. Click the **View** button to switch to the Form view.

   Notice that the Page footer you created does *not* display in the Form view of the form. Page Headers and Footers only display when the form is printed.

6. On the Form View toolbar, click the **Print Preview** button. Locate your name in the Page footer at the lower edge of the page in Print Preview.

7. On the Print Preview toolbar, click the **Print** button to print the form.

   Three pages will print; the last page will contain only the page footer.

8. To the right of *Type a question for help*, click the small **Close Window** button.

9. Click **Yes** when prompted to save changes to the design of the form.

   The Database window, maximized, displays.

Project 2B: School | **Access** 849

Objective 7
Create a Report with the Report Wizard

Recall that a report is a database object that displays the fields and records from a table in an easy-to-read format suitable for printing. Reports are created to summarize information in a database in a professional-looking manner.

The **Report Wizard** assists you in creating a professionally designed report. The Report Wizard asks you a series of questions and then creates a report based on your answers.

Activity 2.10 Creating a Report Using the Report Wizard

1 If desired, to the right of the *Type a question for help box*, click the small **Restore Window** button . On the Objects bar, click **Reports**.

2 To the right of the Objects bar, double-click the command icon **Create report by using wizard**.

The Report Wizard displays with its first question. See Figure 2.39. Here you will select the table from which you want to get information, and then select the fields that you want to include in the report.

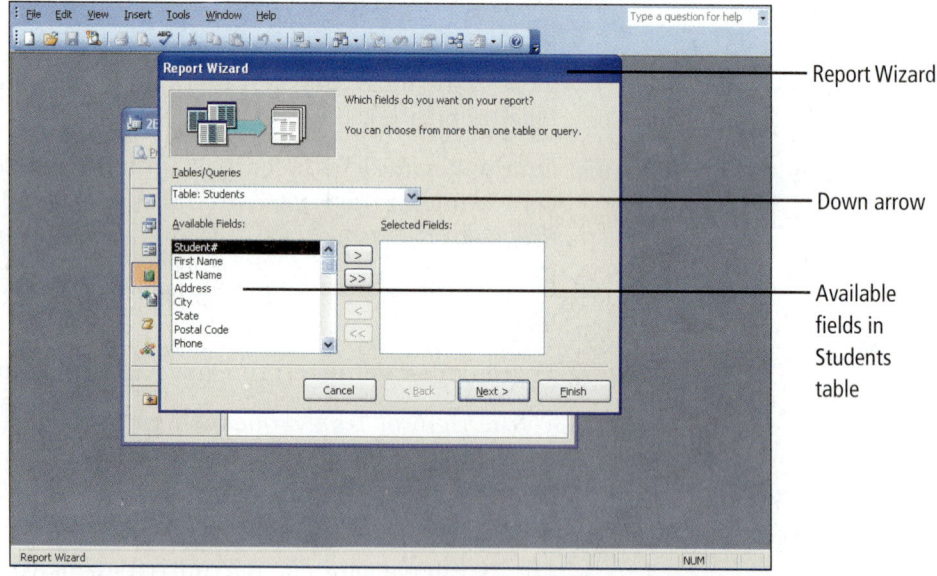

Figure 2.39

3 Under **Tables/Queries**, click the **down arrow**.

A list of tables and queries available for this database displays. Currently, only one object, the Students table, has been created in this database.

4 Click **Table: Students**.

Under Available Fields, a list of the fields in the Students table displays.

5 To the right of the list of available fields, click the **All Fields** button to move all of the fields from the Students table to the Selected Fields column on the far right.

This action will cause all of the fields to be included in the report.

6 Click the **Next** button.

7 Under **Do you want to add any grouping levels?** click **State** and then to the right, click the **One Field** button.

The preview on the right displays the State field as the field by which to group the records in the report. Grouping data helps you organize and summarize the data in your report. Grouping data in a report places all of the records within the same group field together.

8 In the center column, click the **One Field Back** button.

The State field is removed as the field by which to group the data. Because each of the records in the Students table has the same State information, it would not be useful to group the records by State.

9 Click **First Term** and then click the **One Field** button.

This action will cause the data in the report to be grouped by the First Term field.

10 Click the **Next** button.

11 In the **1** box on the right, click the **down arrow** to select a sort order for the records in the report. See Figure 2.40.

A list of fields in the report displays.

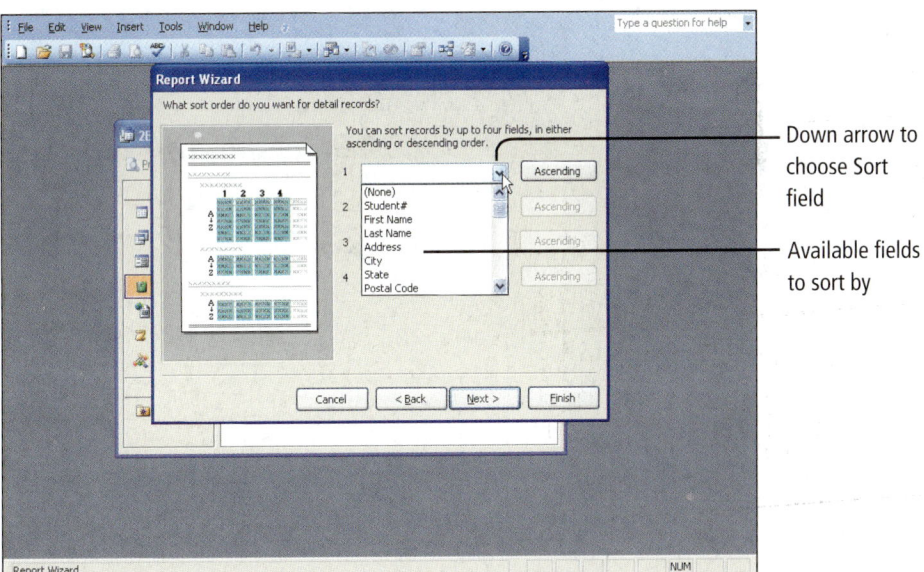

Figure 2.40

12 Click **Student#** and leave the default order as **Ascending**.

This action will cause the records in the report to be sorted numerically by each Student's Student# *within* the grouping option specified, which was First Term. Sorting records in a report presents a more organized report.

Project 2B: School | **Access** 851

13 Click the **Next** button.

14 Under **Layout**, click the **Block** option button and notice the preview on the left. Click the **Outline 1** option button and notice the preview on the left.

15 Click the remaining **Layout** option buttons and view the preview.

The layout you choose for a report determines the arrangement of the data on the printed pages of your report.

16 After you are finished viewing the layout options, click the **Stepped** option button to select it as the layout option for the report.

17 On the right side of the dialog box, under **Orientation**, be sure that **Portrait** is selected, and keep the check mark next to *Adjust the field width so all fields fit on a page.*

18 Click the **Next** button. In the displayed list of styles, click **Soft Gray**.

19 Notice the preview to the left and then click **Compact** to view its preview. Click to view each of the remaining styles and then click **Casual**.

20 Click the **Next** button. In the **What title do you want for your report?** box type **Student Report** and then click the **Finish** button.

The report displays in Print Preview.

21 Maximize the window if necessary. On the toolbar, click the **Zoom arrow** and then click **75%**.

22 If necessary, use the vertical scroll bar to examine the data in the report. Notice that each of the specifications you defined for the report in the Report Wizard is reflected in the Print Preview of the report. Students are grouped by First Term. See Figure 2.41.

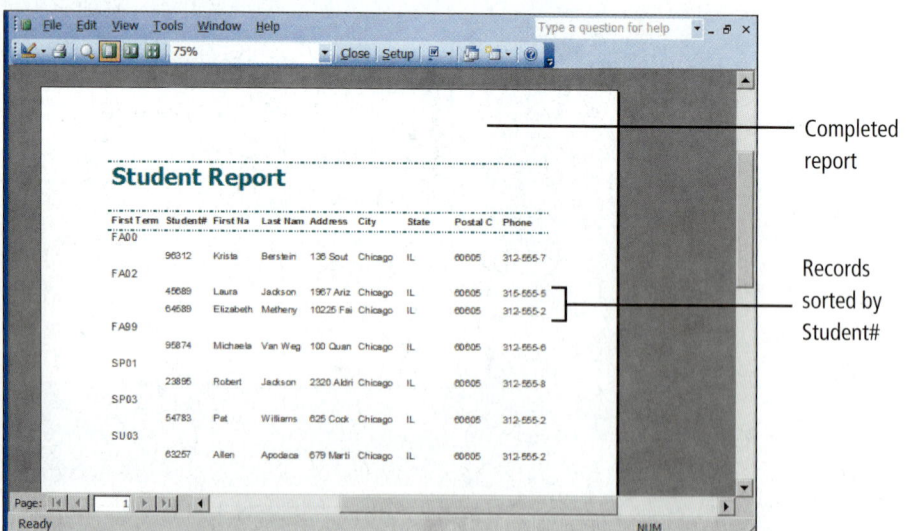

Figure 2.41

Objective 8
Save a Report

You do not need to create a new report each time data in the corresponding table is modified. Once you have created a report and laid it out in a format that is useful to you, you can save the report for future use. Each time the report is opened, any changes made to the table will be automatically reflected in the report.

Activity 2.11 Saving a Report

1 Click the **Close Window** button ☒ to close the report.

The report name, *Student Report*, displays in the Database window. Reports created with the Report Wizard are named in the final step of the wizard. When the report is closed, it is automatically saved.

2 Double-click the **Student Report**.

The report opens in Print Preview.

3 Adjust the zoom to **75%** so you can view the records in the report, and if necessary, maximize the window.

In the displayed report, notice that some of the field names are not completely displayed; they are cut off. For example, the *First Name*, *Last Name*, and *Postal Code* field names are not fully displayed.

4 Leave the report displayed in Print Preview for the next activity.

Objective 9
Modify the Design of a Report

After a report is created, you can still make modifications to its design by opening the report in Design view.

Activity 2.12 Switching Between Report View and Design View

1 On the Print Preview toolbar, click the **View** button to switch to the Design view of the report.

2 In the Design view of the report, examine the sections of the report, and notice that the report contains a Page Header and a Page Footer section. See Figure 2.42.

Design view for a report is similar to the Design view of a form. You can make modifications, and the dotted grid pattern assists you with alignment. Reports created with the Report Wizard contain a Page Header and Page Footer. You do not need to manually add these as you did with the form created with the Form Wizard.

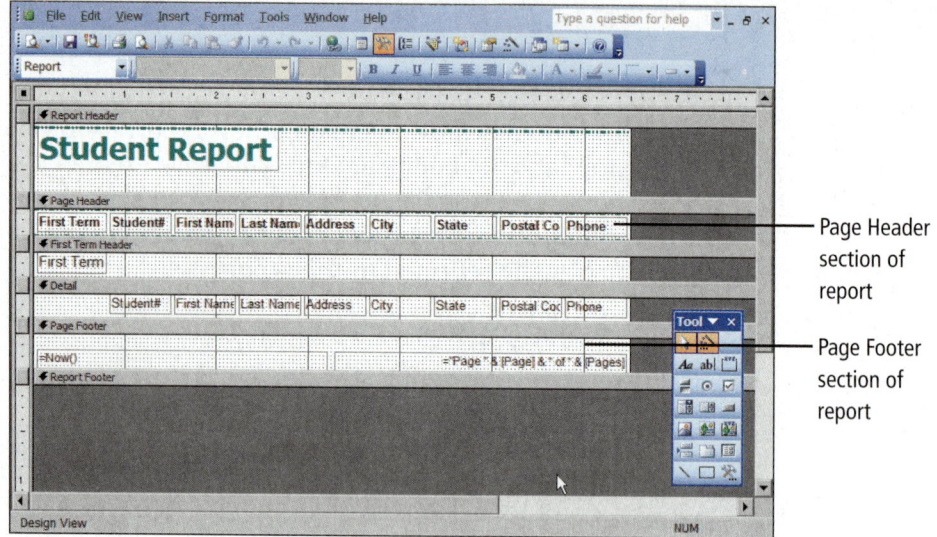

Figure 2.42

3 On the Report Design toolbar, click the **View** button.

The report displays in Print Preview..

4 On the Print Preview toolbar, click the **Setup** button. Alternatively, click File, Page Setup.

5 In the displayed **Page Setup** dialog box, click the **Page tab**. See Figure 2.43.

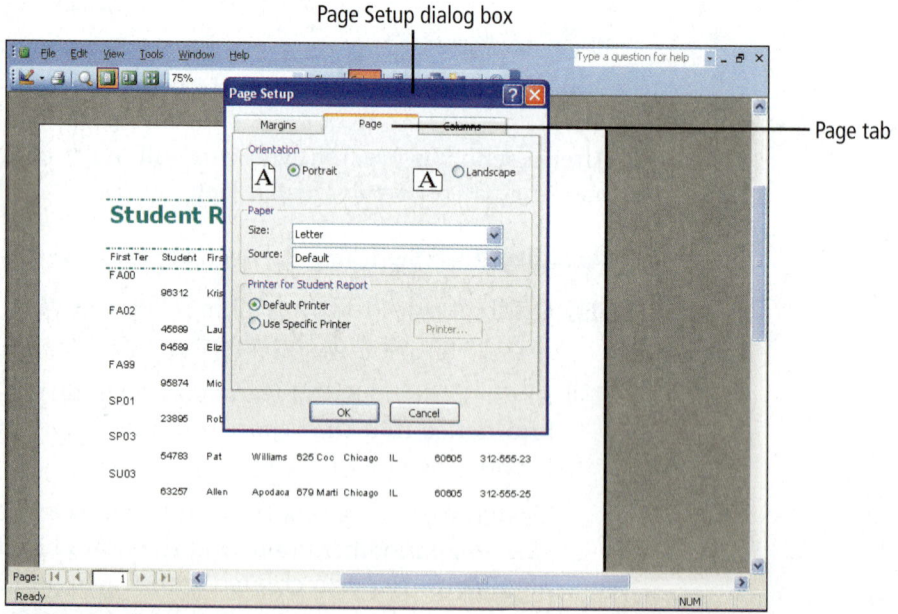

Figure 2.43

6 Under **Orientation**, click the **Landscape** option button and then click **OK**.

The report displays in landscape orientation. Changing the report to landscape orientation will allow more information to print across the page.

7 On the Print Preview toolbar, click the **View** button to switch to Design view, and leave the report open in Design view for the next activity.

Now that you have adjusted the page orientation, you can move to Design view to make additional modifications to the report.

Activity 2.13 Moving and Resizing Fields in a Report

Moving and resizing fields in the Design view of a report is accomplished with the same techniques you practiced when you moved and resized controls in a form in Design view.

1 If necessary, use the horizontal scroll bar to scroll the report to the right so that you can see the 9-inch mark on the horizontal ruler.

2 Position your pointer on the right edge of the report until your pointer changes to a large double arrow, and then drag the right edge of the report to the right to **9 inches on the horizontal ruler**. See Figure 2.44.

The width of the report is increased. By increasing the width of a report, you create more working space to move and reposition fields on the report.

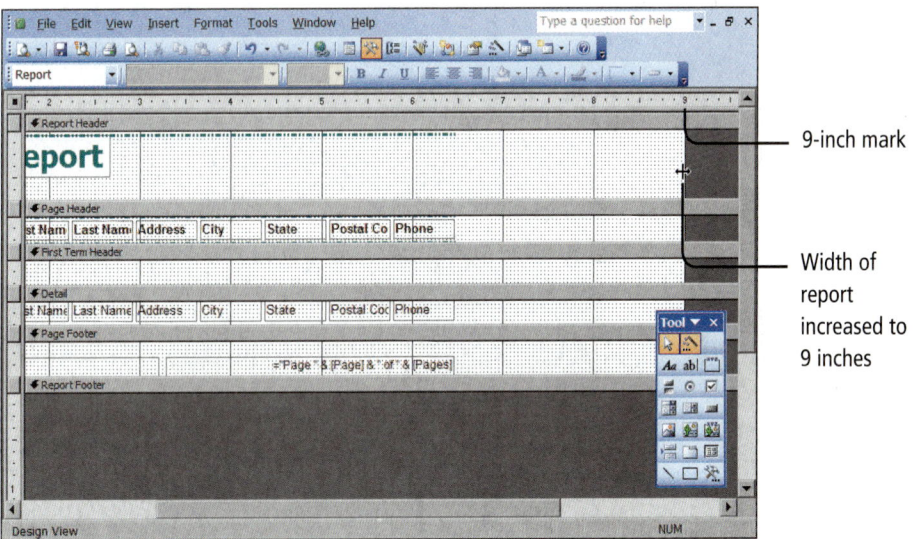

Figure 2.44

3 In the **Detail section**, click to select the **Phone text box control**. See Figure 2.45.

The Phone text box control is selected and handles surround the selected object.

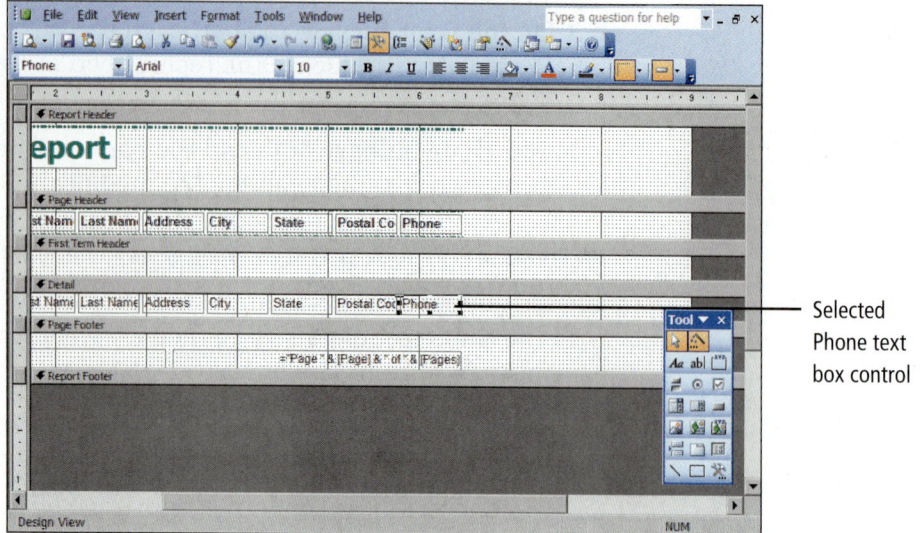

Figure 2.45

[4] Press and hold down Shift. In the **Page Header section**, click the **Phone label control**. Then release the Shift key.

Both the Phone text box control and the Phone label control are selected, as shown in Figure 2.46.

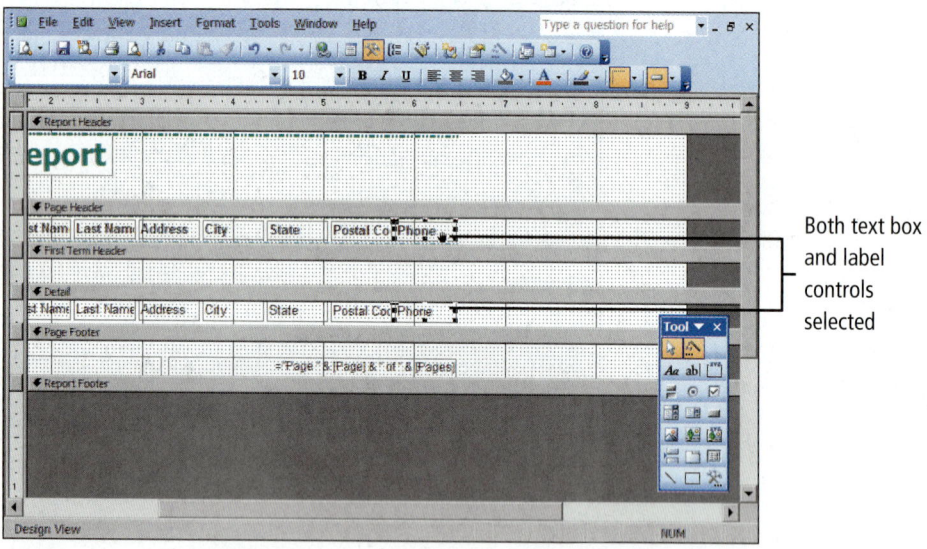

Figure 2.46

[5] In the **Page Header section**, position your pointer in the **Phone label control** until the **hand** pointer displays, and then drag to position the right edge of the two objects, which will move together, at **8.75 inches on the horizontal ruler**.

Both controls are repositioned. Because the text box control and corresponding label control are in different sections of the report, you must use Shift to select both of the controls and then move them together.

856 Access | Chapter 2: Forms and Reports

6 With both controls still selected, resize the controls by dragging the center right handle of either control so that the right edge of the controls is stretched to **9 inches on the horizontal ruler**. See Figure 2.47.

The width of both controls is increased.

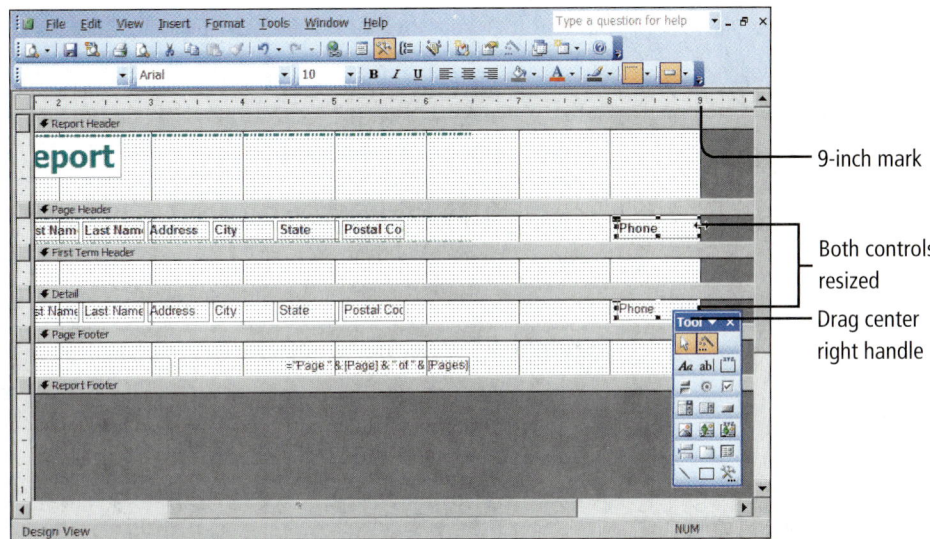

Figure 2.47

7 In the **Detail section**, click the **Postal Code text box control** to select it. Hold down Shift, and then in the **Page Header section**, click the **Postal Code label control**. Release Shift and then point to one of the controls to display the **hand** pointer. Drag to reposition the right edge of the two controls at **7.5 inches on the horizontal ruler**.

8 In the **Detail section**, resize the controls by dragging the center right handle of the **Postal Code text box control** so that the right edge of the control is stretched to **7.75 inches on the horizontal ruler**. See Figure 2.48.

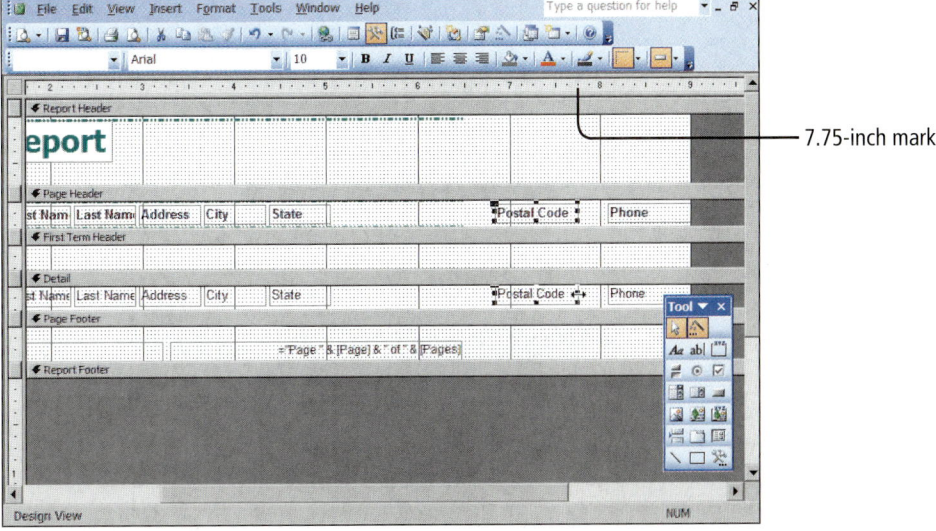

Figure 2.48

9 In the **Detail section**, click the **City text box control**, hold down Shift, and then click the **State text box control**. Continue to hold down Shift, and in the **Page Header section**, click the **City label control** and the **State label control**. Release Shift.

Four controls are selected—the City and State label controls in the Page Header section and the City and State text box controls in the Detail section, as shown in Figure 2.49.

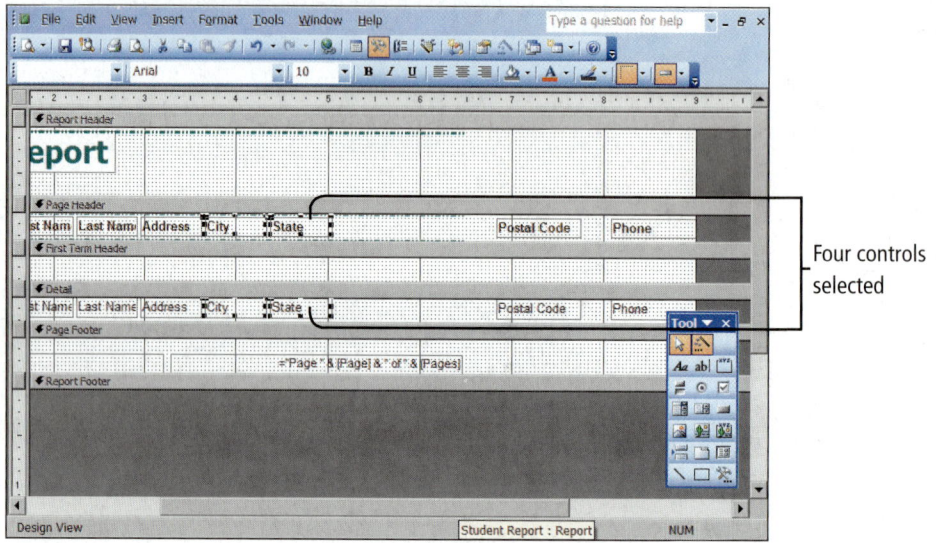

Figure 2.49

10 Position your pointer over any of the selected controls until the **hand pointer** displays. Move the grouped controls to the right until the right edge of the State controls are positioned at **6.75 inches on the horizontal ruler**. See Figure 2.50.

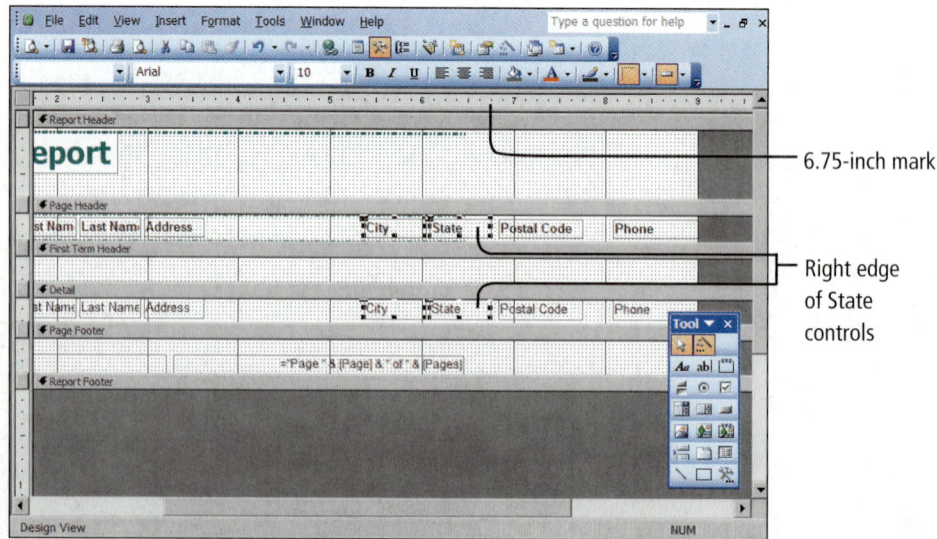

Figure 2.50

---

858 **Access** | Chapter 2: Forms and Reports

11 In the **Detail section**, click the **Address text box control**. Hold down [Shift], and in the Page Header section, click the **Address label control**.

12 Position your pointer over the center right handle of the **Address label control** until the pointer changes to a double horizontal arrow, and then resize the controls by stretching the right edge to **4.25 inches on the horizontal ruler**. See Figure 2.51.

The width of the two controls is increased.

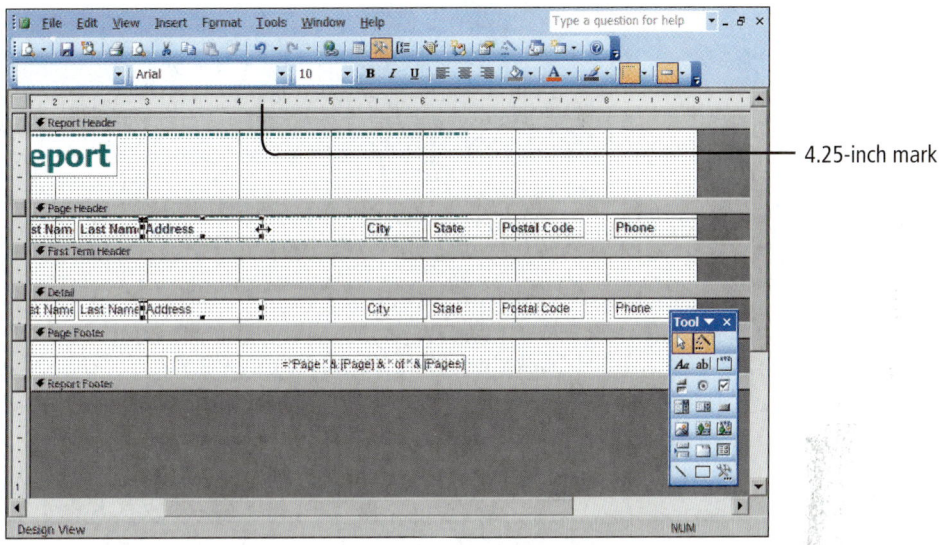

Figure 2.51

13 With the two objects still selected, position the pointer over one of the objects until the **hand** pointer displays, then move the two controls until their right edges are at **5.25 inches on the horizontal ruler**.

The two controls are moved one inch to the right.

14 With the two controls still selected, hold down [Ctrl] and press [→].

The two objects are **nudged**—moved slightly—to the right. Nudging is a useful technique to move controls with precision.

15 Using the [Ctrl] + [→] technique, nudge the selected controls to the right two more times.

16 Using the techniques you have just practiced, select, as a group, the **Last Name text box control** and the **Last Name label control**. Then move the selected objects to the right so that their right edge is at **3.75 inches on the horizontal ruler**. See Figure 2.52.

Project 2B: School | **Access** 859

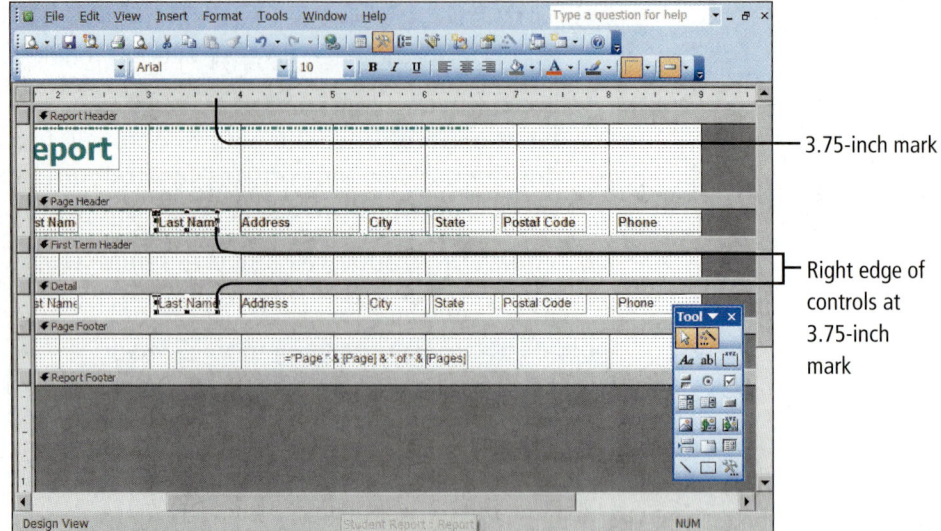

Figure 2.52

17 With the objects still selected, lengthen the controls by dragging their right edge to match Figure 2.53.

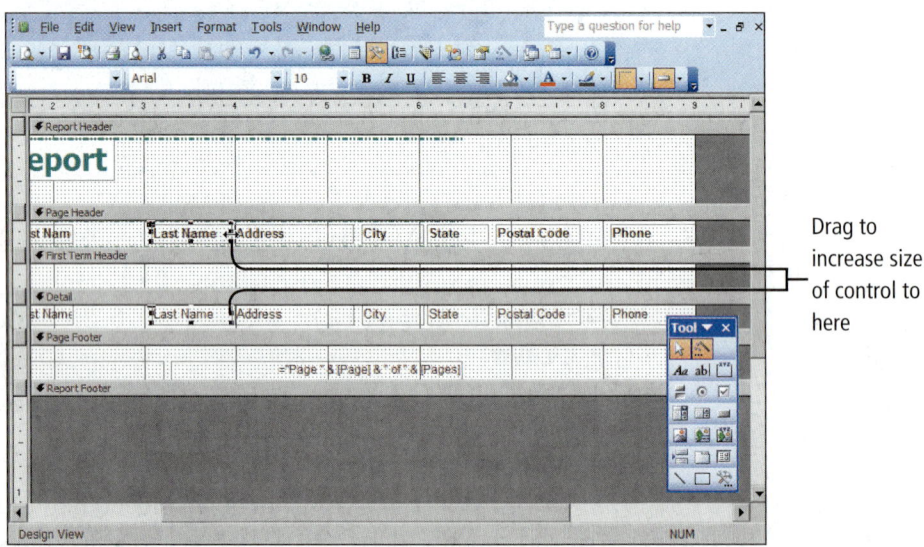

Figure 2.53

18 If necessary, use the horizontal scroll bar to scroll the report so you can see the remainder of the fields to the left. Using the techniques you have practiced to resize the controls, select, then resize the **First Name controls** so their right edge is at **2⅜ inches on the horizontal ruler,** as shown in Figure 2.54.

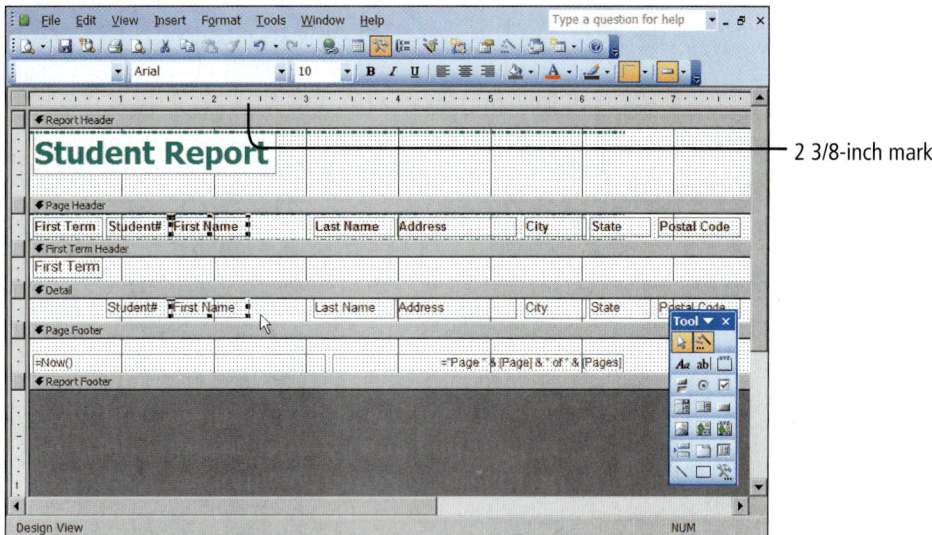

Figure 2.54

19. With the First Name controls still selected, hold Shift and select the **Student# text box control** and the **Student # label control**. Move the fields as a group until the right edge of the First Name field is positioned at **2.75 inches on the horizontal ruler**.

20. On the Report Design toolbar, click the **View** button to switch to the Print Preview of the report. Verify that the changes you made to the report are reflected in the Print Preview of the report, and then compare your screen to Figure 2.55.

> **Note** — Using Graphic Elements on Reports
>
> *Graphic lines can be lengthened.*
>
> The aqua graphic line on the report does not continue across the length of the report. As you progress in your study of Access, you will learn about graphic elements on reports.

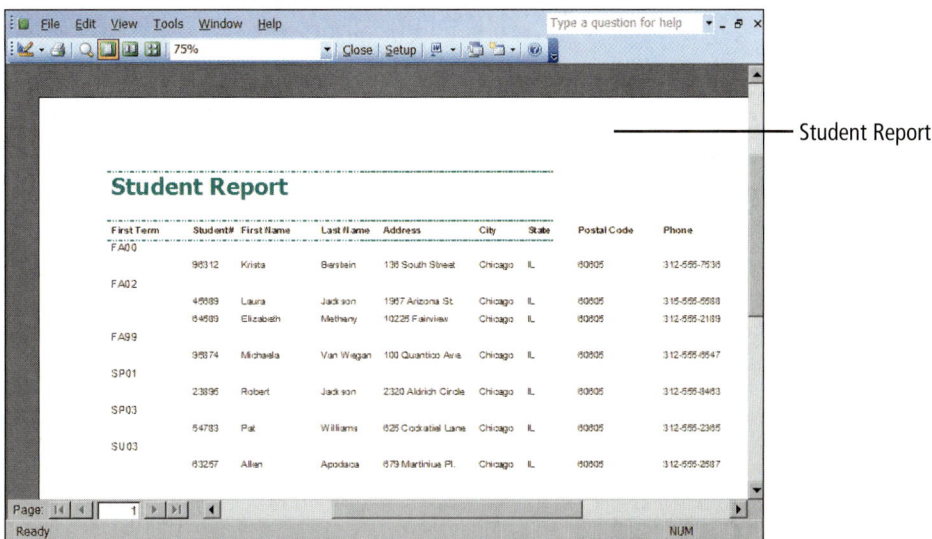

Figure 2.55

Project 2B: School | **Access** 861

21 On the Print Preview toolbar, click the **View** button to switch to the Design view of the report. Leave the report open in Design view for the next activity.

Activity 2.14 Adding a Page Footer and a Report Footer to a Report

1 Locate the **Page Footer** section of the report. Notice that there are two controls in this section. See Figure 2.56.

The control on the left, identified as =*Now( )*, will insert the current date each time the report is opened. The control on the right, identified as =*"Page " & [Page] & " of " & [Pages]*, will insert the page numbers of the pages in the report when the report is displayed in Print Preview or when the report is printed.

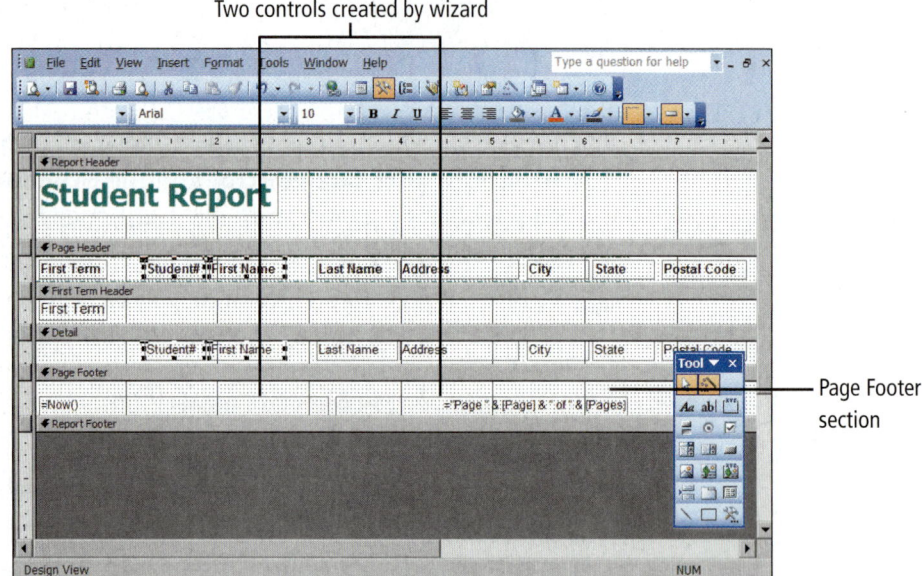

Figure 2.56

2 Click once in the control on the left, the control containing =*Now ( )*, to select it. Shorten this control by dragging its right center handle to the left to **1.5 inches on the horizontal ruler**.

3 Select the control on the right, the control that contains the =*"Page " & [Page] & " of " & [Pages]*. Shorten this control by dragging the left center handle of that control to **4.5 inches on the horizontal ruler**.

4 In the Toolbox, click the **Label** button.

5 Beginning at **2 inches on the horizontal ruler** and aligned with the top of the other two controls, drag down and to the right to **4.25 inches on the horizontal ruler** to draw a new label control, as shown in Figure 2.57.

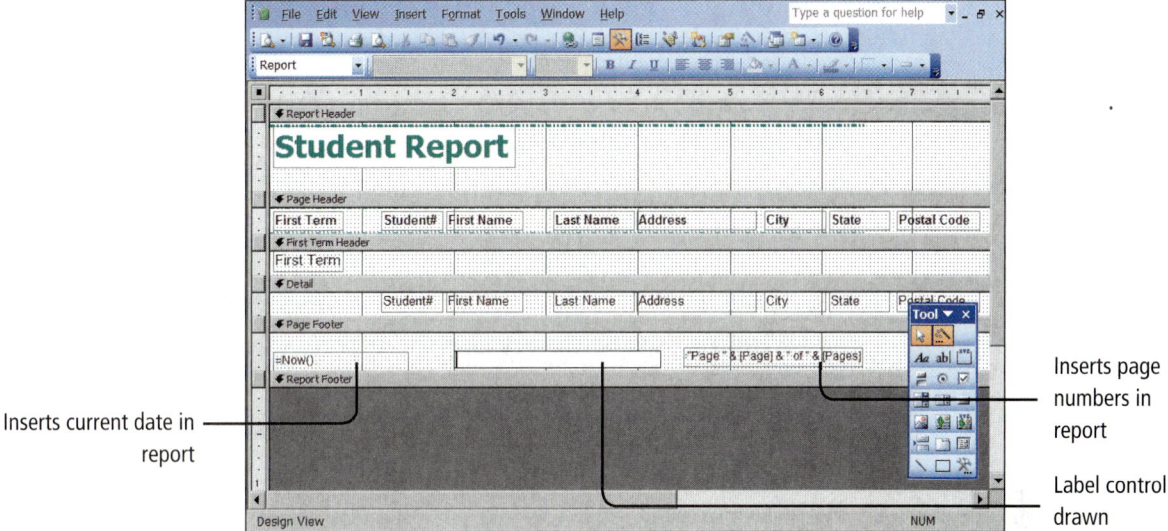

Figure 2.57

6 In the label box you just created, and using your own information, type **2B Students Firstname Lastname** and then press Enter.

An Alert button may display, which when pointed to, indicates *This is a new label and is not associated with a control.*

7 Switch to the Print Preview of the report and verify that your name displays at the lower edge of the report. If you are not satisfied with the positioning of the label control containing your name, return to Design view and use the Nudge feature (Ctrl + any arrow key) to nudge the control into a precise position.

Objective 10
Print a Report

An attractively formatted report printed on paper is much easier to view than looking at the database table on the screen or viewing one record at a time in a form on the screen. Reports are routinely printed for management, staff, or customers who need to look at information. For example, when you visit the Records Office of your college, you probably request a printed copy of your transcript. This is easier than viewing your records on the screen.

Activity 2.15 Printing a Report

1 On the Print Preview toolbar, click the **Print** button .

The report prints on one page.

2 To the right of *Type a question for help*, click the small **Close Window** button ☒ to close the report. Click **Yes** to save your changes.

3 Close the database and then click the **Close** button ☒ to close Access.

End You have completed Project 2B

Summary

A form is a tool for either entering or viewing information in a database. Although you can both enter and view database information in the database table itself, the use of a form is usually preferable for two reasons.

First, for entering data, a form is convenient and time saving, because the person entering the data using a form is not distracted by seeing the entire database table on the screen. He or she sees only the record being entered. Additionally, the fields on the form can be laid out in a manner that is easy for the person entering information to navigate.

Second, for viewing data, a form is easier to view than an entire table of information, because only the record needed is displayed. This is much easier for the person whose job it is to look up information in a database. For example, your college counselor can look at your college transcript in a nicely laid out form on the screen without seeing the records for hundreds of other students at the same time.

Two methods for creating forms in Access are through an AutoForm or through the Form Wizard. Once created, a form can be opened in Design View and further modified to make data entry or viewing even easier. Page headers and footers can be added that will display on each page of the form.

Reports in Access summarize the data in a database in a professional-looking manner suitable for printing. The design of a report can be modified so that the final report is laid out in a format that is useful for the person reading it.

In This Chapter You Practiced How To

- View and Navigate to Records with a Form
- Create an AutoForm
- Save and Close an AutoForm
- Use a Form to Add Records to and Delete Records from a Table
- Create a Form with the Form Wizard
- Modify a Form
- Create a Report with the Report Wizard
- Save a Report
- Modify the Design of a Report
- Print a Report

Concepts Assessments

Matching Match each term in the second column with its correct definition in the first column by writing the letter of the term on the blank line in front of the correct definition.

____ 1. Information that displays at the top of the form when the form is viewed in Form view or is printed.

____ 2. A bar that is used to select an entire record in a form or a table.

____ 3. An object such as a label or text box in a form or report that allows you to view or manipulate information stored in tables or queries.

____ 4. Information that displays at the lower edge of each page of a form or report.

____ 5. An Access feature that guides you step by step to create a form.

____ 6. A toolbar from which you can add various types of controls to forms and reports in Access.

____ 7. A feature in Access that quickly creates a form using the information from one table.

____ 8. A control on a form or report where data from the corresponding table is displayed

____ 9. A feature in Access used to create a professionally designed report.

____ 10. Using a form, the view in which you can enter and modify the information in a record.

____ 11. In the Design view of a form or report, the section that contains the fields and records that display in the form or report.

____ 12. The small squares that surround a selected object.

____ 13. The database object that provides an organized view of the fields in one or more tables or queries.

____ 14. The database object that displays the fields and records from a table in a format suitable for printing.

____ 15. A useful technique to move controls in Design view with precision.

A AutoForm

B Control

C Detail

D Form

E Form header

F Form view

G Form Wizard

H Nudge

I Page footer

J Record selector

K Report

L Report Wizard

M Sizing handles

N Text box

O Toolbox

Concepts Assessments (continued)

Fill in the Blank Write the correct answer in the space provided.

1. Using a form simplifies the data entry process because forms display only _____ record at a time.

2. The navigation buttons on a form include methods to go directly to the next record, last record, first record, and the _____ record in a table, as well as a button to create a new record.

3. Forms and tables are _____ database objects, meaning information entered into one will be automatically entered in the other.

4. A bar in Access used to select an entire record in a form or a table is the _____.

5. Creating a form using the Form Wizard offers more flexibility in the design of the form than creating a form using a(n) _____.

6. To change the layout and arrangement of fields on a form or report you must use the _____ view of the form or report.

7. Two visual aids that guide your placement of controls on a report or form in Design view are the dotted grid pattern and the _____ at the top and left of the screen.

8. Access reports are printed so individuals can view the information in the report without _____ the database itself.

9. To select more than one field simultaneously in the Design view of a form or report, you must hold down the _____ key on the keyboard.

10. The layout that you choose for a report in the Report Wizard determines the _____ of the data in the report.

Access chapter two

Skill Assessments

Project 2C—LMccDepts

Objectives: *View and Navigate to Records with a Form, Create an AutoForm, Save and Close an AutoForm, and Use a Form to Add Records to and Delete Records from a Table.*

In the following Skill Assessment, you will create an AutoForm for use with the database of Department names at Lake Michigan City College. You will use the new form to add records to and delete records from the database. Your completed form will look like the one shown in Figure 2.58. You will rename the database as *2C_LMccDepts_Firstname_Lastname* in the folder you have created for this chapter.

Figure 2.58

(**Project 2C**–LMccDepts continues on the next page)

868   Access | Chapter 2: Forms and Reports

Skill Assessments (continued)

(Project 2C–LMccDepts continued)

1. Open **My Computer** or **Windows Explorer** and navigate to the location where the student files that accompany this textbook are located. Click once to select the file **a02C_LMccDepts**.

2. Copy and paste the **a02C_LMccDepts** file to the folder where you are storing your projects for this chapter.

3. Rename the file **2C_LMccDepts_Firstname_Lastname**

4. Right-click the file you just renamed and click **Properties**. On the displayed **Properties** dialog box, remove the Read-only property from the file and then click **OK**.

5. Close the Windows accessory you are using—either My Computer or Windows Explorer.

6. Start Access and open your **2C_LMccDepts** database. On the Objects bar, click **Forms**.

7. Above the Objects bar, locate and then click the **New** button. On the displayed **New Form** dialog box, click **AutoForm: Columnar**.

8. In the text box to the right of *Choose the table or query where the object's data comes from:*, click the **downward pointing arrow**. There is only one table for this database. Click **Departments** and then click **OK**. A new form based on the information in the Departments table is created and displays on your screen.

   Recall that AutoForm places all of the table's fields into the form. Access will apply the most recently used form formatting; thus, the format displayed on your screen will depend on previous use of the computer at which you are working.

9. At the lower edge of the form, in the navigation area, click the **Last Record** button. The last record in the table, for the Psychology Department, displays.

10. In the navigation area, click the **Previous Record** button once. The previous record, for the Physical Ed. Department, displays. In the navigation area, click the **First Record** button. The first record, for the Accounting Department, displays.

11. Position your mouse pointer in the navigation area over the number of the current record until the pointer turns into an I-beam. Then, drag to select the number. Type **9** and then press [Enter]. The record for the MIS Department displays.

    Recall that if you know the exact number of the record you want to view, this method of navigating to a record in a form is quicker than moving through the records one by one with the navigation buttons.

(Project 2C–LMccDepts continues on the next page)

Skill Assessments (continued)

(Project 2C–LMccDepts continued)

12. On the title bar of the **Departments** form, click the **Close** button. Because you have not previously named or saved this form, a message displays asking you if you want to save the changes to the design of form "*Form1*." Click **Yes**.

13. In the displayed **Save As** dialog box, in the **Form Name** box, accept the default form name of *Departments* by clicking **OK**. For this database, you now have a convenient form with which you can view or enter records, rather than viewing or entering records in the database table itself. Notice that the name of the form displays in the Database window.

14. Click to select the **Departments** form, and then above the Objects bar, click **Design**. The **Departments** form that you created opens in Design view. On the form's title bar, click the **Maximize** button. Maximizing a form in Design view allows you to view the different sections of the form and provides space to make changes to the layout of the form.

15. From the **View** menu, click **Page Header/Footer**. Page Header and Page Footer sections are added to your form.

16. Locate the Toolbox floating on your screen. If necessary, open the Toolbox by displaying the View menu and clicking Toolbox. Recall that the Toolbox is a toolbar that is used to add various types of controls to forms and reports in Access. On the Toolbox, click the **Label** button.

17. Move your pointer into the **Page Footer** section and create a label control approximately **2.75 inches wide**, centered vertically and horizontally in the available space. If you are not satisfied with your result, click the Undo button and begin again. Recall that you can use the Nudge feature ([Ctrl] + any arrow key) to position the object precisely. In the label, using your own information, type **2C LMccDepts Firstname Lastname** and then press [Enter].

18. Switch to Form view. In the navigation area of the form, click the **New Record** button. The fields are cleared and ready to accept a new entry. The record number advances by one to 13.

19. In the blank **Department** field, where the insertion point is blinking, type **General Business** and then press [Tab].

20. In **Extension** field, type **8885** and then press [Tab]. In the **Dept Chair** field, using your own information, type **Firstname Lastname** and then press [Tab].

21. In the **Division** field, type **Business**.

22. Navigate to record 5, the Department of General Mgt. On the left side of the form, locate the record selector bar that contains a right-pointing arrow. Click once in the record selector. The entire record is selected.

(Project 2C–LMccDepts continues on the next page)

Skill Assessments (continued)

(Project 2C–LMccDepts continued)

23. On the Form View toolbar, click the **Delete Record** button, or press . In the displayed alert, click **Yes**. The record is deleted from the Departments table.

24. To the right of *Type a question for help*, click the **Close Window** button. Click **Yes** if prompted to save your changes. The form closes and your changes are saved.

25. On the Objects bar, click **Tables**, and then double-click the **Departments** table to open it in Datasheet view. Examine the table and notice that the changes you made using the form are updated in the corresponding table. The Department of General Business has been added, and the Department of General Mgt. has been deleted. Notice that the records in the table have been sorted by the primary key.

26. To the right of *Type a question for help*, click the **Close Window** button to close the table. On the Objects bar, click **Forms**, and then, if necessary, click the **Departments** form once to select it.

27. On the Database toolbar, click the **Print** button to print the form. Two pages will print, and your name will print in the page footer on each page. Recall that depending on previous use of your computer, the format applied to your form may differ from the one shown in Figure 2.58. To the right of *Type a question for help*, click the **Close Window** button to close the database and then close Access.

End You have completed Project 2C

Project 2D — Office Supplies

Objectives: *Create a Form with the Form Wizard and Modify a Form.*

In the following Skill Assessment, you will use the Form Wizard to create a form for the Office Supplies database at Lake Michigan City College, and then make modifications to the layout of the form. Your completed database objects will look similar to Figure 2.59. You will rename and save your database as *2D_Office_Supplies_Firstname_Lastname*.

1. Open **My Computer** or **Windows Explorer** and navigate to the location where the student files that accompany this textbook are located. Click once to select the file **a02D_Office_Supplies**.

2. Copy and paste the **a02D_Office_Supplies** file to the folder where you are storing your projects for this chapter. Rename the file **2D_Office_Supplies_Firstname_Lastname**

3. Right-click the file you just renamed and click **Properties**. From the displayed **Properties** dialog box, remove the Read-only property from the file, and then click **OK**.

(Project 2D–Office Supplies continues on the next page)

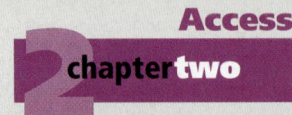

Skill Assessments (continued)

(Project 2D–Office Supplies continued)

Figure 2.59

4. Close the Windows accessory you are using—either My Computer or Windows Explorer. Start Access and open your **2D_Office_Supplies** database. On the Objects bar, click **Forms**.

5. To the right of the Objects bar, double-click the command icon *Create form by using wizard*. The Form Wizard opens requesting information about the table (or query) upon which the form will be based, and the fields from the table to include on the form.

6. Under **Tables/Queries**, click the **down arrow**. A list of tables and queries available for this database displays. Currently only one object, the **Office Inventory** table, has been created in this database. Click **Table: Office Inventory**.

7. To the right of the list of available fields, click the **All Fields** button to move all of the fields from the **Office Inventory** table to the **Selected Fields** column on the right.

(Project 2D–Office Supplies continues on the next page)

Skill Assessments (continued)

(Project 2D–Office Supplies continued)

8. Click the **Next** button. For the layout of the form, make sure the **Columnar** option button is selected, and then click the **Next** button. For the style of the form, click **SandStone**. A preview of the SandStone style displays on the left. Click the **Next** button.

9. With *Office Inventory* highlighted, press Delete to delete the default text. Then, using your own information type **Inventory Firstname Lastname**

10. Click the **Finish** button. Access creates the form using the information you specified in the Wizard screens. The completed form displays in Form view. On the Form View toolbar, click the **View** button to switch to Design view, and then on the form's title bar, click the **Maximize** button.

11. Position your pointer on the horizontal line between the **Form Header section** and the **Detail section** until the pointer changes to a large double arrow. Drag down approximately 0.5 inch. Use your eye and the vertical ruler to determine this distance. The **Form Header** section expands and grid dots display in this area.

12. Locate the **Toolbox** on your screen. (If necessary, display the View menu and click Toolbox.) On the Toolbox, click the **Label** button.

13. Move your pointer into the **Form Header section**, and position the pointer's plus sign at the **left edge of the Form Header area** and centered vertically (use your eye to approximate this distance) in the **Form Header section**. Drag down **about 0.25 inch and to the right to 3.0 inches on the horizontal ruler**. If you are not satisfied with your result, click the Undo button and begin again. In the label box you just created, use your own information to type **Inventory Entry Form (Firstname Lastname)** and then press Enter.

14. On the Form Design toolbar, click the **View** button to switch to the Form view, and notice the Form Header information you added with your name. On the Form View toolbar, click the **View** button to return to Design view. By placing a Form Header on the form, you have created an informative title that will print at the beginning of the form. Someone who reads the printed form will have an indication as to the contents of the form.

15. Position your pointer on the right edge of the form until your pointer changes to a large double arrow. Drag the right edge of the form to the right to **6.5 inches on the horizontal ruler**. The width of the form is expanded. By increasing the dimensions of a form, you create more working space to move and reposition the controls on the form.

16. Click once in the white text box control **Cost**. The Cost text box control is selected and handles surround the selected object. Recall that a text box control on a form is where data from the corresponding table is displayed, or where new data for the table is entered.

(Project 2D–Office Supplies continues on the next page)

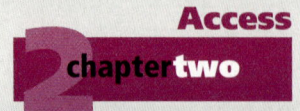

Skill Assessments (continued)

(Project 2D–Office Supplies continued)

17. Position your pointer over any border of the text box until the **hand** pointer displays. Using the grid dots and the horizontal ruler as a guide, drag the **Cost controls** up and to the right of the Inventory# controls—until the right edge of the Cost controls are positioned at approximately **6.0 inches on the horizontal ruler** and aligned with the Inventory# controls, as shown in Figure 2.59.

18. Click once on the white **Quantity on Hand** text box control to select it. Position your pointer over any border of the text box until the **hand** pointer displays. Drag the **Quantity on Hand** controls up and position them directly under the Cost controls—and to the right of the Inventory Item controls. See Figure 2.59.

19. Click once in the white **Unit Measurement** text box control to select it. Position your pointer over the large black handle that is between the **Unit Measurement text box control** and the **Unit Measurement label control** until the **pointing hand** pointer displays. Recall that with this pointer, you can move the text box control independently of the label control. Drag only the **Unit Measurement text box control** to the right, so that its left edge is positioned at **3.5 inches on the horizontal ruler** and its top edge is positioned at **1.0 inch on the vertical ruler**. See Figure 2.59.

20. Position your pointer over the large black handle in the **Unit Measurement label control** until the **pointing hand** pointer displays. Drag the label control until it left edge is positioned at **1.0 inch on the horizontal ruler** and its top edge is positioned at **1.0 inch on the vertical ruler**.

21. Display the **View** menu and click **Page Header/Footer**. On the Toolbox, click the **Label** button. Move your pointer into the **Page Footer** section and create a label control approximately 3 inches wide, centered vertically and horizontally in the available space. Recall that you can use the Nudge feature (Ctrl + any arrow key) to position the object precisely. In the label, using your own information, type **2D Office Supplies Firstname Lastname** and then press Enter.

22. On the Form Design toolbar, click the **View** button to switch to the Form view and then view the changes to your form. The Form Header displays; recall that Page Footers display only when printed or in Print Preview. Then, on the Form View toolbar, click the **Print** button to print the form. Two pages will print.

23. To the right of *Type a question for help*, click the **Restore Window** button. The form is restored to its original size. On the title bar of the form, click the **Close** button. Click **Yes** to save your changes. Close the database and then close Access.

End You have completed Project 2D

874 Access | Chapter 2: Forms and Reports

Access chapter two

Skill Assessments (continued)

Project 2E—Inventory

Objectives: *Create a Report with the Report Wizard, Save a Report, Modify the Design of a Report, and Print a Report.*

The Computer Club at Lake Michigan City College has an inventory of hardware, software, and other equipment that it uses for training and various club events. The club maintains a database of this inventory. In the following Skill Assessment, you will use the Report Wizard to create a report listing the information from a table in the Inventory database. After creating the report, you will modify its design. Your completed report will look like the one shown in Figure 2.60. You will rename and save your database as *2E_Inventory_Firstname_Lastname*.

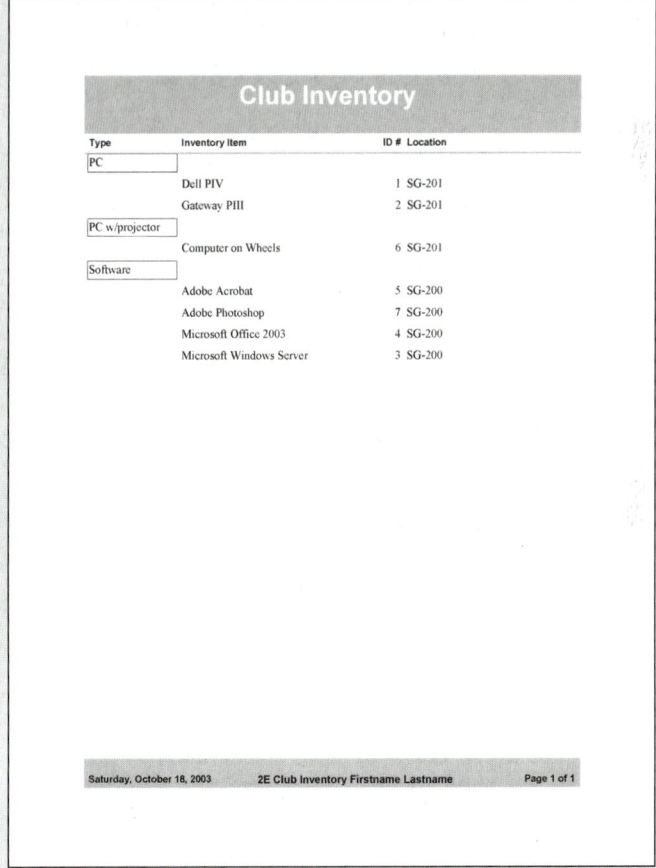

Figure 2.60

1. Open **My Computer** or **Windows Explorer** and navigate to the location where the student files that accompany this textbook are located. Click once to select the file **a02E_Inventory**.

2. Copy and paste the **a02E_Inventory** file to the folder where you are storing your projects for this chapter. Rename the file 2E_Inventory_Firstname_Lastname

(**Project 2E**–Inventory continues on the next page)

Project 2E: Inventory | **Access** 875

Skill Assessments (continued)

(Project 2E–Inventory continued)

3. Right-click the file you just renamed and click **Properties**. From the displayed **Properties** dialog box, remove the Read-only property from the file and then click **OK**.

4. Close the Windows accessory you are using—either My Computer or Windows Explorer. Start Access and open your **2E_Inventory** database. On the Objects bar, click **Reports**.

5. To the right of the Objects bar, double-click **Create report by using wizard**. The Report Wizard opens. The first step in the Report Wizard is to determine from which table (or query) information for the report will be taken, and also what fields from the table to include in the report. Under **Tables/Queries**, click the **down arrow**. A list of tables and queries available for this database displays. Currently only one object, the Inventory table, has been created in this database.

6. Click **Table: Inventory**. A list of the fields in the Inventory table displays in the Available Fields column on the left. To the right of the list of available fields, click the **All Fields** button to move all of the fields from the Inventory table to the Selected Fields column on the far right. All of the fields that were listed under Available Fields display in the Selected Fields list. Click the **Next** button.

7. Recall that it is often useful to group information on a printed report by one or more of the fields in the table. In the displayed list of field names, click **Type**, and then click the **One Field** button. The preview on the right displays the **Type** field, indicating that on the finished report, records will be grouped by type. Click the **Next** button.

8. In this step of the Report Wizard, you can designate an order by which records in the table will be sorted. To the right of the **1** text box, **click** the **down arrow**. In the list of available fields, click **Inventory Item**. Leave the default order as **Ascending**. Click the **Next** button.

9. Under **Layout**, make sure the **Stepped** option button is selected. Under **Orientation**, make sure the **Portrait** option button is selected. Click the **Next** button.

10. From the list of styles that can be applied to the report, click **Soft Gray** and then click the **Next** button. With *Inventory* highlighted, press Delete. Type **Club Inventory** and then click the **Finish** button. The report displays in Print Preview.

11. If necessary, on the Club Inventory title bar, click the **Maximize** button. On the Print Preview toolbar, click the **Zoom arrow** and then click **75%**. Notice that the specifications you defined for the report in the Report Wizard are reflected in the Print Preview of the report. For example, the inventory items are grouped by Type—PC, PC w/projector, and Software. Within each type, the equipment is alphabetized by Inventory Item name.

(Project 2E–Inventory continues on the next page)

Skill Assessments (continued)

(Project 2E–Inventory continued)

12. To the right of *Type a question for help*, click the **Close Window** button. The report closes and the report name displays in the Database window. Reports created with the Report Wizard are named in the final step of the wizard. When the report is closed, it is automatically saved.

13. Double-click the **Club Inventory** report to open the report in Print Preview. On the Print Preview toolbar, click the **View** button to switch to the Design view of the report. If necessary, on the title bar of the report, click the **Maximize** button. The Design view of the report fills the working area.

14. In the **Report Header section**, click the label **Club Inventory**. The label is selected and handles surround the selected object. Position your pointer over a border of the selected object to display the **hand pointer**. Drag the label to the right, until the left edge is positioned at **2.0 inches on the horizontal ruler**, maintaining its vertical placement.

15. In the **Page Footer section** of the report, notice the two controls. The control on the left causes the current date to display in this section each time the report is opened. The control on the right causes the page numbers, as well as the total number of pages, to display in the report.

16. Click to select the **date** control on the left. Drag the center right handle to the left to **2 inches on the horizontal ruler**. Select the page number control on the right. Drag the center left handle to the right to **5.25 inches on the horizontal ruler**.

17. Locate the **Toolbox** floating on your screen. (If necessary, display the View menu and click Toolbox to display it.) Click the **Label** button. In the **Page Footer section**, position the pointer's plus sign near the upper edge of the existing controls at **2.25 inches on the horizontal ruler**. Drag down about **0.25 inch** and to the right to **5.0 inches on the horizontal ruler**.

18. In this label, using your own information, type **2E Club Inventory Firstname Lastname** and then press Enter.

19. On the Report Design toolbar, click the **Print Preview** button to verify that your information displays at the lower edge of the report. If you are not satisfied with the placement of your information, return to Design view, select the label, and use the Nudge feature (Ctrl + any arrow key) to reposition the label.

20. If necessary, return to **Print Preview**. On the Print Preview toolbar, click the **Print** button. One page will print. To the right of *Type a question for help*, click the **Close Window** button. Click **Yes** to save your changes. Close the database and close Access.

 You have completed Project 2E

Access chapter two

Performance Assessments

Project 2F—Music Dept

Objectives: *Create an AutoForm, Save and Close an AutoForm, and Create a Form with the Form Wizard.*

In the following Performance Assessment, you will create two new forms for the Music Department at Lake Michigan City College: one by using the Form Wizard and another by creating an AutoForm. Your completed forms will look similar to Figure 2.61. You will rename and save your database as *2F_Music_Dept_Firstname_Lastname*.

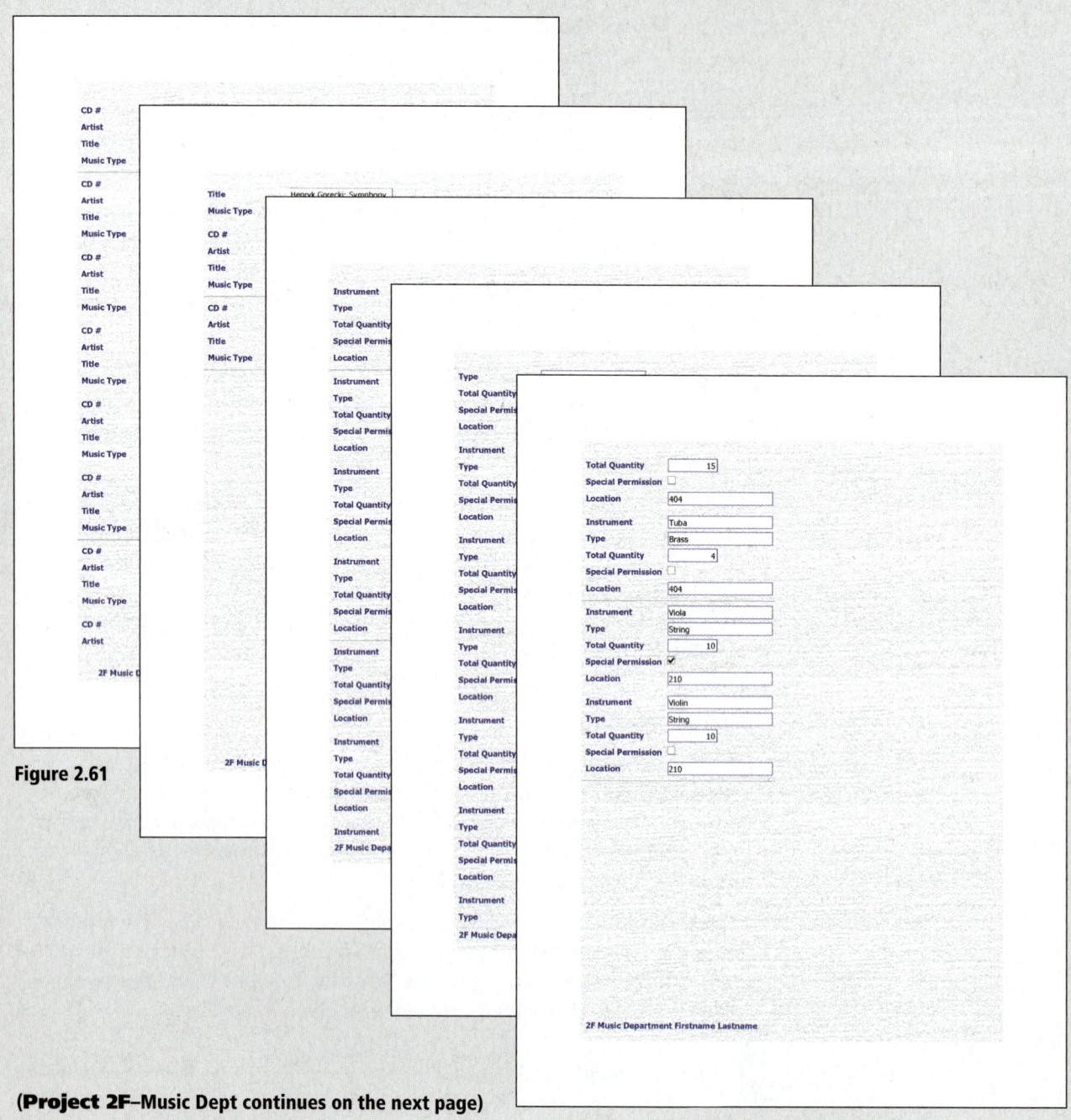

Figure 2.61

(**Project 2F**–Music Dept continues on the next page)

Performance Assessments (continued)

(Project 2F–Music Dept continued)

1. Open **My Computer** or **Windows Explorer** and navigate to the student files for this textbook. Copy and paste the file **a02F_Music_Dept** to the folder where you are storing your projects for this chapter. Rename the file, using your own information, **2F_Music_Dept_Firstname_Lastname** and remove the Read-only property. Close My Computer or Windows Explorer.

2. Start Access and open your **2F_Music_Dept** database. On the Objects bar, click **Forms** and then start the Form Wizard. Under **Tables/Queries**, click the **down arrow**, and then click **Table: CD Collection**. Include all of the fields from the table in the form. Click the **Next** button.

3. Select the **Columnar** layout, click **Next**, and then click the **Sumi Painting** style for the form. Click **Next**. As the title for the form, type **CD Collection Firstname Lastname** and then click **Finish**.

4. Maximize the form and switch to the Design view of the form. Display the **View** menu and then click **Page Header/Footer**.

5. On the Toolbox, click the **Label** button and then move the pointer into the **Page Footer section**. Position the pointer plus sign just below the Page Footer separator at **0.25 inch on the horizontal ruler**. Drag down to the lower edge and to the right to **3 inches on the horizontal ruler**. In the label, and using your own information, type **2F Music Dept Firstname Lastname** and then press Enter.

6. Switch to the Form view and print the form. Two pages will print. Click the **Close Window** button and save your changes.

7. Make sure **Forms** is selected on the Objects bar and then click the **New** button. In the displayed **New Form** dialog box, click **AutoForm: Columnar**. To the right of *Choose the table or query where the object's data comes from*, click the **down arrow**, and then from the displayed list, click **Rental Instruments**. Click **OK**. Click the **Close Window** button and save the form using the default name of *Rental Instruments*.

8. Open the **Rental Instruments** form, switch to the Design View, display the **View** menu, and then click **Page Header/Footer**. In the Toolbox, click the **Label** button. In the **Page Footer** section, just below the Page Footer separator, create a label within the space beginning at the **left edge of the form** and ending at **3.0 inches on the horizontal ruler**. In the label box, use your own information and type **2F Music Dept Firstname Lastname** and then press Enter.

9. Switch to Form view and print the form. Three pages will print. Click the **Close Window** button, save your changes, close the database, and then close Access.

End You have completed Project 2F

Performance Assessments (continued)

Project 2G—Music

Objectives: *Create a Report with the Report Wizard and Save a Report.*

In the following Performance Assessment, you will use the Report Wizard to create a report for the Music Department at Lake Michigan City College. Your completed report will look similar to Figure 2.62. You will save your database as 2G*_Music_Firstname_Lastname.*

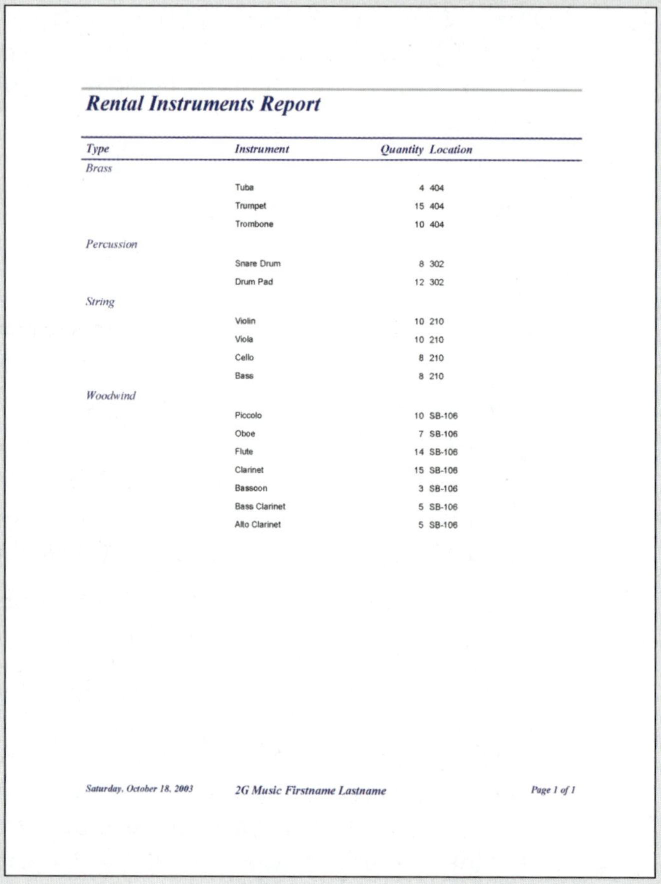

Rental Instruments Report

Type	Instrument	Quantity	Location
Brass			
	Tuba	4	404
	Trumpet	15	404
	Trombone	10	404
Percussion			
	Snare Drum	8	302
	Drum Pad	12	302
String			
	Violin	10	210
	Viola	10	210
	Cello	8	210
	Bass	8	210
Woodwind			
	Piccolo	10	SB-106
	Oboe	7	SB-106
	Flute	14	SB-106
	Clarinet	15	SB-106
	Bassoon	3	SB-106
	Bass Clarinet	5	SB-106
	Alto Clarinet	5	SB-106

Saturday, October 18, 2003 2G Music Firstname Lastname Page 1 of 1

Figure 2.62

1. Open **My Computer** or **Windows Explorer** and navigate to the student files for this textbook. Copy and paste the file **a02G_Music** to the folder where you are storing your projects for this chapter. Rename the file, using your own information, **2G_Music_Firstname_Lastname** and remove the Read-only property. Close My Computer or Windows Explorer.

2. Start Access and open your **2G_Music** database. On the Objects bar, click **Reports** and then start the Report Wizard. Under **Tables/Queries**, click the **down arrow** and then click **Table: Rental Instruments**. Include all of the fields from the **Rental Instruments** table in the report. Click the **Next** button.

(Project 2G–Music continues on the next page)

Performance Assessments (continued)

(Project 2G–Music continued)

3. Group the records by **Type** and click **OneField** button to display Type in the Preview. Click the **Next** button. Sort the records by **Instrument** in **Ascending** order. Click the **Next** button. Select the **Stepped** layout and the **Portrait** orientation. Click the **Next** button. As the style for the report, click **Corporate** and then click the **Next** button. For the name of the report, type **Rental Instruments Report** and then click the **Finish** button.

4. If necessary, maximize the displayed **Print Preview** and then zoom to **75%**. After examining the report, click the **View** button to switch to Design view.

5. In the **Page Footer** section of the report, click the **date control** on the left to select it and then drag the center right handle to the left until the right edge of the control is positioned at **2.0 inches on the horizontal ruler**. Select the **page number control** on the right, and drag its left center handle to **5.25 inches on the horizontal ruler**.

6. In the Toolbox, click the **Label** button. In the **Page Footer** section, starting at approximately the **2.0-inch mark on the horizontal ruler** and vertically aligned with the other controls, drag down and to the right to **5.25 inches on the horizontal ruler**. In the **Label** box, using your own information, type **2G Music Firstname Lastname** and press .

7. Switch to the **Print Preview** of the report and verify that your information displays in the footer. **Print** the report. Click the **Close Window** button and save your changes. Close the database and then close Access.

End You have completed Project 2G

Project 2H—DL Courses

Objectives: *View and Navigate to Records with a Form, Use a Form to Add Records to and Delete Records from a Table, Modify the Design of a Report, and Print a Report.*

In the following Performance Assessment, you will open an existing form for the Distance Learning Courses database at Lake Michigan City College. You will add and delete records using the form. Additionally, you will open an existing report and make changes to the design of the report. Your completed database objects will look similar to Figure 2.63. You will rename and save your database as *2H_DL_Courses_Firstname_Lastname*.

(Project 2H–DL Courses continues on the next page**)**

Access chapter two
Performance Assessments (continued)

(Project 2H–DL Courses continued)

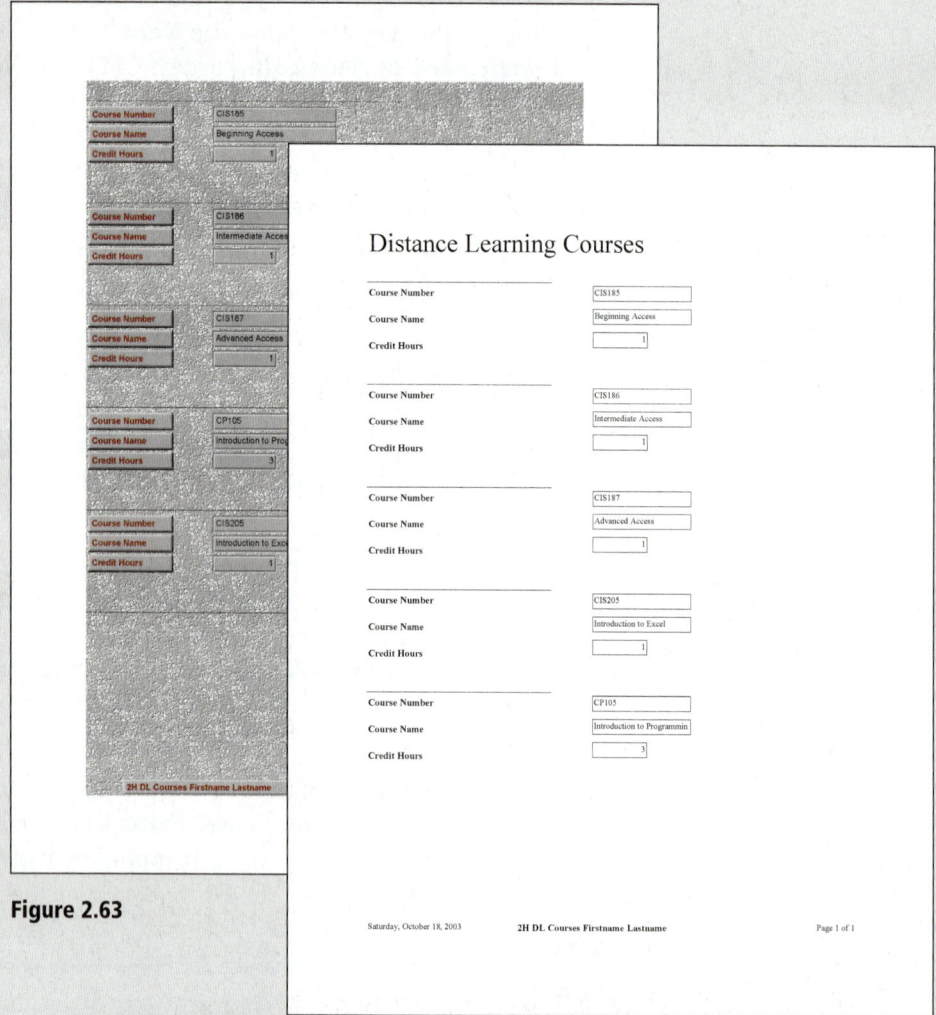

Figure 2.63

1. Open **My Computer** or **Windows Explorer** and navigate to the student files for this textbook. Copy and paste the file a02H_DL_Courses to the folder where you are storing your projects for this chapter. Rename the file, using your own information, **2H_DL_Courses_Firstname_Lastname** and remove the Read-only property. Close My Computer or Windows Explorer.

2. Start Access and open your **2H_DL_Courses** database. On the Objects bar, click **Forms** and then open the **Distance Learning Courses** form. Click the **New Record** button. In the **Course Number** field, type **CIS205** and press Tab. In the **Course Name** field type **Introduction to Excel** and in the **Credit Hours** field type **1**.

3. Navigate to record 1, which has the course name *Introduction to Computers.* Use the record selector bar to select the entire record and then delete the record.

(Project 2H–DL Courses continues on the next page)

Performance Assessments (continued)

(Project 2H–DL Courses continued)

4. Switch to Design view and maximize the form window. Display the **View** menu and then click **Page Header/Footer**. On the Toolbox, click the **Label** button. In the **Page Footer section**, just below the Page Footer separator at **0.5 inch on the horizontal ruler**, drag down to the lower separator and to the right to **3 inches on the horizontal ruler**. In the label box, using your own information, type **2H DL Courses Firstname Lastname** and press Enter.

5. Switch to Form view and print the form. Close the form and save your changes.

6. On the Objects bar, click **Reports** and then open the **Distance Learning Courses** report in Print Preview. If necessary, maximize the window and then zoom to 100%. View the report and notice that the labels and their corresponding text boxes are formatted in a manner that is difficult to read. Switch to Design view. Using the techniques you practiced in this chapter, arrange the label and text box controls to match Figure 2.64.

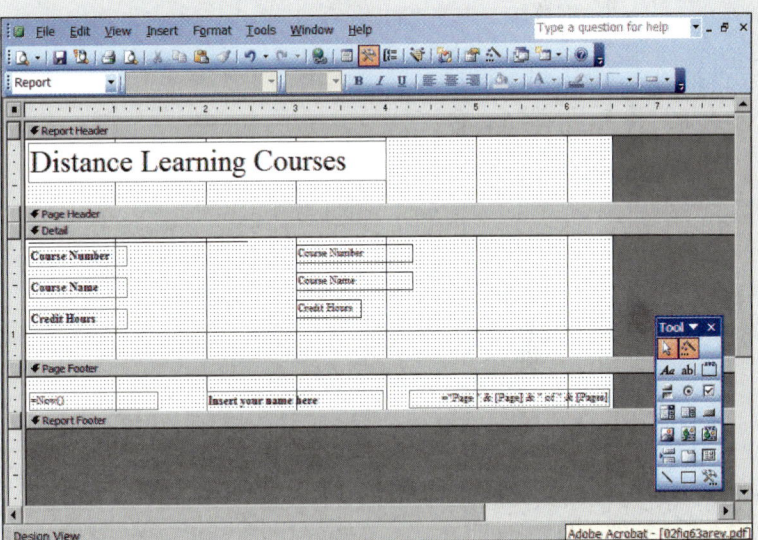

Figure 2.64

7. In the **Page Footer section** of the report, in the control *Insert your name here*, click the control once to select it, and then delete the text in the control. Using your own information, type **2H DL Courses Firstname Lastname** and then press Enter.

8. Switch to the **Print Preview** of the report. Verify that your information is at the lower edge of the report and then print the report. Close the report, save your changes, close the database, and then close Access.

End You have completed Project 2H

Access Chapter Two

Mastery Assessments

Project 2I — Employees

Objectives: *Create an AutoForm, Save and Close an AutoForm, Create a Report with the Report Wizard, Save a Report, and Print a Report.*

In the following Mastery Assessment, you will create an AutoForm and a report that corresponds to the Employees table for Lake Michigan City College. Your completed database objects will look similar to Figure 2.65. You will save your database as *2I_Employees_Firstname_Lastname*.

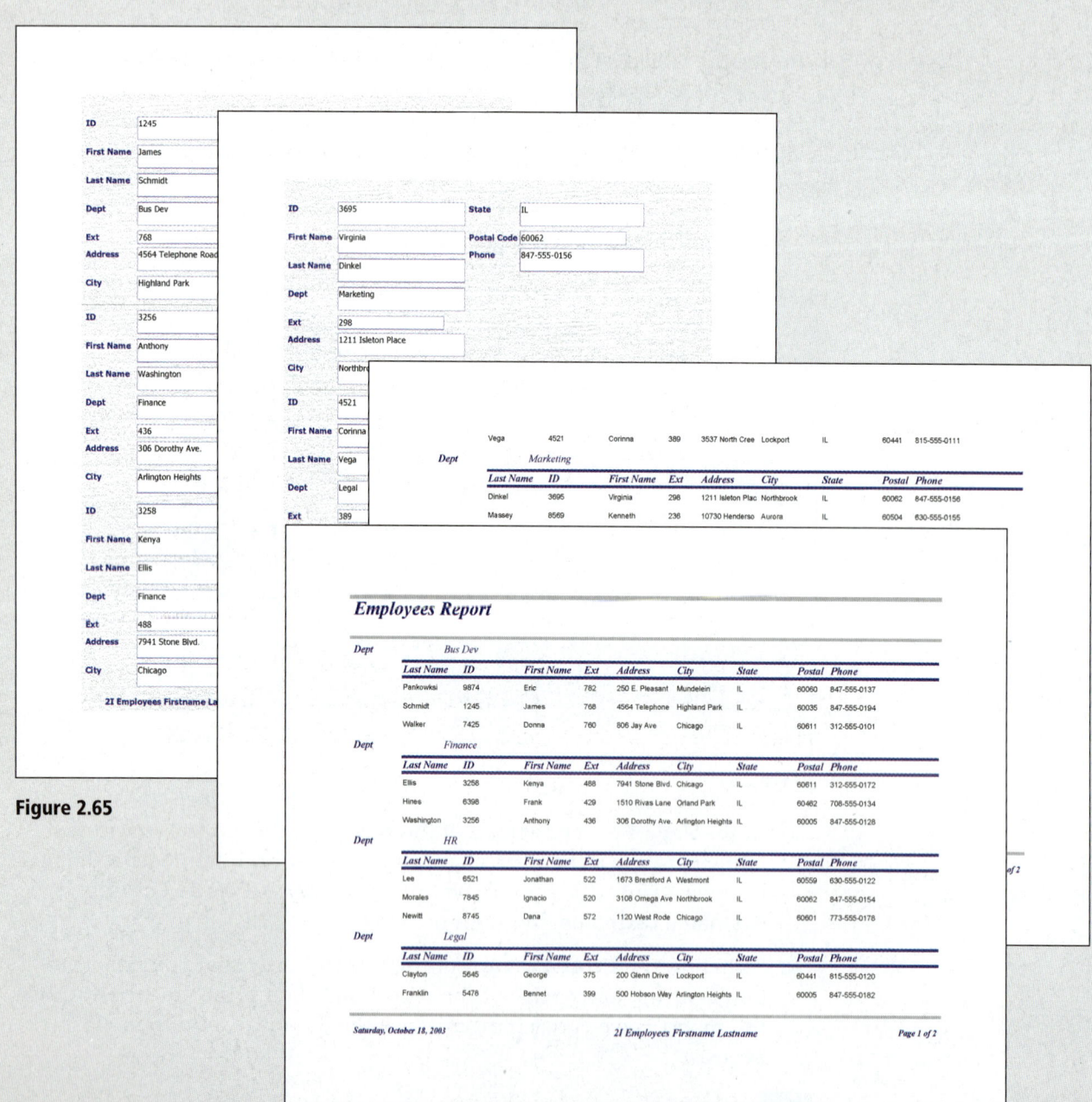

Figure 2.65

(Project 2I–Employees continues on the next page)

884   Access | Chapter 2: Forms and Reports

Access chapter two
Mastery Assessments (continued)

(Project 2I–Employees continued)

1. From the student files that accompany this textbook, copy the file **a02I_Employees** and then paste the file to the folder where you are storing your projects for this chapter. Using your own information, rename this file to **2I_Employees_Firstname_Lastname** and remove the Read-only attribute.

2. Start Access and then open your **2I_Employees** database.

3. Create an AutoForm based on the **Employees** table. Use the **Columnar** format for the form. Add a Page Footer to the form and in it type **2I Employees Firstname Lastname** and then save the AutoForm as **Employees Form** Print the form. Five pages will print.

4. Use the Report wizard to create a report based on the **Employees** table. As you proceed through the wizard, use the following specifications for your report:

   Include all of the fields from the Employees table
   Group the records by Dept
   Sort the records alphabetically by Last Name
   Use the Outline 1 layout for the report in Landscape orientation
   Use the Corporate style for the report
   Save the report as Employees Report

5. In the **Page Footer** section, decrease the width of the control on the right by dragging its left edge to **7.5 inches on the horizontal ruler**. Create a label in the **Page Footer** section, and in it type **2I Employees Firstname Lastname**

6. Print the report. Two pages will print. Close any open database objects, the database, and then close Access.

 End You have completed Project 2I

Project 2J — Suppliers

Objectives: *Use a Form to Add Records to and Delete Records from a Table, Create a Form with the Form Wizard, and Modify a Form.*

In the following Mastery Assessment, you will use the Form Wizard to create a new form for the Suppliers database at Lake Michigan City College. Your completed form will look similar to Figure 2.66. You will save your database as *2J_Suppliers_Firstname_Lastname.*

1. From the student files that accompany this textbook, copy the file a02J_Suppliers and then paste the file to the folder where you are storing your projects for this chapter. Using your own information, rename this file as **2J_Suppliers_Firstname_Lastname** and remove the Read-only attribute.

(Project 2J–Suppliers continues on the next page)

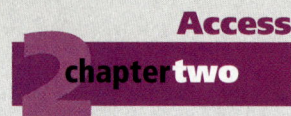

Mastery Assessments (continued)

(Project 2J–Suppliers continued)

Figure 2.66

2. Start Access and then open your **2J_Suppliers** database.

3. Create a form using the Form Wizard based on the **Suppliers** table. Use the following specifications in your form:

   Include all of the fields from the Suppliers table
   Apply the Columnar layout to the form
   Apply the Expedition style to the form
   Accept the default name for the form

(Project 2J–Suppliers continues on the next page)

Mastery Assessments (continued)

(Project 2J–Suppliers continued)

4. Add a **Page Footer** to the form and in it type **2J Suppliers Firstname Lastname**

5. Delete the record for **Jiffy Cleaning Supplies**. Edit the record for **Plastic Warehouse** by changing the name of the contact person from **Debbie Lucero** to **Beau Gellard**.

6. Modify the design of the form by widening it to **6 inches on the horizontal ruler**. Then, instead of one column of eight fields, create two columns of four fields. Begin the second column with the **State** controls, aligning them at **3 inches on the horizontal ruler**. Refer to Figure 2.67. Print and close the form. Two pages will print. Close the database and then close Access.

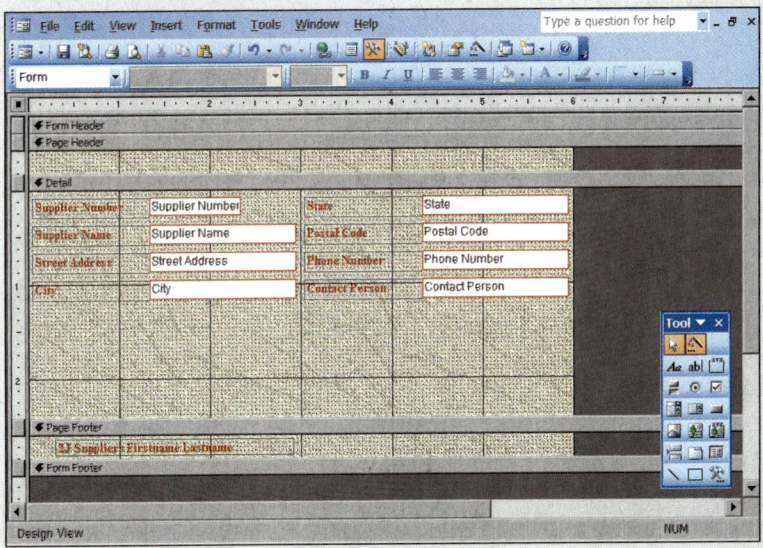

Figure 2.67

 You have completed Project 2J

Project 2J: Suppliers | **Access** 887

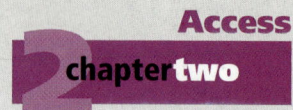

Problem Solving

Project 2K—Employees

Objectives: *Create an AutoForm or Create a Form with the Form Wizard and Modify a Form.*

In this Problem Solving assessment, you will create a form for entering data into the Employees database at Lake Michigan City College.

1. From the student files that accompany this textbook, copy the file *a02K_Employees* and then paste the file to the folder where you are storing your projects for this chapter. Using your own information, rename this file as **2K_Employees_Firstname_Lastname** and remove the Read-only attribute.

2. New employees fill out a paper form similar to the one shown in Figure 2.68. Then, the data entry clerk uses the paper forms to enter the new employees into the database. Create a form, using any method you choose, and then modify the layout of the form so that it closely resembles the layout of the paper form. This will make it much easier and faster to enter new employees into the database.

Lake Michigan City College

Employee Information Form

First Name _____ ID _____

Last Name _____ Dept _____

Address _____ Ext _____

City _____

State _____ Postal Code _____

Figure 2.68

3. Add your name and the project name in a Page Footer on the form and print the form.

 You have completed Project 2K

Problem Solving (continued)

Project 2L—Depts

Objectives: *Create a Report with the Report Wizard, Save a Report, Modify the Design of a Report, and Print a Report.*

In this Problem Solving assessment, you will create a report that faculty and staff members at Lake Michigan City College can consult to obtain information about the departments at the college.

1. From the student files that accompany this textbook, copy the file *a02L_Depts* and then paste the file to the folder where you are storing your projects for this chapter. Using your own information, rename this file as **2L_Depts_Firstname_Lastname** and remove the Read-only attribute.

2. Use the Report Wizard to create a report that includes all the fields in alphabetical order by department name. Arrange the fields on the report in an attractive, easy-to-ready layout. In Design view, create a label in the footer area with the project name and your name. Print the report.

 You have completed Project 2L

On the Internet

Discovering What's New in Access

Working with current database software is an important part of your database training.

Go to **www.microsoft.com** and perform a search to identify the changes from Access 2002 Access 2003.

GO! with Help

Creating a Form in Design View

Besides using the Form Wizard to create a form, you can also create a form from the Design view. Use the Access Help system to find out how to create a form using Design view.

1. Start Access. if necessary, from the **View** menu, click **Task Pane** to display the **Getting Started** task pane. On the task pane, to the right of *Getting Started*, click the **down arrow**. From the displayed list of available task panes, click **Help**.

2. Click in the **Search for** box and type **Create a form**

3. Press [Enter], scroll the displayed list as necessary, and then click **Create a form**.

4. At the lower part of the pane, locate the text *On your own in Design view*, and under this result, click **How?**

5. If you would like to keep a copy of this information, click the **Print** button. One page will print.

6. Click the **Close** button in the top right corner of the Help window to close the Help window and then close Access.

Access 2003

chapter three

Queries

In this chapter, you will: complete these projects and practice these skills.

Project 3A
Creating Queries

Objectives
- Create a New Select Query
- Run, Save, and Close a Query
- Open and Edit an Existing Query
- Specify Text Criteria in a Query

Project 3B
Defining Queries

Objectives
- Use Wildcards in a Query
- Specify Numeric Criteria in a Query
- Use Compound Criteria
- Sort Data in a Query

Project 3C
Using Calculated Fields and Calculating Statistics in a Query

Objectives
- Use Calculated Fields in a Query
- Group Data and Calculate Statistics in a Query

Lake Michigan City College

Lake Michigan City College is located along the lakefront of Chicago—one of the nation's most exciting cities. The college serves its large and diverse student body and makes positive contributions to the community through relevant curricula, partnerships with businesses and nonprofit organizations, and learning experiences that allow students to be full participants in the global community. The college offers three associate degrees in 20 academic areas, adult education programs, and continuing education offerings on campus, at satellite locations, and online.

© Getty Images, Inc.

Queries

Access queries allow you to isolate specific data in a database by asking questions and setting conditions that Access can interpret. The conditions, known as criteria, can be either text or numeric in nature. Wildcard characters can be used when a portion of what you are looking for is unknown.

Access provides comparison operators that, combined with numeric criteria, can further refine the query search. Logical operators such as AND and OR, as well as statistical functions, can be used in queries. In this chapter, you will create and modify queries for an Access database.

Project 3A School

Just like tables, forms, and reports, queries are also database objects. Queries can be used to locate information in an Access database based on certain *criteria* that you specify as part of the query. Criteria are conditions that identify the specific records you are looking for. Queries can also be created to view only certain fields from a table.

Lake Michigan City College uses queries to locate information about the data in their databases that meet certain criteria. In Activities 3.1 through 3.6 you will use queries to locate information about the records in the Students table. Your query result will look similar to Figure 3.1.

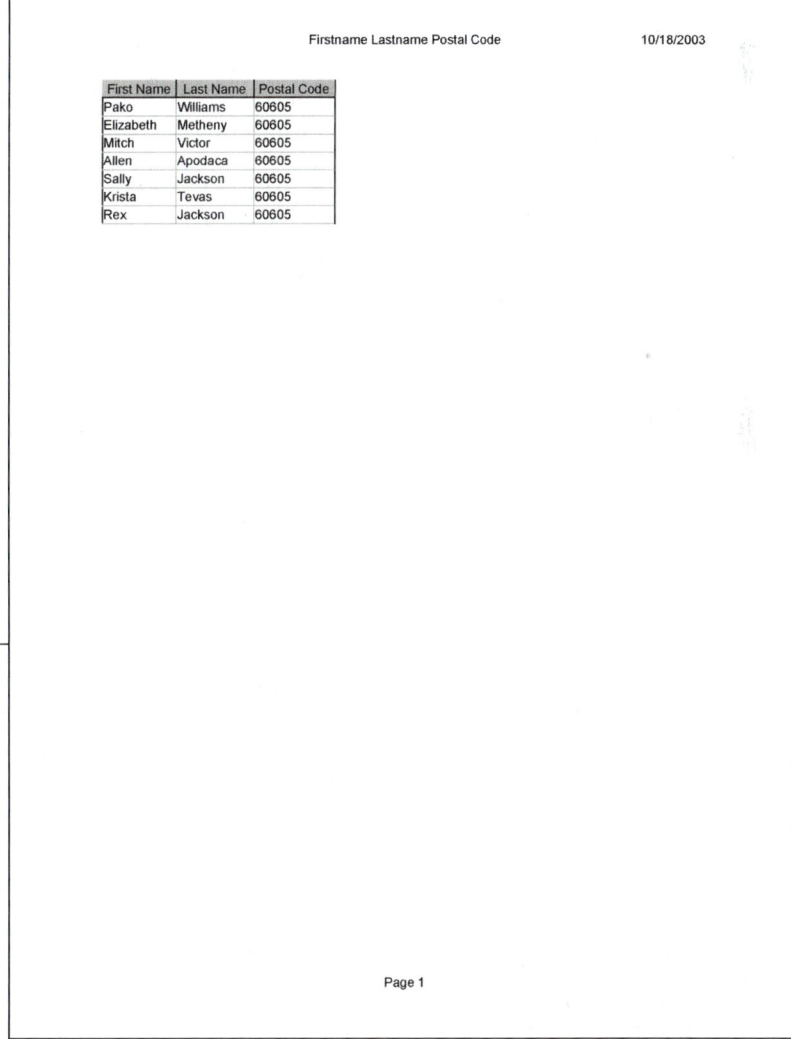

Figure 3.1
Project 3A—School

Project 3A: School | **Access** 893

Objective 1
Create a New Select Query

A ***query*** is a question formed in a manner that Access can interpret. The question that is asked may be simple or complex. For example, you might want to ask, "Which students are Business Majors?" Unless a query has already been set up to ask this question, you must create a new one. A query that retrieves data from one or more tables and then displays the results is called a ***select query***. In the following activity, you will create a simple select query with no criteria specified.

Activity 3.1 Creating a New Query, Using the Select Query Window, and Adding Fields to the Design Grid

1. Using the skills you practiced in Chapter 1, and using either My Computer or Windows Explorer, create a new folder named *Chapter 3* in the location where you will be storing your projects for this chapter.

2. Locate the file **a03A_School** from the student files that accompany this text. Copy and paste the file to the Chapter 3 folder you created in Step 1.

3. Using the technique you practiced in Activity 1.1 of Chapter 1, remove the Read-only property from the file and rename the file as *3A_School_Firstname_Lastname*

4. Close the Windows accessory you are using—either My Computer or Windows Explorer. Start Access and open your **3A_School** database.

5. On the Objects bar, click **Queries**.

   To the right of the Objects bar, two command icons for creating a new query display.

6. Double-click **Create query in Design view**.

   A new Select Query window opens and the **Show Table** dialog box displays. See Figure 3.2. The **Show Table** dialog box lists all of the tables in the database.

> **Note** — Creating Queries in Design View
>
> *Queries in Design view.*
>
> In this chapter, you will create queries only in Design view. Creating queries using the wizard will be addressed as you progress in your study of Access.

Show Table dialog box

Students table

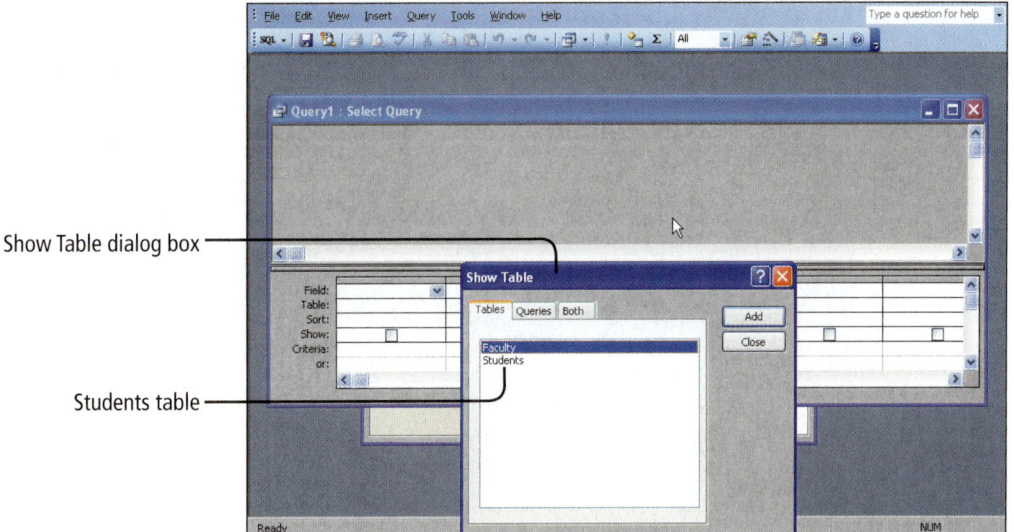

Figure 3.2

7 In the **Show Table** dialog box, click **Students**, click the **Add** button, and then click the **Close** button. See Figure 3.3. Alternatively, you can double-click Students and then click Close.

A list of the fields in the Students table displays in the upper pane of the Select Query window. The **Student#** field is bold, unlike the other fields in the list, because the **Student#** field is the primary key in the Students table.

The Select Query window has two parts: the *table area* (upper pane) and the *design grid* (lower pane). After a table has been selected from the **Show Table** dialog box, it displays in the table area, as shown in Figure 3.4.

Table area

Click to add table to the table area

Closes the Show Table dialog box

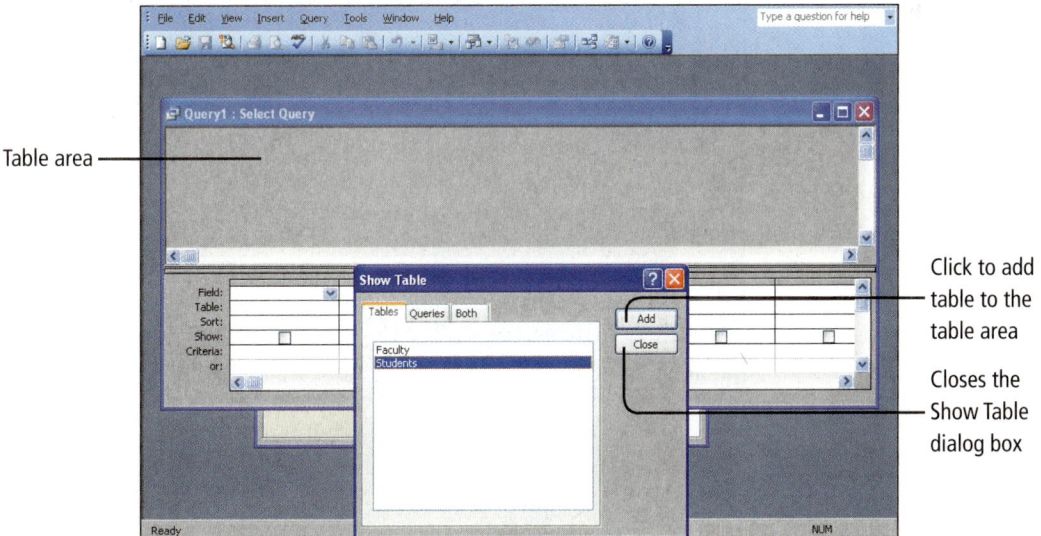

Figure 3.3

Project 3A: School | **Access** 895

8 In the **Students** field list, double-click **Student#**.

The **Student#** field displays in the design grid. See Figure 3.4. The design grid of the Select Query window is where you specify the fields and other criteria to be used in the query.

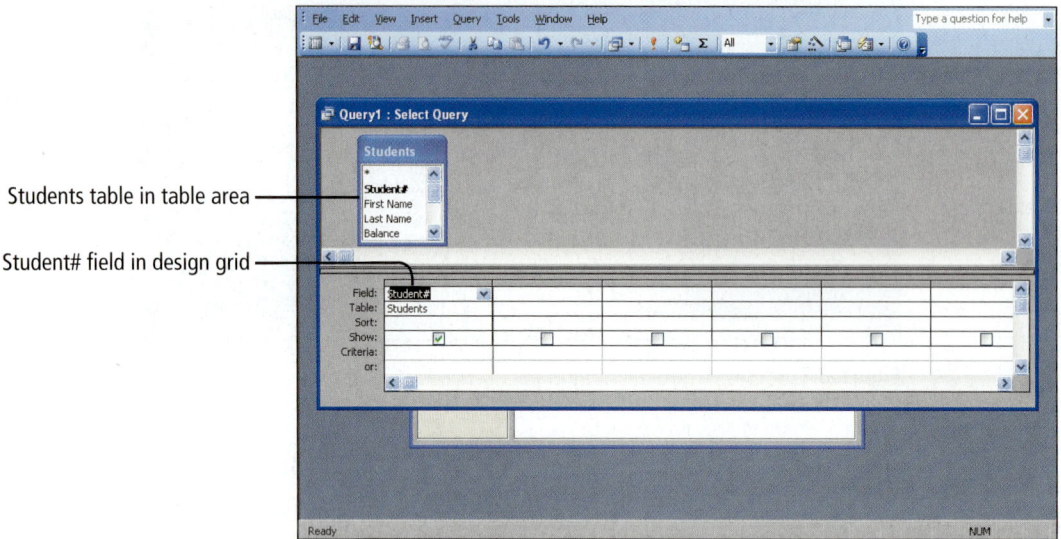

Figure 3.4

9 In the **Students** field list, double-click **First Name**. Repeat this action for all the remaining fields in the field list. Use the vertical scroll bar in the field list window to view the fields toward the end of the list.

As you double-click each field, notice the fields display one by one to the right of the previous field in the design grid. See Figure 3.5.

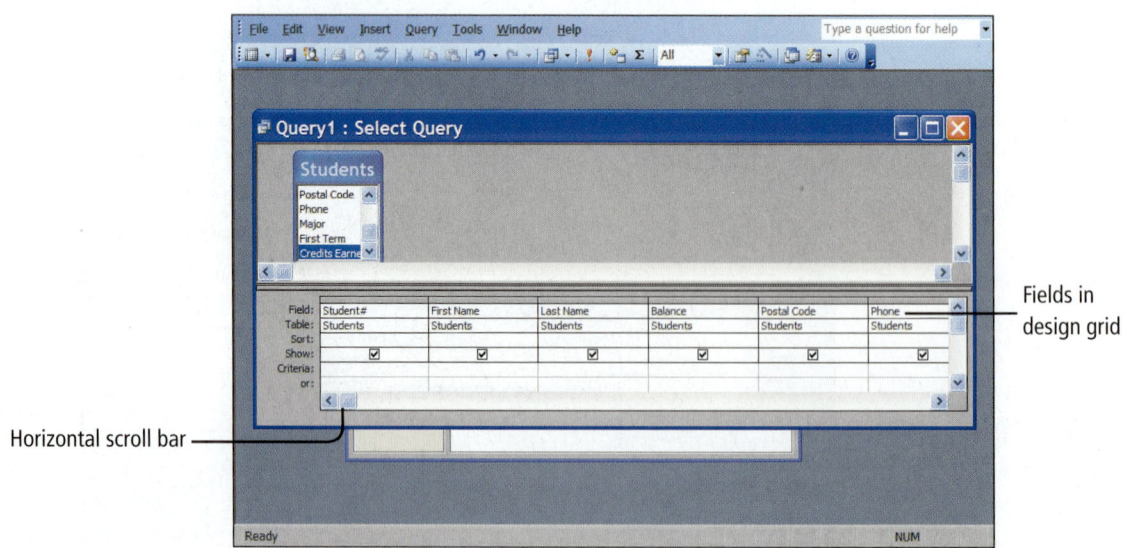

Figure 3.5

10 Use the horizontal scroll bar to scroll to the right to view all the fields in the design grid. Verify that all of the fields from the field list are displayed in the design grid.

Another Way

Adding All Fields to a Query

*Double-click the *.*

You can add all the fields to a query by double-clicking the * at the top of the field list. The field row will display the name of the table followed by .* indicating that all of the fields in the table have been added to the design grid. You will see each field displayed in the datasheet when you run the query.

11 Maximize the Select Query window.

The Select Query window is maximized. The Select Query window can be manipulated like any other window.

12 Position your mouse pointer over the thin gray line in between the table area and the design grid until the pointer changes to a vertical double arrow. See Figure 3.6. Drag the line separating the table area and the design grid down about one inch. See Figure 3.7.

The table area size is increased.

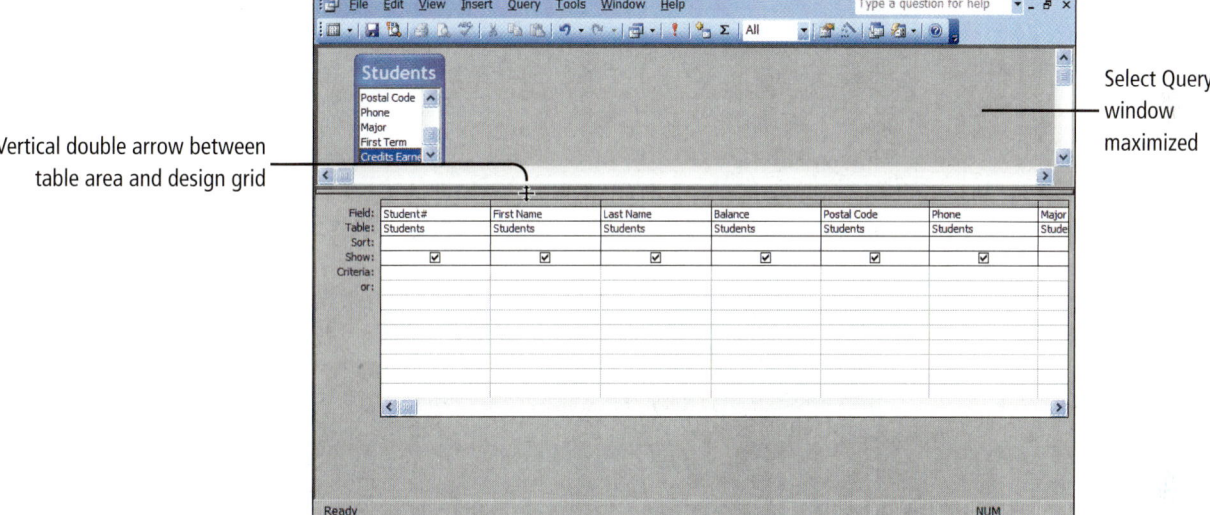

Figure 3.6

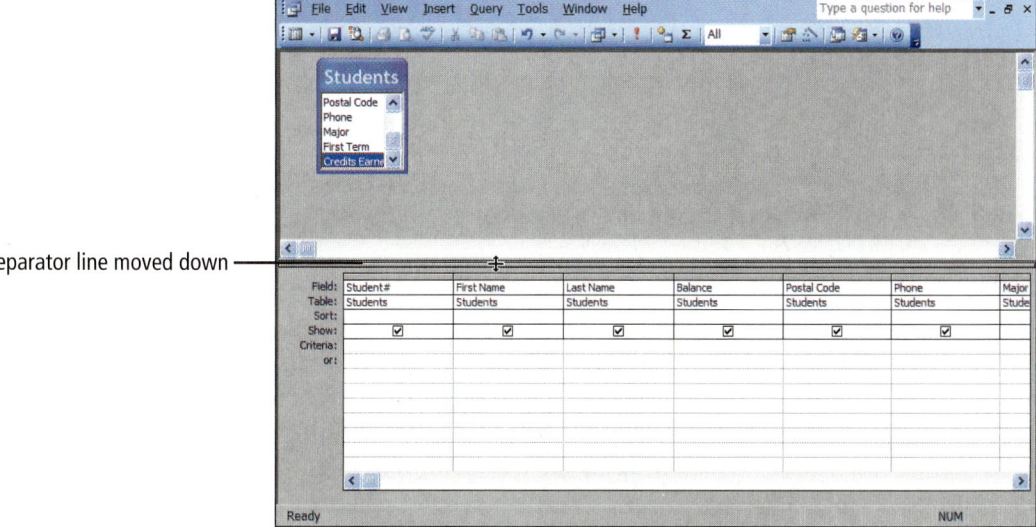

Figure 3.7

13 In the table area, position your mouse pointer on the lower edge of the field list until it displays as a black double arrow, as shown in Figure 3.8. Drag the lower edge of the field list down until all of the fields in the Students table are visible. See Figure 3.9.

The field list displays all of the fields in the table. Use the techniques you just practiced whenever you need to enlarge the upper or lower panes of the Select Query window to gain a better working view.

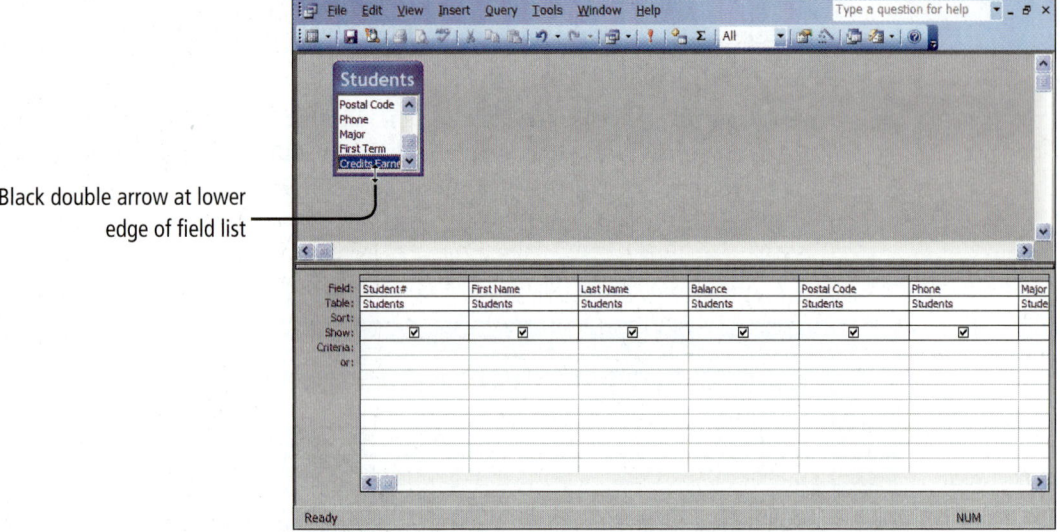

Black double arrow at lower edge of field list

Figure 3.8

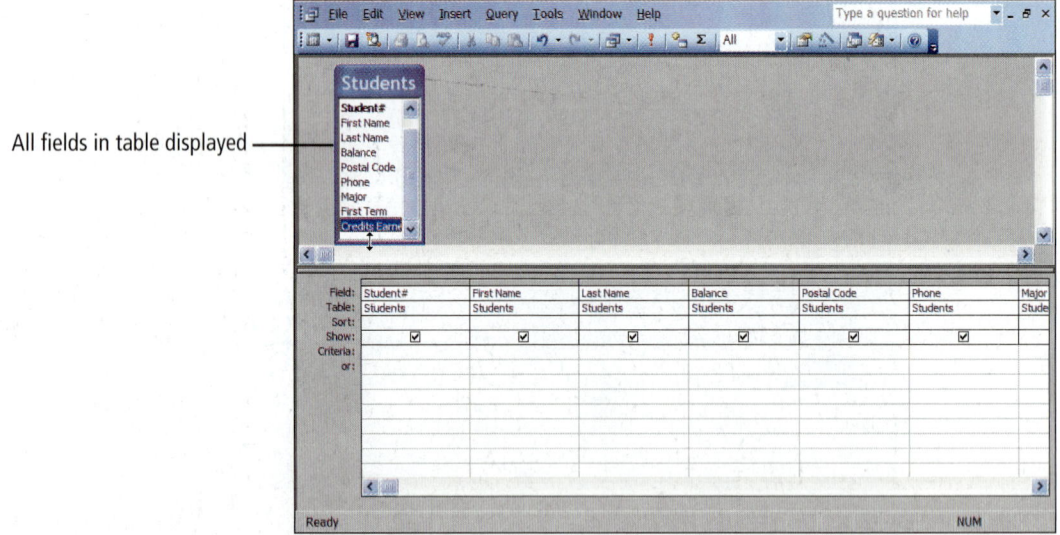

All fields in table displayed

Figure 3.9

14 If desired, resize the elements that you adjusted in Steps 11 through 13 and restore the Select Query window. The following figures show the Select Query window resized to the previous sizes. Leave the query window open for the next activity.

Objective 2
Run, Save, and Close a Query

When you run a query, Access looks at the records in the table (or tables) you have defined, finds the records that match the specified criteria (if any), and displays those records in a table.

Activity 3.2 Running, Saving, and Closing a Query

1 On the Query Design toolbar, click the **Run** button. See Figure 3.10.

The results of the query display in a table in Datasheet view. The fields display in columns, the records display in rows, and a Navigation area displays at the lower edge, in the same manner as in a table. See Figure 3.11. Because no criteria were specified in the design grid of the query, the query results are the same as the data in the Students table.

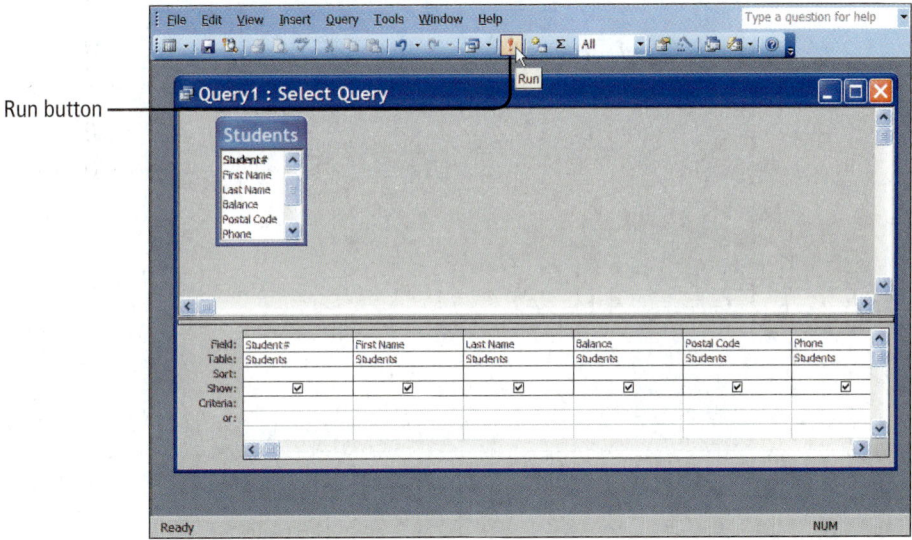

Figure 3.10

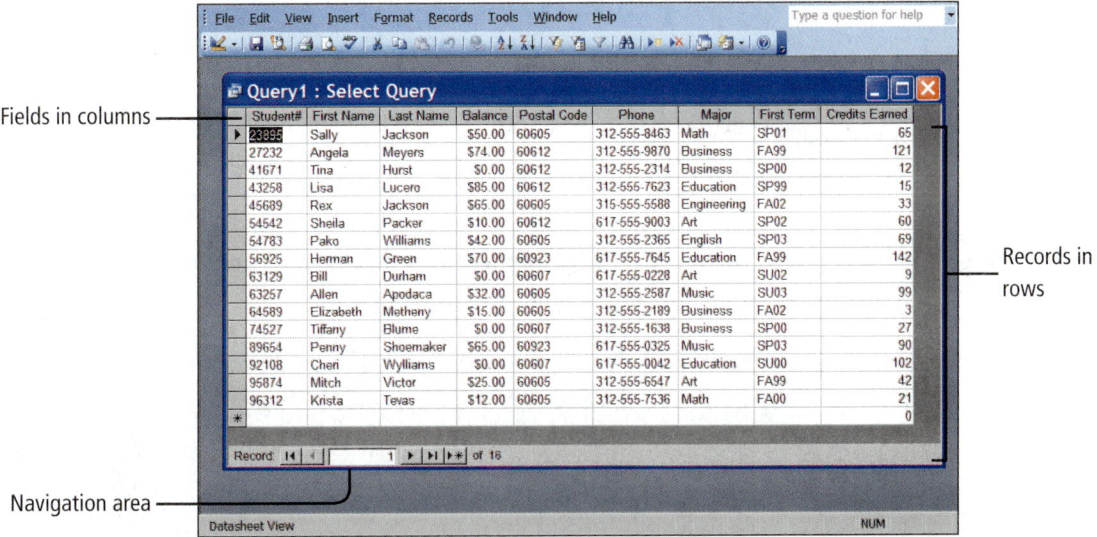

Figure 3.11

2 In the title bar of the query result, click the **Close** button ![X].

Because you have not previously named or saved this query, a message displays asking you if you want to save the changes to the design of query "Query1." The default name of a query created in this manner is "Query" followed by a number, such as "Query1."

3 Click **Yes**.

The Save As dialog box displays. Once created, a query can be run multiple times; thus, queries are frequently saved for future use.

4 In the **Save As** dialog box, in the **Query Name** box, delete the highlighted text. Then using your own information, type **Firstname Lastname Query1** and click **OK**.

The query is saved and closed. The new query name displays in the Database window. See Figure 3.12.

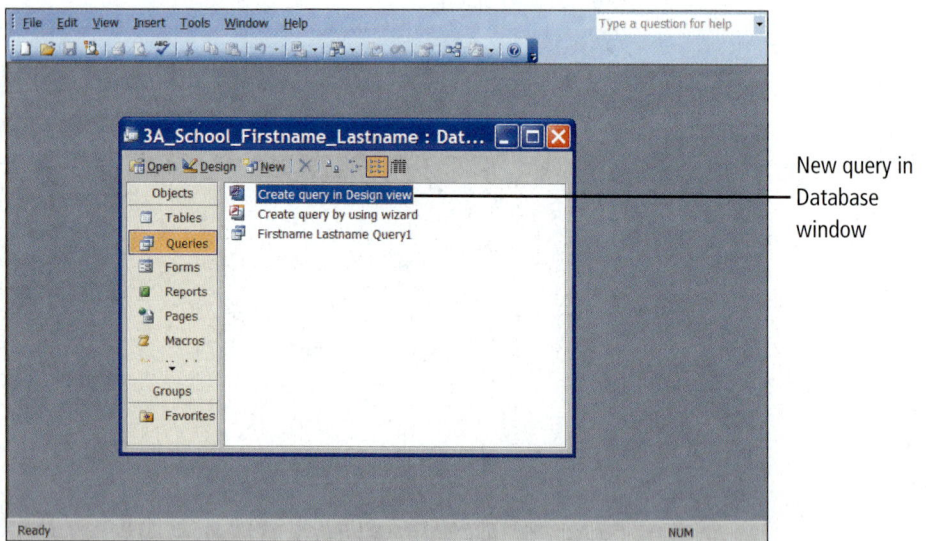

Figure 3.12

Objective 3
Open and Edit an Existing Query

After you have created and saved a query, you can open the query. Opening an existing query will cause the query to run and the results display in Datasheet view. You do not need to create a new query each time data in the corresponding table is modified. Each time the query is run, any changes made to the table will be automatically reflected in the query results.

Activity 3.3 Opening an Existing Query and Switching Between Views

1 In the Database window, be sure **Queries** is selected on the Objects bar and then double-click your **Query1** saved in Activity 3.2.

The query opens in the Datasheet view. If you want to view the records in a query result, use Datasheet view.

900 | Access | Chapter 3: Queries

[2] On the Query Datasheet toolbar, click the **View** button.

The query displays in Design view.

[3] On the title bar of the Query window, click the **Close** button to close the query.

The query closes.

[4] With your **Query1** selected in the Database window, above the Objects bar, click the **Design** button, as shown in Figure 3.13.

Your Query1 query opens directly in Design view. This is another way to display the query in Design view. From the Design view of a query you can make changes to the structure of the query. You can open a query in Design view or Datasheet view, depending on what you want to do with the query. If you want to modify the design of the query, such as the fields included in the query, use Design view.

Leave your query open in Design view for the next activity.

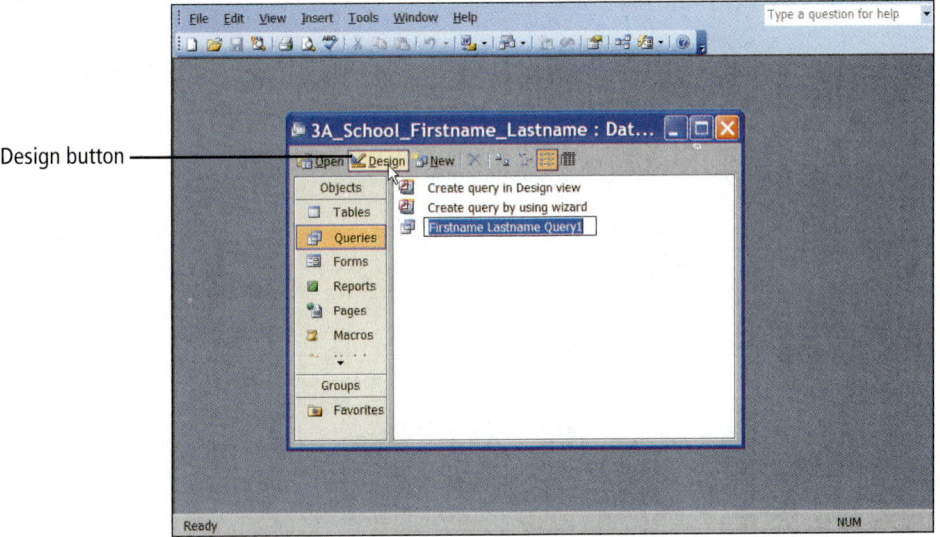

Figure 3.13

Activity 3.4 Editing a Query

A query does not have to contain all the fields from the table.

[1] If necessary, open your **Query1** in Design view. In the design grid, move your pointer above the **Balance** field until it displays as a black downward-pointing arrow and click. See Figure 3.14.

The Balance column is selected (highlighted), as shown in Figure 3.15.

Downward-pointing arrow

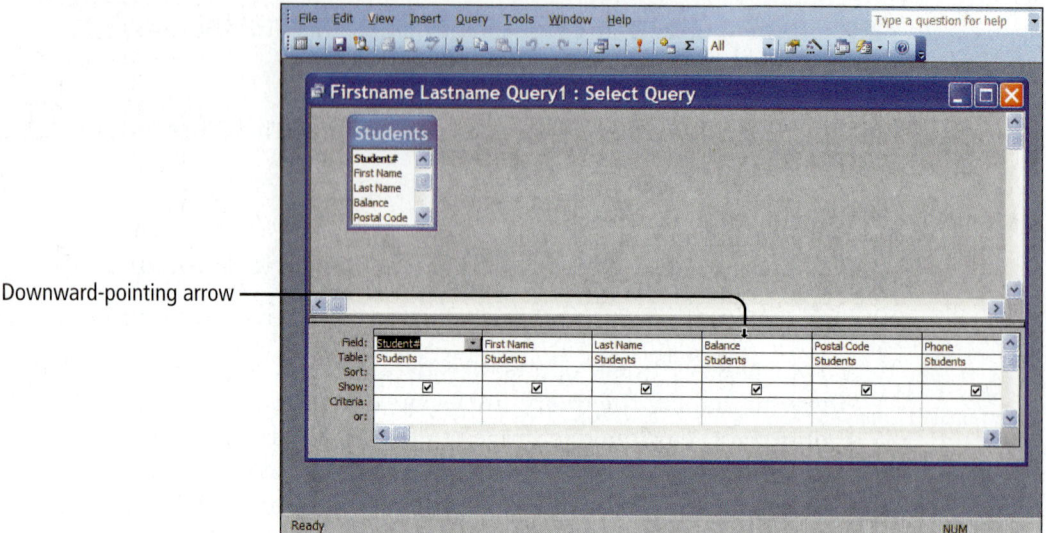

Figure 3.14

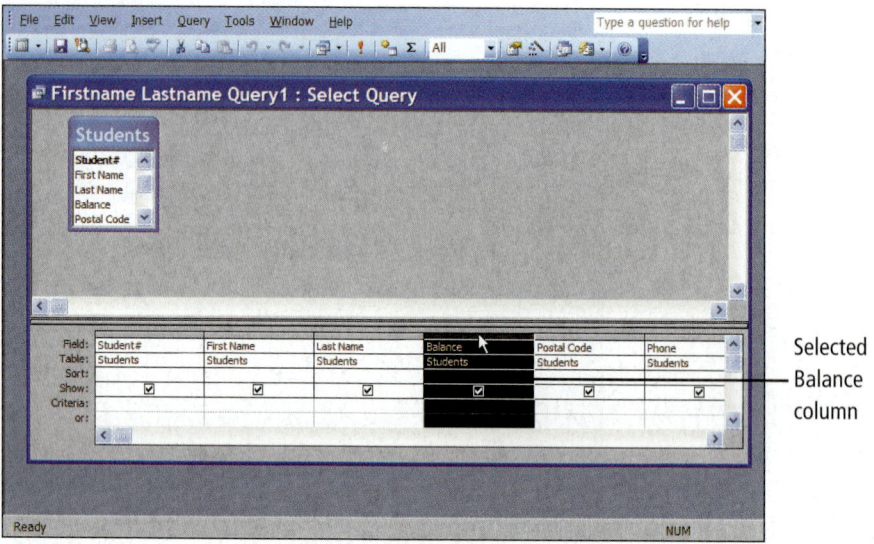

Selected Balance column

Figure 3.15

2 Press Delete.

The Balance field is removed from the design grid, and the remaining fields shift to the left. Removing a field from the design grid of a query does *not* affect the field in its corresponding table.

3 In the design grid, move your pointer above the **Postal Code** field until it displays as a black downward-pointing arrow and click to select the **Postal Code** field.

The Postal Code field is selected (highlighted). See Figure 3.16.

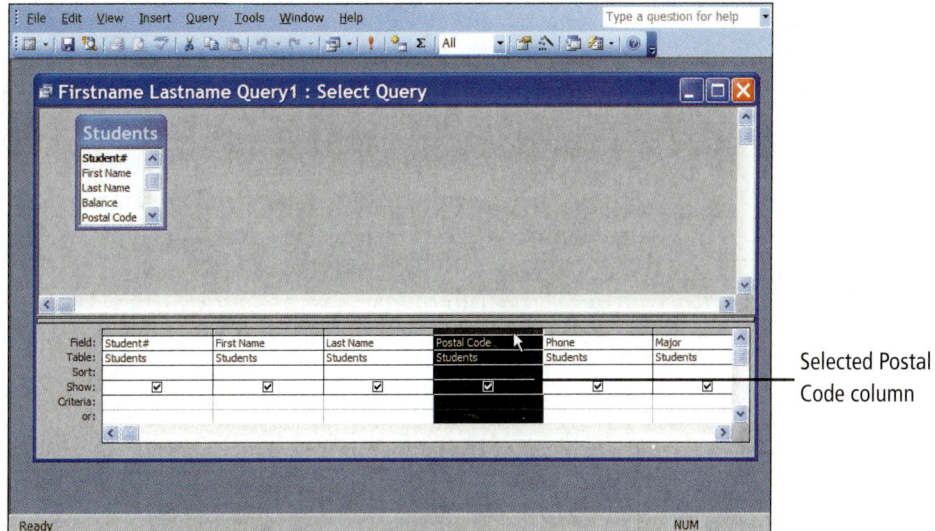

Figure 3.16

4 Press Delete to remove the **Postal Code** field from the design grid.

5 Repeat the technique you have just practiced to remove the **Phone**, **First Term**, and **Credits Earned** fields from the design grid.

The Student#, First Name, Last Name, and Major fields remain in the design grid. See Figure 3.17.

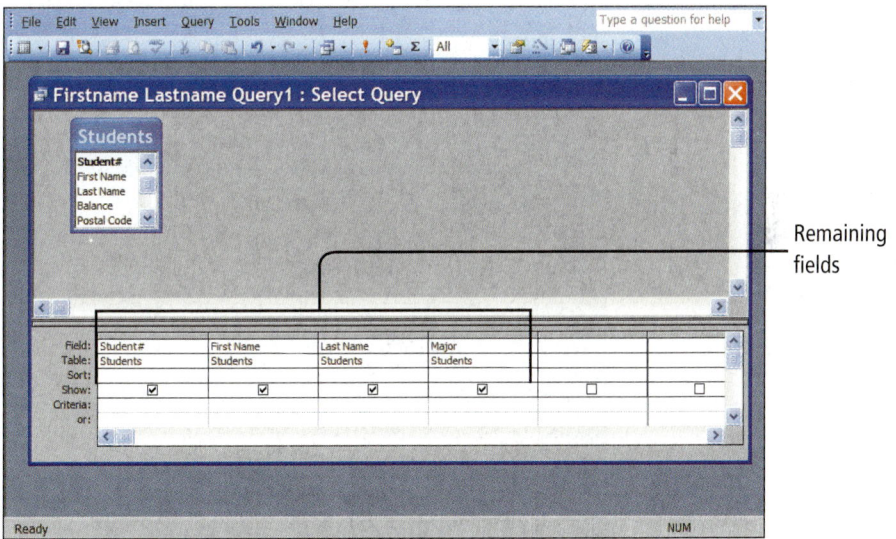

Figure 3.17

6 On the Query Design toolbar, click the **Run** button.

The results of the query display in a table with only the four specified fields displayed. This is a convenient method to use when you want to see only some of the fields from the table.

7 On the Query Datasheet toolbar, click the **View** button to return to Design view. Leave your query open in Design view for the next activity.

Objective 4
Specify Text Criteria in a Query

Specifying criteria in a query will limit the records that display in the query result. Up to this point, the query you created and ran did not limit the number of records displayed by specifying specific criteria; thus all of the records from the corresponding table displayed in the result.

Recall that to query is to ask a question. When criteria is specified in a query, you are asking a more specific question, and therefore you will get a more specific result. For example, suppose you want to find out which students live in a particular area. You could specify a specific Postal Code in the query criteria and only records that match the specified Postal Code will display. Keep in mind that queries do not have to contain all of the fields from a table in order to locate the requested information.

Activity 3.5 Specifying Text Criteria in a Query

In this activity, you will specify the criteria in the query so that only records in the Students table that have *Business* in the Major field display. Records that indicate a major other than Business will not display. You will save the query with a new name.

1 If necessary, open your **Query1** query in Design view. In the design grid, locate the **Criteria** row as indicated in Figure 3.18.

The Criteria row is where you will specify the criteria that will limit the results of the query to your exact specifications.

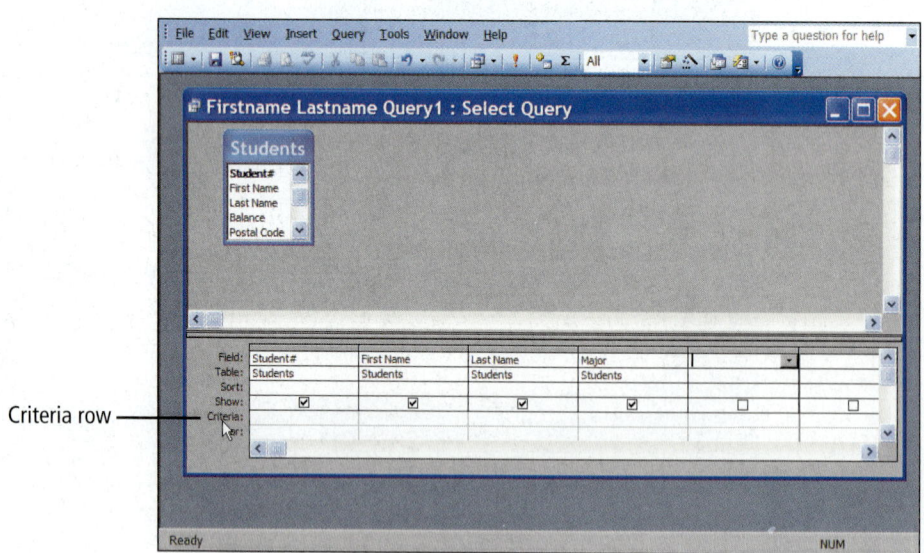

Figure 3.18

2 In the **Criteria** row, under the **Major** field, click and then type **Business** See Figure 3.19.

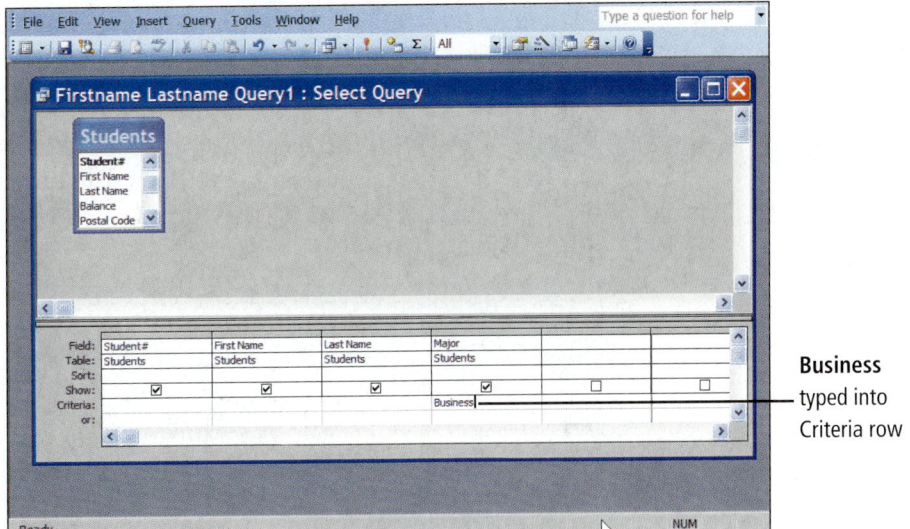

Business typed into Criteria row

Figure 3.19

[3] On the Query Design toolbar, click the **Run** button.

The query runs and the query results display in a table in Datasheet view. See Figure 3.20. Clicking the Run button causes Access to look at all the records in the Students table and locate those records that meet the specified criteria—records that have *Business* in the Major field.

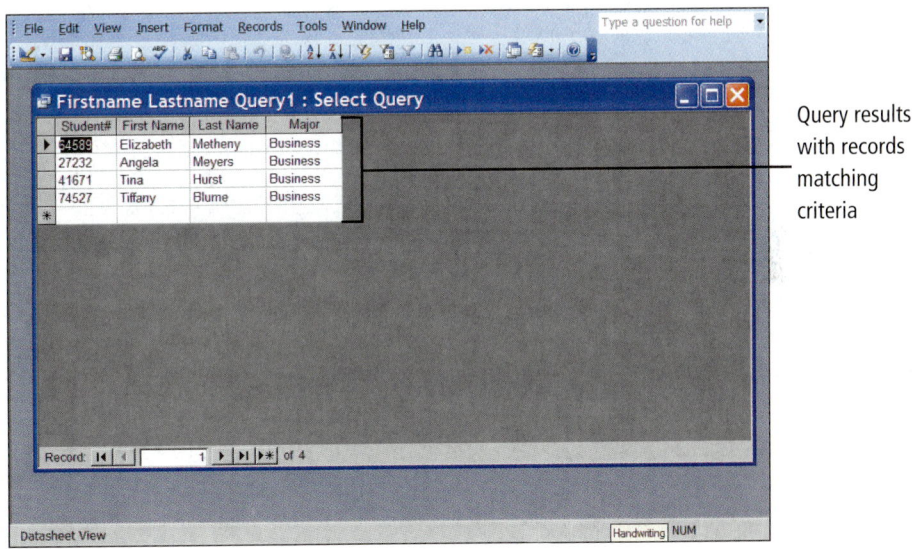

Query results with records matching criteria

Figure 3.20

[4] Examine the records in the query result and verify that the records that display have been limited to those students that have Business as their major.

[5] On the **File** menu, click **Save As**.

The Save As dialog box displays. Here you can give this query a different name from the first query and thus have both as saved queries.

Project 3A: School | **Access**

6. Under **Save Query 'Firstname Lastname Query1' To:**, and using your own information, type **FirstName LastName Business Major** and click **OK**.

The query with the criteria you specified is saved with the new name and the new name displays in the title bar of the query window. See Figure 3.21.

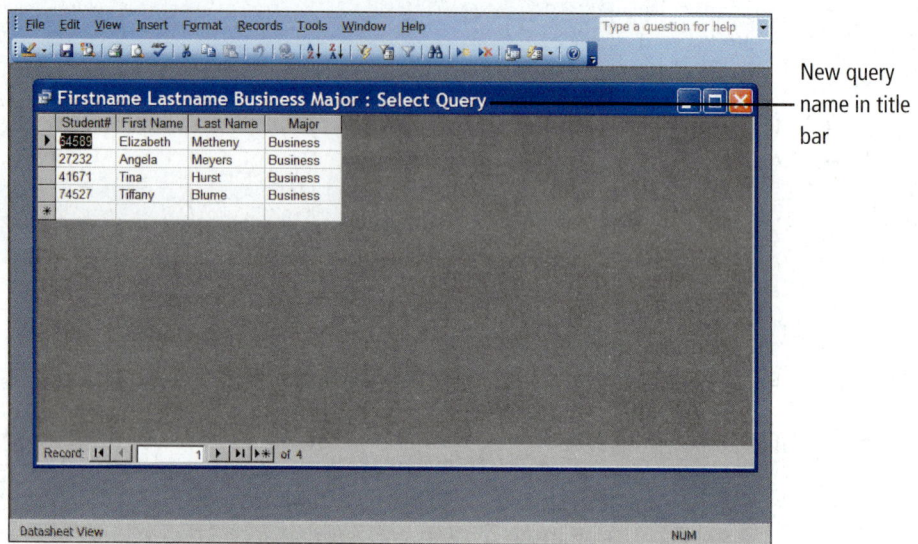

Figure 3.21

7. On the title bar of the query window, click the **Close** button to close the query.

The name of your new query displays in the Database window.

8. If necessary, click **Queries** on the Objects bar and then double-click **Create query in Design view**.

A new query window displays and the Show Table dialog box lists the tables in the database.

9. In the **Show Table** dialog box, click the **Queries tab** shown in Figure 3.22.

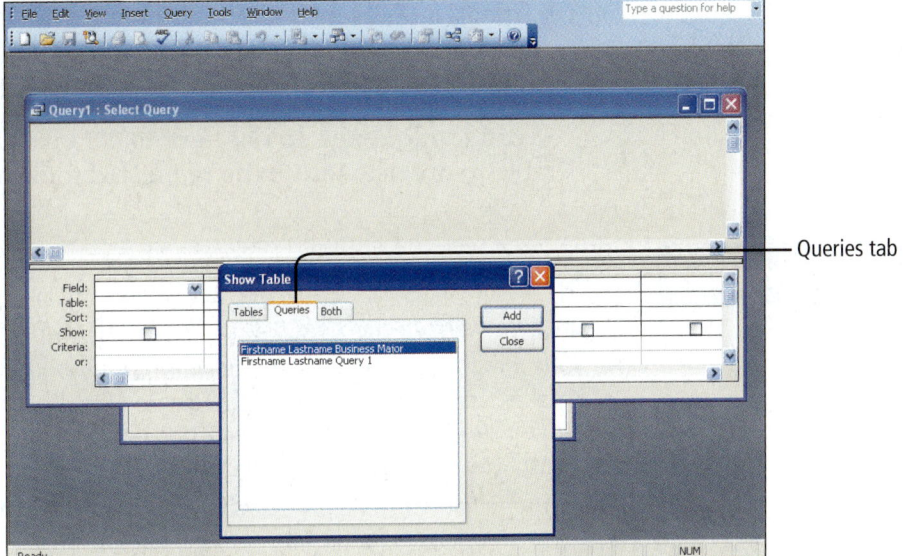

Figure 3.22

10 On the **Queries tab**, notice that the names of the two queries you have created thus far display. Click the **Both tab** and notice that the names of the two tables in the database as well as the names of the two queries you created display. See Figure 3.23.

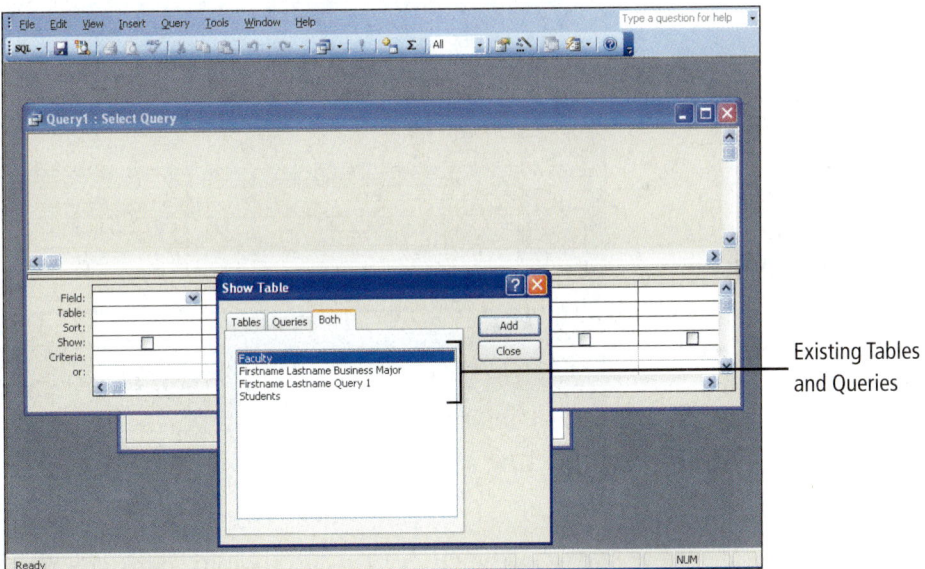

Figure 3.23

11 Click the **Tables tab**, double-click the **Students** table, and then click **Close**.

The field list for the Students table is added to the table area of the query and the Show Table dialog box closes. Next, you will add criteria to the query that will find the records that have a particular Postal Code.

12 In the **Students** field list, double-click the **First Name**, **Last Name**, and **Postal Code** fields to add them to the design grid. If necessary, use the vertical scroll bar to view the **Postal Code** field.

Recall that queries do not have to contain all of the fields from a table in order to locate the requested information.

Another Way

Adding Fields to the Design Grid

Drag fields from the field list or click in the Field row.

You can also add fields to the design grid by dragging the field from the field list and dropping it into the desired location in the design grid. Or, you can click in the field row and then choose the field from the drop-down list.

13 In the **Criteria** row, under **Postal Code**, type **60605** See Figure 3.24.

Although fields such as Postal Code contain numbers, they are considered text because mathematical calculations are not performed on them.

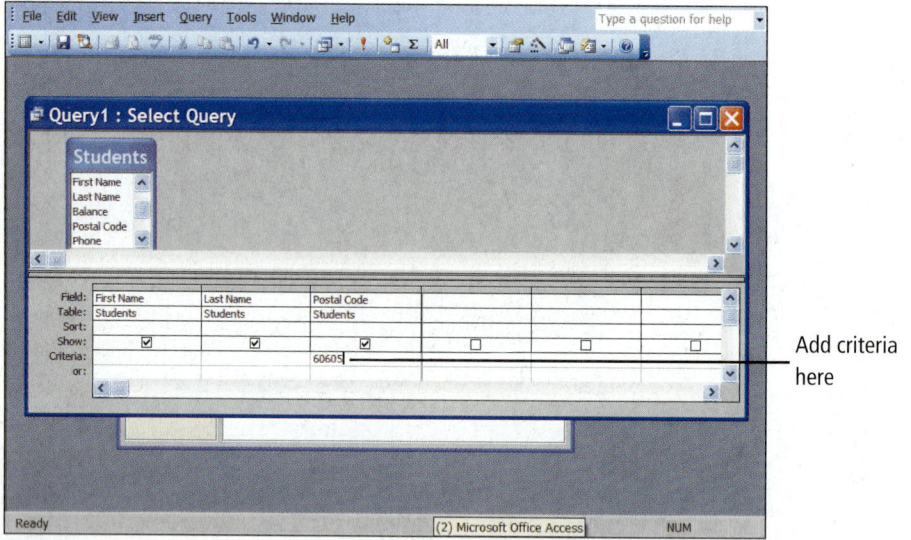

Add criteria here

Figure 3.24

14 On the Query Design toolbar, click the **Run** button.

The query results display only the First Name, Last Name, and Postal Code fields for those records in the Students table that have a Postal Code of 60605. See Figure 3.25.

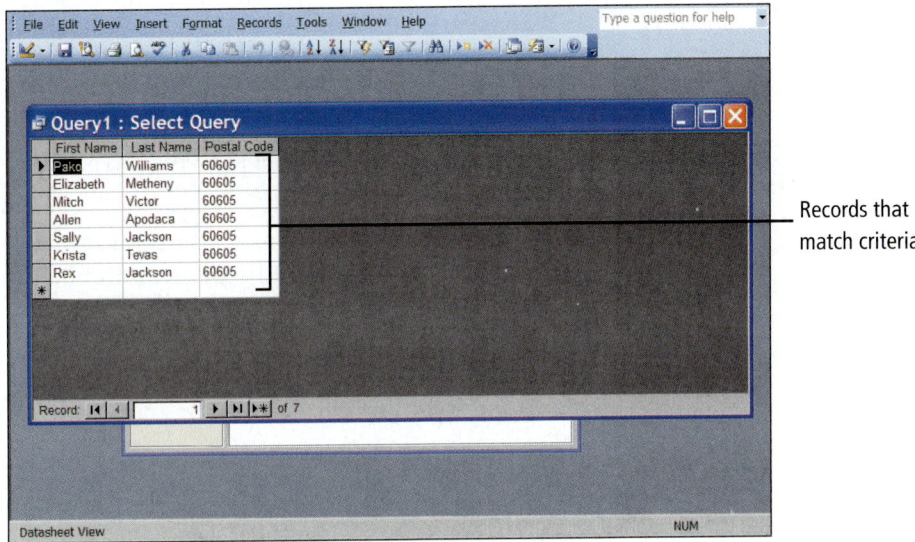

Figure 3.25

15 On the title bar of the query window, click the **Close** button ⊠.

16 When prompted to save the changes to the design of query "Query1", click **Yes**. For the query name, using your own information, type **Firstname_Lastname Postal Code** and click **OK**.

The name of the Postal Code query you created displays in the Database window as shown in Figure 3.26.

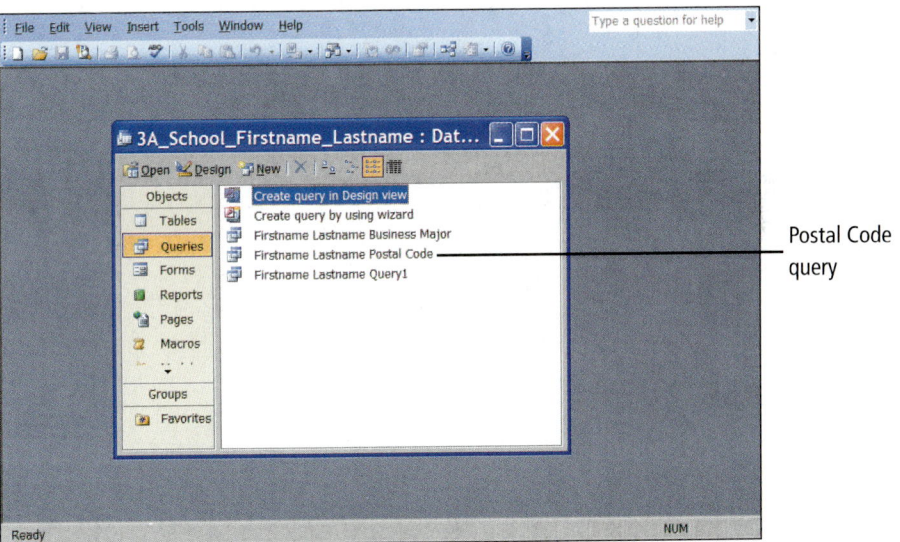

Figure 3.26

Project 3A: School | **Access** 909

Activity 3.6 Printing a Query

Query results in Datasheet view can be printed similar to other database objects.

1 If necessary, on the Objects bar, click **Queries** and then click your **Business Major** query to select it.

2 On the Database toolbar, click the **Print** button. Alternatively, you could display the File menu and click Print.

The query results print with *your* name in the query name at the top of the page.

3 In the Database window, click your **Postal Code** query once to select it.

4 On the Database toolbar, click the **Print** button.

The query results of the Postal Code query print with your name at the top of the page in the query name.

5 Close your **School** database and then close Access.

End You have completed Project 3A

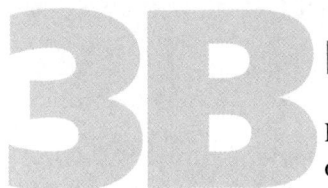

3B Project 3B Students

In this project you will explore new ways to refine queries with more specific information.

In Activities 3.7 through 3.15 you will continue to create new queries and specify criteria in more detail. Your queries will look similar to Figure 3.27.

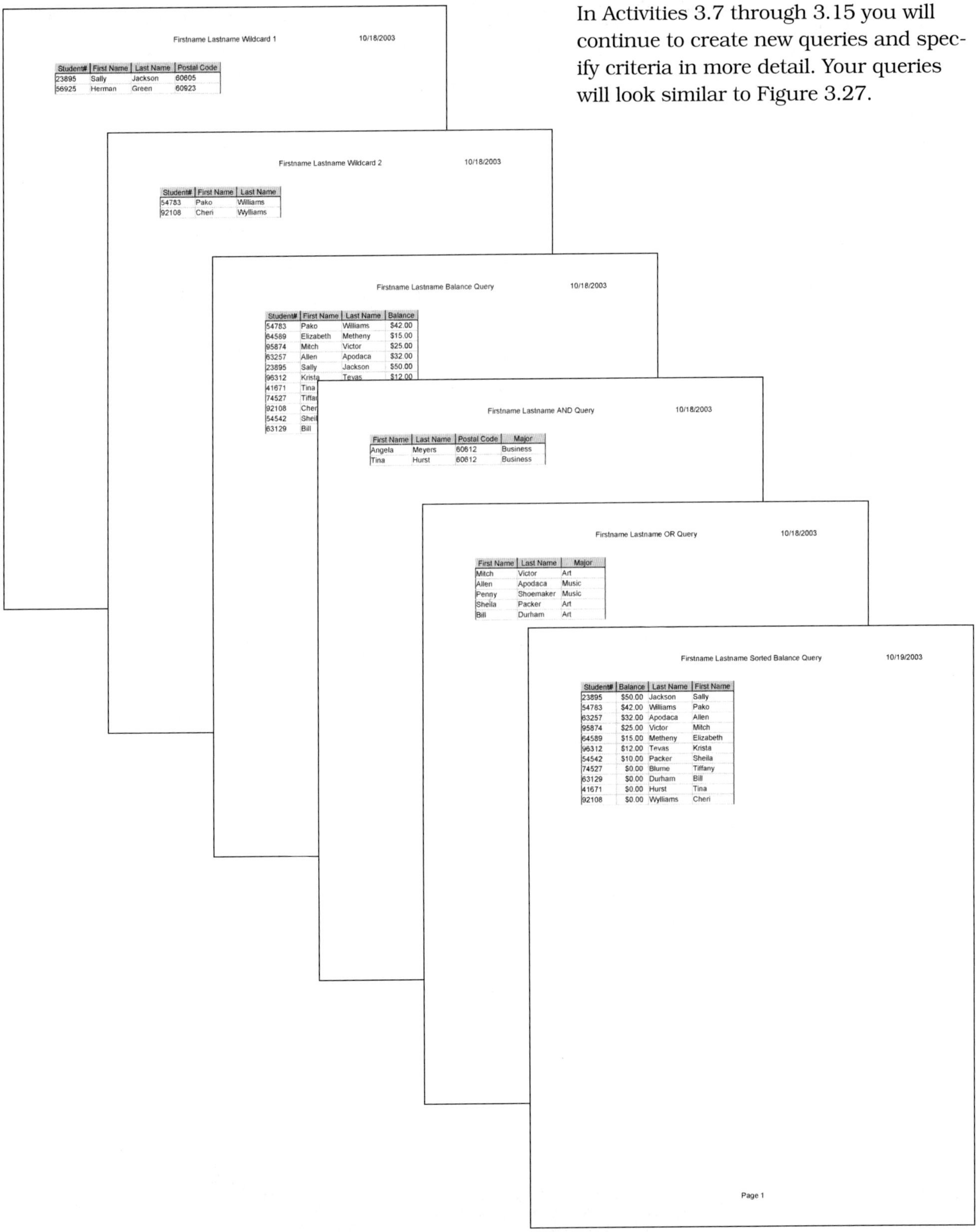

Firstname Lastname Wildcard 1 10/18/2003

Student#	First Name	Last Name	Postal Code
23895	Sally	Jackson	60605
56925	Herman	Green	60923

Firstname Lastname Wildcard 2 10/18/2003

Student#	First Name	Last Name
54783	Pako	Williams
92108	Cheri	Wylliams

Firstname Lastname Balance Query 10/18/2003

Student#	First Name	Last Name	Balance
54783	Pako	Williams	$42.00
64589	Elizabeth	Metheny	$15.00
95874	Mitch	Victor	$25.00
63257	Allen	Apodaca	$32.00
23895	Sally	Jackson	$50.00
96312	Krista	Tevas	$12.00
41671	Tina		
74527	Tiffa		
92108	Cher		
54542	Sheil		
63129	Bill		

Firstname Lastname AND Query 10/18/2003

First Name	Last Name	Postal Code	Major
Angela	Meyers	60612	Business
Tina	Hurst	60612	Business

Firstname Lastname OR Query 10/18/2003

First Name	Last Name	Major
Mitch	Victor	Art
Allen	Apodaca	Music
Penny	Shoemaker	Music
Sheila	Packer	Art
Bill	Durham	Art

Firstname Lastname Sorted Balance Query 10/19/2003

Student#	Balance	Last Name	First Name
23895	$50.00	Jackson	Sally
54783	$42.00	Williams	Pako
63257	$32.00	Apodaca	Allen
95874	$25.00	Victor	Mitch
64589	$15.00	Metheny	Elizabeth
96312	$12.00	Tevas	Krista
54542	$10.00	Packer	Sheila
74527	$0.00	Blume	Tiffany
63129	$0.00	Durham	Bill
41671	$0.00	Hurst	Tina
92108	$0.00	Wylliams	Cheri

Page 1

Figure 3.27
Project 3B—Students

Objective 5
Use Wildcards in a Query

Wildcard characters in a query serve as a placeholder for an unknown character or characters in your criteria. When you are unsure of the particular character or set of characters to include in your criteria, you can use wildcard characters in place of the characters in the criteria of the query.

Activity 3.7 Using the * Wildcard in a Query

The asterisk, *, is used to represent any group of characters. For example, if you use the * wildcard in the criteria *Fo**, the results would return *Foster*, *Forrester*, *Forrest*, *Fossil*, and so forth. In this activity, you will use the * wildcard and specify the criteria in the query so that only records that have a postal code beginning with 606 will display.

1. Locate the file **a03B_School** from the student files that accompany this text. Copy and paste the file to the Chapter 3 folder you created in Project 3A.

2. Using the technique you practiced in Activity 1.1 of Chapter 1, remove the Read-only property from the file and rename the file as **3B_School_Firstname_Lastname**

3. Close the Windows accessory you are using—either My Computer or Windows Explorer. Start Access and open your **3B_School** database.

4. Click **Queries** on the Objects bar and then double-click **Create query in Design view**.

   A new query window displays and the Show Table dialog box lists the tables in the database.

5. In the **Show Table** dialog box, double-click **Students** and then click **Close**.

6. Add the following fields to the design grid by double-clicking the fields in the **Students** field list: **Student#**, **First Name**, **Last Name**, **Postal Code**.

   Four fields are added to the design grid, as shown in Figure 3.28.

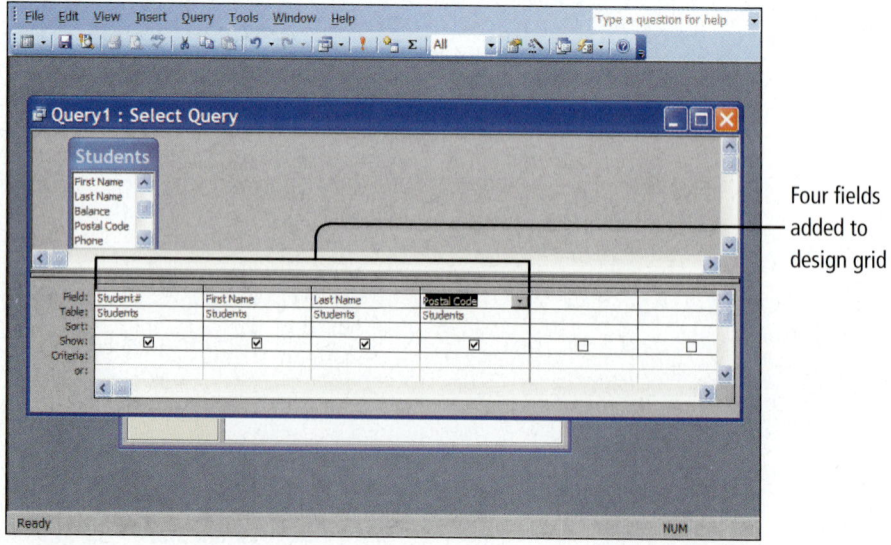

Four fields added to design grid

Figure 3.28

7 In the **Criteria** row, under **Postal Code**, type **606*** as shown in Figure 3.29 and then click the **Run** button.

The query results display 14 records.

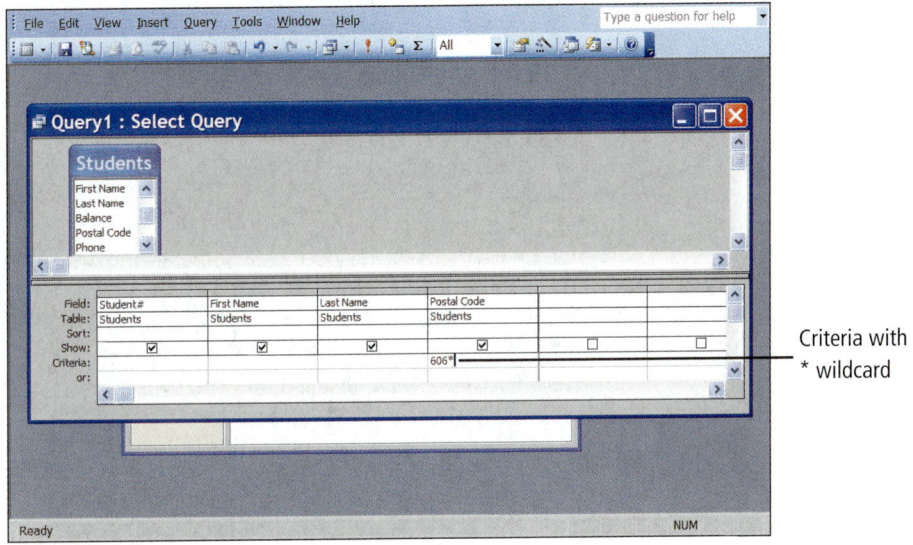

Criteria with * wildcard

Figure 3.29

8 Examine the entries in the **Postal Code** field and notice that each entry begins with *606* but that the last digits vary, as illustrated in Figure 3.30.

The wildcard character, *, is used as a placeholder to match any number of characters.

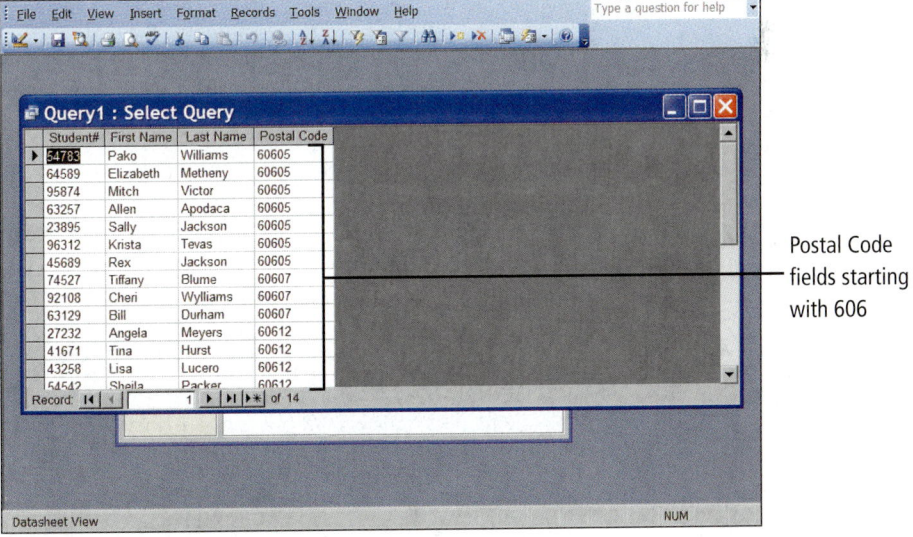

Postal Code fields starting with 606

Figure 3.30

Project 3B: Students | **Access** 913

9 On the Query Datasheet toolbar, click the **View** button to return to Design view.

Notice that Access has inserted the criteria *Like "606*"* in the Criteria row under Postal Code. *Like* is used by Access to compare a sequence of characters and test whether or not the text matches a pattern. Access will automatically insert expressions similar to this when creating queries.

> ### More Knowledge — Structured Query Language
>
> *SQL: Structured Query Language.*
>
> SQL (Structured Query Language) is a language used in querying, updating, and managing relational databases. The term *Like* is used in SQL to compare string expressions. In Access, the term *expression* is the same thing as a formula. A *string expression* looks at a sequence of characters and compares them to the criteria in a query. You will learn more about SQL as you advance in your studies of Access.

10 In the **Criteria** row under **Postal Code**, select and then delete the existing text *Like "606*"*.

11 In the **Criteria** row under **Last Name**, type **m*** as shown in Figure 3.31 and then click the **Run** button.

The query results display two records, both with Last Names that begin with M. This search was not case sensitive; that is, lowercase *m** will find text beginning with either *m* or *M*.

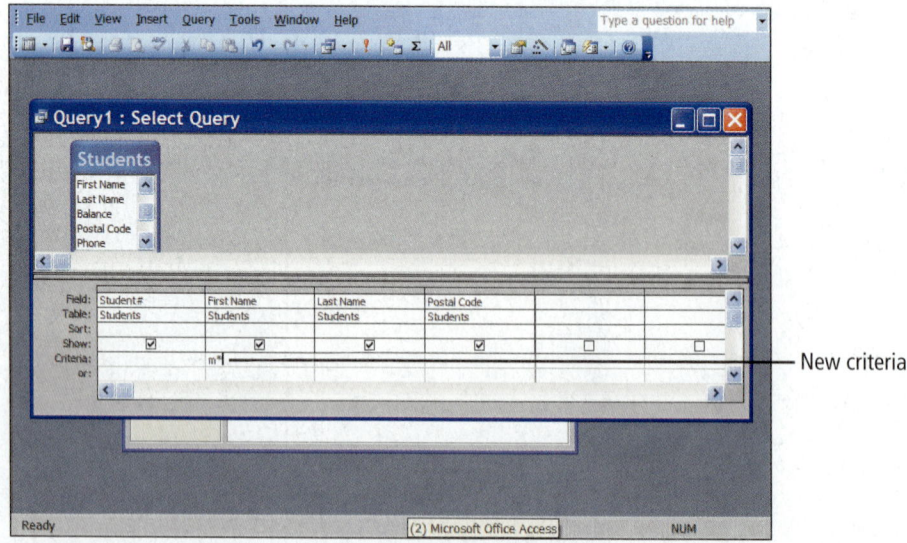

Figure 3.31

12 Notice that *Metheny* and *Meyers* have a different number of characters; *Metheny* contains seven characters and *Meyers* contains six.

The * wildcard can be used to find entries that have a any number of characters.

13 On the Query Datasheet toolbar, click the **View** button to return to Design view. In the **Criteria** row under **Last Name**, select and then delete the existing text *Like "m*"*.

14 In the **Criteria** row under **Student#**, type ***5** as shown in Figure 3.32 and then click the **Run** button.

Two records display, both with Student# entries ending in 5. See Figure 3.33. Wildcard characters can be used either at the beginning or at the end of the criteria.

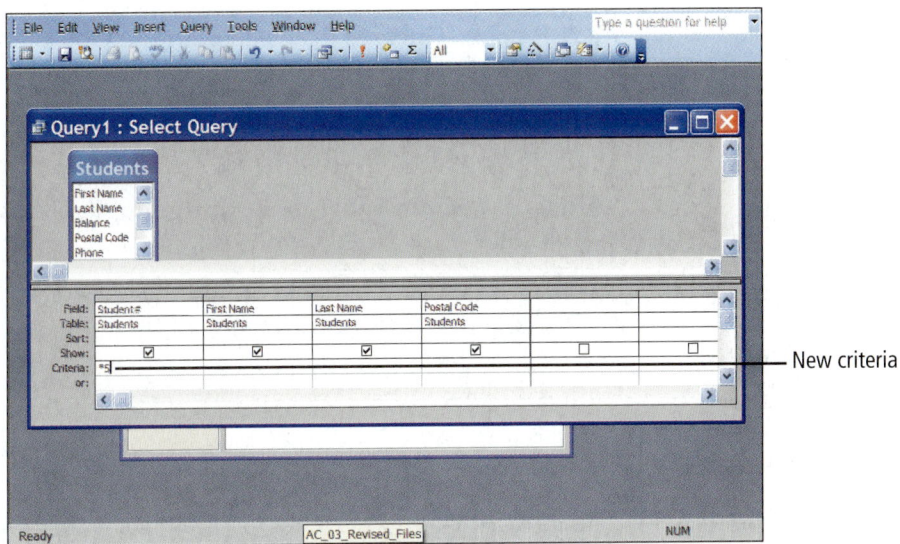

Figure 3.32

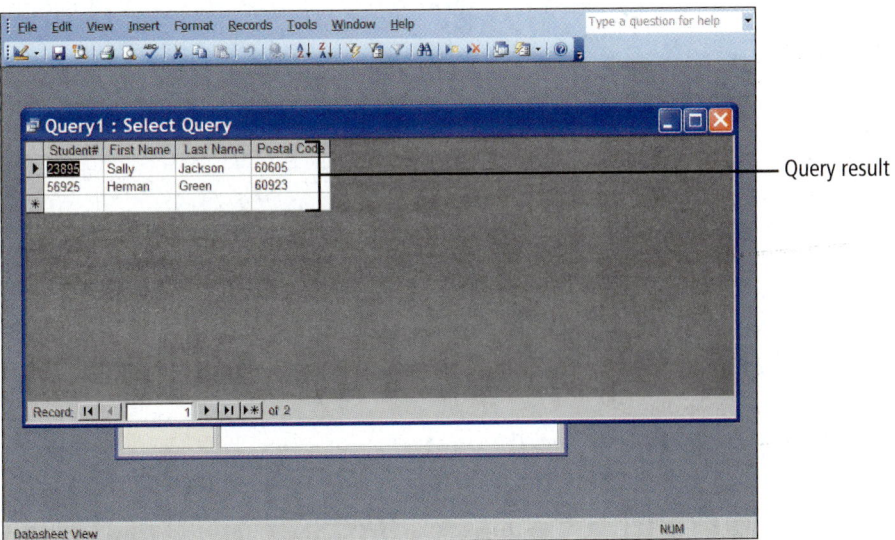

Figure 3.33

15 In the title bar of the query window, click the **Close** button. Click **Yes** to save changes to the query, and then in the **Save As** dialog box and using your own information, type **Firstname Lastname Wildcard 1** as the query name. Click **OK**.

16 In the Database window, select your **Wildcard 1** query and then on the Database toolbar, click the **Print** button.

The query results print.

Activity 3.8 Using the ? Wildcard in a Query

The ? wildcard is a placeholder for only one character in a query. For example, if you use the ? wildcard in the criteria *"l?ne"*, the results could be *lane*, *line*, or *lone*. In this activity, you will use the ? wildcard and specify the criteria in the query so that only those records with either spelling of the last name of *Williams* or *Wylliams* will display.

1 Be sure **Queries** is selected on the Objects bar, then double-click **Create query in Design view**.

A new query window displays and the Show Table dialog box lists the tables in the database.

2 In the **Show Table** dialog box, double-click **Students** and then click **Close**.

3 Add the following fields to the design grid by double-clicking the fields in the **Students** field list: **Student#**, **First Name**, **Last Name**.

Three fields are added to the design grid, as shown in Figure 3.34.

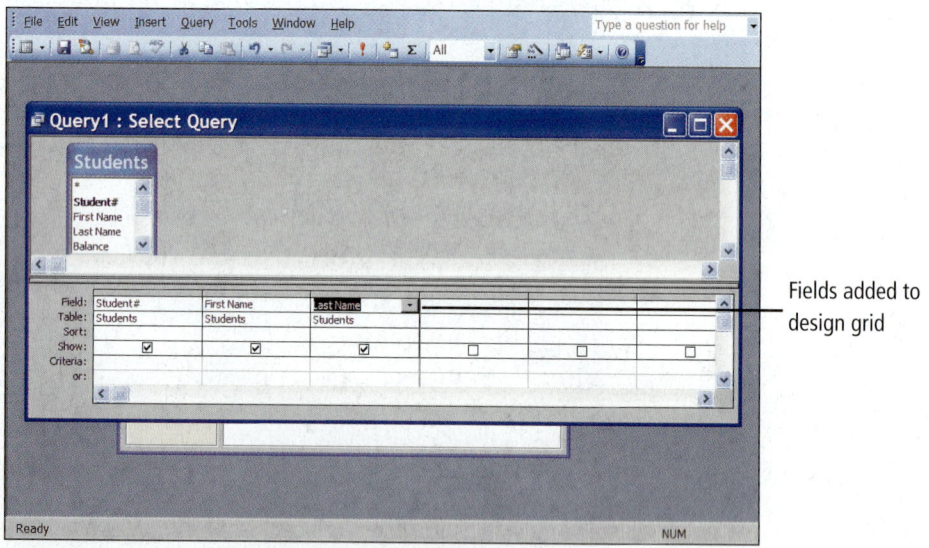

Fields added to design grid

Figure 3.34

4 In the **Criteria** row under **Last Name**, type **w?lliams** as shown in Figure 3.35 and then click the **Run** button.

Two results display with the Last Names of *Williams* and *Wylliams*. See Figure 3.36.

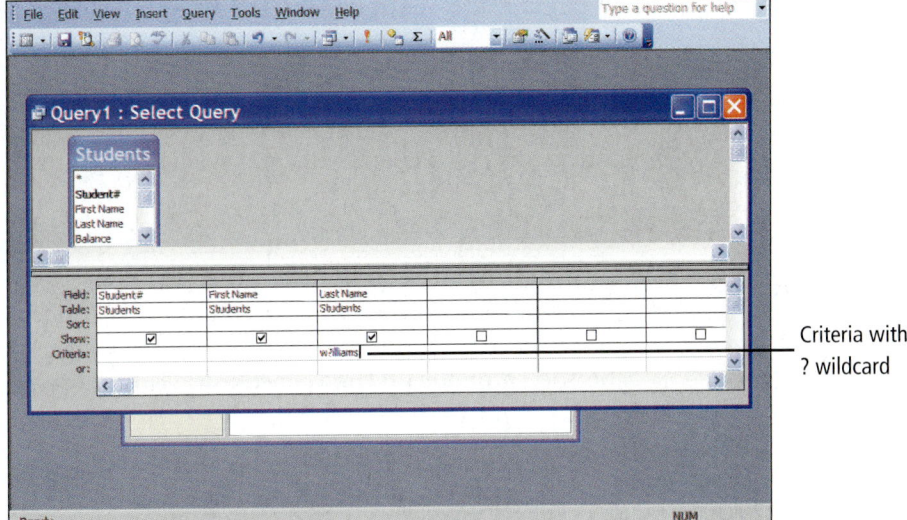

Figure 3.35

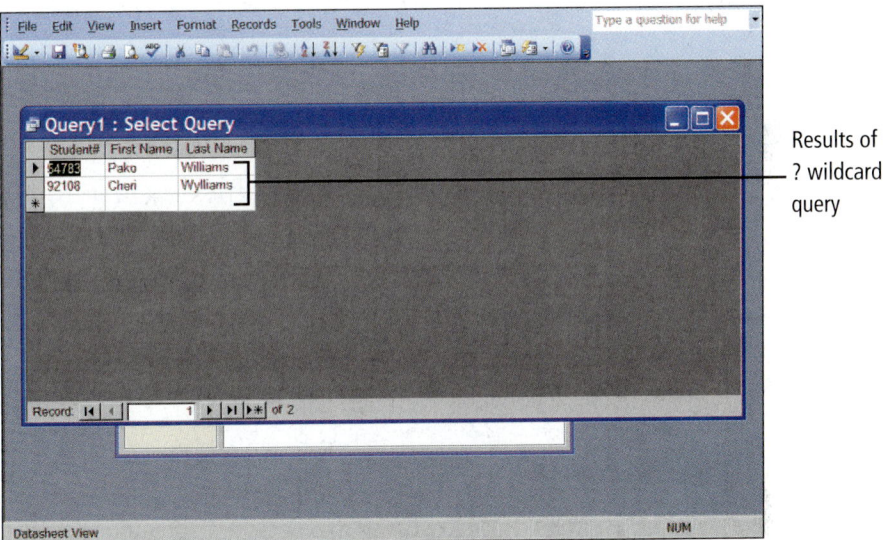

Figure 3.36

5. In the title bar of the query window, click the **Close** button. Click **Yes** to save changes to the query and in the **Save As** dialog box, using your own information, type **Firstname Lastname Wildcard 2** as the query name. Click **OK**.

The Database window displays.

6. Be sure your **Wildcard 2** query is selected and then on the Database toolbar, click the **Print** button.

The query results print.

Project 3B: Students | **Access** 917

Activity 3.9 Specifying Criteria Using a Field Not Displayed in the Query Result

In the queries you have created thus far, all of the fields that you included in the query design have also been included in the query result. It is not required, however, that every field in the query also display in the result, and there will be times when you will not want all the fields to display in the result.

For example, if you were querying your CD Collection database to find out what records in the CD table were performed by a particular artist, you would need the CD Artist field in the query design, but you would not need the field to display in the query result because the artist would be the same for all the records. Including the field would be redundant and not particularly useful.

1. Be sure **Queries** is selected on the Objects bar, then double-click **Create query in Design view**.

   A new query window displays and the Show Table dialog box lists the tables in the database.

2. In the **Show Table** dialog box, double-click **Students** and then click **Close**.

3. Add the following fields to the design grid by double-clicking the fields in the **Students** field list: **Student#**, **First Name**, **Last Name**, and **Major**.

   Four fields are added to the design grid, as shown in Figure 3.37.

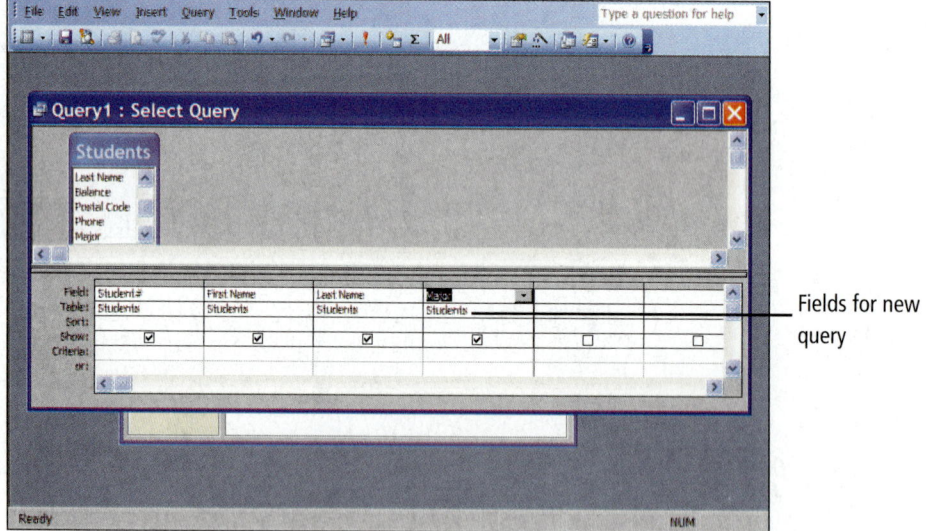

Fields for new query

Figure 3.37

4. In the **Criteria** row under **Major**, type **Music** as shown in Figure 3.38 and then click the **Run** button.

   The query results display the two records in the Students table that have Music as entries in the Major field.

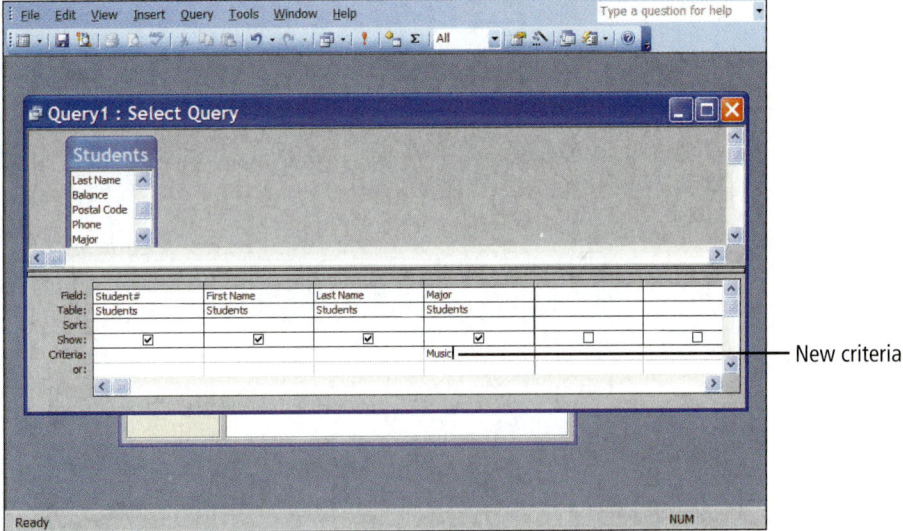
— New criteria

Figure 3.38

5 On the Query Datasheet toolbar, click the **View** button to return to Design view.

6 Directly above the **Criteria** row, in the **Show** row, under **Major**, notice the **Show** check box with a check mark in it. See Figure 3.39.

Fields where the Show check box is checked in the design grid display in the query results.

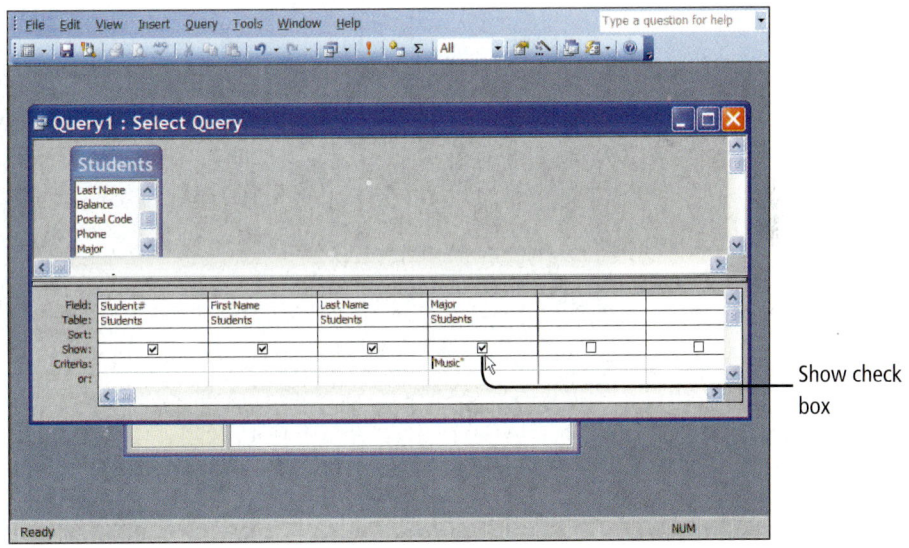
— Show check box

Figure 3.39

7 In the **Show** check box under **Major**, click to clear the **check mark**, as shown in Figure 3.40.

Project 3B: Students | **Access** 919

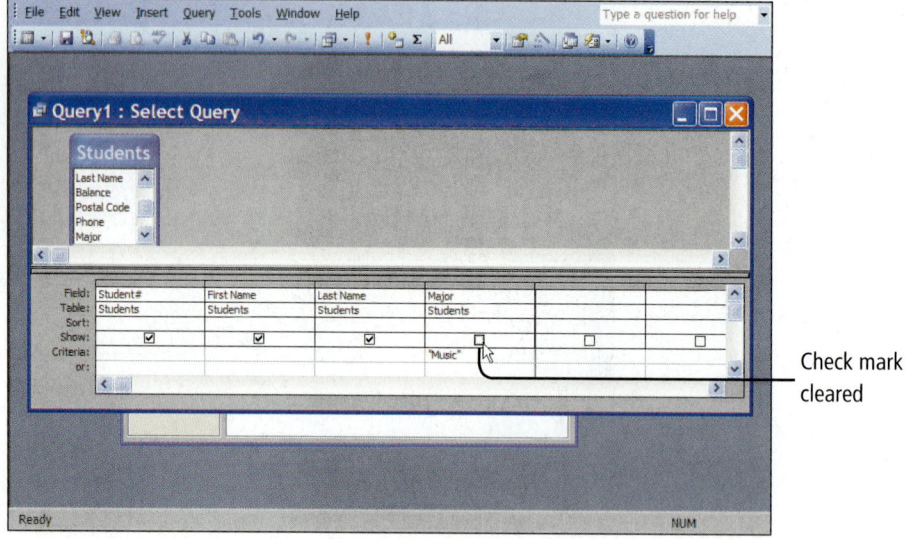

Figure 3.40

8 On the Query Design toolbar, click the **Run** button.

The query results display the same two records but the Major field does not display. See Figure 3.41. Although the Major field was still included in the query criteria for the purpose of identifying specific records, it is not necessary to display the field in the result.

Clear the Show check box when necessary to avoid cluttering the query results with redundant data.

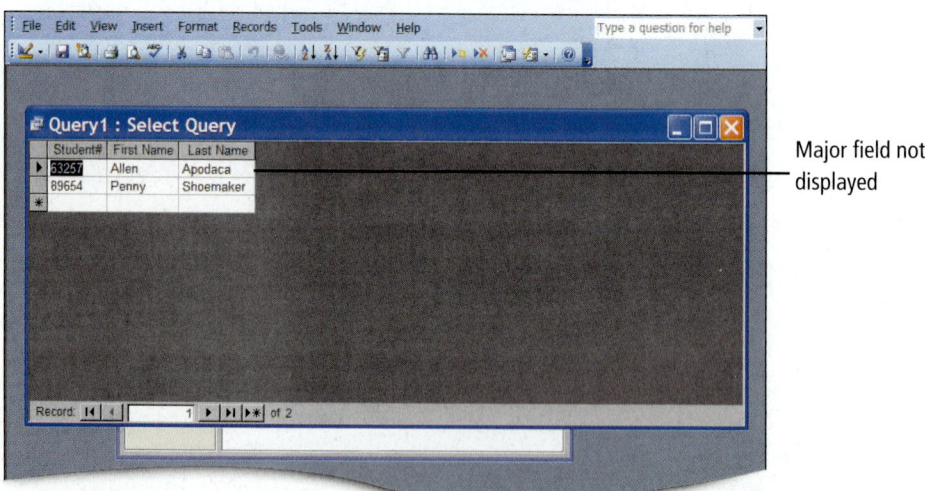

Figure 3.41

9 On the Query Datasheet toolbar, click the **View** button to return to Design view.

10 On the Menu bar, click **Edit**, **Clear Grid**.

The fields are cleared in the design grid. Use this method to quickly clear the design grid to begin a new query. Leave the query open in Design view for the next activity.

Objective 6
Specify Numeric Criteria in a Query

Criteria can be set for fields that contain numeric data as well as text data. Numeric data types are set for fields that will contain numbers on which mathematical calculations will be performed. Because the data is numeric, you can use mathematical symbols to further specify the criteria and locate the desired records.

Activity 3.10 Specifying Numeric Criteria in a Query

In this activity, you will specify the criteria in the query so that only records in the Students table that have a balance of zero will display.

1 With your cleared query window from the previous activity open in Design view, add the following fields to the design grid by double-clicking the fields in the **Students** field list: **Student#**, **First Name**, **Last Name**, and **Balance**.

Four fields are added to the design grid.

2 In the **Criteria** row under **Balance**, type **0** as shown in Figure 3.42 and then click the **Run** button.

Four records display in the query results; each has a balance of $0.00.

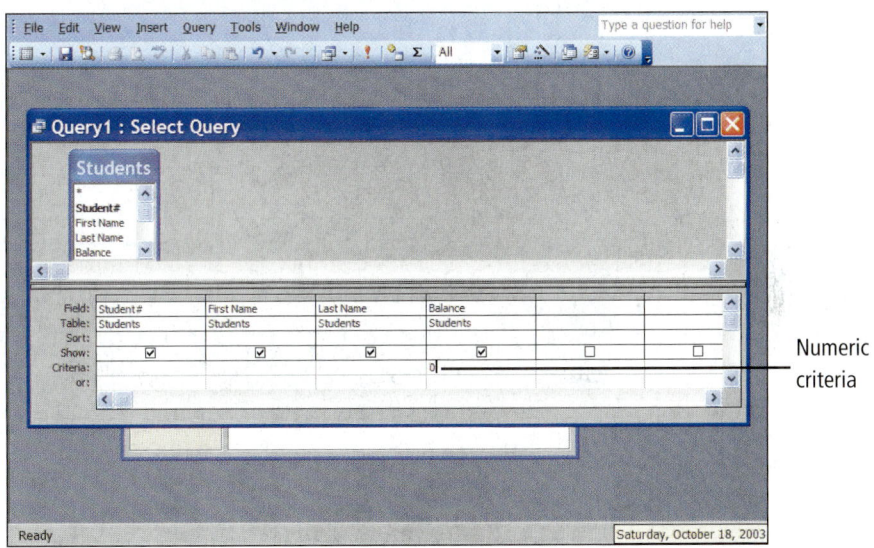

Figure 3.42

3 On the Query Datasheet toolbar, click the **View** button. Leave the query open in Design view for the next activity.

Project 3B: Students | **Access** 921

Activity 3.11 Using Comparison Operators

In Activity 3.10, you created a query to display those records where the student's balance was equal to zero. The equal sign, =, is a comparison operator that, when used in query criteria, causes Access to display those records that have entries equal to the number specified (zero in the previous activity). Other comparison operators can be used in query criteria to cause Access to display a different set of records based on the numeric criteria specified. The most common comparison operators include the < (less than), > (greater than), and the = (equal) signs.

In this activity, you will specify the criteria in the query so that the records in the Students table that have a balance that is greater than $50.00 will display.

1 Be sure your query from the last activity is displayed in Design view.

2 In the **Criteria** row, under **Balance**, select the existing text, *0*, type **>50** as illustrated in Figure 3.43, and then click the **Run** button.

Five records display and each of these has a Balance greater than (but not equal to) $50.00. See Figure 3.44.

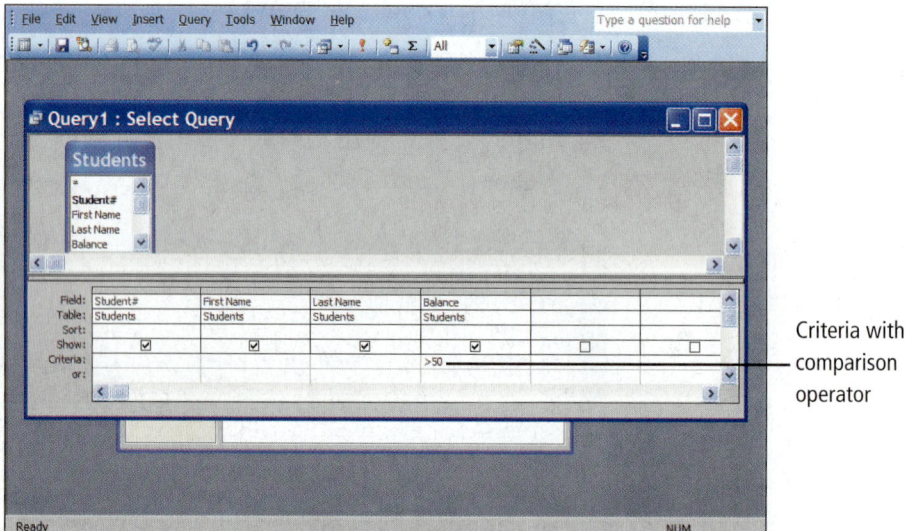

Figure 3.43

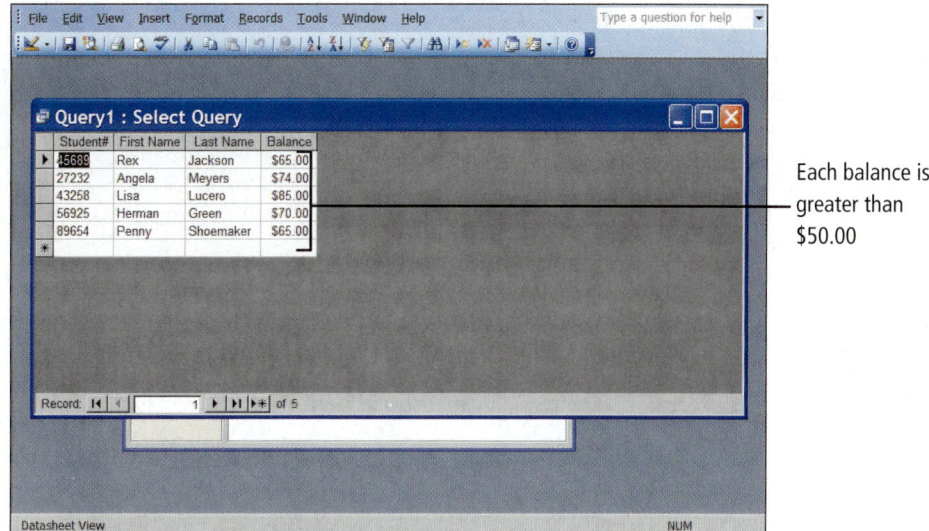

Each balance is greater than $50.00

Figure 3.44

[3] On the Query Datasheet toolbar, click the **View** button.

[4] In the **Criteria** row, under **Balance**, change the greater than sign (>) to the less than sign (<) and then click the **Run** button.

Ten records display and each has a balance less than $50.00. Notice that the results show those records for which the Balance is less than $50.00, but not equal to $50.00. See Figure 3.45.

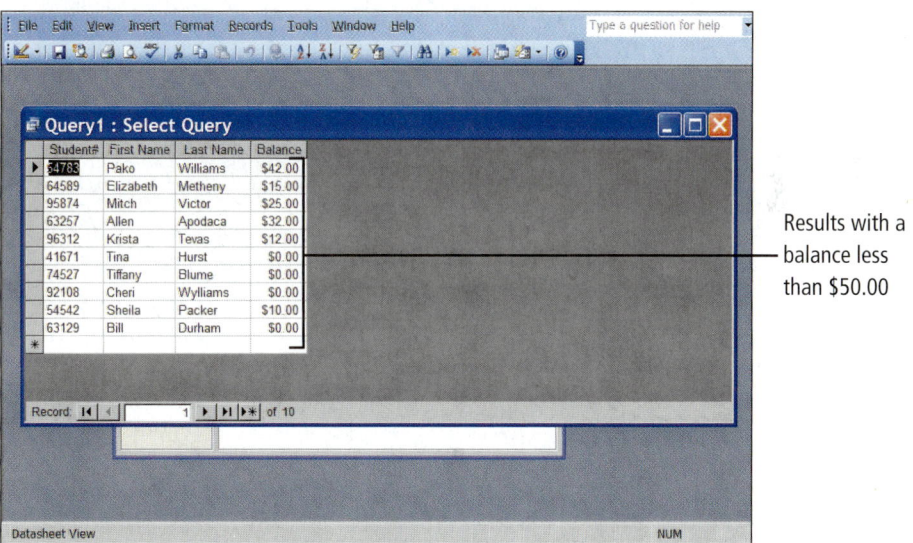

Results with a balance less than $50.00

Figure 3.45

[5] On the Query Datasheet toolbar, click the **View** button.

[6] In the **Criteria** row, under **Balance** and to the right of the less than sign <, type the equal sign, = but do not replace the less than, < sign. See Figure 3.46.

Project 3B: Students | **Access**

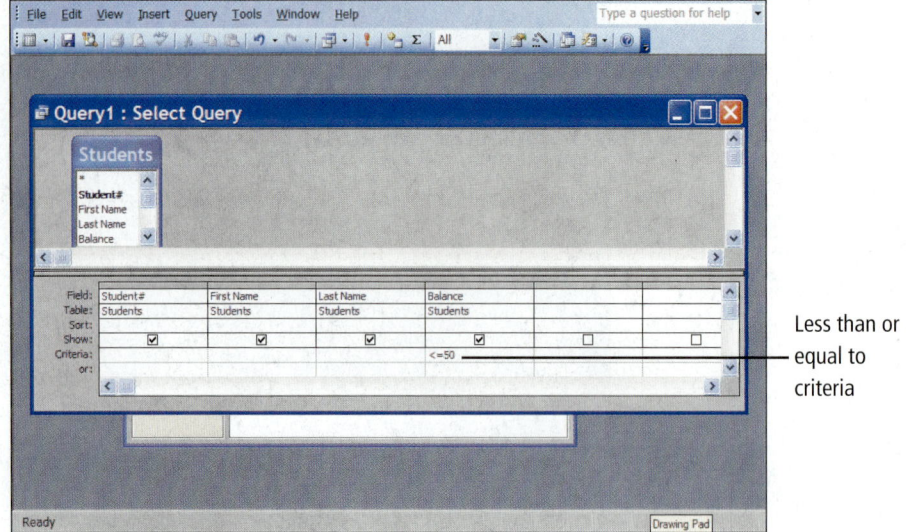

Figure 3.46

7 On the Query Design toolbar, click the **Run** button.

Eleven records display, including the record for Sally Jackson, who has a balance of exactly $50.00. See Figure 3.47. Comparison operators can be combined to form operators, such as the less than or equal to <= symbol.

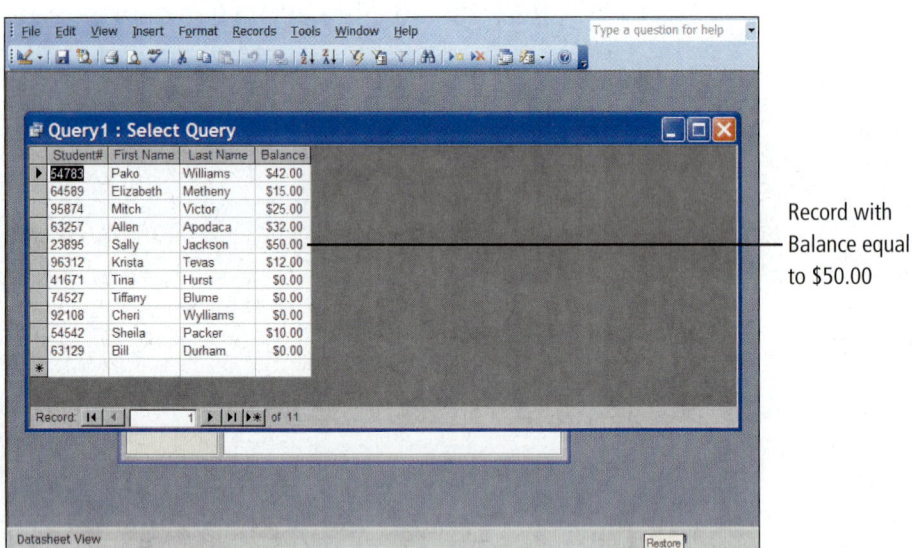

Figure 3.47

8 In the title bar of the query window, click the **Close** button. Click **Yes** to save changes to the query. Then in the **Save As** dialog box and using your own information, type **Firstname Lastname Balance Query** as the query name. Click **OK**.

The Database window displays.

9 Be sure your **Balance Query** is selected and then on the Database toolbar, click the **Print** button .

The query results print.

Objective 7
Use Compound Criteria

You may find that you need to specify more than one condition—criteria—in a query. Two or more criteria are called ***compound criteria***. Compound criteria are used to create more specific criteria and thus further limit the query results. Two types of compound criteria used in queries are AND and OR. Both of these are ***logical operators***. Logical operators allow you to enter criteria for the same field or different fields. For example, suppose you wanted to find those students who have a balance greater than $100.00 *and* who have earned more than 120 credits. You could specify both of those conditions in the same query using AND. Compound criteria that create an AND condition will return those records in the query result that meet *both* parts of the specified criteria.

Activity 3.12 Using AND in a Query

In this activity, you will specify the criteria in the query so that the records in the Students table that have a postal code of 60612 *and* a Business major will display.

1 With **Queries** selected on the Objects bar, double-click **Create query in Design view**.

A new query window displays and the Show Table dialog box lists the tables in the database.

2 In the **Show Table** dialog box, double-click **Students** and then click **Close**.

3 Add the following fields to the design grid by double-clicking the fields in the **Students** field list: **First Name**, **Last Name**, **Postal Code**, and **Major**.

Four fields are added to the design grid.

4 In the **Criteria** row under **Postal Code**, type **60612**

5 In the **Criteria** row under **Major**, type **Business** as shown in Figure 3.48 and then click the **Run** button .

The query results show two records, Angela Meyers and Tina Hurst. These records have *both* the specified Postal Code (60612) *and* the specified Major (Business). The criteria in the above query has two parts: the Postal Code part and the Major part. Criteria specifying an AND condition is always on the same line in the Criteria row.

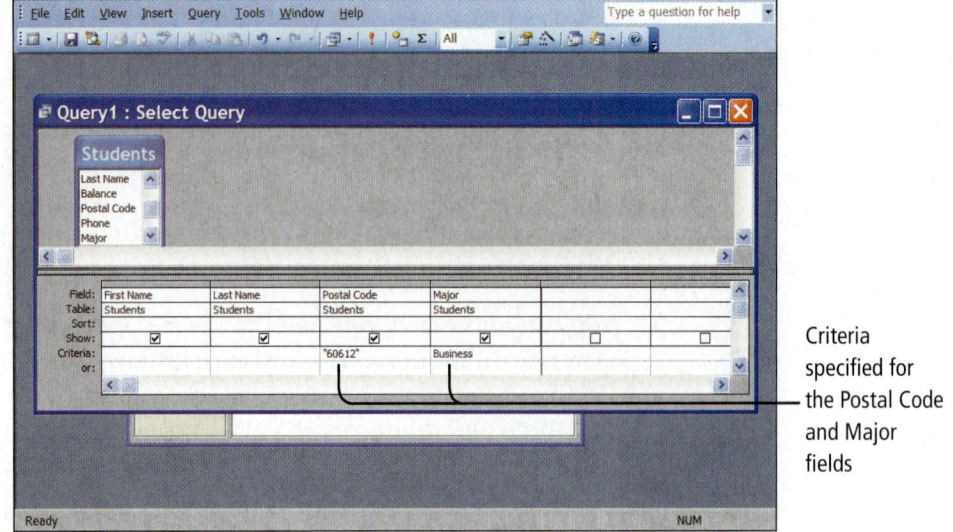

Figure 3.48

◻6 In the title bar of the query window, click the **Close** button ⊠. Click **Yes** to save changes to the query and in the **Save As** dialog box and using your own information, type **Firstname Lastname AND Query** as the query name. Click **OK**.

The Database window displays.

◻7 Be sure your **AND Query** is selected and then, on the Database toolbar, click the **Print** button 🖨.

Activity 3.13 Using OR in a Query

◻1 With **Queries** selected on the Objects bar, double-click **Create query in Design view**. In the **Show Table** dialog box, double-click **Students** and then click **Close**.

◻2 Add the following fields to the design grid by double-clicking the fields in the **Students** field list: **First Name**, **Last Name**, and **Major**.

Three fields are added to the design grid.

◻3 In the **Criteria** row under **Major**, type **Music**

◻4 Under **Major**, below the **Criteria** row, in the **or** row, type **Art** See Figure 3.49.

926   Access | Chapter 3: Queries

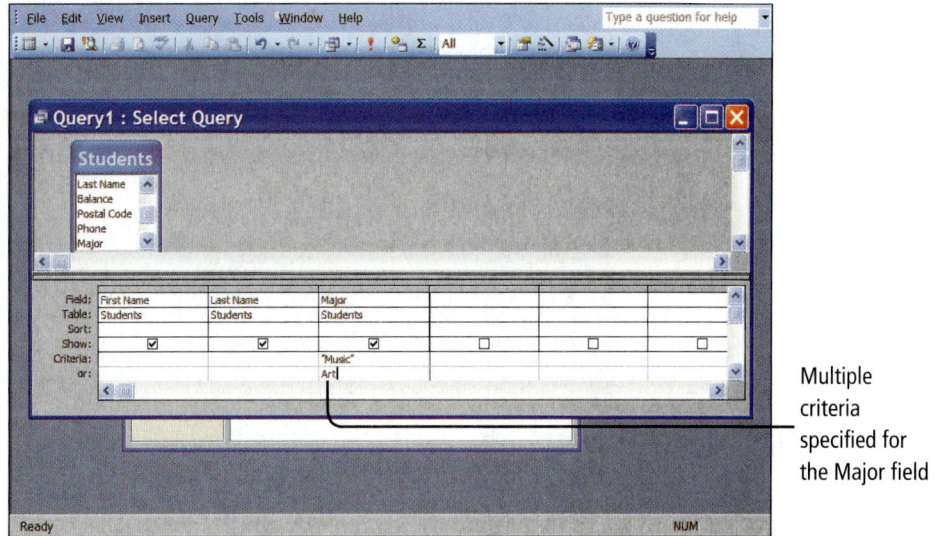

Figure 3.49

5 On the Query Design toolbar, click the **Run** button.

The query results display those records whose Major has an entry that is either Music *or* Art. Use the OR condition to specify multiple criteria for a single field.

6 In the title bar of the query window, click the **Close** button. Click **Yes** to save changes to the query and in the **Save As** dialog box and using your own information, type **Firstname Lastname OR Query** as the query name. Click **OK**.

The Database window displays.

7 Be sure your **OR Query** is selected and then, on the Database toolbar, click the **Print** button. Leave the database open for the next activity.

Objective 8
Sort Data in a Query

To better organize your data, you will find it useful to sort query results. Sorting results in a query is similar to sorting in a table. Records can be sorted in either ascending or descending order. Data in a query can be sorted either from the Datasheet view or from the Design view.

Activity 3.14 Sorting Data in a Query

In this activity, you will sort the results of the Balance Query you created in an earlier activity.

1 With **Queries** selected on the Objects bar, right-click the **Balance Query** that you created in an earlier activity, and then from the displayed shortcut menu, click **Open**.

The query opens in Datasheet view.

2 Click anywhere in the **Last Name column** and then on the Query Datasheet toolbar click the **Sort Ascending** button.

The records are sorted alphabetically by Last Name.

Project 3B: Students | **Access**   927

3 Click anywhere in the **Balance column** and then on the Query Datasheet toolbar, click the **Sort Descending** button.

The records are sorted by the entries in the Balance column from the largest to the smallest balance. See Figure 3.50.

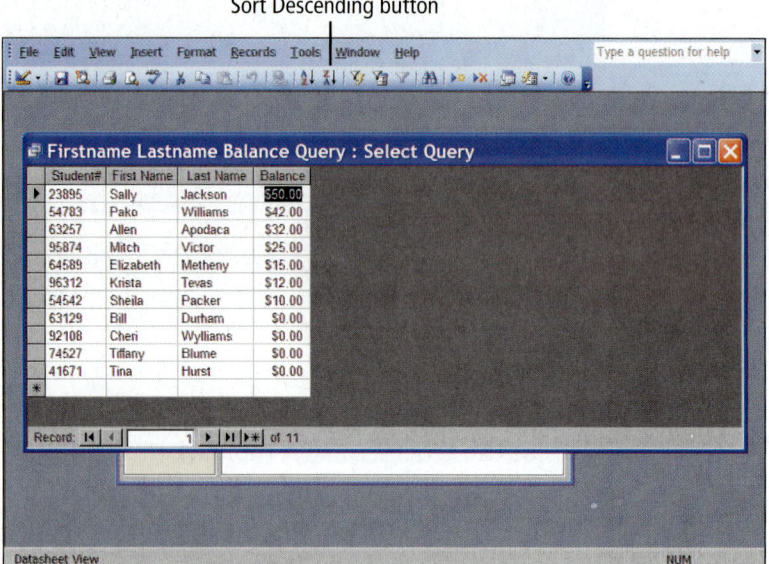

Figure 3.50

4 Switch to the Design view of the query for the next activity.

Activity 3.15 Modifying the Query Design and Sorting Data Using Multiple Fields in a Query

Sorting data in a query using more than one field allows you to further organize your query results. In this activity, you will sort the records in your Balance Query first by balance and then by last name.

1 In the design grid, move your pointer just above the **Balance** column until the pointer displays as a black downward-pointing arrow. See Figure 3.51.

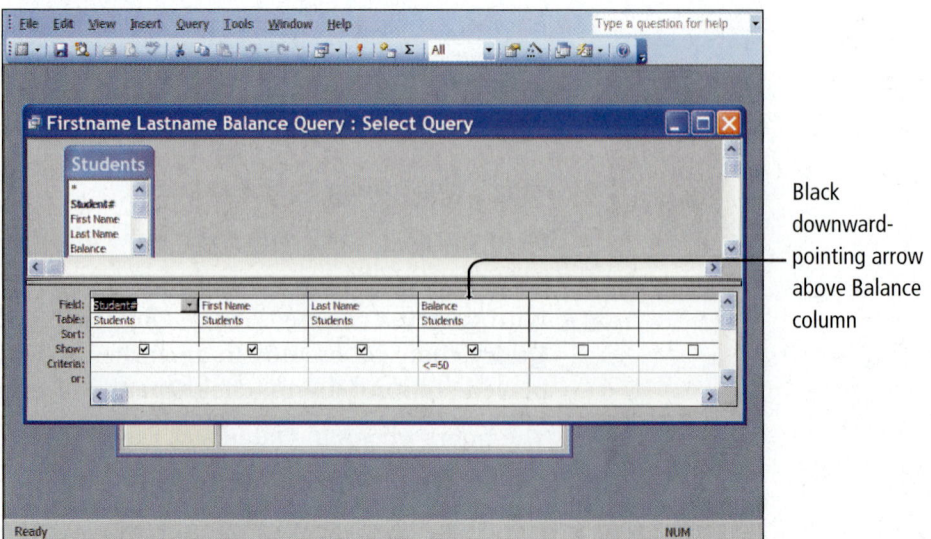

Figure 3.51

928 Access | Chapter 3: Queries

2 With the black downward-pointing arrow displayed, click once to select the **Balance** column.

The Balance column in the design grid is selected.

3 With the **Balance** column selected and your mouse pointer displayed as an arrow and positioned in the black bar above the **Balance** column, click and hold the left mouse button and then drag the **Balance** column to the left until you see a black vertical line between the **Student#** column and the **First Name** column. See Figure 3.52. Release the mouse button.

The Balance column is repositioned in between the Student# field and the First Name field. Recall from Chapter 1 that the field that is to be sorted first (Balance) must be to the left of the field that is sorted next (Last Name).

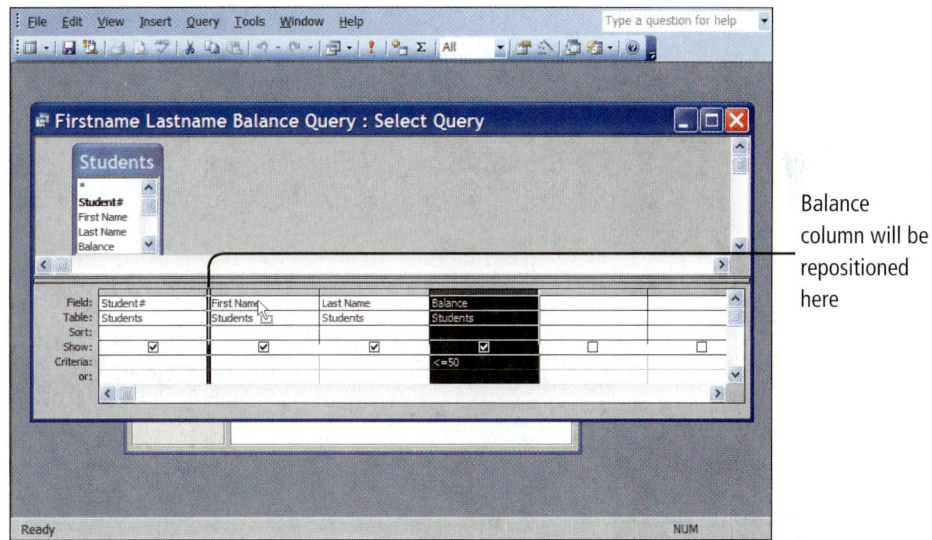

Figure 3.52

4 Repeat this action for the **Last Name** field by moving your pointer just above the **Last Name** column until the pointer displays as a black downward-pointing arrow.

5 With the black downward-pointing arrow displayed, click once to select the **Last Name** column.

The Last Name column in the design grid is selected.

6 With the **Last Name** column selected, click and hold the left mouse button and then drag the **Last Name** column to the left until you see a black vertical line between the **Balance** column and the **First Name** column. Release the mouse button.

The Last Name column is repositioned between the Balance field and the First Name field. See Figure 3.53.

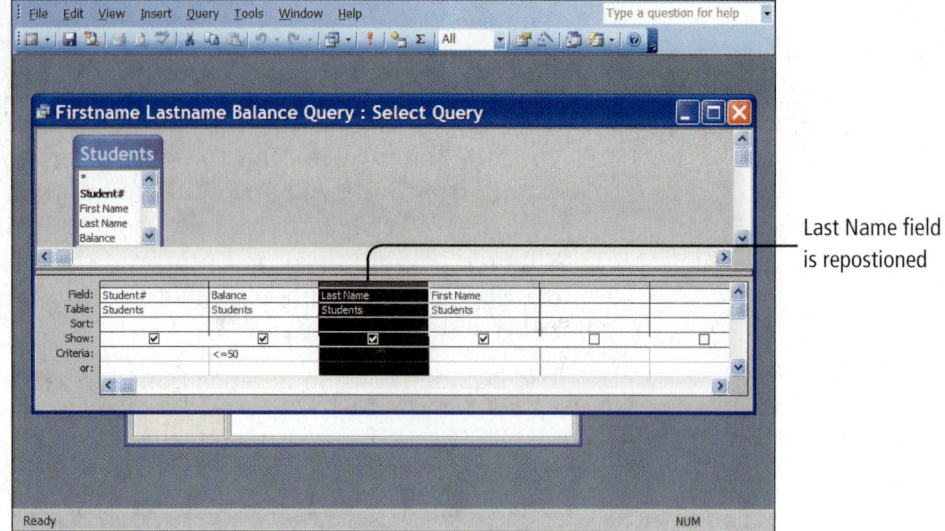

Last Name field is repositioned

Figure 3.53

[7] In the design grid, in the **Sort** row, under **Balance**, click once. See Figure 3.54.

The insertion point is blinking in the Sort row in the Balance field and a downward-pointing arrow displays.

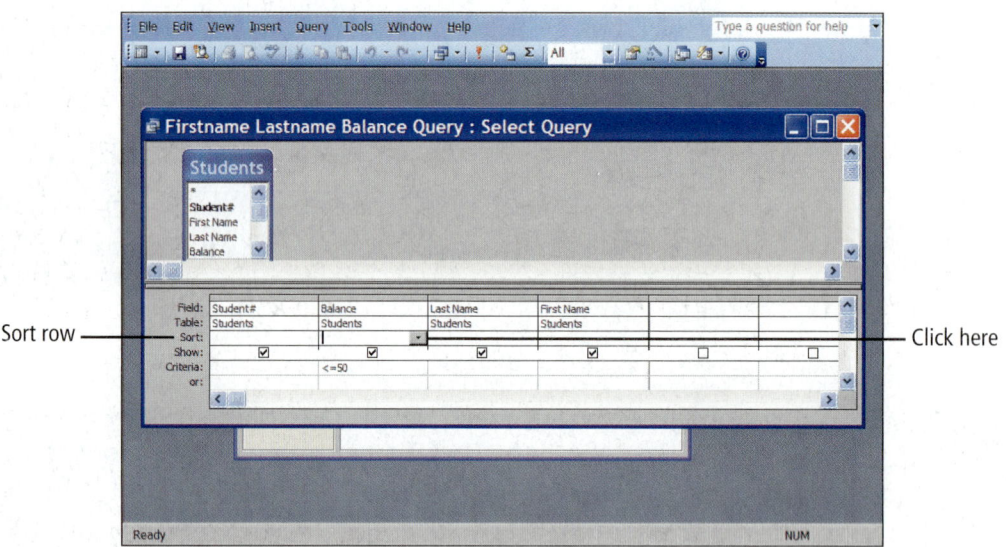

Sort row

Click here

Figure 3.54

[8] Click the **downward-pointing arrow** and then from the displayed list, click **Descending**. See Figure 3.55.

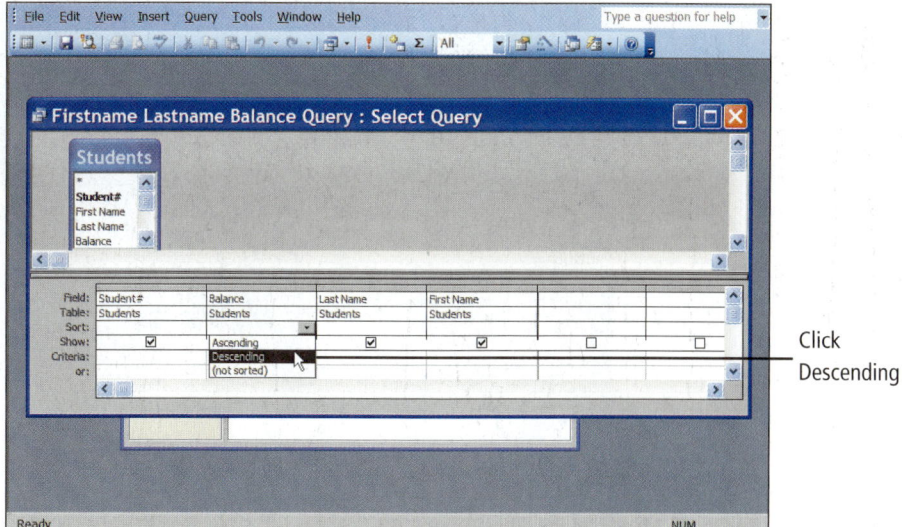

Figure 3.55

9. In the **Sort** row, under **Last Name**, click once.

   The insertion point is blinking in the Sort row in the Last Name field and a downward-pointing arrow displays.

10. Click the **downward-pointing arrow** and then click **Ascending**. See Figure 3.56.

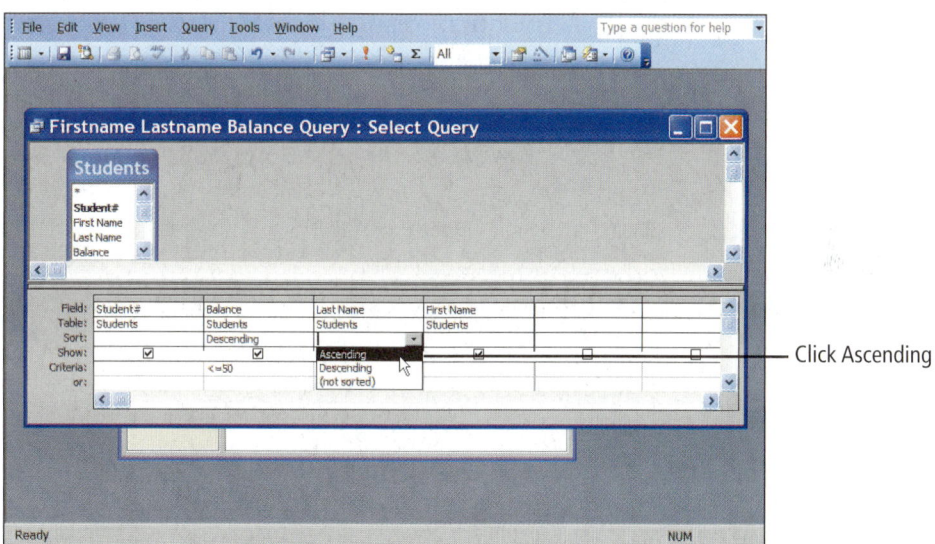

Figure 3.56

11. On the Query Design toolbar, click the **Run** button.

    The query results display with the records sorted first by the Balance field in descending order and then, for those records who have the same balances, the records are further sorted alphabetically by Last Name. See Figure 3.57.

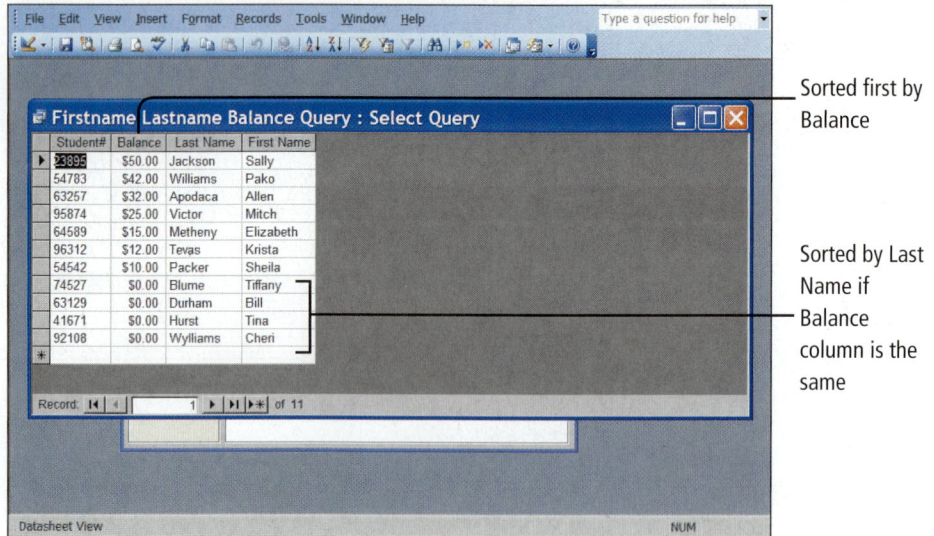

Figure 3.57

12 From the **File** menu, click **Save As**. In the **Save As** dialog box and using your own information, type **Firstname Lastname Sorted Balance Query** and then click **OK**.

The query displays in Datasheet view. The original sorted query remains and now there is a new sorted query.

13 On the Database toolbar, click the **Print** button.

The query results print.

14 Close the query. Close the database and then close Access.

End You have completed Project 3B

Project 3C Faculty

Using calculated fields, statistics, and group data in queries allows you to calculate additional information beyond what is contained in the fields.

In Activities 3.16 through 3.18 you will create queries using calculated fields and statistical functions. Your queries will look like Figure 3.58.

Figure 3.58
Project 3C—Faculty

Objective 9
Use Calculated Fields in a Query

As an example of using calculated fields in queries, you could multiply two fields together, such as Inventory Quantity and Cost per Item and get a Total Cost amount for each Inventory item. Or, as illustrated in the following activity, you could calculate a raise amount for Faculty Salaries by multiplying the salary amount by the raise percentage.

There are two steps to produce a calculated field in a query. First, you must provide a new name for the field that will store the calculated values. Second, you must specify the expression that will perform the calculation. Any field names used in the calculation must be enclosed within square brackets, [ ].

Activity 3.16 Using Calculated Fields in a Query

1. Locate the file **a03C_School** from the student files that accompany this text. Copy and paste the file to the Chapter 3 folder you created in Project 3A of this chapter.

2. Using the technique you practiced in Activity 1.1 of Chapter 1, remove the Read-only property from the file and rename the file as **3C_School_Firstname_Lastname**

3. Close the Windows accessory you are using—either My Computer or Windows Explorer. Start Access and open your **3C_School** database.

4. On the Objects bar, select **Queries** and then double-click **Create query in Design view**. In the **Show Table** dialog box, double-click **Faculty** and then click **Close**.

5. Add the following fields to the design grid by double-clicking the fields in the **Faculty** field list: **First Name**, **Last Name**, and **Salary**.

   Three fields are added to the design grid.

6. In the design grid, in the **Field** row, click in the first empty column on the right, right-click to display a shortcut menu, and then click **Zoom**.

7. In the **Zoom** dialog box, type **Raise Amount: [Salary]*.08** as shown in Figure 3.59.

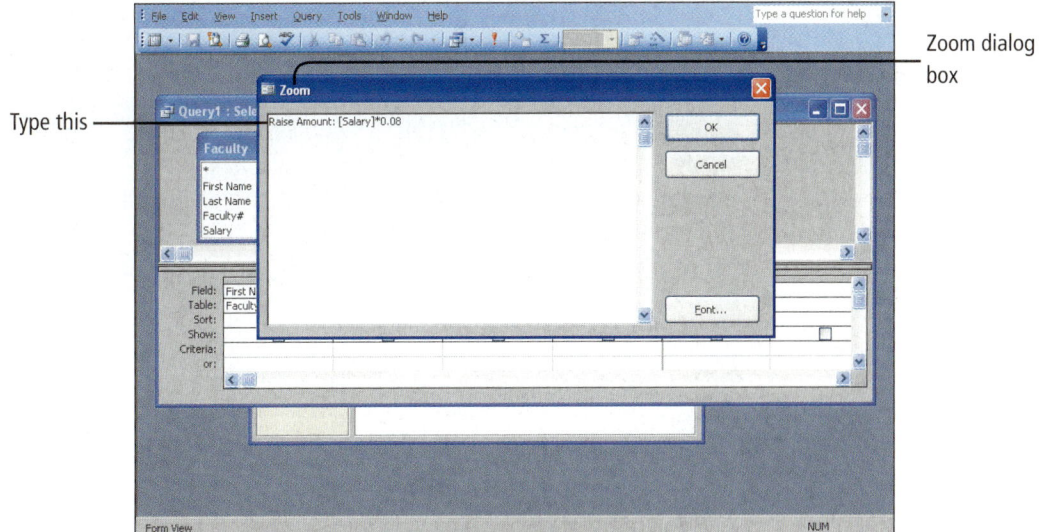

Figure 3.59

8. Look at the expression you have just typed.

    The first element, *Raise Amount*, is the name of the new field where the calculated amounts will display. Following that is a colon (:). A colon in a calculated field separates the new field name from the expression. *Salary* is in square brackets because it is an existing field name from the Faculty table. It contains the information on which the calculation will be performed. Following the square brackets is an asterisk (*), which in math calculations signifies multiplication. Finally, the percentage (8% or .08) is indicated.

> **Alert!**
>
> **Does Your Screen Differ?**
>
> If your calculations in a query do not work, carefully check the expression you typed. Spelling or syntax errors will prevent calculated fields from working properly.

9. In the **Zoom** dialog box, click **OK**, and then click the **Run** button.

    The query results display the three fields from the Faculty table plus a fourth field—*Raise Amount*—in which a calculated amount displays. Each calculated amount equals the amount in Salary field multiplied by .08. See Figure 3.60.

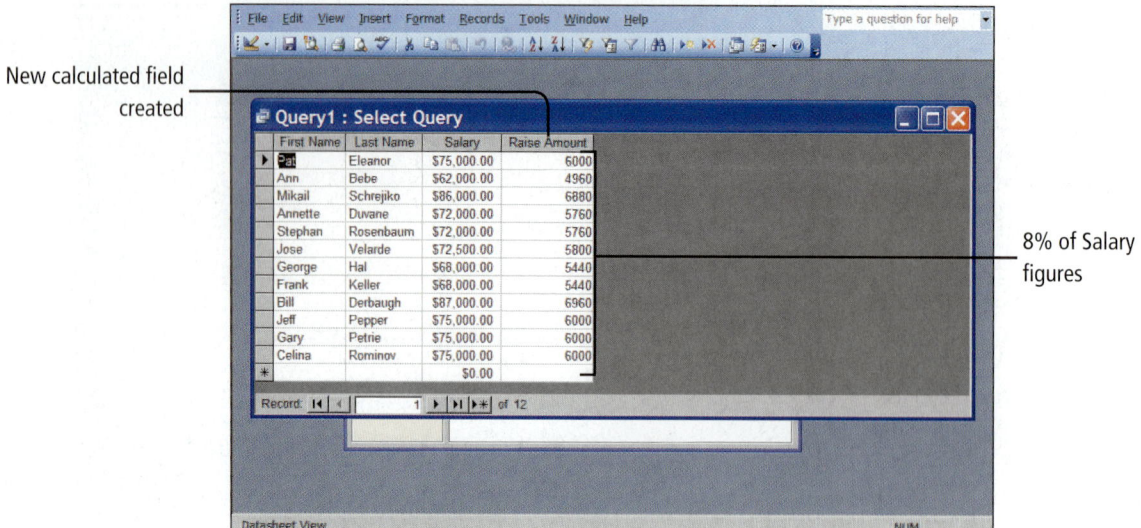

Figure 3.60

10. Notice the formatting of the **Raise Amount** field. There are no dollar signs, commas, or decimal places. You will change this formatting in a later step. Switch to **Design view**. In the **Field** row, in the first empty column, right-click and then click **Zoom**.

    The Zoom dialog box displays. Although you can type directly into the Field box in the column, it is easier to use the Zoom dialog box for a better view of the calculations you want to type.

11. In the **Zoom** dialog box, type **New Salary: [Salary]+[Raise Amount]** and then click **OK**.

12. Click the **Run** button to run the query.

    Access has calculated the New Salary amount by adding together the Salary field and the Raise Amount field. The New Salary column includes dollar signs, commas, and decimal points because the Salary field, on which the calculation was based, uses a format that includes them.

13. Switch to **Design view**. In the **Raise Amount** column, right-click and then click **Properties**. See Figure 3.61.

    The Field Properties dialog box displays. In the Field Properties dialog box, you can customize fields in a query, for example, the format of numbers in the field. As you progress in your study of Access, you will learn more about the Field Properties dialog box.

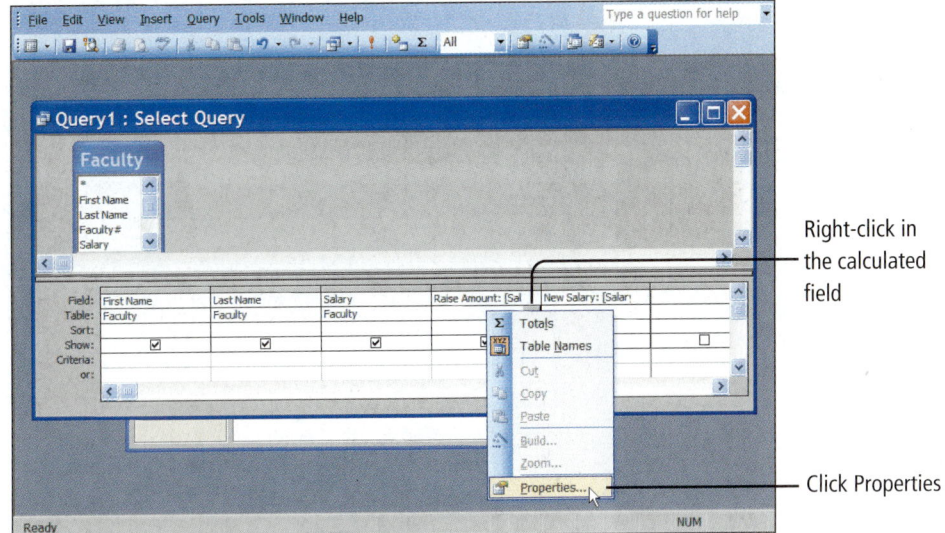

Figure 3.61

14 In the **Field Properties** dialog box, to the right of **Format**, click in the white box and then click the **downward-pointing arrow** that displays. See Figure 3.62.

A list of possible formatting options for this field displays.

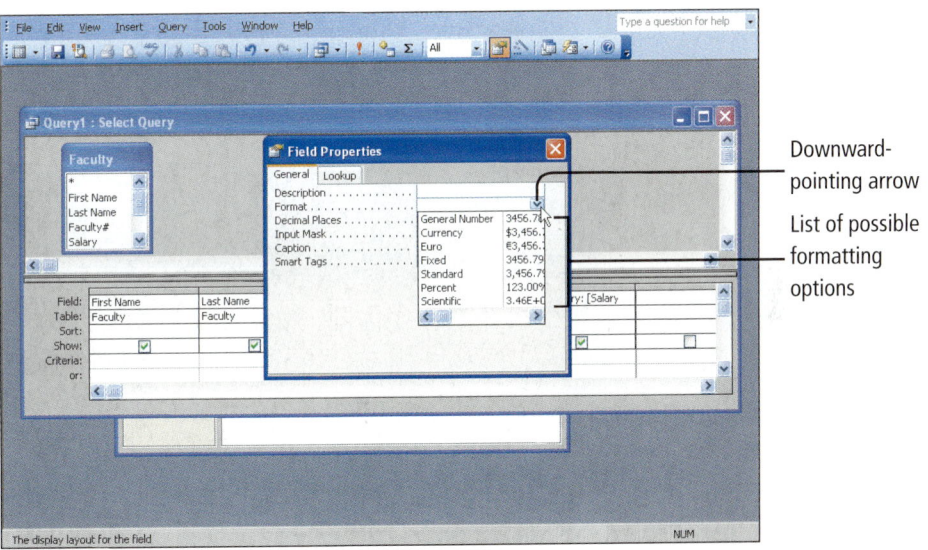

Figure 3.62

15 In the list of formatting options, click **Currency**. Then on the title bar of the **Field Properties** dialog box, click the **Close** button ☒. See Figure 3.63.

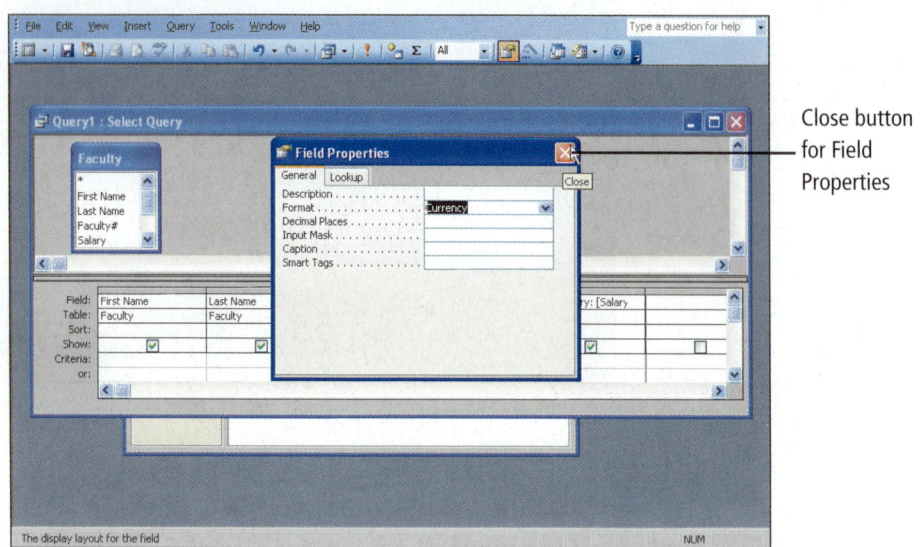

Figure 3.63

16 Click the **Run** button to run the query.

The Raise Amount column displays with Currency formatting—a dollar sign, thousands comma separators, and two decimal places. See Figure 3.64.

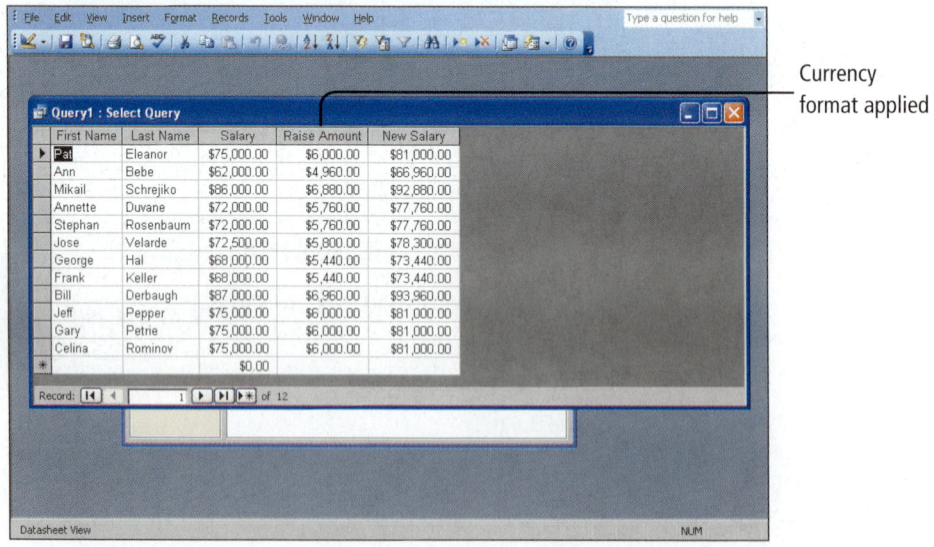

Figure 3.64

17 In the title bar of the query window, click the **Close** button ☒. Click **Yes** to save changes to the query and in the **Save As** dialog box and using your own information, type **Firstname Lastname Faculty Raise** as the query name. Click **OK**.

The Database window displays.

18 Be sure your **Faculty Raise** query is selected and on the Database toolbar, click the **Print** button. Leave the database open for the next activity.

Objective 10
Group Data and Calculate Statistics in a Query

In Access queries, you can perform statistical calculations on a group of records. Statistics that are performed on a group of records are called *aggregate functions*. Access supports the aggregate functions summarized in the table shown in Figure 3.65.

Aggregate Functions

Function Name	What It Does
SUM	Totals the values in a field
AVG	Averages the values in a field
MAX	Locates the largest value in a field
MIN	Locates the smallest value in a field
STDEV	Calculates the Standard Deviation on the values in a field
VAR	Calculates the Variance on the values in a field
FIRST	Displays the First value in a field
LAST	Displays the Last value in a field

Figure 3.65

In the activities that follow, you will use the first four functions in Figure 3.65: SUM, AVG, MAX, and MIN. As you progress in your study of Access, you will use the remaining functions.

Activity 3.17 Grouping Data in a Query

When you want to group records in a query by a specific field, include only that field in the query. For example, if you wanted to group (summarize) the CDs in your CD Collection database by the type of music, you would include only the Type field in your query. To group data in a query, you must insert a Total row in the query design. The Total row does not appear by default. In this activity, you will create a query and group the records by Division.

1 Be sure **Queries** is selected on the Objects bar and then double-click **Create query in Design view**. In the **Show Table** dialog box, double-click **Faculty** and then click **Close**.

2 From the list of fields for the Faculty table, double-click the **Division** field to add it to the design grid.

Project 3C: Faculty | **Access**   939

3 On the Query Design toolbar, click the **Totals** button ∑. See Figure 3.66.

A Total row is inserted as the third row of the design grid. See Figure 3.66.

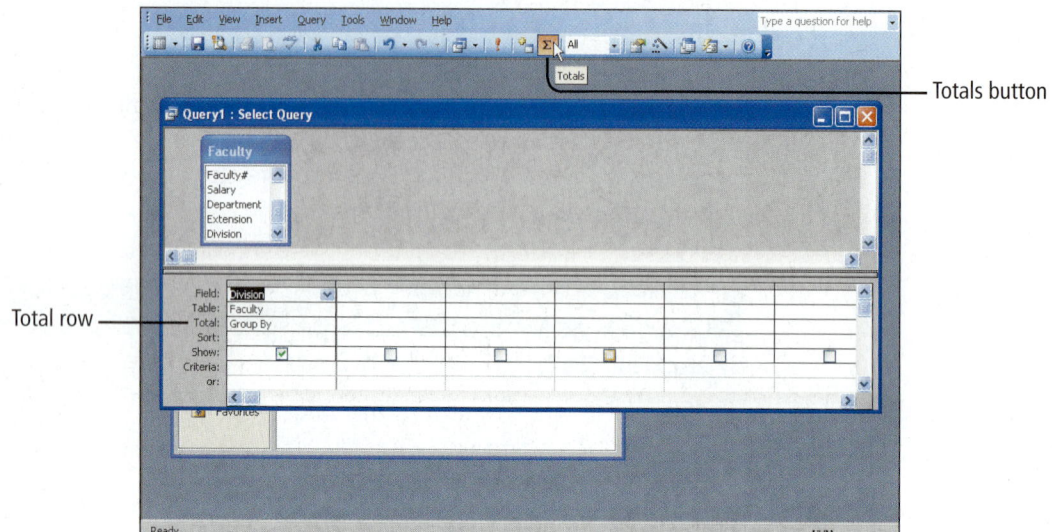

Figure 3.66

4 In the **Total** row, under **Division**, click and then click the arrow that displays to the right of *Group By*.

The list of aggregate functions displays.

5 Click **Group By** and then click the **Run** button to run the query.

The query results display summarized by the entries in the Division field: Business, Education, Fine Arts, and Humanities. See Figure 3.67.

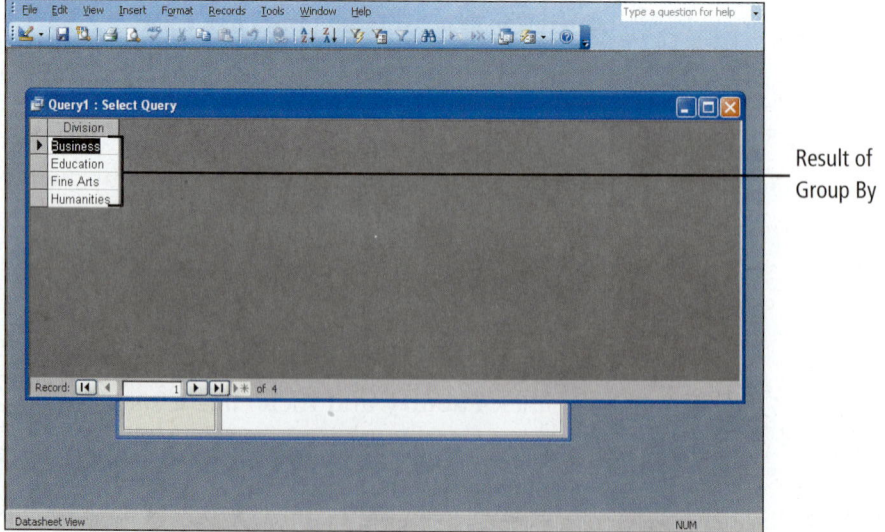

Figure 3.67

Activity 3.18 Using the AVG, SUM, MAX, and MIN Functions in a Query

In this activity, you will create a query that will display the Faculty salary amounts grouped by Division.

1 Switch to **Design view** and then add the **Salary** field to the design grid.

2 Click the **Run** button to run the query.

The query results contain the individual salary amounts, grouped together by division, as shown in Figure 3.68.

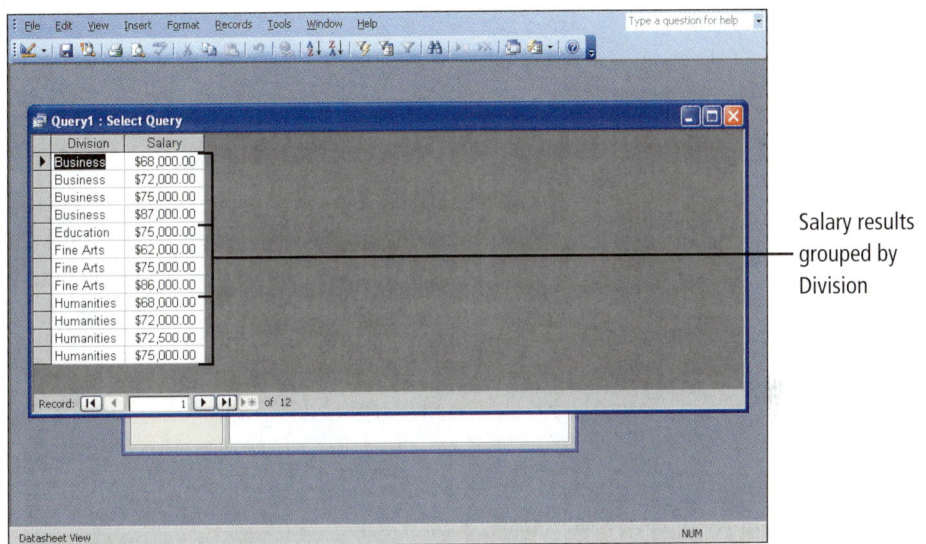

Salary results grouped by Division

Figure 3.68

3 Switch to **Design view**. In the **Total** row, under **Salary**, click and then click the arrow that displays.

4 From the list of functions, click **Avg** as shown in Figure 3.69 and then click the **Run** button.

Access calculates an average salary for each of the four divisions. Notice the field name, *AvgOfSalary*, for the calculation. This query answers the question, "What is the average faculty salary within each division?"

Project 3C: Faculty | **Access** 941

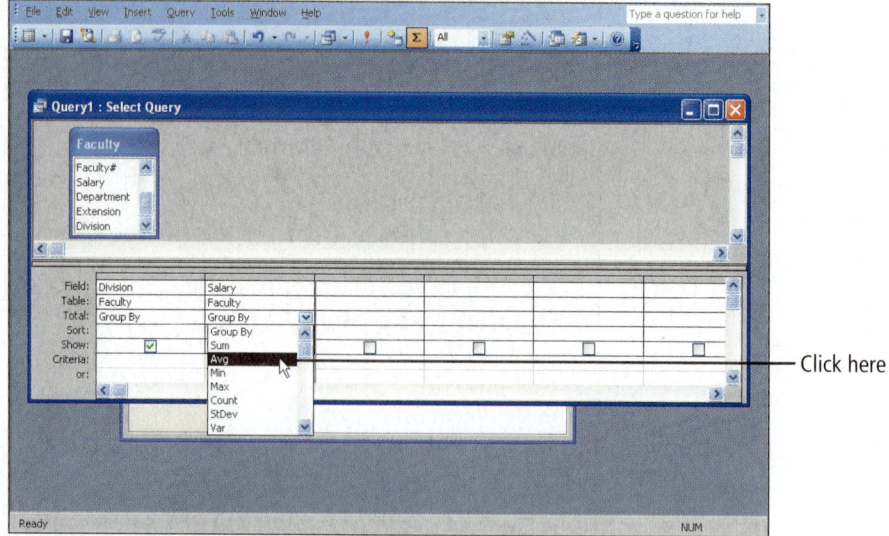

Figure 3.69

5 Switch to **Design view**. In the **Total** row under **Salary**, click and then click the arrow that displays. From the list of functions, click **Sum**.

6 Run the query.

Access sums the Salaries for each of the four Divisions. Notice the field name, *SumOfSalary*, for the calculation. Thus, the total annual salary amount for all of the faculty members in the Business Division is $302,000.00.

7 Switch to **Design view**. In the **Total** row, under **Salary**, click and then click the arrow that displays. From the list of functions, click **Min**.

8 Run the query.

Access locates the smallest value in each of the Divisions and displays the results. Thus, the lowest paid faculty member in the Fine Arts Division earns an annual salary of $62,000.00.

9 Switch to **Design view**. In the **Total** row, under **Salary**, click and then click the arrow that displays. From the list of functions, click **Max**.

10 Run the query.

Access locates the largest value in each of the Divisions and displays the results. See Figure 3.70. Thus, the highest paid faculty member in the Humanities Division earns $75,000.00.

942   **Access** | Chapter 3: Queries

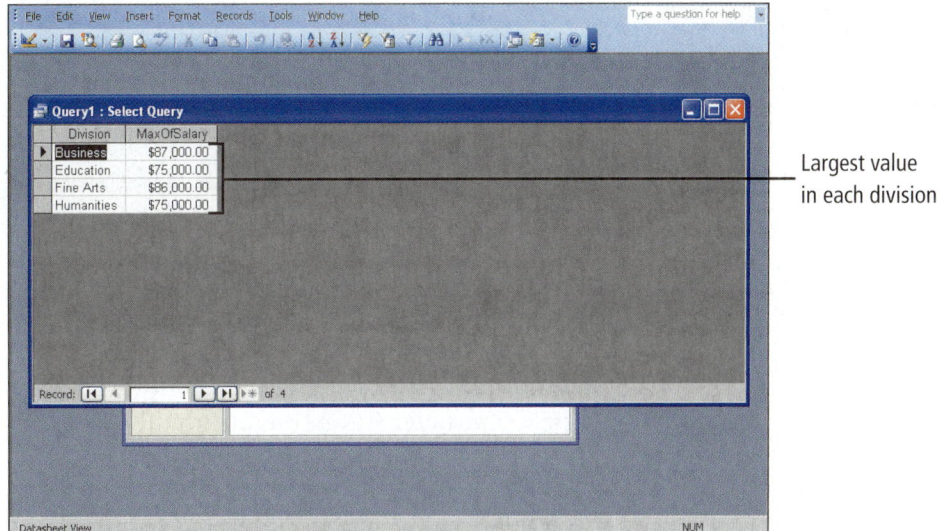

Largest value in each division

Figure 3.70

11 In the title bar of the query window, click the **Close** button. Click **Yes** to save changes to the query and in the **Save As** dialog box and using your own information, type **Firstname Lastname Max Salary** as the query name. Click **OK**.

The Database window displays.

12 Print your **Max Salary** query.

13 Close your **School** database and then close Access.

End You have completed Project 3C

Summary

Queries allow you to ask questions about the data in a database in a manner that Access can interpret. Queries are useful for locating data that matches the criteria, or conditions, that you specify.

Text is one type of criteria that can be specified. Wildcard characters such as the *, which serves as a placeholder for a group of characters, are included as part of the criteria when a portion of what you are looking for is unknown. The wildcard character ? serves as a placeholder for a single character in textual criteria.

Numeric criteria can also be specified in a query. Specifying numeric criteria allows you to use comparison operators, such as less than (<), greater than (>), and equal to (=).

Queries can also have more than one criteria, known as compound criteria, to assist you in locating specific data. There are two types of compound criteria, AND and OR.

Calculations can be performed in a query. Statistical calculations such as SUM, AVG, MAX, and MIN can be used on grouped data in a query.

In This Chapter You Practiced How To

- Create a New Select Query
- Run, Save, and Close a Query
- Open and Edit an Existing Query
- Specify Text Criteria in a Query
- Use Wildcards in a Query
- Specify Numeric Criteria in a Query
- Use Compound Criteria
- Sort Data in a Query
- Use Calculated Fields in a Query
- Group Data and Calculate Statistics in a Query

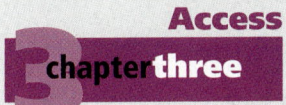

Concepts Assessments

Matching Match each term in the second column with its correct definition in the first column by writing the letter of the term on the blank line in front of the correct definition.

____ 1. The symbols < (less than) > (greater than) and = (equal).

____ 2. The upper portion of the query design grid where selected tables used in the query display.

____ 3. The category that includes AND and OR operators.

____ 4. Statistics performed on a group of records.

____ 5. Two or more conditions in a query.

____ 6. A question formed in a manner that Access can interpret.

____ 7. The conditions that identify the specific records you are looking for.

____ 8. The lower pane of the query window where the fields are added to the query.

____ 9. Characters that serve as a placeholder for an unknown character or characters in a query.

____ 10. Displays the tables available for use in a query.

____ 11. Language used in querying, updating, and managing relational databases.

____ 12. Term used to compare expressions.

____ 13. Examines a sequence of characters and compares them to the criteria in a query.

____ 14. Wildcard character used as a placeholder to match any number of characters.

____ 15. Wildcard character used as a placeholder to match one character.

A Aggregate functions

B Asterisk (*)

C Comparison operators

D Compound criteria

E Criteria

F Design grid

G "Like"

H Logical operators

I Query

J Question mark (?)

K Show Table dialog box

L SQL

M String expression

N Table area

O Wildcard characters

Concepts Assessments | **Access** 945

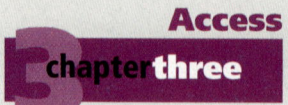

Concepts Assessments (continued)

Fill in the Blank Write the correct answer in the space provided.

1. When a query is run, the results display in a(n) _____.

2. To include, but not display, a field in query results, clear the _____ box in the design grid.

3. In an _____ condition, both parts of the query must be met.

4. In an _____ condition, either part of the query may be met.

5. If sorting records by multiple fields, the field that is to be sorted first must be positioned to the _____ of the field that is sorted next.

6. Use the _____ to better view the calculations entered into a calculated field in a query.

7. To locate the largest value in a group of records, use the _____ function.

8. To display the row in the design grid where you can specify statistical functions, such as Sum or Avg, click the _____ button.

9. To locate the smallest value in a group of records, use the _____ function.

10. To save an existing query with a new name, use the _____ command.

946   **Access** | Chapter 3: Queries

Skill Assessments

Project 3D—Rental Instruments

Objectives: *Create a New Select Query; Run, Save, and Close a Query; and Specify Text Criteria in a Query.*

In the following Skill Assessment, you will create a query that will locate specific information for rental instruments at the Lake Michigan City College Music Department. Your completed query will look similar to the one shown in Figure 3.71. You will rename the database as *3D_Rental_Instruments_Firstname_Lastname* in the folder you have created for this chapter.

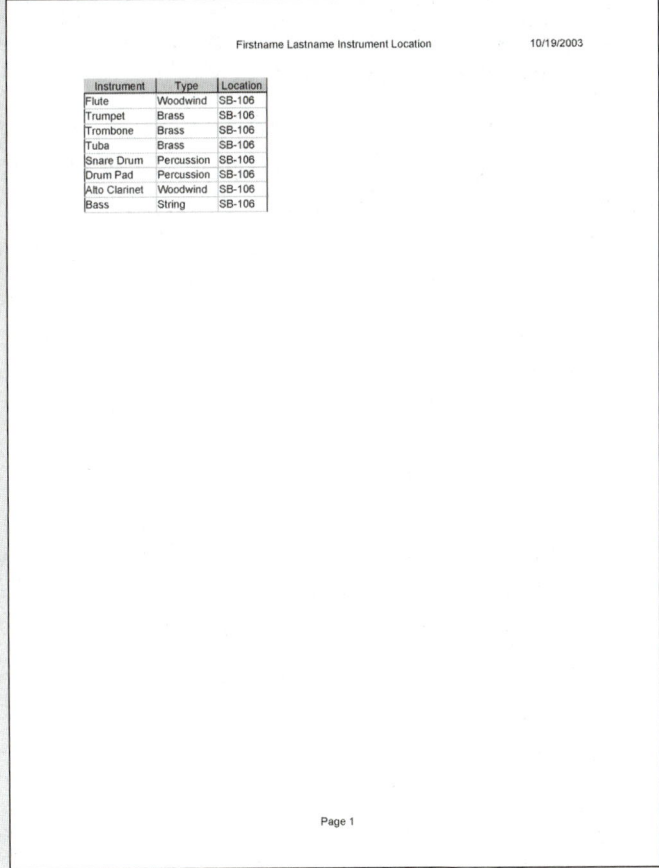

Figure 3.71

1. Locate the file **a03D_Rental_Instruments** from the student files that accompany this text. Copy and paste the file to the Chapter 3 folder you created earlier in this chapter.

2. Using the technique you practiced in Activity 1.1 of Chapter 1, remove the Read-only property from the file and rename the file as **3D_Rental_Instruments_Firstname_Lastname**

(**Project 3D**–Rental Instruments continues on the next page)

Skill Assessments (continued)

(Project 3D–Rental Instruments continued)

3. Close the Windows accessory you are using—either My Computer or Windows Explorer. Start Access and open your **3D_Rental_Instruments** database.

4. On the Objects bar, click **Queries**.

5. Double-click **Create query in Design view**. A new Select Query window opens and the **Show Table** dialog box displays. The Show Table dialog box lists all of the tables in the database.

6. In the **Show Table** dialog box, click **Rental Instruments**, click the **Add** button, and then click the **Close** button. Alternatively, you can double-click Rental Instruments and then click Close.

7. In the **Rental Instruments** field list, double-click **Instrument**. The **Instrument** field displays in the design grid.

8. In the **Rental Instruments** field list, double-click **Type**. Repeat this action for the **Location** field. As you double-click each field, notice the fields display one by one in the design grid.

9. In the **Criteria** row, under the **Location** field, type **SB-106**

10. On the Query Design toolbar, click the **Run** button. The query runs and the query results display in a table in Datasheet view. Clicking the Run button causes Access to look at all the records in the Rental Instruments table and locate only the records that meet the specified criteria, which, in this case, are the records that have SB-106 in the Location field.

11. In the title bar of the query window, click the **Close** button. Click **Yes** to save changes to the query and, in the **Save As** dialog box using your own information, type **Firstname Lastname Instrument Location** as the query name. Click **OK**.

12. Be sure your **Instrument Location** query is selected. Then on the Database toolbar, click the **Print** button.

13. Close the database and then close Access.

 You have completed Project 3D

Project 3E—Inventory

Objectives: Create a New Select Query; Run, Save, and Close a Query; Specify Numeric Criteria in a Query; and Use Compound Criteria.

In the following Skill Assessment, you will create a new query to locate information about the inventory at LMCC. Your completed query will look similar to Figure 3.72. You will rename and save your database as 3E_Inventory_Firstname_Lastname.

(Project 3E–Inventory continues on the next page)

Skill Assessments (continued)

(Project 3E–Inventory continued)

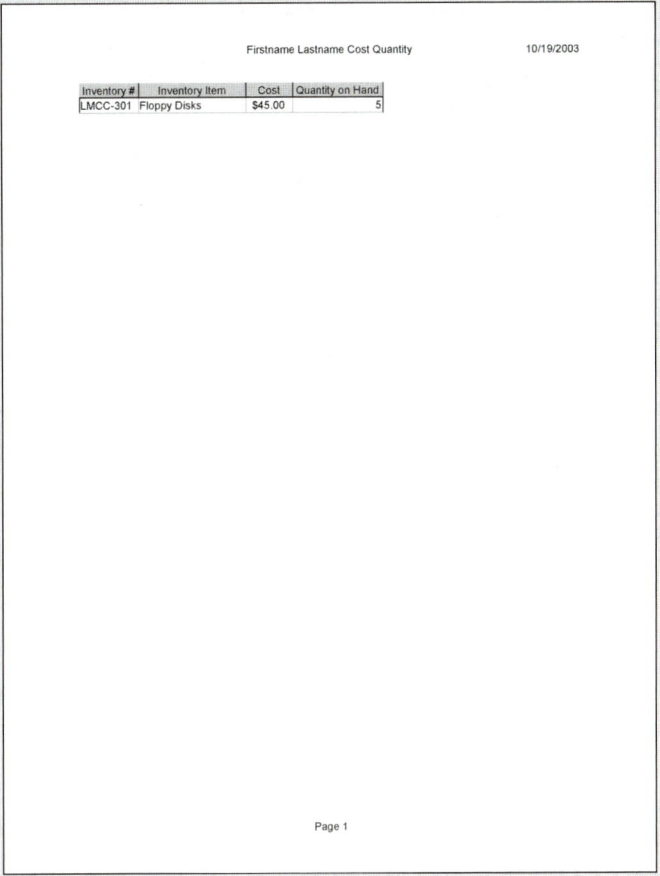

Figure 3.72

1. Locate the file **a03E_Inventory** from the student files that accompany this text. Copy and paste the file to the Chapter 3 folder you created earlier in this chapter.

2. Using the technique you practiced in Activity 1.1 of Chapter 1, remove the Read-only property from the file and rename the file as **3E_Inventory_Firstname_Lastname**

3. Close the Windows accessory you are using—either My Computer or Window Explorer. Start Access and open your **3E_Inventory** database.

4. On the Objects bar, click **Queries**. To the right of the Objects bar, two command icons for creating a new query display.

5. Double-click **Create query in Design view**. A new **Select Query** window opens and the **Show Table** dialog box displays. The Show Table dialog box lists all of the tables in the database.

(Project 3E–Inventory continues on the next page)

Skill Assessments (continued)

(Project 3E–Inventory continued)

6. In the **Show Table** dialog box, double-click **Office Inventory** and then click the **Close** button. A list of the fields in the Office Inventory table displays in the upper pane of the Select Query window. The **Inventory #** field is bold, unlike the other fields in the list, because the Inventory # field is the primary key in the Office Inventory table.

7. In the **Office Inventory** field list, double-click **Inventory #**. The Inventory # field displays in the design grid. The design grid of the Select Query window is where you specify the fields and other criteria to be used in the query.

8. In the **Office Inventory** field list, double-click **Inventory Item**. Repeat this action for the **Cost** and **Quantity on Hand** fields in the field list. Use the vertical scroll bar in the field list window to view the fields toward the end of the list. As you double-click each field, notice the fields display one by one in the design grid.

9. In the **Criteria** row, under **Cost**, type **>40** and then click the **Run** button. Three records display in the query results; each has a Cost greater than $40.00. On the Query Datasheet toolbar, click the **View** button to switch to Design view.

10. In the **Criteria** row, under **Quantity on Hand**, type **>=5** and then click the **Run** button. One record displays for Floppy Disks. This record meets the criteria of a Cost that is greater than $40.00 AND a Quantity on Hand that is greater than or equal to 5.

11. In the title bar of the query window, click the **Close** button. Click **Yes** to save changes to the query and in the **Save As** dialog box using your own information, type **Firstname Lastname Cost Quantity** as the query name. Click **OK**.

12. Be sure your **Cost Quantity** query is selected, then on the Database toolbar, click the **Print** button.

13. Close the database and then close Access.

 End You have completed Project 3E

Project 3F—Computer Inventory

Objectives: *Create a New Select Query; Run, Save, and Close a Query; Use Calculated Fields in a Query; and Group Data and Calculate Statistics in a Query.*

In the following Skill Assessment you will create two queries for the Computer Inventory database at LMCC. Your completed queries will look similar to Figure 3.73. You will rename and save your database as *3F_Computer_Inventory_Firstname_Lastname*.

(Project 3F–Computer Inventory continues on the next page)

Access chapter three

Skill Assessments (continued)

(Project 3F–Computer Inventory continued)

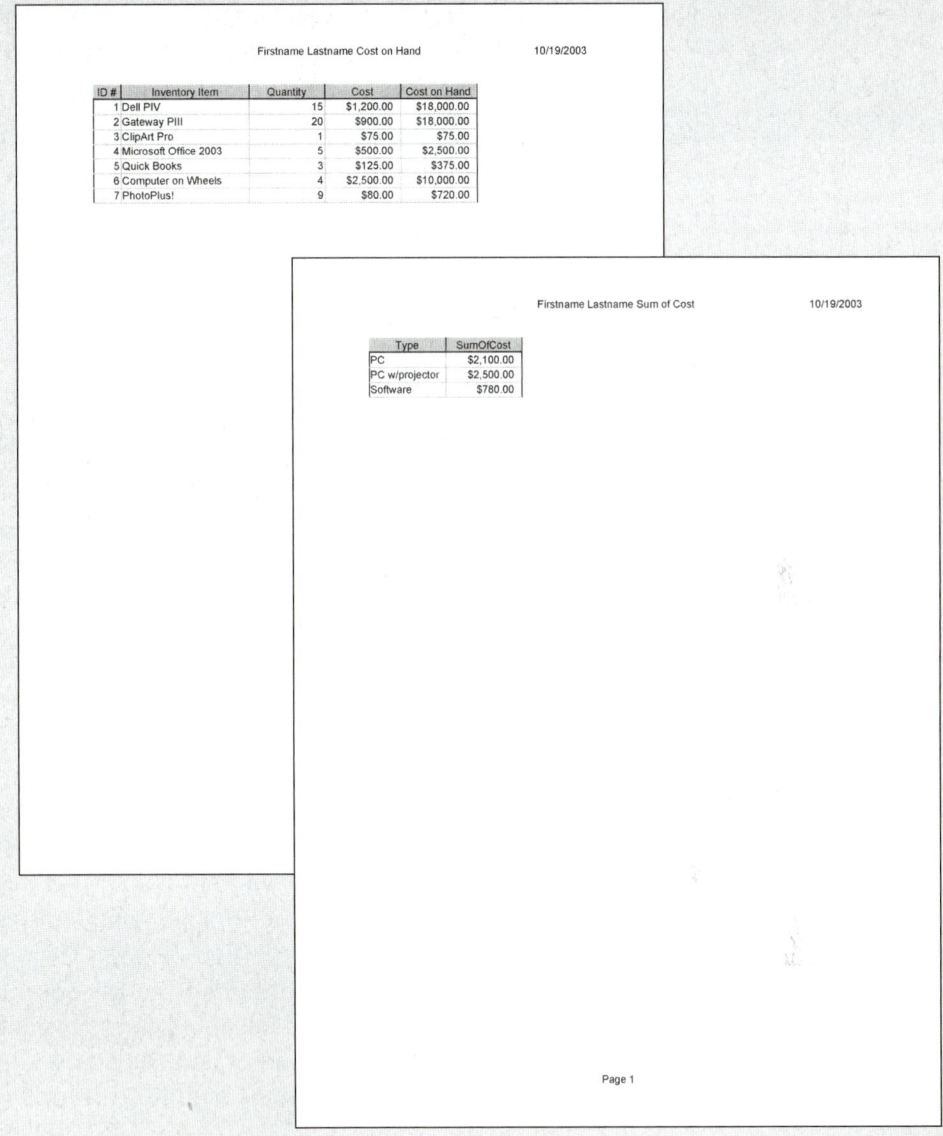

Figure 3.73

1. Locate the file **a03F_Computer_Inventory** from the student files that accompany this text. Copy and paste the file to the Chapter 3 folder you created earlier in this chapter.

2. Using the technique you practiced in Activity 1.1 of Chapter 1, remove the Read-only property from the file and rename the file as **3F_ComputerInventory_Firstname_Lastname**

3. Close the Windows accessory you are using—either My Computer or Windows Explorer. Start Access and open your **3F_ComputerInventory** database.

(Project 3F–Computer Inventory continues on the next page)

Skill Assessments (continued)

(Project 3F–Computer Inventory continued)

4. On the Objects bar, click **Queries**. To the right of the Objects bar, two command icons for creating a new query display.

5. Double-click **Create query in Design view**. A new Select Query window opens and the **Show Table** dialog box displays. The **Show Table** dialog box lists all of the tables in the database.

6. In the **Show Table** dialog box, double-click **Inventory** and then click the **Close** button. A list of the fields in the Inventory table displays in the upper pane of the Select Query window. The ID # field is bold, unlike the other fields in the list, because the ID # field is the primary key in the Inventory table.

7. In the **Inventory** field list, double-click **ID #**. The ID # field displays in the design grid. The design grid of the Select Query window is where you specify the fields and other criteria to be used in the query.

8. In the **Inventory** field list, double-click **Inventory Item**. Repeat this action for the **Quantity** and **Cost** fields in the field list. Use the vertical scroll bar in the field list window to view the fields toward the end of the list. As you double-click each field, notice the fields display one by one in the design grid.

9. In the design grid, in the **Field** row, click in the first empty column on the right, right-click to display the shortcut menu, and then click **Zoom**.

10. In the Zoom dialog box, type **Cost on Hand:[Quantity]*[Cost]**

11. Look at the expression you have just typed. The first element, *Cost on Hand*, is the name of the new field where the calculated amounts will display. Following that is a colon (:). A colon in a calculated field separates the new field name from the equation. *Quantity* and *Cost* are in square brackets because they are existing fields from the Inventory table. In between the fields is an asterisk (*), which in mathematical calculations signifies multiplication.

12. In the **Zoom** dialog box, click **OK** and then click the **Run** button. The query results display the four specified fields from the Inventory table plus a fifth field, *Cost on Hand*, that, for each record, displays a calculated amount that results from multiplying the figure in the *Quantity* field by the figure in the *Cost* field.

13. In the title bar of the query window, click the **Close** button. Click **Yes** to save changes to the query and in the **Save As** dialog box and using your own information, type **Firstname Lastname Cost on Hand** as the query name. Click **OK**. The Database window displays.

14. In the Database window, be sure your **Cost on Hand** query is selected and then on the Database toolbar, click the **Print** button.

(Project 3F–Computer Inventory continues on the next page)

Skill Assessments (continued)

(Project 3F–Computer Inventory continued)

15. If necessary, on the Objects bar, click **Queries**, then double-click **Create query in Design view**.

16. In the **Show Table** dialog box, double-click **Inventory** and then click the **Close** button.

17. In the **Inventory** field list, double-click **Type** and **Cost** to add these fields to the design grid.

18. On the Query Design toolbar, click the **Totals** button. The **Total** row displays in the design grid.

19. In the **Total** row, under **Cost**, click and then click the **arrow** that displays to the right of *Group By*. The list of aggregate functions displays.

20. From the list of functions, click **Sum** and then click the **Run** button to run the query. Access calculates a total cost amount for each type of inventory.

21. In the title bar of the query window, click the **Close** button. Click **Yes** to save changes to the query and in the **Save As** dialog box using your own information, type **Firstname Lastname Sum of Cost** as the query name. Click **OK**. The Database window displays.

22. Be sure your **Sum of Cost** query is selected and on the Database toolbar, click the **Print** button.

23. Close the database. Close Access.

 End You have completed Project 3F

Performance Assessments

Project 3G—Distance Learning

Objectives: *Create a New Select Query; Run, Save, and Close a Query; and Use Wildcards in a Query.*

In the following Performance Assessment, you will create queries to locate information about Distance Learning courses at Lake Michigan City College. Your completed query will look similar to Figure 3.74. You will rename and save your database as *3G_Distance_Learning_Firstname Lastname*.

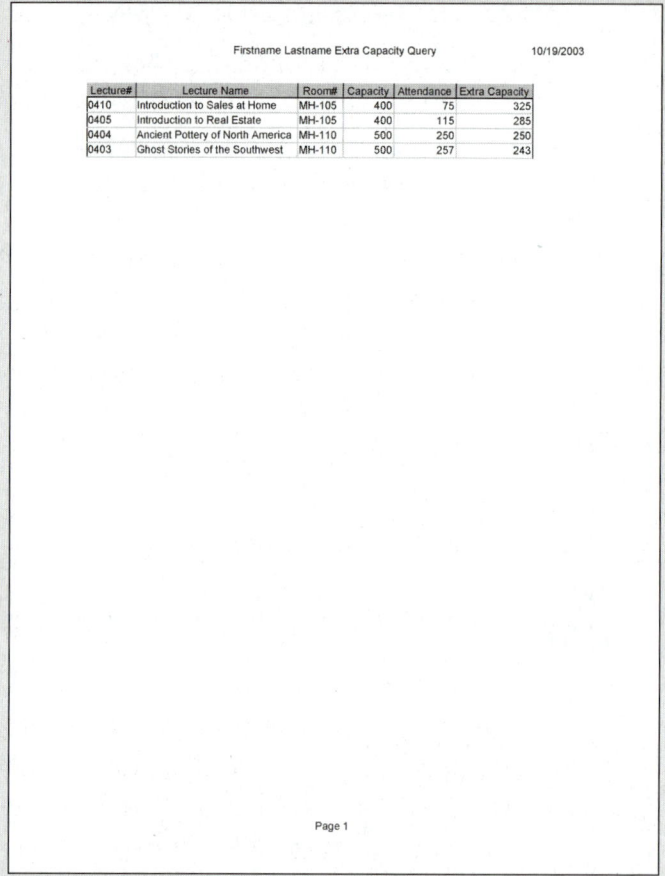

Figure 3.74

1. From the student files that accompany this textbook copy the file **a03G_Distance_Learning** and then paste the file to the folder where you are storing your projects for this chapter. Remove the Read-only attribute and using your own information, rename this file as **3G_Distance_Learning_Firstname_Lastname**

2. Start Access and then open your **3G_Distance_Learning** database.

3. On the Objects bar, click **Queries**, then double-click **Create query in Design view**.

(**Project 3G**–Distance Learning continues on the next page)

954   **Access** | Chapter 3: Queries

Access
chapter three
Performance Assessments (continued)

(Project 3G–Distance Learning continued)

4. In the **Show Table** dialog box, double-click **Distance Learning Courses** and then click the **Close** button.

5. In the **Distance Learning Courses** field list, double-click the following fields to add them to the design grid: **Course Number**, **Course Name**, and **Credit Hours**.

6. Enter the criteria to search for the records whose Course Name contains either Access or Excel by performing the following: In the **Criteria** row, under the **Course Name** field, type *Access and in the **or** row, under the **Course Name** field, type *Excel and then click the **Run** button.

7. In the title bar of the query window, click the **Close** button. Click **Yes** to save the changes to the query and in the **Save As** dialog box using your own information, type **Firstname Lastname Access Excel Query** as the query name. Click **OK**.

8. Print your Access Excel query.

9. Close the database and then close Access.

 You have completed Project 3G

Project 3H—Lecture Series

Objectives: *Open and Edit an Existing Query, Specify Numeric Criteria in a Query, Sort Data in a Query, and Use Calculated Fields in a Query.*

In the following Performance Assessment, you will create a query to locate information about the lectures in the college's new Lecture Series. Your completed query will look similar to Figure 3.75. You will rename and save your database as *3H_Lecture_Series_Firstname_Lastname*.

1. From the student files that accompany this textbook copy the file **a03H_Lecture_Series** and then paste the file to the folder where you are storing your projects for this chapter. Remove the Read-only attribute and using your own information, rename this file as **3H_Lecture_Series_Firstname_Lastname**

2. Start Access and then open your **3H_Lecture_Series** database.

3. Open the **Extra Capacity Query** in Design view.

4. Create a calculated field, called *Extra Capacity*, that will subtract the figures in the **Attendance** field from the figures in the **Capacity** field. (Hint: Capacity—Attendance.) Run the query.

5. Switch to the **Design view**. Add criteria to the query that will limit the query results to those records that have an Extra Capacity that is greater than 200. Sort the records by the **Extra Capacity** field in **Descending** order. Run the query.

(Project 3H–Lecture Series continues on the next page)

Project 3H: Lecture Series | **Access** 955

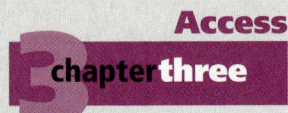

Performance Assessments (continued)

(Project 3H–Lecture Series continued)

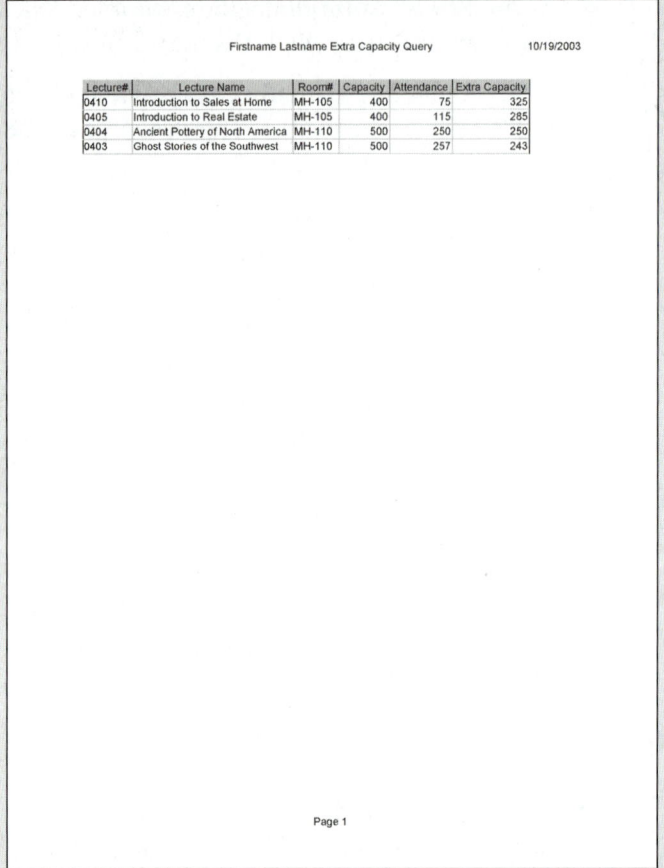

Figure 3.75

6. Using **File**, **Save As**, save the query as **Firstname Lastname Extra Capacity Query**

7. Print your Extra Capacity Query query. Close the database and then close Access.

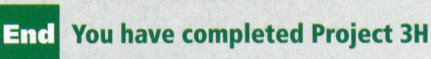

Project 3I—Lecture Hall

Objectives: *Create a New Select Query; Run, Save, and Close a Query; and Group Data and Calculate Statistics in a Query.*

In the following Performance Assessment, you will create a query to locate information about the lectures in LMCC's new Lecture Series. Your completed query will look similar to Figure 3.76. You will rename and save your database as *3I_Lecture_Hall_Firstname_Lastname.*

(Project 3I–Lecture Hall continues on the next page)

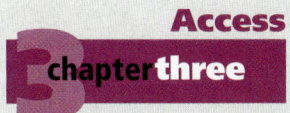

Performance Assessments (continued)

(Project 3I–Lecture Hall continued)

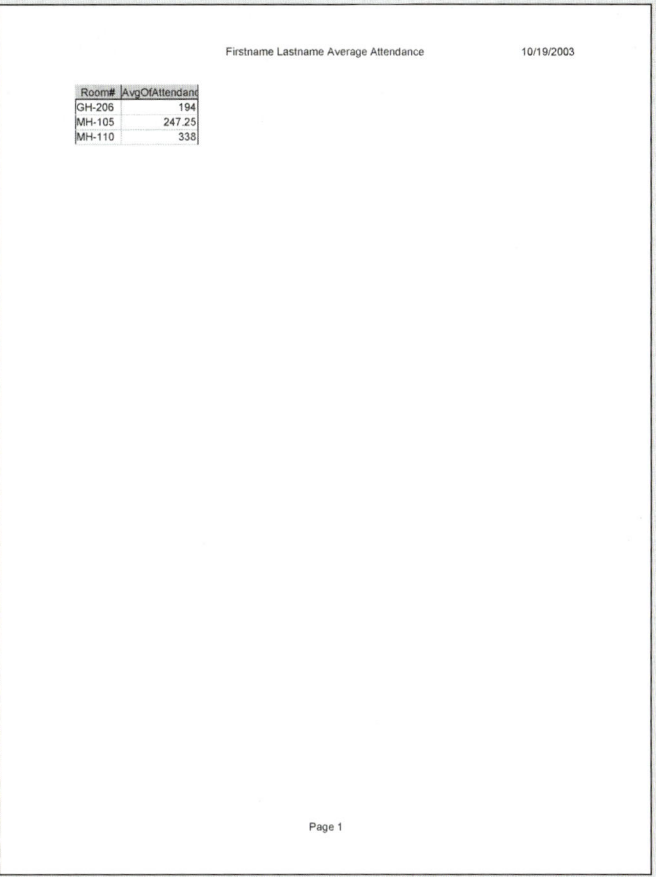

Figure 3.76

1. From the student files that accompany this textbook copy the file **a03I_Lecture_Hall** and then paste the file to the folder where you are storing your projects for this chapter. Remove the Read-only attribute and using your own information, rename this file as **3I_Lecture_Hall_Firstname_Lastname**

2. Start Access and then open your **3I Lecture_Hall** database.

3. Open the **Average Attendance** query in Design view. Click the **Totals** button to display the **Total** row. In the **Total** row, under **Attendance**, click the **arrow** that displays and then click **Avg**. Group the query results by Room#.

4. Run the query. Using **File**, **Save As**, save the query using your own information, as **Firstname Lastname Average Attendance**

5. Print the query you created. Close the database and then close Access.

End You have completed Project 3I

Project 3I: Lecture Hall | **Access** 957

Mastery Assessments

Project 3J—Employees

Objectives: *Create a New Select Query, Run, Save, and Close a Query, Open and Edit an Existing Query, Specify Numeric Criteria in a Query, and Use Calculated Fields in a Query.*

In the following Mastery Assessment, you will create a new query for the Employees database at LMCC. Your completed query will look like Figure 3.77. You will rename and save your database as *3J_Employees_Firstname_Lastname*.

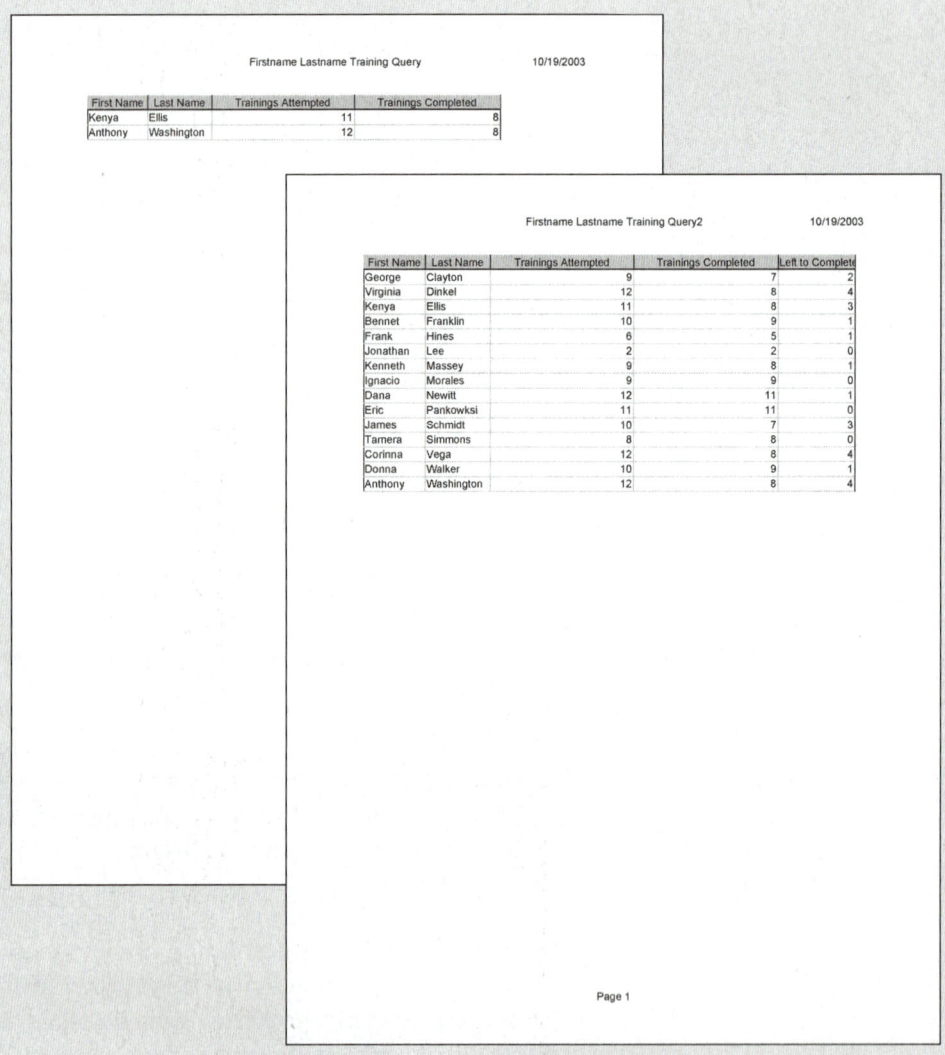

Figure 3.77

1. From the student files that accompany this textbook copy the file **a03J_Employees** and then paste the file to the folder where you are storing your projects for this chapter. Remove the Read-only attribute and using your own information, rename this file as **3J_Employees_Firstname_Lastname** Open your **3J_Employees** database.

(**Project 3J**–Employees continues on the next page)

Mastery Assessments (continued)

(Project 3J–Employees continued)

2. Create a query based on the **Employees** table that will locate the records of the employees in the Finance Department that have completed seven or more trainings. Include the **Trainings Attempted** field in the design grid. (Hint: Trainings Completed is greater than or equal to 7.)

3. Clear the **Show** box for the **Dept** field so it will not display in the query result. Sort the Query alphabetically by the employee's last name. Run the query.

4. Using your own information, save the query as **Firstname Lastname Training Query**

5. Open the **Training** query you just created in Design view. Delete the existing criteria and then remove the **Dept** field from the design grid. Using **File**, **Save As**, save the query with the name **Firstname Lastname Training Query2**

6. Create a calculated field, called *Left to Complete*, which will subtract the figures in the **Trainings Completed** field from the figures in the **Trainings Attempted** field. Run the query. Close the query and save changes.

7. Print both queries. Close the database and then close Access.

End You have completed Project 3J

Project 3K — Employee Training

Objectives: *Open and Edit an Existing Query; Group Data and Calculate Statistics in a Query.*

In the following Mastery Assessment, you will modify an existing query for the Employee Training database at LMCC. Your completed query will look similar to Figure 3.78. You will rename and save your database as *3K_Employee_Training_Firstname_Lastname*.

1. From the student files that accompany this textbook copy the file **a03K_Employee_Training** and then paste the file to the folder where you are storing your projects for this chapter. Remove the Read-only attribute and using your own information, rename this file as **3K_Employee_Training_Firstname_Lastname** Open your **3K Employee Training** database.

2. Open the **Average Trainings** query in Design view. Add a Totals row and calculate an average number of **Trainings Completed** and group them by **Dept**. (Hint: Delete all the fields except Dept and Trainings Completed.)

3. Run the query. Use **File**, **Save As** to save the query with the name (using your own information) **Firstname Lastname Average Trainings** and then close the query.

(**Project 3K**–Employee Training continues on the next page)

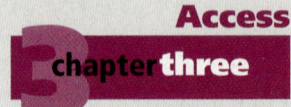

Mastery Assessments (continued)

(Project 3K–Employee Training continued)

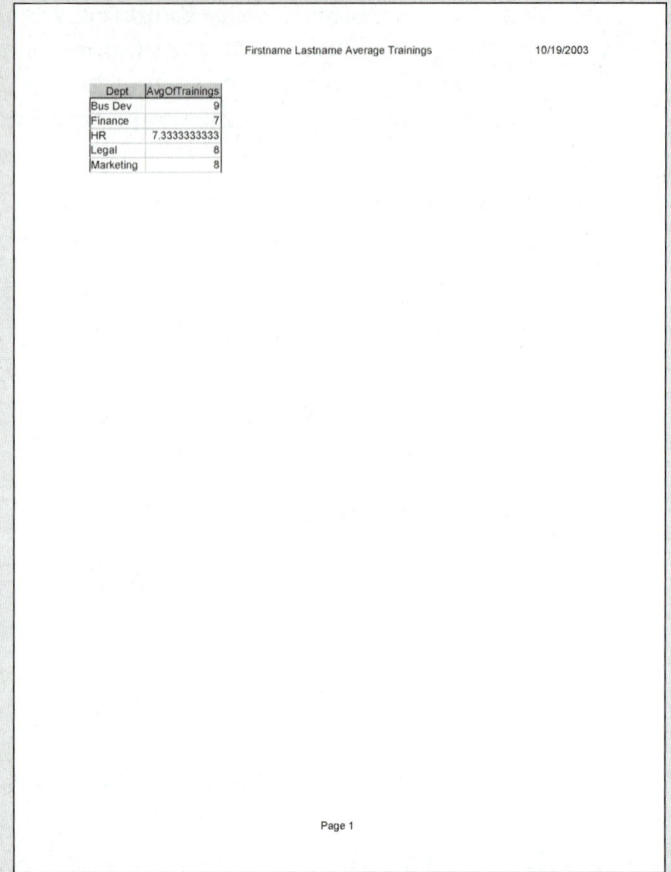

Figure 3.78

4. Print your **Average Trainings** query. Close the database and then close Access.

End You have completed Project 3K

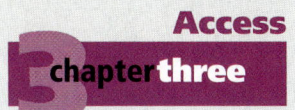

Problem Solving

Project 3L — Bookstore

Objectives: *Open and Edit an Existing Query, Use Calculated Fields in a Query, and Group Data and Calculate Statistics in a Query.*

In the following Problem Solving exercise, you will modify an existing query for the Bookstore database at LMCC.

1. From the student files that accompany this textbook copy the file **a03L_Bookstore** and then paste the file to the folder where you are storing your projects for this chapter. Remove the Read-only attribute and using your own information, rename this file as **3L_Bookstore_FirstName_LastName** Open your **3L Bookstore** database.

2. Modify the **Bookstore Balance** query so that a total sum of all student balances displays in the query result. Run and then save your query as **Firstname Lastname Bookstore Balance** Print the query.

3. Modify the **New Balance Query** using the following information: The manager of the bookstore has decided to give all students a 15% reduction in their bookstore balances. Create the calculated fields in the manner you choose to determine, first, the 15% discount and then to calculate what the students' new balances will be. Run and then save your query as **Firstname Lastname New Balance Query** Print the query.

 You have completed Project 3L

Project 3M — LMCC

Objectives: *Create a New Select Query; Run, Save, and Close a Query; and Specify Text Criteria in a Query.*

In the following Problem Solving exercise, you will modify an existing query for the Bookstore database at LMCC.

1. From the student files that accompany this textbook copy the file **a03M_LMCC** and then paste the file to the folder where you are storing your projects for this chapter. Remove the Read-only attribute and using your own information, rename this file as **3M_LMCC_Firstname_Lastname** Open your **3M_LMCC** database.

2. Create a query that will locate those students who began attending Lake Michigan City College in the FA02 term. Save your query as **Firstname_Lastname_First Term** Print the query.

 You have completed Project 3M

On the Internet

Microsoft Certification Exam

As you progress with your study of Access, you will learn skills necessary to complete the Microsoft certification test for Access 2003. Go to the Microsoft Web site at **www.microsoft.com** and then search the site to locate information regarding the certification exam. Print the core objectives for the Microsoft Access user certification and any additional information about taking the test.

GO! with Help

Getting Help Using Wildcards

There are many types of wildcards that you can use in your queries. Use the Access Help system to find out more about wildcards in Access.

1. Start Access. If necessary, from the **View** menu, click **Task Pane** to display the **Getting Started** task pane. On the task pane, to the right of *Getting Started*, click the **downward-pointing arrow**. From the displayed list of available task panes, click **Help**.

2. Click in the **Search For** box, then type **wildcards**

3. Press [Enter], scroll the displayed list as necessary, and then click **About using wildcard characters**.

4. If you would like to keep a copy of this information, click the **Print** button.

5. Click the **Close** button in the top right corner of the Help window to close the Help window and then close Access.

PowerPoint 2003

chapter one

Getting Started with PowerPoint 2003

In this chapter, you will: complete this project and practice these skills.

Project 1A
Editing and Viewing a Presentation

Objectives
- Start and Exit PowerPoint
- Edit a Presentation Using the Outline/Slides Pane
- Format and Edit a Presentation Using the Slide Pane
- View and Edit a Presentation in Slide Sorter View
- View a Slide Show
- Create Headers and Footers
- Print a Presentation
- Use PowerPoint Help

The City of Desert Park

Desert Park, Arizona, is a thriving city with a population of just under 1 million in an ideal location serving major markets in the western United States and Mexico. Desert Park's temperate year-round climate attracts both visitors and businesses, and it is one of the most popular vacation destinations in the world. The city expects and has plenty of space for long-term growth, and most of the undeveloped land already has a modern infrastructure and assured water supply in place.

© Getty Images, Inc.

Getting Started With PowerPoint 2003

Presentation skills are among the most important skills you will ever learn. Good presentation skills enhance all your communications—written, electronic, and interpersonal. In our fast-paced world of e-mail, pagers, and wireless phones, communicating ideas clearly and concisely is a critical personal skill. Microsoft Office PowerPoint 2003 is a *presentation graphics software* program that you can use to effectively present information to your audience. PowerPoint is used to create electronic slide presentations, black and white or color overhead transparencies, and 35mm slides.

In this chapter, you will edit a presentation and become familiar with the parts of the PowerPoint window. You will also practice using the various views available in PowerPoint.

Project 1A Expansion

The purpose of any presentation is to influence your audience. Whether you are presenting a new product to coworkers, making a speech at a conference, or expressing your opinion to your city council, you want to make a good impression and give your audience a reason to agree with your point of view. How your audience reacts to your message depends on the information you present and how you present yourself.

In Activities 1.1 through 1.24, you will start Microsoft Office PowerPoint 2003 and open a presentation. You will examine the parts of the PowerPoint window, and then edit, print, and view the presentation as a slide show. The six slides of your completed project will look like Figure 1.1. You will save your presentation as 1A_Expansion_Firstname_Lastname.

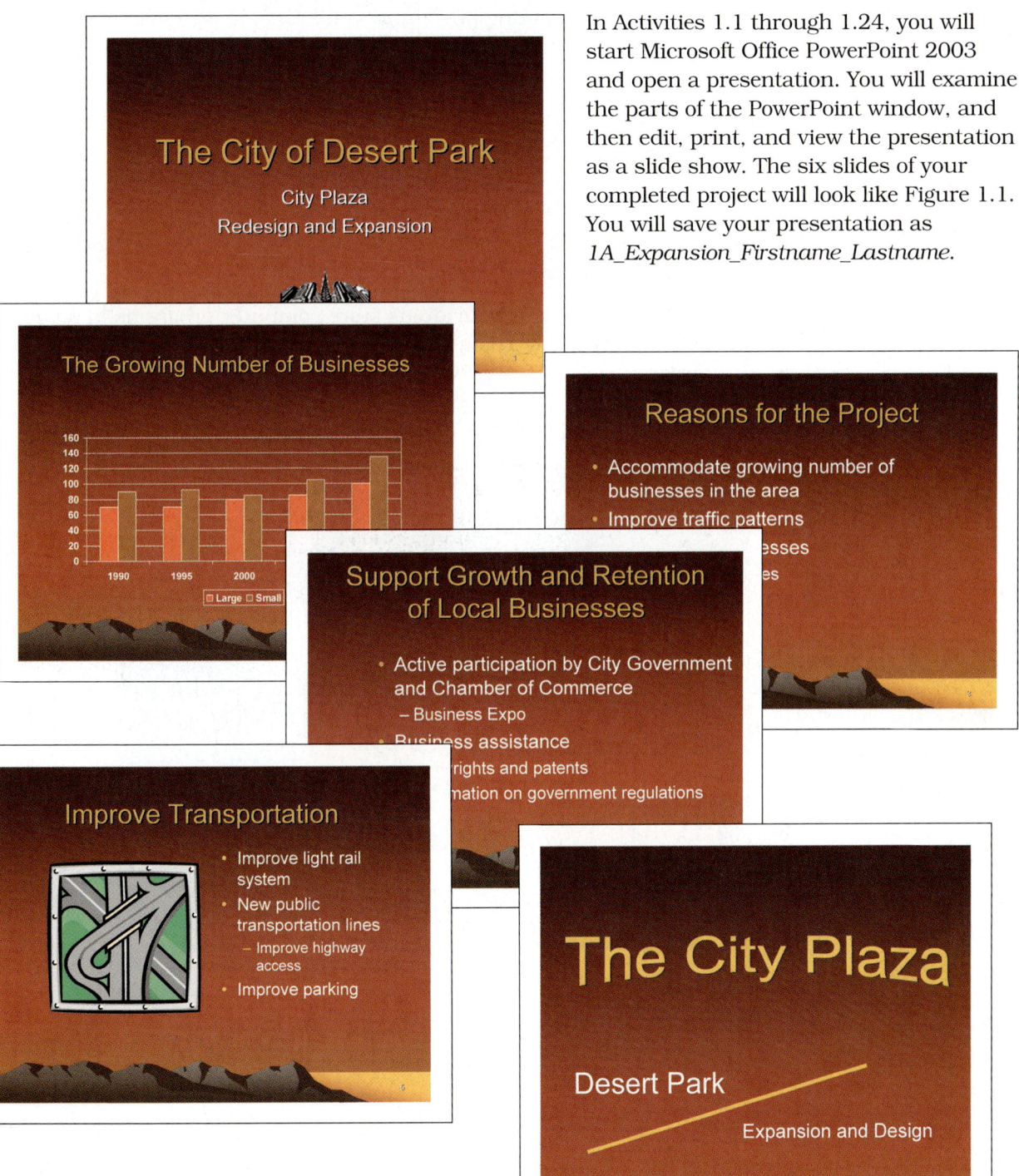

Figure 1.1
Project 1A—Expansion

Project 1A: Expansion | **PowerPoint** 965

Objective 1
Start and Exit PowerPoint

In the following activities, you will start PowerPoint, become familiar with the PowerPoint window, open an existing PowerPoint presentation, close a file, and exit PowerPoint.

Activity 1.1 Starting PowerPoint and Opening a Presentation

You can open an existing presentation file by clicking Open from the File menu, by clicking the Open button on the Standard toolbar, or by Clicking Open or More on the Getting Started task pane.

1 On the left side of the Windows taskbar, point to and then click the **Start** button .

The Start menu displays.

2 On the computer you are using, locate the PowerPoint program and then click **Microsoft Office PowerPoint 2003**.

Organizations and individuals store computer programs in a variety of ways. The PowerPoint program might be located under All Programs, or Microsoft Office, or some other arrangement. See Figure 1.2 for an example.

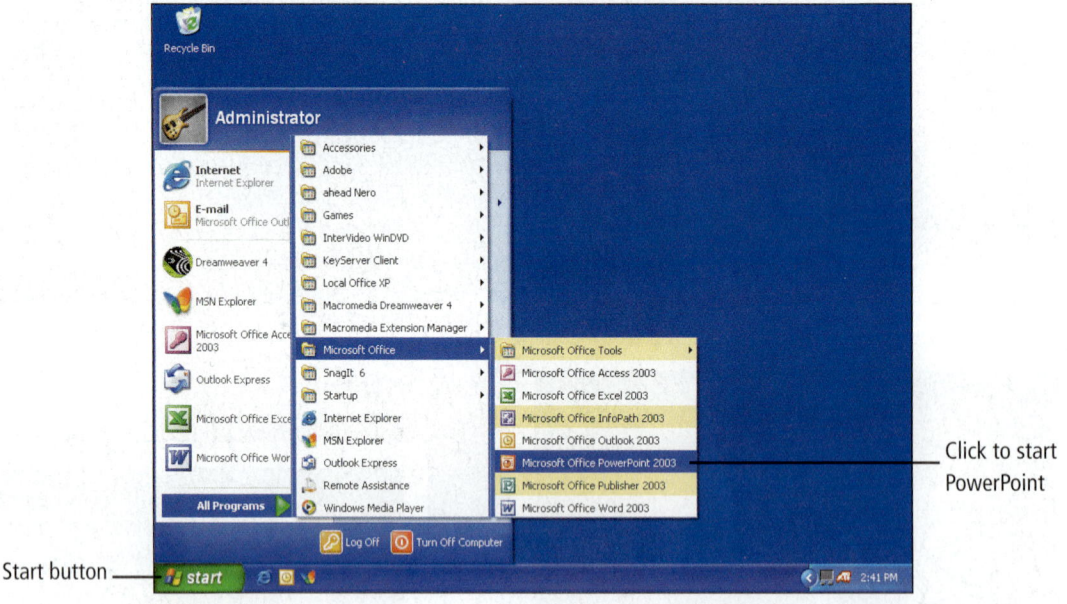

Figure 1.2

966   **PowerPoint** | Chapter 1: Getting Started with PowerPoint 2003

3 Look at the opening PowerPoint screen, and then take a moment to study the main parts of the screen shown in Figure 1.3 and described in the table in Figure 1.4.

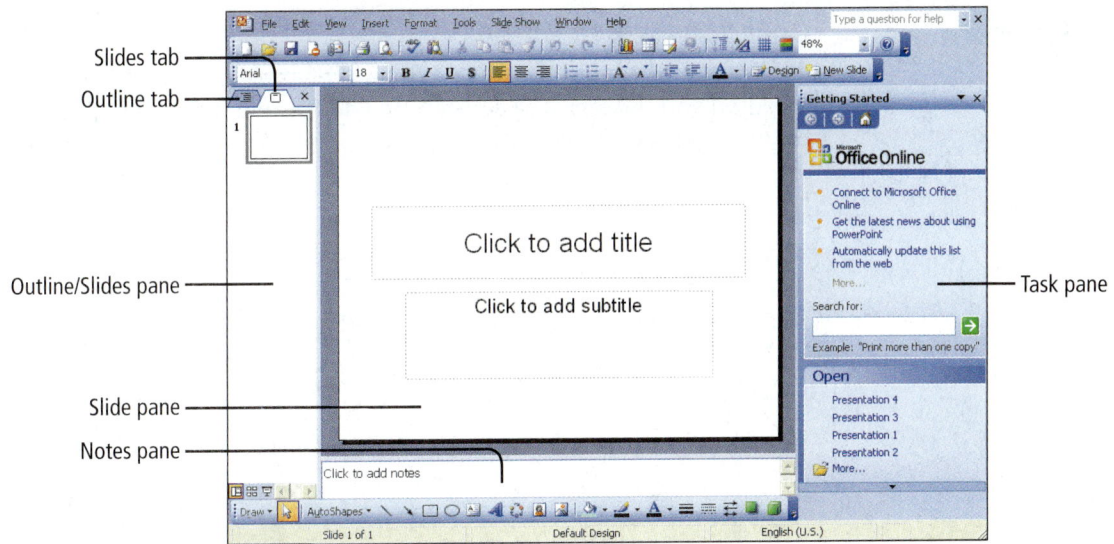

Figure 1.3

Main Parts of the PowerPoint Screen

Screen Element	Description
Outline/Slides pane	Displays either the presentation outline (Outline tab) or all of the slides in the presentation in the form of miniature images called *thumbnails* (Slides tab).
Slide pane	Displays a large image of the active slide.
Notes pane	Displays below the Slide pane and allows you to type notes regarding the active slide.
Task pane	Displays commonly used commands related to the active slide. Its location and small size allow you to use these commands while still working on your presentation.

Figure 1.4

Project 1A: Expansion | **PowerPoint** 967

4 In the lower portion of the **Getting Started** task pane, under **Open**, point to **More...** and notice that your pointer displays as a pointing hand. See Figure 1.5.

Alert! — Does Your Screen Differ?

In most instances, the task pane displays the previous four presentations saved on your system. The settings on *your* system may differ, and instead of these presentations, you may see Open, instead of More. Click Open.

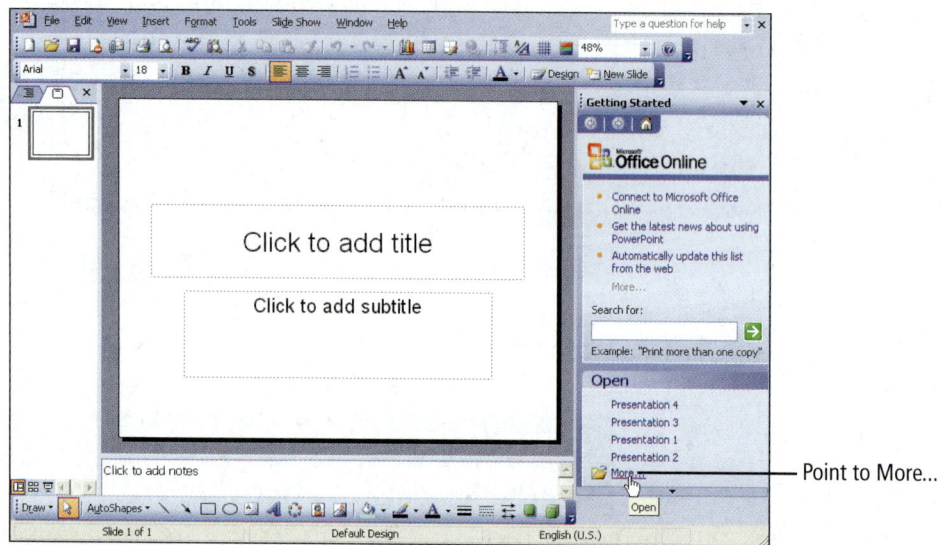

Figure 1.5

5 Click **More...**

The Open dialog box displays.

6 In the **Open** dialog box, at the right edge of the **Look in** box, click the **Look in arrow**, to view a list of the drives available on your system. See Figure 1.6.

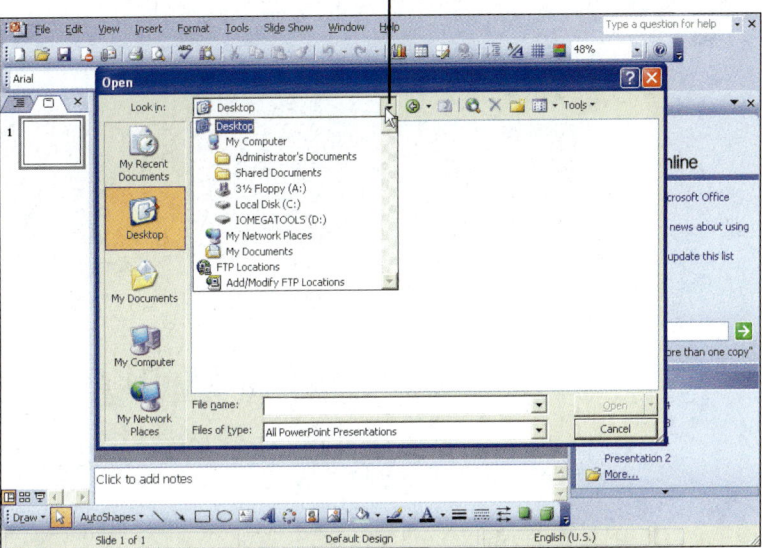

Figure 1.6

7 Navigate to the location where the student files for this textbook are stored.

8 Click **p01A_Expansion** and then click the **Open** button.

Slide 1 of the presentation displays in the PowerPoint window, and the task pane on the right is closed.

Activity 1.2 Identifying Parts of the PowerPoint Window

1 Figures 1.7a and 1.7b identify the parts of the PowerPoint window. Take a moment to familiarize yourself with the parts of the window shown, and notice that the ***status bar*** displays near the bottom of the PowerPoint window.

The status bar indicates that in this presentation, Slide 1 is the active slide and that there are a total of seven slides in the presentation. The first slide of a presentation is the ***title slide***. The title slide frequently contains special formatting that is different from the other slides in the presentation so that it is easily distinguishable as the title slide.

Project 1A: Expansion | **PowerPoint** 969

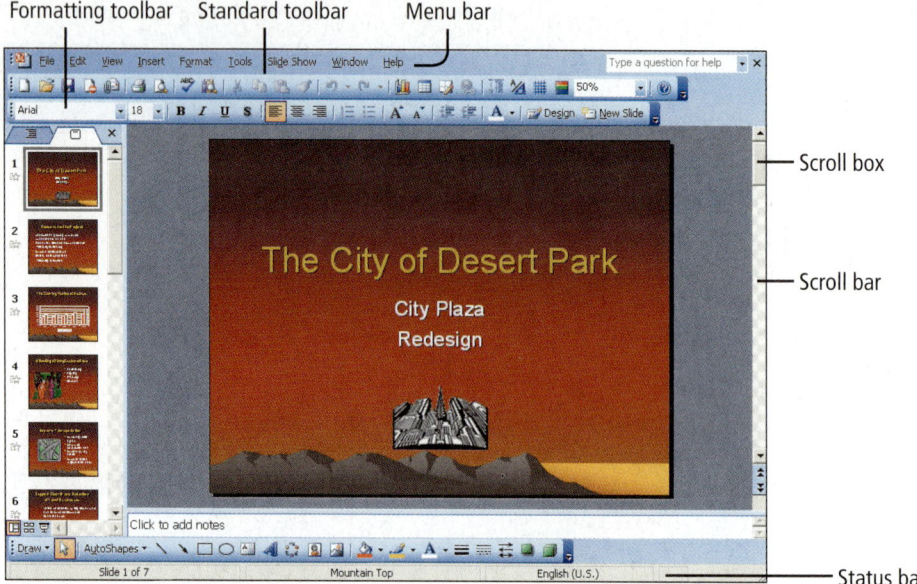

Figure 1.7a

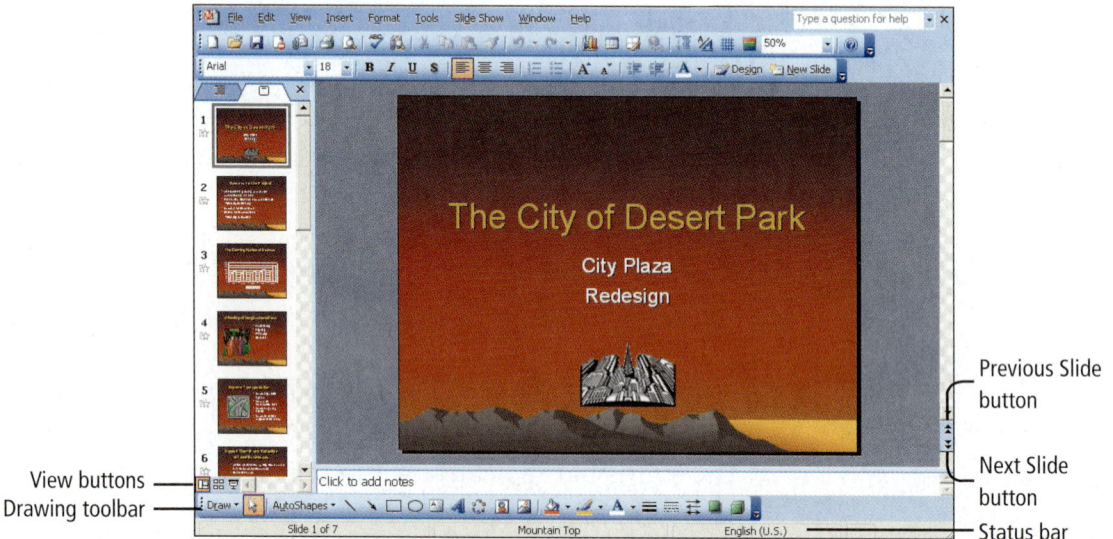

Figure 1.7b

970   PowerPoint | Chapter 1: Getting Started with PowerPoint 2003

Alert!

Does Your Screen Differ?
At the left side of your window in the Outline/Slides pane, your window may display the slide miniatures shown in Figure 1.7, or if the Outline tab is selected, it will display the presentation outline.

2. On the right edge of your screen, at the top of the vertical scroll bar, point to the **scroll** box, and then press and hold down the left mouse button.

   A ***ScreenTip*** is a small box that displays the name of a screen element or, in this instance, the current slide number and the title. The ScreenTip indicates *Slide: 1 of 7 The City of Desert Park*.

3. Drag the **scroll** box down slightly until the ScreenTip *Slide: 2 of 7 Reasons for the Project* displays, and then release the left mouse button.

   In the Slide pane, Slide 2 displays and becomes the active slide. One word on the slide is underlined with a wavy red line, indicating a misspelling. Later in this chapter, you will use PowerPoint's spelling checker tool to correct spelling errors in the presentation.

4. At the bottom of the vertical scroll bar, locate the double, upward-pointing and downward-pointing arrows. Refer to Figure 1.7b, and then without clicking, point to them to display their ScreenTips—*Previous Slide* and *Next Slide*.

5. Click the **Next Slide** button to display **Slide 3** of the presentation, and then click the **Previous Slide** button two times to return to **Slide 1**. At the lower left portion of your screen, check to be sure that *Slide 1 of 7* displays in the status bar.

Project 1A: Expansion | **PowerPoint** 971

6 Near the lower left corner of the window, locate the **View** buttons, as shown in Figure 1.7b. With your mouse, point to each of the three **View** buttons to display their ScreenTips—*Normal View*, *Slide Sorter View*, and *Slide Show from current slide (Shift+F5)*.

These buttons provide three different ways to view your presentation, and you will practice each of these views in this chapter.

Activity 1.3 Accessing the Menu Commands

1 On the menu bar, click **File**.

The File menu displays in either the short format shown in Figure 1.8 or the full format shown in Figure 1.9. PowerPoint's commands are organized in *menus*—lists of commands within a category. A short menu will display fully after a few seconds. Alternatively, you can click the small double arrows at the bottom to display the full menu. The File menu lists the last four to nine presentations used on your computer.

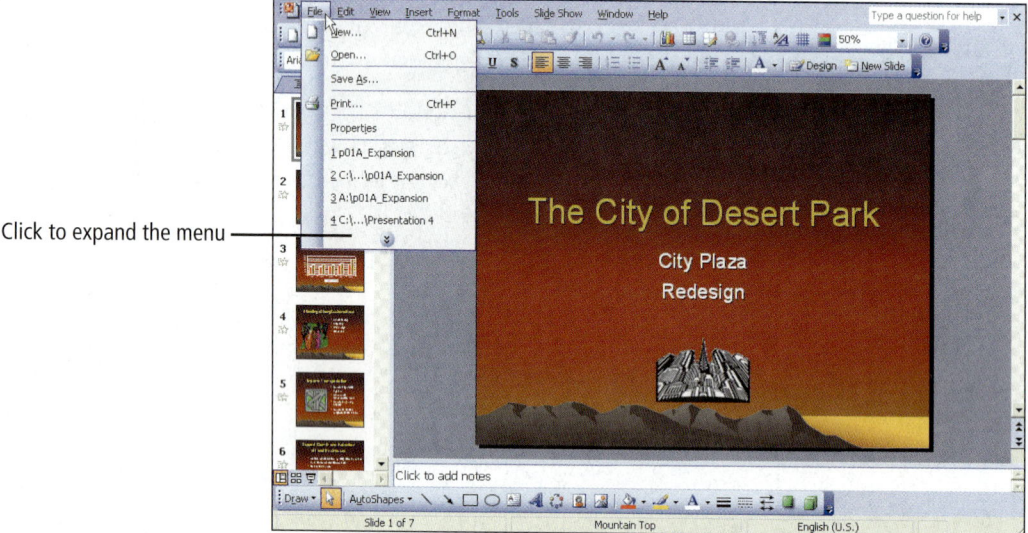

Click to expand the menu

Figure 1.8

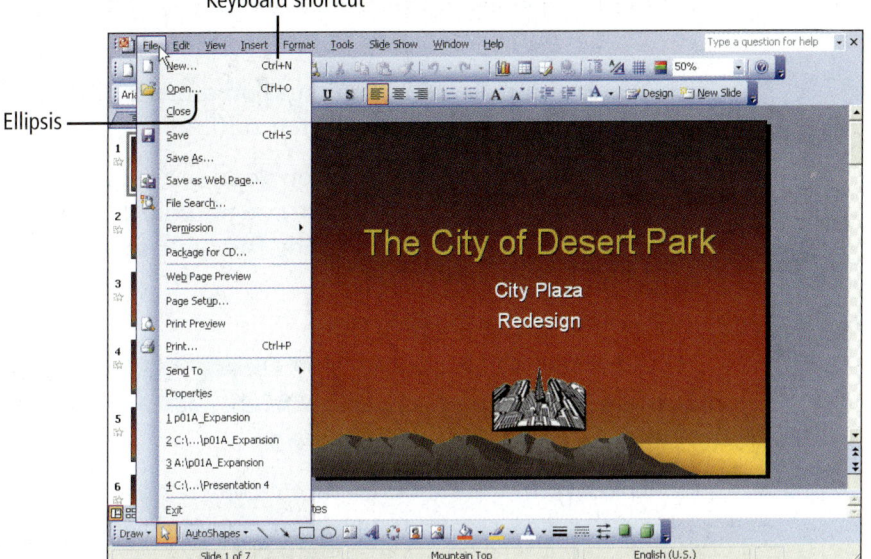

Figure 1.9

> **Note** — **Displaying the Full Menu**
>
> Many individuals prefer the automatic full menu display. To set a system to always display full menus, display the Tools menu, click Customize, and then click the Options tab. Under Personalized Menus and Toolbars, select the Always show full menus check box.

2 Be sure that the full menu is displayed, as shown in Figure 1.9, and notice to the right of some commands there is a keyboard shortcut, for example *Ctrl+N* for the **New** command.

If you press and hold down Ctrl and then press N, the result is the same as clicking File on the menu bar and then clicking New on the File menu. Many commands in PowerPoint can be accomplished in more than one way.

3 On the displayed **File** menu, to the left of some command names, notice that there is an image of the button that represents this command on a toolbar.

This is a reminder that you can initiate the command with one click from a toolbar, rather than from the menu.

Project 1A: Expansion | **PowerPoint** 973

4 On the displayed **File** menu, pause the mouse pointer over **Print**, but do not click.

When you point to a command on a menu, the command is shaded and bordered by a rectangular outline.

5 Look at the full **File** menu on your screen and notice the various symbols and characters that are standard across all Microsoft products. Take a moment to study the table in Figure 1.10 for a description of these elements.

Characteristics of Office Menus

Characteristic	Description	Example
... (ellipsis)	Indicates that either a dialog box requesting more information or a task pane will display.	Print...
▶ (triangle)	Indicates that a submenu—another menu of choices—will display.	Send To ▶
No symbol	Indicates that the command will perform immediately.	Exit
✔ (check mark)	Indicates that a command is turned on or active.	✔ Standard
Gray option name	Indicates that the command is currently unavailable.	Properties

Figure 1.10

6 With the **File** menu still displayed, move your pointer into the menu bar and point to **Insert**.

The Insert menu displays. After a menu from the menu bar is displayed, you can move your pointer over other menu names and they will display without clicking.

7 Move your mouse pointer anywhere into the slide area of your screen, and then click once to close the menu without accessing a command.

Activity 1.4 Identifying and Displaying Toolbars and ScreenTips

Toolbars are the rows of buttons that display below the menu bar. The buttons on the toolbar provide a one-click method to perform commonly used commands and tasks. The three toolbars that you will use most often in PowerPoint are the Standard toolbar, the Formatting toolbar, and the Drawing toolbar.

Depending on how your system is set, you might see the Standard and Formatting toolbars each occupying separate rows as in Figure 1.11. Or, you might see shortened Standard and Formatting toolbars docked side by side below the menu bar. When the Standard and Formatting toolbars share one row, you can click Toolbar Options to view additional buttons. See Figure 1.12. The instruction in this textbook assumes that your toolbars occupy *separate* rows.

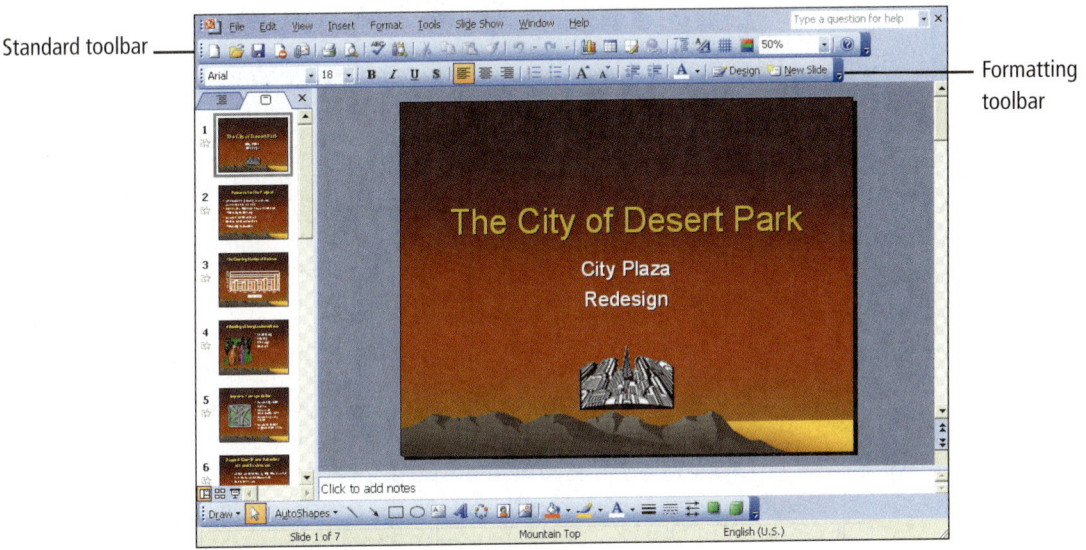

Figure 1.11

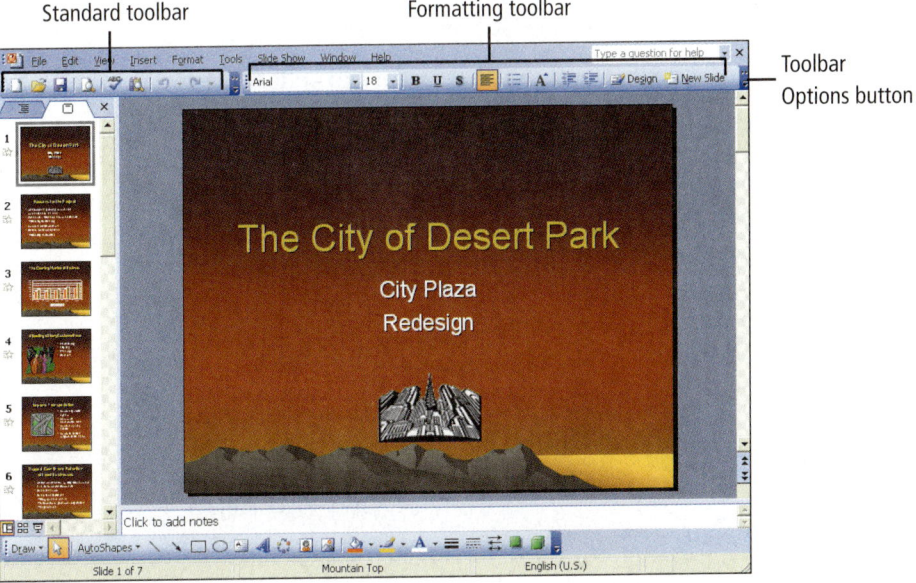

Figure 1.12

1 Look at your screen to determine how toolbars are displayed. On the Standard toolbar, point to, but do not click, any button.

After a few seconds, the ScreenTip for the button displays. Recall that a ScreenTip is a small box that displays the name of a button or part of the PowerPoint window.

2 On the Formatting toolbar, point to, but do not click, any button. The ScreenTip displays.

3 Check your screen to see how your Standard and Formatting toolbars are displayed. If they are *not* displayed on two rows, as shown in Figure 1.11, click the **Toolbar Options** button, as shown in Figure 1.12, and click **Show Buttons on Two Rows**.

> ### More Knowledge — Displaying a Toolbar
> *Right-click any toolbar to select another toolbar.*
> If a toolbar is missing entirely, point to an existing toolbar or to the menu bar and click the right mouse button (also known as *right-clicking*). On the shortcut menu that displays, point to the name of the toolbar you wish to display and click the left mouse button. Alternatively, display the View menu, point to Toolbars, and then click the name of the toolbar you wish to display.

Activity 1.5 Closing and Displaying the Task Pane

Recall that when you opened the PowerPoint program, the **task pane** displayed on the right side of your window. A task pane is a window within a Microsoft Office application that provides commonly used commands. Its location allows you to use these commands while still working on your files. In PowerPoint, the task pane allows you to complete many tasks, including opening and creating files, adding graphic images, and changing the design of your slides. When you opened your presentation, the task pane closed. In this activity, you will redisplay and then close the task pane.

1 On the menu bar, click **View**, and then click **Task Pane**.

The task pane displays at the right side of the window. At the top of the task pane, two buttons display. The Other Task Panes button displays a menu of 16 task panes in PowerPoint. The Close button closes the task pane. See Figure 1.13.

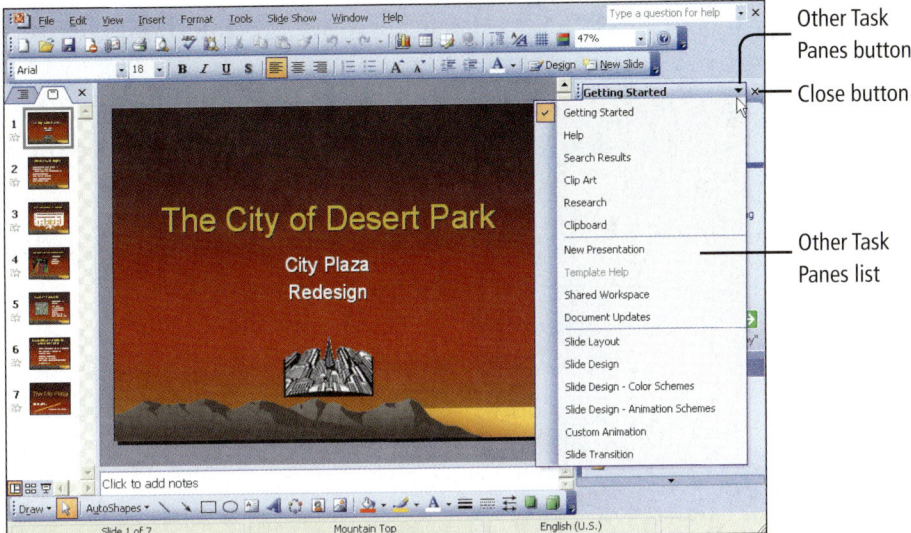

Figure 1.13

[icon] Click **Other Task Panes** [icon] to view the list.

[icon] At the top of the task pane, click **Close** [icon].

Activity 1.6 Creating a New Folder and Saving a File

In the same way that you use file folders to organize your paper documents, Windows uses a hierarchy of electronic folders to keep your electronic files organized. Using Windows' hierarchy of folders, you can group your files in a logical manner. Check with your instructor or lab coordinator to see where you will be storing your presentations (for example, on your own disk or on a network drive) and whether there is any suggested file folder arrangement.

Throughout this textbook, you will be instructed to save your files using the file name followed by your first and last name. Currently, the file p01A_Expansion is displayed in your PowerPoint window. To change the name of the file or its directory or drive location, or to create a new folder in which to store your files, you will use the Save As command on the File menu.

[icon] On the menu bar, click **File**, and then click **Save As**.

The Save As dialog box displays.

[icon] In the **Save As** dialog box, at the right edge of the **Save in** box, click the **Save in arrow** to view a list of the drives available to you.

Project 1A: Expansion | **PowerPoint**   977

3 Navigate to the drive on which you will be storing your folders and presentations—for example, 3½ Floppy (A:), or the drive designated by your instructor or lab coordinator.

4 To the right of the **Save in** box, notice the row of buttons. Click the **Create New Folder** button .

The New Folder dialog box displays, as shown in Figure 1.14.

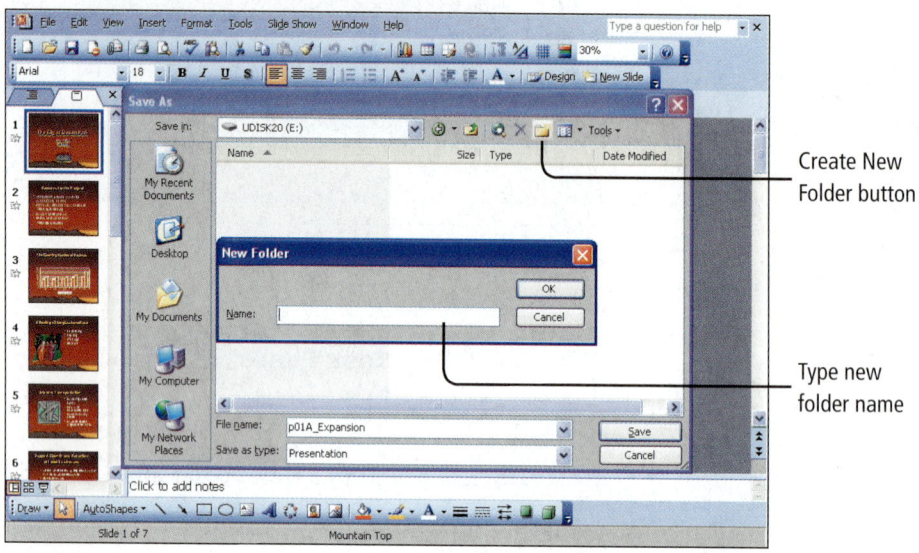

Figure 1.14

5 In the **Name** box, type **Chapter 1** to create a new folder on your disk, and then click **OK**.

6 In the lower portion of the **Save As** dialog box, locate the **File name** box.

The file name *p01A_Expansion* may be highlighted if you selected the default location in the Save in box. If you selected a different location in the Save in box, *p01A_Expansion* may not be highlighted.

7 Click to position your insertion point in the **File name** box and type as necessary to save the file with the name **1A_Expansion_Firstname_Lastname** See Figure 1.15.

978 PowerPoint | Chapter 1: Getting Started with PowerPoint 2003

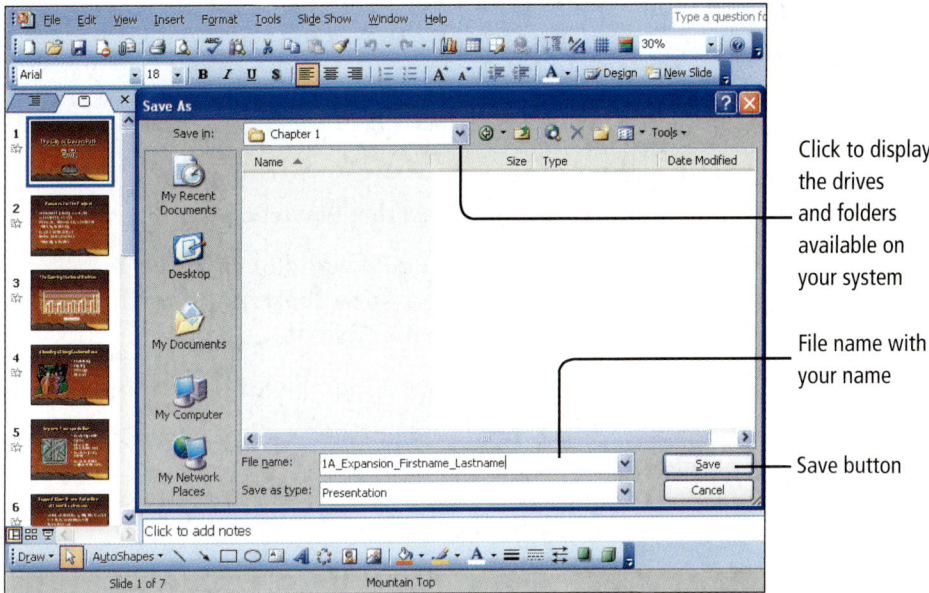

Figure 1.15

8 In the lower right corner, click the **Save** button or press Enter. The new file name displays in the title bar.

> **Note** — Using File Names with Spaces
>
> The Microsoft Windows operating system recognizes file names with spaces. However, some Internet file transfer programs do not. To facilitate sending your files over the Internet using a course management system, in this textbook you will be instructed to save files using an underscore rather than a space.

Activity 1.7 Closing a File

When you are finished working on a presentation, you should save and close it. Closing a file means that you are removing it from your system's random access memory (RAM). You should save a file before closing it, but if you forget to save, PowerPoint will remind you.

1 With your file **1A_Expansion_Firstname_Lastname** still displayed, move your pointer to the menu bar and click **File**.

2 From the **File** menu, click **Close**.

Project 1A: Expansion | **PowerPoint** 979

> **Another Way**
>
> **Using a Button to Close a File**
>
> You can also close a file by clicking the Close Window button.

Activity 1.8 Exiting PowerPoint

You can exit the PowerPoint program by clicking Exit from the File menu or by closing all open presentations and then clicking the Close button at the extreme right edge of the title bar.

1 On the menu bar, click **File**.

2 From the displayed menu, click **Exit** to close PowerPoint.

Objective 2
Edit a Presentation Using the Outline/Slides Pane

In Normal View, the PowerPoint window is divided into three areas—the Slide pane, the Outline/Slides pane, and the Notes pane. When you make changes to the presentation in the Outline/Slides pane, the changes are reflected immediately in the Slide pane. Likewise, when you make changes in the Slide pane, the changes are reflected in the Outline/Slides pane.

Activity 1.9 Editing a Presentation Using the Outline

Editing is the process of adding, deleting, or changing the contents of a slide. In this activity, you will change and delete text in the Outline tab.

1 **Start** PowerPoint. On the Standard toolbar, click the **Open** button.

The Open dialog box displays.

2 In the **Open** dialog box, click the **Look in arrow**, and then navigate to the location where you are storing your files. Click to select your file **1A_Expansion_Firstname_Lastname**. Be sure that you click the file that contains your name.

3 In the lower right corner of the **Open** dialog box, click the **Open** button. Alternatively, you can double-click the name of the file to open it.

4 At the lower left corner of the window, locate the **View** buttons, and check to be sure that your presentation is displayed in **Normal View**.

If necessary, click the **Normal View** button.

In Normal View, the left side of your window displays the Outline/Slides pane. When the Outline tab is active, you can enter and edit text in your presentation. When the Slides tab is active, thumbnails of your presentation display and you can copy, move, and delete entire slides.

5 In the **Outline/Slides** pane, click the **Slides tab** so that the thumbnail image of each slide is displayed.

Alert! Does Your Screen Differ?

When you open a file, the presentation displays in the view in which it was last saved.

6 Click the **Outline tab** to display the text of the presentation in outline format.

The slide numbers in the outline are followed by a small picture called the ***slide icon***. See Figure 1.16. The slide number and slide icon indicate the start of a new slide in your presentation. Notice also that the text displays with indents and bullets similar to an outline that you would type in a word processor. PowerPoint uses these indents to determine the outline level in a slide. Misspelled words are flagged with a wavy red line.

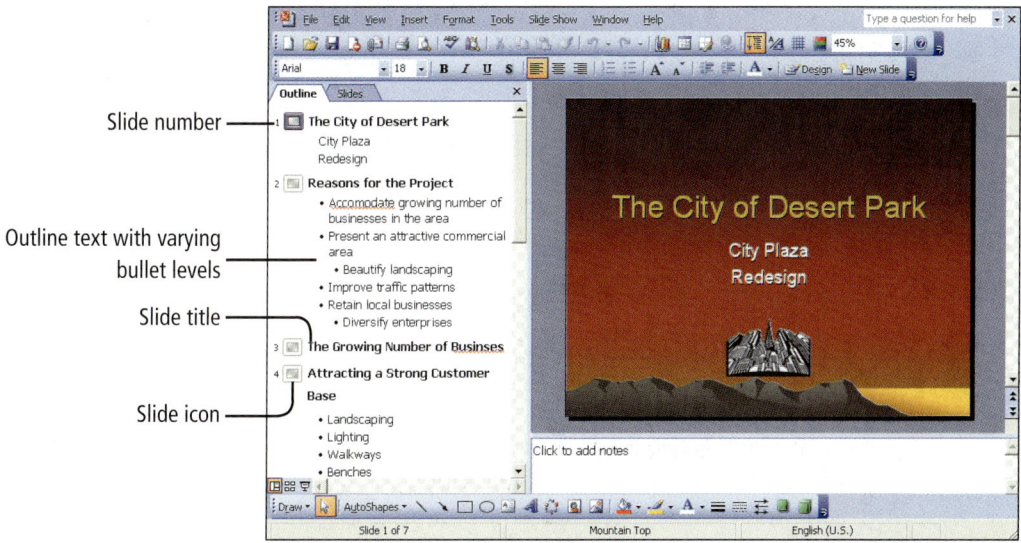

Figure 1.16

7 Move your mouse pointer into the text in the **Outline tab** and notice that your pointer displays as an *I-beam pointer* ⌶.

The I-beam pointer indicates that you are pointing to a text area in the Outline/Slides pane or in the Slide pane.

8 In the **Outline tab**, position your **I-beam** pointer in the first slide after the word *Redesign* and then click the left mouse button to position the *insertion point*—the blinking vertical bar that indicates where text will be inserted when you type—at this location. Press Space and then type **and Expansion**

Notice that as you type, the changes are also made in the Slide pane.

9 In the **Outline tab**, locate **Slide 2**, and then pause the mouse pointer over the second bullet symbol so that a four-headed arrow displays, as shown in Figure 1.17. Click the left mouse button.

Notice that the bulleted item and the subordinate (lower-level) bullet below this item are both *selected* (highlighted in black). Clicking on a bullet selects the bulleted item and all subordinate text.

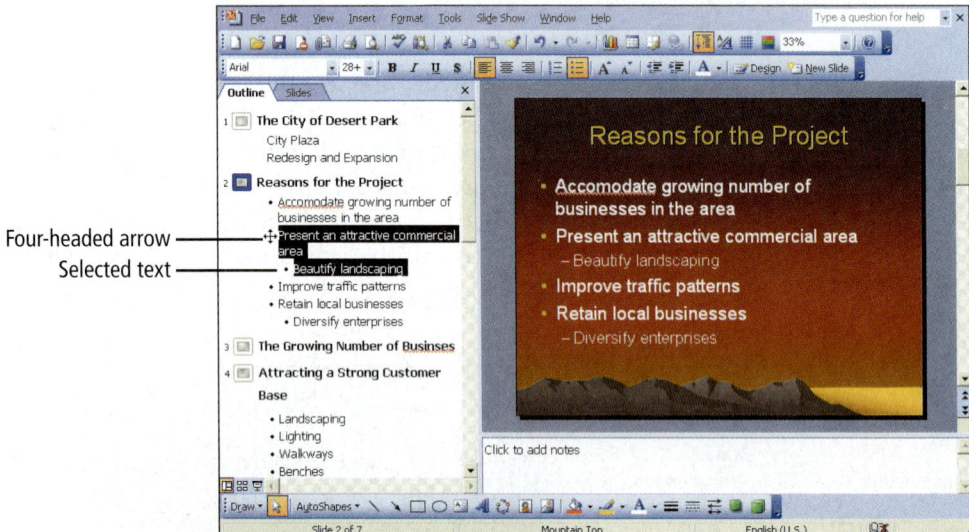

Figure 1.17

10 On your keyboard, press Delete to delete the selected text.

11 On the Standard toolbar, click the **Save** button 🖫.

The changes you have made to your presentation are saved. When you click the Save button, your file is stored to the same drive and folder, with the same file name.

Activity 1.10 Promoting and Demoting Outline Text

Text in a PowerPoint presentation is organized according to outline levels, similar to the outline levels you might make for a book report. The highest level on an individual slide is the title. **Bulleted levels** (outline levels identified by a symbol) are identified in the slides by the indentation and the size of the text. Indented text in a smaller size indicates a lower outline level.

It is easy to change the outline level of text to a higher or lower level. For example, you might create a presentation with four bullets on the same level. Then you might decide that one bulleted item relates to one of the other bullets, rather than to the slide title. In this case, a lower outline level should be applied. You can **demote** text to apply a *lower* outline level, or **promote** text and apply a *higher* outline level. Or, you can begin a new slide by promoting bulleted text to a slide title.

1 On the right side of the **Outline tab**, point to the vertical scroll bar, press and hold down the left mouse button, and then drag down until you can view all of the text in **Slide 6**.

2 In the **Slide 6** text, click to position the insertion point anywhere in the second bulleted line—*Business Expo*. On the Formatting toolbar, click the **Increase Indent** button.

The bulleted item is demoted and displays as a lower outline level under the first bullet. See Figure 1.18.

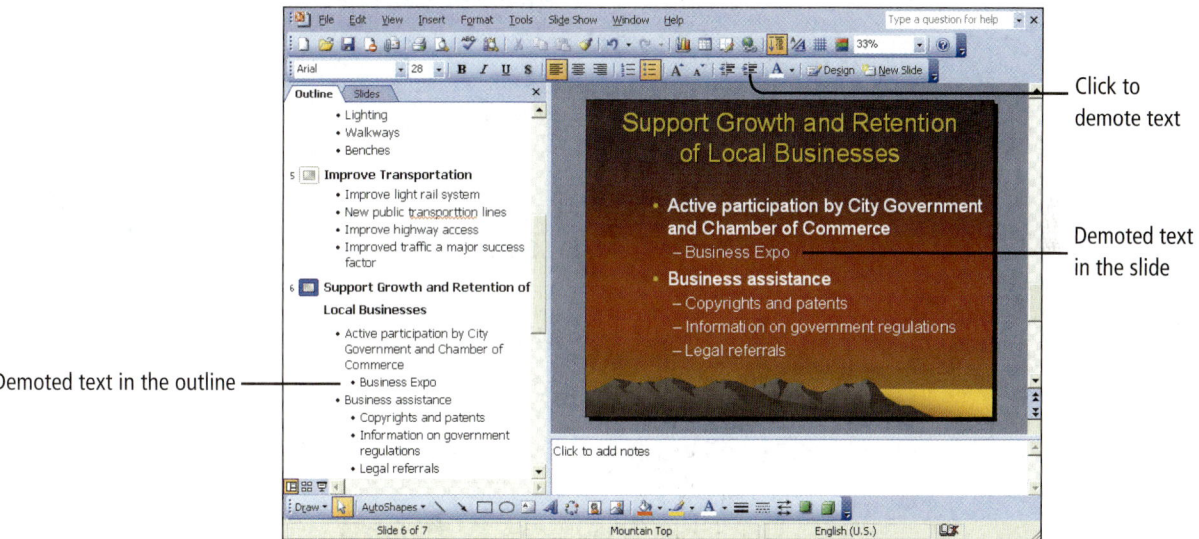

Figure 1.18

3 In the **Outline tab**, locate **Slide 5**, and then click anywhere in the last bulleted item—*Improved traffic a major success factor.*

Slide 5 displays in the Slide pane. Notice that all of the bulleted items are at the highest bullet level, including the last item—*Improved traffic a major success factor.*

4 On the Formatting toolbar, click **Decrease Indent** to promote the item one outline level.

The bulleted item is deleted from the slide, and a new Slide 6 is created with the title *Improved traffic a major success factor.* When a bulleted item at the highest level is promoted, it is promoted to a title slide and a new slide is created. See Figure 1.19.

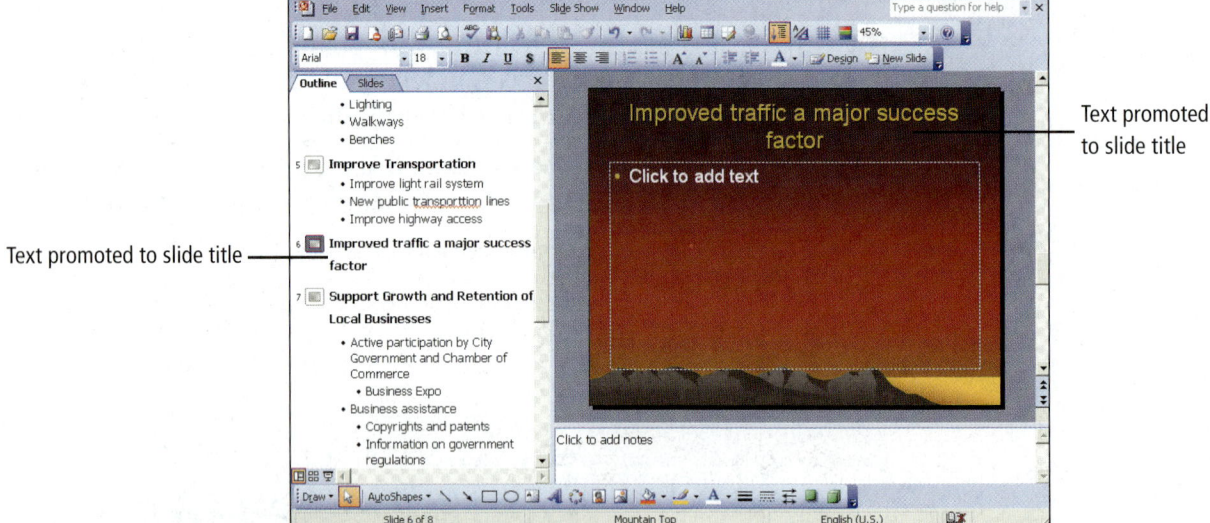

Figure 1.19

5 In the **Outline tab**, on **Slide 7**, click anywhere in the last bulleted line—*Legal referrals.*

Slide 7 displays in the Slide pane.

6 On the Formatting toolbar, click **Decrease Indent** to apply a higher outline level. Click **Decrease Indent** again to create a new **Slide 8** with the title *Legal referrals*.

The newly created Slide 8 displays in the Slide pane.

7 On the Standard toolbar, click the **Save** button to save the changes you have made to your presentation file.

Activity 1.11 Deleting a Slide

In this activity, you will delete Slide 8.

1 In the **Outline/Slides** pane, click the **Slides tab** to display the slide thumbnails.

2 If necessary, click to select **Slide 8**.

Slide 8 is bordered, indicating that it is selected. See Figure 1.20.

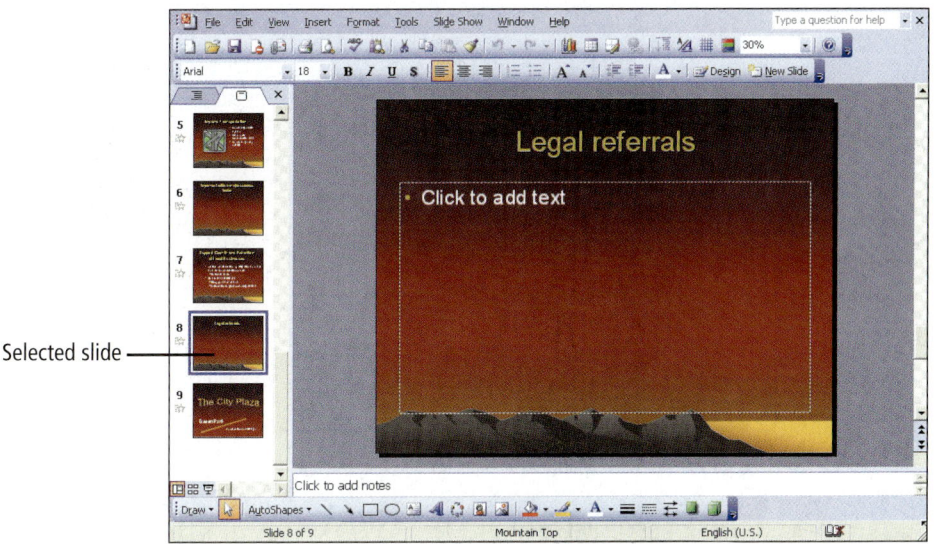

Selected slide

Figure 1.20

3 Press Delete.

The slide is deleted and the remaining slides are renumbered. In the status bar, *Slide 8 of 8* displays.

Another Way — Deleting Slides

When you display a slide that you wish to delete, you can click the Edit menu and then click Delete Slide.

4 On the Standard toolbar, click the **Save** button to save the changes you have made to your presentation file.

Activity 1.12 Moving a Slide

It is easy to change the order of the slides in your presentation using the Slides tab.

1 In the **Outline/Slides** pane, if necessary click the **Slides tab** to display the slide thumbnails. Click to select the thumbnail image for **Slide 7**.

2 Point to the selected slide, press and hold down the left mouse button, drag the mouse upward, and notice the horizontal line that displays as you move the mouse. With the horizontal line positioned between **Slides 4** and **5**, release the left mouse button. See Figure 1.21.

Slide 7 is reordered to become Slide 5.

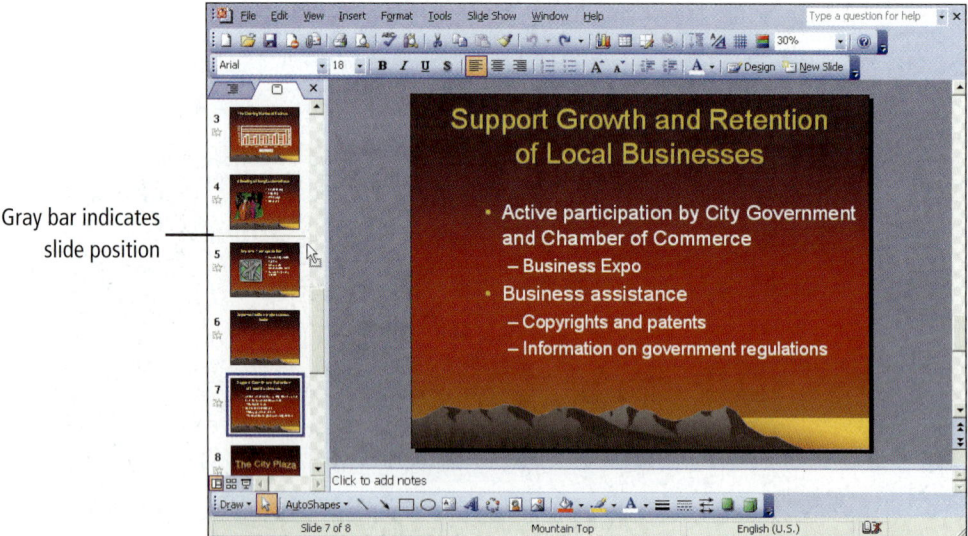

Gray bar indicates slide position

Figure 1.21

3 To close the **Outline/Slides** pane, move your pointer to the right of the **Slides tab**, and then click the **Close** button.

The Outline/Slides pane section of the window closes and the Slide pane fills most of the PowerPoint window.

4 In the lower left corner of your screen, point to the **Normal View** button and notice that the ScreenTip indicates *Normal View (Restore Panes)*.

You can redisplay the Outline/Slides pane by clicking the Normal View button or by displaying the View menu and clicking Normal (Restore Panes).

5 Make sure the **Outline/Slides** pane is still closed, and then, on the Standard toolbar, click the **Save** button to save the changes to your presentation.

Objective 3
Format and Edit a Presentation Using the Slide Pane

You will do most of your *formatting* work in PowerPoint in the Slide pane. Formatting refers to changing the appearance of the text, layout, and design of a slide. You can also edit, promote, and demote text in the Slide pane using the same techniques that you used in the Outline/Slides pane.

Activity 1.13 Editing Text Using the Slide Pane

1 If necessary, **Open** your file **1A_Expansion_Firstname_Lastname**. Be sure that the **Outline/Slides** pane is closed.

Recall that you can close the Outline/Slides tabs by clicking the Close button to the right of the Slides tab.

2 In the vertical scroll bar at the far right edge of the window, point to the scroll box. Press and hold down the left mouse button so that a ScreenTip displays indicating the number and title of the current slide. Drag up or down as necessary to display **Slide 6**.

3 With **Slide 6** displayed in the **Slide** pane, click to position your insertion point at the end of the last bulleted item on the slide—after the word *access*. Press Enter.

A new bullet, displayed in black, is created.

4 Type **Improve parking**

Notice that as you begin to type, the bullet turns to the color of the other bullets on the slide.

5 Click anywhere in the third bulleted line—*Improve highway access*.

On the Formatting toolbar, click **Increase Indent** to apply a lower level bullet. Compare your slide to Figure 1.22.

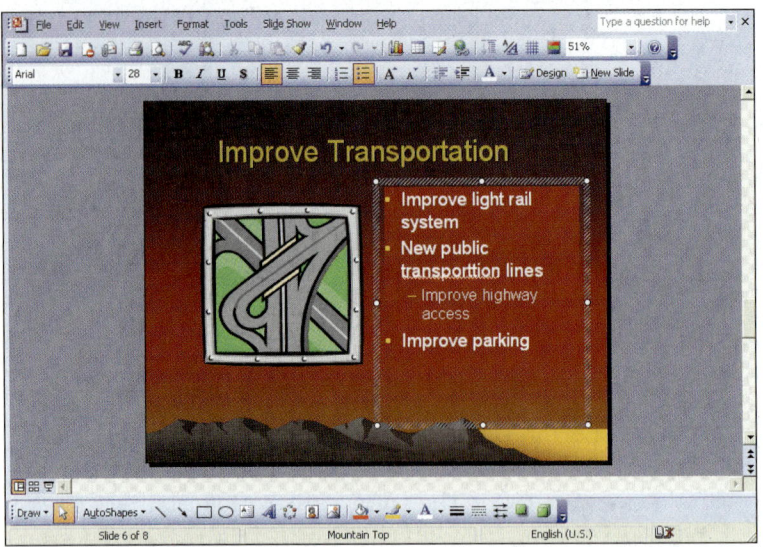

Figure 1.22

6 Save the file.

Activity 1.14 Changing Slide Layout

Layout refers to the placement and arrangement of the text and graphic elements on a slide. For example, a title slide usually has two elements—a title and a subtitle. Additional slide layouts may include a title and a bulleted list or a title and a chart. PowerPoint includes a number of pre-defined layouts that you can apply to your slide for the purpose of rearranging the elements. Changing the layout of a slide is accomplished from the Slide Layout task pane. You can display the Slide Layout task pane by clicking the Format menu and then clicking Slide Layout, or by displaying the task pane, clicking the Other Task Panes arrow, and then clicking Slide Layout.

1 Display **Slide 7** either by clicking the **Next Slide** button or by dragging the vertical scroll box to display **Slide 7**.

This slide contains a title and a ***placeholder*** for bulleted text. A placeholder reserves a portion of a slide and serves as a container for text, graphics, and other slide elements. Recall that this slide was created by promoting a bullet from the previous slide. Promoting a bullet at the highest level results in the creation of a new slide with the bulleted text as the title of the slide.

2 To change the layout of this slide, display the **Format** menu, and then click **Slide Layout**.

The Slide Layout task pane displays all of the predefined layouts available in PowerPoint. See Figure 1.23. The slide layouts are grouped into four categories: *Text Layouts*, *Content Layouts*, *Text and Content Layouts*, and *Other Layouts*.

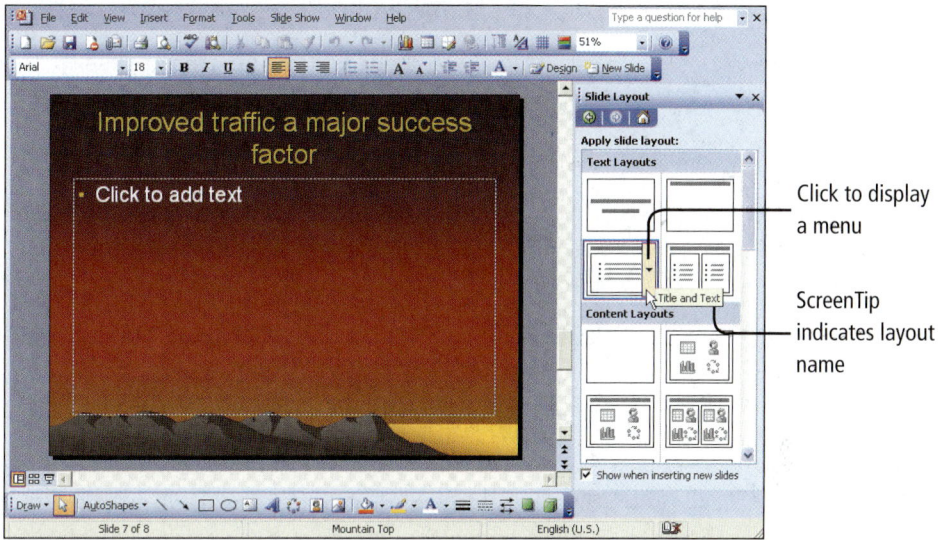

Figure 1.23

3 Take a moment to move the task pane's scroll bar up and down to see the four layout categories and view the layouts. Point to, but do not click, some of the layouts and notice that a ScreenTip displays indicating the name of the layout.

When you point to a slide layout, the right side of the layout displays a bar with an arrow. See Figure 1.23. Clicking the arrow displays a small menu from which you can apply the layout to selected slides or insert a new slide with the layout applied.

4 Scroll to the top to view the four choices under **Text Layouts**, and then click the last layout—**Title and 2-Column Text**.

The slide layout is changed so that there are two side-by-side placeholders on the slide.

5 Click in the **left placeholder**, type **New traffic signals** and then press Enter.

A new bulleted line is created.

6 Type **New street lights** and then press Enter. Type **New crosswalks**

If you inadvertently added an additional bullet by pressing Enter at the end of the bulleted list, press ←Bksp to delete the extra bullet.

7 Click in the **right placeholder**, and then type **Improved parking structures**

8 Press Enter, and then type **Redesigned turn lanes**

9 At the top of the **Slide Layout** task pane, click the **Close** button ☒ to close the **Slide Layout** task pane.

10 Look at the title of this slide and notice that the word *factor* is on the second line of the title by itself.

As a general design rule, you should try to have at least two words on each line of a slide title to create a balanced look.

11 To balance the title, move your pointer into the title placeholder and click after the word *traffic*. Press Enter.

The words *Improved traffic* are on the first line of the slide title and the words *a major success factor* are on the second line of the slide title.

12 Look again at the title of this slide and notice that only the first word of the title—*Improved*—is capitalized.

As a rule, the first letter of each word in a title should be capitalized.

13 Correct the text in the title by clicking in the title placeholder and typing as necessary so that the capitalization matches Figure 1.24. Then, click in a blank area to deselect the placeholder, and compare your slide to Figure 1.24.

Verify title capitalization

Two-column text

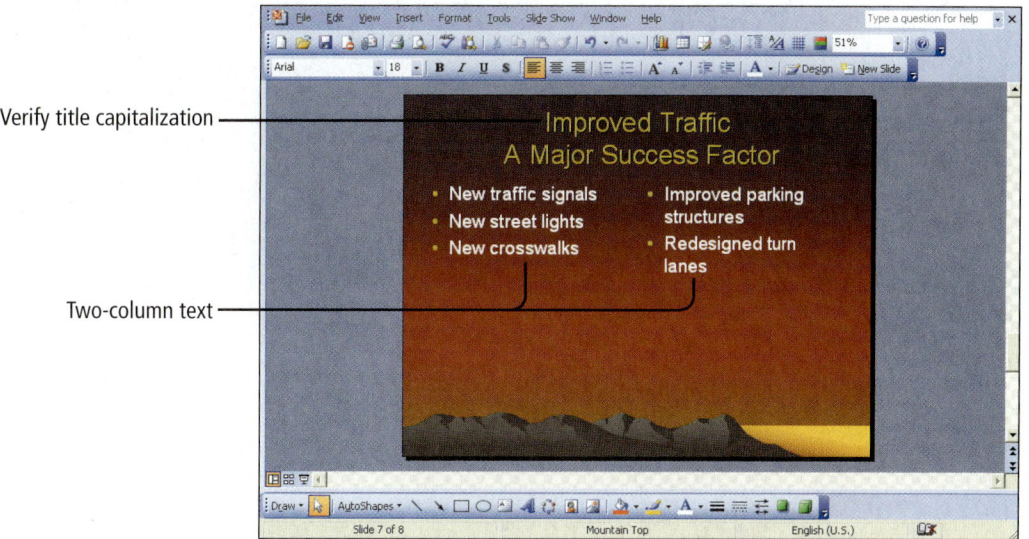

Figure 1.24

14 On the Standard toolbar, click the **Save** button to save the changes you have made to your presentation.

Activity 1.15 Checking the Spelling of a Presentation

As you create a presentation, PowerPoint continually checks spelling by comparing the words in your presentation to the PowerPoint dictionary. A word that is incorrectly spelled or that is not in the dictionary is indicated by a red wavy underline. Spelling errors can be corrected in either the Outline/Slides pane or the Slide pane.

1 Display **Slide 2** by dragging the scroll box in the vertical scrollbar up until the appropriate ScreenTip displays. Notice the red wavy underline in the first bullet of this slide.

Alert!

Enabling Spelling Checker

If the red wavy underline does not display under the incorrectly spelled word, the *Check spelling as you type* feature may not be enabled on your system. To enable this feature, click the Tools menu, and then click Options. Click the Spelling and Style tab and click to place a check mark in the Check spelling as you type check box.

2 Pause the mouse the pointer over the incorrectly spelled word, and then right-click (press the right mouse button).

A shortcut menu displays with several suggested spelling corrections. See Figure 1.25.

Project 1A: Expansion | **PowerPoint** 991

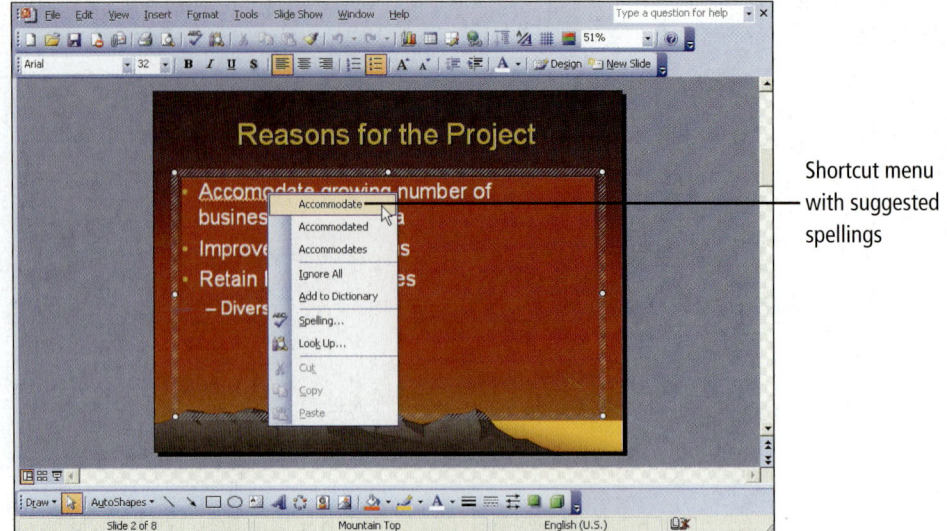

Figure 1.25

[3] In the displayed shortcut menu, click **Accommodate**—the correct spelling of the word.

[4] On the vertical scrollbar, click the **Next Slide** button to display **Slide 3**. Locate the misspelled word in the title, move the pointer over it, and then right-click. From the displayed shortcut menu, click **Businesses** to correct the spelling.

[5] Using the same method that you used to correct the spelling errors on **Slides 2** and **3**, scroll through the presentation and correct spelling on the remaining slides (*transportation* on **Slide 6** and any other spelling errors you might have made).

[6] **Save** the changes you have made to your presentation.

More Knowledge — Checking the Entire Presentation Using the Spelling Command

The Spelling button on the Standard toolbar activates a spelling check of your entire presentation. The spelling checker selects each incorrectly spelled word and displays a dialog box with suggested spellings and the options to ignore the word, change the word, or add the word to the dictionary.

Activity 1.16 Adding Speaker Notes to a Presentation

Recall that when a presentation is displayed in Normal View with the panes displayed, the Notes pane displays below the Slide pane. The Notes pane is used to type speaker's notes that can be printed below a picture of each slide. You can refer to these printouts while making a presentation, thus reminding you of the important points that you wish to make while running an electronic slide show.

1 Drag the scroll box to display **Slide 3**. In the lower left corner of your PowerPoint window, click the **Normal View** button.

The Outline/Slides pane and the Notes pane are restored on your screen.

2 Look at the PowerPoint window and notice the amount of space that is currently dedicated to each of the three panes—the **Outline/Slides** pane, the **Slide** pane, and the **Notes** pane. Locate the horizontal bar and vertical bar that separate the three panes. See Figure 1.26.

These narrow bars are used to adjust the size of the panes. If you decide to type speaker notes, you will want to make the Notes pane larger.

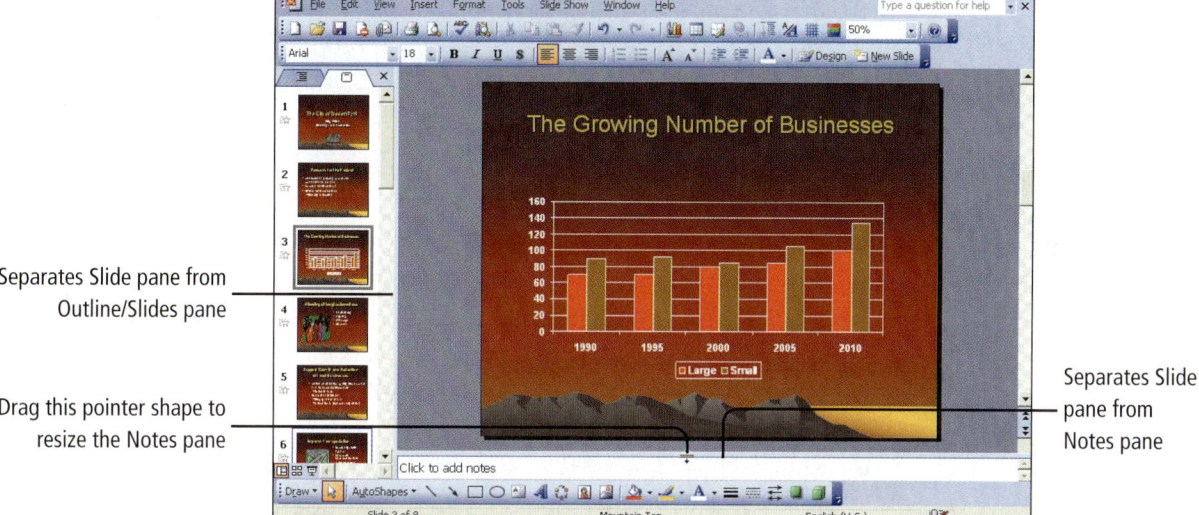

Separates Slide pane from Outline/Slides pane

Drag this pointer shape to resize the Notes pane

Separates Slide pane from Notes pane

Figure 1.26

3 Point to the small bar that separates the **Slide** pane from the **Notes** pane. The pointer displays as an equal sign with an upward-pointing and a downward-pointing arrow, as shown in Figure 1.26.

4 Press and hold down the left mouse button until a pattern of dots displays in the bar, indicating that you can resize the pane. While still holding down the left mouse button, drag the pointer up approximately one inch and then release the left mouse button to resize the pane.

The displayed slide resizes to fit in the Slide pane and the Notes pane expands.

5 With **Slide 3** displayed, click in the **Notes** pane and type **As the population expands, the number of large and small businesses will continue to grow.** Compare your screen to Figure 1.27.

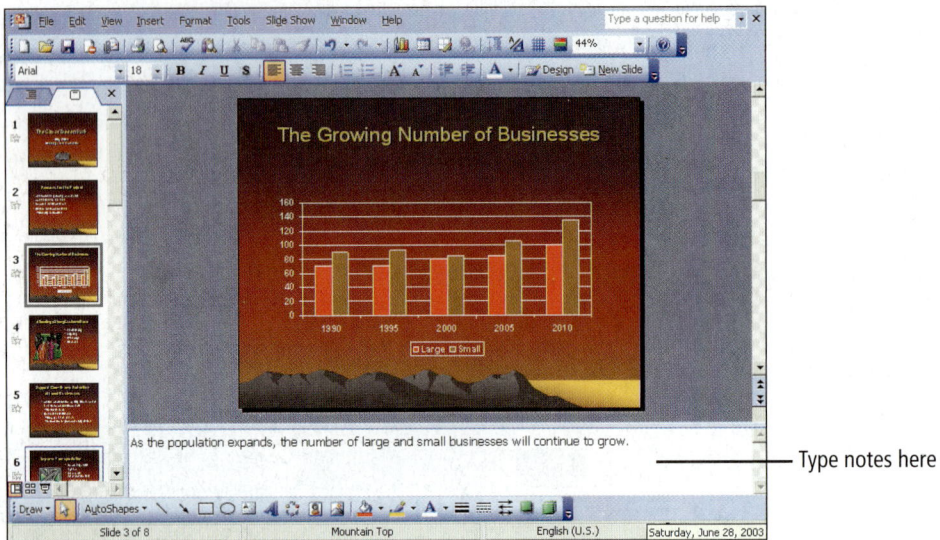

Figure 1.27

6 Display **Slide 7** in the **Slide** pane, and then click in the **Notes** pane. Type **Remember that increased traffic is a major concern for the City. Stress how these changes will improve the traffic flow, not create new problems.**

7 Move to the last slide in the presentation—**Slide 8**. Type the following text in the **Notes** pane: **Stress the importance of the expansion of the City Plaza. Many citizens are working together to create this new space for the benefit of all.**

8 You have finished typing the notes for this presentation. **Save** the presentation.

Objective 4
View and Edit a Presentation in Slide Sorter View

Slide Sorter View displays all of the slides in your presentation in miniature. You can use Slide Sorter View to rearrange and delete slides, apply formatting to multiple slides, and to get an overall impression of your presentation.

Activity 1.17 Selecting Multiple Slides

Selecting more than one slide is accomplished by clicking the first slide that you wish to select, pressing and holding down Shift or Ctrl, and then clicking another slide. Using Shift allows you to select a group of slides that are adjacent (next to each other). Using Ctrl allows you to select a group of slides that are nonadjacent (*not* next to each other). When multiple slides are selected, you can move or delete them as a group. These techniques can also be used when slide miniatures are displayed in the Slides tab.

1 If necessary, **Open** your file **1A_Expansion_Firstname_Lastname**. At the lower left of your window, click the **Slide Sorter View** button.

The Outline/Slides pane is closed, and the eight slides in your presentation display in order from left to right.

2 Point to **Slide 2**, and then click the left mouse button to select it.

An outline surrounds the slide indicating that it is selected.

3 Press and hold down Ctrl, and then click **Slide 4**.

Slides 2 and 4 are selected.

4 Press and hold down Ctrl, and then click **Slide 6**.

Slides 2, 4, and 6 are selected. See Figure 1.28.

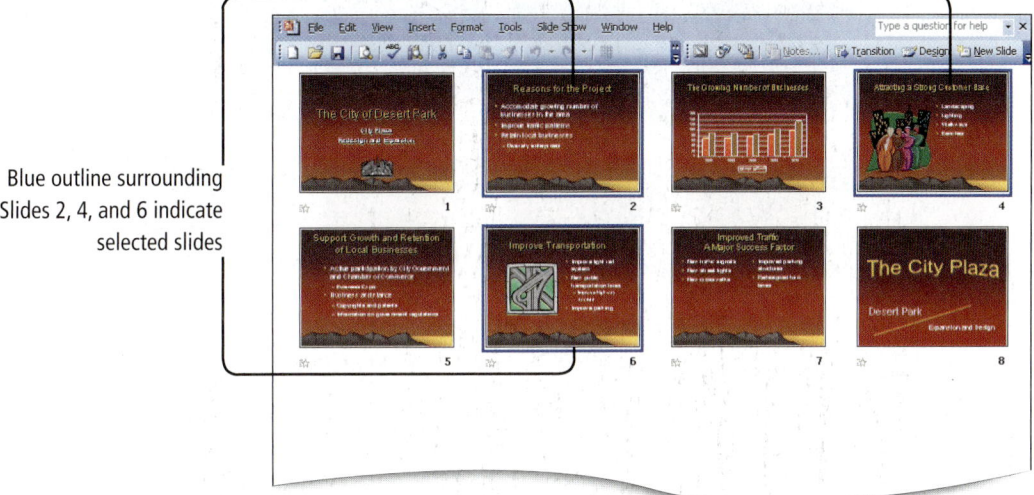

Blue outline surrounding Slides 2, 4, and 6 indicate selected slides

Figure 1.28

5 To deselect **Slide 4** while leaving **Slides 2** and **6** selected, press and hold down Ctrl, and then click **Slide 4**.

Slides 2 and 6 are still selected.

6 Click **Slide 3** *without* holding down Ctrl.

This action deselects Slides 2 and 6, and only Slide 3 is selected.

7 With **Slide 3** still selected, press and hold down Shift, and then click **Slide 6**.

All of the slides between 3 and 6 are selected.

8 Click in the white area below the slides.

The selection is canceled and no slides are selected. Additionally, a large blinking insertion point displays after Slide 8. You can cancel the selection of all slides by clicking anywhere in the white area of the Slide Sorter window.

Project 1A: Expansion | **PowerPoint** 995

Activity 1.18 Moving and Deleting Slides in Slide Sorter View

Slide Sorter view is convenient for deleting and moving slides because you can view a large number of slides at one time.

1 If necessary, display your presentation in Slide Sorter View by clicking the **Slide Sorter View** button.

2 Click to select **Slide 3**.

3 While pointing to **Slide 3**, press and hold down the left mouse button, and then drag the slide to the left until the displayed vertical bar is positioned to the left of **Slide 2**. See Figure 1.29. Release the left mouse button.

The slide with the chart becomes Slide 2.

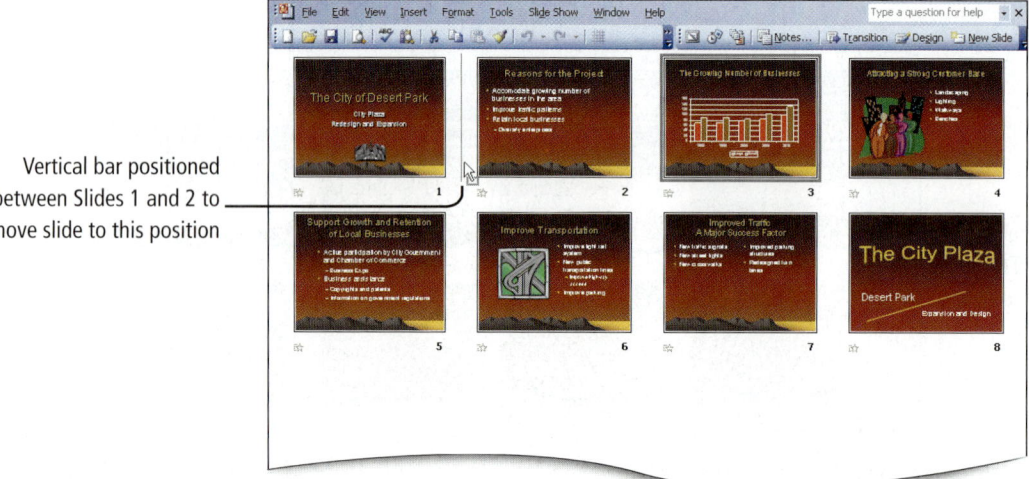

Vertical bar positioned between Slides 1 and 2 to move slide to this position

Figure 1.29

4 Select **Slide 4**, press and hold down Ctrl, and then click **Slide 7**. Make sure that *only* **Slides 4** and **7** are selected, and then press Delete to delete these two slides from the presentation.

5 **Save** the presentation file.

Objective 5
View a Slide Show

When a presentation is viewed as an electronic slide show, the entire slide fills the computer screen, and a large audience can view your presentation if your computer is connected to a projection system. An onscreen slide show may include special effects such as slide *transitions*. Transitions refer to the way that a slide appears or disappears during an onscreen slide show. For example, when one slide leaves the screen, it may fade or dissolve into another slide.

Other special effects that you will see as you run the presentation are text and graphic animations. *Animation effects* introduce individual slide elements so that the slide can be built (displayed) one element at a time. These effects add interest to your slides and draw attention to important features.

Activity 1.19 Viewing a Slide Show

Transitions and animation effects have been applied to the *1A_Expansion* presentation. Clicking the left mouse button allows you to view each animation effect separately on each individual slide. At the end of the slide, you also click the left mouse button to advance to the next slide. You will learn to add special effects to presentations as you progress in this textbook.

1. Display **Slide 1** of your file **1A_Expansion_Firstname_Lastname** in **Normal View**. Then, take a moment to read Steps 2 through 8 to familiarize yourself with what you will see and do as you view the slide presentation. After you have read the steps, in the lower left corner of the screen, click the **Slide Show** button and read the steps again as you proceed through the slide show.

2. Watch for the animation effect on the title of the first slide, and then locate the graphic at the bottom center of the slide.

   This is a graphic file that includes a blinking light at the top of the tall building. The animation in this graphic is not a part of PowerPoint; rather, it is included in the graphic file itself. Upon opening, the title displays an emphasis animation effect—a colored box displays around the title as it expands, and then the colored box disappears as the text reverts to its original size.

3. Click the left mouse button to advance to the next slide, and notice that only the background is visible. Click the left mouse button again to display the title of the slide.

4. Click the left mouse button to display the chart. Click the left mouse button again to display the chart's first bar element.

5. Continue to click the left mouse button until the chart has finished and the third slide displays. When the third slide transitions onto the screen, only the title displays.

6 Click the left mouse button and notice that the first bullet displays toward the bottom of the slide and then bounces into place. Click the left mouse button again and notice that the first bullet dims to a lighter color as the second bullet bounces into place.

Dimming a previous bullet is a type of text animation that keeps the audience focused on the current bullet.

7 Continue to click the left mouse button until the fourth slide displays—entitled *Support Growth and Retention of Local Businesses*. This slide introduces all the text at once.

8 Click the left mouse button to display the fifth slide, and then click again to drop the title onto the screen. Click again so that the graphic spins onto the screen in a pinwheel effect, and then click the left mouse button three more times to display each line of bulleted text.

9 Click to display the sixth and final slide—entitled *The City Plaza*. The elements on this slide do not require that you click the left mouse button to advance the animations. These elements have been set with automatic slide timings. Click the left mouse button one more time to view the last slide, which is a **black slide** that displays the text *End of slide show, click to exit*. PowerPoint inserts a black slide at the end of every slide show to indicate that the presentation is over. Click the left mouse button to return to Normal View.

> **More Knowledge** — Inserting a Formatted Slide at the End of a Presentation
>
> PowerPoint inserts a black slide to signal the end of a presentation. Some presenters prefer to display a blank slide that contains the same background as the other slides in the presentation. If you prefer this method, you can disable the black slide by clicking the Tools menu, and then clicking Options. Click the View tab, and under Slide Show, click to clear the End with black slide check box.

10 Use any method to display **Slide 3**, and then click the **Slide Show** button to start the presentation on **Slide 3**. Click three times, and then after you have viewed the entire third slide, on your keyboard press [Esc] to end the slide show.

You do not have to start a presentation with the first slide. An audience member may ask you a question pertaining to a particular slide. You can begin the slide show on any slide in the presentation by first displaying the slide in Normal View.

11 Save the presentation.

Objective 6
Create Headers and Footers

A ***header*** is text that displays at the top of every slide or that prints at the top of a sheet of ***slide handouts*** or ***notes pages***. Slide handouts are printed images of more than one slide on a sheet of paper. Notes pages are printouts that contain the slide image in the top half of the page and notes that you have created in the Notes pane in the lower half of the page.

In addition to headers, you can also create ***footers***—text that displays at the bottom of every slide or that prints at the bottom of a sheet of slide handouts or notes pages. In this activity, you will add the slide number to the footer on Slides 1 through 5. You will add to the handouts and notes pages a header that includes the current date and a footer that includes your name and the file name.

Activity 1.20 Creating Headers and Footers on Slides

1 If necessary, **Open** your file **1A_Expansion_Firstname_Lastname** and verify that **Slide 1** is displayed in **Normal View**.

2 On the menu bar, click **View**, and then click **Header and Footer** to display the **Header and Footer** dialog box.

At the top of this dialog box, two tabs display—*Slide* and *Notes and Handouts*.

3 Click the **Slide tab**, which contains options to place the header or footer on the actual slide—rather than on the printed handout. Then locate the **Preview** box in the lower right corner of the dialog box and note the pattern of boxes.

As you make changes in the dialog box, the Preview box will change accordingly.

4 Under **Include on slide**, select (click to place a check mark in) the **Slide number** check box, and as you do so, watch the Preview box.

The Preview box in the lower right corner of the dialog box indicates the placeholders on a slide. Recall that a placeholder reserves a location on a slide for text or graphics. The three narrow rectangular boxes at the bottom of the Preview box indicate placeholders for footer text. When you clicked the Slide number check box, the placeholder in the far right corner is filled, indicating the location in which the slide number will display.

5 If necessary, clear the **Date and time** check box so that a check mark does *not* display, and then clear the **Footer** check box.

In the Preview box, the first two small rectangles are no longer solid black.

6 Compare your dialog box to Figure 1.30, and then in the upper right corner of the dialog box, click the **Apply to All** button. This will display the slide number on all the slides in the presentation—not just the selected slides.

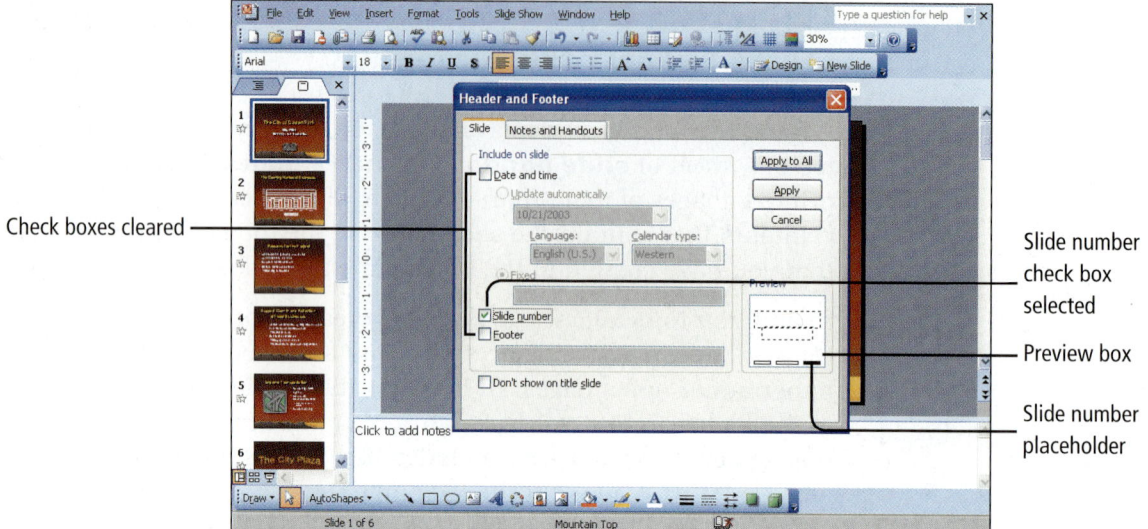

Figure 1.30

7 In the **Slide** pane, at the lower end of the vertical scroll bar, click the **Next Slide** button to display each slide and view the slide number in the lower right corner of each slide—with the exception of **Slide 6**.

8 Display **Slide 6**.

The slide number does not display, and the background formatting is different from the other slides in the presentation. Special formatting on this slide suppresses (prevents from displaying) some elements such as headers and footers and the mountain range border that are present on the first five slides of the presentation. You will learn how to suppress these elements in a later chapter.

9 **Save** the presentation.

Activity 1.21 Creating Headers and Footers on Handouts and Notes Pages

1 Display the **View** menu, and then click **Header and Footer** to display the **Header and Footer** dialog box. Click the **Notes and Handouts tab**, which contains options to apply the header and footer that you create to the notes pages and handouts—and not to the actual slides.

2 Under **Include on page**, make sure there is a check mark in the **Date and time** check box (click to add one if necessary), and then click to select the **Update automatically** option button.

The current date and Language display in the appropriate boxes. The Update automatically option will insert the current date on your printed notes and handouts. The date is determined by your computer's internal calendar and clock. Thus, every time the presentation is opened, the current date displays. Conversely, clicking the Fixed option button inserts a date that you type, and which does *not* update.

More Knowledge — Changing the Date Format

You can change the format of the date that displays by clicking the arrow to the right of the date box, and then choosing a date format. You can also change the Language that you wish to display.

3 If necessary, clear the **Header** and **Page number** check boxes to omit these elements from the header and footer.

In the Preview box, corresponding placeholders are no longer selected.

4 If necessary, select the **Footer** check box, and then click to position the insertion point in the **Footer** box. See Figure 1.31, and then using your own first and last name, type **1A Expansion-Firstname Lastname**

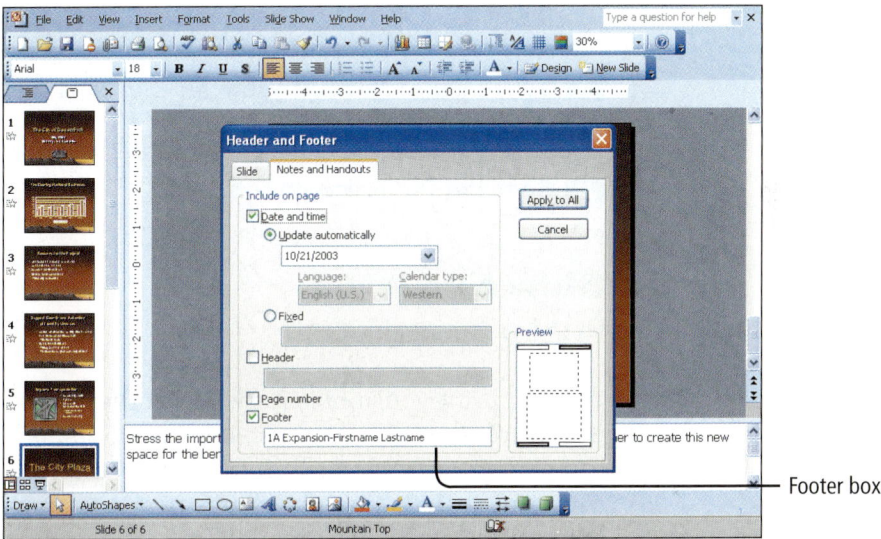

Footer box

Figure 1.31

5 In the upper right corner of the **Header and Footer** dialog box, click **Apply to All** so that each printed sheet displays the header and footer that you created.

6 Display **Slide 2**. From the **View** menu, click **Notes Pages** to display the current slide in the **Notes Page** view. Notice the date in the upper right corner, and the file name in the lower left corner. See Figure 1.32.

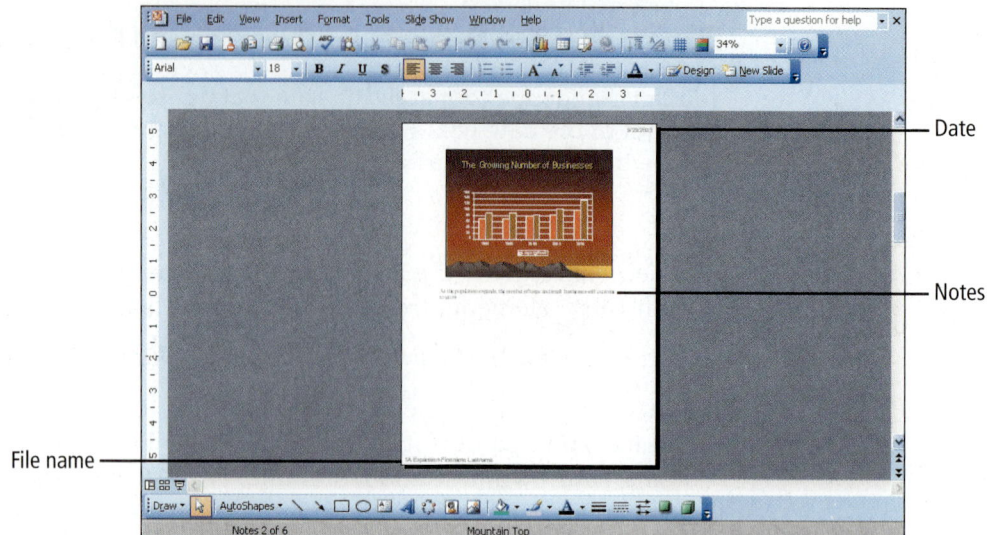

Figure 1.32

7 To return to **Normal View**, in the lower left corner of the PowerPoint window, click the **Normal View** button.

8 **Save** the presentation.

Objective 7
Print a Presentation

You can print your presentation as individual slides so that one slide fills the entire sheet of paper, as slide handouts, or as notes pages. Recall that slide handouts include *several* slides printed on one sheet of paper. You can print 1, 2, 3, 4, 6, or 9 slides per page and then distribute the printed handouts to your audience. The size of the slides on the printout varies, depending on the number of slides that you choose to print per page.

Activity 1.22 Previewing and Printing Handouts and Slides

Clicking the Print button on the Standard toolbar prints one copy of each slide in the presentation—filling the entire page with the slide. Printing a presentation in this manner uses a large amount of ink or toner, depending on the type of printer to which your system is connected. The majority of the projects in this textbook require that you print handouts, *not* slides. This will conserve paper and printer supplies. To change the print options, use the Print dialog box.

1 Display the **File** menu and point to **Print**.

Recall that when a menu option is followed by three small dots (called an ellipsis), it indicates that more information is needed and either a task pane or a dialog box will display.

2 Click **Print** to open the **Print** dialog box. Take a moment to study the table in Figure 1.33, which describes what you can do in each section of the **Print** dialog box.

The Print Dialog Box

Section	Here you can:
Printer	Change the current printer. Information regarding the printer location and the port that the printer is using is included here.
Print range	Choose the slides that you want to print.
Copies	Specify the number of copies that you want to print.
Print what:	Specify the type of output. You can print slides, handouts, notes pages, or outline view (only the text of the slides, in outline format).
Handouts	Specify the number of slides per page and the order in which the slides are arranged on the page.

Figure 1.33

3 In the lower left portion of the dialog box, click the **Print what arrow**, and then from the displayed list, click **Handouts**.

4 Under **Handouts**, click the **Slides per page arrow**. On the displayed list, click **6** to print all six slides in the presentation on one page.

The preview box to the right indicates six slides.

5 In the same dialog box section, click the **Vertical** option button.

The preview changes its order of how the slides will be printed—slides 1–3 in the first column and then slides 4–6 in the second column.

6 At the bottom of the dialog box, click the **Color/grayscale arrow**. Click **Grayscale**. If necessary, click to select the **Frame slides** check box so that a thin border surrounds each slide on the printout, thus giving the printout a finished and professional look.

Selecting *grayscale* optimizes the look of color slides that are printed on a black and white printer, whereas printing in Pure Black and White hides shadows and patterns applied to text and graphics.

7 Under **Print range**, verify that the **All** option button is selected so that all of the slides in the presentation are included in the handouts printout. Under **Copies**, in the **Number of copies** box, verify that **1** displays so that only one copy of the handouts is printed. Compare your dialog box to Figure 1.34.

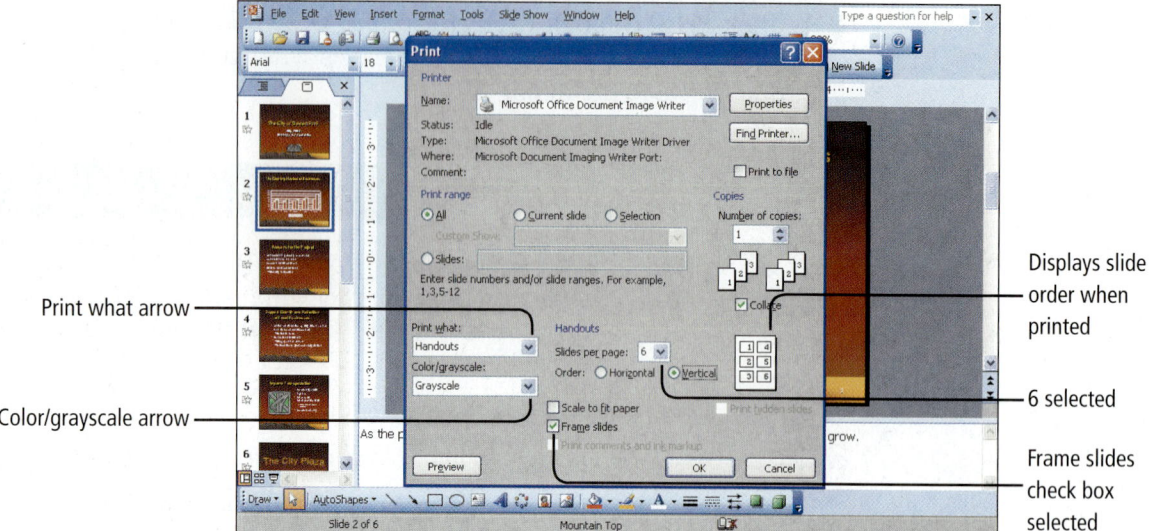

Figure 1.34

8 In the lower left corner of the **Print** dialog box, click **Preview**.

The Print Preview window opens, displaying your presentation as it will look when printed using the print options that you selected. In this window, you can change the print options and then print your presentation.

> **Another Way** — **Displaying the Presentation in the Print Preview Window**
>
> You can display the Print Preview window at any time by clicking the Print Preview button on the Standard toolbar.

9 On the Print Preview toolbar, click **Landscape**.

The presentation displays and will print on paper set up in landscape orientation—11 inches wide by 8½ inches tall.

10 On the Print Preview toolbar, click **Options**, point to **Printing Order**, and then click **Horizontal**.

Slides 1, 2, and 3 display in the top row and slides 4, 5, and 6 display in the bottom row. Compare your Print Preview window to Figure 1.35.

1004 PowerPoint | Chapter 1: Getting Started with PowerPoint 2003

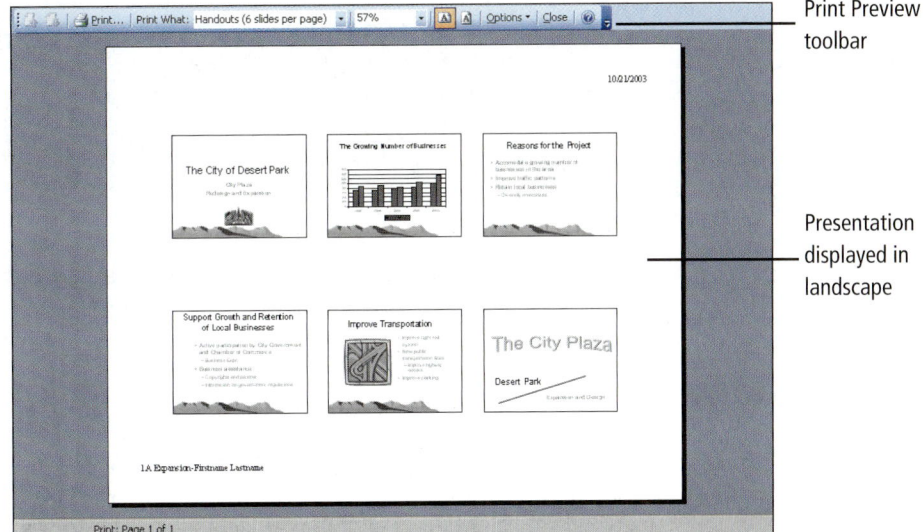

Figure 1.35

[11] On the Print Preview toolbar, click **Portrait**.

The presentation displays and will print on paper set up in portrait orientation—8½ inches wide by 11 inches tall.

[12] On the Print Preview toolbar, click **Print** to return to the print dialog box, and then click **OK**.

All six slides in the presentation are printed on one page, and the printout includes a header with the current date on the right and a footer with the file name on the left.

[13] On the Print Preview toolbar, click **Close**.

The Print Preview window closes and your presentation is displayed in Normal View.

Activity 1.23 Printing Notes Pages

In this activity, you will print Notes Pages for the slides that contain speaker's notes.

[1] Display the **File** menu, and then click **Print**.

[2] In the lower left corner of the **Print** dialog box, click the **Print what arrow**, and then from the displayed list, click **Notes Pages**.

[3] Under **Print range**, click the **Slides** option button and notice that the insertion point is blinking in the **Slides** box.

In this manner, you can choose to print only specific slides by entering the slide numbers that you want to print.

[4] In the **Slides** box, type **2,6**

Note — Printing Several Sequential Slides

You can print several sequential slides by using a hyphen between slide numbers. For example, typing 3–5 in the Slides box results in printouts that include slides 3, 4, and 5.

5 Under **Print what**, click the **Color/grayscale arrow**, and then from the displayed list click **Grayscale**. Compare your dialog box to Figure 1.36.

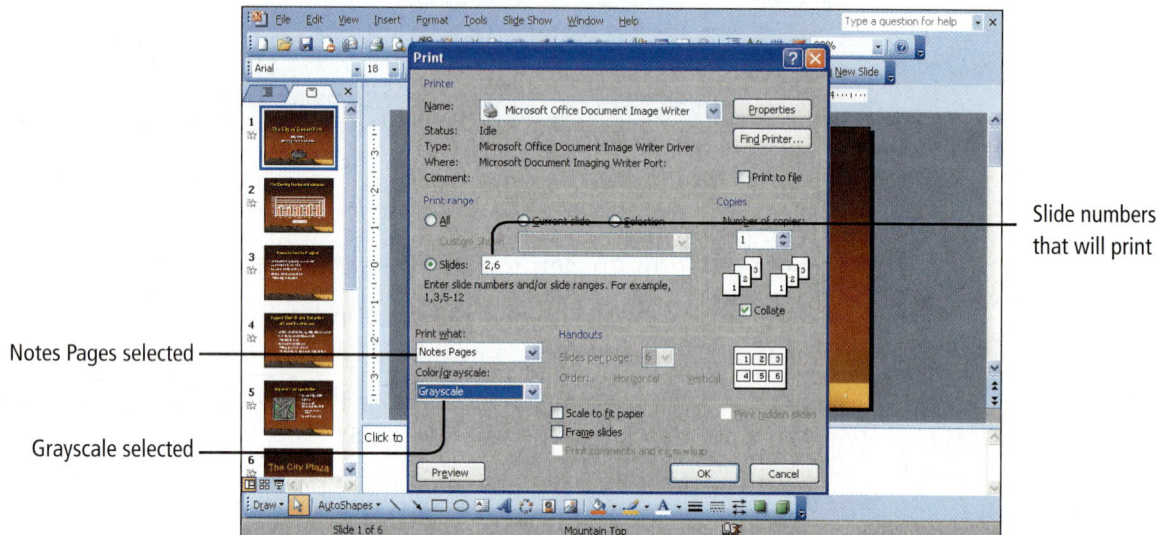

Figure 1.36

6 In the lower right corner of the **Print** dialog box, click **OK** to print the notes.

Two pages will print.

7 **Save** the presentation.

Objective 8
Use PowerPoint Help

As you work with PowerPoint, you can get assistance by using the Help feature. You can ask questions and PowerPoint Help will provide you with information and step-by-step instructions for performing tasks.

Activity 1.24 Using PowerPoint Help

One way to use Help is to type a question in the *Type a question for help* box, located at the right edge of the menu bar.

1 Move your pointer to the right edge of the menu bar and click in the **Type a question for help** box. With the insertion point blinking in the box, type **How do I open a file?** and then press Enter.

The Search Results task pane displays with a list of topics that may answer your question.

2 Point to and then click **Open a file**. See Figure 1.37.

The Microsoft Office PowerPoint Help window opens.

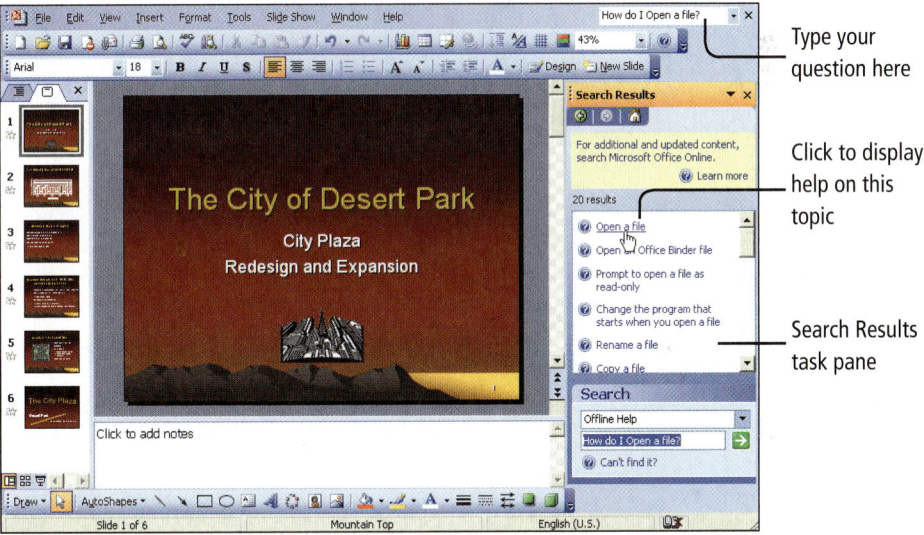

Figure 1.37

3 Read the instructions.

The bulleted items in blue below the Help topic indicate links to related instructions or information.

4 Click the last bullet, **Tips**, to display additional information about opening files.

5 In the second bulleted item, point to and then click the blue words **task pane** to display a green definition of a task pane. Click **task pane** again to close the definition.

6 In the Help window, click the **Close** button ☒, and then **Close** ☒ the **Search Results** task pane.

7 **Save** 🖫 the presentation. In the upper right corner of your screen, to the right of the **Help** box, click the **Close Window** button ☒ to close the presentation. Then, at the far right edge of the title bar, click the **Close** button ☒ to close PowerPoint.

Another Way

Getting Help Using the Task Pane and the Office Assistant

You can access Help by clicking the Microsoft Office PowerPoint Help button on the Standard toolbar. This action opens the Help task pane. In the Search box, type a topic that you want to learn more about and then press [Enter]. Search results are displayed in the same manner as when you used the Type a question for help box.

If installed, the *Office Assistant* provides yet another method for accessing help. This animated character provides tips as you work and when clicked, allows you to ask a question—displaying search results about the topic. You can display the Office Assistant from the Help menu by clicking Show the Office Assistant. When the Office Assistant is displayed, you can hide it by pointing to the Assistant, clicking the right mouse button to display the shortcut menu, and then clicking Hide.

End You have completed Project 1A

Summary

In this chapter, you practiced how to start and exit PowerPoint and how to open a presentation. By working with the different views in PowerPoint, you saw that Normal View is useful for editing and formatting presentation text and that Slide Sorter View is useful to get an overall view of your presentation and to rearrange and delete slides. Using Slide Show view, you practiced running an electronic slide show and became familiar with some of the animation effects that are available in PowerPoint. You also learned how to preview and print a presentation.

As you learn more about PowerPoint, take advantage of the resources available in Help. You can explore a wide variety of topics using the Help feature installed on your system, and you can access Microsoft Office online to find out how other people are using PowerPoint. The more that you use Microsoft Office PowerPoint 2003, the more familiar you will become with all of its features.

In This Chapter You Practiced How To

- Start and Exit PowerPoint
- Edit a Presentation Using the Outline/Slides Pane
- Format and Edit a Presentation Using the Slide Pane
- View and Edit a Presentation in Slide Sorter View
- View a Slide Show
- Create Headers and Footers
- Print a Presentation
- Use PowerPoint Help

Concepts Assessments

Matching Match each term in the second column with its correct definition in the first column by writing the letter of the term on the blank line in front of the correct definition.

_____ 1. A group of slides printed on one sheet of paper, appropriate for audience distribution.

_____ 2. The placement of elements on a slide.

_____ 3. The first slide of a presentation, which often contains distinguishing formatting.

_____ 4. The name used to refer to slide miniatures that display in the Slides tab and also in the Slide Sorter View.

_____ 5. Text that displays at the top of every slide or that prints at the top of a sheet of slide handouts or notes pages.

_____ 6. Effects that are used to introduce individual slide elements so that the slide can be built one element at a time.

_____ 7. A special effect that occurs when a slide is introduced during an onscreen slide show.

_____ 8. A small box that displays the name of a button on a toolbar or some other part of a Windows screen when you pause the mouse pointer over it.

_____ 9. A slide inserted by PowerPoint at the end of every slide show to indicate that the presentation is over.

_____ 10. A box that reserves a location on a slide and serves as a container for text, graphics, and other slide elements.

_____ 11. An animated character that displays tips while you work.

_____ 12. Printed pages that display a picture of the slide at the top of the page and text that the speaker wishes to say during the presentation at the bottom of the page.

_____ 13. Slides that are not next to each other when displayed in the Slide Sorter View.

_____ 14. A command that applies a lower outline level to text.

_____ 15. An option that allows you to choose the slides that you wish to print.

A Animation effects

B Black slide

C Demote

D Handouts

E Headers

F Layout

G Nonadjacent slides

H Notes pages

I Office Assistant

J Placeholder

K Print range

L ScreenTip

M Thumbnails

N Title slide

O Transition

Concepts Assessments (continued)

Fill in the Blank Write the correct answer in the space provided.

1. Microsoft PowerPoint 2003 is a _____ program that you can use to effectively present important information to your audience.

2. _____ is the process of making changes to the text in a presentation.

3. A _____ is text that displays at the bottom of every slide or at the bottom of printed notes pages and handouts.

4. An ellipsis following a menu command indicates that a _____ will follow.

5. The _____ displays at the right side of the PowerPoint window and assists you in completing common tasks.

6. When a bulleted item in a slide is _____, a higher outline level is applied.

7. A _____ is a row of buttons that provides a one-click method to perform common commands that would otherwise require multiple clicks to perform from the menu bar.

8. _____ is the process of changing the appearance of the text, layout, and design of a slide.

9. In the PowerPoint window, the point at which text is inserted is called the _____.

10. To display a shortcut menu, click the _____ mouse button.

PowerPoint chapter one
Skill Assessments

Project 1B—Safety

Objectives: *Start and Exit PowerPoint, Edit a Presentation Using the Outline/Slides Pane, View and Edit a Presentation in Slide Sorter View, View a Slide Show, Create Headers and Footers, and Print a Presentation.*

In the following Skill Assessment, you will edit a presentation created by the Human Resources Department for a new employee orientation concerning fire safety at City Hall. Your completed presentation will look similar to the one shown in Figure 1.38. You will save your presentation as *1B_Safety_Firstname_Lastname*.

Figure 1.38

(**Project 1B**–Safety continues on the next page)

1012   **PowerPoint** | Chapter 1: Getting Started with PowerPoint 2003

Skill Assessments (continued)

(Project 1B–Safety continued)

1. Start PowerPoint. On the Standard toolbar, click the **Open** button. On the displayed **Open** dialog box, click the **Look in arrow** and navigate to the location where the student files for this textbook are stored. Double-click **p01B_Safety**. Alternatively, you can click p01B_Safety once to select it, and then in the lower right corner of the dialog box, click Open.

2. Display the **File** menu, click **Save As**, and then use the **Save in arrow** to navigate to the location where you are storing your projects for this chapter. In the **File name** box, type **1B_Safety_Firstname_Lastname** and then click **Save**.

3. In the **Outline/Slides** pane, click the **Outline tab**. In the **Outline tab**, move your pointer to **Slide 1**. In the subtitle, click to position the insertion point after the word *Hall* and then press [Space] once. Type **Fire**

4. In the **Outline tab**, click anywhere in **Slide 2**. On the menu bar, click **Edit**, and then click **Delete Slide** to delete the second slide. Recall that this is another way to delete a slide. The remaining slides move up and are renumbered accordingly.

5. In the **Outline tab**, click anywhere in **Slide 3** so that it is displayed in the **Slide** pane. Move your pointer into the slide in the **Slide** pane, and then click to position the insertion point at the end of the last bullet after the word *exits*. The placeholder is selected. Press [Enter], and then type **Use stairs to get to safety**

6. Display **Slide 1**. Using the **Outline tab**, the **Next Slide** button, or the scroll bar to the right of the **Slide** pane, scroll through and read the presentation, one slide at a time, and notice the words that are flagged with a red wavy underline indicating incorrect spelling. Point to each misspelled word and click the right mouse button to display the shortcut menu of suggested spellings. Click the correct spelling for each misspelled word. (Hint: You should find two misspelled words—*extinguishers* and *department*.) Alternatively, on the Standard toolbar, click the Spelling button and complete the spelling check.

7. Display **Slide 3**. Point to the small bar between the **Slide** pane and the **Notes** pane until the pointer displays as an upward-pointing and a downward-pointing arrow. If necessary, press and hold down the left mouse button and drag upward slightly to expand the **Notes** pane to approximately one inch high. This should provide adequate space to type notes.

8. Click in the **Notes** pane and type **When a fire alarm is sounded, the elevators stop at the nearest floor. The elevator doors open and remain open so that the elevators cannot be used.**

(Project 1B–Safety continues on the next page)

Skill Assessments (continued)

(Project 1B–Safety continued)

9. In the **View** buttons at the lower left of your window, click the **Slide Sorter View** button to display all four slides. Click **Slide 3** to select it. Press and hold down the left mouse button, and then drag the pointer to the left so that the vertical bar displays to the left of **Slide 2**. Release the left mouse button to drop this slide into position as **Slide 2**.

10. Make sure that **Slide 2**, or any slide, is selected. On the menu bar, click **View**, and then click **Header and Footer**. Click the **Notes and Handouts tab**. If necessary, click to select the **Date and time** check box, and then click the **Update automatically** option button. This will display the current date on printed handouts or notes pages each time the presentation is opened. If necessary, click to select the **Footer** check box, and then in the **Footer** box, using your own first and last name, type **1B Safety-Firstname Lastname**

    If necessary, click to clear (remove the check mark from) the **Header** and **Page number** check boxes, and then click the **Apply to All** button.

11. On the menu bar, click **File**, and then click **Print**. In the displayed **Print** dialog box, click the **Print what arrow**, and then click **Handouts**. Under **Handouts**, click the **Slides per page arrow**, and then click **4**. Under **Handouts**, click the **Horizontal** order option button. Click the **Color/grayscale arrow**, and then click **Grayscale**. Check that the **Frame slides** check box is selected. Click **OK** to print a handout of all four slides on one page.

12. Display the **File** menu again, and then click **Print**. In the displayed **Print** dialog box, click the **Print what arrow**, and then click **Notes Pages**. Click the **Color/grayscale arrow**, and then click **Grayscale**. Under **Print range**, click the **Slides** option button. In the **Slides** box, type **2**

    This action instructs PowerPoint to print only the notes page for Slide 2. Click **OK**.

13. Click **Slide 1** to select it. Move to the **View** buttons at the lower left of your window, and then click the **Slide Show** button to begin viewing the presentation. Click the left mouse button to advance through the slides. Slide transitions (how each new slide displays) and animations (how various slide elements display) have been applied. When the black slide displays, click the left mouse button one more time to close the Slide Show view.

14. On the Standard toolbar, click **Save** to save the changes you have made to your presentation. On the menu bar, click **File**, and then click **Close**.

End You have completed Project 1B

PowerPoint chapter one

Skill Assessments (continued)

Project 1C—Benefits

Objectives: *Start and Exit PowerPoint, Edit a Presentation Using the Outline/Slides Pane, Create Headers and Footers, and Print a Presentation.*

In the following Skill Assessment, you will edit a presentation concerning a new benefits program for City of Desert Park employees. Your completed presentation will look similar to the one shown in Figure 1.39. You will save your presentation as *1C_Benefits_Firstname_Lastname*.

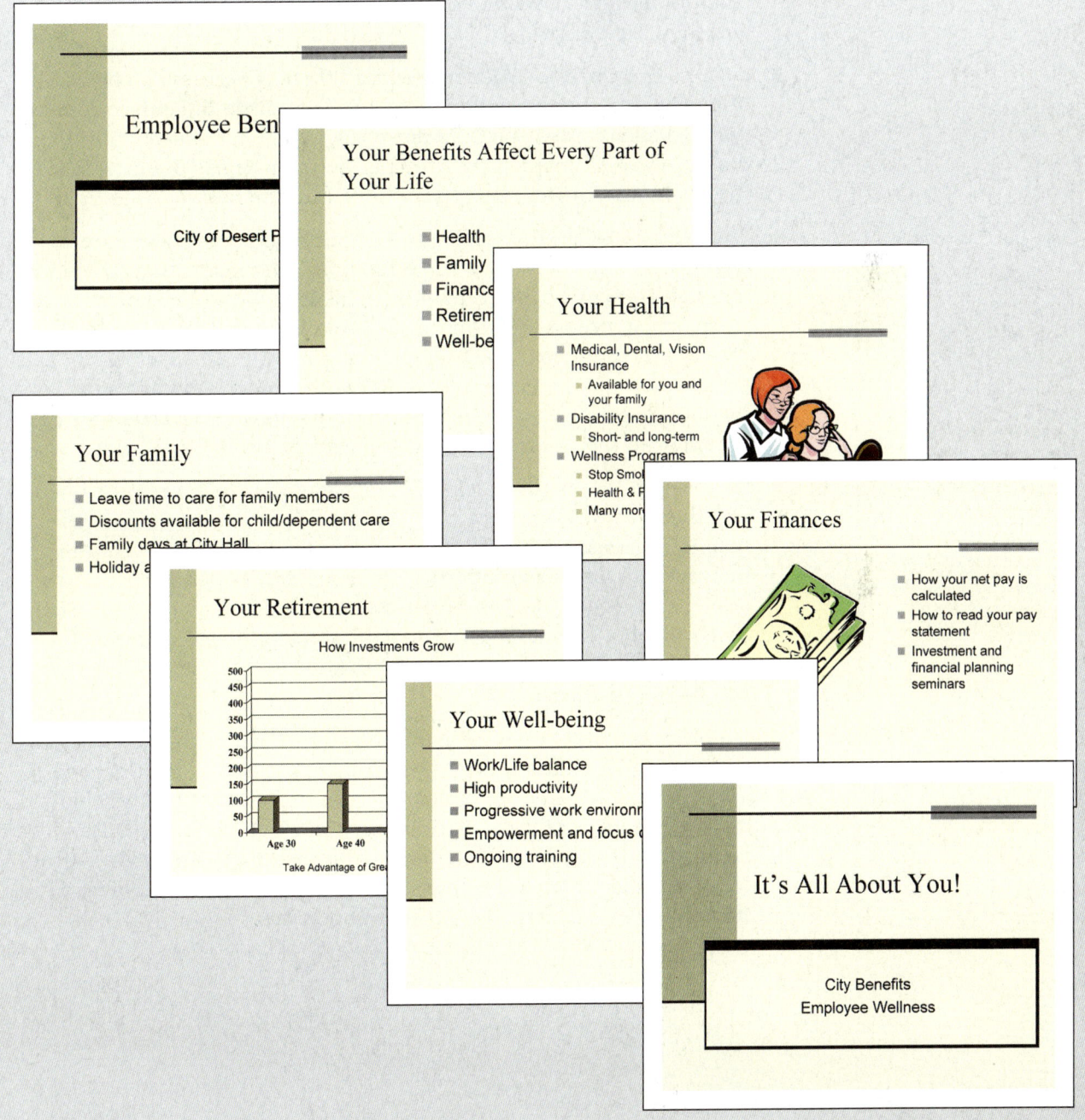

Figure 1.39

(Project 1C–Benefits continues on the next page)

PowerPoint chapter one
Skill Assessments (continued)

(Project 1C–Benefits continued)

1. Start PowerPoint. On the Standard toolbar, click **Open**, and in the displayed **Open** dialog box, use the **Look in arrow** to navigate to the student files that accompany this textbook. Open the file **p01C_Benefits** by double-clicking it. Alternatively, click once to select the file name, and then click the Open button.

2. Display the **File** menu, click **Save As**, and then use the **Save in arrow** to navigate to the location where you are storing your projects for this chapter. In the **File name** box, type **1C_Benefits_Firstname_Lastname** and then click **Save**.

3. Move to the **Outline/Slides** pane, and then, if necessary, click the **Slides tab**. In the **Slides tab**, click to select **Slide 5**. Point to the selected slide, press and hold down the left mouse button, and then drag upward to position the gray bar between Slides 3 and 4. Release the left mouse button to drop the slide into the new location.

4. With **Slide 4** selected, display the **Format** menu, and click **Slide Layout**. Look at the slide in the **Slide** pane, and notice that the current layout includes a bulleted list on the left, and a placeholder to add a clip art picture on the right. In the **Slide Layout** task pane, point to the vertical scroll box, press and hold down the left mouse button, and then drag up to display the **Text Layouts**. Under **Text Layouts**, use the mouse pointer to display ScreenTips to locate the **Title and Text layout**, and then click to apply this layout to the displayed slide.

5. Close the **Slide Layout** task pane. Move to the **Outline/Slides** pane, and then click the **Outline tab**. On **Slide 3**, click anywhere in the second bullet *Available for you and your family*. On the Formatting toolbar, click **Increase Indent** so that this line is demoted to a lower level bullet under the first bulleted line. Click anywhere in the *Short- and long-term* bullet. On the Formatting toolbar, click **Increase Indent** so that this line is demoted to a lower level bullet under *Disability Insurance*.

6. On **Slide 3**, to the left of *Stop Smoking*, position the mouse pointer over the bullet character until the pointer becomes a four-headed arrow. Click to select the bullet and all of its text. Press and hold down [Shift] and then click the bullet to the left of *Many More!* This action selects the two selected lines and the line between for a total of three bulleted lines. On the Formatting toolbar, click **Increase Indent** to demote all three bullets at one time.

(Project 1C–Benefits continues on the next page)

Skill Assessments (continued)

(Project 1C–Benefits continued)

7. Display the last slide—**Slide 7**. In the **Outline tab**, click anywhere in the text of the last bulleted item—*It's All About You!* On the Formatting toolbar, click **Decrease Indent** to promote the bulleted item to a new slide. **Slide 8** is created and the last bulleted item becomes the title of the slide. Press End to move the insertion point to the end of the slide title text, and then press Enter. Notice that a new slide is created. On the Formatting toolbar, click **Increase Indent** to demote by one level, creating the first bullet on **Slide 8**. Type the following two bullets by pressing Enter after the first line. Do *not* press Enter after the last line.

   City Benefits

   Employee Wellness

8. With **Slide 8** as the active slide, display the **Format** menu, and then click **Slide Layout**. In the **Slide Layout** task pane, under **Text Layouts**, click the first layout in the first row—**Title Slide**. In the **Slide** pane, notice that the text is converted to a title and a subtitle. Close the task pane.

9. From the **View** menu, click **Header and Footer**, and then click the **Notes and Handouts tab**. If necessary, select (click to place a check mark in) the **Date and time** check box, and then click the **Update automatically** option button to insert the current date each time notes pages or handouts are printed. Make sure the **Page number** check box is selected, and then clear the **Header** check box. If necessary, select the **Footer** check box, and then click in the **Footer** box. Type **1C Benefits-Firstname Lastname**

10. In the upper right corner of the **Header and Footer** dialog box, click **Apply to All**. Display the **File** menu, and then click **Print**. Click the **Print what arrow**, and then click **Handouts**. Under **Handouts**, click the **Slides per page arrow**, and then click **4**. Next to **Order**, click the **Horizontal** option button. Click the **Color/grayscale arrow**, and then click **Grayscale**. Make sure that the **Frame slides** check box is selected. Click **OK** to print two pages with four slides on each page.

11. On the Standard toolbar, click **Save** to save the changes to your presentation. On the menu bar, click **File**, and then click **Close**.

End You have completed Project 1C

PowerPoint chapter one
Skill Assessments (continued)

Project 1D — Flyer

Objectives: *Start and Exit PowerPoint, Format and Edit a Presentation Using the Slide Pane, View and Edit a Presentation in Slide Sorter View, Create Headers and Footers, and Print a Presentation.*

In the following Skill Assessment, you will edit a presentation to be used as a flyer concerning the City of Desert Park Employee Credit Union. Your completed presentation will look similar to the one shown in Figure 1.40. You will save your presentation as *1D_Flyer_Firstname_Lastname*.

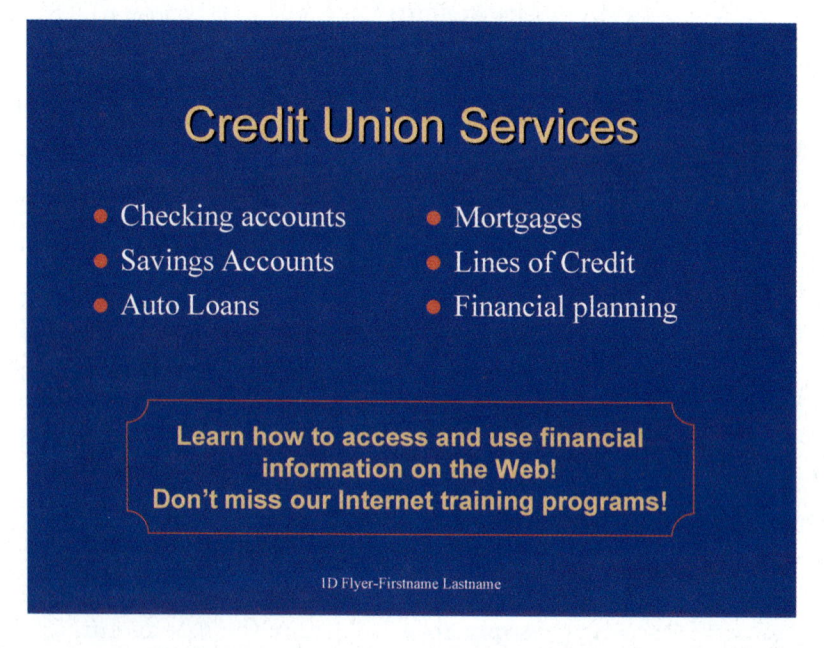

Figure 1.40

(**Project 1D**–Flyer continues on the next page)

1018 **PowerPoint** | Chapter 1: Getting Started with PowerPoint 2003

Skill Assessments (continued)

(Project 1D–Flyer continued)

1. Start PowerPoint. From the **File** menu, click **Open**. On the displayed **Open** dialog box, click the **Look in arrow** and navigate to the location where the student files that accompany this textbook are stored. Double-click **p01D_Flyer**, or click once to select the file name and press Enter.

2. Display the **File** menu, click **Save As**, and then use the **Save in arrow** to navigate to the location where you are storing your projects for this chapter. In the **File name** box, type **1D_Flyer_Firstname_Lastname** and then click **Save**.

3. In the lower left corner of your screen, click the **Slide Sorter View** button to display the three slides in the presentation in Slide Sorter view.

4. Click to select **Slide 1**. Press and hold down Shift and click **Slide 2**. Both Slides 1 and 2 are selected. Press Delete to delete both slides at the same time.

5. In the lower left corner of the screen, click the **Normal View** button. In the **Outline/Slides** pane, click the **Close** button so that only the **Slide** pane displays.

6. In the second column of bulleted items, drag to select the words *and Estate* in the last bulleted line. The placeholder is selected and the background color changes. Press Delete, and then click in the gray area surrounding the slide to deselect the placeholder.

7. On the menu bar, click **View**, and then click **Header and Footer**. In the displayed **Header and Footer** dialog box, click the **Slide tab**. In the **Slide tab**, click to select the **Footer** check box, and then click in the **Footer** box and type **1D Flyer-Firstname Lastname**

8. If necessary, clear any other check boxes in this dialog box. In the upper right corner, click **Apply to All**. Notice that the footer is placed on the slide.

9. This presentation is intended to be used as a flyer and should be printed as a full size slide. From the **File** menu, click **Print**. Click the **Color/grayscale arrow** and then click **Grayscale**. Click **OK**. One full-page copy of the slide prints in grayscale.

10. On the Standard toolbar, click the **Save** button to save your changes to the presentation. On the menu bar, click **File**, and then click **Close**.

End You have completed Project 1D

PowerPoint chapter one
Performance Assessments

Project 1E — Budget

Objectives: *Start and Exit PowerPoint, Edit a Presentation Using the Outline/Slides Pane, Format and Edit a Presentation Using the Slide Pane, View and Edit a Presentation in Slide Sorter View, Create Headers and Footers, and Print a Presentation.*

In the following Performance Assessment, you will edit a presentation to be used by the City of Desert Park Finance Department concerning the City Budget. Your completed presentation will look similar to the one shown in Figure 1.41. You will save your presentation as *1E_Budget_Firstname_Lastname*.

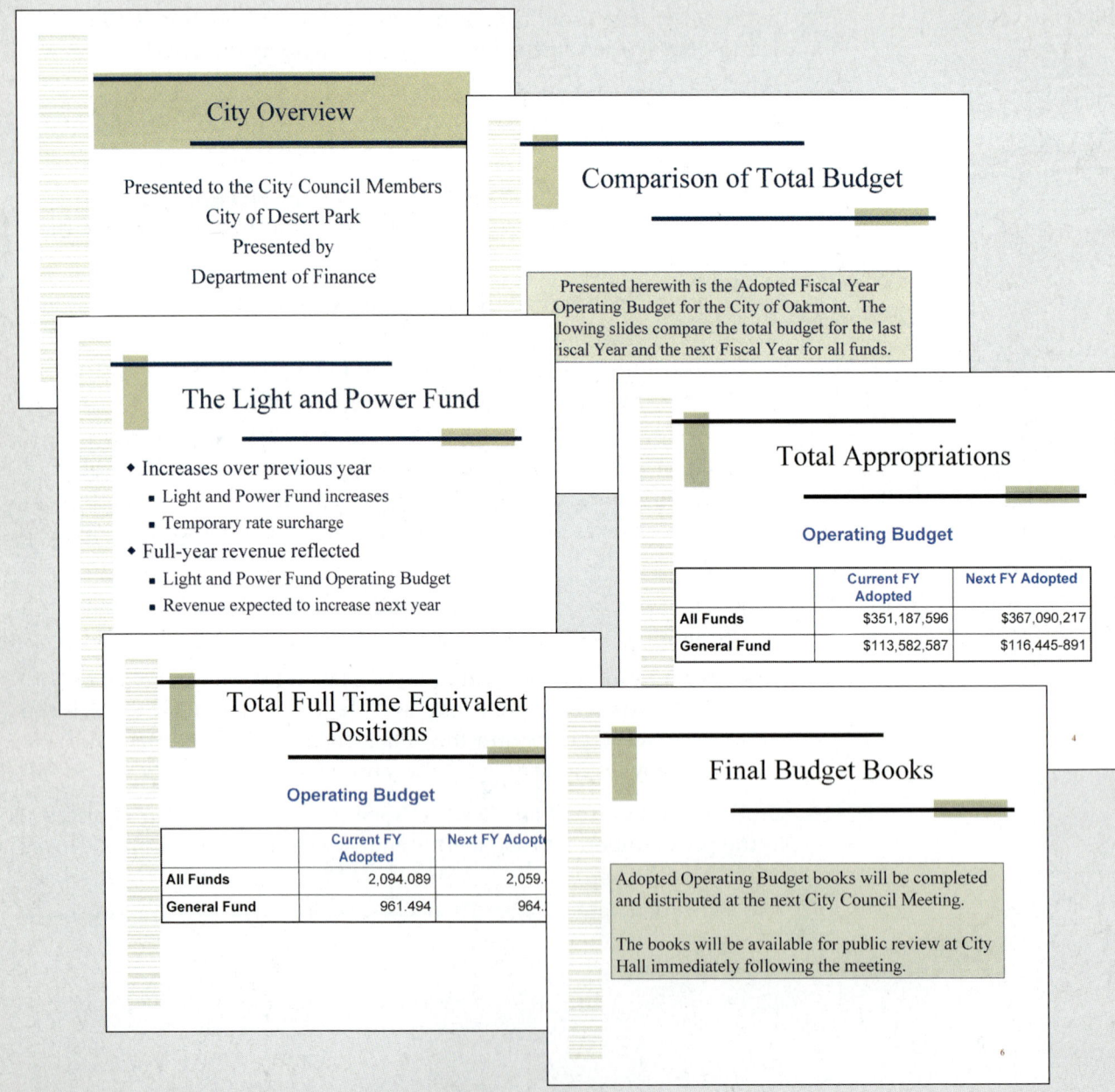

(Project 1E–Budget continues on the next page)

Figure 1.41

PowerPoint chapter one

Performance Assessments (continued)

(Project 1E–Budget continued)

1. Start PowerPoint, navigate to the location where the student files for this textbook are stored, and open the file **p01E_Budget**. Display the **File** menu, click **Save As**, and then use the **Save in arrow** to navigate to the location where you are storing your projects for this chapter. In the **File name** box, type **1E_Budget_Firstname_Lastname**

2. Scroll through the slides to familiarize yourself with the presentation. As you make the editing changes to this presentation, you may work in either the **Outline/Slides** pane or the **Slide** pane. Choose the method with which you feel most comfortable.

3. On **Slide 1**, click after the words *Desert Park* and press [Enter] to start a new line. Type **Presented by**

4. Press [Enter]. Type **Department of Finance** and then display **Slide 4**. Click anywhere in the third bullet, and then click the **Increase Indent** button to demote the third bullet—*Temporary rate surcharge*—to a subordinate level under the first bullet. Click to position the insertion point at the end of the last bullet point in the slide, and press [Enter] to add a new bullet at the end of the slide. Type **Revenue expected to increase next year**

5. On **Slide 4**, increase the height of the **Notes** pane if necessary, and then type the following note:

   The Light and Power Fund is a temporary surcharge that is expected to continue for the next two fiscal years. The City Council will then vote to determine whether or not the surcharge continues to be in effect.

6. Display **Slide 1**, and then on the Standard toolbar, click **Spelling** to check the spelling of the entire presentation. (Hint: There are two misspelled words.) When the spelling check is complete, click **OK** to close the dialog box.

7. Using either the **Slides tab** or the **Slide Sorter View**, move **Slide 4** so that it becomes **Slide 3**. Then move **Slide 6** so that it becomes **Slide 5**.

8. Display the **Header and Footer** dialog box, and click the **Slide tab**. Add numbers to each slide by selecting the **Slide number** check box, and then clear all the other check boxes on this tab. Click **Apply to All**.

(Project 1E–Budget continues on the next page)

PowerPoint
chapter one
Performance Assessments (continued)

(Project 1E–Budget continued)

9. Display the **Header and Footer** dialog box again, and click the **Notes and Handouts tab**. On the **Notes and Handouts tab**, check that the **Footer** check box is selected, click in the **Footer** box, and then create a footer that will print on all the notes and handouts pages as follows: **1E Budget-Firstname Lastname**

10. Clear all the other check boxes on the **Notes and Handouts tab**, and then click the **Apply to All** button.

11. Display the **Print** dialog box. **Print** the presentation as **handouts**, **6** slides per page in **horizontal** order. Set the **Color/grayscale** to **Grayscale**, and if necessary, select the **Frame slides** check box. After printing the handout page, print in **grayscale** the **notes pages** for **Slide 3** only.

12. On the Standard toolbar, click the **Save** button to save the changes to your presentation. **Close** the presentation.

 You have completed Project 1E

1022   **PowerPoint** | Chapter 1: Getting Started with PowerPoint 2003

PowerPoint chapter one
Performance Assessments (continued)

Project 1F — Education

Objectives: *Start and Exit PowerPoint, Edit a Presentation Using the Outline/Slides Pane, Format and Edit a Presentation Using the Slide Pane, View a Slide Show, Create Headers and Footers, and Print a Presentation.*

In the following Performance Assessment, you will edit a presentation for a school district board meeting concerning Community Education Programs in the City of Desert Park. Your completed presentation will look similar to the one shown in Figure 1.42. You will save your presentation as *1F_Education_Firstname_Lastname*.

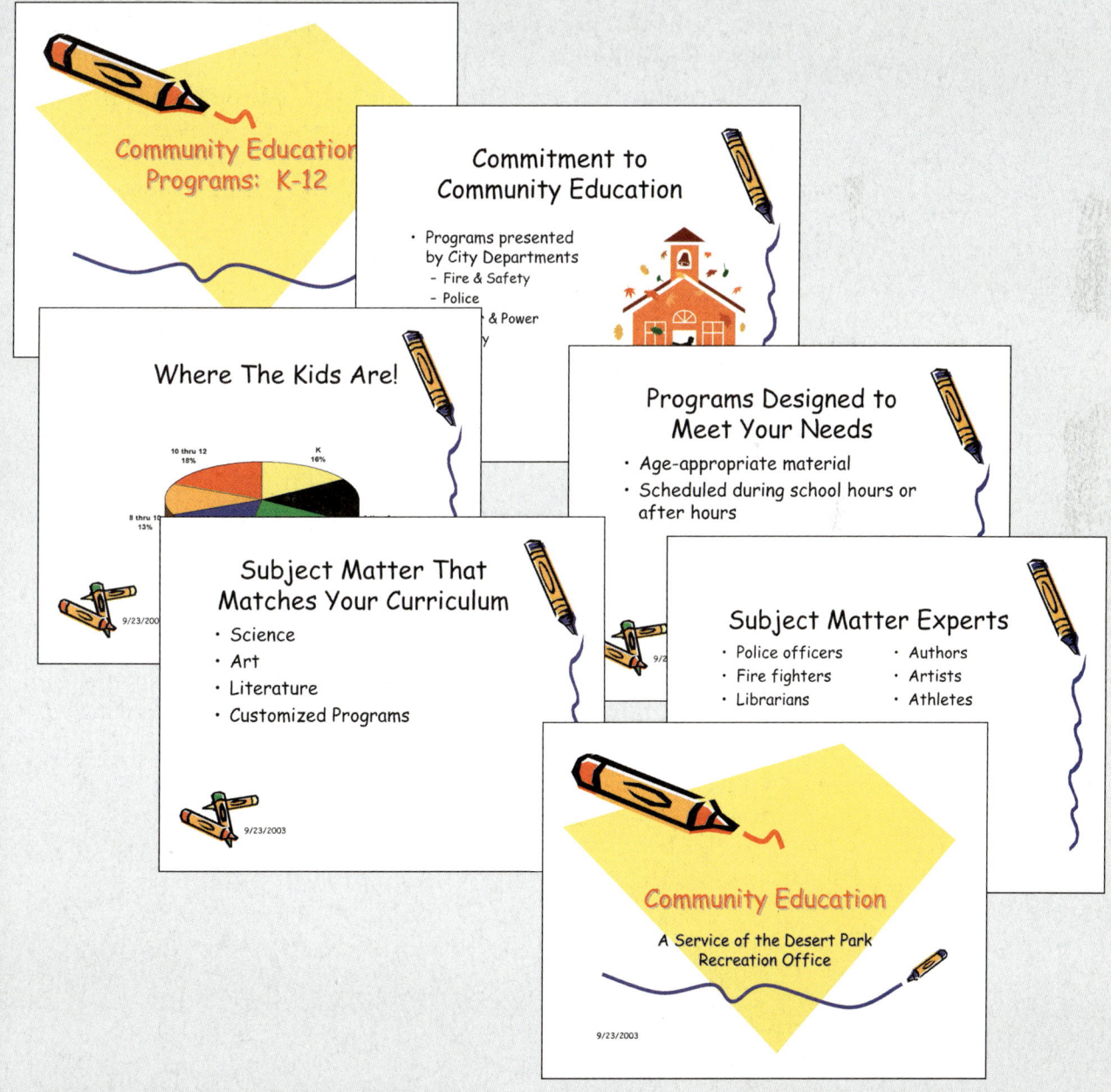

Figure 1.42

(**Project 1F**–Education continues on the next page)

PowerPoint chapter one

Performance Assessments (continued)

(Project 1F–Education continued)

1. Start PowerPoint, and from your student files, open the file **p01F_Education**. Display the **File** menu, click **Save As**, and then use the **Save in arrow** to navigate to the location where you are storing your projects for this chapter. In the **File name** box, type **1F_Education_Firstname_Lastname**

2. Use the **Next Page** button to scroll through the slides. In the **Slide** pane, right-click on any misspelled words that are flagged with a wavy red line, and select the proper spelling. In the **Outline/Slides** pane, click to display the **Outline tab**.

3. Display **Slide 3** and notice that there is no title. In the **Slide** pane, click in the title placeholder and add the following title to the slide: **Where The Kids Are!**

4. In the **Outline tab**, on **Slide 4**, promote the last bulleted item to a new slide title. (Hint: Click anywhere in the bulleted item, and click **Decrease Indent**. This must be done in the Outline tab; the Decrease Indent button is not available when the insertion point is in the Slide pane.)

5. In the new **Slide 5**, in the **Outline tab**, click to position the insertion point after *Curriculum*. Press [Enter] once, and then click the **Increase Indent** button to create the first bulleted item in **Slide 5**. Add the following four bullets to the new slide:

    Science
    Art
    Literature
    Customized Programs

6. Add the following note in the **Notes** pane of **Slide 5**:

    Discuss the activities that the Community Education Outreach program offers in these subject areas.

7. On **Slide 6**, change the **Slide Layout** to **Title and 2–Column Text**. In the **Slide** pane, in the second column, type the following three bullets. Notice that in the **Outline tab**, the two columns are numbered.

    Authors
    Artists
    Athletes

(Project 1F–Education continues on the next page)

Performance Assessments (continued)

(Project 1F–Education continued)

8. In the **Outline tab**, on **Slide 6**, click at the end of the last bullet in the second column, and then press Enter to create a bullet. Then click the **Decrease Indent** button to promote the bullet to a new slide—**Slide 7**. Type the title of the new slide as **Community Education**

9. Change the **Slide Layout** of **Slide 7** to **Title Slide**. Notice that the picture and formatting applied to the **Slide 1** title slide is also applied here. In the **Slide** pane, add the following subtitle: **A Service of the Desert Park Recreation Office**

10. Using the **Header and Footer** command, include on all **slides** the date so that it updates automatically; remove all other header and footer formatting from the slides. On the **Notes and Handouts**, include the **page number** and footer as follows: **1F Education-Firstname Lastname**

11. Clear all other header and footer options on the notes and handouts, and click **Apply to All**. Select **Slide 1**, and then view the presentation as a slide show. Notice that the current date displays on each slide. Slide transitions and animations have been applied.

12. Print the presentation as **handouts**, **4 per page** in **grayscale** and in **horizontal** order. Then, print the **notes page**, in **grayscale**, for **Slide 5** only. Save any changes to your presentation and then close the file.

 You have completed Project 1F

PowerPoint chapter one
Performance Assessments (continued)

Project 1G — Internet

Objectives: *Start and Exit PowerPoint, Edit a Presentation Using the Outline/Slides Pane, Format and Edit a Presentation Using the Slide Pane, View and Edit a Presentation in Slide Sorter View, View a Slide Show, Create Headers and Footers, and Print a Presentation.*

In the following Performance Assessment, you will edit a presentation regarding Internet access at City Hall. Your completed presentation will look similar to the one shown in Figure 1.43. You will save your presentation as *1G_Internet_Firstname_Lastname*.

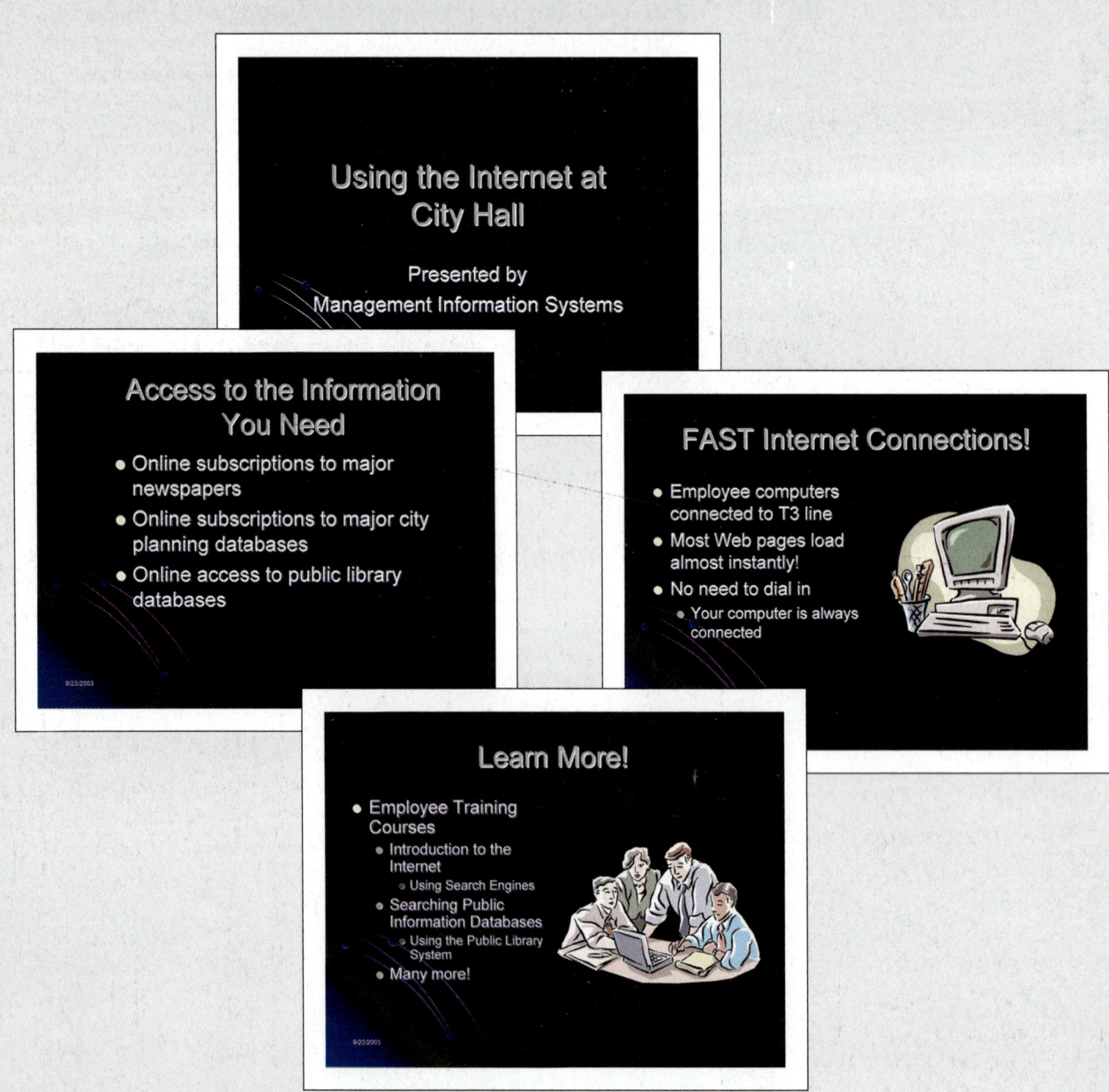

Figure 1.43

(**Project 1G**–Internet continues on the next page)

1026   **PowerPoint** | Chapter 1: Getting Started with PowerPoint 2003

Performance Assessments (continued)

(Project 1G–Internet continued)

1. From your student files, open the file **p01G_Internet**. Display the **File** menu, click **Save As**, and then use the **Save in arrow** to navigate to the location where you are storing your projects for this chapter. In the **File name** box, type 1G_Internet_Firstname_Lastname

2. Use the **Next Page** button or the vertical scroll bar in the **Slide** pane to scroll through the slides to familiarize yourself with the presentation. As you do so, correct any spelling errors.

3. Change the **Slide Layout** for **Slide 1** to **Title Slide**. Click in the subtitle placeholder and type:

   Presented by
   Management Information Systems

4. Close the **Slide Layout** task pane to maximize your viewing area. Display **Slide 2** and open the **Outline tab**. In the last bulleted item, click after the words *dial in* and then press Enter to create a new bullet. Delete the hyphen (-) and any unnecessary spaces. Capitalize the word *your* and then demote the text by one level.

5. Display **Slide 4**. Demote by one level the two bullets—*Using Search Engines* and *Using the Public Library System*. Promote by one level the last bullet—*Many more!*

6. Create a note for **Slide 4** using the following text: **Employees should call MIS for information regarding workshops.**

7. Switch to **Slide Sorter View**. Delete the last slide in the presentation, and then move **Slide 3** so that it becomes **Slide 2**.

8. Display the **Header and Footer** dialog box. On the **Slide tab**, add the **Date** so that it displays and updates automatically. Clear any other formatting on the slides, and apply to *all* slides. On the **Notes and Handouts**, create the footer **1G Internet-Firstname Lastname** and then *clear* all other header and footer options.

9. Click the **Save** button to save the changes you have made to your presentation.

10. Select **Slide 1** and run the slide show. Then, print the presentation as **handouts**, **4** per page in **horizontal** order. Use **grayscale** and **frame** the slides. Print the **notes page** for **Slide 4**. Close the file.

End You have completed Project 1G

PowerPoint Chapter 1

Mastery Assessments

Project 1H — Housing

Objectives: *Start and Exit PowerPoint, Edit a Presentation Using the Outline/Slides Pane, Create Headers and Footers, and Print a Presentation.*

In the following Mastery Assessment, you will edit a presentation regarding access to affordable housing in the City of Desert Park. Your completed presentation will look similar to the one shown in Figure 1.44. You will save your presentation as *1H_Housing_Firstname_Lastname*.

Figure 1.44

(**Project 1H**–Housing continues on the next page)

1028   **PowerPoint** | Chapter 1: Getting Started with PowerPoint 2003

Mastery Assessments (continued)

(Project 1H–Housing continued)

1. From your student files, open the file **p01H_Housing**. Save the file as **1H_Housing_Firstname_Lastname** and then scroll through the slides to familiarize yourself with the presentation. As you do so, correct any spelling errors.

2. On **Slide 1**, apply the **Title Slide** layout. **On Slide 3**, demote the second bullet. In the **Outline tab**, promote the last bullet on **Slide 3** to a new slide, creating **Slide 4**. Using Figure 1.45 as a guide, create **Slide 4** by applying the appropriate slide layout (**Title and 2–Column Text**) and typing the text, demoting text as necessary.

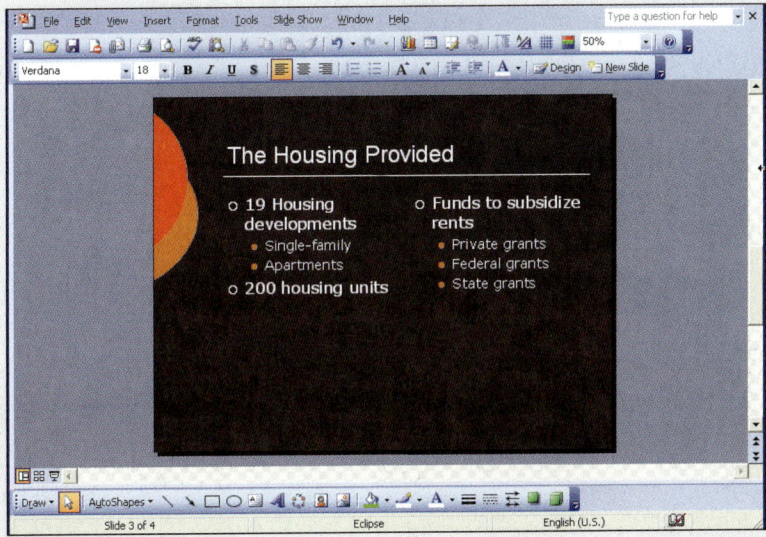

Figure 1.45

3. Move **Slide 2** so that it is the last slide, and then type the following speaker's notes on **Slide 4**:

   Members of the Board of Commissioners serve a three-year term with a maximum of three board members appointed in any given year.

4. Add the slide number to all of the slides, and remove any other slide headers or footers. On the **Notes and Handouts**, include only the date so that it updates automatically, and the footer **1H Housing-Firstname Lastname**

5. Print the presentation as **handouts**, **4** per page in **horizontal** order. Select **Grayscale** and **frame** the slides. Print the notes page for **Slide 4**. Save your changes and close the file.

End You have completed Project 1H

Mastery Assessments (continued)

Project 1I—Membership

Objectives: *Start and Exit PowerPoint, Edit a Presentation Using the Outline/Slides Pane, Format and Edit a Presentation Using the Slide Pane, View a Slide Show, Create Headers and Footers, and Print a Presentation.*

In the following Mastery Assessment, you will edit a presentation regarding membership in the City of Desert Park Nature Center. Your completed presentation will look similar to the one shown in Figure 1.46. You will save your presentation as *1I_Membership_Firstname_Lastname*.

Figure 1.46

(Project 1I–Membership continues on the next page)

Mastery Assessments (continued)

(Project 1I–Membership continued)

1. From your student files, open the file **p01I_Membership**. **Save** the presentation in your storage location as 1I_Membership_Firstname_Lastname On **Slide 1**, change the slide layout to **Title Slide**.

2. On **Slide 3**, demote the second bullet—*Parking is included* and then demote the last two bullets.

3. Display **Slide 5**. Change the slide layout to **Title** and **2–Column Text**. In the second column type the following, indenting the addresses so that the second column is formatted similar to the first column:

   Heron Crest Ranch
   4949 Heron Road
   Pine Creek Canyon
   558 Meadow Lane

4. **Delete Slide 4**. **Move Slide 3** so that it becomes **Slide 2**.

5. Add the **Slide number** to all of the slides, and remove any other header or footer formatting on the slides. Create a footer for the notes and handouts pages by typing 1I Membership-Firstname Lastname. Remove any other header or footer formatting on the notes and handouts pages.

6. Display **Slide 1**, and then view the slide show. Slide transitions and animations have been applied. Print the presentation as **handouts**, **4** per page in **horizontal** order—use **grayscale** and frame the slides. Save your changes and close the file.

End You have completed Project 1I

PowerPoint chapter one
Problem Solving

Project 1J—Park

Objectives: *Start and Exit PowerPoint, Edit a Presentation Using the Outline/Slides Pane, Format and Edit a Presentation Using the Slide Pane, View and Edit a Presentation in Slide Sorter View, Create Headers and Footers, and Print a Presentation.*

Create the content for a presentation regarding a new community park for the City of Desert Park. You will save your presentation as *1J_Park_Firstname_Lastname*.

1. Open the file **p01J_Park**. Save the presentation in your storage location as **1J_Park_Firstname_Lastname** and then notice that this presentation contains two slides—a title slide and a second slide with four bullets.

2. In the **Outline tab**, promote each of the bullets on the second slide to slide titles so that there are a total of six slides. Think about parks in your own community, and then develop at least three bullets for each slide based on the new slide title. The Web site for your local community might be a good source of ideas. Be sure to also develop content for the second slide—*The Westside Community*. Apply an appropriate slide layout to each slide.

3. Create speaker's notes for at least one slide in the presentation. Review the presentation and change the order of the slides if necessary. On the notes and handouts pages, create a footer with the file name and your name in the same manner as the other projects in this chapter.

4. Print notes pages and handouts, 6 slides per page. Save your changes and close the file.

End You have completed Project 1J

PowerPoint chapter one

Problem Solving (continued)

Project 1K — Traveling

Objectives: *Start and Exit PowerPoint, Edit a Presentation Using the Outline/Slides Pane, Format and Edit a Presentation Using the Slide Pane, View and Edit a Presentation in Slide Sorter View, View a Slide Show, Create Headers and Footers, and Print a Presentation.*

Create the content for a presentation regarding tips for parents traveling with children to the Grand Canyon. To create this presentation you will need to conduct research on the Grand Canyon to determine the types of activities that children would like. You should also gather information on traveling by car or train with children. You will save your presentation as *1K_Traveling_Firstname_Lastname*.

1. From your student files, open the file **p01K_Traveling**, and save it to your storage location as **1K_Traveling_Firstname_Lastname** This presentation contains a title slide. Create five additional slides based on your research. Your slides may include general information about the Grand Canyon, methods of travel, weather conditions at various times of the year, activities for children, and keeping children safe and occupied while traveling.

2. Change slide layout as necessary, and create notes for at least two slides in your presentation. Create appropriate footers on the slides and handouts, including your name and the filename on the handouts.

3. Save the changes to your presentation, and then print notes pages and handouts, 6 slides per page.

 End You have completed Project 1K

On the Internet

Preparing for Microsoft Certification

As you progress through this textbook you will learn the skills necessary to complete the Microsoft certification test for PowerPoint 2003. Access your Internet connection and go to the Microsoft certification Web site at **www.microsoft.com/traincert/mcp/officespecialist/requirements.asp** Navigate to the Microsoft PowerPoint objectives for the certification exam. Print the objectives for the Microsoft PowerPoint user certification and any other information about taking the test.

GO! with Help

Getting Help While You Work

The PowerPoint Help system is extensive and can help you as you work. In this exercise, you will view information about getting help as you work in PowerPoint.

1. Start PowerPoint. In the **Type a question for help** box, type **How can I get help while I work?**

2. In the displayed **Search Results** task pane, click the result—**About getting help while you work**. Maximize the displayed window, and below the Help toolbar, click **Show All**. Scroll through and read all the various ways you can get help while working in PowerPoint.

3. On the Help toolbar, click the **Print** button.

PowerPoint 2003

chapter two

Creating a Presentation

In this chapter, you will: complete these projects and practice these skills.

Project 2A
Creating a Marketing Presentation

Objectives
- Create a Presentation
- Modify Slides

Project 2B
Creating a Company History Presentation

Objectives
- Create a Presentation Using a Design Template
- Import Text from Word
- Move and Copy Text

El Cuero Specialty Wares

El Cuero de Mexico is a Mexico City-based manufacturer of high-quality small leather goods for men and women. Their products include wallets, belts, handbags, key chains, and travel bags. The company distributes its products to department and specialty stores in the United States and Canada through its San Diego-based subsidiary, El Cuero Specialty Wares. Plans are currently under way for a new marketing campaign focusing on several new lines that will be unveiled next year.

© Getty Images, Inc.

Creating a Presentation

In this chapter you will create a new presentation and modify slides by changing the presentation design and the location of text. You will also import presentation text from existing presentations and from a word processor outline.

When creating a presentation, keep your audience in mind. Find out the size of the audience and the level of knowledge your audience has about your topic. Learn as much as you can about the age, educational level, occupation, and cultural background of your audience. This information will help you develop a great presentation.

Project 2A Teenagers

There are a variety of methods that you can use to create a new presentation in Microsoft Office PowerPoint 2003. The method that you choose will depend on your content and design ideas. Well-defined content may be created in the PowerPoint outline, and then a design may be applied. Alternatively, a design may be created first and content entered later. You may also decide to use content derived from one of the many PowerPoint AutoContent templates. Choose the method that works best for you.

In Activities 2.1 through 2.6 you will create a new presentation for Richard Kelly, the Vice President of Marketing for El Cuero Specialty Wares. You will also modify the presentation by inserting new and existing slides. The six slides of your completed project will look similar to Figure 2.1. You will save your presentation as *2A_Teenagers_Firstname_Lastname*.

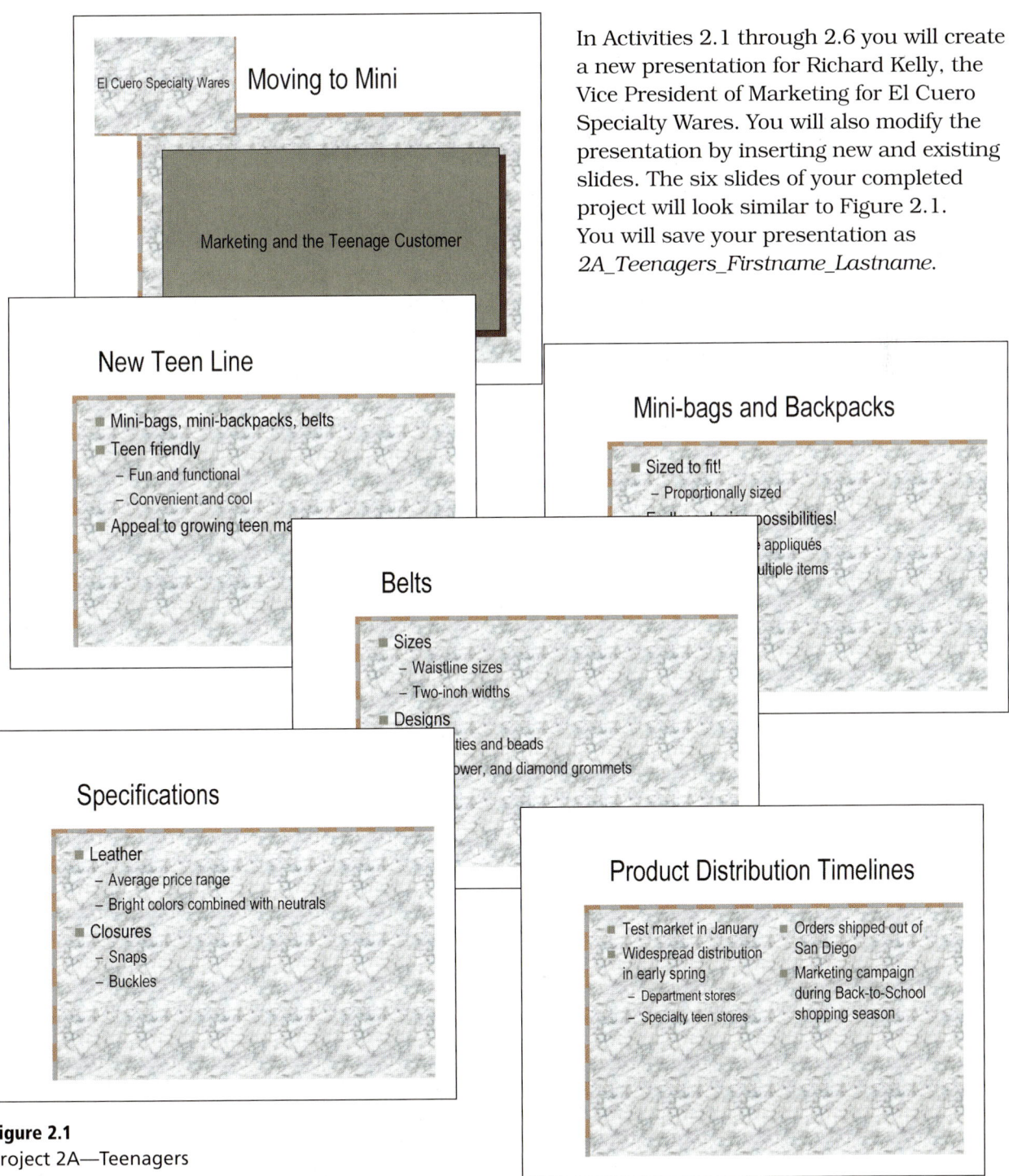

Figure 2.1
Project 2A—Teenagers

Objective 1
Create a Presentation

In the following activities, you will create a new presentation using the **AutoContent Wizard**. The AutoContent Wizard is a feature that leads you step-by-step through the creation of a presentation by asking you questions about the presentation that you want to create. You will also create new slides and insert slides from an existing presentation.

Activity 2.1 Creating a Presentation Using the AutoContent Wizard

In this activity, you will create a presentation using the AutoContent Wizard. You will edit the content of several slides and delete several that are unnecessary to the presentation.

1 **Start** *start* Microsoft Office PowerPoint 2003. On the menu bar, click the **File** menu, and then click **New**.

The New Presentation task pane displays. This task pane provides five methods that you can use to start a new presentation. The table in Figure 2.2 describes each of these methods.

Methods for Starting a New Presentation

Method	Description
Blank presentation	A simple method in which you type your text in a blank presentation using the Outline or the Slides pane.
From design template	A model on which a presentation is based, including graphic elements, animations, and a *color scheme*—a coordinated palette of eight colors that includes background, text, bullet, and accent colors.
From AutoContent wizard	A feature that leads you step-by-step through the creation of a presentation by asking you questions about the presentation that you want to create.
From existing presentation	A presentation that already contains design and content that you want to use, which is then opened and saved with a new name.
Photo album	A presentation containing pictures that fill every slide.

Figure 2.2

2 In the **New Presentation** task pane, click **From AutoContent wizard**.

The AutoContent Wizard displays, as shown in Figure 2.3. If the Office Assistant displays asking if you would like help with this feature, click *No, don't provide help now*. On the left side of the AutoContent Wizard box is a roadmap indicating the steps that you will complete in order to generate a presentation. As you proceed through the Wizard, the green box moves to the next step in the process. At any time, you can click the Next or Back buttons to change the responses that you have made.

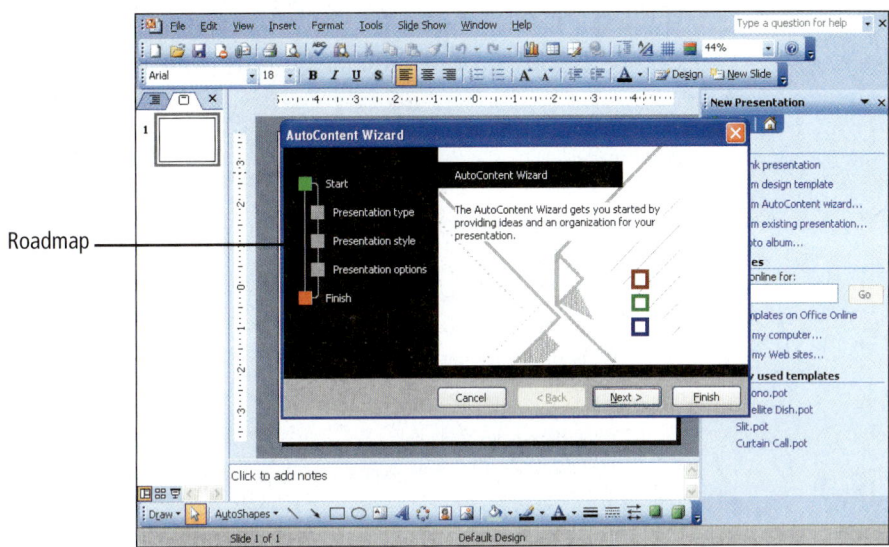

Roadmap

Figure 2.3

3 In the lower right corner, click the **Next** button to proceed to the Presentation type step.

In the Presentation type step, you choose the type of presentation that most closely resembles the presentation that you want to create. Notice that in the center of the dialog box there are five buttons that indicate the categories into which the presentations are grouped.

4 Click the **General** button, notice the types of presentations listed for this presentation category, and then take a moment to click each of the buttons to view the types of presentations listed to the right.

5 When you have finished clicking each category button, click the **Sales/Marketing** button. In the list to the right, click **Product/Services Overview**, and then in the lower right corner, click **Next**.

The Presentation style step displays. Notice that the green box moves to indicate that the Presentation style step is active. In the Presentation style step, you can choose the output that you want to create. Recall that you can use PowerPoint to create presentations on the Web, black-and-white or color transparencies, or 35 mm slides. This will be an on-screen presentation.

6 If necessary, click **On-screen presentation**, and then click **Next**.

The Presentation options step displays.

Project 2A: Teenagers | **PowerPoint** 1039

7 Click in the **Presentation title** box and type **Moving to Mini** so that this text will display on the title slide in the title placeholder. If necessary, delete any text that displays in the **Footer** box, and click to *clear* the **Date last updated** and **Slide number** check boxes so that these do *not* display on the slides. Compare your screen to Figure 2.4.

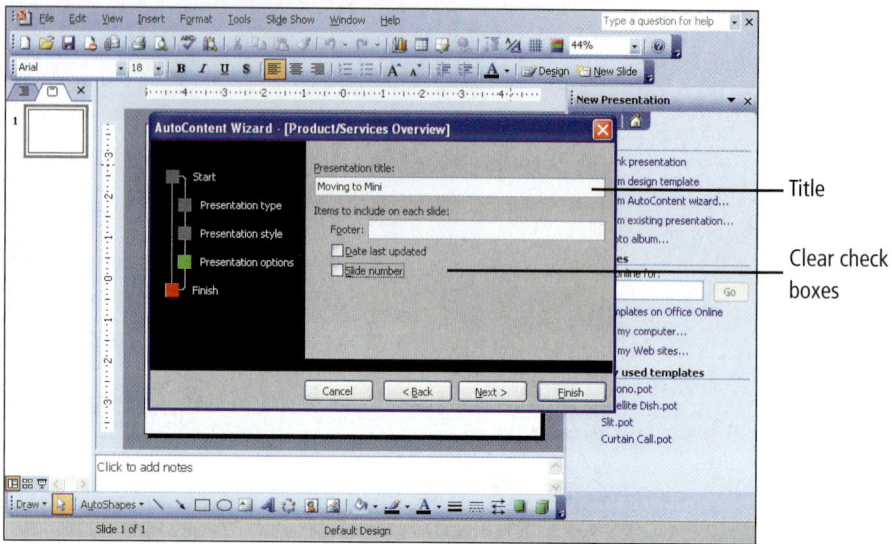

Figure 2.4

8 Click **Next**, and then click **Finish** to create the presentation.

A new presentation displays in Normal view. Depending on your system configuration, a name or other text may display in the subtitle placeholder located in the center of the slide.

9 On the menu bar, click the **File** menu, and then click **Save As**. Navigate to the drive and directory in which you are storing your projects for this chapter, and then create a new Chapter 2 folder if you want to do so. In the **File name** box, type **2A_Teenagers_Firstname_Lastname** and then click **Save** or press [Enter]. Be sure to type your name in the **file name** box, not Firstname_Lastname. Keep the file open for the next activity.

Activity 2.2 Modifying AutoContent Presentation Text

In this activity, you will modify the text in your presentation according to the suggestions in your AutoContent presentation.

1 If necessary, display the presentation Outline by moving to the **View** buttons and then clicking **Normal View**. In the **Outline/Slides** pane, click the **Outline tab**.

2 Look at the **Status bar** and notice that this presentation contains 7 slides. In the vertical scrollbar, use the **Next Slide** button to scroll through the presentation and view each slide. On each slide, read the suggested content in the titles and text placeholders. This is one way that PowerPoint helps you to think about the information you want to include in your presentation. When you have finished reading each slide, display **Slide 1**.

3 The text *Your Logo Here* displays in the upper left corner of **Slide 1** in the **Slide** pane. Click anywhere in the text *Your Logo Here* to activate the placeholder.

Recall that a placeholder reserves a portion of a slide and serves as a container for text, graphics, and other slide elements.

4 Point to the text *Your Logo Here*, press and hold down Ctrl, and then click the left mouse button.

The text *Your Logo Here* is selected.

5 Type **El Cuero Specialty Wares** and notice that *Your Logo Here* is deleted as you type the text. Do not be concerned if the text extends outside the boundaries of the placeholder.

6 If necessary, select and delete the text in the subtitle placeholder and type **Marketing and the Teenage Customer** to create a subtitle for the slide. Compare your slide to Figure 2.5.

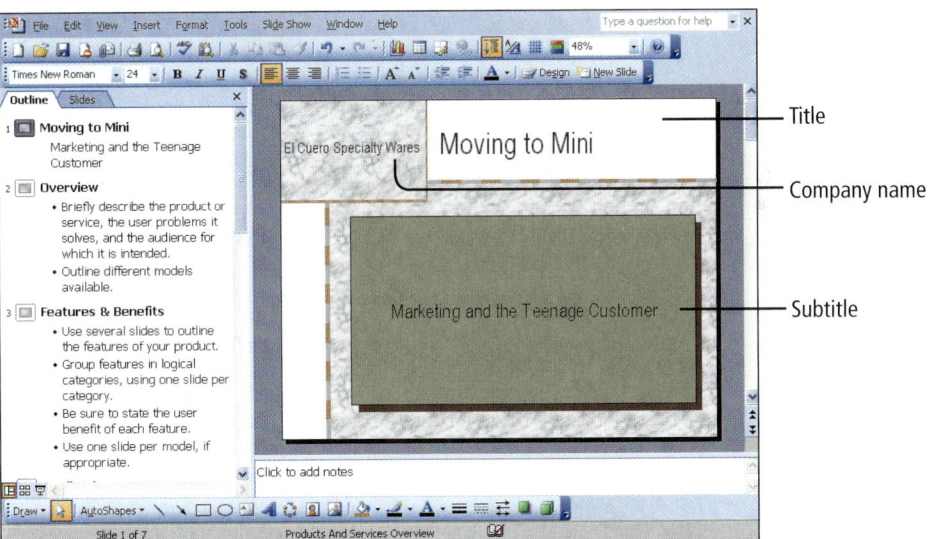

Figure 2.5

Project 2A: Teenagers | **PowerPoint** 1041

7 Display **Slide 2**.

Recall that the purpose of this presentation is to give an overview of a product or service. Thus, the content suggested for Slide 2 is a brief description of the product.

8 Move your pointer into the **Outline** pane and point to the title of **Slide 2**—*Overview*. Double-click to select the word *Overview*. Alternatively, you can drag to select the word. Type **New Teen Line** to create a new title for **Slide 2**.

9 In the **Outline** pane on **Slide 2**, point to the first bullet so that the four-headed arrow displays, and then click the left mouse button.

The entire first bullet point is selected.

10 With the first bullet point selected, press and hold down [Shift], and then on **Slide 2**, click the second bullet.

All of the bulleted text on Slide 2 is selected.

11 On your keyboard, press [Delete]. Type **Mini-bags, mini-backpacks, belts** and then press [Enter].

12 Type the text in the outline in Figure 2.6, demoting and promoting text as necessary. Recall that on the Formatting toolbar, the **Increase Indent** and **Decrease Indent** buttons can be used to demote and promote text, respectively.

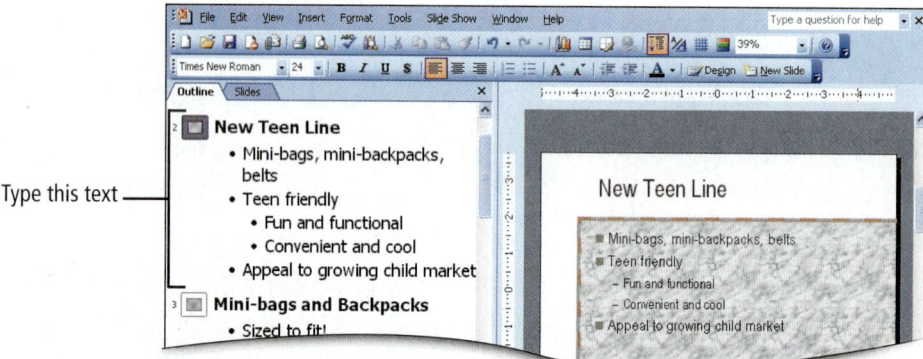

Figure 2.6

[13] Display **Slide 5**. Delete the bulleted text on this slide and type the text in Figure 2.7. **Save** your file.

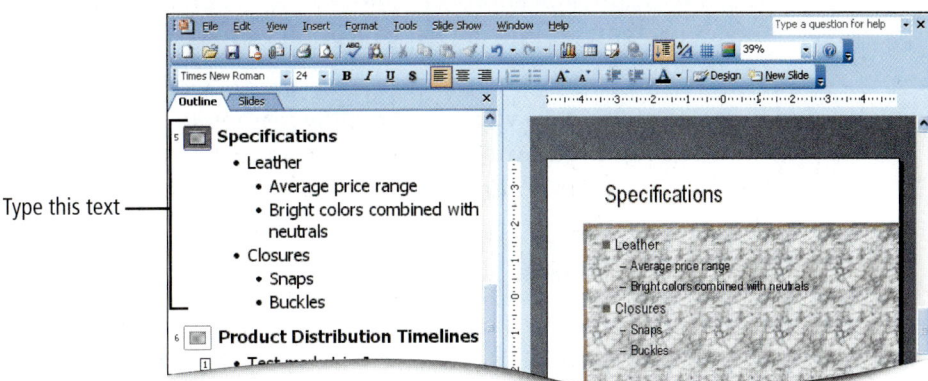

Type this text

Figure 2.7

[14] Several of the slides generated by the AutoContent Wizard are not necessary in this presentation. Recall that you can delete slides using Slide Sorter View. Click **Slide Sorter View**.

All of the slides in the presentation are displayed.

[15] Click **Slide 4** so that a border surrounds it, indicating that it is selected. Press and hold down Ctrl, and then click **Slide 6**. Recall that this action allows you to select nonadjacent slides. Press and hold down Ctrl, and then click **Slide 7**.

[16] With **Slides 4**, **6**, and **7** selected, press Delete.

The three selected slides are removed from the presentation and four slides remain.

[17] Double-click **Slide 1**.

Slide 1 displays in Normal view. Alternatively, click Normal View and then display Slide 1.

[18] On the Standard toolbar, click **Save** to save the changes you have made to your presentation.

Activity 2.3 Inserting Slides from an Existing Presentation

Teamwork is an important aspect of all organizations, and presentations are often shared among employees. Another employee may create several slides for a presentation that you are developing. Rather than re-creating the slides, you can insert slides from an existing presentation into the current presentation.

In this activity, you will delete a slide from your presentation and insert two slides from an existing presentation into your 2A_Teenagers presentation. The slides you insert will become the third and fourth slides in the presentation.

1 Display **Slide 3**.

To insert slides from an existing presentation into the current presentation, display the slide that will precede—*come before*—the slide or slides to be inserted. The content suggested for this slide includes the features of the product. The features for the new products are contained in the presentation p02A_Content.

2 On the menu bar, click **Insert**, and then click **Slides from Files**. In the **Slide Finder** dialog box, click the **Find Presentation tab**, and then click the **Browse** button. Navigate to your student files, and then double-click the file name **p02A_Content**. Alternatively, you can click the file name p02A_Content and then click Open.

In the Slide Finder dialog box under Select slides, the three slides in the p02A_Content presentation display. See Figure 2.8.

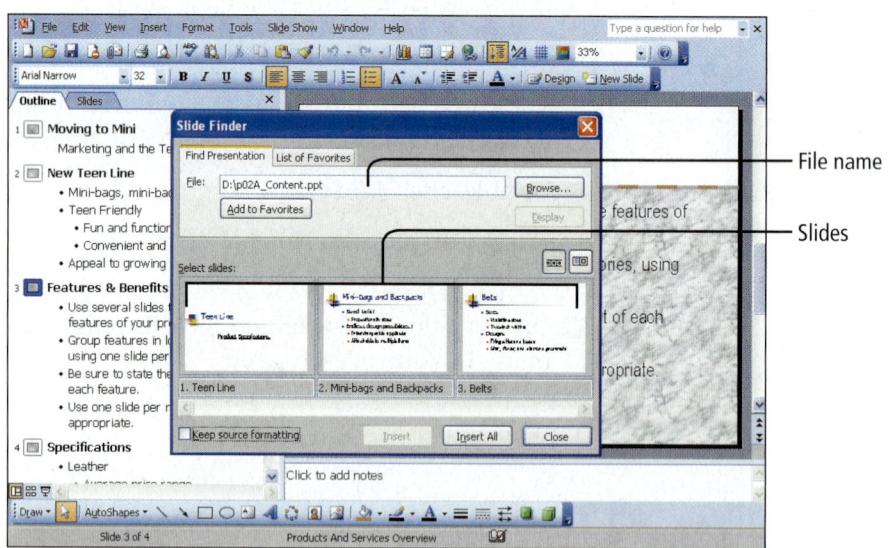

Figure 2.8

3 Under **Select slides**, click **Slides 1**, **2**, and **3**.

Each slide is selected, indicated by the border surrounding each slide.

4 If necessary, *clear* the **Keep source formatting** check box at the lower left corner.

Clearing this check box ensures that when you insert slides from another presentation, the formatting, design, and color of your presentation override the formatting, design, and color of the slides from which the presentation was derived.

5 Click **Slide 1** again and notice that the slide is no longer selected. In the lower center of the dialog box, click the **Insert** button.

The second and third slides of the p02A_Content presentation are inserted as the fourth and fifth slides of the 2A_Teenagers presentation.

6 In the displayed **Slide Finder** dialog box, click the **Close** button.

> **Note** — Inserting All Slides
>
> To insert all of the slides from a presentation displayed in the Slide Finder dialog box, click the Insert All button.

7 Display **Slide 3**. On the **Edit** menu, click **Delete Slide**.

Slide 3 is deleted.

8 **Save** the changes you have made to your presentation.

Activity 2.4 Inserting a New Slide

You can insert a new slide into a presentation using one of four techniques. You can click the New Slide button on the Formatting toolbar, you can click New Slide on the Insert menu, you can press [Ctrl] and press [M], or you can position the insertion point in the last placeholder on a slide and press [Ctrl] and press [Enter]. In this activity, you will use the New Slide button to insert a new, sixth slide.

1 Display **Slide 5** so that you can create a new **Slide 6**. On the Formatting toolbar, click the **New Slide** button.

A new Slide 6 is inserted. Depending on your system settings, the Slide Layout task pane may display.

2 If necessary, display the **Slide Layout** task pane by clicking the **Format** menu and then clicking **Slide Layout**.

3 Under **Text Layouts**, in the second row, click **Title and 2-Column Text**. **Close** the task pane, and then **Close** the Outline/Slides pane.

4 Click in the title placeholder and type **Product Distribution Timelines**

5 Type the slide text shown in Figure 2.9.

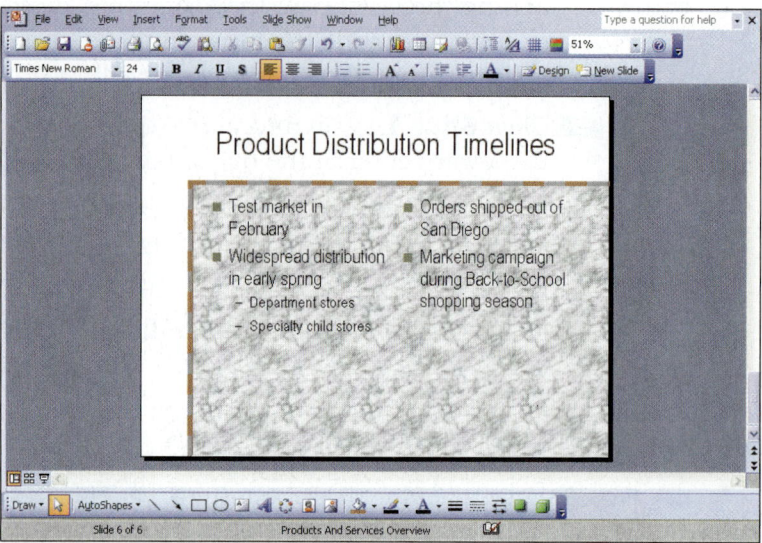

Figure 2.9

6 Save the presentation.

Objective 2
Modify Slides

In the following activities, you will modify slides by finding and replacing text and by using the Undo and Redo commands.

Activity 2.5 Finding and Replacing Text

Throughout this presentation, the word *child* is used to describe the new product line. The word *teen* more accurately describes the product. You could scroll through the presentation and change each occurrence of *child* to *teen*. PowerPoint provides an easier method for you to change all of the occurrences of a word to another word by using the Replace command.

1 Display **Slide 1**. On the menu bar, click the **Edit** menu, and then click **Replace**.

2 In the displayed **Replace** dialog box, in the **Find what** box, type **child** to instruct PowerPoint to search for all occurrences of the word *child*.

3 Press Tab to move the insertion point to the **Replace with** box, and then type **teen**

[4] In the lower left corner of the dialog box, if necessary, *clear* the **Match case** check box.

The Match case option instructs PowerPoint to match the capitalization in the Find what and Replace with boxes. In this instance, you are instructing PowerPoint to replace all occurrences of *child* with *teen*, regardless of the capitalization.

[5] Click to place a check mark in the **Find whole words only** check box.

When the Find whole words only option is checked, PowerPoint finds the word *child*. It will not find a word in which the word *child* is contained, such as *children*. Compare your dialog box to Figure 2.10.

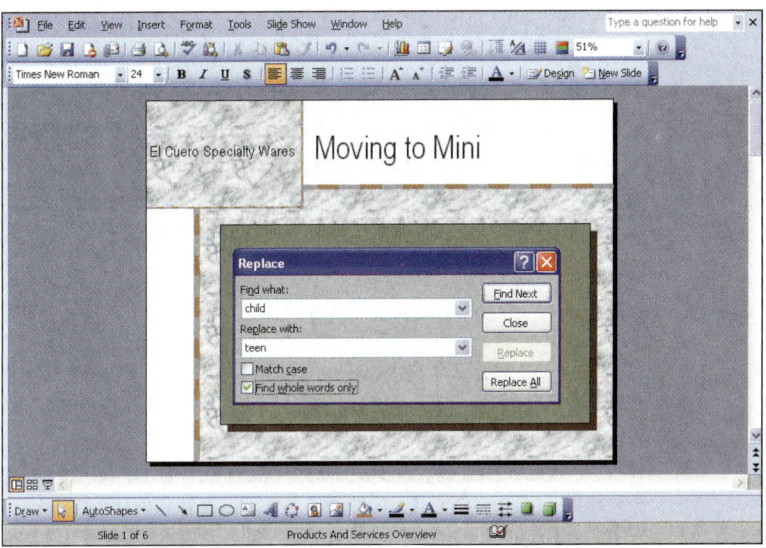

Figure 2.10

[6] In the lower right corner of the **Replace** dialog box, click the **Replace All** button.

PowerPoint searches the presentation and indicates that two replacements were made.

[7] Click **OK** to close the box indicating the number of replacements. Click **Close** to close the **Replace** dialog box.

More Knowledge — Replacing Text

To replace some, but not all, occurrences of a word, use the Find Next button in the Replace dialog box to instruct PowerPoint to stop at each occurrence of the *Find what* text. Then click Replace if you want to replace the selected occurrence, or click Find Next to skip to the next occurrence without replacing.

[8] **Save** the presentation.

Project 2A: Teenagers | **PowerPoint** 1047

Activity 2.6 Using the Undo and Redo Commands

A useful feature in PowerPoint is the ability to undo a change that you have made. PowerPoint remembers each change so that you can undo these commands if you have changed your mind or performed an action by mistake. You can change your mind again and reverse an undo by using the Redo command.

1. Display **Slide 6**. In the first bullet point, select the word *February*, and then type **January** to replace the selected word.

2. On the Standard toolbar, click the **Undo** button.

   February displays in the slide.

3. On the Standard toolbar, click the **Redo** button.

   January displays in the slide.

4. On the menu bar, click the **View** menu, and then click **Header and Footer**. Click the **Notes and Handouts tab**. If necessary, click to select the **Date and time** check box and then click to select **Update automatically**. Clear the **Header** and **Page number** check boxes. If necessary, click to select the **Footer** check box, and then in the **Footer** box type **2A Teenagers-Firstname Lastname** In the upper right corner of the dialog box, click **Apply to All**.

5. **Save** the file.

6. Display the **File** menu, and then click **Print**. Click the **Print what** arrow, and then click **Handouts**. Under **Handouts**, click the **Slides per page arrow**, and then click **6**. Next to **Order**, click the **Horizontal** option button. Click the **Color/grayscale arrow**, and then click **Grayscale**. Make sure that the **Frame slides** check box is selected. In the lower left corner, click **Preview** to see how your slides will print. Then, on the Print Preview toolbar, click **Print**, and then click **OK**. One sheet will print, with the current date in the upper right corner.

7. **Close** the file and close PowerPoint.

More Knowledge — Using the Undo and Redo Buttons

The list arrows to the right of the Undo and Redo buttons display a list of the undo and redo actions available. Use caution, however, because if you undo an action in the list, you will undo all actions above that item in the list too!

End You have completed Project 2A

Project 2B History

Microsoft Office PowerPoint 2003 includes a variety of **design templates** that you can apply to your presentation. A design template is a model on which a presentation is based, including graphic elements, animations, and a color scheme—a coordinated palette of eight colors that includes background, text, bullet, and accent colors. Additional templates are available on the Microsoft Office Online Web site.

In Activities 2.7 through 2.15, you will create a presentation for Miguel Hernandez, CEO of El Cuero de Mexico, which provides a history and overview of the company. The presentation will be used at an employee dinner. To create the presentation, you will use a design template. You will modify the presentation by importing an outline from Microsoft Word and by copying and moving text. The six slides of your completed presentation will look similar to Figure 2.11. You will save your presentation as *2B_History_Firstname_Lastname*.

Figure 2.11
Project 2B—History

Objective 3
Create a Presentation Using a Design Template

Recall that when you used the AutoContent Wizard to create a new presentation, PowerPoint suggested presentation text and applied background colors to the presentation. You can also create a new presentation based on a design template that does *not* include text. Recall that a design template is a model on which a presentation is based, including graphic elements, animations, and a color scheme.

Activity 2.7 Creating a Presentation from a Design Template

In this activity, you will create a new presentation based on one of the PowerPoint design templates.

1 If necessary, **Start** *start* PowerPoint. On the menu bar, click **File**, and then click **New**. In the displayed **New Presentation** task pane, click **From design template**.

Thumbnail images of each design template display in the Slide Design task pane grouped into three categories: Used in This Presentation, Recently Used (displays only if any were recently used), and Available For Use.

Alert!

Does Your Screen Differ?

Depending on how this task pane was last displayed, the design templates may display in one column with each design template filling the width of the task pane, or the templates may be displayed as smaller images in two columns.

2 Take a moment to view the various design templates by scrolling down using the scroll bar at the right edge of the **Slide Design** task pane. Point to, but do *not* click, several of the designs and notice that a ScreenTip displays the name of the template.

PowerPoint includes a variety of unique design templates using many different color schemes and graphic elements.

3 Under **Available For Use**, locate the dark blue **Shimmer** template and point to it so that a bar with a downward-pointing arrow displays to the right of the design. Click the arrow to display a menu. Click **Apply to All Slides**. See Figure 2.12.

The Shimmer template is applied to a new presentation, which currently contains only a title slide. This template consists of a blue color scheme with white text.

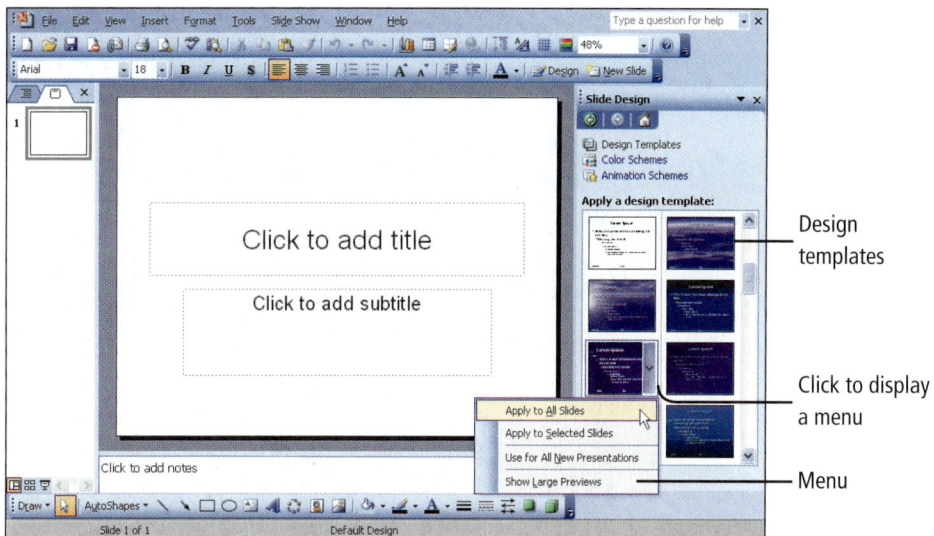

Figure 2.12

Alert! — **Does Your Screen Differ?**

If the Shimmer template does not display, the design templates may need to be installed. Click the Install Additional Templates icon at the lower end of the task pane, to add the template.

4 Close ⊠ the **Slide Design** task pane.

Note — **Locating Design Templates**

If you know the name of a design template, you can quickly locate it by displaying an alphabetical listing of the template names. At the bottom of the Slide Design task pane, click Browse to open the Apply Design Template dialog box. Open the Presentation Designs folder to view the list, and then double click the name of the template that you want to apply to your presentation.

5 Click in the **Title placeholder**, type **El Cuero de Mexico Specialty Wares** and then press and hold down Ctrl and press Enter.

The insertion point moves to the subtitle placeholder. This keyboard shortcut is one of several that allow you to navigate quickly in a presentation.

6 Type **Company History** and then press and hold down Ctrl and press Enter.

A new slide is created with the Title and Text layout. If your insertion point is positioned in the final placeholder on a slide, pressing Ctrl + Enter is a quick method to create a new slide.

Project 2B: History | **PowerPoint** 1051

7 In the Title placeholder, type **How We Started** and then press and hold down [Ctrl] and press [Enter]. Type the text in Figure 2.13.

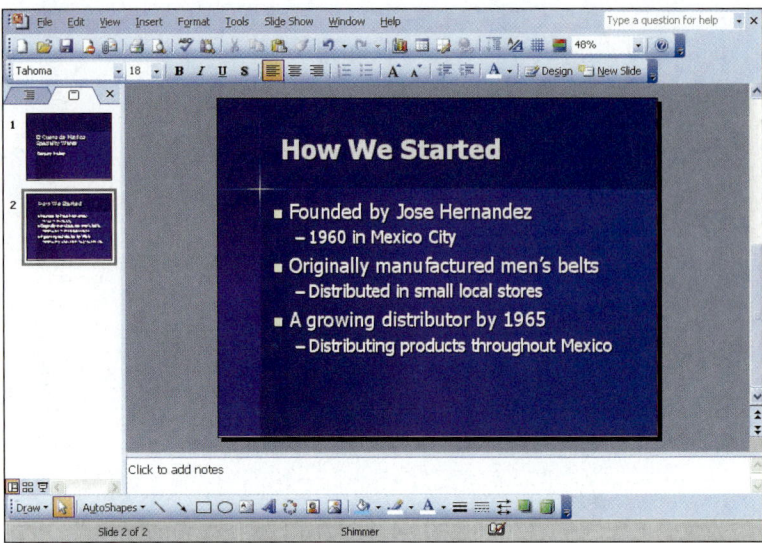

Figure 2.13

8 On the menu bar, click **Insert**, and then click **Slides from Files**.

Recall that in the Slide Finder dialog box, you can navigate to the file that contains the slides that you want to insert.

9 If necessary, click the **Find Presentation tab**, and then click the **Browse** button. Navigate to your student files, and then double-click to open the file name **p02B_Company_History**.

10 At the bottom of the **Slide Finder** dialog box, click **Insert All**, and then click **Close**.

The three slides are inserted into your presentation. This brings the number of slides in your presentation to five.

11 On the menu bar, click **File**, and then click **Save As**. Navigate to the location where your presentations for this chapter are stored. In the **File name** box, type **2B_History_Firstname_Lastname** and then click **Save** or press [Enter].

Activity 2.8 Changing the Design Template for a Single Slide

From the Slide Design task pane, you can change the design template for an entire presentation, for a single slide, or for a selection of slides. In this activity, you will change the design template for the first slide.

1 If the **Outline/Slides** pane is not displayed, click **Normal View**. Click the **Slides tab** to display the slide thumbnails, and then click **Slide 1**.

2 On the Formatting toolbar, click **Slide Design** to display the **Slide Design** task pane.

Another Way — Displaying the Slide Design Task Pane

If another task pane is already displayed, click the Other Task Panes arrow, and then click Slide Design.

3 Locate the **Balance** template and point to it so that a bar with an arrow displays. Click the arrow to display a menu. Click **Apply to Selected Slides**. See Figure 2.14.

Notice on the Slides pane that the Balance template is applied to Slide 1, and the remaining slides still display the Shimmer template.

Figure 2.14

4 Save the presentation.

Activity 2.9 Changing the Design Template for the Entire Presentation

In this activity, you will change the design template for the entire presentation.

1 If necessary, on the Formatting toolbar, click **Design** to display the **Slide Design** task pane.

2 Under **Available For Use**, locate the burgundy colored **Curtain Call** design template and point to it so that a bar with an arrow displays. Click the arrow to display a menu. Click **Apply to All Slides**.

Scroll through the presentation and notice that all of the slides display in the Curtain Call design template.

3 In the **Slide Design** task pane, under **Recently Used**, click **Shimmer**.

Notice that all of the slides in the presentation are formatted with the Shimmer design. If you have not selected any slides, you can click the design template without displaying the menu to apply the template to the entire presentation.

4 **Save** the changes you have made to your presentation.

Activity 2.10 Changing the Design Template for Selected Slides

You can select multiple slides and apply a design to only the slides that you select. In this activity, you will change the design template for Slides 1, 4, and 5.

1 In the **Outline/Slides** pane, click the **Slides tab**. Click **Slide 1** so that a border surrounds it, indicating that the slide is selected. Press and hold down Ctrl, and then click **Slide 4**. Press and hold down Ctrl, and then click **Slide 5**.

Slides 1, 4, and 5 are each surrounded by a border, indicating that all three slides are selected.

2 If necessary, on the Formatting toolbar, click **Design** to display the **Slide Design** task pane.

3 Under **Available For Use**, click the dark blue **Cascade** design template.

The Cascade design template, distinguished by its graphic in the upper left corner, is applied to Slides 1, 4, and 5.

4 **Save** the presentation.

Objective 4
Import Text from Word

A PowerPoint presentation is based on an outline in which bullets are assigned to varying outline text levels. The outline can be typed in PowerPoint or it can be created in a word processing program such as Microsoft Word, and then imported into a PowerPoint presentation. During the import process, PowerPoint converts slide titles and bullet levels based on the indent levels in the imported outline.

Activity 2.11 Importing a Word Outline

In this activity, you will import a Microsoft Word outline that contains text for three of the slides in your presentation.

1 If necessary, **Open** your file **2B_History_Firstname_Lastname** in **Normal View**. Display **Slide 5**. **Close** the task pane if it is open.

2 On the menu bar, click **Insert**, and then click **Slides from Outline**. Navigate to your student files, and then click **p02B_Outline**. In the lower right corner of the **Insert Outline** dialog box, click **Insert**. See Figure 2.15.

The Microsoft Word outline is converted into three new slides—Slides 6, 7, and 8.

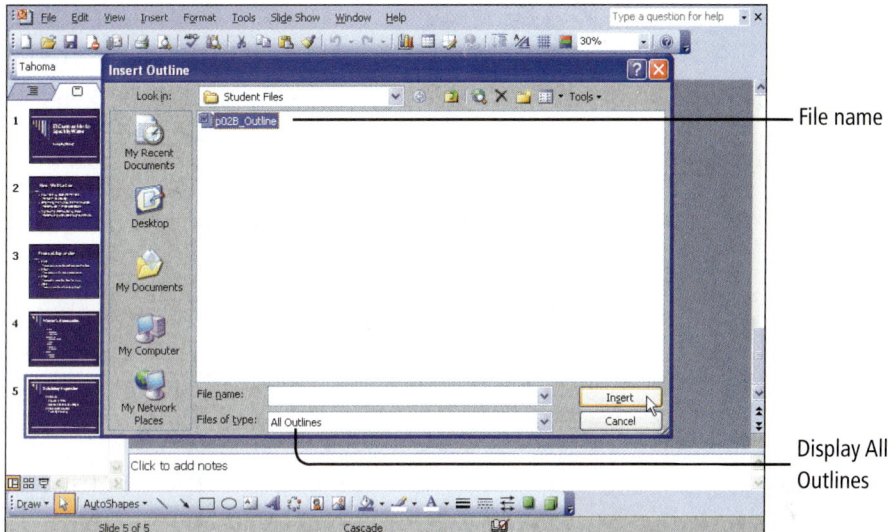

Figure 2.15

> **Note** — Checking the File Type
>
> If the list of files does not display, verify that at the bottom of the Insert Outline dialog box, the Files of type box displays All Outlines.

3 **Save** the presentation.

Project 2B: History | **PowerPoint** 1055

Objective 5
Move and Copy Text

Text that you wish to move or copy (duplicate) can be dragged to another location on a slide or in the outline. You can also rearrange text using the Clipboard task pane. The Clipboard is an area of memory that holds up to 24 selections of text or graphics that you want to copy or move. Additionally, the Clipboard task pane displays the first 50 characters of a selection of text placed there, as well as an icon indicating the source application. The selections of text can be **pasted**—the action of placing text from the Clipboard into a new location—into the same presentation, a different presentation, or another application. You can even place an entire slide on the Clipboard and copy it to another presentation!

Activity 2.12 Moving and Copying Text Using Drag-and-Drop

Drag-and-drop refers to a method of moving or copying selected text or graphics by pointing to the selection and then dragging it to a new location. You can use this method in the Outline/Slides pane and in the Slide pane.

1. If necessary, **Open** your file **2B_History_Firstname_Lastname** in **Normal View**. Display **Slide 4**.

2. In the **Slide** pane, click anywhere in the word *Jewelry*. Then, in the **Slide** pane, point to the *Jewelry* bullet so that a four-headed arrow displays, and click the left mouse button to select the entire bullet point. Press and hold down [Shift] and point to the *Shoes* bullet so that a four-headed arrow displays, and then click the left mouse button.

    The *Jewelry* and *Shoes* bullet points and their subordinate bullet points are selected.

3. Move your pointer over the selected text, and then press and hold down the left mouse button.

    The arrow pointer displays with a small dotted rectangle attached to it, indicating that you may move the selection to a new location. See Figure 2.16.

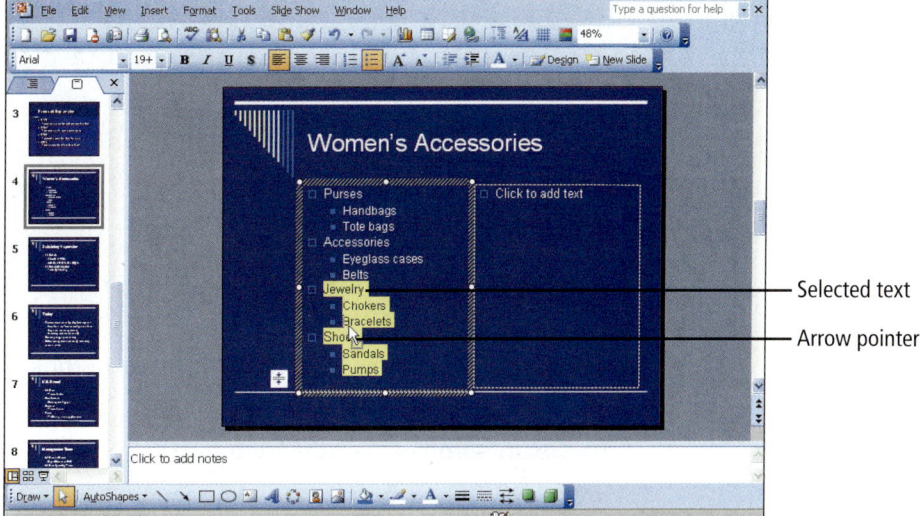

Figure 2.16

4 Continue to press and hold down the left mouse button, and then drag the pointer into the second column. See Figure 2.17.

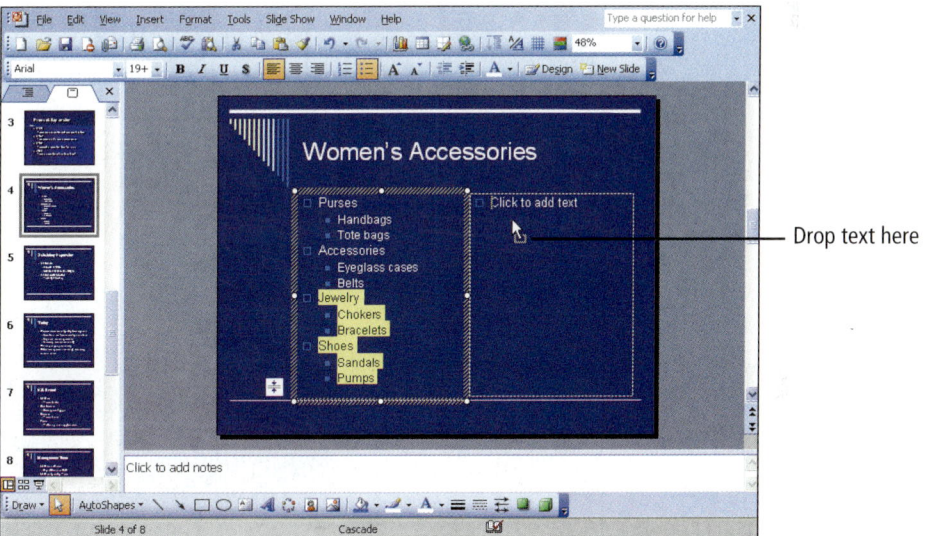

Figure 2.17

5 Release the left mouse button to drop the selection in its new location.

Notice that below the dropped text a button displays. This is the Paste Options *smart tag*. A smart tag is a small button that gives you quick access to relevant commands. In this manner, it is considered to be *context sensitive*. A context-sensitive smart tag or button changes depending on the action.

6 Pause your pointer over the Paste Options smart tag to display its ScreenTip, and then click the **downward-pointing arrow** on the smart tag to display its menu.

Two options display on the menu, allowing you to choose between two types of formatting that you would like to apply to the dropped (pasted) text. You can choose Keep Source Formatting so that the bullets remain at the same levels as the original selection; or, you can choose Keep Text Only, which applies first level bullets to all of the dropped text.

7 From the displayed smart tag menu, click **Keep Source Formatting**.

The Paste Options smart tag will remain on the screen until you perform some other screen action.

8 In the **Outline/Slides** pane, click the **Outline tab**.

9 Display **Slide 1**. Next to the **Slide 1** icon, select the words *El Cuero*.

10 Point to the selection, press and hold down Ctrl, and then press and hold down the left mouse button.

The arrow pointer displays with a small dotted rectangle and a plus sign. The plus sign indicates that you are copying the selection using drag-and-drop.

11 Continue to press Ctrl and drag the pointer down to **Slide 6**. The presentation outline will scroll as you drag down. Position the pointer at the beginning of the title before the word *Today*. See Figure 2.18.

12 Release the left mouse button and then release Ctrl.

The selection is copied to Slide 6.

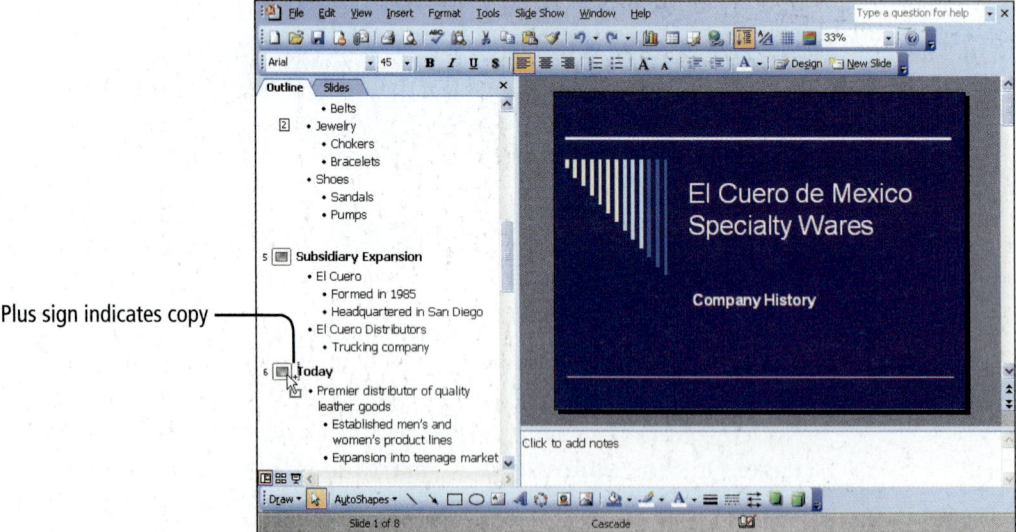

Plus sign indicates copy

Figure 2.18

13 **Save** the presentation.

Alert!

Did You Move the Selection Instead of Copying It?

You must be sure to release the left mouse button before releasing Ctrl. Releasing Ctrl first results in the selection being moved instead of copied. If this happened to you, on the Standard toolbar, click Undo, then repeat the steps.

Activity 2.13 Moving Text Using the Clipboard

The Cut command removes selected text or graphics from your presentation and moves the selection to the Clipboard task pane. From the Clipboard, the selection can be pasted to a new location. You can cut selected text and move it to the Clipboard by clicking the Cut button on the Standard toolbar, by clicking the Edit menu, and then clicking Cut, by using the Ctrl + X keyboard shortcut, or by displaying the shortcut menu and then clicking Cut. In this activity, you will use the Cut button on the Standard toolbar to move a selection of text from the first slide to the last slide.

1 If necessary, **Open** your file **2B_History_Firstname_Lastname** in **Normal View**. Display **Slide 1**.

2 If necessary, display the task pane by clicking the **View** menu and then clicking **Task Pane**. At the top of the task pane, click the **Other Task Panes** arrow, and then click **Clipboard**.

3 In the **Clipboard** task pane, check to see if any items display. When the Clipboard is empty, *Clipboard empty* displays in the task pane.

If items are on the Clipboard, click the **Clear All** button. An empty Clipboard will help you see how the Clipboard stores information that is moved to it.

Note — Using the Clipboard

It is not necessary to display the Clipboard if you are only moving or copying one selection. In this activity, the Clipboard is displayed so that you have a visual indication of how the Clipboard does its work.

4 On **Slide 1** in the title placeholder, drag to select the text *Specialty Wares*. On the Standard toolbar, click the **Cut** button .

The selected text is removed from the slide. Look at the Clipboard and notice that a PowerPoint icon and the text that you cut display. See Figure 2.19.

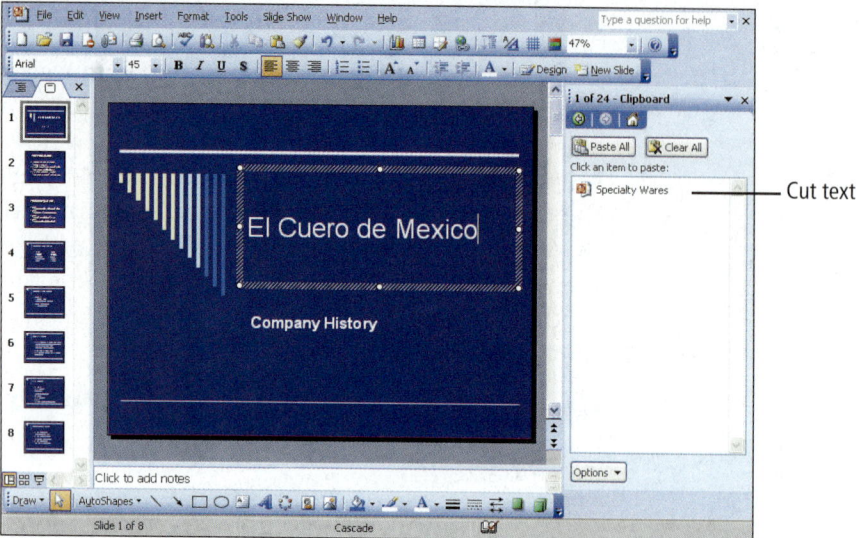

— Cut text

Figure 2.19

5 Display **Slide 5**. In the first bullet point, click after the words *El Cuero*, and then press Spacebar. In the task pane, point to the **Specialty Wares** item and click the left mouse button.

Alternatively, on the Standard toolbar, click **Paste**.

The text that you cut from the first slide is pasted into Slide 5 and the Paste Options smart tag displays. Recall that the Paste Options smart tag is a context-sensitive feature. Here it allows you to choose between two types of formatting that you would like to apply to the pasted text.

6 Point to the **Paste Options** smart tag and click its arrow to display the menu.

In this instance, you can choose Keep Source Formatting—the design template formatting from which the selection originates. The text will retain the large size that it had as title text. Or, you may choose Use Design Template Formatting. This command will match the format of the pasted text to the text surrounding it.

7 From the displayed menu, click **Use Design Template Formatting**.

8 On the task pane, point to the item that you cut so that a bar with a small arrow displays to its right. Click the arrow to display a menu, and from the displayed menu, click **Delete**. See Figure 2.20.

The item is removed from the Clipboard.

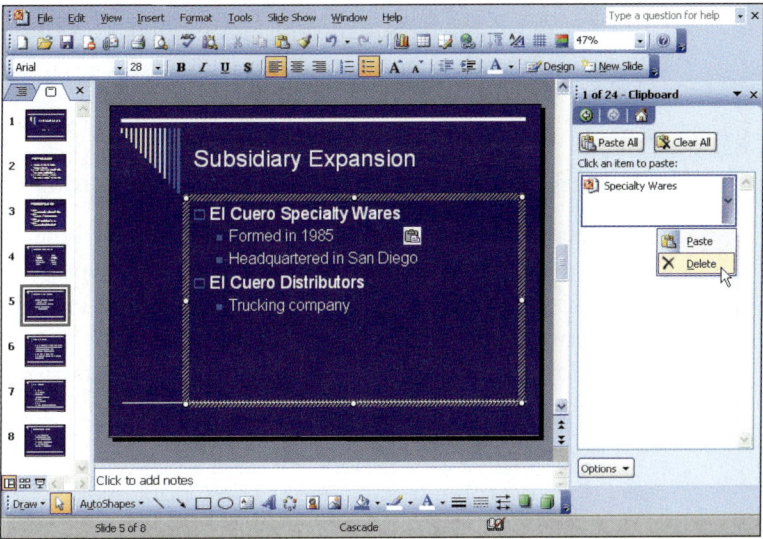

Figure 2.20

9 **Save** your presentation.

Activity 2.14 Copying Text Using the Clipboard

The Copy command duplicates (makes a copy of) selected text or graphics and sends the copy to the Clipboard. From the Clipboard, the copy of selected text can be pasted to another location. You can copy selected text to the Clipboard by clicking the Copy button on the Standard toolbar or on the Clipboard task pane, by clicking the Edit menu, and then clicking Copy, by pressing Ctrl + C, or by displaying the shortcut menu, and then clicking Copy. In this activity, you will use the keyboard shortcut to copy text.

1 Display **Slide 1**. In the title placeholder, select the words *El Cuero*.

2 Press and hold down the Ctrl key and then press C to send a copy of the selection to the **Clipboard** task pane.

Notice that the selection is not removed from its original location. Recall that when you copy text, you are making a *duplicate* of the selection.

3 Display **Slide 4**. In the title placeholder, click to position the insertion point in front of the word *Women's*.

4 On the Standard toolbar, click the **Paste** button to duplicate the selection.

The slide title reads *El Cuero Women's Accessories* and the Paste Options smart tag displays. You will not need the smart tag in this action, and it will clear when another screen action takes place.

Project 2B: History | **PowerPoint** 1061

5 On the **Clipboard** task pane, click the **Clear All** button ![Clear All] to clear the contents of the Clipboard.

6 **Save** the presentation.

Activity 2.15 Moving Multiple Selections Using Collect and Paste

Recall that the Clipboard stores up to 24 selections, and each one can be pasted multiple times. Additionally, groups of items on the Clipboard can be pasted all at one time. The process of cutting or copying multiple items to the Clipboard and then pasting these selections is called ***collect and paste***. In this activity, you will collect and paste several selections from Slide 8.

1 Display the **Clipboard** task pane if it is not already displayed, and if necessary, clear the Clipboard by clicking the **Clear All** button ![Clear All].

2 Display **Slide 8** and select the text *Miguel Hernandez, CEO*.

3 Move the mouse pointer over the selected text, and right-click to display a shortcut menu. From the displayed menu, click **Cut** to move the selection to the Clipboard.

4 Select the text *Alexis Rodriguez, President*. On the Standard toolbar, click the **Cut** button to move the selection to the Clipboard.

Notice that two items display in the task pane.

5 Select the text *Adriana Ramos, President*. Hold down [Ctrl] and press [X] to move the selection to the Clipboard. Compare your task pane to Figure 2.21.

There are many ways to perform commands in PowerPoint. As you have seen, commands are available on the toolbar, on shortcut menus, and with keyboard shortcuts. Use whatever method is convenient for you at the time.

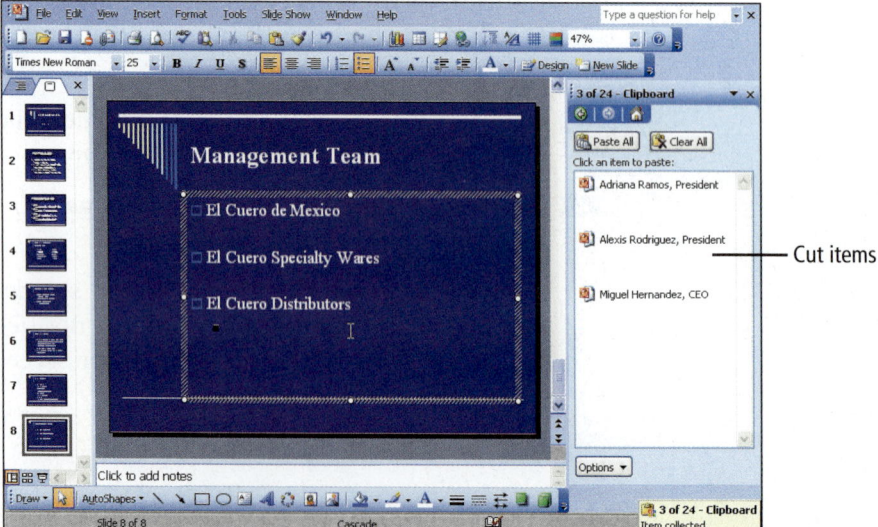

Figure 2.21

6 Display **Slide 2**, and then click in the bulleted list placeholder after the words *Mexico City*. Press [Enter] to create a new bullet.

7 In the **Clipboard** task pane click the **third item—Miguel Hernandez, CEO**.

The selection is pasted to Slide 2 and the Paste Options smart tag displays. Depending on how far you dragged when selecting, an extra bullet may be created; if necessary, press [Bksp] two times to delete it.

8 Display **Slide 5**, click after the words *San Diego*, and then press [Enter]. In the Clipboard task pane click the **second item—Alexis Rodriguez, President**.

The selection is pasted to Slide 5 and the Paste Options smart tag displays. If necessary, press [Bksp] or [Del] to delete any extra bullets.

9 With **Slide 5** still displayed, click after the words *Trucking company*, and then press [Enter]. In the **Clipboard** task pane click the **first item—Adriana Ramos, President**.

The selection is pasted to Slide 5. If necessary, delete any extra bullets.

10 In the **Clipboard** task pane, click **Clear All** [Clear All] to clear the Clipboard, and then **Close** [X] the **Clipboard** task pane.

11 Click the **Slide Sorter View** button. Click **Slide 4**, press and hold down [Ctrl], and then click **Slide 8** so that both slides are selected. On your keyboard, press [Delete].

12 Click the **Normal View** button. Display the **View** menu, and then click **Header and Footer**. Click the **Notes and Handouts tab**. If necessary, click to select the **Date and time** check box and then click to select **Update automatically**. Clear the **Header** and **Page number** check boxes. Make sure the **Footer** check box is selected, and then in the **Footer** box type **2B History-Firstname Lastname** In the upper-right corner, click **Apply to All**.

13 Save the presentation. From the **File** menu, click **Print**. Print the presentation in **grayscale** as **6 handouts** per page in **horizontal** order. In the lower right corner, click **Preview** to preview your print. On the Print Preview toolbar, click **Print**, and then in the **Print** dialog box, click **OK**.

14 Close [X] the presentation, and then close PowerPoint

End You have completed Project 2B

Summary

In this chapter, you created a new presentation by using the AutoContent Wizard and by applying a design template. You also saw that there are multiple ways to create presentation text, including importing slides from existing presentations and from outlines created in a word processor like Microsoft Word. You gained practice in modifying slides by changing the presentation design and the location of text.

In This Chapter You Practiced How To

- Create a Presentation
- Modify Slides
- Create a Presentation Using a Design Template
- Import Text from Word
- Move and Copy Text

Concepts Assessments

Matching Match each term in the second column with its correct definition in the first column by writing the letter of the term on the blank line in front of the correct definition.

____ 1. The action of creating a duplicate of a selection of text.

____ 2. A task pane that holds selections of text or graphics that you want to copy or move.

____ 3. A method of moving or copying selected text or graphics by pointing to the selection, and then dragging it to a new location.

____ 4. A feature that leads you step-by-step through the creation of a presentation by asking you questions about the presentation that you want to create.

____ 5. The command that reverses an Undo action.

____ 6. The process of cutting or copying multiple items to the Clipboard and then pasting these selections.

____ 7. A model on which a presentation is based, including graphic elements, animations, and a color scheme.

____ 8. The action of placing text from the Clipboard into a new location including into the same presentation, a different presentation, or another application.

____ 9. A small button that displays as a result of a specific screen action and that gives you quick access to relevant commands.

____ 10. A coordinated palette of eight colors that includes background, text, bullet, and accent colors.

____ 11. A presentation that is displayed as an electronic slide show.

____ 12. A button, smart tag, or other feature that changes depending on the current action.

____ 13. A command that reverses previous actions.

____ 14. A dialog box that displays slides from other presentations that you can insert into the current presentation.

____ 15. A command that uses the Clipboard to move text from one location to another.

A AutoContent Wizard
B Clipboard
C Color scheme
D Collect and paste
E Context sensitive
F Copy
G Cut
H Design template
I Drag-and-drop
J On-screen presentation
K Paste
L Redo
M Slide Finder
N Smart tag
O Undo

Concepts Assessments (continued)

Fill in the Blank Write the correct answer in the space provided.

1. The keyboard shortcut for moving from one placeholder to another is _____ + _____.

2. When you insert slides from another presentation, the _____ button in the Slide Finder dialog box allows you to navigate to the file containing the slides that you want to insert.

3. The keyboard shortcut for inserting a new slide is _____ + _____.

4. The action of pressing the left mouse button two times rapidly is called _____.

5. To copy a selection using drag-and-drop, the _____ key must be pressed while dragging the mouse.

6. The _____ command allows you to reverse an undo.

7. The Clipboard holds up to _____ selections that can be pasted to other locations.

8. An outline can be imported into a PowerPoint presentation from a _____ program.

9. The Clipboard displays the first _____ characters of a text selection.

10. The keyboard shortcut for cutting selected text is _____ + _____.

PowerPoint chapter two — Skill Assessments

Project 2C — Workshop

Objectives: *Create a Presentation, Move and Copy Text, and Modify Slides.*

In the following Skill Assessment, you will create for Eduardo Terat, Director of Training for El Cuero Specialty Wares, a presentation to be used at a training workshop for managers. Your completed presentation will look similar to the one shown in Figure 2.22. You will save your presentation as *2C_Workshop_Firstname_Lastname*.

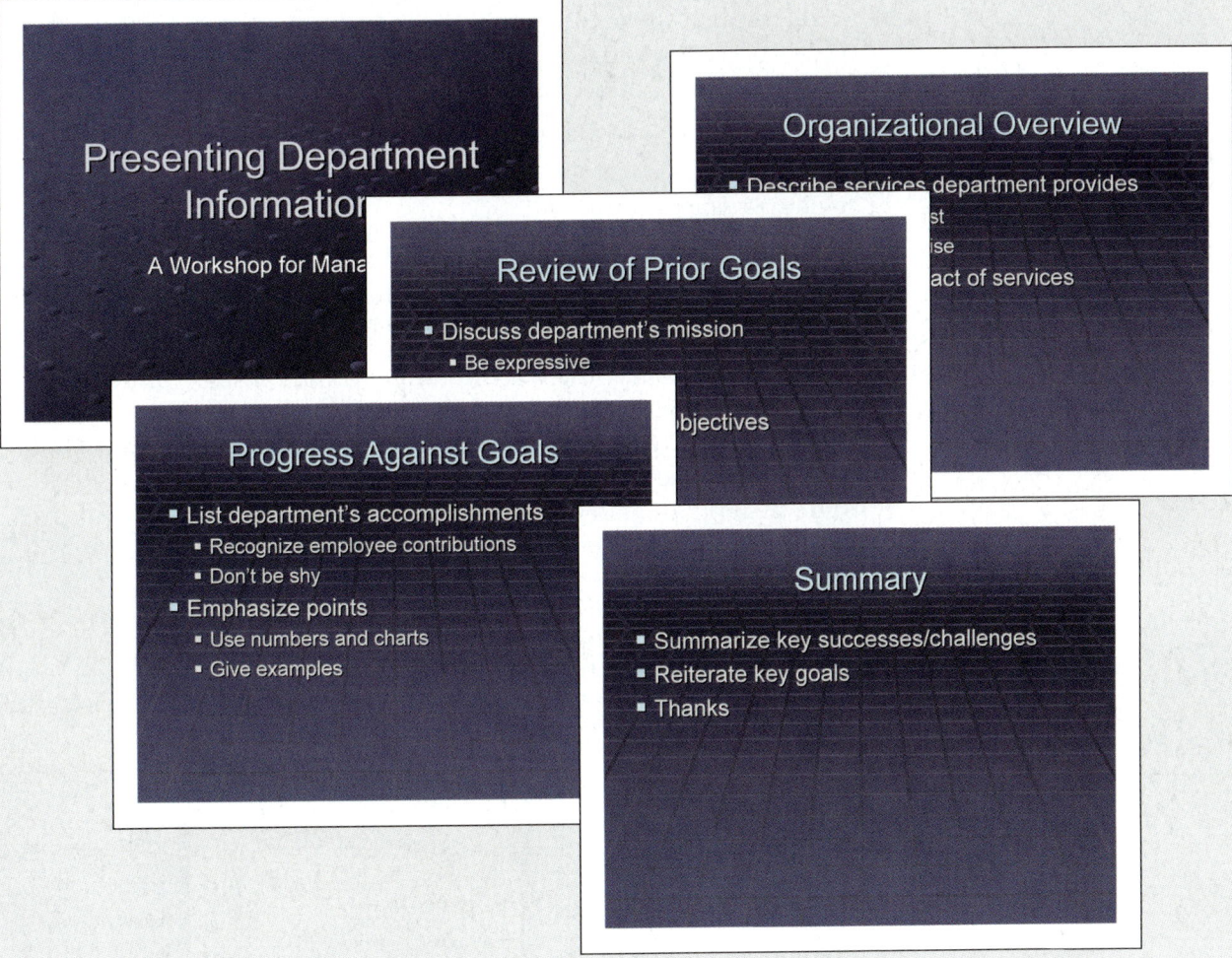

Figure 2.22

1. Start PowerPoint. On the menu bar, click **File** and then click **New**. In the **New Presentation** task pane, click **From AutoContent wizard**. If necessary, close the Office Assistant character. In the first wizard screen, click **Next**.

2. In the **Presentation type** step, click **Corporate**, and then click **Company Meeting**. Click **Next**, and in the **Presentation style** step, click **On-screen presentation**. Click **Next**.

(Project 2C–Worskhop continues on the next page)

Skill Assessments (continued)

(Project 2C–Workshop continued)

3. Click in the **Presentation title** box, and then type **Presenting Department Information** Clear the **Date last updated** and **Slide number** check boxes, and then click **Next**. Click **Finish** to create a new presentation with 13 slides.

4. From the **File** menu, click **Save As**. Use the **Save in arrow** to navigate to the location where you are storing your projects for this chapter. In the **File name** box, type **2C_Workshop_Firstname_Lastname** and click **Save**.

5. Scroll through the presentation and view the suggested content. Click **Slide Sorter View** to view all of the slides in the presentation. Several of the slides are not necessary to the presentation and must be deleted.

6. Click **Slide 2**. Press and hold down Ctrl, and then click **Slides 3**, **4**, **6**, **9**, **10**, **11**, and **12**. On you keyboard, press Delete. Five slides remain in the presentation.

7. Double-click **Slide 1** so that it displays in Normal view. Select any text that displays in the subtitle placeholder and press Delete. In the subtitle placeholder, type **A Workshop for Managers**

8. If necessary, display the **Outline tab** and then display **Slide 2**. In the **Outline tab**, point to the first bullet on **Slide 2** so that a four-headed arrow displays. Click the left mouse button to select the entire bullet point. Press and hold down Shift, and then click the last bullet on **Slide 2**. With all of the bulleted text in the slide selected, press Delete. Type the text for **Slide 2** shown in Figure 2.23, promoting and demoting text as necessary.

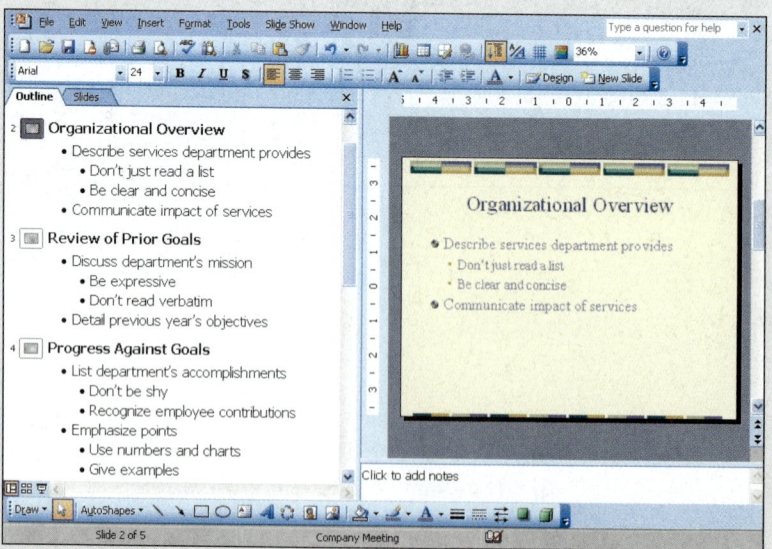

Figure 2.23

(Project 2C–Worskhop continues on the next page)

Skill Assessments (continued)

(Project 2C–Workshop continued)

9. In the **Outline tab**, delete all the bulleted text in **Slides 3** and **4** and refer to Figure 2.23 to create the text for each of these slides.

10. Make sure that **Slide 4** is displayed. In this slide you will use drag-and-drop to rearrange the bulleted text. Point to the third bullet, *Recognize employee contributions*, so that a four-headed arrow displays. Click the left mouse button to select the text. Point to the selected text, and then press and hold down the left mouse button and drag up so that the pointer is positioned in front of the word *Don't*. Release the left mouse button to move the text to its new location.

11. On the Formatting toolbar, click **Design** to display the **Slide Design** task pane. Under **Available For Use**, locate and then click the blue **Fading Grid** design to apply the template to all of the slides in the presentation.

12. Display **Slide 1**. In the **Slide Design** task pane, point to the blue **Digital Dots** template, and then click the arrow bar that displays to the right of the template. Click **Apply to Selected Slides** to apply the design to **Slide 1**.

13. On the menu bar, click **View**, and then click **Header and Footer**. In the displayed **Header and Footer** dialog box, click the **Notes and Handouts tab**. If necessary, click to place a check mark in the **Date and time** check box, and then click **Update automatically**. If necessary, click to select the **Footer** check box, and then click in the **Footer** box and type **2C Workshop-Firstname Lastname** Clear the **Header** and **Page number** check boxes, and then click **Apply to All**. On the Standard toolbar, click **Save** to save the changes you have made to your presentation.

14. Display the **File** menu, and then click **Print**. Click the **Print what arrow**, and then click **Handouts**. Under **Handouts**, click the **Slides per page** arrow, and then click **6**. Next to **Order**, click the **Horizontal** option button. Click the **Color/grayscale arrow**, and then click **Grayscale**. Make sure that the **Frame slides** check box is selected. In the lower left corner, click **Preview** to view how your presentation will print. On the Print Preview toolbar, click **Print**. Click **OK** to print the presentation.

15. On the menu bar, click **File**, and then click **Close**. Close PowerPoint.

End You have completed Project 2C

PowerPoint chapter two

Skill Assessments (continued)

Project 2D—Logo

Objectives: *Create a Presentation Using a Design Template, Modify Slides, Import Text from Word, and Move and Copy Text.*

In the following Skill Assessment, you will create a presentation used by the Marketing Department to promote the sale of logo products. Your completed presentation will look similar to the one shown in Figure 2.24. You will save your presentation as 2D_Logo_Firstname_Lastname.

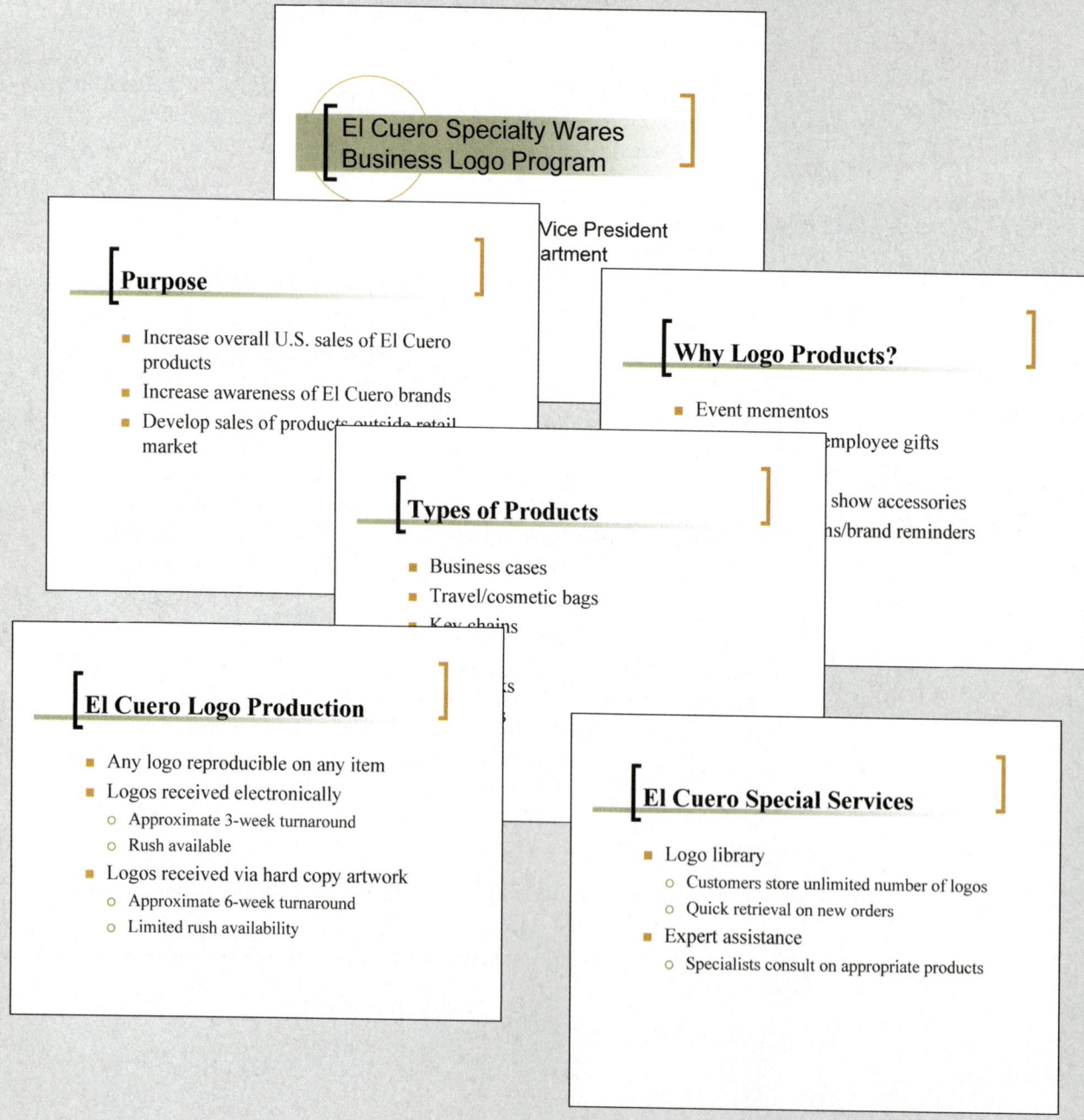

Figure 2.24

(Project 2D–Logo continues on the next page)

1070　**PowerPoint** | Chapter 2: Creating a Presentation

Skill Assessments (continued)

(Project 2D–Logo continued)

1. Start PowerPoint. On the menu bar, click **File** and then click **New**. In the **New Presentation** task pane, click **From design template**. Under **Available For Use**, locate and click the white **Blends** design to display a title slide with the **Blends** template applied.

2. To create the title slide, click the in the title placeholder, and type **El Cuero Specialty Wares** and then press Enter. Type **Business Logo Program** and then press and hold down Ctrl and press Enter to move the insertion point to the subtitle placeholder. Type **Richard Kelly, Vice President Marketing Department**

3. The remaining slides in the presentation are contained in a Microsoft Word outline. To insert the slides, click the **Insert** menu, and then click **Slides from Outline**. Navigate to the location where your student files are stored. Double-click the file **p02D_Products** to convert the outline to PowerPoint slides. Alternatively, click the file p02D_Products, and then click Insert. Your presentation now has six slides.

4. In the task pane, click the **Other Task Panes arrow**, and if necessary, click **Slide Design**. Point to the white **Axis** template, and then click the arrow bar to display the menu. From the displayed menu, click **Apply to All Slides** to change the design template for the entire presentation. Close the task pane.

5. There are several instances in the presentation in which the word *Design* should be changed to *Logo*. To quickly change these occurrences, display **Slide 1**, and then display the **Edit** menu. Click **Replace**. In the **Find what** box, type **Design** and then press Tab to move the insertion point to the **Replace with** box. Type **Logo** and then click to place a check mark in the **Match case** check box. If necessary, clear the **Find whole words only** check box. Click **Replace All**. Click **OK** to close the information box indicating that three replacements were made, and then click **Close** to close the Replace dialog box.

6. Make sure that **Slide 1** is displayed. In the title placeholder, select the words *El Cuero*. On the Standard toolbar, click the **Copy** button. You will copy this text to **Slides 5** and **6**.

7. Display **Slide 5**. Click in the title placeholder in front of the word *Logo*. On the Standard toolbar, click the **Paste** button. Click the **Paste Options** smart tag, and then click **Keep Text Only** so that the text formatting matches the formatting in the title placeholder.

8. Display **Slide 6**. Click in the title placeholder in front of the word *Special*. On the Standard toolbar, click the **Paste** button. Click the **Paste Options** smart tag, and then click **Keep Text Only** so that the text formatting matches the formatting in the title placeholder.

(Project 2D–Logo continues on the next page)

Skill Assessments (continued)

(Project 2D–Logo continued)

9. On the menu bar, click **View**, and then click **Header and Footer**. In the displayed **Header and Footer** dialog box, click the **Notes and Handouts tab**. If necessary, click to place a check mark in the **Date and time** check box, and then click **Update automatically**. Make sure that the **Footer** check box is selected, and then click in the **Footer** box and type **2D Logo-Firstname Lastname** Clear the **Header** and **Page number** check boxes, and then click **Apply to All**.

10. On the Standard toolbar, click the **Save** button to display the **Save As** dialog box. Navigate to the location where you are storing your projects for this chapter, and in the **File name** box type **2D_Logo_Firstname_Lastname** Click the **Save** button. Display **Slide 1** and click the **Slide Show** view button.

11. Display the **File** menu, and then click **Print**. Click the **Print what arrow**, and then click **Handouts**. Under **Handouts**, click the **Slides per page arrow**, and then click **6**. Next to **Order**, click the **Horizontal** option button. Click the **Color/grayscale arrow**, and then click **Grayscale**. Make sure that the **Frame slides** check box is selected. In the lower right corner, click **Preview** to view how your slides will print. Then, on the Print Preview toolbar, click **Print**. Click **OK** to print the presentation. Close the file, and then close PowerPoint.

End You have completed Project 2D

PowerPoint chapter two
Skill Assessments (continued)

Project 2E — Benefits

Objectives: *Create a Presentation Using a Design Template, Modify Slides, and Move and Copy Text.*

In the following Skill Assessment, you will create a presentation introducing a new employee benefits program. Your completed presentation will look similar to the one shown in Figure 2.25. You will save your presentation as *2E_Benefits_Firstname_Lastname*.

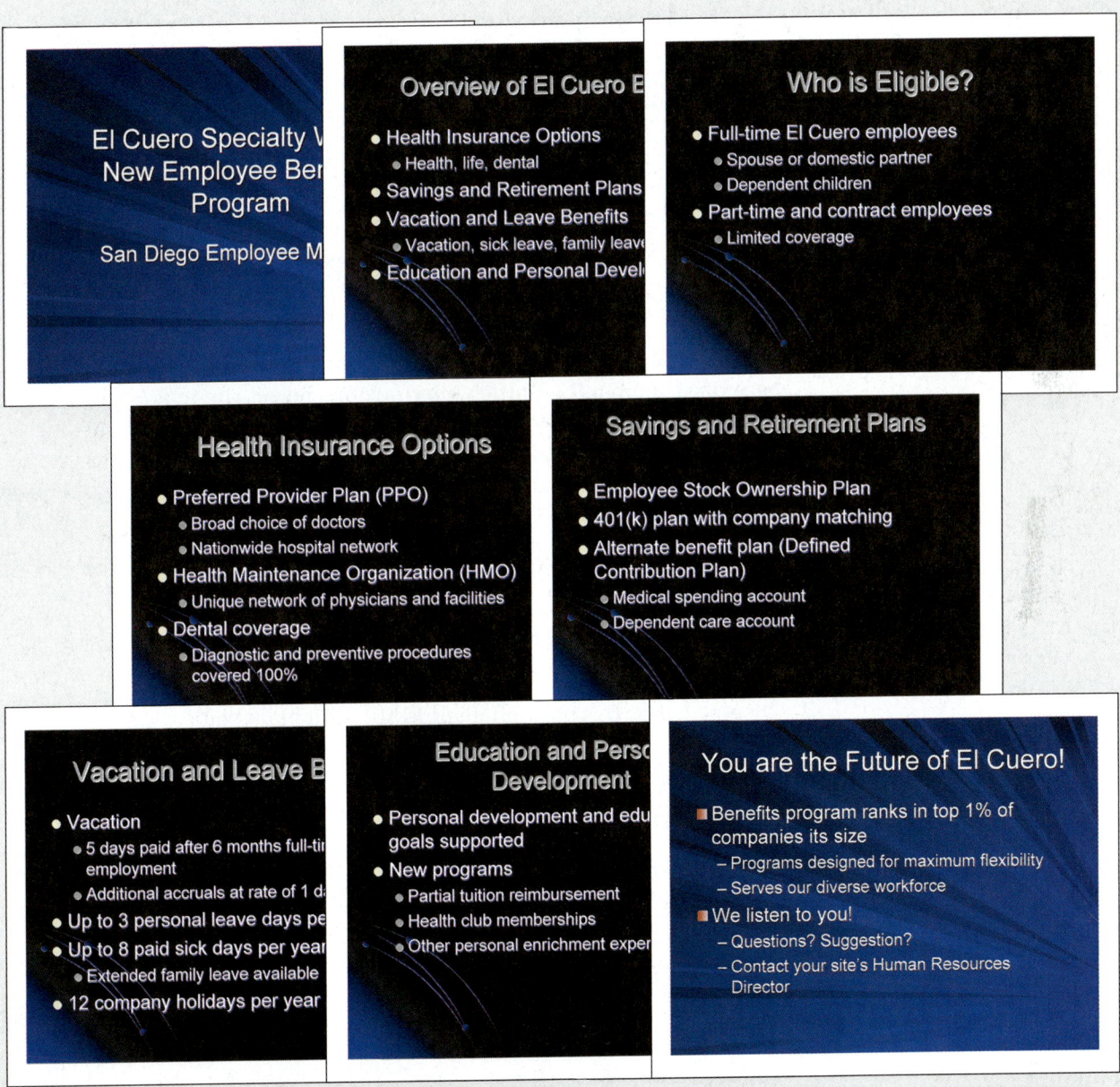

Figure 2.25

(**Project 2E**–Benefits continues on the next page)

PowerPoint chapter two
Skill Assessments (continued)

(Project 2E–Benefits continued)

1. Start PowerPoint. On the menu bar, click **File** and then click **New**. In the **New Presentation** task pane, click **From design template**. Under **Available For Use**, click the dark blue **Beam** design to display a title slide with the **Beam** template applied.

2. Click in the title placeholder, and type **El Cuero Specialty Wares** and then press [Enter]. Type **New Employee Benefits Program** Click in the subtitle box and type **San Diego Employee Meeting**

3. To insert the slides that contain the content for the presentation, click the **Insert** menu, and then click **Slides from Files**. Click the **Browse** button, navigate to your student files, and then double-click **p02E_Benefits**. In the **Slide Finder** dialog box, click **Insert All**, and then click **Close**. Your presentation contains eight slides.

4. Display **Slide 2**. This slide contains an overview of the presentation. Each of the first level bullets is the title of another slide in the presentation. You will use collect and paste to copy the text to the slide titles. Click the **Other Task Panes arrow**, and then click **Clipboard** to display the **Clipboard** task pane. If necessary, on the **Clipboard** task pane, click **Clear All** to delete any items on the Clipboard.

5. On **Slide 2**, select the text *Health Insurance Options*. On the Standard toolbar, click the **Copy** button. Select the text *Savings and Retirement Plans*. On the Standard toolbar, click the **Copy** button. Select the text *Vacation and Leave Benefits* and then click the **Copy** button. Select the text *Education and Personal Development* and click the **Copy** button. The Clipboard displays four items.

6. Display **Slide 4**, and then click in the title placeholder. On the **Clipboard** task pane, click **Health Insurance Options**.

7. Display **Slide 5**, and then click in the title placeholder. On the **Clipboard** task pane, click **Savings and Retirement Plans**.

8. Display **Slide 6**, and then click in the title placeholder. On the **Clipboard** task pane, click **Vacation and Leave Benefits**.

9. Display **Slide 7**, and then click in the title placeholder. On the **Clipboard** task pane, click **Education and Personal Development**.

10. You have finished copying and pasting items in this presentation. On the **Clipboard** task pane, click **Clear All** to delete all of the items stored on the Clipboard.

(Project 2E–Benefits continues on the next page)

Skill Assessments (continued)

(Project 2E–Benefits continued)

11. On the task pane, click the **Other Task Panes arrow,** and then click **Slide Design**. Click **Slide Sorter View** to display all of your slides. Click **Slide 2**, press and hold down , and then click **Slide 7** so that **Slides 2** through **7** are selected. On the task pane, under **Available For Use**, locate and click **Orbit** to apply a different template to the selected slides. Using Slide Sorter View allows you to see a better view of all of your slides than does the Outline/Slides pane.

12. Click **Normal View**. On the menu bar, click **View**, and then click **Header and Footer**. In the displayed **Header and Footer** dialog box, click the **Notes and Handouts tab**. Make sure the **Date and time** check box is selected, and then click **Update automatically**. Check to make sure the **Footer** check box is selected, and then click in the **Footer** box and type 2E Benefits-Firstname Lastname Clear the **Header** and **Page number** check boxes, and then click **Apply to All**.

13. On the Standard toolbar, click the **Save** button to display the **Save As** dialog box. Navigate to the location where you are storing your projects for this chapter, and then in the **File name** box type 2E_Benefits_Firstname_Lastname Click the **Save** button. Display **Slide 1** and click the **Slide Show** view button.

14. Display the **File** menu, and then click **Print**. Click the **Print what arrow**, and then click **Handouts**. Under **Handouts**, click the **Slides per page arrow**, and then click **4**. Next to **Order**, click the **Horizontal** option button. Click the **Color/grayscale arrow**, and then click **Grayscale**. Make sure that the **Frame slides** check box is selected. In the lower right corner, click **Preview** to view how your slides will print. Then, on the Print Preview toolbar, click **Print**. Click **OK** to print the presentation. Close the file and close PowerPoint.

End You have completed Project 2E

PowerPoint chapter two
Performance Assessments

Project 2F—Promotional Events

Objectives: *Create a Presentation Using a Design Template, Modify Slides, Move and Copy Text, and Import Text from Word.*

In the following Performance Assessment, you will create a presentation to be used by the marketing department to advertise upcoming retail promotions. Your completed presentation will look similar to the one shown in Figure 2.26. You will save your presentation as *2F_Promotional_Events_Firstname_Lastname*.

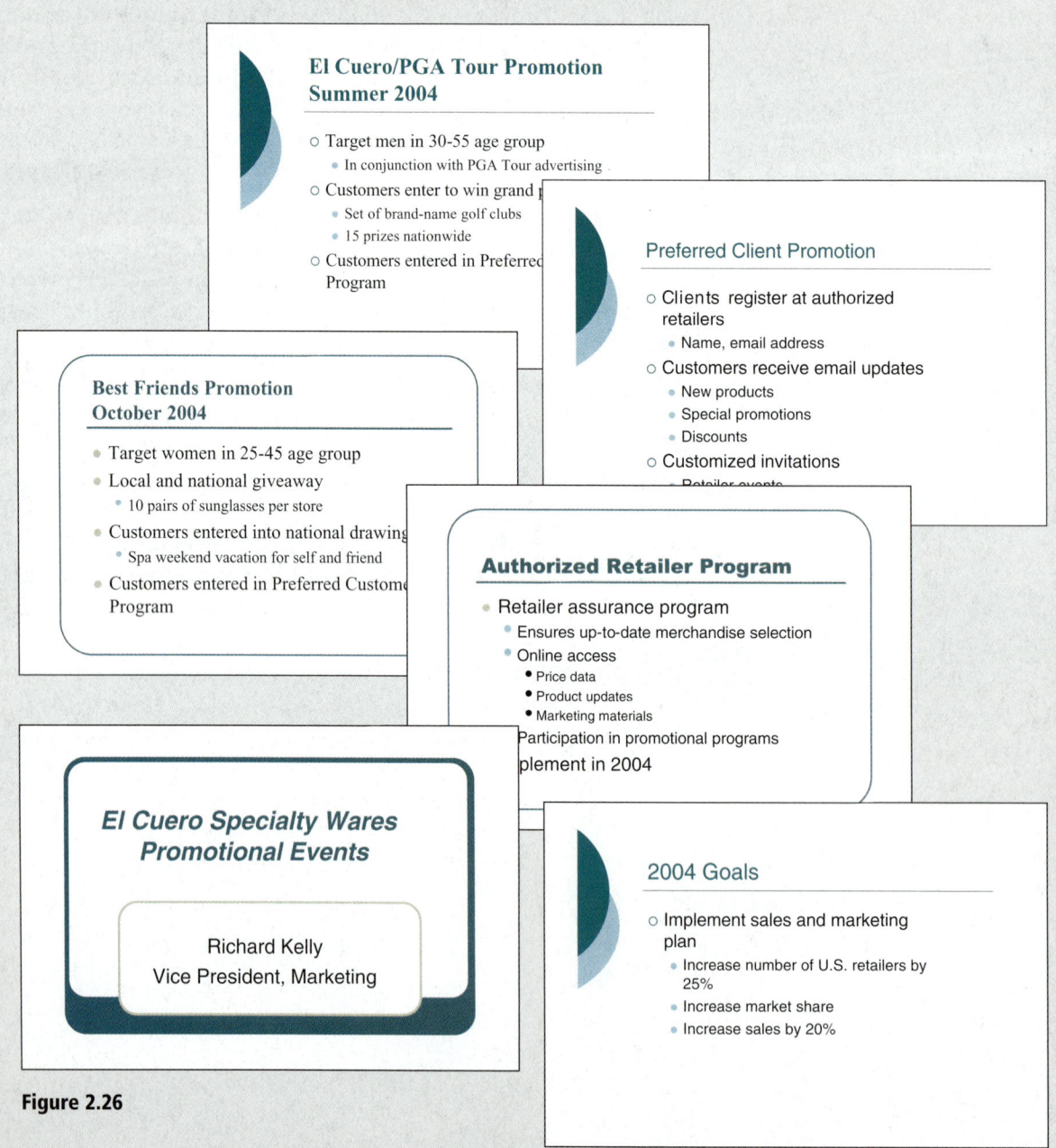

Figure 2.26

(**Project 2F**–Promotional Events continues on the next page)

PowerPoint chapter two
Performance Assessments (continued)

(Project 2F–Promotional Events continued)

1. Start PowerPoint. On the **File** menu, click **New** and in the **New Presentation** task pane, click **From design template**. Under **Available For Use**, locate and click the white and teal **Studio** design template. Close the task pane.

2. In the title placeholder, type **El Cuero Specialty Wares Promotional Events** In the Subtitle placeholder type **Richard Kelly** and then press [Enter]. Type **Vice President, Marketing**

3. Insert a new slide by clicking **New Slide** on the Formatting toolbar. In the **Slide** pane type the text shown in Figure 2.27.

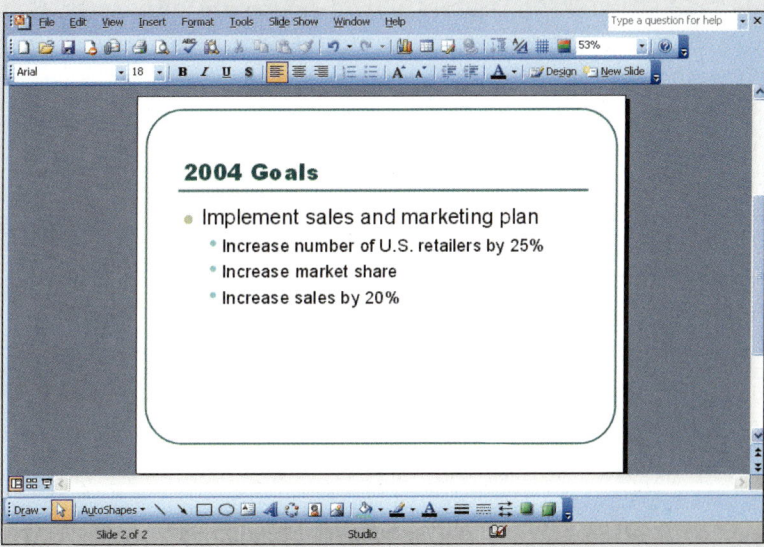

Figure 2.27

4. To insert the next two slides from an existing presentation, display the **Insert** menu, and then click **Slides from Files**. In the **Slide Finder** dialog box, use the **Browse** button to locate your student file **p02F_Retailer**. Click **Insert All** to add the two slides to your presentation. Close the **Slide Finder** dialog box.

5. To create the remainder of the presentation, you will insert slides from a Microsoft Word outline. Display **Slide 4**, and then display the **Insert** menu. Click **Slides from Outline**. From your student files, double-click **p02F_Promotion**.

6. Display **Slide 5** and select the last bullet point—*Customers entered in Preferred Customer Program*. Click the **Copy** button, and then display **Slide 6**. Click at the end of the last bullet point—*Spa weekend vacation for self and friend*. Press [Enter], and then click the **Paste** button. If an additional bullet displays, press [Bksp] to delete the bullet.

(Project 2F–Promotional Events continues on the next page)

Performance Assessments (continued)

(Project 2F–Promotional Events continued)

7. In the **Outline/Slides** pane, click the **Slides tab**, and select **Slides 2**, **4**, and **5**. (Hint: Use .) On the Formatting toolbar, click the **Slide Design** button, and then apply the white and teal **Eclipse** template to the selected slides.

8. Create a header and footer for the notes and handouts that contains a date that updates automatically. As the footer, type **2F Promotional Events-Firstname Lastname** Clear the **Header** and **Page number** check boxes. Run the slide show.

9. Save the file as **2F_Promotional_Events_Firstname_Lastname** in the location in which your projects for this chapter are stored. Print the presentation as **grayscale handouts**, **6** slides per page, in **horizontal** order. Close the file and close PowerPoint.

End You have completed Project 2F

PowerPoint chapter two
Performance Assessments (continued)

Project 2G—Yearly Summary

Objectives: *Create a Presentation and Modify Slides.*

In the following Performance Assessment, you will create a presentation that recaps El Cuero's achievements during the past year. Your completed presentation will look similar to the one shown in Figure 2.28. You will save your presentation as *2G_Yearly_Summary_Firstname_Lastname*.

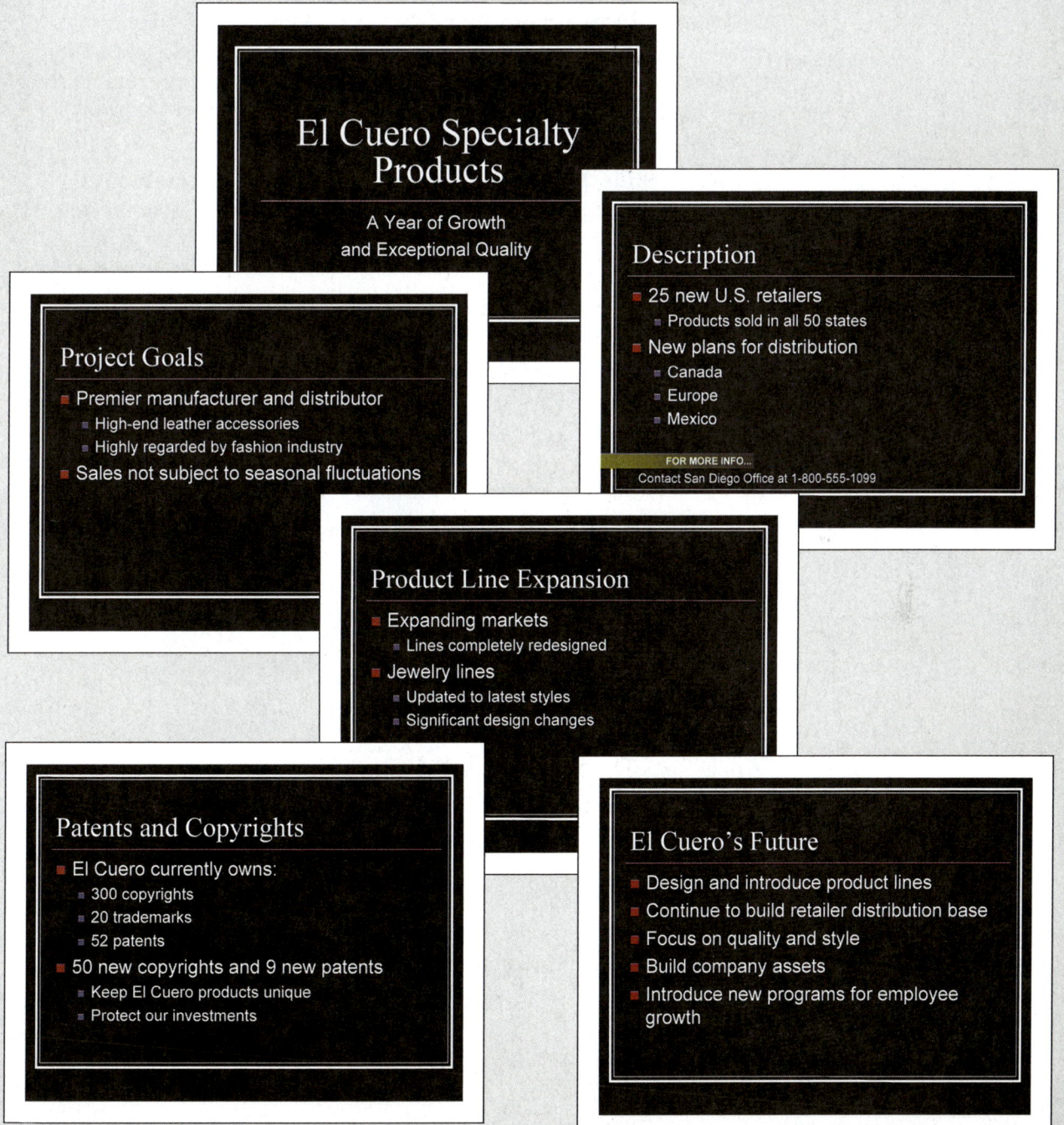

(Project 2G–Yearly Summary continues on the next page) Figure 2.28

Performance Assessments (continued)

(Project 2G–Yearly Summary continued)

1. Start PowerPoint and display the **New Presentation** task pane. Click **From AutoContent wizard**, and then click **Next**. In the **Presentation type** step, click **Projects**, and then click **Project Overview**. Click **Next**, and then click **On-screen presentation**. Click **Next**, and then type the Presentation title **El Cuero Specialty Products** Clear the **Date last updated** and **Slide number** check boxes. Click **Finish** to create the presentation.

2. Delete any subtitle text that displays on **Slide 1**, and then in the subtitle placeholder type **A Year of Growth and Exceptional Quality** Notice that only the word *Quality* displays on the second line of the subtitle. To more evenly distribute the title, click after the word *Growth*, and then press Enter.

3. Display **Slide 2**. The AutoContent wizard suggests that Project Goals be discussed in this slide and that a description of the project be discussed in Slide 3. Figure 2.29 contains the text for Slides 2 and 3. Be sure to delete the existing AutoContent text before typing the new text.

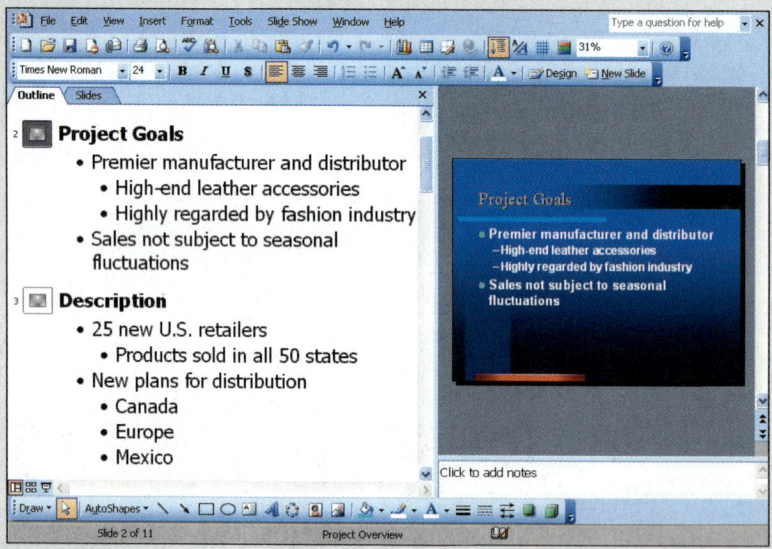

Figure 2.29

(Project 2G–Yearly Summary continues on the next page)

PowerPoint chapter two

Performance Assessments (continued)

(Project 2G–Yearly Summary continued)

4. In the placeholder at the bottom of **Slide 3**, select the text *List location or contact for specification (or other related documents) here*, and then press [Delete]. Type **Contact San Diego Office at 1-800-555-1099**

5. Scroll through the remainder of the presentation and notice the content suggested by the AutoContent Wizard. You will be replacing these slides with similar content contained in another presentation. Display the presentation in **Slide Sorter** view. Click **Slide 4**, and then press and hold down and click **Slide 11** to select **Slides 4** through **11**. Press [Delete].

6. Return your presentation to **Normal View**, and then display **Slide 3**. On the **Insert** menu, click **Slides from Files** and use the **Browse** button to navigate to your student files. Double-click **p02G_Summary**, and then insert **Slides 2**, **3**, and **4**. Close the **Slide Finder** dialog box.

7. Display the **Slide Design** task pane, and change the design template to **Refined**, for the entire presentation. (Hint: The Refined template contains a black background.)

8. Create a header and footer for the notes and handouts that contains a date that updates automatically and the footer **2G Yearly Summary-Firstname Lastname** Clear the **Header** and **Page number** check boxes. Run the Slide Show.

9. Save the file as **2G_Yearly_Summary_Firstname_Lastname** in the location in which your student files are stored. Print the presentation as **grayscale handouts**, **6** slides per page, in **Horizontal** order. Close the file.

End You have completed Project 2G

PowerPoint chapter two
Performance Assessments (continued)

Project 2H—Meeting

Objectives: *Move and Copy Text and Modify Slides.*

In the following Performance Assessment, you will create a presentation detailing the agenda for the annual El Cuero company meeting. Your completed presentation will look similar to the one shown in Figure 2.30. You will save your presentation as *2H_Meeting_Firstname_Lastname*.

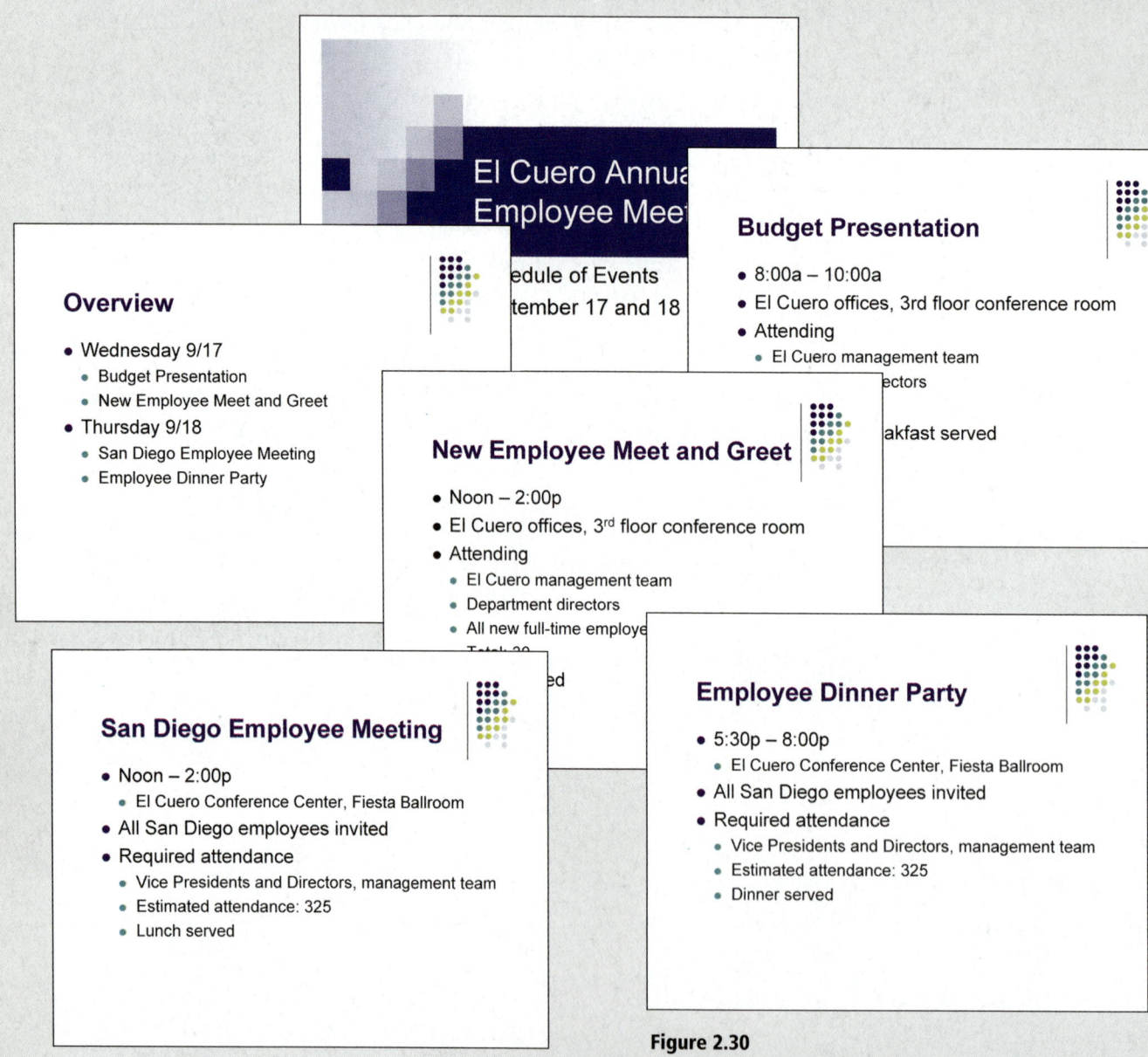

Figure 2.30

1. Start PowerPoint and from your student files, open the presentation **p02H_Meeting**. Display the **Slide Design** task pane and on **Slide 1**, change the design template to **Pixel**. The Pixel template consists of a white background with blue rectangular graphics.

(Project 2H–Meeting continues on the next page)

1082 **PowerPoint** | Chapter 2: Creating a Presentation

Performance Assessments (continued)

(Project 2H–Meeting continued)

2. Display **Slide 2**. This slide provides an overview of the two-day meeting. Each of the second-level bullet points is a title for Slides 3 through 6. Display the **Clipboard** task pane, and clear all items.

3. Individually select and copy each of the *second level* bullet points to the Clipboard. The Clipboard displays four items.

4. Display **Slide 3**. Click in the title placeholder, and then paste the *Budget Presentation* item. Click the **Paste Options** smart tag, and click **Keep Text Only**. If the insertion point is blinking below the pasted item, backspace to delete the extra line.

5. Display **Slide 4**. Click in the title placeholder, then paste the *New Employee Meet and Greet* item. Click the **Paste Options** smart tag, and click **Keep Text Only**. If the insertion point is blinking below the pasted item, backspace to delete the extra line.

6. Repeat this process on **Slides 5** and **6**, pasting the *San Diego Employee Meeting* item to **Slide 5**, and the *Employee Dinner Party* item to **Slide 6**. Clear all items from the Clipboard.

7. Display **Slide 3**. Click to select the *El Cuero executive committee* bullet, and then press and hold down Shift and click the *Department directors* bullet. Click **Copy**, and then display **Slide 4**. Click at the end of the word *Attending* and then press Enter. Click **Paste**. Click the **Paste Options** smart tag and click **Keep Source Formatting**. If necessary, delete any extra bullets that display.

8. Display **Slide 5**. Click in the bulleted list placeholder, and then point to the *Required attendance* bullet so that a four-headed arrow displays. Click the left mouse button to select the bullet point and all of its subordinate bullet points. Click **Copy**. Display **Slide 6** and click at the end of the last bullet point. Press Enter, and then click **Paste**. Click the **Paste Options** smart tag, and click **Keep Source Formatting**. If the insertion point is blinking below the pasted item, backspace to delete the extra line. In the last bullet point, delete the word *Lunch* and type **Dinner**

9. Display **Slide 1**. On the **Edit** menu, click **Replace**, and in the **Find what** box, type **executive committee** In the **Replace with** box, type **management team** Click **Replace All** to replace the four occurrences in the presentation. Close both the message box and the **Replace** dialog box.

10. Create a header and footer for the notes and handouts that contains a date that updates automatically and the footer **2H Meeting-Firstname Lastname** Clear the **Header** and **Page number** check boxes.

11. Save the file as **2H_Meeting_Firstname Lastname** in the location in which your student files are stored. Run the Slide Show. Print the presentation as **grayscale handouts**, 6 slides per page, in **Horizontal** order. Close the file.

End You have completed Project 2H

PowerPoint chapter two
Mastery Assessments

Project 2I—Teamwork

Objectives: *Create a Presentation, Move and Copy Text, and Modify Slides.*

In the following Mastery Assessment, you will create a presentation used by the El Cuero Human Resources Department for a team-training workshop. Your completed presentation will look similar to the one shown in Figure 2.31. You will save your presentation as *2I_Teamwork_Firstname_Lastname*.

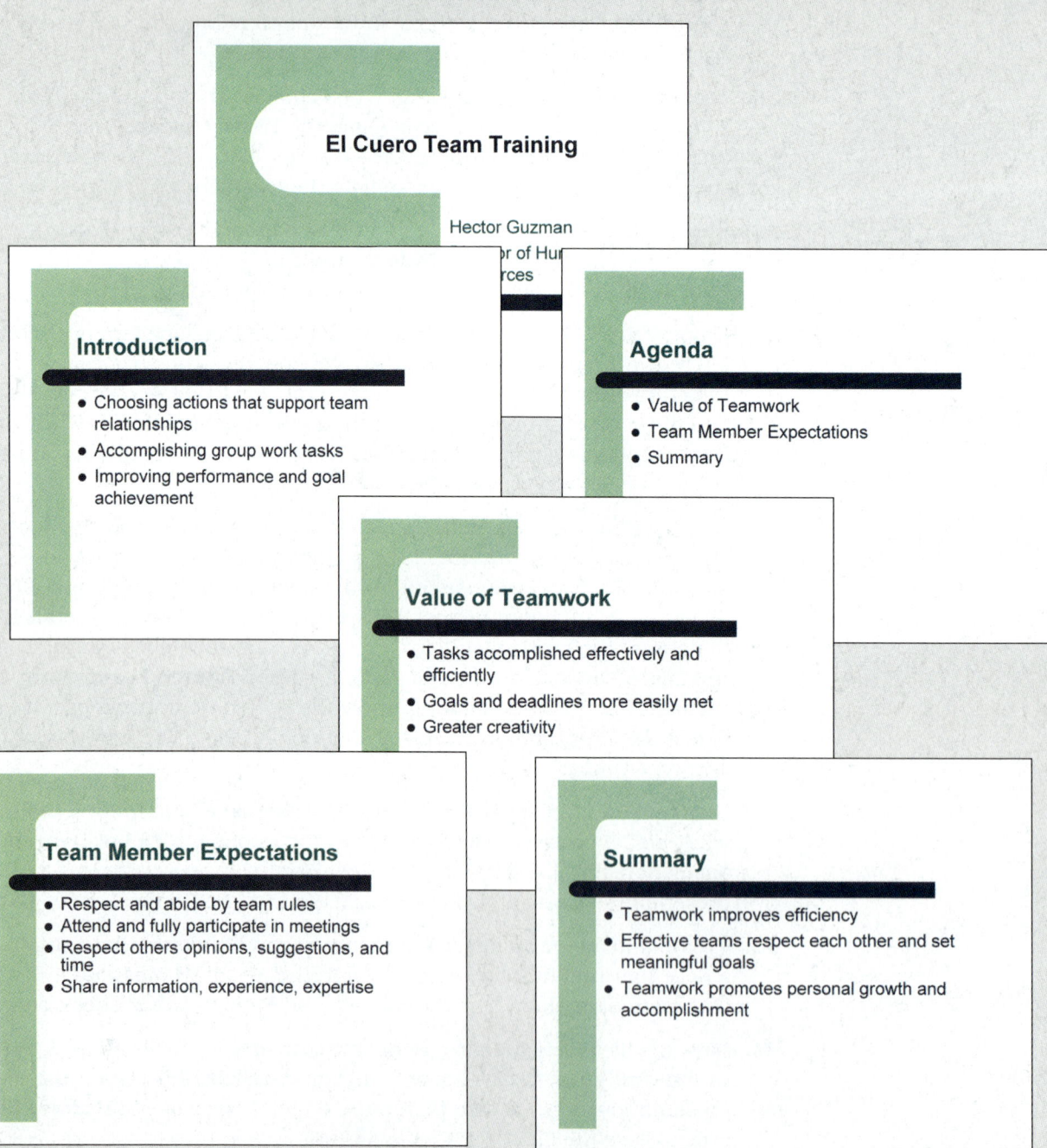

(**Project 2I**–Teamwork continues on the next page) Figure 2.31

Mastery Assessments (continued)

(Project 2I–Teamwork continued)

1. Start a new presentation using the **AutoContent wizard**. Create an on-screen presentation using the **Training presentation** type. The title of the presentation is **El Cuero Team Training**. Do not include the date last updated or the slide numbers. Refer to Figure 2.32 to create **Slides 1** through **3**, deleting any existing **AutoContent** text as necessary. Save the file as **2I_Teamwork_Firstname_Lastname**

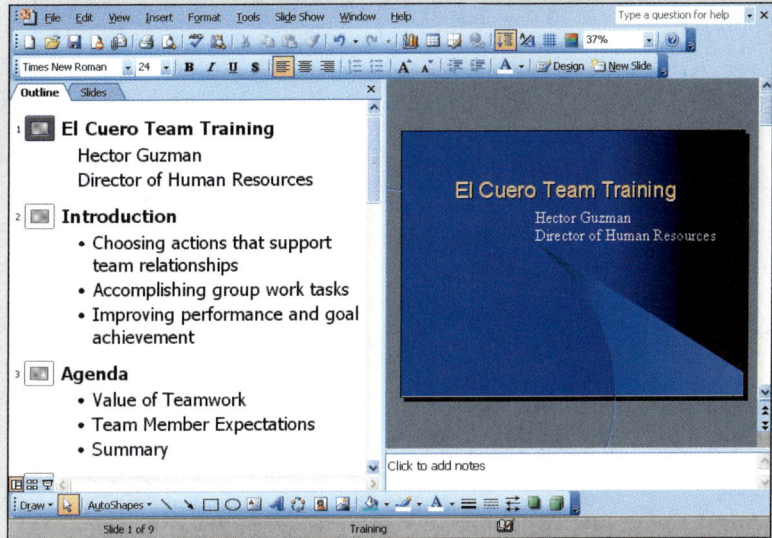

Figure 2.32

2. Scroll through the remainder of the presentation slides to familiarize yourself with the suggested content, and then delete **Slides 4** through **9**. The content for these slides is contained in another PowerPoint presentation.

3. Display **Slide 3**, and then insert all the slides from the file **p02I_Training**.

4. Display **Slide 3** and display the **Clipboard** task pane. Clear all items from the Clipboard, and then select and copy each bullet point individually so that three items display on the Clipboard.

(Project 2I–Teamwork continues on the next page)

Mastery Assessments (continued)

(Project 2I–Teamwork continued)

5. In the **Slide 4** title placeholder, paste the *Value of Teamwork* item. In the **Slide 5** title placeholder, paste the *Team Member Expectations* item. In the **Slide 6** title placeholder, paste the *Summary* item. Be sure to select **Use Design Template Formatting** if the **Paste Options** smart tag displays. Delete any additional lines that display in the titles.

6. Display **Slide 6** and use either drag-and-drop or copy and paste to move the last bullet point so that it is the second bullet point.

7. Change the template for the entire presentation to **Capsules**, which has a white background and green and navy blue designs.

8. Create a header and footer for the notes and handouts that contains a date that updates automatically and the footer **2I Teamwork-Firstname Lastname** Clear the **Header** and **Page number** check boxes.

9. Save the file, and then print the presentation as **grayscale handouts**, 6 slides per page, in **Horizontal** order. Close the file.

End You have completed Project 2I

Mastery Assessments (continued)

Project 2J—Proposal

Objectives: *Create a Presentation Using a Design Template, Import Text from Word, and Modify Slides.*

In the following Mastery Assessment, you will create a marketing presentation for a San Diego City Council Meeting proposing the establishment of an El Cuero retail store in a new outlet center. Your completed presentation will look similar to the one shown in Figure 2.33. You will save your presentation as *2J_Proposal_Firstname_Lastname*.

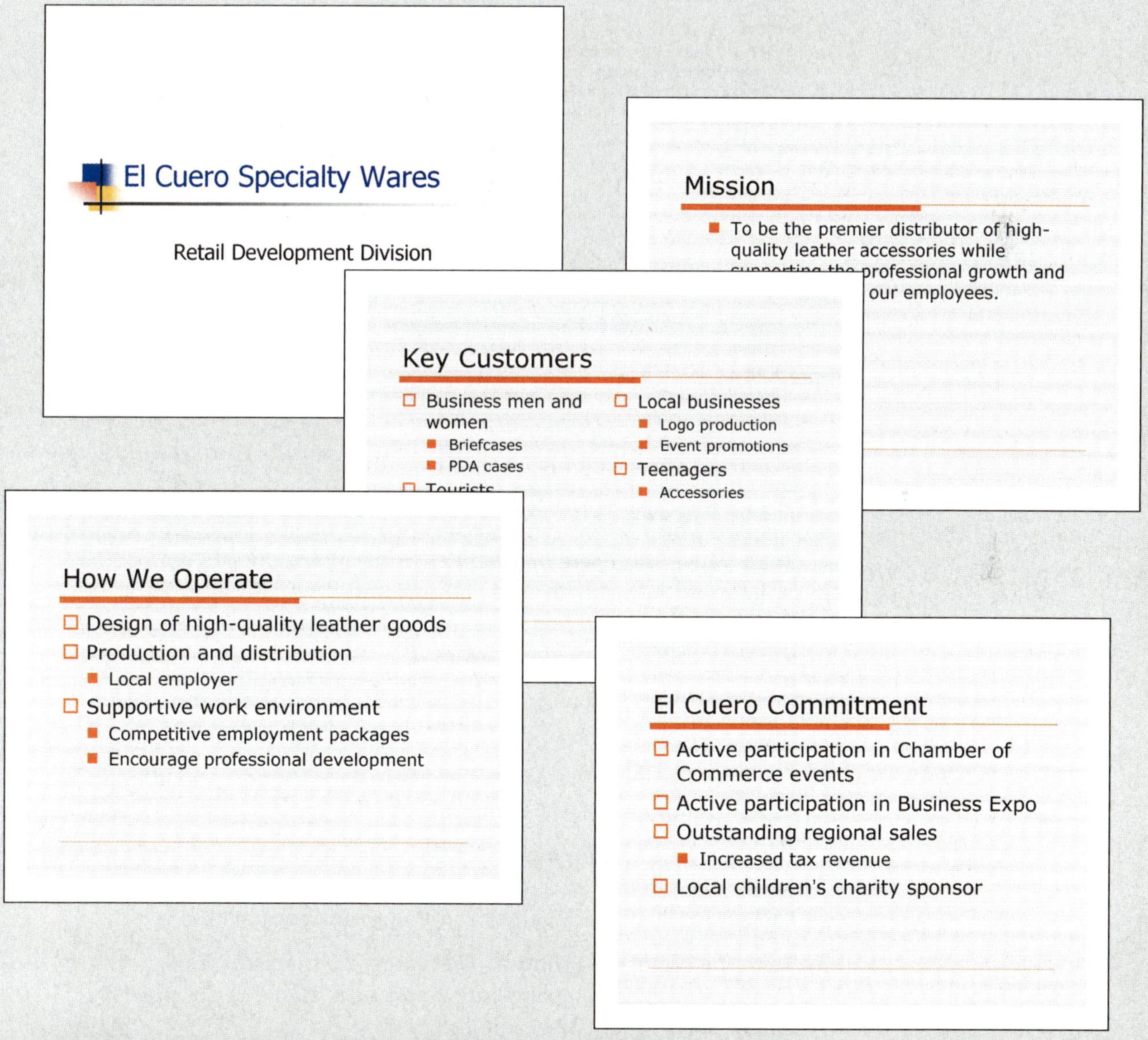

El Cuero Specialty Wares
Retail Development Division

Mission
- To be the premier distributor of high-quality leather accessories while supporting the professional growth and our employees.

Key Customers
- Business men and women
  - Briefcases
  - PDA cases
- Tourists
- Local businesses
  - Logo production
  - Event promotions
- Teenagers
  - Accessories

How We Operate
- Design of high-quality leather goods
- Production and distribution
  - Local employer
- Supportive work environment
  - Competitive employment packages
  - Encourage professional development

El Cuero Commitment
- Active participation in Chamber of Commerce events
- Active participation in Business Expo
- Outstanding regional sales
  - Increased tax revenue
- Local children's charity sponsor

Figure 2.33

(Project 2J–Proposal continues on the next page)

Mastery Assessments (continued)

(Project 2J–Proposal continued)

1. Start PowerPoint and create a new presentation from the **Echo** design template, which consists of a white background and three circles and a line to the left of the title placeholder. Insert a new slide, and type the text for the first two slides shown in Figure 2.34.

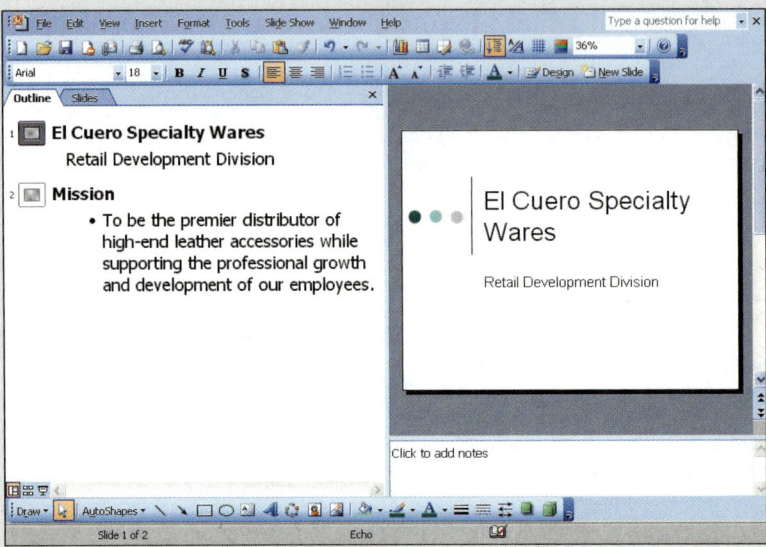

Figure 2.34

2. **Slides 3**, **4**, and **5** are contained in a Microsoft Word outline. Insert the slides from the **p02J_Proposal** outline.

3. Display **Slide 3** and change the slide layout to **Title and 2-Column Text**. Move the *Local businesses* bullet point and its subordinate bullet points to the second column and then add a bullet at the same level as *Local businesses*. Type **Teenagers** Press Enter and demote the new bullet. Type **Accessories**

4. Replace all occurrences of the words *high-end* with the words *high-quality*.

5. Change the design template for **Slide 1** to **Blends** and change the design template for the remainder of the presentation to **Profile**.

6. Create a header and footer for the notes and handouts that contains a date that updates automatically and the footer **2J Proposal-Firstname Lastname** Clear the **Header** and **Page number** check boxes.

7. Save the file as **2J_Proposal_Firstname_Lastname** and then print the presentation as **grayscale handouts**, 6 slides per page, in **Horizontal** order. Close the file.

End You have completed Project 2J

Problem Solving

Project 2K — 2K Plan

Objectives: *Create a Presentation and Modify Slides.*

Start a new presentation using the AutoContent Wizard. In the Corporate category, choose the Business Plan—creating an on-screen presentation with the title **El Cuero Business Plan**. Create an appropriate subtitle. Create content for your presentation based on Slides 1, 2, 3, and 4 and delete the remaining slides. Create an appropriate footer for your notes and handouts and save your presentation as *2K_Plan_Firstname_Lastname*. Print the presentation as handouts, 4 slides per page, in grayscale.

End You have completed Project 2K

Project 2L — Accessory

Objectives: *Create a Presentation Using a Design Template and Modify Slides.*

Start a new presentation based on a design template of your choice. Choose a fashion accessory such as wallets, boots, shoes, luggage, and so on, that might be marketed by a company such as El Cuero. Create four slides that include information such as designs, colors, market, and pricing. You can get ideas for this presentation by researching a variety of fashion magazines on the Internet. Create an appropriate footer for your notes and handouts and save your presentation as *2K_Accessory_Firstname_Lastname*. Print the presentation as handouts, 4 slides per page, in grayscale.

End You have completed Project 2L

On the Internet

Locating Company Mission Statements

Access your Internet connection and visit the home pages of several large companies with which you are familiar. Explore their Web sites to view their mission statements, business plans, and human resources information. Compare the information that you gathered for at least two companies and prepare a four-slide presentation that summarizes the companies' mission and services.

GO! with Help

Using AutoCorrect

The AutoCorrect feature in PowerPoint corrects many misspelled words as you type them, corrects incorrect capitalization, and corrects the accidental usage of the Caps Lock key. In this Help activity, you will learn more about the AutoCorrect feature.

1. Start PowerPoint. In the **Type a question for help** box, type **What is the AutoCorrect feature?**

2. In the displayed **Search Results** task pane, click to display each of the AutoCorrect links.

3. To see how AutoCorrect works, start a new **Blank Presentation**. In the title placeholder, you will intentionally type some words incorrectly. Type **Teh Nwe Feature** and notice that the incorrectly spelled words *Teh* and *Nwe* are corrected. Close the file without saving.

PowerPoint 2003

chapter three

Formatting a Presentation

In this chapter, you will: complete these projects and practice these skills.

Project 3A
Emergency Preparedness Presentation

Objectives
- Format Slide Text
- Modify Placeholders
- Modify Slide Master Elements

Project 3B
Volunteer Opportunities Presentation

Objectives
- Apply Bullets and Numbering
- Customize a Color Scheme
- Modify the Slide Background
- Apply an Animation Scheme

University Medical Center Office of Public Affairs

The University Medical Center is a premier patient-care and research institution serving Orange Beach, Florida. To promote and maintain the Center's sterling reputation, the Office of Public Affairs (OPA) publishes both locally and nationally the Center's services, achievements, and professional staff. The OPA staff interacts with the media, writes press releases and announcements, prepares marketing materials, develops public awareness campaigns, maintains a speakers bureau of experts, and conducts media training for physicians and researchers.

© Photosphere Images Ltd.

Formatting a Presentation

A PowerPoint presentation is a visual *aid* in which well-designed slides help the audience to understand complex information while keeping them focused on the message. When planning the *text* for your slides, use the following guidelines: First, limit the amount of information on a slide. One rule you could follow is the 6x6 rule: no more than 6 lines on a slide, and no more than 6 words per line. Second, include key words, not complete sentences. Use consistent grammar throughout the presentation. If one title begins with a verb, all the titles should begin with verbs. If one bullet point is written in present tense, all the bullet points should be written in present tense.

Color is another important element that provides uniformity and visual interest. When used correctly, color enhances your slides and draws the audience's interest by creating focus. Use the following tips when designing the background and element colors for your presentation: First, use a consistent look throughout the presentation. Second, be sure that the colors you use provide contrast so that the text is visible on the background.

Project 3A Emergency

After you have created the content for a presentation, you can concentrate on improving its format and appearance. You can create focal elements on your slides by formatting text and by changing the size and location of placeholders. Attention to details will take your presentation from good to great!

In Activities 3.1 through 3.13, you will modify a presentation regarding emergency preparedness plans developed by the University Medical Center. You will name the file *3A_Emergency_Firstname_Lastname*. See Figure 3.1.

Figure 3.1
Project 3A—Emergency

Objective 1
Format Slide Text

Recall that formatting is the process of changing the appearance of the text, layout, and design of a slide. Formatting text includes changing the style and size of the text, applying bold, italic, and underline, and enhancing text with effects such as shadows and embossing.

Activity 3.1 Changing Fonts and Font Sizes

A *font* is a set of characters with the same design and shape. Examples of fonts include Arial, Times New Roman, and Tahoma. Fonts are measured in *points* (abbreviated as pt.), with one point equal to $1/72$ of an inch. A greater point size indicates a larger font size. Formatting changes are easier to view when the Slide pane is the only pane active in your PowerPoint window. Thus, in this activity you will change fonts and font sizes using the Slide pane.

1 Start PowerPoint and from your student files, **Open** the file **p03A_Emergency**. If you want, create a Chapter 3 folder. From the **File** menu, click **Save As**. Save the file as **3A_Emergency_Firstname_Lastname** and be sure to use *your* name in place of the words *Firstname Lastname*. **Close** the **Outline/Slides** pane.

2 Display **Slide 2**. In the title, double-click anywhere in the word *Mission*.

The entire word is selected.

3 On the Formatting toolbar, click the **Font arrow**.

The current font is Tahoma. The font list displays the fonts available on your system. Each font name is displayed in its actual style so that you have an immediate picture of how the font will appear in your slide show and on your printed page. See Figure 3.2.

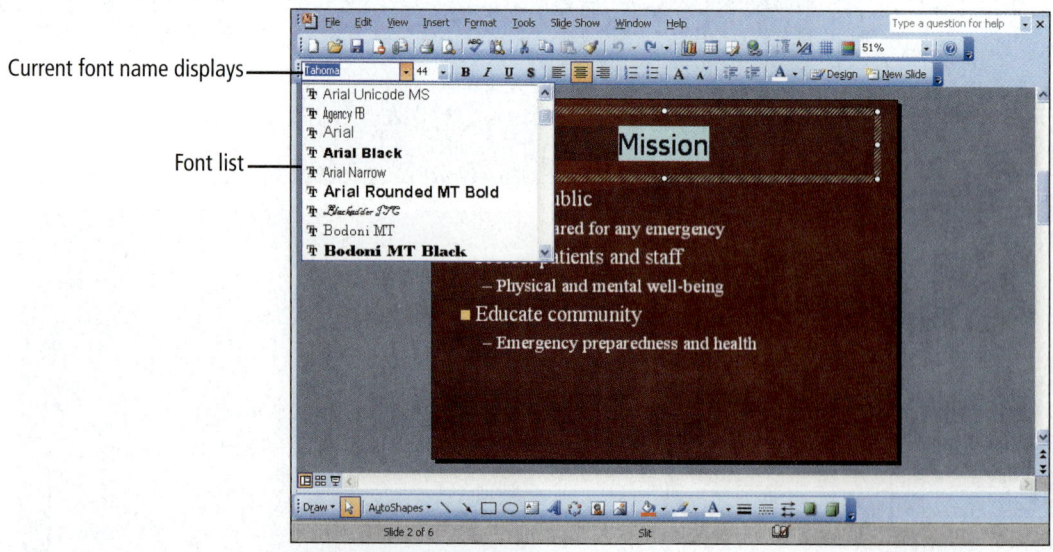

Figure 3.2

1094 PowerPoint | Chapter 3: Formatting a Presentation

4 Take a moment to view the various fonts available on your system by dragging the scroll box in the font list. The fonts are listed alphabetically. In the Font list, click **Times New Roman**.

The selected text is formatted in the Times New Roman font.

5 With the text in the title placeholder still selected, on the Formatting toolbar, click the **Font Size arrow** . Scroll down the **Font Size** list, and then click **48**.

Recall that a greater point size indicates a larger font. The font size is increased by 4 points.

> **Note** — Sizing the Font
>
> The Font Size list displays default values for applying font sizes. You can click in the Font size box and type any font size directly into the box.

6 Save the file.

Activity 3.2 Replacing Fonts

In this presentation, much of the text is formatted in the Times New Roman font. Rather than selecting the text on each slide and changing it to the Arial font, you can use the Replace Fonts command to change all occurrences of a font to a different font.

1 On the menu bar, click **Format**, and then click **Replace Fonts**.

The Replace Font dialog box displays.

2 Click the **Replace arrow** to display the fonts currently applied in the presentation. Click **Times New Roman** to indicate the font that you wish to replace.

3 Click the **With arrow**, and then scroll the font list. Click **Arial** to indicate the new font to be used in the presentation. See Figure 3.3. Click **Replace**, and then click **Close**.

Scroll through your slides and notice the change in the fonts on each slide.

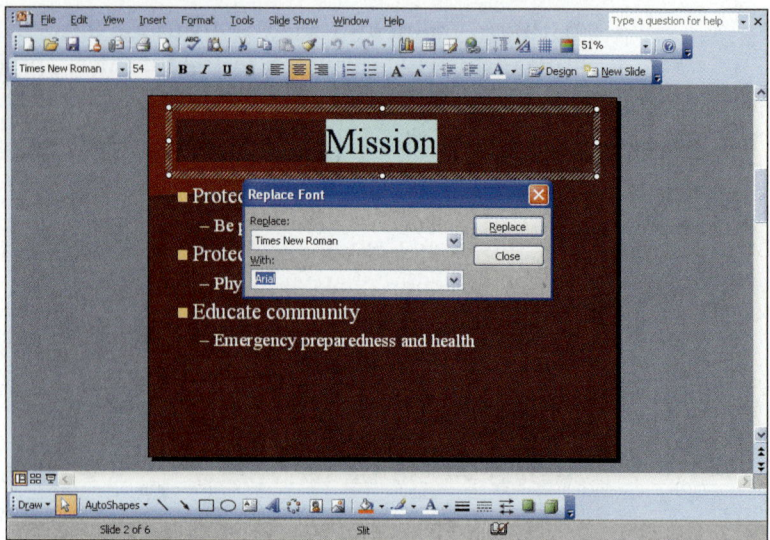

Figure 3.3

4 **Save** the file.

Activity 3.3 Changing Font Styles and Font Effects

Font styles and font effects are used to emphasize text using bold, italic, underline, and shadows. You can apply font formatting options by using the Font dialog box, keyboard shortcuts, or by using the Bold, Italic, Underline, or Shadow buttons on the Formatting toolbar. The Bold, Italic, Underline, and Shadow buttons are *toggle* buttons on the toolbar. A toggle button works similar to a light switch. The button is clicked once to turn the feature on, and the button is clicked again to turn the feature off. Other font effects such as embossing, superscript, and subscript can be accessed from the Font dialog box.

1 Display **Slide 2** and click anywhere in the bulleted list placeholder. Press and hold down Ctrl and then click in the first bullet point—*Protect public.* Do not click the bullet in front of the text.

The first bulleted line is selected. Recall that pressing and holding down Ctrl and then clicking in a line selects the entire line. This action does not include subordinate bullet points in the selection.

2 On the Formatting toolbar, click **Bold** B to apply bold to the selection. Click anywhere on the slide to cancel the selection.

Notice the formatting applied to the first line.

3 Double-click the title to select it, and then on the Formatting toolbar, click **Shadow** S. Click to cancel the selection.

Notice the slight shadowing effect applied to the title. In this presentation, the dark background does not provide sufficient contrast to view the text shadow effectively.

4 Recall that the **Shadow** button is a toggle button. Double-click the title again to reselect it. On the Formatting toolbar, click **Shadow** to remove the shadow effect.

5 You can apply more than one font style or effect to a selection. Select the first bullet point—*Protect public*. Do not select the subordinate bullet. On the Formatting toolbar, click **Italic**, and then click **Underline**. Click to cancel the selection.

Notice that the entire line is formatted in bold, italic, and underline.

6 To use the keyboard shortcut to remove some of the font formatting that you have applied, select the first bullet point—*Protect public* again. Press and hold down [Ctrl] and then press [U] once to remove the underline from the selection. Click to cancel the selection.

7 In the first bullet, select the word *public* but do not select the word *Protect*. Press and hold down [Ctrl] and then press [B] once to remove the bold formatting. With the text still selected, on the Formatting toolbar click **Italic** to remove the italic formatting. Click to cancel the selection and view the first bullet.

The word *Protect* is the only text that contains the bold and italic formatting.

8 Double-click the word *Mission* to select it. On the menu bar, click the **Format** menu, and then click **Font**. Under **Effects**, click to place a check mark in the **Emboss** check box. See Figure 3.4. Click **OK** to apply the formatting to the selection, and then click to cancel the selection, noticing the formatting that is applied to the selection.

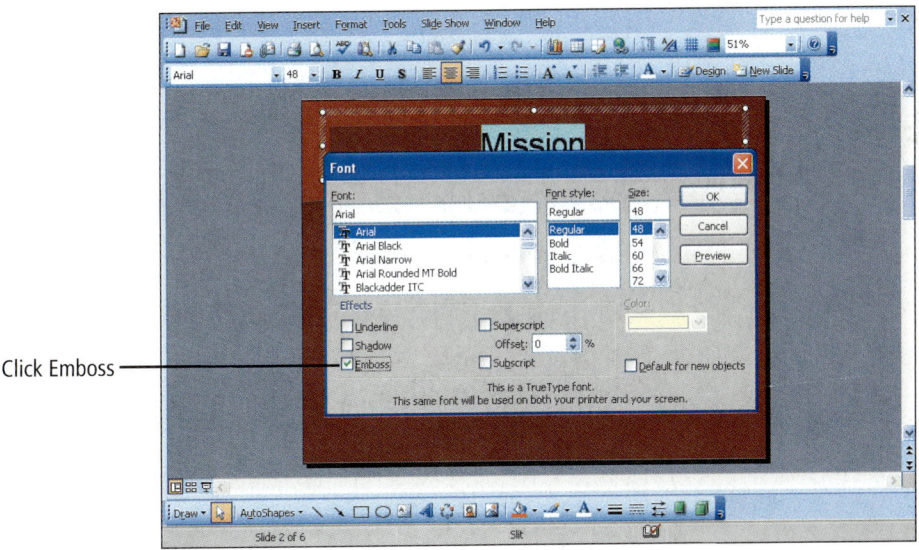

Click Emboss

Figure 3.4

Project 3A: Emergency | **PowerPoint** 1097

9 The Emboss formatting is not effective on this background. On the Standard toolbar, click **Undo** to remove the format.

10 **Save** the file.

Activity 3.4 Using the Repeat Key

You can use the F4 function key to repeat the last command or series of keystrokes that you have performed. If you type a word and press F4, the word will be repeated. Similarly, you can apply bold to a selection of text, and then, using the repeat function, apply bold to a different selection of text.

1 If necessary, display **Slide 2**, and then in the third bullet point, select the first word—*Protect*.

2 On the menu bar, click **Format**, and then click **Font**. Under **Font style**, click **Bold Italic**, and then click **OK**.

3 In the fifth bullet point, select the first word—*Educate*—and then press F4.

The word *Educate* is formatted in bold and italic. Because the formatting was applied from the dialog box, both the bold and italic formats were repeated—the two formats were treated as one action. The first words of each of the first-level bullet points are now formatted with bold and italic.

4 **Save** your file.

Activity 3.5 Changing Font Colors

Recall that every design template consists of a color scheme—a palette of eight coordinated colors that includes background, text, fill, and accent colors. The color scheme for this template includes placeholder text in white. As you view Slide 2, notice that the first word of each bullet is emphasized with the bold and italic formatting that you applied. To further emphasize these words, you can change the font color.

1 Display **Slide 2** and then, in the first bullet point, select the first word—*Protect*. On the Formatting toolbar, click the **Font Color arrow** to display the eight colors in the design template color scheme. See Figure 3.5.

> **Note** — Displaying the Color Palette
>
> *Click the arrow!*
>
> Be sure to click the arrow, not the button itself. Clicking the Font Color button applies to your selected text the color that displays below the letter *A* on the button.

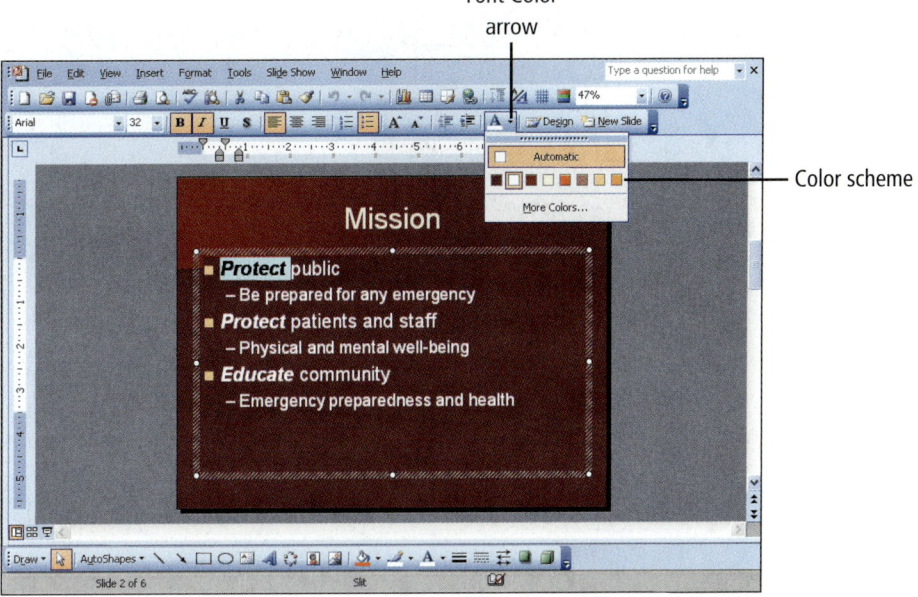

Figure 3.5

2 Point to each of the colors in the color scheme and read the ScreenTip that displays, indicating the usage of each of the colors in the template.

You are not limited to using these colors, but if you use one of the colors in the color scheme, you can be sure that it will coordinate with all of the other colors in the presentation.

3 Below the color palette, click **More Colors**, and, if necessary, click the **Standard tab**.

The Colors dialog box, with a honeycomb of colors, displays providing a variety of color options.

4 In the first row of the honeycomb, click the first color—**dark blue**. See Figure 3.6. Click **OK**.

Click to cancel the selection and view your color change. Notice that this color is very dark and does not draw focus to the selection.

Project 3A: Emergency | **PowerPoint** 1099

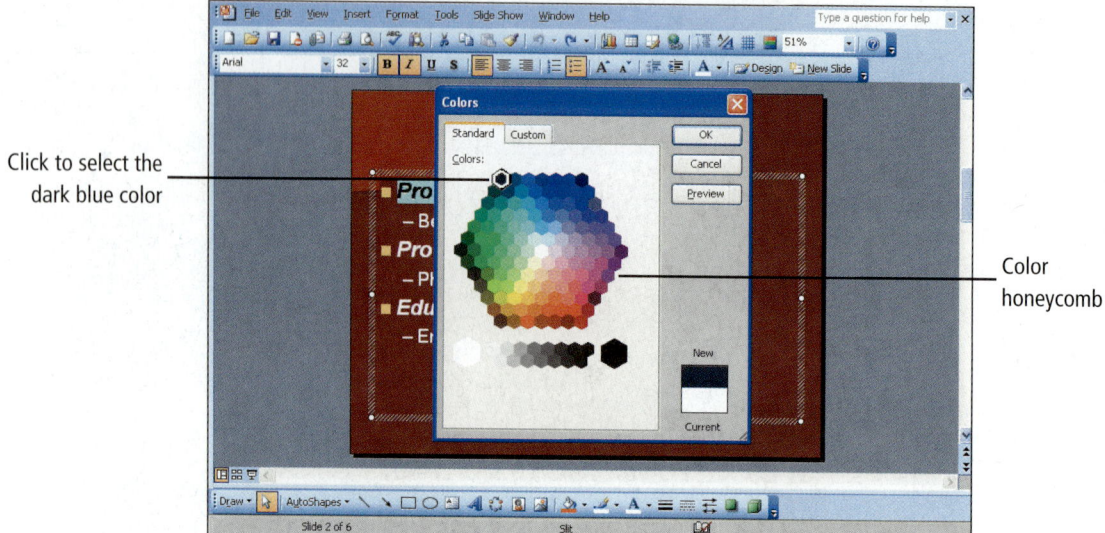

Figure 3.6

5 Select the word *Protect* again and on the Formatting toolbar, click the **Font Color arrow**.

Notice that the dark blue color that you applied displays below the original color palette indicating that this color was applied somewhere in the presentation. The ScreenTip *Custom Color* displays when you point to this color.

6 In the original color scheme palette, click the last color square—**orange**—and then click elsewhere in the slide to cancel the selection.

Notice that this color emphasizes the word *Protect* and creates a focal element on the slide.

7 In the third bullet point, select the word *Protect* and then press F4 to repeat the font color selection. In the fifth bullet point, select the word *Educate*, and then press F4 again to repeat the font color selection. Click elsewhere in the slide to cancel the selection, and then compare your slide to Figure 3.7.

As you read this slide, notice the difference in tone that the orange, bold, and italic create when applied to the first word of each bullet. Using color and font styles, you can effectively create emphasis and focus, and you can change the tone of your presentation.

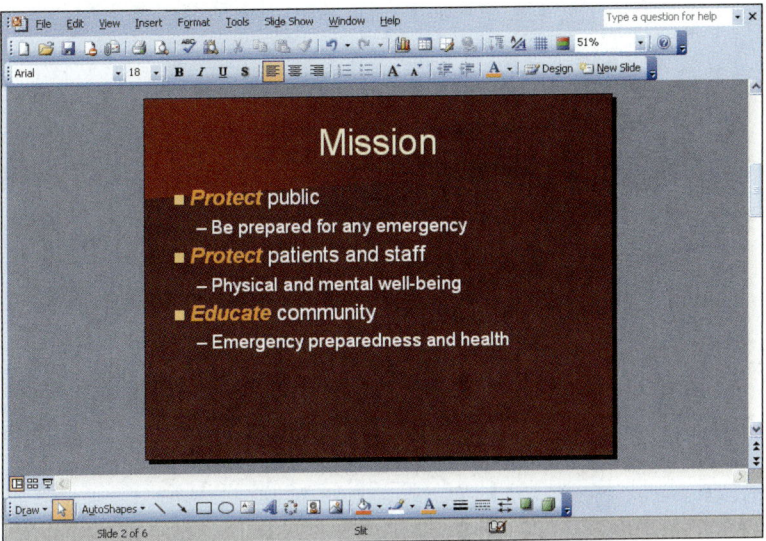

Figure 3.7

8 **Save** the file.

Activity 3.6 Copying Formatting Using Format Painter

Format Painter copies *formatting* from one selection of text to another. This differs from copy and paste in that the text itself is not copied. Instead, only the formatting of the selected text is copied.

In this activity, you will use Format Painter to copy formatting to a single selection of text and also to multiple selections of text.

1 If necessary, **Open** your file **3A_Emergency_Firstname_Lastname**.

2 Display **Slide 2**, and in the first bullet point, double-click to select the first word—*Protect*. This word is formatted in bold and italic, and the font color is orange.

3 On the Standard toolbar, click the **Format Painter** button.

Move the pointer away from the Format Painter button and notice that the Format Painter button is highlighted. Additionally, the mouse pointer appears as an I-beam with a small paintbrush attached to it. See Figure 3.8.

Project 3A: Emergency | **PowerPoint** 1101

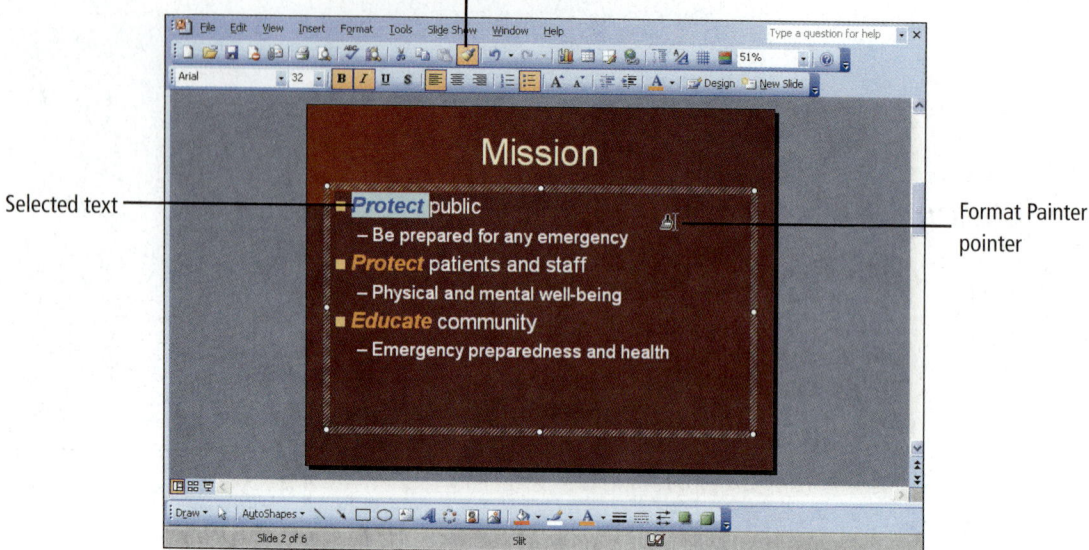

Figure 3.8

[4] Do *not* click anywhere in the slide. Instead, move the pointer to the vertical scroll bar and notice that the pointer displays as a left-pointing arrow. Drag the scroll box down so that **Slide 5** displays. Move the pointer back into the **Slide** pane and notice that the **Format Painter** pointer displays again.

[5] In the first bullet point, drag to the right to select *Mobile emergency trailers*. Release the mouse button and click elsewhere on the slide to cancel the selection.

The Format Painter button is no longer highlighted and the words *Mobile emergency trailers* are formatted with the same formatting as the word *Protect* in Slide 2.

[6] If necessary, display **Slide 5**, and in the first bullet point select the first word—*Mobile*. On the Standard toolbar, double-click the **Format Painter** button.

Double-clicking the Format Painter button will cause it to remain active until it is clicked again to turn it off.

[7] In the second, first-level bullet point, drag the pointer over the words *Rapid response* and then release the mouse button.

The format is applied to the selection. Move your pointer anywhere away from the selection and verify that the paintbrush is still attached to the pointer. This indicates that Format Painter is still active.

Alert!

Has the Paintbrush Disappeared from Your Pointer?
If you do not see the paintbrush, it is likely that your hand moved slightly when you attempted your double-click of the Format Painter button, and it was interpreted as a single click. Double-click the Format Painter button again.

1102 PowerPoint | Chapter 3: Formatting a Presentation

8 Drag your pointer over the words *Teams ready to deploy* and then release the mouse button to apply the formatting.

9 Click the **Format Painter** button once to turn it off, and then click elsewhere on your slide to cancel the selection and view the formatting changes.

10 **Save** your file.

> **Alert!** — **Don't Forget to Turn Off Format Painter!**
>
> When you use Format Painter for multiple selections, do not forget to click the Format Painter button or press Esc to turn it off. Otherwise you will continue to *paint* your presentation text!

Activity 3.7 Changing Text Case

Text Case refers to text capitalization. Text can be changed to all lowercase, all uppercase, sentence case, or title case. You can change text case using the Change Case command on the Format menu, or you can use the Shift + F3 keyboard shortcut. The table in Figure 3.9 describes each case option in PowerPoint.

Text Case Options

Case option	Description
Sentence case	The first letter of the sentence is capitalized.
Lowercase	Text is not capitalized.
Uppercase	Text is in all capital letters.
Title case	The first letter of every word is capitalized.
Toggle case	Uppercase letters in the selection are changed to lowercase, and lowercase letters are changed to uppercase.

Figure 3.9

1 If necessary, **Open** your file **3A_Emergency_Firstname_Lastname**.

2 Display **Slide 1** and select the text in the subtitle placeholder—*Keeping our community safe*. On the menu bar, click the **Format** menu, and then click **Change Case**. Click **Title Case** to capitalize the first letter of each word. Click **OK**.

3 Select the title text. Press and hold down Shift and then press F3.

The title text displays in uppercase.

4 Press and hold down Shift and then press F3 again.

The title text displays in all lowercase.

5 Press and hold down Shift and then press F3 again.

The text displays in title case. The keyboard shortcut rotates through these three case options. Click to cancel the selection and then compare your slide to Figure 3.10.

Figure 3.10

6 Save your file.

Activity 3.8 Changing Text Alignment

Alignment refers to the horizontal position of the text between the left and right edges of a placeholder. There are four alignment options in PowerPoint—Align Left, Center, Align Right, and Justify. You can change alignment by using the alignment button on the Formatting toolbar, by clicking the Format menu and then clicking Alignment, or by using a keyboard shortcut. In this activity, you will change the alignment of the title placeholder on the first and last slides.

1 Display **Slide 6**, and then click in the title placeholder.

Notice in the Formatting toolbar that the Center button is highlighted. This indicates that the line in which the insertion point is positioned is center aligned.

2 On the Formatting toolbar, click **Align Right**.

Although the title displays on two lines, it is treated as one line because when it was typed, the Enter key was not pressed after the word *Response*. Thus, the entire title is right aligned. Aligning the title at the right edge of the slide is a subtle change that makes the slide more interesting.

3 Display **Slide 1**, and then click in the title placeholder. Press and hold down Ctrl, and then press E.

The title is centered within the placeholder.

4 Save the file.

1104 PowerPoint | Chapter 3: Formatting a Presentation

Objective 2
Modify Placeholders

The design template applied to the presentation and the layout applied to the slide determine the initial size of a placeholder on a slide. You can change the size and position of a placeholder so that the text displays more effectively. You can also select the placeholder itself and modify all of the text contained within it at one time.

Activity 3.9 Selecting Placeholder Text

When you click inside a placeholder, a boundary box consisting of diagonal slash marks surrounds it. This boundary box indicates that you can make editing changes to the text in the placeholder. Clicking the boundary box changes the slash marks to a pattern of dots. This dotted pattern indicates that all of the text in the placeholder is selected, allowing you to apply formatting to all of the text in the placeholder without actually selecting the text.

1 Display **Slide 3**, and click anywhere in the bulleted list placeholder.

Notice the diagonal slash marks surrounding the placeholder.

2 Point to the outer edge of the placeholder so that a four-headed arrow displays. See Figure 3.11. Click the left mouse button.

The placeholder is surrounded by a pattern of dots.

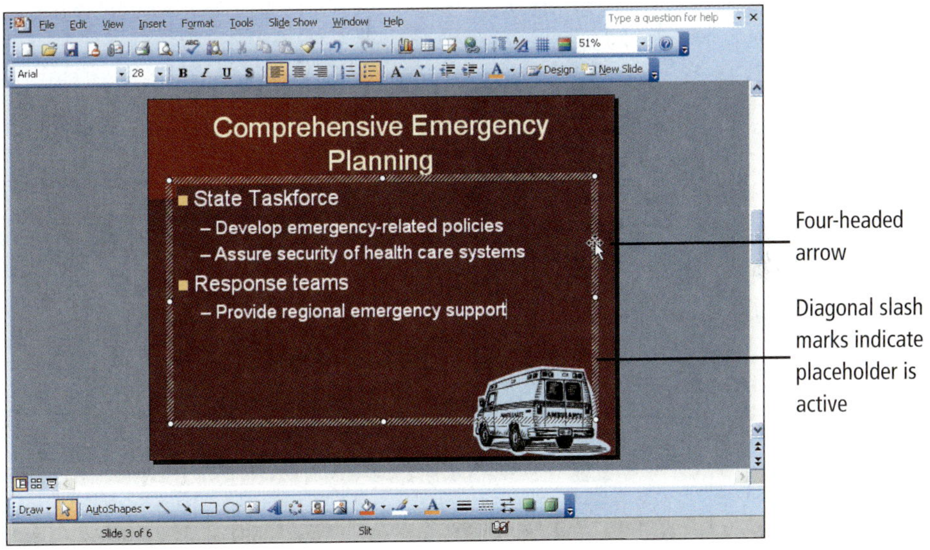

Figure 3.11

3 On the Formatting toolbar, click **Italic** [I].

All of the text in the placeholder is formatted in italic.

4 **Save** your file.

Activity 3.10 Sizing a Placeholder

When you select a placeholder, the boundary box that displays includes small white circles called sizing handles. The sizing handles are used to adjust the size of the placeholder. Depending on the sizing handle to which you point, the pointer displays as a left and right, up and down, or diagonal pointing arrow, indicating that you can size the placeholder. When you reduce the size of a placeholder, PowerPoint may display the AutoFit smart tag, giving you the option to AutoFit the text to the size of the placeholder.

1 If necessary, **Open** your file **3A_Emergency_Firstname_Lastname**.

2 Display **Slide 1**. Click anywhere in the title so that the placeholder boundary displays. The text in this placeholder displays on two lines with only one word on the second line. The title would display more attractively if all of the text fit within one line in the placeholder.

3 At the left edge of the placeholder, point to the center sizing handle so that the pointer displays as a left-and-right-pointing arrow. See Figure 3.12.

Figure 3.12

4 Press and hold down the left mouse button, and then drag to the left. Notice that a dashed box displays. This box indicates the new dimensions and position of the placeholder. Continue to drag to the left so that the edge of the placeholder extends to the left edge of the slide, and then release the mouse button to resize the placeholder.

5 At the right edge of the placeholder, point to the center sizing handle so that the pointer again displays as a left-and-right-pointing arrow. Press and hold down the left mouse button, and then drag to the right edge of the slide. Release the mouse button.

6 Select the title text, and on the Formatting toolbar, click the **Decrease Font Size** button.

The font size decreases to 48 and the text displays on one line.

7 Display **Slide 3**, and then click anywhere in the title placeholder. Point to the center right sizing handle so that a left-and-right sizing arrow displays. Press and hold down the left mouse button, and then drag to the right until the dashed box extends to the right edge of the slide. Release the mouse button to resize the placeholder.

8 Point to the center left sizing handle so that a left-and-right sizing arrow displays. Press and hold down the left mouse button, and then drag to the left until the dashed box extends to the left edge of the slide. Release the mouse button to resize the placeholder.

The text is positioned on a single line.

9 As you view **Slide 3**, notice that the ambulance picture in the lower right corner provides balance for the text elements, but that the text is still heavily weighted on the left side of the slide. To balance this slide more attractively, click in the bulleted text placeholder, and then point to the lower left sizing handle so that a diagonal arrow displays.

10 With the diagonal arrow displayed, press and hold down the left mouse button and drag up and to the right so that the left edge of the placeholder aligns with the letter *p* in *Comprehensive* and the lower edge of the placeholder aligns above the ambulance. See Figure 3.13. Release the left mouse button to resize the placeholder.

Notice that the elements are balanced more attractively on the slide.

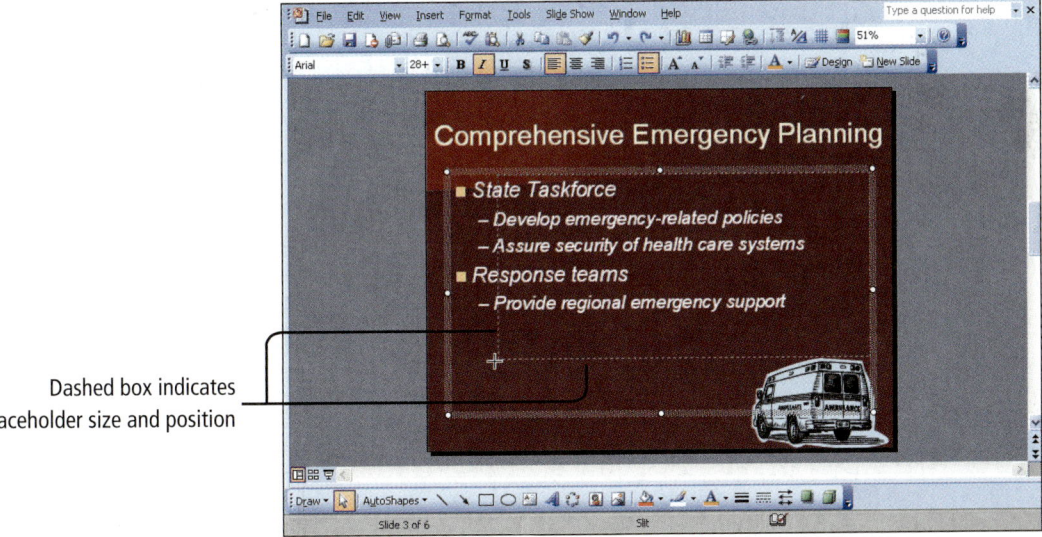

Dashed box indicates placeholder size and position

Figure 3.13

11 **Save** the file.

Activity 3.11 Moving a Placeholder

A placeholder can be positioned anywhere on a slide by dragging it to a new location. Subtle changes in the placement of a placeholder provide visual interest and variety in your presentations. In this activity, you will reposition the subtitle on Slide 1 and the bulleted list placeholder in Slide 6.

1 Display **Slide 6**, and then click anywhere in the bulleted list to select the placeholder.

2 Point anywhere on the outer edge of the placeholder so that a four-headed arrow displays. Do *not* point to one of the sizing handles as this would result in sizing the placeholder instead of moving the placeholder. Press and hold down the left mouse button, and then drag down until the lower edge of the dashed box aligns with the bottom of the slide. See Figure 3.14. Release the mouse button to reposition the placeholder.

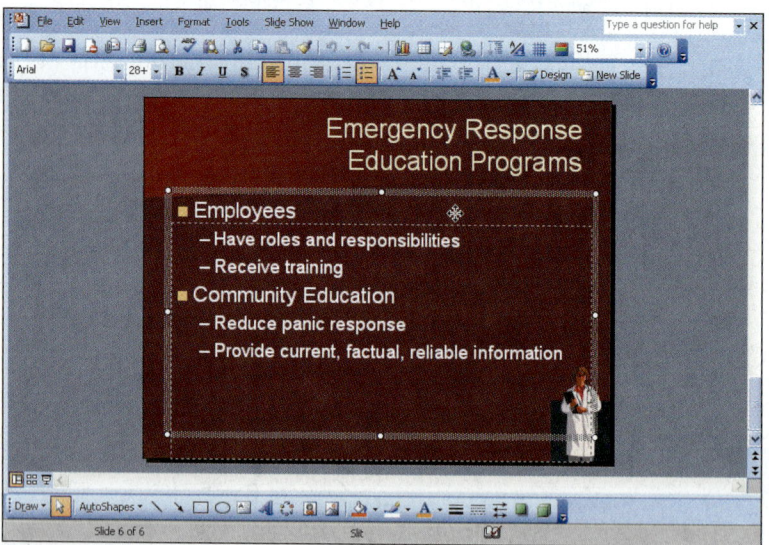

Figure 3.14

3 Display **Slide 1** and click in the subtitle placeholder. Point to the center bottom sizing handle so that an up-and-downward-pointing arrow displays. Press and hold down the left mouse button and drag up so that the bottom edge of the placeholder is just below the text. See Figure 3.15. Release the mouse button to resize the placeholder.

Figure 3.15

[4] Point to the outer edge of the subtitle boundary box so that a four-headed arrow displays. Do not point to a sizing handle. Press and hold down the left mouse button and drag down and to the right so that the lower left corner of the dashed box is positioned in the corner of the hospital building. See Figure 3.16. Release the left mouse button to move the placeholder.

Figure 3.16

[5] **Save** the file.

Project 3A: Emergency | **PowerPoint** 1109

Objective 3
Modify Slide Master Elements

The **slide master** is a slide that holds the information about formatting and text that displays on every slide in your presentation. The slide master is not an actual slide in a presentation; rather, it exists "behind the scenes" of the presentation to help you control the look of your presentation. For example, if your organization has a logo that you wish to display on every slide in your presentation, you can position the logo on the slide master and the logo will display on every slide. Other elements that display on every slide include the graphics and bullets from the design template and the headers and footers. The slide master also includes formatting information such as font and bullet color, size, and text alignment. You can override slide master formatting by changing the formatting on an individual slide.

Activity 3.12 Displaying and Modifying the Title Master

In addition to the slide master, there are several other masters with which you can work, one of which is the title master. In this activity, you will modify the title master and then add a new slide with the Title Slide layout.

1 If necessary, **Open** your file **3A_Emergency_Firstname_Lastname**.

2 Display **Slide 1**. Press and hold down Shift, and point to **Normal View**. Notice that the ScreenTip *Slide Master View* displays. With the Shift key pressed, click **Slide Master View**.

The title master displays because Slide 1 was active. Notice that the status bar indicates that the title master is active. See Figure 3.17. Additionally, the Slide Master View toolbar displays, somewhere on your screen.

> **Note** — The Slide Master Toolbar
>
> As you progress in your study of PowerPoint you will use this toolbar, which is most useful when using multiple slide masters.

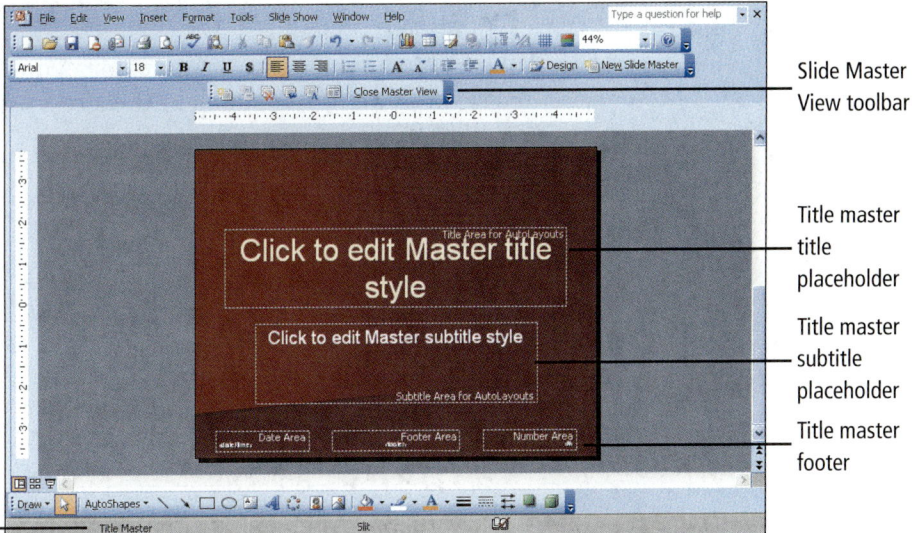

Figure 3.17

3. Click anywhere in the text *Click to edit Master subtitle style*.

   The entire subtitle is selected.

4. On the Formatting toolbar, click the **Font Color arrow**. Click the fifth color in the color scheme—**red-orange**.

   Click to cancel the selection and notice that the font color is changed in the subtitle.

5. To view the change on the title slide, click **Normal View**.

   Slide 1 displays the subtitle in the new font color.

6. Display **Slide 6** and then on the Formatting toolbar, click **New Slide**. In the **Slide Layout** task pane, click **Title Slide**.

   A new slide displays with the title slide layout. Notice that the font formatting (red-orange color) is applied to the subtitle.

7. In the title placeholder, type **Emergency Preparedness** In the subtitle placeholder type **University Medical Center** and then press Enter. Type **We're Here For You!**

8. **Close** the **Slide Layout** task pane, and then **Save** the file.

Project 3A: Emergency | **PowerPoint** 1111

Activity 3.13 Displaying and Modifying the Slide Master

In this activity, you will change font colors on the slide master and then view the effect on all of the slides in the presentation.

1 Display **Slide 2**. Press and hold down [Shift] and click **Slide Master View** to display the slide master. Click in the title placeholder to select the Master title text.

> **More Knowledge** — Displaying Master Slides
>
> When the slide or title master is displayed, notice that a vertical scroll bar displays to the right of the master. Dragging the scroll box down displays the title master, dragging the scroll box up displays the slide master. The toolbar that displays provides options for adding new slide and title masters, deleting masters, and changing the name and layout of master slides.

2 On the Formatting toolbar, click the **Font Color arrow** to display the color scheme. Click the seventh color—**gold**—to change the font color of all of the titles that are not formatted with the title slide layout.

3 To view the effect of the changes that you have made, return to Normal View by clicking the **Normal View** button. Scroll through the presentation and view the titles on each slide, noticing that each title is formatted in the gold color you selected on the slide master.

4 Create a footer for the notes and handouts that includes the date updated automatically and a footer with the text **3A Emergency-Firstname Lastname**. Clear all other header and footer options, and then click **Apply to All**.

5 **Save** the file, and then print the presentation as **handouts**, **4** slides per page in **horizontal** order. **Close** the file.

End You have completed Project 3A

Project 3B Volunteers

Recall that the design template that you apply to a presentation includes a color scheme, background graphics and designs, and bullets. You can modify the color scheme and slide backgrounds, and you can insert new bullets that include shapes and pictures in a variety of colors and sizes.

In Activities 3.14 through 3.23, you will format a presentation regarding volunteer opportunities at University Medical Center. You will name the file *3B_Volunteers_Firstname_Lastname*. See Figure 3.18.

Figure 3.18
Project 3B—Volunteers

Objective 4
Apply Bullets and Numbering

Bullets and numbering are used in a PowerPoint presentation to emphasize important points on a slide. A design template includes bullets for up to five outline levels, and these outline levels determine the shape, size, color, and indentation of the bullet character. You can modify the bullets for an entire presentation by changing the bullet character, color, or size on the slide master, or you can modify bullets on an individual slide.

Activity 3.14 Modifying Bullet Characters

In this activity, you will change the bullet character, the color of the bullet, and the bullet size for the entire presentation by modifying the Slide Master.

1. From your student files, **Open** the file **p03B_Volunteers** and display **Slide 2**. Save the file as **3B_Volunteers_Firstname_Lastname** and then **close** the **Outline/Slides** pane.

2. Press and hold down Shift and then point to the **Normal View** button, noticing that the ScreenTip **Slide Master View** displays. Click to display the slide master.

   If the title master displays, drag the scroll box in the vertical scroll bar up so that the slide master displays.

3. In the bulleted list placeholder, click in the first line—*Click to edit Master text styles*. On the menu bar, click the **Format** menu, and then click **Bullets and Numbering**.

   The Bullets and Numbering box displays six default bullets and two additional bullet boxes—None and Custom. You can use None to remove the bullets from a selection. The Custom box is selected, indicating that the selected bullet is not one of the default bullets, but was instead chosen from one of the symbol fonts.

4. In the second row, click the first bullet—the **shadowed square**. Currently, the **Size** box indicates that the bullet is 60% of the size of the text. To enlarge the bullet, click the **up spin arrow** in the **Size** box three times to increase the size to **75**. Alternatively, select the number in the Size box and type 75.

> **Alert!** — **Is Your Dialog Box Different?**
>
> If the shadowed square does not display in the dialog box, then the bullet has been replaced by another user. To display the shadowed square, click the first bullet in the second row. Then, in the lower left corner of the dialog box, click Reset. The default shadowed square bullet will display.

5️⃣ Below the **Size** box, click the **Color arrow** to display the eight colors in the design template's color scheme. Click the seventh square—**red**. Compare your dialog box to Figure 3.19, and then click **OK**. The Slide Master reflects the changes to the bullet.

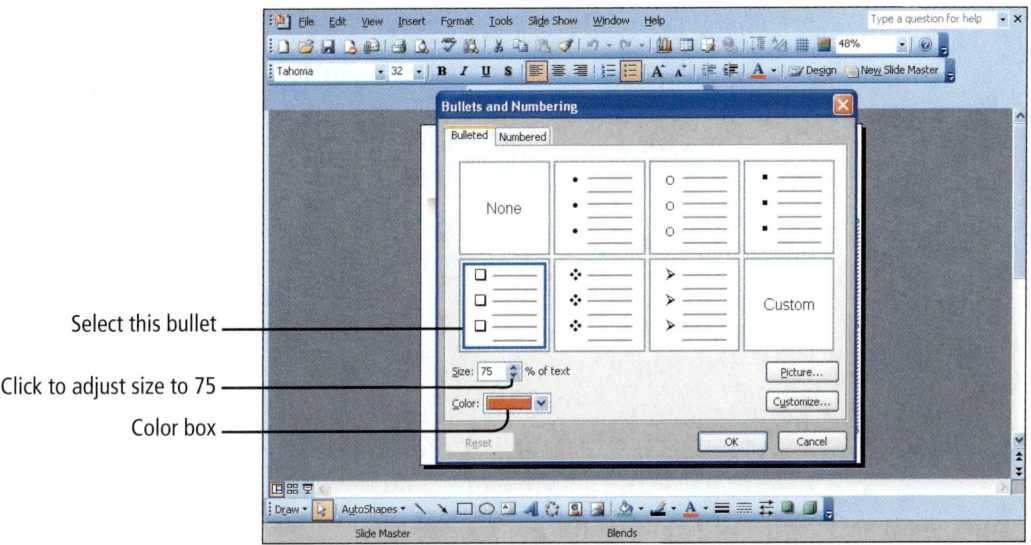

Figure 3.19

6️⃣ Click the **Second level** bullet line. On the **Format** menu, click **Bullets and Numbering**. In the lower right corner of the **Bullets and Numbering** dialog box, click the **Customize** button.

The Symbol dialog box displays characters from the Wingdings font. You can choose any of these symbols as bullet characters.

7️⃣ Scroll to the bottom of the list of symbols, and in the last row, click the first bullet character—a **right-pointing arrow**. See Figure 3.20. Click **OK** to return to the **Bullets and Numbering** dialog box.

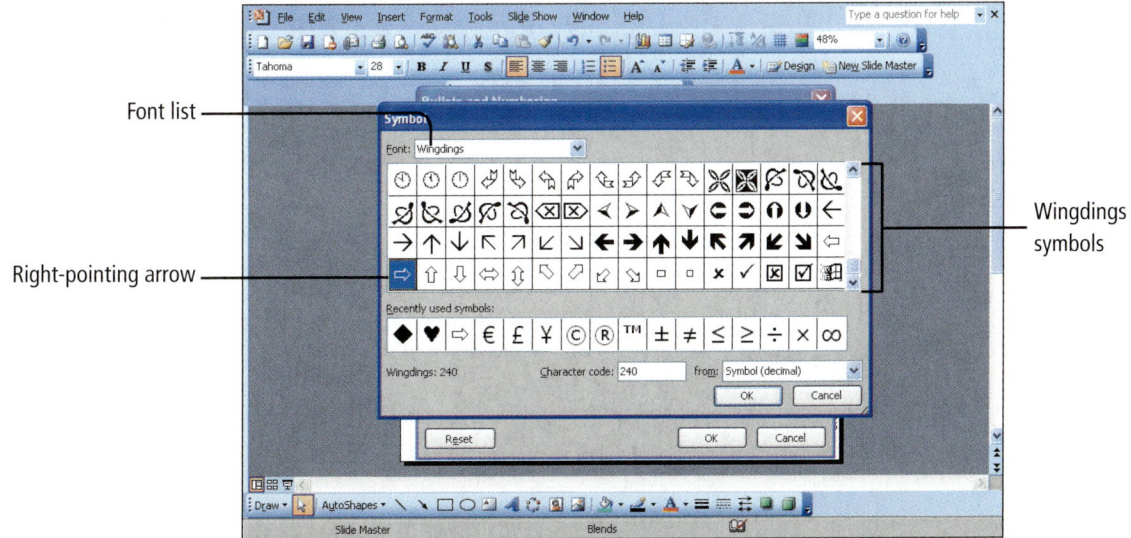

Figure 3.20

Project 3B: Volunteers | **PowerPoint** 1115

8 Click the **Color arrow** and then click **More Colors**. In the last row of the honeycomb, click the last color—**dark red**. Click **OK**, and then click **OK** again to apply your changes to the slide master.

9 Click **Normal View** to close the slide master and to return to the presentation. Display **Slide 4** to view the changes to the first and second level bullets.

10 Display **Slide 5**, and then click the bulleted list placeholder. Point to the outer edge of the placeholder so that a four-headed arrow displays, and then click so that the boundary box surrounding the placeholder changes to a pattern of dots.

Recall that when a placeholder is surrounded by a dotted pattern, formatting changes are applied to all of the text in the placeholder. Rather than making a global change on the slide master, you will modify the bullet color on this individual slide. Changes made to individual slides override the formatting on the slide master.

11 On the menu bar, click the **Format** menu, and then click **Bullets and Numbering**. Click the **Color arrow**, and in the color scheme palette, click the sixth color—**gold**. Click **OK** to change the bullet color for the text in the selected placeholder.

12 **Save** the file.

Activity 3.15 Inserting Picture Bullets

In this activity, you will use the Slide Master View to apply a picture bullet to the second level bullet.

1 Display **Slide 4** and then click **Slide Master View**—[Shift] + . Click the **Second level** bullet.

2 From the **Format** menu, click **Bullets and Numbering**, and then in the lower right corner, click the **Picture** button.

The Picture Bullet dialog box displays a variety of images that can be used as bullets. Use the vertical scroll bar to view the bullets. You can search for bullets that match a keyword or you can scroll through the bullets and choose one that you wish to use.

3 Click in the **Search text** box, type **squares**, and then click **Go**.

The dialog box displays only square bullets.

4 Click the **green bullet** shown in Figure 3.21, then click **OK**.

The picture bullet is applied to the second level bullet.

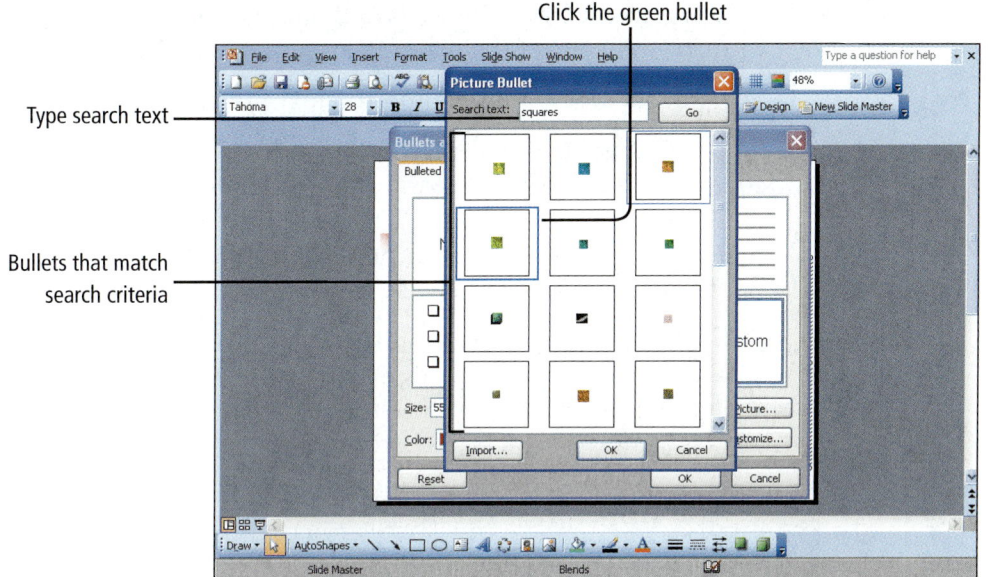

Figure 3.21

5 Click **Normal View** to close the slide master, and then display **Slide 4**.

Notice the picture bullet that displays in the slide. Later in this chapter, you will change the color scheme so that the green bullet coordinates with the presentation.

6 **Save** the file.

Activity 3.16 Removing Bullets from Slide Text

Occasionally you may need to remove the bullet character from a line or paragraph of text. For example, your presentation may include a slide that contains a quote that you would like to display as a paragraph without a bullet. In this instance, the bullet character can be turned off. The Bullets button on the Formatting toolbar is a toggle button. Recall that a toggle button is like a light switch. You can click the button once to turn it on, and then you can click it again to turn it off. In this activity, you will turn off the bullet character in the last slide and then adjust the alignment for the text in the placeholder.

1 Display **Slide 6**. Click anywhere in the bulleted paragraph. On the Formatting toolbar, click **Bullets** to remove the bullet.

2 On the Formatting toolbar, click **Center** to center the lines.

Project 3B: Volunteers | **PowerPoint** 1117

3 Notice that the word *You!* is the only word on the last line, leaving the slide with a poor design. To size the placeholder and adjust the text flow, point to the center left sizing handle so that a left-and-right-pointing arrow displays. Press and hold down the left mouse button and drag to size the placeholder so that its left edge aligns with the left edge of the slide. Release the left mouse button.

The placeholder is resized and the text fits on three lines.

4 Notice that the text is centered within the placeholder but it is not centered on the slide. To correct the alignment, point to the center right sizing handle so that a left-and-right-pointing arrow displays. Press and hold down the left mouse button, and then drag to the right edge of the slide. Release the left mouse button.

The placeholder extends from the right edge to the left edge of the slide and the text is correctly centered on the slide. Compare your slide to Figure 3.22.

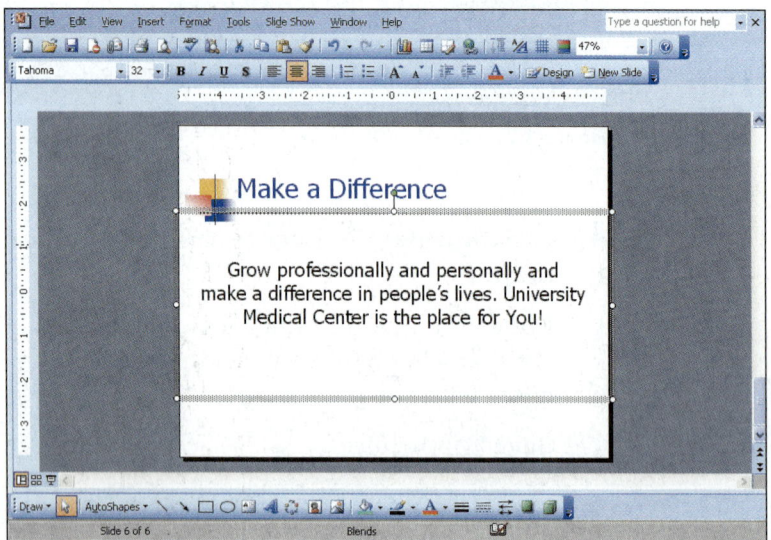

Figure 3.22

5 Save the file.

Activity 3.17 Applying Numbering to a List

Slide text commonly contains bulleted items, but you can also create numbered items by applying numbers, roman numerals, uppercase, or lowercase alphabetic characters. When you move, delete, or add items to a numbered list, PowerPoint automatically reorders the numbers in the list.

1 Display **Slide 5**, and then click anywhere in the bulleted list placeholder. Move the pointer over the outer edge of the placeholder so that a four-headed arrow displays. Click the left mouse button so that the edge of the placeholder displays a pattern of dots, indicating that the placeholder and all of the text within it are selected.

2 On the Formatting toolbar, click **Numbering** to replace the bullets with a numbered list.

Note — **Creating Numbered Lists**

You can automatically create a numbered list in a PowerPoint placeholder by typing a number followed by a parenthesis or period, and then pressing Tab. Type the text and then press Enter. The next number in the sequence is inserted.

3 Click the number **4** so that the line is selected. Press Delete and notice that the list renumbers.

4 Move the pointer over the outer edge of the placeholder so that a four-headed arrow displays. Click the left mouse button so that the edge of the placeholder displays a pattern of dots, indicating that all of the text within the placeholder is selected.

5 On the menu bar, click the **Format** menu, and then click **Bullets and Numbering**. If necessary, click the **Numbered tab**. Notice the various numbering schemes that are available in PowerPoint. In the first row, click the third numbering option—numbers followed by parentheses. Click the **Color arrow**, and then click the last color—**blue**. Compare your dialog box to Figure 3.23. Click **OK** to apply the new numbering scheme.

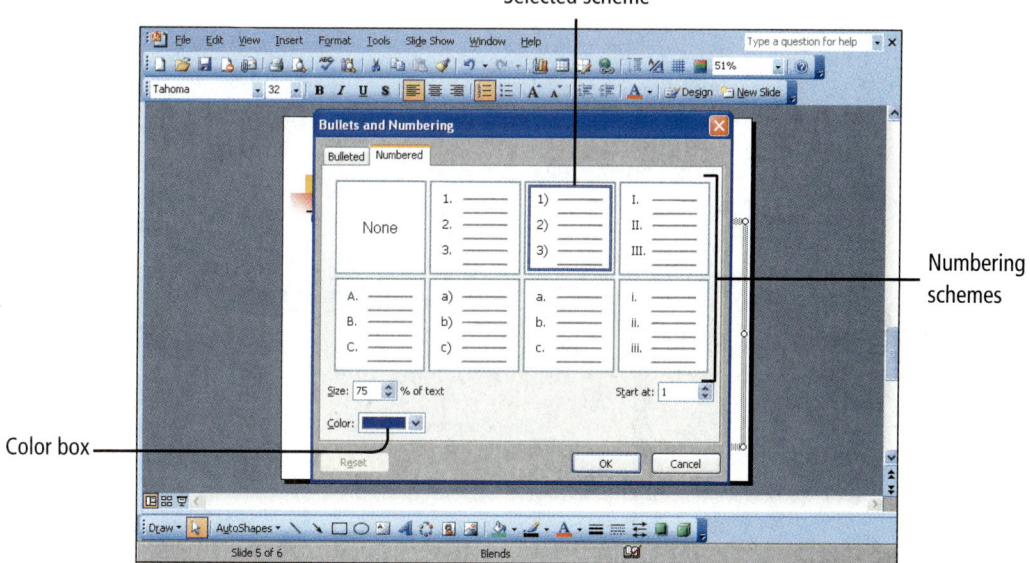

Figure 3.23

6 Click anywhere on the slide to deselect the placeholder. **Save** the file.

Note — **Changing the Start Number**

You can start a numbered list with any number by changing the value in the **Start at** box in the lower right corner of the Bullets and Numbering dialog box.

Project 3B: Volunteers | **PowerPoint** 1119

Objective 5
Customize a Color Scheme

Recall that a color scheme is a palette of eight colors that is applied to various slide elements. Every PowerPoint design template includes a number of color schemes that coordinate with the template's background graphics. For example, the Blends design template includes six color schemes with black, blue, or white backgrounds and a variety of colored elements. You can pick another overall color scheme for a presentation but still keep the background graphics, fonts, and font sizes that are applicable to the design template that you are using.

In addition to choosing a new color scheme, you can customize a color scheme by changing individual color scheme elements. Thus, you can apply a design template to a presentation, and then change color elements to coordinate with the presentation that you are creating.

Activity 3.18 Applying a Slide Color Scheme

1 If necessary, **Open** the file **3B_Volunteers_Firstname_Lastname**, and click **Normal View** to display the **Outline/Slides** pane. Click the **Slides tab** to display the slide thumbnails.

2 On the Formatting toolbar, click **Slide Design** and then in the upper section of the **Slide Design** task pane, click **Color Schemes**.

The six color schemes associated with the Blends design template display. Notice that the first color scheme in the second row is selected, indicating that it is the currently applied scheme. See Figure 3.24.

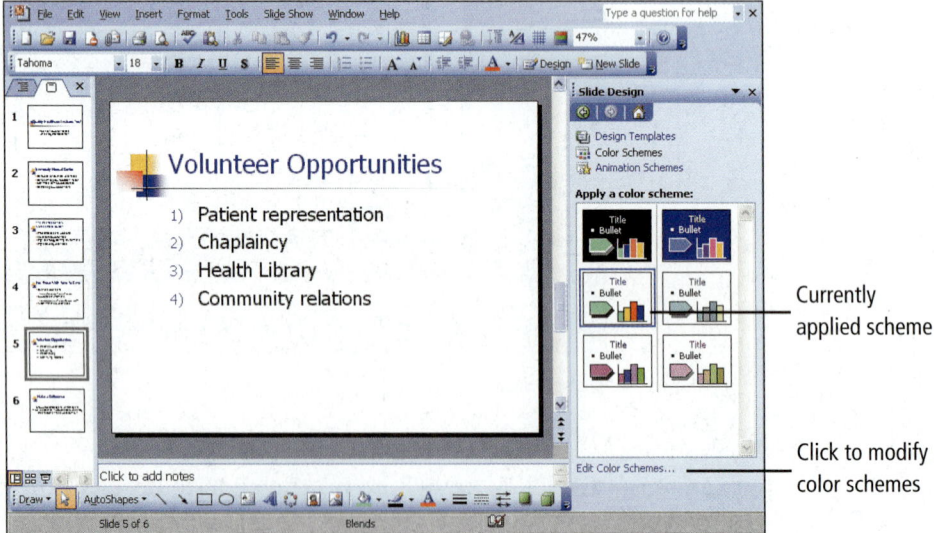

Figure 3.24

3 Click the color scheme that contains a white background with lavender, blue, and green accents.

Notice in the Outline/Slides pane that the color scheme is applied to the entire presentation.

4 Save the file.

> **Note** — Applying Color Schemes to Individual or Selected Slides
>
> The new color scheme can be applied to an individual slide or to a selection of slides. Select the slide(s) and then point to the desired scheme so that an arrow displays. Click the arrow to display a menu, and then click Apply to Selected Slides.

Activity 3.19 Modifying a Slide Color Scheme

To modify an individual color within the color scheme, use the Custom tab in the Edit Color Scheme dialog box. Recall that any changes you make to a color scheme can be applied to a single slide or to the entire presentation.

1 If necessary, display the **Slide Design** task pane. At the bottom of the task pane, click **Edit Color Schemes**. In the **Edit Color Schemes** dialog box click the **Custom tab**.

The Edit Color Schemes dialog box displays the scheme colors and the associated slide elements. The current color scheme includes Title text that is a very dark blue. You can change this color to a lighter blue so that it contrasts with the bulleted text.

2 Under **Scheme colors**, click the fourth box—**Title text**—and then click **Change Color**. See Figure 3.25.

The Standard colors honeycomb displays.

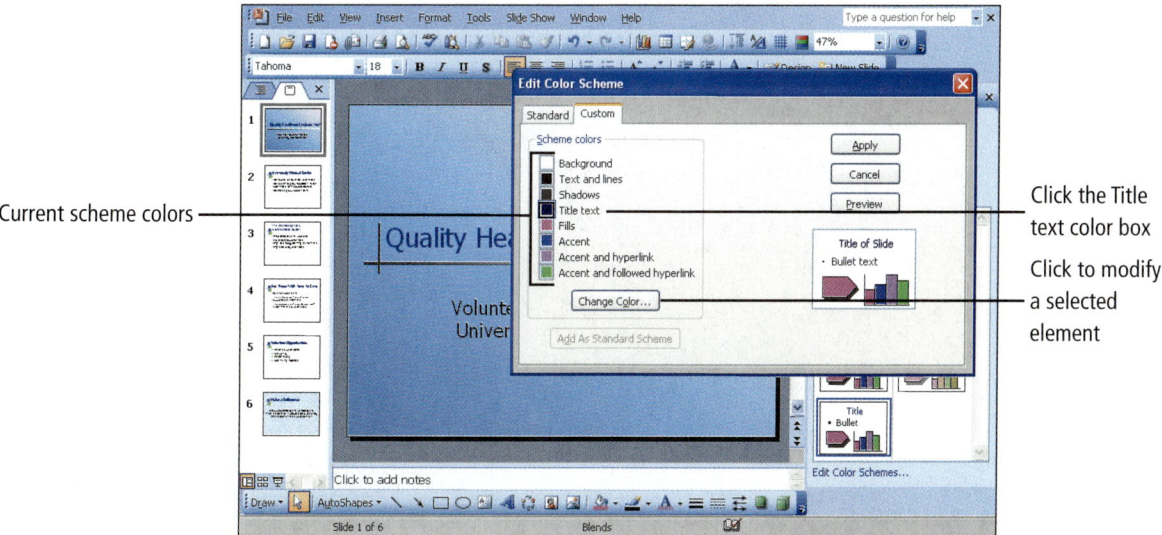

Figure 3.25

Project 3B: Volunteers | **PowerPoint** 1121

3 In the first row, click the **fourth color**, and then click **OK**. Click **Apply** to change the title color.

Scroll through your presentation to view the changes to the title.

4 **Save** the file.

Objective 6
Modify the Slide Background

The Blends design template color schemes include background colors such as white, black, and blue. There are many other background options, called *fill effects*, that can be applied to the background of slides—including textures, patterns, gradient fills, and pictures. A *gradient fill* is a color combination in which one color fades into another. Some of the textures that you can apply to a background are denim, sand, marble, and oak. To modify the slide background effect, use the Background command on the Format menu. As with color scheme options, you can apply a new background effect to a single slide or to an entire presentation.

Activity 3.20 Applying a Gradient Fill Background

There are three types of gradient fills that can be applied to a slide background—one color, two color, and preset. In this activity, you will experiment with each of these gradients and then apply a preset gradient background to the title slide.

1 If necessary, **Open** the file **3B_Volunteers_Firstname_Lastname**.

2 Display **Slide 1**. On the menu bar, click the **Format** menu, and then click **Background**. In the **Background** dialog box, under **Background fill**, click the **downward-pointing arrow**. See Figure 3.26. Click **Fill Effects**, and if necessary, click the **Gradient tab**.

Under Colors, notice that you can choose a One color gradient, in which a single color fades into a lighter or darker shade, or you can choose a Two color gradient, in which one color fades into another color. You can also choose a Preset, which contains color combinations chosen by Microsoft.

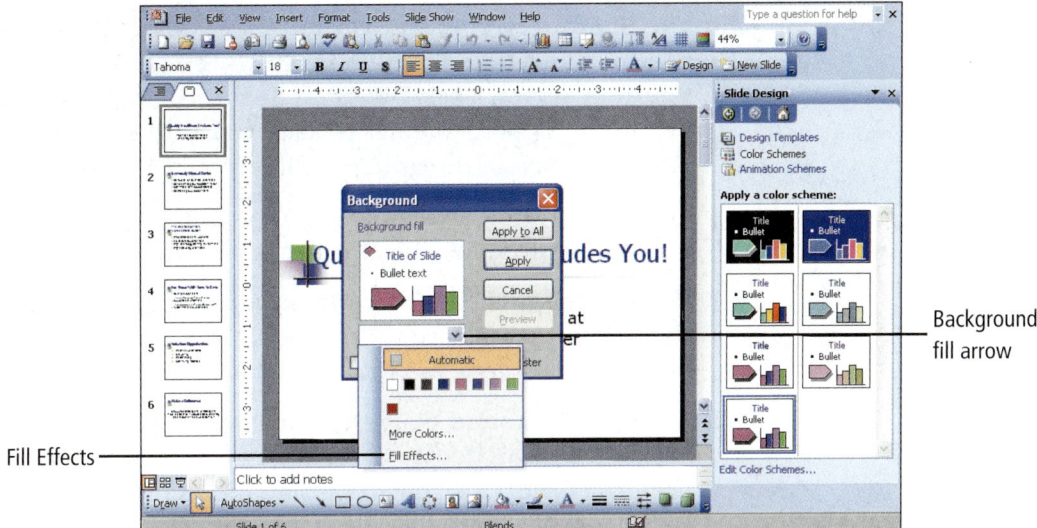

Figure 3.26

3. Under **Colors**, click the **One color** option button and then click the **Color 1 arrow**. Click the last color in the color palette—**green**.

In the lower right corner of the dialog box, notice the Sample that displays.

4. Below the color box, a Dark/Light scale displays. By dragging the scroll box in this scale, you can adjust the intensity of the color that you have chosen. Point to the scroll box and drag it to the right toward the light end of the scale, as shown in Figure 3.27.

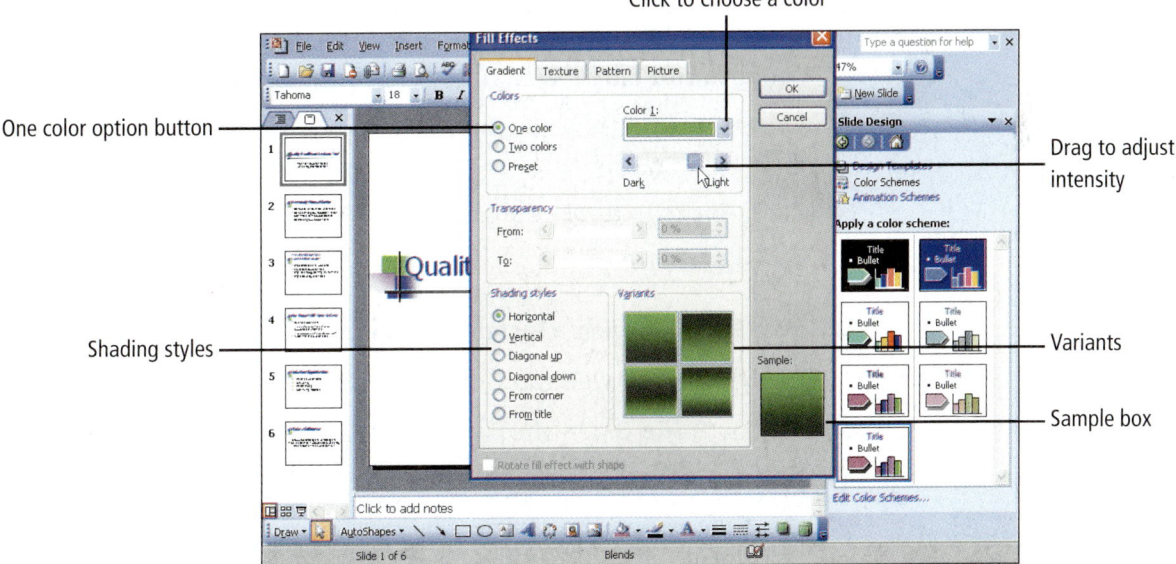

Figure 3.27

Project 3B: Volunteers | **PowerPoint** 1123

5 The **Shading styles** and **Variants** sections of the dialog box allow you to change the direction in which the gradient is applied. Under **Shading styles**, click **Diagonal down**. Under **Variants**, click the first box in the upper left corner. Click **OK**, and then click **Preview** to view the effect of the gradient fill on the title slide.

The Background dialog box displays in the center of the slide, making it difficult to see the effect that the gradient fill has on the slide.

6 Point to the title bar of the **Background** dialog box, and then drag the box to the right so that it overlaps the task pane. Release the mouse button to view the fill effect.

7 In the **Background** dialog box, click the **Background fill arrow**, and then click **Fill Effects**. Click the **Two colors** option button, and then click the **Color 1 arrow** to display the color palette. You can choose a color from the color palette or you can click **More Colors** to choose a custom color. In the color scheme palette, click the second color—**black**. Click the **Color 2 arrow** and then in the color palette, click the fourth color—**dark blue**.

8 Under **Shading styles**, click **From title**. Under **Variants**, click the second variant. Click **OK**, and then click **Preview**.

Notice that this gradient fill is very dark, providing no contrast for the title. To correct the lack of contrast, choose a lighter background.

9 In the **Background** dialog box, click the **Background fill arrow**, and then click **Fill Effects** again. Click **Preset** and then click the **Preset colors arrow** to display the list of preset color designs. Scroll through the list and click on several of the designs to view the Preset color schemes. Click **Daybreak**.

10 Under **Shading styles**, click **Diagonal down**. Under **Variants**, in the first row click the second variant. Click **OK** to return to the **Background** dialog box, and then click **Preview**.

The Daybreak gradient fill provides ample contrast to display the title effectively.

11 Click **Apply** to apply the gradient fill to the title slide only.

12 Save the file.

Activity 3.21 Applying a Textured Background

In this activity, you will apply a textured background to Slide 6.

1 Display **Slide 6**. On the menu bar, click the **Format** menu, click **Background**, and then click the **Background fill arrow**. Click **Fill Effects**, and then click the **Texture tab**.

The Texture tab includes 24 textures that can be applied to the slide background. Drag the scroll box in the vertical scroll bar to view the various textures that are available. As you click on different textures, the texture name displays beneath the grid, and the texture displays in the Sample box.

2 In the third row, click the first texture—**Blue tissue paper**. See Figure 3.28. Click **OK** and then click **Apply**.

The textured background is applied to Slide 6.

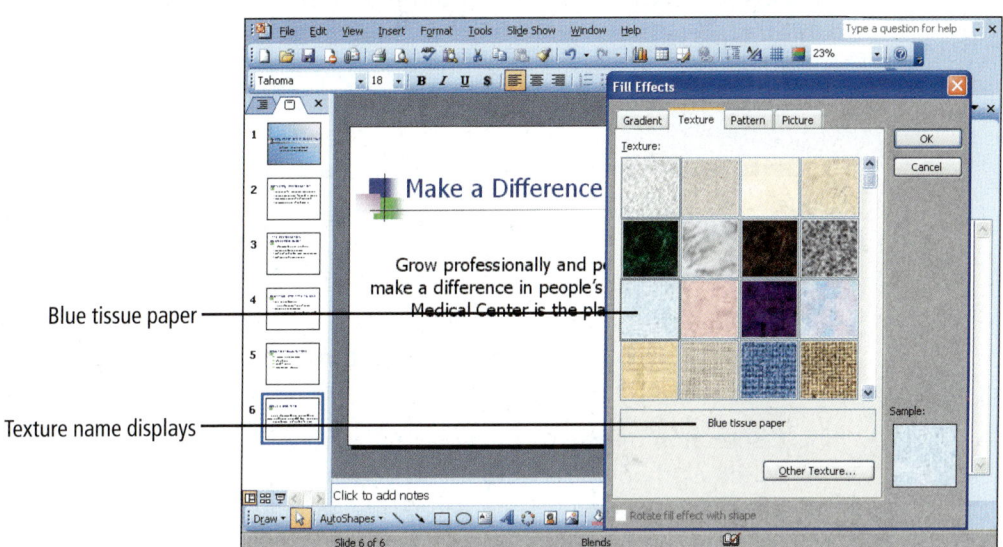

Blue tissue paper

Texture name displays

Figure 3.28

3 Save the file.

Activity 3.22 Omitting Background Graphics from a Slide

Slides often contain elements in addition to text. For example, tables, charts, pictures, and shapes are used to enhance and emphasize text. Sometimes these elements conflict with background graphics that are a part of the applied design template. In the Blends design template, three squares display to the left of the title that are a part of the design template. In this activity, you will turn these elements off on Slide 1.

1 Display **Slide 1**. On the menu bar, click the **Format** menu, and then click **Background**. Select the **Omit background graphics from master** check box. Click **Apply** and notice that the background graphics are removed from this slide.

2 Save the file.

> **Note — Omitting Background Graphics**
>
> When you omit background graphics that are on the master, you must omit all of the graphics. You cannot choose the graphics that you wish to omit.

Objective 7
Apply an Animation Scheme

Animation refers to the movement of slides and slide elements on and off the screen during an electronic slide show. An ***animation scheme*** contains predefined animations for slide placeholders, including titles, subtitles, and bulleted lists. You can apply an animation scheme to individual slides, selected slides, or all of the slides in a presentation.

Activity 3.23 Applying Animation Schemes to Slides

1 If necessary, **Open** the file **3B_Volunteers_Firstname_Lastname** in **Normal view**. In the **Outline/Slides** pane, click the **Slides tab**.

2 Display **Slide 1**. If necessary, display the **Slide Design** task pane. In the upper section of the **Slide Design** task pane, click **Animation Schemes**.

Depending on the recent usage of your computer, the animation schemes display recently used schemes. Scroll down and you will also see Subtle schemes, Moderate schemes and Exciting schemes.

3 At the lower left corner of the task pane, verify that the **AutoPreview** check box is selected so that you can view the animations that you select. Then, take a moment to scroll through the animation schemes. Click several schemes and notice the animation that displays. Under **Exciting**, click **Title arc**. See Figure 3.29.

Notice that the title zooms in and the subtitle wipes from the left to the right.

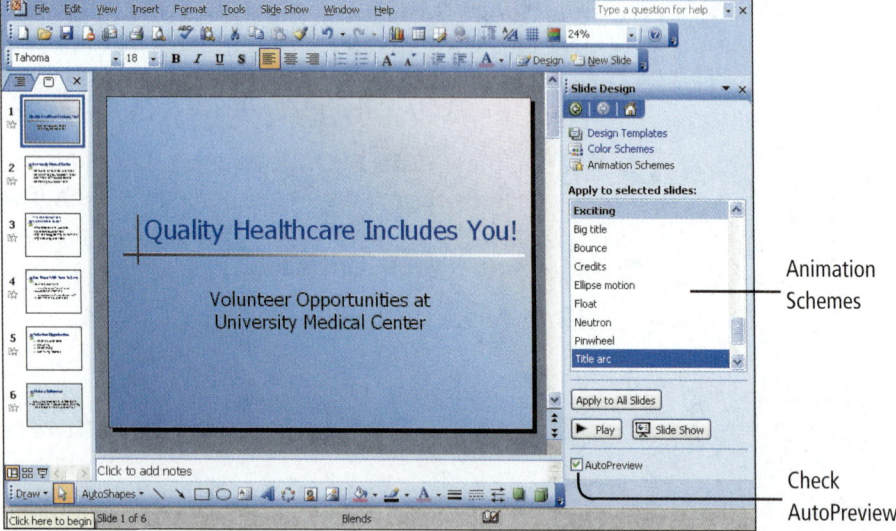

Figure 3.29

4 In the **Outline/Slides** pane, select **Slides 2** through **6**. In the **Slide Design** task pane, under **Moderate**, click **Elegant** to apply the animation scheme to the five selected slides.

Notice that in the Outline/Slides pane, a moving star graphic displays to the left of the slides. This graphic indicates that the slide contains animation.

5 To view your presentation display **Slide 1**. In the lower right corner of the task pane, click **Slide Show**. Press the [Spacebar] or click the left mouse button after each animation to advance through your slides.

6 Create a footer for the notes and handouts that includes the date updated automatically and a footer with the text **3B Volunteers-Firstname Lastname** Clear all other header and footer options.

7 **Save** the file, and then print the presentation as **grayscale handouts**, **6** slides per page in **horizontal** order. **Close** the file.

End **You have completed Project 3B**

Summary

In this chapter you learned how to format slides by changing fonts, font colors, and font sizes, changing text case, and text alignment. By formatting slide text, you created focal elements on your slides that provided emphasis. Thus, you learned how to use font formatting to draw the audience's attention to the important points on your slides.

In addition to font formatting, you learned how to apply and modify bullets and numbering, and how to change color schemes. As you try out new colors and bullets, you can create an endless array of design possibilities. Just remember that the color schemes associated with each design template are designed to coordinate with each other. Make sure that the colors that *you* choose coordinate with the existing colors in the template.

The process that you follow as you create presentations always begins with accurate and appropriate content. When you are satisfied with your content, you can address design and color considerations and then fine-tune your presentation by modifying placeholder size and position. As a final step in creating your presentation, you can apply an animation scheme to control the movement of your slide elements on and off the screen. Then practice your presentation so that you are a confident and composed speaker.

In This Chapter You Practiced How To

- Format Slide Text
- Modify Placeholders
- Modify Slide Master Elements
- Apply Bullets and Numbering
- Customize a Color Scheme
- Modify the Slide Background
- Apply an Animation Scheme

PowerPoint chapter three: Concepts Assessments

Matching Match each term in the second column with its correct definition in the first column by writing the letter of the term on the blank line in front of the correct definition.

____ 1. A set of characters with the same design and shape.

____ 2. A formatting feature that refers to the horizontal position of text between the left and right edges of a placeholder.

____ 3. A button that is clicked once to turn the feature on and then clicked again to turn the feature off.

____ 4. Small white circles on the outer edges of placeholders, graphics, and other slide elements that are used to adjust the size.

____ 5. The unit in which fonts are measured.

____ 6. The movement of slides and slide elements on and off the screen during an electronic slide show.

____ 7. A slide that contains formatting and text that displays on every slide in your presentation.

____ 8. A color combination in which one color fades into another.

____ 9. A feature that copies all formatting from one selection to another selection.

____ 10. Predefined animations for slide placeholders, including titles, subtitles, and bulleted lists.

____ 11. Capitalization in which all letters in a selection are capitalized.

____ 12. Capitalization in which none of the letters in a selection are capitalized.

____ 13. Formatting that includes superscript, subscript, and embossing.

____ 14. Capitalization in which the first letter of every word in a selection is capitalized.

____ 15. Capitalization in which the first word in a sentence is capitalized.

A Alignment
B Animation
C Animation scheme
D Font
E Font effects
F Format Painter
G Gradient fill
H Lowercase
I Point
J Sizing handles
K Slide master
L Sentence case
M Title case
N Toggle
O Uppercase

Concepts Assessments (continued)

Fill in the Blank   Write the correct answer in the space provided.

1. The keyboard shortcut for changing text case is _____ + _____.

2. _____ are used to emphasize important points on a slide.

3. The _____ displays formatting and text that is applied to slides containing the Title Slide layout.

4. A _____ gradient fill contains color combinations chosen by Microsoft.

5. One point is equal to _____ of an inch.

6. The _____ function key is the Repeat key in PowerPoint.

7. To copy formatting to multiple selections, _____ Format Painter.

8. When the outside of a placeholder displays as a pattern of _____, all of the text within the placeholder is selected and can be formatted.

9. When creating the text for your slides, it is a good idea to include no more than _____ words per line and no more than _____ lines per slide.

10. To access the slide master, press and hold down _____ and then click the Normal View button.

1130   **PowerPoint** | Chapter 3: Formatting a Presentation

Skill Assessments

Project 3C—Office Shutdown

Objectives: *Format Slide Text, Modify Placeholders, Apply Bullets and Numbering, Modify Slide Master Elements, and Apply an Animation Scheme.*

In the following Skill Assessment, you will modify a presentation that describes the evening administrative office shutdown procedures at University Medical Center. Your completed presentation will look similar to the one shown in Figure 3.30. You will save your presentation as *3C_Office_Shutdown_Firstname_Lastname*.

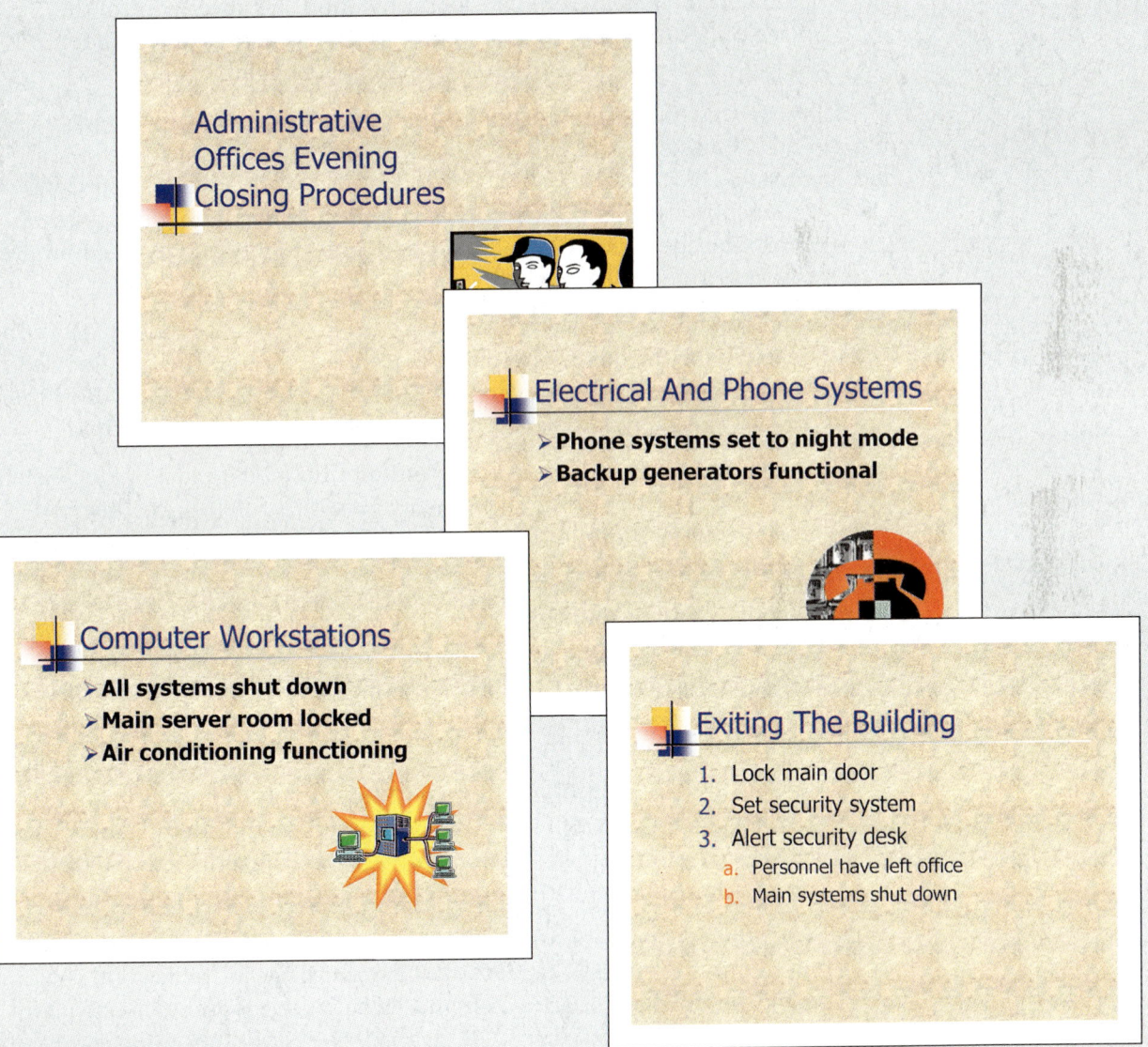

Figure 3.30

(**Project 3C–Office Shutdown** continues on the next page)

PowerPoint
chapter three
Skill Assessments (continued)

(Project 3C–Office Shutdown continued)

1. From your student files, open the file **p03C_Office_Shutdown**. **Save** the file as **3C_Office_Shutdown_Firstname_Lastname** Close the **Outline/Slides** pane and then scroll through the presentation to familiarize yourself with the four slides.

2. On **Slide 1**, click anywhere in the title placeholder. Point to the outer edge of the placeholder so that a four-headed arrow displays. (Be sure that you do not point to a sizing handle.) Press and hold down the left mouse button and drag the placeholder up and to the right so that the left edge of the placeholder aligns with the right edge of the yellow rectangle in the design template's graphic, and the lower edge of the placeholder touches the horizontal line in the center of the slide. Release the mouse button to move the placeholder.

3. Verify that the title placeholder boundary displays as a pattern of dots. If it does not, click in the title placeholder, point to its outer edge so that a four-headed arrow displays, and then click the left mouse button. On the menu bar, click the **Format** menu, and then click **Change Case**. Click **Title Case**, and then click **OK** to capitalize the first letter of each word.

4. Display **Slide 2**, and then click in the bulleted list placeholder. Move the pointer over the outer edge of the placeholder so that the four-headed arrow displays, and then click the left mouse button to select all of the text within the placeholder. On the Formatting toolbar, click **Bold**.

5. Display **Slide 3**, and then click in the bulleted list placeholder. Select all of the text within the placeholder using the technique that you used in Steps 3 and 4. Press [F4] to repeat the bold formatting that you applied in Step 4.

6. Display **Slide 4**, and then select the three, first-level bullet points. You will need to drag the pointer over the bullet points to select them so that the two, second-level bullet points are *not* selected. On the Formatting toolbar, click **Numbering** to convert the bullets to numbers.

7. Select the last two bullet points on **Slide 4**. On the Formatting toolbar, click **Numbering** to convert the bullets to numbers. Notice that because the bullets are second-level, PowerPoint has restarted the numbering scheme with the number 1.

8. With the last two bullets on **Slide 4** still selected, click the **Format** menu, and then click **Bullets and Numbering**. In the second row, click the third numbering scheme—lowercase alphabetic characters followed by a period. Click **OK** to apply the new numbering scheme.

(Project 3C–Office Shutdown continues on the next page)

PowerPoint chapter three
Skill Assessments (continued)

(Project 3C–Office Shutdown continued)

9. On the menu bar, click the **Format** menu, and then click **Background**. Click the **Background fill arrow**, and then click **Fill Effects**. Click the **Texture tab**, and then in the first row, click the last texture—**Stationery**. Click **OK**, and then click **Apply to All** to apply the textured background to all of the slides in the presentation.

10. Press and hold down Shift, and then move the pointer to the **Normal View** button and verify that the ScreenTip *Slide Master View* displays. Click **Slide Master View**.

11. In the bulleted list placeholder, click in the first line—*Click to edit Master text styles*. On the **Format** menu, click **Bullets and Numbering**. Click the **Bulleted tab**. In the second row, click the third bullet—the arrowhead—and then click **OK**.

12. Click **Normal View**, and then scroll through your presentation to view the changes that resulted from the modifications you made on the slide master.

13. Display **Slide 1**. On the Formatting toolbar, click the **Slide Design** button to display the **Slide Design** task pane. Click **Animation Schemes**. Scroll as necessary, and under **Exciting**, click **Float**. Click **Apply to All Slides**. In the lower right corner of the task pane, click **Slide Show** to view the animation applied to your presentation, pressing Spacebar to advance through your slides.

14. Create a footer for the notes and handouts that includes the date updated automatically and a footer with the text **3C Office Shutdown-Firstname Lastname** Clear all other header and footer options.

15. **Save** the file and then print the presentation as **grayscale handouts**, **4** slides per page, in **horizontal** order. **Close** the file.

End You have completed Project 3C

PowerPoint chapter three
Skill Assessments (continued)

Project 3D — Services

Objectives: *Format Slide Text, Modify Placeholders, Modify Slide Master Elements, Apply Bullets and Numbering, Customize a Color Scheme, and Apply an Animation Scheme.*

In the following Skill Assessment, you will format a presentation describing emergency and urgent care medical services at University Medical Center. Your completed presentation will look similar to the one shown in Figure 3.31. You will save your presentation as 3D_Services_Firstname_Lastname.

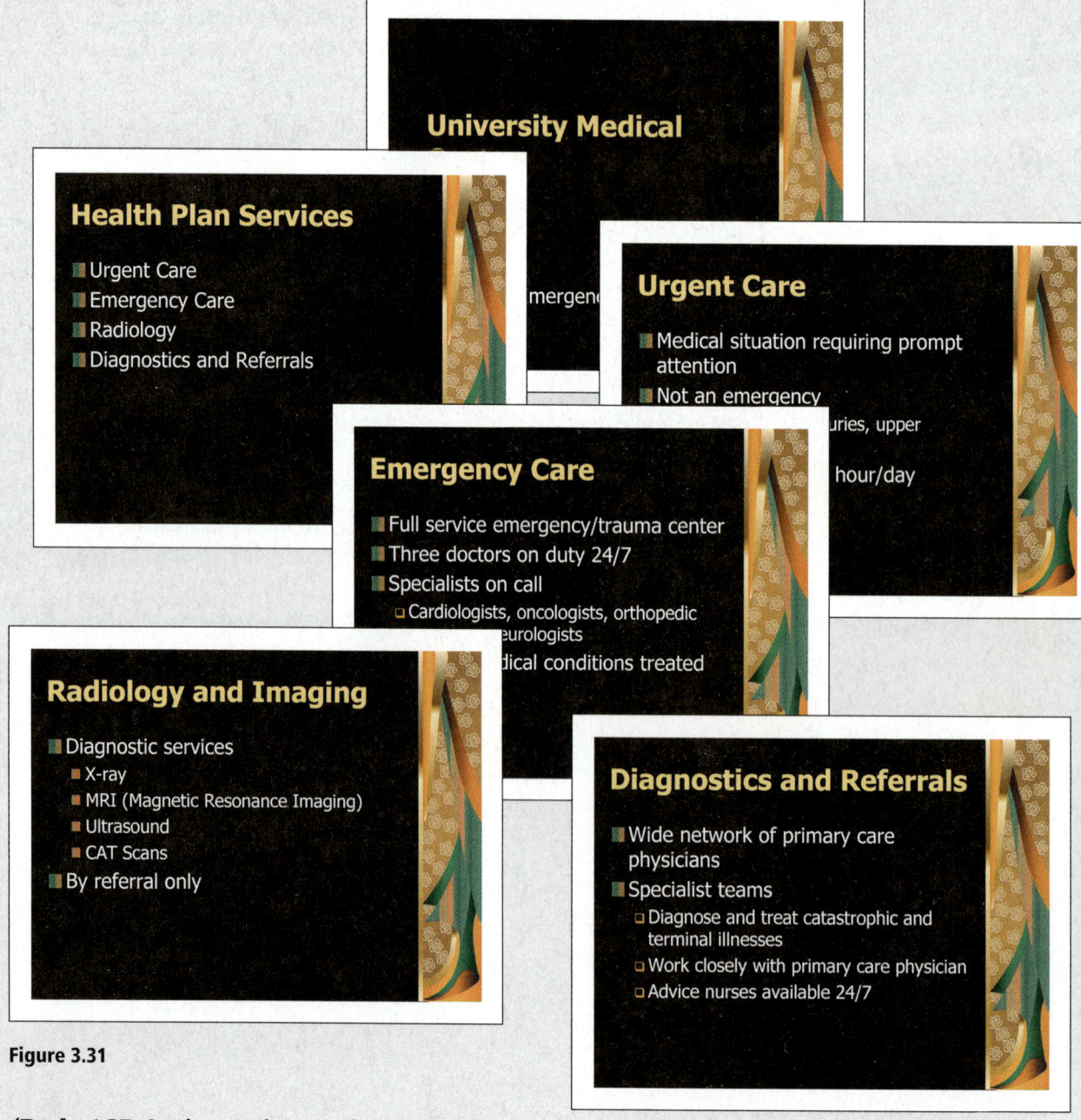

Figure 3.31

(**Project 3D**–Services continues on the next page)

1134   **PowerPoint** | Chapter 3: Formatting a Presentation

Skill Assessments (continued)

PowerPoint chapter three

(Project 3D–Services continued)

1. From your student files, open the file **p03D_Services** and close the **Outline/Slides** pane. **Save** the file as 3D_Services_Firstname_Lastname

2. The font used in the presentation is Arial. To change the font to Tahoma, click the **Format** menu, and then click **Replace Fonts**. If necessary, click the **Replace arrow** and then click **Arial** to indicate the font that you wish to replace. Click the **With arrow** and then scroll through the font list and click **Tahoma**. Click **Replace** to change each occurrence of the Arial font to Tahoma. Close the **Replace Fonts** dialog box.

3. On the Formatting toolbar, click **Slide Design** to display the **Slide Design** task pane. Near the top of the task pane, click **Color Schemes** to display the eight color schemes associated with the Kimono design template. Click the scheme that contains the black background.

4. Display **Slide 1**. Click in the subtitle placeholder, and then on the Formatting toolbar, click **Align Right** so that the two-line subtitle aligns with the right edge of the placeholder.

5. With the subtitle placeholder still selected, point to its outer edge so that a four-headed arrow displays, but do *not* point to a sizing handle! With the four-headed arrow displayed, press and hold down the left mouse button and drag down and to the right. Align the lower edge of the placeholder with the lower edge of the slide and the right edge of the placeholder with the left edge of the graphic image.

6. Display **Slide 3**, and then click in the third bullet point—*Earaches, minor injuries, upper respiratory*. On the menu bar, click the **Format** menu, and then click **Bullets and Numbering**. Click the **Bulleted tab**. In the second row, click the first bullet—the shadowed square. Click the **Color arrow** and in the displayed color scheme, click the seventh color—**gold**. In the **Size** box, click the **downward-pointing arrow** to adjust the bullet size to **70%**. Click **OK**.

7. Display **Slide 4**, and then click in the fourth bullet point—*Cardiologists, oncologists, orthopedic surgeons, neurologists*. Press [F4] to repeat the bullet format.

(Project 3D–Services continues on the next page)

Skill Assessments (continued)

(Project 3D—Services continued)

8. Display **Slide 6** and select the last three bullet points. Press [F4] to repeat the bullet format.

9. Press and hold down [Shift] and click the **Slide Master View** button (Hint: Normal View button) to display the slide master. If the title master displays, drag the vertical scroll bar up to display the slide master. Click in the title placeholder to select the *Click to edit Master title style* text. On the Formatting toolbar, click **Bold**. Click the **Font Size arrow**, and then click **44**.

10. Click the **Normal View** button to return to your presentation, and then display **Slide 1**. If necessary, on the Formatting toolbar click **Slide Design** to display the **Slide Design** task pane. At the top of the task pane, click **Animation Schemes**. Under **Subtle**, click **Dissolve in**, and then click **Apply to All Slides**. Click the **Slide Show** button to view the presentation, pressing [Spacebar] to advance through the slides.

11. Create a footer for the notes and handouts that includes the date updated automatically and a footer with the text **3D Services-Firstname Lastname** Clear all other header and footer options.

12. **Save** the file and then print the presentation as **grayscale handouts**, **6** slides per page, in **horizontal** order. **Close** the file.

End You have completed Project 3D

PowerPoint chapter three

Skill Assessments (continued)

Project 3E — Cholesterol

Objectives: *Format Slide Text, Modify Placeholders, Modify Slide Master Elements, Apply Bullets and Numbering, Customize a Color Scheme, and Modify the Slide Background.*

In the following Skill Assessment, you will format a presentation that is a part of the ongoing community education program at University Medical Center. Your completed presentation will look similar to the one shown in Figure 3.32. You will save your presentation as 3E_Cholesterol_Firstname_Lastname.

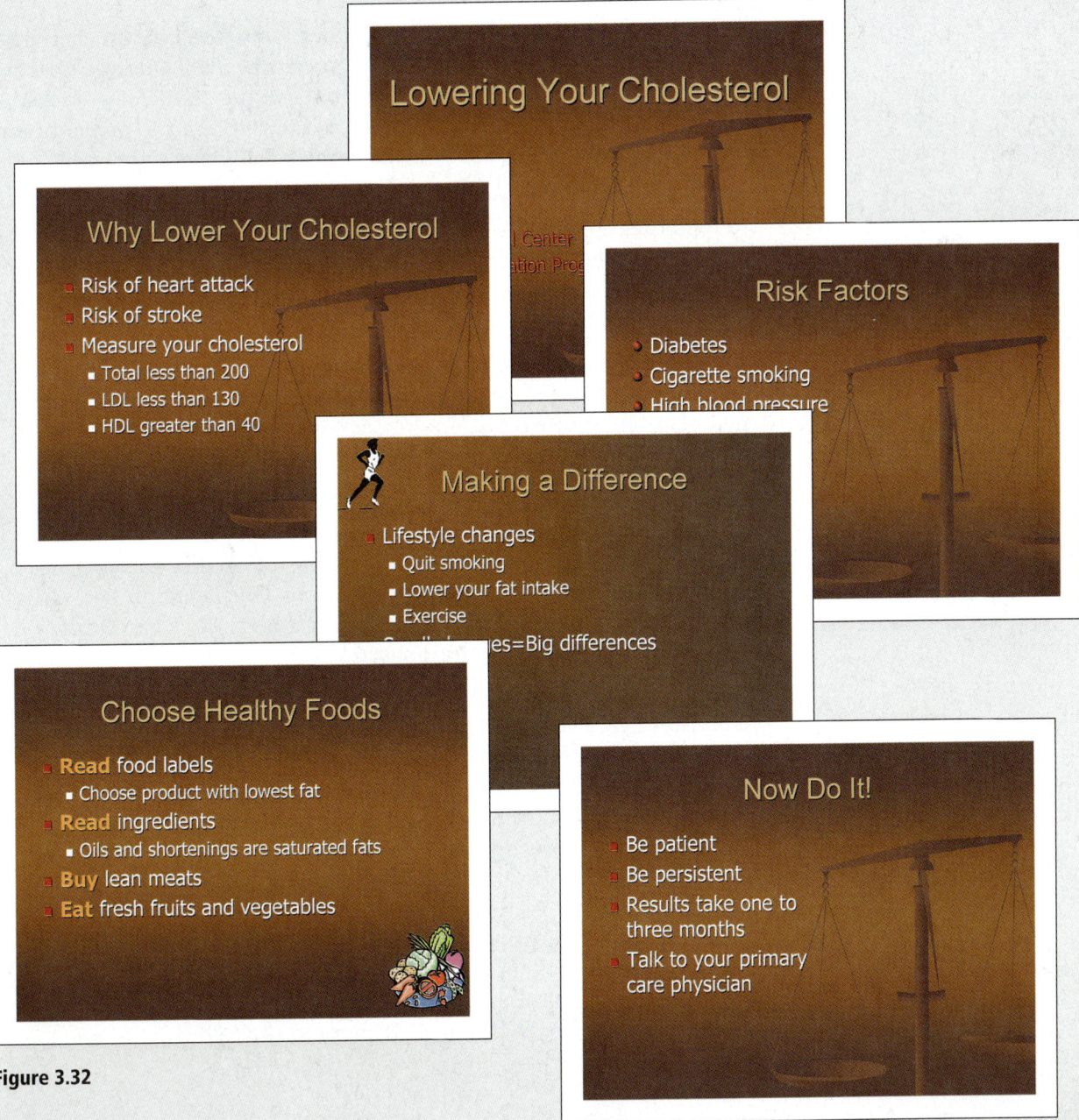

Figure 3.32

(Project 3E–Cholesterol continues on the next page)

Project 3E: Cholesterol | **PowerPoint** 1137

PowerPoint
chapter three
Skill Assessments (continued)

(Project 3E–Cholesterol continued)

1. From your student files, open the file **p03E_Cholesterol**. **Save** the file as **3E_Cholesterol_Firstname_Lastname** and then close the **Outline/Slides** Pane. Scroll through the presentation to familiarize yourself with the six slides.

2. On the Formatting toolbar, click **Slide Design** to display the **Slide Design** task pane. Near the top of the task pane, click **Color Schemes** to display the eight color schemes associated with the Balance design template. At the bottom of the task pane, click **Edit Color Schemes**.

3. If necessary, click the **Custom tab**. Under **Scheme colors**, click the seventh color square—**Accent and hyperlink**. Click **Change Color**. In the last row of the color honeycomb, click the sixth color—**dark red**. Click **OK**, and then click **Apply**. Scroll through the presentation and notice that the first level bullets on each slide are dark red.

4. Display **Slide 3** and then click in the bulleted list placeholder. Point to the outer edge of the placeholder so that a four-headed arrow displays. Click the left mouse button so that the placeholder boundary box displays as a pattern of dots, indicating that formatting will be applied to all of the text in the placeholder.

5. On the menu bar, click the **Format** menu, click **Bullets and Numbering**, and then click the **Bulleted tab**. In the lower right corner, click the **Picture** button. In the **Search text** box, type **ball** and then click **Go** to display bullets that are either spheres or balls. Click the **first bullet**, the large dark red sphere, and then click **OK** to apply the picture bullet to each bullet point in the placeholder.

6. Display **Slide 4**. The background on this slide makes the text and graphic in the upper corner difficult to see. On the menu bar, click the **Format** menu, and then click **Background**. Click the **Omit background graphics from master** check box.

7. Click the **Background fill arrow**, and then click **Fill Effects**. In the **Gradient tab**, click the **One color** option button, and then click the **Color 1 arrow**. In the displayed color scheme, click the first color. Drag the **Dark/Light** scroll box slightly to the right to lighten the color a small amount, using the Sample in the lower right corner of the dialog box as your guide. Under **Shading style**, click **From corner**. Under **Variants**, click the first variant in the first row so that the lighter color displays in the upper left corner of the slide. Click **OK**, and then click **Apply**. (Hint: The background should provide enough contrast to display the graphic image in the upper left corner of the slide. If it does not, display the **Gradient tab** again and drag the **Dark/Light** scroll box slightly more to the right.)

(Project 3E–Cholesterol continues on the next page)

Skill Assessments (continued)

(Project 3E–Cholesterol continued)

8. Display **Slide 5**. The background graphic on this slide interferes with the graphic in the lower corner. On the menu bar, click the **Format** menu, and then click **Background**. Select the **Omit background graphics from master** check box, and then click **Apply**.

9. In the first bullet point, select the word *Read*. On the Formatting toolbar, click **Bold**. With *Read* still selected, on the Formatting toolbar, click the **Font Color arrow**. Click the **fifth color**.

10. To apply the bold and font color change to the first word in each of the first level bullets on **Slide 5**, you will use Format Painter. If necessary, in the first bullet point, select the word *Read*. On the Standard toolbar, double-click **Format Painter**. In each of the first level bullet points, click the words *Read*, *Buy*, and *Eat* to apply consistent formatting. Click **Format Painter** to turn it off.

11. Display **Slide 6**. The text on this slide overlaps the background graphic, making the slide confusing to view. Click in the bulleted list placeholder. Point to the center right sizing handle so that a left-and-right-pointing arrow displays. Press and hold down the left mouse button and drag to the left so that the right edge of the placeholder aligns under the *o* in the word *Do* in the title. Release the left mouse button. The text in the last bullet point should wrap to two lines with the words *care physician* on the last line.

12. Display **Slide 1** and click in the subtitle placeholder. Point to the outer edge of the placeholder so that a four-headed arrow displays. Click the left mouse button so that the placeholder boundary box displays as a pattern of dots, indicating that formatting will be applied to all of the text in the placeholder. On the Formatting toolbar, click the **Font Color arrow**, and then in the color scheme, click the seventh color—**dark red**.

13. Point to the outer edge of the subtitle placeholder so that a four-headed arrow displays. Press and hold down the left mouse button and drag to the left so that the left edge of the placeholder aligns with the left edge of the slide. Release the left mouse button. On the Formatting toolbar, click **Align Left** and then click the **Font Size arrow**. Click **28** to change the font size for all of the text in the subtitle placeholder.

14. Create a footer for the notes and handouts that includes the date updated automatically and a footer with the text **3E Cholesterol-Firstname Lastname** Clear all other header and footer options.

15. **Save** the file and then print the presentation as **grayscale handouts**, **6** slides per page in **horizontal** order. **Close** the file.

End You have completed Project 3E

PowerPoint chapter three
Performance Assessments

Project 3F — Employment

Objectives: *Format Slide Text, Modify Placeholders, Modify Slide Master Elements, Apply Bullets and Numbering, Customize a Color Scheme, Modify the Slide Background, and Apply an Animation Scheme.*

In the following Performance Assessment, you will format a presentation for the Human Resources Department at University Medical Center that is part of a recruitment effort for nurses and administrative staff. Your completed presentation will look similar to the one shown in Figure 3.33. You will save your presentation as *3F_Employment_Firstname_Lastname*.

Figure 3.33

(**Project 3F**–Employment continues on the next page)

1140 PowerPoint | Chapter 3: Formatting a Presentation

PowerPoint chapter three

Performance Assessments (continued)

(Project 3F–Employment continued)

1. From your student files, open the file **p03F_Employment**. Display the **Slide Design** task pane and apply the **Competition** design template. **Save** the file as **3F_Employment_Firstname_Lastname**

2. In the **Outline/Slides** pane, display the slide thumbnails. Select **Slides 2** through **5** and in the **Slide Design** task pane, click **Color Schemes** to display the eight color schemes associated with the **Competition** design template. Apply the color scheme with the red background to the selected slides.

3. With **Slides 2** through **5** still selected, display the **Format** menu, and then click **Background**. Omit the background graphics from the master so that the image of the runner and the lanes do not display. Click the **Background fill arrow** and then click **Fill Effects**. Apply a two-color gradient fill. Change **Color 2** to the sixth color in the color scheme. Change the **Shading style** to **Diagonal up** and under **Variants**, in the first row, click the first option. Click **OK**, and then click **Apply**.

4. Display the **Slide Master** and click anywhere in the first bullet point—*Click to edit Master text styles*. Use the **Font Color arrow** to change the font color to the last color in the color scheme. On the **Format** menu, click **Bullets and Numbering** to display the **Bullets and Numbering** dialog box. In the second row, click the second bullet, and then click **OK**.

5. Click in the **Second level** line. In the **Bullets and Numbering** dialog box, click the **arrowhead bullet style**—in the second row, the third bullet. Change the **Size** to **75**, and change the **Color** to the fourth color. Click **OK**.

6. Click in the title placeholder, and change the text alignment to **Left Align**. Click **Normal View** to display the presentation and view your changes.

7. On the **Format** menu, click **Replace Fonts**, and then replace the **Verdana** font with the **Tahoma** font.

8. Display **Slide 5**. Change the bullets in the bullet list placeholder to numbers. In the **Bullets and Numbering** dialog box, apply the numbering scheme that includes a parenthesis after the number. Point to the center right sizing handle so that a left-and-right-pointing arrow displays, and then size the placeholder so that it fits tightly around the text, but be sure that none of the text wraps to two lines.

(Project 3F–Employment continues on the next page)

PowerPoint chapter three
Performance Assessments (continued)

(Project 3F–Employment continued)

9. Point to the outer edge of the placeholder so that a four-headed arrow displays and then drag the placeholder to the right so that its left edge is positioned under the *s* in *Administrative*. **Center** the title.

10. Display **Slide 6** and then display the **Slide Layout** task pane. Change the slide layout to **Title Slide**. In the title placeholder, change the alignment to **Center**, change the font size to **60**, and then change the font color to **Black**. (Hint: Click **More Colors**.) In the subtitle placeholder, change the font color to **White**.

11. Click the outer edge of the title placeholder so that the boundary consists of a pattern of dots, then use **Format Painter** to copy the formatting of the title placeholder from **Slide 6** to **Slide 1**. Use the same technique to copy the formatting of the *Subtitle* placeholder from **Slide 6** to **Slide 1**.

12. Display the **Slide Design** task pane and click **Animation Schemes**. Apply the **Moderate** scheme—**Rise up**—to **Slides 2** through **5**. Apply the **Exciting** scheme—**Pinwheel**—to **Slides 1** and **6**. Display **Slide 1** and then view the slide show.

13. Create a footer for the notes and handouts that includes the date updated automatically and a footer with the text **3F Employment-Firstname Lastname** Clear all other header and footer options.

14. **Save** the file and then print the presentation as **grayscale handouts**, **6** slides per page, in **horizontal** order. **Close** the file.

End You have completed Project 3F

PowerPoint chapter three
Performance Assessments (continued)

Project 3G — Education

Objectives: *Format Slide Text, Modify Slide Master Elements, Apply Bullets and Numbering, and Customize a Color Scheme.*

In the following Performance Assessment, you will create a one-page presentation to be used as a flyer to be posted on the University Medical Center Web site regarding the hospital's health education program. Your completed presentation will look similar to the one shown in Figure 3.34. You will save your presentation as *3G_Education_Firstname_Lastname*.

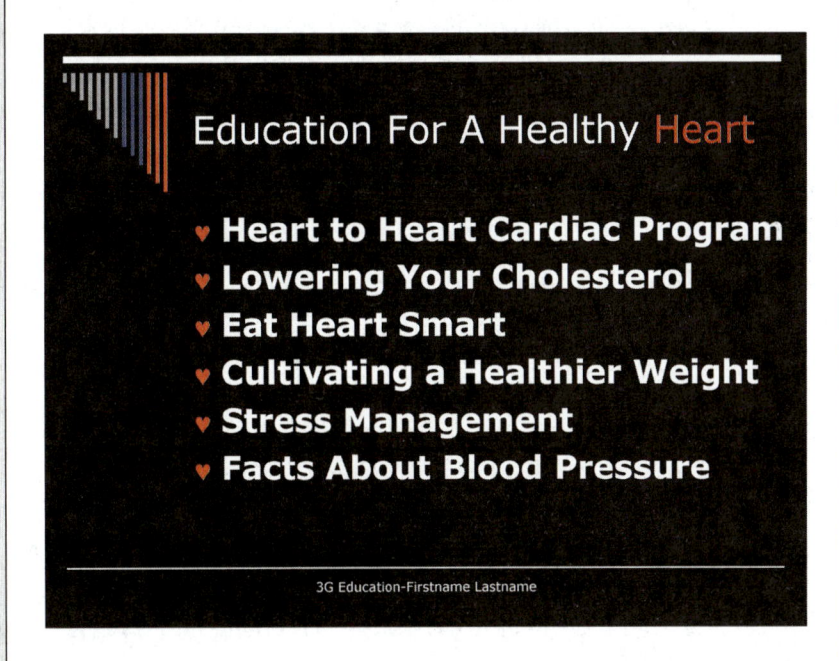

Figure 3.34

(**Project 3G**–Education continues on the next page)

PowerPoint chapter three

Performance Assessments (continued)

(Project 3G–Education continued)

1. Start PowerPoint, and create a new presentation based on the blue **Cascade** design template. Change the **Slide Layout** for the first slide to **Title and Text**.

2. In the title placeholder, type **Education For A Healthy Heart** and in the bulleted list placeholder type each of the following bullet points:

   Heart to Heart Cardiac Program
   Lowering Your Cholesterol
   Eat Heart Smart
   Cultivating a Healthier Weight
   Stress Management
   Facts About Blood Pressure

3. Display the **Slide Design–Color Schemes** task pane, and change the color scheme to the one that contains the black background with the red accents.

4. On the **Format** menu, use the **Replace Fonts** command to replace the **Arial** font with the **Verdana** font.

5. Notice that only one word in the title displays on the second line. To fit the title to one line, select the title text and change the **Font Size** to **35**. Recall that you can type any number in the **Font Size** box if it does not display on the list.

6. In the title placeholder, select the word *Heart* and then click the **Font Color arrow** to display the color scheme. Click the fifth color—**red**—to create a distinctive title on the slide.

7. Display the presentation in **Slide Master** view. Change the first level bullet to a heart. (Hint: In the **Bullets and Numbering** dialog box, click **Customize**. The heart is found in the **Symbol** font.)

8. In the *Click to edit Master text styles* line, change the **font size** to **30** and apply **bold**. Return the presentation to **Normal View**.

9. Click in the bulleted list placeholder and resize the placeholder so that its right edge extends to the right edge of the slide. This action will prevent the first bullet point from wrapping to two lines.

10. Because this is a one-slide presentation, create a footer for the slide (click the **Slide tab** in the **Header and Footer** dialog box) that includes the footer text **3G Education-Firstname Lastname** Clear all other header and footer options.

11. **Save** the file as **3G_Education_Firstname_Lastname** and then print the presentation as a **grayscale slide**. **Close** the file.

 You have completed Project 3G

PowerPoint chapter three
Performance Assessments (continued)

Project 3H — Training

Objectives: *Format Slide Text, Modify Placeholders, Modify Slide Master Elements, Apply Bullets and Numbering, Customize a Color Scheme, and Apply an Animation Scheme.*

In the following Performance Assessment, you will format a presentation regarding a trauma training program being implemented at University Medical Center. Your completed presentation will look similar to the one shown in Figure 3.35. You will save your presentation as 3H_Training_Firstname_Lastname.

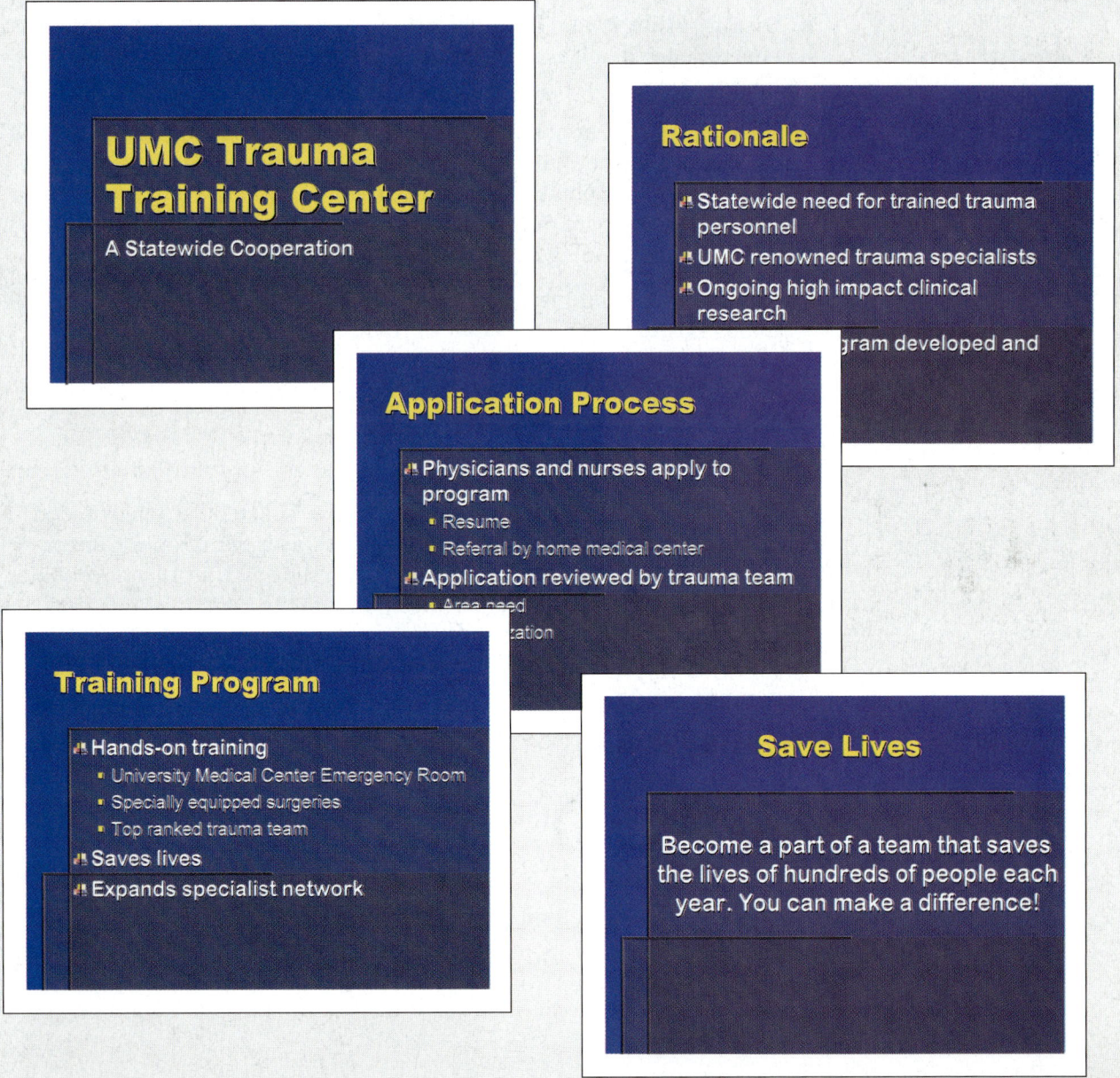

Figure 3.35

(**Project 3H**–Training continues on the next page)

PowerPoint chapter three

Performance Assessments (continued)

(Project 3H–Training continued)

1. From your student files, open the file **p03H_Training**. Display the **Slide Design** task pane and apply the green, **Glass Layers** design template. **Save** the file as 3H_Training_Firstname_Lastname

2. Display the color schemes, click the arrow on the royal blue background color scheme, and then apply the color scheme to all of the slides in your presentation. In the lower section of the **Slide Design** task pane, click **Edit Color Schemes**, and in the **Custom tab**, click **Title text**. Click **Change Color**, and then in the honeycomb, in the third row from the bottom, click the third color—**yellow**.

3. Display **Slide 2**, and then click **Slide Master View**. Be sure that the slide master displays, *not* the title master! Click in the title placeholder and remove the bold format.

4. Click in the first level bullet line and change the font to **Arial Rounded MT Bold**. Use the **Bullets and Numbering** dialog box to insert a picture bullet that contains gold, red, and blue squares blended together. If you are unsure of the bullet that you should choose, refer to Figure 3.35 at the beginning of this Performance Assessment.

5. Click in the second level bullet and use the **Bullets and Numbering** dialog box to change the color of the bullet to yellow. Return the presentation to **Normal View** and scroll through the slides to view your changes.

6. Display **Slide 1** and change the **font size** for the title to **60**. Select the subtitle text and use [Shift] + [F3] to change the subtitle to title case.

7. Display **Slide 5** and center the title. In the bulleted list placeholder, remove the bullet so that the text displays as a paragraph. **Center** the text, and then click elsewhere on the slide so that the placeholder is not selected. Notice that the design template contains lines that create a box in the center of the slide. The paragraph text would display nicely vertically centered within the box. To achieve this effect, you will size and move the placeholder as outlined in the next step.

(Project 3H–Training continues on the next page)

Performance Assessments (continued)

(Project 3H–Training continued)

8. Click in the paragraph placeholder and then, using the center right sizing handle, extend the placeholder to the right edge of the slide. Reduce the size of the placeholder by dragging the bottom center sizing handle up so that the lower edge of the placeholder is just below the last line of text. Drag the placeholder down about ½ inch so that the text is centered vertically within the box in the center of the slide. Refer to Figure 3.35. Change the **font size** to **36**.

9. Display **Slide 1**, and apply the **Compress** animation scheme to all of the slides in the presentation. View the slide show.

10. Create a footer for the notes and handouts that includes the date updated automatically and a footer with the text **3H Training-Firstname Lastname** Clear all other header and footer options.

11. **Save** the file and then print the presentation as **grayscale handouts**, **6** slides per page, in **horizontal** order. **Close** the file.

End You have completed Project 3H

PowerPoint chapter three
Mastery Assessments

Project 3I—Fitness

Objectives: *Format Slide Text, Modify Placeholders, Modify Slide Master Elements, Apply Bullets and Numbering, and Apply an Animation Scheme.*

In the following Mastery Assessment you will format a presentation regarding a study conducted by the Pediatric Research Department at University Medical Center. Your completed presentation will look similar to the one shown in Figure 3.36. You will save your presentation as *3I_Fitness_Firstname_Lastname*.

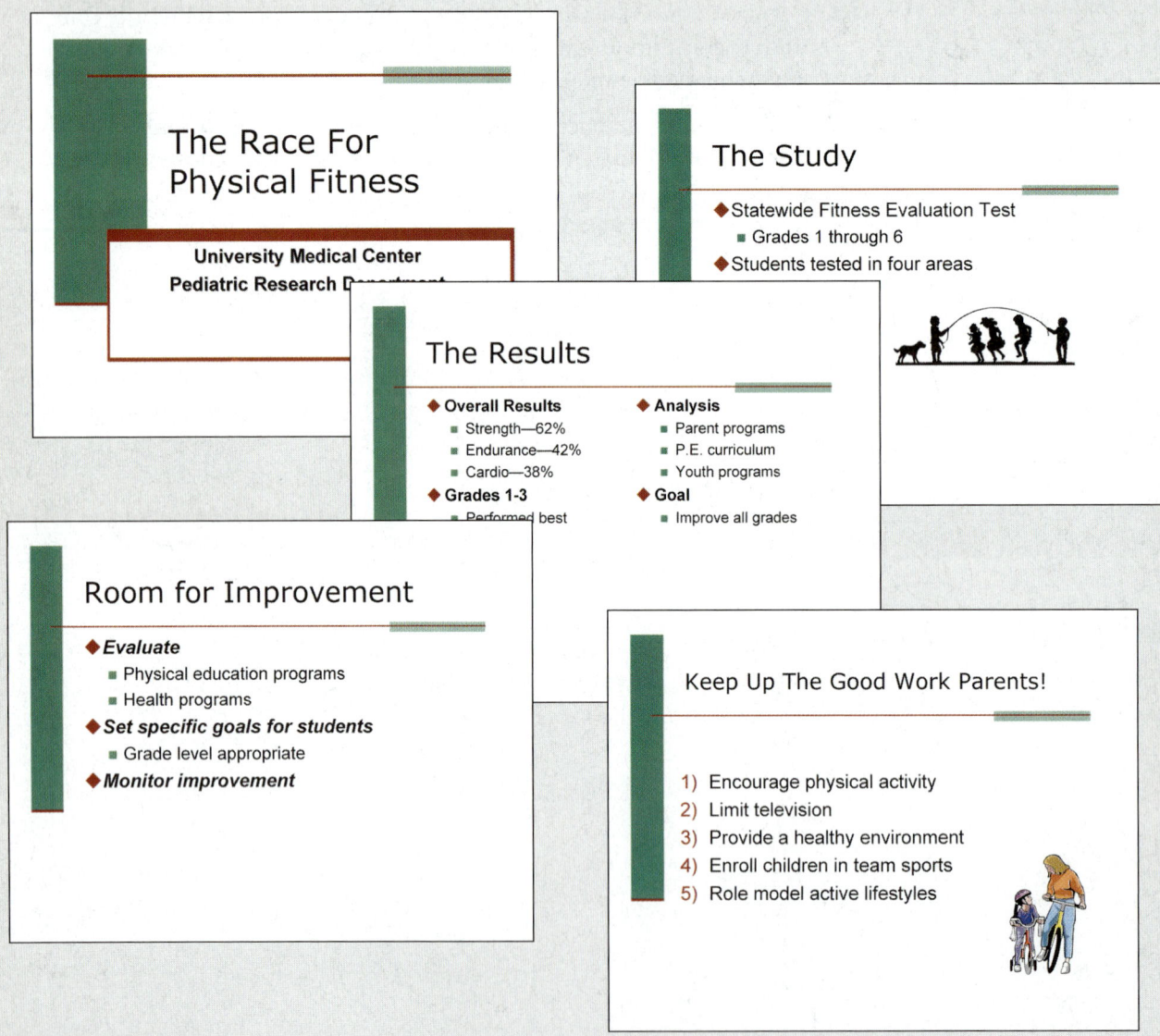

Figure 3.36

(*Project 3I*–Fitness continues on the next page)

Mastery Assessments (continued)

(Project 3I–Fitness continued)

1. From your student files, open the file **p03I_Fitness**. Apply the **Layers** design template (*not Glass Layers*) and then apply the color scheme that contains a white background and a teal arrow with a red shadow. Replace the **Times New Roman** font with **Verdana**. **Save** the file as 3I_Fitness_Firstname_Lastname

2. On **Slide 1**, format the title with bold, shadow, and then italic.

3. Display the slide master (not the title master) and customize the first level bullet using the large diamond in the **Wingdings** font. Change the color of the diamond bullet to dark red and make it 100 percent the size of the text. Return the presentation to **Normal View** and scroll through the slides to view your changes.

4. Display **Slide 3** and apply bold to the bullet point—*Overall Results*. Do not bold the subordinate bullet points. Use the repeat key to apply bold to the three remaining first level bullet points. Be sure that you do not bold any of the subordinate bullet points.

5. Display **Slide 4** and apply bold and italic to the first bullet point—*Evaluate*. Do not apply the formatting to the subordinate bullet points. Use **Format Painter** to copy the formatting from the word *Evaluate* to the two remaining first level bullet points.

6. Display **Slide 5** and apply numbering to the bulleted list. Change the numbering scheme so that the numbers are followed by a parenthesis. Size the numbered list placeholder so that its boundary box fits tightly around the text without any of the text wrapping to the second line. Drag the placeholder down so that the last numbered point aligns with the lower edge of the teal bar. The placeholder should be approximately vertically centered on the slide. Change the title text **font size** to **32**.

7. Apply the **Bounce** animation scheme to **Slide 1**, and then apply the **Float** animation scheme to **Slides 2** through **5**. View your presentation.

8. Create a footer for the notes and handouts that includes the date updated automatically and a footer with the text **3I Fitness-Firstname Lastname** Clear all other header and footer options.

9. **Save** the file and then print the presentation as **grayscale handouts**, 6 slides per page, in **horizontal** order. **Close** the file.

End You have completed Project 3I

PowerPoint
chapter three
Mastery Assessments (continued)

Project 3J—Radiology

Objectives: *Format Slide Text, Modify Placeholders, Modify Slide Master Elements, Apply Bullets and Numbering, Customize a Color Scheme, Modify the Slide Background, and Apply an Animation Scheme.*

In the following Mastery Assessment, you will create a presentation regarding the use of a new radiology procedure for the emergency room at University Medical Center. Your completed presentation will look similar to the one shown in Figure 3.37. You will save your presentation as *3J_Radiology_Firstname_Lastname*.

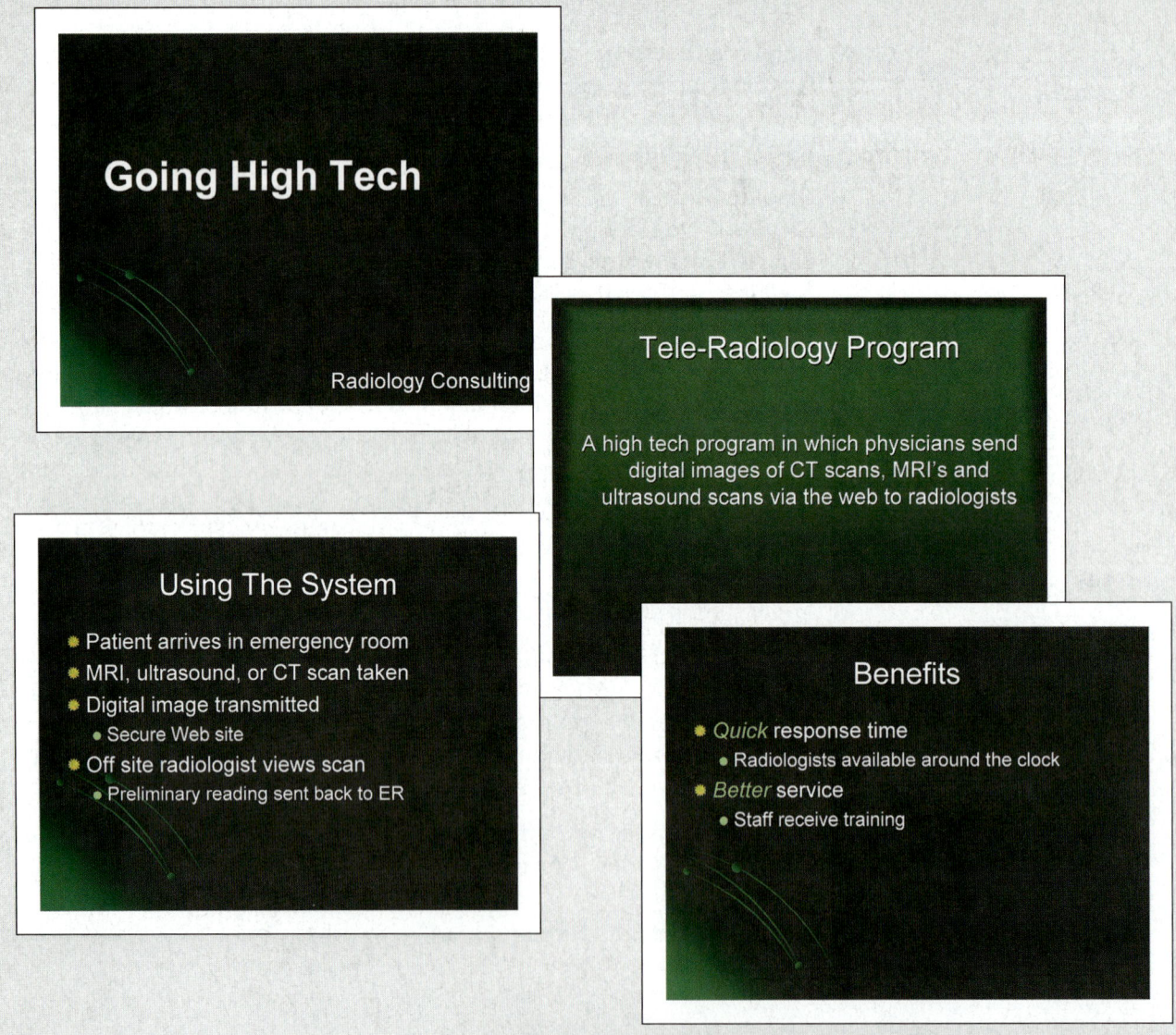

Figure 3.37

(**Project 3J**–Radiology continues on the next page)

1150   **PowerPoint** | Chapter 3: Formatting a Presentation

Mastery Assessments (continued)

(Project 3J–Radiology continued)

1. Start a new presentation based on the dark blue **Orbit** design template. Insert slides from the Microsoft Word file **p03J_Technology**. In the **Outline/Slides** pane, notice that the first slide is blank. Delete the first slide and then apply the **Title Slide** layout to the new first slide. **Save** the file as 3J_Radiology_Firstname_Lastname

2. Apply the dark green color scheme with the lighter green accents to the presentation. Edit the color scheme so that the Title text displays in white, located in the center of the color honeycomb.

3. Display **Slide 1**. Change the **font size** for the title to **60** and apply **bold**. Drag the placeholder so that its left edge aligns with the left edge of the slide.

4. Size the subtitle placeholder so that the boundary box fits tightly to the text, then position the placeholder in the lower right corner of the slide. Change the subtitle text to title case.

5. Display **Slide 2** and remove the bullet from the text. **Center** the text and then adjust the size of the placeholder so that the text displays on three lines. Drag the placeholder down approximately 1 inch, and then deselect the placeholder.

6. Format the background of **Slide 2** by applying a two-color gradient fill. For **Color 1**, choose the first color—**dark green**—and for **Color 2**, choose the sixth color in the color scheme. Apply the **Shading style From title** and choose the second **Variant**. Omit the background graphics from this slide.

7. Display the **Slide Master**. Change the first level bullet to a picture bullet using the search text **geared up factory** Choose the **large yellow starburst**. Change the color of the second level bullet to the last color in the color scheme—**light green**. Return to **Normal view**.

8. Display **Slide 4** and demote the second and fourth bullet points. Select the word *Quick*, apply **italic** and change the **font color** to **light green**—the last color in the color scheme. Use **Format Painter** to copy the format to the word *Better*.

9. Apply an animation scheme of your choice to the presentation and then view the slide show.

10. Create a footer for the notes and handouts that includes the date updated automatically and a footer with the text **3J Radiology-Firstname Lastname** Clear all other header and footer options.

11. **Save** the file and then print the presentation as **grayscale handouts**, **4** slides per page, in **horizontal** order. **Close** the file.

End You have completed Project 3J

PowerPoint chapter three
Problem Solving

Project 3K — Specialty

Objectives: *Format Slide Text, Modify Slide Master Elements, Apply Bullets and Numbering, Customize a Color Scheme, and Modify the Slide Background.*

Start a new presentation based on a design template. Research a medical specialty in which you are interested, such as pediatrics or neurology, and create a four- to six-slide presentation with information that you feel is relevant to the topic. Change the color scheme for your presentation, replace at least one font, and on the Slide Master, change the first level bullet to a picture bullet. On at least one slide, omit the background graphics and apply a gradient fill. Create an appropriate footer for your notes and handouts and save your presentation as *3K_Specialty_Firstname_Lastname*. Print the presentation as handouts, six slides per page, in grayscale.

 You have completed Project 3K ────────────

Project 3L — Nutrition

Objectives: *Format Slide Text, Modify the Slide Background, and Apply an Animation Scheme.*

Start a new presentation based on a design template of your choice. Research current information regarding the food pyramid and create a presentation regarding healthy nutrition choices for someone your age. Create a minimum of four slides that include changes in fonts, font sizes, font colors, and text alignment. Apply a textured background to at least one slide, and apply an animation scheme to the entire presentation. Create an appropriate footer for your notes and handouts and save your presentation as *3L_Nutrition_Firstname_Lastname*. Print the presentation as handouts, six slides per page, in grayscale.

 You have completed Project 3L ────────────

On the Internet

Monster.com

Use your Web browser to access the site **http://www.monster.com**. **Monster.com** lists jobs all over the United States and in several other countries. It provides other services as well, such as a résumé-building feature, career advice, research on companies, and features on specific companies. Explore the Career Advice link site and find an article that pertains to a career in which you might be interested or information about résumé writing and interviewing.

GO! with Help

Slide Orientation

A PowerPoint slide can be designed in portrait or landscape orientation. The default orientation for a slide is landscape, in which the slide is wider than it is tall. Sometimes it is useful to set up a slide in portrait orientation—the slide is taller than it is wide—particularly if you are using PowerPoint to create a one-page flyer. It is also possible to link presentations with different orientations. Use PowerPoint Help to learn about changing orientation.

1. Click in the **Type a question for** help box, type **How do I set up a slide in portrait?** and then press Enter.

2. Click **Use portrait and landscape orientation in the same presentation**, and then click **Select a fill effect or picture**. Read each step and click each link that displays.

Task Guides

Each book in the *GO! Series* is designed to be kept beside your computer as a handy reference, even after you have completed all the activities. Any time you need to recall a sequence of steps or a shortcut needed to achieve a result, look up the general category in the alphabetized listing that follows and then find your task. To review how to perform a task, turn to the page number listed in the second column to locate the step-by-step exercise or other detailed description. Additional entries without page numbers describe tasks that are closely related to those presented in the chapters.

Word 2003

Word Task	Page	Mouse	Menu Bar	Shortcut Menu	Shortcut Keys
Align, center	248	on Formatting toolbar	Format | Paragraph | Indents and Spacing tab, Alignment	Right-click, Paragraph | Indents and Spacing tab, Alignment	Ctrl + E
Align, justify	248	on Formatting toolbar	Format | Paragraph | Indents and Spacing tab, Alignment	Right-click, Paragraph | Indents and Spacing tab, Alignment	Ctrl + J
Align, left	248	on Formatting toolbar	Format | Paragraph | Indents and Spacing tab, Alignment	Right-click, Paragraph | Indents and Spacing tab, Alignment	Ctrl + L
Align, right	248	on Formatting toolbar	Format | Paragraph | Indents and Spacing tab, Alignment	Right-click, Paragraph | Indents and Spacing tab, Alignment	Ctrl + R
Arrow, insert and format	347	on Drawing toolbar	Format | Auto-Shape| Colors and Lines tab	Right-click arrow, Format | AutoShape	
AutoComplete, use	196				Type the first few letters of a month (or other AutoComplete text); when a ScreenTip displays, press Enter
AutoCorrect, record entries	283		Tools | AutoCorrect Options | AutoCorrect tab		
AutoCorrect, use shortcuts	286				Type shortcut text and press Enter, Spacebar, or Tab, or add punctuation mark
AutoFormat, table	384	on Tables and Borders toolbar	Table | Table AutoFormat	Select table, right-click, Table AutoFormat	

1155

Word Task	Page	Mouse	Menu Bar	Shortcut Menu	Shortcut Keys
AutoShape, insert	349	AutoShapes on Drawing toolbar	Insert | Picture | AutoShapes		
AutoText, insert	288		Insert | AutoText		Type the first few letters of AutoText text; when a ScreenTip displays, press Enter
AutoText, insert in header or footer	281	Insert AutoText on Header and Footer toolbar	Insert | AutoText		
AutoText, record entries	288		Tools | AutoCorrect Options | AutoText tab		Select, Alt + F3
Border, add to paragraph	433	on Formatting toolbar	Format | Borders and Shading | Borders tab, Box		
Border, insert custom	426		Format | Borders and Shading | Borders tab, Custom		
Browse, select browse object	463	on vertical scroll bar, select object on palette, use for next object			
Browse, by comment	463	on vertical scroll bar,	Edit | Go To, Comment		Ctrl + G
Browse, by edits	463	on vertical scroll bar,			
Browse, by endnote	463	on vertical scroll bar,	Edit | Go To, Endnote		Ctrl + G
Browse, by field	463	on vertical scroll bar,	Edit | Go To, Field		Ctrl + G
Browse, by footnote	463	on vertical scroll bar,	Edit | Go To, Footnote		Ctrl + G
Browse, by graphic	463	on vertical scroll bar,	Edit | Go To, Graphic		Ctrl + G
Browse, by heading	463	on vertical scroll bar,	Edit | Go To, Heading		Ctrl + G
Browse, by page	463	on vertical scroll bar,	Edit | Go To, Page		Ctrl + G
Browse, by section	463	on vertical scroll bar,	Edit | Go To, Section		Ctrl + G
Browse, by table	463	on vertical scroll bar,	Edit | Go To, Table		Ctrl + G
Browse, find	463	on vertical scroll bar,	Edit | Find		Ctrl + F
Browse, go to	463	on vertical scroll bar,	Edit | Go To		Ctrl + G

Word Task	Page	Mouse	Menu Bar	Shortcut Menu	Shortcut Keys
Bulleted list, create	271	on Formatting toolbar	Format | Bullets and Numbering	Select text, right-click, Bullets and Numbering	
Bulleted list, customize	276		Select list, Format | Bullets and Numbering | Bulleted tab; select style and then click Customize	Select list, right-click, Bullets and Numbering | Bulleted tab; select style and then click Customize	
Clip art, insert	334	on Drawing toolbar; in task pane and then click Clip Art	Insert | Picture | Clip Art		
Clip art, resize	341	Drag sizing handle; on Picture toolbar	Format | Picture | Size tab	Right-click image, Format Picture | Size tab	
Clip art, wrap text around	338	on Picture toolbar; Draw ▾ on Drawing toolbar, Text Wrapping	Format | Picture | Layout tab	Right click image, Format Picture | Layout tab	
Clipboard, clear	451	Clear All in Clipboard task pane			
Clipboard, clear individual items	458	Click arrow next to item in Clipboard, click Delete		Right-click item in Clipboard, Delete	
Clipboard, collect and paste	451, 458	Display Clipboard task pane, or multiple objects; in new location(s), click objects on Clipboard to paste or Paste All	Collect objects on Clipboard using Edit | Copy; Edit | Cut; then paste in new location	Display Clipboard; right-click objects in document, Copy or Cut; right-click objects in Clipboard and Paste	Ctrl + C (copy) or Ctrl + X (cut)
Clipboard, collect from other documents	454	Display Clipboard, document selections to Clipboard	Collect objects on Clipboard using Edit | Copy; Edit | Cut	Display Clipboard; right-click objects in documents, Copy or Cut	Ctrl + C (copy) or Ctrl + X (cut)
Clipboard, display task pane	451	in any task pane and then click Clipboard	Edit | Office Clipboard		Ctrl + F1, and click Clipboard; Ctrl + C twice
Close, document	454	X on menu bar			
Close, file	210	X on menu bar	File | Close		Ctrl + F4 or Ctrl + W
Close, header or footer	188	Close on Header and Footer toolbar; Double-click in text area of document			

Word Task	Page	Mouse	Menu Bar	Shortcut Menu	Shortcut Keys
Close, print preview	196	Close or ✕			
Collect and paste, multiple selections	451, 458	Display Clipboard task pane, 📋 or ✂ multiple objects; in new location(s), click objects on Clipboard to paste or 📋 Paste All	Collect objects on Clipboard using Edit | Copy; Edit | Cut; then paste in new location	Display Clipboard; right-click objects in document, Copy or Cut; right-click objects in Clipboard, Paste	Ctrl + C (copy) or Ctrl + X (cut)
Columns, balancing breaks	431		Insert | Break, Continuous		
Columns, change number	428	▦ on Standard toolbar	Format | Columns		
Columns, insert break	431		Insert | Break, Column break		
Copy	264	📋 on Standard toolbar	Edit | Copy	Right-click selected text, Copy	Ctrl + C
Create, new document	195	Start Word (opens blank document) 📄 on Standard toolbar Click *Create a new document* in Getting Started task pane Click *Blank document* in New Document task pane	File | New		Ctrl + N
Create, new folder	190	📁 in Open or Save As dialog box			
Create, new table	365	▦▾ on Standard toolbar	Table | Insert | Table		
Cut	261, 266	✂ on Standard toolbar	Edit | Cut	Right-click selected text or object, Cut	Ctrl + X
Date and time, insert in header or footer	282	📅 🕐 on Header and Footer toolbar	Insert | Date and Time		Alt + Shift + D and Alt + Shift + T
Delete, text	201, 259		Edit | Clear | Contents		Bksp or Delete
Display, ScreenTip	175	Point to a screen element			
Display, toolbar	166		View | Toolbars	Right-click any toolbar, click toolbar name	
Display/hide, task pane	171		View | Task Pane		Ctrl + F1

1158 Office Brief | Word 2003 Task Guide

Word Task	Page	Mouse	Menu Bar	Shortcut Menu	Shortcut Keys
Document, create new	195	Start Word (opens blank (opens blank document)) on Standard toolbar Click Create a new document in Getting Started task pane Click Blank document in New Document task pane	File | New		Ctrl + N
Document, save	196		File | Save		Ctrl + S
Drag-and-drop, turn off/on	266		Tools | Options | Edit tab		
Drawing canvas, hide	344		Tools | Options | General tab		
Em dash, insert	290		Insert | Symbols | Special Characters tab		Alt + Ctrl + −
Endnote insert	292		Insert | Reference | Endnote		Alt + Ctrl + F
Exit Word	193		File | Exit		Alt + F4
File, close	210	on menu bar	File | Close		
Find and replace text	257	on Select Browse Object palette and then click Replace tab	Edit | Replace		Ctrl + H
Folder, create new	190	in Open or Save As dialog box			
Font, apply style	209	B I U	Format | Font, Font style	Right-click and then click Font	Ctrl + B or Ctrl + I or Ctrl + U
Font, change	206	Times New Roman on Formatting toolbar	Format | Font	Right-click and then click Font	
Font, change size	206	12 on Formatting toolbar	Format | Font, Size	Right-click and then click Font	
Font, color	436	A on Formatting toolbar	Format | Font, Font color	Right-click and then click Font	
Font, effects	437		Format | Font, Effects, select effect	Right-click and then click Font	
Footnote, insert	292		Insert | Reference | Footnote		Alt + Ctrl + F
Format Painter	256	on Standard toolbar			Ctrl + Shift + C and Ctrl + Shift + V

Word 2003 Task Guide | **Office Brief** 1159

Word Task	Page	Mouse	Menu Bar	Shortcut Menu	Shortcut Keys
Formatting marks, display/hide	179	¶ on Standard toolbar	Tools | Options | View tab, Formatting marks		
Graphic image, move	343	Drag image; ✂ and 📋 on Standard toolbar	Edit | Cut Edit | Paste	Right-click image, Cut, and then right-click at new location and choose Paste	Ctrl + X and Ctrl + V Select image ← → ↑ ↓
Header or footer, add to document	188	Double-click in a header or footer area on a page (only if header or footer is not empty)	View | Header and Footer; position insertion point in header or footer area and then enter text		
Header or footer, close and return to document	188	Close on Header and Footer toolbar Double-click in text area of document			
Header or footer, insert date and time	282	📅 🕐 on Header and Footer toolbar	Insert | Date and Time		Alt + Shift + D and Alt + Shift + T
Header or footer, insert page numbers	279	# on Header and Footer toolbar	Insert | Page Numbers		Alt + Shift + P
Header or footer, switch between	188	on Header and Footer toolbar			
Help, display in Word	213	❓ on Standard toolbar Click the *Type a question for help* box; type text and press Enter	Help | Microsoft Office Word Help		F1
Help, hide Office Assistant	170		Help | Hide the Office Assistant	Right-click Office Assistant and then click Hide	
Help, show Office Assistant	213		Help | Show the Office Assistant		
Hyperlink, graphic	444	on Standard toolbar	Insert | Hyperlink	Right-click and then click Hyperlink	Ctrl + K
Hyperlink, modify	445	on Standard toolbar	Insert | Hyperlink	Right-click and then click Edit Hyperlink	Ctrl + K
Hyperlink, text	441	on Standard toolbar	Insert | Hyperlink	Right-click and then click Hyperlink	Ctrl + K
Indent, decrease left indent	359	on Formatting toolbar	Format | Paragraph | Indents and Spacing tab, Left	Right-click, Paragraph | Indents and Spacing tab | Left	Ctrl + Shift + M

1160 Office Brief | Word 2003 Task Guide

Word Task	Page	Mouse	Menu Bar	Shortcut Menu	Shortcut Keys
Indent, first line	255	on ruler	Format | Paragraph | Indents and Spacing tab, Special	Right-click, Paragraph | Indents and Spacing tab, Special	
Indent, hanging	298	on ruler	Format | Paragraph | Indents and Spacing tab, Special	Right-click, Paragraph | Indents and Spacing tab, Special	Ctrl + T
Indent, increase left indent	359	on Formatting toolbar Drag Left Indent marker on ruler	Format | Paragraph | Indents and Spacing tab, Left	Right-click, Paragraph | Indents and Spacing tab | Left	Ctrl + M
Indent, left	255	hanging	Format | Paragraph | Indents and Spacing tab, left	Right-click, Paragraph | Indents and Spacing tab, left	
Insert mode, toggle between overtype/insert	202	Double-click OVR in status bar			Ins
Insert, clip art	334	on Drawing toolbar in task pane, then click Clip Art	Insert | Picture | Clip Art		Ctrl + F1, then choose Clip Art
Insert, text box	344	on Drawing toolbar	Insert | Text Box		
Keyboard shortcut	171				Press and hold down the first key, such as Ctrl, and then press the second key (if any), such as F1
Line spacing	250	on Formatting toolbar	Format | Paragraph | Indents and Spacing tab, Line spacing	Right-click, Paragraph | Indents and Spacing tab, Line spacing	Ctrl + 1 (single) Ctrl + 2 (double) Ctrl + 5 (space and one half)
Margins, set	246	Double-click at right of ruler and then click	File | Page Setup | Margins tab		
Menu bar, use	171	Click menu name and then click a command			Alt + underlined letter on menu and then underlined letter of command
Menu, display full	171	Double-click menu name in menu bar Wait a few seconds after displaying menu Click expand arrows at bottom of menu	Tools | Customize | Options tab, Always show full menus		

Word 2003 Task Guide | **Office Brief** 1161

Word Task	Page	Mouse	Menu Bar	Shortcut Menu	Shortcut Keys
Menu, display full always	171		Tools | Customize | Options tab, Always show full menus	Right-click any toolbar and then click Customize; on Options tab, select Always show full menus	
Menu, use keyboard shortcut shown on menu	171				Press and hold down the first key, such as Ctrl, and then press the second key (if any), such as F1
Move, graphic image	343	Drag image; ✂ and 📋 on Standard toolbar	Edit | Cut and Edit | Paste	Right-click image, Cut, and then right-click at new location and choose Paste	Ctrl + X and Ctrl + V
Move, text	261, 266	✂ and 📋 on Standard toolbar; Drag selected text to new location	Edit | Cut Edit | Paste	Right-click selected text, Cut, and then right-click at new location and choose Paste	Ctrl + X and Ctrl + V
Navigate, down, a line at a time	175	▼ at the bottom of vertical scroll bar			↓
Navigate, up/down, screen at a time	175	Click in gray area above/below scroll box on vertical scroll bar			Page Up PageDown
Navigate, to beginning of current line	178	Click at beginning of line			Home
Navigate, to beginning of document	178	Drag vertical scroll bar to top, click before first line			Ctrl + Home
Navigate, to beginning of next word	178	Click at beginning of next word			Ctrl + →
Navigate, to beginning of previous word	178	Click at beginning of previous word			Ctrl + ←
Navigate, to end of current line	178	Click at end of line			End
Navigate, to end of document	178	Drag vertical scroll bar to lower end, click after last line			Ctrl + End
Navigate, up a line at a time	175	▲ at the top of the vertical scroll bar			↑
Normal view, display	180	≡ in lower left corner of Word window	View | Normal		Alt + Ctrl + N
Numbered list, create	272	≣ on Formatting toolbar	Format | Bullets and Numbering	Select text, right-click, Bullets and Numbering	

1162　**Office Brief** | Word 2003 Task Guide

Word Task	Page	Mouse	Menu Bar	Shortcut Menu	Shortcut Keys
Open, existing document	170	on Standard toolbar More or document name in Getting Started task pane	File | Open File | document name at bottom of File menu		Ctrl + O
Outline view, display	180	in lower left corner of Word window	View | Outline		Alt + Ctrl + O
Page break, insert manual	292		Insert | Break, Page break		Ctrl + Enter
Page numbers, different on first page	279	on Header and Footer toolbar	File | Page Setup | Layout tab		
Page numbers, format in header or footer	279	on Header and Footer toolbar			
Page numbers, in header or footer	279	on Header and Footer toolbar	Insert | Page Numbers		Alt + Shift + P
Page setup	196	Double-click left or right of ruler	File | Page Setup		
Paragraph, border	433	on Formatting toolbar	Format | Borders and Shading | Borders tab, Box		
Paragraph, decrease left indent	274	on Formatting toolbar	Format | Paragraph | Indents and Spacing tab, Left	Right-click, Paragraph | Indents and Spacing tab, Left	Ctrl + Shift + M
Paragraph, increase left indent	274	on Formatting toolbar	Format | Paragraph | Indents and Spacing tab, Left	Right-click, Paragraph | Indents and Spacing tab, Left	Ctrl + Shift + M
Paragraph, hanging indent	298	on ruler	Format | Paragraph | Indents and Spacing tab, Special	Right-click, Paragraph | Indents and Spacing tab, Special	Ctrl + T
Paragraph, indent first line	255	on ruler	Format | Paragraph | Indents and Spacing tab, Special	Right-click, Paragraph | Indents and Spacing tab, Special	
Paragraph, Indent left margin	255	on ruler	Format | Paragraph | Indents and Spacing tab, left	Right-click, Paragraph | Indents and Spacing tab, left	
Paragraph, line spacing	250	on Formatting toolbar	Format | Paragraph | Indents and Spacing tab, Line spacing	Right-click, Paragraph | Indents and Spacing tab, Line spacing	Ctrl + 1 (single) Ctrl + 2 (double) Ctrl + 5 (space and one half)
Paragraph, shading	435		Format | Borders and Shading | Shading tab		
Paragraph, spacing	252, 274		Format | Paragraph | Indents and Spacing tab, Before/After	Right-click, Paragraph | Indents and Spacing tab, Before/After	

Word Task	Page	Mouse	Menu Bar	Shortcut Menu	Shortcut Keys
Paste	261	on Standard toolbar Click item in Office Clipboard	Edit | Paste	Right-click, then choose Paste	Ctrl + V
Paste options	261	after Paste			
Picture, insert	336	on Drawing toolbar then choose	Insert | Picture | From File		Ctrl + F1 and then choose Clip Art
Picture, resize	341	Drag sizing handle on Picture toolbar	Format | Picture | Size tab	Right-click image, Format Picture | Size tab	
Picture, wrap text around	338	on Picture toolbar Draw on Drawing toolbar, Text Wrapping	Format | Picture | Layout tab	Right-click image, Format Picture | Layout tab	
Preview, as Web page	447		File | Web Page Preview		
Print Layout view, display	180	in lower left corner of Word window	View | Print Layout		Alt + Ctrl + P
Print, document	193, 210	on Standard toolbar	File | Print		Ctrl + P
Print, from preview	349	on Print Preview toolbar			
Print, preview	196	on Standard toolbar	File | Print Preview		Ctrl + F2
Reading Layout view, close	180	Close on Reading Layout toolbar			
Reading Layout view, display	180	in lower left corner of Word window Read on Standard toolbar	View | Reading Layout		
Redo an action (after Undo)	268	on Standard toolbar	Edit | Redo		Ctrl + Y
Research	455	on Standard toolbar, type a search topic and select a source	Tools | Research		Alt + click word(s)
Ruler, display/hide	246		View | Ruler		
Save, document	196		File | Save		Ctrl + S
Save, document (new name, location, or type)	190		File | Save As		F12

1164 Office Brief | Word 2003 Task Guide

Word Task	Page	Mouse	Menu Bar	Shortcut Menu	Shortcut Keys
Save, document as Web page	448		File | Save as Web Page		
ScreenTip, display	175	Point to a screen element			
Sort, paragraphs	298	[A-Z] or [Z-A] on Tables and Borders toolbar	Table | Sort		
Spelling and Grammar, check entire document	185	[ABC] on Standard toolbar	Tools | Spelling and Grammar, then choose an action for each suggestion		F7
Spelling and Grammar, check individual errors	183			Right-click word or phrase with red or green wavy underline and then choose a suggested correction or other action	
Spelling and Grammar, turn on/off features	183		Tools | Options | Spelling & Grammar tab, then choose Check spelling as you type and/or Check grammar as you type		
Start Word	166	[start] on Windows task-bar and then locate and click Microsoft Office Word 2003	Start | All Programs | Microsoft Office | Microsoft Office Word 2003		
Symbols, insert	290		Insert | Symbols | Special Characters tab		
Tab stops, clear	357	Drag tab stop off ruler	Format | Tabs, Clear or Clear All		
Tab stops, dot leaders	359		Format | Tabs, Leader		
Tab stops, format	357		Format | Tabs, Set		
Tab stops, move	362	Drag markers on ruler	Format | Tabs, Set		
Tab stops, set	354	[L] on ruler; click to cycle tab types, then click ruler	Format | Tabs, Set		
Tab stops, use	359				Tab while typing
Table, align	380	Select table, [icon] or [icon] or [icon] on Formatting toolbar	Table | Table Properties | Table tab	Right-click, Table Properties, Table tab	
Table, align cells	385	[icon] on Tables and Borders toolbar	Table | Table Properties | Cell tab	Right-click in cell, Cell Alignment	
Table, AutoFormat	384	[icon] on Tables and Borders toolbar	Table | Table AutoFormat	Select table, right-click, Table AutoFormat	
Table, change border	377	[icon] on Tables and Borders toolbar	Format | Borders and Shading | Borders tab	Right-click, Borders and Shading | Borders tab	

Word 2003 Task Guide | **Office Brief**

Word Task	Page	Mouse	Menu Bar	Shortcut Menu	Shortcut Keys
Table, column width	370	Drag column boundary	Table | Table Properties | Column tab, Preferred width	Right-click in column, Table Properties | Column tab, Preferred width	
Table, convert from text	381		Table | Convert | Text to Table		
Table, create new	365	on Standard toolbar	Table | Insert | Table		
Table, format cell text	373	Formatting toolbar			
Table, insert column	371	arrow on Tables and Borders toolbar, Insert Columns to the Left or Insert Columns to the Right	Table | Insert | Columns to the Left or Columns to the Right	Right-click in selected column, Insert Columns	
Table, insert row	368	arrow on Tables and Borders toolbar, Insert Rows Above or Insert Rows Below	Table | Insert | Rows Above or Rows Below	Right-click to left of row, Insert Rows	
Table, merge selected cells	385	on Tables and Borders toolbar	Table | Merge Cells	Right-click in selected cells, Merge Cells	
Table, move between cells	365	Click in cell			Tab, Shift + Tab, → ← ↑ ↓
Table, select	380	Click table move handle in Print Layout view	Table | Select | Table		Alt + 5
Table, shading cells	375	on Tables and Borders toolbar	Format | Borders and Shading | Shading tab	Right-click in selected cells, Borders and Shading | Shading tab	
Tables and Borders toolbar, display		on Standard toolbar	View | Toolbars | Tables and Borders	Right-click in any toolbar, click Tables and Borders	
Task pane, display/hide	171		View | Task Pane		Ctrl + F1
Text box, insert	344	on Drawing toolbar	Insert | Text Box		
Text box, move	346	Drag border; and on Standard toolbar	Edit | Cut and Edit | Paste	Right-click border, Cut, then right-click at new location and choose Paste	Ctrl + X and Ctrl + V ← → ↑ ↓
Text box, resize	346	Drag sizing handle	Format | Text Box | Size tab	Right-click border, Format Text Box | Size tab	
Text, align	248		Format | Paragraph | Indents and Spacing tab, Alignment	Right-click, Paragraph | Indents and Spacing tab, Alignment	Ctrl + L (left) Ctrl + E (center) Ctrl + R (right) Ctrl + J (justify)

1166 **Office Brief** | Word 2003 Task Guide

Word Task	Page	Mouse	Menu Bar	Shortcut Menu	Shortcut Keys
Text, cancel selection	204	Click anywhere in document			
Text, change font	206	Times New Roman on Formatting toolbar	Format | Font	Right-click and then click Font	
Text, change font size	206	12 on Formatting toolbar	Format | Font	Right-click and then click Font	
Text, copy	264	on Standard toolbar	Edit | Copy	Right-click selected text, Copy	Ctrl + C
Text, delete	201, 259		Edit | Clear | Contents		Bksp or Delete
Text, enter	196	Click to place insertion point and then type text			
Text, find and replace	257	on Select Browse Object palette and then click Replace tab	Edit | Replace		Ctrl + H
Text, move (cut)	261, 266	and on Standard toolbar Drag selected text to new location	Edit | Cut Edit | Paste	Right-click selected text, Cut, click at new location, and choose Paste	Ctrl + X Ctrl + V
Text, new paragraph or blank line	196				Enter once or twice
Text, overtype/ insert	202	Double-click OVR in status bar, then type			Insert and then type
Text, paste	261	on Standard toolbar	Edit | Paste	Right-click and then choose Paste	Ctrl + V
Text, paste options	261	after pasting			
Text, select	204	Drag over text			Click at beginning, Shift + click at end of selection
Text, select consecutive lines	204				Shift + ↑ or ↓
Text, select consecutive paragraphs	204				Shift + Ctrl + ↑ or ↓
Text, select entire document (including objects)	204	Triple-click in selection bar	Edit | Select All		Ctrl + A
Text, select line	204	Click next to line in selection bar			

Word Task	Page	Mouse	Menu Bar	Shortcut Menu	Shortcut Keys
Text, select one character at a time	204				Shift + → or ←
Text, select one word at a time	204, 259				Shift + Ctrl + → or ←
Text, select paragraph	204	Triple-click in paragraph Double-click in selection bar next to paragraph			
Text, select sentence	204				Ctrl + click sentence
Text, select word	204	Double-click word			
Thesaurus	461	on Standard toolbar, select Thesaurus in Research task pane	Tools | Language | Thesaurus	Right-click a word, Synonyms | Thesaurus	Shift + F7
Toolbar, display	166		View | Toolbars	Right-click any toolbar, click toolbar name	
Toolbars, show on one or two rows	166	on Standard or Formatting toolbar, Show Buttons on One Row / Two Rows	Tools | Customize | Options tab, Show Standard and Formatting toolbars on two rows View | ToolbarsCustomize | Options tab, Show Standard and Formatting toolbars on two rows	Right-click any toolbar and then click Customize; on Options tab, select or clear Show Standard and Formatting toolbars on two rows	
Undo an action	268	on Standard toolbar	Edit | Undo		Ctrl + Z
View, Normal	180	in lower left corner of Word window	View | Normal		Alt + Ctrl + N
View, Outline	180	in lower left corner of Word window	View | Outline		Alt + Ctrl + O
View, Print Layout	180	in lower left corner of Word window	View | Print Layout		Alt + Ctrl + P
View, Reading Layout	180	in lower left corner of Word window Read on Standard toolbar	View | Reading Layout		
View, Web Layout	180	in lower left corner of corner of Word window	View | Web Layout		
Web Layout view, display	180	in lower left corner of Word window	View | Web Layout		
Web page, save document	448		File | Save as Web Page		

1168 Office Brief | Word 2003 Task Guide

Word Task	Page	Mouse	Menu Bar	Shortcut Menu	Shortcut Keys
WordArt, alignment	424	on WordArt toolbar			
WordArt, change shape	424	on WordArt toolbar			
WordArt, character spacing	424	on WordArt toolbar			
WordArt, display toolbar	424	Click the WordArt image	View	Toolbars	WordArt		
WordArt, edit text	424	Edit Text... on WordArt toolbar		Right-click WordArt, Edit Text	
WordArt, format	424	on WordArt toolbar	Format	WordArt	Right-click WordArt, Format WordArt	
WordArt, gallery	424	on WordArt toolbar			
WordArt, insert	422	on Drawing toolbar	Insert	Picture	WordArt		
WordArt, same letter heights	424	on WordArt toolbar			
WordArt, text wrapping	424	on WordArt toolbar	Format WordArt	Layout tab	Right-click WordArt, Format WordArt	Layout tab	
WordArt, vertical text	424	on WordArt toolbar			
Zoom, magnify or shrink the view of a document	181	100% arrow on Standard toolbar and then choose a display percentage Click in Zoom box 100% and then type a percentage	View	Zoom		
Zoom, maximum page width	181	100% arrow on Standard toolbar and then choose Page Width	View	Zoom, Page Width		

Excel 2003

Excel Task	Page	Mouse	Menu Bar	Shortcut Menu	Shortcut Keys
Absolute reference, create	635	Edit cell reference to precede the column letter and/or row number with $, such as $B$6			While typing formula, select cell, press F4 In Formula Bar, click cell reference, press F4 (repeat to cycle through options)
Align, cell contents	675		Format | Cells | Alignment tab	Format Cells | Alignment tab	Ctrl + 1 Press Alt + Enter to move specific text to the next line in the cell
Align, center across selection	678		Format | Cells | Alignment tab, Horizontal: Center Across Selection	Format Cells | Alignment tab	Ctrl + 1 Press Alt + Enter to move specific text to the next line in the cell
Align, fill cell(s) with character(s)	677		Format | Cells | Alignment tab, Horizontal: Fill	Format Cells | Alignment tab	Ctrl + 1 Press Alt + Enter to move specific text to the next line in the cell
Align, indent cell contents	675	increase, or decrease on Formatting toolbar	Format | Cells | Alignment tab, Indent	Format Cells | Alignment tab	Ctrl + 1 Press Alt + Enter to move specific text to the next line in the cell
Align, left-align cell contents	602	on Formatting toolbar	Format | Cells | Alignment tab, Horizontal: Left (Indent)	Format Cells | Alignment tab	Ctrl + 1 Press Alt + Enter to move specific text to the next line in the cell
Align, merge and center cells	603, 678	on Formatting toolbar	Format | Cells | Alignment tab, Horizontal: center Merge cells	Format Cells | Alignment tab	Ctrl + 1 Press Alt + Enter to move specific text to the next line in the cell
Align, merge cells	689	on Formatting toolbar (also centers)	Format | Cells | Alignment tab, Merge cells	Format Cells | Alignment tab	Ctrl + 1 Press Alt + Enter to move specific text to the next line in the cell
Align, right-align cell contents	602	on Formatting toolbar	Format | Cells | Alignment tab, Horizontal: Right (Indent)	Format Cells | Alignment tab	Ctrl + 1 Press Alt + Enter to move specific text to the next line in the cell

Excel Task	Page	Mouse	Menu Bar	Shortcut Menu	Shortcut Keys
Align, rotate cell contents	681	In Format Cells dialog box, Alignment tab, Orientation, drag red diamond	Format	Cells	Alignment tab, Orientation or Degrees	Format Cells	Alignment tab	Ctrl + 1 Press Alt + Enter to move specific text to the next line in the cell
Align, shrink to fit cell contents	684		Format	Cells	Alignment tab, Shrink to fit	Format Cells	Alignment tab	Ctrl + 1 Press Alt + Enter to move specific text to the next line in the cell
Align, vertically	679		Format	Cells	Alignment tab, Vertical	Format Cells	Alignment tab	Ctrl + 1 Press Alt + Enter to move specific text to the next line in the cell
Align, wrap text in cell	682		Format	Cells	Alignment tab, Wrap text	Format Cells	Alignment tab	Ctrl + 1 Press Alt + Enter to move specific text to the next line in the cell
AutoFill Options, smart tag	592	Use AutoFill, click to select a fill option			
AutoComplete, use	540				Begin typing the first few letters; when a ScreenTip displays, press Enter
AutoFill, ascending	592	Select cell fill handle, drag + down or right	Edit	Fill	Down Edit	Fill	Right		
AutoFill, descending	592	Select cell fill handle, drag + up or left	Edit	Fill	Up Edit	Fill	Left		
AutoFill, duplicate data	594	Use AutoFill, click , click Copy Cells			
AutoFit, fit column(s) to widest entry	618	Double-click vertical bar at right of column heading	Format	Column	AutoFit Selection		
AutoSum, insert	553	Σ ▾ on Standard toolbar	Insert	Function	SUM		Alt + =
AutoSum, select range	623	Select range, Σ ▾ on Standard toolbar Σ ▾ on Standard toolbar, and then drag to select range	Insert	Function	SUM function		Alt + =

1172 **Office Brief** | Excel 2003 Task Guide

Excel Task	Page	Mouse	Menu Bar	Shortcut Menu	Shortcut Keys
Bold, apply to font	684	**B** on Formatting toolbar	Format | Cells | Font, Font style: Bold	Format Cells | Font tab	Ctrl + B
Border, apply to cell(s)	690	on Formatting toolbar; click arrow for predefined border style	Format | Cells | Border tab; choose a preset style or choose line style, color, and position	Format Cells | Border tab	Ctrl + Shift + 7 (outline border) Ctrl + 1 | Border tab, then Alt + T (top) or Alt + B (bottom) or Alt + L (left) or Alt + R (right)
Cancel an entry	542, 545	X on Formula bar			Esc (entire entry) or Bksp (characters left of insertion point)
Chart, change value(s)	523	Edit value(s) in worksheet			
Clear, cell contents	548		Edit | Clear | Contents	Clear Contents	Del
Clear, cell contents and formatting	697		Edit | Clear | All		
Clear, cell formats	697		Edit | Clear | Formats		
Clipboard, clear	604	Clear All in Clipboard task pane			
Clipboard, collect and paste	608	Display Clipboard task pane, or multiple objects; in new location(s), click objects on Clipboard to paste or Paste All	Collect objects on Clipboard using Edit | Copy or Edit | Cut or Insert | Picture | Clip Art; and then paste in new location (must use clipboard task pane)	Display Clipboard; right-click objects, Copy or Cut; right-click objects in Clipboard, Paste	With Clipboard displayed, Ctrl + C or Ctrl + X, and then paste (must use Clipboard task pane)
Clipboard, display task pane	604	in any task pane, and then click Clipboard	Edit | Office Clipboard		Ctrl + F1, choose Clipboard
Close, task pane	502, 534	X in task pane	View | Task Pane		Ctrl + F1

Excel 2003 Task Guide | **Office Brief** 1173

Excel Task	Page	Mouse	Menu Bar	Shortcut Menu	Shortcut Keys
Close, workbook	509, 559	✕ on menu bar	File | Close		Ctrl + F4 or Ctrl + W
Collect and paste, multiple selections	608	Display Clipboard task pane, 📋 or ✂ multiple objects; in new location(s), click objects on Clipboard to paste or Paste All	Collect objects on Clipboard using Edit | Copy or Edit | Cut or Insert | Picture | Clip Art; and then paste in new location (must use Clipboard task pane)	Display Clipboard; right-click objects, Copy or Cut; right-click objects in Clipboard, Paste	With Clipboard displayed, Ctrl + C or Ctrl + X, and then paste (must use Clipboard task pane)
Color, fill	693	🎨 on Formatting toolbar	Format | Cells | Patterns tab, Color	Format Cells | Patterns tab	Ctrl + 1 | Patterns tab
Column width, change	596	Drag vertical bar at right of column heading left or right	Format | Column | Width	Right-click vertical bar to right of column heading, and then click Column Width	
Column, delete	599		Edit | Delete | Entire column	Right-click column heading; click Delete	Ctrl + −
Column, insert	599		Insert | Columns	Right-click column heading; click Insert	Ctrl + Shift + +
Columns, select multiple	596	Point to column heading until pointer changes to ↓, drag over column headings			
Comment, insert in cell	712	📁 on Reviewing toolbar	Insert | Comment	Insert Comment	
Comment, view	712	Point to cell containing red triangle	View | Comments		
Copy and paste, multiple ranges from another workbook	610	Display Clipboard, 📋; in source workbook, Edit | Copy workbook ranges. In destination workbook paste (click) each Clipboard item	Display Clipboard, 📋; in source workbook, Edit | Copy workbook ranges. In destination workbook paste (click) each Clipboard item	Display Clipboard, 📋; in source workbook, Edit | Copy workbook ranges. In destination workbook paste (click) each Clipboard item	Ctrl + C
Copy, cell contents	604	📋 on Standard toolbar	Edit | Copy	Copy	Ctrl + C
Copy, formula with absolute cell references	635	For cell references that should not change, create absolute references in formula; copy (and paste)			
Copy, formula with relative cell references	633	Point to fill handle of formula cell; drag + to copy formula to adjacent cell(s)	Select formula cell, Edit | Copy; click another cell, Edit | Paste	Right-click formula cell, click Copy; click another cell, right-click, and then click Paste	Ctrl + C and then, in another cell, Ctrl + V
Copy, worksheet	609	Click sheet tab, hold down Ctrl, drag to location	Click sheet tab, Edit | Move or Copy Sheet	Right-click sheet tab, Move or Copy	

1174 Office Brief | Excel 2003 Task Guide

Excel Task	Page	Mouse	Menu Bar	Shortcut Menu	Shortcut Keys
Create, new folder	530	in Open or Save As dialog box			
Create, new workbook	534	Start Excel (opens blank workbook) on Standard toolbar Click Create a new workbook in Getting Started task pane Click Blank workbook in in New Workbook task pane	File | New		Ctrl + N
Cut, cell contents	614	on Standard toolbar	Edit | Cut	Cut	Ctrl + X
Date, enter in cell	543	Type date in allowed format, such as m/d/yy, and click another cell			Type date in allowed format, such as m/d/yy, and press Enter or Tab
Decimal places, decrease (for selected styles)	621	on Formatting toolbar	Format | Cells | Number tab	Format Cells | Number tab	Ctrl + 1 | Number tab
Decimal places, increase (for selected styles)	621	on Formatting toolbar	Format | Cells | Number tab	Format Cells | Number tab	Ctrl + 1 | Number tab
Delete, row or column	599		Edit | Delete | Entire row or Entire column	Right-click row heading or column heading; click Delete	Ctrl + –
Deselect, row or column	512	Click any cell			
Display, underlying formulas	640				Ctrl + ` (below Esc); repeat to return display to normal
Edit, data in cell	545, 632	Double-click cell, type changes, in Formula bar			F2, type and use ←, →, Bksp, Del as needed, and then Enter
Edit, data in Formula bar	629	Click in Formula bar, and then type Double-click cell reference in Formula bar, click a cell, and press Enter			In Formula bar, type and use ←, →, Bksp, Del as needed, and then Enter
Edit, overtype mode	545				Ins
Exit Excel	530	X	File | Exit		Alt + F4

Excel Task	Page	Mouse	Menu Bar	Shortcut Menu	Shortcut Keys
File name, view on taskbar	534	Point to taskbar button, view ScreenTip			
Font, apply style	684	**B** *I* on Formatting toolbar	Format | Cells | Font, Font style	Format Cells | Font tab	Ctrl + B or Ctrl + I
Font, apply underline	684	U on Formatting toolbar	Format | Cells | Font, Underline	Format Cells | Font tab	Ctrl + U
Font, change (face)	684	Arial on Formatting toolbar	Format | Cells | Font, Font	Format Cells | Font tab	
Font, change size	684	10 on Formatting toolbar	Format | Cells | Font, Size	Format Cells | Font tab	
Format numbers	670		Format | Cells | Number tab, choose Category	Format Cells | Number tab	Ctrl + 1 | Number tab
Format numbers, comma style	622, 670	, on Formatting toolbar	Format | Cells | Number tab, Category: Currency, Symbol: None	Format Cells | Number tab	Ctrl + 1 | Number tab
Format numbers, currency style	618, 674	$ on Formatting toolbar (precisely, accounting style)	Format | Cells | Number tab, Category: Currency	Format Cells | Number tab	Ctrl + Shift + 4 Ctrl + 1 | Number tab
Format numbers, percent style	620	% on Formatting toolbar	Format | Cells | Number tab, Category: Percentage	Format Cells | Number tab	Ctrl + Shift + 5 Ctrl + 1 | Number tab
Format Painter	695	on Standard toolbar (double-click to apply repeatedly)			
Formula Bar, edit within	629	Click in Formula bar, and then type Double-click cell reference in Formula bar, click a cell, press Enter			In Formula bar, type and use ←, →, Bksp, Del as needed, and then Enter
Formula, display underlying	640				Ctrl + ` (below Esc); repeat to return display to normal
Formula, enter in cell	549	Type = followed by formula			
Formula, enter using point-and-click method	551	Type = and then click cells and type operators to enter formula			

1176 **Office Brief** | Excel 2003 Task Guide

Excel Task	Page	Mouse	Menu Bar	Shortcut Menu	Shortcut Keys
Header/footer, create	525, 590, 703		View	Header and Footer, Custom Header or Custom Footer File	Page Setup	Header/Footer tab, Custom Header or Custom Footer		
Header/footer, insert picture	703	in Header dialog box or Footer dialog box	View	Header and Footer, Custom Header or Custom Footer		
Help, close window	559	in Help window			
Help, display in Excel	559	on Standard toolbar Click the *Type a question for help* box; type text and press Enter	Help	Microsoft Excel Help		F1
Help, print help topic	559	in Help window		Print	Ctrl + P in Help window
Insert, row or column	599		Insert	Rows or Columns	Right-click row or column heading; click Insert	Ctrl + Shift + +
Italic, apply to font	684	on Formatting toolbar	Format	Cells	Font, Font style: Italic	Format Cells	Font tab	Ctrl + I
Menus, display full	506	Double-click menu name in menu bar Wait a few seconds after displaying menu Click double arrows at bottom of menu	Tools	Customize	Options tab, Always show full menus		
Move active cell, down one cell	520	Click cell			Enter
Move active cell, down one full screen	520				PgDn
Move active cell, left one cell	520	Click cell			Shift + Tab
Move active cell, left one full screen	520				Alt + Page Up
Move active cell, left/right/up/down one cell	520	Click cell			← or → or ↑ or ↓
Move active cell, right one cell	520	Click cell			Tab

Excel 2003 Task Guide | **Office Brief** 1177

Excel Task	Page	Mouse	Menu Bar	Shortcut Menu	Shortcut Keys
Move active cell, right one full screen	520				Alt + PgDn
Move active cell, to cell A1	520				Ctrl + Home
Move active cell, to column A of current row	520				Home
Move active cell, up one cell	520	Click cell			Shift + Enter
Move active cell, up one full screen	520				PgUp
Move active cell, use Name box	520	Click Name box (left of Formula bar); type cell reference, Enter			
Move to last cell of active area	520				Ctrl + End
Move, cell contents	614, 616	on Standard toolbar and then, in new location, . Select range, drag to new location, drop (release mouse button)	Edit | Cut and then, in new location, Edit | Paste	Cut and then, in new location, right-click and then click Paste	Ctrl + X and then, in new location, Ctrl + V
Move, to another worksheet	522	Click sheet tab			
Number, enter in cell	542	Type number in cell, click another cell			Type number in cell, press Enter or Tab
Open, workbook	509	on Standard toolbar More or workbook name in Getting Started task pane	File | Open File | workbook name at bottom of File menu		Ctrl + O
Page setup, center worksheet on page	699		File | Page Setup | Margins tab, Horizontally and/or Vertically		
Page setup, header or footer	703		View | Header and Footer, Custom Header or Custom Footer File | Page Setup | Header/Footer tab, Custom Header or Custom Footer		
Page setup, header or footer margins	708		File | Page Setup | Margins tab, Header or Footer		
Page setup, margins	699		File | Page Set-up | Margins tab; Top, Bottom, Left, Right		

1178 **Office Brief** | Excel 2003 Task Guide

Excel Task	Page	Mouse	Menu Bar	Shortcut Menu	Shortcut Keys
Page setup, page settings (orientation, scaling, paper size)	641, 699		File | Page Setup | Page tab		
Page setup, sheet settings (print area, rows/columns to repeat, gridlines, row/column headings, page order)	710		File | Page Set-up | Sheet tab		
Paste (after Cut or Copy)	604	on Standard toolbar Click item in Office Clipboard	Edit | Paste	Paste	Ctrl + V
Paste options	604	after pasting			
Pattern, apply to cell(s)	693		Format | Cells | Patterns tab, Pattern	Format Cells | Patterns tab	Ctrl + 1 | Patterns tab
Print, entire workbook	616	Click first sheet tab, Shift + click last sheet tab, then	File | Print, Entire workbook		Ctrl + P | Entire workbook
Print, Preview	529, 558	on Standard toolbar	File | Print Preview File | Print, click Preview button in the dialog box		
Print, worksheet(s)	529	on Standard toolbar	File | Print, Active sheet(s)		Ctrl + P
Redo	548	on Standard toolbar	Edit | Redo		Ctrl + Y
Row height, change	596	Drag horizontal line between row headings up or down	Format | Row | Height	Right-click horizontal line between row headings, and then click Row Height	
Row, delete	599		Edit | Delete | Entire row	Right click row heading; click Delete	Ctrl + −
Row, insert	599		Insert | Rows	Right-click row heading; click Insert	Ctrl + Shift + +
Save, new workbook	536		File | Save As		Ctrl + S or F12
Save, workbook	536		File | Save		Ctrl + S
Save, workbook (new name, location, or type)	530		File | Save As		F12

Excel Task	Page	Mouse	Menu Bar	Shortcut Menu	Shortcut Keys
Scroll, multiple columns to right/left	518	Click between scroll box and scroll arrow on horizontal scroll bar			
Scroll, multiple rows down/up	518	Click between scroll box and scroll arrow on vertical scroll bar			
Scroll, one column to right/left	518	Click right/left scroll arrow on horizontal scroll bar			
Scroll, one row down/up	518	Click down/up scroll arrow on vertical scroll bar			
Select, all cells	512	Click Select All button (where row and column headings intersect)			Ctrl + A
Select, multiple columns	596	Point to column heading until the pointer changes to ↓, drag over column headings			
Select, multiple rows	598	Point to row heading until the pointer changes to →, drag over row headings			
Select, nonadjacent cells	512				Click first cell, Ctrl + click remaining cells
Select, range (adjacent cells)	512	Click first cell, drag to last cell			Click first cell, Shift + click last cell
Select, row or column	512	Click row or column heading in worksheet frame			Shift + Spacebar (row); Ctrl + Spacebar (column)
Spelling check	557	on Standard toolbar	Tools	Spelling		F7
Start Excel	502	start on Windows taskbar, and then locate and click Microsoft Office Excel 2003	Start	All Programs	Microsoft Office	Microsoft Office Excel 2003		
Text, enter in cell	537	Type in cell, click another cell			Type in cell, press Enter or Tab
Toolbar buttons, identify	506	Point to button, view ScreenTip			
Toolbars, show on one or two rows	506	on Standard or Formatting toolbar, Show Buttons on One Row / Two Rows	Tools	Customize	Options tab, Show Standard and Formatting toolbars on two rows View	Toolbars	Customize	Options tab, Show Standard and Formatting toolbars on two rows	Right-click any toolbar, and then click Customize; on Options tab, select or clear Show Standard and Formatting toolbars on two rows	

Excel Task	Page	Mouse	Menu Bar	Shortcut Menu	Shortcut Keys
Trace Error, smart tag	629	Click cell containing green triangle; point to smart tag, read error in ScreenTip, and then click and select an option			
Underline, apply to font	684	[U] on Formatting toolbar	Format | Cells | Font, Underline	Format Cells | Font tab	Ctrl + U
Undo	548, 559	[↶] on Standard toolbar	Edit | Undo		Ctrl + Z
Workbook, close	509, 559	[X] on menu bar	File | Close		Ctrl + F4 or Ctrl + W
Workbook, create new	534	Start Excel (opens blank workbook) [ ] on Standard toolbar Click Create a new workbook in Getting Started task pane Click Blank workbook in New Workbook task pane	File | New		Ctrl + N
Workbook, open	509	[ ] on Standard toolbar More or workbook name in Getting Started task pane	File | Open File | workbook name at bottom of File menu		Ctrl + O
Worksheet, copy	609	Click sheet tab, hold down Ctrl, drag to location	Click sheet tab, Edit | Move or Copy Sheet	Right-click sheet tab, Move or Copy	
Worksheet, rename	524	Double-click sheet tab, type new name		Right-click sheet tab, click Rename, type new name	
Worksheet, select all (group)	525	Click first sheet, hold down Shift and click last sheet		Right-click sheet tab, click Select All Sheets	
Worksheet, ungroup multiple worksheets	525	Click an inactive sheet tab		Right-click a grouped worksheet tab, click Ungroup Sheets	
Zoom	555	[100% ▼] on Standard toolbar	View | Zoom		

Excel 2003 Task Guide | **Office Brief** 1181

Access 2003

Access Task	Page	Mouse	Menu Bar	Shortcut Menu	Shortcut Keys
AutoForm, close	827	✖ in form window	File | Close		Ctrl + F4 or Ctrl + W
AutoForm, create	825	On Objects bar, click Forms, and then click New and select an AutoForm. Select a table, and then click [icon] on Database toolbar	Insert | Form, and then select an AutoForm		
Close, database	792	✖ in the Database window	File | Close		Ctrl + F4 or Ctrl + W
Close, Database window	761	✖ in Database window	File | Close		Ctrl + F4 or Ctrl + W
Close, query	758, 899	✖ in query window	File | Close		Ctrl + F4 or Ctrl + W
Close, table	756	✖ in table window	File | Close		Ctrl + F4 or Ctrl + W
Create, new blank database	766	[icon] then click Blank database in New File task pane	File | New		Ctrl + N
Create, table in Design view	767	On Objects bar, click Tables; double-click *Create table in Design view* or click New, and then click Design View	Insert | Table, Design View	Right-click Create table in Design view command, and then click Open	
Data type, select	767	In Table Design view, click a field's Data Type column, and then select from drop-down list			
Database window, close	761	✖ in Database window			
Database window, restore	761	[icon]			
Database, clear Read-only property	742		File | Properties (in My Computer); clear Read-only	In My Computer, right-click database file name, and then click Properties; clear Read-only	

1183

Access Task	Page	Mouse	Menu Bar	Shortcut Menu	Shortcut Keys
Database, close	792	X in the Database window	File | Close		
Database, copy	742		Edit | Copy, and then Edit | Paste in same or other folder (in My Computer)	In My Computer, right-click database file name, and then click Copy; right-click in file name area of destination folder, and then click Paste	Ctrl + C and Ctrl + V
Database, create new (blank)	766	and then click Blank database in New File task pane	File | New		Ctrl + N
Database, open existing	744		File | Open		Ctrl + O
Database, rename	742		File | Rename (in My Computer)	In My Computer, right-click database file name, and then click Rename	
Delete, record	783	in Table Datasheet view	Edit | Delete Record, and then click Yes to confirm	Right-click selected record, and then click Delete Record	Delete
Delete, table field	777	In Table Design view, click record selector and then	Edit | Delete Rows Edit | Delete	Right-click a field name, and then click Delete Rows	Delete
Display, first record in form	822		Edit | Go To | First		Ctrl + Home
Display, last record in form	822		Edit | Go To | Last		Ctrl + End
Display, next record in form	759		Edit | Go To | Next		PageDown
Display, previous record in form	822		Edit | Go To | Previous		Page Up
Display, print preview of form	848		File | Print Preview	Right-click form name, and then click Print Preview	
Display, Total row in query design grid	939	Σ	View | Totals	Totals	
Display/close, field list	853	X to close	View | Field List		
Display/hide report's page header/footer	862		View | Page Header/Footer	Page Header/Footer	

1184 Office Brief | Access 2003 Task Guide

Access Task	Page	Mouse	Menu Bar	Shortcut Menu	Shortcut Keys
Display/hide report's report header/footer	862		View | Report Header/Footer	Report Header/Footer	
Display/hide, form header/footer	836, 848		View | Form Header/Footer	Form Header/Footer	
Edit, record	782	In Table Datasheet view, click in a field, and then type			Delete or Bksp to delete text
Exit, Access	792	✕ in the Access window	File | Exit		Alt + F4
Field list, display/close	853	[icon] ✕ to close	View | Field List		
Field, add to table	779	In Table Design view, [icon], and then type field name Click in first field of next available row, and then type field name	Insert | Rows (Design view)	Right-click a field name or blank row, and then click Insert Rows	
Form, add label	836	[Aa icon] on Toolbox in Design view			
Form, add form footer	848	Add a label to Form Footer section (Design view)			
Form, add form header	836	Add a label to Form Header section (Design view)			
Form, add new record	828	[icon]	Insert | New Record (in Datasheet view)		Ctrl + +
Form, close	759, 822	✕ in form window	File | Close		Ctrl + F4 or Ctrl + W
Form, close AutoForm	827	✕ in form window	File | Close		Ctrl + F4 or Ctrl + W
Form, close when maximized	848	✕	Close (on form Program menu)	Right-click title bar, and then click Close	
Form, create AutoForm	825	On Objects bar, click Forms, and then click [New] and select an AutoForm Select a table, and then click [icon] on Database toolbar	Insert | Form, and then select an AutoForm		

Access 2003 Task Guide | Office Brief 1185

Access Task	Page	Mouse	Menu Bar	Shortcut Menu	Shortcut Keys
Form, create with Form Wizard	833	On Objects bar, click Forms, and then click [New], Form Wizard Double-click *Create form by using wizard*	Insert | Form, Form Wizard		
Form, delete record	829	on Formatting toolbar	Edit | Delete Record	Right-click record selector, and then click Cut	Delete
Form, display first	822		Edit | Go To | First		Ctrl + Home
Form, display last record	822		Edit | Go To | Last		Ctrl + End
Form, display next record	759		Edit | Go To | Next		PageDown
Form, display previous record	822		Edit | Go To | Previous		Page Up
Form, display print preview	848		File | Print Preview	Right-click form name, and then click Print Preview	
Form, display/hide form header/footer	836, 848		View | Form Header/Footer	Form Header/Footer	
Form, display/hide rulers	836		View | Ruler (Design view)	Ruler	
Form, display/hide Toolbox	836	on Form Design toolbar	View | Toolbox	Toolbox	
Form, maximize window	836	Double-click title bar			
Form, move a field	841	Display , drag border (Design view)			
Form, move text box control separately from label	841	Display , drag large black handle (Design view)			
Form, open in Design view	759	Click form name and then [Design]		Right-click form name, and then click Design View	
Form, open in Form view	759, 822	Click form name and then [Open] Double-click form name		Right-click form name, and then click Open	

1186 Office Brief | Access 2003 Task Guide

Access Task	Page	Mouse	Menu Bar	Shortcut Menu	Shortcut Keys
Form, print	848		File | Print	Right-click form name, and then click Print	Ctrl + P
Form, resize a field	841	Drag a selection handle (Design view)	Format | Size	Right-click field, and then click Size	
Form, save design	827	on Form design toolbar	File | Save		Ctrl + S
Form, switch to Design view	759, 836		View | Design View	Right-click form title bar, and then click Form Design	
Form, switch to Form view	759, 836		View | Form View	Right-click form title bar, and then click Form View	
Go to, first field of first record in datasheet	791	Click in first field			Ctrl + Home
Go to, first record in datasheet	791		Edit | Go To | First		Ctrl + Page Up and then Ctrl + Home
Go to, last field of last record in datasheet	791	Click in last field			Ctrl + End
Go to, last record in datasheet	791		Edit | Go To | Last		Ctrl + PageDown and then Ctrl + End
Go to, next record in datasheet	790, 791		Edit | Go To | Next		↓
Go to, previous record in datasheet	790, 791		Edit | Go To | Previous		↑
Move, field in form	841	Display , drag border (Design view)			
Move, query field	928	Drag column selector left or right			
Move, report field and label in different sections in Design view	855	Select using Shift, and then drag			→, ←, ↑, ↓

Access Task	Page	Mouse	Menu Bar	Shortcut Menu	Shortcut Keys
Open, existing database	744	[icon]	File | Open		Ctrl + O
Open, form in Design view	759	Click form name and then [Design icon]		Right-click form name, and then click Design View	
Open, form in Form view	759, 822	Click form name and then [Open icon] Double-click form name		Right-click form name, and then click Open	
Open, query in Datasheet view	758, 900, 927	Click query name and then [Open icon] Double-click query name		Right-click query name, and then click Open	
Open, query in Design view	758, 900	Click query name and then [Design icon] and then click		Right-click query name, and then click Design View	
Open, report in Design view	761	Click report name and then [Design icon]		Right-click report name, and then click Design View	
Open, table in Datasheet view	752, 776	Click table name and then [Open icon] Double-click table name		Right-click table name, and then click Open	
Open, table in Design view	752	Click table name and then [Design icon]		Right-click table name, and then click Design View	
Page setup, check margins	780	In Print dialog box, click Setup	File | Page Setup		
Primary key, create	772	In Table Design view, click a field name, and then [key icon]	Edit | Primary Key	Right-click a field name, and then click Primary Key	
Print, table	780	[printer icon] in Table Datasheet view	File | Print	Right-click table name, and then click Print	Ctrl + P
Print, form	848	[printer icon]	File | Print	Right-click form name, and then click Print	Ctrl + P
Print, landscape/ portrait orientation	780	In Print dialog box, click Properties, Layout tab, and then Landscape or Portrait	File | Properties | Layout tab, Landscape or Portrait		
Print, query results	910	[printer icon]	File | Print		Ctrl + P
Print, report	761	[printer icon] on Print Preview toolbar	File | Print	Right-click on report, and then click Report	Ctrl + P

1188 **Office Brief** | Access 2003 Task Guide

Access Task	Page	Mouse	Menu Bar	Shortcut Menu	Shortcut Keys
Query, add calculated field	934	Type expression in Field row, enclosing field names in brackets		Right-click in Field row, Field row, choose Zoom, type expression	
Query, add fields to design grid	894	Double-click field name in field list Drag field to grid Click in Field row, and then select from list			
Query, add table in Design view	894	, click Add	Query | Show Table, Add	Show Table	
Query, clear the design grid	918		Edit | Clear Grid		
Query, close	758, 899	in query window	File | Close		Ctrl + F4 or Ctrl + W
Query, create in Design view	894	On Objects bar, click Queries; click New ; click Design View double-click *Create query in Design view*	Insert | Query, Design View		
Query, delete selected field(s)	901		Edit | Delete Columns	Cut	Delete
Query, display Total row	939	Σ	View | Totals	Totals	
Query, format calculated field	934		View | Properties	Properties	Alt + Enter
Query, group data	939	In Total row, click Group By			
Query, hide field from result	918	In the Show row under the field, clear the check box			
Query, move field	928	Drag column selector left or right			
Query, open in Datasheet view	758, 900, 927	Click query name and then Open Double-click query name		Right-click query name, and then click Open	
Query, open in Design view	758, 900	Click query name and then Design		Right-click query name, and then click Design View	

Access 2003 Task Guide | **Office Brief** 1189

Access Task	Page	Mouse	Menu Bar	Shortcut Menu	Shortcut Keys
Query, print results	910	🖨	File | Print		Ctrl + P
Query, run	899	❗ in Design view			
Query, save design	899	💾	File | Save		Ctrl + S
Query, save to new name	904		File | Save As	Right-click report name, and then click Save As	
Query, sort by multiple fields in Design view	928	Move fields in order of sort; in Sort row, select Ascending or Descending for each sort field			
Query, sort in Datasheet view	927	A↓ or Z↓			
Query, sort in Design view	928	In Sort row, select Ascending or Descending			
Query, specify * wildcard criteria	912	Type under field in Criteria row, substituting * for multiple characters			
Query, specify ? wildcard criteria	916	Type under field in Criteria row, substituting ? for single characters (Design view)			
Query, specify criteria using AND	925	Type under each field in Criteria row			
Query, specify criteria using comparison operators	922	Type under field in Criteria row with < > <= >= operators			
Query, specify criteria using OR	926	Type under field in Criteria and *or* rows			
Query, specify text or numeric criteria	904, 921	Type under field in Criteria row			
Query, switch to Datasheet view	758	▦ ▾ on Query Design toolbar	View | Datasheet View	Right-click query title bar, and then click Datasheet View	
Query, switch to Design view	758, 900	✏ ▾	View | Design View	Right-click query title bar, and then click Query Design	
Query, use functions	941	In Total row, click Sum, Avg, Min, Max, etc.			

1190 **Office Brief** | Access 2003 Task Guide

Access Task	Page	Mouse	Menu Bar	Shortcut Menu	Shortcut Keys
Record, add to table	774	In Table Datasheet view, [icon], and then type Click in first field of next available record, and then type Click in last field of last record, and then press Tab and type	Insert | New Record (Datasheet view)	Right-click selected record, and then click New Record	Ctrl + +
Record, delete	783	[icon] in Table Datasheet view	Edit | Delete Record, and then click Yes to confirm	Right-click selected record, and then click Delete Record	Delete
Record, edit	782	In Table Datasheet view, click in a field, and then type			Delete or Bksp to delete text
Report, add page footer or report	867	[Aa icon], drag in Page Footer or Report Footer section			
Report, change setup	853	[Setup icon] on Print Preview toolbar	File | Page Setup		
Report, change width	855	Drag right edge of report [icon], click Format tab, Width			
Report, close	761	[X icon] in report window	File | Close		Ctrl + F4 or Ctrl + W
Report, create with Report Wizard	850	On Objects bar, click Report; click [New icon], Report Wizard double-click *Create report by using wizard*	Insert | Report, Report Wizard		
Report, display/hide page header/footer	867		View | Page Header/Footer	Page Header/Footer	
Report, display/hide report header/footer	867		View | Report Header/Footer	Report Header/Footer	
Report, maximize window	761	[icon], Double-click title bar			
Report, move field and label in different sections in Design view	855	Select using Shift, and then drag			→, ←, ↑, ↓
Report, nudge object in Design view	855				Ctrl + (→, ←, ↑, ↓)

Access Task	Page	Mouse	Menu Bar	Shortcut Menu	Shortcut Keys
Report, open in Design view	761	Click report name and then Design		Right-click report name, and then click Design View	
Report, preview	761	Click report name, and then Preview or [icon] Double-click report name		Right-click report name, and then click Print Preview	
Report, print	761	[icon] on Print Preview toolbar	File | Print	Right-click on report, and then click	Ctrl + P
Report, save design	853	[icon] on Database toolbar	File | Save		Ctrl + S
Report, switch to Design view	761, 853	[icon]	View | Design View	Right-click report title bar, and then click Report Design	
Report, switch to Print preview	761, 853	[icon] or [icon]	View | Print Preview	Right-click report title bar, and then click Print Preview	
Report, zoom to size	761	Fit [dropdown] on Print Preview toolbar	View | Zoom	Right-click on report, and then choose zoom setting	
Resize, column	784	Drag vertical line between column headings left or right	Format | Column Width	Right-click column heading, and then click Column Width	
Resize, column to fit widest entry	784	Double-click vertical line between column headings at right of field	Format | Column Width, Best Fit	Right-click column heading, and then click Column Width; choose Best Fit	
Resize, form field	841	Drag a selection handle (Design view)	Format | Size	Right-click field, and then click Size	
Resize, multiple columns	784	Select multiple columns; drag vertical line between column headings left or right	Format | Column Width	Right-click column heading, and then click Column Width	
Resize, multiple row heights	784	Select multiple rows; drag horizontal line between row headings up or down	Format | Row Height	Right-click row heading, and then click Row Height	
Resize, row height	784	Drag horizontal line between row headings up or down	Format | Row Height	Right-click row heading, and then click Row Height	
Resize, row height to default	784		Format | Row Height, Standard Height	Right-click row heading, and then click Row Height; choose Standard Height	
Save, form design	827	[icon] on Form Design toolbar	File | Save		Ctrl + S
Save, query design	899	[icon] on Query Design toolbar	File | Save		Ctrl + S

Access Task	Page	Mouse	Menu Bar	Shortcut Menu	Shortcut Keys
Save, query design to new name	904		File | Save As	Right-click report name, and then click Save As	
Save, report design	853	on toolbar	File | Save		Ctrl + S
Save, table design	771	on Table Design toolbar Switch views, and then click Yes	File | Save		Ctrl + S
Sort, query by multiple fields in Design view	928	Move fields in order of sort; in Sort row, select Ascending or Descending for each sort field			
Sort, query in Datasheet view	927	or			
Sort, query in Design view	928	In Sort row, select Ascending or Descending			
Sort, records in ascending order	789	Select one or more adjacent columns, and then click	Records | Sort | Sort Ascending	Right-click anywhere in selected column(s), and then click Sort Ascending	
Sort, records in descending order	789	Select one or more adjacent columns, and then click	Records | Sort | Sort Descending	Right-click anywhere in selected column(s), and then click Sort Descending	
Start, Access	744	start on Windows taskbar, and then locate and click Microsoft Office Access 2003	Start | All Programs | Microsoft Office | Microsoft Office Access 2003		
Table, add field	779	In Table Design view, click , and then type field name Click in first field of next available row, and then type field name	Insert | Rows (Design view)	Right-click a field name or blank row, and then click Insert Rows	
Table, add record	774	In Table Datasheet view, click , and then type Click in first field of next available record, and then type Click in last field of last record, and then press Tab and type	Insert | New Record (Datasheet view)	Right-click selected record, and then click New Record	Ctrl + +
Table, close	756	in table window	File | Close		Ctrl + F4 or Ctrl + W

Access Task	Page	Mouse	Menu Bar	Shortcut Menu	Shortcut Keys
Table, create in Design view	767	On Objects bar, click Tables; double-click Create table in Design view or click New, and then click Design View	Insert | Table, Design View	Right-click Create table in Design view command, and then click Open	
Table, delete field	777	In Table Design view, click record selector and then	Edit | Delete Rows Edit | Delete (Design view)	Right-click a field name, and then click Delete Rows	Delete
Table, deselect	784	Click anywhere in the table			
Table, enter description for field	767	In Table Design view, click a field's Description column, and then type text			
Table, hide columns	787		Format | Hide Columns	Right-click column heading, and then click Hide Columns	
Table, move down one screen	791	Click below scroll box in vertical scroll bar			PageDown
Table, move to first field in datasheet	791	Click in first field			Ctrl + Home
Table, move to first record in datasheet	791		Edit | Go To | First		Ctrl + Page Up and then Ctrl + Home
Table, move to last field in datasheet	791	Click in last field			Ctrl + End
Table, move to last record in datasheet	791		Edit | Go To | Last		Ctrl + PageDown and then Ctrl + End
Table, move to next record in datasheet	790, 791		Edit | Go To | Next		↓
Table, move to previous record in datasheet	790, 791		Edit | Go To | Previous		↑
Table, move up one screen	791	Click above scroll box in vertical scroll bar			Page Up
Table, open in Datasheet view	752, 776	Click table name and then Open Double-click table name		Right-click table name, and then click Open	
Table, open in Design view	752	Click table name and then Design		Right-click table name, and then click Design View	

Access Task	Page	Mouse	Menu Bar	Shortcut Menu	Shortcut Keys
Table, print	780	in Table Datasheet view	File | Print	Right-click table name, and then click Print	Ctrl + PrtScr
Table, remove sort	789		Records | Remove Filter/Sort	Right-click anywhere in table, and then click Remove Filter/Sort	
Table, save design	771	on Table Design toolbar Switch views, and then click Yes	File | Save		Ctrl + S
Table, select column	752	Click column heading			
Table, select data type	767	In Table Design view, click a field's Data Type column, and then select from drop-down list			
Table, select row	752	Click row selector			
Table, sort records in ascending order	789	Select one or more adjacent columns, and then click	Records | Sort | Sort Ascending	Right-click anywhere in selected column(s), and then click Sort Ascending	
Table, sort records in descending order	789	Select one or more adjacent columns, and then click	Records | Sort | Sort Descending	Right-click anywhere in selected column(s), and then click Sort Descending	
Table, switch to Datasheet view	756, 771		View | Datasheet View	Right-click table title bar, and then click Datasheet View	
Table, switch to Design view	756		View | Design View	Right-click table title bar, and then click Design View	
Table, unhide columns	787		Format | Unhide Columns, and then select boxes for columns to unhide	Right-click table title bar, and then click Unhide Columns	

PowerPoint 2003

PowerPoint Task	Page	Mouse	Menu Bar	Shortcut Menu	Shortcut Keys
Animation scheme, apply to selected slides	1126	Click Animation Schemes in Slide Design task pane	Slide Show | Animation Schemes	Right-click slide, then choose Slide Design, and click Animation Schemes	
Bullet point, create new	1062				[Enter] after bullet point
Bullet point, select	1056	Click the bullet			
Bullet, delete extra	1062				[Bksp] twice
Bullet, insert picture	1116	on Formatting toolbar, and then click Picture	Format | Bullets and Numbering | Bulleted tab, Picture	Right-click selected bullet point(s), click Bullets and Numbering, and then click Picture	
Bullet, modify character	1114		Format | Bullets and Numbering | Bulleted tab	Right-click selected bullet point(s), and then click Bullets and Numbering	
Bullets, add or remove	1117	on Formatting toolbar	Format | Bullets and Numbering | Bulleted tab	Right-click selected text, and then click Bullets and Numbering	
Clipboard, clear all	1059	Clear All in Clipboard task pane			
Clipboard, delete item	1059	Point to item in Clipboard task pane; click arrow, and then click Delete		Right-click item in Clipboard task pane, and then click Delete	
Clipboard, display task pane	1059	in any task pane, and then click Clipboard	Edit | Office Clipboard		[Ctrl] + [F1], choose Clipboard
Close, file (presentation)	979	[X]	File | Close		[Ctrl] + [F4] or [Ctrl] + [W]
Close, Outline/Slides pane	986	[X] in Outline/Slides pane			
Close, task pane	976	[X] in task pane	View | Task Pane		[Ctrl] + [F1]
Color scheme, apply	1120	Click Color Schemes in Slide Design task pane	Format | Slide Design | Color Schemes	Right-click slide or slide icon, click Slide Design, and then click Color Schemes	
Color scheme, edit	1121	Design on Formatting toolbar; click Color Schemes, then Edit Color Schemes in Slide Design task pane	Format | Slide Design | Color Schemes, Edit Color Schemes	Right-click slide or slide icon, click Slide Design, and then Color Schemes, Edit Color Schemes	

1197

PowerPoint Task	Page	Mouse	Menu Bar	Shortcut Menu	Shortcut Keys
Create, new folder	977	in Save As or Open dialog box			
Create, presentation from AutoContent wizard	1038	Click *From AutoContent wizard* in New Presentation task pane	File	New, From AutoContent wizard		Ctrl + N
Create, presentation from design template	1050	Click *From design template* in New Presentation task pane	File	New, From design template		Ctrl + N
Date and time, add to slide(s)	999		View	Header and Footer	Slide tab, Date and time		
Delete, Clipboard item	1059	Point to item in Clipboard task pane; click arrow, and then click Delete		Right-click item in Clipboard task pane, and then click Delete	
Delete, slide	985		Edit	Delete Slide	Right-click an icon in Outline/Slides pane, and then click Delete Slide	Select slide, then press Delete
Delete, slide in Slide Sorter view	996		Edit	Delete Slide	Right-click slide icon, and then click Delete Slide	Select slide, then press Delete
Design template, change for a single slide	1052	Click slide design's arrow in Slide Design task pane, and then click Apply to Selected Slides		Right-click design in Slide Design task pane, and then click Apply to Selected Slides	
Design template, change for entire presentation	1053	Click slide design icon's arrow in Slide Design task pane, and then click Apply to All Slides		Right-click design in Slide Design task pane, and then click Apply to All Slides	
Design template, change for selected slides	1054	Click slide design icon's arrow in Slide Design task pane, and then click Apply to Selected Slides		Right-click design in Slide Design task pane, and then click Apply to Selected Slides	
Design template, use to create presentation	1050	Click *From design template* in New Presentation task pane	File	New, From design template		
Display, Clipboard task pane	1059	in any task pane, and then click Clipboard	View	Task Pane, Clipboard		
Display, full menus	972		Tools	Customize	Options tab, Always show full menus		
Display, next slide (Normal view)	969	at bottom of Slide pane's vertical scroll bar Drag Slide pane's scroll box down until ScreenTip displays next slide			PageDown

1198 **Office Brief** | PowerPoint 2003 Task Guide

PowerPoint Task	Page	Mouse	Menu Bar	Shortcut Menu	Shortcut Keys
Display, Normal view	980	in lower-left corner of PowerPoint window	View	Normal		
Display, Outline tab	980	Click Outline tab			
Display, previous slide (Normal view)	969	at bottom of Slide pane's vertical scroll bar Drag Slide pane's scroll box up until ScreenTip displays next slide			Page Up
Display, Slide Design task pane	1052	Design on Formatting toolbar Double-click design template name in status bar in task pane, and then click Slide Design	Format	Slide Design		
Display, Slide Layout task pane	1045	in task pane, and then click Slide Layout	Format	Slide Layout	Right-click in Slide pane or on an icon on the Slides tab; click Slide Layout	
Display, Slide Sorter view	996	in lower-left corner of PowerPoint window	View	Slide Sorter		
Display, task pane	976		View	Task Pane		
Display, toolbar	975		View	Toolbars	Right-click any toolbar, and then click toolbar name	
Exit PowerPoint	980		File	Exit		Alt + F4
Folder, create new	977	in Save As or Open dialog box			
Font, change (face)	1094	Arial on Formatting toolbar	Format	Font	Right-click selected text, and then click Font	Ctrl + Shift + F
Font, change color	1098	on Formatting toolbar	Format	Font, Color	Right-click selected text, and then click Font	
Font, change size	1094	32 on Formatting toolbar (select or type in box)	Format	Font, Size	Right-click selected text, and then click Font	Ctrl + Shift + P
Font, decrease size	1096	on Formatting toolbar	Format	Font, Size		Ctrl + Shift + <
Font, increase size	1096	on Formatting toolbar	Format	Font, Size		Ctrl + Shift + >

PowerPoint 2003 Task Guide | **Office Brief**

PowerPoint Task	Page	Mouse	Menu Bar	Shortcut Menu	Shortcut Keys
Fonts, replace	1095		Format	Replace Fonts		
Footer, add to slide(s)	999		View	Header and Footer	Slide tab; select Footer, and then type text in box		
Format, keep source formatting after pasting	1056	, Keep Source Formatting			
Format, use design template formatting after pasting	1056	, Use Design Template Formatting			
Handouts, print	1002		File	Print, then in Print what list, choose Handouts		
Header or footer, add to notes or handouts	1000		View	Header and Footer	Notes and Handouts tab, select Header or Footer, and then type text in box		
Header or footer, change date format	1000		View	Header and Footer	choose tab, Date and time, then Update automatically; select a date format		
Help, display in PowerPoint	1007	on Standard toolbar Click the *Type a question for help* box; type text and press Enter	Help	Microsoft PowerPoint Help		F1
Help, display Office Assistant	1007		Help	Show the Office Assistant		
Import, Word outline	1054		Insert	Slides from Outline, Insert		
Master view, close	1110	 Close Master View button on Slide Master View toolbar	View	Normal		
Master view, display	1110	Press Shift and then click	View	Master	Slide Master		
Master view, scroll to slide or title master	1110	Display master view, drag scroll box in vertical scroll bar			
Menu commands, use	972	Point to menu, click command	Menu name	Command name		Press keys shown next to command on menu

1200   **Office Brief** | PowerPoint 2003 Task Guide

PowerPoint Task	Page	Mouse	Menu Bar	Shortcut Menu	Shortcut Keys
Menu, display full	972	Double-click menu name in menu bar Wait a few seconds after displaying menu Click double arrows at bottom of menu	Tools | Customize | Options tab, Always show full menus		
Move, slide	986	In Slides tab or Slide Sorter view, drag slide to new position			
Normal view, activate from Slide Sorter view	1040	Double-click an icon in Slide Sorter view			
Normal view, display	980	▦ in lower-left corner of PowerPoint window	View | Normal		
Normal view, display next slide	969	▼ at bottom of Slide pane's vertical scroll bar Drag Slide pane's scroll box down until ScreenTip displays next slide			PageDown
Normal view, display previous slide	969	▲ at bottom of Slide pane's vertical scroll bar Drag Slide pane's scroll box up until ScreenTip displays next slide			Page Up
Notes pane, resize	992	Drag pane separator bar up toward Slides pane			
Notes, enter speaker notes	992	Click in Notes pane, and then type text	View | Notes Page; type in notes box		
Numbering, add or remove	1118	▤ on Formatting toolbar	Format | Bullets and Numbering | Numbered tab	Right-click selected text, then click Bullets and Numbering	
Numbering, change start number	1118		Format | Bullets and Numbering, Start at	Right-click selected numbered line(s), click Bullets and Numbering, Start at	
Numbering, modify format	1118		Format | Bullets and Numbering | Numbered tab	Right-click selected numbered line(s), and then click Bullets and Numbering	
Open, presentation	966	📂 on Standard toolbar Click More or the presentation name in Getting Started task pane	File | Open File | presentation name at bottom of File menu		Ctrl + O
Outline tab, display	980	Click Outline tab			

PowerPoint Task	Page	Mouse	Menu Bar	Shortcut Menu	Shortcut Keys
Outline tab, select slide	980	Click slide icon			
Outline, enter text	980	In Outline tab, click to place insertion point, and then type			
Outline/Slides pane, close	986	☒ in Outline/Slides pane			
Paste options	1056	📋 after pasting			
Placeholder, move	1108	Click in placeholder, and then drag border with four-headed arrow pointer	Format | Placeholder | Position	Right-click placeholder border, and then click Format Placeholder | Position tab	
Placeholder, select	1105	Click in placeholder, and then click placeholder border			
Placeholder, size	1106	Drag sizing handle on placeholder	Format | Placeholder | Size	Right-click placeholder border, and then click Format Placeholder | Size tab	
Print, grayscale	1005		File | Print, then in Color/grayscale list, choose Grayscale		
Print, handouts	1002		File | Print, then in Print what list, choose Handouts		
Print, notes pages	1005		File | Print, then in Print what list, choose Notes Pages		
Print, presentation with current settings	1002	🖨 on Standard toolbar	File | Print		Ctrl + P
Print, slides	1002		File | Print, then in Print what list, choose Slides		
Redo an action (after undo)	1048	↻ on Standard toolbar	Edit | Redo		Ctrl + Y
Repeat, last action	1098		Edit | Repeat		F4 or Ctrl + Y
Save, file (new name, location, or type)	977		File | Save As		F12
Save, file (presentation)	977	💾 on Standard toolbar	File | Save		Ctrl + S
Slide Design, display task pane	1052	Design on Formatting toolbar Double-click design template name in status bar ▼ in task pane, then click Slide Design	Format | Slide Design		

PowerPoint Task	Page	Mouse	Menu Bar	Shortcut Menu	Shortcut Keys
Slide Layout, apply	988	▼ in task pane, then click Slide Layout	Format | Slide Layout	Right-click in Slide pane or on an icon on the Slides tab; click Slide Layout	
Slide Layout, display task pane	1045	▼ in task pane, then click Slide Layout	Format | Slide Layout	Right-click in Slide pane or on an icon on the Slides tab; click Slide Layout	
Slide number, add to slide(s)	999		View | Header and Footer | Slide tab, Slide number		
Slide Show, activate starting with current slide	997	in lower-left corner of PowerPoint window			Shift + F5
Slide Show, activate starting with first slide	997	in lower-left corner of PowerPoint window	Slide Show | View Show View | Slide Show		F5
Slide Show, end	997			Right-click, then click End Show	Esc
Slide Sorter view, display	996	in lower-left corner of PowerPoint window	View | Slide Sorter		
Slide, change background	1122, 1124		Format | Background	Right-click slide icon in Slide Sorter view, Slides tab or Slide pane, and then click Background	
Slide, delete	985		Edit | Delete Slide	Right-click an icon in Outline/Slides pane, and then click Delete Slide	Select slide, then press Delete
Slide, delete in Slide Sorter view	996		Edit | Delete Slide	Right-click slide, and then click Delete Slide	Select slide, then press Delete
Slide, insert all slides from another presentation	1044		Insert | Slides from Files, Insert All		
Slide, insert from another presentation	1044		Insert | Slides from Files, Insert		
Slide, insert new	1045	New Slide on Formatting toolbar	Insert | New Slide	Right-click slide icon in Slide Sorter view, Slides tab, or Outline tab; then click New Slide	Ctrl + M Ctrl + Enter from last placeholder on slide
Slide, move	986	In Slides tab or Slide Sorter view, drag slide to new position			
Slide, omit background graphics	1125		Format | Background, Omit background graphics from master	Right-click slide icon in Slide Sorter view, Slides tab, or Slide pane; click Background, and then click Omit background graphics from master	

PowerPoint 2003 Task Guide | **Office Brief**

PowerPoint Task	Page	Mouse	Menu Bar	Shortcut Menu	Shortcut Keys
Slides, print	1002		File	Print, then in Print what list, choose Slides		
Slides, select multiple	994, 1054	Click slide, then press [Ctrl] and click additional slides			Select slide, then press [Ctrl] and select additional slides
Speaker notes, enter	992	Click in Notes pane, and then type text	View	Notes Page; type in notes box		
Spelling checker, enable feature	991		Tools	Options	Spelling and Style tab, Check spelling as you type		
Spelling, check	991	on Standard toolbar	Tools	Spelling	Right-click word with red wavy line, and then click correct spelling	[F7]
Start PowerPoint	966	start on Windows taskbar, then locate and click Microsoft Office PowerPoint 2003	Start	All Programs	Microsoft Office	Microsoft Office PowerPoint 2003		
Task pane, close	976	in task pane	View	Task Pane		
Task pane, display	976	in task pane	View	Task Pane		
Text, align left	1104	on Formatting toolbar	Format	Alignment	Align Left		[Ctrl] + [L]
Text, align right	1104	on Formatting toolbar	Format	Alignment	Align Right		[Ctrl] + [R]
Text, apply bold	1096	B on Formatting toolbar	Format	Font, Font style	Right-click selected text, and then click Font	[Ctrl] + [B]
Text, apply italic	1096	I on Formatting toolbar	Format	Font, Font style	Right-click selected text, and then click Font	[Ctrl] + [I]
Text, apply shadow	1096	S on Formatting toolbar	Format	Font, Font style	Right-click selected text, and then click Font	
Text, apply underline	1096	U on Formatting toolbar	Format	Font, Font style	Right-click selected text, and then click Font	
Text, center	1104	on Formatting toolbar	Format	Alignment	Center		[Ctrl] + [E]
Text, change case	1103		Format	Change Case		[Shift] + [F3]
Text, change font (face)	1094	Arial on Formatting toolbar	Format	Font	Right-click selected text, and then click Font	[Ctrl] + [Shift] + [F]
Text, change font color	1098	A on Formatting toolbar	Format	Font, Color	Right-click selected text, and then click Font	

PowerPoint Task	Page	Mouse	Menu Bar	Shortcut Menu	Shortcut Keys
Text, change font size	1094	32 ▼ on Formatting toolbar (select or type in box)	Format | Font, Size	Right-click selected text, and then click Font	Ctrl + Shift + P
Text, copy	1056, 1061	on Standard toolbar Press Ctrl and drag selected text to new location	Edit | Copy	Right-click selected text, and then click Copy	Ctrl + C Ctrl + drag
Text, copy formatting	1101	on Standard toolbar			Ctrl + Shift + C, select text, Ctrl + Shift + V
Text, decrease font size	1096	on Formatting toolbar	Format | Font, Size		Ctrl + Shift + <
Text, demote (increase indent)	983	on Formatting toolbar			Tab
Text, enter	987	Click in placeholder, and then type text			
Text, enter in outline	980	In Outline tab, click to place insertion point, and then type text			
Text, increase font size	1096	on Formatting toolbar	Format | Font, Size		Ctrl + Shift + >
Text, justify	1104		Format | Alignment | Justify		Ctrl + J
Text, move (cut)	1056, 1059	on Standard toolbar Drag selected text to new location	Edit | Cut	Right-click selected text, and then click Cut	Ctrl + X
Text, move multiple selections	1062	Cut text and/or objects, then display Clipboard; in new location(s), click items to paste			
Text, paste	1056, 1059	on Standard toolbar Drop dragged text at new location Click item(s) in Clipboard task pane	Edit | Paste	Right-click at new location, and then click Paste Right-click item in Clipboard task pane, and then click Paste	Ctrl + V
Text, paste options	1056	after pasting			
Text, promote (decrease indent)	983	on Formatting toolbar			Shift + Tab
Text, replace	1046		Edit | Replace		Ctrl + H
Text, replace fonts	1095		Format | Replace Fonts		

PowerPoint 2003 Task Guide | **Office Brief**

PowerPoint Task	Page	Mouse	Menu Bar	Shortcut Menu	Shortcut Keys
Text, select a bullet point	1056	Click the bullet			
Text, select a bullet point and its subordinate points	1056	Press Ctrl and click the bullet			Ctrl + click bullet
Text, select all in placeholder	1040	Click placeholder boundary box	Edit | Select All (in selected placeholder)		
Toolbar and View buttons, identify	969	Point to button, view ScreenTip			
Toolbar, display	975		View | Toolbars	Right-click any toolbar, and then click toolbar name	
Toolbars, show on one or two rows	975	on Standard or Formatting toolbar, Show Buttons on One Row / Two Rows	Tools | Customize | Options tab, Show Standard and Formatting toolbars on two rows View | Toolbars | Customize | Options tab, Show Standard and Formatting toolbars on two rows	Right-click any toolbar, then click Customize; on Options tab, select or clear Show Standard and Formatting toolbars on two rows	
Undo an action	1048	on Standard toolbar	Edit | Undo		Ctrl + Z

Glossary

Absolute cell reference A cell address in which both the column letter and the row number of the cell are preceded with dollar signs. An absolute cell reference in a formula, such as $A$1, always refers to a cell in a specific location. When an absolute cell reference is used in a formula and the formula is copied to another cell, the cell references in the new cell are not adjusted to fit the new location of the formula; they remain as they are in the source cell.

Accounting format A format for numbers in which the currency symbol displays flush with the left boundary of the cell, a format which conforms to formats necessary for creating profit and loss statements and balance sheets.

Active area The rectangle formed by all the rows and columns in a worksheet that contain or contained entries.

Active cell The cell in which the next keystroke or command will take place. A black border surrounds the cell when it is active.

Aggregate functions A function that groups and performs calculations on multiple fields.

Aligned left The most common alignment, with the left edge of the text straight, and the right edge uneven.

Aligned right The right edge of the text is straight, and the left edge is uneven.

Alignment The horizontal position of data or text within a cell in relation to its left and right boundary or placeholder.

Anchor Indicates that the image is attached to the nearest paragraph.

Animation effects A command that introduces individual slide elements so that the slide can be displayed one element at a time.

Animation scheme Predefined animations for slide placeholders, including titles, subtitles, and bulleted lists.

Animation The movement of slides and slide elements on and off the screen during an electronic slide show.

Applications software Computer programs that enable you to accomplish specific tasks using a computer.

Arithmetic/logic unit The unit that processes data by performing mathematical calculations and sorting data alphabetically or numerically, filtering data that meets specific criteria, and so forth.

Arrow keys Keys on a keyboard that move the insertion point to a different position in text and numbers.

Ascending order Sorts text alphabetically (A to Z) and sorts numbers from the lowest number to the highest number.

Asterisk The term used to refer to the * symbol.

AutoComplete A feature in Excel and Word that speeds your typing and lessens the likelihood of errors by automatically suggesting words or phrases. For example, in Excel, if the first few characters you type in a cell match an existing entry in the column, Excel fills in the remaining characters for you.

AutoContent Wizard A feature that leads you step-by-step through the creation of a presentation by asking you questions about the presentation that you want to create.

AutoCorrect A feature that corrects common typing and spelling errors, and can also be used as a shortcut for typing commonly used text.

AutoFill Extending values into adjacent cells based on the values of selected cells. Can be completed using the AutoFill Options button.

AutoForm A feature that creates a form, with minimal formatting, using all available fields from an existing table.

AutoFormat Table Uses predefined formats to create a professional-looking table.

AutoNumber A data type that assigns a number to each record as it is entered into the table.

AutoSum A function (predefined formula) that adds a series of cell values by selecting a range.

AutoText A feature that stores commonly used text and graphics for easy retrieval.

Black slide A slide that displays at the end of a slide presentation indicating the end of the slide show.

Bridge A network device that connects two networks that contain similar hardware and other devices such as a LAN from a company office in one city with a LAN for the same company office in another city.

Bulleted list A group of items formatted in a similar manner and preceded by a symbol, called a bullet.

Bus network A network topography in which each computer, printer, and other device connects to a central high-speed line with no host or server, and only one computer or device can transmit over the network at a time.

Byte One character, such as a letter, number digit, space, tab, and so forth.

Calendar item Information about appointments stored in a folder named Calendar within the Calendar module.

Cathode ray tubes (CRT) Standard monitors that range from about 10 inches deep to about 14 inches deep, have a curved screen or a flat screen, and are relatively inexpensive.

CD-ROM Compact Disc-Read Only Memory. An optical storage device used to permanently store data and from which you can read and open files. Also referred to as a CD-R.

CD-RW A compact disc that can be used over and over again to read and save files.

Cell address The intersecting column letter and row number of a cell.

Cell content Anything typed into a cell.

Cell reference The intersecting column letter and row number of a cell. Also referred to as a cell address.

Cell The intersection of a row and column in a table.

Center alignment Text is spaced equally between the left and right margins.

Central processing unit (CPU) The unit that gets data from memory and processes that data by performing mathematical or logical operations.

Chart A visual representation of your data using graphics.

Client A computer that connect to servers or hosts.

Clip art Graphic images included with the Microsoft Office program or obtained from other sources.

Clip A media file, such as sound, art, animation, or movies.

Clipboard A storage location that stores up to 24 selections of text or graphics to be copied or moved.

Clock speed The speed at which the CPU is capable of processing data measured in megahertz.

Collapse Hide items contained in a subfolder or list.

Collect and paste The process of copying a group of items to the Office Clipboard and then pasting them into various locations in a worksheet.

Color scheme A coordinated palette of eight colors that includes background, text, bullet, and accent colors.

Column heading The heading that appears above the topmost cell in a column and that is identified by a unique letter.

Column selector In My Computer or Windows Explorer, the headings at the top of the list of files. These headings include Name, Size, Type, and Date Modified.

Column A vertical group of cells in a worksheet.

Comma style A cell style in which Excel sets the formatting of a cell to display numeric values with two decimal places and with commas in the thousand, million, and billion (and higher) places.

Comment A note attached to a cell and which is separate from other cell content.

Compound criteria Two or more criteria in a query. Compound criteria are used to create more specific criteria and refine the query's results.

Computer network Two or more computers connected together in some way so that they can share hardware (printers, storage devices), software programs, data, and other resources.

Computer A machine that computes or an electronic system that accepts, stores, processes, and reports data in a format that provides useful information.

Console The main computer unit that houses the processor as well as other hardware units.

Constant value Numbers, text, dates, or times of day that are typed into a cell.

Contact items Names, addresses, and phone numbers of personal and business associates stored within the Contacts folder in the Contacts module.

Contact The information about a person or organization.

Contacts module The Outlook module that holds folders for storing contacts.

Context sensitive A command, smart tag, or button that changes depending on the action.

Control unit The part of the CPU that retrieves data from memory so that it can be processed and sends it back to memory when the CPU is finished with it.

Control An object such as a label or text box in a form or report that allows you to view or manipulate information stored in tables or queries.

Copy Send a graphic or block of text to the Office Clipboard, while also leaving it in its original location.

Copyright Laws that protect the rights of authors of original works, including text, art, photographs, and music.

Criteria The conditions specified to Access so it can find matching fields and records.

Currency style A cell style in which Excel sets the formatting of a cell to display numeric values with two decimal places, with commas in the thousand, million, and billion (and higher) places, and with a leading dollar sign. Also referred to as currency format.

Cut A command in which selected data is removed from its original location and placed on the Office Clipboard.

Data entry Typing data into the database.

Data type The type of data that can be entered in a field: text, memo, number, date/time, currency, AutoNumber, Yes/No, OLE object, and hyperlink. Specifies how Access organizes and stores data in a field.

Data Refers to facts about people, events, things, or ideas.

Database window The window from which all database objects can be manipulated or accessed. The Database window displays when a database is open.

Database A collection of data related to a particular topic or purpose.

Datasheet view The view in which the information in a table or query can be viewed and manipulated. Datasheet view displays all the records in a table in a format of columns (fields) and rows (records).

Date Navigator The monthly calendar palette that displays at the top of the Calendar Navigation pane.

Demote A command that applies a lower outline level to text.

Descending order Sorts text in reverse alphabetic order (Z to A) and sorts numbers from the highest number to the lowest.

Deselect To cancel the selection of one or more cells.

Design grid The lower pane of the Select Query window.

Design template A model on which a presentation is based, including graphic elements, animations, and a color scheme.

Design view The view in which the structure of a table or query can be viewed and manipulated.

Design The number and content of the fields in the table. Good design ensures that a database is easy to maintain.

Desktop publisher A program, such as Microsoft Publisher, that is used to create newsletters, posters, greeting cards, and even Web pages.

Desktop 1. Microcomputer that sits on a desktop, floor, table, or other flat surface and has a detachable keyboard, mouse, monitor, and other pieces of equipment. 2. The basic screen from which Windows and applications are run. The desktop consists of program icons, a taskbar, a Start button, and a mouse pointer.

Detail In Design view of a form or report, the section that contains the fields and records that display in the form or report.

Dialog box A box that asks you to make a decision about an individual object or topic. Dialog boxes do not have Minimize buttons.

Displayed value The value that appears in a formatted cell.

Domain name The name of a location on the World Wide Web (www) and the type of site that contains the Web site.

Dots per inch (dpi) The unit of measure to identify resolution in printed output.

Double-click The act of clicking the left mouse button twice in rapid succession without moving the position of the mouse pointer.

Download To save a copy of a Web page or file on your computer hard drive or floppy disk so that you can review page contents after ending your Internet connection.

Drag Holding down the left mouse button and moving the mouse pointer over text to select it.

Drag-and-drop A method of moving or copying selected text or graphics in which you point to the selection, then click and hold the mouse button to drag it to a new location.

Drawing canvas A work area for creating and editing complex figures created using the drawing tools.

Edit The process of adding, deleting, or changing the contents of a document, worksheet, or slide.

Em dash A long dash that separates distinct phrases in a sentence. It is about four times as long as a hyphen.

Endnote A reference placed at the end of a section or the end of the document. Excel treats a selected area as a single unit; thus, you can make the same change or combination of changes to more than one cell at a time.

Expand Display items contained in a subfolder or list.

Expansion cards Removable circuit cards for adding new peripherals or increasing computer capabilities.

Expansion slots The slots on the motherboard that hold expansion cards.

Extender keys Ctrl and Alt keys on a keyboard that are used in combination with other keys to access menus, control onscreen mouse actions, and perform other special actions.

Extracting Pulling out specific information from a database based on the specified criteria.

Favorites Web addresses for sites you visit frequently that you intentionally save for easy access.

Field An individual item of information that describes a record and is the same type for all records in the table. In Access, fields are located in vertical columns.

File extension The three characters to the right of the period in a file name. Extensions tell the computer the program to use to open the file. File extensions can be displayed or hidden.

File transfer protocol (ftp) A protocol used primarily to post files to a Web site.

File Work that you save and store on a drive, such as a Word document or a PowerPoint presentation.

Fill effects Formatting options that include textures, patterns, gradient fills, and pictures.

Fill handle The small black square in the lower right corner of a selected cell.

Fit An entire page of a report displays onscreen at one time, giving an overall view of what the printed pages will look like.

Flat panel monitors Slim monitors that range in depth from one or two inches to three or four inches and use LCD (liquid crystal display) technology, which many people believe offers good resolution and a faster refresh rate.

Glossary | **Office Brief** 1209

Floating image A graphic that moves independently of the surrounding text.

Floppy disk drive A removable storage device that holds a limited amount of information, usually used to back up or transport files.

Font size The size of characters in a font, measured in points.

Font style Bold, italic, or underline emphasis added to characters.

Font A set of characters with the same design, size, and shape.

Footer Area reserved at the bottom of each page for text and graphics that appear at the bottom of each page in a document or section of a document. Displays only in Print Preview or on the page when it is printed.

Footnote A reference placed at the bottom of a page.

Form Footer Displays only at the end of a form when it is viewed in Form view or when the form is printed.

Form Header Displays only at the beginning of a form when the form is viewed in Form view or when the form is printed.

Form Wizard Creates a form in a manner that gives you much more flexibility in the design, layout, and number of fields included in the form. The Form Wizard asks the user questions and then creates a form based on the answers provided.

Form A database object used to enter, edit, and manipulate information in a table.

Format painter A feature that copies formatting from one selection of text to another.

Format text The process of establishing the overall appearance of text in a document.

Formatting marks Characters that display on the screen, but do not print, indicating where the Enter key, the Spacebar, and the Tab key were pressed. Also called nonprinting characters.

Formatting toolbar Contains buttons for some of the most common formatting tasks in Word. It may occupy an entire row or share a row with the Standard toolbar.

Formatting Changing the appearance of the text, layout, and design of a slide.

Formula An equation that you type into a cell and that acts as an instruction to Excel to perform mathematical operations (such as adding and subtracting) on data within a worksheet.

Function keypad The keys F1 through F12 on a keyboard, which perform special functions for different programs.

Function A predefined formula that performs calculations by using specific values, called arguments, in a particular order or structure.

Gateway A network device that enables hardware on one network to communicate with hardware and other resources on a different type of network.

General format The default number format in Excel, which formats numbers exactly as you type them, with no commas or decimal points.

Gigabyte (GB) Roughly one billion bytes or characters.

Gigahertz Speed of a computer measured in billions of actions per second.

Gradient fill A color combination in which one color fades into another.

Graphical user interface (GUI) A computer environment in which icons with pictures on them are used to issue computer commands rather than written word commands.

Grave accent The ` symbol on the keyboard.

Grid A pattern of horizontal and vertical lines.

Handheld Microcomputer that varies in size but is designed to fit in your hand and provide a convenient resource for maintaining an organized calendar and list of business and personal associates.

Hanging indent A paragraph where the first line extends to the left of the rest of the lines in the same paragraph. Hanging indents are often used for bibliographic entries.

Hard copy A permanent paper printout of data and information generated by a computer.

Hard disk drive Generally referred to as a hard drive, the main storage device on your computer. It stores the programs that run on your computer, as well as the files that you save.

Hardware The physical pieces, both inside and outside the computer, that make up the computer system.

Header Area reserved at the top of each page for text and graphics that appear at the top of each page in a document or section of a document. Displays only in Print Preview or on the printed page of a worksheet.

Home page The screen that opens each time you start Internet Explorer when you are connected to the Internet.

Horizontal alignment The alignment of data within a cell relative to the left and right cell boundaries.

Horizontal scroll bar The bar at the bottom of a window that enables you to move left and right to view information that extends beyond the left and right edges of the screen.

Host A computer to which other computers are connected to share data contained on the server and/or to access other computers or the Internet.

Hub Computer or other connection device that allows multiple network resources to connect to other devices.

1210 Office Brief | Glossary

Hyperlinks Text, buttons, pictures, and other objects displayed on Web pages that access other Web pages or display other sections of the active page when you click on them. Hyperlinks are usually a different color (usually blue) than the surrounding text and are often underlined.

Hypertext markup language (HTML) The computer language used to format Web pages.

Hypertext transfer protocol (HTTP) The standard protocol for retrieving Web sites on the Internet.

I-beam Pointer A mouse pointer that indicates that you are pointing to a text area in the Outline/Slides pane or in the Slide pane.

Icon A graphic representation; often a small image on a button that enables you to run a program or program function.

Inbox The folder Outlook uses to store incoming Email message items from your connected mail server.

Indent Adding space between the cell data and its left or right cell boundaries.

Indicator lights Lights on a keyboard that identify active number lock, caps lock, and scroll lock keys.

Information Data that has been organized in a useful manner.

Ink-jet printer A printer that prints by shooting colored or black ink through a jet stream onto the paper.

Inline image A graphic that acts like a character in a sentence.

Input devices Pieces of hardware used to get data into the computer in a format that the computer can understand.

Input The means of getting data—facts and figures—into a computer.

Insert mode The default mode in which characters move to the right to make space for new characters.

Insertion point The blinking vertical bar that indicates where text will be inserted when you type.

Internet protocol (IP) A numeric address assigned to Internet domains that appears in a format, such as 206.44.183.67.

Internet service provider (ISP) Companies such as AT&T, AOL, and Earthlink that set up large computers which act as servers or hosts to connect client computers to the Internet via telephone lines, cable, and DSL lines.

Internet The largest online computer network in the world that provides a way for mainframes to communicate with other mainframes and PCs to communicate with many types of computers.

Item Each appointment, mail message, address book entry, note, and task that you record in Outlook.

Justified alignment Both the left and right margins are straight (aligned). Text in books and magazines is nearly always justified.

Keyboard shortcut A combination of keys on the keyboard, usually using the Ctrl key or the Alt key, that provides a quick way to activate a command.

Kilobyte (KB) Roughly 1000 bytes or characters.

Landscape orientation A page orientation in which the printed page is wider than it is tall.

Laptop Microcomputer, also known as notebook computer, that is smaller than a desktop computer and is designed to fit comfortably on your lap and normally has the keyboard, pointing device, and monitor screen built in so that you can take it with you when you travel.

Laser printer Printer that creates copies using a laser beam to transfer toner from a drum inside the printer onto the paper.

Layout The placement and arrangement of the text and graphic elements on a slide.

Left-align A cell formats in which data is aligned with the left boundary of the cell.

Local area network (LAN) Network established to connect computers and other hardware resources that are physically located in a relatively close space, such as the same room, on the same floor of a building, or within the same building.

Logical operators Boolean operators: AND, OR, and NOT.

Mail module The Outlook module used for communication.

Mail server A computer that stores and distributes Email messages.

Mainframe Large computer often found in businesses and colleges, where thousands of people use the computer to process huge volumes of data.

Manual column break An artificial end to a column to balance columns or to provide space for the insertion of other objects.

Margin The white space at the top, bottom, left, and right sides of a page.

Masthead The large title at the top of a newsletter.

Maximize To increase the size of a window to fill the screen.

Mega Speed or storage capacity of a computer measured in millions.

Megabyte (MB) Roughly one million bytes or characters.

Megahertz (MHz) Processing speed of the computer.

Memory slots The slots on the motherboard into which you add memory (RAM) chips to increase the computer memory (RAM).

Memory The temporary holding area inside the computer, also known as RAM, where data is stored electronically to make it accessible for processing.

Menu bar The bar, just under the title bar, that contains command options. These commands are words, not icons.

Menu A list of commands within a category.

Merge and Center The process of combining cells in a row or column into one cell and then centering the cell contents within the new cell.

Microcomputers The smallest of the main categories of computers, ranging in size from servers that have the storage capability of minicomputers (and small mainframes) to handheld devices that fit into your pocket.

Microprocessors The small, powerful chip inside the computer system unit that processes the data.

Minicomputers Mid-sized computers often used in medium-sized businesses with smaller data storage requirements than businesses using mainframe computers.

Minimize To remove the window from the screen without closing it. Minimized windows can be reopened by clicking the associated button in the taskbar.

Modules Separate storage areas named to identify the type of information they hold, such as Email messages, calendar appointments and due dates, notes, and lists of tasks to accomplish.

Monitor An essential piece of computer hardware used to display data, text, and graphics on a television-like screen.

Motherboard The component that is contained inside the system unit that ties everything inside the system unit together.

Mouse pointer The arrow, I-beam, or other symbol that shows the location or position of the mouse on your screen. Also called the pointer.

Mouse A small, hand-sized unit that acts as a pointing device.

Multimedia buttons and knobs Keys and buttons on a keyboard that play, pause, stop, fast forward, and otherwise manipulate multimedia audio and video items and sometimes connect directly to the Internet.

Multimedia keyboard Keyboards that contain buttons and knobs for interacting with the Internet, controlling sound settings, and adjusting screen settings in addition to all the keys found on the enhanced keyboard.

Multimedia A term often associated with visual and audio media.

Multitask Perform many different types of tasks at the same time.

My Computer A window that gives you access to the files and folders on your computer.

Navigate The act of moving from one point to another within a program or file. For example, moving the cursor down the page in a Word document.

Network A group of computers connected in some way to each other.

Nonprinting characters Characters that display on the screen, but do not print, indicating where the Enter key, the Spacebar, and the Tab key were pressed. Also called formatting marks.

Normal view A simplified view of a document that does not show graphics, margins, headers, or footers.

Notebook Microcomputer, also known as laptop, that is smaller than a desktop computer, is designed to fit in a briefcase, and normally has the keyboard, pointing device, and monitor screen built in so that you can take it with you when you travel.

Notes module The Outlook module that contains the Notes folder, which stores notes that resemble sticky notes.

Notes pages Printouts that contain the slide image in the top half of the page and speaker's notes in the lower half of the page.

Notes pane An area of the PowerPoint window that displays below the Slide pane and allows you to type notes regarding the active slide.

Nudge Move slightly. Nudging is a useful technique to move controls with precision.

Number formats The various ways that Excel displays numbers.

Numbered list A group of items formatted in a similar manner, and preceded by a number. Numbered lists are used for items that have some relationship (chronological or sequential).

Numeric keypad Numeric and operational keys on a keyboard used to enter numbers and calculation operations such as multiply (*), divide (/), add (+), and subtract (-).

Object The primary component of an Access database, such as a table, form, query, or report.

Objects bar Located on the left side of the Database window and contains the buttons to access the objects in the database.

Office Assistant An animated character that provides tips and access to Help.

Office Clipboard A memory area that can hold up to 24 graphics or blocks of text. Items are place in the Office Clipboard when the Cut or Copy features are used.

Operating system A set of instructions that coordinates the activities of your computer. Microsoft Windows XP is an operating system.

Operating systems software The operating software that contains the instructions the computer needs to start up and run[md]in essence, it enables the computer to operate.

Operator A symbol that represents a mathematical operation in a formula.

Option buttons The round buttons to the left of each magnification options in the zoom dialog box.

Order of operations The mathematical rules for performing multiple calculations within a formula.

Outline view A document view that shows headings and subheadings, which can be expanded or collapsed.

Outline/Slides pane An area of the PowerPoint window that displays either the presentation. outline (Outline tab) or all of the slides in the presentation in the form of miniature images called thumbnails (Slides tab).

Output devices Pieces of hardware used to get data and information from the computer in a format that the users can understand.

Output The means of getting data and information out of the computer.

Overtype mode A mode for entering text in which existing text is replaced as you type.

Page Footer Contains information that displays at the bottom of every page of a form or report in Print Preview or when printed.

Page Header Contains information that displays at the top of every page of a form or report in Print Preview or when printed.

Paste The action of placing text from the Clipboard into a new location.

Peripherals Devices that attach to the outside of the main computer unit.

Personal digital assistants (PDA) Handheld microcomputers that vary in size but are designed to fit in your hand and provide a convenient resource for maintaining an organized calendar and list of business and personal associates.

Personal Information Management (PIM) A program that helps you get organized to communicate efficiently with others.

Pixels Points of light measured in dots per square inch that appear on a monitor screen.

Placeholder A slide element that reserves a portion of a slide and serves as a container for text, graphics, and other slide elements.

Point A measurement of the size of a font. There are 72 points in an inch, with 10-12 points being the most commonly used font size.

Pointer See mouse pointer.

Populate Fill a table with data.

Pop-up windows Onscreen windows that open as you navigate pages and sites on the Web to display information related to the site.

Portals Home page ISPs and other sources that make accessing Email and other frequently used features easier by acting as launching sites to other Web pages.

Portrait orientation The page orientation in which the printed page is taller than it is wide.

Presentation graphics software A program used to effectively present information to an audience.

Primary key One or more fields that uniquely identifies a record in a table.

Primary sort field The field that Access sorts by initially during a sort operation.

Print Layout view A view of a document that looks like a sheet of paper. It displays margins, headers, footers, and graphics.

Process Performing an arithmetic calculation or logical operation such as alphabetizing or sorting the data to change it into useful information.

Promote A command that applies a higher outline level to selected text.

Protocol A method for posting and retrieving Web sites.

Pt. Abbreviation for point in terms of font size.

Quarters A three-month period within a fiscal year.

Query 1. A database object that locates information based on specified criteria so that the information can be viewed, changed, or analyzed in various ways. 2. A question formed in a manner that Access can interpret.

Quick Launch toolbar An area to the right of the Start button that contains shortcut icons for commonly used programs.

Random access memory (RAM) The temporary holding area inside the computer, also known as memory, where data is stored electronically to make it accessible for processing.

Range A group of adjacent cells.

Reading Layout view Displays easy-to-read pages that fit on the screen.

Reading pane The Inbox pane that displays the active message when a mail folder is open or the active item in other modules.

Recognizer A purple dotted underscore beneath a date or address indicating that the information could be placed into another Microsoft Office application program such as Outlook.

Record selector The gray bar along the left edge of a table or form, that when clicked, selects the entire record.

Record All the items of information (fields) that pertain to one particular thing such as a customer, employee, or course. In Access, records are located in horizontal rows.

Recycle bin A storage area for files that have been deleted. Files can be recovered from the Recycle bin or permanently removed.

Reference A mark indicating information taken verbatim or paraphrased from another source. References can be placed at the bottom of each page (footnote) or the end of the section or document (endnote).

Refresh rate The rate at which objects appear onscreen.

Relative cell reference In a formula, the address of a cell based on the relative position of the cell that contains the formula and the cell referred to.

Report Wizard Creates a report by asking a series of questions and then constructs the report based on the answers provided.

Report A database object that displays the fields and records from the table (or query) in an easy-to-read format suitable for printing or viewing on the screen.

Resolution The number of points of light per square inch that appear on a monitor screen and control the quality of the image.

Restore Return a window to the size it was before it was maximized, using the Restore Down button.

Right-alignment A cell format in which the data aligns with the right boundary of the cell.

Right-click The action of clicking the right mouse button once, usually to display a shortcut menu.

Ring network A network topography where all devices connect to a circular line around which data travels in only one direction.

Rotate handle Rotates the image clockwise or counterclockwise.

Row heading The heading that appears to the left of the leftmost cell in a row and that is identified by a unique number.

Row selector The small gray box at the left end of a row that, when clicked, selects all the cells in the row.

Row A horizontal group of cells in a worksheet.

Ruler Displays the exact location of paragraph margins, indents, and tab stops.

Sample area A preview area of cell formats within the Format Cells dialog box.

Sans serif font A font with no lines or extensions on the ends of characters.

Scaling The ability of Excel to increase or decrease the size of printed characters so that the worksheet will fit within a specific number of pages.

ScreenTip A small box, activated by holding the pointer over a button or other screen object, that displays its corresponding name and/or function.

Scroll box The box in the vertical and horizontal scroll bars that provides a visual indication of your location in a document. It can also be used with the mouse to reposition the document on the screen. The size of the scroll box also indicates the relative size of the document.

Scroll The action of moving the workbook window either vertically (from top to bottom) or horizontally (from left to right) to bring different areas of the worksheet into view on your screen.

Search engines Programs designed to search the Internet for sites containing specific text.

Secondary sort field The field that Access uses to sort records that have matching primary sort fields during a sort operation.

Select query A query that retrieves data from one or more tables and then displays the results.

Selecting text Highlighting text so that it can be formatted, deleted, copied, or moved.

Separator character A character used to identify column placement in text; usually a tab or a comma.

Serif font A font that contains extensions or lines on the ends of the characters; usually the easiest type of font to read for large blocks of text.

Server A computer to which other computers are connected to share data contained on the server and/or to access other computers or the Internet.

Sheet tab A label located at the lower border of the worksheet window. It identifies each worksheet in a workbook and is used to navigate between worksheets.

Shortcut menu A context-sensitive menu that offers a quick way to activate the most commonly used commands for a selected area. The menu is activated by placing the pointer over an object and clicking the right mouse button.

Sizing handle A small square or circle in the corners and the middle of the sides of a graphic that can be used to increase or decrease the size of the graphic.

Slide handouts Printed images of more than one slide on a sheet of paper.

Slide icon An icon that displays next to the slide number in the Outline indicating the beginning of a new slide.

Slide master A slide that holds the information about formatting and text that displays on every slide in your presentation.

Slide pane An area of the PowerPoint window that displays a large image of the active slide.

Small caps Text format, usually used in titles, that changes lower-case text into capital letters using a reduced font size.

Smart tag 1. A small button that gives you quick access to relevant commands. 2. A button that displays when Excel recognizes a specific type of data.

Soft copy Printed data and images that disappear when you turn off the computer.

Software The programs installed on computers that contain instructions which tell the computer what to do.

Sorting The process of rearranging records in a specific order. Records can be sorted either ascending or descending.

Special keys Keys on a keyboard that move to specific locations such as home and next page and delete and insert text.

1214 Office Brief | Glossary

Spin box arrow The up and down arrows in an option box that enable you to move a value up or down incrementally.

Standard toolbar Contains buttons for some of the most common commands in Word. It may occupy an entire row or share a row with the Formatting toolbar.

Star network A network topography that includes a host computer to which all other computers (clients or workstations), printers, and other devices are connected.

Start button The button on the left side of the taskbar that is used to start programs, change system settings, find Windows help, or shut down the computer.

Status bar The bar at the bottom of a window that gives additional information about the window. In PowerPoint, the status bar indicates the current and total number of slides in the presentation and the applied design template. In Word, the status bar provides information about the current state of what you are viewing in the window, including the page number, and whether overtype or track changes are on or off.

Storage devices Pieces of hardware used to store data and information inside and outside the computer.

Storage medium The disk or tape that actually holds data and is inserted into or contained inside the storage device.

Storage Storing data for future use.

Submenu A second-level menu activated by selecting a menu option.

Supercomputers Large, powerful computers normally devoted to performing specialized tasks.

System board The component that is contained inside the system unit that ties everything inside the system unit together.

System tray A notification area on the right side of the taskbar that keeps you informed about processes that are occurring in the background, such as antivirus software, network connections, and other utility programs. It also displays the time.

System unit The main computer unit that houses the processor as well as other hardware units.

Tab stop A mark on the ruler bar to which the insertion point will jump when the Tab key is pressed.

Table area The upper pane of the Select Query window.

Table Design toolbar The toolbar that displays when a table is displayed in Design view.

Table Horizontal rows and vertical columns of text or numbers, used to organize data and present it effectively. In Excel, rows are referred to as records and columns are referred to as fields.

Task pane A window within a Microsoft Office application that provides commonly used commands.

Taskbar A bar, usually at the bottom of the screen, that contains the Start button, buttons representing open programs, and other buttons that will activate programs.

Tasks module The Outlook module that contains the Tasks folder in which you can store "to do" items.

Text box control A control on a form or report where data from the corresponding table is displayed when the form or report is viewed.

Text case Type of text capitalization, including uppercase, lowercase, sentence case, and title case.

Thumbnails Miniature images of each slide.

Title bar Displays the program icon, the name of the document, and the name of the program. The Minimize, Maximize/Restore Down, and Close buttons are grouped on the right side of the title bar.

Title slide The first slide in a presentation that frequently contains special formatting.

Toggle button A button that when clicked once is turned on and when clicked again is turned off.

Toolbar Options Button that enables you to see all of the buttons associated with a toolbar. It also enables you to place the Standard and Formatting toolbars on separate rows or on the same row.

Toolbar A row of buttons that displays below the menu bar and provides a one-click method (using the left mouse button) to perform commonly used commands and tasks. These commands are buttons with icons, not words.

Toolbox The toolbar that contains the controls that can be added to forms or reports.

Topography The arrangements of computers on a network.

Trace error A message displayed by Excel when anomalies in formulas are recognized.

Transitions The way that a slide appears or disappears during an onscreen slide show.

Truncate To cut off or shorten.

Typing keypad Alphabetic and numeric keys on a keyboard that are arranged in the same order as keys on a typewriter and are used to enter text and other data.

Underlying formula The formula entered in a cell and visible only on the Formula Bar.

Uniform resource locator (URL) The address on the World Wide Web that accesses a Web site.

Value Numbers, text, dates, or times of day that are typed into a cell. Also referred to as a constant value.

Vertical alignment The alignment of data in a cell relative to its top and bottom boundaries.

Vertical scroll bar The bar at the right side of a window that enables you to move up and down to view information that extends beyond the top and bottom of the screen.

View A view is a way of looking at something for a specific purpose, such as Design view or Datasheet view.

Web browser Software that enables you to use the Web and navigate from page to page and site to site.

Web Layout view A document view that shows how the document would look if viewed with a Web browser.

Web page an individual page of information, similar to a page of a document, that displays as a screen containing links, frames, pictures, and other features of interest to many users.

Web site a group of related Web pages published to a specific location on the World Wide Web.

What-if analysis A process of changing the values in cells to see how those changes affect the outcome of formulas on the worksheet, for example, varying the interest rate used in an amortization table to determine the amount of the payments at different rates.

Wide area networks (WAN) Networks established to connect computers and other hardware resources across a broader geographic area, such as across campus, across town, or across the country.

Wildcard A character, such as an asterisk, that can be used to match any number of characters in a file search.

Window A box that displays information or a program, such as a letter, Excel, or a calculator. Windows usually consist of title bars, toolbars, menu bars, and status bars. A window will always have a Minimize button.

Wireless network A network topography in which devices connect to other computers and network resources using radio signals, microwaves, satellite signals, and other wireless media.

Word wrap Automatically moves text from the right edge of a paragraph to the beginning of the next line as necessary to fit within the margins.

WordArt A Microsoft Office drawing tool that enables you to turn text into graphics.

Workbook An Excel file that contains one or more worksheets.

Worksheet A page formatted as a pattern of uniformly spaced horizontal and vertical lines.

Workstation A computer that connects to servers or hosts.

World Wide Web A vast network of computers connected together for the purpose of sharing information.

Wrap text An Excel feature in which the content of a cell is split onto two or more lines when the width of the cell is not sufficient to display all the content on one line.

Zoom An option to make the page view larger or smaller.

Index

Symbols

* (asterisk)
    adding fields to queries, 897
    search wildcard, 39
    multiplication operator, 552–553
    query wildcard, 912
✓ (check mark), menu command characteristic, 174, 508, 974
: (colon), using calculated fields in queries, 935
... (ellipsis), menu command characteristic, 174, 508, 974
= (equal) comparison operator, 922
` (grave accent), 640
> (greater than) comparison operator, 922–924
< (less than) comparison operator, 922–924
+ (plus) signs, folder pane, 27–34
? (question mark) wildcard, 916–917
▶ (right arrow), 174
[ ] (square brackets), using calculated fields in queries, 934–935

A

absolute cell reference, copying formulas, 635–638
Access, 153
    closing, 792
    commands. *See* commands, Access
    databases. *See* databases
    dialog boxes. *See* dialog boxes, Access
    help system, 793–795
    keyboard shortcuts, navigating records, 791
    parts of Access window, 745–746, 749–750
    starting, 744–745
    toolbars
        Database. See Database toolbar
        Form Design. See Form Design toolbar
        Form View. See Form View toolbar
        Print Preview. See Print Preview toolbar
        Query Datasheet. See Query Datasheet toolbar
        Query Design. See Query Design toolbar
        Report Design. See Report Design toolbar
        Table Datasheet. See Table Datasheet toolbar
        Table Design. See Table Design toolbar
        Toolbox. See Toolbox toolbar
accessing
    headers and footers, 188–189
    menu commands, 171–175, 973–974
Accessories, 12–13
Accounting format, 674
accounting software, 154
activating the spelling/grammar checkers, 183
active cells, 504–505, 513–514, 538–539
    clearing formats, 697
    Clipboard, 611
    moving to location of
        keyboard shortcuts, 521
        using Enter key for, 540
active documents, 169
active folder, 55–56, 60–61
active message (Reading pane), 55–56
active modules, 55–56
    banners, 55–56, 60–61
    buttons, 55–56
    colors, 56
    Contacts module, 60–61
    creating new folders, 59
    folders listed, 55–56
Add button (Internet Explorer Favorites pane), 113
Add Favorite dialog box (Internet Explorer), 113
Add Text shortcut menu, 351
Add to Dictionary button (Word), 186
adding
    borders, 426–427, 433–434
    emphasis to text, 209
    graphics, 332
    hyperlinks to graphics, 444–445
    shading to paragraphs, 435
    special paragraph formatting, 433
Address bar, 97–105
addresses
    storing, 60–65
    Web sites, 97. *See also* URLs
adjacent slides, selecting, 994–995
Adjust to spin box, 701
Adobe software, 154
Advanced Micro Devices®, 142
After spin box, 274
aggregate functions, 939–943
Align Left button (Formatting toolbar)
    Excel, 602
    Word, 248, 250
Align Right button (Formatting toolbar)
    Excel, 603, 687
    PowerPoint, 1104
    Word, 248, 279, 374
aligning
    cell contents, 675–678
        fill, 678–679
        Format Cells dialog box (Excel), 675–678
        horizontal, 602–603
        left, 538
        right, 542, 602–603
        vertical, 679–681

text, 248–249, 353
   placeholders, 1104, 1118
   tables, 385–388
All Fields button (Access), 834, 851
All Programs command (Windows XP), 12
Always show full menus (check box), 973
anchors, 341
AND logical operator, 925–926
animated character (Office Assistant), 215, 793, 1008
   turning off, 171
animation effects
   applying animation schemes, 1126–1127
   displaying in slide shows, 997–998
   previewing, 1126
animation schemes, 1126–1127
Apple Macintosh computers, 142, 151
application software, 150–154
Apply to All button (PowerPoint), 999
applying font styles, 209–210
appointments
   opening New Appointment window, 72–73
   scheduling, 69–74
Approach® (Lotus), 153
arithmetic/logic unit, 142
arithmetic processing, 142
arrow pointers. *See also* **pointers**
   four-headed arrow, 1108
   resizing arrows, 1106–1107
arrows, 144
   double-headed
      resizing Form Header section, 838
      resizing table columns/rows, 784–786
   down, 16, 175, 520
   inserting, 347–349
   right-pointing, in database tables, 753
   up, 17, 176, 520
ascending order, 789
ask a question, 758
assistance. *See* **help**
asterisks (*)
   adding fields to queries, 897
   multiplication operator, 552–553
   query wildcard, 912
   search wildcard, 39
Athlon® processors, 142
attachments, e-mail, 41
Auto Fill Options button (Excel), 593–595
AutoComplete
   entering/editing
      data, 540–541, 590
      text, 196
   text display, 446
AutoContent Wizard, 1038–1040
   deleting unnecessary slides, 1043
   modifying AutoContent text, 1040–1043
   roadmap, 1038
   specifying presentation options, 1039–1040

AutoCorrect
   recording entries, 283–286
   shortcuts, 286–288
   Spelling and Grammar dialog box (Word), 186
AutoCorrect dialog box (Word), 283–288
AutoCorrect Options smart tag, 285, 297
AutoFill
   constant values generated by, 590
   duplicating data with, 594
   series created with, 592–594
AutoFit Selection command (Format menu, Excel), 597, 628, 634
AutoFit to contents option button (Word), 382
AutoForms, 825
   closing, 827
   creating, 825–827
   saving, 827
AutoNumber data type, 773
AutoPreview (check box), 1126
AutoShapes, inserting, 349–351
AutoShapes button (Word), 349
AutoSum function, 553–554, 623–628, 677
AutoText, inserting, 282–283, 288–290
AVG aggregate function, 939, 941–942

B

Back button (Internet Explorer), 100
background color of forms, 826
Background dialog box (PowerPoint), 112–1124
background graphics
   gradient fill, 1122–1124
   omitting, 1125
   textured, 1122–1125
Backspace key, 192, 201–202, 366
   versus using Delete key or Cut command, 261
balancing column breaks, 433
bar tab stops. *See* **tabs**
beginning a new document. *See* **new, documents**
bibliographies, 297–300
black slides, 998
blank pages, removing, 439
blinking vertical line, 169
Bold button (Formatting toolbar)
   Excel, 685, 687
   PowerPoint, 1096
   Word, 209–210, 351, 374, 436
bold format, folder names, 57
borders
   adding border lines, 426–427
   adding to text, 433–434
   applying to cells, 690–692
   changing, 377–379
Borders and Shading dialog box (Word), 375–377, 426, 433–435
boundary boxes of placeholders
   diagonal slash marks, 1105
   dotted pattern, 1105

four-headed arrow, 1108
sizing handles, 1106
boxes. *See also* **dialog boxes**
    Address Bar, 97–105
    File name, 192
    Search in, 335
    scroll, 17–18, 169, 511, 519, 970
    Type a question for help, 213, 559–561, 745–746, 794, 1007
brackets ([ ]), using calculated fields in queries, 196–197
Break dialog box (Word), 431
bridges, 156
Browse by Graphic button (Word), 464–465
Browse by Page button (Word), 464, 466
Browser toolbar (Word), Close button, 448
bulleted levels, 983
bulleted lists, 271–272. *See also* **numbered lists**
    customizing bullets, 276–278
    Decrease Indent button (PowerPoint), 984
    formatting bullets
        bullet characters, 1114–1116
        picture bullets, 1116–1117
        removing bullets from text, 1117–1118
        symbols as bullet characters, 1115
    Increase Indent button (PowerPoint), 983
    outlines and outline levels, 966
    promoting and demoting items, 983–985
Bullets and Numbering dialog box
    PowerPoint, 1114–1116, 1119
    Word, 276–277
bus network, 155
buttons. *See also* **toolbars**
    displayed with menu commands, 973
    for records, 760
    in database window, 749–750
    navigating to records, 791, 823–824
    toggling, 687
bytes, 142–143, 149

C

.ca (in URLs), 101
calculated fields, in queries, 934–939
calculations, in worksheet, 549–551
calculator, 12–14, 21
Calendar module (Outlook)
    Calendar folder pane, 69–72, 75
    changing views, 69–71
    Date Navigator. *See* Date Navigator
    printing, 74
    scheduling appointments, 69–74
    screen elements, 70
    Standard toolbar, 69–70
        Day button, 71
        Month, 71
        New Appointment button, 72
        Work Week button, 70

Cancel button (Excel), 545–546
canceling text selection, 206
capitalization. *See* **case of text**
case of text
    changing, 1103–1104
    matching when finding and replacing text, 1047
    slide titles, 990
catalogs, 101
cathode ray tubes (CRTs), 147
CDs, 138, 149
CD-ROM (Compact Disc-Read Only Memory) discs, 4
CD-RW (Compact Disc-Read-Write) discs, 4
Celeron® processors, 142
cells, 537. *See also* **relative cell reference**
    active, 538–539. *See also* active cells
    address or reference, 513–514, 550
    aligning, 602–603, 675–678
    borders, 690–692
    clearing, 548
    copying and moving, 604–616
        formulas containing absolute, 635–638
    cutting and pasting, 604–607
    editing data in, 545–547
    fill handles, 592–594
    filling, 678–679
    formatting, 670–674
        Comma Style button (Excel), 622–623
        Currency Style button (Excel), 618–619
        Percent Style button (Excel), 620–621
        text in, 373–375
    gridlines, 710
    indenting, 677–678
    locking in data, 538–540
    merging, 385, 603–604, 689
    moving between, 366–368
    range, 514
    selecting, 512
    shading, 375–376, 693
    tables, 365
    truncated values, 592
    typing formula in, 549–550
    view and insert comments, 712
    worksheet, 502. *See also* worksheets
Cells command (Format menu, Excel), 672, 677
Center button (Formatting toolbar)
    Excel, 602, 676, 687, 695
    PowerPoint, 1104
    Word, 248–249, 298, 346, 351, 374, 388
Center Tab button (Word), 356
Center tab stops. *See* **tabs**
centering
    cell contents, 602–603, 675–678
    tables, 380–381
    text, 248
    worksheets, 701–702
central processing unit (CPU), 141–143

Change All button (Word), 186
Change button
   Excel, 558
   Word, 186
Change Case command (Format menu, PowerPoint), 1103–1104
character, animated (Office Assistant), 1008
Character command button (Word), 277
characters. *See also* fonts
   bullet characters, 277, 1114–1116
   nonprinting, 179, 381, 439
   removing, 202
   selecting single, 206
   separator, 381
   spaces and underscores in file names, 979
   special character formats, 436–439
   Special Characters tab, 291
Chart Wizard, 825
charts, viewing, 523–524
Check Address dialog box (Outlook), 64
Check Full Name dialog box (Outlook), 63–64
check mark (✓), menu command characteristic, 174, 508, 974
Check spelling as you type (check box), 991
checking spelling. *See also* spelling and grammar checkers
   checking entire presentation, 992
   continuous spell checking, 991–992
   red wavy underline, 991–992
   Spelling button (PowerPoint Standard toolbar), 992
circles, white, on placeholder boundary boxes, 1105–1106
Clear All button, Clipboard task pane
   Excel, 604
   PowerPoint, 1062
Clear All command (Edit menu, Excel), 670
Clear button (Word), 357
Clear command (Edit menu, Excel), 548–549
Clear Contents command, keyboard shortcut (Excel), 549
Clear Formats command (Edit menu, Excel), 670, 697
Clear Grid command (Edit menu, Access), 920
clearing
   cells, 548
   design grid, 920
clicking mouse buttons, 10
   cut and paste, 33–34
   left mouse button, 10–11
   right-clicking, 8–9
   selecting multiple files, 31
client computers, 155
clients, 96
clip art, 332
   inserting, 334–338, 453–455
   missing images, 335
   modifying, 338, 340–351
   moving, 343–344
   wrapping text around, 339–340

Clip Art task pane, 335, 452
Clipboard, 1056–1058. *See also* Office Clipboard
   collecting and pasting, 1062–1063
   copying cell contents, 604–605, 607–615
   moving text, 1059–1063
Clipboard task pane. *See also* Office Clipboard task pane
   Excel, 604–605, 608
   PowerPoint, 1056–1058
   Word, 263, 452–453, 457–460
clips, 332
clock speed, 142
Close button
   Access
     Access window, 831
     Database window, 792, 831
     Field Properties dialog box, 938
     forms, 824
     query result, 900
     query window, 915, 917, 909, 927, 938, 943
     table, 758
   Excel
     Print Preview toolbar, 691
     task panes, 503
     title bar, 532
   PowerPoint
     program, 980
     task pane, 976–977
   Word
     Browser toolbar, 448
     Clip Art task pane, 338
     Clipboard task pane, 460
     Header and Footer toolbar, 269
     Print Preview toolbar, 200, 431, 530
     Research task pane, 462
     title bar, 213
Close command (File menu, PowerPoint), 979
Close Window button
   Excel, 511
   PowerPoint, 980
closing
   Access, 792
     AutoForms, 827
     databases, 792
     queries, 899–900
     tables, 775–776
   Excel, 532
     task pane, 503
     workbooks, 559
   Internet Explorer, 124
   Outlook, 59
   PowerPoint, 980
     Outline/Slides pane, 986
     presentations, 979–980
     slide shows, 998
   windows, 18–22
   Word, 210–213

collect and paste, 451–452, 608–609, 612, 1062–1063
colon (:), using calculated fields in queries, 935
color
   active module, 56
   applying to cell borders, 692. *See also* shading
   design guidelines for presentations, 1092
   font color, changing, 436–437, 1098–1100
   palette
     changing font color, 1099
     displaying, 1098
     modifying color schemes, 1121–1122
     using colors outside color scheme, 1099
   schemes, 1038, 1120–1122
     applying to slides, 1120–1121
     modifying colors, 1121–1122
     using colors outside color scheme, 1099
color laser printers, 148
Colors dialog box (PowerPoint), 1099
columns
   adding (Word), 371–372
   balancing breaks (Word), 433
   changing one column to two (Word), 428–429
   database tables, 753–754
   deselecting (Excel), 516
   formatting multiple (Word), 429–430
   headings
     Access, 779
     Excel, 512, 590–591
   hiding (Access), 787–788
   inserting and deleting
     Excel, 599–601
     Word, 431–432
   printing headings (Excel), 710–711
   selecting (Excel), 512
   width
     Access, 784–786
     Excel, 596–598, 607
     Word, 370–371
Columns button (Word), 428
Columns command (Insert menu, Excel), 599
Columns tab, in Page Setup dialog box (Access), 830
Comma Style button (Excel), 622–623, 674
command characteristics, 174
command icons (Access)
   Create form by using wizard, 833
   Create query in Design view, 894
   Create report by using wizard, 850
   Create table in Design view, 768
commands
   Access
     Edit menu. See Edit menu commands
     File menu. See File menu commands
     Format menu. See Format menu commands
     Records menu, Remove Filter/Sort, 790
     Tools menu. See Tools menu commands
     View menu. See View menu commands
   accessing in menus, 171–175, 973–974
   displayed in task pane, 967
   Excel
     Edit menu. See Edit menu commands
     Fill Series, 595
     Fill Without Formatting, 634–635
     File menu. See File menu commands
     Format menu. See Format menu commands
     Ignore Error, 632
     Insert menu. See Insert menu commands
     Select All Sheets, 590, 613, 618, 641, 699
     Tools menu. See Tools menu commands
     Ungroup Sheets, 591
     View menu. See View menu commands
   keyboard shortcuts. *See* keyboard shortcuts
   Outlook
     Current View, 66–68
     File menu. See File menu commands
     View menu. See View menu commands
   PowerPoint
     Copy, 1061
     Cut, 1059
     Edit menu. See Edit menu commands
     File menu. See File menu commands
     Format menu. See Format menu commands
     Insert menu. See Insert menu commands
     View menu. See View menu commands
   repeating last command, 1098
   toolbar buttons. *See* toolbars
   unavailable menu commands, 974
   Windows XP
     All Programs, 12
     Compressed (zipped) Folder, 43
     New, 23
   Word
     Copy, 451
     current task, 169
     Cut, 261, 451
     Edit menu. See Edit menu commands
     File menu. See File menu commands
     Format menu. See Format menu commands
     Insert menu. See Insert menu commands
     Table menu. See Table menu commands
     Tools menu. See Tools menu commands
     Track Changes, 464
     Undo/Redo, 268–269
     View menu. See View menu commands
comments
   hiding/unhiding, 713
   printing, 713
   view and insert in cell, 712
communications software, 149, 154
comparison operators, 922–924
compound criteria, 925–927
compressing files, 3–4, 41–47
computer networks
   components, 154
   local area networks (LANs), 155–156

Index | **Office Brief** 1221

topography, 155–156
wide area networks (WANs), 155–156
computer programs. *See* **software**
computer storage media, 143
computer system components, 136–138
computers
    components, 136–138
    definition, 137
    hardware devices, 140–149
    networks, 154–156
    software, 149–154
    types, 138–139
connections to servers, 54
consective lines/paragraphs, selecting, 206
console unit, 140
constant value
    cell content, 537
    generated with AutoFill, 590
Contacts module (Outlook)
    Contact form, 61–65
    contact item, 60–61
    Contacts folder, 60–61, 66
    Contacts module banner, 60–61
    Contacts view options, 60–61
    creating contacts, 60–65
    Current View command, 66–68
    editing and printing contacts, 60, 66–68
    Folder contents pane, 60–61
    managing contacts, 53
    Navigation pane, 60, 66, 69–71
    screen elements, 60–61
    searching for contacts, 63
    Standard toolbar, 61
        New Contact, 61
        Print, 66
        Save and Close button, 64–65
    storing addresses, 53, 60–65
    tabs, 60–61
Contents pane, 23
    sorting files, 28
context-sensitive
    menus, 9, 24
    tags or buttons, 593, 1057
Control Panel, Regional and Language Options, 544
control unit, 8
controls in forms, 838
converting text to tables, 381–388
Copy button (Standard toolbar)
    Excel, 605, 610
    PowerPoint, 1061
    Word, 454
Copy command (Edit menu)
    PowerPoint, 1061
    Word, 451
Copy command (shortcut menu, PowerPoint), 1061
copying. *See also* **moving**
    between applications, 22
    cell contents, 604–607

    databases, 742
    entire worksheet, 609–610
    files, 27–34
    formatting
        using Format Painter, 1101–1103
        using repeat key, 1098
    formulas, 633–638
    text, 257, 264–265, 1056–1058
        Copy button (PowerPoint Standard toolbar), 1061
        using Clipboard, 1061–1062
        using collect and paste, 608–609
        using Format Painter, 695–696
    Web pages, 119. *See also* downloading files
copyright issues, 457
cordless mouse, 145
Corel® Software, 152–154
corner-sizing handles, 341
CPU (central processing unit), 141–143
Create form by using wizard command icon, 833
Create New Folder button
    Excel, 531
    PowerPoint, 978
    Word, 191
Create New Folder dialog box (Outlook), 57–58
Create query in Design view command icon, 894
Create report by using wizard command icon, 850
Create table in Design view command icon, 768
criteria, 892–893
    compound, 925–927
    for record query, 759
    from field not in query result, 918–920
    numeric, 921
    text, 904–909
    using calculated fields, 934–939
    using comparison operators, 922–924
    using wildcard characters, 912–917
Criteria row, in query design grid, 904
crosshair pointer, 344
CRTs (cathode ray tubes), 147
Currency
    data type, 774
    formatting, 938
    selecting and applying, 674–675
Currency Style button (Excel), 618–619, 671
current date
    in report footers, 862
    viewing, 69–70
Current View command (View menu, Outlook)
    Address Cards option, 67–68
    Detailed Address Cards option, 68
    Phone List button, 66–67

Custom Footer button (Excel), 526, 538, 590, 618, 672, 699, 710–711
Custom Header button (Excel), 707
Customize button (Windows XP), 11
Customize command (Tools menu)
    Access, 748
    Excel, 507
    Word, 172
Customize dialog box
    PowerPoint, 973
    Word, 172
Customized Bullet List dialog box (Word), 277–278
customizing
    bullets (bulleted lists), 276–278
    toolbars, 508
cut and paste
    moving files, 33–34
    text/data between applications, 22
Cut button (Standard toolbar)
    Excel, 614
    PowerPoint, 1059–1060
    Word, 261–263
Cut command (Edit menu)
    PowerPoint, 1059
    Word, 261, 451
Cut command (shortcut menu, PowerPoint), 1059
cutting/moving, 257, 261–263, 1059–1061.
See also **deleting**
    cell contents, 614–615

D

data, 741
    editing, 545–547
    entering, 537–544, 822
    formatting. *See* formatting, cells
    locking in cells, 538–540
    sorting, 927–932
data entry, 822
Data Type column, 769
data types, 770
    AutoNumber, 773
    Currency, 774
    Number, 769
        as criteria in queries, 921
    Text, 769
        as criteria in queries, 904
Database toolbar (Access)
    in Access window, 745–746
    New button, 766
    New Object AutoForm button, 827
    Open button, 746
    Print button, 831, 910, 916–917, 927, 932
database wizard, 766
databases, 153, 741
    closing, 792
    copying, 742
    creating, 765–767
    file extension, 742
    opening, 744–749
    renaming, 742–744
    saving, 792
    viewing the window, 750–752
Datasheet view (Access)
    adding records, 771
    opening a table, 776
    viewing a table, 756–757
Date Navigator (Outlook), 69–72
    displaying dates, 75
    Next Month button, 71
    printing calendars, 74
dates
    changing format, 1001
    default format, 544
    displaying, 75
    entering, 544
    headers/footers, 281
        reports, 862
    navigating to specific, 69
    scheduling events, 53
    typing into worksheet, 543–544
    viewing current dates, 69–70
decimal places, increasing and decreasing, 621
Decimal places spin box, 674
Decimal tab stops. *See* **tabs**
decorative mastheads, creating, 422–427
Decrease Decimal button (Excel), 622
Decrease Font Size button (PowerPoint Formatting toolbar), 1107
Decrease Indent button (Formatting toolbar)
    PowerPoint, 984, 1042
    Word, 274–275
defaults, 111
    alignment, 538
    format for dates, 544
    Outlook
        History lists, 109
        home pages, 97–98
    PowerPoint, 981
    tab stops, 353
Degrees spin box, 682
Delete command (Edit menu, Word), 599
Delete key, 201–202
    versus using Backspace or Cut command, 261
Delete Record button (Access), 784, 830
Delete Slide command (Edit menu, PowerPoint), 985
deleting
    blank pages, 439
    fields, 777–779
    files, 27–34
        recovering deleted files, 34
        Recycle bin, 6
    records from tables, 784
    rows and columns, 599, 601

Index | **Office Brief** 1223

slides
    in Slide Sorter view, 996
    in Slides tab, 985
    unnecessary AutoContent slides, 1043
tab stops, 357–359
text, 201–202, 259–260, 1059–1061
versus using backspace or cut, 261
Web sites from Favorites list, 114–115

demoting outline text, 983–985
descending order, 789
Description column, 770
deselecting
    columns, 516
    slides, 995
    text, 272
design, tables, 777
Design button
    Access, 777, 901
    PowerPoint, 1053–1054
design grid
    adding fields to query, 908
    clearing, 920
    of Select Query window, 894–896
design guidelines, in presentations, 1092
design templates, 1038, 1049. *See also* **formatting**
    changing
        for a single slide, 1052–1053
        for entire presentation,
            1053–1054
        for selected slides, 1054
    color schemes, 1120–1122
    creating presentations, 1050–1052
Design view (Access)
    creating a new table, 767–768
    creating queries, 894, 896
    of forms, 836–837, 841
    of reports, 853–855
        moving and resizing fields, 855–862
    opening a table, 776
    viewing a table, 756–757
desktop, 6–7
    viewing from Access, 750–751
desktop computers, 139
desktop publishing programs, 420
Detail section, of forms, 837
diagonal sizing box, 511
diagonal-pointing arrow pointer, 1106–1107
dialog boxes, 174
    Access
        Field Properties, 936–938
        File New Database, 767
        Form Wizard, 833
        New Form, 825
        Open, 748
        Page Setup, 782, 830, 854
        Print, 780, 795
        Properties, 743, 781
        Row Height, 786

        Save As, 827, 900, 905, 915, 917,
            926–927, 943
        Show Table, 894–895, 906, 912, 916, 918,
            925, 939
        Unhide Columns, 787
        Zoom, 934–936
    Excel
        Font, 527, 705, 707
        Footer, 526–528, 591, 618, 711
        Format Cells, 670–678, 681–685, 689–693
        Format Picture, 705–706
        Function, 505
        Header, 704
        Insert Function, 553
        Insert Picture, 705–706
        Move or Copy, 609
        New Folder, 531
        Open, 509, 672, 699, 710
        Options, 506, 540–541
        Page Setup, 526–528, 538, 590, 641,
            699–701, 707, 710
        Print, 558
        Row Height, 679
        Save As, 530–532, 536–537, 591, 672, 699
        Spelling, 557
        Zoom, 555–556
    Internet Explorer
        Add Favorite, 113
        Internet Options, 98
        Organize Favorites, 114
        Print, 122–123
        Save Web Page, 119–121
    Outlook
        Check Address, 64
        Check Full Name, 63–64
        Create New Folder, 57–58
        New Appointment, 71
        Print, 66, 68, 74
        Server Connection, 54
    PowerPoint
        AutoContent Wizard, 1038–1040
        Background, 1122–1124
        Bullets and Numbering, 1114–1116, 1119
        Colors, 1099
        Customize, Options tab, 973
        Edit Color Scheme, 1121–1122
        Fill Effects, 1124
        Font, 1096–1098
        Header and Footer, 999–1001
        Insert Outline, 1055
        New Folder, 978
        Open, 968, 980
        Options, Spelling tab, 991
        Picture Bullet, 1116
        Print, 1003, 1006
        Replace, 1046
        Replace Fonts, 1095
        Save As, 977
        Symbol, 1115

Windows XP
- *Compressed (zipped) Folder command, 43*
- *Extraction Wizard, 46–47*
- *password requests, 7*

Word, 174
- *AutoCorrect, 283, 285–286, 288*
- *Borders and Shading, 375–377, 426, 433–435*
- *Break, 431*
- *Bullets and Numbering, 276–277*
- *Convert Text to Table, 382*
- *Customize, 172*
- *Customized Bullet List, 277–278*
- *Edit Hyperlink, 445–446*
- *Edit WordArt Text, 423–424*
- *Favorites-Microsoft Clip organizer, 453*
- *Find and Replace, 258, 289, 461, 464–465*
- *Font, 209, 437*
- *Footnote and Endnote, 293*
- *Format AutoShape, 349*
- *Format Picture, 339*
- *Format WordArt, 424, 426*
- *Header and Footer, 338*
- *Insert Hyperlink, 442–444*
- *Insert Symbol, 283*
- *New Folder, 191*
- *Open, 170, 246, 271, 334, 354, 422, 441*
- *Options, 186*
- *Page Setup, 199–200, 247, 279*
- *Paragraph, 252–254, 274–275, 362*
- *Print, 193, 213*
- *Save As, 190–191, 200, 246, 271, 334, 354, 422, 441, 448*
- *Set Hyperlink ScreenTip, 442–445*
- *Set Page Title, 448–449*
- *Sort Text, 299*
- *Spelling and Grammar, 185–186*
- *Symbol, 277–278, 291*
- *Table AutoFormat, 384*
- *Table Properties, 380, 387*
- *Tabs, 357–358*
- *WordArt Gallery, 422–423*

dictionary
- adding names to, 558
- suggestions list, 186, 557

digital cameras, 143
directories to Web sites, 101
displayed value, 640–641
displaying
- active documents, 169
- Clipboard task pane, 452–453
- favorite Web sites, 112–113
- file extensions, 29
- formatting marks, 179–180
- linked pages, 109
- page/section number/Word settings, 169
- task pane, 171–175
- text, scroll bars, 169
- underlying formulas, 640–641

documents
- active, 169
- changing layouts, 246–257
- checking spelling and grammar, 185
- creating/editing, 194–203
- finding elements, 463–464
- folders, creating, 190–192
- navigating, 175–178
- organizing/saving/printing, 190–193
- previewing/saving as Web pages, 447–449
- printing, 193
- selecting text, 206
- viewing, 179–183
- Word document window, 169

domain names, 101
dot leaders, 358, 361. *See also* **tabs**
dots per inch (dpi), 148
double-click, within cells, 545
double-headed arrow
- resizing Form Header section, 838
- resizing table columns/rows, 784

double spacing
- paragraphs, 250
- sentence end, 198

down arrow, 16, 175, 520
downloading files, 119–121
drag-and-drop technique
- fields in query design grid, 908
- moving
  - cell contents with, 616
  - text, 1056–1058
- turning on, 266–267

dragging, 177. *See also* **drag-and-drop technique; scroll bar**
- documents, 169
- resizing windows, 16

Drawing button (Word), 344
drawing canvas, 344
- deactivating, 347

Drawing Canvas toolbar, 347
Drawing toolbar
- PowerPoint, 970
- Word, 332, 344
  - *Arrow button, 347*
  - *AutoShapes button, 349*
  - *Text Box button, 344*

duplicating
- data with AutoFill, 594–595
- text. *See* copying, text

Duron® chips, 142
DVDs, 149

E

Edit Color Scheme dialog box (PowerPoint), 1121–1122
Edit Hyperlink dialog box (Word), 446
Edit Hyperlink shortcut menu (Word), 445

Edit menu commands
   Access
      Clear Grid, 920
   Excel
      Clear, 548–549
      Clear All, 670
      Clear Formats, 670, 697
      Delete, 599
      Move or Copy Sheet, 609
      Office Clipboard, 604, 608
      Paste Special, 606
      Redo, 548
      Undo, 548
   PowerPoint
      Copy, 1061
      Cut, 1059
      Delete Slide, 985
      Replace, 1046
   Word
      Office Clipboard, 452
      Replace, 258
Edit Text button (Word), 424
Edit WordArt Text dialog box (Word), 423–424
editing. *See also* **Edit menu commands**
   contacts, 66–68
   data in cells, 545–547
   files (removing read-only status), 35
   formulas, 623–633
   headers and footers, 189
   information in a record, 782–783
   new documents, 194–203
   presentations, 980–987
   queries, 901–903
   workbooks, 501
editing text. *See also* **formatting text**
   checking spelling, 991–992
   copying text, 1056–1058
      Copy button (PowerPoint Standard toolbar), 1061
      using Clipboard, 1061–1062
   deleting text, 1059–1061
   finding and replacing text, 1046–1047
   in Outline tab, 982
   in Slide pane, 987–988, 990
   modifying AutoContent text, 1040–1043
   moving text, 1056–1058
      multiple selections, 1062–1063
      using Clipboard, 1059–1063
      using collect and paste, 1062–1063
      using drag-and-drop, 1056–1058
   placeholders. *See* placeholders
   Redo button (PowerPoint Standard toolbar), 1048
   Spelling button (PowerPoint Standard toolbar), 992
   Undo button (PowerPoint Standard toolbar), 1048
   undoing or redoing edits, 1048

.edu (in URLs), 101
effects
   animation effects, 997–998, 1126–1127
      applying animation schemes, 1126–1127
      displaying in slide shows, 997–998
      previewing, 1126
   fill effects
      gradient fill backgrounds, 1122–1124
      omitting background graphics, 1125
      textured backgrounds, 1122–1125
   font effects, 1097
   transitions, 997–998
ellipsis (...), menu command characteristic, 174, 508, 974
e-mail
   addresses, registering, 59
   attachments, 41
   messages
      identifying unread items, 57
      organizing, 54, 56–59
      sending, 59–60
      storing, 57–59
em dashes, 291
emphasizing text. *See* **formatting text**
End with black slide (check box), 998
ending slide shows, 998
Enter button (Excel Formula Bar), 546–547, 634, 636–637, 682
Enter key, 366
   for making active cell, 540
envelope icons, unread messages, 55–56
equations, in calculated fields, 934
events
   all-day, 73
   scheduling dates for, 53
Excel, 152
   closing, 532
   commands. *See* commands, Excel
   dialog boxes. *See* dialog boxes, Excel
   formula editing buttons, 505
   Help, 559–561
   keyboard shortcuts
      bold, 685
      Clear Contents command, 549
      Copy, 635
      Copy command, 606
      displayed values, 640
      entering dates, 544
      formatting cells, 673
      italic, 685
      new workbook, 536
      Paste, 635
      starting commands, 507
      underline, 685
      Undo, 548
   mathematical operators, 552
   parts of Excel window, 503–505, 510–511
   starting, 502, 505

toolbars
- *Formatting toolbar*, 505. See also *Formatting toolbar, Excel*
- *Header and Footer*, 705
- *Print Preview*. See *Print Preview toolbar, Excel*
- *Standard Toolbar*. See *Standard toolbar, Excel*
- worksheets. *See* worksheets

Exit command (File menu)
- Outlook, 59
- PowerPoint, 980

exiting. *See* closing
expand arrows, menus, 507
expansion cards, 141
expansion slots, 141
Explain (grammar) button (Word), 186
expression, 914
extender keys, 144
extensions. *See* files, extensions
extracting information from database, 758
Extraction Wizard, 46–47

F

Fair Use guidelines, 457
Favorites list, 111
- adding addresses, 111–113
- deleting addresses, 114–115

Favorites menu, 98
Favorites pane, 113
- Organize, 114

Favorites-Microsoft Clip Organizer dialog box (Word), 453
Field descriptions in database table, 770
Field Properties dialog box (Access), 936–938
field row, in query design grid, 897, 908, 934
fields, 754
- adding, 779
- adding to query design grid, 908
- deleting, 777–779
- moving and resizing
  - in forms, 841–847
  - in reports, 855–862
- removing from query table, 901–903

file extensions. *See* files, extensions
file folders, organizing, 190
File menu
- closing workbook, 559
- displayed in full, 506–507

File menu commands, 972
- Access
  - *New, Folder*, 742
  - *Open*, 748
  - *Page Setup*, 854
  - *Print*, 780, 910
- Excel
  - *New*, 536
  - *Open*, 509
  - *Page Setup*, 641
  - *Print Preview*, 558
  - *Save As*, 530, 591
- Outlook
  - *Exit*, 59
  - *Folder, New Folder*, 57
  - *New, Appointment*, 72
  - *Print*, 67
- PowerPoint
  - *Close*, 979
  - *Exit*, 980
  - *New*, 1038
  - *Open*, 966
  - *Print*, 1002, 1005, 1048
  - *Save As*, 977, 1094
- Word
  - *Close*, 213
  - *Save As*, 190, 246
  - *Save As Web Page*, 448
  - *Web Page Preview*, 447

File name box, 192
file names
- using spaces, 743
- visible in task bar, 535

File New Database dialog box (Access), 767
files
- associations, 43–47
- closing, 979–980
- compressing, 41–47
- copying, 27–34
- deleting, 6, 33–34
- downloading, 119–121
- extensions
  - .doc, 29
  - hiding, 29
  - .mdb, 742
  - .ppt, 29
  - search restrictions, 39–40
  - .xls, 29
  - .zip, 43
- finding, 35–39
- moving, 977
- name restrictions, 34
- opening, 966, 968
- renaming, 978
- searching for, 35–39
- sending over the Internet, 192
- sorting, 27
- spaces in file names, 743, 979
- storing, 3–4

fill alignment, within cell, 678–679
Fill Color arrow (Excel), 693
fill effects
- gradient fill backgrounds, 1122–1124
- omitting background graphics, 1125

fill handle
- cells, 592–594
- copying cells, 636
- copying formulas, 634, 637

Fill Series command (Excel), 595
Fill Without Formatting command (Excel), 634–635
Find and Replace dialog box (Word), 258, 289, 461, 464–465
Find Next button (PowerPoint), 1047
Find whole words only (check box), 1047
finding
    and replacing text, 1046–1047
    objects, 463–466
    text, 257–259
Finish button (Access), 835
FIRST aggregate function, 939
First Line Indent tab stops. *See* tabs
First Record button (Access), 823
Fit, 762
flat-panel monitors, 147
flat-screen monitors, 147
floating images, 338. *See also* clip art
floppy disks, 149
    drives, 4
    formatting, 23
    sending files to, 31
Folder, New Folder command (File menu, Outlook), 57
Folder contents pane (Contacts module), 60–61
folders, 977
    active, 55–56, 60–61
    banners, 55–56, 60–61
    Calendar module (Outlook), 69–72, 75
    Contacts (Outlook module), 60–61
    creating new
        Excel, 530–532
        Outlook, 57–59
        PowerPoint, 978
        Windows XP, 22–26
        Word, 190–192
    downloads, 119
    Inbox, 55–56
    Mail module (Outlook), 57–58
    naming, 191
        in Web site directories, 101
        renaming, 25–26, 532
    Notes (Outlook module), 75, 78
    organizing, 190
        e-mail messages, 56–59
    searching for, 35–39
    Tasks (Outlook module), 75
Folders button (My Computer), 22
Font button arrow (Formatting toolbar)
    Excel, 527, 685, 695, 707
    PowerPoint, 1094
    Word, 208, 429
Font Color arrow (Formatting toolbar)
    PowerPoint, 1098–1100, 1111–1112
    Word, 436

Font dialog box
    Excel, 527, 705, 707
    PowerPoint, 1096–1098
    Word, 209, 437
Font Size button arrow (Formatting toolbar)
    Excel, 686–687
    Word, 207–208, 351, 429, 436
fonts
    applying styles, 209–210
    changing, 206–209, 684–688, 1094–1095
    color, changing, 436–437, 1098–1100
    effects, changing, 1097
    replacing all occurrences of a font, 1095
    size, changing, 1094–1095
        and column width, 596
        and row height, 599
        changing, 684–688
    style, changing, 1096–1098
Footer dialog box (Excel), 526–528, 591, 618, 711
footers, 999. *See also* headers and footers
    creating, 525–526, 528, 703–704, 706–708
    in forms, 837, 848
    inserting
        and formatting page numbers, 279–280
        AutoText, 281
        Current Date and Time, 282
    margin setting, 708
    on handouts or notes pages, 1000–1001
    on slides, 999–1000
    viewing, 188
Footnote and Endnote dialog box (Word), 293
footnotes
    formatting, 296
    inserting, 292–295
Form Design toolbar (Access)
    Toolbox button, 839
    View button, 847
Form Footer section, 837
Form Header section, 837
form headers, 837–840
Form Name box, 827
form types, by wizard creation, 825
Form view, of forms, 836
Form View toolbar (Access)
    Delete Record button, 830
    Print Preview button, 849
    View button, 836, 840
Form Wizard, 832
    creating forms, 833–835
Format AutoShape dialog box (Word), 349
Format Cells dialog box (Excel), 670–678, 681–685, 689–693
Format menu commands
    Access
        Hide Columns, 787–788
        Row Height, 786
        Unhide Columns, 787–788

Excel
   AutoFit Selection, 597, 628, 634
   Cells, 672, 677
PowerPoint
   Alignment, 1104
   Background, 1122–1124
   Bullets and Numbering, 1114–1116, 1119
   Change Case, 1103–1104
   Replace Fonts, 1095
   Slide Layout, 989, 1045
Word
   Borders and Shading, 375–377, 426, 433, 435
   Bullets and Numbering, 276
   Paragraph, 254, 298
   Picture, 339–340
   Tabs, 357

Format Painter
   Excel, 695–697
   PowerPoint
      copying formatting, 1101–1103
      turning off, 1103
   Word, 256–257

Format Picture dialog box
   Excel, 705–706
   Word, 339

Format WordArt dialog box (Word), 424–425, 426

formatting, 204–210, 987–996, 1094. *See also*
   Formatting toolbar
   bullets
      bullet characters, 1114–1116
      numbered lists, 1118–1119
      picture bullets, 1116–1117
      removing bullets from text, 1117–1118
   cells
      aligning. See aligning, cell contents
      applying, 684–697
      Comma Style button (Excel), 622–623
      Currency Style button (Excel), 618
      Percent Style button (Excel), 620–621
   copying, 1101–1103
      copying with Format Painter, 695–696
   floppy disks, 23
   footnotes, 296
   headers and footers, 279–280
   lists, 274–275
   marks
      displaying, 179–180
      Show/Hide ¶ button. See Show/Hide ¶ button
   multiple columns, 429–430
   numbers
      with Format Cells dialog box (Excel), 670–674
      with toolbar, 618–622
   paragraphs, 274
   placeholders
      moving, 1108
      resizing, 1106, 1118
      selecting, 1105–1106
      text alignment, 1104, 1118
   repeating commands, 1098
   slides. *See also* design templates
      applying animation schemes, 1126–1127
      applying color schemes, 1120–1121
      backgrounds, 1122–1124
      changing slide layouts, 988–991
      final slides in presentations, 998
      inserting existing slides, 1045
      Slide Design button (PowerPoint Formatting toolbar), 1120
      slide master, 1110–1112
      title master, 1110–1111
   special
      character, 436–439
      paragraph, 433–435
   tab stops, 357–359
   tables, 373–381
      predefined, 384–385
   text. *See also* editing edit
      aligning, 542, 602–603, 1104, 1118
      applying formatting to pasted text, 1058–1060
      balancing slide titles visually, 990
      capitalizing slide titles, 990
      changing date format, 1001
      converting to tables, 382–383
      fonts. See fonts
      removing bullets from text, 1117–1118
      text case, 1103–1104
   workbooks, 699–702
   worksheets, 537

Formatting toolbar
   Excel, 505
      Align Left button, 602
      Align Right button, 603, 687
      Bold button, 685, 687
      Borders arrow, 692
      Borders button, 690
      Center button, 602, 676, 687, 695
      Comma Style button, 622–623, 674
      Currency Style button, 618–619, 671
      Decrease Decimal button, 622
      Fill Color arrow, 693
      Font button arrow, 685, 695
      Font Size arrow, 686–687
      Format Painter button, 697
      Increase Decimal button, 621
      Increase Indent button, 678, 697
      Italic button, 685, 687, 695
      Merge and Center button, 603–604, 624
      Percent Style button, 620–621, 674
      Print Preview button, 691
      Underline button, 685, 687
   PowerPoint, 970
      Align Right button, 1104
      Bold button, 1096
      Decrease Font Size button, 1107

Decrease Indent button, 984, 1042
  Design button, 1053–1054
  displaying, 975
  Font button arrow, 1094
  Font Color arrow, 1098-1100, 1111–1112
  Increase Indent button, 983, 1042
  Italic button, 1097, 1105
  New Slide button, 1045, 1111
  Numbering button, 1118
  Shadow, 1096
  Slide Design, 1120
  Underline button, 1097
  Word, 169
    Align Left button, 248, 250
    Align Right button, 248, 279, 374
    Bold button, 209, 351, 374, 436
    Bullets button, 272
    Center button, 248–249, 298, 346, 351, 374, 380, 388
    Decrease Indent button, 274–275
    Font button arrow, 208, 429
    Font Color button, 436
    Font Size button arrow, 207–208, 429, 436
    Increase Indent button, 362
    Italic button, 209
    Justify button, 249, 430
    Line Spacing button, 250–252
    Numbering button, 272
    Toolbar Options button, 167
forms, 820–821
  adding
    form headers, 837–840
    page footers, 848–849
    records to tables, 828–829
  background color, 826
  creating with Form Wizard, 833–835
  deleting records from tables, 829–831
  entering information, ease of use, 820, 822
  modifying, 836
  moving and resizing fields, 841–847
  navigating to records, 822–824
  style, 834
  switching between views, 836, 840–841
  viewing, 759–760
  viewing information, ease of use, 820, 822
Forms button (Access), 759, 822
formula, 914
Formula Bar (Excel)
  AutoSum, 625
  Cancel button, 545–546
  displaying
    buttons, 550
    formulas, 554, 632–633, 640–641
    text, 539
  Enter button, 546–547, 634, 636–637, 682
  examining formulas, 637
  Excel, 505

formulas
  cell content as, 537
  copying, 633–638
  creating, 549–553
  editing, 623–633
    buttons, 505
  entering cell references in, 551, 553
  locking in, 637
  prebuilt. *See* functions
  underlying. *See* underlying formula
Forward button (Internet Explorer), 100
four-headed arrow pointer, 346, 1108
.fr (in URLs), 101
Freelance Graphics® (Lotus), 153
frequently used text, inserting, 283–290, 292
FTP (File Transfer Protocol), 101
full justified text, 248, 429
full menus, 746–748
  displaying, 507
  turning on, 172
Function dialog box (Excel), 505
function keypad, 144
functions. *See also* **formulas**
  aggregate or statistical, 939, 941–943
  AutoSum, 553–554, 623–628
  Trace Error, 636

G

gateway, 156
getting help. *See* **help**
Getting Started task pane
  closing, 534, 590
  creating new files
    document, 195–196
    workbook, 536
  opening a presentation, 966
  viewing, 175
gigabytes (GB), 142
gigahertz (GHz), 142
.gov (in URLs), 101
gradient fill backgrounds, 1122–1124
grammar checker. *See* **spelling and grammar checkers**
grammar rules, 186
graphic lines on reports, 861
graphic presentations, 153
graphical user interface (GUI), 2, 150
graphics. *See also* **clip art**
  adding, 332
  adding hyperlinks, 444–445
  text boxes, 344–345
  wrapping text around, 339–340
grave (`) accent, 640
grayed menu commands, 174, 974
grayed toolbar buttons (Excel), 535
grayscale printing, 1003
greater than (>) comparison operator, 922–924

grid pattern
    in Detail section of forms, 837
    in reports, 853
gridlines, 710
    printing, 711
Group indicator on title bar, 525, 529
    removing, 529
grouping data in queries, 939–940
groups bar in database window, 749–750
Groupwise (Corel), 154
GUI (graphical user interface), 150

H

hand pointer. *See also* **pointers**
    on control borders, 842–843, 845
handheld computers, 139
handles
    rotate, 341
    sizing, 339, 341
handouts, 999
    adding headers and footers, 1000–1001
    printing, 1002–1006
hanging indent, 299. *See also* **tabs**
hard disk, 3–4, 143, 149
hard-copy printout, 148
hardware devices, 140–149
    input devices, 143–146
    keyboards, 143–144
    output devices, 147–149
    storage devices, 149
    system unit, 140–142
Header and Footer command (View menu)
    Excel, 538, 590, 618, 672, 699, 703, 710–711
    PowerPoint, 999–1000, 1048
    Word, 188, 210, 269, 279, 338, 430, 466
Header and Footer dialog box
    PowerPoint, 999
        Notes and Handouts tab, 1000–1001
    Word, 338
Header and Footer toolbar, 189, 300, 705
    Excel, 705
    Word
        Close button, 189, 269, 282, 338, 359, 430, 446, 466
        Insert AutoText button, 281, 338, 359, 430, 446, 466
        Insert Date button, 282
        Insert Page Number button, 279
        Insert Time button, 282
        Page Setup button, 279
        Switch Between Header and Footer button, 188, 210, 269, 281, 338, 359, 430, 446
Header dialog box (Excel), 704
headers, 999
    creating, 525–528, 703–704, 706–708
    in forms, 837, 848
    margin setting, 708
    on handouts or notes pages, 1000–1001
    on slides, 999–1000
headers and footers
    accessing, 188–189
    viewing, 188–189
    working with, 279, 281–283
headings (Excel)
    columns, 512, 590, 598, 601
    printing, 710–711
    rows, 512, 598
Height spin box, 706
Help
    Access, 745, 793–795
    Excel, 559–561
    PowerPoint, 1007–1008
        Office Assistant, 1008
    Word, 213–215
        Office Assistant, 171
Hide button (Word), 171
Hide Columns command (Format menu, Access), 787–788
hiding
    columns, 787–788
    file extensions, 29
highlighting
    cell shading, 375–376
    selecting worksheet items, 512–517
History list, 109–115. *See also* **Favorites list**
Home button (Internet Explorer), 100
Home Edition, 11
home pages, 97–98
    default for Internet Explorer, 98
    setting options, 111
horizontal alignment
    cell contents, 602–603
    changing with Format Cells dialog box (Excel), 675–678
horizontal rulers, in Design view of forms, 839
Horizontal Scroll banner button (Word), 350
horizontal scroll bar, 14, 519
horizontal window split box, 511
hosts, 96
HTML (hypertext markup language), 120
http (Hypertext Transfer Protocol), 101
hub computers, 156
Hyperlink command (Insert menu, Word), 442–444
hyperlinks, 105–109, 295, 441
    expanding information, 793
    inserting, 441–446
    modifying, 445–446
    Type a question for help box, 560

I

I-beam pointer. *See also* **pointers**
    Access, 823
    Excel, 520, 547

PowerPoint, 982
    with paintbrush attached, 1101
Windows XP, 6
Word, 204, 256
icons, 6
    envelope, unread messages, 55–56
    My Computer, 6, 14
Ignore All button
    Excel, 557
    Word, 186
Ignore Error command (Excel), 632
Ignore Once button Word), 186–187
Ignore Rule (Grammar) button (Word), 186
images. *See also* **clip art**
    gathering, 451–452
importing Microsoft Word outlines, 1054–1055
Inbox folder, 55–56
Increase Decimal button (Excel), 621
Increase Indent button (Formatting toolbar)
    Excel, 678, 697
    PowerPoint, 983, 1042
    Word, 362
Indent spin box, 678
indenting
    cell contents, 677–678
    items within table cells, 373
    paragraphs, 255
indents, 169
    hanging, 299
    versus tab stops, 362
indicator lights, 144
information, 741. *See also* **help**
    expanding (hyperlinks), 793
    extracting from database, 758
    locating supporting, 451–462
    pasting from Clipboard task pane, 458–460
ink-jet printers, 148
inline images, 338. *See also* **clip art**
input, 137
input devices, 143–146
    keyboards, 143–144
    multimedia input devices, 146
    scanners, 146
Insert All button (PowerPoint), 1045
Insert AutoText button (Word), 281, 338, 359, 430, 446, 466
Insert button (Word), 336
Insert command (Table menu, Word), 369, 371
Insert Comment command (Excel), 712
Insert Date button (Word), 282
Insert Function dialog box (Excel), 553
Insert Hyperlink dialog box (Word), 442–444
Insert menu commands
    Excel
        Columns, 599
        Rows, 599
    PowerPoint, 974
        New Slide, 1045
        Slides from Files, 1057
        Slides from Outlines, 1055

    Word
        Break, 431
        Hyperlink, 442, 444
        Picture, 335, 452
        Reference, Footnote, 293–295
        Symbol, 291
insert mode, 202
    in worksheet, 547
Insert Options button (Excel), 600–601
Insert Outline dialog box (PowerPoint), 1055
Insert Page Number button (Word), 279
Insert Picture dialog box (Excel), 705–706
Insert Symbol dialog box (Word), 283
Insert Table button (Word), 365
Insert Time button (Word), 282
inserting
    arrows, 347–349
    AutoShapes, 349–351
    AutoText, 282–283, 288–290
    clip art and pictures, 334–338, 453–455
    column breaks, 431–432
    comments in cell, 712
    frequently used text, 283–290, 292
    hyperlinks, 441–446
    manual column breaks, 428
    references, 292–300
    rows and columns, 599–601
    slides
        existing, 1044–1045
        new, 1045–1046, 1051
    symbols, 290–292
    WordArt, 422–426
insertion point, 169, 505, 526, 539, 982
instructions. *See* **help**
Intel® processors, 142
Internet, 156
    connection to, 448. *See also under* Web
    mail server, 54
    navigating, 99–105
    searching, 116–118
    start (origin) of, 94
Internet Explorer
    closing, 124
    dialog boxes. *See* dialog boxes, Internet Explorer
    screen elements, 97–98
    starting/opening, 96
Internet Options dialog box (Internet Explorer), 98
Internet Service Providers (ISPs), 96
ISP (Internet Service Provider), 96
Italic button (Formatting toolbar)
    Excel, 685, 687, 695
    PowerPoint, 1097, 1105
    Word, 209–210, 296

J-K

Justify button (Word), 249, 430
justifying text, 248, 1104

Keep source formatting (check box), 1045
keyboard indicator area, 505
keyboards, 143–144
    navigating documents, 178
    selecting text, 204–205
keyboard shortcuts
    Access, navigating records, 791
    Excel
        bold, 685
        Clear Contents command, 549
        Copy command, 606, 635
        displayed values, 640
        entering dates, 544
        formatting cells, 673
        italic, 685
        new workbook, 536
        Paste, 635
        underline, 685
        Undo, 548
    Outlook
        closing Outlook, 59
        creating contacts, 61
        opening New Appointment window, 72
    PowerPoint
        Change Case, 1103–1104
        changing font styles, 1097
        Copy, 1061
        Cut, 1059
        inserting new slides, 1051
        menu commands, 974
        navigating between placeholders, 1051
        New command, 973
        New Slide, 1045
        repeating last command or keystrokes, 1098
    starting commands, 507
    Word
        cutting/copying/pasting text, 257
        navigating documents, 178
        text formatting, 209
keystrokes, 179. *See also* **nonprinting characters**
kilobytes (KB), 143, 149

L

Label button (Access Toolbox toolbar), 838, 848
label controls, in Design view of forms, 840, 842
landscape orientation, 641–642, 699, 701, 781
    Print Preview toolbar (PowerPoint), 1004
    reports, 854
LANs (local area networks), 155–156
laptop computers, 139, 143

laser mouse, 145
laser printers, 148
LAST aggregate function, 939
Last Record button (Access), 791, 823, 829
laws, copyright, 457
layouts
    changing
        document and paragraph, 246–257
        slides, 988–991
    master slides
        slide master, 1110–1112
        title master, 1110–1111
    placeholders. *See* placeholders
    predefined, 989
        tables, 384–385
left alignment
    cell data, 538, 603
    text, 248, 1104
left mouse button, 10–11
left scroll arrow, 520
Left Tab button (Word), 355
Left tab stops. *See* **tabs**
less than (<) comparison operator, 922–924
Like term in SQL, 914
lines
    changing spacing between, 250–252
    selecting, 206
links, 105–109, 1007. *See also* **hyperlinks**
    unavailable, 118
Linux operating system, 151
lists
    bulleted, 983–985, 1114–1118
    creating/modifying, 271–278
    formatting, 274–275
    modifying, 271–278
    numbered, 1118–1119
local area networks (LANs), 155–156
locating and replacing text, 1046–1047
locating supporting information, 451–462
logical operators, 925
logical processing, 142
losing work, 191–192
Lotus software, 153–154
low-quality copy, 148

M

Macintosh computers, 142, 151
Mail module (Outlook)
    default setup, 54
    folders, 57–58
    Navigation pane, 55–58
mail servers, 54
mainframe computers, 94, 138
Make available offline check box, 114
manual column breaks, inserting, 428
margins, 169, 246
    changing, 247
    header and footer, 708
    setting, 247, 701–702

master slides
    slide master, 1110–1112
    title master, 1110–1111
mastheads, 420
    creating decorative, 422–427
Match case (check box), 1047
mathematical operators, 552–553
MAX aggregate function, 939, 941–942
Maximize button
    Access, 751, 761–762
    Excel, 511
Maximize/Restore Down button (Word), 169
maximizing
    database window, 751–752
    windows, 18–22
megabytes (MB), 143, 149
megahertz (MHz), 142
memory, 142–143
    RAM chips, 141
    RAM slots, 141
menu bar, 8, 169, 171
    Access window, 745–746
    Edit menu commands, 697
    Excel, 505
        toolbars available, 508
    Favorites, 97
        MSN.com, 97
    File menu commands, 708
    Format menu commands, Cells, 673
    Start, Internet, 97
    Tools, Internet Options, 97
menus, 8, 970. *See also* **commands; specific menu names**
    accessing commands, 171–175, 973–974
    command characteristics, 174, 508, 974
    displaying full menus, 507, 973
    My Recent Documents, 11
    shortcuts, 9–10, 973. *See also* keyboard shortcuts
        in worksheet, 516–518
    toolbar buttons. *See* toolbars
Merge and Center command (Excel), 603–604, 624
Merge Cells command (Table menu, Word), 386
merging cells, 603–604, 689
messages
    delivery, 59
    envelopes, 55–56
    warning
        Confirm File Rename, 743
        Security Warning, 749
        There is no primary key defined, 772
microcomputers, 138
microphones, 146, 149
microprocessors, 141
Microsoft Help system. *See* **help**
Microsoft Office. *See* **Office**

Microsoft software
    Access, 153. *See also* Access
    communications and organization, 154
    database, 153
    Excel, 152. *See also* Excel
    Office, 151
    Outlook, 154. *See also* Outlook
    PhotoEditor, 154
    PowerPoint, 153. *See also* PowerPoint
    presentations, 153
    suites, 154
    Word, 152. *See also* Word
Microsoft Word outlines, importing, 1054–1055
.mil (in URLs), 101
MIN aggregate function, 939, 941–942
minicomputers, 138
Minimize button
    Access, 750
    Excel, 511
    Word, 169
minimizing
    Access window, 750–751
    windows, 18–22
misspelled words. *See* **spelling and grammar checkers**
module buttons, 55–56
modules, 53
monitors, 147
motherboard, 140–141
Motorola® processors, 142
mouse, 143, 145, 171
    cut and paste, 33–34
    moving cursor using keyboard shortcuts, 178
    right-clicking, 8–9, 168, 976
    selecting
        multiple files, 31
        text, 204–205
    using wheel button, 177
mouse pointer, 6, 505, 517, 844. *See also* **pointers**
    crosshair, 344
    diagonal two-headed arrows, 14
    double-headed arrow, 596, 598
    dragging and releasing, 514
    four-headed arrow pointer, 346
    I-beam, 630. *See also* I-beam pointer
    magnifying glass, 67
    pointing to hyperlinks, 98
    resize pointer, 370
    right-clicking, 516
    Select Column black arrow, 512
    Select Row black arrow, 512
    white cross, 596
Move or Copy dialog box (Excel), 609
Move or Copy Sheet command (Edit menu, Excel), 609

moving. *See also* **copying**
   cell contents with Cut command, 614–616
   files, 27–34, 977
   graphic objects, 343–344
   mouse cursor, keyboard shortcuts, 178
   placeholders, 1108
   slides, 986–987, 996
   tab stops, 362–364
   text, 1056–1058
     scroll bars, 169
     using Clipboard, 1059–1063
     using collect and paste, 1062–1063
     using drag-and-drop, 1056–1058
   text boxes, 346–347
   to headers or footers, 189
   windows, 14–18
multicolumn text
   creating, 428–433
   formatting, 429–430
multimedia, 146
   buttons, 144
   input devices, 146
   keyboards, 143
   output devices, 147, 149
   projectors, 149
multiple files, selecting, 31
multitasking, 138
.mus (in URLs), 101
My Computer icon, 6
My Computer window (Windows XP), 14
   Maximize button, 18, 20
   Minimize button, 20
   Restore Down button, 19
My Recent Documents menu, 11

N

Name Box, 505, 538
   navigating with, 520–521
names. *See also* **Contacts module (Outlook)**
   renaming files, 978
   spaces and underscores in file names, 979
naming
   files, 743
     restrictions, 34
   folders, 191
navigating
   between placeholders, 1051
   documents
     using keyboard, 178
     using vertical scroll bar, 175–177
   Next Slide button (PowerPoint), 970–971
   Previous Slide button (PowerPoint), 970–971
   scroll bar and scroll box, 970
   scrolling in Slide pane, 971
   tables, 368
   the Internet, 99–105
   to records
     in tables, 790–792
     using a form, 822–824
   to specific dates, 69
   using object elements, 463
   Word window, 165–178
navigation area, results from query, 899
Navigation pane
   banner, 56
   Contacts module, 60, 66, 69–71
   Mail module, 55–58
.net (in URLs), 101
networking, 96. *See also* **computer networks**
New Appointment dialog box (Outlook), 71
New Blank Document button (Word), 196
New button
   Database toolbar (Access), 766
   Excel, 509, 535
New command (File menu)
   Access, Folder, 742
   Excel, 536
   Outlook, Appointment, 72
   PowerPoint
     presentation, 1038
     Slide, 1045
   Windows XP, 23
new documents, creating/editing, 194–203
New File task pane, 766
New Folder dialog box
   Excel, 531
   PowerPoint, 978
   Word, 191
new folders, creating, 22–26, 121
New Form dialog box (Access), 825
New Form wizards, 825
New Object AutoForm button (Access), 827
New Presentation task pane, 1038, 1050
New Record button (Access), 824, 828
New Slide button (PowerPoint Formatting toolbar), 1045, 1111
new text, inserting, 202–203
New Workbook task pane, 536
Next button (Excel), 530, 700
Next Record button (Access), 760, 791, 829
Next Sentence (grammar) button (Word), 186
Next Slide button (PowerPoint), 970–971, 1000, 1041
nonadjacent slides, selecting, 994–995
nonprinting characters, 179, 381, 439
Normal view
   PowerPoint, 981, 987, 993, 1040, 1110, 1114
   Word, 180, 439
notebook computers, 139
Notes and Handouts tab (Header and Footer), 1000–1001
Notes module (Outlook)
   Notes folder, 75, 78
   recording notes, 75–78
   storing notes, 53

notes pages, 999
    adding headers and footers, 1000–1001
    adding notes in Notes pane, 994
    printing, 1005–1006
    speaker's notes, 992–994
Notes pane, 967
    adding notes, 994
    resizing, 993
notes. *See* **notes pages**
nudging objects in Design view of reports, 859, 863
Number (numeric) data types, 769
    as criteria in queries, 921
numbered lists, 272–273. *See also* **bulleted lists**
    applying numbering, 1118–1119
    changing start number, 1119
    creating, 1119
Numbering button (Formatting toolbar)
    PowerPoint, 1118
    Word, 272
numbers
    changing formats, 670–675
    entering in cell, 542–543
    formatting with
        Format Cells dialog box, 670–674
        toolbar, 618–622
numeric keypad, 144
    entering numbers with, 542–543

O

objects, 750, 752
    finding, 463–466
Objects bar (Access)
    Forms, 759
    in database window, 749–750, 752
    Queries, 758, 894
    Reports, 761
    Tables, 752
Office (Microsoft), 151
Office Assistant, 215, 793, 1008
    turning off, 171
Office Clipboard, 257, 261, 451
Office Clipboard command (Edit menu)
    Excel, 604, 608
    Word, 452
Office Clipboard task pane, 265
Omit background graphics from master (check box), 1125
One Field Back button (Access), 851
One Field button (Access), 834, 851
Open button (Standard toolbar)
    Access, 746, 752, 822
    Excel, 509
    PowerPoint, 980
    Word, 246, 271, 354, 422, 441, 451, 454

Open command (File menu)
    Access, 748
    PowerPoint, 966
Open dialog box
    Access, 748
    Excel, 509, 672, 699, 710
    PowerPoint, 968, 980
    Word, 170, 246, 271, 334, 354, 422, 441
opening
    databases, 744–749
    Internet Explorer, 96–98
    Open button. *See* Open button (Standard toolbar)
    Outline/Slides pane, 986
    Outlook, 54
        Mail module, 54
        New Appointment window, 72–73
    panes, 976
    PowerPoint, 966
    presentations, 966, 968
    queries, 900–901
    tables, 752–756, 776–777
operating systems software, 150–151
operators, 892
    comparison, 922–924
    logical, 925
    mathematical, 552–553
optical travel mouse, 145
option buttons, 555
    spelling and grammar, 186
option names, gray, 174
Options command (Tools menu)
    Excel, 506, 540
    PowerPoint, 973
    Word, 266, 344
Options dialog box
    Excel, 506, 540–541, 640
    PowerPoint, 991
    Word, 183, 186
.org (in URLs), 101
OR logical operator, 925–927
order of operations, 552
Organize clips (Clip Art task pane), 335
Organize Favorites dialog box (Internet Explorer), 114
Other Task Panes button (PowerPoint), 976–977
Outline/Slides pane, 967, 971, 981, 986
Outline tab, 966–967, 971, 981
    creating new slides, 984
    editing text, 982
    entering text, 982
    modifying AutoContent suggested text, 1040–1043
    selecting text, 982, 1042
Outline view, 180

outlines and outline levels, 981, 983–985. *See also* **Outline tab**
    creating new slides, 984
    Decrease Indent button, 984
    importing Microsoft Word outlines, 1054–1055
    Increase Indent button, 983
    promoting and demoting text, 983–985
Outlook, 154
    closing, 59
    commands. *See* commands, Outlook
    dialog boxes. *See* dialog boxes, Outlook
    keyboard shortcuts
        closing Outlook, 59
        creating contacts, 61
        opening New Appointment window, 72
    opening
        Mail module, 54
        New Appointment window, 72–73
    screen elements, 54–56
    title bar
        Close button, 59
        Maximize button, 54
    toolbars
        Print Preview, 66–67
        Standard. See Standard toolbar, Outlook
output, 137
output devices, 147–149
    monitors, 147
    multimedia output devices, 147, 149
    printers, 148
overtype mode, 202–203
    in worksheet, 547

P

page breaks, 431
Page Footer
    adding to forms, 848–849
    reports, 862–863
    reports created by Report Wizard, 853–854
Page Header, in reports created by Report Wizard, 853–854
Page Header/Footer command (View menu, Access), 848. *See also* **Header and Footer command (View menu)**
page names in Web site directories, 101
page numbers
    headers and footers, 279–280
    in report footers, 862
page orientation
    changing, 641–642
    selecting, 699–701
Page Setup command (File menu)
    Access, 854
    Excel, 641
Page Setup dialog box
    Access, 782, 830, 854
    Excel, 526, 528, 538, 590, 641, 699–701, 707, 710
    Word, 199–200, 247, 279

Pagemaker® (Adobe), 154
pages
    headers and footers. *See* headers and footers
    inserting breaks, 431
    removing blank, 439
pane dividers (Outlook), 55–56
panes. *See also* **task panes**
    Notes pane, 967
    opening and closing, 976
    Outline/Slides pane, 967, 971, 981, 986
    resizing, 993
    scrolling, 971
    Search, 116
    Slide pane, 967
paper size, selecting, 699–701
paperclip, 793
Paradox® (Corel), 153
Paragraph dialog box (Word), 252–254, 274–275, 298, 362
paragraphs
    adding
        shading, 435
        space after, 252–254
        special formatting, 433
    aligning, 248–249
    changing layouts, 246–257
    formatting, 274
    indenting, 255
    line spacing, 250–252
    selecting, 206
passwords, 7
Paste All button (Excel), 608
Paste button
    Excel, 605
    PowerPoint, 1061
    Word, 262–263, 265
Paste Options button (Excel), 605, 607
Paste Options menu, 263
Paste Options smart tag, 291, 1057–1060
Paste Special command (Excel), 606
pasting. *See also* **copying; cut and paste**
    copying text
        Copy button (PowerPoint Standard toolbar), 1061
        using Clipboard, 1061–1062
    cutting and pasting, 261–265
    formatting pasted text, 1058–1060
    keyboard shortcuts, 257
    moving text
        using Clipboard, 1059–1063
        using drag-and-drop, 1056–1058
    multiple times, 265
    workbook data into another workbook, 610–614
paths in URLs, 101
Peachtree® Accounting, 154
pencil image, in database tables, 755–756
Pentium processors, 142

people. *See* Contacts module (Outlook)
Percent Style button (Excel), 620–621, 674
Period key, 361
peripherals, 140
personal digital assistants (PDAs), 139
Personal Folders, 57–58
phone numbers. *See* Contacts module (Outlook)
photo albums, creating presentations, 1038
PhotoEditor (Microsoft), 154
Photoshop® (Adobe), 154
Picture Bullet dialog box (PowerPoint), 1116
picture bullets, 1116–1117
Picture button (PowerPoint), 1116
Picture command (Format menu, Word), 339–340
Picture command (Insert menu, Word), 335, 452
pictures
   headers and footers created with inserted, 703–704, 706–708
   inserting, 334–338
   modifying, 338, 340–351
   moving, 343–344
pixels, 147
placeholders, 988. *See also* wildcard characters
   AutoContent suggested content, 1041
   boundary boxes
      diagonal slash marks, 1105
      dotted pattern, 1105
      four-headed arrow, 1108
      sizing handles, 1106
   creating new slides, 1051
   modifying, 1105–1109
   moving, 1108
   navigating between placeholders, 1051
   resizing, 1106, 1118
   selecting placeholder text, 1105
   selecting placeholders, 1106
   text alignment in placeholders, 1104, 1118
plus (+) signs, folder pane, 27–34
plus sign and letter A pointer, 839
point (pt.), 207, 596, 684, 1094–1095
point and click, for entering cell references in formula, 551, 553
point size. *See* fonts
pointers, 6. *See also* mouse pointers
   four-headed arrow, 1108
   hand, on control borders, 842–843, 845
   I-beam. *See* I-beam pointer
   pointing hand, 844
   plus sign and letter A, 839
   pointing hand, 844
   resizing arrows, 1106
   Select Column black arrow, 512
   Select Row black arrow, 512
   selecting rows, 516

pop-up windows, 105
populate a table, 767
portals, 98
Portrait button (PowerPoint Print Preview toolbar), 1005
portrait orientation, 641–642, 699, 701, 781
positioning. *See* moving
posting files to Web sites, 101
PowerPoint, 153
   commands. *See* commands, PowerPoint
   defaults, 981
   dialog boxes. *See* dialog boxes, PowerPoint
   exiting, 980
   help, 1007–1008
   keyboard shortcuts
      Change Case, 1103–1104
      changing font styles, 1097
      Copy, 1061
      Cut, 1059
      inserting new slides, 1051
      menu commands, 974
      navigating between placeholders, 1051
      New command, 973
      New Slide, 1045
      repeating last command or keystrokes, 1098
   parts of PowerPoint window, 967–972
   presentations. *See* presentations
   slides. *See* slides
   starting, 966
   toolbars
      Drawing, 970
      Formatting. See *Formatting toolbar*
      Print Preview, 1004–1005
      Slide Master, 1110
      Standard. See *Standard toolbar*
predefined formats
   applying to tables, 384–385
   presentations, 989
Presentation options step, AutoContent Wizard, 1039–1040
presentation outline. *See* outlines and outline levels
presentation software, 153
Presentation type step, AutoContent Wizard, 1039
presentations. *See also* slide shows
   checking spelling, 991–992
   closing, 979–980
   creating, 1037
      from design templates, 1038
      from existing presentations, 1038
      from photo albums, 1038
      using AutoContent Wizard, 1038–1040
      using design templates, 1050–1052
   design guidelines
      color, 1092
      text, 1092
   editing, 980–987
   ending slide shows, 998

final slides, 998
opening, 966, 968
printing, 1002–1006
Presentations® (Corel), 153
previewing
  animation effects, 1126
  documents, 210–213
    as Web pages, 447–449
  Print Preview button (PowerPoint Standard toolbar), 1004
  printed presentations, 1004
  slide shows, 997–998
Previous button (Excel), 700
Previous Record button (Access), 823
Previous Slide button (PowerPoint), 970–971
primary key, 772–773
primary sort field, 790
Print button, 193, 351, 530, 697
  Access
    in Access Help window, 795
    Database toolbar, 831, 910, 916–917, 927, 932
    Print Preview toolbar, 849, 864
    queries, 910
    reports, 763
    Standard toolbar, 780
  Excel, Print Preview toolbar, 708
  PowerPoint, Print Preview toolbar, 1004–1005
  Standard toolbar, 193
  Word
    Print Preview toolbar, 388
Print command (File menu)
  Access, 780, 910
  Outlook, 67
  PowerPoint, 1002, 1005, 1048
Print dialog box
  Access, 780, 795
  Excel, 558
  Internet Explorer, 122
  PowerPoint, 1003, 1006
  Outlook, 66, 68, 74
  Word, 193, 213
Print Layout view, 180–181, 433, 439
Print Preview button
  Access (Form View toolbar), 849
  Excel, 529, 641–642, 691, 699, 710–711
  PowerPoint (Standard toolbar), 1004
  Word, 199–200, 209, 211, 351, 388, 431
Print Preview command (File menu, Excel), 558
Print Preview toolbar
  Access
    Print button, 849, 864
    View button, 853
  Excel
    Close button, 530, 691, 700
    Margins button, 702
    Next button, 530, 700

    Previous button, 700
    Print button, 642, 697, 708
    Setup button, 701, 707
    Zoom button, 558
  Outlook, 66–67, 74
  PowerPoint
    Landscape button, 1004
    Portrait button, 1005
    Print button, 1005
  Word
    Close button, 431
    Print button, 193, 388
Print Preview window, 1004
print quality, setting, 710–711
printers, 148
printing
  appointments, 69
  calendars, 74
  contacts, 60, 66–68
  documents, 193, 210–213
  grayscale copies, 1003
  gridlines and row and column headings, 710–711
  handouts, 1002–1006
  notes pages, 1005–1006
  previewing printed presentation, 1004
  Print Preview button. *See* Print Preview button
  query results, 910
  reports, 761–764, 864
  slides, 1002–1006
  tables, 780–782
  underlying formulas, 640–641
  Web pages, 122–123
printouts. *See* **printing**
processors, 141–142
programs, shortcut buttons, 169
projecting slide shows, 997–998
promoting text in outlines, 983–985
Properties button (Access), 781
Properties dialog box (Access), 743, 781
Publisher (Microsoft), 154
publishing programs, 154

Q

QuarkXPress™, 154
quarters (year division), 601
QuattroPro® (Corel), 152
queries, 892, 894
  adding all fields, 897–898
  calculated fields, 934–939
  creating, 894–898
  criteria
    compound, 925–927
    from field not in query result, 918–920
    numeric, 921
    text, 904–909
    with comparison operators, 922–924
    with wildcard characters, 912–917

design modification, 928–930, 932
grouping data, 939–940
opening, 900–901
printing results, 910
removing fields from table, 901–903
running, saving, and closing, 899–900
sorting data
    with multiple fields, 928–930, 932
    with single field, 927–928
switching between views, 900–901
viewing, 758–759

Queries object, 758
Query Datasheet toolbar (Access)
Sort Ascending button, 927
Sort Descending button, 928
View button, 901, 903, 914–915, 919–920, 923
Query Design toolbar (Access)
Run button, 899, 903–905, 908, 915, 920–921, 924, 927, 931, 936–941
Totals button, 940
question mark (?) wildcard, 916–917
questions. *See also* **help**
Type a question for help box, 213, 1007
Quick Launch toolbar (Windows XP), 6
QuickBooks, 154

R

ragged right alignment, 248, 429
random access memory (RAM), 141–142
ranges (cells), 514
Read button (Word), 181
read only memory (ROM), 142
Read-Only
attribute on databases, 743–744
files, 525
status, removing from a file, 35
Reading Layout view, 180–181
Reading pane, 55–56
recognizers, 197
record selector in forms, 830
recording
AutoCorrect entries, 283–286
AutoText, 288–290
tasks and notes, 75–78
records
adding to tables, 774–775
    using forms, 828–829
changing information, 782–783
deleting from tables, 783–784
    using forms, 829–831
editing, 782–783
in a form, 760
in database tables, 754

navigating
    and viewing using forms, 822–824
    using keyboard, 791–792
    using navigation area, 790
Records menu commands (Access)
Remove Filter/Sort, 790
recovering deleted files, 34
Recycle bin, 6
red wavy underline, 991–992
Redo button (Standard toolbar)
Excel, 548
PowerPoint, 1048
Word, 268
Redo command (Edit menu)
Excel, 548
Word, 268–269
redoing edits, 1048
reference cell, 550
reference pages, creating, 297–300
Reference, Footnote command (Insert menu, Word), 293–295
references, inserting, 292–300
relative cell reference, 633–635
Remove Filter/Sort command (Records menu, Access), 790
removing
blank pages, 439
characters, 202
tab stops, 357–359
Rename command (Excel), 524–525
renaming
databases, 742–744
files, 27–34, 978
folders, 25–26, 532
sheet tabs, 524
reordering slides, 986–987, 996
reorganizing text, 257–269
Replace All button (PowerPoint), 1047
Replace button (PowerPoint), 1047
Replace command (Edit menu)
PowerPoint, 1046
Word, 258
Replace dialog box (PowerPoint), 1046
Replace Fonts dialog box (PowerPoint), 1095
replacing text, 257–259, 1046–1047. *see also* **editing text**
Report Design toolbar (Access), View button, 854
Report Footer, 862–863
Report view, 853
Report Wizard (Access), 850–852
reports, 761, 820
creating with Report Wizard, 850–852
Design view, 853–855
ease of use, 820
moving and resizing fields in Design view, 855–862
Page and Report Footers, 862–863

1240 Office Brief | Index

printing, 761–764, 864
Report view, 853
saving, 853
viewing, 761–764
Reports button (Access), 761
repositioning. *See* **copying; moving**
Research task pane, 455, 457, 462
Research tool, 455–458
resize pointer, 370
resizing
columns and rows, 784–786
fields in forms, 841–847
fields in reports, 855–862
graphic objects, 341–342
panes, 993
placeholders, 1106, 1118
text boxes, 346–347
windows, 14–18
resolution, monitors, 147
Restore button (Access), 850
Restore Window button (Excel), 752, 764
restoring windows, 18–22
restrictions
file names, 34
search, 39–40
right alignment
cell data, 542, 602–603
text, 248, 429, 1104
right arrow (▸), menus, 174, 519
Right Tab button (Word), 355
Right tab stops. *See* **tabs**
right-clicking, 8–9, 168, 976
cut and paste, 33–34
in worksheet, 516, 518
selecting multiple files, 31
right-pointing arrows in database tables, 753
ring network, 155
roadmap, AutoContent Wizard, 1038
ROM (read only memory), 142
rotate handles, 341
rotating text, 681–682
Row Height dialog box
Access, 786
Excel, 679
rows
adding, 368–370
database tables, 753–754
headings, 511
printing, 710
height
adjusting, 596, 598–599
resizing, 784–786
inserting and deleting, 599–601
selecting, 512
row selector in database tables, 755
Rows command (Insert menu, Excel), 599
ruler, 169
Ruler command (View menu, Access), 839

rulers
Design view of forms, 839
height, 341
rules, grammar, 186
Run button (Access Query Design toolbar), 899, 903–905, 908, 915, 920–921, 924, 927, 931, 936–941
running queries, 899–901

S

sans serif fonts, 206–207, 684–688
Save As command (File menu)
Excel, 530, 591
PowerPoint, 977, 1094
Word, 190, 246
Save As dialog box
Access, 827, 900, 905, 915, 917, 926–927, 943
Excel, 530–532, 536–537, 591, 672, 699
PowerPoint, 977
Word, 190, 200, 246, 271, 334, 354, 422, 448
Save As Web Page command (File menu, Word), 448
Save button (Excel), 536
Save in box, 767
saving
AutoForms, 827
databases, 792
documents, 190–192
as Web pages, 447–449
new workbook, 536
queries, 899–900
reports, 853
tables, 771, 775–776
Web pages, 119–121
Make Available Offline, 114
workbooks, 534
scaling, selecting, 699–701
scanners, 146
scheduling
appointments in calendar, 69–74
dates for events, 53
screen elements, 98, 169
Access, 745–746, 749–750
Excel, 503–505, 510–511
Internet Explorer, 97–98
Outlook, 54–56
Calendar module, 70
Contact form (Contacts module), 62
Contacts module, 60–61
PowerPoint, 967–972
Windows XP, 6
Word, 167–169
ScreenTips, 8–9, 176–177, 971
Access
Open, 746
Zoom, 762

Index | **Office Brief** **1241**

Excel
- *AutoFill Options button, 593*
- *AutoSum function, 554*
- *Borders button, 692*
- *buttons without, 527*
- *column width information, 596*
- *command activation, 509*
- *displaying, 509*
- *displaying months, 593*
- *Insert Options button, 600*
- *moving cell contents, 616*
- *pixel counts, 596, 598–599*
- *Trace Error, 631, 636*
- *workbook name, 535*

PowerPoint
- *buttons, 976*
- *color palette, 1099*
- *Custom Color, 1100*
- *Formatting toolbar, 976*
- *Paste Options smart tag, 1058*
- *Slide Master View, 1110, 1114*

Word
- *AutoComplete, 196*
- *AutoCorrect, 290*
- *line spacing, 251*
- *Paste Options, 262*
- *Set Hyperlink, 442*
- *tab selection, 354*
- *tab type, 363*
- *WordArt, 424*

scroll arrows, 511, 519
scroll bar, 511, 970
- navigating worksheets, 518, 520
- vertical/horizontal, 169, 175–177, 519

scroll boxes, 17–18, 169, 511, 519, 970
scrolling, 14–18
- in Slide pane, 971

Search Companion, 116
search engines, 116
Search in box, 335
Search pane, 116
Search Results task pane
- Access, 793
- Excel, 560
- PowerPoint, 1007
- Word, 214

Search, in Help system, 793
searching. *See also* **finding text**
- for and replacing text, 1046–1047
- for contacts, 63
- for files, 35–39
- the Internet, 116–118

secondary sort field, 790
Security Warning message, 749. *See also* **messages, warning**
Select All, worksheets, 511, 518
Select All Sheets command (Excel), 590, 618, 641, 699
Select Browse Object button (Word), 463–465

Select Cell command (Table menu, Word), 378
Select Column black arrow, 512
select queries, 894
Select Query window, 894–897
Select Row black arrow, 512
Select Table command (Table menu, Word), 388
selecting. *See also* **highlighting**
- and formatting text, 204–210
- consecutive lines/paragraphs, 206
- multiple files, 31
- paper size, 600–701
- slides, 994–995
- tab stop marks, 363
- text, 204–206, 259–260. *See also* text, selecting
  - entire bullet points, 1056
  - entire lines, 1096
  - in outlines, 982, 1042
  - placeholder text, 1105

sending
- files to floppy drives, 31
- messages, 59

Sentence Case option, 1103
sentences
- selecting, 206
- spacing at end, 198

separator characters, 381
- between columns, 383

series, creating with AutoFill, 592–594
serif fonts, 206–207, 684–688
server, 155
Server Connection dialog box (Outlook), 54
servers, 96
Set Hyperlink ScreenTip dialog box (Word), 442–445
Set Page Title dialog box (Word), 448–449
settings
- History options, 111
- home pages, 111
- Internet options, 111

Setup button (Excel)
- Print dialog box, 782
- Print Preview toolbar, 701, 707

shading
- adding to paragraphs, 435
- applying to cells, 375–376, 693

Shadow button (PowerPoint Formatting toolbar), 1096
sheet tabs
- renaming, 524
- workbook, 511
- worksheet, 522–523

shift key, 192
short menu, 746–747
shortcut menus
- Access, Properties, 743
- Excel
  - *Clear Contents, 603*
  - *Delete, 599, 601*

1242 Office Brief | Index

    formatting cells, 673, 675–676, 678
    Hide Comments, 713
    Insert, 599–600, 608
    Insert Comment, 712
    Paste Special, 606
    Rename command, 524–525
    Row Height, 679
    Select All Sheets, 525, 529, 537
    worksheets, 516–518
  PowerPoint
    Copy, 1061
    Cut, 1059
    spelling, 991–992
  Windows XP
    Format, 23
    sending files to floppy drives, 31
  Word
    Add Text, 351
    Edit Hyperlink, 445
    Format AutoShape, 349
    Synonyms, 462
    table alignment, 387
    Toolbars, 344
shortcuts. *See also* **keyboard shortcuts; shortcut menus**
  AutoCorrect, 286–288
  AutoFill, 590
  Internet Explorer
    Favorites menu, 98
    Standard Buttons toolbar, 98
  keyboard, 172, 178
    cutting/copying/pasting text, 257
Show check box, 919
Show Table dialog box, 894–895, 906, 912, 916, 918, 925, 939
Show/Hide ¶ button (Word Standard toolbar), 179, 196, 246, 271–272, 334, 381, 438–439, 441
side-sizing handles, 341
single-spaced paragraphs, 250
size of fonts. *See* **fonts, size**
sizing
  Access window, 745–746, 749
  database window, 749–750
  graphic objects, 341–342
  handles, 339, 341, 1106
    on label box in Design view of forms, 840
  images, 338
Slide Design button (PowerPoint Formatting toolbar), 1120
Slide Design task pane, 1050, 1052–1053
Slide Finder dialog box (PowerPoint), 1044–1045, 1052
slide handouts. *See* **handouts**
slide icon, 981
Slide Layout command (Format menu, PowerPoint), 1045
Slide Layout task pane, 988–991

slide master, 1110–1114
slide numbers
  displayed in ScreenTips, 971
  in Outline pane, 981
Slide pane, 967
  editing text, 987–988, 990
  formatting text, 987–988
  scrolling, 971
Slide Show button (PowerPoint), 997
slide shows, 997–998. *See also* **presentations**
  animation. *See* animation effects
  ending slide shows, 998
  final slides, 998
  transitions, 997–998
  viewing, 997–998
Slide Sorter view, 994–996
  deleting slides, 996
  moving slides, 996
  selecting slides, 994–995
Slide Sorter View button (PowerPoint), 995–996, 1043, 1063
Slide tab (Header and Footer), 999
slide titles
  balancing visually, 990
  capitalizing, 990
  displayed in ScreenTips, 971
  promoting bulleted items, 984–985
slides
  adding headers and footers, 999–1000
  black slides, 998
  changing design templates
    for a single slide, 1052–1053
    for entire presentation, 1053–1054
    for selected slides, 1054
  changing slide layouts, 988–991
  creating
    from imported outline, 1054–1055
    promoting bulleted items, 984
    title slides, 984, 1053
    using Ctrl+Enter keyboard shortcut, 1051
    using New Slide button, 1045
  deleting
    in Slide Sorter view, 996
    in Slides tab, 985
    unnecessary AutoContent slides, 1043
  editing. *See* editing text
  formatting. *See also* design templates
    applying animation schemes, 1126–1127
    applying color schemes, 1120–1121
    backgrounds, 1122–1124
    changing slide layouts, 988–991
    final slides in presentations, 998
    inserting existing slides, 1045
    Slide Design button (Formatting toolbar), 1120
    slide master, 1110–1112
    title master, 1110–1111

inserting
- *existing slides, 1044–1045*
- *new slides, 1045–1046, 1051*

moving, 986–987, 996

printing, 1002–1006

selecting
- *deselecting slides, 995*
- *multiple slides, 994–995*

title slide, 969

Slides from Files command (Insert menu, PowerPoint), 1057

Slides from Outlines command (Insert menu, PowerPoint), 1055

Slides tab, 967, 981
- deleting slides, 985
- moving slides, 986–987
- reordering slides, 986–987
- selecting slides, 994–995

small caps, 437–438

smart tags, 262, 594, 1057
- Auto Fill Options button (Excel), 593
- AutoCorrect Options, 285, 297
- Paste Options, 291
- Trace Error, 630

software, 150–154. *See also under* **software application titles**
- accounting software, 154
- application software, 150–154
- communications software, 149, 154
- systems software, 150

Sort Ascending button (Access Query Design toolbar), 789–790, 927

Sort Descending button (Access Query Design toolbar), 928

Sort Text dialog box (Word), 299

sorting
- data
  - *with multiple fields in queries, 928–930, 932*
  - *with single field, 927–928*
- files, 27
- records in tables, 789–790

spaces in file names, 743, 979

spacing
- after paragraphs, 252–254
- around graphic objects, 338
- changing line, 250–252
- end of sentences, 198

speaker's notes, 992–994
- adding in Notes pane, 994
- notes pages, 999
  - *adding headers and footers, 1000–1001*
  - *printing, 1005–1006*

speakers, 149

Special Characters tab, 291

special effects
- animation effects
  - *applying animation schemes, 1126–1127*
  - *displaying in slide shows, 997–998*
  - *previewing, 1126*

fill effects
- *gradient fill backgrounds, 1122–1124*
- *omitting background graphics, 1125*
- *textured backgrounds, 1122–1125*

font effects, 1097

transitions, 997–998

special keys, 144

specifications, criteria for record query, 759

Spelling and Grammar button (Word), 185

spelling and grammar checkers, 183–187

Spelling and Style tab (Options, PowerPoint), 991

Spelling button (Standard toolbar)
- Excel, 557, 558
- PowerPoint, 992

spelling checker, 555–558, 991–992
- Change button (Word), 185
- Check spelling as you type, 991
- checking entire presentation, 992
- continuous spell checking, 991–992
- red wavy underline, 991–992
- Spelling button. *See* spelling button (Standard toolbar)
- Suggestions list, 557

Spelling dialog box (Excel), 557

spelling errors, 935

spreadsheets, 152. *See also* **worksheets**

SQL (Structured Query Language), 914

square brackets ([ ]), using calculated fields in queries, 934–935

Standard Buttons toolbar (Internet Explorer), 99–100
- Back, 99, 103, 106
- Favorites, 111–113
- Forward, 99, 103
- History, 110–111
- Home, 99, 104, 109
- Print, 122–123
- Search, 116–118

Standard Height check box, 786–787

standard mouse, 145

Standard toolbar, 56, 169, 970, 975
- Access
  - *Print button, 780*
- Excel, 505
  - *AutoSum button, 553, 623–628*
  - *Copy button, 605, 610*
  - *Cut button, 614*
  - *Font list, 685*
  - *Format Painter button, 695–696*
  - *New button, 509, 535*
  - *Paste button, 605*
  - *Print button, 530*
  - *Print Preview button, 529, 699, 711*
  - *Redo button, 548*
  - *Save button, 536*
  - *Spelling button, 557, 992*
  - *Zoom button, 556*

Internet Explorer
   Back, 99, 103, 106
   Favorites, 111–113
   Forward, 99, 103
   History, 110–111
   Home, 99, 104, 109
   Print, 122–123
   Search, 116–118
Outlook
   Day button (Calendar module), 71
   Month (Calendar module), 71
   New Appointment button (Calendar module), 72
   New Contact (Contacts module), 61
   Print (Contacts module, 66
   Save and Close button (Contacts module), 64–65
   Work Week button (Calendar module), 70
PowerPoint
   Copy button, 1061
   Cut button, 1059–1060
   Format Painter button, 1101–1103
   Help button, 1008
   Open button, 980
   Paste button 1061
   Print Preview button, 1004
   Redo button, 1048
   Undo button, 1048
Word
   Bold button, 209
   Close button, 200
   Columns button, 428
   Copy button, 454
   Cut button, 261, 263
   Drawing button, 344
   Format Painter button, 256–257
   Insert Hyperlink button, 442
   Insert Table button, 365
   Italic button, 209
   New Blank Document button, 196
   Open button, 170, 246, 271, 334, 354, 422, 441, 451, 454
   Paste button, 262–263, 265
   Print button, 66, 68, 193
   Print Preview button, 199–200, 209, 211, 351, 388, 431
   Read button, 181
   Redo button, 268
   Research button, 455
   Show/Hide ¶ button, 179, 196, 246, 271, 334, 381, 438–439, 441
   Spelling and Grammar button, 185
   Underline button, 209
   Undo button, 268, 342, 548, 615
   Zoom button arrow, 181–183, 247, 271, 346
star network, 155

Stars and Banners menu (Word), Horizontal Scroll banner button, 350
Start button, 4–5, 11, 166, 169, 502, 966
Start menu, 166, 744
starting
   Access, 744–745
   Excel, 502, 505
   Internet Explorer, 96–98
   Outlook, 54
   PowerPoint, 966
   programs, Quick Launch toolbar, 6
   Word, 166–169
statistical functions in queries, 939, 941–943
status area, Excel, 505
Status bar
   Access window, 745–746
   Outlook, 55–56
   PowerPoint, 970
   Windows XP, 8
   Word, 169
STDEV aggregate function, 939
storage, 137–138
   devices, 3–4, 149
   media, 143, 149
storing
   addresses, 60–65
   documents, 190–192
      Office Clipboard, 257
   e-mail messages, 57–59
   files, 3–4
   notes and tasks, 53
string expression, 914
Structured Query Language (SQL), 914
student files, 453–455
style of forms, 834
styles, applying font, 209–210
submenus, 11
suffixes in URLs, 101
Suggestions list in spelling checker, 557
SUM aggregate function, 939, 941–942
supercomputers, 138
supporting information, locating, 451–462
Switch Between Header and Footer button (Word Header and Footer toolbar), 188, 210, 269, 281, 338, 359, 430, 446
switching between views
   forms, 836, 840–841
   queries, 900–901
   reports, 853–855
   tables, 771
Symbol dialog box
   PowerPoint, 1115
   Word, 277–278, 291
symbols
   inserting, 290–292
   text, 271
   using as bullets, 276
System tray, 6

Index | **Office Brief** **1245**

system unit, 140–142
systems software, 150

T

tab scrolling buttons, 511
tab split box, 511
tab stops, 169, 332. *See also* tabs
table area, of Select Query window, 895
Table AutoFormat dialog box (Word), 384
Table Datasheet toolbar (Access), View button, 756–757, 773
Table Design toolbar (Access), 772
  View button, 757, 771
Table menu commands (Word)
  Convert, 382
  Insert, 369, 371
  Merge Cells, 386
  Select Cell, 378
  Select Table, 388
  Table AutoFormat, 384
  Table Properties, 380, 387
Table Properties command (Table menu, Word), 380, 387
Table Properties dialog box (Word), 380, 387
tables, 332, 744, 750
  adding
    columns, 371–372
    rows, 368–370
  adding records, 774–775
    using forms, 828–829
  applying predefined formats, 384–385
  centering, 380–381
  changing
    borders, 377–379
    column widths, 370–371
  closing, 775–776
  creating, 365–373, 767–771
    from existing text, 381–388
  deleting records using forms, 829–831
  formatting, 373–381
  merging cells, 385–388
  modifying design, 777–779
  moving between cells, 366–367
  navigating, 368
  opening, 752–756, 776–777
  printing, 780–782
  resizing columns and rows, 784–786
  saving, 771, 775–776
  shading cells, 375–376
  sorting records, 789–790
  switching between views, 771
  using tabs in, 373
  viewing, 756–758
tabs, 98
  alignment options, 353, 355–359, 361–364
  between columns, 383
  moving, 362–364

  setting, 354–356
  using in tables, 373
  versus indent, 362
Tabs dialog box (Word), 357–358
Tabs option button (Word), 382
task bar
  location, 6–7
  Start button, 54
  switching to other open workbooks, 611
Task form, 76–77
Task pane, 169, 171–175, 745
Task Pane command (View menu, PowerPoint), 976
task panes, 8, 967–968. *See also* panes
  Access window, 745–746
  button to activate, 976–977
  Clear All button (Excel), 609
  Clip Art, 335, 452
  Clipboard, 263, 452–453, 457–460, 604–605, 608
  Clipboard task pane, 1056–1058. *See also* Clipboard task pane
  Close button
    Excel, 503, 534, 561, 609, 614
    Word, 195
  Excel window, 502
  Help task pane, 1008
  Getting Started, 175, 195–196, 534–536, 590, 966
  New Blank Document, 196
  New Presentation task pane, 1038, 1050
  Office Clipboard, 265
  opening and closing, 976
  Research, 455, 457, 462
  Search Results task pane, 214, 560, 793, 1007
  Slide Design task pane, 1050, 1052–1053
  Slide Layout task pane, 988–991
Taskbar, 169, 970
TaskPad command (View menu, Outlook), 75–76
Tasks module (Outlook), 75
  recording, 75–78
  scheduling events, 53
  storing, 52
  Tasks folder, 75
templates. *See* design templates
text
  adding
    borders, 433–434
    emphasis, 209
  aligning, 248–249, 353
    in tables, 385–388
  changing/reorganizing, 257–269
  copying, 1056–1058
    and pasting, 264–265
    Copy button (PowerPoint Standard toolbar), 1061
    using Clipboard, 1061–1062

1246 Office Brief | Index

creating
  multicolumn, 428–433
  tables from, 381–388
cutting and pasting, 261–263
deleting, 1059–1061
deselecting, 272
design guidelines for presentations, 1092
editing, 201–202. *See also* editing text
entering
  into cell, 537, 540–541
  using tab stops, 359–362
finding/replacing, 257–259
formatting, 987–996, 1094. *See also* formatting
inserting
  frequently used, 283–290, 292
  new, 202–203
  text hyperlinks, 441–442
insertion point, 169
justification, 429
moving, 1056–1058
  multiple selections, 1062–1063
  using Clipboard, 1059–1063
  using collect and paste, 1062–1063
  using drag-and-drop, 1056, 1058
outlines. *See* outlines and outline levels
pasting. *See* pasting text
rotating, 681–682
selecting
  and deleting, 259–260
  and formatting, 204–210
  canceling, 206
  entire bullet points, 1056
  entire lines, 1096
  in outlines, 982, 1042
  placeholder text, 1105
wrapping, 682–683
Text Box button (Word), 344
text box control, on forms, 841–842
Text Box toolbar (Word), 345
text boxes, 344–345
  moving/resizing, 346–347
text case, changing, 1103–1104
text criteria in queries, 904–909
Text data type, 769
text symbols, 271
Texture tab (Fill Effects), 1124
textured backgrounds, 1122–1125
Thesaurus, 450–451, 461–462
thumbnails, 967, 981. *See also* **Slide Sorter view**
time, inserting in headers/footers, 281
Tips (help). *See* **help**
Title bar, 98, 169, 970
title bar
  Access, 745–746
  Excel, 505, 511
    Close button, 532, 561
    [Group], 613–614

Windows XP, 8
Word, 169
Title Case option, 1103
title slides, 969
  creating, 984, 1053
  title master, 1110–1111
titles, worksheets, 590
toggle buttons, 210, 687, 1096–1098
toggle switch, 273
toggling text case, 1103
toolbar buttons. *See* **buttons; toolbars**
toolbar names, 772
Toolbar Options
  Excel, 505, 508
  PowerPoint, 975
  Word, 169
toolbars, 8, 975
  Access
    Database. See Database toolbar
    Form Design. See Form Design toolbar
    Form View. See Form View toolbar
    Print Preview. See Print Preview toolbar
    Query Datasheet. See Query Datasheet toolbar
    Query Design. See Query Design toolbar
    Report Design. See Report Design toolbar
    Standard. See Standard toolbar
    Table Datasheet. See Table Datasheet toolbar
    Table Design. See Table Design toolbar
    Toolbox. See Toolbox toolbar
  buttons. *See* buttons
  Excel
    customizing, 508
    displayed list, 508
    formatting numbers with, 618–622
    Formatting. See Formatting toolbar
    Print Preview. See Print Preview toolbar
    Standard. See Standard toolbar
  Internet Explorer, Standard. *See* Standard toolbar
  Outlook
    Contact form, 62, 68
    Print Preview, 67, 74
    Standard. See Standard toolbar
  PowerPoint
    displaying, 976
    Drawing, 970
    Slide Master, 1110
    Standard. See Standard toolbar
  Windows XP, Quick Launch, 6
  Word
    Browser, Close button, 448
    Drawing, 332, 344
    Drawing Canvas, 347
    Formatting. See Formatting toolbar

*Header and Footer, 189, 300. See also
Header and Footer toolbar, Word
Print Preview. See Print Preview toolbar
printing documents from, 193
Standard. See Standard toolbar
Text Box, 345
View menu, 173
WordArt, 424–426*
Toolbars command (View menu, Word), 425
Toolbox command (View menu, Access), 839
Toolbox toolbar (Access)
    in forms Design view, 836–838
    Label button, 838, 848
Tools, Internet Options, 98
Tools menu commands
    Access
        Customize, 748
    Excel
        Customizing, 507
        Options, 506, 540, 640
    Word
        AutoCorrect Options, 283–288
        Customize, 172
        Options, 183, 266, 344
topography, 155–156
Total row, in query design, 939–940
touch-screen monitors, 147
Trace Error smart tag, 630–631, 636
Track Changes command (Word), 464
tracking sites. *See History list*
transitions, 997–998. *See also special effects*
triangle, menu command characteristic, 508, 974
TrueType fonts, 686
truncated value in cells, 592
Two page view, 182
Type a question for help box
    Access, 745–746, 794
    Excel, 559–561
    PowerPoint, 1007
    Word, 213
types of domains, 101
typing keypad, 144

U

unavailable
    links, 118
    menu command characteristic, 174, 508, 974
    toolbar buttons, 535
Underline button (Formatting toolbar)
    Excel, 685–687
    PowerPoint, 1097
    Word. 209–210
underline, red wavy, 991–992
underlying formulas, 550–551
    displaying and printing, 640–641
underscore key, 192

underscores in file names, 743, 979
Undo button (Standard toolbar)
    Excel, 548, 596, 615
    PowerPoint, 1048
    Word, 268, 342
Undo command (Edit menu)
    Excel, 548
    Word, 268–269
undoing edits, 1048
Ungroup Sheets command (Excel), 591
Unhide Columns dialog box (Access), 787–788
unread messages, identifying, 57
up arrows, 17, 176, 520
up-and-down-pointing arrow pointer, 1106
updating contacts, 66–68
uploading files, 101
Uppercase option, 1103
URLs (Uniform Resource Locators), 97, 101–105
    Favorites list, 111
USB ports, 144
Use advanced search options check box, 40
Use Current button (setting home pages, Internet Explorer), 98

V

value. *See constant value*
VAR aggregate function, 939
vertical alignment, cell contents, 679–681
vertical line, blinking, 169
vertical rulers, in Design view of forms, 839
vertical scroll bars, 14, 169, 175–177, 519
vertical split window box, 511
video cameras, 146, 149
View button
    Access
        Form Design toolbar, 847
        Form View toolbar, 836, 840
        Print Preview toolbar, 853
        Query Datasheet toolbar, 901, 903, 914–915, 919–920, 923
        Report Design toolbar, 854
        Table Datasheet toolbar, 756–757, 773
        Table Design toolbar, 757, 771
    PowerPoint, 970, 972
View menu commands
    Access
        Page Header/Footer, 848
        Ruler, 839
        Toolbox, 839
    Excel
        Header and Footer, 538, 590, 618, 672, 699, 703, 710–711
        Zoom, 555
    Outlook
        Current View, 66–68
        TaskPad, 75–76

PowerPoint
  Header and Footer, 999–1000, 1048, 1063
  Task Pane, 976
Word, 171
  Header and Footer, 188, 210, 269, 279, 338
  Toolbars, 173, 425
viewing
  Contacts module option buttons, 60–61
  current date, 69–70
  database window, 750–752
  documents, 179–183. *See also* displaying
  forms, 759–760
  headers and footers, 188–189
  queries, 758–759
  records, 822–824
  reports, 761–764
  slide shows, 997–998
  tables, 756–758
views
  changing, 69–71, 180–181
  Normal, 180
  outline, 180
  Print Layout, 180
  Reading layout, 180–181
  switching between, 756
    in forms, 836, 840–841
    in queries, 900–901
    in reports, 853–855
    in tables, 771
  Two page, 182
  Web Layout, 180
Views button (My Computer), 26
virus protection programs, 119
voice-input devices, 146

W

wavy red underline, 183, 991–992
Web addresses, 101–105, 295
  adding to Favorites list, 111–112
  deleting from Favorites, 114
  Favorites list, 111
Web browser, 447
Web Layout view, 180
Web Page Preview command (File menu, Word), 447
Web pages, 97
  downloading, 119–121
  previewing/saving documents as, 447–449
  printing, 122–123
  saving, 119–121
Web sites
  directories, 101
  displaying favorites, 112–113
  nonappearing, 106
Weight spin box, 349
What would you like to do? box, 793
what-if analysis, conducting, 639

wheel button (mouse), 177
white circles on placeholder boundary boxes, 1105–1106
wide area networks (WANs), 155–156
Width spin box, 706
wildcard characters,
  using in queries, 912–917
  using in searches, 39
Window Control, workbooks, 511
Windows, 4–5, 7–11, 13–14, 150–151
  Control Panels, 544
  Start button, 4–5, 54, 166, 169, 502, 966
  Start Menu, 502, 744
windows
  applications, 22
  Access features, 745–746, 749–750
  closing, 18–22
  diagonal sizing box, 511
  dragging for resizing, 16
  Excel features, 503–505, 510–511
  horizontal split, 511
  maximizing, 18–22
  minimizing, 18–22
  moving, 14–18
  My Computer window, 14
    Maximize button, 18
    Minimize button, 20
    Restore Down button, 19
  opening Web sites in new, 109
  parts of, 8
  parts of a Windows screen, 6
  pop-up, 105
  PowerPoint features, 967–972
  resizing, 14–18
  restoring, 18–22
  scrolling, 14–18
  versus Windows, 2
  vertical split, 511
  Word features, 166–169
  workbook, 505
Windows operating system, 2
Windows XP operating system, 2
  desktop, 150
  dialog boxes. *See* dialog boxes, Windows XP
  Home Edition, 11
  screen elements, 6
  versus windows, 2
wireless network, 155
wizards
  AutoContent Wizard, 1038–1040
    deleting unnecessary slides, 1043
    modifying AutoContent text, 1040–1043
    roadmap, 1038
    specifying presentation options, 1039–1040
  Chart, 825
  database, 766
  Extraction Wizard, 46–47
  Form, 832–835
  forms, 825
  Report, 850–852

Index | **Office Brief** 1249

Word, 152
    closing, 210–213
    commands. *See* commands, Word
    dialog boxes. *See* dialog boxes, Word
    documents. *See* documents
    exploring/navigating Word window, 165–169, 171–178
    importing outlines, 1054–1055
    keyboard shortcuts
        cutting/copying/pasting text, 257
        navigating documents, 178
        text formatting, 209
    parts of Word window, 166–169
    starting, 166
    toolbars
        Browser, Close button, 448
        Drawing, 332, 344
        Drawing Canvas, 347
        Header and Footer, 189, 300, 705. See also Header and Footer toolbar, Word
        printing documents from, 193
        Text Box, 345
        View menu, 173
        WordArt, 424–426
word processing programs, 165
WordArt Gallery dialog box (Word), 422–423
WordArt toolbar (Word), 424–426
    activating, 425
    Edit Text button, 424
    Format WordArt button, 425
words
    misspelled. *See* spelling and grammar checkers
    selecting, 206
wordwrap, 198
workbooks
    beginning new, 536
    existing, opening, 511
    navigating, 501, 504–507, 509–526, 529–532, 538
    new, creating, 533–537
    previewing and printing, 529
    Read-Only files, 525
    window elements, 505
    worksheets in, 502
worksheets, 152, 502
    copying to new worksheet, 609–610
    entering and editing data, 537–549
    highlighting in, 512, 515, 517
    inserting titles and headings, 590
    previewing, 558
    selecting all cells, 518
    sheet tabs, 522–523
    typing dates into, 543–544
    ungrouping, 614
    window elements, 511
    zooming, 555–556
workspace, in Access window, 745–746
workstations, 155
World Wide Web, 95
wrapping text
    around images, 339–340
    in cells, 682–683

X-Z

zipping (compressing) files, 41–47
Zoom button arrow
    Access, 762
    Excel, 555–558
    Word, 181, 247, 271, 346, 438–439
Zoom dialog box
    Excel, 555–556
    PowerPoint, 934–936